Plate 1 Attributed to Bishan Das, *Birth of a Prince,* India, c. 1620. Believed to depict the birth of Jahangir, this work is attributed to the artist whom the emperor esteemed as the greatest portrait painter of the age. The women, who by custom were segregated from the men (though some peek around the screen at the lower left) and were therefore usually portrayed as types in earlier painting, here have strikingly individual features. Next to the woman thought to be Jahangir's mother, who was Indian, sits his grand-mother, Akbar's mother, whose Central-Asian heritage is suggested by her dress. (Birth of a Prince *from an illustrated manuscript of the Jahangir-nama, Bishndas [Attributed to], Northern India, Mughal, c. 1620. Frances Bartlett Donation of 1912 and Picture Fund [14.657], Museum of Fine Arts, Boston.*)

Plate 2 Guler School, *Lady with a Hawk,* northern India, c. 1750. Freely mixing realism and symbolism, the artist shows a woman contemplating a majestic hawk who stands in for her absent lover, the bright red of the background symbolizing their passion, as her servant and confidante looks on from the side. The woman is portrayed as a distinct individual observed in a quiet moment, one sandal off as she braces a foot against a couch, but the scene also illustrates the ancient Indian theme of love in separation. *(Victoria and Albert Museum, London / Art Resource, New York.)*

Plate 3 Illuminated *tughra* (signature) of Sultan Suleiman the Magnificent, Turkey, mid-16th century. Reflecting the intertwining of writing and painting in Islamic art, the sultan's signature is elaborated into a visual image of his authority and the splendor of his reign. In Islam as in Judaism, a prohibition on graven images was often understood to prohibit portraiture. *(Suleiman the Magnificent, mid-16th century. The Metropolitan Museum of Art, Rogers Fund, 1938 [38.149.1]; photograph © 1986 The Metropolitan Museum of Art / The Metropolitan Museum of Art, New York, NY, U.S.A. Image copyright © The Metropolitan Museum of Art.)*

Plate 4 *Portrait of a Nobleman and His Wife,* China, mid-1700s. Jia Baoyu's mother and father in *The Story of the Stone* may well have resembled the solemn pair in this Qing dynasty hanging scroll. The work displays the opulent simplicity favored by the aristocrats of the day, and it embodies a harmonious union of nature and culture: the husband and wife are both indoors and outdoors on their viewing porch, poised between the artworks behind them and the artistically arranged tree, birds, and deer in front of them. *(With permission of the Royal Ontario Museum © ROM.)*

Plate 5 Marcellus Laroon, *Charles II as President of the Royal Society,* England, 1684. In this portrait of the king painted a year before his death, the traditional trappings of royalty—crown, throne, and orb—literally take a back seat (in the background at left) to the advancements of the new science. Charles gestures toward the instruments of seeing, modeling, mapping, and calibrating that the Royal Society he sponsored had done much to devise and develop. By their placement, the painter suggests that these tools make possible the naval commerce and conquest depicted in the distance—as though the telescope were the world's new scepter, and the globe the monarch's proper sphere. *(Eileen Tweedy / Christ's Hospital / The Art Archive / Picture Desk, Inc. / Kobal Collection.)*

Plate 6 Carle Van Loo, *Madame de Pompadour as a Sultana*, France, 1752. Wearing "Turkish dress," especially when sitting for one's portrait, was all the rage among the European elite of the eighteenth century. Here the powerful mistress of Louis XV is shown in a setting inspired by descriptions of harems, such as those of Lady Mary Wortley Montagu and the Baron de Montesquieu. Accepting a cup of coffee from a devoted, dark-skinned slave while holding a Turkish pipe, Madame de Pompadour grandly enjoys the exotic luxuries that Europeans were importing from the East. *(The State Hermitage Museum, St. Petersburg, Russia.)*

Plate 7 Johann Zoffany, *Queen Charlotte with Her Two Eldest Sons,* England, 1764. Zoffany's conversation piece counterpoises the grandeur of the royal family with its sentimental intimacy. The queen's beauty is reflected in the mirror on her vanity, even as she neglects the business of self-adornment in favor of the first duty of all women, to educate good citizens; a new era of majesty as good example of private domesticity has commenced. The scene opens out to the wider world as well, both through the royal park seen through the open French doors (complete with grazing deer, as in the Chinese portrait in Plate 4), and in the imported Chinese figurines behind the queen. Her children, meanwhile, combine East and West, past and present, with imperial politics played out as sibling rivalry between the sons in Roman armor and Turkish costume. *(A. C. Cooper Ltd. / The Royal Collection © Her Majesty Queen Elizabeth II.)*

INDÉPENDANCE DES ÉTATS-UNIS.

e A Juillet 1776, les Treize Colonies Confederées nnues depuis sous le nom d'Etats-Unis) sont larées, par le Congrès, libres et independantes. Gerard, porteur des pouvoirs de LOUIS XVI, Roi France, Benjamin Franklin, pour les États-Unis,

désastre accélère la Paix L'indépendance des États-Unis est reconnue par les Traités de Paix Pénétrés de reconnoissance pour les services que LOUIS XVI leur a rendus, les États-Unis ont de-puis fait élever à Philadelphie un monument qui

Plate 8   *Indépendence des États-Unis*, France, 1786. Symbols of France and a portrait of King Louis XVI surmount portraits of Benjamin Franklin and George Washington on a monument whose inscription reads, "America and the oceans, O Louis! Acknowledge you as their liberator." On the right, a native American (symbol of his continent) tramples on the defeated British lion, while a banner on the palm tree beside him proclaims, "In raising myself up, I adorn myself." Louis XVI was soon overtaken by the revolutionary ferment he guides here, and seven years after this print was made he was guillotined by his own subjects. *(Spencer Collection / Astor, Lenox and Tilden Foundations / The New York Public Library.)*

EXPLICATION.

Plate 9 *An Army of Jugs*, France, 1793. Commissioned by the French revolutionary government, this engraving shows the British King George III at the head of his jug-shaped army, himself led by a turkey, with a goose bringing up the rear. Although well equipped, the group advances uselessly against the determined French fighters known as sans-culottes—literally, "without pants"—who are positioned atop the arch on the left, wearing the revolutionary Phrygian cap. British cannons—shaped like the devices used to give enemas—only seem to increase the barrage of feces being fired in their direction by the mocking French. *(Musée de la Révolution Française, Vizille, France / Visual Arts Library, London, UK / The Bridgeman Art Library.)*

The Longman Anthology
of World Literature

VOLUME D

THE SEVENTEENTH AND EIGHTEENTH CENTURIES

David Damrosch

COLUMBIA UNIVERSITY

The Ancient Near East; Mesoamerica

David L. Pike

AMERICAN UNIVERSITY

Rome and the Roman Empire; Medieval Europe

☙

April Alliston

PRINCETON UNIVERSITY

The Age of the Enlightenment

Marshall Brown

UNIVERSITY OF WASHINGTON

The Nineteenth Century

Page duBois

UNIVERSITY OF CALIFORNIA, SAN DIEGO

Classical Greece

Sabry Hafez

UNIVERSITY OF LONDON

Arabic and Islamic Literatures

Ursula K. Heise

STANFORD UNIVERSITY

The Twentieth Century

Djelal Kadir

PENNSYLVANIA STATE UNIVERSITY

The Twentieth Century

Sheldon Pollock

COLUMBIA UNIVERSITY

South Asia

Bruce Robbins

COLUMBIA UNIVERSITY

The Nineteenth Century

Haruo Shirane

COLUMBIA UNIVERSITY

Japan

Jane Tylus

NEW YORK UNIVERSITY

Early Modern Europe

Pauline Yu

AMERICAN COUNCIL OF LEARNED SOCIETIES

China

The Longman Anthology of World Literature

SECOND EDITION

David Damrosch

David L. Pike

General Editors

VOLUME D

THE SEVENTEENTH AND EIGHTEENTH CENTURIES

April Alliston

with contributions by
David Damrosch, Sabry Hafez,
Sheldon Pollock, Haruo Shirane, and Pauline Yu

PEARSON
Longman

New York   San Francisco   Boston
London   Toronto   Sydney   Tokyo   Singapore   Madrid
Mexico City   Munich   Paris   Cape Town   Hong Kong   Montreal

Editor-in-Chief: *Joseph Terry*
Associate Development Editor: *Erin Reilly*
Executive Marketing Manager: *Joyce Nilsen*
Senior Supplements Editor: *Donna Campion*
Production Manager: *Ellen MacElree*
Project Coordination, Text Design, and Page
    Makeup: *GGS Book Services PMG*
Senior Cover Design Manager: *Nancy Danahy*
On the Cover: Detail from *Portrait of a*

Negro Man, Olaudah Equiano, 1780s,
English school, 18th century, previously
attributed to Joshua Reynolds. Royal
Albert Memorial Museum, Exeter, Devon,
UK/The Bridgeman Art Library.
Image Permission Coordinator: *Joanne Dippel*
Senior Manufacturing Buyer: *Alfred C. Dorsey*
Printer and Binder: *LSC Communications*
Cover Printer: *LSC Communications*

For permission to use copyrighted material, grateful acknowledgment is made to the copyright holders on pages 617–619, which are hereby made part of this copyright page.

Library of Congress Cataloging-in-Publication Data

The Longman anthology of world literature / David Damrosch, David L. Pike, general editors.—2nd ed.
    p.   cm.
    Includes bibliographical references and index.
    Contents: v. A. The ancient world—v. B. The medieval era—v. C. The early modern period—v. D. The seventeenth and eighteenth centuries—v. E. The nineteenth century—v. F. The twentieth century.
    ISBN 978-0-205-62595-6 (v. A).—ISBN 978-0-205-62596-3 (v. B).— 978-0-205-62597-0 (v. C).— 978-0-205-62590-1 (v. D).— 978-0-205-62591-8 (v. E).— 978-0-205-62594-9 (v. F).
    1. Literature—Collections.   2. Literature—History and criticism.
I. Damrosch, David.   II. Pike, David L. (David Lawrence), 1963–
PN6013.L66   2009
808.8—dc22

2008015921

Please visit us at http://www.ablongman.com/damrosch.

To place your order, please use the following ISBN numbers:

Volume A, *The Ancient World:* ISBN 13: 978-0-205-62595-6; ISBN 10: 0-205-62595-9
    A la Carte Edition: ISBN 13: 978-0-13-450864-1; ISBN 10: 0-13-450864-5

Volume B, *The Medieval Era:* ISBN 13: 978-0-205-62596-3; ISBN 10: 0-205-62596-7
    A la Carte Edition: ISBN 13: 978-0-13-450670-8; ISBN 10: 0-13-450670-7

Volume C, *The Early Modern Period:* ISBN 13: 978-0-205-62597-0; ISBN 10: 0-205-62597-5
    A la Carte Edition: ISBN 13: 978-0-13-450669-2; ISBN 10: 0-13-450669-3

Volume D, *The Seventeenth and Eighteenth Centuries:* ISBN 13: 978-0-205-62590-1;
    ISBN 10: 0-205-62590-8
    A la Carte Edition: ISBN 13: 978-0-13-450863-4; ISBN 10: 0-13-450863-7

Volume E, *The Nineteenth Century:* ISBN 13: 978-0-205-62591-8; ISBN 10: 0-205-62591-6
    A la Carte Edition: ISBN 13: 978-0-13-450667-8; ISBN 10: 0-13-450667-7

Volume F, *The Twentieth Century:* ISBN 13: 978-0-205-62594-9; ISBN 10: 0-205-62594-0
    A la Carte Edition: ISBN 13: 978-0-13-450862-7; ISBN 10: 0-13-450862-9

CONTENTS

The Age of the Enlightenment   185

JEAN-BAPTISTE POQUELIN [MOLIÈRE]
(1622–1673)   199

⇒⊢ PERSPECTIVES ⊣⇐
Court Culture and Female Authorship   253

On the Cover

Portrait of Olaudah Equiano, English, 1780s. This glowing portrait shows Equiano as an Enlightenment gentleman, visually supporting the eloquent testimony of his *Interesting Narrative* (page 441) that a freed African slave can fully share all "the Rights of Man" being sought for European citizens.

ADDITIONAL AUDIO AND ONLINE RESOURCES

Voices of World Literature, Disk 2 (ISBN: 0-321-22518-X)

An audio CD to accompany *The Longman Anthology of World Literature,* Volume 2. Throughout most of history, literature was created to be read, recited, or sung aloud. The selections on this CD, which can be ordered/packaged with the anthology, present a range of the many voices of world literature from the seventeenth century to the modern day and open up a range of cultural contexts for student discussion and writing. The following selections are available for Volume D.

The Seventeenth and Eighteenth Centuries

1. Tanburi Isak: Guilizar Agir Sema'i
Performed by the Lalezar Ensemble (2:45)

An example of the sophisticated music composed at the Ottoman court in Constantinople in the seventeenth through nineteenth centuries. Singers and musicians would perform their songs far into the night during banquets, their free-form rhythms and shifting harmonies inducing a meditative, reflective pleasure in the gathered listeners.

2. Johann Sebastian Bach: from *The Well-Tempered Clavier,* Book 1: Prelude and Fugue #1 in C Major, BWV 846
Performed by Jeno Jando, piano (4:32)

One of the world's great composers, J. S. Bach (1685-1750), was deeply interested in the ordered modulations of harmony and the patterned rhythms of counterpoint. He composed his Well-tempered Clavier *for his elder children, to illustrate the principles of counterpoint and the modern system of musical keys—a classically Enlightenment project of rationalizing music's mysterious harmonies. This delightful prelude begins with open chords, brilliantly harmonized in the fugue that follows it.*

3. Georg Friedrich Handel: from the *Messiah:* "O Death, where is thy sting."
Performed by the Scholars Baroque Ensemble (3:30)

This recording uses period instruments and the small chorus Handel favored, bringing out the compelling blend of lightness and magnificence of this great oratorio from 1742. In words taken from Paul's first letter to the Corinthians, a playful duet between a tenor and a countertenor celebrates Christ's triumph over death: "O Death, where is thy sting, O grave, where is thy victory? This sting of death is sin, and the strength of sin is the law." Then the full chorus rejoices: "But thanks be to God, who giveth us the victory through our Lord Jesus Christ."

4. Jonathan Swift: from "The Lady's Dressing Room"
Read by Patrick Deer (3:40)

A love-smitten shepherd tiptoes into his beloved Celia's dressing room, where he finds more than he has bargained for.

5. Lady Mary Wortley Montagu: from "The Reasons that Induced Dr. S to Write a Poem Called 'The Lady's Dressing Room'"
Read by Elizabeth Richmond-Garza (3:02)

Matching Swift witticism for witticism and obscenity for obscenity, Montagu reveals the "true" story behind Swift's poem.

6. Priest Jinbo: from "Jinbo Sanya"
Performed by Ronnie Nyogetsu Reishin Seldin (2:37)

A composition for solo bamboo flute (shakuhachi), *expressing a free-floating spiritual state, composed in the early seventeenth century by a wandering Zen priest who spent his life perfecting this single piece of music.*

7. Wolfgang Amadeus Mozart and Lorenzo da Ponte: from *Don Giovanni*: "La ci darem la mano"
Performed by bass soloist Bo Skovhus, soprano Ildiko Raimondi, and the Estherházy Sinfonia (3:18)

This famous duet from Mozart and Da Ponte's opera is a tour de force *of enticement by the rake Don Giovanni and melting resistance from the peasant girl Zerlina.*

Companion Website for *The Longman Anthology of World Literature,* Second Edition

www.ablongman.com/damrosch

Our Companion Website for the second edition has been enhanced with the addition of an interactive timeline, practice quizzes for major periods and authors, author biographies, research links, a glossary of literary terms, an audio glossary that provides the accepted pronunciations of author, character, and selection names from the anthology, audio recordings of our Translations features, and sample syllabi.

RESOURCES FOR VOLUME D

Practice Quizzes

Period Quizzes

- The Seventeenth and Eighteenth Centuries
- The Age of Enlightenment

Quizzes on Major Texts

- *Tartuffe*
- *Oroonoko*
- *Gulliver's Travels*
- *Candide*
- *The Rape of the Lock*
- An Answer to the Question: What Is Enlightenment

- The poetry of Matsuo Bashō
- *The Story of the Stone*
- "The Lady's Dressing Room" and responses
- *The Love Suicides at Amijima*

Author Biographies

- Ihara Saikaku
- Aphra Behn
- Alexander Pope
- Lorenzo da Ponte
- Cao Xueqin

- Jean-Baptiste Poquelin (Molière)
- Jonathan Swift
- François-Marie Arouet (Voltaire)
- Chikamatsu Mon'zaemon

Research Links

Author and Major Texts

- Aphra Behn
- Cao Xueqin and Shen Fu
- Giacomo Casanova
- Chikamatsu Mon'zaemon
- Mary, Lady Chudleigh
- Denis Diderot
- Olaudah Equiano
- Jonathan Swift
- Eliza Haywood
- Ihara Saikaku
- Immanuel Kant
- Matsuo Bashō
- Lady Mary Wortley Montagu
- Jean Baptiste Poquelin (Molière)
- Marie-Madeleine Pioche de la Vergne, Comtesse de Lafayette
- Charles de Secondat, Baron de la Brède et de Montesquieu

- The Ottoman Empire
- Elisabeth Charlotte Von Der Pfalz, Duchesse d'Orléans
- Katherine Philips
- Alexander Pope
- Jean-Jacques Rousseau
- Marie de Rabutin-Chantal, Marquise de Sévigné
- Anne Finch, Countess of Winchilsea
- Tsangyang Gyatso
- François Marie Arouet (Voltaire)
- John Wilmot, Earl of Rochester
- Mary Wollstonecraft
- Ann Yearsley
- Maria de Zayas y Sotomayor

Translations

- Voltaire's *Candide*

PREFACE

Our world today is both expanding and growing smaller at the same time. Expanding, through a tremendous increase in the range of cultures that actively engage with each other; and yet growing smaller as well, as people and products surge across borders in the process known as globalization. This double movement creates remarkable opportunities for cross-cultural understanding, as well as new kinds of tensions, miscommunications, and uncertainties. Both the opportunities and the uncertainties are amply illustrated in the changing shape of world literature. A generation ago, when the term "world literature" was used in North America, it largely meant masterworks by European writers from Homer onward, together with a few favored North American writers, heirs to the Europeans. Today, however, it is generally recognized that Europe is only part of the story of the world's literatures, and only part of the story of North America's cultural heritage. An extraordinary range of exciting material is now in view, from the earliest Sumerian lyrics inscribed on clay tablets to the latest Kashmiri poetry circulated on the Internet. Many new worlds—and newly visible *older* worlds of classical traditions around the globe—await us today.

How can we best approach such varied materials from so many cultures? Can we deal with this embarrassment of riches without being overwhelmed by it, and without merely giving a glancing regard to less familiar traditions? This anthology has been designed to help readers successfully navigate "the sea of stories"—as Salman Rushdie has described the world's literary heritage.

The enthusiastic reception of the first edition attests to the growing relevance of a truly global approach to world literature. Drawing from the insight of instructors across the country, we have updated and further improved our anthology. We've gone about this challenging, fascinating task in several ways.

NEW TO THIS EDITION

- In our new Translations features, a brief selection is presented in the original language accompanied by two or three translations, chosen to show differing strategies translators have used to convey the sense of the original in new and powerful ways.
- Each of the Perspectives sections is now followed by our new Crosscurrents feature, which will highlight additional connections for students to explore.
- In response to reviewer requests, we have reevaluated each selection and streamlined our coverage to focus on the readings most frequently taught in the world literature course. We have also added several important works in their entirety, including Sophocles' *Antigone,* Shakespeare's *Othello,* Moliere's *Tartuffe,* Tolstoy's *The Death of Ivan Ilych,* and Silko's "Yellow Woman."

- Pull-out quotations in our period introductions and new headings in our author introductions have been added to help draw student interest and highlight important information.
- We have enhanced our Companion Website with the addition of a multitude of resources, including an interactive timeline, practice quizzes for major periods and authors, author biographies, research links, a glossary of literary terms, an audio glossary that provides the accepted pronunciations of author, character, and selection names from the anthology, audio recordings of our translations features, and sample syllabi. Visit www.ablongman.com/damrosch to explore these and other resources.
- We have improved our table of contents through the addition of a new media index—enabling you to locate all available resources quickly.

CONNECTING DISTINCTIVE TRADITIONS

Works of world literature engage in a double conversation: with their culture of origin and with the varied contexts into which they travel away from home. To look broadly at world literature is therefore to see patterns of difference as well as points of contact and commonality. The world's disparate traditions have developed very distinct kinds of literature, even very different ideas as to what should be called "literature" at all. This anthology uses a variety of means to showcase what is most distinctive and also what is commonly shared among the world's literatures. Throughout the anthology, we employ two kinds of grouping:

☞ PERSPECTIVES: **Groupings that provide cultural context for major works, illuminating issues of broad importance.**

☞ RESONANCES: **Sources for a specific text or responses to it, often from a different time and place.**

Throughout the anthology, our many "Perspectives" sections provide cultural context for the major works around them, giving insight into such issues as the representation of death and immortality (in the ancient Near East); the meeting of Christians, Muslims, and Jews in medieval Iberia; the idea of the national poet in the nineteenth century; and "modernist memory" in the twentieth. Perspectives sections give a range of voices and views, strategies and styles, in highly readable textual groupings. The Perspectives groupings serve a major pedagogical as well as intellectual purpose in making these selections accessible and useful within the time constraints of a survey course. New to the second edition is "Crosscurrents," a feature that concludes each "Perspectives" section with connections to related selections within the same volume and in other volumes of the anthologies. "Crosscurrents" opens up the focused grouping of the "Perspectives," facilitating the study of specific themes and issues across cultures and across time.

Our "Resonances" perform the crucial function of linking works across time as well as space. For Homer's *Iliad*, a Resonance shows oral composition as it is still practiced today north of Greece, while for the *Odyssey* we have Resonances giving modern responses to Homer by Franz Kafka, Derek Walcott, and the Greek poet George Seferis. Accompanying the traditional Navajo "Story of the Emergence" (Volume E) is an extended selection from *Black Elk Speaks* which shows how ancient imagery infused the dream visions of the Sioux healer and warrior Nicholas Black Elk, helping him deal with the crises of lost land and independence that his people were facing. Resonances for Conrad's *Heart of Darkness* (Volume F) give selections from Conrad's diary of his own journey upriver in the Congo, and a speech by Henry Morton Stanley, the explorer-journalist who was serving as publicist for King Leopold's exploitation of his colony in the years just before Conrad went there. Stanley's surreal speech—in which he calculates how much money the Manchester weavers can make providing wedding dresses and burial clothes for the Congolese—gives a vivid instance of the outlook, and the rhetoric, that Conrad grimly parodies in Mr. Kurtz and his associates.

PRINCIPLES OF SELECTION

Beyond our immediate groupings, our overall selections have been made with an eye to fostering connections across time and space: a Perspectives section on "Courtly Women" in medieval Japan (Volume B) introduces themes that can be followed up in "Court Culture and Female Authorship" in Enlightenment-era Europe (Volume D), while the ancient Mediterranean creation myths at the start of Volume A find echoes in later cosmic-creation narratives from Mesoamerica (Volume C) and indigenous peoples today (Volume E). Altogether, we have worked to create an exceptionally coherent and well-integrated presentation of an extraordinary variety of works from around the globe, from the dawn of writing to the present.

Recognizing that different sorts of works have counted as literature in differing times and places, we take an inclusive approach, centering on poems, plays, and fictional narratives but also including selections from rich historical, religious, and philosophical texts like Plato's *Apology* and the Qur'an that have been important for much later literary work, even though they weren't conceived as literature themselves. We present many complete masterworks, including *The Epic of Gilgamesh* (in a beautiful verse translation), Homer's *Odyssey*, Dante's *Inferno*, and Chinua Achebe's *Things Fall Apart*, and we have extensive, teachable selections from such long works as *The Tale of Genji*, *Don Quixote*, and both parts of Goethe's *Faust*.

Along with these major selections we present a great array of shorter works, some of which have been known only to specialists and only now are entering into world literature. It is our experience as readers and as teachers that the established classics themselves can best be understood when they're set in a varied literary landscape. Nothing is included here, though, simply to make a point: whether world-renowned or recently rediscovered, these are compelling works to read. Throughout our work on this book, we've tried to be highly inclusive in principle and yet carefully selective in practice, avoiding tokenism and also its inverse, the piling up of an unmanageable array of heterogeneous material. If we've succeeded as we hope, the result will be coherent as well as capacious, substantive as well as stimulating.

LITERATURE, ART, AND MUSIC

One important way to understand literary works in context is to read them in conjunction with the broader social and artistic culture in which they were created. Literature has often had a particularly close relation to visual art and to music. Different as the arts are in their specific resources and techniques, a culture's artistic expressions often share certain family resemblances, common traits that can be seen across different media—and that may even come out more clearly in visual or musical form than in translations of literature itself. This anthology includes dozens of black-and-white illustrations and a suite of color illustrations in each volume, chosen to work in close conjunction with our literary selections. Some of these images directly illustrate literary works, while others show important aspects of a culture's aesthetic sensibility. Often, writing actually appears on paintings and sculptures, with represented people and places sharing the space with beautifully rendered Mayan hieroglyphs, Arabic calligraphy, or Chinese brushstrokes.

Music too has been a close companion of literary creation and performance. Our very term "lyric" refers to the lyres or harps with which the Greeks accompanied poems as they were sung. In China, the first major literary work is the *Book of Songs*. In Europe too, until quite recent times poetry was often sung and even prose was usually read aloud. We have created two audio CDs to accompany the anthology, one for Volumes A through C and one for Volumes D through F. These CDs give a wealth of poetry and music from the cultures we feature in the anthology; they are both a valuable teaching resource and also a pure pleasure to listen to.

AIDS TO UNDERSTANDING

A major emphasis of our work has been to introduce each culture and each work to best effect. Each major period and section of the anthology, each grouping of works, and each individual author has an introduction by a member of our editorial team. Our goal has been to write introductions informed by deep knowledge worn lightly. Neither talking down to our readers nor overwhelming them with masses of unassimilable information, our introductions don't seek to "cover" the material but instead try to uncover it, to provide ways in and connections outward. Similarly, our footnotes and glosses are concise and informative, rather than massive or interpretive. Time lines for each volume, and maps and pronunciation guides throughout the anthology, all aim to foster an informed and pleasurable reading of the works. The second edition of *The Longman Anthology of World Literature* has added highlighted quotations in the period introductions and additional headings to the author introductions to help draw student interest and clarify key ideas.

GOING FURTHER

The second edition makes connections beyond its covers as well as within them. Bibliographies at the end of each volume point the way to historical and critical readings for students wishing to go into greater depth for term papers. The Companion Website we've developed for the course (www.ablongman.com/damrosch) gives a wealth of links to excellent Web resources on all our major texts and many related historical and cultural movements and events. The Website includes an audio version of our printed pronunciation guides: you can simply click on a name to hear it pronounced. Each of our new Translations features is also available on the Website, where you can listen to readings of works in their original language and in translation. This rich resource will give you extensive exposure to the aural dimension of many of the languages represented in the anthology. We have also enhanced the Website for this edition, with the addition of practice quizzes for each period and for major selections, an interactive timeline, author biographies, a searchable glossary of literary terms, and sample syllabi. For instructors, we have also created an extensive instructor's manual, written directly by the editors themselves, drawing on years of experience in teaching these materials. Finally, our audio CDs remain available, providing a library of music and readings to augment your world literature course.

TRANSLATION ACROSS CULTURES

The circulation of world literature is always an exercise in cultural translation, and one way to define works of world literature is that they are the works that gain in translation. Some great texts remain so intimately tied to their point of origin that they never read well abroad; they may have an abiding importance at home, but don't play a role in the wider world. Other works, though, gain in resonance as they move out into new contexts, new conjunctions. Edgar Allan Poe found his first really serious readers in France, rather than in the United States. *The Thousand and One Nights,* long a marginal work in Arabic traditions oriented toward poetry rather than popular prose, gained new readers and new influence abroad, and Scheherazade's intricately nested tales now help us in turn to read the European tales of Boccaccio and Marguerite de Navarre with new attention and appreciation. A Perspectives section on *"The Thousand and One Nights* in the Twentieth Century" (Volume F) brings together a range of Arab, European, and American writers who have continued to plumb its riches to this day.

As important as cultural translation in general is the issue of actual translation from one language to another. We have sought out compelling translations for all our foreign-language works, and periodically we offer our readers the opportunity to think directly about the issue of translation. Sometimes we offer distinctively different translations of differing works from a single author or source: for the Bible, for example, we give Genesis 1–11 in Robert Alter's lively, oral-style translation, while we give selected psalms in the magnificent King James Version and the Joseph story in the lucid New International Version. Our selections from Homer's *Iliad* appear in Richmond Lattimore's stately older translation, while Homer's *Odyssey* is given in Robert Fagles's eloquent new version.

At other times, we give alternative translations of a single work. So we have Chinese lyrics translated by the modernist poet Ezra Pound and by a contemporary scholar; and we have Petrarch sonnets translated by the Renaissance English poet Thomas Wyatt and also by contemporary translators. These juxtapositions can show some of the varied ways in which translators over the centuries have sought to carry works over from one time and place to another—not so much by mirroring and reflecting an unchanged meaning, as by refracting it, in a prismatic process that can add new highlights and reveal new facets in a classic text. At times, when we haven't found a translation that really satisfies us, we've translated the work ourselves—an activity we recommend to all who wish to come to know a work from the inside.

To help focus on the many issues involved in translation, we have incorporated a new Translations feature into the second edition. In each volume of the anthology, two major works are followed by a selection in the original language and in several different translations. By studying the different choices made by translators in different times and cultural contexts, we not only discover new meaning in the original work but in the ways in which literature is transformed as it is translated for each generation of readers.

We hope that the results of our years of work on this project will be as enjoyable to use as the book has been to create. We welcome you now inside our pages.

David Damrosch
David L. Pike

ACKNOWLEDGMENTS

In the extended process of planning and preparing the second edition of this anthology, the editors have been fortunate to have the support, advice, and assistance of many people. Our editor, Joe Terry, and our publisher, Roth Wilkofsky, have supported our project in every possible way and some seemingly impossible ones as well, helping us produce the best possible book despite all challenges to budgets and well-laid plans in a rapidly evolving field. Their associates Mary Ellen Curley and Joyce Nilsen have shown unwavering enthusiasm and constant creativity in developing the book and its related Web site and audio CDs and in introducing the results to the world. Our development editors, first Adam Beroud and then Erin Reilly, have shown a compelling blend of literary acuity and quiet diplomacy in guiding thirteen far-flung editors through the many stages of work. Peter Meyers brought great energy and creativity to work on our CDs. Donna Campion and Dianne Hall worked diligently to complete the instructor's manual. A team of permissions editors cleared hundreds and hundreds of text permissions from publishers in many countries.

Once the manuscript was complete, Ellen MacElree, the production manager, oversaw the simultaneous production of six massive books on a tight and shifting schedule. Valerie Zaborski, managing editor in production, also helped and, along the way, developed a taste for the good-humored fatalism of Icelandic literature. Our copyeditor, Stephanie Magean, and then Doug Bell and his colleagues at GGS Book Services PMG, worked overtime to produce beautiful books accurate down to the last exotic accent.

Our plans for this edition have been shaped by the comments, suggestions, and thoughtful advice of our reviewers. Charles Bane (University of Central Arkansas); Laurel Bollinger (University of Alabama in Huntsville); Patricia Cearley (South Plains College); Ed Eberhart (Troy University); Fidel Fajardo-Acosta (Creighton University); Gene C. Fant (Union University); Kathy Flann (Eastern Kentucky University); Katona D. Hargrave (Troy University); Nainsi J. Houston (Creighton University); Marta Kvande (Valdosta State University); Wayne Narey (Arkansas State University); Kevin R. Rahimzadeh (Eastern Kentucky University); Elizabeth L. Rambo (Campbell University); Gavin Richardson (Union University); Joseph Rosenblum (University of North Carolina at Greensboro); Douglass H. Thomson (Georgia Southern University); and Tomasz Warchol (Georgia Southern University).

We remain grateful as well for the guidance of the many reviewers who advised us on the creation of the first edition: Roberta Adams (Fitchburg State College); Adetutu Abatan (Floyd College); Magda al-Nowaihi (Columbia University); Nancy Applegate (Floyd College); Susan Atefat-Peckham (Georgia College and State University); Evan Balkan (CCBC-Catonsville); Michelle Barnett (University of Alabama, Birmingham); Colonel Bedell (Virginia Military Institute); Thomas Beebee (Pennsylvania State University); Paula Berggren (Baruch College); Mark Bernier (Blinn College); Ronald Bogue (University of Georgia); Terre Burton (Dixie State College); Patricia Cearley (South Plains College); Raj Chekuri (Laredo Community College); Sandra Clark (University of Wyoming); Thomas F. Connolly (Suffolk University); Vilashini Cooppan (Yale University); Bradford Crain (College of the Ozarks); Robert W. Croft (Gainesville College); Frank Day (Clemson University); Michael Delahoyde (Washington State University);

Elizabeth Otten Delmonico (Truman State University); Jo Devine (University of Alaska Southeast); Gene Doty (University of Missouri—Rolla); James Earle (University of Oregon); R. Steve Eberly (Western Carolina University); Walter Evans (Augusta State University); Fidel Fajardo-Acosta (Creighton University); Mike Felker (South Plains College); Janice Gable (Valley Forge Christian College); Stanley Galloway (Bridgewater College); Doris Gardenshire (Trinity Valley Community College); Jonathan Glenn (University of Central Arkansas); Dean Hall (Kansas State University); Dorothy Hardman (Fort Valley State University); Elissa Heil (University of the Ozarks); David Hesla (Emory University); Susan Hillabold (Purdue University North Central); Karen Hodges (Texas Wesleyan); David Hoegberg (Indiana University-Purdue University—Indianapolis); Sheri Hoem (Xavier University); Michael Hutcheson (Landmark College); Mary Anne Hutchinson (Utica College); Raymond Ide (Lancaster Bible College); James Ivory (Appalachian State University); Craig Kallendorf (Texas A & M University); Bridget Keegan (Creighton University); Steven Kellman (University of Texas—San Antonio); Roxanne Kent-Drury (Northern Kentucky University); Susan Kroeg (Eastern Kentucky University); Tamara Kuzmenkov (Tacoma Community College); Robert Lorenzi (Camden County College—Blackwood); Mark Mazzone (Tennessee State University); David McCracken (Coker College); George Mitrenski (Auburn University); James Nicholl (Western Carolina University); Roger Osterholm (Embry-Riddle University); Joe Pellegrino (Eastern Kentucky University); Linda Lang-Peralta (Metropolitan State College of Denver); Sandra Petree (University of Arkansas); David E. Phillips (Charleston Southern University); Terry Reilly (University of Alaska); Constance Relihan (Auburn University); Nelljean Rice (Coastal Carolina University); Colleen Richmond (George Fox University); Gretchen Ronnow (Wayne State University); John Rothfork (West Texas A & M University); Elise Salem-Manganaro (Fairleigh Dickinson University); Asha Sen (University of Wisconsin Eau Claire); Richard Sha (American University); Edward Shaw (University of Central Florida); Jack Shreve (Allegany College of Maryland); Jimmy Dean Smith (Union College); Floyd C. Stuart (Norwich University); Eleanor Sumpter-Latham (Central Oregon Community College); Ron Swigger (Albuquerque Technical Vocational Institute); Barry Tharaud (Mesa State College); Theresa Thompson (Valdosta State College); Teresa Thonney (Columbia Basin College); Charles Tita (Shaw University); Scott D. Vander Ploeg (Madisonville Community College); Marian Wernicke (Pensacola Junior College); Sallie Wolf (Arapahoe Community College); and Dede Yow (Kennesaw State University).

We also wish to express our gratitude to the reviewers who gave us additional advice on the book's companion Web site: Nancy Applegate (Floyd College); James Earl (University of Oregon); David McCracken (Coker College); Linda Lang-Peralta (Metropolitan State College of Denver); Asha Sen (University of Wisconsin—Eau Claire); Jimmy Dean Smith (Union College); Floyd Stuart (Norwich University); and Marian Wernicke (Pensacola Junior College).

The editors were assisted in tracking down texts and information by wonderfully able research assistants: Kerry Bystrom, Julie Lapiski, Katalin Lovasz, Joseph Ortiz, Laura B. Sayre, and Lauren Simonetti. April Alliston wishes to thank Brandon Lafving for his invaluable comments on her drafts and Gregory Maertz for his knowledge and support. Marshall Brown would like to thank his research assistant Françoise Belot for her help and Jane K. Brown for writing the Goethe introduction. Sheldon Pollock would like to thank Whitney Cox, Rajeev Kinra, Susanne Mrozik, and Guriqbal Sahota for their assistance and Haruo Shirane thanks Michael Brownstein for writing the introduction to Hozumi Ikan, and Akiko Takeuchi for writing the introductions to the Noh drama.

It has been a great pleasure to work with all these colleagues both at Longman and at schools around the country. This book exists for its readers, whose reactions and suggestions we warmly welcome, as the second edition of *The Longman Anthology of World Literature* moves out into the world.

ABOUT THE EDITORS

David Damrosch (Columbia University). His books include *The Narrative Covenant: Transformations of Genre in the Growth of Biblical Literature* (1987), *Meetings of the Mind* (2000), *What Is World Literature?* (2003), and *How to Read World Literature* (2009). He has been president of the American Comparative Literature Association (2001–2003) and is founding general editor of *The Longman Anthology of British Literature* (third edition, 2006).

David L. Pike (American University). Author of *Passage Through Hell: Modernist Descents, Medieval Underworlds* (1997), *Subterranean Cities: The World Beneath Paris and London, 1800–1945* (2005), and *Metropolis on the Styx: The Underworlds of Modern Urban Culture* (2007). He is co-author of the forthcoming *A World of Writing: Poems, Stories, Drama, Essays*.

April Alliston (Princeton University). Author of *Virtue's Faults: Correspondences in Eighteenth-Century British and French Women's Fiction* (1996), and editor of Sophia Lee's *The Recess* (2000). Her book on concepts of character, gender, and plausibility in Enlightenment historical narratives is forthcoming.

Marshall Brown (University of Washington). Author of *The Shape of German Romanticism* (1979), *Preromanticism* (1991), *Turning Points: Essays in the History of Cultural Expressions* (1997), *The Gothic Text* (2005), and *The Tooth That Nibbles at the Soul: Essays on Music and Poetry* (forthcoming). Editor of *Modern Language Quarterly: A Journal of Literary History,* and the *Cambridge History of Literary Criticism,* Vol. 5: Romanticism.

Page duBois (University of California, San Diego). Her books include *Centaurs and Amazons* (1982), *Sowing the Body* (1988), *Torture and Truth* (1991), *Sappho Is Burning* (1995), *Trojan Horses* (2001), and *Slaves and Other Objects* (2003).

Sabry Hafez (University of London). Author of several books in Arabic on poetry, drama, the novel, and on a number of major Arab writers, including works on Mahfouz, Idris, and Mahmoud Darwish. His books in English include *The Genesis of Arabic Narrative Discourse* (1993), *The Quest for Identies: The Arabic Short Story* (2007), and the edited volumes *A Reader of Modern Arabic Short Stories* and *Modern Arabic Criticism*. He is the editor of the on-line bilingual Arabic/English monthly journal, *Al-Kalimah/The World.*

Ursula K. Heise (Stanford University). Author of *Chronoschisms: Time, Narrative, and Postmodernism* (1997) and of *Sense of Place and Sense of Planet: The Environmental Imagination of the Global* (2008).

Djelal Kadir (Pennsylvania State University). His books include *Columbus and the Ends of the Earth* (1992), *The Other Writing: Postcolonial Essays in Latin America's Writing Culture* (1993), and *Other Modernisms in an Age of Globalizations* (2002). He served in the 1990s as editor of *World Literature Today* and is coeditor of the *Comparative History of Latin America's Literary Cultures* (2004). He is the founding president of the International American Studies Association.

Sheldon Pollock (Columbia University). His books include *The Language of the Gods in the World of Men* (2006). He recently edited *Literary Cultures in History: Reconstructions from South Asia* (2003). He is general editor of the Clay Sanskrit Library.

Bruce Robbins (Columbia University). His books include *The Servant's Hand: English Fiction from Below* (1986), *Secular Vocations* (1993), *Feeling Global: Internationalism in Distress* (1999), and *Upward Mobility and the Common Good: Toward a Literary History of the Welfare State* (2007). Edited volumes include *Cosmopolitics: Thinking and Feeling Beyond the Nation* (1998).

Haruo Shirane (Columbia University). Author of *The Bridge of Dreams: A Poetics of "The Tale of Genji"* (1987) and of *Traces of Dreams: Landscape, Cultural Memory, and the Poetry of Bashō* (1998). He is coeditor of *Inventing the Classics: Modernity, National Identity, and Japanese Literature* (2000) and has recently edited *Early Modern Japanese Literature: An Anthology 1600–1900*.

Jane Tylus (New York University). Author of *Writing and Vulnerability in the Late Renaissance* (1993), coeditor of *Epic Traditions in the Contemporary World* (1999), and editor and translator of Lucrezia Tornabuoni de' Medici's *Sacred Narratives* (2001). Her study on late medieval female spirituality and the origins of humanism is forthcoming.

Pauline Yu (American Council of Learned Societies). President of the American Council of Learned Societies, she is the author of *The Poetry of Wang Wei* (1980) and *The Reading of Imagery in the Chinese Poetic Tradition* (1987), the editor of *Voices of the Song Lyric in China* (1994), and coeditor of *Culture and State in Chinese History* (1997) and *Ways with Words: Writing about Reading Texts from Early China* (2000).

David Damrosch
COLUMBIA UNIVERSITY
The Ancient Near East; Mesoamerica

David L. Pike
AMERICAN UNIVERSITY
Rome and the Roman Empire; Medieval Europe

April Alliston
PRINCETON UNIVERSITY
The Age of the Enlightenment

Marshall Brown
UNIVERSITY OF WASHINGTON
The Nineteenth Century

Page duBois
UNIVERSITY OF CALIFORNIA, SAN DIEGO
Classical Greece

Sabry Hafez
UNIVERSITY OF LONDON
Arabic and Islamic Literatures

Ursula K. Heise
STANFORD UNIVERSITY
The Twentieth Century

Djelal Kadir
PENNSYLVANIA STATE UNIVERSITY
The Twentieth Century

Sheldon Pollock
COLUMBIA UNIVERSITY
South Asia

Bruce Robbins
COLUMBIA UNIVERSITY
The Nineteenth Century

Haruo Shirane
COLUMBIA UNIVERSITY
Japan

Jane Tylus
NEW YORK UNIVERSITY
Early Modern Europe

Pauline Yu
AMERICAN COUNCIL OF LEARNED SOCIETIES
China

The Longman Anthology
of World Literature

VOLUME D

THE SEVENTEENTH AND EIGHTEENTH CENTURIES

LE ROY DE FRANCE.

l'Home immortel Chef de la Ste Ligue.

Mon soleil par sa force eclaira l'heretique.
Il chassa tout d'un coup les brouillards de Calvin:
Non pas par un Zele divin,
Mais a fin de cacher ma fine Politique.

Anonymous drawing of Louis XIV as the "Sun King." The verses below the image are a masterpiece of propaganda, describing the French king's conservative Counter-Reformation policy, reversing earlier religious tolerance in the new terms of the Enlightenment: the power of Louis' "Sun" will enlighten heretics, evaporating the mists of John Valving's Protestant teachings——not because of any religious zeal but to conceal his subtle political strategy.

The Seventeenth and Eighteenth Centuries

The middle decades of the 1600s marked a time of transition in many parts of the world. The Manchu people came to power in China in 1644; their Qing dynasty would continue to rule the world's most populous country until 1911. In Japan, the Tokugawa clan of warlords, or shoguns, had begun to establish themselves in 1600; they cemented their control over the country in the next few decades. By midcentury they had succeeded in their ambition of closing Japan to outside influence, and after 1641 the sole foreign presence in Japan was a small Dutch trade mission confined to an island in Nagasaki Harbor—a situation that wouldn't change for over two hundred years. Both local and colonial rule began to assume new forms in Africa and the Americas: the great Bambara kingdom was established in midcentury along the upper reaches of the Niger River, and in 1652 Dutch settlers founded a colony at Capetown in what would become the English colony of South Africa. While the Dutch gained in Africa, they lost in the Western hemisphere: in 1654 Portugal took back Brazil from them, and a decade later the English expelled them from their colony of New Amsterdam, renaming it New York.

Europe too saw sweeping changes during these years. A long period of conflict in and around Germany, the Thirty Years' War finally ended in 1648, while in France the "Sun King" Louis XIV ascended the throne at age five in 1643 and began to rule in his own right in 1661; he remained the dominant political figure of the era until his death in 1715, after a record-breaking reign of seventy-two years. Gathering the French nobility into the gilded cage of his lavish palace complex at Versailles, Louis proclaimed absolute authority granted by divine right, asserting "L'état, c'est moi"—"I am the state." The Mughal Empire reached its height under a similarly absolutist monarch, Aurangzeb (r. 1685–1707), who extended his realm to include most of India and what is now Pakistan. Yet neither monarch bequeathed a stable situation to his successors: Louis's unrestrained spending on frequent wars and on lavish palaces left France's treasuries depleted on his death, while his insistence on Catholicism as the sole permitted religion led to the departure of tens of thousands of French Protestants, many of them enterprising small manufacturers and artisans, seriously weakening the French economy. Growing popular discontent in France would lead to revolution by the end of the century. In India, Aurangzeb tried to unify his widened realm by making Islam the state religion and repressing the practice of Hinduism; his restless Hindu subjects repeatedly revolted and his sons fought each other, and the empire declined after his death.

The splendor of courts like Versailles in France, Saint Petersburg in Russia, and Delhi in India was underwritten by the growing economic contributions of traders and manufacturers, who provided new sources of wealth beyond the traditional base of peasant agriculture. A new "middle class" was growing up between the aristocracy and the peasantry, often congregating in towns and known on the Continent as Bürger or bourgeois (from the German and French terms for "town"). This volume begins with an extensive selection of readings on courts and commoners, giving a range of the literature that probed these new relations, from China and Japan to India and the

1

Ottoman Empire. The section that follows on the Enlightenment begins with the great bourgeois court playwright Molière and continues with a Perspectives section on court culture and female authorship.

The new bourgeoisie often favored self-government and flexibility over aristocratic authority, and increasingly proposed that laws, not monarchs, should have the final say. As the philosopher John Locke wrote in 1690, "Wherever Law ends, Tyranny begins." Or as an antiroyal rebel, Richard Rumbold, declared in 1685, as he stood on the scaffold to be executed: "I never could believe that Providence had sent a few men into the world, ready booted and spurred to ride, and millions ready saddled and bridled to be ridden." The literature of the period often explores the new possibilities for individual liberty— and the dangers of unrestrained self-indulgence symbolized by the figure of the "libertine," the focus of the Perspectives section included here on liberty and libertines.

COMMERCE AND INDUSTRY

Some small countries, like Holland and Switzerland, asserted their freedom by abolishing monarchy altogether and became republics. In England, the unpopular monarch Charles I was beheaded by Puritan rebels in 1649; though the monarchy was restored in 1660, Charles II and his successors were increasingly subject to parliamentary control. Elsewhere, monarchs like Russia's Peter the Great prospered by working closely with the bourgeoisie to modernize agriculture and establish the rudiments of modern industry. In Persia, the ruler Karim Khan developed his capital of Shiraz as a commercial center accessible to the Persian Gulf and trade with India. A driving force in the changing expectations of middle-class subjects, in fact, was the opening up of the world through rapidly expanding travel and trade. Though the Dutch East India Company maintained only a tenuous foothold in Japan, it assumed greater and greater influence in Indonesia, while French and British trading companies jostled for influence in India. In 1661 the British East India Company took control of Bombay, and in 1690 the company founded the major city of Calcutta. Gradually the East India Company became the de facto ruler of much of the Indian subcontinent. Trade steadily increased as well between Europe and the Americas, which now provided not only gold and silver but also a growing bulk of goods like sugar, cotton, hides, and timber. England and other nations developed a further trade, in human bodies, to support these enterprises: the "triangular trade" of slaves from Africa to the Americas and of slave-produced sugar and cotton from the Americas to Europe, which in turn manufactured finished goods to sell back to Africa and the Americas.

This was a new sort of empire: developed and maintained less by governments and guns than by companies and invoices.

This was a new sort of empire: developed and maintained less by governments and guns than by companies and invoices. As the Scottish economic theorist Adam Smith said in his 1776 book *The Wealth of Nations,* "To found a great empire for the sole purpose of raising up a people of customers, may at first sight appear a project fit only for a nation of shopkeepers. It is, however, a project altogether unfit for a nation of shopkeepers; but extremely fit for a nation whose Government is influenced by shopkeepers." Elsewhere in the world too, there was a growing sense of social life as a changing and changeable reality, subject to personal initiative more than to inherited status or direct divine intervention. As Ihara Saikaku said in his book *Japan's Eternal Storehouse,*

Heaven says nothing, and the whole earth grows rich beneath its silent rule. Men, too, are touched by heaven's virtue; yet, in their greater part, they are creatures of deceit. They are born, it seems, with an emptiness of soul, and must take their qualities wholly from things without. To be born thus empty into this modern age, this mixture of good and ill, and yet to steer through life in an honest course to the splendors of success—this is a feat reserved for the paragons of our kind, a task beyond the nature of the normal man.

The writers of the era responded to these new circumstances, in realistic accounts of the new social mobility and in fictional or literal travel narratives as well. Voltaire's comic hero Candide ventures from a Europe torn by war to South America, searching for happiness and security in what his teacher Pangloss asserts is "the best of all possible worlds." The worst of all possible commercial worlds—that of the slave trade—provides the backdrop for Aphra Behn's dramatic fictional narrative *Oroonoko,* as well as for the real-life autobiography of Olaudah Equiano. His is one of many gripping travel accounts written in many parts of the world during this period. In the same Perspectives section on journeys in search of the self, the great Japanese poet and traveler Matsuo Bashō sees travel as the condition of life itself, shared even by the passing seasons: "The months and days are the travelers of eternity. The years that come and go are also voyagers. . . . I too for years past have been stirred by the sight of a solitary cloud drifting with the wind to ceaseless thoughts of roaming."

SCIENCE AND TECHNOLOGY

The growth of commerce and industry was fed by rapid developments in science and technology, and commerce fed the advance of science in turn. The scientific revolution inaugurated during the early modern period took on new force in the late seventeenth century. In a period of three years in the 1660s, for example, England's Isaac Newton made three major discoveries: he developed the theory of gravitation; determined that white light is composed of colored rays; and invented calculus. Far from resting on his laurels, Newton continued to press for new understanding. As he famously remarked,

> *The growth of commerce and industry was fed by rapid developments in science and technology, and commerce fed the advance of science in turn.*

I do not know what I may appear to the world; but to myself I seem to have been only like a boy playing on the seashore, and diverting myself in now and then finding a smoother pebble or a prettier shell than ordinary, whilst the great ocean of truth lay all undiscovered before me.

Major practical advances in technology followed from the new research. The spinning and weaving of cloth, formerly laborious handwork, became mechanized with the invention of the flying shuttle in 1733 and the spinning jenny in 1764. The first modern factories were built, and their output grew enormously with the invention of the steam engine, perfected by James Watt in 1769. Steam power vastly multiplied the work that an individual could accomplish, and humanity seemed poised to rise above its traditional limits—literally so, when the Montgolfier brothers launched the first hot air balloon in France in 1783.

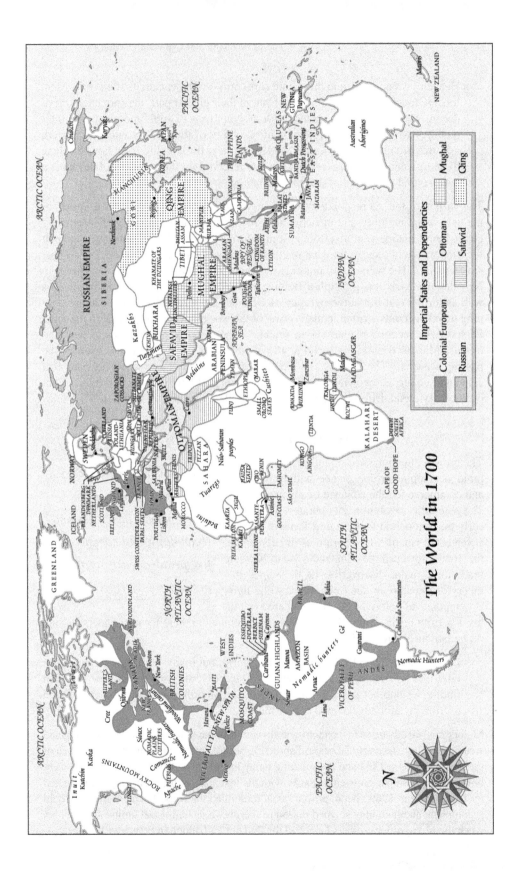

The World in 1700

The rapidly increasing grasp of the laws of nature prompted major shifts in religious understanding. Many scientists—Newton included—saw their discoveries as illuminating God's sublime handiwork; as one early scientist, Sir Thomas Pope Blount, asserted in 1693, "Every flower of the field, every fiber of a plant, every particle of an insect, carries with it the impress of its Maker, and can—if duly considered—read us lectures of ethics or divinity." Others took a more skeptical view, and increasingly began to view religious beliefs as projections of human needs and understandings: as the French philosopher Montesquieu put it in 1721, "If triangles had a god, he would have three sides."

Many scientists—Newton included—saw their discoveries as illuminating God's sublime handiwork.

Increasingly the ideals of science and of rational planning came to be applied to the social world as well as to the world of nature. In Europe, this broad movement became known as "the Enlightenment," a process that will be discussed in detail in the introduction to "The Age of the Enlightenment" later in this volume. By the late eighteenth century, Enlightenment ideas of political, economic, and intellectual liberty stimulated and shaped the revolutionary movements that led to America's declaration of independence from England in 1776 and the French Revolution of 1789. The outlines of our modern world were beginning to emerge, along with the increasingly visible figure of the modern artist as a skeptical observer, independent of royal patronage or received ideas, even of received literary forms. Alexander Pope used the mock-epic to satirize English court culture, and Cao Xueqin transformed popular prose romance into a vivid portrait of an aristocratic Chinese culture in decay. Enlightenment ideals themselves came under scrutiny: Jonathan Swift sent his imaginary traveler Gulliver to encounter strange satiric worlds like the ideal order of the philosopher-horses the Houyhnhnms, while Lady Mary Wortley Montagu used sharply pointed couplets to mock Swift's own mockery of women. Everywhere the period's writers vanquished their enemies in print if not in fact: as Voltaire wrote to a friend, late in life: "I have never made but one prayer to God, a very short one: 'O Lord, make my enemies ridiculous.' And God granted it."

THE SEVENTEENTH AND EIGHTEENTH CENTURIES

YEAR	THE WORLD	LITERATURE
1600		
	1603 Death of Elizabeth I of England, accession of James I	**1605, 1615** Cervantes, *Don Quixote*
	1605 Death of Akbar; Jahangir ascends Mughal throne	
	1607 British settlement of Virginia	
	1608–1648 Marquise de Rambouillet's "Blue Room," first important Parisian salon	
	1609 Tokugawa Shogunate founded in Japan	
1610		
		1616 Death of Shakespeare
	1618 Bohemian revolt against Habsburgs initiates Thirty Years' War	
	1619 First African slaves taken to Virginia	
1620		
	1620 English Pilgrims begin migration to New England	**1624** Babur, *Memoirs of Babur*
1630		
	1633 Tokugawa shoguns close Japan to foreigners	
	1634 First official meeting of the Académie Française	**1637** Maria de Zayas, *Amorous and Exemplary Novellas*
1640		
		1641 René Descartes, *Meditations on First Philosophy;* Banarasidas, *Half a Life*
	1642 English Civil War begins; Tasman discovers New Zealand and Tasmania	
	1643 Shah Jahan rules much of India; Taj Mahal completed	
	1644 Qing Dynasty begins in China (to 1912)	
	1648 The Fronde, civil war in France; Treaty of Westphalia ends Thirty Years' War	
	1649 Execution of Charles I of England, which becomes a republic under Oliver Cromwell and Parliament	
1650		
		1651 Thomas Hobbes, *Leviathan*
	1652 Dutch establish colony in South Africa	
	1653 Louis XIV returns to Paris from exile with his powerful minister Cardinal Mazarin, ending the Fronde rebellion	**1654–1660** Madeleine de Scudéry, *Clélie*
	1658 Oliver Cromwell dies	
1660		
	1660 Restoration of Charles II to the English throne; Royal Society founded; rise of Bambara kingdom on upper Niger River	**1660** Pierre Corneille, collected plays and discourses on the art of the theater
	1661 Louis XIV, aged 23, assumes the full government of France after the death of his protector Cardinal Mazarin and the arrest of his finance minister, Fouquet	
	1662 English Royal Society receives its charter from Charles II	

YEAR	THE WORLD	LITERATURE
	1663 Brazil becomes Portuguese Viceroyalty	
	1664 England seizes New Amsterdam from Dutch, changes name to New York	**1664** Molière, *Tartuffe*
	1665 Last "Great Plague" in England	**1665** Katherine Philips, *Poems;* George Warren, *An Impartial Description of Surinam*
	1666 Great Fire of London destroys the city, which is rebuilt on a neoclassical plan; Isaac Newton formulates the law of gravity	**1667** John Milton, *Paradise Lost*
		1668 Jean de la Fontaine, *Fables*
1670	**1670** Hudson's Bay Company incorporated in London to conduct trade in North America	
		1678 Comtesse de Lafayette, *The Princess of Clèves*
1680		**1680** Unauthorized posthumous edition of the Earl of Rochester's poems
	1683 Ottoman siege of Vienna fails after intervention of the Poles	
	1685 Death of Charles II of England, accession of James II; Louis XIV revokes the Edict of Nantes, ending tolerance for Protestants in France	
	1686 The English establish Calcutta as a factory and port settlement in Bengal	**1686** Ihara Saikaku, *Life of a Sensuous Woman*
	1688 "Glorious Revolution" in England: Mary, daughter of James II of England, and her spouse the Dutch Prince William of Orange oust her father in a bloodless coup	**1687** Isaac Newton, *Principia Mathematica*
		1688 Aphra Behn, *Oroonoko;* Ihara Saikaku, *Japan's Eternal Storehouse*
	1689 Treaty of Nerchinsk between Russian and Qing empires	
1690		**1690** John Locke, *Essay Concerning Human Understanding*
		1694 *Dictionary* of the French Academy
		1697 Charles Perrault, *Tales of Past Times, with Morals* (*Mother Goose Tales*); Pierre Bayle, *Historical and Critical Dictionary*
	1698 Omani Arabs capture Mombasa and Zanzibar in Africa	
1700	**1700** Charles II of Spain dies, leaving the kingdom to the French duke of Anjou	**1701** Mary Chudleigh, *The Ladies Defence*
	1702 War of Spanish Succession; Holy Roman Emperor Charles XII invades Poland; death of William III of England and accession of Queen Anne	
	1703 St. Petersburg founded by Czar Peter the Great, who has just visited Western Europe and vowed to modernize Russia	
	1704 English capture Gibraltar (in War of the Spanish Succession)	**1704–1717** Galland's French translation of *1001 Nights,* its first translation into a European language
	1707 United Kingdom links formerly separate kingdoms of England and Scotland; death of Aurangzeb in India, leading to the decline of the Mughal Empire; first pipe organ built by Gottfried Silbermann in Germany	
	1708 Robert Walpole, first to use title of Prime Minister, takes charge of the Whig government in London	

YEAR	THE WORLD	LITERATURE
	1709 Technique for making Chinese porcelain first replicated in Europe, Meissen factory established the following year; modern piano invented in Padua by Bartolomeo Cristofori	
1710		
		1710 Gottfried Wilhelm von Leibniz, *Theodicy*
	1712 German composer Georg Friedrich Händel moves permanently to London	1712, 1717 Alexander Pope, *The Rape of the Lock*
	1713 Treaty of Utrecht ends the War of the Spanish Succession for Britain and the Netherlands: France cedes most Canadian holdings to Britain; Pope Clement XI condemns the powerful Jansenist sect as heretical	1713 Anne Finch, Countess of Winchilsea, *Miscellaneous Poems on Several Occasions, Written by a Lady*
	1714 Death of Queen Anne and accession of George I of Great Britain; Tripoli becomes independent from the Ottoman Empire; France makes peace with Austria, Bavaria, and the Holy Roman Empire; Fahrenheit invents the mercury thermometer	
	1715 Death of Louis XIV; partisans of the exiled Stuart heir (Jacobites) rebel and are suppressed in Britain	
	1716 Ottoman Turks defeated by forces of the Holy Roman Empire at the Battle of Peterwardein	
	1717 France, Britain and Holland form the Triple Alliance; Walpole resigns as Prime Minister of Great Britain	1717–1724 Lady Mary Wortley Montagu, *The Turkish Embassy Letters*
	1718 Ottoman and Holy Roman Empires sign Treaty of Passarowitz; Triple Alliance becomes Quadruple Alliance when Holy Roman Emperor Charles VI joins it	1718, 1724 Comtesse de Lafayette, *The Countess of Tende* (published posthumously)
1720		
	1720 "South Sea Bubble" bursts in Britain, ruining many; Manchus seize control of Xinjiang	1721 Chikamatsu Mon'zaemon, *The Love Suicides at Amijima;* Baron de Montesquieu, *Persian Letters*
	1722 Dutch East India Company founded by Holy Roman Emperor Charles VI	
	1723 French Regency ends with majority of Louis XV; Ottoman Empire attacks Persia	
	1724 Treaty of Constantinople: Russian and Ottoman Empires partition Persia	1724 Eliza Haywood, *Fantomina*
		1725, 1754 Marquise de Sévigné, *Correspondence* (written 1648–1696)
		1726 Jonathan Swift, *Gulliver's Travels; Dictionary* of the Spanish Academy
	1727 Oxygen isolated by Stephen Hales in England	
	1728 Bering Strait first explored by Europeans	
		1729 First secular Turkish literature published in Constantinople
1730		
	1730 Ottoman Emperor Achmet III deposed in favor of Mahmud I	
	1731 John Hadley invents the sextant, improving navigation	
	1733 War of the Polish Succession	1732 Swift, "The Lady's Dressing Room"
		1733–1734 Alexander Pope, *An Essay on Man*

YEAR	THE WORLD	LITERATURE
		1734 Lady Mary Wortley Montagu, "The Reasons that Induced Doctor S. to Write a Poem called *The Lady's Dressing Room*"
		1735 Alexander Pope, *Epistle II: To a Lady (Of the Characters of Women)*
	1736 War between Ottoman, Holy Roman, and Russian empires	
	1738 War of the Polish Succession ends	
	1739 Nadir Shah of Persia sacks Delhi; slave rebellion in South Carolina	
1740		
	1740 Holy Roman Emperor Charles VI dies; Frederick II the Great crowned king of Prussia; invading Silesia, he begins the War of the Austrian Succession	**1740** Samuel Richardson, *Pamela*
	1742 Händel's *Messiah* first performed in Dublin	
	1746 Uprising in western Szechuan province, China; French conquer Madras, India	
	1747 Achmed Khan Abdali establishes kingdom of Afghanistan and invades India	**1747** Françoise de Graffigny, *Letters of a Peruvian Woman*
	1748 War of the Austrian Succession ends, confirming the taking of Silesia from Austria by Prussia, while Britain surrenders Asiento (Italy) to Spain	**1748** Baron de Montesquieu, *The Spirit of the Laws*
1750		
	1750s Emergence of Wahhabi movement in Arabia	**1750–1760** Cao Xueqin, *The Story of the Stone*
	1751 Chinese invade Tibet; Portugal and Spain divide their South American colonies by treaty	**1751** First volume of Diderot's *Encyclopedia* published
	1752 Benjamin Franklin proves that lightning is electricity; start of Konbuang Dynasty in Burma	
	1753 British Museum founded; Swedish Academy of Letters founded	
		1754 Etienne Bonnot de Condillac, *Treaty on the senses*
	1755 Lisbon earthquake kills 30,000–40,000 people	**1755** Samuel Johnson, *Dictionary of the English Language*
	1756 Seven Years' War begins when Frederick the Great of Prussia invades Saxony; English lose settlement at Calcutta to the nawab of Bengal, suffering great loss of life in the "Black Hole of Calcutta"	
	1757 British regain Calcutta; start of British imperial rule in India	
	1758 Invention of the threshing machine	
		1759 Voltaire, *Candide*
		1759–1767 Laurence Sterne, *Tristram Shandy*
1760		
	1760s Start of Industrial Revolution, inventions of Hargreaves's "spinning jenny" in 1765 and Watt's improved steam engine in 1769 help to mechanize the textile industry	
	1760 George III succeeds George II as King of Great Britain	
	1762 Catherine II the Great crowned Empress of Russia	**1762** Jean-Jacques Rousseau, *The Social Contract*

YEAR	THE WORLD	LITERATURE
	1763 Seven Years' War ends; France is awarded Guadeloupe, Martinique, and parts of Africa and India; Britain takes over Canada and Florida; Spain takes Cuba and the Philippines	**1763** Lady Mary Wortley Montagu, *The Turkish Embassy Letters* (written 1716–1718)
	1764 Jesuits expelled from France	**1764** Voltaire, *Philosophical Dictionary*; Horace Walpole, *The Castle of Otranto*
	1765 British East India Company wins control of Bengal and Bihar	
	1766 Britain occupies the Falkland Islands; hydrogen discovered by Henry Cavendish	
	1766–1769 Louis Antoine de Bougainville circumnavigates the world	
	1767 Jesuits expelled from Spain, Parma, and Sicily	
	1768–1771 Captain James Cook explores Australia and New Zealand	
1770		
	1770 The Boston Massacre; Spain seizes Falklands from Britain; famine in Bengal kills one-third of the population	**1771** Louis Antoine de Bougainville, *Voyage Around the World*
	1772 War between Russian and Ottoman Empires ends with First Partition of Poland; nitrogen discovered by Daniel Rutherford; Captain James Cook begins a three-year voyage of the South Seas	**1772** Gotthold Lessing, *Emilia Galotti*
	1773 Boston Tea Party; Jesuit order abolished by Pope Clement XIV	
	1774 Louis XVI succeeds Louis XV in France; Joseph Priestley isolates oxygen; Karl Scheele identifies chlorine; Nguyen Anh becomes emperor of Vietnam	**1774** Johann Wolfgang Goethe, *The Sufferings of Young Werther*
	1775 Start of American Revolution	**1775** Pierre de Beaumarchais, *The Barber of Seville*
	1776 Declaration of Independence adopted by the Continental Congress in Philadelphia; first submarine, David Bushnell's *Turtle;* the following year he invents the torpedo	
	1778 War of the Bavarian Succession begins; hypnotism first used by Friedrich Mesmer in Paris	**1778** Frances Burney, *Evelina*
	1779 Captain James Cook killed in Hawaii; First Kaffir War between Dutch Boer settlers and the Xhosa of South Africa	
1780		
	1780 Anti-Catholic "Gordon Riots" in England; waltz invented in Germany and Austria	
	1781 Continental Army defeats British at Yorktown, Virginia; Uranus, first planet discovered since antiquity, identified by William Herschel	**1781** First Polish encyclopedia; Sauda, *Satires*
	1782 Irish gain legislative independence	**1782** Pierre Choderlos de Laclos, *Les Liaisons dangereuses*; first volume of Jean-Jacques Rousseau's *Confessions*
	1783 Treaty of Versailles ends war between Britain, France, and Spain, recognizes American independence and extends borders of the United States as far as the Mississippi River and the Great Lakes; first demonstrations of the hot air balloon and the steamboat	

YEAR	THE WORLD	LITERATURE
	1784 Ottoman Empire cedes Crimea to Russians	**1784** Immanuel Kant, "An Answer to the Question: What Is Enlightenment?"
		1785 Charles Wilkins translates the *Bhagavad-Gita* into English (first translation of an important Sanskrit text into a European language); Ann Yearsley, *Poems, on Several Occasions*
	1786 Death of Frederick the Great of Prussia	**1786** Robert Burns, *Poems Chiefly in the Scottish Dialect*; Ann Yearsley, *Poems, on Various Subjects*
	1787 Constitution of the United States of America; British begin to settle freed slaves in Sierra Leone	**1787** Lorenzo Da Ponte and Wolfgang Amadeus Mozart, *Don Giovanni*
	1788 First British settlement in Australia	**1789** Olaudah Equiano, *Interesting Narrative of the Life of Olaudah Equiano*
	1789 Declaration of the Rights of Man and Citizen adopted by the French National Assembly; storming of the Bastille political prison in Paris; Antoine Lavoisier creates first table of elements; start of French Revolution	**1789–1792** Benedikte Naubert, *New German Folk Tales*
1790		
	1791 French National Assembly abolishes royal censorship; start of Haitian Revolution	
	1792 France declared a republic; Revolutionary Assembly legalizes divorce; Manchus invade Nepal	**1792** Mary Wollstonecraft, *A Vindication of the Rights of Woman*
	1793 Execution of Louis XVI of France; the Louvre palace becomes a public art gallery; France at war against Britain, Holland, Spain, Portugal, Tuscany, and the Holy Roman Empire; Second Kaffir War between Boer settlers and Xhosa of South Africa	
	1794 Fall of Robespierre ends French "Reign of Terror"; Qajar Dynasty founded in Persia (to 1925); Eli Whitney invents the cotton gin in the United States	**1794** Ann Radcliffe, *The Mysteries of Udolpho*
	1795 White Lotus Uprising in China; Mungo Park explores West Africa and River Niger	**1795** Anna Letitia Barbauld, "The Rights of Woman"; Marquis de Sade, *Philosophy in the Boudoir*
	1796 Death of Russian Empress Catherine the Great; Edward Jenner introduces smallpox vaccine; first exhibition of paintings by J. M.W. Turner	**1796** Denis Diderot, *Supplement to the Voyage of Bougainville* (written 1772)
	1798–1799 Napoleon's expedition to Egypt results in discovery of Rosetta Stone and naval defeat by British	**1798** William Wordsworth and Samuel Taylor Coleridge, *Lyrical Ballads*
	1799 War of the Second Coalition (Great Britain, Portugal, and Naples, with the Holy Roman, Russian, and Ottoman empires) against France, where the Directory Government is overthrown and Napoleon Bonaparte is named First Consul	

The Taj Mahal. Mughal Emperor Shah Jahan's monument to his wife, Mumtaz Mahal, constructed at Agra, India, in 1632–1643.

The World the Mughals Made

If we think of India as part of greater Eurasia, and not the sovereign state it has become in modern times, and remember that even before modernity this was a place of remarkable mobility, we may understand its history not as one of "invasions of foreigners" but of movements of peoples

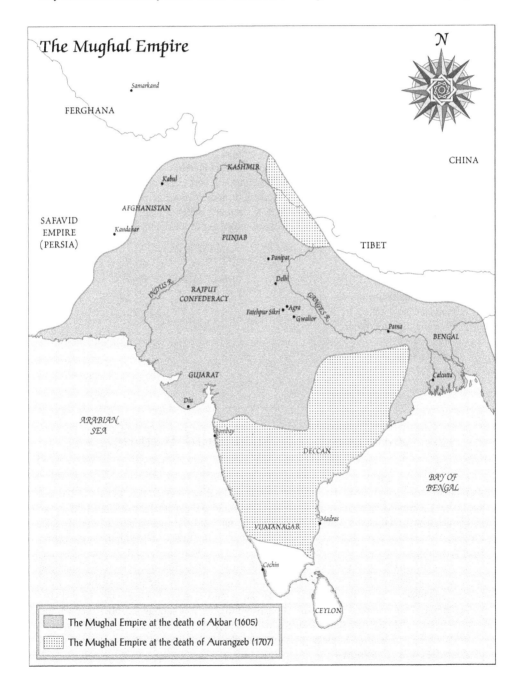

The Mughal Empire

- Samarkand
- FERGHANA
- CHINA
- KASHMIR
- Kabul
- AFGHANISTAN
- SAFAVID EMPIRE (PERSIA)
- Kandahar
- PUNJAB
- TIBET
- INDUS R.
- Panipat
- Delhi
- RAJPUT CONFEDERACY
- GANGES R.
- Fatehpur Sikri
- Agra
- Gwalior
- Patna
- BENGAL
- GUJARAT
- Calcutta
- Diu
- ARABIAN SEA
- Bombay
- DECCAN
- BAY OF BENGAL
- VIJAYANAGAR
- Madras
- Cochin
- CEYLON

The Mughal Empire at the death of Akbar (1605)

The Mughal Empire at the death of Aurangzeb (1707)

seeking new opportunities, while giving and taking cultural goods as they moved. Greeks and Persians, Kushans and Scythians—to say nothing of the Vedic *aryas* or Aryans themselves— were earlier peoples on the move through southern Eurasia. So were Muslim Arabs, from the seventh century on, and, from the eleventh, Central Asian Turks. Among the latter was a tribe of Turkicized Mongols of the Ferghana Valley (in today's Uzbekistan), descendents of Timur (Tamerlane, 1336–1405) and, more distantly, Genghis Khan. They spoke a Turki dialect called Chaghatay and had ostensibly converted to Islam in the fourteenth century. People to their west in Samarkand and Bukhara called them, somewhat disdainfully, "Mughals" (though their relationship to the Mongols was now a distant memory), the appellation adopted by European travelers in the seventeenth century, and from them by western historiography.

In the early sixteenth century, the Mughals under their leader Babur made their way to India, and built one of the most remarkable, if short-lived, empires in history. Over the period from 1526 to 1761 the Mughals not only extended their sway over the greater part of South Asia, bringing a kind of peace that allowed economy and society to flourish everywhere. They also stimulated a wide range of cultural interactions and transformations that were to enrich the Indian world in remarkable ways, in everything from architecture and miniature painting (see Color Plate 1 for a lively example) to cuisine (the *tandoor* and the *nan* bread cooked in it are Mughal gifts). Equally important if less well-known in the West is the magnificent literature the Mughals produced and patronized, first in the imperial language of Persian that was adopted in the late sixteenth century, and, from the early eighteenth century, in Urdu, a north Indian language closely related to Hindi but indebted to Persian for its script, some of its vocabulary, many of its genres, and much of its aesthetic. The selections that follow aim to suggest something of the rich variety of this literature.

PRONUNCIATIONS:
> *Akbar:* UHK-buhr
> *Babur:* BAH-boor
> *Banarasidas:* buh-NAHR-see-dahs
> *Humayun:* hoo-MA-yoon
> *Jahangir:* juh-HAHN-geer
> *nama:* NAH-muh
> *Nur Jahan:* NOOR juh-HAHN

⊶⊷ ⚖ ⊶⊷

Zahiruddin Muhammad Babur
1483–1530

Zahiruddin Muhammad Babur ascended the throne of Samarkand when he was twelve. Driven out by the Uzbeks, he made his way south to Afghanistan and eventually to India. At the time of his death in Kabul at the age of forty-seven, he had laid the foundations of the Mughal Empire. The *Baburnama* (Book or Memoirs of Babur) is the first autobiography in the entire Islamic world, and a work to be set beside Augustine and Rousseau—and Banarasidas—for its uncommon candor in the presentation of self. How vividly Babur's personality emerges from the small details (like his correcting the spelling mistakes in the letters of his son Humayun) and his catalog of likes and dislikes. He liked gardens with flowing water; he disliked India. "It is a strange country," he writes. "Compared to ours, it is another world . . . unpleasant and inharmonious India." He did not long remain there. But his descendents did. They gradually forgot Fergana, their old homeland, and the Chaghatay Turkish they once spoke, and made this "strange country" their own.

from The Memoirs of Babur[1]

I have not written all this to complain: I have simply written the truth. I do not intend by what I have written to compliment myself: I have simply set down exactly what happened. Since I have made it a point in this history to write the truth of every matter and to set down no more than the reality of every event, as a consequence I have reported every good and evil I have seen of father and brother and set down the actuality of every fault and virtue of relative and stranger. May the reader excuse me; may the listener take me not to task.

HINDUSTAN

Hindustan lies in the first, second, and third climes, with none of it in the fourth clime. It is a strange country. Compared to ours, it is another world. Its mountains, rivers, forests, and wildernesses, its villages and provinces, animals and plants, peoples and languages, even its rain and winds are altogether different. Even if the Kabul[2] dependencies that have warm climates bear a resemblance to Hindustan in some aspects, in others they do not. Once you cross the Indus, the land, water, trees, stones, people, tribes, manners, and customs are all of the Hindustani fashion. The mountain range in the north that has been mentioned—as soon as the Indus is crossed these mountains are dependent provinces to Kashmir. Although as of this date the provinces in this range, like Pakhli and Shahmang, mostly are not obedient to Kashmir, nonetheless they used to be inside Kashmir. Once past Kashmir, there are innumerable peoples, tribes, districts, and provinces in this range. There are people continuously in these mountains all the way to Bengal, even to the ocean. * * *

The cities and provinces of Hindustan are all unpleasant. All cities, all locales are alike. The gardens have no walls, and most places are flat as boards.

On the banks of some large rivers and riverbeds, due to the monsoon rains, are gullies that prevent passage. In some places in the plains are forests of thorny trees in which the people of those districts hole up and obstinately refuse to pay tribute. In Hindustan there is little running water aside from the great rivers. Occasionally in some places there are still waters. All the cities and provinces live from well or pond water, which is collected from the monsoon rains. In Hindustan the destruction and building of villages and hamlets, even of cities, can be accomplished in an instant. Such large cities in which people have lived for years, if they are going to be abandoned, can be left in a day, even half a day, so that no sign or trace remains. If they have a mind to build a city, there is no necessity for digging irrigation canals or building dams. Their crops are all unirrigated. There is no limit to the people. A group gets together, makes a pond, or digs a well. There is no making of houses or raising of walls. They simply make huts from the plentiful straw and innumerable trees, and instantly a village or city is born.

* * *

I always thought one of the chief faults of Hindustan was that there was no running water. Everywhere that was habitable it should be possible to construct waterwheels, create running water, and make planned, geometric spaces. A few days after coming to Agra, I crossed the Jumna with this plan in mind and scouted around for places to build gardens, but everywhere I looked was so unpleasant and desolate that

---

1. Translated by Wheeler M. Thackston.
2. Kabul (in today's Afghanistan) served as merely a base from which Babur undertook periodic raids into the subcontinent. Once he had vanquished the Lodi dynasty and taken over its capital Agra, the Kabul region was kept as a dependency of the emerging empire.

I crossed back in great disgust. Because the place was so ugly and disagreeable I abandoned my dream of making a *charbagh*.[3]

Although there was no really suitable place near Agra, there was nothing to do but work with the space we had. The foundation was the large well from which the water for the bathhouse came. Next, the patch of ground with tamarind trees and octagonal pond became the great pool and courtyard. Then came the pool in front of the stone building and the hall. After that came the private garden and its outbuildings, and after that the bathhouse. Thus, in unpleasant and inharmonious India, marvelously regular and geometric gardens were introduced. In every corner were beautiful plots, and in every plot were regularly laid out arrangements of roses and narcissus.

We suffered from three things in Hindustan. One was the heat, another the biting wind, and the third the dust. The bathhouse was a refuge from all three. Of course, a bathhouse has no dust or wind, and in the hot weather it is so cool that one almost feels chill. One chamber of the bath, the one in which the warm-water reservoir was, was finished completely in stone. The dado was of white stone; otherwise the floor and ceiling were of red stone from Bayana. Khalifa, Shaykh Zayn, Yunus Ali, and all who had acquired lands on the river also built geometric and beautifully planned gardens and ponds. As is done in Lahore and Dipalpur, they made running water with waterwheels. Since the people of India had never seen such planned or regular spaces, they nicknamed the side of the Jumna on which these structures stood, "Kabul."

Babur Encourages His Troops

During this same time, as has been mentioned before, great and small were suffering from trepidation and fear over past events. Manly words or courageous ideas were being heard from no one—neither from ministers who should have been speaking eloquently or from amirs who should have been devouring provinces. Neither their strategies nor their tactics were noble. During this campaign Khalifa performed several outstanding feats, and there was no shortcoming in his earnestness or seriousness in maintaining order. Finally, having realized such fears and seen such weakness, I formulated a plan. I invited all the *begs*[4] and warriors and said, "Begs and warriors,

> Whoever comes into the world is mortal;
> he who remains forever is God.

Whoever enters the assembly of matter will, in the end, quaff the cup of death; and every person who comes to the way station of life will, in the end, pass from the abode of sorrow that is this world. It is better to die with a good name than to live with a bad one.

> If I die with good repute, it is well.
> I must have a good name, for the body belongs to death.

God has allotted us the happiness and has given us the good fortune that those who die are martyrs and those who kill are holy warriors. All must swear by God's Word that they will not dream of turning their faces from this battle or leaving this contest and struggle while there is life left in their bodies."

Beg and liege man, great and small alike, all willingly took Korans in their hands and swore oaths to this effect. It was a really good plan, and it had favorable propagandistic effect on friend and foe.

---

3. Probably a garden constructed from a series of terraces with a central waterway (literally a four-sided garden).

4. Mughal nobility (pronounced *bayg*).

Babur Takes the Pledge of Temperance

On Monday the twenty-third of Jumada 1 [February 25], I mounted for a tour. During my excursion it occurred to me that the thought of repenting from drinking had long been on my mind, and that my heart had continually been clouded by committing this illegal act. I said, "O soul,

> How long will you taste of sin? Temperance is not unpalatable. Have a taste! / How long will you be polluted by sin? How long will you stay comfortable in deprivation? / How long will you follow your lusts? How long will you waste your life? / When you march intent upon raiding the infidels you see your own death before you. / You know that he who is resolved to die will attain this state: / He throws off all these forbidden things from himself and cleanses himself of all sin! / I rid myself of this transgression and repented of wine drinking. / Gold and silver vessels and goblets, all the implements of the assembly / I had brought and broke them all. Abandoning wine, I gave my heart rest.

The broken pieces of the gold and silver vessels and implements were distributed among the deserving and the poor. The one who joined me in my repentance was Asas.[5] He had also joined me in letting our beards grow.[6] That night and the next morning nearly three hundred begs and ichkis [retainers], soldiers and civilians, repented. All the wine on hand was poured out, and into the wine Baba Dost[7] had brought we ordered salt put to turn it into vinegar. In the place where the wine was poured out a stepwell was dug, and I made an intention to have it finished in stone and a charitable building built next to it.

A Letter to Humayun

I wrote letters to Humayun and Kamran.[8] On Friday the fourteenth [November 27], when the letters and documents were ready, they were handed posthaste to Buyan Shaykh,[9] and he was given leave to depart. On Saturday the fifteenth he was escorted out of Agra.

This is a copy of the letter to Humayun:

> To Humayun. Thinking of you with much longing, I greet you. My words are these: On Monday the tenth of Rabiδ 1 [November 23], Begginä,[1] and Buyan Shaykh came. From your letters and reports we have become acquainted with the situation on both sides of the Hindu Kush.
>
> I give thanks for your son, a son to you and a beloved one to me.
>
> May God ever grant me and you such joy. Amen, O Lord of the Universe. You have named him "al-Aman."[2] May God bless him. However, although you yourself may write it thus, you have not considered the fact that frequently the common people will say either "Alaman" or "Ilaman." Moreover, names with "al-" are rare. Nonetheless, may God bless and keep both him and his name. For my sake and yours, may He keep al-Aman in fortune and happiness for many years, for many decades. God has ordered our affairs through his great grace and generosity. Such an event has not happened in how many decades?
>
> Item: On Tuesday the eleventh rumors were heard to the effect that the people of Balkh had summoned Qurban[3] and let him in.

---

5. Abdullah Asas was a close friend of the emperor's and his companion on many expeditions.
6. Vows would be taken before a campaign against infidels not to shave until victory was achieved.
7. A functionary in Babur's court.
8. Humayun Mirza and Kamran Mirza were two of Babur's five children. Humayun (1508–1556) later became the second emperor of the Mughal dynasty.
9. One of Humayun's servants who acted as a messenger between Babur and Humayun while they were separated.
1. The messenger who reported to Babur that Humayun's son Akbar (1542–1605) had been born.
2. "Peace, tranquility."
3. One of Babur's subjects.

Item: Kamran and the Kabul begs were ordered to go join you, and you all will proceed to Hissar or Samarkand or whichever direction is in our best interests. Through God's grace you will defeat your enemies, take their territory, and make your friends happy by overthrowing the foe. God willing, this is your time to risk your life and wield your sword. Do not fail to make the most of an opportunity that presents itself. Indolence and luxury do not suit kingship.

Conquest tolerates not inaction; the world is his who hastens most. When one is master one may rest from everything—except being king.

If, by God's grace and favor, Balkh and Hissar are won and subdued, let one of your men stay in Hissar and one of Kamran's in Balkh. If, by God's grace and favor, Samarkand is also subdued, you stay there yourself and, God willing, I will make Hissar royal demesne. If Kamran thinks Balkh is small, write me. God willing, I will make up the deficiency to him out of those other territories.

Item: You know that this rule has always been observed: six parts to you and five to Kamran. Always observe this rule yourself and do not break it.

Item: Conduct yourself well with your younger brother. Elder brothers need to have restraint. It is my hope that you will get along well with him, for he has grown up to be a religiously observant and fine young man. Let him also display no deficiency in homage and respect for you.

Item: I have a few complaints of you. For two or three years now none of your men has come. The man I sent returned exactly a year later. Is this proper?

Item: In your letters you keep talking about being alone. Solitude is a flaw in kingship, as has been said, "If you are fettered, resign yourself; but if you are a lone rider, your reins are free." There is no bondage like the bondage of kingship. In kingship it is improper to seek solitude.

Item: As I asked, you have written your letters, but you didn't read them over, for if you had had a mind to read them, you would have found that you could not. After reading them you certainly would have changed them. Although your writing can be read with difficulty, it is excessively obscure. Who has ever heard of prose designed to be an enigma? Your spelling is not bad, although it is not entirely correct either. You wrote *iltifat* with the wrong *t;* you wrote *qulinj* with a *y*. Your handwriting can be made out somehow or other, but with all these obscure words of yours the meaning is not entirely clear. Probably your laziness in writing letters is due to the fact that you try to make it too fancy. From now on write with uncomplicated, clear, and plain words. This will cause less difficulty both for you and for your reader.

Item: You are going on a great mission. Consult the experienced begs for strategy and tactics and do what they say. If you want to make me happy, stop sitting by yourself and avoiding people. Don't leave the decision to your brother and your begs, but invite them in twice a day, consult with them on whatever has come up, and make your decisions with the agreement of these supporters of yours.

Item: Khwaja Kalan[4] learned to be free and easy with me through constant contact. So should you mingle with others as I did with him. If, through God's grace, the situation over there should demand less attention and you do not need Kamran, station trustworthy men in Balkh and let him come to me.

Item: There were such conquests and victories while we were in Kabul that I consider Kabul my lucky piece and have made it royal demesne. Let none of you covet it.

Item: Conduct yourself well. Make friends with Sultan Ways.[5] Bring him in and act upon his opinion, for he is an experienced man. Keep the army disciplined and in training. Buyan Shaykh has had verbal instructions from me that he will communicate to you. With longing, peace. Written on Wednesday the thirteenth of Rabiδ 1 [November 26].

---

4. An important Mughal noble who served Babur, Humayun, and also the young Akbar. He died fighting for the Mughals in Afghanistan.

5. The ruler of Swat (one of the dependencies of Kabul), who previously allied himself with Babur against Afghan forces.

┅ ⊫ ◈ ⊐┅ ┅

Jahangir
1569–1627

India was truly home for the fourth Mughal emperor, Jahangir. He was the son of Akbar and a Rajasthani princess, and was fluent in Hindi, though he composed his autobiography in Persian. His *Book* or memoir (covering his life from 1605 to 1624) may not have the literary excellence of that of his great-grandfather Babur, but the remarkable character of the man who wrote it comes through just as vividly. And this is a character strangely contemporary, even familiar, to us, in his struggle with substance abuse (opium and wine), his quest for knowledge from spiritual teachers regardless of whether they were Muslim or Hindu (he preferred their company to that of kings), his childlike fascination with the natural world (and especially exotic things like pineapples, zebras, and American turkeys), and his passion for art, even to the point of sketching a friend, a drug-addict, as he lay dying before him ("It was so strange I ordered the artists to draw his likeness"). For his obsessions and flaws, and for his everyday involvement with the minutiae of the world around him, like his miscalculated advice to a lovesick blacksmith who sought audience with him, the "Grasper of the World"—the meaning of Jahangir, his accession name—comes across as human, all too human.

from The Memoirs of Jahangir[1]

ACCESSION TO THE FIRST NAWROZ[2]

By God's boundless mercy, one sidereal hour had elapsed of Thursday the twentieth of Jumada II A.H. 1014 [23 October 1605] when I ascended the throne of the sultanate in the capital Agra at the age of thirty-eight.

Until my father[3] was twenty-eight years old, none of his children had survived and he was always soliciting dervishes and hermits (who have spiritual proximity to the divine court) for the survival of a child. Since the great Khwaja Mu'inuddin Chishti was the fountainhead of most of the saints of India, it occurred to my father that in order to attain his wish he should resort to the khwaja's blessed threshold, and therefore he decided that if God would grant him a son he would travel from Agra to his blessed tomb, a distance of one hundred forty kos, on foot in thanksgiving.[4]

DATE OF BIRTH

In the year 977, on Wednesday the seventeenth of Rabi' 1 [30 August 1569], at seven *gharis*,[5] with the ascendant in the twenty-fourth degree of Libra, God brought me forth into existence from the recesses of the unseen.

HIS HOLINESS SHAYKH SALIM

During the days when my exalted father was seeking a son, an ecstatic dervish named Shaykh Salim, who had traversed many stages of life, lived on a mountain next to Sikri, a

---

1. Translated by Wheeler M. Thackston.
2. This refers to the period between Jahangir's accession to the throne and the first Persian New Year day (*nawroz*) that happened during his reign.
3. Jalaluddin Muhammad Akbar (1542–1605), the third emperor of the Mughal dynasty.
4. The tomb of the medieval spiritual master and founder of a Sufi order, Khwaja Mu'inuddin Chishti, is

located in Ajmer, Rajasthan. The Chishtis were respected for their austerity and aloofness from secular power. Akbar set the tone of tolerance and pluralism for his regime by identifying himself with the Chishtis over the more orthodox Naqshbandi order with which his family had been long associated.
5. One-eighth part of a watch (a day consisted of eight watches of three hours).

dependency of Agra. The people in the vicinity believed in the shaykh implicitly. Because my father was a devotee of dervishes, he visited this one too. One day while Shaykh Salim was in a trance, my father asked him, "How many sons will I have?"

"He who bestows without obligation will grant you three sons," he replied.

"I vow to turn my first son over to you for training and attention," my father said, "and to put him under the protection and guardianship of your compassion and kindness."

The shaykh accepted and said, "May he be blessed. We have named him after ourself."

PLACE OF BIRTH

When my mother was near the time of delivery, she was sent to the shaykh's house so that my birth might take place there. After my birth I was named Sultan Salim, although I never heard my father, either drunk or sober, call me Sultan Salim or Muhammad Salim. He always called me "Shaykhu Baba."[6]

FATEHPUR-SIKRI

My exalted father considered the village of Sikri, my birth place, auspicious and made it his capital. For fourteen or fifteen years those mountains and jungles filled with wild beasts became a city replete with buildings, gardens, pleasure spots, and delightful places. After the conquest of Gujarat it was named Fatehpur.[7]

DESIGNATION OF NAME AND HONORIFIC

When I became emperor it occurred to me that I should change my name lest it be confused with the caesars of Anatolia.[8] An inspiration from the beyond suggested to me that the labor of emperors is world domination (*jahangiri*) so I named myself Jahangir and made my honorific Nuruddin [light of religion] because my accession occurred at the time of the rising of the majestic greater luminary, at a time when the world was being illuminated.

While a prince I heard from the sages of India that when the time of Jalaluddin Muhammad Akbar Padishah's rule was over, one named Nuruddin would succeed to the rule. This had also remained in my mind, and therefore I named myself Nuruddin Muhammad Jahangir.

JAHANGIR'S DRINKING HABITS

I myself did not drink until the age of eighteen, except during my infancy, when two or three times my mother and nurses asked my exalted father for liquor to treat infantile complaints and gave me a tola[9] of it mixed with rose water and water as cough medicine. Then, when my exalted father's entourage was camped to deal with the Yusufzai Afghans[1] in the Attock fortress on the banks of the Nilab River, one day I mounted to go hunting. Since I overdid it and got exhausted, a wonderful gunner named Ustad Shah-Quli, the chief of my uncle Mirza Muhammad-Hakim's gunners,

---

6. "Dear little shaykh."
7. "Fatehpur" means "City of Victory." Akbar had defeated all resistance to the Mughal regime and was declared the sovereign of Gujarat in 1572.
8. The 16th-century Ottoman Sultans Selim I and Selim II.

9. A measure equal to about 13 grams.
1. Pacification campaigns directed against these and other rebels were undertaken after Akbar transferred his capital to Lahore, Panjab, in 1585.

said to me, "If you drink a beaker of wine, it will relieve the exhaustion." Since I was young and my nature was inclined to do these things, I ordered Mahmud the water-carrier to go to Hakim Ali's house and bring some alcoholic syrup. The physician sent a phial and a half of yellow-colored, sweet-tasting wine in a small bottle. I drank it and liked the feeling I got.

After that I started drinking wine, increasing it day by day until I no longer got a kick out of grape wine and started drinking liquor. Little by little, over nine years, it increased to twenty phials of double-distilled spirits, fourteen during the day and rest at night. By weight that much is six Hindustani seers, which is equivalent to one and a half Iranian maunds.[2] During those days my only food was the equivalent of one meal with bread and radishes. In this state no one had the power to stop me. Things got so bad that in my hangovers my hands shook and trembled so badly I couldn't drink myself but had to have others help me. Finally I summoned Hakim Humam, Hakim Abu'l-Fath's brother and one of my exalted father's confidants, and informed him of my condition. In perfect sincerity and compassion he said, with no beating around the bush, "Highness, the way you're drinking, in another six months—God forbid—things will be so bad it will be beyond remedy." Since his words were spoken in benevolence, and life is precious, it made a great impression on me.

From that date I began to decrease the amount and started taking philonium, increasing it by the amount I decreased the wine. Then I ordered the spirits mixed with grape wine, two parts wine to one part spirits, and I kept decreasing the amount I drank every day. Over a period of seven years I got it down to six phials, the weight of a phial being seventeen and three-quarters mithcals. I have now been drinking like this for fifteen years without increase or decrease. I only drink at night, but not on Thursday, the day of my accession, or on Friday eve, a blessed night of the week. Out of these two considerations I drink at the end of the day because I don't like to let the night go by in negligence without rendering thanks to the True Benefactor. On Thursdays and Sundays I don't eat meat—Thursday because it is the day of my accession, and Sunday, my exalted father's birthday, because he venerated it greatly.

After a while I substituted opium for the philonium. Now that I am forty-six years and four months old by solar reckoning, or forty-seven years and nine months by lunar reckoning, I have eight surkhs of opium after the elapse of five *gharis* of the day and six surkhs after the first watch of the night.

A VISIT TO THE HERMIT JADRUP

It had been repeatedly heard that near the town of Ujjain an ascetic sanyasi[3] named Jadrup Ashram had been living for several years in an out-of-the-way spot in the country far from civilization, where he worshiped the true deity. I very much desired to meet him and had wanted to summon him and see him while I was in Agra, but in view of the trouble it would have caused him I didn't do it. Now that we were in the vicinity, I got out of the boat and went an eighth of a kos on foot to visit him.

The place he had chosen for his abode was a pit dug out in the middle of a hill. The entrance was shaped like a *mihrab*,[4] one ell tall and ten *girihs* in width.[5] The distance from the entrance to the hole in which he sat was two ells five *girihs* long, eleven and a quarter *girihs* wide, and one ell three *girihs* high from the ground to the

2. About ten pounds.
3. Renouncer.

4. An archway, often marking the principal place of a mosque.
5. An ell is about a yard; a girih is about two inches.

roof. The hole that gave entrance to his sitting place was five and a half *girihs* tall and three and a half *girihs* wide. A skinny person would have great difficulty getting in. The length and width of the pit were the same. He had neither mat nor straw strewn underfoot as other dervishes do. He spends his time alone in that dark, narrow hole. In winter and cold weather, although he is absolutely naked and has no clothing except a piece of rag with which he covers himself in front and behind, he never lights a fire. As Mulla Rumi[6] says, speaking in the idiom of dervishes: "Our clothing is the heat of the sun by day, and moonlight is our pillow and quilt by night."

Twice a day he goes to make ablutions in the river nearby, and once a day he goes into Ujjain, enters the houses of only three Brahmins out of the seven married persons with children he has chosen and in whose asceticism and contentment he has confidence, takes in his hand like a beggar five morsels of food they have prepared for themselves, and swallows them without chewing lest he derive any enjoyment from the taste—this provided that no calamity has occurred in any of the three houses, no birth has taken place, and there be no menstruating women. This is how he lives.

He desires no intercourse with people, but since he has acquired a great reputation, people go to see him. He is not devoid of learning and has studied well the science of the Vedanta,[7] which is the science of Sufism.

I held conversation with him for six gharis, and he had such good things to say that he made a great impression on me. He also liked my company. When my exalted father had conquered the fortress of Asir and the province of Khandesh[8] and was on his way back to Agra, he also paid him a visit in this very place and often mentioned it with fondness.

ANOTHER VISIT TO JADRUP

On previous pages something has been written about Gosain[9] Jadrup, who lived as a hermit in Ujjain. Recently he had moved from Ujjain to Mathura, one of the major temple sites of the Hindus, and worshiped the true deity on the banks of the Jumna River. Since I was anxious to talk to him, I went to see him and spent a long time alone with him without interruption. He is truly a great resource, and one can enjoy and derive much benefit from sitting with him.

On Saturday the tenth [October 23] the scouts reported a lion in the vicinity that was harassing *ryots*[1] and travelers. I immediately ordered lots of elephants taken out and the forest closely surrounded. Toward the end of the day I rode out along with the ladies of the harem. Since I had sworn not to harm a living creature with my own hand, I told Nur Jahan Begam[2] to fire the musket. The elephant sensed the lion and wouldn't keep still, and to shoot a gun from on top of an elephant without missing is a very difficult task. (After me, Mirza Rustam[3] has no equal in marksmanship, but it has often happened that he has shot three or four times from atop an elephant and still missed.) Nur Jahan Begam hit it so well on the first shot that it died of the wound.

On Monday the twelfth [October 25] I had another overwhelming desire to see Gosain Jadrup. I went to his hut without any ceremony and had a discussion with

---

6. Jalaluddin Rumi (1207–1273), one of the most prominent Sufi poets.
7. A Hindu monistic philosophy based on the Upanishads. That Jahangir equates this with Sufism, an Islamic tradition, is striking.
8. In the Deccan region of south central India.
9. Title for a respected Hindu spiritual master.

1. Peasants.
2. Nur Jahan ("Light of the World"), born Mehrunissa, was the young widow of a Mughal officer when Jahangir married her in 1611. She exerted great influence over the emperor and the royal court in general. Begam is a lady of noble rank.
3. One of Jahangir's favorite courtiers (d. 1641).

him. Lofty things were spoken of. God has bestowed upon him a rare ability and given him a fine understanding, elevated mind, and quick comprehension together with knowledge. He has freed his heart from attachment to material things and turned his back on the world and everything in it, seated in a corner by himself in need of no one and nothing. Of worldly goods he has only a half a yard of old cotton to cover his private parts and a piece of pottery with which to take a sip of water. Winter, summer, and monsoon, he lives naked, head and feet bare, and has taken up residence in a hole in which it is extremely difficult to fit, with a passage so narrow a nursing babe would have trouble getting through. The following few lines by Hakim Sana'i are appropriate to his condition: "Luqman's cell was small and narrow to boot, / Like the throat of a pipe, or the breast of a lute. / A foolish one said to the grand old man— / 'What house is this—three feet and six span?' / With tears and emotion the sage made reply— / 'Ample for him whose task is to die.'"

On Wednesday the fourteenth [October 27] I went off again to meet Gosain Jadrup and bid him farewell. Without exaggeration, it was hard for me to part from him.

On Thursday the fifteenth [October 28] we marched and camped opposite Bindraban.[4] Here my son Shah Parvez was given leave to depart for Allahabad and his *jagir* estates.[5] I had desired that he should accompany me on this trip, but since he was already showing signs of distress, I had no choice but to let him go. He was given a topchaq horse, a mottled, striated girth dagger, a personal sword, and a personal shield. I hope he will come to see me again soon and in good health.

MUQUARRAB KHAN BRINGS RARITIES FROM GOA

On the sixteenth of Farvardin [March 25], Muqarrab Khan, one of the most important and long-serving Jahangirid servants, who had been promoted to the rank of 3000/2000, arrived from the port of Cambay to pay homage. I had ordered him to go to the port of Goa on several items of business and see the vice-rei, the governor of Goa, and to purchase any rarities he could get hold of there for the royal treasury. As ordered, he went to Goa with all preparedness and stayed there a while. Without consideration for cost, he paid any price the Franks asked for whatever rarities he could locate. When he returned from there to court, he presented the rarities he had brought for my inspection several times. He had every sort of thing and object. He had brought several very strange and unusual animals I had not seen before. No one even knew what their names were. Although His Majesty Firdaws-Makani [Babur] wrote in his memoirs of the shapes and forms of some animals, apparently he did not order the artists to depict them. Since these animals looked so extremely strange to me, I both wrote of them and ordered the artists to draw their likenesses in the *Jahangirnama* so that the astonishment one has at hearing of them would increase by seeing them.

One of the animals was larger in body than a peahen and significantly smaller than a peacock. Sometimes when it displays itself during mating it spreads its tail and its other feathers like a peacock and dances. Its beak and legs are like a rooster's. Its head, neck, and wattle constantly change color. When it is mating they are as red as can be—you'd think it had all been set with coral. After a while these same places become white and look like cotton. Sometimes they look turquoise. It keeps changing color like a chameleon. The piece of flesh it has on its head resembles a cock's comb. The strange part about it is that when it is mating, the piece of flesh hangs down a

---

4. Vrindavan, near the city of Mathura, a region associated with the Hindu deity Krishna.

5. Estates whose tax revenue was granted to an individual by the emperor as a reward for service.

span from its head like an elephant's trunk, but then when it pulls it up it stands erect a distance of two fingers like a rhinoceros' horn. The area around its eyes is always turquoise-colored and never changes. Its feathers appear to be of different colors, unlike a peacock's feathers. * * *

THE DEATH OF INAYAT KHAN

On this date news came of the death of Inayat Khan. He was one of my closest servants and subjects. In addition to eating opium he also drank wine when he had the chance. Little by little he became obsessed with wine, and since he had a weak frame, he drank more than his body could tolerate and was afflicted with diarrhea. While so weakened he was overcome two or three times by something like epileptic fits. By my order Hakim Rukna treated him, but no matter what he did it was to no avail. In addition, Inayat Khan developed a ravenous appetite, and although the doctor insisted that he not eat more than once a day, he couldn't restrain himself and raged like a madman. Finally he developed cachexia and dropsy and grew terribly thin and weak.

Several days prior to this he requested that he be taken ahead to Agra. I ordered him brought to me to be given leave to depart. He was put in a palanquin and brought. He looked incredibly weak and thin. "Skin stretched over bone." Even his bones had begun to disintegrate. Whereas painters employ great exaggeration when they depict skinny people, nothing remotely resembling him had ever been seen. Good God! how can a human being remain alive in this shape? The following two lines of poetry are appropriate to the situation: "If my shadow doesn't hold my leg, I won't be able to stand until Doomsday. / My sigh sees my heart so weak that it rests a while on my lip."

It was so strange I ordered the artists to draw his likeness. At any rate, I found him so changed that I said, "At this time you mustn't draw a single breath without remembrance of God, and don't despair of His graciousness. If death grants you quarter, it should be regarded as a reprieve and means for atonement. If your term of life is up, every breath taken with remembrance of Him is a golden opportunity. Do not occupy your mind or worry about those you leave behind, for with us the slightest claim through service is much." Since his distress had been reported to me, I gave him a thousand rupees for traveling expenses and gave him leave to depart. He died the second day.

HIS HOLINESS SHAYKH SALIM CHISHTI

On Thursday night, the eve of Friday the thirteenth [January 21], I went to the holy shrine of Shaykh Salim Chishti, a bit about whose good qualities was recorded in the introduction to this auspicious book, and there I recited the Fatiha.[6] Although producing miracles and supernatural occurrences is displeasing to those chosen of God's court—and in fact they consider it beneath their dignity and try to avoid it—occasionally they produce them involuntarily while in a trance or stupor in order to guide someone. One such event happened before I was born, when Shaykh Salim made His Majesty Arsh-Ashyani[7] hopeful of the birth of me and my two brothers.

Another happened one day when His Majesty Arsh-Ashyani asked Shaykh Salim, "How old are you, and when will you be translated to the abode of eternity?" In answer he said, "God—exalted be he—knows all mysteries and hidden things." After much insistence and persistence, he pointed to me and said, "When the prince, either by instruction of a teacher or someone else, memorizes something and speaks it aloud, this

---

6. The first chapter of the Qur'an, often recited at holy places.

7. A title of Akbar.

will be the sign of our demise." Of course, His Majesty commanded those who were in my service absolutely not to teach me to memorize anything either in prose or poetry.

Two years and seven months passed. One day one of the worthy women who was in the harem and always burned wild rue to keep away the evil eye—and because of this she had access to my quarters and was on the receiving end of my charitable contributions—found me alone. Unaware of the prediction, she taught me this line of poetry: "O God, open the bud of hope and show me a rose from the garden of eternity."

I went off to my master and recited the line for him. The master involuntarily leapt up from his place and ran to His Majesty Arsh-Ashyani to tell him of this event. As it happened, that very night traces of a fever appeared [in the shaykh]. The next day he sent someone to His Majesty to ask for Tan Sen Kalawant, an unrivaled singer. Tan Sen went to him and began to sing. After that he sent someone to summon His Majesty Arsh-Ashyani, and when His Majesty arrived, he said, "The time of death is here. I bid you farewell." Taking his turban from his head, he placed it on my head and said, "We have made Sultan Salim our successor and entrust him to God the protector and pre-server." His illness lasted a very, very long time, and it became more and more obvious that he was dying. Finally he achieved union with his real beloved.

A SELF-SACRIFICING LOVER

At this time it was reported that a blacksmith named Kalyan had fallen desperately in love with a woman from his own caste and was constantly following her around and acting love-crazed. Although she was a widow, the woman refused him absolutely, for the lovesick wretch's love had made no impression on her whatsoever. I summoned them both for an investigation. No matter how I tried to placate the woman and per-suade her to accept him, she refused. Then the blacksmith said, "If I knew for certain that you would give her to me, I'd throw myself off the top of the Shah Burj tower."

Just as a joke I said, "Never mind the Shah Burj. If your claim of love has any truth to it, you'll have to throw yourself off the roof of this building. Then I'll give her to you by command." These words were scarcely out of my mouth when he raced like a streak of lightning and threw himself down. As soon as he hit the ground blood be-gan to stream from his eyes and mouth.

I really regretted having spoken in jest and was dreadfully sorry. I ordered Asaf Khan to take him home and tend to him. However, since the cup of his life was full, he died of his injuries.

A lover who sacrifices himself at that threshold dies of ecstasy using fate as a pretext.

Mirza Muhammad Rafi "Sauda"
1713–1781

Like Persian, with which it shares many linguistic and cultural traits, Urdu is a cosmopolitan language of South Asia, spoken and written across the subcontinent (with local variations), principally but by no means exclusively among Muslims. Although the earlier history of the language and its literature is unclear, the eighteenth century witnessed an efflorescence of ex-quisite Urdu poetry, the epoch that marks the effective beginning of Urdu's literary history. This is a conservative literary culture, marked by master-pupil training, as well as public and often highly competitive recitation gatherings (*mushairas*). It is also a keenly intellectual culture, presupposing knowledge of Persian literature and a mastery of a very wide range of conventions and precedents. Yet one of the most remarkable writers of this era, Sauda, was anything but tradition-bound. Sauda wrote with extraordinary independence of mind, and little in the world around him, including the Mughal emperor himself, escaped his critical gaze or caustic wit. Sauda was once interviewed by the emperor: "How many poems do you compose in a day?" "Three or four couplets, if I am inspired." "I can compose four whole poems in the bathroom," said the king. "They smell like it," replied the poet.

PRONUNCIATION:
  Sauda: SAW-dah

from Satires[1]

[HOW TO EARN A LIVING IN HINDUSTAN]

Better to keep silent than try to answer such a question, for even the tongues of angels cannot do justice to the answer. There are many professions which you could adopt, but let us see what difficulties will beset you in each of them these days. You could buy a horse and offer yourself for service in some noble's army. But never in this world will you see your pay, and you will rarely have both sword and shield by you, for you must pawn one or the other to buy fodder for your horse; and unless the moneylender is kind to you, you or your wife must go hungry, for you will not get enough to feed you both. You could minister to the needs of the faithful in a mosque, but you would find asses tethered there and men young and old sitting there idle and unwilling to be disturbed. Let the muezzin give the call to prayer and they will stop his mouth, for no one cares for Islam these days ... You could become the courtier of some great man, but your life would not be worth living. If he does not feel like sleeping at night, you too must wake with him, though you are ready to drop, and until he feels inclined to dine, you may not, though you are faint with hunger and your belly is rumbling. Or you could become his physician; but if you did, your life would be passed in constant apprehension, for should the Navvab sneeze, he will glare at you as though you ought to have given him a sword and buckler to keep off the cold wind. You will live through torture as you watch him feed. He will stuff himself with sweet melon and cream and then fish, and then cow's tongue, and, with it all, fancy breads of all kinds; and if at any stage he feels the slightest pain in his stomach, then you, you ignorant fool, are to blame, though you were Bu Ali Sina[2] himself. Why not become a merchant then? But if you do, you must reckon with the possibility that the wares you buy in Ispahan[3] will not find a market in Hindustan, and you will have to take them as far afield as the Deccan.[4] You never know in the morning whether you will ever reach your destination for the day, and your evenings will be passed in anxious reckonings of gain and loss. When you take your wares to some great man, you will be astonished at the way he speaks to you, and an observer, noting the price you are compelled to accept, would conclude that you are suspected of selling stolen property. Moreover, you will not get your money right away, but must go to the great man's agent for it, and though you show him authorisation to pay, he will tell you that he has not got the

---

1. Translated by Ralph Russell and Khurshidul Islam.
2. A celebrated Iranian physician and philosopher (980–1037), known in Europe as Avicenna.

3. A major historic city in central Iran.
4. The southern region of the Indian subcontinent.

money to do so. So back you must go to his master, only to be told, "Take your goods back; my steward says they are too dear." But when you go for them, they are not to be found. So you lose both the goods and their price, and you must stand outside the great man's fortress hoping to waylay him as he comes out in his palanquin and lay your petition for redress before him. And do not think you can make a living from the land, for only if the rains are good can you survive, and you pass your days in dread of drought or floods . . . But perhaps you have thought of becoming a poet, for are not poets said to enjoy freedom from all care? You will find it is not so. No one is such a prey to worry as he. He cannot even concentrate on his Id[5] prayer, for he is trying all the time to compose an ode to his patron. No sooner is it rumoured that the noble lord has fertilised his lady's womb than he must rack his brains for a chronogram, ready for the birth of the child, and if she should miscarry, he must write such an elegy on the abortion that no one ever after will want to read those on Imam Husain.[6] If you think of becoming a teacher, bear this in mind, that men able to teach the greatest works of Persian literature today get paid no more than what will give them a cup of cheap lentils and two rounds of coarse bread to dine on. Calligraphers could once command great honours. But nobody appreciates their art these days, and even the greatest masters of the art must sit in the open street, soliciting work and selling their talents for a song. . . . Perhaps, then, in the end you will forsake all wordly professions and, taking no thought for the morrow, repose your trust in God. But do you know what will happen then? Your wife will think you a lazy good-for-nothing; your son will despise you; your daughter will think you have gone mad. And when your children begin to die of hunger, you must run after every great man's carriage and ask for the charity that your holiness deserves. And perhaps you may get a few coppers and a little chit saying, "This man merits your charity; he is a truly religious man and is learned in religious lore." In short, you will not find in Hindustan any means of earning a decent living. Peace and plenty have become empty words in this world. Some say that we shall know them in the next, but who can persuade himself that it is so? For my part, I think it only wishful thinking. Here, there is nothing but the struggle to live; there, nothing but the tumult of Judgement Day. Peace and plenty is an empty recollection: you will not find it either on earth or in heaven.

* * *

The ministers of the Empire have been summoned for consultation. See how they consult for the welfare of the state. The Imperial Paymaster is thinking up some scheme to stay at home doing nothing and still draw his pay, while the Chief Minister has his eyes on the silver knobs on the poles of the royal tent, and is calculating how much they will fetch in the market. They are all of them strangers to any sense of shame. They spend their time in gambling and only come when summoned. A lifetime of their counsel has resulted only in this, that men who once lived in well-built houses now inhabit mud huts. Yet each of them is in his own estimation a veritable paragon. If war comes they creep out of their fortresses just long enough to draw up an army which, you may depend on it, will turn and run from every battle, soldiers who quake with fear even when they see the barber take out his razor to shave them, horsemen who fall out of their beds at night even at the dream of a horse rearing under them.

---

5. The day that marks the end of the month-long fast of Ramadan.
6. The grandson of the Prophet Muhammad, who was martyred at Karbala, in present-day Iraq. The *marsiya*, or elegy, is one of the major forms of Urdu verse typically about the martyrdom of Imam Hussein.

The royal treasury is empty: nothing comes in from the crown lands; the state of the Office of Salaries defies description. Soldiers, clerks, all alike are without employment. Documents authorising payment to the bearer are so much waste paper: the pharmacist tears them up to wrap his medicines in. Men who once held jagirs or posts paid from the royal treasury are looking for jobs as village watchmen. Their sword and shield have long since gone to the pawnshop, and when they next come out, it will be with a beggar's staff and bowl. Words cannot describe how some of these once great ones live. Their wardrobe has ended up at the rag merchant's. If the cow's tongue which comes out of their oven could speak, it would say, "Before my master could buy me, he had to do without three meals and sell his sable robe for next to nothing." Ask the steward who has charge of his beasts and cattle; he will tell you that there is neither grain nor fodder for them to eat and their condition is pitiable. The noble lord boasts of his elephants, but go to look at them and you will find an old blind she and a one-eyed bull, both without any hope of being fed and resigned to the prospect of death. The servants' hunger has made them bold and insolent. The doorkeeper, who should protect his master's privacy, cares nothing for his duties, and all and sundry get access to him. The cooks are told to prepare *pulao,* but send up broth instead.[7] If the servant is told to straighten out the carpet on which his master is sitting, he will not wait for his master to rise, but will give a tug at the carpet there and then. But the truth is that servants and courtiers alike are weak from hunger and are not fit to perform even the lightest duties.

The *salatin*[8] are in such desperate straits that their clothes are all threadbare. They are ashamed to admit visitors to their homes and will slam the door in their faces rather than do so. Some are saying that if they are such a burden to maintain, it would be better to give them poison to take. In short, poverty has overtaken all, and a man may try his utmost for employment and still find none, unless he is prepared to emigrate as far afield as Ispahan or Istambul. * * *

How can I describe the desolation of Delhi? There is no house from where the jackal's cry cannot be heard. The mosques at evening are unlit and deserted, and only in one house in a hundred will you see a light burning. Its citizens do not possess even the essential cooking pots, and vermin crawl in the places where in former days men used to welcome the coming of spring with music and rejoicing. The lovely buildings which once made the famished man forget his hunger are in ruins now. In the once-beautiful gardens where the nightingale sang his love songs to the rose, the grass grows waist-high around the fallen pillars and ruined arches. In the villages round about, the young women no longer come to draw water at the wells and stand talking in the leafy shade of the trees. The villages are deserted, the trees themselves are gone, and the wells are full of corpses. Jahanabad,[9] you never deserved this terrible fate, you who were once vibrant with life and love and hope, like the heart of a young lover, you for whom men afloat upon the ocean of the world once set their course as to the promised shore, you from whose dust men came to gather pearls. Not even a lamp of clay now burns where once the chandelier blazed with light. Those who once lived in great mansions now eke out their lives among the ruins. Thousands of hearts once full of hope are sunk in despair. Women of noble birth, veiled from head to foot, stand in the streets carrying in their arms their little children, lovely as fresh flowers; they are ashamed to beg outright, and offer for sale rosaries made from the holy clay of Karbala.

---

7. Pulāo is a rich dish prepared from rice, meat, and spices; apparently the servants are stealing the food.

8. The many relatives of the imperial family.

9. Delhi.

But Sauda, still your voice, for your strength fails you now. Every heart is aflame with grief, every eye brimming with tears. There is nothing to be said but this: We are living in a special kind of age. So say no more.

Mir Muhammad Taqi "Mir"
1723–1810

Mir Muhammad Taqi "Mir" was revered as one of the greatest Urdu poets of his day; his complete works were the first by an Urdu poet to be typeset and printed, in the year after his death. He was a courtier of the Mughal elite during the melancholy decades of the waning of their power, when, as the contemporary quip had it, "the realm of the 'Emperor of the World' reaches from Delhi to Palam" (a suburb of today's Delhi). The selections of his poetry offered here are composed in the *ghazal* form, of which he was the acknowledged master. This is a refined, highly compact, and allusive genre, which shares many traits with the larger world of Indian love poetry. The full range of references and allusions will inevitably escape the nonspecialist reader, but the aesthetic and emotional power of his verse is unmistakable, and shows the capacity of good literature to slip the bonds of convention and context, however tightly they may be tied. In addition to his poetry, Mir left us an autobiography, the first of an Urdu poet (the work is written in Persian, since Urdu had not yet become a language of expository prose). The new kind of self-presentation and introspection of the early modern era in India, particularly evident in the autobiographies of Babur and Jahangir, as in Banarasidas (page 36), do not in fact continue to reverberate in Mir's life story, which is nonetheless fascinating in its obsessions. In addition to the notable account it provides of the misery of public life in Delhi and Lucknow, the portrait of private life with his father, an eccentric Sufi mystic (a dervish), offers precious materials for understanding the psychology of a brilliant and strange poet from a very different world.

PRONUNCIATION:
Mir Taqi Mir: MEER tah-ki MEER

Selected Couplets[1]

Live in the chains of slavery, and die in jail
But do not fall into the snare of love.

I was all fire when first I fell in love:
Now at the last nothing but ash remains.

Man's eyes and heart have plunged him in disaster—
If only he could go and make his home
Where no one ever looks into another's eyes,
And what is meant by "heart" is still unknown!

Mir's last behest to me was only this:
"Do what you will, my son, but do not love!"

I caught a glimpse of you with hair dishevelled
And my distracted heart was yours for life.

---

1. Translated by Ralph Russell and Khurshidul Islam.

She came but once, but do not ask what left me as she went—
My strength, and faith, and fortitude, and will and heart and soul.

Morning and night mean nothing any more
To him whose eyes have seen her hair and face.

The nightingale fell quiet, the tulip blushed, the rose turned pale
The cypress stood like one amazed, the eglantine distraught.
I too walked with my mistress in the garden yesterday
And all around I saw the changes that her beauty wrought.

Her glowing, radiant face confronts the candle
And overwhelmed with shame, it melts away.

Perhaps when it passed by that way my love was combing out her hair:
The scented breeze of morning brings a fragrance into every lane.

Drinking, worshipping beauty, revelry—
These three have occupied me all my days.
I am an old, old man, but what of that?
After so long, I cannot change my ways.

I cannot sit down quietly to die.
Yes, even now my heart will not be still.
While I have breath, with each returning spring
I must go out—my eyes must look their fill.

The way she looks has conquered all men's hearts—
Muslims and Brahmins, Christians and Jews.

Yes, we and you and Mir[2] are all her captives;
The beauty of her tresses binds us fast.

God knows what magic power her red lips hold;
Their still fire raises tumult in the world.

Since first I saw the form of that sweet infidel,[3] my idol
I cannot find it in my heart to contemplate Islam.

The very men who thought it blasphemy to worship idols
Sit now before the mosque and put the caste mark on their brow.

True Musalman am I, for to these idols
I pledge my love. "There is no god but God."[4]

Shaikh, pawn your prayer mat—for its price you'll get a glass of wine or so;
Yes, sell the gear of piety so that the rose-red wine may flow.
Or else unroll your worthless mat for drunkards to recline upon.
Sing praises to almighty wine! All honour to the bottle show!

2. The pen name (*takhallus*) assumed by most Urdu poets may or may not have some connection with the poet's real name but it is often a meaningful word. Mir's *takhallus* is the same as the name given to him at birth and, meaning "leader," marks his Sayyid roots as it also served as the title for descendants of the family of Muhammad. In the *ghazal* the pen name is expected to appear in the closing verse and can appear elsewhere as well.

3. One convention of the genre is that the infidel (*kafir*) is seductively attractive.

4. In this verse and the two preceding, a particularly risqué quality of Mir's poetry and the *ghazal* in general is evident as the celebration of idolatry challenges Islamic orthodoxy.

Let the wine stain your spotless robe! Pester the pretty serving boys!
50 They'll swear at you, and that will be a fresh delight for you to know!
Come on now, say a quick goodbye to good repute. Your heart and faith
Present as an unworthy gift to her in whom all beauties glow.
Yes, let your good name go to hell. Be like the lads, and spread your wings.
Shout to the *sāqi*,[5] "Bring more wine!"—and scold him if he comes too slow.
55 Stand up! The flagon bows its head to serve the revelers. You too
Proffer your services. You too in token of respect bow low.
The harpist comes to play and sing. You've nothing to reward him with?
Then be like us: take off your shirt and give him that. He won't say no.
Under the rosebush in the shade set down the wine jar by the stream.
60 Go on, take up your glass and drink. Disgrace yourself with high and low.
Too long the mosque and monastery have stifled you. One day at least
Set out at dawn and spend the day in gardens where red roses grow.

from The Autobiography[1]

Now says this humble man, Mir Muhammad Taqi whose *takhallus* is Mir, that being unemployed these days and confined to my solitary corner, I wrote down my story, containing the events of my life, the incidents of my times and some other anecdotes and tales. And I concluded this book entitled *Zikr-i Mīr* with some witty anecdotes. I hope my friends, should they notice any mistake therein, will not deny me their forgiveness and seek only to set me right.

My ancestors, beset with hard times when even mornings appear dark as nights, left Hejaz with their wives and dependants and travelled to the border of the Deccan. After suffering what none should suffer and experiencing what none should experience, they moved to Ahmedabad, Gujarat, where some of them chose to settle down. Others, however, decided to be more resolute and pressed on to seek their fortune elsewhere. And so my great-grandfather came to the capital, Akbarabad,[2] and made it his home. The climate of the place did not suit him; he fell ill and eventually bid farewell to this world of dust and water. He left one son, who was my grandfather. Girding his loins, my grandfather set about looking for a job and after much struggle gained honour by being made a "Faujdar"[3] in the neighbourhood of Akbarabad. He lived a decent life, but when he came to be fifty his disposition became unbalanced. For some days he treated himself with cooling drinks. However, he had not yet fully recovered when he went to Gwalior. The rigors of the journey were fatal to his weakened body; he collapsed and died, leaving two sons. The older of the two was not without a disturbed mind; he died young and that ended his story.

The younger son, i.e. my father, withdrew from the world. He studied those mundane subjects which are necessary for one to reach the "world of meaning," with Shah Kalimullah Akbarabadi[4]—who was one of the most perfect men of God at that place—and strove hard to tread the path of inner knowledge. He suffered a great deal in his pursuit of renunciation and abstinence, but under the guidance of that master he eventually reached the acme of saintliness.

5. The cupbearer, one of the stock figures of the Urdu *ghazal*.
1. Translated by C. M. Naim.
2. That is, Agra, the Mughal capital until 1648, when it was shifted to the new city, Delhi.
3. An important administrative officer.
4. A Sufi scholar and teacher who died in Agra in 1697.

After much suffering the heart reached its goal.

He was a virtuous man, given to love and possessing a passionate heart, and gained fame by receiving the name Ali Muttaqi.[5]

* * *

My father remained busy day and night in the remembrance of God, and God too did not forsake him. Whenever he would come out of his state of absorption, he would say to me: "My son, practice love, for it is love that holds sway over everything. But for love, nothing would have taken shape. Without love, life is a burden. To give one's heart to love, that is perfection. Love creates and love consumes. Whatever exists in the world is a manifestation of love. Fire is love's ardour; wind is love's agitation. Water is the flow of love; earth is the repose of love. Death is love's inebriated state; life is love's sober state. Night is the sleep of love; day is the wakefulness of love. The Muslim is the comforting beauty of love; the infidel is the awesome grandeur of love. Virtue lies in the proximity of love; sin arises in separation from love. Paradise is for love; hell is for love. The state of love is above the states of worship, gnostic knowing, asceticism, companionship, sincerity, desirefulness, friendship, or being loved. All agree that the movement of the heavens is caused by love—they keep going round in circles and never reach their desired one.

One cannot be without love; one cannot live without love.
Even the Prophet of Canaan[6] is filled with love for his son.

During the day my father was oblivious to one and all, and at night he remained awake, alert to His call. Much of the time he would lie prostrate in submission; all the time he was drunk with desire but pure and chaste. His glorious face adorned the ranks of the devotees who rise at dawn; he was a sun, but he avoided even his own shadow. When he was himself he would say: "My son, this world is but a momentary excitement, turn your back on it. Do not let its attachment soil your hands. Practice only love of God; a day awaits you, give yourself some thought. A worthy person knows that the world is a trifle, and life, merely a conjecture. To use a conjecture for foundation is like holding water with a piece of rope. If one pursues the amplitude of worldly boons, one is running with a yardstick after the moon. You are a transient here, don't neglect that fact; prepare well for the journey, lest you later come under attack. Turn your face towards Him whose mirror the universe is said to be, and put yourself in the hands of Him whom everyone seeks within himself. Although the goal has already been reached, it is still obligatory to seek it. Everything is Him, yet one must be proper and not speak of it. (Subtle point:) God is with His creation, like soul is with body. You don't exist without Him, and He is not manifest without you. Before creation, the world was his essence; and after creation, He is the world's essence.

How terrible a paradox! Every particle is His essence;
and yet none of us can dare to disclose His presence."

He was a dervish, and himself devoted to dervishes. He possessed a suffering heart but was ever eager for more suffering. A man of unusual humility, he lived like a stranger in his own city. Free of prejudice, a perfect Sufi, he identified with every

---

5. Ali, the God-fearing one.
6. Jacob, father of Joseph. This couplet may be by Mir

himself. The second line can also be translated: "Even the Prophet of Canaan is filled with the love for a boy."

hue of life like water in any colour. Sometimes he would hold me in his embrace and, affectionately looking at my pale countenance, say: "Treasure of my life, what fire lies hidden in your heart? What passion has become your life's inseparable part?" I would then laugh, but he would shed tears. I didn't recognise his worth while he was here. He was a man lost to his own self, and was never a burden to anyone else.

Once after the late morning prayers, he looked for me but saw me busy in some game. He said to me, "Son, Time flows very fast; it leaves you with little opportunity. So don't neglect the task of improving yourself. This road is full of ups and downs, tread it with extreme care.

> Your footprints are an account of your life's progress—
> so count every step you take in this ancient dust-heap.

"What is this game that you have chosen for yourself, and what is this impropriety that you have preferred for yourself? Devote yourself to One to whom the heavens are devoted, and give your heart to Him whom every heart adores. Be a nightingale to that rose whose spring has no end; and love that simple beauty whose colourful ways are without end. The ever-changing heavens tolerate no delay—hurry, count this little time a boon and strive to find yourself." * * *

Then suddenly my father, even though he had no provisions for a journey, set out again—placing his trust in God—and in ten or twelve days reached Shahjahanabad Dihli. There he stayed at the house of Fakhruddin Khan,[7] son of Shaikh Abdul 'Aziz 'Izzat, who was the Divan of that region and also closely related to my father. Excellent people of the city came to that residence and with great devotion sought to serve [my father] who was intoxicated by the wine of love. When seated, he was like an enraptured person, and when standing, he appeared as if drunk. His speech was similarly inebriated, and his passionate breath set afire many a desirous heart. A great many people placed their hands in his hand and became his disciples, and many of them were transformed when his glance fell upon them. When he did his ablutions, people saved the [used] water and gave it to the sick. Those who drank it became well. My father wept so much that he would choke, and when he let out a cry it would pierce the heavens. News spread throughout the city that a dervish of such eminence had come into town. Now even nobles sought permission to visit him. My father refused: "I am a faqir and you are an emir[8]—we have nothing in common." Amir-ul-Umara Samsam-ud-Daulah, on account of his previous claims on my father, persisted and said, "You shouldn't deny me the boon of looking at you. Be kind, and let this ignoble person join the company of those who are truly noble." My father smiled and sent back the following reply: "Something common must be there for two persons to meet. I hope you will accept my excuse and leave me alone." When the crowds began to bother him too much, he got up one midnight and after performing his *tahajjud* prayers, left the city. People strained themselves looking for him but couldn't find even a trace. * * *

The dervish "Aziz Murda" [my father] made every effort to console me and never did anything that would make me feel bad. Sometimes he said to me, "My son, I love you greatly. But I am also much anguished by the thought that I too must soon depart." Then at other times he said, "My moon, you are not a baby anymore. Allah

---

7. A close and generous friend of Mir's family whose widow took care of Mir during his period of madness. The title "divan" was reserved for a Mughal revenue officer.

8. A faqir is an ascetic; an emir is a nobleman.

be praised, you are ten years old. Why are you in despair? After all, you are the son of a dervish. Keep your heart strong and put yourself in God's hands. Live happily; keep smiling. You should know that I'm always ready to fulfil your every desire. *Ai* soul of mine, are you an infant that you cry all the time? Why must you worry for yourself when you have a guardian and protector in God? Those who go away do not come back; those who passed away will never again show their face. *Ai* son, this world is transitory; everyone you see is bound to depart. Do not consider this world to be a permanent place for you; nay, it is just a momentary assembly. Those who were present here, have moved on; those who were seated here, are gone. Do not clench your brow like a bud; smile, open up like a flower. Spring in this garden is transitory, so don't for nothing put yourself in torture. He made this gambling house of a world in such a way that there are scores of you who have gambled their hearts away. Do not set foot on this path until you have learned how to walk. Among astute gamblers there is a well-known proverb: "There is gambling, and then there is a way to gamble."

That is how he talked to me every day and nurtured me with great care. * * *

A soul-consuming anecdote: One day, at midday, the dervish "Aziz Murda" [my father] went to Alamganj, a well-known neighbourhood in Akbarabad, to visit with Muhammad Ba'ith who was ill. The latter was the nephew of Mir Amanullah, and himself a learned man and a perfect Sufi. When evening began to darken the sky, the dervish turned homeward and, arriving at his mosque, performed there the two combined evening prayers. When he finally lay down on his bed and I presented myself before him, he said, "*Ai* son, the heat of the day has affected me. I have a severe headache, and it seems that I'm going to have a fever." He didn't eat the evening meal and went to sleep. When he woke up the next morning, he was running a very high temperature. Abul Fath, his regular physician [*hakim*], came and gave him a cooling potion to drink, but it brought him no relief. He then gave him stronger coolants—some excessively so—but to no avail. The fever set in, that is, it gripped the dervish every evening and lasted the night through. Then they tried many other ways to break the fever's grip but none succeeded. After a month it was diagnosed that the fever had taken hold of his heart and had even penetrated into the bones. In other words, that enfeebled dervish who was no more than a handful of bone was dying of consumption.

He then said to me, "*Ai* son, my soul is all submission and my body is burning away. I feel no desire for food. If I eat anything it sits heavy with me. The medicine that the *hakim* gives me in the morning suffices me till the next day. I now wish not to have any food till the day I die. Send for a few bunches of dried narcissus flowers from the market so that, life permitting, I may smell their fragrance every so often." I followed his orders and, getting the flowers, kept them near him all the time. Whenever he would open his eyes he would hold the bunch in his hand and smell the flowers, then he would say, "Allah be praised! Now I feel satiated."

When he stopped eating he caused us miserable ones to lose all hopes for his recovery. His legs and arms lost what strength they had, and weakness overwhelmed him. He spoke very little and used only gestures when praying. On the twenty-first of Rajab,[9] the *hakim* as usual brought him a bowl of the cooling potion; but the dervish became angry and didn't drink it. He hurled it to the ground and said, "You wretch,

---

9. The seventh month of the Muslim calendar.

from the first day it has been clear just how effective your medicine is! I have been taking it only out of consideration for you. But you don't seem to learn a thing. Now go away and leave me alone. Your foolishness is cureless."

Then he sent for Hafiz Muhammad Hasan, who was my half-brother and older to me, and said to him, "I am a faqir; except for three hundred books I have no possessions. Bring them here and divide them up with your brothers." He replied, "I am a student, and I am diligent in my work. These brothers have no interest in books. They will only tear pages out of them; one will use them for kites, the other will make paper boats out of them. It will be better if you leave the books in my trust—otherwise, you are the master."

My father was well aware of his bad nature, so he admonished him and said, "It makes no difference if you have put on a new garb, your meanness has not left you. You only wish to cheat these boys and cause them trouble after I am gone. But you should know that Almighty God jealously guards His honour and also loves the people who similarly guard theirs. I strongly believe that Mir Muhammad Taqi will never have to stretch his hand before you. If you treat him wrongly he will expose you in public. Your name will matter little before this child's fame. If you gain your aim you will see that he will punish you severely. No one trusts a stingy person, and meanness and jealousy lead only to disgrace. All right, take the books and look after them."

Then my father turned to me and said, "*Ai* son, I owe three hundred rupees to the shopkeepers in the market. I hope you will not bury me until you have paid off that debt, for I have been a man of integrity and never in my life did I cheat anyone." I humbly replied, "There is nothing worth anything in the house except for the books, and those you have already given to my elder brother. How am I going to pay off the debt?" Tears came into his eyes as he said, "God is munificent. Do not despair. A bill of payment is on its way; it should reach here very soon. I wish I could stay alive until it arrives, but I cannot. I must depart." He then prayed for my welfare and entrusted me to God, then took the remaining few breaths he still had to account for and passed away.

The inhumanity of the brother: When the dervish closed his eyes, the world darkened before my eyes. It was a terrible calamity; the sky fell upon me. My tears poured out in torrents. Losing all self-control, I rolled in the dirt and struck my head against the walls. There was so much noise and such turmoil that you might have thought the day of reckoning had arrived. My elder brother gave up all pretensions of civility and behaved shamelessly. Seeing that our father had been indigent and died in poverty and that his creditors were going to make their demands, he separated himself from us, saying, "They who had received favours and affection from the deceased should now take care of their responsibility. I had no say in any matter while my father was alive; and now I renounce even my claims as a son. May they live long who now sit on his prayer-rug [as his spiritual heirs]. They are tearing their hair and scratching their faces—they shall do whatever is needed."

When I, who had just been made utterly helpless, heard his senseless remarks, I felt tremendous anger and pain. But I didn't plead with him; instead, I girded my waist in readiness and waited, setting my eyes only on God. The market people came with another two hundred rupees and pleaded with me to accept the money, but I didn't. I was bound to honour the dervish's last wish. I didn't, however, wish to hurt their feelings and so I mollified them with kind words. Just then a man sent by Sayyid Mikmal Khan, a disciple of my revered "uncle," arrived with a bill of payment worth five hundred rupees, newly minted, and joined me in my grief. I gave three hundred rupees to the creditors and obtained a full receipt of clearance; then I spent another hundred rupees and had the dervish properly buried next to his spiritual master.

My wretched state after the death of the dervish: I suffered the inhumanities of the heavens and experienced the cruelties of the times. No, no, that was neither a fault of the heavens nor a crime of the times. Whatever happened was my misfortune. It was in my stars that I should lose the comforting warmth of that sun. I discovered that I was my own guardian, there was no one else to look after me. So I relied only on my sense of honour and never went to stand at another man's door. Not a word of asking touched my lips; and no glance of mine went chasing after things. I did not seek anyone's help, and no one came to hold my hand. In short, the munificent God did not let me be burdened by anyone's favours; nor did He make me depend on my mean and hostile older brother. I distributed the "sweets of mourning" for the dervish, then placed all my affairs in the generous hands of God. Putting my younger brother in my place at home, I strained my limbs roaming the environs of the city for some means to earn a living, but I did not find any. Not obtaining any relief in my city I was compelled to leave home and resign myself to the hardships of a journey.

━━ ⇥⬧⬩⇤ ━━

Banarasidas
mid-17th century

The Old Hindi *Half a Tale* is one of the most remarkable examples of autobiography in pre-modern South Asia. Written in 1641 at the height of the Mughal Empire, it contains a memorable account of the author's sorrow as a young man over the death of Emperor Akbar in 1605. Banarasidas belonged to the Jain community, whose lay members typically engaged in commerce. It seems hardly coincidental that the work comes from the pen of a merchant. Like his wealth, a merchant's life is something he creates for himself; there is no pregiven, mythic paradigm to which it is expected to conform, like the lives of heroes or holy men, nor is its narrative dictated by the mere succession of years, as in the royal annals of the *Memoirs of Babur*. Banarasidas's quest is not only for worldly success but also for spiritual fulfillment, although the tone of the work carries little of the fervent devotionalism that characterizes so much of the vernacular literature of the period. Altogether, the writer's sense of himself and his world suggests, even more strongly than in the case of Jahangir, that if the transition to modernity consists in part of new forms of self-awareness, then modernity began in seventeenth-century India no less than in seventeenth-century Europe.

PRONUNCIATIONS:
    Banarasidas: buh-NAHR-see-dahs
    Jain: JAYN

from Half a Tale[1]

My name is Banarasi, a name which carries the stamp of the city that gave birth to two Tirthankaras.[2] I will now relate to you the story of my life because it occurred to me that I should make my history public.

---

1. Translated by Mukund Lath.
2. Benares was the birthplace of Suparshanath and

Parshvanath, two of the 24 *tirthankaras* or Jain saints.

I will speak of my life from my early childhood to the present, describing what I saw and experienced; and to this narrative I will also sometimes add things I have heard from others. In this manner. I will relate the events of my past in broad outlines, but the future I do not know; only the All-knowing can know that.

I will narrate my story in the common language of middle India (*madhyadesa*), freely revealing all that lies concealed. And though I will speak to you of my virtues, I will also disclose my sins and follies.

Listen attentively, friends, as I unveil my past.

I am a Jain belonging to the clan of Srimals, who were once princely Rajputs living in Biholi, a village near the town of Rohtak in the region known as Madhyadesa of our good land of Bharat.[3] These Rajputs were converted to Jainism under the influence of a great teacher, and, giving up their earlier life of violence, they took to the practice of wearing a *mala,* a garland, inscribed with the true mantra; hence they came to be called Srimals. My ancestors bore the gotra-name[4] Biholia, for they had once been defenders of Biholi.

* * *

I was now fourteen and began to develop a keen desire to pursue further studies, and so I went to Pandit Devadutt, who was a knowledgeable scholar. I studied with him a number of standard works on a wide variety of subjects. My studies included two lexical texts, the *Namamala* and the *Anekarthakosa.* I also took lessons in *jyotisa* (astronomy cum astrology), *alankara* (poetics), and erotics, in which latter subject I read a work called *Laghukoka* by Pandit Koka. In addition, I also studied the *Khandasphuta* which is a work in four hundred verses. I spent the whole of Vikram 1657[5] intent upon studying and reflecting deeply on whatever I had learnt.

But I had also another, equally strong, passion. For I was in love and I gave myself up to this consuming passion with the whole-hearted yearning and devotion of a sufi fakir. Single-mindedly I meditated upon the object of my desire. My beloved occupied my entire vision. Forever I thought of her, paying no heed to propriety or family honour. I even stooped to stealing money and jewels from my father so that I could buy her costly presents and offer her the choicest sweets. Following the right etiquette in such matters, I called myself the "slave" of my beloved, always referring to myself as the "poor one."

After four months of summer had passed, the weather turned cool. During this pleasant season, two Jain sadhus[6] named Bhanchand and Ramchand came to sojourn in Jaunpur. Both were disciples of a great teacher called Abhaydharma, who was a Svetambara[7] monk of the Kharataragaccha sect of Jainism, a religion which reveals the path of fearlessness. Bhanchand was the more intelligent and knowledgeable of the two. Ramchand was yet a young boy; he still wore the attire of householders, such as novice sadhus do. Devotees of the sect to which they belonged often came piously to visit these two. I, too, followed the custom of my community and went to see them at the *upasraya,* a religious building where Jain sadhus stay. I became friendly with Bhanchand and my attachment to him grew so much that I spent all my days in his company, often returning home quite late at night. With him I began earnestly to study the sacred texts of Jainism. I studied a large number of works including hymns to various Tirthankaras, hundreds of well-known verses on different religious topics

---

3. The ancient family name that has come to be the official name of India today.
4. I.e., family name.
5. 1600 C.E. The Vikram era, named after a king of Ujjain,

began in 57 B.C.E.
6. Holy men.
7. "White-clothed," one of the two sects of Jainism, the other being Digambara, "Sky-clothed,"—that is, naked.

and a treatise on the proper ritual for bathing a Jina image. I also studied texts dealing with *samayika*[8] meditation and penances for sin. Besides Jain texts I also studied lexicons and works on prosody. An important work I studied was the famous *Srutabodha*. Another was the *Chandakosa*. I was a diligent student and spent much time memorising texts and reciting them with the right enunciation. I had become quite religious and did my best to acquire the eight merits[9] of a good Jain.

I also began to write and commenced work on a book called *Pancasandhi* dealing with an important aspect of Sanskrit grammar. But I was still leading a dual life. Though I was fully devoted to the task of acquiring knowledge, yet I did not give up my amorous pursuits. I composed a book of poems containing a thousand verses with love as the central theme, though, ostensibly, the book was about all the major human sentiments, which have been classified as the nine *rasas*. Reflecting back, I realize that I had become a false poet, an author of words and sentiments expressing falsehood.

Devoted thus entirely to my two consuming passions, I was doing nothing to earn money. I was so lost in the labours of love and learning that often I even forgot to eat my meals. Where then was the time for thinking of paltry things like money?

I spent two whole years in this state of abandon, despite severe admonitions from my parents. By Vikram 1659, however, I was satiated with books and amour. I now set out to fetch my bride from her father's home. I put on all my finery, and attended by a livery of servants, travelled happily in a palanquin to Khairabad, the home of my father-in-law.

I was now fifteen years and ten months old. After a month in Khairabad, I suddenly fell sick with a disgusting disease caused by a morbid condition of the windy humour. The skin all over my body became like that of a leper. My very bones ached and my hair began to fall out. Innumerable eruptions appeared all over my arms and legs and soon I was so unsightly that people shunned my company. My father-in-law and my brother-in-law refused to sit with me at meals. I was so repellant that none wanted even to come near me. My sins were bearing fruit once again.

* * *

In Vikram 1662 [1605 C.E.], during the month of Kartik, after the monsoon was over, the great emperor Akbar breathed his last in Agra. The alarming news of his death spread fast and soon reached Jaunpur. People felt suddenly orphaned and insecure without their sire. Terror raged everywhere; the hearts of men trembled with dire apprehension, their faces became drained of colour.

I was sitting upon a flight of stairs in my house when I heard the dreadful news, which came as a sharp and sudden blow. It made me shake with violent, uncontrollable agitation. I reeled, and losing my balance, fell down the stairs in a faint. My head hit the stone floor and began to bleed profusely, turning the courtyard red. Everyone present rushed to my help. My dear parents were in utter agony. My mother put my head in her lap and applied a piece of burnt cloth to my wound in order to stop the flow of blood. I was then quickly put to bed with my sobbing mother at my side.

The whole town was in a tremor. Everyone closed the doors of his house in panic; shop-keepers shut down their shops. Feverishly, the rich hid their jewels and costly attire underground; many of them quickly dumped their wealth and their ready capital on carriages and rushed to safe, secluded places. Every householder began stocking his home with weapons and arms. Rich men took to wearing thick, rough

---

8. Jain religious activities.
9. The "eight merits" likely include the five major vows

of Jainism: nonviolence, truthfulness, refraining from stealing, celibacy, and renunciation.

clothes such as are worn by the poor, in order to conceal their status, and walked the streets covered in harsh woolen blankets or coarse cotton wrappers. Women shunned finery, dressing in shabby, lustreless clothes. None could tell the status of a man from his dress and it became impossible to distinguish the rich from the poor. There were manifest signs of panic everywhere although there was no reason for it since there were really no thieves or robbers about.

The commotion subsided after ten days, when a letter arrived from Agra bearing news that all was well in the capital. The situation returned to normal. Let me give you the gist of the news the letter carried. Akbar had died in the month of Kartik, in the year 1662 Vikram, after a reign of fifty-two years; now Akbar's eldest son, Prince Salim, had been enthroned as king to rule from Agra, like his father. Salim had assumed the title of Sultan Nuruddin Jahangir; his power reigned supreme and unchallenged throughout the land.

This news came as a great relief and people heartily hailed the new king.

To the joy of my parents, I, too, soon regained my health. We celebrated the end of the days of gloom with much festivity, distributing alms to the poor and gifts to friends and relations.

Soon after these events I went alone one day to my room at the roof-top and sat down to think and reflect. I began seriously to question the state of my faith and belief.

"I have been an ardent devotee of Siva," I said to myself, "but when I fell down the stairs and was severely hurt, Siva did not come to my aid." This thought nagged me constantly and made me neglect my daily ritual to Siva. My heart was no longer in it, and one day I simply put the Siva-conch away.

Indeed, a strange mood had come over me. For that conch was not the only thing I put away. One day, in the company of a few close friends, I strolled down to the bridge over the Gomti, taking with me the manuscript of my book of poems on love, and began reciting verses from it to my friends. But as I read, a sudden thought violently perturbed me: "A man who utters a single lie," I reflected, "suffers in hell; yet here I am with a whole book full of nothing but falsehood—how can I ever be redeemed?" I looked down at the flowing waters, and on the spur of the moment, flung away the manuscript into the river, as though it was so much waste paper. My friends rushed to stop me from this impulsive act, but the deed was done. The folios of my poems were lying scattered over waters running deep and fearful. The book was now beyond retrieval. My friends were greatly distressed, but all they could do was to lament over the quirks of destiny.

My father was glad to hear the news. "Perhaps this is a sign that my son is undergoing a real change for the better," he happily remarked, "there is yet hope for the future of my family."

* * *

I had made two good friends, both very close and dear to me. One was Narottamdas, the grandson of Benidas of the Khobra gotra.[1] The other was Thanmal Badaliya. The three of us were greatly attached to each other. We made a merry trio, spending all our time in each other's company.

One day, taking a carriage we went together to offer worship at a Jain shrine. After performing the usual rites of propitiation, the three of us approached the deity with folded palms and, in unison, made the following supplication: "O Lord, grant us wealth, for then we shall have occasion to come and offer worship at your shrine again."

1. Lineage.

After that day the three of us became still more attached to each other, one in body and soul. We began to spend every hour of the day together in sweet conversation.

Then, during that year, in the spring month of Phalgun, a rich friend of ours named Tarachand Mothiya, who was a son of Nema, invited me to join him in a marriage party which was soon to proceed out of town. Balchand was the groom. Narottamdas was travelling with it and I, too, was prevailed upon to go. I began to look for some money to take with me, and sold a few pearls which I had put aside for bad times. They fetched me thirty-two rupees, which sum I took with me on my journey.

When I returned I had no money left. I hastened to sell my stock of cloth for whatever I could get and had to be satisfied with four rupees less than my cost price. I used this money to pay off some interest that had fallen due. I was free of debt but a pauper once again.

I went to see Narottam at his house. He welcomed me warmly and forced me to share his meal. I told him I was bankrupt, with nothing left and nowhere to go. He implored me to come and live with him. He assured me that I was like a brother to him and that whatever was his was also mine. His house, he added, was always open to those whom he loved. I was hesitant and protested that others in his family, especially his wife, may not like my being there. But he silenced me with these words: "Can you think of anyone in my family who will say anything to hurt you?"

He insisted that I could not refuse. He now made it a habit to address me as "brother"; he also treated me like one, and we were always inseparable.

One day, when Narottamdas was with Tarachand Mothiya, Tarachand offered him some work. He asked Narottam to travel as his agent to Patna, taking me with him. He gave us money and we began making preparations for our departure. Then, on an auspicious day, we performed the propitiatory rites customary for people setting out on a long journey and crossed the Yamuna[2] with tilak-marks[3] on our foreheads.

We were three of us, Narottam, I, and his father-in-law: all young, able Srimal[4] men. We hired a carriage for our journey but took no serving men.

We had hired our carriage at Firozabad and we were to travel on it up to Shahzadpur, about half way on the road to Patna. When we reached Shahzadpur we paid our fare and decided to cover the rest of the journey on foot, hiring a porter to carry our luggage.

We decided to leave Shahzadpur as early in the morning as possible. That night, about five hours after sunset, the moonlight suddenly became very bright and we were deceived into thinking that day was about to dawn. So we immediately set out on our way. But as the light was yet dim, we could not properly make out our path. We strayed towards the south and soon entered a thick forest. It was not long before we realized that we were completely lost in the middle of a desolate jungle. Our porter suddenly lost his wits and began to scream and howl in panic. He threw down the luggage he was carrying and ran away into the wilderness. We had no choice but to carry the load ourselves. We divided it into three bundles, one for each of us. But the journey now became an ordeal. We tried to ease our burden by constantly shifting the weight from head to shoulders, but this was hardly of any help. Soon it was midnight and yet we were still far away from anywhere. We were miserable and almost

2. The same river referred to earlier as Jumna.
3. Here a mark, made usually of saffron or sandalwood   paste, applied after worship in a temple.
4. Srimal was Banarasi's clan name.

demented with fatigue, singing and crying in the same breath like men who have suddenly gone mad.

After a little while, we entered a part of the forest where robbers lived in little hamlets of their own. A man espied us and shouted: "Who goes there?" We were seized with terror. Our lips were parched and suddenly glued together. We could not bring ourselves to utter a single word and began fervently to pray to God.

The man we had encountered was the chief of the robbers himself. Seeing him, I had a timely inspiration. I pronounced a benediction upon the man, chanting a sacred verse in Sanskrit in the manner of a pious Brahman. My trick worked. The robber chief took us for learned Brahmans, and approaching us, humbly bowed at our feet with deep respect. He also offered to give us shelter for the night.

"Consider me your humble servant, O venerable ones," he said. "Come with me and I will take you to my village where you can spend the night in the *chaupal*.[5] Do not be afraid of me, for as God is my witness, I mean you no harm."

We quietly followed the robber chief to his village, and, true to his word, he gave us a place for the night.

But we were still trembling violently with fear, our hearts pounding and our faces drained of all colour. As soon as we were alone, we hurriedly hunted for some loose yarn and quickly spun it into four sacred threads such as every Brahman must wear.[6] We then hung three of the sacred threads across our shoulders, and kept the fourth conspicuously out for all to see. Then, fetching some mud and a little water from a nearby pond, we smeared our foreheads with holy tilak-marks befitting pious Brahmans. Our disguise now complete, we waited quietly for the morning to come. But we were still seized with fear and remained huddled together in a crouching position till about six hours later when light dawned and the rising sun turned the clouds red.

The robber chief approached us on a horse with a retinue of twenty men. When he came near us, he folded his palms and deeply bowed his head in veneration. I blessed him, again loudly intoning a sacred benedictory verse.

"Come venerable Brahmans, let me lead you out of the forest and show you the road," the chief said.

Obediently, we followed him with our bundles on our head. The man meant well and took us along a path that led out of the forest. After we had walked for about three kos,[7] we reached the road to Fatehpur.

"This road will take you to your destination," the robber chief assured us. Pointing to a clump of trees in the distance, he added: "There, across those trees, lies Fatehpur."

He then begged leave of us and we blessed him heartily, chanting "May you live long," and began to walk towards Fatehpur.

* * *

In Vikram 1696, my third son, the only surviving child I had, also died. His death rent my heart with agony. I was wretched and miserable with sorrow. Worldly attachments are powerful bonds, for they bind both the ignorant and the knowing. Two years have now passed since my son's death, and I still feel desolate. I find myself unable to overcome my sorrow and my attachment to his memory remains an unbearable pain.

---

5. Assembly hall.
6. A woven thread is worn by high-caste Hindus, especially when engaged in sacred studies, such as Banarasi

and his friends were pretending to be.
7. About two miles.

My story is now complete. I am fifty-five years of age, and I live in Agra with my wife in reasonably comfortable circumstances. I married thrice, and had two daughters and seven sons. But all my children died. And now my wife and I are alone like winter trees that have shed all their greenery, standing bare and denuded. Looking at it in the light of the absolute vision, you may declare that as a man takes unto himself, so he sheds. But can any man rooted in this world ever see things in such a light? A man feels enriched when he takes something unto himself and utterly lost when he is deprived of even a trifle.

I will now end. But before I do so, I would like to speak to you of my present good and bad attributes.

First, then, my good points. As a poet I am matchless in composing verses on spiritual themes, which I recite with great art and impact. I know Prakrit and Sanskrit and can intone these languages with faultless pronunciation. I also know many vernacular languages. In my use of language I am ever alive to nuances of words and meanings.

My temper is naturally forgiving. I am easily content, and not readily moved by worldly cares. I am sweet of tongue and good at mixing with people for I have great forbearance and shun harsh language. My intentions are unsullied; so the counsel I give usually proves helpful to others. I have no foul or vicious habits, and I do not run after other men's wives. I have a true, unwavering faith in Jainism, and a steadfast mind which remains unshaken in its determination. I am pure in heart and always strive for equanimity.

These are my various virtues, both small and big. None of them really touch supreme heights and none are quite without shortcomings.

Now for my bad points. I said I have little of anger, pride or cunning, yet my greed for money is great. A little gain makes me inordinately happy and a little loss plunges me into the depths of despair. I am indolent by nature and slow in my work, hardly ever wanting to stir out of my house.

I do not perform sacred religious rituals; I never utter the holy mantras, never sit for meditations and never exercise self-restraint. Neither do I perform *puja*[8] nor practise charity.

I am overfond of laughter, and love to poke fun at everything. I delight in playing the clown and acting the buffoon, indulging in these capers with great relish and gusto. I often utter things that should not be said without any sense of shame, revelling in narrating unutterable stories and escapades with much glee. I love to relate fictitious stories, often quite scandalous, and try to pass them off as true especially when I am in the midst of a large gathering. When I am in the mood for fun, nothing can restrain me from telling fanciful lies or untruths.

I sometimes break into a dance when I am alone. Yet I am also prone to sudden, irrational feelings of sheer dread.

Such is my temper. The good in my character alternates with the bad.

I have now done with all that I had to say about myself. Yet what I have said pertains mostly to my visible conduct and actions: things that could be seen or discovered by all. But in a man's life there is much that is too subtle to be so palpable. Of this, however, only God can know.

Also, I must confess that I spoke mostly of things I could best recollect. I have also deliberately remained silent about certain of my deeds which were perversities of such gross proportions that I cannot speak of them to anyone. Yet you must grant that

8. Worship.

I have not entirely shied away from speaking of my faults and follies. This at least is something quite unusual since people are careful to conceal even their smallest misdoings although they be petty things of common occurrence. A man who confesses to his faults is a Kevalin,[9] a realized soul.

But none can report all that happens, not even the all-knowing Kevalin. Even in the tiny span of a day, a man passes through myriad states of consciousness. The all-knowing Kevalin can perceive them, but even he cannot describe them in their fulness. And who can know more than the Kevalin? The wisest, most occult of sages can know only a part of what the Kevalin knows. Compared to them I am nothing but a primitive earthworm with no more than the haziest of awareness. How could I have revealed all? A man's life has much that is subtly secret and profoundly beyond grasp. What I have reported is certainly the grossest of the gross part of my life. For as I said, I have spoken mainly of my outward conduct and behaviour.

I have narrated to you the story of fifty-five years of my life. The full span of a man's life is a hundred and ten years. I have lived only half of this span. I do not know what is to come in the future. God alone can know that.

All men at all times can be divided into three categories; the truly praiseworthy, the utterly despicable, and those who fall between these two.

The truly praiseworthy men are those who, in speaking of others, speak only of their merits, deliberately drawing a veil over their faults. When such men speak of themselves, they speak only of faults and never of their merits.

The utterly despicable have just the contrary traits. They only speak of faults in others while boasting of their own merits. Never do they utter a word about their own blemishes.

I am one who falls in between. I speak unreservedly of both faults and merits in others as well as myself.

Today, as I complete my tale, it is Monday, the fifth of the bright half of the month Agrahayana, Vikram 1698 [1641 C.E.]. I now live in Agra and I am, let me repeat, a Jain of the Srimal clan, Banarasi Biholia by name and an Adhyatmi[1] by conviction. It occurred to me that I should make the story of my life public, and so I have narrated the events that have happened during these last fifty-five years. The future I do not know; I shall face it as it comes.

The story of the last fifty-five years of my life covers half the number of days allotted to man. I have, therefore, named my story "Half a Tale."

Wicked men will mock at my tale. But friends will surely give it a glad and attentive ear and recite it to each other.

Before I finish I would like to extend my good wishes to all who may read my story or listen to it or recite it to others.

[END OF THE WORLD THE MUGHALS MADE]

---

9. One who has attained liberation beyond the dualism of spirit and matter, entering into a state of oneness (*kaivalyam*) with the absolute. Such a state is one of inactivity, complete knowledge, and everlasting peace.
1. One who believes in the identity between *atman* or the soul and the *brahman* or supreme being.

‒‧ ⸝◇⸏ ‧‒

Chikamatsu Mon'zaemon
1653–1725

Japanese puppet theater emerged in the early seventeenth century and flourished thereafter as popular entertainment. In contrast to Noh—a medieval dramatic genre that continued to be staged but whose audience was largely samurai or merchant elite—puppet theater was aimed at a wide audience. Puppet theater consists of three elements that are closely coordinated: the puppets, the music (played by a banjo-like *shamisen*), and the chanting (*jōruri*) performed by a chanter who sits to the side of the stage and who speaks or sings all the roles of the puppets, including the third-person narration. Puppet theater began with one-man puppets, but by the eighteenth century it had evolved into a complex art with three-man puppets whose handlers are visible to the audience: the head puppeteer controls the head and right hand, the second manipulates the left hand, and the third is in charge of the feet. Of the three elements—puppets, music, and chanting—the chanting is the most important, so much so that the chanter is usually the star performer and the chanting is sometimes performed alone, without the puppets.

Chikamatsu Mon'zaemon was the greatest of the puppet theater playwrights. He came from a relatively well-off samurai (warrior) family and served in the households of royalty and aristocrats in Kyoto in his youth, before going into the theater and moving to Osaka, the city of merchants and urban commoners. One consequence is that Chikamatsu describes the life of townspeople but is deeply interested in samurai values and society. Chikamatsu's earliest play on contemporary social life was the one-act *Love Suicides at Sonezaki* (1703), which depicts an actual incident of the time and which became a model for subsequent contemporary life plays.

The Love Suicides at Amijima, first performed at the Takemoto Theater in Osaka in 1721, is widely considered to be Chikamatsu Mon'zaemon's best puppet play concerning contemporary life. The source for the play is unclear, but the incident inspired a number of later plays. In the play, Kamiya (literally, "paper merchant") Jihei, an Osaka paper merchant with a wife and children, falls in love with Koharu, a prostitute under contract to the Kinokuniya House in Sonezaki (a licensed quarter in Osaka). Forced into tragic circumstances, the two of them commit suicide at a temple in Amijima, in Osaka.

About half of Chikamatsu's twenty-four contemporary-life plays focus on an incident concerning an Osaka urban commoner. Almost all the male protagonists are young and of low social station, either an adopted son or a shop clerk, and most of them become involved with a low-level prostitute. In that the lovers have already decided to commit double suicide at the beginning, *The Love Suicides at Amijima* differs from such double-suicide plays as *The Love Suicides at Sonezaki,* which show the tragic chain of events that lead to death. Instead, the focus in *Amijima* is on the desperate efforts of those who attempt to prevent the suicide of the two lovers. Chikamatsu places the tragedy in a tight web of urban commoner social relationships and obligations, particularly the hierarchical relations between master and apprentice, parent and child, and husband and wife, as well as in the context of the new monetary economy and commercial life of Osaka. Jihei and Koharu bear a great social burden, particularly as Jihei is a pillar of the family business, and the tragic result pulls down not only the two lovers but others in the family. Here Chikamatsu develops one of the central themes of his contemporary-life plays: the conflict between those who try to preserve the family *and* the individual, driven by his or her own desires, who works against that social order.

Chikamatsu focuses on *giri*, or sense of social obligation, including that between women, between Koharu and Jihei's wife Osan, whose conflicted relationship develops into a tense mutual understanding. Not only does Chikamatsu create complex conflicts between individual

Puppeteers performing *The Love Suicides at Amijima*. Koharu attempting to persuade the samurai (Magoemon, in a hood, to hide his identity) to become her customer so that she and Jihei can avoid committing suicide.

desire and obligation, he focuses on conflicts between competing obligations that result in extreme pathos. Desire and obligation are also reflected in the settings: the first act occurs in the pleasure quarters, a world of desire, passion, and the individual; and the second act takes place in the paper shop, a world of responsibility, reason, and the family, with Jihei caught between the two. The third act focuses on a journey in which the lovers leave behind both places and travel toward death.

In the poetic journey in the third act there is a double movement: a downward movement, the Buddhist cycle of *samsara*, of birth and death, of suffering, which leads to hell; and an upward movement, leading from hell to possible salvation. The fundamental assumption behind the two movements, which is symbolically mapped out, is that awakening is the result of some profound crisis or suffering. Accordingly, the lovers initially pass such places as Tenma Bridge and the River of the Three Fords—which represent places in hell—before they cross over Kyō (Sutra) Bridge and Onari (Becoming a Buddha) Bridge. The final scene has the added function of praying for the spirits of the dead—that is, the play implicitly recalls to this world the spirits or ghosts of the two lovers, who have recently died a gruesome death, and now sends them off again to the world of the dead.

PRONUNCIATIONS:
Chikamatsu Mon'zaemon: chi-ka-mah-tsu mon-ZAH-e-mon
Gozaemon: go-zah-e-mon
Jihei: ji-hay
Koharu: ko-hah-reu
Osan: o-sahn
Tahei: tah-hay

The Love Suicides at Amijima[1]

Characters

JIHEI, *aged twenty-eight, a paper merchant*
MAGOEMON, *his brother, a flour merchant*
GOZAEMON, *Jihei's father-in-law*
TAHEI, *a rival for Koharu*
DENBEI, *proprietor of the Yamato House*
SANGORŌ, *Jihei's servant*
KANTARŌ, *aged six, Jihei's son*
KOHARU, *aged nineteen, a courtesan belonging to the Kinokuni House in Sonezaki,*
    a new licensed quarter in the north part of Ōsaka
OSAN, *Jihei's wife*
OSAN'S MOTHER (*who is also Jihei's aunt*), *aged fifty-six*
OSUE, *aged four, Jihei's daughter*

ACT 1

[*In an opening scene, which is rarely performed and is omitted here, Koharu makes her way to the Kawashō Teahouse in Sonezaki licensed quarter to meet Tahei, a samurai customer. We learn that Koharu is in love with Jihei and that Tahei, a man that she dislikes immensely, is trying to buy out her contract. Koharu sees Tahei in the street and flees.*]

The Kawashō, a Teahouse in Sonezaki.

CHANTER: Koharu slips away, under cover of the crowd, and hurries into the Kawashō Teahouse.

[PROPRIETRESS]: Well, well, I hadn't expected you so soon—It's been ages since I've even heard your name mentioned. What a rare visitor you are, Koharu! And what a long time it's been!

CHANTER: The proprietress greets Koharu cheerfully.

[KOHARU]: Oh—you can be heard as far as the gate. Please don't call me Koharu in such a loud voice. That horrible Ri Tōten[2] is out there. I beg you, keep your voice down.

CHANTER: Were her words overheard? In bursts a party of three men.

[TAHEI]: I must thank you first of all, dear Koharu, for bestowing a new name on me, Ri Tōten. I never was called *that* before. Well, friends, this is the Koharu I've confided to you about—the good-hearted, good-natured, good-in-bed Koharu. Step up and meet the whore who's started all the rivalry! Will I soon be the lucky man and get Koharu for my wife? Or will Kamiya Jihei ransom her?

CHANTER: He swaggers up.

[KOHARU]: I don't want to hear another word. If you think it's such an achievement to start unfounded rumors about someone you don't even know, go ahead; say what you please. But I don't want to hear.

CHANTER: She steps away suddenly, but he sidles up again.

[TAHEI]: You may not want to hear me, but the clink of my gold coins will make you listen! What a lucky girl you are! Just think—of all the many men in Tenma and

---

the rest of Ōsaka, you chose Jihei the paper dealer, the father of two children, with his cousin for his wife and his uncle for his father-in-law! A man whose business is so tight he's at his wits' end every sixty days merely to pay the wholesalers' bills! Do you think he'll be able to fork over nearly ten *kanme* to ransom you? That reminds me of the mantis who picked a fight with an oncoming vehicle![3] But look at me—I don't have a wife, a father-in-law, a father, or even an uncle, for that matter. Tahei the Lone Wolf—that's the name I'm known by. I admit that I'm no match for Jihei when it comes to bragging about myself in the Quarter, but when it comes to money, I'm an easy winner. If I pushed with all the strength of my money, who knows what I might conquer?—How about it, men?—Your customer tonight, I'm sure, is none other than Jihei, but I'm taking over. The Lone Wolf's taking over. Hostess! Bring on the saké! On with the saké!

[PROPRIETRESS]: What are you saying? Her customer tonight is a samurai, and he'll be here any moment. Please amuse yourself elsewhere.

CHANTER: But Tahei's look is playful.

[TAHEI]: A customer's a customer, whether he's a samurai or a townsman. The only difference is that one wears swords and the other doesn't. But even if this samurai wears his swords, he won't have five or six—there'll only be two, the broadsword and dirk. I'll take care of the samurai and borrow Koharu afterward. [*To Koharu.*] You may try to avoid me all you please, but some special connection from a former life must have brought us together. I owe everything to that ballad-singing priest—what a wonderful thing the power of prayer is! I think I'll recite a prayer of my own. Here, this ashtray will be my bell, and my pipe the hammer. This is fun.

> *Chan Chan Cha Chan Chan.*
> *Ei Ei Ei Ei Ei.*
> *Jihei the paper dealer—*
> *Too much love for Koharu*
> *Has made him a foolscap,*
> *He wastepapers sheets of gold*
> *Till his fortune's shredded to confetti*
> *And Jihei himself is like scrap paper*
> *You can't even blow your nose on!*
> *Hail, Hail Amida Buddha!*
> *Namaida Namaida Namaida.*

CHANTER: As he prances wildly, roaring his song, a man appears at the gate, so anxious not to be recognized that he wears, even at night, a wicker hat.[4]

[TAHEI]: Well, Toilet Paper's showed up! That's quite a disguise! Why don't you come in, Toilet Paper? If my prayer's frightened you, say a Hail Amida![5] Here, I'll take off your hat!

CHANTER: He drags the man in and examines him: it is the genuine article, a two-sworded samurai, somber in dress and expression, who glares at Tahei through his woven hat, his eyeballs round as gongs. Tahei, unable to utter either a Hail or an Amida, gasps "Haaa!" in dismay, but his face is unflinching.

---

3. A simile, derived from ancient Chinese texts, for someone who doesn't know his own limitations.
4. Customers visiting the licensed quarter by day wear these deep wicker hats (which virtually conceal the face) in order to preserve the secrecy of their visits. But this customer wears a hat even at night.
5. A play on words centering on the syllables *ami*, part of the name Amida Buddha, and on *amigasa*, meaning "woven hat."

[TAHEI]: Koharu, I'm a townsman. I've never worn a sword, but I've lots of New Silver[6] at my place, and I think that the glint could twist a mere couple of swords out of joint. Imagine that wretch from the toilet paper shop, with a capital as thin as tissue, trying to compete with the Lone Wolf! That's the height of impertinence! I'll wander down now from Sakura Bridge to Middle Street, and if I meet that Wastepaper along the way, I'll trample him under foot. Come on, men.

CHANTER: Their gestures, at least, have a cavalier assurance as they swagger off, taking up the whole street. The samurai customer patiently endures the fool, indifferent to his remarks because of the surroundings, but every word of gossip about Jihei, whether for good or ill, affects Koharu. She is so depressed that she stands there blankly, unable even to greet her guest. Sugi, the maid from the Kinokuni House, runs up from home, looking annoyed.

[SUGI]: When I left you here a while ago, Miss Koharu, your guest hadn't appeared yet, and they gave me a terrible scolding when I got back for not having checked on him. I'm very sorry, sir, but please excuse me a minute.

CHANTER: She lifts the woven hat and examines the face.

[SUGI]: Oh—it's not him! There's nothing to worry about, Koharu. Ask your guest to keep you for the whole night, and show him how sweet you can be. Give him a barrelful of nectar![7] Good-bye, madam, I'll see you later, honey.

CHANTER: She takes her leave with a cloying stream of puns. The extremely hard baked[8] samurai is furious.

[SAMURAI]: What's the meaning of this? You'd think from the way she appraised my face that I was a tea canister or a porcelain cup! I didn't come here to be trifled with. It's difficult enough for me to leave the residence even by day, and in order to spend the night away I had to ask the senior officer's permission and sign the register. You can see how complicated the regulations make things. But I'm in love, miss, just from hearing about you, and I wanted very badly to spend a night with you. I came here a while ago without an escort and made the arrangements with the teahouse. I had been looking forward to your kind reception, a memory to last me a lifetime, but you haven't so much as smiled at me or said a word of greeting. You keep your head down as if you were counting money in your lap. Aren't you afraid of getting a stiff neck? Madam—I've never heard the like. Here I come to a teahouse, and I must play the part of night nurse in a maternity room!

[PROPRIETRESS]: You're quite right, sir. Your surprise is entirely justified, considering that you don't know the reasons. This girl is deeply in love with a customer named Kamiji. It's been Kamiji today and Kamiji tomorrow, with nobody else allowed a chance at her. Her other customers have scattered in every direction, like leaves in a storm. When two people get so carried away with each other, it often leads to trouble, for both the customer and the girl. In the first place, it interferes with business, and the owner, whoever he may be, must prevent it. That's why all her guests are examined. Koharu is naturally depressed—it's only to be expected. You are annoyed, which is equally to be expected. But speaking as the proprietress here, it seems to me that the essential thing is for you to meet each other halfway and cheer up. Come, have a drink.—Act a little more lively, Koharu.

CHANTER: Koharu, without answering, lifts her tear-stained face.

---

6. Good-quality coinage of about 1720.
7. The imagery used by the maid has been altered from puns on saltiness (soy sauce, green vegetables, and so forth) to puns on sweetness.
8. A technical term of pottery making, meaning "hard-fired."

[KOHARU]: Tell me, samurai, they say that if you're going to kill yourself anyway, people who die during the Ten Nights[9] are sure to become Buddhas. Is that really true?

[SAMURAI]: How should I know? Ask the priest at your family temple.

[KOHARU]: Yes, that's right. But there's something I'd like to ask a samurai. If you're committing suicide, it'd be a lot more painful, wouldn't it, to cut your throat rather than hang yourself?

[SAMURAI]: I've never tried cutting my throat to see whether or not it hurt. Please ask more sensible questions.—What an unpleasant girl!

CHANTER: Samurai though he is, he looks nonplussed.

[PROPRIETRESS]: Koharu, that's a shocking way to treat a guest the first time you meet him. I'll go and get my husband. We'll have some saké together. That ought to liven things up a bit.

CHANTER: The gate she leaves is lighted by the evening moon low in the sky; the clouds and the passers in the street have thinned.

For long years there has lived in Tenma, the seat of the mighty god,[1] though not a god himself, Kamiji,[2] a name often bruited by the gongs of worldly gossip, so deeply, hopelessly, is he tied to Koharu by the ropes[3] of an ill-starred love. Now is the tenth moon, the month when no gods will unite them;[4] they are thwarted in their love, unable to meet. They swore in the last letters they exchanged that if only they could meet, that day would be their last. Night after night Jihei, ready for death, trudges to the Quarter, distracted, as though his soul had left a body consumed by the fires of love.

At a roadside eating stand he hears people gossiping about Koharu. "She's at Kawashō with a samurai customer," someone says, and immediately Jihei decides, "It will be tonight!"

He peers through the latticework window and sees a guest in the inside room, his face obscured by a hood. Only the moving chin is visible, and Jihei cannot hear what is said.

[JIHEI]: Poor Koharu! How thin her face is! She keeps it turned away from the lamp. In her heart she's thinking only of me. I'll signal her that I'm here, and we'll run off together. Then which will it be—Umeda or Kitano?[5] Oh—I want to tell her I'm here. I want to call her.

CHANTER: He beckons with his heart, his spirit flies to her; but his body, like a cicada's cast-off shell, clings to the latticework. He weeps with impatience. The guest in the inside room gives a great yawn.

[SAMURAI]: What a bore, playing nursemaid to a prostitute with worries on her mind!—The street seems quiet now. Let's go to the end room. We can at least distract ourselves by looking at the lanterns. Come with me.

CHANTER: They go together to the outer room. Jihei, alarmed, squeezes into the patch of shadow under the lattice window. Inside they do not realize that anyone is eavesdropping.

9. A period in the Tenth Month when special Buddhist services were conducted in temples of the Pure Land (Jōdo) sect. It was believed that persons who died during this period immediately became Buddhas.

1. Tenma, one of the principal districts of Ōsaka, was the site of the Tenjin Shrine, for the worship of the deified Sugawara no Michizane (845–903).

2. The word kami, for "paper," sounds like kami, "god."

We have thus "Kami who is not a kami"—the paper dealer who isn't a god.

3. The sacred ropes at a Shintō shrine.

4. The Tenth Month was a time when the gods were believed to gather at Izumo; they thus were absent from the rest of Japan.

5. Both places had well-known cemeteries.

[SAMURAI]: I've been noticing your behavior and the little things you've said this evening. It's plain to me that you intend a love suicide with Kamiji, or whatever his name is—the man the hostess mentioned. I'm sure I'm right. I realize that no amount of advice or reasoning is likely to penetrate the ears of somebody bewitched by the god of death, but I must say that you're exceedingly foolish. The boy's family won't blame him for his recklessness, but they will blame and hate you. You'll be shamed by the public exposure of your body. Your parents may be dead, for all I know, but if they're alive, you'll be punished in hell as a wicked daughter. Do you think you'll become a buddha? You and your lover won't even be able to fall smoothly into hell together! What a pity—and what a tragedy! This is only our first meeting, but as a samurai, I can't let you die without trying to save you. No doubt money's the problem. I'd like to help, if five or ten *ryō* would be of service. I swear by the god Hachiman and by my good fortune as a samurai that I will never reveal to anyone what you tell me. Open your heart without fear.

CHANTER: He whispers these words. She joins her hands and bows.

[KOHARU]: I'm extremely grateful. Thank you for your kind words and for swearing an oath to me, someone you've never had for a lover or even a friend. I'm so grateful that I'm crying.—Yes, it's as they say, when you've something on your mind it shows on your face. You were right. I have promised Kamiji to die with him. But we've been completely prevented from meeting by my master, and Jihei, for various reasons, can't ransom me at once. My contracts with my former master[6] and my present one still have five years to run. If somebody else claimed me during that time, it would be a blow to me, of course, but a worse disgrace to Jihei's honor. He suggested that it would be better if we killed ourselves, and I agreed. I was caught by obligations from which I could not withdraw, and I promised him before I knew what I was doing. I said, "We'll watch for a chance, and I'll slip out when you give the signal." "Yes," he said, "slip out somehow." Ever since then I've been leading a life of uncertainty, never knowing from one day to the next when my last hour will come.

I have a mother living in a back alley south of here. She has no one but me to depend on, and she does piecework to eke out a living. I keep thinking that after I'm dead she'll become a beggar or an outcast, and maybe she'll die of starvation. That's the only sad part about dying. I have just this one life. I'm ashamed that you may think me a coldhearted woman, but I must endure the shame. The most important thing is that I don't want to die. I beg you, please help me stay alive.

CHANTER: As she speaks, the samurai nods thoughtfully. Jihei, crouching outside, hears her words with astonishment; they are so unexpected to his manly heart that he feels like a monkey who has tumbled from a tree. He is frantic with agitation.

[JIHEI, *to himself*]: Then was everything a lie? Ahhh—I'm furious! For two whole years I've been bewitched by that rotten she-fox! Shall I break in and kill her with one blow of my sword? Or shall I satisfy my anger by shaming her to her face?

CHANTER: He gnashes his teeth and weeps in chagrin. Inside the house Koharu speaks through her tears.

[KOHARU]: It's a curious thing to ask, but would you please show the kindness of a samurai and become my customer for the rest of this year and into next spring? Whenever Jihei comes, intent on death, please step in and force him to postpone

---

6. The master at the bathhouse where Koharu formerly worked.

his plan. In this way our relations can be broken quite naturally. He won't have to kill himself, and my life will also be saved.—What evil connection from a former existence made us promise to die? How I regret it now!

CHANTER: She weeps, leaning on the samurai's knee.

[SAMURAI]: Very well, I'll do as you ask. I think I can help you.—But I feel a breeze. Somebody may be watching.

CHANTER: He slams shut the latticework *shōji*. Jihei, listening outside, is in a frenzy.

[JIHEI]: Exactly what you'd expect from a whore, a cheap whore! I misjudged her foul nature. She robbed the soul from my body, the thieving harlot! Shall I slash her or run her through? What am I to do?

CHANTER: The shadows of two profiles fall on the *shōji*.

[JIHEI]: I'd like to give her a taste of my fist and trample her.—What are they chattering about? See how they nod to each other! Now she's bowing to him, whispering and sniveling. I've tried to control myself—I've pressed my chest, I've stroked it—but I can't stand any more. This is too much to endure!

CHANTER: His heart pounds wildly as he unsheathes his dirk, a Magoroku of Seki. "Koharu's side must be here," he judges, and stabs through an opening in the latticework. But Koharu is too far away for his thrust, and although she cries out in terror, she remains unharmed. Her guest instantly leaps at Jihei, grabs his hands, and jerks them through the latticework. With his sword knot he quickly and securely fastens Jihei's hands to the window upright.

[SAMURAI]: Don't scream, Koharu. Don't look at him.

CHANTER: At this moment the proprietor and his wife return. They exclaim in alarm.

[SAMURAI]: This needn't concern you. Some ruffian ran his sword through the *shōji*, and I've tied his arms to the latticework. I have my own way of dealing with him. Don't untie the cord. If you attract a crowd, the place is sure to be thrown in an uproar. Let's all go inside. Come with me, Koharu. We'll go to bed.

CHANTER: Koharu answers yes, but she recognizes the handle of the dirk, and the memory—if not the blade—transfixes her breast.

[KOHARU]: There're always people doing crazy things in the Quarter when they've had too much to drink. Why don't you let him go without making any trouble? I think that's best, don't you?

[SAMURAI]: Out of the question. Do as I say—inside, all of you. Koharu, come along.

CHANTER: Jihei can still see their shadows even after they enter the inner room, but he is bound to the spot, his hands held in fetters that grip him more tightly as he struggles, his body beset by suffering as he tastes a living shame worse than a dog's.[7] More determined than ever to die, he sheds tears of blood, a pitiful sight.

Tahei the Lone Wolf returns from his carousing.

[TAHEI]: That's Jihei standing by Kawashō's window. I'll give him a thrashing.

CHANTER: He catches Jihei by the collar and starts to lift him over his back.

[JIHEI]: Owww!

[TAHEI]: Owww? What kind of weakling are you? Oh, I see—you're tied here. You must've been pulling off a robbery. You dirty pickpocket! You rotten pickpocket!

CHANTER: He beats Jihei mercilessly.

[TAHEI]: You burglar! You convict!

CHANTER: He kicks him wildly.

---

7. A proverb of Buddhist origin: "Suffering follows one like a dog."

[TAHEI]: Kamiya Jihei's been caught burgling, and they've tied him up!

CHANTER: Passersby and people of the neighborhood, attracted by his shouts, quickly gather. The samurai rushes from the house.

[SAMURAI]: Who's calling him a burglar? You? Tell me what Jihei's stolen! Out with it!

CHANTER: He seizes Tahei and forces him into the dirt. Tahei rises to his feet only for the samurai to kick him down again and again. He grabs Tahei.

[SAMURAI]: Jihei! Kick him to your heart's content!

CHANTER: He pushes Tahei under Jihei's feet. Bound though he is, Jihei stamps furiously on Tahei's face. Tahei, thoroughly kicked and covered with muck, gets to his feet and glares around him.

[TAHEI, *to bystander*]: How could you fools just stand there and let him step on me? I know every one of your faces, and I intend to pay you back. Remember that!

CHANTER: He makes his escape, still determined to have the last word. The spectators burst out laughing.

[VOICES]: Listen to him brag, even after he's been beaten up! Let's throw him from the bridge and give him a drink of water! Don't let him get away!

CHANTER: They chase after him. When the crowd has dispersed, the samurai goes to Jihei and unfastens the knots. He shows his face with his hood removed.

[JIHEI]: Magoemon! My brother! How shameful!

CHANTER: He sinks to the ground and weeps, prostrating himself in the dirt.

[KOHARU]: Are you his brother, sir?

CHANTER: Koharu runs to them. Jihei, catching her by the front of the kimono, forces her to the ground.

[JIHEI]: Beast! She-fox! I'd sooner kick you than Tahei!

CHANTER: He raises his foot, but Magoemon calls out.

[MAGOEMON]: That's the kind of foolishness that's gotten you into all this trouble. A prostitute's business is to deceive men. Are you just realizing that? I could see to the bottom of her heart the very first time I met her, but you're so scatterbrained that in more than two years of sleeping with this woman you never figured out what she was thinking. Instead of kicking Koharu, why don't you use your feet on your own misguided disposition?—It's deplorable. You may be my younger brother, but you're almost thirty, and you've got a six-year-old boy and a four-year-old girl, Kantarō and Osue. You run a shop with a thirty-six-foot frontage,[8] but you don't seem to realize that your whole fortune's collapsing. You shouldn't have to be lectured to by your brother. Your father-in-law is your aunt's husband, and your mother-in-law is your aunt. They've always been like real parents to you. Your wife Osan is my cousin, too. The ties of marriage are multiplied by those of blood. But when the family has a reunion, the only subject of discussion is our mortification over your incessant visits to Sonezaki. I feel sorry for our poor aunt. You know what a stiff-necked gentleman of the old school her husband Gozaemon is. He's forever flying into a rage and saying, "We've been tricked by your nephew. He's deserted our daughter. I'll take Osan back and ruin Jihei's reputation throughout Tenma." Our aunt, with all the heartache to bear herself, sometimes sides with him and sometimes with you. She's worried herself sick. What an ingrate not to appreciate how she's defended you in your shame! This one offense is enough to make you the target for Heaven's future punishment!

8. A large shop.

I realized that your marriage couldn't last much longer at this rate. So I decided, in the hopes of relieving our aunt's worries, that I'd see with my own eyes what kind of woman Koharu was and work out some sort of solution afterward. I consulted the proprietor here, then came myself to investigate the cause of your sickness. I see now how easy it was for you to desert your wife and children. What a faithful prostitute you discovered! I congratulate you!

And here I am, Magoemon the Miller,[9] known far and wide for my paragon of a brother, dressed up like a masquerader at a festival or maybe a lunatic! I put on swords for the first time in my life and announced myself, like a bit player in a costume piece, as an officer at a residence. I feel like an absolute idiot with these swords, but there's nowhere I can dispose of them now.—It's so infuriating—and ridiculous—that it's given me a pain in the chest.

CHANTER: He gnashes his teeth and grimaces, attempting to hide his tears. Koharu, choking all the while with emotion, can only say:

[KOHARU]: Yes, you're entirely right.

CHANTER: The rest is lost in tears. Jihei pounds the ground with his fist.

[JIHEI]: I was wrong. Forgive me, Magoemon. For three years I've been possessed by that witch. I've neglected my parents, relatives—even my wife and children—and wrecked my fortune, all because I was deceived by Koharu, that sneak thief! I'm utterly mortified. But I'm through with her now, and I'll never set foot here again. Weasel! Vixen! Sneak thief! Here's proof that I've broken with her!

CHANTER: He pulls out the amulet bag that has rested next to his skin.

[JIHEI]: Here are the written oaths we've exchanged, one at the beginning of each month, twenty-nine in all. I am returning them. This means our love and affection are over. Take them.

CHANTER: He flings the notes at her.

[JIHEI]: Magoemon, get my pledges from her. Please make sure you get them all. Then burn them with your own hands. [*To Koharu.*] Give them to my brother.

[KOHARU]: As you wish.

CHANTER: In tears, she surrenders the amulet bag. Magoemon opens it.

[MAGOEMON]: One, two, three, four . . . ten . . . twenty-nine. They're all here. There's also a letter from a woman. What's this?

CHANTER: He starts to unfold it.

[KOHARU]: That's an important letter. I can't let you see it.

CHANTER: She clings to Magoemon's arm, but he pushes her away. He holds the letter to the lamplight and examines the address, "To Miss Koharu from Kamiya Osan." As soon as he reads the words, he casually thrusts the letter into his kimono.

[MAGOEMON]: Koharu. A while ago I swore by my good fortune as a samurai, but now Magoemon the Miller swears by his good fortune as a businessman that he will show this letter to no one, not even his wife. I alone will read it, then burn it with the oaths. You can trust me. I will not break this oath.

[KOHARU]: Thank you. You save my honor.

CHANTER: She bursts into tears again.

[JIHEI *laughs contemptuously*]: Save your honor! You talk like a human being! [*To Magoemon.*] I don't want to see her cursed face another minute. Let's go. No—I

---

9. Magoemon is a dealer in flour (for noodles). His shop name Konaya—"the flour merchant"—is used almost as a surname.

can't hold so much resentment and bitterness! I'll kick her one in the face, a memory to treasure for the rest of my life. Excuse me, please.

CHANTER: He strides up to Koharu and stamps on the ground.

[JIHEI]: For three years I've loved you, delighted in you, longed for you, adored you; but today my foot will say my only farewells.

CHANTER: He kicks her sharply on the forehead and bursts into tears. The brothers leave, forlorn figures. Koharu, unhappy woman, raises her voice in lament as she watches them go. Is she faithful or unfaithful? Her true feelings are hidden in the words penned by Jihei's wife, a letter that no one has seen. Jihei goes his separate way without learning the truth.

ACT 2

Scene 1

Scene: The house and shop of Kamiya Jihei. Time: Ten days later.

CHANTER: The busy street that runs straight to Tenjin Bridge,[1] named for the god of Tenma, bringer of good fortune, is known as the Street Before the Kami,[2] and here a paper shop does business under the name Kamiya Jihei. The paper is honestly sold, and the shop is well situated; it is a long-established firm, and customers come thick as raindrops.

Outside, crowds pass in the street, on their way to the Ten Nights service, while inside, the husband dozes in the kotatsu,[3] shielded from drafts by a screen at his pillow. His wife Osan keeps solitary, anxious watch over shop and house.

[OSAN]: The days are so short—it's dinnertime already, but Tama still hasn't returned from her errand to Ichinokawa.[4] I wonder what can be keeping her. That scamp Sangorō isn't back either. The wind is freezing. I'm sure both the children will be cold. He doesn't even realize that it's time for Osue to be nursed. Heaven preserve me from ever becoming such a fool! What an infuriating creature!

CHANTER: She speaks to herself.

[KANTARŌ]: Mama, I've come back all by myself.

CHANTER: Her son, the older child, runs up to the house.

[OSAN]: Kantarō—is that you? What's happened to Osue and Sangorō?

[KANTARŌ]: They're playing by the shrine. Osue wanted her milk, and she was bawling her head off.

[OSAN]: I was sure she would. Oh—your hands and feet are frozen stiff as nails! Go and warm yourself at the kotatsu. Your father's sleeping there.—What am I to do with that idiot?

CHANTER: She runs out impatiently to the shop just as Sangorō shuffles back, alone.

[OSAN]: Come here, you fool! Where have you left Osue?

[SANGORŌ]: You know, I must've lost her somewhere. Maybe somebody's picked her up. Should I go back for her?

[OSAN]: How could you! If any harm has come to my precious child, I'll beat you to death!

CHANTER: But while she is screaming at him, the maid Tama returns with Osue on her back.

---

1. The reference is to Tenma Tenjin, a deified form of Sugawara no Michizane.
2. Again, a play on the words *kami* (god) and *kami* (paper).

3. A source of heat in which a charcoal burner is placed under a low, quilt-covered table.
4. The site of a large vegetable market near the north end of Tenjin Bridge.

[TAMA]: The poor child—I found her in tears at the corner. Sangorō, when you're supposed to look after the child, do it properly.

[OSAN]: You poor dear. You must want your milk.

CHANTER: She joins the others by the kotatsu and nurses the child.

[OSAN]: Tama—give that fool a taste of something that he'll remember![5]

CHANTER: Sangorō shakes his head.

[SANGORŌ]: No, thanks. I gave each of the children two tangerines just a while ago at the shrine, and I tasted five myself.

CHANTER: Fool though he is, bad puns come from him nimbly enough, and the others can only smile despite themselves.

[TAMA]: Oh—I've become so involved with this half-wit that I almost forgot to tell you, ma'am, that Mr. Magoemon and his aunt[6] are on their way here from the west.

[OSAN]: Oh dear! In that case, I'll have to wake Jihei. [To Jihei] Please get up. Mother and Magoemon are coming. They'll be upset again if you let them see you, a businessman, sleeping in the afternoon, with the day as short as it is.

[JIHEI]: All right.

CHANTER: He struggles to a sitting position and, with his abacus in one hand, pulls his account book to him with the other.

[JIHEI]: Two into ten goes five, three into nine goes three, three into six goes two, seven times eight is fifty-six.

CHANTER: His fifty-six-year-old aunt enters with Magoemon.

[JIHEI]: Magoemon, aunt. How good of you. Please come in. I was in the midst of some urgent calculations. Four nines makes thirty-six *monme*. Three sixes make eighteen *fun*. That's two *monme* less two *fun*.[7] Kantarō! Osue! Granny and Uncle have come! Bring the tobacco tray! One times three makes three. Osan, serve the tea.[8]

CHANTER: He jabbers away.

[AUNT]: We haven't come for tea or tobacco. Osan, you're young, I know, but you're the mother of two children, and your excessive forbearance does you no credit. A man's dissipation can always be traced to his wife's carelessness. Remember, it's not only the man who's disgraced when he goes bankrupt and his marriage breaks up. You'd do well to take notice of what's going on and assert yourself a bit more.

[MAGOEMON]: It's foolish to hope for any results, aunt. The scoundrel deceives even me, his elder brother. Why should he take to heart criticism from his wife? Jihei—you played me for a fool. After showing me how you returned Koharu's pledges, here you are, not ten days later, redeeming her! What does this mean? I suppose your urgent calculations are of Koharu's debts! I've had enough!

CHANTER: He snatches away the abacus and flings it clattering into the hallway.

[JIHEI]: You're making an enormous fuss without any cause. I haven't left the house since the last time I saw you, except to go twice to the wholesalers in Imabashi and once to the Tenjin Shrine. I haven't even thought of Koharu, much less redeemed her.

[AUNT]: None of your evasions! Last evening at the Ten Nights service I heard the people in the congregation gossiping. Everybody was talking about the great patron from Tenma who'd fallen in love with a prostitute named Koharu from the Kinokuni House in Sonezaki. They said he'd driven away her other guests and was

---

5. A pun on the two meanings of *kurawasu:* "to cause to eat" and "to beat."
6. Magoemon's (and Jihei's) aunt but Osan's mother.

7. Meaningless calculations. Twenty *fun* made two *monme.*
8. The name Osan echoes the word *san* (three).

going to ransom her in the next couple of days. There was all kinds of gossip about the abundance of money and fools even in these days of high prices.

My husband Gozaemon has been hearing about Koharu constantly, and he's sure that her great patron from Tenma must be you, Jihei. He told me, "He's your nephew, but to me he's a stranger, and my daughter's happiness is my chief concern. Once he ransoms the prostitute he'll no doubt sell his wife to a brothel. I intend to take her back before he starts selling her clothes."

He was halfway out of the house before I could stop him. "Don't get so excited. We can settle this calmly. First we must make sure whether or not the rumors are true."

That's why Magoemon and I are here now. He was telling me a while ago that the Jihei of today was not the Jihei of yesterday—that you'd broken all connections with Sonezaki and completely reformed. But now I hear that you've had a relapse. What disease can this be?

Your father was my brother. When the poor man was on his deathbed, he lifted his head from the pillow and begged me to look after you, as my son-in-law and nephew. I've never forgotten those last words, but your perversity has made a mockery of his request!

CHANTER: She collapses in tears of resentment. Jihei claps his hands in sudden recognition.

[JIHEI]: I have it! The Koharu everybody's gossiping about is the same Koharu, but the great patron who's to redeem her is a different man. The other day, as my brother can tell you, Tahei—they call him the Lone Wolf because he hasn't any family or relations—started a fight and was beaten up. He gets all the money he needs from his home town, and he's been trying for a long time to redeem Koharu. I've always prevented him, but I'm sure he's decided that now is his chance. I have nothing to do with it.

CHANTER: Osan brightens at his words.

[OSAN]: No matter how forbearing I might be—even if I were an angel—you don't suppose I'd encourage my husband to redeem a prostitute! In this instance at any rate there's not a word of untruth in what my husband has said. I'll be a witness to that, Mother.

CHANTER: Husband's and wife's words tally perfectly.

[AUNT]: Then it's true?

CHANTER: The aunt and nephew clap their hands with relief.

[MAGOEMON]: Well, I'm happy it's over, anyway. To make us feel doubly reassured, will you write an affidavit that will dispel any doubts your stubborn uncle may have?

[JIHEI]: Certainly. I'll write a thousand if you like.

[MAGOEMON]: Splendid! I happen to have bought this on the way here.

CHANTER: Magoemon takes from the fold of his kimono a sheet of oath-paper from Kumano, the sacred characters formed by flocks of crows.[9] Instead of vows of eternal love, Jihei now signs under penalty of Heaven's wrath an oath that he will sever all ties and affections with Koharu. "If I should lie, may Bonten and Taishaku above, and the Four Great Kings below, afflict me!"[1] So the text runs and

---

9. The charms issued by the Shintō shrine at Kumano were printed with six Chinese characters, whose strokes were in the shape of crows. The reverse side of these charms was used for writing oaths.

1. A formal oath. Bonten (Brahma) and Taishaku (Indra), though Hindu gods, were considered to be protective deities of the Buddhist law. The four Deva kings served under Indra and were also protectors of Buddhism.

to it is appended the names of many Buddhas and gods. He signs his name, Kamiya Jihei, in bold characters, seals the oath with blood, and hands it over.

[OSAN]: It's a great relief to me too. Mother, I have you and Magoemon to thank. Jihei and I have had two children, but this is his firmest pledge of affection. I hope you share my joy.

[AUNT]: Indeed we do. I'm sure that Jihei will settle down and his business will improve, now that he's in this frame of mind. It's been entirely for his sake and for love of the grandchildren that we've intervened. Come, Magoemon, let's be on our way. I'm anxious to set my husband's mind at ease.—It's become chilly here. See that the children don't catch cold.—This, too, we owe to the Buddha of the Ten Nights. I'll say a prayer of thanks before I go. Hail, Amida Buddha!

CHANTER: She leaves, her heart innocent as Buddha's. Jihei is perfunctory even about seeing them to the door. Hardly have they crossed the threshold than he slumps down again at the kotatsu. He pulls the checked quilting over his head.

[OSAN]: You still haven't forgotten Sonezaki, have you?

CHANTER: She goes up to him in disgust and tears away the quilting. He is weeping; a waterfall of tears streams along the pillow, deep enough to bear him afloat. She tugs him upright and props his body against the kotatsu frame. She stares into his face.

[OSAN]: You're acting outrageously, Jihei. You shouldn't have signed that oath if you felt so reluctant to leave her. The year before last, on the middle day of the boar of the Tenth Month,[2] we lit the first fire in the kotatsu and celebrated by sleeping here together, pillow to pillow. Ever since then—did some demon or snake creep into my bosom that night?—for two whole years I've been condemned to keep watch over an empty nest. I thought that tonight at least, thanks to Mother and Magoemon, we'd share sweet words in bed as husbands and wives do, but my pleasure didn't last long. How cruel of you, how utterly heartless! Go ahead, cry your eyes out, if you're so attached to her. Your tears will flow into Shijimi River, and Koharu, no doubt, will ladle them out and drink them! You're ignoble, inhuman.

CHANTER: She embraces his knees and throws herself over him, moaning in supplication. Jihei wipes his eyes.

[JIHEI]: If tears of grief flowed from the eyes and tears of anger from the ears, I could show my heart without saying a word. But my tears all pour in the same way from my eyes, and there's no difference in their color. It's not surprising that you can't tell what's in my heart. I have not a shred of attachment left for that vampire in human skin, but I bear a grudge against Tahei. He has all the money he wants and no wife or children. He's schemed again and again to redeem her, but Koharu refused to give in, at least until I broke with her. She told me time and again, "You have nothing to worry about. I'll never let myself be redeemed by Tahei, not even if my ties with you are ended and I can no longer stay by your side. If my master is induced by Tahei's money to deliver me to him, I'll kill myself in a way that'll do you credit!" But think—not ten days have passed since I broke with her, and she's to be redeemed by Tahei! That rotten whore! That animal! No, I haven't a trace of affection left for her, but I can just hear how Tahei will be boasting. He'll spread the word around Ōsaka that my business has come to a standstill and I'm hard pressed for money. I'll meet with contemptuous stares from the wholesalers. I'll be dishonored. My heart is broken, and my body burns with shame. What a disgrace!

2. It was customary to light the first fire of the winter on this day.

How maddening! I've passed the stage of shedding hot tears, tears of blood, sticky tears—my tears now are of molten iron!

CHANTER: He collapses, weeping. Osan turns pale with alarm.

[OSAN]: If that's the situation, poor Koharu will surely kill herself.

[JIHEI]: You're too well bred, despite your intelligence, to understand someone like her! What makes you suppose that faithless creature would kill herself? Far from it—she's probably taking moxa treatments and medicine to prolong her life!

[OSAN]: No, that's not true. I was determined never to tell you so long as I lived, but I'm afraid of the crime I'd be committing if I concealed the facts and let her die with my knowledge. I will reveal my great secret. There is not a grain of deceit in Koharu. It was I who schemed to end the relations between you. I could see signs that you were drifting toward suicide. I felt so unhappy that I wrote a letter, begging her as one woman to another to break with you, even though I knew how painful it would be. I asked her to save your life. The letter must have moved her. She answered that she would give you up, even though you were more precious than life itself, because she could not shirk her duty to me. I've kept her letter with me ever since—it's been like a protective charm. Would such a noble-hearted woman break her promise and brazenly marry Tahei? When a woman—I no less than another—has given herself completely to a man, she does not change. I'm sure she'll kill herself. I'm sure of it. Ahhh—what a dreadful thing to have happened! Save her, please.

CHANTER: Her voice rises in agitation. Her husband is thrown into a turmoil.

[JIHEI]: There was a letter in an unknown woman's hand among the written oaths she surrendered to my brother. It must have been from you. If that's the case, Koharu will surely commit suicide.

[OSAN]: Alas! I'd be failing in the obligations I owe her as another woman if I allowed her to die. Please go to her at once. Don't let her kill herself.

CHANTER: Clinging to her husband, she melts in tears.

[JIHEI]: But what can I possibly do? It'd take half the amount of her ransom in earnest money merely to keep her out of Tahei's clutches. I can't save Koharu's life without administering a dose of 750 *monme* in New Silver.[3] How could I raise that much money in my present financial straits? Even if I crush my body to powder, where will the money come from?

[OSAN]: Don't exaggerate the difficulties. If that's all you need, it's simple enough.

CHANTER: She goes to the wardrobe, and opening a small drawer takes out a bag fastened with cords of twisted silk. She unhesitatingly tears it open and throws down a packet which Jihei retrieves.

[JIHEI]: What's this? Money? Four hundred *monme* in New Silver? How in the world—

CHANTER: He stares astonished at this money he never put there.

[OSAN]: I'll tell you later where this money came from. I've scraped it together to pay the bill for Iwakuni paper that falls due the day after tomorrow. We'll have to ask Magoemon to help us keep the business from going bankrupt. But Koharu comes first. The packet contains 400 *monme*. That leaves 350 *monme* to raise.

CHANTER: She unlocks a large drawer. From the wardrobe lightly fly kite-colored Hachijō silks; a Kyōto crepe kimono lined in pale brown, insubstantial as her

---

3. Koharu's plight is described as a sickness. If 750 *me* is half the sum needed to redeem Koharu, the total of 1,500 *me* (or 6,000 *me* in Old Silver) is considerably less than the 10 *kanme*, or 10,000 *me* in Old Silver, mentioned by Tahei.

husband's life, which flickers today and may vanish tomorrow; a padded kimono of Osue's, a flaming scarlet inside and out—Osan flushes with pain to part with it; Kantarō's sleeveless, unlined jacket—if she pawns this, he'll be cold this winter. Next comes a garment of striped Gunnai silk lined in pale blue and never worn, and then her best formal costume—heavy black silk dyed with her family crest, an ivy leaf in a ring. They say that those joined by marriage ties can even go naked at home, although outside the house clothes make the man: she snatches up even her husband's finery, a silken cloak, making fifteen articles in all.

[OSAN]: The very least the pawnshop can offer is 350 *monme* in New Silver.

CHANTER: Her face glows as though she already held the money she needs; she hides in the one bundle her husband's shame and her own obligation and puts her love in besides.

[OSAN]: It doesn't matter if the children and I have nothing to wear. My husband's reputation concerns me more. Ransom Koharu. Save her. Assert your honor before Tahei.

CHANTER: But Jihei's eyes remain downcast all the while, and he is silently weeping.

[JIHEI]: Yes, I can pay the earnest money and keep her out of Tahei's hands. But once I've redeemed her, I'll either have to maintain her in a separate establishment or bring her here. Then what will become of you?

CHANTER: Osan is at a loss to answer.

[OSAN]: Yes, what shall I do? Shall I become your children's nurse or the cook? Or perhaps the retired mistress of the house?

CHANTER: She falls to the floor with a cry of woe.

[JIHEI]: That would be too selfish. I'd be afraid to accept such generosity. Even if the punishment for my crimes against my parents, against Heaven, against the gods and the Buddhas fails to strike me, the punishment for my crimes against my wife alone will be sufficient to destroy all hope for the future life. Forgive me, I beg you.

CHANTER: He joins his hands in tearful entreaty.

[OSAN]: Why should you bow before me? I don't deserve it. I'd be glad to rip the nails from my fingers and toes, to do anything that might serve my husband. I've been pawning my clothes for some time in order to scrape together the money for the paper wholesalers' bills. My wardrobe is empty, but I don't regret it in the least. But it's too late now to talk of such things. Hurry, change your cloak and go to her with a smile.

CHANTER: He puts on an underkimono of Gunnai silk, a robe of heavy black silk, and a striped cloak. His sash of figured damask holds a dirk of middle length worked in gold: Buddha surely knows that tonight it will be stained with Koharu's blood.

[JIHEI]: Sangorō! Come here!

CHANTER: Jihei loads the bundle on the servant's back, intending to take him along. Then he firmly thrusts the wallet next to his skin and starts toward the gate.

[VOICE]: Is Jihei at home?

CHANTER: A man enters, removing his fur cap. They see—good heavens!—that it is Gozaemon.

[OSAN and JIHEI]: Ahhh—how fortunate that you should come at this moment!

CHANTER: Husband and wife are upset and confused. Gozaemon snatches away Sangorō's bundle and sits heavily. His voice is sharp.

[GOZAEMON]: Stay where you are, harlot!—My esteemed son-in-law, what a rare pleasure to see you dressed in your finest attire, with a dirk and a silken cloak! Ahhh—that's how a gentleman of means spends his money! No one would take you for a paper dealer. Are you perchance on your way to the New Quarter? What commendable perseverance! You have no need for your wife, I take it.—Give her a divorce. I've come to take her home with me.

CHANTER: He speaks needles and his voice is bitter. Jihei has not a word to reply.

[OSAN]: How kind of you, Father, to walk here on such a cold day. Do have a cup of tea.

CHANTER: Offering the teacup serves as an excuse for edging closer.

[OSAN]: Mother and Magoemon came here a while ago, and they told my husband how much they disapproved of his visits to the New Quarter. Jihei was in tears and he wrote out an oath swearing he had reformed. He gave it to Mother. Haven't you seen it yet?

[GOZAEMON]: His written oath? Do you mean this?

CHANTER: He takes the paper from his kimono.

[GOZAEMON]: Libertines scatter vows and oaths wherever they go, as if they were monthly statements of accounts. I thought there was something peculiar about this oath, and now that I am here I can see I was right. Do you still swear to Bonten and Taishaku? Instead of such nonsense, write out a bill of divorcement!

CHANTER: He rips the oath to shreds and throws down the pieces. Husband and wife exchange looks of alarm, stunned into silence. Jihei touches his hands to the floor and bows his head.

[JIHEI]: Your anger is justified. If I were still my former self, I would try to offer explanations, but today I appeal entirely to your generosity. Please let me stay with Osan. I promise that even if I become a beggar or an outcast and must sustain life with the scraps that fall from other people's chopsticks, I will hold Osan in high honor and protect her from every harsh and bitter experience. I feel so deeply indebted to Osan that I cannot divorce her. You will understand that this is true as time passes and I show you how I apply myself to my work and restore my fortune. Until then please shut your eyes and allow us to remain together.

CHANTER: Tears of blood stream from his eyes and his face is pressed to the matting in contrition.

[GOZAEMON]: The wife of an outcast! That's all the worse. Write the bill of divorcement at once! I will verify and seal the furniture and clothes Osan brought in her dowry.

CHANTER: He goes to the wardrobe. Osan is alarmed.

[OSAN]: All my clothes are here. There's no need to examine them.

CHANTER: She runs up to stop him, but Gozaemon pushes her aside and jerks open a drawer.

[GOZAEMON]: What does this mean?

CHANTER: He opens another drawer: it too is empty. He pulls out every last drawer, but not so much as a foot of patchwork cloth is to be seen. He tears open the wicker hampers, long boxes, and clothes chests.

[GOZAEMON]: Stripped bare, are they?

CHANTER: His eyes set in fury. Jihei and Osan huddle under the striped kotatsu quilts, ready to sink into the fire with humiliation.

[GOZAEMON]: This bundle looks suspicious.

CHANTER: He unties the knots and dumps out the contents.

[GOZAEMON]: As I thought! You were sending these to the pawnshop, I take it. Jihei—you'd strip the skin from your wife's and your children's bodies to squander the money on your whore! Dirty thief! You're my wife's nephew, but an utter stranger to me, and I'm under no obligation to suffer for your sake. I'll explain to Magoemon what has happened and ask him to make good on whatever you've already stolen from Osan's belongings. But first, the bill of divorcement!

CHANTER: Even if Jihei could escape through seven padlocked doors, eight layers of chains, and a hundred retention walls, he could not escape so stringent a demand.

[JIHEI]: I won't use a brush to write the bill of divorcement. Here's what I'll do instead! Good-bye, Osan.

CHANTER: He lays his hand on his dirk, but Osan clings to him.

[OSAN]: Father—Jihei admits that he's done wrong and he's apologized in every way. You press your advantage too hard. Jihei may be a stranger, but his children are your grandchildren. Have you no affection for them? I will not accept a bill of divorcement.

CHANTER: She embraces her husband and raises her voice in tears.

[GOZAEMON]: Very well. I won't insist on it. Come with me, woman.

CHANTER: He pulls her to her feet.

[OSAN]: No, I won't go. What bitterness makes you expose to such shame a man and wife who still love each other? I will not suffer it.

CHANTER: She pleads with him, weeping, but he pays her no heed.

[GOZAEMON]: Is there some greater shame? I'll shout it through the town!

CHANTER: He pulls her up, but she shakes free. Caught by the wrist she totters forward when—alas!—her toes brush against her sleeping children. They open their eyes.

[CHILDREN]: Mother dear, why is Grandfather, the bad man, taking you away? Whom will we sleep beside now?

CHANTER: They call out after her.

[OSAN]: My poor dears! You've never spent a night away from Mother's side since you were born. Sleep tonight beside your father. [*To Jihei.*] Please don't forget to give the children their tonic before breakfast.—Oh, my heart is broken!

CHANTER: These are her parting words. She leaves her children behind, abandoned as in the woods; the twin-trunked bamboo of conjugal love is sundered forever.

ACT 3

Scene 1

In Sonezaki, in front of the Yamato Teahouse.

CHANTER: This is Shijimi River, the haunt of love and affection. Its flowing water and the feet of passersby are stilled now at two in the morning, and the full moon shines clear in the sky. Here in the street a dim doorway lantern is marked "Yamatoya Denbei" in a single scrawl. The night watchman's clappers take on a sleepy cadence as he totters by on uncertain legs. The very thickness of his voice crying, "Beware of fire! Beware of fire!" tells how far advanced the night is. A serving woman from the upper town comes along, followed by a palanquin. "It's terribly late," she remarks to the bearers as she clatters open the side door of the Yamato Teahouse and steps inside.

[SERVANT]: I've come to take back Koharu of the Kinokuni House.

CHANTER: Her voice is faintly heard outside. A few moments later, after hardly time enough to exchange three or four words of greeting, she emerges.

[SERVANT]: Koharu is spending the night. Bearers, you may leave now and get some rest. [*To proprietress, inside the doorway.*] Oh, I forgot to tell you, madam. Please keep an eye on Koharu. Now that the ransom to Tahei has been arranged and the money's been accepted, we're merely her custodians. Please don't let her drink too much saké.

CHANTER: She leaves, having scattered at the doorway the seeds that before morning will turn Jihei and Koharu to dust.

At night between two and four even the teahouse kettle rests; the flame flickering in the low candle stand narrows; and the frost spreads in the cold river-wind of the deepening night. The master's voice breaks the stillness.

[DENBEI, *to Jihei*]: It's still the middle of the night. I'll send somebody with you. [*To the servants.*] Mr. Jihei is leaving. Wake Koharu. Call her here.

CHANTER: Jihei slides open the side door.

[JIHEI]: No, Denbei, not a word to Koharu. I'll be trapped here until dawn if she hears I'm leaving. That's why I'm letting her sleep and slipping off this way. Wake her up after sunrise and send her back then. I'm returning home now and will leave for Kyōto immediately on business. I have so many engagements that I may not be able to return in time for the interim payment.[4] Please use the money I gave you earlier this evening to clear my account. I'd like you also to send 150 *me* of Old Silver to Kawashō for the moon-viewing party last month. Please get a receipt. Give Saietsubō[5] from Fukushima one piece of silver as a contribution to the Buddhist altar he's bought, and tell him to use it for a memorial service. Wasn't there something else? Oh yes—give Isoichi a tip of four silver coins. That's the lot. Now you can close up and get to bed. Good-bye. I'll see you when I return from Kyōto.

CHANTER: Hardly has he taken two or three steps than he turns back.

[JIHEI]: I forgot my dirk. Fetch it for me, won't you?—Yes, Denbei, this is one respect in which it's easier being a townsman. If I were a samurai and forgot my sword, I'd probably commit suicide on the spot!

[DENBEI]: I completely forgot that I was keeping it for you. Yes, here's the knife with it.

CHANTER: He gives the dirk to Jihei, who fastens it firmly into his sash.

[JIHEI]: I feel secure as long as I have this. Good night!

CHANTER: He goes off.

[DENBEI]: Please come back to Ōsaka soon! Thank you for your patronage!

CHANTER: With this hasty farewell Dembei rattles the door bolt shut; then not another sound is heard as the silence deepens. Jihei pretends to leave, only to creep back again with stealthy steps. He clings to the door of the Yamato Teahouse. As he peeps inside he is startled by shadows moving toward him. He takes cover at the house across the way until the figures pass.

Magoemon the Miller, his heart pulverized with anxiety over his younger brother, comes first, followed by the apprentice Sangorō with Jihei's son Kantarō on his back. They hurry along until they see the lantern of the Yamato Teahouse. Magoemon pounds on the door.

[MAGOEMON]: Excuse me. Kamiya Jihei's here, isn't he? I'd like to see him a moment.

CHANTER: Jihei thinks, "It's my brother!" but dares not stir from his place of concealment. From inside a man's sleep-laden voice is heard.

[DENBEI]: Jihei left a while ago saying he was going up to Kyōto. He's not here.

CHANTER: Not another sound is heard. Magoemon's tears fall unchecked.

[MAGOEMON, *to himself.*]: I ought to have met him on the way if he'd been going home. I can't understand what would take him to Kyōto. Ahhh—I'm shivering all over with worry. I wonder whether he took Koharu with him.

CHANTER: The thought pierces his heart; unable to bear the pain, he pounds again on the door.

[DENBEI]: Who is it, so late at night? We've gone to bed.

---

4. On the last day of the Tenth Month, one of the times during the year for making payments.

5. The name of a male entertainer in the quarter. Fukushima was west of Sonezaki.

[MAGOEMON]: I'm sorry to disturb you, but I'd like to ask one more thing. Has Koharu of the Kinokuni House left? I was wondering whether she might have gone with Jihei.

[DENBEI]: What's that? Koharu's upstairs, sound asleep.

[MAGOEMON]: That's a relief, anyway. There's no fear of a lovers' suicide. But where is he hiding himself, causing me all this anxiety? He can't imagine the agony of suspense that the whole family is going through on his account. I'm afraid that bitterness toward his father-in-law may make him forget himself and do something rash. I brought Kantarō along, hoping he would help to dissuade Jihei, but the gesture was in vain. I wonder why I never saw him?

CHANTER: He murmurs to himself, his eyes wet with tears. Jihei's hiding place is close enough for him to hear every word. He chokes with emotion but can only swallow his tears.

[MAGOEMON]: Sangorō! Where does the fool go night after night? Don't you know anywhere else?

CHANTER: Sangorō imagines that he himself is the fool referred to.

[SANGORŌ]: I know a couple of places, but I'm too embarrassed to mention them.

[MAGOEMON]: You know them? Where are they? Tell me.

[SANGORŌ]: Please don't scold me when you've heard. Every night I wander down below the warehouses by the market.

[MAGOEMON]: Imbecile! Who's asking about that? Come on, let's search the back streets. Don't let Kantarō catch a chill. The poor kid's having a hard time of it, thanks to that useless father of his. Still, if the worst the boy experiences is the cold, I won't complain. I'm afraid that Jihei may cause him much greater pain. The scoundrel!

CHANTER: But beneath the rancor in his heart of hearts is profound pity.

[MAGOEMON]: Let's look at the back street!

CHANTER: They pass on. As soon as their figures have gone off a distance, Jihei runs from his hiding place. Standing on tiptoes he gazes with yearning after them and cries out in his heart.

[JIHEI]: He cannot leave me to my death, even though I am the worst of sinners! I remain to the last a burden to him! I'm unworthy of such kindness!

CHANTER: He joins his hands and kneels in prayer.

[JIHEI]: If I may make one further request of your mercy, look after my children!

CHANTER: These are his only words; for a while he chokes with tears.

[JIHEI]: At any rate, our decision's been made. Koharu must be waiting.

CHANTER: He peers through a crack in the side door of the Yamato Teahouse and glimpses a figure.

[JIHEI]: That's Koharu, isn't it? I'll let her know I'm here.

CHANTER: He clears his throat, their signal. "Ahem, ahem"—the sound blends with the clack of wooden clappers as the watchman comes from the upper street, coughing in the night wind. He hurries on his round of fire warning, "Take care! Beware!" Even this cry has a dismal sound to one in hiding. Jihei, concealing himself like the god of Katsuragi,[6] lets the watchman pass. He sees his chance and rushes to the side door, which softly opens from within.

[JIHEI]: Koharu?

---

6. The god was so ashamed of his ugliness that he ventured forth only at night.

[KOHARU]: Were you waiting? Jihei—I want to leave quickly.

CHANTER: She is all impatience, but the more quickly they open the door, the more likely people will be to hear the casters turning. They lift the door; it makes a moaning sound that thunders in their ears and in their hearts. Jihei lends a hand from the outside, but his fingertips tremble with the trembling of his heart. The door opens a quarter of an inch, a half, an inch—an inch ahead are the tortures of hell, but more than hell itself they fear the guardian-demon's eyes. At last the door opens, and with the joy of New Year's morning[7] Koharu slips out. They catch each other's hands. Shall they go north or south, west or east? Their pounding hearts urge them on, though they know not to what destination: turning their backs on the moon reflected in Shijimi River, they hurry eastward as fast as their legs will carry them.

Scene 2

The farewell journey of many bridges.

CHANTER: *The running hand in texts of nō is always Konoe style;*
                    An actor in a woman's part is sure to wear a purple hat.
                    Does some teaching of the Buddha as rigidly decree
                    That men who spend their days in evil haunts must end like this?

Poor creatures, although they would discover today their destiny in the Sutra of Cause and Effect,[8] tomorrow the gossip of the world will scatter like blossoms the scandal of Kamiya Jihei's love suicide, and carved in cherry wood,[9] his story to the last detail will be printed in illustrated sheets.

Jihei, led on by the spirit of death—if such there be among the gods—is resigned to this punishment for neglect of his trade. But at times—who could blame him?—his heart is drawn to those he has left behind, and it is hard to keep walking on. Even in the full moon's light, this fifteenth night of the Tenth Month,[1] he cannot see his way ahead—a sign perhaps of the darkness in his heart? The frost now falling will melt by dawn, but even more quickly than this symbol of human frailty, the lovers themselves will melt away. What will become of the fragrance that lingered when he held her tenderly at night in their bedchamber?

This bridge, Tenjin Bridge, he has crossed every day, morning and night, gazing at Shijimi River to the west. Long ago, when Tenjin, then called Michizane,[2] was exiled to Tsukushi, his plum tree, following its master, flew in one bound to Dazaifu, and here is Plum-Field Bridge.[3] Green Bridge recalls the aged pine that followed later, and Cherry Bridge the tree that withered away in grief over parting. Such are the tales still told, demonstrating the power of a single poem.[4]

---

7. Mention of New Year is connected with Koharu's name, in which *haru* means "spring."

8. A sacred text of Buddhism, which states: "If you wish to know the past cause, look at the present effect; if you wish to know the future effect, look at the present cause."

9. The blocks from which illustrated books were printed were frequently made of cherry wood. The illustrated sheets mentioned here featured current scandals, such as lovers' suicides.

1. November 14, 1720. In the lunar calendar the full moon occurs on the fifteenth of the month.

2. Sugawara no Michizane, unfairly abused at court, was exiled to Dazaifu in Kyūshū. When he was about to depart, he composed a poem of farewell to his favorite plum tree. The tree, moved by this honor, flew after him to Kyūshū. The cherry tree in his garden withered away in grief. Only the pine seemed indifferent, as Michizane complained in another poem. The pine thereupon also flew to Kyūshū.

3. Umeda Bridge. "Green Bridge" is Midori-bashi.

4. The poem by Michizane bewailing the inconstancy of his pine tree.

[JIHEI]: Though born the parishioner of so holy and mighty a god, I shall kill you and then myself. If you ask the cause, it was that I lacked even the wisdom that might fill a tiny Shell Bridge.[5] Our stay in this world has been short as an autumn day. This evening will be the last of your nineteen, of my twenty-eight years. The time has come to cast away our lives. We promised we'd remain together faithfully until you were an old woman and I an old man, but before we knew each other three full years, we have met this disaster. Look, there is Ōe Bridge. We will follow the river from Little Naniwa Bridge to Funairi Bridge. The farther we journey, the closer we approach the road to death.

CHANTER: He laments. She clings to him.

[KOHARU]: Is this already the road to death?

CHANTER: Falling tears obscure from each the other's face and threaten to immerse even the Horikawa bridges.

[JIHEI]: A few steps north and I could glimpse my house, but I will not turn back. I will bury in my breast all thoughts of my children's future, all pity for my wife. We cross southward over the river. Why did they call a place with as many buildings as a bridge has piers "Eight Houses"? Hurry, we want to arrive before the downriver boat from Fushimi comes—with what happy couples sleeping aboard!

Next is Tenma Bridge, a frightening name[6] for us about to depart this world. Here the two streams Yodo and Yamato join in one great river, as fish with water, and as Koharu and I, dying on one blade, will cross together the River of Three Fords.[7] I would like this water for our tomb offering!

[KOHARU]: What have we to grieve about? Although in this world we could not stay together, in the next and through each successive world to come until the end of time we shall be husband and wife. Every summer for my devotions[8] I have copied the All Compassionate and All Merciful Chapter of the Lotus Sutra, in the hope that we may be reborn on one lotus.

CHANTER: They cross over Sutra Bridge and reach the opposite shore.[9]

[KOHARU]: If I can save living creatures at will when once I mount a lotus calyx in Paradise and become a Buddha, I want to protect women of my profession, so that never again will there be love suicides.

CHANTER: This unattainable prayer stems from worldly attachment, but it touchingly reveals her heart. They cross Onari Bridge.[1] The waters of Noda Creek are shrouded with morning haze; the mountain tips show faintly white.

[JIHEI]: Listen—the voices of the temple bells begin to boom. How much farther can we go on this way? We are not fated to live any longer—let us end it quickly. Come this way.

CHANTER: Tears are strung with the 108 beads of the rosaries in their hands. They have come now to Amijima, to the Daichō Temple. The overflowing sluice gate of a little stream beside a bamboo thicket will be their place of death.

---

5. The lovers' journey takes them along the north bank of Shijimi River ("Shell River") to Shijimi Bridge, where they cross to Dōjima. At Little Naniwa Bridge they cross back again to Sonezaki. Continuing eastward, they cross Horikawa, then cross the Tenma Bridge over the Ōkawa. At "Eight Houses" (Hakkenya) they journey eastward along the south bank of the river as far as Kyō Bridge. They cross this bridge to the tip of land at Katamachi and then take the Onari Bridge to Amijima.

6. The characters used for "Tenma" literally mean "demon."

7. A river in the Buddhist underworld that had to be crossed to reach the world of the dead. This is arithmetic association: one blade plus two people equals three fords.

8. It was customary for Buddhist monks to observe a three-month summer retreat during which they practiced various austerities.

9. Kyōbashi is literally "Sutra Bridge." "Opposite Shore" implies the Buddhist term for nirvana.

1. The name Onari means "to become a Buddha."

Scene 3

Amijima.

[JIHEI]: No matter how far we walk, there'll never be a spot marked "For Suicides." Let us kill ourselves here.

CHANTER: He takes her hand and sits on the ground.

[KOHARU]: Yes, that's true. One place is as good as another to die. But I've been thinking on the way that if they find our dead bodies together, people will say that Koharu and Jihei committed a lovers' suicide. Osan will think then that I treated as mere scrap paper the letter I sent promising her, when she asked me not to kill you, that I would not and vowing to break off all relations with you. She will be sure that I lured her precious husband into a lovers' suicide. She will despise me as a one-night prostitute, a false woman with no sense of decency. I fear her contempt more than the slander of a thousand or ten thousand strangers. I can imagine how she will resent and envy me. That is the greatest obstacle to my salvation. Kill me here, then choose another spot, far away, for yourself.

CHANTER: She leans against him. Jihei joins in her tears of pleading.

[JIHEI]: What foolish worries! Osan has been taken back by my father-in-law. I've divorced her. She and I are strangers now. Why should you feel obliged to a divorced woman? You were saying on the way that you and I will be husband and wife through each successive world until the end of time. Who can criticize us, who can be jealous if we die side by side?

[KOHARU]: But who is responsible for your divorce? You're even less reasonable than I. Do you suppose that our bodies will accompany us to the afterworld? We may die in different places, our bodies may be pecked by kites and crows, but what does it matter as long as our souls are twined together? Take me with you to heaven or to hell!

CHANTER: She sinks again in tears.

[JIHEI]: You're right. Our bodies are made of earth, water, fire, and wind, and when we die they revert to emptiness. But our souls will not decay, no matter how often they're reborn. And here's a guarantee that our souls will be married and never part!

CHANTER: He whips out his dirk and slashes off his black locks at the base of the topknot.

[JIHEI]: Look, Koharu. As long as I had this hair, I was Kamiya Jihei, Osan's husband, but cutting it has made me a monk. I have fled the burning house of the three worlds of delusion; I am a priest, unencumbered by wife, children, or worldly possessions. Now that I no longer have a wife named Osan, you owe her no obligations either.

CHANTER: In tears he flings away the hair.

[KOHARU]: I am happy.

CHANTER: Koharu takes up the dirk and ruthlessly, unhesitatingly, slices through her flowing Shimada coiffure. She casts aside the tresses she has so often washed and combed and stroked. How heartbreaking to see their locks tangled with the weeds and midnight frost of this desolate field!

[JIHEI]: We have escaped the inconstant world, a nun and a priest. Our duties as husband and wife belong to our profane past. It would be best to choose quite separate places for our deaths, a mountain for one, the river for the other. We will pretend that the ground above this sluice gate is a mountain. You will die there. I shall hang myself by this stream. The time of our deaths will be the same, but the method and place will differ. In this way we can honor to the end our duty to Osan. Give me your undersash.

CHANTER: Its fresh violet color and fragrance will be lost in the winds of impermanence; the crinkled silk long enough to wind twice round her body will bind two worlds, this and the next. He firmly fastens one end to the crosspiece of the sluice, then twists the other into a noose for his neck. He will hang for love of his wife like the "pheasant in the hunting grounds."[2] Koharu watches Jihei prepare for his death. Her eyes swim with tears, her mind is distraught.

[KOHARU]: Is that how you're going to kill yourself?—If we are to die apart, I have only a little while longer by your side. Come near me.

CHANTER: They take each other's hands.

[KOHARU]: It's over in a moment with a sword, but I'm sure you'll suffer. My poor darling!

CHANTER: She cannot stop the silent tears.

[JIHEI]: Can suicide ever be pleasant, whether by hanging or cutting the throat? You mustn't let worries over trifles disturb the prayers of your last moments. Keep your eyes on the westward-moving moon, and worship it as Amida himself.[3] Concentrate your thoughts on the Western Paradise. If you have any regrets about leaving the world, tell me now, then die.

[KOHARU]: I have none at all, none at all. But I'm sure you must be worried about your children.

[JIHEI]: You make me cry all over again by mentioning them. I can almost see their faces, sleeping peacefully, unaware, poor dears, that their father is about to kill himself. They're the one thing I can't forget.

CHANTER: He droops to the ground with weeping. The voices of the crows leaving their nests at dawn rival his sobs. Are the crows mourning his fate? The thought brings more tears.

[JIHEI]: Listen to them. The crows have come to guide us to the world of the dead. There's an old saying that every time somebody writes an oath on the back of a Kumano charm, three crows of Kumano die on the holy mountain. The first words we've written each New Year have been vows of love, and how often we've made oaths at the beginning of the month! If each oath has killed three crows, what a multitude must have perished! Their cries have always sounded like "beloved, beloved," but hatred for our crime of taking life makes their voices ring tonight "revenge, revenge!"[4] Whose fault is it they demand revenge? Because of me you will die a painful death. Forgive me!

CHANTER: He takes her in his arms.

[KOHARU]: No, it's my fault!

CHANTER: They cling to each other, face pressed to face; their sidelocks, drenched with tears, freeze in the winds blowing over the fields. Behind them echoes the voice of the Daichō Temple.

[JIHEI]: Even the long winter night seems as short as our lives.

CHANTER: Dawn is already breaking, and matins can be heard. He draws her to him.

[JIHEI]: The moment has come for our glorious end. Let there be no tears on your face when they find you later.

[KOHARU]: There won't be any.

2. A reference to a poem by Ōtomo no Yakamochi (718–785): "The pheasant foraging in the fields of spring reveals his whereabouts to man as he cries for his mate."
3. Amida's paradise lies in the west. The moon is often used as a symbol of Buddhist enlightenment.
4. The cries have always sounded like *kawai, kawai* (beloved), but now they sound like *mukui, mukui* (revenge).

CHANTER: She smiles. His hands, numbed by the frost, tremble before the pale vision of her face, and his eyes are first to cloud. He is weeping so profusely that he cannot control the blade.

[KOHARU]: Compose yourself—but be quick!

CHANTER: Her encouragement lends him strength; the invocations to Amida carried by the wind urge a final prayer. *Namu Amida Butsu*. He thrusts in the savaging sword.[5] Stabbed, she falls backward, despite his staying hand, and struggles in terrible pain. The point of the blade has missed her windpipe, and these are the final tortures before she can die. He writhes with her in agony, then painfully summons his strength again. He draws her to him and plunges his dirk to the hilt. He twists the blade in the wound, and her life fades away like an unfinished dream at dawning.

He arranges her body with her head to the north, face to the west, lying on her right side,[6] and throws his cloak over her. He turns away at last, unable to exhaust with tears his grief over parting. He pulls the sash to him and fastens the noose around his neck. The service in the temple has reached the closing section, the prayers for the dead. "Believers and unbelievers will equally share in the divine grace," the voices proclaim, and at the final words Jihei jumps from the sluice gate.

[JIHEI]: May we be reborn on one lotus! Hail Amida Buddha!

CHANTER: For a few moments he writhes like a gourd swinging in the wind, but gradually the passage of his breath is blocked as the stream is dammed by the sluice gate, where his ties with this life are snapped. Fishermen out for the morning catch find the body in their net.[7]

[FISHERMEN]: A dead man! Look, a dead man! Come here, everybody!

CHANTER: The tale is spread from mouth to mouth. People say that they who were caught in the net of Buddha's vow immediately gained salvation and deliverance, and all who hear the tale of the Love Suicides at Amijima are moved to tears.

⸎

RESONANCE

Hozumi Ikan, Preface to *Souvenirs of Naniwa*[1]
CHIKAMATSU ON THE ART OF PUPPET THEATER

PREFACE

When I was visiting Chikamatsu at his home many years ago, he told me the following:

"*Jōruri* is a living thing: the most important consideration is that these are plays written for puppets, so *jōruri* differs from other kinds of fiction; the words must create movement. What's more, *jōruri* competes with the artistry of live actors at nearby kabuki theaters, but since *jōruri* tries to capture the sympathies of the audience by

---

5. The invocation of Amida's name freed one from spiritual obstacles, just as a sword freed one from physical obstacles. Here the two images are blended.
6. The dead were arranged in this manner because Shakyamuni Buddha chose this position when he died.
7. "Net" (*ami*) is echoed a few lines later in the name Amijima. The vow of the Buddha to save all living creatures is likened to a net that catches people in its meshes.

1. Translated by Michael Brownstein. *Souvenirs of Naniwa* was published in 1738, fourteen years after Chikamatsu's death. It is best remembered for the preface written by Hozumi Ikan (1692–1769), a Confucian scholar and devotee of puppet theater, because it contains the only extended comments we have on *jōruri* or puppet theater in Chikamatsu's own words.

endowing inanimate puppets with a variety of feelings, the usual plays can hardly be called superb literary works.

"When I was young, I read a story about Heian court life describing how on the occasion of a festival, the snow had piled up rather deeply. An attendant was ordered to clear the snow off the branches of an orange tree, but when he did so, the branches of a nearby pine tree, also bent with snow, recoiled as if in resentment.[2] The stroke of a pen animated a soulless tree. That is because the pine tree, envious at seeing the snow cleared from the orange tree, recoiled its branches in resentment and dumped the snow that was weighing them down. Isn't that just how a living, moving thing would feel? With this model, I understood how to breathe life into the characters of my plays. It is essential, therefore, that even the words describing the scenery of the *michiyuki*, not to mention the narrative passages and the dialogue, be charged with feeling. If a writer does not bear that in mind, his plays will have little emotional impact.

"What poets call 'evocative imagery' is the same thing. For example, a poet may describe in a verse the marvelous scenery of Matsushima or Miyajima, but if it lacks the sense of wonder that comes from immersing oneself in the scene, it would be as if the poet were just looking idly at the portrait of a beautiful woman. A playwright, therefore, must keep in mind that his words should be based on feelings. . . .

"The old *jōruri* was the same as those tales sung by scandalmongers in the streets today; it had neither fruit nor flower. After I left Kaganojō and began writing plays for Takemoto Gidayū,[3] I took more care with my words, so my plays were a cut above those of the past.

"For example, my first principle is to distinguish between the social position of each and every character, from the nobility and the samurai on down, and to depict them accordingly, from their demeanor to the way they speak. By the same token, even among the samurai, there are daimyō, chief retainers, and others whose stipends vary according to their rank, so I distinguish one from the other based on their social position. This is because it is essential that readers sympathize with the feelings of each character.

"The words of *jōruri* depict reality as it is, but being a form of art it also contains elements that are not found in real life. Specifically, female characters often say things a real woman would not say, but such instances are examples of art. Since they speak openly of things that a real woman would not talk about, the character's true feelings are revealed. Thus, when a playwright models a female character on the feelings of a real woman and conceals such things, her deepest thoughts will not be revealed, and contrary to his hopes, the play will not be entertaining. It follows that when one watches a play without paying attention to the artistry, one will probably criticize it on the grounds that the female characters say many discomfiting things that are inappropriate for a woman to say. However, such instances should be regarded as art. There are, in addition, many other aspects that one should regard as art rather than reality, such as when a villain acts too cowardly or the humor is actually buffoonery. People should understand this when watching a play.

"Some playwrights, thinking that sadness is essential to a *jōruri*, often put in words like 'How sad it is!' or the lines are chanted tearfully, as in the Bunyabushi

---

2. The passage appears in "The Safflower" chapter of *The Tale of Genji.*
3. Kaganojō and Takemoto Gidayū were pioneer *jōruri* chanters. Chikamatsu wrote his first play for Takemoto Gidayū in 1686, after which he wrote only three more plays for Kaganojō, the last in 1699.

style,[4] but that is not how I write plays. The sadness in all my plays is based entirely on reason [*giri*]. Since the audience will be moved when the logic of the dramatization is convincing, the more restrained the words and the chanting are, the more moving the play will be. Thus, when one says of a moment of pathos 'How sad it is!' the connotations are lost, and in the end, the feeling conveyed is weak. It is essential that the moment be filled with pathos in and of itself, without having to say 'How sad it is!' For example, when you praise a landscape such as Matsushima by saying 'Oh, what a beautiful scene!' you have said all you can about it in a few words but to no avail. If you wish to praise a scene, pointing out all its features objectively will reveal its intrinsic appeal naturally, without having to say 'it is a beautiful scene.' This applies to everything of this sort."

Someone said that in this day and age, people won't accept a play unless it is very realistic and logically convincing, so there are many things in the old stories that people will not stand for now. It is precisely for this reason that people are apt to think kabuki actors are skillful when their acting resembles real life. They think the most important thing is for the actor playing a chief retainer to imitate a real chief retainer and the actor playing a daimyō to imitate a real daimyō. They will not accept the sort of childish antics of the past.

Chikamatsu answered: "That argument seems quite reasonable, but it fails to grasp the true method of art. Art is something that lies between the skin and the flesh [*hiniku*], between the make-believe and the real. In today's world, of course, given the preference for realistic acting, an actor playing a chief retainer may imitate the speech and mannerisms of a real chief retainer, but if that's the case, would a real chief retainer of a daimyō wear makeup on his face like an actor? Or would it be entertaining if an actor, saying that a real chief retainer does not use makeup, appeared on stage and performed with his beard growing wild and his own bald head? This is what I mean by 'between the skin and the flesh.' Art is make-believe and not make-believe; it is real and not real; entertainment lies between the two.

"In this connection, a lady-in-waiting in the old imperial court was in love with a certain man. The two communicated their feelings for each other with passion, but the woman lived deep within the palace. The man was unable to visit her in the women's quarters, so she could see him only on rare occasions through the gaps of the hanging blinds at court. She longed for him so much that she had a wooden image carved in his likeness. It was unlike ordinary dolls in that its face was exactly like the man's down to the tiniest hair, even the color of his complexion. The pores of his skin, the holes for the ears and nose, and even the number of teeth in his mouth were reproduced exactly. Since the image was made with the man right next to it, the only difference between the man and the doll was the presence of a soul in the one but not the other. Even so, when the woman drew near and gazed at it, because the man's body had been duplicated exactly, her passion cooled; she found it somehow repulsive and frightening. Court lady that she was, her love for the man cooled as well. Just keeping the doll around became annoying, and it appears that she soon threw it away.

"With this example in mind, if we duplicate a living person exactly, even if it is Yang Gueifei,[5] we will become disgusted with it. For this reason, whether painting an image or carving it in wood, there will be places where the artist takes liberties, even

---

4. A style of chanting used by Okamoto Bunya in the late 17th century. Chikamatsu preferred the style used by Takemoto Gidayū (Gidayubushi), which became the standard.

5. A concubine of the Tang dynasty's Emperor Xuanzong (r. 712–756), remembered for her great beauty.

while copying the original form, on the grounds that it is a fabrication; but in the end, this is what people love. It is the same with new plot situations: even though the story resembles the original version, there will be places where the artist takes liberties, but in the end, this is what makes it art and entertaining. There are many instances where the dialogue in a play should also be viewed with this in mind."

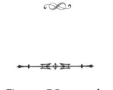

Cao Xueqin
c.1715–1763

Scholars and readers alike have agreed that *The Story of the Stone* is the greatest Chinese novel, but about the nature of its greatness lively differences of opinion have swirled from its first appearance. Uncertainty and controversy surround its very authorship. Of its 120 chapters, only the first eighty were written by its supposed author, Cao Xueqin, the descendant of a family of distinguished generals and government officials whose fortunes had recently drastically declined. Copies of the unfinished manuscript circulated among the author's circle of friends for decades, augmented by a running commentary penned by someone clearly familiar with details of his life and identified only as Red Inkstone, along with additional remarks by several other readers. When the novel was finally published in 1791, long after Cao's death, it was accompanied by the prefaces of two other individuals who also claimed to have found a fragmentary conclusion that they edited and completed. These additional forty chapters recount a dizzying set of events whose correspondence to the author's original intention was almost immediately debated. Even the title of the novel has been subject to discussion. Cao refers to it as *The Story of the Stone* in his first chapter, but it has been more commonly known in China by another title drawn from a list of alternatives he also provides there, *Dream of the Red Chamber.*

Subsequent generations of amateurs and scholars have generated a cottage industry of "*Red* studies" arguing about the facts and the merits of the novel's authorship and its themes. Early readers assumed a close connection to Cao Xueqin's own life, about which surprisingly little is known for certain, given the prominence of his family. Even before the conquest of China by the Manchus, his forefathers had been captured by the future rulers of the Qing Empire (1644–1911) and entered into their service. Cao's grandfather held the relatively powerful post of Imperial Textile Commissioner in Nanjing and was succeeded by his son. The family's fortunes shifted, however, when a struggle for the throne after the emperor's death found it allied with the losing side. Its considerable estate was confiscated, and it was forced to live largely off the kindness of relatives in Beijing. Cao's pampered childhood thus became a distant memory. He worked as a clerk in the imperial school, may have passed a low-level civil service examination and held minor office, and appears to have also supported himself by selling his own paintings (although not well enough to pay off rather hefty drinking debts). *The Story of the Stone,* which he drafted between 1740 and 1750 and revised five times, was clearly his major accomplishment and appears to have drawn heavily upon his family's experiences.

The novel has successfully resisted the dogged efforts of generations of Chinese critics to establish precise correspondences between its characters and events and those of the author's own life. Cao Xueqin was the first major author to base his novel on personal history, but he was also clearly fascinated by the many possibilities for manipulating illusion and reality opened up by fiction. An often-cited couplet from the novel proclaims that "Truth becomes fiction when the fiction's true; / Real becomes not-real where the unreal's real," and the work plays with both language and plot to test the patience of would-be literary detectives. The surname of its main family, for example, Jia, is a homophone for "false," and a second family introduced late in the novel is surnamed Zhen, which sounds like the word "true"; their fortunes mirror in reverse those of the protagonists. Two minor characters are named Zhen Shiyin and Jia Yucun, puns on phrases meaning "true things hidden" and "false words preserved."

The opening chapter of *The Story of the Stone* literally contains the novel in its entirety. A stone rejected by a goddess who was repairing the sky is picked up by a Buddhist monk and a Daoist priest and taken into the world of mortals, to be found eons later in the same place by another Daoist, with the long story of its worldly experiences inscribed upon it. The story of the stone, then, is on the stone itself. In addition to situating the novel's origins within the realm of myth, perhaps seeking to deflect in some measure the suspicions of some readers who might want to discern political allegory or critique within it, this first chapter provides an opportunity for Cao to foreground his interest in the nature of fiction, which is the topic of a conversation between the second Daoist and the inscribed stone itself. It also explains the dynamic of the novel's most important relationship, for before going into the world the stone tenderly waters with sweet dew a lovely flower, who thus incurs a karmic debt of a lifetime of tears. As it turns out, this will be repaid in the rest of the novel by the young Lin Dai-yu, whose love for her cousin Jia Bao-yu ("Precious Jade"), the protagonist born with a jade stone in his mouth, is cause for constant weeping throughout the story. Other elements of this narrative envelope, like the Buddhist and Daoist priests, appear at crucial moments of the boy's life as well.

Vanitas (*Kongkong daoren,* or the Daoist of Emptiness) is the name of the second Daoist, suggesting the importance of understanding *The Story of the Stone* within a religious or philosophical framework that would insist on the vain and transitory nature of the material world. Curious nonetheless about the human world of sentiments and attachments, the stone is given the opportunity to be reincarnated as the adolescent Bao-yu, whose nine years of embroilment in a panoply of pleasures and sorrows are a necessary prerequisite to eventual detachment, enlightenment and return from that world. Yet the vivid and loving detail of his experiences recorded in this five-volume novel belies such an unequivocal commitment to disengagement from it.

Indeed, no other traditional Chinese novel provides such a richly depicted account of both the emotions and the contexts of human interaction. Jia Bao-yu is the scion of an extended family that occupies two large and complex households in some unspecified city with characteristics of both Nanjing and Beijing. His father is a rising official and his older sister an honored imperial concubine, but the family's position and wealth decline, first gradually and then precipitously, over the course of the novel. His early "golden" days are spent cavorting with cousins and friends, mostly girls, in a vast garden constructed by the family to honor a rare visit home by his sister and in which the children have afterward been given permission to reside. Parties, opera performances and poetry contests punctuate the leisurely daily rhythms of rich meals, sexual experimentation, and intrigues between and among the children and their personal servants. As the years go by Bao-yu, with the frequent protection of his doting grandmother, must resist two pressures to abandon these carefree pursuits: his father's stern, rigidly Confucian injunctions to study hard for the civil service examinations and a successful career as a bureaucrat, and his mother's concern that he find an appropriate match for his own sake and that of the family line. Bao-yu's affection for his cousin Dai-yu feels predetermined to him (as indeed it is), but worries about her frail health lead the adults to focus on another differently attractive cousin, both sturdier and less temperamental, Xue Baochai. Having been given a gold locket at her birth by a strange monk, with the instruction to seek a mate of jade, she seems equally destined for Bao-yu. The charged and complicated interactions within this triangle, captured with unprecedented psychological depth and animation, have captivated the attention and allegiances of readers for generations.

Genealogy of the Ning-guo and Rong-guo Houses of the Jia Clan

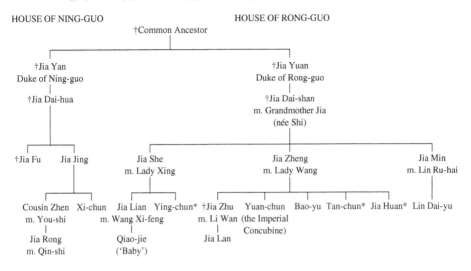

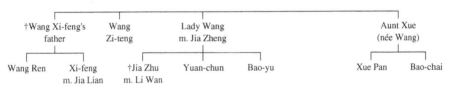

The Wang Family

m. Married   †Dead before the beginning of the novel   *Son or daughter by a concubine

The Story of the Stone also serves as a veritable encyclopedia of late imperial Chinese society and culture. Over four hundred characters enter its pages, hailing from all walks of life and involved in subplots of often considerable intricacy. Detailed descriptions of buildings, gardens, furniture, medicines, food, and drink are matched by exquisitely described clothing, jewelry, makeup, and coiffures. There is a wealth of information regarding family structure, rituals, etiquette, games, performances, and other pastimes of the aristocracy, as well as the extraordinary complexity of running such vast domains. With the exception of Bao-yu himself, the novel focuses on the fate of the family's numerous young women. They are both the most talented and capable characters of the lot and the most vulnerable; indeed, the lives of most end miserably, in unhappy marriages, nunneries, suicides, or painful deaths.

The fate of the Jia family as a whole unfolds inexorably over the first eighty chapters, its decline attributable to a number of factors such as overindulgence, corruption, and Bao-yu's own weakness, not to mention the narrative frame that requires it. During the last third of the novel, the pace of events quickens markedly as the family's fortune and position are lost and its property confiscated, before the novel finally ends in the renunciation provided for in the beginning of *The Story of the Stone*. Only a small portion of this vast work could be included here, but the process of excerpting does less damage than might be expected, since the work is shaped as much by sequences of vignettes as it is by the forward movement of plot. If Cao

Xueqin wants the reader to take heed of the risks of attachment to this world, he provides at the same time lessons worth lingering over.

PRONUNCIATIONS:

Cao Xueqin: TSAO shweh-CHIN
Jia Bao-yu: GEE-ah BOW yü
Lin Dai-yu: LIN DIE-yü
Xue Bao-chai: SHWEH BOW-chai

from The Story of the Stone[1]

CHAPTER 1

Zhen Shi-yin makes the Stone's acquaintance in a dream
And Jia Yu-cun finds that poverty is not incompatible with romantic feelings

GENTLE READER,

What, you may ask, was the origin of this book?

Though the answer to this question may at first seem to border on the absurd, re-flection will show that there is a good deal more in it than meets the eye.

Long ago, when the goddess Nü-wa was repairing the sky, she melted down a great quantity of rock and, on the Incredible Crags of the Great Fable Mountains, moulded the amalgam into thirty-six thousand, five hundred and one large building blocks, each measuring seventy-two feet by a hundred and forty-four feet square. She used thirty-six thousand five hundred of these blocks in the course of her building operations, leaving a single odd block unused, which lay, all on its own, at the foot of Greensickness Peak in the aforementioned mountains.

Now this block of stone, having undergone the melting and moulding of a goddess, possessed magic powers. It could move about at will and could grow or shrink to any size it wanted. Observing that all the other blocks had been used for celestial repairs and that it was the only one to have been rejected as unworthy, it became filled with shame and resentment and passed its days in sorrow and lamentation.

One day, in the midst of its lamentings, it saw a monk and a Taoist approaching from a great distance, each of them remarkable for certain eccentricities of manner and appearance. When they arrived at the foot of Greensickness Peak, they sat down on the ground and began to talk. The monk, catching sight of a lustrous, translucent stone—it was in fact the rejected building block which had now shrunk itself to the size of a fan-pendant and looked very attractive in its new shape—took it up on the palm of his hand and addressed it with a smile:

"Ha, I see you have magical properties! But nothing to recommend you. I shall have to cut a few words on you so that anyone seeing you will know at once that you are something special. After that I shall take you to a certain

brilliant

successful

poetical

---

1. Translated by David Hawkes.

cultivated

aristocratic

elegant

delectable

luxurious

opulent

locality on a little trip."

The stone was delighted.

"What words will you cut? Where is this place you will take me to? I beg to be enlightened."

"Do not ask," replied the monk with a laugh. "You will know soon enough when the time comes."

And with that he slipped the stone into his sleeve and set off at a great pace with the Taoist. But where they both went to I have no idea.

Countless aeons went by and a certain Taoist called Vanitas in quest of the secret of immortality chanced to be passing below that same Greensickness Peak in the Incredible Crags of the Great Fable Mountains when he caught sight of a large stone standing there, on which the characters of a long inscription were clearly discernible.

Vanitas read the inscription through from beginning to end and learned that this was a once lifeless stone block which had been found unworthy to repair the sky, but which had magically transformed its shape and been taken down by the Buddhist mahāsattva Impervioso and the Taoist illuminate Mysterioso into the world of mortals, where it had lived out the life of a man before finally attaining nirvana and returning to the other shore. The inscription named the country where it had been born, and went into considerable detail about its domestic life, youthful amours, and even the verses, mottoes and riddles it had written. All it lacked was the authentication of a dynasty and date. On the back of the stone was inscribed the following quatrain:

> Found unfit to repair the azure sky
> Long years a foolish mortal man was I.
> My life in both worlds on this stone is writ:
> Pray who will copy out and publish it?

From his reading of the inscription Vanitas realized that this was a stone of some consequence. Accordingly he addressed himself to it in the following manner:

"Brother Stone, according to what you yourself seem to imply in these verses, this story of yours contains matter of sufficient interest to merit publication and has been carved here with that end in view. But as far as I can see (a) it has no discoverable dynastic period, and (b) it contains no examples of moral grandeur among its characters—no statesmanship, no social message of any kind. All I can find in it, in fact, are a number of females, conspicuous, if at all, only for their passion or folly or for some trifling talent or insignificant virtue. Even if I were to copy all this out, I cannot see that it would make a very remarkable book."

"Come, your reverence," said the stone (for Vanitas had been correct in assuming that it could speak) "must you be so obtuse? All the romances ever written have an artificial period setting—Han or Tang for the most part. In refusing to make use of that stale old convention and telling my *Story of the Stone* exactly as it occurred, it seems to me that, far from *depriving* it of anything, I have given it a freshness these other books do not have.

"Your so-called 'historical romances,' consisting, as they do, of scandalous anecdotes about statesmen and emperors of bygone days and scabrous attacks on the reputations of long-dead gentlewomen, contain more wickedness and immorality than I care to mention. Still worse is the 'erotic novel,' by whose filthy obscenities our young folk are all too easily corrupted. And the 'boudoir romances,' those dreary stereotypes with their volume after volume all pitched on the same note and their different characters undistinguishable except by name (all those ideally beautiful young ladies and ideally eligible young bachelors)—even they seem unable to avoid descending sooner or later into indecency.

"The trouble with this last kind of romance is that it only gets written in the first place because the author requires a framework in which to show off his love-poems. He goes about constructing this framework quite mechanically, beginning with the names of his pair of young lovers and invariably adding a third character, a servant or the like, to make mischief between them, like the *chou*[2] in a comedy.

"What makes these romances even more detestable is the stilted, bombastic language—inanities dressed in pompous rhetoric, remote alike from nature and common sense and teeming with the grossest absurdities.

"Surely my 'number of females,' whom I spent half a lifetime studying with my own eyes and ears, are preferable to this kind of stuff? I do not claim that they are better people than the ones who appear in books written before my time; I am only saying that the contemplation of their actions and motives may prove a more effective antidote to boredom and melancholy. And even the inelegant verses with which my story is interlarded could serve to entertain and amuse on those convivial occasions when rhymes and riddles are in demand.

"All that my story narrates, the meetings and partings, the joys and sorrows, the ups and downs of fortune, are recorded exactly as they happened. I have not dared to add the tiniest bit of touching-up, for fear of losing the true picture.

"My only wish is that men in the world below may sometimes pick up this tale when they are recovering from sleep or drunkenness, or when they wish to escape from business worries or a fit of the dumps, and in doing so find not only mental refreshment but even perhaps, if they will heed its lesson and abandon their vain and frivolous pursuits, some small arrest in the deterioration of their vital forces. What does your reverence say to that?"

For a long time Vanitas stood lost in thought, pondering this speech. He then subjected the *Story of the Stone* to a careful second reading. He could see that its main theme was love; that it consisted quite simply of a true record of real events; and that it was entirely free from any tendency to deprave and corrupt. He therefore copied it all out from beginning to end and took it back with him to look for a publisher.

As a consequence of all this, Vanitas, starting off in the Void (which is Truth) came to the contemplation of Form (which is Illusion); and from Form engendered Passion; and by communicating Passion, entered again into Form; and from Form awoke to the Void (which is Truth). He therefore changed his name from Vanitas to Brother Amor, or the Passionate Monk (because he had approached Truth by way of Passion), and changed the title of the book from *The Story of the Stone* to *The Tale of Brother Amor*.

2. A buffoon.

Old Kong Mei-xi from the homeland of Confucius called the book *A Mirror for the Romantic.* Wu Yu-feng called it *A Dream of Golden Days.* Cao Xueqin in his Nostalgia Studio worked on it for ten years, in the course of which he rewrote it no less than five times, dividing it into chapters, composing chapter headings, renaming it *The Twelve Beauties of Jinling,* and adding an introductory quatrain. Red Inkstone restored the original title when he recopied the book and added his second set of annotations to it.

This, then, is a true account of how *The Story of the Stone* came to be written.

> Pages full of idle words
> Penned with hot and bitter tears:
> All men call the author fool;
> None his secret message hears.

The origin of *The Story of the Stone* has now been made clear. The same cannot, however, be said of the characters and events which it recorded. Gentle reader, have patience! This is how the inscription began:

Long, long ago the world was tilted downwards towards the south-east; and in that lower-lying south-easterly part of the earth there is a city called Soochow; and in Soochow the district around the Chang-men Gate is reckoned one of the two or three wealthiest and most fashionable quarters in the world of men. Outside the Chang-men Gate is a wide thoroughfare called Worldly Way; and somewhere off Worldly Way is an area called Carnal Lane. There is an old temple in the Carnal Lane area which, because of the way it is bottled up inside a narrow *cul-de-sac,* is referred to locally as Bottle-gourd Temple. Next door to Bottle-gourd Temple lived a gentleman of private means called Zhen Shi-yin and his wife Feng-shi, a kind, good woman with a profound sense of decency and decorum. The household was not a particularly wealthy one, but they were nevertheless looked up to by all and sundry as the leading family in the neighbourhood.

Zhen Shi-yin himself was by nature a quiet and totally unambitious person. He devoted his time to his garden and to the pleasures of wine and poetry. Except for a single flaw, his existence could, indeed, have been described as an idyllic one. The flaw was that, although already past fifty, he had no son, only a little girl, just two years old, whose name was Ying-lian.

Once, during the tedium of a burning summer's day, Shi-yin was sitting idly in his study. The book had slipped from his nerveless grasp and his head had nodded down onto the desk in a doze. While in this drowsy state he seemed to drift off to some place he could not identify, where he became aware of a monk and a Taoist walking along and talking as they went.

"Where do you intend to take that thing you are carrying?" the Taoist was asking.

"Don't you worry about him!" replied the monk with a laugh. "There is a batch of lovesick souls awaiting incarnation in the world below whose fate is due to be decided this very day. I intend to take advantage of this opportunity to slip our little friend in amongst them and let him have a taste of human life along with the rest."

"Well, well, so another lot of these amorous wretches is about to enter the vale of tears," said the Taoist. "How did all this begin? And where are the souls to be reborn?"

"You will laugh when I tell you," said the monk. "When this stone was left unused by the goddess, he found himself at a loose end and took to wandering about all over the place for want of better to do, until one day his wanderings took him to the place where the fairy Disenchantment lives.

"Now Disenchantment could tell that there was something unusual about this stone, so she kept him there in her Sunset Glow Palace and gave him the honorary title of Divine Luminescent Stone-in-Waiting in the Court of Sunset Glow.

"But most of his time he spent west of Sunset Glow exploring the banks of the Magic River. There, by the Rock of Rebirth, he found the beautiful Crimson Pearl Flower, for which he conceived such a fancy that he took to watering her every day with sweet dew, thereby conferring on her the gift of life.

"Crimson Pearl's substance was composed of the purest cosmic essences, so she was already half-divine; and now, thanks to the vitalizing effect of the sweet dew, she was able to shed her vegetable shape and assume the form of a girl.

"This fairy girl wandered about outside the Realm of Separation, eating the Secret Passion Fruit when she was hungry and drinking from the Pool of Sadness when she was thirsty. The consciousness that she owed the stone something for his kindness in watering her began to prey on her mind and ended by becoming an obsession.

"'I have no sweet dew here that I can repay him with,' she would say to herself. 'The only way in which I could perhaps repay him would be with the tears shed during the whole of a mortal lifetime if he and I were ever to be reborn as humans in the world below.'

"Because of this strange affair, Disenchantment has got together a group of amorous young souls, of which Crimson Pearl is one, and intends to send them down into the world to take part in the great illusion of human life. And as today happens to be the day on which this stone is fated to go into the world too, I am taking him with me to Disenchantment's tribunal for the purpose of getting him registered and sent down to earth with the rest of these romantic creatures."

"How very amusing!" said the Taoist. "I have certainly never heard of a debt of tears before. Why shouldn't the two of us take advantage of this opportunity to go down into the world ourselves and save a few souls? It would be a work of merit."

"That is exactly what I was thinking," said the monk. "Come with me to Disenchantment's palace to get this absurd creature cleared. Then, when this last batch of romantic idiots goes down, you and I can go down with them. At present about half have already been born. They await this last batch to make up the number."

"Very good, I will go with you then," said the Taoist. Shi-yin heard all this conversation quite clearly, and curiosity impelled him to go forward and greet the two reverend gentlemen. They returned his greeting and asked him what he wanted.

"It is not often that one has the opportunity of listening to a discussion of the operations of *karma* such as the one I have just been privileged to overhear," said Shi-yin. "Unfortunately I am a man of very limited understanding and have not been able to derive the full benefit from your conversation. If you would have the very great kindness to enlighten my benighted understanding with a somewhat fuller account of what you were discussing, I can promise you the most devout attention. I feel sure that your teaching would have a salutary effect on me and—who knows—might save me from the pains of hell."

The reverend gentlemen laughed. "These are heavenly mysteries and may not be divulged. But if you wish to escape from the fiery pit, you have only to remember us when the time comes, and all will be well."

Shi-yin saw that it would be useless to press them. "Heavenly mysteries must not, of course, be revealed. But might one perhaps inquire what the 'absurd creature' is that you were talking about? Is it possible that I might be allowed to see it?"

"Oh, as for that," said the monk: "I think it is on the cards for you to have a look at *him*," and he took the object from his sleeve and handed it to Shi-yin.

Shi-yin took the object from him and saw that it was a clear, beautiful jade on one side of which were carved the words "Magic Jade." There were several columns of smaller characters on the back, which Shi-yin was just going to examine more closely when the monk, with a cry of "Here we are, at the frontier of Illusion," snatched the stone from him and disappeared, with the Taoist, through a big stone archway above which

THE LAND OF ILLUSION

was written in large characters. A couplet in smaller characters was inscribed vertically on either side of the arch:

> Truth becomes fiction when the fiction's true;
> Real becomes not-real where the unreal's real.

Shi-yin was on the point of following them through the archway when suddenly a great clap of thunder seemed to shake the earth to its very foundations, making him cry out in alarm.

And there he was sitting in his study, the contents of his dream already half forgotten, with the sun still blazing on the ever-rustling plantains outside, and the wet-nurse at the door with his little daughter Ying-lian in her arms. Her delicate little pink-and-white face seemed dearer to him than ever at that moment, and he stretched out his arms to take her and hugged her to him.

After playing with her for a while at his desk, he carried her out to the front of the house to watch the bustle in the street. He was about to go in again when he saw a monk and a Taoist approaching, the monk scabby-headed and barefoot, the Taoist tousle-haired and limping. They were behaving like madmen, shouting with laughter and gesticulating wildly as they walked along.

When this strange pair reached Shi-yin's door and saw him standing there holding Ying-lian, the monk burst into loud sobs. "Patron," he said, addressing Shi-yin, "what are you doing, holding in your arms that ill-fated creature who is destined to involve both her parents in her own misfortune?"

Shi-yin realized that he was listening to the words of a madman and took no notice. But the monk persisted:

"Give her to me! Give her to me!"

Shi-yin was beginning to lose patience and, clasping his little girl more tightly to him, turned on his heel and was about to re-enter the house when the monk pointed his finger at him, roared with laughter, and then proceeded to intone the following verses:

> "Fond man, your pampered child to cherish so—
> That caltrop-glass which shines on melting snow!
> Beware the high feast of the fifteenth day,
> When all in smoke and fire shall pass away!"

Shi-yin heard all this quite plainly and was a little worried by it. He was thinking of asking the monk what lay behind these puzzling words when he heard the Taoist say, "We don't need to stay together. Why don't we part company here and each go about his own business? Three *kalpas* from now I shall wait for you on Bei-mang Hill. Having joined forces again there, we can go together to the Land of Illusion to sign off."

"Excellent!" said the other. And the two of them went off and soon were both lost to sight.

"There must have been something behind all this," thought Shi-yin to himself. "I really ought to have asked him what he meant, but now it is too late."

* * *

One day a desire to savour country sights and sounds led him[3] outside the city walls, and as he walked along with no fixed destination in mind, he presently found himself in a place ringed with hills and full of murmuring brooks and tall stands of bamboo where a temple stood half-hidden among the trees. The walled approach to the gateway had fallen in and parts of the surrounding wall were in ruins. A board above the gate announced the temple's name:

THE TEMPLE OF PERFECT KNOWLEDGE

while two cracked and worn uprights at the sides of the gate were inscribed with the following couplet:

> (on the right-hand side)
> As long as there is a sufficiency behind you, you press greedily forward.

> (on the left-hand side)
> It is only when there is no road in front of you that you think of turning back.

"The wording is commonplace to a degree," Yu-cun reflected, "yet the sentiment is quite profound. In all the famous temples and monasteries I have visited, I cannot recollect having ever seen anything quite like it. I shouldn't be surprised to find that some story of spectacular downfall and dramatic conversion lay behind this inscription. It might be worth going in and inquiring."

But when he went inside and looked around, he saw only an ancient, wizened monk cooking some gruel who paid no attention whatsoever to his greetings and who proved, when Yu-cun went up to him and asked him a few questions, to be both deaf and partially blind. His toothless replies were all but unintelligible, and in any case bore no relation to the questions.

Yu-cun walked out again in disgust. He now thought that in order to give the full rural flavour to his outing he would treat himself to a few cups of wine in a little country inn and accordingly directed his steps towards the near-by village. He had scarcely set foot inside the door of the village inn when one of the men drinking at separate tables inside rose up and advanced to meet him with a broad smile.

"Fancy meeting you!"

It was an antique dealer called Leng Zi-xing whom Yu-cun had got to know some years previously when he was staying in the capital. Yu-cun had a great admiration for Zi-xing as a practical man of business, whilst Zi-xing for his part was tickled to claim acquaintanceship with a man of Yu-cun's great learning and culture. On the basis of this mutual admiration the two of them had got on wonderfully well, and Yu-cun now returned the other's greeting with a pleased smile.

"My dear fellow! How long have you been here? I really had no idea you were in these parts. It was quite an accident that I came here today at all. What an extraordinary coincidence!"

"I went home at the end of last year to spend New Year with the family," said Zi-xing. "On my way back to the capital I thought I would stop off and have a few words with a friend of mine who lives hereabouts, and he very kindly invited me to spend a

---

3. Zhen Shi-yin's neighbor, a student named Jia Yu-cun.

few days with him. I hadn't got any urgent business waiting for me, so I thought I might as well stay on a bit and leave at the middle of the month. I came out here on my own because my friend has an engagement today. I certainly didn't expect to run into *you* here."

Zi-xing conducted Yu-cun to his table as he spoke and ordered more wine and some fresh dishes to be brought. The two men then proceeded, between leisurely sips of wine, to relate what each had been doing in the years that had elapsed since their last meeting.

Presently Yu-cun asked Zi-xing if anything of interest had happened recently in the capital.

"I can't think of anything particularly deserving of mention," said Zi-xing. "Except, perhaps, for a very small but very unusual event that took place in your own clan there."

"What makes you say that?" said Yu-cun, "I have no family connections in the capital."

"Well, it's the same name," said Zi-xing. "They must be the same clan."

Yu-cun asked him what family he could be referring to.

"I fancy you wouldn't disown the Jias of the Rong-guo mansion as unworthy of you."

"Oh, you mean them," said Yu-cun. "There are so many members of my clan, it's hard to keep up with them all. Since the time of Jia Fu of the Eastern Han dynasty there have been branches of the Jia clan in every province of the empire. The Rong-guo branch is, as a matter of fact, on the same clan register as my own; but since they are exalted so far above us socially, we don't normally claim the connection, and nowadays we are completely out of touch with them."

Zi-xing sighed. "You shouldn't speak about them in that way, you know. Nowadays both the Rong and Ning mansions are in a greatly reduced state compared with what they used to be."

"When I was last that way the Rong and Ning mansions both seemed to be fairly humming with life. Surely nothing could have happened to reduce their prosperity in so short a time?"

"Ah, you may well ask. But it's a long story."

"Last time I was in Jinling," went on Yu-cun, "I passed by their two houses one day on my way to Shi-tou-cheng to visit the ruins. The Ning-guo mansion along the eastern half of the road and the Rong-guo mansion along the western half must between them have occupied the greater part of the north side frontage of that street. It's true that there wasn't much activity outside the main entrances, but looking up over the outer walls I had a glimpse of the most magnificent and imposing halls and pavilions, and even the rocks and trees of the gardens beyond seemed to have a sleekness and luxuriance that were certainly not suggestive of a family whose fortunes were in a state of decline."

"Well! For a Palace Graduate Second Class, you ought to know better than that! Haven't you ever heard the old saying, 'The beast with a hundred legs is a long time dying'? Although I say they are not as prosperous as they used to be in years past, of course I don't mean to say that there is not still a world of difference between *their* circumstances and those you would expect to find in the household of your average government official. At the moment the numbers of their establishment and the activities they engage in are, if anything, on the increase. Both masters and servants all lead lives of luxury and magnificence. And they still have plenty of plans and projects under way. But they can't bring themselves to economize or make any adjustment in their accustomed style of living. Consequently, though outwardly they still manage to keep up appearances, inwardly they are beginning to feel the pinch. But that's a small matter. There's something much more seriously wrong with them than that. They are not able to turn out good sons, those stately houses, for all their pomp and show. The males in the family get more degenerate from one generation to the next."

"Surely," said Yu-cun with surprise, "it is inconceivable that such highly cultured households should not give their children the best education possible? I say nothing of other families, but the Jias of the Ning and Rong households used to be famous for the way in which they brought up their sons. How could they come to be as you describe?"

"I assure you, it is precisely those families I am speaking of. Let me tell you something of their history. The Duke of Ning-guo and the Duke of Rong-guo were two brothers by the same mother. Ning-guo was the elder of the two. When he died, his eldest son, Jia Dai-hua, inherited his post. Dai-hua had two sons. The elder, Jia Fu, died at the age of eight or nine, leaving only the second son, Jia Jing, to inherit. Nowadays Jia Jing's only interest in life is Taoism. He spends all his time over retorts and crucibles concocting elixirs, and refuses to be bothered with anything else.

"Fortunately he had already provided himself with a son, Jia Zhen, long before he took up this hobby. So, having set his mind on turning himself into an immortal, he has given up his post in favour of this son. And what's more he refuses outright to live at home and spends his time fooling around with a pack of Taoists somewhere outside the city walls.

"This Jia Zhen has got a son of his own, a lad called Jia Rong, just turned sixteen. With old Jia Jing out of the way and refusing to exercise any authority, Jia Zhen has thrown his responsibilities to the winds and given himself up to a life of pleasure. He has turned that Ning-guo mansion upside down, but there is no one around who dares gainsay him.

"Now I come to the Rong household—it was there that this strange event occurred that I was telling you about. When the old Duke of Rong-guo died, his eldest son, Jia Dai-shan, inherited his emoluments. He married a girl from a very old Nanking family, the daughter of Marquis Shi, who bore him two sons, Jia She and Jia Zheng.

"Dai-shan has been dead this many a year, but the old lady is still alive. The elder son, Jia She, inherited; but he's only a very middling sort of person and doesn't play much part in running the family. The second son, though, Jia Zheng, has been mad keen on study ever since he was a lad. He is a very upright sort of person, straight as a die. He was his grandfather's favourite. He would have sat for the examinations, but when the emperor saw Dai-shan's testamentary memorial that he wrote on his death bed, he was so moved, thinking what a faithful servant the old man had been, that he not only ordered the elder son to inherit his father's position, but also gave instructions that any other sons of his were to be presented to him at once, and on seeing Jia Zheng he gave him the post of Supernumerary Executive Officer, brevet rank, with instructions to continue his studies while on the Ministry's payroll. From there he has now risen to the post of Under Secretary.

"Sir Zheng's lady was formerly a Miss Wang. Her first child was a boy called Jia Zhu. He was already a Licensed Scholar at the age of fourteen. Then he married and had a son. But he died of an illness before he was twenty. The second child she bore him was a little girl, rather remarkable because she was born on New Year's day. Then after an interval of twelve years or more she suddenly had another son. He was even more remarkable, because at the moment of his birth he had a piece of beautiful, clear, coloured jade in his mouth with a lot of writing on it. They gave him the name 'Bao-yu' as a consequence. Now tell me if you don't think that is an extraordinary thing."

"It certainly is," Yu-cun agreed. "I should not be at all surprised to find that there was something very unusual in the heredity of that child."

"Humph," said Zi-xing. "A great many people have said that. That is the reason why his old grandmother thinks him such a treasure. But when they celebrated the First Twelve-month and Sir Zheng tested his disposition by putting a lot of objects in front of him and seeing which he would take hold of, he stretched out his little hand and started playing with some women's things—combs, bracelets, pots of rouge and powder and the like—completely ignoring all the other objects. Sir Zheng was very displeased. He said he would grow up to be a rake, and ever since then he hasn't felt much affection for the child. But to the old lady he's the very apple of her eye.

"But there's more that's unusual about him than that. He's now rising ten and unusually mischievous, yet his mind is as sharp as a needle. You wouldn't find one in a hundred to match him. Some of the childish things he says are most extraordinary. He'll say, 'Girls are made of water and boys are made of mud. When I am with girls I feel fresh and clean, but when I am with boys I feel stupid and nasty.' Now isn't that priceless! He'll be a lady-killer when he grows up, no question of that."

* * *

Everyone's attention now centred on Dai-yu.[4] They observed that although she was still young, her speech and manner already showed unusual refinement. They also noticed the frail body which seemed scarcely strong enough to bear the weight of its clothes, but which yet had an inexpressible grace about it, and realizing that she must be suffering from some deficiency, asked her what medicine she took for it and why it was still not better.

"I have always been like this," said Dai-yu. "I have been taking medicine ever since I could eat and been looked at by ever so many well-known doctors, but it has never done me any good. Once, when I was only three, I can remember a scabby-headed old monk came and said he wanted to take me away and have me brought up as a nun; but of course, Mother and Father wouldn't hear of it. So he said, 'Since you are not prepared to give her up, I am afraid her illness will never get better as long as she lives. The only way it might get better would be if she were never to hear the sound of weeping from this day onwards and never to see any relations other than her own mother and father. Only in those conditions could she get through her life without trouble.' Of course, he was quite crazy, and no one took any notice of the things he said. I'm still taking Ginseng Tonic Pills."

"Well, that's handy," said Grandmother Jia. "I take the Pills myself. We can easily tell them to make up a few more each time."

She had scarcely finished speaking when someone could be heard talking and laughing in a very loud voice in the inner courtyard behind them.

"Oh dear! I'm late," said the voice. "I've missed the arrival of our guest."

"Everyone else around here seems to go about with bated breath," thought Dai-yu. "Who can this new arrival be who is so brash and unmannerly?"

Even as she wondered, a beautiful young woman entered from the room behind the one they were sitting in, surrounded by a bevy of serving women and maids. She was dressed quite differently from the others present, gleaming like some fairy princess with sparkling jewels and gay embroideries.

---

4. Lin Dai-yu, a young girl whom Jia Yu-cun tutored. After her mother's death she has been sent to live with her maternal grandmother Jia, whose family has just been described.

Her chignon was enclosed in a circlet of gold filigree and clustered pearls. It was fastened with a pin embellished with flying phoenixes, from whose beaks pearls were suspended on tiny chains.

Her necklet was of red gold in the form of a coiling dragon.

Her dress had a fitted bodice and was made of dark red silk damask with a pattern of flowers and butterflies in raised gold thread.

Her jacket was lined with ermine. It was of a slate-blue stuff with woven insets in coloured silks.

Her under-skirt was of a turquoise-coloured imported silk crêpe embroidered with flowers.

She had, moreover,

> eyes like a painted phoenix,
> eyebrows like willow-leaves,
> a slender form,
> seductive grace;
> the ever-smiling summer face
> of hidden thunders showed no trace;
> the ever-bubbling laughter started
> almost before the lips were parted.

"You don't know her," said Grandmother Jia merrily. "She's a holy terror this one. What we used to call in Nanking a 'peppercorn.' You just call her 'Peppercorn Feng.' She'll know who you mean!"

Dai-yu was at a loss to know how she was to address this Peppercorn Feng until one of the cousins whispered that it was "Cousin Lian's wife," and she remembered having heard her mother say that her elder uncle, Uncle She, had a son called Jia Lian who was married to the niece of her Uncle Zheng's wife, Lady Wang. She had been brought up from earliest childhood just like a boy, and had acquired in the school-room the somewhat boyish-sounding name of Wang Xi-feng. Dai-yu accordingly smiled and curtseyed, greeting her by her correct name as she did so.

Xi-feng took Dai-yu by the hand and for a few moments scrutinized her carefully from top to toe before conducting her back to her seat beside Grandmother Jia.

"She's a beauty, Grannie dear! If I hadn't set eyes on her today, I shouldn't have believed that such a beautiful creature could exist! And everything about her so *distingué!* She doesn't take after your side of the family, Grannie. She's more like a Jia. I don't blame you for having gone on so about her during the past few days—but poor little thing! What a cruel fate to have lost Auntie like that!" and she dabbed at her eyes with a handkerchief.

"I've only just recovered," laughed Grandmother Jia. "Don't you go trying to start me off again! Besides, your little cousin is not very strong, and we've only just managed to get *her* cheered up. So let's have no more of this!"* * *

Dai-yu had long ago been told by her mother that she had a boy cousin who was born with a piece of jade in his mouth and who was exceptionally wild and naughty. He hated study and liked to spend all his time in the women's apartments with the girls; but because Grandmother Jia doted on him so much, no one ever dared to correct him. She realized that it must be this cousin her aunt was now referring to.

"Do you mean the boy born with the jade, Aunt?" she asked. "Mother often told me about him at home. She told me that he was one year older than me and that his name was Bao-yu. But she said that though he was very wilful, he always behaved very nicely to girls. Now that I am here, I suppose I shall be spending all my time with my girl cousins and not in the same part of the house as the boys. Surely there will be no danger of *my* provoking him?"

Lady Wang gave a rueful smile. "You little know how things are here! Bao-yu is a law unto himself. Because your grandmother is so fond of him she has thoroughly spoiled him. When he was little he lived with the girls, so with the girls he remains now. As long as they take no notice of him, things run quietly enough. But if they give him the least encouragement, he at once becomes excitable, and then there is no end to the mischief he may get up to. That is why I counsel you to ignore him. He can be all honey-sweet words one minute and ranting and raving like a lunatic the next. So don't believe anything he says."

Dai-yu promised to follow her aunt's advice. * * *

Lady Wang now led Dai-yu along a gallery, running from east to west, which brought them out into the courtyard behind Grandmother Jia's apartments. Entering these by a back entrance, they found a number of servants waiting there who, as soon as they saw Lady Wang, began to arrange the table and chairs for dinner. The ladies of the house themselves took part in the service. Li Wan brought in the cups, Xi-feng laid out the chopsticks, and Lady Wang brought in the soup.

The table at which Grandmother Jia presided, seated alone on a couch, had two empty chairs on either side. Xi-feng tried to seat Dai-yu in the one on the left nearer to her grandmother—an honour which she strenuously resisted until her grandmother explained that her aunt and her elder cousins' wives would not be eating with them, so that, since she was a guest, the place was properly hers. Only then did she ask permission to sit, as etiquette prescribed. Grandmother Jia then ordered Lady Wang to be seated. This was the cue for the three girls to ask permission to sit. Ying-chun sat in the first place on the right opposite Dai-yu, Tan-chun sat second on the left, and Xi-chun sat second on the right.

While Li Wan and Xi-feng stood by the table helping to distribute food from the dishes, maids holding fly-whisks, spittoons, and napkins ranged themselves on either side. In addition to these, there were numerous other maids and serving-women in attendance in the outer room, yet not so much as a cough was heard throughout the whole of the meal.

When they had finished eating, a maid served each diner with tea on a little tray. Dai-yu's parents had brought their daughter up to believe that good health was founded on careful habits, and in pursuance of this principle, had always insisted that after a meal one should allow a certain interval to elapse before taking tea in order to avoid indigestion. However, she could see that many of the rules in this household were different from the ones she had been used to at home; so, being anxious to conform as much as possible, she accepted the tea. But as she did so, another maid proferred a spittoon, from which she inferred that the tea was for rinsing her mouth with. And it was not, in fact, until they had all rinsed out their mouths and washed their hands that another lot of tea was served, this time for drinking.

Grandmother Jia now dismissed her lady servers, observing that she wished to enjoy a little chat with her young grand-children without the restraint of their grown-up presence.

Lady Wang obediently rose to her feet and, after exchanging a few pleasantries, went out, taking Li Wan and Wang Xi-feng with her.

Grandmother Jia asked Dai-yu what books she was studying.

"*The Four Books,*"[5] said Dai-yu, and inquired in turn what books her cousins were currently engaged on.

"Gracious, child, they don't study books," said her grandmother; "they can barely read and write!"

While they were speaking, a flurry of footsteps could be heard outside and a maid came in to say that Bao-yu was back.

"I wonder," thought Dai-yu, "just what sort of graceless creature this Bao-yu is going to be!"

The young gentleman who entered in answer to her unspoken question had a small jewel-encrusted gold coronet on the top of his head and a golden headband low down over his brow in the form of two dragons playing with a large pearl.

He was wearing a narrow-sleeved, full-skirted robe of dark red material with a pattern of flowers and butterflies in two shades of gold. It was confined at the waist with a court girdle of coloured silks braided at regular intervals into elaborate clusters of knotwork and terminating in long tassels.

Over the upper part of his robe he wore a jacket of slate-blue Japanese silk damask with a raised pattern of eight large medallions on the front and with tasselled borders.

On his feet he had half-length dress boots of black satin with thick white soles.

> As to his person, he had:
> a face like the moon of Mid-Autumn,
> a complexion like flowers at dawn,
> a hairline straight as a knife-cut,
> eyebrows that might have been painted by an artist's brush,
> a shapely nose, and
> eyes clear as limpid pools,
> that even in anger seemed to smile,
> and, as they glared, beamed tenderness the while.

Around his neck he wore a golden torque in the likeness of a dragon and a woven cord of coloured silks to which the famous jade was attached.

Dai-yu looked at him with astonishment. How strange! How very strange! It was as though she had seen him somewhere before, he was so extraordinarily familiar. Bao-yu went straight past her and saluted his grandmother, who told him to come after he had seen his mother, whereupon he turned round and walked straight out again.

Quite soon he was back once more, this time dressed in a completely different outfit.

The crown and circlet had gone. She could now see that his side hair was dressed in a number of small braids plaited with red silk, which were drawn round to join the long hair at the back in a single large queue of glistening jet black, fastened at intervals from the nape downwards with four enormous pearls and ending in a jewelled gold clasp. He had changed his robe and jacket for a rather more worn-looking rose-coloured gown, sprigged with flowers. He wore the gold torque and his jade as before, and she observed that the collection of objects round his neck had been further augmented by a padlock-shaped amulet and a lucky charm. A pair of ivy-coloured embroidered silk trousers were partially visible beneath his gown, thrust into black and white socks trimmed with brocade. In place of the formal boots he was wearing thick-soled crimson slippers. * * *

---

5. Four texts central to Confucianism: *Analects, Mencius, Doctrine of the Mean* and *The Great Learning.*

"Fancy changing your clothes before you have welcomed the visitor!" Grandmother Jia chided indulgently on seeing Bao-yu back again. "Aren't you going to pay your respects to your cousin?"

Bao-yu had already caught sight of a slender, delicate girl whom he surmised to be his Aunt Lin's daughter and quickly went over to greet her. Then, returning to his place and taking a seat, he studied her attentively. How different she seemed from the other girls he knew!

Her mist-wreathed brows at first seemed to frown, yet were not frowning;

> Her passionate eyes at first seemed to smile, yet were not merry.
> Habit had given a melancholy cast to her tender face;
> Nature had bestowed a sickly constitution on her delicate frame.
> Often the eyes swam with glistening tears;
> Often the breath came in gentle gasps.
> In stillness she made one think of a graceful flower reflected in the water;
> In motion she called to mind tender willow shoots caressed by the wind.
> She had more chambers in her heart than the martyred Bi Gan;[6]
> And suffered a tithe more pain in it than the beautiful Xi Shi.[7]

Having completed his survey, Bao-yu gave a laugh.

"I have seen this cousin before."

"Nonsense!" said Grandmother Jia. "How could you possibly have done?"

"Well, perhaps not," said Bao-yu, "but her face seems so familiar that I have the impression of meeting her again after a long separation."

"All the better," said Grandmother Jia. "That means that you should get on well together."

Bao-yu moved over again and, drawing a chair up beside Dai-yu, recommenced his scrutiny.

Presently: "Do you study books yet, cousin?"

"No," said Dai-yu. "I have only been taking lessons for a year or so. I can barely read and write."

"What's your name?"

Dai-yu told him.

"What's your school-name?"

"I haven't got one."

Bao-yu laughed. "I'll give you one, cousin. I think 'Frowner' would suit you perfectly."

"Where's your reference?" said Tan-chun.

"In the *Encyclopedia of Men and Objects Ancient and Modern* it says that somewhere in the West there is a mineral called 'dai' which can be used instead of eye-black for painting the eye-brows with. She has this 'dai' in her name and she knits her brows together in a little frown. I think it's a splendid name for her!"

"I expect you made it up," said Tan-chun scornfully.

"What if I did?" said Bao-yu. "There are lots of made-up things in books—apart from the *Four Books*, of course."

He returned to his interrogation of Dai-yu.

---

6. When Bi Gan scolded his nephew, the tyrannical last ruler of the Shang dynasty, for his barbarous behavior, the king responded that people said that a sage had a heart with seven openings, and that he would have to tear his uncle's heart out to see if he qualified.

7. A legendary beauty known for a slight frown.

"Have you got a jade?"

The rest of the company were puzzled, but Dai-yu at once divined that he was asking her if she too had a jade like the one he was born with.

"No," said Dai-yu. "That jade of yours is a very rare object. You can't expect everybody to have one."

This sent Bao-yu off instantly into one of his mad fits. Snatching the jade from his neck he hurled it violently on the floor as if to smash it and began abusing it passionately.

"Rare object! Rare object! What's so lucky about a stone that can't even tell which people are better than others? Beastly thing! I don't want it!"

The maids all seemed terrified and rushed forward to pick it up, while Grandmother Jia clung to Bao-yu in alarm.

"Naughty, naughty boy! Shout at someone or strike them if you like when you are in a nasty temper, but why go smashing that precious thing that your very life depends on?"

"None of the girls has got one," said Bao-yu, his face streaming with tears and sobbing hysterically. "Only I have got one. It always upsets me. And now this new cousin comes here who is as beautiful as an angel and she hasn't got one either, so I *know* it can't be any good."

"Your cousin did have a jade once," said Grandmother Jia, coaxing him like a little child, "but because when Auntie died she couldn't bear to leave her little girl behind, they had to let her take the jade with her instead. In that way your cousin could show her mamma how much she loved her by letting the jade be buried with her; and at the same time, whenever Auntie's spirit looked at the jade, it would be just like looking at her own little girl again.

"So when your cousin said she hadn't got one, it was only because she didn't want to boast about the good, kind thing she did when she gave it to her mamma. Now you put yours on again like a good boy, and mind your mother doesn't find out how naughty you have been."

So saying, she took the jade from the hands of one of the maids and hung it round his neck for him. And Bao-yu, after reflecting for a moment or two on what she had said, offered no further resistance. * * *

CHAPTER 5

Jia Bao-yu visits the Land of Illusion
And the fairy Disenchantment performs the "Dream of Golden Days"

From the moment Lin Dai-yu entered the Rong mansion, Grandmother Jia's solicitude for her had manifested itself in a hundred different ways. The arrangements made for her meals and accommodation were exactly the same as for Bao-yu. The other three granddaughters, Ying-chun, Tan-chun and Xi-chun, were relegated to a secondary place in the old lady's affections, and the objects of her partiality themselves began to feel an affection for each other which far exceeded what they felt for any of the rest. Sharing each other's company every minute of the day and sleeping in the same room at night, they developed an understanding so intense that it was almost as if they had grown into a single person.

And now suddenly this Xue Bao-chai[8] had appeared on the scene—a young lady who, though very little older than Dai-yu, possessed a grown-up beauty and aplomb

---

8. Another of Bao-yu's cousins, the daughter of his mother's sister.

in which all agreed Dai-yu was her inferior. Moreover, in contrast to Dai-yu with her air of lofty self-sufficiency and total obliviousness to all who did not move on the same exalted level as herself, Bao-chai had a generous, accommodating disposition which greatly endeared her to subordinates, so that even the tiniest maid looked on Miss Bao-chai as a familiar friend. Dai-yu could not but feel somewhat put out by this—a fact of which Bao-chai herself, however, was totally unaware.

As for Bao-yu, he was still only a child—a child, moreover, whom nature had endowed with the eccentric obtuseness of a simpleton. Brothers, sisters, cousins, were all one to him. In his relationships with people he made no distinction between one person and another. If his relationship with Dai-yu was exceptional, it was because greater proximity—since she was living with him in his grandmother's quarters—made her more familiar to him than the rest; and greater familiarity bred greater intimacy.

And of course, with greater intimacy came the occasional tiffs and misunderstandings that are usual with people who have a great deal to do with each other.

One day the two of them had fallen out over something or other and the argument had ended with Dai-yu crying alone in her room and Bao-yu feeling remorsefully that perhaps he had spoken too roughly. Presently he went in to make his peace with her and gradually, very gradually, Dai-yu's equanimity was restored.

The winter plum in the gardens of the Ning Mansion was now at its best, and this particular day Cousin Zhen's wife, You-shi, had some wine taken into the gardens and came over in person, bringing her son Jia Rong and his young wife with her, to invite Grandmother Jia, Lady Xing and Lady Wang to a flower-viewing party.

Grandmother Jia and the rest went round as soon as they had finished their breakfast. The party was in the All-scents Garden. It began with tea and continued with wine, and as it was a family gathering confined to the ladies of the Ning and Rong households, nothing particularly worth recording took place.

At one point in the party Bao-yu was overcome with tiredness and heaviness and expressed a desire to take an afternoon nap. Grandmother Jia ordered some of the servants to go back to the house with him and get him comfortably settled, adding that they might return with him later when he was rested; but Qin-shi, the little wife of Jia Rong, smilingly proposed an alternative.

"We have got just the room here for Uncle Bao. Leave him to me, Grannie dear! He will be quite safe in my hands."

She turned to address the nurses and maidservants who were in attendance on Bao-yu.

"Come, my dears! Tell Uncle Bao to follow me."

Grandmother Jia had always had a high opinion of Qin-shi's trustworthiness— she was such a charming, delightful little creature, the favourite among her great-granddaughters-in-law—and was quite content to leave the arrangements to her.

Qin-shi conducted Bao-yu and his little knot of attendants to an inner room in the main building. As they entered, Bao-yu glanced up and saw a painting hanging above them on the opposite wall. The figures in it were very finely executed. They represented Scholarly Diligence in the person of the Han philosopher Liu Xiang at his book, obligingly illuminated for him by a supernatural being holding a large flaming torch. Bao-yu found the painting—or rather its subject—distasteful. But the pair of mottoes which flanked it proved the last straw:

True learning implies a clear insight into human activities.
Genuine culture involves the skilful manipulation of human relationships.

In vain the elegant beauty and splendid furnishings of the room! Qin-shi was given to understand in no uncertain terms that her uncle Bao-yu wished to be out of it *at once.*

"If this is not good enough for you," said Qin-shi with a laugh, "where *are* we going to put you?—unless you would like to have your rest in my bedroom."

A little smile played over Bao-yu's face and he nodded. The nurses were shocked.

"An uncle sleep in the bedroom of his nephew's wife! Who ever heard of such a thing!"

Qin-shi laughed again.

"He won't misbehave. Good gracious, he's only a little boy! We don't have to worry about that sort of thing yet! You know my little brother who came last month: he's the same age as Uncle Bao, but if you stood them side by side I shouldn't be a bit surprised if he wasn't the taller of the two."

"Why haven't I seen your brother yet?" Bao-yu demanded. "Bring him in and let me have a look at him!"

The servants all laughed.

"Bring him in? Why, he's ten or twenty miles away! But I expect you'll meet him one of these days."

In the course of this exchange the party had made its way to Qin-shi's bedroom. As Bao-yu entered, a subtle whiff of the most delicious perfume assailed his nostrils, making a sweet stickiness inside his drooping eyelids and causing all the joints in his body to dissolve.

"What a lovely smell!"

He repeated the words several times over.

Inside the room there was a painting by Tang Yin[9] entitled 'Spring Slumber' depicting a beautiful woman asleep under a crab-apple tree, whose buds had not yet opened. The painting was flanked on either side by a pair of calligraphic scrolls inscribed with a couplet from the brush of the Song poet Qin Guan:[1]

> (on one side)
> The coldness of spring has imprisoned the soft buds in a wintry dream;

> (on the other side)
> The fragrance of wine has intoxicated the beholder with imagined flower-scents.

On a table stood an antique mirror that had once graced the tiring-room of the lascivious empress Wu Ze-tian.[2] Beside it stood the golden platter on which Flying Swallow[3] once danced for her emperor's delight. And on the platter was that very quince which the villainous An Lu-shan threw at beautiful Yang Gui-fei,[4] bruising her plump white breast. At the far end of the room stood the priceless bed on which Princess Shou-yang was sleeping out of doors under the eaves of the Han-zhang Palace when the plum-flower lighted on her forehead and set a new fashion for coloured patches. Over it hung a canopy commissioned by Princess Tong-chang entirely fashioned out of ropes of pearls.

"I like it here," said Bao-yu happily.

"My room," said Qin-shi with a proud smile, "is fit for an immortal to sleep in." And she unfolded a quilted coverlet, whose silk had been laundered by the fabulous

---

9. A well-known Ming dynasty painter (1470–1523).
1. A major composer of song lyrics (1049–1100).
2. A Tang imperial consort who managed to gain control of the government through her son and rule China from 684 to 705.
3. A consort of a Han dynasty emperor, said to be so light

she could dance on a platter.
4. Yang Gui-fei, the beloved consort of the Tang emperor Xuanzong, was blamed for distracting him from his proper job, which allowed the general An Lu-shan to mount a successful rebellion in 755.

Xi Shi, and arranged the double head-rest that Hong-niang[5] once carried for her amorous mistress.

The nurses now helped Bao-yu into bed and then tiptoed out, leaving him attended only by his four young maids: Aroma, Skybright, Musk, and Ripple. Qin-shi told them to go outside and stop the cats from fighting on the eaves.

As soon as Bao-yu closed his eyes he sank into a confused sleep in which Qin-shi was still there yet at the same time seemed to be drifting along weightlessly in front of him. He followed her until they came to a place of marble terraces and vermilion balustrades where there were green trees and crystal streams. Everything in this place was so clean and so pure that it seemed as if no human foot could ever have trodden there or floating speck of dust ever blown into it. Bao-yu's dreaming self rejoiced. "What a delightful place!" he thought. "If only I could spend all my life here! How much nicer it would be than living under the daily restraint of my parents and teachers!"

These idle reflections were interrupted by someone singing a song on the other side of a hill:

> "Spring's dream-time will like drifting clouds disperse,
> Its flowers snatched by a flood none can reverse.
> Then tell each nymph and swain
> 'Tis folly to invite love's pain!"

It was the voice of a girl. Before its last echoes had died away, a beautiful woman appeared in the quarter from which the voice had come, approaching him with a floating, fluttering motion.

* * *

Observing delightedly that the lady was a fairy, Bao-yu hurried forward and saluted her with a smile.

"Madam Fairy, I don't know where you have come from or where you are going to, but as I am quite lost in this place, will you please take me with you and be my guide?"

"I am the fairy Disenchantment," the fairy woman replied. "I live beyond the Realm of Separation, in the Sea of Sadness. There is a Mountain of Spring Awakening which rises from the midst of that sea, and on that mountain is the Paradise of the Full-blown Flower, and in that paradise is the Land of Illusion, which is my home. My business is with the romantic passions, love-debts, girlish heartbreaks and male philanderings of your dust-stained, human world. The reason I have come here today is that recently there has been a heavy concentration of love-*karma* in this area, and I hope to be able to find an opportunity of distributing a quantity of amorous thoughts by implanting them in the appropriate breasts. My meeting you here today is no accident but a part of the same project.

"This place where we are now is not so very far from my home. I have not much to offer you, but would you like to come back with me and let me try to entertain you? I have some fairy tea, which I picked myself. You could have a cup of that. And I have a few jars of choice new wine of my own brewing. I have also been rehearsing a fairy choir and a troupe of fairy dancers in a twelve-part suite which I recently composed called 'A Dream of Golden Days.' I could get them to perform it for you. What do you think?'

5. The maid Crimson, who facilitated a tryst between her mistress Yingying and a young student Zhang in *The Story of the Western Wing*, a well-known Yuan dynasty romantic comedy.

Bao-yu was so excited by this invitation that he quite forgot to wonder what had become of Qin-shi in his eagerness to accompany the fairy. As he followed her, a big stone archway suddenly loomed up in front of them on which

THE LAND OF ILLUSION

was written in large characters. A couplet in smaller characters was inscribed on either side of the arch:

> Truth becomes fiction when the fiction's true;
> Real becomes not-real when the unreal's real.

Having negotiated the archway, they presently came to the gateway of a palace. The following words were inscribed horizontally above the lintel:

SEAS OF PAIN AND SKIES OF PASSION

whilst the following words were inscribed vertically on the two sides:

> Ancient earth and sky
> Marvel that love's passion should outlast all time,
> Star-crossed men and maids
> Groan that love's debts should be so hard to pay.

"I see," said Bao-yu to himself. "I wonder what the meaning of 'passion that outlasts all time' can be. And what are 'love's debts'? From now on I must make an effort to understand these things."

He could not, of course, have known it, but merely by thinking this he had invited the attentions of the demon Lust, and at that very moment a little of the demon's evil poison had entered Bao-yu's body and lodged itself in the innermost recesses of his heart.

Wholly unconscious of his mortal peril, Bao-yu continued to follow the fairy woman. They passed through a second gateway, and Bao-yu saw a range of palace buildings ahead of them on either hand. The entrance to each building had a board above it proclaiming its name, and there were couplets on either side of the doorways. Bao-yu did not have time to read all of the names, but he managed to make out a few, viz.:

DEPARTMENT OF FOND INFATUATION

DEPARTMENT OF CRUEL REJECTION

DEPARTMENT OF EARLY MORNING WEEPING

DEPARTMENT OF LATE NIGHT SOBBING

DEPARTMENT OF SPRING FEVER

DEPARTMENT OF AUTUMN GRIEF

"Madam Fairy," said Bao-yu, whose interest had been whetted by what he had managed to read, "couldn't you take me inside these offices to have a look around?"

"In these offices," said the fairy woman, "are kept registers in which are recorded the past, present and future of girls from all over the world. It is not permitted that your earthly eyes should look on things that are yet to come."

Bao-yu was most unwilling to accept this answer, and begged and pleaded so persistently that at last Disenchantment gave in.

"Very well. You may make a very brief inspection of this office here."

Delighted beyond measure, Bao-yu raised his head and read the notice above the doorway:

DEPARTMENT OF THE ILL-FATED FAIR

The couplet inscribed vertically on either side of the doorway was as follows:

> Spring griefs and autumn sorrows were by yourselves provoked.
> Flower faces, moonlike beauty were to what end disclosed?

Bao-yu grasped enough of the meaning to be affected by its melancholy.

* * *

At once she ordered the remains of the feast to be removed and conducted Bao-yu to a dainty bedroom. The furnishings and hangings of the bed were more sumptuous and beautiful than anything he had ever seen. To his intense surprise there was a fairy girl sitting in the middle of it. Her rose-fresh beauty reminded him strongly of Bao-chai, but there was also something about her of Dai-yu's delicate charm. As he was pondering the meaning of this apparition, he suddenly became aware that Disenchantment was addressing him.

"In the rich and noble households of your mortal world, too many of those bowers and boudoirs where innocent tenderness and sweet girlish fantasy should reign are injuriously defiled by coarse young voluptuaries and loose, wanton girls. And what is even more detestable, there are always any number of worthless philanderers to protest that it is woman's beauty alone that inspires them, or loving feelings alone, unsullied by any taint of lust. They lie in their teeth! To be moved by woman's beauty is itself a kind of lust. To experience loving feelings is, even more assuredly, a kind of lust. Every act of love, every carnal congress of the sexes is brought about precisely because sensual delight in beauty has kindled the feeling of love.

"The reason I like you so much is because you are full of lust. You are the most lustful person I have ever known in the whole world!"

Bao-yu was scared by the vehemence of her words.

"Madam Fairy, you are wrong! Because I am lazy over my lessons, Mother and Father still have to scold me quite often; but surely that doesn't make me *lustful?* I'm still too young to know what they do, the people they use that word about."

"Ah, but you *are* lustful!" said Disenchantment. "In principle, of course, all lust is the same. But the word has many different meanings. For example, the typically lustful man in the common sense of the word is a man who likes a pretty face, who is fond of singing and dancing, who is inordinately given to flirtation; one who makes love in season and out of season, and who, if he could, would like to have every pretty girl in the world at his disposal, to gratify his desires whenever he felt like it. Such a person is a mere brute. His is a shallow, promiscuous kind of lust.

"But your kind of lust is different. That blind, defenceless love with which nature has filled your being is what we call here 'lust of the mind.' 'Lust of the mind' cannot be explained in words, nor, if it could, would you be able to grasp their meaning. Either you know what it means or you don't.

"Because of this 'lust of the mind' women will find you a kind and understanding friend; but in the eyes of the world I am afraid it is going to make you seem unpractical and eccentric. It is going to earn you the jeers of many and the angry looks of many more.

"Today I received a most touching request on your behalf from your ancestors the Duke of Ning-guo and the Duke of Rong-guo. And as I cannot bear the idea of your being rejected by the world for the greater glory of us women, I have brought you here. I have made you drunk with fairy wine. I have drenched you with fairy tea. I have admonished you with fairy songs. And now I am going to give you my little sister Two-in-one—'Ke-qing' to her friends—to be your bride.

"The time is propitious. You may consummate the marriage this very night. My motive in arranging this is to help you grasp the fact that, since even in these immortal precincts love is an illusion, the love of your dust-stained, mortal world must be doubly an illusion. It is my earnest hope that, knowing this, you will henceforth be able to shake yourself free of its entanglements and change your previous way of thinking, devoting your mind seriously to the teachings of Confucius and Mencius and your person wholeheartedly to the betterment of society."

Disenchantment then proceeded to give him secret instructions in the art of love; then, pushing him gently inside the room, she closed the door after him and went away.

Dazed and confused, Bao-yu nevertheless proceeded to follow out the instructions that Disenchantment had given him, which led him by predictable stages to that act which boys and girls perform together—and which it is not my intention to give a full account of here.

Next morning he lay for a long time locked in blissful tenderness with Ke-qing, murmuring sweet endearments in her ear and unable to tear himself away from her. Eventually they emerged from the bedroom hand in hand to walk together out-of-doors.

Their walk seemed to take them quite suddenly to a place where only thorn-trees grew and wolves and tigers prowled around in pairs. Ahead of them the road ended at the edge of a dark ravine. No bridge connected it with the other side. As they hesitated, wondering what to do, they suddenly became aware that Disenchantment was running up behind them.

"Stop! Stop!" she was shouting. "Turn back at once! Turn back!"

Bao-yu stood still in alarm and asked her what place this was.

"This is the Ford of Error," said Disenchantment. "It is ten thousand fathoms deep and extends hundreds of miles in either direction. No boat can ever cross it; only a raft manned by a lay-brother called Numb and an acolyte called Dumb. Numb holds the steering-paddle and Dumb wields the pole. They won't ferry anyone across for money, but only take those who are fated to cross over.

"If you had gone on walking just now and had fallen in, all the good advice I was at such pains to give you would have been wasted!"

CHAPTER 17

The inspection of the new garden becomes a test of talent
And Rong-guo House makes itself ready for an important visitor 6

One day Cousin Zhen came to Jia Zheng with his team of helpers to report that work on the new garden had been completed.

"Uncle She has already had a look," said Cousin Zhen. "Now we are only waiting for you to look round it to tell us if there is anything you think will need altering and also to decide what inscriptions ought to be used on the boards everywhere."

Jia Zheng reflected a while in silence.

---

6. Bao-yu's sister Yuan-chun, who has become an Imperial Concubine, is returning home for a visit, in honor of which the family is constructing a magnificent garden complete with dwellings of all sorts.

"These inscriptions are going to be difficult," he said eventually. "By rights, of course, Her Grace should have the privilege of doing them herself; but she can scarcely be expected to make them up out of her head without having seen any of the views which they are to describe. On the other hand, if we wait until she has already visited the garden before asking her, half the pleasure of the visit will be lost. All those prospects and pavilions—even the rocks and trees and flowers will seem somehow incomplete without that touch of poetry which only the written word can lend a scene."

"My dear patron, you are so right," said one of the literary gentlemen who sat with him. "But we have had an idea. The inscriptions for the various parts of the garden obviously cannot be dispensed with; nor, equally obviously, can they be decided in advance. Our suggestion is that we should compose provisional names and couplets to suit the places where inscriptions are required, and have them painted on rectangular paper lanterns which can be hung up temporarily—either horizontally or vertically as the case may be—when Her Grace comes to visit. We can ask her to decide on the permanent names after she has inspected the garden. Is not this a solution of the dilemma?"

"It is indeed," said Jia Zheng. "When we look round the garden presently, we must all try to think of words that can be used. If they seem suitable, we can keep them for the lanterns. If not, we can call for Yu-cun to come and help us out."

"Your own suggestions are sure to be admirable, Sir Zheng," said the literary gentlemen ingratiatingly. "There will be no need to call in Yu-cun."

Jia Zheng smiled deprecatingly.

"I am afraid it is not as you imagine. In my youth I had at best only indifferent skill in the art of writing verses about natural objects—birds and flowers and scenery and the like; and now that I am older and have to devote all my energies to official documents and government papers, I am even more out of touch with this sort of thing than I was then; so that even if I were to try my hand at it, I fear that my efforts would be rather dull and pedantic ones. Instead of enhancing the interest and beauty of the garden, they would probably have a deadening effect upon both."

"That doesn't matter," the literary gentlemen replied. "We can *all* try our hands at composing. If each of us contributes what he is best at, and if we then select the better attempts and reject the ones that are not so good, we should be able to manage all right."

"That seems to me a very good suggestion," said Jia Zheng. "As the weather today is so warm and pleasant, let us all go and take a turn round the garden now!"

So saying he rose to his feet and conducted his little retinue of literary luminaries towards the garden. Cousin Zhen hurried on ahead to warn those in charge that they were coming.

As Bao-yu was still in very low spirits these days because of his grief for Qin Zhong, Grandmother Jia had hit on the idea of sending him into the newly made garden to play. By unlucky chance she had selected this very day on which to try out her antidote. He had in fact only just entered the garden when Cousin Zhen came hurrying towards him.

"Better get out of here!" said Cousin Zhen with an amused smile. "Your father will be here directly!"

Bao-yu streaked back towards the gate, a string of nurses and pages hurrying at his heels. But he had only just turned the corner on coming out of it when he almost ran into the arms of Jia Zheng and his party coming from the opposite direction. Escape was impossible. He simply had to stand meekly to one side and await instructions.

Jia Zheng had recently received a favourable report on Bao-yu from his teacher Jia Dai-ru in which mention had been made of his skill in composing couplets. Although the boy showed no aptitude for serious study, Dai-ru had said, he nevertheless possessed a certain meretricious talent for versification not undeserving of commendation. Because of this report, Jia Zheng ordered Bao-yu to accompany him into the garden, intending to put his aptitude to the test. Bao-yu, who knew nothing either of Dai-ru's report or of his father's intentions, followed with trepidation.

As soon as they reached the gate they found Cousin Zhen at the head of a group of overseers waiting to learn Jia Zheng's wishes.

"I want you to close the gate," said Jia Zheng, "so that we can see what it looks like from outside before we go in."

Cousin Zhen ordered the gate to be closed, and Jia Zheng stood back and studied it gravely.

It was a five-frame gate-building with a hump-backed roof of half-cylinder tiles. The wooden lattice-work of the doors and windows was finely carved and ingeniously patterned. The whole gatehouse was quite unadorned by colour or gilding, yet all was of the most exquisite workmanship. Its walls stood on a terrace of white marble carved with a pattern of passion-flowers in relief, and the garden's whitewashed circumference wall to left and right of it had a footing made of black-and-white striped stone blocks arranged so that the stripes formed a simple pattern. Jia Zheng found the unostentatious simplicity of this entrance greatly to his liking, and after ordering the gates to be opened, passed on inside.

A cry of admiration escaped them as they entered, for there, immediately in front of them, screening everything else from their view, rose a steep, verdure-clad hill.

"Without this hill," Jia Zheng somewhat otiosely observed, "the whole garden would be visible as one entered, and all its mystery would be lost."

The literary gentlemen concurred. "Only a master of the art of landscape could have conceived so bold a stroke," said one of them.

As they gazed at this miniature mountain, they observed a great number of large white rocks in all kinds of grotesque and monstrous shapes, rising course above course up one of its sides, some recumbent, some upright or leaning at angles, their surfaces streaked and spotted with moss and lichen or half concealed by creepers, and with a narrow, zig-zag path only barely discernible to the eye winding up between them.

"Let us begin our tour by following this path," said Jia Zheng. "If we work our way round towards the other side of the hill on our way back, we shall have made a complete circuit of the garden."

He ordered Cousin Zhen to lead the way, and leaning on Bao-yu's shoulder, began the winding ascent of the little mountain. Suddenly on the mountainside above his head, he noticed a white rock whose surface had been polished to mirror smoothness and realized that this must be one of the places which had been prepared for an inscription.

"Aha, gentlemen!" said Jia Zheng, turning back to address the others who were climbing up behind him. "What name are we going to choose for this mountain?"

"Emerald Heights," said one.

"Embroidery Hill," said another.

Another proposed that they should call it "Little Censer" after the famous Censer Peak in Kiangsi. Another proposed "Little Zhong-nan." Altogether some twenty or thirty names were suggested—none of them very seriously, since the literary gentlemen were aware that Jia Zheng intended to test Bao-yu and were anxious not to make the boy's task too difficult. Bao-yu understood and was duly grateful.

When no more names were forthcoming Jia Zheng turned to Bao-yu and asked him to propose something himself.

"I remember reading in some old book," said Bao-yu, "that 'to recall old things is better than to invent new ones; and to recut an ancient text is better than to engrave a modern.' We ought, then, to choose something old. But as this is not the garden's principal 'mountain' or its chief vista, strictly speaking there is no justification for having an inscription here at all—unless it is to be something which implies that this is merely a first step towards more important things ahead. I suggest we should call it 'Pathway to Mysteries' after the line in Chang Jian's[7] poem about the mountain temple:

> A path winds upwards to mysterious places.

A name like that would be more distinguished."

There was a chorus of praise from the literary gentlemen:

"Exactly right! Wonderful! Our young friend with his natural talent and youthful imagination succeeds immediately where we old pedants fail!"

Jia Zheng gave a deprecatory laugh:

"You mustn't flatter the boy! People of his age are adept at making a little knowledge go a long way. I only asked him as a joke, to see what he would say. We shall have to think of a better name later on."

As he spoke, they passed through a tunnel of rock in the mountain's shoulder into an artificial ravine ablaze with the vari-coloured flowers and foliage of many varieties of tree and shrub which grew there in great profusion. Down below, where the trees were thickest, a clear stream gushed between the rocks. After they had advanced a few paces in a somewhat northerly direction, the ravine broadened into a little flat-bottomed valley and the stream widened out to form a pool. Gaily painted and carved pavilions rose from the slopes on either side, their lower halves concealed amidst the trees, their tops reaching into the blue. In the midst of the prospect below them was a handsome bridge:

> In a green ravine
> A jade stream sped.
> A stair of stone
> Plunged to the brink.
> Where the water widened
> To a placid pool,
> A marble baluster
> Ran round about.
> A marble bridge crossed it
> With triple span,
> And a marble lion's maw
> Crowned each of the arches.

Over the centre of the bridge there was a little pavilion, which Jia Zheng and the others entered and sat down in.

"Well, gentlemen!" said Jia Zheng. "What are we going to call it?"

7. A Tang dynasty poet of the 8th century.

"Ou-yang Xiu[8] in his *Pavilion of the Old Drunkard* speaks of 'a pavilion poised above the water,'" said one of them. "What about 'Poised Pavilion'?"

"'Poised Pavilion' is good," said Jia Zheng, "but *this* pavilion was put here in order to dominate the water it stands over, and I think there ought to be some reference to water in its name. I seem to recollect that in that same essay you mention Ou-yang Xiu speaks of the water 'gushing between twin peaks.' Could we not use the word 'gushing' in some way?"

"Yes, yes!" said one of the literary gentlemen. "'Gushing Jade' would do splendidly."

Jia Zheng fondled his beard meditatively, then turned to Bao-yu and asked him for *his* suggestion.

"I agreed with what you said just now, Father," said Bao-yu, "but on second thoughts it seems to me that though it may have been all right for Ou-yang Xiu to use the word 'gushing' in describing the source of the river Rang, it doesn't really suit the water round this pavilion. Then again, as this is a Separate Residence specially designed for the reception of a royal personage, it seems to me that something rather formal is called for, and that an expression taken from the *Drunkard's Pavilion* might seem a bit improper. I think we should try to find a rather more imaginative, less obvious sort of name."

"I hope you gentlemen are all taking this in!" said Jia Zheng sarcastically. "You will observe that when we suggest something original we are recommended to prefer the old to the new, but that when we *do* make use of an old text we are 'improper' and 'unimaginative'!—Well, carry on then! Let's have your suggestion!"

"I think 'Drenched Blossoms' would be more original and more tasteful than 'Gushing Jade.'"

Jia Zheng stroked his beard and nodded silently. The literary gentlemen could see that he was pleased and hastened to commend Bao-yu's remarkable ability.

"That's the two words for the framed board on top," said Jia Zheng. "*Not* a very difficult task. But what about the seven-word lines for the sides?"

Bao-yu glanced quickly round, seeking inspiration from the scene, and presently came up with the following couplet:

> "Three pole-thrust lengths of bankside willows green,
> One fragrant breath of bankside flowers sweet."

Jia Zheng nodded and a barely perceptible smile played over his features. The literary gentlemen redoubled their praises.

They now left the pavilion and crossed to the other side of the pool. For a while they walked on, stopping from time to time to admire the various rocks and flowers and trees which they passed on their way, until suddenly they found themselves at the foot of a range of whitewashed walls enclosing a small retreat almost hidden among the hundreds and hundreds of green bamboos which grew in a dense thicket behind them. With cries of admiration they went inside. A cloister-like covered walk ran round the walls from the entrance to the back of the forecourt and a cobbled pathway led up to the steps of the terrace. The house was a tiny three-frame one, two parts latticed, the third part windowless. The tables, chairs and couches which furnished it seemed to have been specially made to fit the interior. A door in the rear wall opened

---

8. Song dynasty scholar and statesman (1007–1072).

onto a garden of broad-leaved plantains dominated by a large flowering pear-tree and overlooked on either side by two diminutive lodges built at right angles to the back of the house. A stream gushed through an opening at the foot of the garden wall into a channel barely a foot wide which ran to the foot of the rear terrace and thence round the side of the house to the front, where it meandered through the bamboos of the forecourt before finally disappearing through another opening in the surrounding wall.

"This must be a pleasant enough place at any time," said Jia Zheng with a smile. "But just imagine what it would be like to sit studying beside the window here on a moonlight night! It is pleasures like that which make a man feel he has not lived in vain!"

As he spoke, his glance happened to fall on Bao-yu, who instantly became so embarrassed that he hung his head in shame. He was rescued by the timely intervention of the literary gentlemen who changed the subject from that of study to a less dangerous topic. Two of them suggested that the name given to this retreat should be a four-word one. Jia Zheng asked them what four words they proposed.

"'Where Bends the Qi'" said one of them, no doubt having in mind the song in the *Poetry Classic* which begins with the words

> See in that nook where bends the Qi,
> The green bamboos, how graceful grown![9]

"No," said Jia Zheng. "Too obvious!"

"'North of the Sui,'" said the other, evidently thinking of the ancient Rabbit Garden of the Prince of Liang in Suiyang—also famous for its bamboos and running water.

"No," said Jia Zheng. "Still too obvious!"

"You'd better ask Cousin Bao again," said Cousin Zhen, who stood by listening.

"He always insists on criticizing everyone else's suggestions before he will deign to make one of his own," said Jia Zheng. "He is a worthless creature." * * *

They had been moving on meanwhile, and he now led them into the largest of the little thatched buildings, from whose simple interior with its paper windows and plain deal furniture all hint of urban refinement had been banished. Jia Zheng was inwardly pleased. He stared hard at Bao-yu:

"How do you like *this* place, then?"

With secret winks and nods the literary gentlemen urged Bao-yu to make a favourable reply, but he wilfully ignored their promptings.

"Not nearly as much as 'The Phoenix Dance.'"

His father snorted disgustedly.

"Ignoramus! You have eyes only for painted halls and gaudy pavilions—the rubbishy trappings of wealth. What can *you* know of the beauty that lies in quietness and natural simplicity? This is a consequence of your refusal to study properly."

"Your rebuke is, of course, justified, Father," Bao-yu replied promptly, "but then I have never really understood what it was the ancients *meant* by 'natural.'"

The literary gentlemen, who had observed a vein of mulishness in Bao-yu which boded trouble, were surprised by the seeming naïveté of this reply.

---

9. From *The Book of Songs,* poem 55.

"Why, fancy not knowing what 'natural' means—you who have such a good understanding of so much else! 'Natural' is that which is *of nature,* that is to say, that which is produced by nature as opposed to that which is produced by human artifice."

"There you are, you see!" said Bao-yu. "A farm set down in the middle of a place like this is obviously the product of human artifice. There are no neighbouring villages, no distant prospects of city walls; the mountain at the back doesn't belong to any system; there is no pagoda rising from some tree-hid monastery in the hills above; there is no bridge below leading to a near-by market town. It sticks up out of nowhere, in total isolation from everything else. It isn't even a particularly remarkable view—not nearly so 'natural' in either form or spirit as those other places we have seen. The bamboos in those other places may have been planted by human hand and the streams diverted out of their natural courses, but there was no *appearance* of artifice. That's why, when the ancients use the term 'natural' I have my doubts about what they really meant. For example, when they speak of a 'natural painting,' I can't help wondering if they are not referring to precisely that forcible interference with the landscape to which I object: putting hills where they are not meant to be, and that sort of thing. However great the skill with which this is done, the results are never quite . . ."

His discourse was cut short by an outburst of rage from Jia Zheng.

"Take that boy out of here!"

Bao-yu fled.

"Come back!"

He returned.

"You still have to make a couplet on this place. If it isn't satisfactory, you will find yourself reciting it to the tune of a slapped face!"

Bao-yu stood quivering with fright and for some moments was unable to say anything. At last he recited the following couplet:

> "Emergent buds swell where the washerwoman soaks her cloth.
> A fresh tang rises where the cress-gatherer fills his pannier."

Jia Zheng shook his head: "Worse and worse."

* * *

Leaving the place of many fragrances behind them, they had not advanced much further when they could see ahead of them a building of great magnificence which Jia Zheng at once identified as the main reception hall of the Residence.

> Roof above roof soared,
> Eye up-compelling,
> Of richly-wrought chambers
> And high winding galleries.
> Green rafts of dark pine
> Brushed the eaves' edges.
> Milky magnolias
> Bordered the buildings.
> Gold-glinting cat-faces,
> Rainbow-hued serpents' snouts
> Peered out or snarled down
> From cornice and finial.

"It is rather a showy building," said Jia Zheng. But the literary gentlemen reassured him:

"Although Her Grace is a person of simple and abstemious tastes, the exalted position she now occupies makes it only right and proper that there should be a certain amount of pomp in her reception. This building is in no way excessive."

Still advancing in the same direction, they presently found themselves at the foot of the white marble memorial arch which framed the approach to the hall. The pattern of writhing dragons protectively crouched over its uppermost horizontal was so pierced and fretted by the sculptor's artistry as to resemble lacework rather than solid stone.

"What inscription do we want on this arch?" Jia Zheng inquired.

"'Peng-lai's Fairy Precincts' is the only name that would do it justice," said the literary gentlemen.

Jia Zheng shook his head and said nothing.

The sight of this building and its arch had inspired a strange and unaccountable stir of emotion in Bao-yu which on reflection he interpreted as a sign that he must have known a building somewhat like this before—though where or when he could not for the life of him remember. He was still racking his brains to recall what it reminded him of, when Jia Zheng ordered him to produce a name and couplet for the arch, and he was quite unable to give his mind to the task of composition. The literary gentlemen, not knowing the nature of his preoccupation, supposed that his father's incessant bullying had worn him out and that he had finally come to the end of his inspiration. They feared that further bullying might once more bring out the mulish streak in him, thereby provoking an explosion which would be distasteful for everybody. Accordingly they urged Jia Zheng to allow him a day's grace in which to produce something suitable. Jia Zheng, who was secretly beginning to be apprehensive about the possible conquences of Grandmother Jia's anxiety for her darling grandson, yielded, albeit with a bad grace:

"Jackanapes! So even you have your off moments it seems. Well, I'll give you a day to do it in. But woe betide you if you can't produce something tomorrow! And it had better be something good, too, because this is the most important building in the garden."

After they had seen over the building and come out again, they stopped for a while on the terrace to look at a general view of the whole garden and attempted to make out the places they had already visited. They were surprised to find that even now they had covered little more than half of the whole area. Just at that moment a servant came up to report that someone had arrived with a message from Yu-cun.

"I can see that we shan't be able to finish today," said Jia Zheng. "However, if we go out by the way I said, we should at least be able to get some idea of the general layout."

He conducted them to a large bridge above a crystal curtain of rushing water. It was the weir through which the water from the little river which fed all the pools and watercourses of the garden ran into it from outside. Jia Zheng invited them to name it.

"This is the source of the 'Drenched Blossoms' stream we looked at earlier on," said Bao-yu. "We should call it "Drenched Blossoms Weir.'"

"Rubbish!" said Jia Zheng. "You may as well forget about your 'Drenched Blossoms,' because we are not going to use that name!"

Their progress continued past many unexplored features of the garden, viz.:

    a summer lodge
    a straw-thatched cot
    a dry-stone wall
    a flowering arch
    a tiny temple nestling beneath a hill
    a nun's retreat hidden in a little wood
    a straight gallery

a crooked cave
a square pavilion
and a round belvedere.

But Jia Zheng hurried past every one of them without entering. However, he had now been walking for a very long time without a rest and was beginning to feel somewhat footsore; and so, when the next building appeared through the trees ahead, he proposed that they should go in and sit down, and led his party towards it by the quickest route possible. They had to walk round a stand of double-flowering ornamental peach-trees and through a circular opening in a flower-covered bamboo trellis. This brought them in sight of the building's whitewashed enclosing wall and the contrasting green of the weeping willows which surrounded it. A roofed gallery ran from each side of the gate round the inner wall of the forecourt, in which a few rocks were scattered. On one side of it some green plantains were growing and on the other a weeping variety of Szechwan crab, whose pendant clusters of double-flowering carmine blossoms hung by stems as delicate as golden wires on the umbrella-shaped canopy of its boughs.* * *

He led them inside the building. Its interior turned out to be all corridors and alcoves and galleries, so that properly speaking it could hardly have been said to have *rooms* at all. The partition walls which made these divisions were of wooden panelling exquisitely carved in a wide variety of motifs: bats in clouds, the "three friends of winter"—pine, plum and bamboo, little figures in landscapes, birds and flowers, scrollwork, antique bronze shapes, "good luck" and "long life" characters, and many others. The carvings, all of them the work of master craftsmen, were beautified with inlays of gold, mother-o'-pearl and semi-precious stones. In addition to being panelled, the partitions were pierced by numerous apertures, some round, some square, some sunflower-shaped, some shaped like a fleur-de-lis, some cusped, some fan-shaped. Shelving was concealed in the double thickness of the partition at the base of these apertures, making it possible to use them for storing books and writing materials and for the display of antique bronzes, vases of flowers, miniature tray-gardens and the like. The overall effect was at once richly colourful and, because of the many apertures, airy and graceful.

The *trompe-l'œil* effect of these ingenious partitions had been further enhanced by inserting false windows and doors in them, the former covered in various pastel shades of gauze, the latter hung with richly-patterned damask portières. The main walls were pierced with window-like perforations in the shape of zithers, swords, vases and other objects of virtù.

The literary gentlemen were rapturous:

"Exquisite!" they cried. "What marvellous workmanship!"

Jia Zheng, after taking no more than a couple of turns inside this confusing interior, was already lost. To the left of him was what appeared to be a door. To the right was a wall with a window in it. But on raising its portière he discovered the door to be a bookcase; and when, looking back, he observed—what he had not noticed before—that the light coming in through the silk gauze of the window illuminated a passageway leading to an open doorway, and began walking towards it, a party of gentlemen similar to his own came advancing to meet him, and he realized that he was walking towards a large mirror. They were able to circumvent the mirror, but only to find an even more bewildering choice of doorways on the other side.

"Come!" said Cousin Zhen with a laugh. "Let me show you the way! If we go out here we shall be in the back courtyard. We can reach the gate of the garden much more easily from the back courtyard than from the front."

He led them round the gauze hangings of a summer-bed, then through a door into a garden full of rambler roses. Behind the rose-trellis was a stream running between green banks. The literary gentlemen were intrigued to know where the water came from. Cousin Zhen pointed in the direction of the weir they had visited earlier:

"The water comes in over that weir, then through the grotto, then under the lea of the north-east 'mountain' to the little farm. There a channel is led off it which runs into the southeast corner of the garden. Then it runs round and rejoins the main stream here. And from here the water flows out again underneath that wall."

"How very ingenious!"

They moved on again, but soon found themselves at the foot of a tall "mountain."

"Follow me!" said Cousin Zhen, amused at the bewilderment of the others, who were now completely at sea as to their whereabouts. He led them round the foot of the "mountain"—and there, miraculously, was a broad, flat path and the gate by which they had entered, rising majestically in front of them.

"Well!" exclaimed the literary gentlemen. "This beats everything! The skill with which this has all been designed is quite out of this world!"

Whereupon they all went out of the garden.[1]

from CHAPTER 23

One day after lunch—it was round about the Midwash of the third month, as our fore-fathers, who measured the passage of time by their infrequent ablutions, were wont to say—Bao-yu set off for Drenched Blossoms Weir with the volumes of *Western Chamber*[2] under his arm, and sitting down on a rock underneath the peach-tree which grew there beside the bridge, he took up the first volume and began, very attentively, to read the play. He had just reached the line

    The red flowers in their hosts are falling

when a little gust of wind blew over and a shower of petals suddenly rained down from the tree above, covering his clothes, his book and all the ground about him. He did not like to shake them off for fear they got trodden underfoot, so collecting as many of them as he could in the lap of his gown, he carried them to the water's edge and shook them in. The petals bobbed and circled for a while on the surface of the water before finally disappearing over the weir. When he got back he found that a lot more of them had fallen while he was away. As he hesitated, a voice behind him said,

"What are you doing here?"

He looked round and saw that it was Dai-yu. She was carrying a garden hoe with a muslin bag hanging from the end of it on her shoulder and a garden broom in her hand.

"You've come just at the right moment," said Bao-yu, smiling at her. "Here, sweep these petals up and tip them in the water for me! I've just tipped one lot in myself."

"It isn't a good idea to tip them in the water," said Dai-yu. "The water you see here is clean, but farther on beyond the weir, where it flows past people's houses, there are all sorts of muck and impurity, and in the end they get spoiled just the same. In that corner over there I've got a grave for the flowers, and what I'm doing now is sweeping them up and putting them in this silk bag to bury them there, so that they can gradually turn back into earth. Isn't that a cleaner way of disposing of them?"

---

1. After the Imperial Concubine's visit, Bao-yu and his young female relatives are allowed to move into the garden's dwellings.

2. The comic play also known as *The Story of the Western Wing*.

Bao-yu was full of admiration for this idea.

"Just let me put this book somewhere and I'll give you a hand."

"What book?" said Dai-yu.

"Oh . . . The *Doctrine of the Mean* and *The Greater Learning*,"[3] he said, hastily concealing it.

"Don't try to fool *me!*" said Dai-yu. "You would have done much better to let me look at it in the first place, instead of hiding it so guiltily."

"In your case, coz, I have nothing to be afraid of," said Bao-yu; "but if I do let you look, you must promise not to tell anyone. It's marvellous stuff. Once you start reading it, you'll even stop wanting to eat!"

He handed the book to her, and Dai-yu put down her things and looked. The more she read, the more she liked it, and before very long she had read several acts. She felt the power of the words and their lingering fragrance. Long after she had finished reading, when she had laid down the book and was sitting there rapt and silent, the lines continued to ring on in her head.

"Well," said Bao-yu, "is it good?"

Dai-yu smiled and nodded.

Bao-yu laughed:

> "How can I, full of sickness and of woe,
> Withstand that face which kingdoms could o'erthrow?"

Dai-yu reddened to the tips of her ears. The eyebrows that seemed to frown yet somehow didn't were raised now in anger and the lovely eyes flashed. There was rage in her crimson cheeks and resentment in all her looks.

"You're *hateful!*"—she pointed a finger at him in angry accusal—"deliberately using that horrid play to take advantage of me. I'm going straight off to tell Uncle and Aunt!"

At the words "take advantage of me" her eyes filled with tears, and as she finished speaking she turned from him and began to go. Bao-yu rushed after her and held her back:

"Please, *please* forgive me! Dearest coz! If I had the slightest intention of taking advantage of you, may I fall into the water and be eaten up by an old bald-headed turtle! When you have become a great lady and gone at last to your final resting-place, I shall become the stone turtle that stands in front of your grave and spend the rest of eternity carrying your tombstone on my back as a punishment!"

His ridiculous declamation provoked a sudden explosion of mirth. She laughed and simultaneously wiped the tears away with her knuckles:

"Look at you—the same as ever! Scared as anything, but you still have to go on talking nonsense. Well, I know you now for what you are:

> "Of silver spear the leaden counterfeit"!'

"Well! *You* can talk!" said Bao-yu laughing. "Listen to *you!* Now I'*m* going off to tell on *you!*"

"You needn't imagine you're the only one with a good memory," said Dai-yu haughtily. "I suppose I'm allowed to remember lines too if I like."

Bao-yu took back the book from her with a good-natured laugh:

---

3. Two of what were known as the Four Books, important Confucian texts.

"Never mind about all that now! Let's get on with this flower-burying!"

And the two of them set about sweeping together the fallen flower-petals and putting them into the bag. They had just finished burying it when Aroma came hurrying up to them:

"So there you are! I've been looking for you everywhere. Your Uncle She isn't well and the young ladies have all gone over to visit him. Her Old Ladyship says you are to go as well. You'd better come back straight away and get changed!"

Bao-yu picked up his book, took leave of Dai-yu, and accompanied Aroma back to his room.

And there, for the moment, we shall leave him.

CHAPTER 27

We now return to Dai-yu, who, having slept so little the night before, was very late getting up on the morning of the festival.[4] Hearing that the other girls were all out in the garden 'speeding the fairies' and fearing to be teased by them for her lazy habits, she hurried over her toilet and went out as soon as it was completed. A smiling Bao-yu appeared in the gateway as she was stepping down into the courtyard.

"Well, coz," he said, "I hope you *didn't* tell on me yesterday. You had me worrying about it all last night."

Dai-yu turned back, ignoring him, to address Nightingale inside:

"When you do the room, leave one of the casements open so that the parent swallows can get in. And put the lion doorstop on the bottom of the blind to stop it flapping. And don't forget to put the cover back on the burner after you've lighted the incense."

She made her way across the courtyard, still ignoring him.

Bao-yu, who knew nothing of the little drama that had taken place outside his gate the night before, assumed that she was still angry about his unfortunate lapse earlier on that same day, when he had offended her susceptibilities with a somewhat risqué quotation from *The Western Chamber*. He offered her now, with energetic bowing and hand-pumping, the apologies that the previous day's emergency had caused him to neglect. But Dai-yu walked straight past him and out of the gate, not deigning so much as a glance in his direction, and stalked off in search of the others.

Bao-yu was nonplussed. He began to suspect that something more than he had first imagined must be wrong.

"Surely it can't only be because of yesterday lunchtime that she's carrying on in this fashion? There must be something else. On the other hand, I didn't get back until late and I didn't see her again last night, so how *could* I have offended her?"

Preoccupied with these reflections, he followed her at some distance behind.

Not far ahead Bao-chai and Tan-chun were watching the ungainly courtship dance of some storks. When they saw Dai-yu coming, they invited her to join them, and the three girls stood together and chatted. Then Bao-yu arrived. Tan-chun greeted him with sisterly concern:

"How have you been keeping, Bao? It's three whole days since I saw you last."

Bao-yu smiled back at her.

4. The festival of Grain in Ear marked the beginning of summer, which young girls would celebrate by fashioning miniature coaches and banners of twigs and brocade to speed the flower fairies on their way.

"How have *you* been keeping, sis? I was asking Cousin Wan about you the day before yesterday."

"Come over here a minute," said Tan-chun. "I want to talk to you."

He followed her into the shade of a pomegranate tree a little way apart from the other two.

"Has Father asked to see you at all during this last day or two?" Tan-chun began.

"No."

"I thought I heard someone say yesterday that he had been asking for you."

"No," said Bao-yu, smiling at her concern. "Whoever it was was mistaken. He certainly hasn't asked for *me*."

Tan-chun smiled and changed the subject.

"During the past few months," she said, "I've managed to save up another ten strings or so of cash. I'd like you to take it again like you did last time, and next time you go out, if you see a nice painting or calligraphic scroll or some amusing little thing that would do for my room, I'd like you to buy it for me."

"Well, I don't know," said Bao-yu. "In the trips I make to bazaars and temple fairs, whether it's inside the city or round about, I can't say that I ever see anything *really* nice or out of the ordinary. It's all bronzes and jades and porcelain and that sort of stuff. Apart from that it's mostly dress-making materials and clothes and things to eat."

"Now what would I want things like that for?" said Tan-chun. "No, I mean something like that little wickerwork basket you bought me last time, or the little box carved out of bamboo root, or the little clay burner. I thought they were sweet. Unfortunately the others took such a fancy to them that they carried them off as loot and wouldn't give them back to me again."

"Oh, if *those* are the sort of things you want," said Bao-yu laughing, "it's very simple. Just give a few strings of cash to one of the boys and he'll bring you back a whole cartload of them."

"What do the boys know about it?" said Tan-chun. "I need someone who can pick out the interesting things and the ones that are in good taste. You get me lots of nice little things, and I'll embroider a pair of slippers for you like the ones I made for you last time—only this time I'll do them more carefully."

"Talking of those slippers reminds me," said Bao-yu. "I happened to run into Father once when I was wearing them. He was Most Displeased. When he asked me who made them, I naturally didn't dare to tell him that *you* had, so I said that Aunt Wang had given them to me as a birthday present a few days before. There wasn't much he could do about it when he heard that they came from Aunt Wang; so after a very long pause he just said, 'What a pointless waste of human effort and valuable material, to produce things like that!' I told this to Aroma when I got back, and she said, 'Oh, that's nothing! You should have heard your Aunt Zhao complaining about those slippers. She was *furious* when she heard about them: "Her own natural brother so down at heel he scarcely dares show his face to people, and she spends her time making things like that!"'"

Tan-chun's smile had vanished:

"How *can* she talk such nonsense? Why should *I* be the one to make shoes for him? Huan gets a clothing allowance, doesn't he? He gets his clothing and footwear provided for the same as all the rest of us. And fancy saying a thing like that in front of a roomful of servants! For whose benefit was this remark made, I wonder? I make an occasional pair of slippers just for something to do in my spare time; and if I give a pair to someone I particularly like, that's my own affair. Surely no one else has any business to start telling me who I should give them to? Oh, she's so petty!"

Bao-yu shook his head:

"Perhaps you're being a bit hard on her. She's probably got her reasons."

This made Tan-chun really angry. Her chin went up defiantly:

"Now you're being as stupid as her. Of *course* she's got her reasons; but they are ignorant, stupid reasons. But she can think what she likes: as far as *I* am concerned, Sir Jia is my father and Lady Wang is my mother, and who was born in whose room doesn't interest me—the way I choose my friends inside the family has nothing to do with that. Oh, I know I shouldn't talk about her like this; but she is *so* idiotic about these things. As a matter of fact I can give you an even better example than your story of the slippers. That last time I gave you my savings to get something for me, she saw me a few days afterwards and started telling me how short of money she was and how difficult things were for her. I took no notice, of course. But later, when the maids were out of the room, she began attacking me for giving the money I'd saved to other people instead of giving it to Huan. Really! I didn't know whether to laugh or get angry with her. In the end I just walked out of the room and went round to see Mother."

There was an amused interruption at this point from Bao-chai, who was still standing where they had left her a few minutes before:

"Do finish your talking and come back soon! It's easy to see that you two are brother and sister. As soon as you see each other, you get into a huddle and start talking about family secrets. Would it *really* be such a disaster if anything you are saying were to be overheard?"

Tan-chun and Bao-yu rejoined her, laughing.

Not seeing Dai-yu, Bao-yu realized that she must have slipped off elsewhere while he was talking.

"Better leave it a day or two," he told himself on reflection. "Wait until her anger has calmed down a bit."

While he was looking downwards and meditating, he noticed that the ground where they were standing was carpeted with a bright profusion of wind-blown flowers—pomegranate and balsam for the most part.

"You can see she's upset," he thought ruefully. "She's neglecting her flowers. I'll bury this lot for her and remind her about it next time I see her."

He became aware that Bao-chai was arranging for him and Tan-chun to go with her outside.

"I'll join you two presently," he said, and waited until they were a little way off before stooping down to gather the fallen blossoms into the skirt of his gown. It was quite a way from where he was to the place where Dai-yu had buried the peach-blossom on that previous occasion, but he made his way towards it, over rocks and bridges and through plantations of trees and flowers. When he had almost reached his destination and there was only the spur of a miniature "mountain" between him and the burial-place of the flowers, he heard the sound of a voice, coming from the other side of the rock, whose continuous, gentle chiding was occasionally broken by the most pitiable and heart-rending sobs.

"It must be a maid from one of the apartments," thought Bao-yu. "Someone has been ill-treating her, and she has run here to cry on her own."

He stood still and endeavoured to catch what the weeping girl was saying. She appeared to be reciting something:

The blossoms fade and falling fill the air,
Of fragrance and bright hues bereft and bare.
Floss drifts and flutters round the Maiden's bower,
Or softly strikes against her curtained door.

The Maid, grieved by these signs of spring's decease,
Seeking some means her sorrow to express,
Has rake in hand into the garden gone,
Before the fallen flowers are trampled on.

Elm-pods and willow-floss are fragrant too;
Why care, Maid, where the fallen flowers blew?
Next year, when peach and plum-tree bloom again,
Which of your sweet companions will remain?

This spring the heartless swallow built his nest
Beneath the eaves of mud with flowers compressed.
Next year the flowers will blossom as before,
But swallow, nest, and Maid will be no more.

Three hundred and three-score the year's full tale:
From swords of frost and from the slaughtering gale
How can the lovely flowers long stay intact,
Or, once loosed, from their drifting fate draw back?

Blooming so steadfast, fallen so hard to find!
Beside the flowers' grave, with sorrowing mind,
The solitary Maid sheds many a tear,
Which on the boughs as bloody drops appear.

At twilight, when the cuckoo sings no more,
The Maiden with her rake goes in at door
And lays her down between the lamplit walls,
While a chill rain against the window falls.

I know not why my heart's so strangely sad,
Half grieving for the spring and yet half glad:
Glad that it came, grieved it so soon was spent.
So soft it came, so silently it went!

Last night, outside, a mournful sound was heard:
The spirits of the flowers and of the bird.
But neither bird nor flowers would long delay,
Bird lacking speech, and flowers too shy to stay.

And then I wished that I had wings to fly
After the drifting flowers across the sky:
Across the sky to the world's farthest end,
The flowers' last fragrant resting-place to find.

But better their remains in silk to lay
And bury underneath the wholesome clay,
Pure substances the pure earth to enrich,
Than leave to soak and stink in some foul ditch.

Can I, that these flowers' obsequies attend,
Divine how soon or late *my* life will end?

> Let others laugh flower-burial to see:
> Another year who will be burying me?
>
> As petals drop and spring begins to fail,
> The bloom of youth, too, sickens and turns pale.
> One day, when spring has gone and youth has fled,
> The Maiden and the flowers will both be dead.

All this was uttered in a voice half-choked with sobs; for the words recited seemed only to inflame the grief of the reciter—indeed, Bao-yu, listening on the other side of the rock, was so overcome by them that he had already flung himself weeping upon the ground.

But the sequel to this painful scene will be told in the following chapter.

CHAPTER 28

A crimson cummerbund becomes a pledge of friendship
And a chaplet of medicine-beads becomes a source of embarrassment

On the night before the festival, it may be remembered, Lin Dai-yu had mistakenly supposed Bao-yu responsible for Sky-bright's refusal to open the gate for her. The ceremonial farewell to the flowers of the following morning had transformed her pent-up and still smouldering resentment into a more generalized and seasonable sorrow. This had finally found its expression in a violent outburst of grief as she was burying the latest collection of fallen blossoms in her flower-grave. Meditation on the fate of flowers had led her to a contemplation of her own sad and orphaned lot; she had burst into tears, and soon after had begun a recitation of the poem whose words we recorded in the preceding chapter.

Unknown to her, Bao-yu was listening to this recitation from the slope of the near-by rockery. At first he merely nodded and sighed sympathetically; but when he heard the words

> "Can I, that these flowers' obsequies attend,
> Divine how soon or late *my* life will end?"

and, a little later,

> "One day when spring has gone and youth has fled,
> The Maiden and the flowers will both be dead."

he flung himself on the ground in a fit of weeping, scattering the earth all about him with the flowers he had been carrying in the skirt of his gown.

Lin Dai-yu dead! A world from which that delicate, flower-like countenance had irrevocably departed! It was unutterable anguish to think of it. Yet his sensitized imagination *did* now consider it—went on, indeed, to consider a world from which the others, too—Bao-chai, Caltrop, Aroma and the rest—had also irrevocably departed. Where would *he* be then? What would have become of him? And what of the Garden, the rocks, the flowers, the trees? To whom would they belong when he and the girls were no longer there to enjoy them? Passing from loss to loss in his imagination, he plunged deeper and deeper into a grief that seemed inconsolable. As the poet says:

> Flowers in my eyes and bird-song in my ears
> Augment my loss and mock my bitter tears.

Dai-yu, then, as she stood plunged in her own private sorrowing, suddenly heard the sound of another person crying bitterly on the rocks above her.

"The others are always telling me I'm a 'case,'" she thought. "Surely there can't be another 'case' up there?"

But on looking up she saw that it was Bao-yu.

"Pshaw!" she said crossly to herself. "I thought it was another girl, but all the time it was that cruel, hate—"

"Hateful" she had been going to say, but clapped her mouth shut before uttering it. She sighed instead and began to walk away.

By the time Bao-yu's weeping was over, Dai-yu was no longer there. He realized that she must have seen him and have gone away in order to avoid him. Feeling suddenly rather foolish, he rose to his feet and brushed the earth from his clothes. Then he descended from the rockery and began to retrace his steps in the direction of Green Delights. Quite by coincidence Dai-yu was walking along the same path a little way ahead.

"Stop a minute!" he cried, hurrying forward to catch up with her. "I know you are not taking any notice of me, but I only want to ask you one simple question, and then you need never have anything more to do with me."

Dai-yu had turned back to see who it was. When she saw that it was Bao-yu still, she was going to ignore him again; but hearing him say that he only wanted to ask her one question, she told him that he might do so.

Bao-yu could not resist teasing her a little.

"How about *two* questions? Would you wait for two?"

Dai-yu set her face forwards and began walking on again.

Bao-yu sighed.

"If it has to be like this now," he said, as if to himself, "it's a pity it was ever like it was in the beginning."

Dai-yu's curiosity got the better of her. She stopped walking and turned once more towards him.

"Like *what* in the beginning?" she asked. "And like what now?"

"Oh, the *beginning!*" said Bao-yu. "In the *beginning,* when you first came here, I was your faithful companion in all your games. Anything I had, even the thing most dear to me, was yours for the asking. If there was something to eat that I specially liked, I had only to hear that you were fond of it too and I would religiously hoard it away to share with you when you got back, not daring even to touch it until you came. We ate at the same table. We slept in the same bed. I used to think that because we were so close then, there would be something special about our relationship when we grew up—that even if we weren't particularly affectionate, we should at least have more understanding and forbearance for each other than the rest. But how wrong I was! Now that you *have* grown up, you seem only to have grown more touchy. You don't seem to care about *me* any more at all. You spend all your time brooding about outsiders like Feng and Chai. I haven't got any *real* brothers and sisters left here now. There are Huan and Tan, of course; but as you know, they're only my half-brother and half-sister: they aren't my mother's children. I'm on my own, like you. I should have thought we had so much in common—But what's the use? I try and try, but it gets me nowhere; and nobody knows or cares."

At this point—in spite of himself—he burst into tears.

The palpable evidence of her own eyes and ears had by now wrought a considerable softening on Dai-yu's heart. A sympathetic tear stole down her own cheek, and she hung her head and said nothing. Bao-yu could see that he had moved her.

"I know I'm not much use nowadays," he continued, "but however bad you may think me, I would never wittingly do anything in your presence to offend you. If I *do* ever slip up in some way, you ought to tell me off about it and warn me not to do it again, or shout at me—hit me, even, if you feel like it; I shouldn't mind. But you don't do that. You just ignore me. You leave me utterly at a loss to know what I'm supposed to have done wrong, so that I'm driven half frantic wondering what I ought to do to make up for it. If I were to die now, I should die with a grievance, and all the masses and exorcisms in the world wouldn't lay my ghost. Only when you explained what your reason was for ignoring me should I cease from haunting you and be reborn into another life."

Dai-yu's resentment for the gate incident had by now completely evaporated. She merely said:

"Oh well, in that case why did you tell your maids not to let me in when I came to call on you?"

"I honestly don't know what you are referring to," said Bao-yu in surprise. "Strike me dead if I ever did any such thing!"

"Hush!" said Dai-yu. "Talking about death at this time of the morning! You should be more careful what you say. If you did, you did. If you didn't, you didn't. There's no need for these horrible oaths."

"I really and truly didn't know you had called," said Bao-yu. "Cousin Bao came and sat with me a few minutes last night and then went away again. That's the only call I know about."

Dai-yu reflected for a moment or two, then smiled.

"Yes, it must have been the maids being lazy. Certainly they can be very disagreeable at such times."

"Yes, I'm sure that's what it was," said Bao-yu. "When I get back, I'll find out who it was and give her a good talking-to."

"I think some of your young ladies could *do* with a good talking-to," said Dai-yu, "—though it's not really for me to say so. It's a good job it was only me they were rude to. If Miss Bao or Miss Cow were to call and they behaved like that to *her,* that would be really serious."

She giggled mischievously. Bao-yu didn't know whether to laugh with her or grind his teeth. But just at that moment a maid came up to ask them both to lunch and the two of them went together out of the Garden and through into the front part of the mansion, calling in at Lady Wang's on the way.

"How did you get on with that medicine of Dr Bao's," Lady Wang asked Dai-yu as soon as she saw her, "—the Court Physician? Do you think you are any better for it?"

"It didn't seem to make very much difference," said Dai-yu. "Grandmother has put me back on Dr Wang's prescription."

"Cousin Lin has got a naturally weak constitution, Mother," said Bao-yu. "She takes cold very easily. These strong decoctions are all very well provided she only takes one or two to dispel the cold. For regular treatment it's probably best if she sticks to pills."

"The doctor was telling me about some pills for her the other day," said Lady Wang, "but I just can't remember the name."

"I know the names of most of those pills," said Bao-yu. "I expect he wanted her to take Ginseng Tonic Pills."

"No, that wasn't it," said Lady Wang.

"Eight Gem Motherwort Pills?" said Bao-yu. "Zhang's Dextrals? Zhang's Sinistrals? If it wasn't any of them, it was probably Dr Cui's Adenophora Kidney Pills."

"No," said Lady Wang, "it was none of those. All I can remember is that there was a 'Vajra' in it."

Bao-yu gave a hoot and clapped his hands:

"I've never heard of 'Vajra Pills.' If there are 'Vajra Pills,' I suppose there must be 'Buddha Boluses!'"

The others all laughed. Bao-chai looked at him mockingly.

"I should think it was probably 'The Deva-king Cardiac Elixir Pills,'" she said.

"Yes, yes, that's it!" said Lady Wang. "Of course! How stupid of me!"

"No, Mother, not stupid," said Bao-yu. "It's the strain. All those Vajra-kings and Bodhisattvas have been overworking you!"

"You're a naughty boy to make fun of your poor mother," said Lady Wang. "A good whipping from your Pa is what you need."

"Oh, Father doesn't whip me for that sort of thing nowadays," said Bao-yu.

"Now that we know the name of the pills, we must get them to buy some for your Cousin Lin," said Lady Wang.

"None of those things are any good," said Bao-yu. "You give me three hundred and sixty taels of silver and I'll make up some pills for Cousin Lin that I guarantee will have her completely cured before she has finished the first boxful."

"Stuff!" said Lady Wang. "Whoever heard of a medicine that cost so much?"

"No, honestly!" said Bao-yu. "This prescription is a very unusual one with very special ingredients. I can't remember all of them, but I know they include

> the caul of a first-born child;
> a ginseng root shaped like a man, with the leaves still on it;
> a turtle-sized polygonum root;

and

> lycoperdon from the stump of a thousand-year-old pine-tree.

—Actually, though, there's nothing so *very* special about those ingredients. They're all in the standard pharmacopoeia. For 'sovereign remedies' they use ingredients that would *really* make you jump. I once gave the prescription for one to Cousin Xue. He was more than a year begging me for it before I would give it to him, and it took him another two or three years and nearly a thousand taels of silver to get all the ingredients together. Ask Bao-chai if you don't believe me, Mother."

"I know nothing about it," said Bao-chai. "I've never heard it mentioned. It's no good telling Aunt to ask *me*."

"You see! Bao-chai is a *good* girl. *She* doesn't tell lies," said Lady Wang.

Bao-yu was standing in the middle of the floor below the kang. He clapped his hands at this and turned to the others appealingly.

"But it's the *truth* I'm telling you. This is no lie."

As he turned, he happened to catch sight of Dai-yu, who was sitting behind Bao-chai, smiling mockingly and stroking her cheek with her finger—which in sign-language means, "You are a great big liar and you ought to be ashamed of yourself."

But Xi-feng, who happened to be in the inner room supervising the laying of the table and had overheard the preceding remarks, now emerged into the outer room to corroborate:

"It's quite true, what Bao says. I don't think he *is* making it up," she said. "Not so long ago Cousin Xue came to me asking for some pearls, and when I asked him what he wanted them for, he said, 'To make medicine with.' Then he started grumbling about the trouble he was having in getting the right ingredients and how he had half a mind not to make this medicine up after all. I said, 'What medicine?' and he told me that it was a prescription that Cousin Bao had given him and reeled off a lot of ingredients—I can't remember them now. 'Of course,' he said, 'I could easily enough *buy* a few pearls; only these have to be ones that have been worn. That's why I'm asking *you* for them. If you haven't got any loose ones,' he said, 'a few pearls broken off a bit of jewellery would do. I'd get you something nice to replace it with.' He was so insistent that in the end I had to break up two of my ornaments for him. Then he wanted a yard of Imperial red gauze. That was to put over the mortar to pound the pearls through. He said they had to be ground until they were as fine as flour."

"You see!" "You see!" Bao-yu kept interjecting throughout this recital.

"Incidentally, Mother," he said, when it was ended, "even *that* was only a substitute. According to the prescription, the pearls ought really to have come from an ancient grave. They should really have been pearls taken from jewellery on the corpse of a long-buried noblewoman. But as one can't very well go digging up graves and rifling tombs every time one wants to make this medicine, the prescription allows pearls worn by the living as a second-best."

"Blessed name of the Lord!" said Lady Wang. "What a *dreadful* idea! Even if you *did* get them from a grave, I can't believe that a medicine made from pearls that had been come by so wickedly—desecrating people's bones that had been lying peacefully in the ground all those hundreds of years—could possibly do you any good."

Bao-yu turned to Dai-yu.

"Did you hear what Feng said?" he asked her. "I hope you're not going to say that *she* was lying."

Although the remark was addressed to Dai-yu, he winked at Bao-chai as he made it.

Dai-yu clung to Lady Wang.

"Listen to him, Aunt!" she wailed. "Bao-chai won't be a party to his lies, but he still expects *me* to be."

"Bao-yu, you are very unkind to your cousin," said Lady Wang.

Bao-yu only laughed.

"You don't know the reason, Mother. Bao-chai didn't know a half of what Cousin Xue got up to, even when she was living with her mother outside; and now that she's moved into the Garden, she knows even less. When she said she didn't know, she *really* didn't know: she wasn't giving me the lie. What you don't realize is that Cousin Lin was all the time sitting behind her making signs to show that she didn't believe me."

Just then a maid came from Grandmother Jia's apartment to fetch Bao-yu and Dai-yu to lunch.

Without saying a word to Bao-yu, Dai-yu got up and, taking the maid's hand, began to go. But the maid was reluctant.

"Let's wait for Master Bao and we can go together."

"He's not eating lunch today,' said Dai-yu. 'Come on, let's go!"

"Whether he's eating lunch or not," said the maid, "he'd better come with us, so that he can explain to Her Old Ladyship about it when she asks."

"All right, you wait for him then," said Dai-yu. "I'm going on ahead."

And off she went.

"I think I'd rather eat with *you* today, Mother," said Bao-yu.

"No, no, you can't," said Lady Wang. "Today is one of my fast-days: I shall only be eating vegetables. You go and have a proper meal with your Grandma."

"I shall share your vegetables," said Bao-yu. "Go on, you can go," he said, dismissing the maid; and rushing up to the table, he sat himself down at it in readiness.

"You others had better get on with your own lunch," Lady Wang said to Bao-chai and the girls. "Let him do as he likes."

"You really ought to go," Bao-chai said to Bao-yu. "Whether you have lunch there or not, you ought to keep Cousin Lin company. She is very upset, you know. Why don't you?"

"Oh, leave her alone!" said Bao-yu. "She'll be all right presently."

Soon they had finished eating, and Bao-yu, afraid that Grandmother Jia might be worrying and at the same time anxious to rejoin Dai-yu, hurriedly demanded tea to rinse his mouth with. Tan-chun and Xi-chun were much amused.

"Why are you always in such a hurry, Bao?" they asked him. "Even your eating and drinking all seems to be done in a rush."

"You should let him finish quickly, so that he can get back to his Dai-yu," said Bao-chai blandly. "Don't make him waste time here with us."

Bao-yu left as soon as he had drunk his tea, and made straight for the west courtyard where his Grandmother Jia's apartment was. But as he was passing by the gateway of Xi-feng's courtyard, it happened that Xi-feng herself was standing in her doorway with one foot on the threshold, grooming her teeth with an ear-cleaner and keeping a watchful eye on nine or ten pages who were moving potted plants about under her direction.

"Ah, just the person I wanted to see!" she said, as soon as she caught sight of Bao-yu. "Come inside. I want you to write something down for me."

Bao-yu was obliged to follow her indoors. Xi-feng called for some paper, an inkstone and a brush, and at once began dictating:

"Crimson lining-damask forty lengths, dragonet figured satin forty lengths, miscellaneous Imperial gauze one hundred lengths, gold necklets four,—"

"Here, what *is* this?" said Bao-yu. "It isn't an invoice and it isn't a presentation list. How am I supposed to write it?"

"Never you mind about that," said Xi-feng. "As long as I know what it is, that's all that matters. Just put it down anyhow."

Bao-yu wrote down the four items. As soon as he had done so, Xi-feng took up the paper and folded it away.

"Now," she said, smiling pleasantly, "there's something I want to talk to you about. I don't know whether you'll agree to this or not, but there's a girl in your room called 'Crimson' whom I'd like to work for me. If I find you someone to replace her with, will you let me have her?"

"There are so many girls in my room," said Bao-yu. "Please take any you have a fancy to. You really don't need to ask me about it."

"In that case," said Xi-feng, "I'll send for her straight away."

"Please do," said Bao-yu, and started to go.

"Hey, come back!" said Xi-feng. "I haven't finished with you yet."

"I've got to see Grandma now," said Bao-yu. "If you've got anything else to say, you can tell me on my way back."

When he got to Grandmother Jia's apartment, they had all just finished lunch. Grandmother Jia asked him if he had had anything nice to eat with his mother.

"There wasn't anything nice," he said. "But I had an extra bowl of rice."

Then, after the briefest pause:

"Where's Cousin Lin?"

"In the inner room," said Grandmother Jia.

In the inner room a maid stood below the kang[5] blowing on a flat-iron. Up on the kang two maids were marking some material with a chalked string, while Dai-yu, her head bent low over her work, was engaged in cutting something from it with her shears.

"What are you making?" he asked her. "You'll give yourself a headache, stooping down like that immediately after your lunch."

Dai-yu took no notice and went on cutting.

"That corner looks a bit creased still," said one of the maids. "It will have to be ironed again."

"Leave it alone!" said Dai-yu, laying down her shears. *"It will be all right presently."*

Bao-yu found her reply puzzling.

Bao-chai, Tan-chun and the rest had now arrived in the outer room and were talking to Grandmother Jia. Presently Bao-chai drifted inside and asked Dai-yu what she was doing; then, when she saw that she was cutting material, she exclaimed admiringly.

"What a lot of things you can do, Dai! Fancy, even dressmaking now!"

Dai-yu smiled malignantly.

"Oh, it's all lies, really. I just do it to fool people."

"I've got something to tell you that I think will amuse you, Dai," said Bao-chai pleasantly. "When our cousin was holding forth about that medicine just now and I said I didn't know about it, I believe actually he was rather wounded."

"Oh, leave him alone!" said Dai-yu. *"He will be all right presently."*

"Grandma wants someone to play dominoes with," said Bao-yu to Bao-chai. "Why don't you go and play dominoes?"

"Oh, is *that* what I came for?" said Bao-chai; but she went, notwithstanding.

"Why don't *you* go?" said Dai-yu. "There's a tiger in this room. You might get eaten."

She said this still bending over her cutting, which she continued to work away at without looking up at him.

Finding himself once more ignored, Bao-yu nevertheless attempted to remain jovial.

"Why don't you come out for a bit too? You can do this cutting later."

Dai-yu continued to take no notice.

Failing to get a response from her, he tried the maids:

"Who told her to do this dress-making?"

"Whoever told her to do it," said Dai-yu, "it has nothing whatever to do with Master Bao."

Bao-yu was about to retort, but just at that moment someone came in to say that he was wanted outside, and he was obliged to hurry off.

Dai-yu leaned forward and shouted after him:

"Holy name! By the time you get back, I shall be dead."

* * *

She[6] ordered a little maid to get out Bao-yu's share of the things sent. There were two Palace fans of exquisite workmanship, two strings of red musk-scented medicine-beads, two lengths of maidenhair chiffon and a grass-woven "lotus" mat to lie on in the hot weather.

---

5. A brick platform, often carpeted, that could be sat and slept on.
6. Aroma, Bao-yu's personal maid. The Imperial Concubine has sent gifts to mark the Double Fifth festival, a celebration of the summer solstice on the fifth day of the fifth lunar month.

"Did the others all get the same?" he asked.

"Her Old Ladyship's presents were the same as yours with the addition of a per-fume-sceptre and an agate head-rest, and Sir Zheng's, Lady Wang's and Mrs Xue's were the same as Her Old Ladyship's but without the head-rest; Miss Bao's were ex-actly the same as yours; Miss Lin, Miss Ying-chun, Miss Tan-chun and Miss Xi-chun got only the fans and the beads; and Mrs Zhu and Mrs Lian both got two lengths of gauze, two lengths of chiffon, two perfume sachets and two moulded medicine-cakes."

"Funny!" said Bao-yu. "I wonder why Miss Lin didn't get the same as me and why only Miss Bao's and mine were the same. There must have been some mistake, surely?"

"When they unpacked them yesterday, the separate lots were all labelled," said Aroma. "I don't see how there could have been any mistake. Your share was in Her Old Ladyship's room and I went round there to get it for you. Her Old Ladyship says she wants you to go to Court at four o'clock tomorrow morning to give thanks."

"Yes, of course," said Bao-yu inattentively, and gave Ripple instructions to take his presents round to Dai-yu:

"Tell Miss Lin that I got these things yesterday and that if there's anything there she fancies, I should like her to keep it."

Ripple went off with the presents. She was back in a very short time, however.

"Miss Lin says she got some yesterday too, and will you please keep these for yourself."

Bao-yu told her to put them away. As soon as he had washed, he left to pay his morning call on Grandmother Jia; but just as he was going out he saw Dai-yu coming towards him and hurried forward to meet her.

"Why didn't you choose anything from the things I sent you?"

Yesterday's resentments were now quite forgotten; today Dai-yu had fresh mat-ter to occupy her mind.

"I'm not equal to the honour," she said. "You forget, I'm not in the gold and jade class like you and your Cousin Bao. I'm only a common little wall-flower!"

The reference to gold and jade immediately aroused Bao-yu's suspicions.

"I don't know what anyone else may have been saying on the subject," he said, "but if any such thought ever so much as crossed *my* mind, may Heaven strike me dead, and may I never be reborn as a human being!"

Seeing him genuinely bewildered, Dai-yu smiled in what was meant to be a reas-suring manner.

"I wish you wouldn't make these horrible oaths. It's so disagreeable. Who *cares* about your silly old 'gold and jade,' anyway?"

"It's hard to make you *see* what is in my heart," said Bao-yu. "One day perhaps you will know. But I can tell you this. My heart has room for four people only. Grannie and my parents are three of them and Cousin Dai is the fourth. I swear to you there isn't a fifth."

"There's no need for you to swear," said Dai-yu. "I know very well that Cousin Dai has a place in your heart. The trouble is that as soon as Cousin Chai comes along, Cousin Dai gets forgotten."

"You imagine these things," said Bao-yu. "It really isn't as you say."

"Yesterday when Little Miss Bao wouldn't tell lies for you, why did you turn to *me* and expect *me* to? How would you like it if I did that sort of thing to you?"

Bao-chai happened to come along while they were still talking and the two of them moved aside to avoid her. Bao-chai saw this clearly, but pretended not to notice and hurried by with lowered eyes. She went and sat with Lady Wang for a while and from there went on to Grandmother Jia's. Bao-yu was already at his grandmother's when she got there.

Bao-chai had on more than one occasion heard her mother telling Lady Wang and other people that the golden locket she wore had been given her by a monk, who had insisted that when she grew up the person she married must be someone who had "a jade to match the gold." This was one of the reasons why she tended to keep aloof from Bao-yu. The slight embarrassment she always felt as a result of her mother's chatter had yesterday been greatly intensified when Yuan-chun singled her out as the only girl to receive the same selection of presents as Bao-yu. She was relieved to think that Bao-yu, so wrapped up in Dai-yu that his thoughts were only of her, was unaware of her embarrassment.

But now here was Bao-yu smiling at her with sudden interest.

"Cousin Bao, may I have a look at your medicine-beads?"

She happened to be wearing one of the little chaplets on her left wrist and began to pull it off now in obedience to his request. But Bao-chai was inclined to plumpness and perspired easily, and for a moment or two it would not come off. While she was struggling with it, Bao-yu had ample opportunity to observe her snow-white arm, and a feeling rather warmer than admiration was kindled inside him.

"If that arm were growing on Cousin Lin's body," he speculated, "I might hope one day to touch it. What a pity it's hers! Now I shall never have that good fortune."

Suddenly he thought of the curious coincidence of the gold and jade talismans and their matching inscriptions, which Dai-yu's remark had reminded him of. He looked again at Bao-chai—

> that face like the full moon's argent bowl;
> those eyes like sloes;
> those lips whose carmine hue no Art contrived;
> and brows by none but Nature's pencil lined.

This was beauty of quite a different order from Dai-yu's. Fascinated by it, he continued to stare at her with a somewhat dazed expression, so that when she handed him the chaplet, which she had now succeeded in getting off her wrist, he failed to take it from her.

Seeing that he had gone off into one of his trances, Bao-chai threw down the chaplet in embarrassment and turned to go. But Dai-yu was standing on the threshold, biting a corner of her handkerchief, convulsed with silent laughter.

"I thought you were so delicate," said Bao-chai. "What are you standing there in the draught for?"

"I've been in the room all the time," said Dai-yu. "I just this moment went to have a look outside because I heard the sound of something in the sky. It was a gawping goose."

"Where?" said Bao-chai. "Let *me* have a look."

"Oh," said Dai-yu, "as soon as I went outside he flew away with a *whir-r-r—*"

She flicked her long handkerchief as she said this in the direction of Bao-yu's face.

"Ow!" he exclaimed—She had flicked him in the eye.

* * *

from CHAPTER 29

Cousin Zhen was aware that, though Abbot Zhang[7] had started life a poor boy and entered the Taoist church as "proxy novice" of Grandmother Jia's late husband, a former Emperor had with his own Imperial lips conferred on him the title "Doctor Mysticus," and he now held the seals of the Board of Commissioners of the Taoist Church, had been awarded the title "Doctor Serenissimus" by the reigning sovereign, and was addressed as "Holiness" by princes, dukes and governors of provinces. He was therefore not a man to be trifled with. Moreover he was constantly in and out of the two mansions and on familiar terms with most of the Jia ladies. Cousin Zhen at once became affable.

"Oh, *you're* one of the family, Papa Zhang, so let's have no more of that kind of talk, or I'll take you by that old beard of yours and give it a good pull. Come on, follow me!"

Abbot Zhang followed him inside, laughing delightedly.

Having found Grandmother Jia, Cousin Zhen ducked and smiled deferentially.

"Papa Zhang has come to pay his respects, Grannie."

"Help him, then!" said Grandmother Jia; and Cousin Zhen hurried back to where Abbot Zhang was waiting a few yards behind him and supported him by an elbow into her presence. The abbot prefaced his greeting with a good deal of jovial laughter.

"Blessed Buddha of Boundless Life! And how has Your Old Ladyship been all this while? In rude good health, I trust? And Their Ladyships, and all the younger ladies?—also flourishing? It's quite a while since I was at the mansion to call on Your Old Ladyship, but I declare you look more blooming than ever!"

"And how are *you*, old Holy One?" Grandmother Jia asked him with a pleased smile.

"Thank Your Old Ladyship for asking. I still keep pretty fit. But never mind about that. What *I* want to know is, how's our young hero been keeping, eh? We were celebrating the blessed Nativity of the Veiled King here on the twenty-sixth. Very select little gathering. Tasteful offerings. I thought our young friend might have enjoyed it; but when I sent round to invite him, they told me he was out."

"He really *was* out," said Grandmother Jia, and turned aside to summon the "young hero"; but Bao-yu had gone to the lavatory. He came hurrying forward presently.

"Hallo, Papa Zhang! How are you?"

The old Taoist embraced him affectionately and returned his greeting.

"He's beginning to fill out," he said, addressing Grandmother Jia.

"He looks well enough on the outside," said Grandmother Jia, "but underneath he's delicate. And his Pa doesn't improve matters by forcing him to study all the time. I'm afraid he'll end up by *making* the child ill."

"Lately I've been seeing calligraphy and poems of his in all kinds of places," said Abbot Zhang, "—all quite remarkably good. I really can't understand why Sir Zheng is concerned that the boy doesn't study enough. If you ask me, I think he's all right as he is." He sighed. "Of course, you know who this young man reminds me of, don't you? Whether it's his looks or the way he talks or the way he moves, to me he's the spit and image of Old Sir Jia."

The old man's eyes grew moist, and Grandmother Jia herself showed a disposition to be tearful.

"It's quite true," she said. "None of our children or our children's children turned out like him, except my Bao. Only my little Jade Boy is like his grandfather."

---

7. An old acquaintance of the family who has stopped by for a visit.

"Of course, your generation wouldn't remember Old Sir Jia," Abbot Zhang said, turning to Cousin Zhen. "It's before your time. In fact, I don't suppose even Sir She and Sir Zheng can have a very clear recollection of what their father was like in his prime."

He brightened as another topic occurred to him and once more quaked with laughter.

"I saw a most attractive young lady when I was out visiting the other day. Fourteen this year. Seeing her put me in mind of our young friend here. It must be about time we started thinking about a match for him, surely? In looks, intelligence, breeding, background this girl was ideally suited. What does Your Old Ladyship feel? I didn't want to rush matters. I thought I'd better first wait and see what Your Old Ladyship thought before saying anything to the family."

"A monk who once told the boy's fortune said that he was not to marry young," said Grandmother Jia; "so I think we had better wait until he is a little older before we arrange anything definite. But do by all means go on inquiring for us. It doesn't matter whether the family is wealthy or not; as long as the girl *looks* all right, you can let me know. Even if it's a poor family, we can always help out over the expenses. Money is no problem. It's looks and character that count."

"Now come on, Papa Zhang!" said Xi-feng when this exchange had ended. "Where's that new amulet for my little girl? You had the nerve to send someone round the other day for gosling satin, and of course, as we didn't want to embarrass the old man by refusing, we had to send you some. So now what about that amulet?"

Abbot Zhang once more quaked with laughter.

"Ho! ho! ho! You can tell how bad my eyes are getting; I didn't even see you there, dear lady, or I should have thanked you for the satin. Yes, the amulet has been ready for some time. I was going to send it to you two days ago, but then Her Grace unexpectedly asked us for this *Pro Viventibus* and I stupidly forgot all about it. It's still on the high altar being sanctified. I'll go and get it for you."

He went off, surprisingly nimbly, to the main hall of the temple and returned after a short while carrying the amulet on a little tea-tray, using a red satin book-wrap as a tray-cloth. Baby's nurse took the amulet from him, and he was just about to receive the little girl from her arms when he caught sight of Xi-feng laughing at him mockingly.

"Why didn't you bring it in your hand?" she asked him.

"The hands get so sweaty in this weather," he said. "I thought a tray would be more hygienic."

"You gave me quite a fright when I saw you coming in with that tray," said Xi-feng. "I thought for one moment you were going to take up a collection!"

There was a loud burst of laughter from the assembled company. Even Cousin Zhen was unable to restrain himself.

"Monkey! Monkey!" said Grandmother Jia. "Aren't you afraid of going to the Hell of Scoffers when you die and having your tongue cut out?"

"Oh, Papa and I say what we like to each other," said Xi-feng. "*He*'s always telling *me* I must 'acquire merit' and threatening me with a short life if I don't pay up quickly. That's right, isn't it Papa?"

"As a matter of fact I *did* have an ulterior motive in bringing this tray," said Abbot Zhang, laughing, "but it wasn't in order to make a collection, I assure you. I wanted to ask this young gentleman here if he would be so very kind as to lend me the famous jade for a few minutes. The tray is for carrying it outside on, so that my Taoist friends, some of whom have travelled long distances to be here, and my old students, and *their* students, all of whom are gathered here today, may have the privilege of examining it."

"My dear good man, in that case let the boy go with it round his neck and show it to them himself!" said Grandmother Jia. "No need for all this running to and fro with trays—at your age, too!"

"Most kind! Most considerate!—But Your Old Ladyship is deceived," said the abbot. "I may look my eighty years, but I'm still hale and hearty. No, the point is that with so many of them here today and the weather so hot, the smell is sure to be somewhat overpowering. Our young friend here is certainly not used to it. We shouldn't want him to be overcome by the—ah—effluvia, should we?"

Hearing this, Grandmother Jia told Bao-yu to take off the Magic Jade and put it on the tray. Abbot Zhang draped the crimson cloth over his hands, grasped the tray between satin-covered thumbs and fingers, and, holding it like a sacred relic at eye level in front of him, conveyed it reverently from the courtyard.

Grandmother Jia and the others now continued their sightseeing. They had finished with everything at ground level and were about to mount the stairs into the galleries when Cousin Zhen came up to report that Abbot Zhang had returned with the jade. He was followed by the smiling figure of the abbot, holding the tray in the same reverential manner as before.

"Well, they've all seen the jade now," he said, "—and very grateful they were. They agreed that it really is a most remarkable object, and they regretted that they had nothing of value to show their appreciation with. Here you are!—this is the best they could do. These are all little Taoist trinkets they happened to have about them. Nothing very special, I'm afraid; but they'd like our young friend to keep them, either to amuse himself with or to give away to his friends."

Grandmother Jia looked at the tray. It was covered with jewellery. There were golden crescents, jade thumb-rings and a lot of "motto" jewellery—a tiny sceptre and persimmons with the rebus-meaning "success in all things," a little quail and a vase with corn-stalks meaning "peace throughout the years," and many other designs—all in gold- or jade-work, and much of it inlaid with pearls and precious stones. Altogether there must have been about forty pieces.

"What have you been up to, you naughty old man?" she said. "Those men are all poor priests—they can't afford to give things like *this* away. You really shouldn't have done this. We can't possibly accept them."

"It was their own idea, I do assure you," said the abbot. "There was nothing I could do to stop them. If you refuse to take these things, I am afraid you will destroy my credit with these people. They will say that I cannot really have the connection with your honoured family that I have always claimed to have."

After this Grandmother Jia could no longer decline. She told one of the servants to receive the tray.

"We obviously can't refuse, Grannie, after what Papa Zhang has just said," said Bao-yu; 'but I really have no use for this stuff. Why not let one of the boys carry it outside for me and I'll distribute it to the poor?"

"I think that's a very good idea," said Grandmother Jia.

But Abbot Zhang thought otherwise and hastily intervened:

"I'm sure it does our young friend credit, this charitable impulse. However, although these things are, as I said, of no especial value, they are—what shall I say— objects of *virtù,* and if you give them to the poor, in the first place the poor won't have much use for them, and in the second place the objects themselves will get spoiled. If you want to give something to the poor, a largesse of money would, I suggest, be far more appropriate."

"Very well, look after this stuff for me, then," said Bao-yu to the servant, "and this evening you will distribute a largesse."∗ ∗ ∗

For Bao-yu the whole of the previous day had been spoilt by Abbot Zhang's proposal to Grandmother Jia to arrange a match for him. He came home in a thoroughly bad temper and kept telling everyone that he would "never see Abbot Zhang again as long as he lived." Not associating his ill-humour with the abbot's proposal, the others were mystified.

Grandmother Jia's unwillingness was further reinforced by the fact that Dai-yu, since her return home yesterday, had been suffering from mild sunstroke. What with one thing and another, the old lady declined absolutely to go again, and Xi-feng had to make up her own party and go by herself.

But Xi-feng's play-going does not concern us.

Bao-yu, believing that Dai-yu's sunstroke was serious and that she might even be in danger of her life, was so worried that he could not eat, and rushed round in the middle of the lunch-hour to see how she was. He found her neither as ill as he had feared nor as responsive as he might have hoped.

"Why don't you go and watch your plays?" she asked him. "What are you mooning about at home for?"

Abbot Zhang's recent attempt at match-making had profoundly distressed Bao-yu and he was shocked by her seeming indifference.

"I can forgive the others for not understanding what has upset me," he thought; "but that *she* should want to trifle with me at a time like this . . . !"

The sense that she had failed him made the annoyance he now felt with her a hundred times greater than it had been on any previous occasion. Never could any other person have stirred him to such depths of atrabilious rage. Coming from other lips, her words would scarcely have touched him. Coming from hers, they put him in a passion. His face darkened.

"It's all along been a mistake, then," he said. "You're not what I took you for."

Dai-yu gave an unnatural little laugh.

"Not what you took me for? That's hardly surprising, is it? I haven't got that *little something* which would have made me worthy of you."

Bao-yu came right up to her and held his face close to hers:

"You do realize, don't you, that you are deliberately willing my death?"

Dai-yu could not for the moment understand what he was talking about.

"I swore an oath to you yesterday," he went on. "I said that I hoped Heaven might strike me dead if this 'gold and jade' business meant anything to me. Since you have now brought it up again, it's clear to me that you *want* me to die. Though what you hope to gain by my death I find it hard to imagine."

Dai-yu now remembered what had passed between them on the previous day. She knew that she was wrong to have spoken as she did, and felt both ashamed and a little frightened. Her shoulders started shaking and she began to cry.

"May Heaven strike *me* dead if I ever willed your death!" she said. "But I don't see what you have to get so worked up about. It's only because of what Abbot Zhang said about arranging a match for you. You're afraid he might interfere with your precious 'gold and jade' plans; and because you're angry about that, you have to come along and take it out on me—That's all it is, isn't it?"

Bao-yu had from early childhood manifested a streak of morbid sensibility, which being brought up in close proximity with a nature so closely in harmony with his own had done little to improve. Now that he had reached an age when both his experience and the reading of forbidden books had taught him something about "worldly matters," he had begun to take a rather more grown-up interest in girls. But although there were plenty of young ladies of outstanding beauty and breeding among the Jia family's numerous acquaintance, none of them, in his view, could remotely compare with Dai-yu. For some time now his feeling for her had been a very special one; but precisely because of this same morbid sensibility, he had shrunk from telling her about it. Instead, whenever he was feeling particularly happy or particularly cross, he would invent all sorts of ways of probing her to find out if this feeling for her was reciprocated. It was unfortunate for him that Dai-yu herself possessed a similar streak of morbid sensibility and disguised her real feelings, as he did his, while attempting to discover what *he* felt about *her*.

Here was a situation, then, in which both parties concealed their real emotions and assumed counterfeit ones in an endeavour to find out what the real feelings of the other party were. And because

When false meets false the truth will oft-times out,

there was the constant possibility that the innumerable little frustrations that were engendered by all this concealment would eventually erupt into a quarrel.

Take the present instance. What Bao-yu was actually thinking at this moment was something like this:

"In my eyes and in my thoughts there is no one else but you. I can forgive the others for not knowing this, but surely *you* ought to realize? If at a time like this you can't share my anxiety—if you can think of nothing better to do than provoke me with that sort of silly talk, it shows that the concern I feel for you every waking minute of the day is wasted: that you just don't care about me at all."

This was what he *thought;* but of course he didn't *say* it. On her side Dai-yu's thoughts were somewhat as follows:

"I know you must care for me a little bit, and I'm sure you don't take this ridiculous 'gold and jade' talk seriously. But if you cared *only* for me and had absolutely no inclination at all in another direction, then every time I mentioned 'gold and jade' you would behave quite naturally and let it pass almost as if you hadn't noticed. How is it, then, that when I do refer to it you get so excited? It shows that it must be on your mind. You *pretend* to be upset in order to allay my suspicions."

Meanwhile a quite different thought was running through Bao-yu's mind:

"I would do anything—absolutely *anything*," he was thinking, "if only you would be nice to me. If you would be nice to me, I would gladly die for you this moment. It doesn't really matter whether you know what I feel for you or not. Just be nice to me, then at least we shall be a little closer to each other, instead of so horribly far apart."

At the same time Dai-yu was thinking:

"Never mind me. Just be your own natural self. If *you* were all right, *I* should be all right too. All these manoeuverings to try and anticipate my feelings don't bring us any closer together; they merely draw us farther apart."

The percipient reader will no doubt observe that these two young people were already of one mind, but that the complicated procedures by which they sought to draw together were in fact having precisely the opposite effect. Complacent reader! Permit us to remind you that your correct understanding of the situation is due solely to the fact that we have been revealing to you the secret, innermost thoughts of those two young persons, which neither of them had so far ever felt able to express.

Let us now return from the contemplation of inner thoughts to the recording of outward appearances.

When Dai-yu, far from saying something nice to him, once more made reference to the "gold and jade," Bao-yu became so choked with rage that for a moment he was quite literally bereft of speech. Frenziedly snatching the "Magic Jade" from his neck and holding it by the end of its silken cord he gritted his teeth and dashed it against the floor with all the strength in his body.

"*Beastly* thing!" he shouted. "I'll smash you to pieces and put an end to this once and for all."

But the jade, being exceptionally hard and resistant, was not the tiniest bit damaged. Seeing that he had not broken it, Bao-yu began to look around for something to smash it with. Dai-yu, still crying, saw what he was going to do.

"Why smash a dumb, lifeless object?" she said. "If you want to smash something, let it be me."

The sound of their quarrelling brought Nightingale and Snowgoose hurrying in to keep the peace. They found Bao-yu apparently bent on destroying his jade and tried to wrest it from him. Failing to do so, and sensing that the quarrel was of more than usual dimensions, they went off to fetch Aroma. Aroma came back with them as fast as she could run and eventually succeeded in prising the jade from his hand. He glared at her scornfully.

"It's my own thing I'm smashing," he said. "What business is it of yours to interfere?"

Aroma saw that his face was white with anger and his eyes wild and dangerous. Never had she seen him in so terrible a rage. She took him gently by the hand:

"You shouldn't smash the jade just because of a disagreement with your cousin," she said. "What do you think she would feel like and what sort of position would it put her in if you really *were* to break it?"

Dai-yu heard these words through her sobs. They struck a responsive chord in her breast, and she wept all the harder to think that even Aroma seemed to understand her better than Bao-yu did. So much emotion was too much for her weak stomach. Suddenly there was a horrible retching noise and up came the tisane of elsholtzia leaves she had taken only a short while before. Nightingale quickly held out her handkerchief to receive it and, while Snowgoose rubbed and pounded her back, Dai-yu continued to retch up wave upon wave of watery vomit, until the whole handkerchief was soaked with it.

"However cross you may be, Miss, you ought to have more regard for your health," said Nightingale. "You'd only just taken that medicine and you were beginning to feel a little bit better for it, and now because of your argument with Master Bao you've gone and brought it all up again. Suppose you were to be *really* ill as a consequence. How do you think Master Bao would feel?"

When Bao-yu heard these words they struck a responsive chord in *his* breast, and he reflected bitterly that even Nightingale seemed to understand him better than Dai-yu. But then he looked again at Dai-yu, who was sobbing and panting by turns, and whose red and swollen face was wet with perspiration and tears, and seeing how pitiably frail and ill she looked, his heart misgave him.

"I shouldn't have taken her up on that 'gold and jade' business," he thought. "I've got her into this state and now there's no way in which I can relieve her by sharing what she suffers." As he thought this, he, too, began to cry.

Now that Bao-yu and Dai-yu were both crying, Aroma instinctively drew towards her master to comfort him. A pang of pity for him passed through her and she squeezed his hand sympathetically. It was as cold as ice. She would have liked to tell him not to cry but hesitated, partly from the consideration that he might be suffering from some deep-concealed hurt which crying would do something to relieve, and partly from the fear that to do so in Dai-yu's presence might seem presumptuous. Torn between a desire to speak and fear of the possible consequences of speaking, she did what girls of her type often do when faced with a difficult decision: she avoided the necessity of making one by bursting into tears.

As for Nightingale, who had disposed of the handkerchief of vomited tisane and was now gently fanning her mistress with her fan, seeing the other three all standing there as quiet as mice with the tears streaming down their faces, she was so affected by the sight that she too started crying and was obliged to have recourse to a second handkerchief.

There the four of them stood, then, facing each other; all of them crying; none of them saying a word. It was Aroma who broke the silence with a strained and nervous laugh.

"You ought not to quarrel with Miss Lin," she said to Bao-yu, "if only for the sake of this pretty cord she made you."

At these words Dai-yu, ill as she was, darted forward, grabbed the jade from Aroma's hand, and snatching up a pair of scissors that were lying nearby, began feverishly cutting at its silken cord with them. Before Aroma and Nightingale could stop her, she had already cut it into several pieces.

"It was a waste of time making it," she sobbed. "He doesn't really care for it. And there's someone else who'll no doubt make him a better one!"

"What a shame!" said Aroma, retrieving the jade. "It's all my silly fault. I should have kept my mouth shut."

"Go on! Cut away!" said Bao-yu. "I shan't be wearing the wretched thing again anyway, so it doesn't matter."

Preoccupied with the quarrel, the four of them had failed to notice several old women, who had been drawn by the sound of it to investigate. Apprehensive, when they saw Dai-yu hysterically weeping and vomiting and Bao-yu trying to smash his jade, of the dire consequences to be expected from a scene of such desperate passion, they had hurried off in a body to the front of the mansion to report the matter to Grandmother Jia and Lady Wang, hoping in this way to establish in advance that whatever the consequences might be, *they* were not responsible for them. From their precipitate entry and the grave tone of their announcement Grandmother Jia and Lady Wang assumed that some major catastrophe had befallen and hurried with them into the Garden to find out what it was.

Their arrival filled Aroma with alarm. "What did Nightingale want to go troubling Their Ladyships for?" she thought crossly, supposing that the talebearer had been sent to them by Nightingale; while Nightingale for her part was angry with Aroma, thinking that the talebearer must have been one of Aroma's minions.

Grandmother Jia and Lady Wang entered the room to find a silent Bao-yu and a silent Dai-yu, neither of whom, when questioned, would admit that anything at all was the matter. They therefore visited their wrath on the heads of the two unfortunate maids, insisting that it was entirely owing to their negligence that matters had got so much out of hand. Unable to defend themselves, the girls were obliged to endure a long and abusive dressing-down, after which Grandmother Jia concluded the affair by carrying Bao-yu off to her own apartment.

Next day, the third of the fifth month, was Xue Pan's birthday and there was a family party with plays, to which the Jias were all invited. Bao-yu, who had still not seen Dai-yu since his outburst—which he now deeply regretted—was feeling far too dispirited to care about seeing plays, and declined to go on the ground that he was feeling unwell.

Dai-yu, though somewhat overcome on the day previous to this by the sultry weather, had by no means been seriously ill. Arguing that if *she* was not ill, it was impossible that *he* should be, she felt sure, when she heard of Bao-yu's excuse, that it must be a false one.

"He usually enjoys drinking and watching plays," she thought. "If he's not going, it must be because he is still angry about yesterday; or if it isn't that, it must be because he's heard that I'm not going and doesn't want to go without me. Oh! I should *never* have cut that cord! Now he won't ever wear his jade again—unless I make him another cord to wear it on."

So she, too, regretted the quarrel.

Grandmother Jia knew that Bao-yu and Dai-yu were angry with each other, but she had been assuming that they would see each other at the Xues' party and make it up there. When neither of them turned up at it, she became seriously upset.

"I'm a miserable old sinner," she grumbled. "It must be my punishment for something I did wrong in a past life to have to live with a pair of such obstinate, addle-headed little geese! I'm sure there isn't a day goes by without their giving me some fresh cause for anxiety. It must be fate. That's what it says in the proverb, after all:

> 'Tis Fate brings foes and lo'es tegither.

I'll be glad when I've drawn my last breath and closed my old eyes for the last time; then the two of them can snap and snarl at each other to their hearts' content, for *I* shan't be there to see it, and 'what the eye doesn't see, the heart doesn't grieve.' The Lord knows, it's not *my* wish to drag on this wearisome life any longer!"

Amidst these muttered grumblings the old lady began to cry.

In due course her words were transmitted to Bao-yu and Dai-yu. It happened that neither of them had ever heard the saying

> 'Tis Fate brings foes and lo'es tegither,

and its impact on them, hearing it for the first time, was like that of a Zen "perception": something to be meditated on with bowed head and savoured with a gush of tears. Though they had still not made it up since their quarrel, the difference between them had now vanished completely:

> In Naiad's House one to the wind made moan,
> In Green Delights one to the moon complained,

to parody the well-known lines. Or, in homelier verses:

> Though each was in a different place,
> Their hearts in friendship beat as one.

On the second day after their quarrel Aroma deemed that the time was now ripe for urging a settlement.

"Whatever the rights and wrongs of all this may be," she said to Bao-yu, "*you* are certainly the one who is *most* to blame. Whenever in the past you've heard about a quarrel between one of the pages and one of the girls, you've always said that the boy was a brute for not understanding the girl's feelings better—yet here you are behaving in exactly the same way yourself! Tomorrow will be the Double Fifth. Her Old Lady-ship will be really angry if the two of you are still at daggers drawn on the day of the festival, and that will make life difficult for *all* of us. Why not put your pride in your pocket and go and say you are sorry, so that we can all get back to normal again?"* * *

from CHAPTER 30

Dai-yu, as we have shown, regretted her quarrel with Bao-yu almost as soon as it was over; but since there were no conceivable grounds on which she could run after him and tell him so, she continued, both day and night, in a state of unrelieved depression that made her feel almost as if a part of her was lost. Nightingale had a shrewd idea how it was with her and resolved at last to tackle her:

"I think the day before yesterday you were too hasty, Miss. *We* ought to know what things Master Bao is touchy about, if no one else does. Look at all the quarrels we've had with him in the past on account of that jade!"

"Poh!" said Dai-yu scornfully. "You are trying to make out that it was my fault because you have taken his side against me. Of course I wasn't too hasty."

Nightingale gave her a quizzical smile.

"No? Then why did you cut that cord up? If three parts of the blame was Bao-yu's, I'm sure at least seven parts of it was yours. From what I've seen of it, he's all right with you when you allow him to be; it's because you're so prickly with him and always trying to put him in the wrong that he gets worked up."

Dai-yu was about to retort when they heard someone at the courtyard gate calling to be let in. Nightingale turned to listen:

"That's Bao-yu's voice," she said. "I expect he has come to apologize."

"I forbid you to let him in," said Dai-yu.

"There you go again!" said Nightingale. "You're going to keep him standing outside in the blazing sun on a day like this. Surely *that*'s wrong, if nothing else is?"

She was moving outside, even as she said this, regardless of her mistress's in-junction. Sure enough, it *was* Bao-yu. She unfastened the gate and welcomed him in with a friendly smile.

"Master Bao! I was beginning to think you weren't coming to see us any more. I certainly didn't expect to see you here again so soon."

"Oh, you've been making a mountain out of a molehill," said Bao-yu, returning her smile. "Why ever shouldn't I come? Even if I died, my *ghost* would be round here a hundred times a day. How is my cousin? Quite better now?"

"Physically she's better," said Nightingale, "but she's still in very poor spirits."

"Ah yes—I know she's upset."

This exchange took place as they were crossing the forecourt. He now entered the room. Dai-yu was sitting on the bed crying. She had not been crying to start with, but the bittersweet pang she experienced when she heard his arrival had started the tears rolling. Bao-yu went up to the bed and smiled down at her.

"How are you, coz? Quite better now?"

As Dai-yu seemed to be too busy wiping her eyes to make a reply, he sat down close beside her on the edge of the bed:

"I know you're not *really* angry with me," he said. "It's just that if the others no-ticed I wasn't coming here, they would think we had been quarrelling; and if we waited for them to interfere, we should be allowing other people to come between us. It would be better to hit me and shout at me now and get it over with, if you still bear any hard feelings, than to go on ignoring me. Coz dear! Coz dear!—"

He must have repeated those same two words in the same tone of passionate entreaty upwards of twenty times. Dai-yu had been meaning to ignore him, but what he had just been saying about other people "coming between" them seemed to prove that he must in *some* way feel closer to her than the rest, and she was unable to maintain her silence.

"You don't have to treat me like a child," she blurted out tearfully. "From now on I shall make no further claims on you. You can behave exactly as if I had gone away."

"Gone away?" said Bao-yu laughingly. "Where would you go to?"

"Back home."

"I'd follow you."

"As if I were dead then."

"If you died," he said, "I should become a monk."

Dai-yu's face darkened immediately:

"What an utterly idiotic thing to say! Suppose your own sisters were to die? Just how many times can one person become a monk? I think I had better see what the others think about that remark."

Bao-yu had realized at once that she would be offended; but the words were already out of his mouth before he could stop them. He turned very red and hung his head in silence. It was a good thing that no one else was in the room at that moment to see him. Dai-yu glared at him for some seconds—evidently too enraged to speak, for she made a sound somewhere between a snort and a sigh, but said nothing—then, seeing him almost purple in the face with suppressed emotion, she clenched her teeth, pointed her finger at him, and, with an indignant "Hmn!", stabbed the air quite savagely a few inches away from his forehead:

"You—!"

But whatever it was she had been going to call him never got said. She merely gave a sigh and began wiping her eyes again with her handkerchief.

Bao-yu had been in a highly emotional state when he came to see Dai-yu and it had further upset him to have inadvertently offended her so soon after his arrival. This angry gesture and the unsuccessful struggle, ending in sighs and tears, to say what she wanted to say now affected him so deeply that he, too, began to weep. In need of a handkerchief but finding that he had come out without one, he wiped his eyes on his sleeve.

Although Dai-yu was crying, the spectacle of Bao-yu using the sleeve of his brand-new lilac-coloured summer gown as a handkerchief had not escaped her, and while continuing to wipe her own eyes with one hand, she leaned over and reached with the other for the square of silk that was draped over the head-rest at the end of the bed. She lifted it off and threw it at him—all without uttering a word—then, once more burying her face in her own handkerchief, resumed her weeping. Bao-yu picked up the handkerchief she had thrown him and hurriedly wiped his eyes with it. When he had dried them, he drew up close to her again and took one of her hands in his own, smiling at her gently.

"I don't know why you go on crying," he said. "I feel as if all my insides were shattered. Come! Let's go and see Grandmother together."

Dai-yu flung off his hand.

"Take your hands off me! We're not children any more. You really can't go on mauling me about like this all the time. Don't you understand *anything*—?"

"Bravo!"

The shouted interruption startled them both. They spun round to look just as Xi-feng, full of smiles, came bustling into the room.

"Grandmother has been grumbling away something *awful*," she said. "She insisted that I should come over and see if you were both all right. 'Oh' I said, 'there's no need to go and look, Grannie; they'll have made it up by now without any interference from *us*.'" So she told me I was lazy. Well, here I am—and of course it's *exactly* as I said it would be. *I* don't know. I don't understand you two. What is it you find to argue about? For every three days that you're friends you must spend at least two days quarrelling. You really are a couple of babies. And the older you get, the worse you get. Look at you *now*—holding hands crying! And a couple of days ago you were glaring at each other like fighting-cocks. Come on! Come with me to see Grandmother. Let's put the old lady's mind at rest."

from CHAPTER 34

Bao-yu kept thinking about Dai-yu and wanted to send someone over to see her, but he was afraid that Aroma would disapprove, so, as a means of getting her out of the way, he sent her over to Bao-chai's place to borrow a book. As soon as she had gone, he summoned Skybright.

"I want you to go to Miss Lin's for me," he said, "Just see what she's doing, and if she asks about me, tell her I'm all right."

"I can't go rushing in there bald-headed without a reason," said Skybright. "You'd better give me *some* kind of a message, just to give me an excuse for going there."

"I have none to give," said Bao-yu.

"Well, give me something to take, then," said Skybright, "or think of something I can ask her for. Otherwise it will look so silly."

Bao-yu thought for a bit and then, reaching out and picking up two of his old handkerchiefs, he tossed them towards her with a smile.

"All right. Tell her I said you were to give her these."

"That's an odd sort of present!" said Skybright. "What's she going to do with a pair of your old handkerchiefs? Most likely she'll think you're making fun of her and get upset again."

"No she won't," said Bao-yu. "She'll understand."

Skybright deemed it pointless to argue, so she picked up the handkerchiefs and went off to the Naiad's House. Little Delicate, who was hanging some towels out to dry on the verandah railings, saw her enter the courtyard and attempted to wave her away.

"She's gone to bed."

Skybright ignored her and went on inside. The lamps had not been lit and the room was in almost total darkness. The voice of Dai-yu, lying awake in bed, spoke to her out of the shadows.

"Who is it?"

"Skybright."

"What do you want?"

"Master Bao has sent me with some handkerchiefs, Miss."

Dai-yu seemed to hesitate. She found the gift puzzling and was wondering what it could mean.

"I suppose they must be very good ones," she said. "Probably someone gave them to him. Tell him to keep them and give them to somebody else. I have no use for them just now myself."

Skybright laughed.

"They're not new ones, Miss. They're two of his old, everyday ones."

This was even more puzzling. Dai-yu thought very hard for some moments. Then suddenly, in a flash, she understood.

"Put them down. You may go now."

Skybright did as she was bid and withdrew. All the way back to Green Delights she tried to make sense of what had happened, but it continued to mystify her.

Meanwhile the message that eluded Skybright had thrown Dai-yu into a turmoil of conflicting emotions.

"I feel so happy," she thought, "that in the midst of his own affliction he has been able to grasp the cause of all *my* trouble.

"And yet at the same time I am sad," she thought; "because how do I know that my trouble will end in the way I want it to?

"Actually, I feel rather amused," she thought. "Fancy his sending a pair of old handkerchiefs like that! Suppose I hadn't understood what he was getting at?

"But I feel alarmed that he should be sending presents to me in secret.

"Oh, and I feel so ashamed when I think how I am forever crying and quarrelling," she thought, "and all the time he has understood! . . ."

And her thoughts carried her this way and that, until the ferment of excitement within her cried out to be expressed. Careless of what the maids might think, she called for a lamp, sat herself down at her desk, ground some ink, softened her brush, and proceeded to compose the following quatrains, using the handkerchiefs themselves to write on:

1

Seeing my idle tears, you ask me why
These foolish drops fall from my teeming eye:
Then know, your gift, being by the merfolk made,
In merman's currency must be repaid.

2

Jewelled drops by day in secret sorrow shed
Or, in the night-time, in my wakeful bed,
Lest sleeve or pillow they should spot or stain,
Shall on these gifts shower down their salty rain.

3

Yet silk preserves but ill the Naiad's tears:
Each salty trace of them fast disappears.
Only the speckled bamboo stems that grow
Outside the window still her tear-marks show.

She had only half-filled the second handkerchief and was preparing to write another quatrain, when she became aware that her whole body was burning hot all over and her cheeks were afire. Going over to the dressing-table, she removed the brocade cover from the mirror and peered into it.

"Hmn! 'Brighter than the peach-flower's hue,'" she murmured complacently to the flushed face that stared out at her from the glass, and, little imagining that what she had been witnessing was the first symptom of a serious illness, went back to bed, her mind full of handkerchiefs.[8]

---

8. The next 60 chapters recount daily activities of Bao-yu and his relatives, while intrigue, scandal, and financial troubles—and now an unusual natural occurrence—disturb the Jia household.

from CHAPTER 94

When Dai-yu heard that Grandmother Jia was coming, she got up to change and sent Snowgoose on ahead, telling her to report back the moment Her Old Ladyship arrived. She soon came running back.

"Her Old Ladyship and Her Ladyship and a lot of the other ladies have all arrived! Hurry, Miss!"

Dai-yu took a brief look in the mirror, passed a comb quickly through her hair and set off with Nightingale in the direction of Green Delights. She arrived to find Grandmother Jia installed on Bao-yu's day-couch, and after greeting her and Lady Xing and Lady Wang went on to say hello to Li Wan, Tan-chun, Xi-chun and Xing Xiu-yan. She noticed that several people were absent: Xi-feng was ill in bed, Shi Xi-ang-yun had gone home to see her uncle who was in the capital on transfer, while Bao-qin had stayed at home with Bao-chai, and the two Li sisters, Wen and Qi, had been taken to live elsewhere by their mother, whom recent events had convinced that Prospect Garden was a rather unsuitable environment for her daughters.

They were all chatting away, each propounding a different interpretation of the strange phenomenon of the winter-flowering crab-trees.

"They usually flower in the third month, I know," Grandmother Jia was saying. "And we are in the eleventh month now. But then the movable terms in the calendar are rather late this year, so we could say this is more like the tenth month, which is after all sometimes called 'Little Spring.' With the exceptionally warm weather we have been having, a little blossom is only to be expected."

"You are quite right, Mother," agreed Lady Wang. "We need someone of your experience to show us that this is really nothing out of the ordinary."

Lady Xing however was not so easily convinced.

"I heard that these trees had already been struck by the blight for almost a year . . . How do you explain the fact that half-dead trees should start flowering now, at such an odd time of the year?"

Li Wan spoke next.

"I think you are both right," she said with a smile. "My own humble suggestion is that they have flowered specially to tell us of some happy event that is about to take place in Bao-yu's life."

Tan-chun, although she remained silent, was secretly thinking to herself:

"This must be an ill-omen. Everything that is in harmony with nature prospers, and things out of season, out of time, fade and die. Plants and trees obey a natural cycle. If a tree flowers out of season, it must be an ill-omen."

She kept all this to herself, however. It was Dai-yu who spoke next. She had been struck by Li Wan's mention of a happy event, and said with some excitement:

"There was once a family of farmers who had a thornbush. There were three sons in the family, and one day these three sons decided to leave home and go their separate ways. No sooner had they gone than the thornbush began to fade away and die. But some time later the brothers began to yearn for each other's company, returned home and were reunited. And at once the thornbush began to flourish again. So you see plants follow closely the fortunes of the people to whom they are attached. Now Cousin Bao is devoting himself seriously to his studies, which pleases Uncle Zheng, which pleases the crab-trees, which is why they are flowering!"

This went down very well with Grandmother Jia and Lady Wang.

"What a well-chosen story! Such an interesting idea!"

Jia She and Jia Zheng now arrived to view the flowers, accompanied by Jia Huan and Jia Lan. Jia She spoke first.

"Cut them down. That's what I say. There's evil work afoot here."

"On the contrary," said Jia Zheng. "Leave them alone. Evil manifestations thrive on such superstition. Ignore them and they disappear."

"What's all this?" interrupted Grandmother Jia testily. "We're all gathered here to witness a happy event. Why do you have to start talking about manifestations and what-have-you? When there's good luck then enjoy it while you can. I'll take care of any bad luck. I forbid you to utter another word of such gloomy nonsense."

This silenced Jia Zheng, and he and Jia She effected an awkward departure. Grandmother Jia was unperturbed and determined to enjoy herself.

"Send someone to the kitchen," she said. "We want wine and some nice things to eat. We'll have a little party. I should like you, Bao-yu, Huan and Lan, each to write a poem to celebrate the occasion. Miss Lin has been unwell so she can be excused. If she feels up to it she can help you boys polish yours."

Turning to Li Wan she continued:

"You and the others come up and have some wine with me."

"Yes Grannie," said Li Wan, then turning to Tan-chun she laughed and said:

"This is all your fault, Tan!"

"What do you mean?" protested Tan-chun. "We've been let off the poetry-writing—my fault for what?"

"Aren't you the founder of the Crab-flower Club?" replied Li Wan. "I know *that* crab was an Autumn Crab—but can't you see? Now the *real* crab-blossom wants to join in too . . ."

Everyone laughed at the idea.

Food and wine were now served, and they all drank and did their best to humour the old lady with light-hearted conversation. Bao-yu came up to pour himself some wine, and standing there thought up a quatrain which he then wrote out and recited for his grandmother.

> I asked the crab-tree why at blossom-time it failed,
> Yet now profusely bloomed so long before the spring?
> The tree replied: "Midwinter marks the birth of light.
> Glad tidings to the Mistress of this House I bring."

It was Huan's turn next. He wrote his out and began to recite:

> Plants should put out buds in spring:
> Our crab tree's timing's topsy-turvy.
> Of all the wonders of the world
> Ours is the only winter-flowering tree.

Then Jia Lan made a careful copy of his poem, in immaculate *kai-shu* calligraphy, and presented it to his great-grandmother, who asked Li Wan to read it out for her.

> Your mist-congealed beauty blighted in the spring,
> Your frosted petals blush now in the snow.
> Hail Tree of Wisdom! Whose Rebirth
> Adds lustre to our Family Hearth.

When she reached the end, Grandmother Jia commented:

"I don't know much about poetry, but I should judge Lan's good, while I should say that Huan's was poor. Come on now, everybody come and have something to eat."

* * *

Earlier that day, Bao-yu had been lounging around indoors, casually dressed in a fur-lined gown with slits at the sides. When he caught sight of the flowering crab-trees through the window, he went out to look at them. The more he gazed at the blossom the more lovely and poignant it seemed, the more strangely it seemed to reflect the mysterious vagaries of destiny, the joy and pathos of life. It was the embodiment of his own thoughts and feelings. Then, when he heard that Grandmother Jia was coming over, he hurried in to change into more formal attire, choosing a pale fox-lined robe with cut-away archer's sleeves and a darker jacket, also fox-lined, to go with it. He emerged again properly dressed to receive his grandmother, and in his hurry quite forgot to put on his Magic Jade.

When Grandmother Jia left he went in again to change back into his comfortable clothes, and it was then that Aroma detected the absence of the jade and asked him where it was.

"I was in such a rush when I came in to change," he replied. "I took it off and left it on the kang-table. Then I forgot to put it on again."

Aroma looked but it was not on the table. She searched everywhere but could see no sign of it. She began to feel frightened, and broke into a cold sweat.

"Please don't worry," Bao-yu begged her. "It must be somewhere in the room. It's bound to turn up. Ask the others—they might know."

It occurred to Aroma that Musk or one of the other maids might have hidden it somewhere as a practical joke and she bore down on them with an expression of playful accusation:

"You mean lot! Can't you think of a better way of amusing yourselves? Come on, where have you hidden it? Don't take this too far! If it really did get lost we'd be in real trouble, all of us!"

But Musk replied with a straight face:

"What on earth do you mean? We'd know better than to play a trick like that. We're not that silly. You're the one who should stop and think a minute. Try to remember where you put it, instead of laying the blame on us!"

Aroma could tell that Musk was in earnest and cried out in alarm:

"Heaven save us then! Oh little ancestor, where *can* you have put it? You must try to remember!"

"I do," replied Bao-yu, "I remember quite clearly putting it on the kang-table. Have another look for it."

The maids were too scared to tell anyone else, and joined together in a furtive search. This went on for most of the day but there was still no sign of the jade. They emptied every box, and rummaged in every trunk, until there simply was nowhere left to look and they began to wonder if perhaps one of the visitors might have picked it up earlier in the day.

"How would anyone dare do such a thing?" said Aroma. "Everyone knows how important it is, and that Master Bao's very life hinges on it. Ask about it, but be very discreet. If you find out that one of the maids has taken it and is playing a trick on us, kowtow to her and beg for it back. If it's a junior maid who's stolen it, don't tell a soul, just do whatever is necessary to get it back. Give her whatever you like in exchange.

This is very serious. It would be terrible if we lost the jade, worse even than losing Master Bao himself!"[9]

from CHAPTER 96

The time had come round for the triennial review of civil servants stationed in the capital. Jia Zheng's Board gave him a high commendation, and in the second month the Board of Civil Office presented him for an audience with the Emperor. His Majesty, in view of Jia Zheng's record as a "diligent, frugal, conscientious and prudent servant of the Throne," appointed him immediately to the post of Grain Intendant for the province of Kiangsi. The same day, Jia Zheng offered his humble acceptance and gratitude for the honour, and suggested a day for his departure. Friends and relatives were all eager to celebrate, but he was not in festive mood. He was loath to leave the capital at a time when things were so unsettled at home, although at the same time he knew that he could not delay his departure.

He was pondering this dilemma, when a message came to summon him to Grandmother Jia's presence. He made his way promptly to her apartment, where he found Lady Wang also present, despite her illness. He paid his respects to Grandmother Jia, who told him to be seated and then began:

"In a few days, you will be leaving us to take up your post. There is something I should like to discuss with you, if you are willing."

The old lady's eyes were wet with tears. Jia Zheng rose swiftly to his feet, and said:

"Whatever you have to say, Mother, please speak: your word is my command."

"I shall be eighty-one this year," said Grandmother Jia, sobbing as she spoke. "You are going away to a post in the provinces, and with your elder brother still at home, you will not be able to apply for early retirement to come and look after me. When you are gone, of the ones closest to my heart I shall only have Bao-yu left to me. And he, poor darling, is in such a wretched state, I don't know what we can do for him! The other day I sent out Lai Sheng's wife to have the boy's fortune told. The man's reading was uncanny. What he said was: 'This person must marry a lady with a destiny of gold, to help him and support him. He must be given a marriage as soon as possible to turn his luck. If not, he may not live.' Now I know you don't believe in such things, which is why I sent for you, to talk it over with you. You and his mother must discuss it among yourselves. Are we to save him, or are we to do nothing and watch him fade away?"

Jia Zheng smiled anxiously.

"Could I, who as a child received such tender love and care from you, Mother, not have fatherly feelings myself? It is just that I have been exasperated by his repeated failure to make progress in his studies, and have perhaps been too ambitious for him. You are perfectly right in wanting to see him married. How could I possibly wish to oppose you? I am concerned for the boy, and his recent illness has caused me great anxiety. But as you have kept him from me, I have not ventured to say anything. I should like to see him now for myself, and form my own impression of his condition."

Lady Wang saw that his eyes were moist, and knew that he was genuinely concerned. She told Aroma to fetch Bao-yu and help him into the room. He walked in, and when Aroma told him to pay his respects to his father, did exactly as she said. Jia

---

9. Having lost his jade, Bao-yu has lost his wits as well and become seriously ill.

Zheng saw how emaciated his face had grown, how lifeless his eyes were. His son was like some pathetic simpleton. He told them to take him back to his room.

"I shall soon be sixty myself," he mused. "With this provincial posting, it is difficult to tell how many years it will be before I return. If anything were to happen to Bao-yu, I should be left without an heir in my old age. I have a grandson, but that is not the same. And then Bao-yu is the old lady's favourite. If anything untoward occurred, I should be still more deeply at fault."

He glanced at Lady Wang. Her face was wet with tears. He thought of the sorrow it would cause her too, and stood up again to speak.

"If, from your wealth of experience, you have thought of a way to help him, Mother, then how could I possibly raise any objection? We should do whatever you think is best. But has Mrs. Xue been informed?"

"My sister has already expressed her agreement," replied Lady Wang. "We have only been biding our time because Pan's court-case has still not been settled."

"Yes, that is certainly the first obstacle," commented Jia Zheng. "How can a girl be given in marriage while her elder brother is in jail? And besides there is Her Grace's death. Although that does not strictly entail any such prohibition, Bao-yu should at least abide by the set term of mourning for a deceased elder sister, which would mean a period of nine months during which marriage would be highly irregular. And then, my own date of departure has already been reported to the throne, and I cannot postpone it now. That only leaves us a few days. There is not enough time."

Grandmother Jia pondered her son's words. "What he says is true," she thought to herself. "If we wait for all of these conditions to be fulfilled, his father will have left, and who knows to what state the boy's health may deteriorate. And then it may be too late. We shall have to put aside the rules for once. There is no other way."

Having reached this conclusion in her own mind, she spoke to Jia Zheng again.

"If you will agree to this for him, I shall take care of any problems that may arise. There is nothing that cannot be ironed out, of that I am confident. His mother and I shall go over and put the matter personally to Mrs. Xue. As for Pan, I shall ask young Ke to go to him and explain that we are doing this to save Bao-yu's life. When he knows the reason, I am sure he will agree. As for marrying during a period of mourning, strictly speaking one shouldn't, I know. And besides, it is not right for him to marry while he is so ill. But it's a question of turning his luck. Both families are willing, and as the children have the bond of gold and jade to justify their union, we can dispense with the usual reading of horoscopes. We just need to choose an auspicious day to exchange presents in proper style, and then set a date for the wedding itself, possibly afterwards. No music during the wedding itself, but otherwise we can follow court practice: twelve pairs of long-handled lanterns and an eight-man palanquin for the bride. We shall have the ceremony in our southern form, and keep our old customs of throwing dried fruit onto the bridal bed and so forth. That will be enough to make it quite a proper wedding. Bao-chai is a sensible girl. We need not worry on her account. And Aroma is a very reliable person. We can count on her to have a calming influence on Bao-yu. She gets on well with Bao-chai too.

"One other thing: Mrs. Xue once told us that a monk said Bao-chai should only marry someone with a jade to match her golden locket. Perhaps when she comes to live as Bao-yu's wife, her locket will draw the jade back. Once they are married, things will look up and the whole family will benefit. So, we must prepare a courtyard and decorate it nicely—I should like you to choose it. We shan't be inviting any friends or relations to the wedding, and we can have the party later, when

Bao-yu is better and the mourning period is over. This way, everything will be done in time, and you will be able to see the young people married and set off with an easy mind."

Jia Zheng had grave doubts about the proposal. But as it was Grandmother Jia's, he knew he could not go against it. He smiled dutifully, and hastened to reply:

"You have thought it all out very well, Mother, and have taken everything into account. We must tell the servants not to go talking about this to everyone they meet. It would hardly redound to our credit if people knew. And personally I doubt if Mrs. Xue will agree to the idea. But if she does, then I suppose we should do as you suggest."

"You need not worry about Mrs. Xue," said the old lady. "I can explain things to her. Off you go then."

Jia Zheng took his leave. He felt extremely uneasy about the whole idea. Official business soon engulfed him, however—acceptance of his new papers of appointment, recommendations of staff from friends and relatives, an endless round of social gatherings of one sort or another—and he delegated all responsibility for the marriage plans to Grandmother Jia, who in turn left the arrangements to Lady Wang and Xi-feng. Jia Zheng's only contribution was to designate a twenty-frame building in a courtyard behind the Hall of Exalted Felicity, to the side of Lady Wang's private apartment, as Bao-yu's new home. Grandmother Jia's mind was now quite made up, and when she sent someone to communicate this to Jia Zheng he just replied: "Very well." But of this, more later.

Bao-yu, after his brief interview with his father, was escorted back by Aroma to his kang in the inner room. Intimidated by the Master's presence in the next room, none of the maids dared speak to him and he soon fell into a deep sleep. As a consequence he did not hear a word of the conversation between his father and Grandmother Jia. Aroma and the others did, however, and stood in complete silence taking it all in. Aroma had heard rumours of this marriage-plan, rumours whose likelihood, it is true, had been strengthened by Bao-chai's repeated absence from family gatherings. Now that she knew it for a fact, all became crystal clear. She was glad.

"They've shown some sense at last!" she thought to herself. "Those two will make by far the better match. And I shall be better off too. With Miss Chai here I'll be able to unload a lot of my responsibilities. The only trouble is, Master Bao still thinks of no one but Miss Lin . . . It's a good thing he didn't hear just now. If he knew what they are planning, I dread to think what trouble we'd have."

This cast a shadow over her previous optimism. "What's to be done?" she continued to brood to herself. "Her Old Ladyship and Her Ladyship obviously don't know about the secret feelings Master Bao and Miss Lin have for each other, and in their enthusiasm they could tell him their plan, to try and cure him. But if he still feels as he did—when he first saw Miss Lin, for instance, and hurled his jade to the ground and wanted to smash it to pieces; or last summer in the Garden, when he mistook me for her and poured his heart out to me; or when Nightingale teased him by saying that Miss Lin was going away, and had him in such floods of tears—and if they go and tell him now that he's betrothed to Miss Chai and will have to give Miss Lin up for ever, so far from turning his luck they'll probably kill him! (Unless of course he's going through one of his deaf-and-dumb spells, in which case he probably won't even notice.) I'd better tell them what I know, or three people may suffer!"

Aroma's mind was made up. As soon as Jia Zheng had taken his leave of the ladies, she left Ripple to look after Bao-yu, and went into the outer room. She walked over to Lady Wang and whispered that she would like a word with her privately in the room to the rear of Grandmother Jia's apartment. Grandmother Jia imagined it to be some message from Bao-yu and did not pay much attention, but continued to engross herself in the wedding arrangements. Lady Wang rose to leave, and Aroma followed her into the rear chamber, where she at once fell on her knees and began crying. Lady Wang had no idea what it was all about, and taking her by the hand, said:

"Come now! What is all this? Has someone done you wrong? If so, stand up, and tell me."

"It is something I shouldn't really say, but in the circumstances I feel I must."

"Well, tell me then. And take your time."

"You and Her Old Ladyship have made an excellent decision, in choosing Miss Bao-chai as Bao-yu's future bride . . ." began Aroma. "But, I wonder, ma'am, if you have noticed which of the two young ladies Bao-yu is more closely attached to, Miss Chai, or Miss Lin?"

"As they have lived together since they were children," replied Lady Wang, "I suppose he would be a little closer to Miss Lin."

"More than a little!" protested Aroma, and went on to give Lady Wang a detailed history of how things had always stood between Bao-yu and Dai-yu, and of the various incidents that had occurred between them.

"These are all things that you would have seen for yourself, ma'am," she added, "with the exception of his outburst during the summer, which I have not mentioned to a soul until now."

Lady Wang drew Aroma toward her.

"Yes, most of what you have told me I have been able to deduce for myself. What you have said simply bears out my own observations. But you must all have heard the Master's words. Tell me, how did Bao-yu react?"

"As things are at present, ma'am, Bao-yu smiles if someone talks to him, but otherwise he just sleeps. He heard nothing."

"In that case, what are we to do?"

"It is not my place to say," replied Aroma. "Your Ladyship should inform Her Old Ladyship of what I have said, and think of a suitable way of solving the problem."

"Then you had better go," said Lady Wang, "and leave it to me. Now would not be a good moment to bring it up; there are too many people in the room. I shall wait for an opportunity to tell Her Old Ladyship, and we will discuss what to do."

Lady Wang returned to Grandmother Jia's apartment. The old lady was talking to Xi-feng, and when she saw Lady Wang come in, asked:

"What did Aroma want? What was all that mysterious whispering about?"

Lady Wang answered her directly, and told the whole story of Bao-yu's love for Dai-yu, as Aroma had told it her. When she had finished, Grandmother Jia was silent for a long while. Neither Lady Wang nor Xi-feng dared say a word. At last, Grandmother Jia sighed and said:

"Everything else seemed somehow soluble. It does not matter so much about Dai-yu. But if Bao-yu really feels this way about her, it seems we have run into an insoluble problem."

Xi-feng looked very thoughtful for a minute, then said:

"Not insoluble. I think I can see a solution. But I am not sure if you would agree to it or not, Aunt."

"Whatever your idea is," said Lady Wang, "speak up and let Mother know. Then we can all discuss it together."

"There is only one solution that I can think of," said Xi-feng. "It involves two things: a white lie, and a piece of discreet substitution."

"Substitution? What do you mean?" asked Grandmother Jia.

"First of all," replied Xi-feng, "whether Bao-yu knows anything yet or not, we let it be known that Sir Zheng proposes to betroth him to Miss Lin. We must watch for his reaction. If he is quite unaffected, then there is no need to bother with my plan. But if he does seem at all pleased at the news, it will make things rather more complicated."

"Supposing he is pleased?" asked Lady Wang. "What then?"

Xi-feng went over and whispered at some length in Lady Wang's ear. Lady Wang nodded, smiled and said:

"Well, well . . . An ingenious idea, I must say!"

"Come on, you two!" exclaimed Grandmother Jia. "Let me in on the secret: what are you whispering about?"

Xi-feng was afraid that Grandmother Jia might not grasp her idea at once, and might inadvertently give the game away. She leant across and whispered in the old lady's ear. Grandmother Jia did seem rather puzzled at first. Xi-feng smiled, and added a few more words of explanation. Grandmother Jia finally said with a smile:

"Why not? But isn't it rather hard on Bao-chai? And what about Miss Lin? What if she gets to hear of it?"

"We shall only tell Bao-yu," replied Xi-feng. "No one else will be allowed to mention it. That way no one need know."

* * *

A day or two after these events, Dai-yu, having eaten her breakfast, decided to take Nightingale with her to visit Grandmother Jia. She wanted to pay her respects, and also thought the visit might provide some sort of distraction for herself. She had hardly left the Naiad's House, when she remembered that she had left her handkerchief at home, and sent Nightingale back to fetch it, saying that she would walk ahead slowly and wait for her to catch up. She had just reached the corner behind the rockery at Drenched Blossoms Bridge—the very spot where she had once buried the flowers with Bao-yu—when all of a sudden she heard the sound of sobbing. She stopped at once and listened. She could not tell whose voice it was, nor could she distinguish what it was that the voice was complaining of, so tearfully and at such length. It really was most puzzling. She moved forward again cautiously and as she turned the corner, saw before her the source of the sobbing, a maid with large eyes and thick-set eyebrows.

Before setting eyes on this girl, Dai-yu had guessed that one of the many maids in the Jia household must have had an unhappy love-affair, and had come here to cry her heart out in secret. But now she laughed at the very idea. "How could such an ungainly creature as this know the meaning of love?" she thought to herself. "This must be one of the odd-job girls, who has probably been scolded by one of the senior maids." She looked more closely, but still could not place the girl. Seeing Dai-yu, the maid ceased her weeping, wiped her cheeks, and rose to her feet.

"Come now, what are you so upset about?" inquired Dai-yu.

"Oh Miss Lin!" replied the maid, amid fresh tears. "Tell me if you think it fair. *They* were talking about it, and how was I to know better? Just because I say one thing wrong, is that a reason for sister to start hitting me?"

Dai-yu did not know what she was talking about. She smiled, and asked again:

"Who is your sister?"

"Pearl," answered the maid.

From this, Dai-yu concluded that she must work in Grandmother Jia's apartment.

"And what is your name?"

"Simple."

Dai-yu laughed. Then:

"Why did she hit you? What did you say that was so wrong?"

"That's what I'd like to know! It was only to do with Master Bao marrying Miss Chai!"

The words struck Dai-yu's ears like a clap of thunder. Her heart started thumping fiercely. She tried to calm herself for a moment, and told the maid to come with her. The maid followed her to the secluded corner of the garden, where the Flower Burial Mound was situated. Here Dai-yu asked her:

"Why should she hit you for mentioning Master Bao's marriage to Miss Chai?"

"Her Old Ladyship, Her Ladyship and Mrs Lian," replied Simple, "have decided that as the Master is leaving soon, they are going to arrange with Mrs. Xue to marry Master Bao and Miss Chai as quickly as possible. They want the wedding to turn his luck, and then . . ."

Her voice tailed off. She stared at Dai-yu, laughed and continued:

"Then, as soon as those two are married, they are going to find a husband for you, Miss Lin."

Dai-yu was speechless with horror. The maid went on regardless:

"But how was I to know that they'd decided to keep it quiet, for fear of embarrassing Miss Chai? All I did was say to Aroma, that serves in Master Bao's room: 'Won't it be a fine to-do here soon, when Miss Chai comes over, or Mrs. Bao . . . what *will* we have to call her?' That's all I said. What was there in that to hurt sister Pearl? Can *you* see, Miss Lin? She came across and hit me straight in the face and said I was talking rubbish and disobeying orders, and would be dismissed from service! How was I to know their Ladyships didn't want us to mention it? Nobody told me, and she just hit me!"

She started sobbing again. Dai-yu's heart felt as though oil, soy-sauce, sugar and vinegar had all been poured into it at once. She could not tell which flavour predominated, the sweet, the sour, the bitter or the salty. After a few moments' silence, she said in a trembling voice:

"Don't talk such rubbish. Any more of that, and you'll be beaten again. Off you go!"

She herself turned back in the direction of the Naiad's House. Her body felt as though it weighed a hundred tons, her feet were as wobbly as if she were walking on cotton-floss. She could only manage one step at a time. After an age, she still had not reached the bank by Drenched Blossoms Bridge. She was going so slowly, with her feet about to collapse beneath her, and in her giddiness and confusion had wandered off course and increased the distance by about a hundred yards. She reached Drenched Blossoms Bridge only to start drifting back again along the bank in the direction she had just come from, quite unaware of what she was doing.

Nightingale had by now returned with the handkerchief, but could not find Dai-yu anywhere. She finally saw her, pale as snow, tottering along, her eyes staring straight in front of her, meandering in circles. Nightingale also caught sight of a maid disappearing in the distance beyond Dai-yu, but could not make out who it was. She was most bewildered, and quickened her step.

"Why are you turning back again, Miss?" she asked softly. "Where are you heading for?"

Dai-yu only heard the blurred outline of this question. She replied:

"I want to ask Bao-yu something."

Nightingale could not fathom what was going on, and could only try to guide her on her way to Grandmother Jia's apartment. When they came to the entrance, Dai-yu seemed to feel clearer in mind. She turned, saw Nightingale supporting her, stopped for a moment, and asked:

"What are you doing here?"

"I went to fetch your handkerchief," replied Nightingale, smiling anxiously. "I saw you over by the bridge and hurried across. I asked you where you were going, but you took no notice."

"Oh!" said Dai-yu with a smile. "I thought you had come to see Bao-yu. What else did we come here for?"

Nightingale could see that her mind was utterly confused. She guessed that it was something that the maid had said in the garden, and only nodded with a faint smile in re-ply to Dai-yu's question. But to herself she was trying to imagine what sort of an en-counter this was going to be, between the young master who had already lost his wits, and her young mistress who was now herself a little touched. Despite her apprehensions, she dared not prevent the meeting, and helped Dai-yu into the room. The funny thing was that Dai-yu now seemed to have recovered her strength. She did not wait for Nightingale but raised the portière herself, and walked into the room. It was very quiet inside. Grand-mother Jia had retired for her afternoon nap. Some of the maids had sneaked off to play, some were having forty winks themselves and others had gone to wait on Grandmother Jia in her bedroom. It was Aroma who came out to see who was there, when she heard the swish of the portière. Seeing that it was Dai-yu, she greeted her politely:

"Please come in and sit down, Miss."

"Is Master Bao at home?" asked Dai-yu with a smile.

Aroma did not know that anything was amiss, and was about to answer, when she saw Nightingale make an urgent movement with her lips from behind Dai-yu's back, pointing to her mistress and making a warning gesture with her hand. Aroma had no idea what she meant and dared not ask. Undeterred, Dai-yu walked on into Bao-yu's room. He was sitting up in bed, and when she came in made no move to get up or wel-come her, but remained where he was, staring at her and giving a series of silly laughs. Dai-yu sat down uninvited, and she too began to smile and stare back at Bao-yu. There were no greetings exchanged, no courtesies, in fact no words of any kind. They just sat there staring into each other's faces and smiling like a pair of half-wits. Aroma stood watching, completely at a loss.

Suddenly Dai-yu said:

"Bao-yu, why are you sick?"

Bao-yu laughed.

"I'm sick because of Miss Lin."

Aroma and Nightingale grew pale with fright. They tried to change the subject, but their efforts only met with silence and more senseless smiles. By now it was clear to Aroma that Dai-yu's mind was as disturbed as Bao-yu's.

"Miss Lin has only just recovered from her illness," she whispered to Nightin-gale. "I'll ask Ripple to help you take her back. She should go home and lie down." Turning to Ripple, she said: "Go with Nightingale and accompany Miss Lin home. And no stupid chattering on the way, mind."

Ripple smiled, and without a word came over to help Nightingale. The two of them began to help Dai-yu to her feet. Dai-yu stood up at once, unassisted, still star-ing fixedly at Bao-yu, smiling and nodding her head.

"Come on, Miss!" urged Nightingale. "It's time to go home and rest."

"Of course!" exclaimed Dai-yu. "It's time!"

She turned to go. Still smiling and refusing any assistance from the maids, she strode out at twice her normal speed. Ripple and Nightingale hurried after her. On leaving Grandmother Jia's apartment, Dai-yu kept on walking, in quite the wrong direction. Nightingale hurried up to her and took her by the hand.

"This is the way, Miss."

Still smiling, Dai-yu allowed herself to be led, and followed Nightingale towards the Naiad's House. When they were nearly there, Nightingale exclaimed:

"Lord Buddha be praised! Home at last!"

She had no sooner uttered these words when she saw Dai-yu stumble forwards onto the ground, and give a loud cry. A stream of blood came gushing from her mouth.

from CHAPTER 97

Next day, Xi-feng came over after breakfast. Wishing to sound out Bao-yu according to her plan, she advanced into his room and said:

"Congratulations, Cousin Bao! Uncle Zheng has already chosen a lucky day for your wedding! Isn't that good news?"

Bao-yu stared at her with a blank smile, and nodded his head faintly.

"He is marrying you," went on Xi-feng, with a studied smile, "to your cousin Lin. Are you happy?"

Bao-yu burst out laughing. Xi-feng watched him carefully, but could not make out whether he had understood her, or was simply raving. She went on:

"Uncle Zheng says, you are to marry Miss Lin, *if* you get better. But not if you carry on behaving like a half-wit."

Bao-yu's expression suddenly changed to one of utter seriousness, as he said:

"I'm not a half-wit. You're the half-wit."

He stood up.

"I am going to see Cousin Lin, to set her mind at rest."

Xi-feng quickly put out a hand to stop him.

"She knows already. And, as your bride-to-be, she would be much too embarrassed to receive you now."

"What about when we're married? Will she see me then?"

Xi-feng found this both comic and somewhat disturbing.

"Aroma was right," she thought to herself. "Mention Dai-yu, and while he still talks like an idiot, he at least seems to understand what's going on. I can see we shall be in real trouble, if he sees through our scheme and finds out that his bride is not to be Dai-yu after all."

In reply to his question, she said, suppressing a smile:

"If you behave, she will see you. But not if you continue to act like an imbecile."

To which Bao-yu replied:

"I have given my heart to Cousin Lin. If she marries me, she will bring it with her and put it back in its proper place."

Now this was madman's talk if ever, thought Xi-feng. She left him, and walked back into the outer room, glancing with a smile in Grandmother Jia's direction. The old lady too found Bao-yu's words both funny and distressing.

"I heard you both myself," she said to Xi-feng. "For the present, we must ignore it. Tell Aroma to do her best to calm him down. Come, let us go."

* * *

Dai-yu meanwhile, for all the medicine she took, continued to grow iller with every day that passed. Nightingale did her utmost to raise her spirits. Our story finds her standing once more by Dai-yu's bedside, earnestly beseeching her:

"Miss, now that things have come to this pass, I simply must speak my mind. We know what it is that's eating your heart out. But can't you see that your fears are groundless? Why, look at the state Bao-yu is in! How can he possibly get married, when he's so ill? You must ignore these silly rumours, stop fretting and let yourself get better."

Dai-yu gave a wraithlike smile, but said nothing. She started coughing again and brought up a lot more blood. Nightingale and Snowgoose came closer and watched her feebly struggling for breath. They knew that any further attempt to rally her would be to no avail, and could do nothing but stand there watching and weeping. Each day Nightingale went over three or four times to tell Grandmother Jia, but Faithful, judging the old lady's attitude towards Dai-yu to have hardened of late, intercepted her reports and hardly mentioned Dai-yu to her mistress. Grandmother Jia was preoccupied with the wedding arrangements, and in the absence of any particular news of Dai-yu, did not show a great deal of interest in the girl's fate, considering it sufficient that she should be receiving medical attention.

Previously, when she had been ill, Dai-yu had always received frequent visits from everyone in the household, from Grandmother Jia down to the humblest maidservant. But now not a single person came to see her. The only face she saw looking down at her was that of Nightingale. She began to feel her end drawing near, and struggled to say a few words to her:

"Dear Nightingale! Dear sister! Closest friend! Though you were Grandmother's maid before you came to serve me, over the years you have become as a sister to me . . ."

She had to stop for breath. Nightingale felt a pang of pity, was reduced to tears and could say nothing. After a long silence, Dai-yu began to speak again, searching for breath between words:

"Dear sister! I am so uncomfortable lying down like this. Please help me up and sit next to me."

"I don't think you should sit up, Miss, in your condition. You might get cold in the draught."

Dai-yu closed her eyes in silence. A little later she asked to sit up again. Nightingale and Snowgoose felt they could no longer deny her request. They propped her up on both sides with soft pillows, while Nightingale sat by her on the bed to give further support. Dai-yu was not equal to the effort. The bed where she sat on it seemed to dig into her, and she struggled with all her remaining strength to lift herself up and ease the pain. She told Snowgoose to come closer.

"My poems . . ."

Her voice failed, and she fought for breath again. Snowgoose guessed that she meant the manuscripts she had been revising a few days previously, went to fetch them and laid them on Dai-yu's lap. Dai-yu nodded, then raised her eyes and gazed in the direction of a chest that stood on a stand close by. Snowgoose did not know how to interpret this and stood there at a loss. Dai-yu stared at her now with feverish impatience. She began to cough again and brought up another mouthful of blood. Snowgoose went to fetch some water, and Dai-yu rinsed her mouth and spat into the spittoon. Nightingale wiped her lips with a handkerchief. Dai-yu took the handkerchief from her and pointed to the chest. She tried to speak, but was again seized with an attack of breathlessness and closed her eyes.

"Lie down, Miss," said Nightingale. Dai-yu shook her head. Nightingale thought she must want one of her hand-kerchiefs, and told Snowgoose to open the chest and bring her a plain white silk one. Dai-yu looked at it, and dropped it on the bed. Making a supreme effort, she gasped out:

"The ones with the writing on . . ."

Nightingale finally realized that she meant the handkerchiefs Bao-yu had sent her, the ones she had inscribed with her own poems. She told Snowgoose to fetch them, and herself handed them to Dai-yu, with these words of advice:

"You must lie down and rest, Miss. Don't start wearing yourself out. You can look at these another time, when you are feeling better."

Dai-yu took the handkerchiefs in one hand and without even looking at them, brought round her other hand (which cost her a great effort) and tried with all her might to tear them in two. But she was so weak that all she could achieve was a pathetic trembling motion. Nightingale knew that Bao-yu was the object of all this bitterness but dared not mention his name, saying instead:

"Miss, there is no sense in working yourself up again."

Dai-yu nodded faintly, and slipped the handkerchiefs into her sleeve.

"Light the lamp," she ordered.

Snowgoose promptly obeyed. Dai-yu looked into the lamp, then closed her eyes and sat in silence. Another fit of breathlessness. Then:

"Make up the fire in the brazier."

Thinking she wanted it for the extra warmth, Nightingale protested:

"You should lie down, Miss, and have another cover on. And the fumes from the brazier might be bad for you."

Dai-yu shook her head, and Snowgoose reluctantly made up the brazier, placing it on its stand on the floor. Dai-yu made a motion with her hand, indicating that she wanted it moved up onto the kang. Snowgoose lifted it and placed it there, temporarily using the floor-stand, while she went out to fetch the special stand they used on the kang. Dai-yu, far from resting back in the warmth, now inclined her body slightly forward—Nightingale had to support her with both hands as she did so. Dai-yu took the handkerchiefs in one hand. Staring into the flames and nodding thoughtfully to herself, she dropped them into the brazier. Nightingale was horrified, but much as she would have liked to snatch them from the flames, she did not dare move her hands and leave Dai-yu unsupported. Snowgoose was out of the room, fetching the brazier-stand, and by now the handkerchiefs were all ablaze.

"Miss!" cried Nightingale. "What are you doing?"

As if she had not heard, Dai-yu reached over for her manuscripts, glanced at them and let them fall again onto the kang. Nightingale, anxious lest she burn these too, leaned up against Dai-yu and freeing one hand, reached out with it to take hold of them. But before she could do so, Dai-yu had picked them up again and dropped them in the flames. The brazier was out of Nightingale's reach, and there was nothing she could do but look on helplessly.

Just at that moment Snowgoose came in with the stand. She saw Dai-yu drop something into the fire, and without knowing what it was, rushed forward to try and save it. The manuscripts had caught at once and were already ablaze. Heedless of the danger to her hands, Snowgoose reached into the flames and pulled out what she could, throwing the paper on the floor and stamping frantically on it. But the fire had done its work, and only a few charred fragments remained.

from CHAPTER 98

His brief access of clarity enabled Bao-yu to understand the gravity of his illness. When the others had gone and he was left alone with Aroma, he called her over to his side and taking her by the hand said tearfully:

"Please tell me how Cousin Chai came to be here? I remember Father marrying me to Cousin Lin.[1] Why has *she* been made to go? Why has Cousin Chai taken her place? She has no right to be here! I'd like to tell her so, but I don't want to offend her. How has Cousin Lin taken it? Is she very upset?'

Aroma did not dare tell him the truth, but merely said:

"Miss Lin is ill."

"I must go and see her," insisted Bao-yu. He wanted to get up, but days of going without food and drink had so sapped his strength that he could no longer move, but could only weep bitterly and say:

"I know I am going to die! There's something on my mind, something very important, that I want you to tell Grannie for me. Cousin Lin and I are both ill. We are both dying. It will be too late to help us when we are dead; but if they prepare a room for us now and if we are taken there before it is too late, we can at least be cared for together while we are still alive, and be laid out together when we die. Do this for me, for friendship's sake!"

Aroma found this plea at once disturbing, comical and moving. Bao-chai, who happened to be passing with Oriole, heard every word and took him to task straight away.

"Instead of resting and trying to get well, you make yourself iller with all this gloomy talk! Grandmother has scarcely stopped worrying about you for a moment, and here you are causing more trouble for her. She is over eighty now and may not live to acquire a title because of your achievements; but at least, by leading a good life, you can repay her a little for all that she has suffered for your sake. And I hardly need mention the agonies Mother has endured in bringing you up. You are the only son she has left. If you were to die, think how she would suffer! As for me, I am wretched enough as it is; you don't need to make a widow of me. Three good reasons why even if you want to die, the powers above will not let you and you will not be able to. After four or five days of proper rest and care, your illness will pass, your strength will be restored and you will be yourself again."

For a while Bao-yu could think of no reply to this homily. Finally he gave a silly laugh and said:

"After not speaking to me for so long, here you are lecturing me. You are wasting your breath."

Encouraged by this response to go a step further, Bao-chai said:

"Let me tell you the plain truth, then. Some days ago, while you were unconscious, Cousin Lin passed away."

With a sudden movement, Bao-yu sat up and cried out in horror:

"It can't be true!"

"It is. Would I lie about such a thing? Grandmother and Mother knew how fond you were of each other, and wouldn't tell you because they were afraid that if they did, you would die too."

---

1. The marriage has taken place during the previous chapter, thanks to Xi-feng's idea of disguising Bao-chai as Dai-yu.

Bao-yu began howling unrestrainedly and slumped back in his bed. Suddenly all was pitch black before his eyes. He could not tell where he was and was beginning to feel very lost, when he thought he saw a man walking towards him and asked in a bewildered tone of voice:

"Would you be so kind as to tell me where I am?"

"This," replied the stranger, "is the road to the Springs of the Nether World. Your time is not yet come. What brings you here?"

"I have just learned of the death of a friend and have come to find her. But I seem to have lost my way."

"Who is this friend of yours?"

"Lin Dai-yu of Soochow."

The man gave a chilling smile:

"In life Lin Dai-yu was no ordinary mortal, and in death she has become no ordinary shade. An ordinary mortal has two souls which coalesce at birth to vitalize the physical frame, and disperse at death to rejoin the cosmic flux. If you consider the impossibility of tracing even such ordinary human entities in the Nether World, you will realize what a futile task it is to look for Lin Dai-yu. You had better return at once."

After standing for a moment lost in thought, Bao-yu asked again:

"But if as you say, death is a dispersion, how can there be such a place as the Nether World?"

"There is," replied the man with a superior smile, "and yet there is not, such a place. It is a teaching, devised to warn mankind in its blind attachment to the idea of life and death. The Supreme Wrath is aroused by human folly in all forms—whether it be excessive ambition, premature death self-sought, or futile self-destruction through debauchery and a life of overweening violence. Hell is the place where souls such as these are imprisoned and made to suffer countless torments in expiation of their sins. This search of yours for Lin Dai-yu is a case of futile self-delusion. Dai-yu has already returned to the Land of Illusion and if you really want to find her you must cultivate your mind and strengthen your spiritual nature. Then one day you will see her again. But if you throw your life away, you will be guilty of premature death self-sought and will be confined to Hell. And then, although you may be allowed to see your parents, you will certainly never see Dai-yu again."

When he had finished speaking, the man took a stone from within his sleeve and threw it at Bao-yu's chest. The words he had spoken and the impact of the stone as it landed on his chest combined to give Bao-yu such a fright that he would have returned home at once, if he had only know which way to turn. In his confusion he suddenly heard a voice, and turning, saw the figures of Grandmother Jia, Lady Wang, Bao-chai, Aroma and his other maids standing in a circle around him, weeping and calling his name. He was lying on his own bed. The red lamp was on the table. The moon was shining brilliantly through the window. He was back among the elegant comforts of his own home. A moment's reflection told him that what he had just experienced had been a dream. He was in a cold sweat. Though his mind felt strangely lucid, thinking only intensified his feeling of helpless desolation, and he uttered several profound sighs.

Bao-chai had known of Dai-yu's death for several days. While Grandmother Jia had forbidden the maids to tell him for fear of further complicating his illness, she felt she knew better. Aware that it was Dai-yu who lay at the root of his illness and that the loss of his jade was only a secondary factor, she took the opportunity of breaking the news of her death to him in this abrupt manner, hoping that by severing his attachment once and for all she would enable his sanity and health to be restored. Grandmother Jia, Lady Wang and company were not aware of her intentions and at first reproached her for her lack of caution. But when they saw Bao-yu regain consciousness, they were all greatly relieved and went at once to the library to ask doctor Bi to come in and examine his patient again. The doctor carefully took his pulses.

"How odd!" he exclaimed. "His pulses are deep and still, his spirit calm, the oppression quite dispersed. Tomorrow he must take a regulative draught, which I shall prescribe, and he should make a prompt and complete recovery."

The doctor left and the ladies all returned to their apartments in much improved spirits.

Although at first Aroma greatly resented the way in which Bao-chai had broken the news, she did not dare say so. Oriole, on the other hand, reproved her mistress in private for having been, as she put it, too hasty.

"What do you know about such things?" retorted Bao-chai. "Leave this to me. I take full responsibility."

Bao-chai ignored the opinions and criticisms of those around her and continued to keep a close watch on Bao-yu's progress, probing him judiciously, like an acupuncturist with a needle.

A day or two later, he began to feel a slight improvement in himself, though his mental equilibrium was still easily disturbed by the least thought of Dai-yu. Aroma was constantly at his side, with such words of consolation as:

"The Master chose Miss Chai as your bride for her more dependable nature. He thought Miss Lin too difficult and temperamental for you, and besides there was always the fear that she would not live long. Then later Her Old Ladyship thought you were not in a fit state to know what was best for you and would only be upset and make yourself iller if you knew the truth, so she made Snowgoose come over, to try and make things easier for you."

This did nothing to lessen his grief, and he often wept inconsolably. But each time he thought of putting an end to his life, he remembered the words of the stranger in his dream; and then he thought of the distress his death would cause his mother and grandmother and knew that he could not tear himself away from them. He also reflected that Dai-yu was dead, and that Bao-chai was a fine lady in her own right; there must after all have been some truth in the bond of gold and jade. This thought eased his mind a little. Bao-chai could see that things were improving, and herself felt calmer as a result. Every day she scrupulously performed her duties towards Grandmother Jia and Lady Wang, and when these were completed, did all she could to cure Bao-yu of his grief. He was still not able to sit up for long periods, but often when he saw her sitting by his bedside he would succumb to his old weakness for the fairer sex. She tried to rally him in an earnest manner, saying:

"The important thing is to take care of your health. Now that we are married, we have a whole lifetime ahead of us."

He was reluctant to listen to her advice. But since his grandmother, his mother, Aunt Xue and all the others took it in turns to watch over him during the day, and since Bao-chai slept on her own in an adjoining room, and he was waited on at night by one or two maids of Grandmother Jia's, he found himself left with little choice but to rest and get well again. And as time went by and Bao-chai proved herself a gentle and devoted companion, he found that a small part of his love for Dai-yu began to transfer itself to her. But this belongs to a later part of our story.

⤬

RESONANCE

Shen Fu: from *Six Records of a Floating Life*[1]

THE JOYS OF THE WEDDING CHAMBER

I was born in the winter of the 27th year of the reign of the Emperor Chien Lung [1763], on the second and twentieth day of the eleventh month. Heaven blessed me, and life then could not have been more full. It was a time of great peace and plenty, and my family was an official one that lived next to the Pavilion of the Waves in Soochow. As the poet Su Tung-po wrote, "All things are like spring dreams, passing with no trace." If I did not make a record of that time, I should be ungrateful for the blessings of heaven.

The very first of the three hundred chapters of the *Book of Odes* concerns husbands and wives, so I too will write of other matters in their turn. Unfortunately I never completed my studies, so my writing is not very skilful. But here my purpose is merely to record true feelings and actual events. Criticism of my writing will be like the shining of a bright light into a dirty mirror.

When I was young I was engaged to Chin Sha-yu, but she died when she was eight years old. Eventually I married Chen Yün, the daughter of my uncle, Mr. Chen Hsin-yü. Her literary name was Shu-chen.[2]

Even while small, she was very clever. While she was learning to talk she was taught the poem *The Mandolin Song*[3] and could repeat it almost immediately.

Yün's father died when she was four years old, leaving her mother, whose family name was Chin, and her younger brother, Ko-chang. At first they had virtually nothing, but as Yün grew older she became very adept at needlework, and the labour of her ten fingers came to provide for all three of them. Thanks to her work, they were always able to afford to pay the tuition for her brother's teachers.

One day Yün found a copy of *The Mandolin Song* in her brother's book-box and, remembering her lessons as a child, was able to pick out the characters one by one. That is how she began learning to read. In her spare moments she gradually learned how to write poetry, one line of which was, "We grow thin in the shadows of autumn, but chrysanthemums grow fat with the dew."

When I was thirteen, my mother took me along on a visit to her relatives. That was the first time I met my cousin Yün, and we two children got on well together. I had a chance to see her poems that day, and though I sighed at her brilliance I privately feared she was too sensitive to be completely happy in life. Still, I could not forget her, and I remember saying to my mother, "If you are going to choose a wife for me, I will marry no other than Yün."

Mother also loved her gentleness, so she was quick to arrange our engagement, sealing the match by giving Yün a gold ring from her own finger. This was in the 39th year of the reign of the Emperor Chien Lung [1775], on the 16th day of the seventh month.

---

1. Translated by Leonard Pratt and Chiang Su-hui. Little is known of Shen Fu, other than that he was born in 1763, pursued a largely unsuccessful career as a minor bureaucrat, and was at work on these *Six Records* (of which two have been lost) in 1809. This memoir owes much to the interest spurred by *The Story of the Stone* in romantic love and its detailed narrative of daily life, though of a differ-

ent social class.
2. Educated Chinese would take a "literary name," often expressing a desired attribute (Shu-chen likely means "precious virtue").
3. A poem by Bo Juyi (772–864), about the meeting between an exiled official and a courtesan who has been abandoned by her husband.

That winter mother took me to their home once again, for the marriage of Yün's cousin. Yün and I were born in the same year, but because she was ten months older than I, I had always called her "elder sister," while she called me "younger brother." We continued to call one another by these names even after we were engaged.

At her cousin's wedding the room was full of beautifully dressed people. Yün alone wore a plain dress; only her shoes were new. I noticed they were skilfully embroidered, and when she told me she had done them herself I began to appreciate that her cleverness lay not only in her writing.

Yün had delicate shoulders and a stately neck, and her figure was slim. Her brows arched over beautiful, lively eyes. Her only blemish was two slightly protruding front teeth, the sign of a lack of good fortune. But her manner was altogether charming, and she captivated all who saw her.

I asked to see more of her poems that day, and found some had only one line, others three or four, and most were unfinished. I asked her why.

"I have done them without a teacher," she replied, laughing. "I hope you, my best friend, can be my teacher now and help me finish them." Then as a joke I wrote on her book, "The Embroidered Bag of Beautiful Verses." I did not then realize that the origin of her early death already lay in that book.

That night after the wedding I escorted my relatives out of the city, and it was midnight by the time I returned. I was terribly hungry and asked for something to eat. A servant brought me some dried plums, but they were too sweet for me. So Yün secretly took me to her room, where she had hidden some warm rice porridge and some small dishes of food. I delightedly picked up my chopsticks, but suddenly heard Yün's cousin Yu-heng call, "Yün, come quickly!"

Yün hurriedly shut the door and called back, "I'm very tired. I was just going to sleep." But Yu-heng pushed open the door and came in anyway.

He saw me just about to begin eating the rice porridge, and chuckled, looking out of the corner of his eye at Yün. "When I asked you for some rice porridge just now, you said there wasn't any more! But I see you were just hiding it in here and saving it for your 'husband'!"

Yün was terribly embarrassed, and ran out. The whole household broke into laughter. I was also embarrassed and angry, roused my servant, and left early.

Every time I returned after that, Yün would hide. I knew she was afraid that everyone would laugh at her.

On the night of the 22nd day of the first month in the 44th year of the reign of the Emperor Chien Lung [1780], I saw by the light of our wedding candles that Yün's figure was as slim as before. When her veil was lifted we smiled at each other. After we had shared the ceremonial cup of wine and sat down together for the wedding banquet, I secretly took her small hand under the table. It was warm and it was soft, and my heart beat uncontrollably.

I asked her to begin eating, but it turned out to be a day on which she did not eat meat, a Buddhist practice which she had followed for several years. I thought to myself that she had begun this practice at the very time I had begun to break out with acne, and I asked her, "Since my skin is now clear and healthy, couldn't you give up this custom?" Her eyes smiled amusement, and her head nodded agreement.

That same night of the 22nd there was a wedding-eve party for my elder sister. She was to be married on the 24th, but the 23rd was a day of national mourning[4] on

4. Probably the anniversary of a previous emperor's death.

which all entertaining was forbidden and the holding of the wedding-eve party would have been impossible. Yün attended the dinner, but I spent the time in our bedroom drinking with my sister's maid of honour. We played a drinking game which I lost frequently, and I wound up getting very drunk and falling asleep. By the time I woke up the next morning, Yün was already putting on her make-up.

During the day a constant stream of relatives and friends came to congratulate Yün and me on our marriage. In the evening there were some musical performances in honour of the wedding, after the lamps had been lit.

At midnight I escorted my sister to her new husband's home, and it was almost three in the morning when I returned. The candles had burned low and the house was silent. I stole quietly into our room to find my wife's servant dozing beside the bed and Yün herself with her make-up off but not yet asleep. A candle burned brightly beside her; she was bent intently over a book, but I could not tell what it was that she was reading with such concentration. I went up to her, rubbed her shoulder, and said, "You've been so busy these past few days, why are you reading so late?"

Yün turned and stood up. "I was just thinking of going to sleep, but I opened the bookcase and found this book, *The Romance of the Western Chamber*.[5] Once I had started reading it, I forgot how tired I was. I had often heard it spoken of, but this was the first time I had had a chance to read it. The author really is as talented as people say, but I do think his tale is too explicitly told."

I laughed and said, "Only a talented writer could be so explicit."

Yün's servant then urged us to go to sleep, but we told her she should go to sleep first, and to shut the door to our room. We sat up making jokes, like two close friends meeting after a long separation. I playfully felt her breast and found her heart was beating as fast as mine. I pulled her to me and whispered in her ear, "Why is your heart beating so fast?" She answered with a bewitching smile that made me feel a love so endless it shook my soul. I held her close as I parted the curtains and led her into bed. We never noticed what time the sun rose in the morning.

As a new bride, Yün was very quiet. She never got angry, and when anyone spoke to her she always replied with a smile. She was respectful to her elders and amiable to everyone else. Everything she did was orderly, and was done properly. Each morning when she saw the first rays of the sun touch the top of the window, she would dress quickly and hurry out of bed, as if someone were calling her. I once laughed at her about it; "This is not like that time with the rice porridge! Why are you still afraid of someone laughing at you?"

"True," she answered, "my hiding the rice porridge for you that time has become a joke. But I'm not worried about people laughing at me now. I am afraid your parents will think I'm lazy."

While I would have liked it if she could have slept more, I had to agree that she was right. So every morning I got up early with her, and from that time on we were inseparable, like a man and his shadow. Words could not describe our love.

We were so happy that our first month together passed in the twinkling of an eye. At that time my father, the Honourable Chiafu, was working as a private secretary in the prefectural government office at Kuichi. He sent for me, having enrolled me as a

---

5. A classic drama, also known as *The Story of the Western Wing*, by Wang Shifu, a ribald version of the Tang tale by Yuan Zhen (776–831), "The Story of Yingying," in which a young woman submits to the desires of a student.

student of Mr. Chao Sheng-chai at Wulin. Mr. Chao taught me patiently and well; the fact that I can write at all today is due to his efforts.

I had, however, originally planned to continue my studies with my father after my marriage, so I was disappointed when I received his letter. I feared Yün would weep when she heard of it, but she showed no emotion, encouraged me to go, and helped me pack my bag. The night before I left she was slightly subdued, but that was all. When it was time for me to go, though, she whispered to me, "There will be no one there to look after you. Please take good care of yourself."

My boat cast off just as the peach and the plum flowers were in magnificent bloom. I felt like a bird that had lost its flock. My world was shaken. After I arrived at the offices where my father worked, he immediately began preparations to go east across the river.

Our separation of three months seemed as if it were ten years long. Yün wrote to me frequently, but her letters asked about me twice as often as they told me anything about herself. Most of what she wrote was merely to encourage me in my studies, and the rest was just polite chatter. I really was a little angry with her. Every time the wind would rustle the bamboo trees in the yard, or the moon would shine through the leaves of the banana tree outside my window, I would look out and miss her so terribly that dreams of her took possession of my soul.

My teacher understood how I felt, and wrote to tell my father about it. He then assigned me ten compositions and sent me home for a while to write them. I felt like a prisoner who has been pardoned.

Once I was on the boat each quarter of an hour seemed to pass as slowly as a year. After I got home and paid my respects to my mother, I went into our room and Yün rose to greet me. She held my hands without saying a word. Our souls became smoke and mist. I thought I heard something, but it was as if my body had ceased to exist.

It was then the sixth month, and steamy hot in our room. Fortunately we lived just west of the Pavilion of the Waves' Lotus Lovers' Hall, where it was cooler. By a bridge and overlooking a stream there was a small hall called My Desire, because, as desired, one could "wash my hat strings in it when it is clean, and wash my feet in it when it is dirty."[6] Almost under the eaves of the hall there was an old tree that cast a shadow across the windows so deep that it turned one's face green. Strollers were always walking along the opposite bank of the stream. This was where my father, the Honourable Chia-fu, used to entertain guests privately, and I obtained my mother's permission to take Yün there to escape the summer's heat. Because it was so hot, Yün had given up her embroidery. She spent all day with me as I studied, and we talked of ancient times, analysed the moon, and discussed the flowers. Yün could not take much drink, and would accept at the most three cups of wine when I forced her to. I taught her a literary game, in which the loser has to drink a cup. We were certain two people had never been happier than we were.

One day Yün asked me, "Of all the ancient literary masters, who do you think is the best?"

"*The Annals of the Warring States* and *Chuang Tsu* are known for their liveliness," I replied. "Kuang Heng and Liu Hsiang are known for their elegance. Shih Chien and Pan Ku are known for their breadth. Chang Li is known for his extensive

6. From an ancient fisherman's song that advises one to adjust to one's circumstances.

knowledge, and Liu Chou for his vigorous style. Lu Ling is known for his originality, and Su Hsün and his two sons for their essays. There are also the policy debates of Chia and Tung, the poetic styles of Yü and Hsü, and the Imperial memorials of Lu Chih.[7] I could never give a complete list of all the talented writers there have been. Besides, which one you like depends upon which one you feel in sympathy with."

"It takes great knowledge and a heroic spirit to appreciate ancient literature," said Yün. "I fear a woman's learning is not enough to master it. The only way we have of understanding it is through poetry, and I understand but a bit of that."

"During the Tang Dynasty all candidates had to pass an examination in poetry before they could become officials," I remarked. "Clearly the best were Li Pai and Tu Fu.[8] Which of them do you like best?"

Yün said her opinion was that "Tu Fu's poetry is very pure and carefully tempered, while Li Pai's is ethereal and open. Personally, I would rather have Li Pai's liveliness than Tu Fu's strictness."

"But Tu Fu was the more successful, and most scholars prefer him. Why do you alone like Li Pai?"

"Tu Fu is alone," Yün replied, "in the detail of his verse and the vividness of his expression. But Li Pai's poetry flows like a flower tossed into a stream. It's enchanting. I would not say Li Pai is a better poet than Tu Fu, but only that he appeals to me more."

I smiled and said, "I never thought you were such an admirer of Li Pai's."

Yün smiled back. "Apart from him, there is only my first teacher, Mr. Pai Lo-tien.[9] I have always had a feeling in my heart for him that has never changed."

"Why do you say that?" I asked.

"Didn't he write *The Mandolin Song?*"

I laughed. "Isn't that strange! You are an admirer of Li Pai's, and Pai Lo-tien was your first tutor. And as it happens, the literary name of your husband is San-pai. What is this affinity you have for the character *pai?*"[1]

Yün laughed and said, "Since I do have an affinity for the character *pai,* I'm afraid that in the future my writing will be full of *pai* characters." (Our Kiangsu accent pronounces the character *pieh* as *pai.*)[2] We both shook with laughter.

"Since you know poetry," I said, "you must know the good and bad points of the form called *fu.*"[3]

"I know it's descended from the ancient Chu Tzu poetry,"[4] Yün replied, "but I have only studied it a little and it's hard to understand. Of the *fu* poets of the Han and Chin Dynasties, who had the best meter and the most refined language, I think Hsiang-ju was the best."

I jokingly said, "So perhaps Wen-chün did not fall in love with Hsiang-ju[5] because of the way he played the lute after all, but because of his poetry?" The conversation ended with us both laughing loudly.

---

7. Shen Fu mentions both classic writers and those who later defended the classic tradition against the more florid styles.

8. Li Bo (pronounced *Bai* in modern Chinese, 701–762) and Du Fu (712–770), the two great poets of the Tang dynasty.

9. The Tang poet Bo (or Bai) Juyi, who was her "first teacher" because his poem was the first work she ever read.

1. Meaning "white" in all three names.

2. By saying she feared she would write many *pai* characters, Yün is making a dialect pun to say she fears she would write many *pieh* characters—that is, characters written incorrectly.

3. A long mixed prose-verse form known as rhymeprose or rhapsody.

4. The "Songs of the South," from the 4th and 3rd centuries B.C.E.

5. Famous lovers of the Han dynasty. The recently widowed Zhuo Wenjun fell in love with the *fu* poet Sima Xiangru after hearing him play the lute.

I am by nature candid and unconstrained, but Yün was scrupulous and meticulously polite. When I would occasionally put a cape over her shoulders or help her adjust her sleeves, she would invariably say, "I beg your pardon." If I gave her a handkerchief or a fan, she would always stand to take it. At first I did not like her acting like this, and once I said to her, "Do you think that by being so polite you can make me do as you like? For it is said that 'Deceit hides behind too much courtesy.'"

Yün blushed. "Why should respect and good manners be called deceit?"

"True respect comes from the heart, not from empty words," I said.

"There is no one closer to us than our parents," Yün said, arguing with me now. "But how could we merely respect them in our hearts while being rude in our treatment of them?"

"But I was only joking," I protested.

"Most arguments people have begin with a joke," Yün said. "Don't ever argue with me for the fun of it again—it makes me so angry I could die!"

I pulled her close to me, patted her back, and comforted her. Her anger passed and she began to smile. From then on, the polite phrases "How dare I?" and "I beg your pardon" became mere expressions to us. We lived together with the greatest mutual respect for three and twenty years, and as the years passed we grew ever closer.

Whenever we would meet one another in a darkened room or a narrow hallway of the house, we would hold hands and ask, "Where are you going?" We felt furtive, as if we were afraid others would see us. In fact, at first we even avoided being seen walking or sitting together, though after a while we thought nothing of it. If Yün were sitting and talking with someone and saw me come in, she would stand up and move over to me and I would sit down beside her. Neither of us thought about this and it seemed quite natural; and though at first we felt embarrassed about it, we gradually grew accustomed to doing it. The strangest thing to me then was how old couples seemed to treat one another like enemies. I did not understand why. Yet people said, "Otherwise, how could they grow old together?" Could this be true? I wondered.

On the evening of the 7th day of the seventh month that year, Yün lit candles and set out fruit on the altar by the Pavilion of My Desire, and we worshipped Tien Sun[6] together. I had had two matching seals engraved with the inscription, "May we remain husband and wife in all our lives to come"; on mine the characters were raised and on hers they were incised. We used them to sign the letters we wrote one another. That night the moonlight was very lovely, and as it was reflected in the stream it turned the ripples of the water as white as silk. We sat together near the water wearing light robes and fanned ourselves gently as we looked up at the clouds flying across the sky and changing into ten thousand shapes.

Yün said, "The world is so vast, but still everyone looks up at the same moon. I wonder if there is another couple in the world as much in love as we are."

"Naturally there are people everywhere who like to enjoy the night air and gaze at the moon," I said, "and there are more than a few women who enjoy discussing the sunset. But when a man and wife look at it together, I don't think it is the sunset they will wind up talking about." The candles soon burned out, and the moon set. We took the fruit inside and went to bed.

6. The Weaving Girl (the constellation Vega), who was separated from her lover the Herdboy because of excessive affection; the one night of the year they are allowed to meet (the seventh day of the seventh month) is a day for lovers and hopeful brides.

The 15th day of the seventh month, when the moon is full, is the day called the Ghost Festival. Yün had prepared some small dishes, and we had planned to invite the moon to drink with us. But when night came, clouds suddenly darkened the sky.

Yün grew melancholy and said, "If I am to grow old together with you, the moon must come out."

I also felt depressed. On the opposite bank I could see will-o'-the-wisps winking on and off like ten thousand fireflies, as their light threaded through the high grass and willow trees that grew on the small island in the stream. To get ourselves into a better mood Yün and I began composing a poem out loud, with me offering the first couplet, her the second, and so on. After the first two couplets we gradually became less and less restrained and more and more excited, until we were saying anything that came into our heads. Yün was soon laughing so hard that she cried, and had to lean up against me, unable to speak a word. The heavy scent of jasmine in her hair assailed my nostrils, so to stop her laughing I patted her on the back and changed the subject, saying, "I thought women of ancient times put jasmine flowers in their hair because they resembled pearls. I never realized that the jasmine is so attractive when mixed with the scent of women's make-up, much more attractive than the lime."

Yün stopped laughing. "Lime is the gentleman of perfumes," she said, "and you notice its scent unconsciously. But the jasmine is a commoner that has to rely on a woman's make-up for its effect. It's suggestive, like a wicked smile."

"So why are you avoiding the gentleman and taking up with the commoner?"

"I'm only making fun of gentlemen who love commoners," she replied.

Just as we were speaking, the water clock showed midnight. The wind gradually began to sweep the clouds away, and the full moon finally came out. We were delighted, and drank some wine leaning against the windowsill. But before we had finished three cups we heard a loud noise from under the bridge, as if someone had fallen into the water. We leaned out of the window and looked around carefully. The surface of the stream was as bright as a mirror, but we saw not a thing. We only heard the sound of a duck running quickly along the river bank. I knew that the ghosts of people who had drowned often appeared by the river near the Pavilion of the Waves, but I was worried that Yün would be afraid and so I did not dare tell her.

"Yi!" she said, none the less frightened for my silence. "Where did that sound come from?"

We could not keep ourselves from trembling. I closed the window and we took the wine into the bedroom. The flame in the lamp was as small as a bean, and the curtains around the bed cast shadows that writhed like snakes. We were still frightened. I turned up the lamp and we got into bed, but Yün was already suffering hot and cold attacks from the shock. I caught the same fever, and we were ill for twenty days. It is true what people say, that happiness carried to an extreme turns into sadness. The events of that day were another omen that we were not to grow old together. * * *

My younger brother Chi-tang's wife is the granddaughter of Wang Hsü-chou. As the time for their marriage approached, she discovered she did not have enough pearl flowers.[7] Yün took out her own pearls that she had been given when we were married, and gave them to my mother for her to give to my brother's fiancée. The servants thought it was a pity that she should give up her own jewellery.

---

7. Hair ornaments in the shape of flowers, made from small pearls.

"Women are entirely *yin* in nature," Yün told them, "and pearls are the essence of *yin*. If you wear them in your hair, they completely overcome the spirit of *yang*. So why should I value them?"[8]

On the other hand, she prized shabby old books and tattered paintings. She would take the partial remnants of old books, separate them all into sections by topic, and then have them rebound. These she called her "Fragments of Literature." When she found some calligraphy or a painting that had been ruined, she felt she had to search for a piece of old paper on which to remount it. If there were portions missing, she would ask me to restore them. These she named the "Collection of Discarded Delights." Yün would work on these projects the whole day without becoming tired, whenever she could take time off from her sewing and cooking. If, in an old trunk or a shabby book, she came across a piece of paper with something on it, she acted as if she had found something very special. Every time our neighbour, old lady Fung, got hold of some scraps of old books, she would sell them to Yün.

Yün's habits and tastes were the same as mine. She understood what my eyes said, and the language of my brows. She did everything according to my expression, and everything she did was as I wished it.

Once I said to her, "It's a pity that you are a woman and have to remain hidden away at home. If only you could become a man we could visit famous mountains and search out magnificent ruins. We could travel the whole world together. Wouldn't that be wonderful?"

"What is so difficult about that?" Yün replied. "After my hair begins to turn white, although we could not go so far as to visit the Five Sacred Mountains, we could still visit places nearer by. We could probably go together to Hufu and Lingyen, and south to the West Lake and north to Ping Mountain."[9]

"By the time your hair begins to turn white, I'm afraid you will find it hard to walk," I told her.

"Then if we can't do it in this life, I hope we will do it in the next."

"In our next life I hope you will be born a man," I said. "I will be a woman, and we can be together again."

"That would be lovely," said Yün, "especially if we could still remember this life."

I laughed. "We still haven't finished talking about that business with the rice porridge when we were young. If in the next life we can still remember this one, we will have so much to talk about on our wedding night that we will never get to sleep!"

"People say that marriages are arranged by the 'Old Man of the Moon,'" said Yün. "He has already pulled us together in this life, and in the next we will have to depend on him too. Why don't we have a picture of him painted so we can worship him?"

At that time the famous portraitist Chi Liu-ti, whose literary name was Chun, was living in Tiaohsi, and we asked him to paint the picture for us. He portrayed the old man carrying his red silk cord[1] in one hand, while with the other he grasped his walking stick with the *Book of Marriages* tied to the top of it. Though his hair was white, his face was that of a child, and he was striding through mist and fog. This was the best painting that Mr. Chi ever did. My friend Shih Cho-tang wrote a complimentary inscription at the top of the painting, and I hung it in our room. On the 1st and the

---

8. *Yin*, the female principle, and *yang*, the male, should be kept in balance, neither one overshadowing the other.
9. The Five Sacred Mountains are scattered throughout

the country. The other scenic spots Yün mentions would have been an easy trip from Soochow.
1. With which he joins the couple together.

15th days of each month, Yün and I would light incense and worship in front of it. Later, because of the many things that happened to our family, the painting was somehow lost and I have no idea in whose home it hangs now. "Our next life is not known, while this life closes." Our passion was so great. Will the Old Man understand and help us once again?

* * *

When Chien Shih-chu of Wuchiang County fell ill and died, my father wrote and ordered me to represent him at the funeral. Hearing this, Yün took me aside. "If you are going to Wuchiang, you have to cross Lake Tai. I would love to go with you and see something more of the world."

"I had just been thinking how lonely it would be going by myself," I said, "and that if you could come with me it would be lovely. But there is no excuse for you to go."

"I could say I wanted to go home for a visit. You could go to the boat first, and I would meet you there."

"Then on the way back we could stop the boat under Ten Thousand-Years Bridge," I said. "We could relax in the moonlight, the way we used to at the Pavilion of the Waves."

It was then the 18th day of the sixth month. In the cool of the morning I took a servant and went ahead to the Hsü River Dock, where we boarded a boat and waited. Yün arrived in a sedan chair shortly afterwards. The boat cast off and left the Tiger's Roar Bridge, and after a while we began to see other sails in the wind, and birds on the sandy shore. The sky and the water became the same colour.

"Is this the Lake Tai that everyone speaks of?" asked Yün. "Now that I see how grand the world is, I have not lived in vain! There are women who have lived their entire lives without seeing a vista like this." It seemed we had only chatted for a little while before we arrived at Wuchiang, where the wind was rustling the willows along the bank.

I went ashore, only to return after the funeral to find the boat empty. I anxiously questioned the boatman, who pointed along the bank and said, "Don't you see them in the shadow of the willows by the bridge watching the cormorants catch fish?"

To my surprise, Yün had gone ashore with the boatman's daughter. When I came up behind her she was still covered with perspiration, leaning against the other girl and lost in watching the birds.

I patted her shoulder and said, "Your clothes are soaked through!"

Yün turned her head to look at me. "I was afraid someone from the Chien family would come to the boat with you," she said, "so I came here for a while to keep them from seeing me if they did. Why did you come back so quickly?"

I laughed. "So I could recapture you."

We walked to the boat hand in hand, and sailed back to Ten Thousand-Years Bridge. The sun had not yet set by the time we reached the bridge, so we let down the windows of the boat to admit a breeze, then changed into silk clothes and, fanning ourselves, ate some melon to cool off. Before long the setting sun turned the bridge red, and the twilight mist enveloped the willows in darkness. The silver moon was just rising and the river quickly filled up with the lights of night fishermen. We sent our servant to the stern to drink with the boatman.

The boatman's daughter was named Su-yün, and she had had several cups of wine with me once before. She was quite nice, so I called her over and asked her to sit with Yün. There was no light in the bow of the boat, so we were able to enjoy the moon and drink happily. We began to play a literary drinking game, at which Su-yün could only blink her eyes. She listened to us for quite a while, then said, "I know a lot about drinking games, but I have never heard of this one. Will you teach it to me?"

Yün thought up several examples to try to explain it to her, but after some time the boat girl still did not understand.

I laughed and said, "Stop it, lady teacher. I have a comparison that will explain the problem."

"What kind of an example are you going to give?" Yün asked.

"A crane can dance but cannot plough, while an ox can plough but cannot dance. That is just the nature of things. Wouldn't it be a waste of time if you tried to teach each of them to play the other's game?"

Su-yün laughed playfully, hit me on the shoulder, and said, "Are you making fun of me?"

At this Yün ordered us to stop. "From now on we allow only talking. No more hitting! Whoever breaks the rule has to drink a big cup of wine."

Su-yün had quite a capacity for wine, so she poured a big cup and downed it at one gulp.

"No hitting," I then said, "but surely it's all right if we caress one another."

Yün laughed and pushed Su-yün over to me. "Caress her to your heart's content, then."

"Don't misunderstand me," I said laughing. "The whole point of caressing someone is to carry it off nonchalantly. Only a country boy would be rough about it."

By this time the scent of jasmine in their hair had mixed with the aroma of the wine, all of it overlaid by the smell of perspiration in their make-up. It was quite overpowering.

"The stink of commoners fills the bow of this boat," I joked. "It's enough to make a man sick."

At this Su-yün could not be stopped from hitting me repeatedly. "Who told you to sniff around?" she shouted.

"You broke the rule," Yün called out to her. "I sentence you to two big cups!"

"But he called me a commoner. Why shouldn't I hit him?"

"He had a reason for using the word 'commoner,'" Yün told her. "Drink these and I'll tell you." So Su-yün drank the two big cups of wine one after the other, and Yün told her how we had joked about the jasmine one night when we lived at the Pavilion of the Waves.

"If that's what he was talking about," Su-yün said, "I should not have blamed him. The sentence should be carried out once again." She then drank a third big cup of wine.

"I have heard what a beautiful voice you have," Yün said as she put the cup down. "Could I hear one of your songs?"

Su-yün immediately began to sing, beating time on a small plate with her ivory chopsticks. Yün was having so much fun she forgot how much she was drinking. She became tipsy without even realizing it, so that she had to take a sedan chair and go home ahead of me. I stayed a few moments longer for some tea and conversation with Su-yün, and then walked home in the moonlight.

At that time we were living with my friend Lu Pan-fang, at his home, the Villa of Serenity. A few days after our trip Mrs. Lu heard some gossip, and took Yün aside. "Yesterday I heard that your husband had been seen drinking with two courtesans in a boat by the Ten Thousand-Years Bridge. Did you know that?"

"It happened all right," Yün replied, "but one of those courtesans was me." Because she had brought it up, Yün then told her in detail about our trip together. Hearing the explanation, Mrs. Lu laughed heartily and dropped the subject.

In the seventh month of the Chiayen year of the reign of the Emperor Chien Lung [1794], I returned from Yüehtung with my friend Hsü Hsiu-feng, who was my cousin's husband. He brought a new concubine back with him, raving about her beauty to everyone, and one day he invited Yün to go and see her. Afterwards Yün said to Hsiu-feng, "She certainly is beautiful, but she is not the least bit charming."

"If your husband were to take a concubine," Hsiu-feng asked, "would she have to be charming as well as beautiful?"

"Naturally," said Yün.

From then on, Yün was obsessed with the idea of finding me a concubine, even though we had nowhere near enough money for such an ambition.

There was a courtesan from Chekiang named Wen Leng-hsiang then living in Soochow. She was something of a poet, and had written four stanzas on the theme of willow catkins that had taken the city by storm, many talented writers composing couplets in response to her originals. My friend from Wuchiang, Chang Hsienhan, had long admired Leng-hsiang, and asked us to help him write some verses to accompany hers. Yün thought little of her and so declined, but I longed to write, and thus composed some verses to her rhyme. One couplet that Yün liked very much was, "They arouse my springtime wistfulness, and ensnare her wandering fancy."

A year later, on the 5th day of the eighth month, mother was planning to take Yün on a visit to Tiger Hill, when my friend Hsien-han suddenly arrived at our house. "I am going to Tiger Hill too," he said, "and today I came especially to invite you to go with me and admire some flowers[2] along the way."

I then asked mother to go on ahead, and said I would meet her at Pantang near Tiger Hill. Hsien-han took me to Leng-hsiang's home, where I discovered that she was already middle-aged.

However, she had a daughter named Han-yüan, who, though not yet fully mature, was as beautiful as a piece of jade. Her eyes were as lovely as the surface of an autumn pond, and while they entertained us it became obvious that her literary knowledge was extensive. She had a younger sister named Wen-yüan who was still quite small.

At first I had no wild ideas and wanted only to have a cup of wine and chat with them. I well knew that a poor scholar like myself could not afford this sort of thing, and once inside I began to feel quite nervous. While I did not show my unease in my conversation, I did quietly say to Hsien-han, "I'm only a poor fellow. How can you invite these girls to entertain me?"

Hsien-han laughed. "It's not that way at all. A friend of mine had invited me to come and be entertained by Han-yüan today, but then he was called away by an important visitor. He asked me to be the host and invite someone else. Don't worry about it."

At that, I began to relax. Later, when our boat reached Pantang, I told Han-yüan to go aboard my mother's boat and pay her respects. That was when Yün met Han-yüan and, as happy as old friends at a reunion, they soon set off hand in hand to climb the hill in search of all the scenic spots it offered. Yün especially liked the height and

2. Visit courtesans.

vista of Thousand Clouds, and they sat there enjoying the view for some time. When we returned to Yehfangpin, we moored the boats side by side and drank long and happily.

As the boats were being unmoored, Yün asked me if Han-yüan could return aboard hers, while I went back with Hsien-han. To this, I agreed. When we returned to the Tuting Bridge we went back aboard our own boats and took leave of one another. By the time we arrived home it was already the third night watch.

"Today I have met someone who is both beautiful and charming," said Yün. "I have just invited Han-yüan to come and see me tomorrow, so I can try to arrange things for you."

"But we're not a rich family," I said, worried. "We cannot afford to keep someone like that. How could people as poor as ourselves dare think of such a thing? And we are so happily married, why should we look for someone else?"

"But I love her too," Yün said, laughing. "You just let me take care of everything."

The next day at noon, Han-yüan actually came. Yün entertained her warmly, and during the meal we played a game—the winner would read a poem, while the loser had to drink a cup of wine. By the end of the meal still not a word had been said about our obtaining Han-yüan.

As soon as she left, Yün said to me, "I have just made a secret agreement with her. She will come here on the 18th, and we will pledge ourselves as sisters. You will have to prepare animals for the sacrifice."

Then, laughing and pointing to the jade bracelet on her arm, she said, "If you see this bracelet on Han-yüan's arm then, it will mean she has agreed to our proposal. I have just told her my idea, but I am still not very sure what she thinks about it all."

I only listened to what she said, making no reply.

It rained very hard on the 18th, but Han-yüan came all the same. She and Yün went into another room and were alone there for some time. They were holding hands when they emerged, and Han-yüan looked at me shyly. She was wearing the jade bracelet!

We had intended, after the incense was burned and they had become sisters, that we should carry on drinking. As it turned out, however, Han-yüan had promised to go on a trip to Stone Lake, so she left as soon as the ceremony was over.

"She has agreed," Yün told me happily. "Now, how will you reward your go-between?" I asked her the details of the arrangement.

"Just now I spoke to her privately because I was afraid she might have another attachment. When she said she did not, I asked her, 'Do you know why we have invited you here today, little sister?'

"'The respect of an honourable lady like yourself makes me feel like a small weed leaning up against a great tree,' she replied, 'but my mother has high hopes for me, and I'm afraid I cannot agree without consulting her. I do hope, though, that you and I can think of a way to work things out.'

"When I took off the bracelet and put it on her arm I said to her, 'The jade of this bracelet is hard and represents the constancy of our pledge; and like our pledge, the circle of the bracelet has no end. Wear it as the first token of our understanding.' To which she replied, 'The power to unite us rests entirely with you.' So it seems as if we have already won over Han-yüan. The difficult part will be convincing her mother, but I will think of a plan for that."

I laughed, and asked her, "Are you trying to imitate Li-weng's *Pitying the Fragrant Companion?*"[3]

"Yes," she replied.

From that time on there was not a day that Yün did not talk about Han-yüan. But later Han-yüan was taken off by a powerful man, and all the plans came to nothing. In fact, it was because of this that Yün died. * * *

THE SORROWS OF MISFORTUNE

Why are there misfortunes in life? They are usually the retributions for one's own sins, but this was not so with me! I always have been friendly, frank, and open, and kept my word to others, but these qualities only became the reasons for my troubles. My father, the Honourable Chia-fu, was also a most generous gentleman, anxious to help those in trouble, to assist anyone in need, to marry off other people's daughters and to bring up their sons. There are countless examples. He spent money like dirt, most of it for other people.

When my wife and I were living at home, we could not avoid pawning our belongings if we had unforeseen expenses; at first we somehow found ways to make ends meet, but later we were always in need. As people say, "Without money, you cannot both run a household and mix with friends." First our circumstances aroused talk amongst local gossips, and later scorn from our family. The ancients were right: "Lack of talent in a woman is a virtue."

Although I was the eldest son in the family, I was the third child, and so at first everyone called Yün "third lady." Later, however, they suddenly started calling her "third wife." It began as a joke, but then became usual practice, so that everyone from the elders to the servants was calling her "third wife."[4] I wonder, was this the beginning of the disagreements in our family?

[*Shen Fu's father becomes furious with Yün, accusing her of disrespect and of mishandling money. Overcome with worry, Yün has increasingly serious bouts of illness, and Shen Fu cannot afford proper treatment, food, or lodging.*]

Her illness worsened daily. Finally I was about to call a doctor to treat her, but she stopped me. "My illness began because of my terribly deep grief over my brother's running away and my mother's death," said Yün. "It continued because of my affections, and now it has returned because of my indignation. I have always worried too much about things, and while I have tried my best to be a good daughter-in-law, I have failed.

"These are the reasons why I have come down with dizziness and palpitations of the heart. The disease has already entered my vitals, and there is nothing a doctor can do about it. Please do not spend money on something that cannot help.

"I have been happy as your wife these twenty-three years. You have loved me and sympathized with me in everything, and never rejected me despite my faults. Having had for my husband an intimate friend like you, I have no regrets over this life. I have had warm cotton clothes, enough to eat, and a pleasant home. I have strolled among streams and rocks, at places like the Pavilion of the Waves and the

---

3. In this play by Li Yu, or Li Liweng (1611–c. 1680), a married woman falls in love with a young girl and obtains her as a concubine for her husband.

4. "Third lady" is a title of respect, and what Yün would normally have been called in the house. While "third wife" is not impolite, it falsely and insultingly implied that the author had two wives senior to Yün.

Villa of Serenity. In the midst of life, I have been just like an Immortal. But a true Immortal must go through many incarnations before reaching enlightenment. Who could dare hope to become an Immortal in only one lifetime? In our eagerness for immortality, we have only incurred the wrath of the Creator, and brought on our troubles with our passion. Because you have loved me too much, I have had a short life!"

Later she sobbed and spoke again. "Even someone who lives a hundred years must still die one day. I am only sorry at having to leave you so suddenly and for so long, halfway through our journey. I will not be able to serve you for all your life, or to see Feng-sen's wedding with my own eyes." When she finished, she wept great tears.

I forced myself to be strong and comforted her saying, "You have been ill for eight years, and it has seemed critical many times. Why do you suddenly say such heartbreaking things now?"

"I have been dreaming every night that my parents have sent a boat to fetch me," said Yün. "When I shut my eyes it feels as if I'm floating, as if I were walking in the mist. Is my spirit leaving me, while only my body remains?"

"That is only because you are upset," I said. "If you will relax, drink some medicine, and take care of yourself, you will get better."

Yün only sobbed again and said, "If I thought I had the slightest thread of life left in me I would never dare alarm you by talking to you like this. But the road to the next world is near, and if I do not speak to you now there will never be a day when I can.

"It is all because of me that you have lost the affection of your parents and drifted apart from them. Do not worry, for after I die you will be able to regain their hearts. Your parents' springs and autumns are many, and when I die you should return to them quickly. If you cannot take my bones home, it does not matter if you leave my coffin here for a while until you can come for it. I also want you to find someone who is attractive and capable, to serve our parents and bring up my children. If you will do this for me, I can die in peace."

When she had said this a great sad moan forced itself from her, as if she was in an agony of heartbreak.

"If you part from me half way I would never want to take another wife," I said. "You know the saying, 'One who has seen the ocean cannot desire a stream, and compared with Wu Mountain there are no clouds anywhere.'"[5]

Yün then took my hand and it seemed there was something else she wanted to say, but she could only brokenly repeat the two words "next life." Suddenly she fell silent and began to pant, her eyes staring into the distance. I called her name a thousand times, but she could not speak. Two streams of agonized tears flowed from her eyes in torrents, until finally her panting grew shallow and her tears dried up. Her spirit vanished in the mist and she began her long journey. This was on the 30th day of the third month in the 7th year of the reign of the Emperor Chia Ching [1803]. When it happened there was a solitary lamp burning in the room. I looked up but saw nothing, there was nothing for my two hands to hold, and my heart felt as if it would shatter. How can there be anything greater than my everlasting grief?

My friend Hu Ken-tang loaned me ten golds, and by selling every single thing remaining in the house I put together enough money to give my beloved a proper burial.

Alas! Yün came to this world a woman, but she had the feelings and abilities of a man. After she entered the gate of my home in marriage, I had to rush about daily to

---

5. A couplet from a poem by the Tang poet Yuan Zhen.

earn our clothing and food, there was never enough, but she never once complained. When I was living at home, all we had for entertainment was talk about literature. What a pity that she should have died in poverty and after long illness. And whose fault was it that she did? It was my fault, what else can I say? I would advise all the husbands and wives in the world not to hate one another, certainly, but also not to love too deeply. As it is said, "An affectionate couple cannot grow old together." My example should serve as a warning to others.

The Ottoman Empire

The Ottoman Empire derives its name from its founder 'Uthman or Othman, who founded a fairly powerful principality in Asia Minor in the thirteenth century and began to unite the Turcomans of western Anatolia and expand to the Byzantine territory. By 1326 the Ottoman principality began to expand into Macedonia, Serbia, and Bulgaria. These conquests were strongly motivated by Islamic religious fervour and regulated by *Shari'a,* Islamic law. They were greatly strengthened by their success in the Balkans and started to expand westward to the Danube River and southward.

The Ottoman state was further expanded at the time of Murad II, who in 1413 introduced a highly developed Turkish-Islamic system of central government. When Mehmed II, the Conqueror, ascended the Ottoman throne in 1451 at the age of nineteen, he needed a great victory to assert his power. He embarked on planning a campaign to conquer Constantinople to secure the safety and integration of the Ottoman State. In 1453 the siege of Constantinople took only forty-four days, and the conquest of the city turned Mehmed II overnight into the most celebrated sultan in the Muslim world. He began to see himself as the heir to a worldwide Muslim Empire, and devoted thirty years of his reign to the realization of this aim. He extended his empire to the borders of Hungary and Austria and to the Black Sea and Moldavia. Indeed it was Mehmed the Conqueror who established the distinctive character and nature of the Ottoman Empire, which remained unshaken for four centuries.

When Mehmed II died in 1481, at the age of forty-nine, the expeditions to Egypt, Italy, and the Mediterranean were left unfinished. After a period of inner strife, Selim I (r. 1512–1520) resumed his unfinished expeditions and proceeded to expand the Empire to the east. By 1517, he conquered Syria, Egypt, and the Hijaz in the Arabian Peninsula, claiming that the last Abbasid caliph, al-Mutawakkil III, had relinquished the caliphate. Selim consolidated the grip of the Ottoman Empire over most of the present Middle East and most of North Africa. By the time of Sulaiman the Magnificent (r. 1520–1566) the Ottoman Empire extended from the Atlantic Ocean to the steppes of Russia and controlled most of the Muslim world in the present Middle East including Iraq, Iran, and the Arabian Peninsula.

Between the fifteenth and seventeenth centuries, the Ottoman Empire achieved great cultural and social developments in terms of wealth, literary output, and architectural monuments, reaching its peak during the time of Salim and Sulaiman. But when the power shifted from the Sultan's palace to the grand vizier's office, known as the Sublime Port, signs of decline began to appear. The first came in 1571 when the Ottomans lost control of the western Mediterranean. They besieged Vienna in 1683 but were driven back by the King of Poland.

The Ottoman Empire, 1672

North Sea
Baltic Sea
RUSSIA
HOLY ROMAN EMPIRE
POLAND
Paris
Vienna
Buda
TRANSYLVANIA
FRANCE
Venice
HUNGARY
WALLACHIA
Bucharest
CRIMEA
BOSNIA
SERBIA
Kosovo
ITALY
Rome
BULGARIA
Black Sea
Madrid
SPAIN
Constantinople
GREECE
Bursa
ANATOLIA
Ankara
Athens
OTTOMAN EMPIRE
Algiers
Tunis
ALGIERS
TUNIS
Mediterranean Sea
CRETE
CYPRUS
SYRIA
Damascus
SAFAVID EMPIRE
Baghdad
Tripoli
Jerusalem
TRIPOLI
EGYPT
Cairo
ARABIA
HEJAZ
SAHARA DESERT
Medina
Mecca
AFRICA
Aden
ATLANTIC OCEAN
INDIAN OCEAN
Don R.
Volga R.
Caspian Sea
Euphrates R.
Tigris R.
Persian Gulf
Red Sea
Nile R.

Though the era of Ottoman expansion had ended, Ottoman power remained considerable through the eighteenth century, before entering a long final period of decline in the nineteenth and early twentieth centuries. Throughout the seventeenth and eighteenth centuries, Constantinople was a major link in trade and cultural exchange between east and west, north and south. The court and upper classes patronized art and poetry, and European visitors like Lady Mary Wortley Montagu wrote of their fascination with a culture so rich, and so

non-European, so close to home. The following selections give a range of poetry and prose
from and about this magnetic culture.

Mihri Khatun
1445–1512

Mihri (or Mihrimah) Khatun is the most distinguished Turkish woman poet of the end of the
fifteenth and the beginning of the sixteenth century. She comes from a glorious Sufi family, for
she was a descendant of Pir Ilyas, the sheikh of Amasya, the area in which she spent most of
her life. Her father was a famous judge who was erudite and wrote poetry under the pen name
Belayi. Educated at home, she availed herself of the rich family library and her father's learned
contacts. For a woman of her age she was highly educated and mastered both Persian poetry
and Turkish rhetorical devices. Her knowledge extended to the realm of Islamic jurisprudence
and theology, and she wrote several treatises in this field, which was not open to women at her
time. But her major talent was in the realm of poetry, in which she left an important though not
voluminous *Diwan* or collection. She saw herself as equal to the major poets of her time and
entered into a poetic dialogue with the leading Turkish poet Nejati (d. 1509), and wrote many
naza'ir (parallel poems) responding to his major ones. Some of her parallel poems were superior to his—to the extent that he was irritated by the freshness, unattainable simplicity and emotional richness of her *naza'ir*.

Mihri Khatun was the leading light of the literary salon of the governor of Amasya, Prince
Ahmad, son of Bayezid II, to whom she addressed most of her poems. She was the center of attention of the men of this salon, for she was blessed with beauty and an ardent temperament. But
she remained unmarried despite the many men who sought her love and attention. She seems to
have reciprocated in a manner appropriate to her time, and to have fallen in love repeatedly. Her
ghazals (love poems) were an expression of her amatory experience and platonic love, particularly for a certain leading army officer and Iskender Celbi, the son of the famous Ottoman archi-
tect Sinan Pasha. This was a time when women practiced chastity and virtuous behaviour, and
Khatun's innocent *ghazal* poetry is a clear reflection of this. She preserved her chastity in order
to preserve her personal and literary independence and to use her access to literary circles to defend and praise women. Yet the subtlety of her poems and their rich emotional expression of real
experiences reveal originality and a delicate and lyrical poetic structure.

I opened my eyes from sleep[1]

I opened my eyes from sleep, and suddenly raised my head
There I saw the moon-face[2] of the love-thief, shining

My star of good luck had risen—I was thus exalted
When in my chamber I saw this Jupiter rise to the evening sky

5   He appeared to be a Muslim, but by his dress an infidel[3]
And divine light poured from the beauty of his face

I opened, then closed my eyes, but he had vanished from my sight
All I know of him—he was an angel or a faery

---

1. Translated by Walter Andrews, Mehmet Kalpakli, and
Najaat Black.
2. A standard reference to the beloved.

3. This is a unique modification of the Roman god Jupiter
to a Muslim one despite the mythological dress that
makes him an infidel.

Now she knows the water of life,
   Mihrî will not die until the Judgement Day[4]
10 For she has seen that visible Alexander
   in the eternal dark of night

At times, my longing for the beloved slays me

At times, my longing for the beloved slays me
At times, union with him and the passing of time slay me too

My enemy laughs at my condition, but I cry
   on and on
How can my spirit endure this sorrow which kills us all?

5 Oh you who doctors the sick heart with his image
The trouble is medicines, like poison, kill me

This day, all my friends and enemies, come crying
I've not yet met my fated end, but these perplexities kill me

Oh my rival, if Mihrî dies on the thorn of love, why grieve?
10 You dog! The grave-keeper stones you, but the rose-mouthed one slays him too

My heart burns in flames of sorrow

My heart burns in flames of sorrow
Sparks and smoke rise turning to the sky

Within me, the heart has taken fire like a candle
My body, whirling, is a lighthouse illuminated by your image[1]

5 See the rope-dancer of the soul, reaching for your ruby lips
Spinning, descending the twist of your curl

The sun and moon came to your quarter, circling in the sky
Bowing to you, faces in the dust before your feet

Oh you with the bright face, radiant as Venus
10 The moon twisted into a crescent to resemble your arching brow

When longing for an image of your lips had befallen my heart
Oh Mihrî, then my heart burned in flames of sorrow

Fuzuli
1480–1556

Fuzuli is the pen name of Muhammad or Mehmed Ibn Sulayman, one of the most distinguished writers of classical Turkish literature. Ironically, Fuzuli lived all of his life in Iraq, writing in

4. Having seen this Roman/Muslim god (heavenly form of her beloved Alexander/Iskender). the poet feels sure of immortality.

1. A Sufi reference to the beloved.

three different languages—Turkish, Arabic, and Persian. Although he wrote several works in Arabic that reveal his erudition and literary skills, his literary reputation rests on his Turkish work written under the Ottomans, and to a lesser extent on his Persian works for their insight and penetrating depth.

He was born in Iraq to a pious and learned Shi'ite Muslim family that provided him with a traditionally solid and comprehensive literary education. His studies in Iraq commenced at Karbala, the center of Shi'ite learning, and continued in Hilla and Baghdad. He started writing poetry at a very early age, and it is reported that he fell in love with the daughter of his master, Rahmat-Allah, and took to poetry to express his love for her. By the age of twenty he established himself as a talented poet. When Sultan Suleyman the Magificent conquered Iraq in 1534, Fuzuli hastened to address several poems to him and composed panegyrics in honor of members of his entourage, from his grand vizier, Ibrahim Pasha, to his military commander, Qadir Celebi. This led the Sultan to promise Fuzuli a pension. When this didn't materialize after the Sultan's departure from Baghdad, Fuzuli wrote a poetic work of complaint that proved highly effective and resulted in prompt payment. Yet he continued to write panegyrics for successive governors of Baghdad. After securing a stable income and a steady patronage, Fuzuli turned his attention to more elaborate composition. It was during this period that he wrote his famous *Layla wa Majnun* (Layla and Her Lover). Although he spoke in his poetry of travel and longed to visit many places in Persia, India, and Asia Minor, Fuzuli never left Iraq. He died in 1556 during the plague epidemic of that year and was buried in Karbala, Iraq.

Fuzuli had a long and prolific literary career in which he wrote poetry in Turkish, Arabic, and Persian, as well as several treatises on religious and literary issues. But it was his work in Turkish that kept his name for posterity, with works that demonstrate the originality of his topics and his artistry, mastery of style, and learning. His most accomplished works are the ones in which he deals with themes of emotions, mystic love, wisdom, Sufism and the tragic events of Karbala's history. Although he derives many of his themes from classical Arabic and Persian literature, he succeeded in his Turkish works in distinguishing himself and stamping his original mark and unique personality on his treatment of common subject matter. His Turkish work is marked by a sensitive, lyrical, and delicate quality that no other Turkish poet has attained.

Oh God, don't let anyone be like me[1]

Oh God, don't let anyone be like me,
    crying and disheveled
Oh God, don't let anyone be an addict of love's
    pain and separation's blow

Always I have been oppressed by those merciless
    idols, those beloveds
Oh God, don't let a Muslim be a slave
    to those infidels

5   I see the moon-faced one, thinking of killing me
    with her love

---

1. Translated by Walter Andrews, Mehmet Kalpakli, and Najaat Black.

I'm unafraid, oh God, just don't let her change
    her mind

When they want to draw from my body the arrowhead
    of the cypress-bodied one
Oh God, let it be my wounded heart they take,
    but not her arrow

I'm accustomed to misery and cruelty—how would
    life be without them?
10   Oh God, don't let my suffering be limited
    nor her tyranny end

Don't say that she shows no justice, that she is
    so unfair
Oh God, let no one but her be sultan
    on the throne of my heart

In the corner of this tavern Fuzûlî found a treasure
    of delight
Oh God, this is a holy place, may it never
    be brought to ruin

If my heart were a wild bird

If my heart were a wild bird, it would nest in your twisted curl
Wherever I am, oh jinn, my love is by your side

I'm happy with my suffering, take your hand
    from the medicine that will cure me
Oh doctor, do not heal me, the poison
    that destroys me is your cure!

5   Don't be shy and pull your skirts from the hands
    of those fallen with love—take care!
For the hands which hold your hem, if suddenly
    emptied, may pray evilly to the sky

The fragments of my shattered heart lie pierced
    on the spearpoints of your lashes
Go to sleep, drunk on your own beauty, and mend
    my heart by the closing of your eyes

Separation from you is death, beloved, the end
    of life itself
10   I am bewildered by others who live long
    apart from you

The wick of your spirit is twisted
    like the hyacinth curl of the beloved
Hey Fuzûlî, you can't hope for release
    until you burn like a candle with love's flame

For long years we have been haunting the quarter

For long years we have been haunting the quarter
   of those who call us vagrants
We are the soldiers of the sultan of the spiritually wise,
   waiting for God to befriend us

Night and day we crouch in the dust at the threshold
   of the tavern
Don't think we are begging, we are waiting for promotion
   at prosperity's door

5   We are not like those vultures, hunting
   for the world-corpse
We are the contented Phoenix, waiting
   on the summit of Kâf mountain

Our eyes see no sleep, we are troubled by those
   who keep us from her
We are the night-guard, watching over the treasure
   of the secrets of love

Surprised by your love, we stand still as the stones
   of the wall
10   While others wander through the garden, we wait
   at our place of torment

We are the caravan on the path of isolation,
   we fear danger along the way
Sometimes Mejnûn keeps our vigil, sometimes it is I,
   we are sentries through the night

Don't think our nightly crying out is in vain!
We stand sentinel in the tower of devotion
   over the country of love

15   Ferhâd and Mejnûn lay down, drunk
   on the full cup of love
Hey Fuzûlî, while they sleep, it's our turn
   to speak of the heart

The pointed reproach of the enemy

The pointed reproach of the enemy
   cannot harm me
The arrowheads of your glances
   protect me with an iron skin

I am also safe from the striking stones of blame
For the chains which bind the madman
   are an iron fortress around me

5   The wounds of your sword have covered me
        in a shirt of blood
But my tears have worn the shirt away,
        I am naked and ashamed

Oh light of my eye, were my eye not shining
        from the candle of your beauty
My worldly vision would be no use to me at all

The pleasure of wondering when I will be near you
10   Keeps me from calling any place my home

Oh keeper of the garden, it is useless to wander
        in the rose-garden of many delights
When I burn for union with the cypress
        of the jasmine breast

Oh Fuzûlî, let the throne of power
        go up in flames!
God knows, far better are homeless nights
        in the warm ashes of the hamam°   *Turkish Bath*

Nedîm
1681–1730

Nedîm, a word meaning drinking companion or intimate friend and confidant, is the pen name of Ahmed Mehmed Nadîm, one of the greatest Ottoman poets of the early eighteenth century. The late seventeenth and early eighteenth centuries witnessed an Ottoman cultural revival and the peak of Ottoman poetry which by then had acquired its pure Turkish style and unique lyrical features. It distinguished itself from classical Arabic and Persian poetry on which it relied for so long, and developed its particular imagery, pure Turkish diction, new themes, and poetic characteristics. Nedîm played an important role in developing these characteristics and provided Turkish poetry with one of its most cherished bodies of poetry.

Little is known about Nedîm's early life or his date of birth, apart from the fact that he was born in Istanbul and was the son of a judge named Mehmed Bey. This put him in the class of the *'ulama'*, learned men, and ensured that he attained a traditional religiously based education. But to perceive him as a traditional intellectual would do him grave injustice. Though he started his life as a teacher in a traditional religious school, he was one of the enlightened *'ulama'* of his time who encouraged and participated in the cultural revival and active Westernization of Mustapha II and Ahmed III. In fact, Nedîm acquired his sobriquet from his long and close association with the court of Sultan Ahmed III (r. 1703–1730) and his grand vizier and son-in-law, Damad Ibrahim Pasha (r. 1718–1730).

Nedîm was the poet laureate of his period, serving as the official poet of the sultan's court, enjoying the sultan's patronage, and formulating cultural policies. He also was the librarian of a national library established under the auspices of the grand vizier. The innovative cultural politics of Ahmed III bred opposition, however, and this led eventually to his downfall. On hearing of the end of Damad Pasha and the deposition of the sultan in October 1730, Nedîm fled the palace and lost his life in a horrible accident. While escaping from the mob leaving the grand vizier's palace, he fell from the roof and died instantly.

Unlike many of the exponents of the period's cultural revival, who came from the ranks of the Ottoman bureaucrat class and lacked a thorough traditional education, and thus were easily dismissed by the conservative traditionalists, Nedîm was considered one of the *'ulama'*. Yet he was more interested in innovating Turkish poetry and culture than in earning the support of the traditionalists. Although he eventually paid with his life for this, his reputation and poetry outlived the work of his opponents. His literary works extol a life of dalliance and worldly pleasures and are highly appreciated for their pure and exquisite language and elegant style. His poetry is today still considered among the most highly regarded literary works in the long span of Turkish culture.

At the gathering of desire[1]

At the gathering of desire you made me a wine-cup
    with your sugar smile[2]
Oh saki,[3] give me only half a cup of wine,
    you've made me drunk enough

You crushed me under the hoof of a wild horse
    that runs like fire
In those places flames rise up from my ashes
    like cypress trees

5   Ah, east wind, you came to me with the scent
    of my lover's hair
You made me love-bewildered like the hyacinth's curl

With your beauteous grace my hair has been standing
    like a jinn
With love you've made me mirror-colored from head
    to foot

Don't make your crying Nedîm drunk and devastated
    like that
10   Saki, give me only half a cup of wine, you've made
    me drunk enough

When the east wind leaves that curl

When the east wind leaves that curl,
    it carries the scent of musk
And when it opens the knot of your gown,
    it carries the scent of rose

On that rose-petal lip, I would find the taste
    of sugar

---

1. Translated by Walter Andrews, Mehmet Kalpakli, and Najaat Black.

2. A Sufi reference to the spirituality of love.
3. The cup-bearer, in this case the beloved.

On that rosebud mouth, I would discover
    the scent of wine

5   At what party did you stay up all night
    in conversation?
Your drunken narcissus-eye is still perfumed
    with sleep

Alas, we were unable to see her without her veil
A shame that my rival should smell that silver
    neck unveiled

My tormented flesh became ash in the searing
    heat of love
10 The grass that grows there smells of burning
    until the Judgment Day

The rose-charm of coquettishness brought rosewater
    to your brow[1]
Oh rose, the small apple of your chin smelled sweet!

Oh Nedîm, are you again cutting open and revealing
    meaning?
The point of the sword of the pen[2] smells of the blood
    of difficult choice

As the morning wind blows

As the morning wind blows, you are disheveled,
    my heart
You are imprisoned in the curls of the beloved,
    my heart

In this time of the rose, we are both ashamed
Ashamed for having given up wine, my heart

5   Why are the tears like a flame within my eye?
Are you hidden in the fire of weeping, my heart?

Did I say, "Drink no wine"?
    Did I say, "Don't love the beloved"?
Why do you run from me, my heart?

Your behavior is a stranger to wisdom
    and good sense
10 You are a guest in the depths of my breast,
    my heart

Looking at you in wonder, the mirror melts
    to a silver pool

---

1. A drop of sweat.   2. A standard Arabic reference to the traditional relationship between writing and fighting.

Oh God, what a harshly burning flame you are,
    my heart

Like the lanterns of the caravan along the pilgrims' road
You shine among the people of love, my heart

15   Within you, the sun of talent shows itself,
    you are the nest of divine light
You are the border of the morning of passion,
    my heart

Since you have offered the cup of love to Nedîm,
    don't take the cup away
Let him quench his thirst before you,
    my heart

Take yourself to the rose-garden

Take yourself to the rose-garden, it's the season
    of our wandering
Oh swaying cypress, give back the ruined spring
    its reign
Pour down your dark curls, let your cheek
    be dressed in sable
Oh swaying cypress, give back the ruined spring
    its reign

5   Come rose-mouthed one, your nightingales
    are calling
Come to the garden, that we might forget
    the rose has gone
Come, before the meadow is ravaged
    by winter
Oh swaying cypress, give back the ruined spring
    its reign

Cast your black down onto that red cheek
10   This year, border your crimson shawl in mink
And if the tulip cups are lacking, bring wine cups
    in their stead
Oh swaying cypress, give back the ruined spring
    its reign

The world is a Paradise, it is the season
    of plentiful fruit
Won't you make the fruit of union ours as well?
15   Secretly bless your lovers, give each of them
    a kiss
Oh swaying cypress, give back the ruined spring
    its reign

Oh my heart-brightening beauty, I heard
    a line of verse
It was lovely, though I don't know what
    it meant
Oh Nedîm; I suppose you spoke the line
    knowingly . . . it is this
20   Oh swaying cypress, give back the ruined spring
    its reign

Delicacy was drawn out like the finest wine

Delicacy was drawn out like the finest wine
    and became your slender body
Wine poured from the bottle and became
    your crimson cheek

The scent of the rose was distilled,
    a perfumed bead upon your cheek
The thorn embroidered your handkerchief,
    your veil of shyness

5   Oh reed pen, your hollowed center is filled
    with magic and with spells
Your center, secret within you, can be named black,
    the locks of Hârût[1]

Dark crusaders surrounded the temple
    of your face
They came to the altar of your brow,
    became the mole upon your cheek

That heretic asked—"Would you like
    to drink wine?"
10   The most difficult question she has asked you,
    God have mercy, oh heart!

Of what cup are you the drunkard?
    Whose love-bewildered one are you?
You have deceived yourself, my heart,
    you know not what has befallen you

Your lips will be wounded on the teeth
    of the "s" of kiss
Thus is it impossible for you to let
    your ruby mouth be kissed

15   Nedîm, you speak of a beloved not found
    in this city

1. The poet's beloved.

Perhaps she was some sweet illusion
with a faery's luring face

━•━ ≖◆≕ ━•━

Lady Mary Wortley Montagu
1689–1762

Lady Mary Pierrepont, as she was called upon becoming a countess at age one, educated her-self only slightly later on to become a classical scholar, translator, and poet. She also learned to follow in the footsteps of Madame de Sévigné (see page 268), establishing her lasting literary fame on the basis of personal letters to close relations carefully edited for posthumous publica-tion, rather than publishing her translations or poetry. For at twenty she already knew that "there is hardly a character in the world more despicable, or more liable to universal ridicule than that of the Learned Woman."

Having lost her mother, Mary Fielding, in infancy, Lady Mary studied in her father's li-brary under the guidance of mentors including Mary Astell (whose famous plan to establish a Protestant convent to educate women she thought of implementing), Bishop Burnet, and Anne Montagu. When the latter died in 1709, Edward Wortley Montagu continued his sister's epis-tolary mentorship of Lady Mary. After three years of sober, rational discourse, he persuaded her to elope with him against her father's wishes. Wortley Montagu was soon named ambas-sador to Constantinople (modern Istanbul), where Lady Mary used the veil like a mask to wan-der the streets with far greater freedom and independence than she ever could in London. Her sex also allowed her to visit a real harem—about which contemporary male Western writers could only fantasize (and indeed did copiously; see Montesquieu's *Persian Letters,* page 427). The letters she wrote home during her two years in Constantinople provide an intimate glimpse of women's lives in both worlds, illuminated by her thoughtful comparisons and contrasts. Af-ter returning home, she set a persuasive example to the Western public, fearful then as now of the risks of vaccination, by inoculating her own two children against smallpox. Thus she helped introduce to the West a Turkish custom that would eventually eradicate that dreaded plague.

Like the French *précieuses,* Lady Mary Wortley Montagu circulated her poetry to friends, but unlike them she was more interested in satire, wit, and sex than in sentiment. Her ladylike avoid-ance of publication during her lifetime did not prevent her from being active in literary and politi-cal life, nor save her from becoming, like Aphra Behn before her, a subject of her contemporaries' scandalized admiration. She did publish journalism, producing an edition of *The Spectator* for her friends Joseph Addison and Richard Steele, as well as her own periodical, *The Nonsense of Com-mon Sense* (1737–1738). She wielded some of her influence in London literary circles to promote the career of her cousin, the satirical novelist Henry Fielding. Alexander Pope was her great friend, and became her greatest enemy. They wrote poetry together, wrote letters to one another, and wrote satires against each other until he attacked her in his famous *Epistle II: To a Lady* (1735). In it Pope insults Wortley Montagu by calling her a "Sappho"—the same name voluntarily adopted by Madeleine de Scudéry in the previous century to exalt her literary reputation (see page 256).

In 1739, at age fifty, Montagu broke off her friendship with Pope, married off her daugh-ter, and ran off to Italy with a bisexual writer, Francesco Algarotti, of no more than half her age. She remained in Italian exile for over twenty years—for the rest of both their lives. Living in Italy independently of both Algarotti and her husband, she returned to England only in the final year of her life. From Italy she continued writing letters home about her alienation, as a foreigner and a woman, from all the worlds she tried to inhabit. Her final comment was: "It has all been most interesting."

Title page of Baudier's
*General History of the Seraglio
and of the Court of the Noble
Lord Emperor of the Turks,*
1631. The French mind imagines the Turkish harem, reflecting fantasy more than
reality.

For one of Lady Mary Wortley Montagu's retorts to her age's satires on women, see
page 292.

from The Turkish Embassy Letters

To Alexander Pope 1 April [1717]

Adrianople, Ap. 1. O.S.[1]

I dare say you expect at least something very new in this letter after I have gone a journey not undertaken by any Christian of some 100 years. The most remarkable accident
that happen'd to me was my being very near overturn'd into the Hebrus; and if I had
much regard for the glories that one's name enjoys after death I should certainly be

---

1. Old Style. In the early 18th century most of Europe used the Gregorian ("New Style") calendar, introduced by Pope
Gregory XIII in 1582, while England continued to use the Julian (or "Old Style," established by Julius Caesar) calendar
until 1752. The two calendars were 10 to 11 days apart.

sorry for having miss'd the romantic conclusion of swimming down the same river in which the musical head of Orpheus repeated verses so many ages since.

> –Caput a cervice revulsum,
> Gurgite cum medio portans Oeagrius Hebrus
> Volveret, Euridicen vox ipsa, et frigida lingua,
> Ah! Miseram Euridicen! anima fugiente vocabat,
> Euridicen toto referebant flumine ripaeæ.[2]

Who knows but some of your bright wits might have found it a subject affording many poetical turns, and have told the world in a heroic elegy that

> As equal were our Souls, so equal were our fates?

I dispair of ever having so many fine things said of me as so extraodinary a death would have given occasion for.

I am at this present writing in a house situate on the banks of the Hebrus, which runs under my chamber window. My garden is full of tall cypress trees, upon the branches of which several Couple of true turtles[3] are saying soft things to one another from morning till night. How naturally do boughs and vows come into my head at this minute! And must not you confess to my praise that 'tis more than an ordinary discretion that can resist the wicked suggestions of poetry in a place where truth for once furnishes all the ideas of pastoral? The summer is already far advanc'd in this part of the world, and for some miles round Adrianople the whole ground is laid out in gardens, and the banks of the river set with rows of fruit trees, under which all the most considerable Turks divert themselves every evening; not with walking, that is not one of their pleasures, but a set party of 'em choose out a green spot where the shade is very thick, and there they spread a carpet on which they sit drinking their coffee and generally attended by some slave with a fine voice or that plays on some instrument. Every 20 paces you may see one of these little companies listening to the dashing of the river, and this taste is so universal that the very gardeners are not without it. I have often seen them and their children siting on the banks and playing on a rural instrument perfectly answering the description of the ancient fistula, being compos'd of unequal reeds, with a simple but agreable softness in the sound. Mr. Addison might here make the experiment he speaks of in his travels,[4] there not being one instrument of music among the Greek or Roman statues that is not to be found in the hands of the people of this country. The young lads gennerally divert themselves with making garlands for their favourite lambs, which I have often seen painted and adorn'd with flowers, lying at their feet while they sung or play'd. It is not that they ever read romances, but these are the ancient amusements here, and as natural to them as cudgel playing and football to our British swains, the softness and warmth of the climate forbidding all rough exercises, which were never so much as heard of amongst 'em, and naturally inspiring a laziness and aversion to labour, which the great plenty indulges. These gardeners are

---

2. From Virgil's *Georgics*, iv. 523–27, describing Orpheus's dismemberment by Thracian women while he mourned the loss of his wife, Eurydice: "Then, when his Head, from his fair Shoulders torn, / Wash'd by the Waters, was on Hebrus born; / Ev'n then his trembling Tongue invok'd his Bride; / With his last Voice, Eurydice, he cry'd, / Eurydice, the Rocks and River-banks reply'd" (John Dryden trans.).

3. Faithful turtledoves.

4. Joseph Addison's *Remarks on Several Parts of Italy, &c.* (1705).

the only happy race of country people in Turkey. They furnish all the city with fruit and herbs, and seem to live very easily. They are most of 'em Greeks and have little houses in the midst of their gardens where their wives and daughters take a liberty not permitted in the town: I mean, to go unveil'd. These wenches are very neat and handsome, and pass their time at their looms under the shade of their trees. I no longer look upon Theocritus as a romantic Writer; he has only given a plain image of the way of life amongst the peasants of his country, which before oppresion had reduc'd them to want, were I suppose all employ'd as the better sort of 'em are now.[5] I don't doubt had he been born a Briton his Idylliums had been fill'd with descriptions of threshing and churning, both which are unknown here, the corn being all trod out by oxen, and butter (I speak it with sorrow) unheard of.

I read over your Homer[6] here with an infinite pleasure, and find several little passages explain'd that I did not before entirely comprehend the beauty of, many of the customs and much of the dress then in fashion being yet retain'd; and I don't wonder to find more remains here of an age so distant than is to be found in any other country, the Turks not taking that pains to introduce their own manners as has been generally practis'd by other nations that imagine themselves more polite. It would be too tedious to you to point out all the passages that relate to the present customs, but I can assure you that the princesses and great ladies pass their time at their looms embrodiering veils and robes, surrounded by their maids, which are always very numerous, in the same manner as we find Andromache and Helen describ'd. The description of the belt of Menelaüs exactly ressembles those that are now worn by the great men, fasten'd before with broad golden clasps and embrodier'd round with rich work. The snowy veil that Helen throws over her face is still fashionable; and I never see (as I do very often) half a dozen old bashaws with their reverend beards siting basking in the sun, but I recollect Good King Priam and his councellors. Their manner of dancing is certainly the same that Diana is sung to have danc'd by Eurotas.[7] The great lady still leads the dance and is follow'd by a troop of young girls who imitate her steps, and if she sings, make up the chorus. The tunes are extreme gay and lively, yet with something in 'em wonderful soft. The steps are vary'd according to the pleasure of her that leads the dance, but always in exact time and infinitely more agreeable than any of our dances, at least in my opinion. I sometimes make one in the train, but am not skilfull enough to lead. These are Grecian dances, the Turkish being very different.

I should have told you in the first place that the Eastern manners give a great light into many scripture passages that appear odd to us, their phrases being commonly what we should call scripture language. The vulgar Turk is very different from what is spoke at Court or amongst the people of figure, who always mix so much Arabic and Persian in their discourse that it may very well be call'd another language; and 'tis as ridiculous to make use of the expressions commonly us'd, in speaking to a great man or a lady, as it would be to talk broad Yorkshire or Sommersetshire in the drawing-room. Besides this distinction they have what they call the sublime, that is, a style proper for poetry, and which is the exact scripture style.

---

5. The *Idylls* of the Greek poet Theocritus (c. 308–c. 240 B.C.E.) serve as the archetype of pastoral poetry, offering an idealized portrayal of rural life.
6. The second volume of Pope's translation of the *Iliad*

had appeared in March of 1716.
7. In Homer's *Odyssey* (bk. 6), the goddess Diana dances near the river Erymanthus, but Lady Mary puts her beside another Greek river.

I believe you would be pleas'd to see a genuine example of this, and I am very glad I have it in my power to satisfy your curiosity by sending you a faithful copy of the verses that Ibrahim Bassa,[8] the reigning favourite, has made for the young Princess, his contracted wife, whom he is not yet permitted to visit without witnesses, thô she is gone home to his house. He is a man of wit and learning, but whether or no he is capable of writing good verse himself, you may be sure that on such an occasion he would not want the assistance of the best poets in the Empire. Thus the verses may be look'd upon as a sample of their finest poetry, and I don't doubt you'll be of my Mind that it is most wonderfully ressembling the Song of Solomon, which was also address'd to a royal bride.

Turkish Verses address'd to the Sultana, eldest daughter of S[ultan] Achmet 3rd

Stanza 1st

The nightingale now wanders in the vines,
Her passion is to seek roses.
I went down to admire the beauty of the vines,
The sweetness of your charms has ravish'd my soul.
Your eyes are black and lovely
But wild and disdainful as those of a stag.

Stanza 2nd

The wish'd possession is delayed from day to day,
The cruel Sultan Achmet will not permit me to see those cheeks more vermillion
    than roses.
I dare not snatch one of your kisses,
The sweetness of your charms has ravish'd my soul.
Your eyes are black and lovely
But wild and disdainful as those of a stag.

Stanza 3rd

The wretched Bassa Ibrahim sighs in these verses,
One dart from your eyes has pierc'd through my heart.
Ah, when will the hour of possession arrive?
Must I yet wait a long time?
The sweetness of your charms has ravish'd my soul.
Ah Sultana stag-ey'd, an angel amongst angels,
I desire and my desire remains unsatisfy'd.
Can you take delight to prey upon my heart?

Stanza 4th

My cries pierce the heavens,
My eyes are without sleep;
Turn to me, Sultana, let me gaze on thy beauty.
Adieu, I go down to the grave;
If you call me I return.
My heart is hot as sulphur; sigh and it will flame.
Crown of my life, fair light of my eyes, my Sultana, my Princess,
I rub my face against the earth, I am drown'd in scalding tears—I rave!
Have you no compassion? Will you not turn to look upon me?

---

8. Ibraham Pasha was an accomplished writer.

I have taken abundance of pains to get these verses in a literal translation, and if you were acquainted with my interpreters, I might spare myself the trouble of assuring you that they have receiv'd no poetical touches from their hands. In my opinion (allowing for the inevitable faults of a prose translation into a language so very different) there is a good deal of beauty in them. The epithet of stag-ey'd (thô the sound is not very agreeable in English) pleases me extremely, and is, I think, a very lively image of the fire and indifference in his mistress's Eyes. Monsieur Boileau[9] has very justly observ'd, we are never to judge of the elevation of an expression in an ancient author by the sound it carrys with us, which may be extremely fine with them, at the same time it looks low or uncouth to us. You are so well acquainted with Homer, you cannot but have observ'd the same thing, and you must have the same indulgence for all Oriental poetry. The repetitions at the end of the 2 first stanzas are meant for a sort of chorus and agreeable to the ancient manner of writing. The music of the verses apparently changes in the 3rd stanza where the burden is alter'd, and I think he very artfully seems more passionate at the conclusion as 'tis natural for people to warm themselves by their own discourse, especially on a subject where the heart is concern'd, and is far more touching than our modern custom of concluding a song of passion with a turn which is inconsistent with it. The 1st verse is a description of the season of the year, all the country being now full of nightingales, whose amours with roses is an Arabian fable as well known here as any part of Ovid amongst us, and is much the same thing as if an English poem should begin by saying: Now Philomela[1] sings—Or what if I turn'd the whole into the style of English poetry to see how twould look?

Stanza 1

Now Philomel renews her tender strain,
Indulging all the night her pleasing pain.
I sought the groves to hear the wanton sing,
There saw a face more beauteous than the spring.
Your large stag's-eyes where 1,000 glories play,
As bright, as lively, but as wild as they.

2

In vain I'm promis'd such a heavenly prize,
Ah, cruel Sultan who delays my joys!
While piercing charms transfix my amorous heart
I dare not snatch one kiss to ease the smart.
Those eyes like etc.

3

Your wretched lover in these lines complains,
From those dear beauties rise his killing pains.
When will the hour of wish'd-for bliss arrive?
Must I wait longer? Can I wait and live?
Ah, bright Sultana! Maid divinely fair!
Can you unpitying see the pain I bear?

9. Nicholas Despréaux Boileau (1636–1711), French literary critic and poet.

1. The nightingale. In Greek myth, Philomela was transformed into a nightingale after being raped and having her tongue cut out by her brother-in-law, Tereus.

Stanza 4th

The heavens relenting hear my peircing cries,
I loath the light and sleep forsakes my eyes.
Turn thee, Sultana, ere thy lover dies.
Sinking to earth, I sigh the last adieu—
Call me, my Goddess, and my life renew.
My Queen! my Angel! my fond heart's desire,
I rave—my bosom burns with heavenly fire.
Pity that passion which thy charms inspire.

I have taken the Liberty in the 2nd verse of following what I suppose is the true sense of the author, thô not literally express'd. By saying he went down to admire the beauty of the vines and her charms ravish'd his soul, I understand by this a poetical fiction of having first seen her in a garden where he was admiring the beauty of the spring; but I could not forbear retaining the comparison of her eyes to those of a stag, thô perhaps the novelty of it may give it a burlesque sound in our language. I cannot determine upon the whole how well I have succeeded in the translation. Neither do I think our English proper to express such violence of passion, which is very seldom felt amongst us; and we want those compound words which are very frequent and strong in the Turkish language.—You see I am pretty far gone in Oriental learning, and to say truth I study very hard. I wish my studies may give me occasion of entertaining your curiosity, which will be the utmost advantage hop'd from it by etc.

To Sarah Chiswell 1 April [1717]

Adrianople, Ap. 1. O.S.

In my opinion, dear S[arah], I ought rather to quarrel with you for not answering my Nimeguen[1] letter of Aug't till December, than to excuse my not writing again till now. I am sure there is on my side a very good excuse for silence, having gone such tiresome land journeys, thô I don't find the conclusion of 'em so bad as you seem to imagine. I am very easy here and not in the solitude you fancy me; the great quantity of Greeks, French, English and Italians that are under our protection make their court to me from morning till night, and I'll assure you are many of 'em very fine ladies, for there is no possibility for a Christian to live easily under this government but by the protection of an ambassador, and the richer they are the greater their danger.

Those dreadfull stories you have heard of the plague have very little foundation in truth. I own I have much ado to reconcile myself to the sound of a word which has allways given me such terrible Ideas, thô I am convinc'd there is little more in it than a fever, as a proof of which we past through 2 or 3 towns most violently infected. In the very next house where we lay, in one of 'em, 2 persons dy'd of it. Luckily for me I was so well deceiv'd that I knew nothing of the matter, and I was made believe that our 2nd cook who fell ill there had only a great cold. However, we left our doctor to take care of him, and yesterday they both arriv'd here in good health and I am now let into the secret that he has had the plague. There are many that 'scape of it, neither is

---

1. A Dutch city near the German border.

the air ever infected. I am persuaded it would be as easy to root it out here as out of Italy and France, but it does so little mischief, they are not very solicitous about it and are content to suffer this distemper instead of our variety, which they are utterly unacquainted with.

A propos of distempers, I am going to tell you a thing that I am sure will make you wish yourself here. The small pox so fatal and so general amongst us is here entirely harmless by the invention of engrafting (which is the term they give it). There is a set of old women who make it their business to perform the operation. Every autumn in the month of September, when the great heat is abated, people send to one another to know if any of their family has a mind to have the small pox. They make parties for this purpose, and when they are met (commonly 15 or 16 together) the old woman comes with a nutshell full of the matter of the best sort of small-pox and asks what veins you please to have open'd. She immediately rips open that you offer to her with a large needle (which gives you no more pain than a common scratch) and puts into the vein as much venom as can lie upon the head of her needle, and after binds up the little wound with a hollow bit of shell, and in this manner opens 4 or 5 veins. The Grecians have commonly the superstition of opening one in the middle of the forehead, in each arm and on the breast to mark the sign of the cross, but this has a very ill effect, all these wounds leaving little scars, and is not done by those that are not superstitious, who choose to have them in the legs or that part of the arm that is conceal'd. The children or young patients play together all the rest of the day and are in perfect health till the 8th. Then the fever begins to seize 'em and they keep their beds 2 days, very seldom 3. They have very rarely above 20 or 30 in their faces, which never mark, and in 8 days time they are as well as before their illness. Where they are wounded there remains running sores during the distemper, which I don't doubt is a great releif to it. Every year thousands undergo this operation, and the French Ambassador says pleasantly that they take the small pox here by way of diversion as they take the waters in other countries. There is no example of any one that has died in it, and you may beleive I am very well satisfy'd of the safety of the experiment since I intend to try it on my dear little Son.[2] I am patriot enough to take pains to bring this useful invention into fashion in England, and I should not fail to write to some of our doctors very particularly about it if I knew any one of 'em that I thought had virtue enough to destroy such a considerable branch of their revenue for the good of mankind, but that distemper is too beneficial to them not to expose to all their resentment the hardy wight that should undertake to put an end to it. Perhaps if I live to return I may, however, have courage to war with 'em. Upon this Occasion, admire the heroism in the heart of your friend, etc.

To Lady Mar 18 April [1717]

Adrianople, Ap. 18. O.S.

I writ to you (dear sister) and all my other English correspondants by the last ship, and only Heaven can tell when I shall have another opportunity of sending to you, but I cannot forbear writing, thô perhaps my letter may lie upon my hands this 2 months. To confess the truth my head is so full of my entertainment yesterday that 'tis

2. Lady Mary had her son vaccinated against smallpox the following year and was instrumental in introducing the practice into England.

absolutely necessary for my own repose to give it some vent. Without farther preface I will then begin my story.

I was invited to dine with the Grand Vizier's lady and twas with a great deal of pleasure I prepar'd myself for an entertainment which was never given before to any Christian. I thought I should very little satisfy her curiosity (which I did not doubt was a considerable motive to the invitation) by going in a dress she was us'd to see, and therefore dress'd my selfe in the Court habit of Vienna, which is much more magnificent than ours. However, I chose to go incognito to avoid any disputes about ceremony, and went in a Turkish coach only attended by my woman that held up my train and the greek lady who was my interpretress. I was met at the Court door by her black eunuch, who help'd me out of the coach with great respect and conducted me through several rooms where her she slaves, finely dress'd, were rang'd on each side. In the innermost, I found the lady siting on her sofa in a sable vest. She advanc'd to meet me and presented me half a dozen of her friends with great civility. She seem'd a very good woman, near 50 year old. I was surpriz'd to observe so little magnificence in her house, the furniture being all very moderate, and except the habits and number of her slaves nothing about her that appear'd expensive. She guess'd at my thoughts and told me that she was no longer of an Age to spend either her time or money in superfluities, that her whole expense was in charity and her employment praying to God. There was no affectation in this speech; both she and her husband are entirely given up to devotion.[1] He never looks upon any other woman, and what is much more extraodinary touches no bribes, notwithstanding the example of all his predecessors. He is so scrupulous in this point, he would not accept Mr. W[ortley]'s present till he had been assur'd over and over twas a settle'd perquisite of his place at the entrance of every ambassador.

She entertain'd me with all kind of civility till dinner came in, which was serv'd one dish at a time, to a vast number, all finely dress'd after their manner, which I do not think so bad as you have perhaps heard it represented. I am a very good Judge of their eating, having liv'd 3 weeks in the house of an Effendi[2] at Belgrade who gave us very magnificent dinners dress'd by his own cooks, which the first week pleas'd me extremely, but I own I then begun to grow weary of it and desir'd my own cook might add a dish or 2 after our manner, but I attribute this to custom. I am very much enclin'd to beleive an Indian that had never tasted of either would prefer their cookery to ours. Their sauces are very high, all the roast very much done. They use a great deal of rich spice. The soup is serv'd for the last dish, and they have at least as great variety of ragoûts as we have. I was very sorry I could not eat of as many as the good lady would have had me, who was very earnest in serving me of every thing. The treat concluded with coffee and perfumes, which is a high mark of respect. 2 slaves kneeling cens'd my hair, clothes, and handkerchief. After this ceremony she commanded her slaves to play and dance, which they did with their guitars in their hands, and she excus'd to me their want of skill, saying she took no care to accomplish them in that art. I return'd her thanks and soon after took my leave.

I was conducted back in the same manner I enter'd, and would have gone straight to my own house, but the Greek lady with me earnestly solicited me to visit

---

1. Armand Khalil Pasha had been Grand Vizier since 1716 and was reputed a devout and temperate ruler.

2. A Turkish title of respect applied to government officials and members of learned professions.

the Kahya's lady, saying he was the 2nd officer in the Empire and ought indeed to be look'd upon as the first, the Grand Vizier having only the name while he exercis'd the authority. I had found so little diversion in this harem that I had no mind to go into another, but her importunity prevail'd with me, and I am extreme glad that I was so complaisant. All things here were with quite another air than at the Grand Vizier's, and the very house confess'd the difference between an old devote and a young beauty. It was nicely clean and magnificent. I was met at the door by 2 black eunuchs who led me through a long gallery between 2 ranks of beautiful young girls with their hair finely plaited almost hanging to their feet, all dress'd in fine light damasks brocaded with silver. I was sorry that decency did not permit me to stop to consider them nearer, but that thought was lost upon my entrance into a large room, or rather pavilion, built round with gilded sashes which were most of 'em thrown up; and the trees planted near them gave an agreeable shade which hinder'd the sun from being troublesome, the jess'mins and honeysuckles that twisted round their trunks sheding a soft perfume encreas'd by a white marble fountain playing sweet water in the lower part of the room, which fell into 3 or 4 basons with a pleasing sound. The roof was painted with all sort of flowers falling out of gilded baskets that seem'd tumbling down.

On a sofa rais'd 3 steps and cover'd with fine Persian carpets sat the Kahya's lady, leaning on cushions of white satin embrodier'd, and at her feet sat 2 young girls, the eldest about 12 year old, lovely as angels, dress'd perfectly rich and almost cover'd with jewels. But they were hardly seen near the fair Fatima (for that is her name), so much her beauty effac'd everything. I have seen all that has been call'd lovely either in England or Germany, and must own that I never saw anything so gloriously beautiful, nor can I recollect a face that would have been taken notice of near hers. She stood up to receive me, saluting me after their fashion, putting her hand upon her heart with a sweetness full of majesty that no court breeding could ever give. She order'd cushions to be given me and took care to place me in the corner, which is the place of honour. I confess, thô the Greek lady had before given me a great opinion of her beauty I was so struck with admiration that I could not for some time speak to her, being wholly taken up in gazing. That surprizing harmony of features! that charming result of the whole! that exact proportion of body! that lovely bloom of complexion unsully'd by art! the unutterable enchantment of her smile! But her eyes! large and black with all the soft languishment of the blue! every turn of her face discovering some new charm! After my first surprize was over, I endeavor'd by nicely examining her face to find out some imperfection, without any fruit of my search but being clearly convinc'd of the error of that vulgar notion, that a face perfectly regular would not be agreeable, Nature having done for her with more success what Apelles[3] is said to have essay'd, by a collection of the most exact features to form a perfect face; and to that a behaviour so full of grace and sweetness, such easy motions, with an air so majestic yet free from stiffness or affectation that I am persuaded could she be suddenly transported upon the most polite throne of Europe, nobody would think her other than born and bred to be a queen, thô educated in a country we call barbarous. To say all in a word, our most celebrated English beauties would vanish near her.

---

3. Said to have been the greatest painter of ancient Greece.

She was dress'd in a caftan of gold brocade flowerd with silver, very well fitted to her shape and showing to advantage the beauty of her bosom, only shaded by the thin Gauze of her shift. Her drawers were pale pink, green and silver; her slippers white, finely embroider'd; her lovely arms adorn'd with bracelets of diamonds, and her broad girdle set round with diamonds; upon her head a rich Turkish handkerchief of pink and silver, her own fine black hair hanging a great length in various tresses, and on one side of her head some bodkins of jewels. I am afraid you will accuse me of extravagance in this description. I think I have read somewhere that women always speak in rapture when they speak of beauty, but I can't imagine why they should not be allow'd to do so. I rather think it virtue to be able to admire without any mixture of desire or envy. The gravest writers have spoke with great warmth of some celebrated pictures and statues. The workmanship of Heaven certainly excels all our weak imitations, and I think has a much better claim to our praise. For me, I am not asham'd to own I took more pleasure in looking on the beauteous Fatima than the finest piece of sculpture could have given me. She told me the 2 girls at her feet were her daughters, thô she appear'd too young to be their mother.

Her fair maids were rang'd below the sofa to the number of 20, and put me in mind of the pictures of the ancient nymphs. I did not think all Nature could have furnish'd such a scene of beauty. She made them a sign to play and dance. 4 of them immediately begun to play some soft airs on instruments between a lute and a guitar, which they accompany'd with their voices while the others danc'd by turns. This dance was very different from what I had seen before. Nothing could be more artful or more proper to raise certain ideas, the tunes so soft, the motions so languishing, accompany'd with pauses and dying eyes, half falling back and then recovering themselves in so artful a manner that I am very possitive the coldest and most rigid prude upon earth could not have look'd upon them without thinking of something not to be spoke of. I suppose you may have read that the Turks have no music but what is shocking to the ears, but this account is from those who never heard any but what is play'd in the streets, and is just as reasonable as if a foreigner should take his ideas of the English music from the bladder and string, and marrow bones and cleavers.[4] I can assure you that the music is extremely pathetic.[5] 'Tis true I am enclin'd to prefer the Italian, but perhaps I am partial. I am acquainted with a Greek lady who sings better than Mrs. Robinson,[6] and is very well skill'd in both, who gives the preference to the Turkish. Tis certain they have very fine natural voices; these were very agreeable.

When the dance was over 4 fair slaves came into the room with silver censors in their hands and perfum'd the air with amber, aloes wood and other rich scents. After this they serv'd me coffee upon their knees in the finest Japan china with soûcoupes of silver gilt. The lovely Fatima entertain'd me all this time in the most polite agreeable manner, calling me often Uzelle Sultanam, or the beautifull Sultana, and desiring my Friendship with the best grace in the world, lamenting that she could not entertain me in my own language. When I took my leave 2 maids brought

4. Crude ways to make music in the streets. Butchers would celebrate weddings of their guild members by banging marrow bones against the flat blades of their cleavers. An animal's bladder filled with air was attached to a broomstick, with a string stretched across and bowed like a string bass.
5. Full of pathos.
6. Anastasia Robinson (d. 1755), a celebrated London vocalist.

in a fine silver basket of embrodier'd handkerchiefs. She beg'd I would wear the richest for her sake, and gave the others to my woman and interpretress. I retir'd through the same ceremonies as before, and could not help fancying I had been some time in Mahomet's Paradise, so much I was charm'd with what I had seen. I know not how the relation of it appears to you. I wish it may give you part of my pleasure, for I would have my dear sister share in all the diversions of etc.

[END OF THE OTTOMAN EMPIRE]

Execution of Louis XVI (period engraving). Standing before the dreaded guillotine—erected on the former site of a statue of Louis XV—the executioner dramatically displays the severed head of Louis XVI to a crowd of 80,000 spectators.

The Age of the Enlightenment

The period known as "the Enlightenment," or "the Age of Reason," extends roughly from the English Revolution to the French Revolution—that is, from the beheading of Charles I (1649) to the beheading of Louis XVI (1793). The former monarch was decapitated by sword, the quintessential aristocratic implement; the latter by guillotine, a newfangled democratizing machine for the mass production of death. This telling change in the technology of regicide says much about the social transformations brought about during the intervening century and a half. In the first revolution monarchy, hitherto considered as a divine right, is still respected in the king's person even at his execution by the use of the nobleman's sword. In the later one, the use of the guillotine aptly symbolizes the more permanent overthrow of monarchy as a political system by a middle class who could more successfully manipulate—and entertain—the masses. What remains constant throughout this period of transformation is the spectacular bloodshed that accompanied the process by which Europe became enlightened. The English, French, and American Revolutions are only the best-remembered conflicts amid almost constant warfare. The Age of Reason could just as fittingly be called the Age of Revolution.

> *The Age of Reason could just as fittingly be called the Age of Revolution.*

France and England were the two primary poles generating the massive charge of intellectual and political energy that spread so much "light" all over Europe and beyond. These neighboring societies were different in important ways. France was officially Catholic, with an absolutist monarchy, and philosophers who favored deductive and abstract systematizing. England was officially Protestant, had a more democratic monarchy, and tended philosophically more toward positivism and inductive reasoning from empirical observation. Many other countries contributed to the Enlightenment and experienced its profound influence, but in general all were responding to the political, social, scientific, industrial, and intellectual revolutions that accompanied the political ones in France and England, the two most centralized and powerful nations in Europe at the time. The term Enlightenment, however, is originally French, and Paris was in many ways the capital of what the French call *l'Age des Lumières*. London alone rivaled it as a seat of government and finance, but as a European cultural and intellectual capital there was no equal to the city where the meeting of the minds of the *philosophes*—principally Voltaire, Diderot, and Rousseau—took place.

What eighteenth-century philosophers themselves baptized as "the Enlightenment" was the continued trend in Europe, after the early modern wars of religion, to question received authority—religious, political, moral, and intellectual. Absolute, received authority was to be tempered or even replaced by the guidance of reason, understood as a faculty common to all humankind. Such questioning brought with it an increasing recognition that reason must also master the passions that drove the wars of religion by fostering religious tolerance alongside free intellectual experimentation and argument.

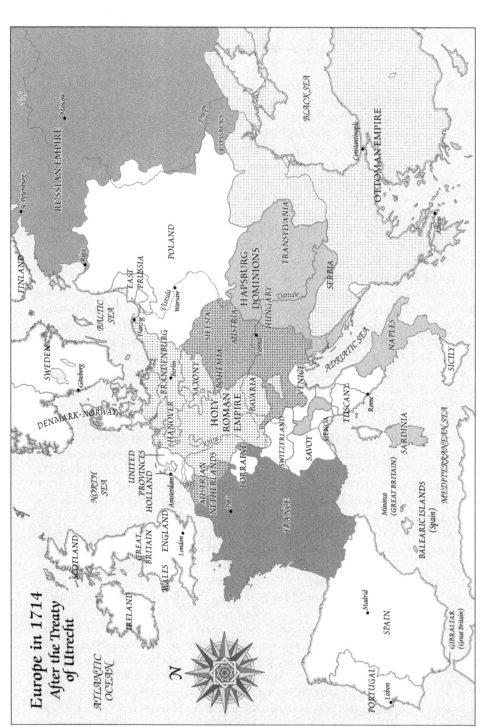

Europe in 1714, after the Treaty of Utrecht.

ORIGINS AND POLITICAL PHILOSOPHY OF THE ENLIGHTENMENT

Of course, the Enlightenment did not emerge out of complete darkness. Its essential impulses arose out of the earlier, bloody struggles over freedom of belief and thought that have been called the Reformation in religion and the "Renaissance" of classical humanist learning. The sixteenth- and seventeenth-century wars of religion left Spain and the Holy Roman Empire—the two major empires of early modern Europe—shattered and weakened by comparison with France and England, which now emerged as its primary nation-states. After Dutch and English forces defeated Spain, crumbling under the weight of its own far-flung colonial empire, the main conflict that continued to divide Europe was the struggle between Louis XIV and Protestant Europe, of which Great Britain emerged as the leading nation. This struggle came to a crisis with the "Glorious Revolution" of 1688, when the Dutch Protestant prince William of Orange supplanted Louis's Catholic Stuart allies on the English throne, banishing the hereditary British king James II and his supporters to permanent exile in France. This Protestant victory was solidified at the next crisis of the British succession, when a German Protestant prince became George I of England (1740), blocking the restoration of the exiled Stuart heir. These foreign princes were served by the philosophers John Locke and Gottfried Wilhelm von Leibniz respectively, each of whom came to characterize the thought of their reigns.

Although they had important philosophical differences, Locke and Leibniz shared fundamental Enlightenment principles. Both called for religious toleration and freedom of thought, and for the crucial role of human reason in understanding even revealed religious truths—in stark contrast to Louis XIV's political absolutism and forced religious conformity. Neither philosopher, on the other hand, advocated freethinking, or "libertinism," to the extent of outright rejection of revealed religious doctrine. "Scriptural doctrine," wrote Leibniz, "is reconcilable with the findings of sheer reason, but it goes beyond them. We believe the Scriptures, because they are authenticated by marks of supernatural intervention in the circumstances of their origin. We believe them, but reason controls our interpretation of them." This statement describes the stance of Christian theism that gradually became the predominant Enlightenment solution to the fundamental tension between religious dogma and freethinking that generated it, from Locke and Leibniz in the late seventeenth century through Voltaire to Rousseau and the leaders of the American Revolution toward the end of the eighteenth century. More radical thinkers, such as David Hume, Denis Diderot, and William Godwin, rejected the authority of revealed religious doctrine altogether, paving the way for Romantic iconoclasm and the "death of God" pronounced by Friedrich Nietzsche in the nineteenth century.

As in the early modern period, religious reformation was tied to political revolution. Jean-Jacques Rousseau described "the social contract" as a bond willingly built up from below by individuals in need of mutual support, rather than imposed upon them from

> *As in the early modern period, religious reformation was tied to political revolution.*

above. His concept crystallized the long-standing critique of monarchical rule by divine right that went back at least as far as John Locke, and prepared the philosophical justification for the French Revolution a century after Locke. The forces that led to the revolution in France were international, and played themselves out in the Americas and

An Emblematical View of the Constitutions of England and France. (Unsigned late 18th-century engraving.)

elsewhere. The German philosopher Immanuel Kant, as well as Rousseau, has been called "the philosopher of the Revolution." Rousseau's rather pessimistic outlook held that humankind had been happiest in a lost state of nature, which had been destroyed by European civilization. Kant's more optimistic view was more representative of the widespread Enlightenment belief in progress and the infinite perfectibility of mankind. As one of his students wrote, "a favorite idea of Professor Kant is that the final end of the human race is the attainment of the most perfect political constitution." Kant was profoundly influenced by Rousseau in his conclusion that all social inequality is unjustifiable, and grounded only in unreasoned prejudice: "[only] the opinion of inequality makes people unequal. Only the teaching of M. R[ousseau] can bring it about that even the most learned philosopher with his knowledge holds himself, uprightly and without the help of religion, no better than the common human being." It was this idea of fundamental human equality, most forcefully formulated by Rousseau and Kant, that gave rise to the concept of inalienable political rights upon which both the French and American revolutions were based, and which still drives the civil rights movement in the United States and human rights activism around the world.

REASON, SCIENCE, AND ENCYCLOPEDIC KNOWLEDGE

Once revealed religious truth was opened to interpretation outside the established ecclesiastical hierarchy and the divine right of kings was stained with the blood of Stuart and Bourbon monarchs, all forms of authority were equally opened to the free interrogation of reason. Alongside the Reformation in religion and the revolutions in politics, the scientific advances and global explorations begun in the early modern period exploded into full-blown industrial revolution and colonial exploitation. The opening up of the whole world, as it seemed to many Europeans, to the power of reason fostered an encyclopedic approach to knowledge. Diderot's and d'Alembert's *Encyclopédie* (1751–1765) was only the most ambitious and influential of a long series of attempts throughout the period to catalogue systematically the entirety of human knowledge and experience, even as knowledge was expanding at a rate hitherto unknown. *The Dictionary of the French Academy* (1694) was followed in France by Pierre Bayle's *Philosophical Dictionary* (1697) and another (1764) by Voltaire, who at the same time was contributing to Diderot's encyclopedia. Voltaire's great comic narrative, *Candide,* is itself a kind of encyclopedic exploration of the uses and limits of reason in a violent and unpredictable world.

In Britain, Samuel Johnson added his famous *Dictionary* (1755) to Chambers' *Cyclopaedia* (London, 1728), followed by the *Encyclopedia Britannica* (Edinburgh, 1768–1771). Modern readers may wonder how such sober reference books could once have been so revolutionary as to provoke lifelong rifts between the *philosophes,* attacks by the clergy, and government censorship. The revolutionary aim of the *Encyclopédie* was the unification of knowledge centered around humankind rather than God. Its anatomical illustrations offended morality. Its descriptions of non-Western cultures called European norms into question. Its explanations of recent scientific discoveries challenged traditional and religious beliefs. Even its detailed descriptions of industrial processes unveiled trade secrets closely guarded by guilds for centuries. The *philosophes* labored at this great project for decades in the hope that the wider dissemination of knowledge of all kinds would be the path of progress toward increased happiness and well-being for all of humanity.

> *Modern readers may wonder how such sober reference books could once have been so revolutionary as to provoke lifelong rifts between the* philosophes, *attacks by the clergy, and government censorship.*

The most revolutionary aspect of encyclopedias and dictionaries was their widespread distribution in print. They bear a complex relationship to the more elitist academies of arts and sciences that sprung up at about the same time all around Europe, nourished by the same general "encyclopedic" project: the unification of human knowledge. The earliest of these Enlightenment institutions, the *Académie Française,* illustrates how the project of unification could lend itself to the centralized control of knowledge, as much as to its democratic circulation.

The *Académie Française,* or French Academy, evolved out of—and away from—the private Parisian salons of the early seventeenth century. Organized and dominated by aristocratic and intellectual women, salons functioned as alternatives to the royal court, and along with wit, civility, and all intellectual pursuits, they fostered strong political opposition to the increasingly centralized royal absolutism of seventeenth-century France. So when in 1634 Cardinal Richelieu, minister of Louis XIII, learned that some of the men associated with the Marquise de Rambouillet's "Blue Room" had recently spun off from her salon to create their own secret, all-male literary society, he wisely offered them government sponsorship. They wisely understood

Supplement.

Antiquités Babyloniennes et Egyptiennes.

Babylonian and Egyptian antiquities, from Denis Diderot's *Encyclopédie*, 1751–1772.

it could be dangerous to refuse. Richelieu excluded women and set his men the task of creating a dictionary that would unify and purify a national literary language out of competing spoken dialects, defining its rules and drawing its vocabulary from literary works they would designate as forming one canonical, national tradition. To this day the *Académie Française* defends the "purity" of the French language from foreign influence.

Soon after the founding of the *Académie Française* a number of sister academies for various arts were also organized, including the Academy of Sciences (founded 1666). Both Catholic and Protestant members were included in all these academies, members of the bourgeoisie as well as aristocrats. Yet women weren't the only French thinkers excluded for reasons other than merit. Descartes, Pascal, La Rochefoucauld, Molière, and Diderot were also among those denied entry—as was anyone whose political, philosophical, or aesthetic views offered too much resistance to government control or tended to subvert the goal of separating literature from politics and religious controversy.

Science, as well as literature, was in constant danger of becoming embroiled in social controversy. A surge of new scientific discoveries arose during the seventeenth century, such as the law of gravity, the circulation of the blood, and improvements in optics, navigation, and printing that allowed for far greater observation of celestial bodies and distant continents. These advances created serious challenges to traditional religious and political authority. King Charles II of Great Britain, who had been forced to spend his youth in exile after his father's execution and thus was keenly aware of the need for damage control in government, he learned from his relatives in Paris the trick of harnessing the potentially disruptive intellectual forces of the Enlightenment. Like Louis XIII's minister Richelieu, Charles discovered an informal club of intellectuals that had been holding meetings on its own for some years—in this case, to discuss "experimental philosophy" at Oxford, and then London, during the years of his exile. Like Richelieu, Charles offered his group a royal charter in 1662, with the title of "Royal Society for the Improving of Natural Knowledge"—as much to control the "scientific revolution" as to promote it. Like the French academies, the Royal Society was open to members of various classes

> *The new experimental method probed experience directly rather than accepting unquestioningly the received wisdom of Christianity and ancient philosophy.*

and religious persuasions. The new experimental method probed experience directly rather than accepting unquestioningly the received wisdom of Christianity and ancient philosophy; the perceived threat of this method was softened by likening the close interpretation of God's "Book of Nature" to the new Protestant exercise of scrutinizing the Scriptures themselves. The now legitimized Royal Society was assigned the same task as the *Académie Française*—to create an authoritative dictionary that would define the national language—but instead its members invented a better pocket watch and a machine to create a vacuum. They also began collecting natural and manmade wonders of all kinds in their "cabinets of curiosities," the first proto-museums. Aphra Behn claims in *Oroonoko* to have contributed some South American "rare flies, of amusing forms and colors" to one of these.

The members of the Royal Society were more interested in the Book of Nature than they were in printed books. It took the literary genius and labor of Dr. Johnson, backed by a commercial publisher, to produce the first great *Dictionary of the English Language.* The Royal Society itself had a consuming interest in technology with commercial potential, and it is no coincidence that in the English-speaking world the first dictionaries emerged as a result of free enterprise, rather than being produced under the auspices of state-sponsored academies as in France, Italy, and Germany. In the new United States of America, Noah Webster followed up his first grammar textbook (1783–1785) with his *American Dictionary of the English Language* (1828)— both, like Johnson's dictionary, highly successful commercial ventures.

While the British Royal Society failed to produce its dictionary, the Berlin Society of Sciences failed to produce the encyclopedia dreamed of by its founder, Gottfried Wilhelm von Leibniz. Although Leibniz's encyclopedia never appeared, the Berlin Academy later harbored and supported the authors of some of the greatest encyclopedias and dictionaries of the age when they were persecuted by more repressive states. Diderot and d'Alembert, excluded from the *Académie Française,* were named to the Berlin Academy in 1751 and to the St. Petersburg Academy of the Arts in 1767. The enlightened monarchs who supported these academies stood behind the *Encyclopédie* as a work of international importance, in the face of French government censorship. The Empress Catherine the Great of Russia even offered to finance its completion personally, once French royal permission to publish it was revoked after years of work. Later, when the Brothers Grimm were exiled from the kingdom of Hanover for their resistance to royal absolutism, the Berlin Academy of Sciences harbored them and gave them the financial support to begin work on their great dictionary (begun 1838)—the goal of which was, once again, to define the rules and vocabulary of a German national literary language. The various national academies, like the encyclopedias and dictionaries they sponsored, thus played a dual, ambiguous role: they were at the same time nationalist in their agenda and transnational in their influence, competing with one another to foster the production of knowledge while attempting to censor or control its circulation.

The various national academies, like the encyclopedias and dictionaries they sponsored, thus played a dual, ambiguous role ... competing with another to foster the production of knowledge while attempting to censor or control its circulation.

THE DEATH OF ABSOLUTISM

The most repressive of the learned academies were those established in France under Louis XIV, who could be called an enlightened despot. He was personally fairly liberal-minded and tolerant in matters of religion and literary expression. He indulgently nudged awake his nominally Catholic sister-in-law, the German Duchesse d'Orléans (see page 271), when she fell asleep during mass each day. He was equally indulgent with Molière, whose works were regularly banned by his government. These outsiders were two of his favorite people. Violating court protocol, the King sometimes even liked to enjoy a simple lunch alone with the middle-class playwright, and later authorized his secret interment in consecrated ground when the Archbishop of Paris denied him Christian burial. He sponsored the arts and sciences in the royal academies, theaters, and elsewhere. Nevertheless, his whole government was devoted to surveillance and repression—because the absolute power of the monarchy was already under siege by the aristocracy and bourgeoisie. During Louis's youth, the powerful minister Cardinal Mazarin, having seen royal authority challenged during the previous reign, attempted to consolidate it on behalf of his young charge by diminishing the ancient prerogatives of the peers. This conflict erupted in the civil war known as the *Fronde* in 1648–1653. Coinciding in time with the English Revolution, it was an uprising of the highest aristocracy against royal absolutism, rather than, as in England, a revolt of a Protestant middle class against their king and his aristocratic or Catholic supporters. The French aristocrats lost, and the result was the establishment of Louis XIV's brilliant royal court at Versailles, where all the aristocracy was required to dance attendance, cut off from the resources of fiscal and military support that could be raised in their provincial seats, and ruining themselves with the expense of the lavish display now expected at court.

Louis XIV's long reign was one of order, decorum, and reason, yet the orderly synthesis of all aspects of life and thought became constraining, and reason itself, like social and economic behavior, came to be regulated by strict and often hypocritical rules of custom and religious dogma. People danced in the streets of Paris at the news of Louis' death in 1715—as they would again near the end of the century at his descendant's execution. The subsequent Regency of Philippe d'Orléans on behalf of Louis' five-year-old great-grandson was a period of liberation, exuberance, and possibility. The modern poet Paul Valéry once described the Regency as a rare opportunity for literature, when a whole civilization was in the throes of disintegration. Freedom came too suddenly, and decorum descended into decadence. If the Enlightenment was an age of revolution—in politics, religion, science, industry, and knowledge—it was so because all this burgeoning progress was not free simply to happen. When control was suddenly released or overcome, decadence, bloodshed, and new abuses of power often ensued.

SATIRE AND REVOLUTION

Literature played a crucial role in these revolutionary power struggles, often deployed directly as a weapon through a revival of the classical genre of satire. Ancient Roman writers like Horace and Juvenal had used literary works as a vehicle for open social critique and civil dissent, and eighteenth-century writers imitated them in form and purpose. It is hard for readers of the twenty-first century to appreciate the power of satire in the eighteenth. It may help to be reminded of the repressive conditions under which literature was produced before "free speech" was considered a right. In order to be published, all French books had to be reviewed by a bureaucracy of government and religious censors, for no printer could distribute them without the *privilège du roi:* to circulate one's writings in print was a privilege granted by the king, not a personal right. Royal spies filled court circles, salons, and coffeehouses, and opened private

> *It is hard for readers of the twenty-first century to appreciate the power of satire in the eighteenth.*

letters, trying to control the circulation of unpublished writings. The theater was such a good medium for Molière's social satire because during his time any material could still be staged at least once—before the theater was shut down. Several of the authors whose works appear in this section were imprisoned at one time or another for their writings (Diderot, Voltaire, Sade). The French kings were right to be afraid, after all: the ideas of such writers would lead to the beheading of Louis XVI during Sade's lifetime, just a few years after the deaths of Voltaire and Diderot.

Writing was dangerous, and therefore important. In addition to official government controls on writers, there still survived more lawless, aristocratic prerogatives, which the centralized monarchies of France and Great Britain sought imperfectly to check. An aristocrat's entourage had long functioned as a small army or band of thugs, and these could be deployed against literary offenders with little recourse. When Voltaire satirized a lord, he was beaten up by the nobleman's retainers. The Earl of Rochester (one of whose own satires appears in this section) wielded both the pen and the thug: when a playwright whom he had previously sponsored dedicated a new play to another nobleman, the Earl had him beaten. A few satirists were aristocrats, like Rochester and Lady Mary Wortley Montagu, but most of the prominent satirists of the age were not: Nicolas Boileau-Despréaux, Molière, and Voltaire in France, and in Britain Jonathan Swift and Alexander Pope, "the Wasp of Twickenham." They judged their targets by the measures of virtue and reason, showing shocking disrespect for social hierarchies. The upper classes weren't their only objects of derision; they attacked vice and folly wherever they found it. And they found it so universally that Dr. Johnson wrote of Swift and Pope: "whoever should form his opinion of the age from their representation, would suppose them to have lived amidst ignorance and barbarity, unable to find among their contemporaries either virtue or intelligence, and persecuted by those that could not understand them." Wortley Montagu echoes Johnson's judgment of Swift and Pope with a satirical exaggeration befitting an aristocrat on the defensive: "it is pleasant to consider that, had it not been for the good nature of the very mortals they contemn, these two superior beings were entitled by their birth and hereditary fortune, to be only a couple of link boys"—golf caddies. Satire was thus a weapon in the class warfare that led to the spectacular revolutions of the period.

Satire was thus a weapon in the class warfare that led to the spectacular revolutions of the period.

THE "BATTLE OF THE BOOKS"

Class warfare wasn't the only political struggle in which literature became embroiled. The Enlightenment was characterized by a public battle over literature itself, a longstanding debate arising from the quintessentially Enlightenment concept of progress in human history, and so it was closely related to the scientific revolution and the beginnings of the feminist revolution, as well as political revolution more properly speaking. Since the fall of Rome Europeans had revered classical learning, but for the first time since then it was undeniable that moderns had surpassed the ancients in scientific achievement. The debate was whether it was possible or desirable to achieve similar progress in the realm of letters—what the Enlightenment first called "literature," which included history and philosophy—that is, in what we would now call the humanities. Proponents of the "Ancients" held that the highest achievement in modern literature was the most perfect imitation of ancient models, perhaps with some adaptation to the needs of modern audiences. The "Moderns," on the other hand, claimed that innovation was just as important in literature as it was in science.

In this literary battle, dubbed in English "the Battle of the Books" by Jonathan Swift, satire was both the primary weapon and one of the main objects of contention, since it was itself a neoclassical form. The debate began as the "quarrel of ancients and moderns" (*querelle des anciens et modernes*) in France, where it intensified throughout the seventeenth century, with even the most celebrated poets occasionally hauled up before the *Académie Française* for violating neoclassical norms of poetic propriety. A more general and international battle erupted around a spat between two poets and French Academicians, Boileau and Charles Perrault. In one of his poems flattering Louis XIV (*The Age of Louis the Great,* 1687), Perrault had the audacity to admire the works of writers who broke with the norms of classical tradition, like Molière, above the ancient classics themselves, arguing that French society and litera-ture had progressed to a higher level of civilization and morality than that of Greece and Rome. The playwright Racine and powerful critic Boileau led the party of the Ancients, defending the classics—in strident satires on their Modern rivals—as mod-els that could never be surpassed. In 1697 Louis himself, disliking controversy, adju-dicated the contest in favor of the conservative Ancients. That very year Swift applied the French king's judgment to British letters in his satire against "modern" writing, "The Battle of the Books." This work is the source of the now pervasive phrase "sweetness and light," which Swift claimed the literary imitators of the ancients drew directly from nature, as the bee draws honey from the flower—while the spider-like Moderns merely spun poisoned webs out of their own guts.

Despite the royal decree and international reaction, Perrault and the Moderns were not to be silenced. The same year he published his still beloved collection of *Tales of Past Times, with Morals* (1697), which he soon retitled *Mother Goose Tales.* It includes such perennial favorites as "Cinderella," "Little Red Riding Hood," "Sleeping Beauty," "Bluebeard," "Tom Thumb," and "Puss in Boots." Perrault per-fected the fairy-tale genre in the literary salons of its most accomplished practitioners, most of whom were female, including Marie Catherine le Jumel de Barneville d'Aulnoy (whose works were often translated into English during the period) and his own niece, Marie-Jeanne L'Heritier de Villandon. Like them, he invested with moral value a new aesthetics of the marvelous and improbable based on medieval northern folklore, and rejected the neoclassical principle that morality could be upheld only through Aristotelian principles of plausibility. Modern moral values included the en-lightened defense of women, in which Perrault had directly engaged with his "De-fense of Women" (1694), directed against Boileau's "Satire against Women" (1694). The form of the fairy tale, along with associated Modern viewpoints and values, be-came prominent in European literature with the Romantic movement.

The example of Perrault's fairy tales shows how the stakes in the debate between Ancients and Moderns included not simply the entrenched literary conventions of neo-classicism, but also nationalism and the access to literacy of women and the lower classes. Implicit in the Moderns' position was a conception of literature and its audience as participating in a nationalist agenda, rather than a European-wide reflection of

From this widespread experimentation in literary prose, the modern novel emerged.

the Roman Empire. They espoused writing in modern national vernacular languages rather than Latin, and especially worked in forms and genres, such as tales and romances, which they viewed as indigenous, northern, medieval, and popular, rather than adapting the more exalted classical genres. This increasingly nationalist consciousness grew up alongside and in productive tension with the call by philosophers like Voltaire and Kant for enlightened thinkers to be citizens of the world, engaged in free debate across national boundaries. It culminated toward the end of the period in the work of the Gothic and Romantic writers. The Modern agenda of innovation and nationalism in literature also encouraged those who had "little Latin and less Greek"—little or no education in classical languages and literary forms—to take advantage of the industrialization of printing to create new, popular forms and to circulate them widely. From this widespread experimentation in literary prose, the modern novel emerged.

"THE WOMAN QUESTION"

From its beginnings in seventeenth-century France, the *quérelle des anciens et modernes* was intimately linked to the *quérelle des femmes,* just as widely debated in England as "the Woman Question," a running interrogation into the nature and proper role of woman at all levels—physical, moral, spiritual, and intellectual— that vexed and preoccupied Western European societies from the seventeenth into the twentieth centuries. The subject had been debated already in the Middle Ages, and was discussed by some ancient philosophers. The Enlightenment, however, brought a new urgency to the ongoing questioning of women's traditional role in society. There had always, of course, been exceptions to the prevailing tendency to keep women uneducated and, in particular, illiterate. In the Middle Ages convents were the primary avenue to literacy for women, and in the sixteenth century the rise of humanism lent new prestige to the knowledge of ancient languages and secular letters, even as the Protestant Reformation, with its emphasis on the importance for all Christians to read the Bible, had already led to an increase in the number of lay and married women who read and wrote. These were still a quite small and wealthy minority of the population, however, and the writings they produced were mainly religious, as had been the case with cloistered learned women of the Middle Ages.

It was during the Enlightenment that women in large numbers began reading and writing secular and imaginative literature in all genres—drama, poetry, letters. Above all, and increasingly as the period wore on, women employed the new experimental and popular genre of plausible prose fiction that came to be called the novel. It may well be that more novels were written by women than by men during the Enlightenment period. Paradoxically, the very age which saw unprecedented access by women to literacy and publishing was also one that transformed the conventional European image of femininity from one of barely controlled sexual power and cunning into one of relatively desexualized passivity combined with a new moral rectitude. This change was so profound, so pervasive, and so lastingly successful that it deserves to be called the "great gender shift." To this day many Westerners take for granted assumptions such as that women's place is in the home, that women's sexual drives are weaker than men's, or that women in general are kinder, gentler, more sympathetic, nurturing, and loyal beings than their husbands, brothers, and fathers. Before the Enlightenment, European women were dangerously sexual creatures, tempting man to sin; weak indeed, but morally as much as physically so, and thus naturally unfaithful and unreliable. And all of them worked—from the brewsters, baxters, and spinsters (feminine terms for the once female-dominated professions of brewing, baking, and spinning) to the noblewomen who managed great households or abbeys the size of towns.

Yet the more women themselves wrote and published over the course of the eighteenth century, the more generally women came to be perceived as the sexually passive and morally superior "angels in the house," to borrow a later phrase, whose image has only very recently begun to be challenged. The shift is perhaps most obvious in English literature, as observed in the transition from the late seventeenth-century Aphra Behn, who associated with rakes and whores (and wrote about them), to Jane Austen, still appreciated for her demurely ironic, detailed portrayals of domestic life in the early nineteenth century. In between, the long literary career of Eliza Haywood illustrates how rapidly and thoroughly the shift took hold: she began by publishing best-selling novels about dangerously desirous heroines in the 1720s, but then the success of Samuel Richardson's sentimental novels of the 1740s forced her to take a sudden turn to similarly domestic and sentimental fiction about passively virtuous heroines, in order to stay in business as a novelist. The more women broke out of their medieval alternatives of illiteracy and childbearing or the cloister, the more they became tamed, domesticated.

This "great gender shift" transformed conventional European masculinity along with femininity. The "angel in the house" needed the libertine—the freethinking, atheistic and very male sexual predator—to domesticate, just as the period required that the political liberties fought for in its bloody revolutions become domesticated in the figure of the isolated and damned sexual transgressor. Of Richardson's two enormously popular libertine protagonists, *Pamela*'s Mr. B. is successfully domesticated, while *Clarissa*'s unredeemed Lovelace is punished by death after tormenting remorse. The transformation of the figure of the libertine over the course of the period nicely illustrates the development of the Enlightenment and its transition into Romanticism, for the Enlightenment's increasing emphasis on the individual, in its revolutions against authority of all kinds, led at its extreme to the Romantic movement after the French Revolution. In the seventeenth century, playwrights Tirso de Molina and Molière had featured a roguish hero named Don Juan, a freethinker who exposes religious hypocrisy and is punished for assailing the sexual and social foundations of aristocratic privilege. By the early nineteenth century, in Byron's hands Don Juan becomes a doomed Promethean individualist gloriously but hopelessly hurling himself against the fortress of stale convention in the name of free love. As that century progressed, the upper- and (increasingly) middle-class European men still in control of political and economic power actually bound themselves more than ever in the chains of social propriety, in an effort to tighten their vulnerable monopoly

> *This "great gender shift" transformed conventional European masculinity along with femininity.*

on social power by keeping everyone else even more tightly entangled in those same chains. The charismatic, cheerfully unfettered aristocratic libertine enjoyed a darkly Romantic last gasp in the career of Lord Byron, "mad, bad, and dangerous to know," before degenerating into the effete Victorian dandy—more a fop than a rake—in the novels of Oscar Wilde and Robert Louis Stevenson: a Dorian Gray forced to hide the hideous portrait of his misdeeds, or a monstrous Mr. Hyde erupting periodically to the torment of the proper Dr. Jekyll.

CONCLUSION: ECHOES OF THE ENLIGHTENMENT

Just as the characteristic concerns of the Enlightenment didn't emerge suddenly with the English Revolution in 1642, neither did they vanish with the French one in 1789. By the end of the Enlightenment period, political liberation was only just beginning in earnest, with the French and American Revolutions—for European men of property at least. It had scarcely begun for women of any class, and for slaves it was only a faint and distant glimmer of hope, represented by appeals like Olaudah Equiano's to the British Parliament in the year of the French Revolution (1789; see page 441). Even for European men of the laboring classes, the famous battle cry of "liberty, equality, fraternity" referred to ideals that remained largely abstract in that year. The struggles of all these groups to realize the best promise of the Enlightenment would continue to gather force over the course of the nineteenth century, with the movements for the abolition of slavery, for women's education and suffrage, and for the liberation of workers from the new capitalist oppression—as analyzed by Karl Marx—that was fast replacing the feudal kind. For better and worse, most of the world is still deeply affected by Enlightenment ideas today. Wherever popular democracy and individual civil liberties are valued, or the scientific method and the technological advances produced by it; wherever debate rages over the effects of colonialism, the economic principles of free trade and enlightened self-interest; wherever the plausible fictional narratives called novels are enjoyed, and even wherever the pervasive fear is expressed that young people cannot help but be corrupted by the bad examples they encounter in fictional representations, from pornography to violent television shows—in all these instances and more, the Enlightenment endures.

> *Just as the characteristic concerns of the Enlightenment didn't emerge suddenly with the English Revolution in 1642, neither did they vanish with the French one in 1789.*

PRONUNCIATIONS:
  Académie Française: ah-kah-day-MEE frahn-SEZ
  l'Age des Lumières: LAHZH day leu-mee-AYR
  d'Alembert: da-lahm-BAYR
  Candide: kahn-DEED
  Pierre Corneille: pee-AYR kohr-NEH
  Denis Diderot: duh-NEE DEE-duh-ROH
  Don Juan: don HWAHN
  Fronde: FROND
  François, duc de La Rochefoucauld: frahnh-SWAH deuk duh lah rohsh-foo-KOH

Gottfried Wilhelm von Leibniz: got-freed vil-helm fon LAIB-nits
Mazarin: MA-za-RANH
Molière: moh-LYEHR
philosophe: fee-loh-ZOF
privilège du roi: pree-vee-LEZH deu RWAH
quérelle des femmes: kay-rel day FUM
Marquise de Rambouillet: mahr-KEEZ duh RAHM-boo-YAY
Jean-Jacques Rousseau: zhahnh-ZHAHK roo-SOH
Versailles: vehr-SAI

Jean-Baptiste Poquelin [Molière]
1622–1673

Molière's great ambition in life was to distinguish himself in the preeminent genre of the golden age of French literature: tragedy. He failed miserably—but just as his stage career seemed to be over for good, he made the king laugh. From that moment, he became one of the greatest French authors of all time by creating a new kind of comedy, which he elevated to the status of high literary art.

Jean-Baptiste Poquelin was born and raised to cover with silk damask the ornate gilded chairs on which the king sat with his court. His father and both grandfathers had amassed such a fortune in upholstery that by 1631 M. Poquelin senior was able to purchase the office of upholsterer-in-ordinary to the King. This meant access to court society and a hereditary monopoly for his eldest son, Jean-Baptiste, who was accordingly groomed to hobnob with the aristocracy through an elite education, including law school. His classical training at a Jesuit college known for freethinking nurtured his independence along with his interest in drama (he is said to have memorized all the Latin comedies of Terence—which owed much to ancient mime show situations that survived in the *commedia dell'arte* so popular in Molière's Paris). Upon graduation at twenty-one he replaced his father in the service of Louis XIII for one year. That was enough. Adopting the stage name "Molière" in 1643, he abandoned the family business to run off to the theater, becoming a founding member of the "Illustre Théâtre." Funded by the Béjart theatrical family and managed by the young actress Madeleine Béjart, this upstart company staged the great neoclassical tragedies in a converted tennis court. The venture failed disastrously. Molière's stutter was no obstacle in *commedia dell'arte* mime, but was a serious one to his ambition as a tragic actor. Within two years, bankrupt, he was thrown into debtor's prison. Released when his father paid off his debts, he fled Paris with other members of the original troupe to tour the southern provinces for the next thirteen years as its star, alongside Madeleine as business manager and female lead. By 1650 he was directing the company, and began writing original plays for it.

Molière's company was at last invited back to Paris in 1658 to perform for the young king Louis XIV at the Louvre. Their production of Corneille's tragedy *Nicomède* did not impress, and Molière was judged a mediocre actor. He snatched victory from the jaws of defeat by persuading the king, in a witty closing speech, to allow his company to close by presenting his original farce *The Doctor in Love,* in which he played the lead. The king couldn't stop laughing, so his courtiers all tittered along with him. The result was that the company was allowed to share a royal theater with an Italian company of *commedia dell'arte* mimes led by the renowned "Scaramouche" (Tiberio Fiorelli), who had been Molière's drama teacher, and who left the space entirely to his former student the following year. That year Molière came through with his first major success, *Les Précieuses ridicules* (1659), in which he satirized ladies who imitated the linguistic and literary pretensions, rarefied manners, and ideals of platonic love cultivated in the salons of such important literary women as the Marquise de Rambouillet, Madeleine de Scudéry, Marie-Madeleine de Lafayette, and the Marquise de Sévigné—known as *précieuses*. No mere farce like his earlier comedies, this play addressed contemporary ideas. So incendiary was it considered that it was temporarily withdrawn, probably under pressure from influential *précieuses* or offended members of their circles. This play was perhaps the first modern comedy of manners, in which Molière's innovation was to employ more recognizably realistic characters, speaking a more straightforward language than was customary in tragedy. His satire of the mannered language of the *précieuses* was also indirectly a satire on the stilted verse of neoclassical tragedy.

A writer who achieves fame by exposing recognizable people to public ridicule is bound to make enemies, and Molière made many powerful ones. The year after his inaugural Parisian success (and its suppression), intriguers against him managed to have his theater demolished. His company moved the following year to the Palais-Royal theater, and followed up with another hit which brought Molière to the peak of his career: *The School for Wives* (1662), about the absurd and futile jealousies of a forty-two-year-old man (rather ancient in those days) who wants to marry a young girl. Molière himself was forty and had just wed nineteen-year-old Armande Béjart, who had replaced Madeleine—probably her mother—as Molière's costar, and the newlyweds played the husband and wife roles in the new piece. His marriage actually was troubled by jealousy and differences in age and temperament. Even during their repeated separations, however, the couple continued to act together on stage. Molière often drew on his personal troubles and vulnerabilities for comic material—making fun not only of jealous husbands but of middle-class men who, like himself, mixed with the aristocracy; playing the hypochondriac in *The Imaginary Invalid* when he was really at death's door; and even making two plays out of the extended controversy that arose in response to *The School for Wives,* which included charges of bad art and bad morals. In March 1663 he published the text of *The School for Wives,* dedicating it to "Madame" (Elizabeth Charlotte, Duchess of Orléans), the king's sister-in-law, which resulted in a generous royal pension, citing Molière as an "excellent comic poet." His company was soon renamed "The King's Company." That December the controversy reached its nadir when a rival actor wrote to the king accusing Molière of having "married the daughter and slept with the mother." This was effectively rebuffed when Louis XIV himself served as godfather in February 1664 to the son Armande had just borne Molière (the baby died soon after).

Tartuffe premiered later in 1664, a satire on religious hypocrisy. Another brilliant success, it added to Molière's roster of powerful enemies the clergy, who now denounced him as a blasphemous libertine. *Dom Juan* (1665), yet another success, was also attacked as impious, so much so that it was withdrawn and never again presented in Molière's lifetime. A daughter, Esprit-Madeleine (his only child to survive), was born the same year. By the next year he was continually ill and estranged from his wife. Yet the several years following saw more than one version of *Tartuffe,* first banned under pressure from the clergy but then revived to acclaim, and another of his greatest plays, *The Bourgeois Gentleman* (1670). In 1672 Madeleine Béjart died, Molière was reconciled with Armande, and a second son was born, who also died in infancy. He wrote *The Imaginary Invalid* so that he could perform the lead role even with his horrible cough. A theatrical rival, Lully, succeeded in having the play rejected for court performance; nevertheless it was a success at the Palais-Royal. Molière was overcome by coughing in the middle of the fourth performance on February seventeenth, and died soon after. Burial in consecrated ground was at first refused by the Archbishop of Paris, as it would be later to Voltaire, but on the King's petition it was permitted, albeit at night and without ceremony. Lully took over the Palais-Royal theater after Molière's death, but in 1680 his former company, having merged with its rivals, formed the *Comédie Française,* which remains to this day France's leading company for classical theater.

TARTUFFE

Tartuffe; or The Impostor (1664–1669), has been considered Molière's masterpiece by many critics ever since its first publication. Voltaire wrote, "*Tartuffe* is a eulogy of Molière that will last as long as the French language." This play exemplifies the original contributions to drama for which all his best work is known, combining poetic yet plain language with the broad, physical routines of farce and the stock situations of the ancient *commedia dell'arte* theater to create plausible plots about recognizably current character types. Tartuffe, the religious hypocrite, is perhaps the most famous of the major satirical character types featured in Molière's mature work, which also include the jealous husband, the spendthrift, the miser, the snob, the vulgar social climber, the learned lady, and the hypochondriac. The aesthetic norms of the period held that literature should instruct as well as delight, rendering comedy morally suspect, as more frivolous and less instructive than tragedy; but Molière sought to teach through the cautionary character types he created.

Molière's innovative, modern approach to theater was fabulously successful in his time but also caused repeated explosive controversies. *Tartuffe* was not the first of his plays to send shock waves of scandal and bitter aesthetic and moral controversy through Parisian society; for it was not the first of his plays to use the combination of stock comic plot devices with recognizable character types to afford commentary on the contemporary social scene. *The Ridiculous Précieuses* had ruffled feathers as early as 1659, while *The School for Wives* engendered a sustained critical controversy, dubbed by one participant "The Comic War," which exploded theatrical as well as literary rivalries while fueling the antagonisms of literary women and religious prudes. These hostile rivalries had everything to do with the immense popular appeal of Molière's plays. The critic Boileau's response to the controversy, addressed to Molière a mere week after the first performance of *The School for Wives*, reassured him, "If you pleased a bit less, you would not displease so much." For several years thereafter, the play was attacked in a whole series of critical dialogues and satirical one-act plays published by numerous rival writers and actors. Molière replied with his own brief plays, in which he rebuts rivals in the established theater by satirizing the mannered and emphatic tragic delivery then in vogue, using his own more natural acting style. The force and duration of the Comic War, and the repeated controversies in response to his later plays, show how new and how threatening to the social and literary status quo were Molière's innovations in creating serious literary drama with broad popular appeal, his alterations to the conventional styles of language and acting then dominating the established theater, and his attacks on powerful social groups.

No group, however, was more powerful than the Church in Molière's time, and those already offended by what they saw as blasphemous elements in *The School for Wives* (principally in a scene where the husband is made to look absurd as he lectures his wife on the ten rules of marriage, which some saw as a mockery of the Ten Commandments) became implacable when he turned his sights from the character type of the jealous husband to that of the religious hypocrite. The court of Louis XIV, as the letters of his sister-in-law Duchess of Orleans collected in this volume so vividly illustrate, was deeply ambivalent about theatrical spectacle, and the early reception of Tartuffe expresses that ambivalence to a degree that may now appear incomprehensibly contradictory. The theater in general was under severe and sustained attack from this period through that of Rousseau for what was seen as its general fostering of immorality, indecency, and irreligion. Yet Louis XIV was known as the Sun King not only for his splendor but also for his enlightened liberality, his fostering of the arts and sciences, and his love of the pleasure and luxury that he lavished in every form on his court, which could itself be seen as one extended theatrical spectacle. Indeed *Tartuffe* was first performed at one of the Sun King's most lavish court entertainments, which he called "The Enchanted Island," where his courtiers were to forget the outside world in a weeklong round of pleasures in the gardens of Versailles. A first version of Molière's play in three acts, entitled *The Hypocrite*, was presented between a ballet and a jousting tournament on 12 May 1664. Although the king may have commissioned the play for the occasion, and in any case certainly permitted it to be performed there, a few days afterward a newspaper reported that he had deemed it "injurious to religion, and capable of producing very dangerous consequences." Pamphlets were published denouncing Molière as a libertine and calling for him to be burned at the stake. While the king's official report declared the play amusing and did not doubt the author's good intentions, he forbade its public performance until it could be examined by the royal censors.

Molière followed the king to his palace at Fontainebleau that summer to plead his own case with his patron. A nephew of the Pope, Cardinal Chigi, was there on a delegation from Rome, and took up the examination of Molière's play. He approved it, finding nothing offensive to Christianity, upon which Molière wrote a formal petition to the king asking for permission to stage a public performance. Molière's request was refused, and yet the play continued to circulate and to be performed and read privately in the homes of the aristocracy for several years. The Versailles version was performed at the palace of the king's brother, and the complete, five-act play was performed two months later at the palace of his wife, the Duchess of Orleans in honor of the prince de Condé, who thereupon declared himself its staunchest defender and Molière's friend and protector. Although the king continued to ban public performances, he compensated Molière and his company for the resulting loss of revenue by instituting a royal pension of 6,000 livres for him in August 1665, increasing it still more soon after. Meanwhile the grandest of the *précieuses*—the group targeted by Molière's first successful satire of a few years earlier—made it the height of fashion to host dramatic readings of a four-act version of the play in their salons.

With his next play, *Dom Juan* (1665), also banned and denounced on similar charges of libertinism, Molière sought to evade the ban on *Tartuffe* by performing a new and altered version of the play at the Palais-Royal theater, re-entitled *The Impostor*, with five acts, a protagonist named Panulphe who represented a higher social class than the Tartuffe character, and a general softening of the play's language and tone. Nevertheless the very next day, on 6 August 1667, the president of the Parisian parliament banned the play until further notice. Molière again took his case to the king himself, closing his theater and actually sending two of his actors to Flanders, where the king was engaged in the siege of Lille, bearing a second formal petition. Still no favorable answer was forthcoming, and meanwhile the archbishop of Paris banned even the private reading of the play. It is speculated that Molière made the play more complex but also made its acceptance more difficult by satirizing not only Tartuffe, the con man who only pretends to be devout, but also Orgon, the sincerely religious man whose subtler fault is to be too rigid and extreme in his virtue. It is possible at the same time that the king was torn between his own fondness for the playwright and the pleasures he offered, on the one hand, and the rigid Catholicism of his mother, Anne of Austria, on the other. In any event, another year and half would pass before the authorities relented and the play was once again put on at the Palais-Royal, where it went through more than thirty performances in its first season, with Molière himself in the role of Orgon and the Béjart sisters as Mme Pernelle and Dorine. As is so often the case, the very prohibition of the play seems to have contributed to its huge success. Molière published it at his own expense after the first performance in 1669; it was snapped up by a publisher who rapidly produced a second edition. After that it was revived frequently in France, and inspired a number of different English adaptations through the middle of the eighteenth century, by such authors as Congreve and Cibber.

That Molière became such a threat within only five years on the Parisian theater scene—beginning with *The Ridiculous Précieuses* and *The School for Wives* and succeeded swiftly by *Tartuffe* and *Dom Juan*—demonstrates how important was the enthusiastic public response to his new brand of comedy. Crucial as was the king's support to Molière's ability to continue producing plays in Paris in the face of scandal, it never would have been sufficient, alone, to make them survive the centuries.

Tartuffe[1]

Characters[2]

MADAME PERNELLE, *Orgon's mother*
ORGON, *Elmire's husband*
ELMIRE, *Orgon's wife*
DAMIS, *Orgon's son, Elmire's stepson*
MARIANE, *Orgon's daughter, Elmire's stepdaughter, in love with Valère*
VALÈRE, *in love with Mariane*
CLÉANTE, *Orgon's brother-in-law*
TARTUFFE, *a hypocrite*
DORINE, *Mariane's lady's-maid*
M. LOYAL, *a bailiff*
A POLICE OFFICER
FLIPOTE, *Mme. Pernelle's maid*

The scene throughout: Orgon's house in Paris

ACT 1

Scene 1[3]

Madame Pernelle and Flipote, her maid, Elmire, Mariane, Dorine, Damis, Cléante

MADAME PERNELLE: Come, come, Flipote; it's time I left this place.
ELMIRE: I can't keep up, you walk at such a pace.
MADAME PERNELLE: Don't trouble, child; no need to show me out.
　　It's not your manners I'm concerned about.
ELMIRE: We merely pay you the respect we owe.
　　But, Mother, why this hurry? Must you go?
MADAME PERNELLE: I must. This house appals me. No one in it
　　Will pay attention for a single minute.
10　I offer good advice, but you won't hear it.
　　Children, I take my leave much vexed in spirit.
　　You all break in and chatter on and on.
　　It's like a madhouse with the keeper gone.
DORINE: If . . .
MADAME PERNELLE: Girl, you talk too much, and I'm afraid
　　You're far too saucy for a lady's-maid.
15　You push in everywhere and have your say.

---

1. Translated by Richard Wilbur.
2. The name Tartuffe has been traced back to an older word associated with liar or charlatan: *truffer,* "to deceive" or "to cheat." Then there was also the Italian actor Tartufo, physically deformed and truffle shaped. Most of the other names are typical of the genre of court comedy and possess rather elegant connotations of pastoral and *bergerie.* Dorine would be a *demoiselle de campagne* and not a mere maid, that is, a female companion to Mariane of roughly the same social status. This in part accounts for the liberties she takes in conversation with Orgon, Madame Pernelle, and others. Her name is short for Théodorine.
3. In French drama, the scene changes every time a character enters or exits.

DAMIS: But . . .

MADAME PERNELLE: You, boy, grow more foolish every day.
        To think my grandson should be such a dunce!
        I've said a hundred times, if I've said it once,
        That if you keep the course on which you've started,
20   You'll leave your worthy father broken-hearted.

MARIANE: I think . . .

MADAME PERNELLE: And you, his sister, seem so pure,
        So shy, so innocent, and so demure.
        But you know what they say about still waters.
        I pity parents with secretive daughters.

ELMIRE: Now, Mother . . .

MADAME PERNELLE: And as for you, child, let me add
        That your behavior is extremely bad,
        And a poor example for these children, too.
        Their dear, dead mother did far better than you.
        You're much too free with money, and I'm distressed
30   To see you so elaborately dressed.
        When it's one's husband that one aims to please,
        One has no need of costly fripperies.

CLÉANTE: Oh, Madam, really . . .

MADAME PERNELLE: You are her brother, Sir,
        And I respect and love you; yet if I were
35   My son, this lady's good and pious spouse,
        I wouldn't make you welcome in my house.
        You're full of worldly counsels which, I fear,
        Aren't suitable for decent folk to hear.
        I've spoken bluntly, Sir; but it behooves us
40   Not to mince words when righteous fervor moves us.

DAMIS: Your man Tartuffe is full of holy speeches . . .

MADAME PERNELLE: And practises precisely what he preaches.
        He's a fine man, and should be listened to.
        I will not hear him mocked by fools like you.

DAMIS: Good God! Do you expect me to submit
        To the tyranny of that carping hypocrite?
        Must we forgo all joys and satisfactions
        Because that bigot censures all our actions?

DORINE: To hear him talk—and he talks all the time—
50   There's nothing one can do that's not a crime.
        He rails at everything, your dear Tartuffe.

MADAME PERNELLE: Whatever he reproves deserves reproof.
        He's out to save your souls, and all of you
        Must love him, as my son would have you do.

DAMIS: Ah no, Grandmother, I could never take
        To such a rascal, even for my father's sake.
        That's how I feel, and I shall not dissemble.

His every action makes me seethe and tremble
With helpless anger, and I have no doubt
60   That he and I will shortly have it out.
DORINE: Surely it is a shame and a disgrace
To see this man usurp the master's place—
To see this beggar who, when first he came,
Had not a shoe or shoestring to his name
65   So far forget himself that he behaves
As if the house were his, and we his slaves.
MADAME PERNELLE: Well, mark my words, your souls would fare far better
If you obeyed his precepts to the letter.
DORINE: You see him as a saint. I'm far less awed;
70   In fact, I see right through him. He's a fraud.
MADAME PERNELLE: Nonsense!
DORINE: His man Laurent's the same, or worse;
I'd not trust either with a penny purse.
MADAME PERNELLE: I can't say what his servant's morals may be;
His own great goodness I can guarantee.
75   You all regard him with distaste and fear
Because he tells you what you're loath to hear,
Condemns your sins, points out your moral flaws,
And humbly strives to further Heaven's cause.
DORINE: If sin is all that bothers him, why is it
80   He's so upset when folk drop in to visit?
Is Heaven so outraged by a social call
That he must prophesy against us all?
I'll tell you what I think: if you ask me,
He's jealous of my mistress' company.
MADAME PERNELLE: Rubbish!
85   [To Elmire.]   He's not alone, child, in complaining
Of all your promiscuous entertaining.
Why, the whole neighborhood's upset, I know,
By all these carriages that come and go,
With crowds of guests parading in and out
90   And noisy servants loitering about.
In all of this, I'm sure there's nothing vicious;
But why give people cause to be suspicious?
CLÉANTE: They need no cause; they'll talk in any case.
Madam, this world would be a joyless place
95   If, fearing what malicious tongues might say,
We locked our doors and turned our friends away.
And even if one did so dreary a thing,
D' you think those tongues would cease their chattering?
One can't fight slander; it's a losing battle;
100   Let us instead ignore their tittle-tattle.
Let's strive to live by conscience clear decrees,
And let the gossips gossip as they please.

DORINE: If there is talk against us, I know the source:
  It's Daphne and her little husband, of course.
105 Those who have greatest cause for guilt and shame
  Are quickest to besmirch a neighbor's name.
  When there's a chance for libel, they never miss it;
  When something can be made to seem illicit
  They're off at once to spread the joyous news,
110 Adding to fact what fantasies they choose.
  By talking up their neighbor's indiscretions
  They seek to camouflage their own transgressions,
  Hoping that others' innocent affairs
  Will lend a hue of innocence to theirs,
115 Or that their own black guilt will come to seem
  Part of a general shady color-scheme.
MADAME PERNELLE: All that is quite irrelevant. I doubt
  That anyone's more virtuous and devout
  Than dear Orante; and I'm informed that she
120 Condemns your mode of life most vehemently.
DORINE: Oh, yes, she's strict, devout, and has no taint
  Of worldliness; in short, she seems a saint.
  But it was time which taught her that disguise;
  She's thus because she can't be otherwise.
125 So long as her attractions could enthrall,
  She flounced and flirted and enjoyed it all,
  But now that they're no longer what they were
  She quits a world which fast is quitting her,
  And wears a veil of virtue to conceal
130 Her bankrupt beauty and her lost appeal.
  That's what becomes of old coquettes today:
  Distressed when all their lovers fall away,
  They see no recourse but to play the prude,
  And so confer a style on solitude.
135 Thereafter, they're severe with everyone,
  Condemning all our actions, pardoning none,
  And claiming to be pure, austere and zealous
  When, if the truth were known, they're merely jealous,
  And cannot bear to see another know
140 The pleasures time has forced them to forgo.
MADAME PERNELLE [Initially to Elmire.]:
  That sort of talk[4] is what you like to hear;
  Therefore you'd have us all keep still, my dear,
  While Madam rattles on the livelong day.
  Nevertheless, I mean to have my say.
145 I tell you that you're blest to have Tartuffe
  Dwelling, as my son's guest, beneath this roof;

---

4. In the original, a reference to a collection of novels about chivalry found in *La Bibliothèque bleue* (The blue library), written for children.

That Heaven has sent him to forestall its wrath
By leading you, once more, to the true path;
That all he reprehends its reprehensible,
150 And that you'd better heed him, and be sensible.
These visits, balls, and parties in which you revel
Are nothing but inventions of the Devil.
One never hears a word that's edifying:
Nothing but chaff and foolishness and lying,
155 As well as vicious gossip in which one's neighbor
Is cut to bits with epee, foil, and saber.
People of sense are driven half-insane
At such affairs, where noise and folly reign
And reputations perish thick and fast.
160 As a wise preacher said on Sunday last,
Parties are Towers of Babylon,[5] because
The guests all babble on with never a pause;
And then he told a story, which, I think . . .
(*To Cléante.*) I heard that laugh, Sir, and I saw that wink!
165 Go find your silly friends and laugh some more!
Enough; I'm going; don't show me to the door.
I leave this household much dismayed and vexed;
I cannot say when I shall see you next.

[*Slapping Flipote.*]

Wake up, don't stand there gaping into space!
170 I'll slap some sense into that stupid face.
Move, move, you slut.

Scene 2

Cléante, Dorine

CLÉANTE: I think I'll stay behind;
I want no further pieces of her mind.
How that old lady . . .
DORINE: Oh, what wouldn't she say
If she could hear you speak of her that way!
5 She'd thank you for the *lady,* but I'm sure
She'd find the *old* a little premature.
CLÉANTE: My, what a scene she made, and what a din!
And how this man Tartuffe has taken her in!
DORINE: Yes, but her son is even worse deceived;
10 His folly must be seen to be believed.
In the late troubles,[6] he played an able part
And served his king with wise and loyal heart,

---

5. Tower of Babel, Madame Pernelle's malapropism is the cause of Cléante's laughter.
6. A series of political disturbances, during the minority of Louis. XIV. Specifically these consisted of the *Fronde* ("opposition") of the Parlement (1648–1649) and the *Frande* of the Princes (1650–1653). Orgon is depicted as supporting Louis XIV in these outbreaks and their resolution.

But he's quite lost his senses since he fell
Beneath Tartuffe's infatuating spell.
15   He calls him brother, and loves him as his life,
Preferring him to mother, child, or wife.
In him and him alone will he confide;
He's made him his confessor and his guide;
He pets and pampers him with love more tender
20   Than any pretty mistress could engender,
Gives him the place of honor when they dine,
Delights to see him gorging like a swine,
Stuffs him with dainties till his guts distend,
And when he belches, cries "God bless you, friend!"
25   In short, he's mad; he worships him; he dotes,
His deeds he marvels at, his words he quotes,
Thinking each act a miracle, each word
Oracular as those that Moses heard.
Tartuffe, much pleased to find so easy a victim,
30   Has in a hundred ways beguiled and tricked him,
Milked him of money, and with his permission
Established here a sort of Inquisition.
Even Laurent, his lackey, dares to give
Us arrogant advice on how to live;
35   He sermonizes us in thundering tones
And confiscates our ribbons and colognes.
Last week he tore a kerchief into pieces
Because he found it pressed in a *Life of Jesus:*
He said it was a sin to juxtapose
40   Unholy vanities and holy prose.

Scene 3

Elmire, Mariane, Damis, Cléante, Dorine

ELMIRE [*To Cléante*]: You did well not to follow; she stood in the door
And said *verbatim* all she'd said before.
I saw my husband coming. I think I'd best
Go upstairs now, and take a little rest.
CLÉANTE: I'll wait and greet him here; then I must go.
I've really only time to say hello.
DAMIS: Sound him about my sister's wedding, please.
I think Tartuffe's against it, and that he's
Been urging Father to withdraw his blessing.
10   As you well know, I'd find that most distressing.
Unless my sister and Valère can marry,
My hopes to wed *his* sister will miscarry,
And I'm determined . . .
DORINE: He's coming.

Scene 4

Orgon, Cléante, Dorine

ORGON: Ah, Brother, good-day.
CLÉANTE: Well, welcome back. I'm sorry I can't stay.
     How was the country? Blooming, I trust, and green?
ORGON: Excuse me, Brother; just one moment.
     [*To Dorine.*]   Dorine . . .
5   [*To Cléante.*] To put my mind at rest, I always learn
     The household news the moment I return.
     [*To Dorine.*] Has all been well, these two days I've been gone?
     How are the family? What's been going on?
DORINE: Your wife, two days ago, had a bad fever,
10   And a fierce headache which refused to leave her.
ORGON: Ah. And Tartuffe?
DORINE: Tartuffe? Why, he's round and red,
     Bursting with health, and excellently fed.
ORGON: Poor fellow!
DORINE: That night, the mistress was unable
     To take a single bite at the dinner-table.
15   Her headache-pains, she said, were simply hellish.
ORGON: Ah. And Tartuffe?
DORINE: He ate his meal with relish,
     And zealously devoured in her presence
     A leg of mutton and a brace of pheasants.
ORGON: Poor fellow!
DORINE: Well, the pains continued strong.
20   And so she tossed and tossed the whole night long,
     Now icy-cold, now burning like a flame.
     We sat beside her bed till morning came.
ORGON: Ah. And Tartuffe?
DORINE: Why, having eaten, he rose
     And sought his room, already in a doze,
25   Got into his warm bed, and snored away
     In perfect peace until the break of day.
ORGON: Poor fellow!
DORINE: After much ado, we talked her
     Into dispatching someone for the doctor.
     He bled her, and the fever quickly fell.
ORGON: Ah. And Tartuffe?
DORINE: He bore it very well.
     To keep his cheerfulness at any cost,
     And make up for the blood *Madame* had lost,
     He drank, at lunch, four beakers full of port.
ORGON: Poor fellow!
DORINE: Both are doing well, in short.
35   I'll go and tell *Madame* that you've expressed
     Keen sympathy and anxious interest.

Scene 5

Orgon, Cléante

CLÉANTE: That girl was laughing in your face, and though
        I've no wish to offend you, even so
        I'm bound to say that she had some excuse.
        How can you possibly be such a goose?
        Are you so dazed by this man's hocus-pocus
5   That all the world, save him, is out of focus?
        You've given him clothing, shelter, food, and care;
        Why must you also . . .
ORGON: Brother, stop right there.
        You do not know the man of whom you speak.
CLÉANTE: I grant you that. But my judgment's not so weak
        That I can't tell, by his effect on others . . .
ORGON: Ah, when you meet him, you two will be like brothers!
        There's been no loftier soul since time began.
        He is a man who . . . a man who . . . an excellent man.
15   To keep his precepts is to be reborn,
        And view this dunghill of a world with scorn.
        Yes, thanks to him I'm a changed man indeed.
        Under his tutelage my soul's been freed
        From earthly loves, and every human tie:
20   My mother, children, brother, and wife could die,
        And I'd not feel a single moment's pain.
CLÉANTE: That's a fine sentiment, Brother; most humane.
ORGON: Oh, had you seen Tartuffe as I first knew him,
        Your heart, like mine, would have surrendered to him.
25   He used to come into our church each day
        And humbly kneel nearby, and start to pray.
        He'd draw the eyes of everybody there
        By the deep fervor of his heartfelt prayer;
        He'd sigh and weep, and sometimes with a sound
30   Of rapture he would bend and kiss the ground;
        And when I rose to go, he'd run before
        To offer me holy-water at the door.
        His serving-man, no less devout than he,
        Informed me of his master's poverty;
35   I gave him gifts, but in his humbleness
        He'd beg me every time to give him less.
        "Oh, that's too much," he'd cry, "too much by twice!
        I don't deserve it. The half, Sir, would suffice."
        And when I wouldn't take it back, he'd share
40   Half of it with the poor, right then and there.
        At length, Heaven prompted me to take him in
        To dwell with us, and free our souls from sin.
        He guides our lives, and to protect my honor
        Stays by my wife, and keeps an eye upon her;
45   He tells me whom she sees, and all she does,

And seems more jealous than I ever was!
And how austere he is! Why, he can detect
A mortal sin where you would least suspect;
In smallest trifles, he's extremely strict.
50   Last week, his conscience was severely pricked
Because, while praying, he had caught a flea
And killed it, so he felt, too wrathfully.[7]

CLÉANTE: Good God, man! Have you lost your common sense—
Or is this all some joke at my expense?
55   How can you stand there and in all sobriety . . .

ORGON: Brother, your language savors of impiety.
Too much free-thinking's made your faith unsteady,
And as I've warned you many times already,
'Twill get you into trouble before you're through.

CLÉANTE: So I've been told before by dupes like you:
Being blind, you'd have all others blind as well;
The clear-eyed man you call an infidel,
And he who sees through humbug and pretense
Is charged, by you, with want of reverence.
65   Spare me your warnings, Brother; I have no fear
Of speaking out, for you and Heaven to hear,
Against affected zeal and pious knavery.
There's true and false in piety, as in bravery,
And just as those whose courage shines the most
70   In battle, are the least inclined to boast,
So those who hearts are truly pure and lowly
Don't make a flashy show of being holy.
There's a vast difference, so it seems to me,
Between true piety and hypocrisy:
75   How do you fail to see it, may I ask?
Is not a face quite different from a mask?
Cannot sincerity and cunning art,
Reality and semblance, be told apart?
Are scarecrows just like men, and do you hold
80   That a false coin is just as good as gold?
Ah, Brother, man's a strangely fashioned creature
Who seldom is content to follow Nature,
But recklessly pursues his inclination
Beyond the narrow bounds of moderation,
85   And often, by transgressing Reason's laws,
Perverts a lofty aim or noble cause.
A passing observation, but it applies.

ORGON: I see, dear Brother, that you're profoundly wise;
You harbor all the insight of the age.
90   You are our one clear mind, our only sage,

---

7. In the *Golden Legend* (*Legenda sanctorum*), a popular collection of the lives of the saints written in the 13th century, it is said of St. Marcarius, the Elder (d. 390) that he dwelt naked in the desert for six months, a penance he felt appropriate for having killed a flea.

The era's oracle, its Cato[8] too,
And all mankind are fools compared to you.
CLÉANTE: Brother, I don't pretend to be a sage,
Nor have I all the wisdom of the age.
95   There's just one insight I would dare to claim:
I know that true and false are not the same;
And just as there is nothing I more revere
Than a soul whose faith is steadfast and sincere,
Nothing that I more cherish and admire
100 Than honest zeal and true religious fire,
So there is nothing that I find more base
Than specious piety's dishonest face—
Than these bold mountebanks, these histrios
Whose impious mummeries and hollow shows
105 Exploit our love of Heaven, and make a jest
Of all that men think holiest and best;
These calculating souls who offer prayers
Not to their Maker, but as public wares,
And seek to buy respect and reputation
110 With lifted eyes and sighs of exaltation;
These charlatans, I say, whose pilgrim souls
Proceed, by way of Heaven, toward earthly goals,
Who weep and pray and swindle and extort,
Who preach the monkish life, but haunt the court,
115 Who make their zeal the partner of their vice—
Such men are vengeful, sly, and cold as ice,
And when there is an enemy to defame
They cloak their spite in fair religion's name,
Their private spleen and malice being made
120 To seem a high and virtuous crusade,
Until, to mankind's reverent applause,
They crucify their foe in Heaven's cause.
Such knaves are all too common; yet, for the wise,
True piety isn't hard to recognize,
125 And, happily, these present times provide us
With bright examples to instruct and guide us.
Consider Ariston and Périandre;
Look at Oronte, Alcidamas, Clitandre;[9]
Their virtue is acknowledged; who could doubt it?
130 But you won't hear them beat the drum about it.
They're never ostentatious, never vain,
And their religion's moderate and humane;
It's not their way to criticize and chide:
They think censoriousness a mark of pride,
135 And therefore, letting others preach and rave,

8. Roman statesman (95–46 B.C.) with an enduring reputation for honesty and incorruptibility.

9. Vaguely Greek and Roman names derived from the
elegant literature of the day.

They show, by deeds, how Christians should behave.
They think no evil of their fellow man,
But judge of him as kindly as they can.
They don't intrigue and wangle and conspire;
140 To lead a good life is their one desire;
The sinner wakes no rancorous hate in them;
It is the sin alone which they condemn;
Nor do they try to show a fiercer zeal
For Heaven's cause than Heaven itself could feel.
145 These men I honor, these men I advocate
As models for us all to emulate.
Your man is not their sort at all, I fear:
And, while your praise of him is quite sincere,
I think that you've been dreadfully deluded.

ORGON: Now then, dear Brother, is your speech concluded?

CLÉANTE: Why, yes.

ORGON: Your servant, Sir.

> [*He turns to go.*]

CLÉANTE: No, Brother; wait.
There's one more matter. You agreed of late
That young Valère might have your daughter's hand.

ORGON: I did.

CLÉANTE: And set the date, I understand.

ORGON: Quite so.

CLÉANTE: You've now postponed it; is that true?

ORGON: No doubt.

CLÉANTE: The match no longer pleases you?

ORGON: Who knows?

CLÉANTE: D'you mean to go back on your word?

ORGON: I won't say that.

CLÉANTE: Has anything occurred
Which might entitle you to break your pledge?

ORGON: Perhaps.

CLÉANTE: Why must you hem, and haw, and hedge?
The boy asked me to sound you in this affair . . .

ORGON: It's been a pleasure.

CLÉANTE: But what shall I tell Valère?

ORGON: Whatever you like.

CLÉANTE: But what have you decided?
What are your plans?

ORGON: I plan, Sir, to be guided
By Heaven's will.

CLÉANTE: Come, Brother, don't talk rot.
You've given Valère your word; will you keep it, or not?

ORGON: Good day.

CLÉANTE: This looks like poor Valère's undoing;
I'll go and warn him that there's trouble brewing.

ACT 2

Scene 1

Orgon, Mariane

ORGON: Mariane.

MARIANE: Yes, Father?

ORGON: A word with you; come here.

MARIANE: What are you looking for?

ORGON [*Peering into a small closet*]: Eavesdroppers, dear.

    I'm making sure we shan't be overheard.

    Someone in there could catch our every word.

5   Ah, good, we're safe. Now, Mariane, my child,

    You're a sweet girl who's tractable and mild,

    Whom I hold dear, and think most highly of.

MARIANE: I'm deeply grateful, Father, for your love.

ORGON: That's well said, Daughter; and you can repay me

10   If, in all things, you'll cheerfully obey me.

MARIANE: To please you, Sir, is what delights me best.

ORGON: Good, good. Now, what d'you think of Tartuffe, our guest?

MARIANE: I, Sir?

ORGON: Yes. Weigh your answer; think it through.

MARIANE: Oh, dear. I'll say whatever you wish me to.

ORGON: That's wisely said, my Daughter. Say of him, then,

    That he's the very worthiest of men,

    And that you're fond of him, and would rejoice

    In being his wife, if that should be my choice.

    Well?

MARIANE: What?

ORGON: What's that?

MARIANE: I . . .

ORGON: Well?

MARIANE: Forgive me, pray.

ORGON: Did you not hear me?

MARIANE: Of *whom*, Sir, must I say

    That I am fond of him, and would rejoice

    In being his wife, if that should be your choice?

ORGON: Why, of Tartuffe.

MARIANE: But, Father, that's false, you know.

    Why would you have me say what isn't so?

ORGON: Because I am resolved it shall be true.

    That it's my wish should be enough for you.

MARIANE: You can't mean, Father . . .

ORGON: Yes, Tartuffe shall be

    Allied by marriage[1] to this family,

---

1. This assertion is important and more than a mere device in the plot of the day. The second *placet* or petition insists that Tartuffe be costumed as a layman, and Orgon's plan for him to marry again asserts Tartuffe's position in the laity. In the 1664 version of the play Tartuffe had been dressed in a cassock suggestive of the priesthood, and Molière was now anxious to avoid any suggestion of this kind.

30   And he's to be your husband, is that clear?
     It's a father's privilege . . .

Scene 2

Dorine, Orgon, Mariane

ORGON (*To Dorine*): What are you doing in here?
     Is curiosity so fierce a passion
     With you, that you must eavesdrop in this fashion?
DORINE: There's lately been a rumor going about—
5   Based on some hunch or chance remark, no doubt—
     That you mean Mariane to wed Tartuffe.
     I've laughed it off, of course, as just a spoof.
ORGON: You find it so incredible?
DORINE: Yes, I do.
     I won't accept that story, even from you.
ORGON: Well, you'll believe it when the thing is done.
DORINE: Yes, yes, of course. Go on and have your fun.
ORGON: I've never been more serious in my life.
DORINE: Ha!
ORGON: Daughter, I mean it; you're to be his wife.
DORINE: No, don't believe your father; it's all a hoax.
ORGON: See here, young woman . . .
DORINE: Come, Sir, no more jokes;
     You can't fool us.
ORGON: How dare you talk that way?
DORINE: All right, then: we believe you, sad to say.
     But how a man like you, who looks so wise
     And wears a moustache of such splendid size,
     Can be so foolish as to . . .
ORGON: Silence, please!
     My girl, you take too many liberties.
     I'm master here, as you must not forget.
DORINE: Do let's discuss this calmly; don't be upset.
     You can't be serious, Sir, about this plan.
25   What should that bigot want with Mariane?
     Praying and fasting ought to keep him busy.
     And then, in terms of wealth and rank, what is he?
     Why should a man of property like you
     Pick out a beggar son-in-law?
ORGON: That will do.
30   Speak of his poverty with reverence.
     His is a pure and saintly indigence.
     Which far transcends all worldly pride and pelf.
     He lost his fortune, as he says himself,
     Because he cared for Heaven alone, and so
35   Was careless of his interests here below.
     I mean to get him out of his present straits
     And help him to recover his estates—

Which, in his part of the world, have no small fame.
Poor though he is, he's a gentleman just the same.
DORINE: Yes, so he tells us; and, Sir, it seems to me
Such pride goes very ill with piety.
A man whose spirit spurns this dungy earth
Ought not to brag of lands and noble birth;
Such worldly arrogance will hardly square
45   With meek devotion and the life of prayer.
. . . But this approach, I see, has drawn a blank;
Let's speak, then, of his person, not his rank.
Doesn't it seem to you a trifle grim
To give a girl like her to a man like him?
50   When two are so ill-suited, can't you see
What the sad consequence is bound to be?
A young girl's virtue is imperilled, Sir,
When such a marriage is imposed on her;
For if one's bridegroom isn't to one's taste,
55   It's hardly an inducement to be chaste,
And many a man with horns upon his brow
Has made his wife the thing that she is now.
It's hard to be a faithful wife, in short,
To certain husbands of a certain sort,
60   And he who gives his daughter to a man she hates
Must answer for her sins at Heaven's gates.
Think, Sir, before you play so risky a role.
ORGON: This servant-girl presumes to save my soul!
DORINE: You would do well to ponder what I've said.
ORGON: Daughter, we'll disregard this dunderhead.
Just trust your father's judgment. Oh, I'm aware
That I once promised you to young Valère;
But now I hear he gambles, which greatly shocks me;
What's more, I've doubts about his orthodoxy.
70   His visits to church, I note, are very few.
DORINE: Would you have him go at the same hours as you,
And kneel nearby, to be sure of being seen?
ORGON: I can dispense with such remarks, Dorine.
[*To Mariane.*] Tartuffe, however, is sure of Heaven's blessing,
75   And that's the only treasure worth possessing.
This match will bring you joys beyond all measure;
Your cup will overflow with every pleasure;
You two will interchange your faithful loves
Like two sweet cherubs, or two turtle-doves.
80   No harsh word shall be heard, no frown be seen,
And he shall make you happy as a queen.
DORINE: And she'll make him a cuckold, just wait and see.
ORGON: What language!
DORINE: Oh, he's a man of destiny;

He's *made* for horns, and what the stars demand
85   Your daughter's virtue surely can't withstand.
ORGON: Don't interrupt me further. Why can't you learn
    That certain things are none of your concern?
DORINE: It's for your own sake that I interfere.

[*She repeatedly interrupts Orgon just as he is turning to speak to his daughter.*]

ORGON: Most kind of you. Now, hold your tongue, d'you hear?
DORINE: If I didn't love you . . .
ORGON: Spare me your affection.
DORINE: I'll love you, Sir, in spite of your objection.
ORGON: Blast!
DORINE: I can't bear, Sir, for your honor's sake,
    To let you make this ludicrous mistake.
ORGON: You mean to go on talking?
DORINE: If I didn't protest
95   This sinful marriage, my conscience couldn't rest.
ORGON: If you don't hold your tongue, you little shrew . . .
DORINE: What, lost your temper? A pious man like you?
ORGON: Yes! Yes! You talk and talk. I'm maddened by it.
    Once and for all, I tell you to be quiet.
DORINE: Well, I'll be quiet. But I'll be thinking hard.
ORGON: Think all you like, but you had better guard
    That saucy tongue of yours, or I'll . . .
    [*Turning back to Mariane.*]   Now, child,
    I've weighed this matter fully.
DORINE [*Aside*]:   It drives me wild
    That I can't speak.

[*Orgon turns his head, and she is silent.*]

ORGON: Tartuffe is no young dandy,
    But, still, his person . . .
DORINE [*Aside.*]: Is as sweet as candy.
ORGON: Is such that, even if you shouldn't care
    For his other merits . . .

[*He turns and stands facing Dorine, arms crossed.*]

DORINE [*Aside.*]: They'll make a lovely pair.
    If I were she, no man would marry me
    Against my inclination, and go scot-free.
110   He'd learn, before the wedding-day was over,
    How readily a wife can find a lover.
ORGON [*To Dorine*]: It seems you treat my orders as a joke.
DORINE: Why, what's the matter? 'Twas not to you I spoke.
ORGON: What *were* you doing?
DORINE: Talking to myself, that's all.
ORGON: Ah! [*Aside.*] One more bit of impudence and gall,
    And I shall give her a good slap in the face.

[*He puts himself in position to slap her; Dorine, whenever he glances at her, stands immobile and silent.*]

    Daughter, you shall accept, and with good grace,
    The husband I've selected . . . Your wedding-day . . .
    [*To Dorine.*] Why don't you talk to yourself?
DORINE: I've nothing to say.
ORGON: Come, just one word.
DORINE: No, thank you, Sir. I pass.
ORGON: Come, speak; I'm waiting.
DORINE: I'd not be such an ass.
ORGON: [*Turning to Mariane.*]
    In short, dear Daughter, I mean to be obeyed,
    And you must bow to the sound choice I've made.
DORINE [*Moving away*]: I'd not wed such a monster, even in jest.

        [*Orgon attempts to slap her, but misses.*]

ORGON: Daughter, that maid of yours is a thorough pest;
    She makes me sinfully annoyed and nettled.
    I can't speak further; my nerves are too unsettled.
    She's so upset me by her insolent talk,
    I'll calm myself by going for a walk.

Scene 3

Dorine, Mariane

DORINE [*Returning*]: Well, have you lost your tongue, girl? Must I play
    Your part, and say the lines you ought to say?
    Faced with a fate so hideous and absurd,
    Can you not utter one dissenting word?
MARIANE: What good would it do? A father's power is great.
DORINE: Resist him now, or it will be too late.
MARIANE: But . . .
DORINE: Tell him one cannot love at a father's whim;
    That you shall marry for yourself, not him;
10   That since it's you who are to be the bride,
    It's you, not he, who must be satisfied;
    And that if his Tartuffe is so sublime,
    He's free to marry him at any time.
MARIANE: I've bowed so long to Father's strict control,
15   I couldn't oppose him now, to save my soul.
DORINE: Come, come, Mariane. Do listen to reason, won't you?
    Valère has asked your hand. Do you love him, or don't you?
MARIANE: Oh, how unjust of you! What can you mean
    By asking such a question, dear Dorine?
20   You know the depth of my affection for him;
    I've told you a hundred times how I adore him.
DORINE: I don't believe in everything I hear;

Who knows if your professions were sincere?

MARIANE: They were, Dorine, and you do me wrong to doubt it;

25   Heaven knows that I've been all too frank about it.

DORINE: You love him, then?

MARIANE: Oh, more than I can express.

DORINE: And he, I take it, cares for you no less?

MARIANE: I think so.

DORINE: And you both, with equal fire,

Burn to be married?

MARIANE: That is our one desire.

DORINE: What of Tartuffe, then? What of your father's plan?

MARIANE: I'll kill myself, if I'm forced to wed that man.

DORINE: I hadn't thought of that recourse. How splendid!

Just die, and all your troubles will be ended!

A fine solution. Oh, it maddens me

To hear you talk in that self-pitying key.

MARIANE: Dorine, how harsh you are! It's most unfair.

You have no sympathy for my despair.

DORINE: I've none at all for people who talk drivel

And, faced with difficulties, whine and snivel.

MARIANE: No doubt I'm timid, but it would be wrong . . .

DORINE: True love requires a heart that's firm and strong.

MARIANE: I'm strong in my affection for Valère,

But coping with my father is his affair.

DORINE: But if your father's brain has grown so cracked

Over his dear Tartuffe that he can retract

45   His blessing, though your wedding-day was named,

It's surely not Valère who's to be blamed.

MARIANE: If I defied my father, as you suggest,

Would it not seem unmaidenly, at best?

Shall I defend my love at the expense

50   Of brazenness and disobedience?

Shall I parade my heart's desires, and flaunt . . .

DORINE: No, I ask nothing of you. Clearly you want

To be Madame Tartuffe, and I feel bound

Not to oppose a wish so very sound.

55   What right have I to criticize the match?

Indeed, my dear, the man's a brilliant catch.

Monsieur Tartuffe! Now, there's a man of weight!

Yes, yes, Monsieur Tartuffe, I'm bound to state,

Is quite a person; that's not to be denied;

60   'Twill be no little thing to be his bride.

The world already rings with his renown;

He's a great noble—in his native town;

His ears are red, he has a pink complexion,

And all in all, he'll suit you to perfection.

MARIANE: Dear God!

DORINE: Oh, how triumphant you will feel

At having caught a husband so ideal!

MARIANE: Oh, do stop teasing, and use your cleverness
    To get me out of this appalling mess.
    Advise me, and I'll do whatever you say.
DORINE: Ah no, a dutiful daughter must obey
    Her father, even if he weds her to an ape.
    You've a bright future; why struggle to escape?
    Tartuffe will take you back where his family lives,
    To a small town as warm with relatives—
75   Uncles and cousins whom you'll be charmed to meet.
    You'll be received at once by the elite,
    Calling upon the bailiff's[2] wife, no less—
    Even, perhaps, upon the mayoress,[3]
    Who'll sit you down in the *best* kitchen chair.[4]
80   Then, once a year, you'll dance at the village fair
    To the drone of bagpipes—two of them, in fact—
    And see a puppet-show, or an animal act.[5]
    Your husband . . .
MARIANE: Oh, you turn my blood to ice!
    Stop torturing me, and give me your advice.
DORINE [*threatening to go*]:
    Your servant, Madam.
MARIANE: Dorine, I beg of you . . .
DORINE: No, you deserve it; this marriage must go through.
MARIANE: Dorine!
DORINE: No.
MARIANE: Not Tartuffe! You know I think him . . .
DORINE: Tartuffe's your cup of tea, and you shall drink him.
MARIANE: I've always told you everything, and relied . . .
DORINE: No. You deserve to be tartuffified.
MARIANE: Well, since you mock me and refuse to care,
    I'll henceforth seek my solace in despair:
    Despair shall be my counsellor and friend,
    And help me bring my sorrows to an end. [*She starts to leave.*]
DORINE: There now, come back; my anger has subsided.
    You do deserve some pity, I've decided.
MARIANE: Dorine, if Father makes me undergo
    This dreadful martyrdom, I'll die, I know.
DORINE: Don't fret; it won't be difficult to discover
100   Some plan of action . . . But here's Valère, your lover.

2. A high-ranking official in the judiciary, not simply a sheriff's deputy as today.
3. The wife of a tax collector (*élue*), an important official controlling imports, elected by the Estates General.
4. In elegant society of Molière's day, there was a hierarchy of seats, and the use of each was determined by rank.

The seats descended from *fauteuils* to *chaises, perroquets, tabourets*, and *plints*. Thus Mariane would get the lowest seat in the room.
5. In the original, *fagotin*, literally "a monkey dressed up in a man's clothing."

Scene 4

Valère, Mariane, Dorine

VALÈRE: Madam, I've just received some wondrous news
    Regarding which I'd like to hear your views.
MARIANE: What news?
VALÈRE: You're marrying Tartuffe.
MARIANE: I find
    That Father does have such a match in mind.
VALÈRE: Your father, Madam . . .
MARIANE: . . . has just this minute said
    That it's Tartuffe he wishes me to wed.
VALÈRE: Can he be serious?
MARIANE: Oh, indeed he can;
    He's clearly set his heart upon the plan.
VALÈRE: And what position do you propose to take,
    Madam?
MARIANE: Why—I don't know.
VALÈRE: For heaven's sake—
    You don't know?
MARIANE: No.
VALÈRE: Well, well!
MARIANE: Advise me, do.
VALÈRE: Marry the man. That's my advice to you.
MARIANE: That's your advice?
VALÈRE: Yes.
MARIANE: Truly?
VALÈRE: Oh, absolutely.
    You couldn't choose more wisely, more astutely.
MARIANE: Thanks for this counsel; I'll follow it, of course.
VALÈRE: Do, do; I'm sure 'twill cost you no remorse.
MARIANE: To give it didn't cause your heart to break.
VALÈRE: I gave it, Madam, only for your sake.
MARIANE: And it's for your sake that I take it, Sir.
DORINE: [*Withdrawing to the rear of the stage.*]
20   Let's see which fool will prove the stubborner.
VALÈRE: So! I am nothing to you, and it was flat
    Deception when you . . .
MARIANE: Please, enough of that.
    You've told me plainly that I should agree
    To wed the man my father's chosen for me,
25   And since you've deigned to counsel me so wisely,
    I promise, Sir, to do as you advise me.
VALÈRE: Ah, no, 'twas not by me that you were swayed.
    No, your decision was already made;
    Though now, to save appearances, you protest
30   That you're betraying me at my behest.
MARIANE: Just as you say.
VALÈRE: Quite so. And I now see

That you were never truly in love with me.
MARIANE: Alas, you're free to think so if you choose.
VALÈRE: I choose to think so, and here's a bit of news:
35   You've spurned my hand, but I know where to turn
        For kinder treatment, as you shall quickly learn.
MARIANE: I'm sure you do. Your noble qualities
        Inspire affection . . .
VALÈRE: Forget my qualities, please.
        They don't inspire you overmuch, I find.
40   But there's another lady I have in mind
        Whose sweet and generous nature will not scorn
        To compensate me for the loss I've borne.
MARIANE: I'm no great loss, and I'm sure that you'll transfer
        Your heart quite painlessly from me to her.
VALÈRE: I'll do my best to take it in my stride.
        The pain I feel at being cast aside
        Time and forgetfulness may put an end to.
        Or if I can't forget, I shall pretend to.
        No self-respecting person is expected
50   To go on loving once he's been rejected.
MARIANE: Now, that's a fine, high-minded sentiment.
VALÈRE: One to which any sane man would assent.
        Would you prefer it if I pined away
        In hopeless passion till my dying day?
55   Am I to yield you to a rival's arms
        And not console myself with other charms?
MARIANE: Go then: console yourself; don't hesitate.
        I wish you to; indeed, I cannot wait.
VALÈRE: You wish me to?
MARIANE: Yes.
VALÈRE: That's the final straw.
60   Madam, farewell. Your wish shall be my law.

[*He starts to leave, and then returns: this repeatedly.*]

MARIANE: Splendid.
VALÈRE [*Coming back again*]: This breach, remember, is of your making;
        It's you who've driven me to the step I'm taking.
MARIANE: Of course.
VALÈRE [*Coming back again*]: Remember, too, that I am merely
        Following your example.
MARIANE: I see that clearly.
VALÈRE: Enough. I'll go and do your bidding, then.
MARIANE: Good.
VALÈRE [*Coming back again*]: You shall never see my face again.
MARIANE: Excellent.
VALÈRE [*Walking to the door, then turning about*]:
                        Yes?
MARIANE: What?
VALÈRE: What's that? What did you say?

MARIANE: Nothing. You're dreaming.

VALÈRE: Ah. Well, I'm on my way.

    Farewell, Madame.

[*He moves slowly away.*]

MARIANE: Farewell.

DORINE [*To Mariane*].:   If you ask me,

70   Both of you are as mad as mad can be.

    Do stop this nonsense, now. I've only let you

    Squabble so long to see where it would get you.

    Whoa there, Monsieur Valère!

[*She goes and seizes Valère by the arm; he makes a great show of resistance.*]

VALÈRE: What's this, Dorine?

DORINE: Come here.

VALÈRE: No, no, my heart's too full of spleen.

75   Don't hold me back; her wish must be obeyed.

DORINE: Stop!

VALÈRE: It's too late now; my decision's made.

DORINE: Oh, pooh!

MARIANE [*Aside*]: He hates the sight of me, that's plain.

    I'll go, and so deliver him from pain.

DORINE [*Leaving Valère, running after Mariane.*]:

    And now *you* run away! Come back.

MARIANE: No, no.

80   Nothing you say will keep me here. Let go!

VALÈRE [*Aside*]: She cannot bear my presence, I perceive.

    To spare her further torment, I shall leave.

DORINE [*Leaving Mariane, running after Valère.*]:

    Again! You'll not escape, Sir; don't you try it.

    Come here, you two. Stop fussing, and be quiet.

[*She takes Valère by the hand, then Mariane, and draws them together.*]

VALÈRE [*To Dorine*]: What do you want of me?

MARIANE [*To Dorine*]: What is the point of this?

DORINE: We're going to have a little armistice.

    [*To Valère.*] Now, weren't you silly to get so overheated?

VALÈRE: Didn't you see how badly I was treated?

DORINE [*To Mariane*]: Aren't you a simpleton, to have lost your head?

MARIANE: Didn't you hear the hateful things he said?

DORINE [*To Valère*]: You're both great fools. Her sole desire, Valère,

    Is to be yours in marriage. To that I'll swear.

    [*To Mariane.*] He loves you only, and he wants no wife

95   But you, Mariane. On that I'll stake my life.

MARIANE [*To Valère*]: Then why you advised me so, I cannot see.

VALÈRE [*To Mariane*]: On such a question, why ask advice of *me*?

DORINE: Oh, you're impossible. Give me your hands, you two.

    [*To Valère.*] Yours first.

VALÈRE [*Giving Dorine his hand*]: But why?

DORINE [*To Mariane*]: And now a hand from you.
MARIANE [*Also giving Dorine her hand.*]:
    What are you doing?
DORINE: There: a perfect fit.
    You suit each other better than you'll admit.

[*Valère and Mariane hold hands for some time without looking at each other.*]

VALÈRE [*Turning toward Mariane.*]:
    Ah, come, don't be so haughty. Give a man
    A look of kindness, won't you, Mariane?

[*Mariane turns toward Valère and smiles.*]

DORINE: I tell you, lovers are completely mad!
VALÈRE [*To Mariane*]: Now come, confess that you were very bad
    To hurt my feelings as you did just now.
    I have a just complaint, you must allow.
MARIANE: *You* must allow that you were most unpleasant . . .
DORINE: Let's table that discussion for the present;
    Your father has a plan which must be stopped.
MARIANE: Advise us, then; what means must we adopt?
DORINE: We'll use all manner of means, and all at once.
    [*To Mariane.*] Your father's addled; he's acting like a dunce.
115   Therefore you'd better humor the old fossil.
    Pretend to yield to him, be sweet and docile,
    And then postpone, as often as necessary,
    The day on which you have agreed to marry.
    You'll thus gain time, and time will turn the trick.
120   Sometimes, for instance, you'll be taken sick,
    And that will seem good reason for delay;
    Or some bad omen will make you change the day—
    You'll dream of muddy water, or you'll pass
    A dead man's hearse, or break a looking-glass.
125   If all else fails, no man can marry you
    Unless you take his ring and say "I do."
    But now, let's separate. If they should find
    Us talking here, our plot might be divined.
    [*To Valère.*] Go to your friends, and tell them what's occurred,
130   And have them urge her father to keep his word.
    Meanwhile, we'll stir her brother into action,
    And get Elmire[6], as well, to join our faction.
    Good-bye.
VALÈRE [*To Mariane*]: Though each of us will do his best,
135   It's your true heart on which my hopes shall rest.
MARIANE [*To Valère*]: Regardless of what Father may decide,
    None but Valère shall claim me as his bride.

---

6. Orgon's second wife.

VALÈRE: Oh, how those words content me! Come what will . . .

DORINE: Oh, lovers, lovers! Their tongues are never still.
     Be off, now.

VALÈRE [*Turning to go, then turning back*]:
     One last word . . .

DORINE: No time to chat:
     You leave by this door; and *you* leave by that.

     [*Dorine pushes them, by the shoulders, toward opposing doors.*]

A C T   3

Scene 1

Damis, Dorine

DAMIS: May lightning strike me even as I speak,
     May all men call me cowardly and weak,
     If any fear or scruple holds me back
     From settling things, at once, with that great quack!

DORINE: Now, don't give way to violent emotion.
     Your father's merely talked about this notion,
     And words and deeds are far from being one.
     Much that is talked about is left undone.

DAMIS: No, I must stop that scoundrel's machinations;
10   I'll go and tell him off; I'm out of patience.

DORINE: Do calm down and be practical. I had rather
     My mistress dealt with him—and with your father.
     She has some influence with Tartuffe, I've noted.
     He hangs upon her words, seems most devoted,
15   And may, indeed, be smitten by her charm.
     Pray Heaven it's true! 'Twould do our cause no harm.
     She sent for him, just now, to sound him out
     On this affair you're so incensed about;
     She'll find out where he stands, and tell him, too,
20   What dreadful strife and trouble will ensue
     If he lends countenance to your father's plan.
     I couldn't get in to see him, but his man
     Says that he's almost finished with his prayers.
     Go, now. I'll catch him when he comes downstairs.

DAMIS: I want to hear this conference, and I will.

DORINE: No, they must be alone.

DAMIS: Oh, I'll keep still.

DORINE: Not you. I know your temper. You'd start a brawl,
     And shout and stamp your foot and spoil it all.
     Go on.

DAMIS: I won't; I have a perfect right . . .

DORINE: Lord, you're a nuisance! He's coming; get out of sight.

     [*Damis conceals himself in a closet at the rear of the stage.*]

Scene 2

Tartuffe, Dorine

TARTUFFE [*Observing Dorine, and calling to his manservant offstage.*]:
　　Hang up my hair-shirt, put my scourge in place,
　　And pray, Laurent, for Heaven's perpetual grace.
　　I'm going to the prison now, to share
　　My last few coins with the poor wretches there.
DORINE [*Aside*]: Dear God, what affectation! What a fake!
TARTUFFE: You wished to see me?
DORINE:　　　　　　　　　　　Yes . . .
TARTUFFE [*Taking a handkerchief from his pocket.*]:
　　　　　　　　　　　　　　　　For mercy's sake,
　　Please take this handkerchief, before you speak.
DORINE: What?
TARTUFFE: Cover that bosom,[1] girl. The flesh is weak,
　　And unclean thoughts are difficult to control.
10　Such sights as that can undermine the soul.
DORINE: Your soul, it seems, has very poor defenses,
　　And flesh makes quite an impact on your senses.
　　It's strange that you're so easily excited;
　　My own desires are not so soon ignited,
15　And if I saw you naked as a beast,
　　Not all your hide would tempt me in the least.
TARTUFFE: Girl, speak more modestly; unless you do,
　　I shall be forced to take my leave of you.
DORINE: Oh, no, it's I who must be on my way;
20　I've just one little message to convey.
　　Madame is coming down, and begs you, Sir,
　　To wait and have a word or two with her.
TARTUFFE: Gladly.
DORINE [*Aside*]:　That had a softening effect!
　　I think my guess about him was correct.
TARTUFFE: Will she be long?
DORINE:　　　　　　　　No: that's her step I hear.
　　Ah, here she is, and I shall disappear.

Scene 3

Elmire, Tartuffe

TARTUFFE: May Heaven, whose infinite goodness we adore,
　　Preserve your body and soul forevermore,
　　And bless your days, and answer thus the plea
　　Of one who is its humblest votary.

---

1. The Brotherhood of the Holy Sacrament practiced alms-giving to prisoner and kept a careful, censorious check on women's clothing if they deemed it lascivious. Thus Molière's audience would have identified Tarruffe as sympathetic—hypocritically—to the aims of the organization.

ELMIRE: I thank you for that pious wish. But please,
    Do take a chair and let's be more at ease.

    [*They sit down.*]

TARTUFFE: I trust that you are once more well and strong?
ELMIRE: Oh, yes: the fever didn't last for long.
TARTUFFE: My prayers are too unworthy, I am sure,
10   To have gained from Heaven this most gracious cure;
    But lately, Madam, my every supplication
    Has had for objects your recuperation.
ELMIRE: You shouldn't have troubled so. I don't deserve it.
TARTUFFE: Your health is priceless, Madam, and to preserve it
15   I'd gladly give my own, in all sincerity.
ELMIRE: Sir, you outdo us all in Christian charity.
    You've been most kind. I count myself your debtor.
TARTUFFE: 'Twas nothing, Madam. I long to serve you better.
ELMIRE: There's a private matter I'm anxious to discuss.
20   I'm glad there's no one here to hinder us.
TARTUFFE: I too am glad; it floods my heart with bliss
    To find myself alone with you like this.
    For just this chance I've prayed with all my power—
    But prayed in vain, until this happy hour.
ELMIRE: This won't take long, Sir, and I hope you'll be
    Entirely frank and unconstrained with me.
TARTUFFE: Indeed, there's nothing I had rather do
    Than bare my inmost heart and soul to you.
    First, let me say that what remarks I've made
30   About the constant visits you are paid
    Were prompted not by any mean emotion,
    But rather by a pure and deep devotion,
    A fervent zeal . . .
ELMIRE: No need for explanation.
    Your sole concern, I'm sure, was my salvation.
TARTUFFE [*Taking Elmire's hand and pressing her fingertips.*]:
35   Quite so; and such great fervor do I feel . . .
ELMIRE: Ooh! Please! You're pinching!
TARTUFFE: 'Twas from excess of zeal.
    I never meant to cause you pain, I swear.
    I'd rather . . .

    [*He places his hand on Elmire's knee.*]

ELMIRE: What can your hand be doing there?
TARTUFFE: Feeling your gown, what soft, fine-woven stuff.
ELMIRE: Please, I'm extremely ticklish. That's enough.

    [*She draws her chair away; Tartuffe pulls his after her.*]

TARTUFFE: [*Fondling the lace collar of her gown.*]
    My, my, what lovely lacework on your dress!
    The workmanship's miraculous, no less.

I've not seen anything to equal it.
ELMIRE: Yes, quite. But let's talk business for a bit.
45   You say my husband means to break his word
        And give his daughter to you, Sir. Had you heard?
TARTUFFE: He did once mention it. But I confess
        I dream of quite a different happiness.
        It's elsewhere, Madam, that my eyes discern
50   The promise of that bliss for which I yearn.
ELMIRE: I see: you care for nothing here below.
TARTUFFE: Ah, well—my heart's not made of stone, you know.
ELMIRE: All your desires mount heavenward, I'm sure,
        In scorn of all that's earthly and impure.
TARTUFFE: A love of heavenly beauty does not preclude
        A proper love for earthly pulchritude;
        Our senses are quite rightly captivated
        By perfect works our Maker has created.
        Some glory clings to all that Heaven has made;
60   In you, all Heaven's marvels are displayed.
        On that fair face, such beauties have been lavished,
        The eyes are dazzled and the heart is ravished;
        How could I look on you, O flawless creature,
        And not adore the Author of all Nature,
65   Feeling a love both passionate and pure
        For you, his triumph of self-portraiture?
        At first, I trembled lest that love should be
        A subtle snare that Hell had laid for me;
        I vowed to flee the sight of you, eschewing
70   A rapture that might prove my soul's undoing;
        But soon, fair being, I became aware
        That my deep passion could be made to square
        With rectitude, and with my bounden duty.
        I thereupon surrendered to your beauty.
75   It is, I know, presumptuous on my part
        To bring you this poor offering of my heart,
        And it is not my merit, Heaven knows,
        But your compassion on which my hopes repose.
        You are my peace, my solace, my salvation;
80   On you depends my bliss—or desolation;
        I bide your judgment and, as you think best,
        I shall be either miserable or blest.
ELMIRE: Your declaration is most gallant, Sir,
        But don't you think it's out of character?
85   You'd have done better to restrain your passion
        And think before you spoke in such a fashion.
        It ill becomes a pious man like you . . .
TARTUFFE: I may be pious, but I'm human too:
        With your celestial charms before his eyes,
90   A man has not the power to be wise,

I know such words sound strangely, coming from me,
But I'm no angel, nor was meant to be,
And if you blame my passion, you must needs
Reproach as well the charms on which it feeds.
95   Your loveliness I had no sooner seen
Than you became my soul's unrivalled queen;
Before your seraph glance, divinely sweet,
My heart's defenses crumbled in defeat,
And nothing fasting, prayer, or tears might do
100   Could stay my spirit from adoring you.
My eyes, my sighs have told you in the past
What now my lips make bold to say at last,
And if, in your great goodness, you will deign
To look upon your slave, and ease his pain,—
105   If, in compassion for my soul's distress,
You'll stoop to comfort my unworthiness,
I'll raise to you, in thanks for that sweet manna,
An endless hymn, an infinite hosanna.
With me, of course, there need be no anxiety,
110   No fear of scandal or of notoriety.
These young court gallants, whom all the ladies fancy,
Are vain in speech, in action rash and chancy;
When they succeed in love, the world soon knows it;
No favor's granted them but they disclose it
115   And by the looseness of their tongues profane
The very altar where their hearts have lain.
Men of my sort, however, love discreetly,
And one may trust our reticence completely.
My keen concern for my good name insures
120   The absolute security of yours;
In short, I offer you, my dear Elmire,
Love without scandal, pleasure without fear.
ELMIRE: I've heard your well-turned speeches to the end,
And what you urge I clearly comprehend.
125   Aren't you afraid that I may take a notion
To tell my husband of your warm devotion,
And that, supposing he were duly told,
His feelings toward you might grow rather cold?
TARTUFFE: I know, dear lady, that your exceeding charity
130   Will lead your heart to pardon my temerity;
That you'll excuse my violent affection
As human weakness, human imperfection;
And that—O fairest!—you will bear in mind
That I'm but flesh and blood, and am not blind.
ELMIRE: Some women might do otherwise, perhaps,
But I shall be discreet about your lapse;
I'll tell my husband nothing of what's occurred
If, in return, you'll give your solemn word

To advocate as forcefully as you can
140   The marriage of Valère and Mariane,
Renouncing all desire to dispossess
Another of his rightful happiness,
And . . .

Scene 4

Damis, Elmire, Tartuffe

DAMIS [*Emerging from the closet where he has been hiding.*]:
No! We'll not hush up this vile affair;
I heard it all inside that closet there,
Where Heaven, in order to confound the pride
Of this great rascal, prompted me to hide.
5   Ah, now I have my long-awaited chance
To punish his deceit and arrogance,
And give my father clear and shocking proof
Of the black character of his dear Tartuffe.
ELMIRE: Ah no, Damis; I'll be content if he
10   Will study to deserve my leniency.
I've promised silence—don't make me break my word;
To make a scandal would be too absurd.
Good wives laugh off such trifles, and forget them;
Why should they tell their husbands, and upset them?
DAMIS: You have your reasons for taking such a course,
And I have reasons, too, of equal force.
To spare him now would be insanely wrong.
I've swallowed my just wrath for far too long
And watched this insolent bigot bringing strife
20   And bitterness into our family life.
Too long he's meddled in my father's affairs,
Thwarting my marriage-hopes, and poor Valère's.
It's high time that my father was undeceived,
And now I've proof that can't be disbelieved—
25   Proof that was furnished me by Heaven above.
It's too good not to take advantage of.
This is my chance, and I deserve to lose it
If, for one moment, I hesitate to use it.
ELMIRE: Damis . . .
DAMIS: No, I must do what I think right
30   Madam, my heart is bursting with delight,
And, say whatever you will, I'll not consent
To lose the sweet revenge on which I'm bent.
I'll settle matters without more ado;
And here, most opportunely, is my cue.[2]

---

2. In the original stage directions, Tartuffe now reads silently from his breviary—in the Roman Catholic Church, the book containing the Divine Office for each day, which those in holy orders are required to recite.

Scene 5

Orgon, Damis, Tartuffe, Elmire

DAMIS: Father, I'm glad you've joined us. Let us advise you
    Of some fresh news which doubtless will surprise you.
    You've just now been repaid with interest
    For all your loving-kindness to our guest.
5   He's proved his warm and grateful feelings toward you;
    It's with a pair of horns he would reward you.
    Yes, I surprised him with your wife, and heard
    His whole adulterous offer, every word.
    She, with her all too gentle disposition,
10   Would not have told you of his proposition;
    But I shall not make terms with brazen lechery,
    And feel that not to tell you would be treachery.
ELMIRE: And I hold that one's husband's peace of mind
    Should not be spoilt by tattle of this kind.
15   One's honor doesn't require it: to be proficient
    In keeping men at bay is quite sufficient.
    These are my sentiments, and I wish, Damis,
    That you had heeded me and held your peace.

Scene 6

Orgon, Damis, Tartuffe

ORGON: Can it be true, this dreadful thing I hear?
TARTUFFE: Yes, Brother, I'm a wicked man, I fear:
    A wretched sinner, all depraved and twisted,
    The greatest villain that has ever existed.
5   My life's one heap of crimes, which grows each minute;
    There's naught but foulness and corruption in it;
    And I perceive that Heaven, outraged by me,
    Has chosen this occasion to mortify me.
    Charge me with any deed you wish to name;
10   I'll not defend myself, but take the blame.
    Believe what you are told, and drive Tartuffe
    Like some base criminal from beneath your roof;
    Yes, drive me hence, and with a parting curse:
    I shan't protest, for I deserve far worse.
ORGON [*To Damis*]: Ah, you deceitful boy, how dare you try
    To stain his purity with so foul a lie?
DAMIS: What! Are you taken in by such a bluff?
    Did you not hear . . . ?
ORGON: Enough, you rogue, enough!
TARTUFFE: Ah, Brother, let him speak: you're being unjust.
20   Believe his story; the boy deserves your trust.
    Why, after all, should you have faith in me?
    How can you know what I might do, or be?
    Is it on my good actions that you base
    Your favor? Do you trust my pious face?

25   Ah, no, don't be deceived by hollow shows;
      I'm far, alas, from being what men suppose;
      Though the world takes me for a man of worth,
      I'm truly the most worthless man on earth.
      [*To Damis.*] Yes, my dear son, speak out now: call me the chief
30   Of sinners, a wretch, a murderer, a thief;
      Load me with all the names men most abhor;
      I'll not complain; I've earned them all, and more;
      I'll kneel here while you pour them on my head
      As a just punishment for the life I've led.
ORGON [*To Tartuffe.*]:
      This is too much, dear Brother.
35   [*To Damis.*]   Have you no heart?
DAMIS: Are you so hoodwinked by this rascal's art . . . ?
ORGON: Be still, you monster.
      [*To Tartuffe.*]   Brother, I pray you, rise.
      [*To Damis.*] Villain!
DAMIS: But . . .
ORGON: Silence!
DAMIS: Can't you realize . . . ?
ORGON: Just one word more, and I'll tear you limb from limb.
TARTUFFE: In God's name, Brother, don't be harsh with him.
      I'd rather far be tortured at the stake
      Than see him bear one scratch for my poor sake.
ORGON [*To Damis.*]: Ingrate!
TARTUFFE: If I must beg you, on bended knee,
      To pardon him . . .
ORGON [*Falling to his knees, addressing Tartuffe.*]
                        Such goodness cannot be!
      [*To Damis.*] Now, *there's* true charity!
DAMIS: What, you . . . ?
ORGON: Villain, be still!
      I know your motives; I know you wish him ill:
      Yes, all of you—wife, children, servants, all—
      Conspire against him and desire his fall,
      Employing every shameful trick you can
50   To alienate me from this saintly man.
      Ah, but the more you seek to drive him away,
      The more I'll do to keep him. Without delay,
      I'll spite this household and confound its pride
      By giving him my daughter as his bride.
DAMIS: You're going to force her to accept his hand?
ORGON: Yes, and this very night, d'you understand?
      I shall defy you all, and make it clear
      That I'm the one who gives the orders here.
      Come, wretch, kneel down and clasp his blessed feet,
60   And ask his pardon for your black deceit.
DAMIS: I ask that swindler's pardon? Why, I'd rather . . .
ORGON: So! You insult him, and defy your father!

A stick! A stick! [*To Tartuffe.*] No, no—release me, do.

[*To Damis.*] Out of my house this minute! Be off with you,

65 And never dare set foot in it again.

DAMIS: Well, I shall go, but . . .

ORGON: Well, go quickly, then.

I disinherit you; an empty purse

Is all you'll get from me—except my curse!

Scene 7

Orgon, Tartuffe

ORGON: How he blasphemed your goodness! What a son!

TARTUFFE: Forgive him, Lord, as I've already done.

[*To Orgon.*] You can't know how it hurts when someone tries

To blacken me in my dear Brother's eyes.

ORGON: Ahh!

TARTUFFE: The mere thought of such ingratitude

Plunges my soul into so dark a mood . . .

Such horror grips my heart . . . I gasp for breath,

And cannot speak, and feel myself near death.

ORGON: [*He runs, in tears, to the door through which he has just driven his son.*]

You blackguard! Why did I spare you? Why did I not

10 Break you in little pieces on the spot?

Compose yourself, and don't be hurt, dear friend.

TARTUFFE: These scenes, these dreadful quarrels, have got to end.

I've much upset your household, and I perceive

That the best thing will be for me to leave.

ORGON: What are you saying!

TARTUFFE: They're all against me here:

They'd have you think me false and insincere.

ORGON: Ah, what of that? Have I ceased believing in you?

TARTUFFE: Their adverse talk will certainly continue,

And charges which you now repudiate

20 You may find credible at a later date.

ORGON: No, Brother, never.

TARTUFFE: Brother, a wife can sway

Her husband's mind in many a subtle way.

ORGON: No, no.

TARTUFFE: To leave at once is the solution;

Thus only can I end their persecution.

ORGON: No, no, I'll not allow it; you shall remain.

TARTUFFE: Ah, well; 'twill mean much martyrdom and pain,

But if you wish it . . .

ORGON: Ah!

TARTUFFE: Enough; so be it.

But one thing must be settled, as I see it.

For your dear honor, and for our friendship's sake,

30 There's one precaution I feel bound to take.

I shall avoid your wife, and keep away . . .

ORGON: No, you shall not, whatever they may say.
    It pleases me to vex them, and for spite
35   I'd have them see you with her day and night.
    What's more, I'm going to drive them to despair
    By making you my only son and heir;
    This very day, I'll give to you alone
    Clear deed and title to everything I own.
    A dear, good friend and son-in-law-to-be
40   Is more than wife, or child, or kin to me.
    Will you accept my offer, dearest son?
TARTUFFE: In all things, let the will of Heaven be done.
ORGON: Poor fellow! Come, we'll go draw up the deed,
    Then let them burst with disappointed greed!

ACT 4

Scene 1

Cléante, Tartuffe

CLÉANTE: Yes, all the town's discussing it, and truly,
    Their comments do not flatter you unduly.
    I'm glad we've met, Sir, and I'll give my view
    Of this sad matter in a word or two.
5   As for who's guilty, that I shan't discuss;
    Let's say it was Damis who caused the fuss;
    Assuming, then, that you have been ill-used
    By young Damis, and groundlessly accused,
    Ought not a Christian to forgive, and ought
10   He not to stifle every vengeful thought?
    Should you stand by and watch a father make
    His only son an exile for your sake?
    Again I tell you frankly, be advised:
    The whole town, high and low, is scandalized;
15   This quarrel must be mended, and my advice is
    Not to push matters to a further crisis.
    No, sacrifice your wrath to God above,
    And help Damis regain his father's love.
TARTUFFE: Alas, for my part I should take great joy
20   In doing so. I've nothing against the boy.
    I pardon all, I harbor no resentment;
    To serve him would afford me much contentment.
    But Heaven's interest will not have it so:
    If he comes back, then I shall have to go.
25   After his conduct—so extreme, so vicious—
    Our further intercourse would look suspicious.
    God knows what people would think! Why, they'd describe
    My goodness to him as a sort of bribe;
    They'd say that out of guilt I made pretense
30   Of loving-kindness and benevolence—

That, fearing my accuser's tongue, I strove
To buy his silence with a show of love.
CLÉANTE: Your reasoning is badly warped and stretched,
And these excuses, Sir, are most far-fetched.
35   Why put yourself in charge of Heaven's cause?
Does Heaven need our help to enforce its laws?
Leave vengeance to the Lord, Sir; while we live,
Our duty's not to punish, but forgive;
And what the Lord commands, we should obey
40   Without regard to what the world may say.
What! Shall the fear of being misunderstood
Prevent our doing what is right and good?
No, no; let's simply do what Heaven ordains,
And let no other thoughts perplex our brains.
TARTUFFE: Again, Sir, let me say that I've forgiven
Damis, and thus obeyed the laws of Heaven;
But I am not commanded by the Bible
To live with one who smears my name with libel.
CLÉANTE: Were you commanded, Sir, to indulge the whim
50   Of poor Orgon, and to encourage him
In suddenly transferring to your name
A large estate to which you have no claim?
TARTUFFE: 'Twould never occur to those who know me best
To think I acted from self-interest.
55   The treasures of this world I quite despise;
Their specious glitter does not charm my eyes;
And if I have resigned myself to taking
The gift which my dear Brother insists on making,
I do so only, as he well understands,
60   Lest so much wealth fall into wicked hands,
Lest those to whom it might descend in time
Turn it to purposes of sin and crime,
And not, as I shall do, make use of it
For Heaven's glory and mankind's benefit.
CLÉANTE: Forget these trumped-up fears. Your argument
Is one the rightful heir might well resent;
It *is* a moral burden to inherit
Such wealth, but give Damis a chance to bear it.
And would it not be worse to be accused
70   Of swindling, than to see that wealth misused?
I'm shocked that you allowed Orgon to broach
This matter, and that you feel no self-reproach;
Does true religion teach that lawful heirs
May freely be deprived of what is theirs?
75   And if the Lord has told you in your heart
That you and young Damis must dwell apart,
Would it not be the decent thing to beat
A generous and honorable retreat,
Rather than let the son of the house be sent,

80   For your convenience, into banishment?
        Sir, if you wish to prove the honesty
        Of your intentions . . .
TARTUFFE: Sir, it is half-past three.
        I've certain pious duties to attend to,
        And hope my prompt departure won't offend you.
CLÉANTE [*Alone.*]: Damn.

Scene 2

Elmire, Mariane, Cléante, Dorine

DORINE: Stay, Sir, and help Mariane, for Heaven's sake!
        She's suffering so, I fear her heart will break.
        Her father's plan to marry her off tonight
        Has put the poor child in a desperate plight.
5   I hear him coming. Let's stand together, now,
        And see if we can't change his mind, somehow,
        About this match we all deplore and fear.

Scene 3

Orgon, Elmire, Mariane, Cléante, Dorine

ORGON: Hah! Glad to find you all assembled here.
        [*To Mariane.*] This contract, child, contains your happiness,
        And what it says I think your heart can guess.
MARIANE [*Falling to her knees.*]:
        Sir, by that Heaven which sees me here distressed,
5   And by whatever else can move your breast,
        Do not employ a father's power, I pray you,
        To crush my heart and force it to obey you,
        Nor by your harsh commands oppress me so
        That I'll begrudge the duty which I owe—
10   And do not so embitter and enslave me
        That I shall hate the very life you gave me.
        If my sweet hopes must perish, if you refuse
        To give me to the one I've dared to choose,
        Spare me at least—I beg you, I implore—
15   The pain of wedding one whom I abhor;
        And do not, by a heartless use of force,
        Drive me to contemplate some desperate course.
ORGON [*Feeling himself touched by her.*]:
        Be firm, my soul. No human weakness, now.
MARIANE: I don't resent your love for him. Allow
20   Your heart free rein, Sir; give him your property,
        And if that's not enough, take mine from me;
        He's welcome to my money; take it, do,
        But don't, I pray, include my person too.
        Spare me, I beg you; and let me end the tale
25   Of my sad days behind a convent veil.
ORGON: A convent! Hah! When crossed in their amours,

All lovesick girls have the same thought as yours.
Get up! The more you loathe the man, and dread him,
The more ennobling it will be to wed him.
30   Marry Tartuffe, and mortify your flesh!
Enough; don't start that whimpering afresh.
DORINE: But why . . . ?
ORGON: Be still, there. Speak when you're spoken to.
Not one more bit of impudence out of you.
CLÉANTE: If I may offer a word of counsel here . . .
ORGON: Brother, in counseling you have no peer;
All your advice is forceful, sound, and clever;
I don't propose to follow it, however.
ELMIRE [*To Orgon.*]:
I am amazed, and don't know what to say;
Your blindness simply takes my breath away.
40   You are indeed bewitched, to take no warning
From our account of what occurred this morning.
ORGON: Madam, I know a few plain facts, and one
Is that you're partial to my rascal son;
Hence, when he sought to make Tartuffe the victim
45   Of a base lie, you dared not contradict him.
Ah, but you underplayed your part, my pet;
You should have looked more angry, more upset.
ELMIRE: When men make overtures, must we reply
With righteous anger and a battle-cry?
50   Must we turn back their amorous advances
With sharp reproaches and with fiery glances?
Myself, I find such offers merely amusing,
And make no scenes and fusses in refusing;
My taste is for good-natured rectitude,
55   And I dislike the savage sort of prude
Who guards her virtue with her teeth and claws,
And tears men's eyes out for the slightest cause:
The Lord preserve me from such honor as that,
Which bites and scratches like an alley-cat!
60   I've found that a polite and cool rebuff
Discourages a lover quite enough.
ORGON: I know the facts, and I shall not be shaken.
ELMIRE: I marvel at your power to be mistaken.
Would it, I wonder, carry weight with you
65   If I could *show* you that our tale was true?
ORGON: Show me?
ELMIRE: Yes.
ORGON: Rot.
ELMIRE: Come, what if I found a way
To make you see the facts as plain as day?
ORGON: Nonsense.
ELMIRE: Do answer me; don't be absurd.
70   I'm not now asking you to trust our word.

Suppose that from some hiding-place in here
You learned the whole sad truth by eye and ear—
What would you say of your good friend, after that?
ORGON: Why, I'd say . . . nothing, by Jehoshaphat!
It can't be true.
ELMIRE: You've been too long deceived,
And I'm quite tired of being disbelieved.
Come now: let's put my statements to the test,
And you shall see the truth made manifest.
ORGON: I'll take that challenge. Now do your uttermost.
We'll see how you make good your empty boast.
ELMIRE [*To Dorine*]: Send him to me.
DORINE: He's crafty; it may be hard
To catch the cunning scoundrel off his guard.
ELMIRE: No, amorous men are gullible. Their conceit
So blinds them that they're never hard to cheat.
Have him come down.
[*To Cléante and Mariane.*] Please leave us, for a bit.

Scene 4

Elmire, Orgon

ELMIRE: Pull up this table, and get under it.
ORGON: What?
ELMIRE: It's essential that you be well-hidden.
ORGON: Why there?
ELMIRE: Oh, Heaven's! Just do as you are bidden.
I have my plans; we'll soon see how they fare.
5   Under the table, now; and once you're there,
Take care that you are neither seen nor heard.
ORGON: Well, I'll indulge you, since I gave my word
To see you through this infantile charade.
ELMIRE: Once it is over, you'll be glad we played.

[*To her husband, who is now under the table.*]

10   I'm going to act quite strangely, now, and you
Must not be shocked at anything I do.
Whatever I may say, you must excuse
As part of that deceit I'm forced to use.
I shall employ sweet speeches in the task
15   Of making that imposter drop his mask;
I'll give encouragement to his bold desires,
And furnish fuel to his amorous fires.
Since it's for your sake, and for his destruction,
That I shall seem to yield to his seduction,
20   I'll gladly stop whenever you decide
That all your doubts are fully satisfied.
I'll count on you, as soon as you have seen
What sort of man he is, to intervene,

And not expose me to his odious lust
25   One moment longer than you feel you must.
Remember: you're to save me from my plight
Whenever . . . He's coming! Hush! Keep out of sight!

Scene 5

Tartuffe, Elmire, Orgon

TARTUFFE: You wish to have a word with me, I'm told.
ELMIRE: Yes. I've a little secret to unfold.
    Before I speak, however, it would be wise
    To close that door, and look about for spies.

[Tartuffe goes to the door, closes it, and returns.]

5   The very last thing that must happen now
    Is a repetition of this morning's row.
    I've never been so badly caught off guard.
    Oh, how I feared for you! You saw how hard
    I tried to make that troublesome Damis
10   Control his dreadful temper, and hold his peace.
    In my confusion, I didn't have the sense
    Simply to contradict his evidence;
    But as it happened, that was for the best,
    And all has worked out in our interest.
15   This storm has only bettered your position;
    My husband doesn't have the least suspicion,
    And now, in mockery of those who do,
    He bids me be continually with you.
    And that is why, quite fearless of reproof,
20   I now can be alone with my Tartuffe,
    And why my heart—perhaps too quick to yield—
    Feels free to let its passion be revealed.
TARTUFFE: Madam, your words confuse me. Not long ago,
    You spoke in quite a different style, you know.
ELMIRE: Ah, Sir, if that refusal made you smart,
    It's little that you know of woman's heart,
    Or what that heart is trying to convey
    When it resists in such a feeble way!
    Always, at first, our modesty prevents
30   The frank avowal of tender sentiments;
    However high the passion which inflames us,
    Still, to confess its power somehow shames us.
    Thus we reluct, at first, yet in a tone
    Which tells you that our heart is overthrown,
35   That what our lips deny, our pulse confesses,
    And that, in time, all noes will turn to yesses.
    I fear my words are all too frank and free,
    And a poor proof of woman's modesty;
    But since I'm started, tell me, if you will—

40 Would I have tried to make Damis be still,
    Would I have listened, calm and unoffended,
    Until your lengthy offer of love was ended,
    And been so very mild in my reaction,
    Had your sweet words not given me satisfaction?
45 And when I tried to force you to undo
    The marriage-plans my husband has in view,
    What did my urgent pleading signify
    If not that I admired you, and that I
    Deplored the thought that someone else might own
50 Part of a heart I wished for mine alone?
TARTUFFE: Madam, no happiness is so complete
    As when, from lips we love, come words so sweet;
    Their nectar floods my every sense, and drains
    In honeyed rivulets through all my veins.
55 To please you is my joy, my only goal;
    Your love is the restorer of my soul;
    And yet I must beg leave, now, to confess
    Some lingering doubts as to my happiness.
    Might this not be a trick? Might not the catch
60 Be that you wish me to break off the match
    With Mariane, and so have feigned to love me?
    I shan't quite trust your fond opinion of me
    Until the feelings you've expressed so sweetly
    Are demonstrated somewhat more concretely,
65 And you have shown, by certain kind concessions,
    That I may put my faith in your professions.
ELMIRE [*She coughs, to warn her husband.*]:
    Why be in such a hurry? Must my heart
    Exhaust its bounty at the very start?
    To make that sweet admission cost me dear,
70 But you'll not be content, it would appear,
    Unless my store of favors is disbursed
    To the last farthing, and at the very first.
TARTUFFE: The less we merit, the less we dare to hope,
    And with our doubts, mere words can never cope.
75 We trust no promised bliss till we receive it;
    Not till a joy is ours can we believe it.
    I, who so little merit your esteem,
    Can't credit this fulfillment of my dream,
    And shan't believe it, Madam, until I savor
80 Some palpable assurance of your favor.
ELMIRE: My, how tyrannical your love can be,
    And how it flusters and perplexes me!
    How furiously you take one's heart in hand,
    And make your every wish a fierce command!
85 Come, must you hound and harry me to death?
    Will you not give me time to catch my breath?
    Can it be right to press me with such force,

Give me no quarter, show me no remorse,
And take advantage, by your stern insistence,
90   Of the fond feelings which weaken my resistance?
TARTUFFE: Well, if you look with favor upon my love,
     Why, then, begrudge me some clear proof thereof?
ELMIRE: But how can I consent without offense
     To Heaven, toward which you feel such reverence?
TARTUFFE: If Heaven is all that holds you back, don't worry.
     I can remove that hindrance in a hurry.
     Nothing of that sort need obstruct our path.
ELMIRE: Must one not be afraid of Heaven's wrath?
TARTUFFE: Madam, forget such fears, and be my pupil,
100   And I shall teach you how to conquer scruple.
     Some joys, it's true, are wrong in Heaven's eyes;
     Yet Heaven is not averse to compromise;
     There is a science, lately formulated,
     Whereby one's conscience may be liberated,[1]
105   And any wrongful act you care to mention
     May be redeemed by purity of intention.
     I'll teach you, Madam, the secrets of that science;
     Meanwhile, just place on me your full reliance.
     Assuage my keen desires, and feel no dread:
110   The sin, if any, shall be on my head.

    [*Elmire coughs, this time more loudly.*]

     You've a bad cough.
ELMIRE: Yes, yes. It's bad indeed.
TARTUFFE [*Producing a little paper bag.*]:
     A bit of licorice may be what you need.
ELMIRE: No, I've a stubborn cold, it seems. I'm sure it
     Will take much more than licorice to cure it.
TARTUFFE: How aggravating.
ELMIRE: Oh, more than I can say.
TARTUFFE: If you're still troubled, think of things this way:
     No one shall know our joys, save us alone,
     And there's no evil till the act is known;
     It's scandal, Madam, which makes it an offense,
120   And it's no sin to sin in confidence.
ELMIRE [*Having coughed once more.*]:
     Well, clearly I must do as you require,
     And yield to your importunate desire.
     It is apparent, now, that nothing less
     Will satisfy you, and so I acquiesce.
125   To go so far is much against my will;
     I'm vexed that it should come to this; but still,
     Since you are so determined on it, since you

---

1. Molière created his own footnote to this line: "It is a scoundrel who speaks."

Will not allow mere language to convince you,
And since you ask for concrete evidence, I
130   See nothing for it, now, but to comply.
If this is sinful, if I'm wrong to do it,
So much the worse for him who drove me to it.
The fault can surely not be charged to me.
TARTUFFE: Madam, the fault is mine, if fault there be,
And . . .
ELMIRE: Open the door a little, and peek out;
I wouldn't want my husband poking about.
TARTUFFE: Why worry about the man? Each day he grows
More gullible; one can lead him by the nose.
To find us here would fill him with delight,
140   And if he saw the worst, he'd doubt his sight.
ELMIRE: Nevertheless, do step out for a minute
Into the hall, and see that no one's in it.

Scene 6

Orgon, Elmire

ORGON [*Coming out from under the table.*]:
That man's a perfect monster, I must admit!
I'm simply stunned. I can't get over it.
ELMIRE: What, coming out so soon? How premature!
Get back in hiding, and wait until you're sure.
5   Stay till the end, and be convinced completely;
We mustn't stop till things are proved concretely.
ORGON: Hell never harbored anything so vicious!
ELMIRE: Tut, don't be hasty. Try to be judicious.
Wait, and be certain that there's no mistake.
10   No jumping to conclusions, for Heaven's sake!

[*She places Orgon behind her, as Tartuffe re-enters.*]

Scene 7

Tartuffe, Elmire, Orgon

TARTUFFE [*Not seeing Orgon.*]:
Madam, all things have worked out to perfection;
I've given the neighboring rooms a full inspection;
No one's about; and now I may at last . . .
ORGON [*Intercepting him*]: Hold on, my passionate fellow, not so fast!
5   I should advise a little more restraint.
Well, so you thought you'd fool me, my dear saint!
How soon you wearied of the saintly life—
Wedding my daughter, and coveting my wife!
I've long suspected you, and had a feeling
10   That soon I'd catch you at your double-dealing.

Just now, you've given me evidence galore;
    It's quite enough; I have no wish for more.
ELMIRE [*To Tartuffe*]: I'm sorry to have treated you so slyly,
    But circumstances forced me to be wily.
TARTUFFE: Brother, you can't think . . .
ORGON: No more talk from you;
    Just leave this household, without more ado.
TARTUFFE: What I intended . . .
ORGON: That seems fairly clear.
    Spare me your falsehoods and get out of here.
TARTUFFE: No, I'm the master, and you're the one to go!
20   This house belongs to me, I'll have you know,
    And I shall show you that you can't hurt *me*
    By this contemptible conspiracy,
    That those who cross me know not what they do,
    And that I've means to expose and punish you,
25   Avenge offended Heaven, and make you grieve
    That ever you dared order me to leave.

Scene 8

Elmire, Orgon

ELMIRE: What was the point of all that angry chatter?
ORGON: Dear God, I'm worried. This is no laughing matter.
ELMIRE: How so?
ORGON: I fear I understood his drift.
    I'm much disturbed about that deed of gift.
ELMIRE: You gave him . . . ?
ORGON: Yes, it's all been drawn and signed.
    But one thing more is weighing on my mind.
ELMIRE: What's that?
ORGON: I'll tell you; but first let's see if there's
    A certain strong-box in his room upstairs.

ACT 5

Scene 1

Orgon, Cléante

CLÉANTE: Where are you going so fast?
ORGON: God knows!
CLÉANTE: Then wait;
    Let's have a conference, and deliberate
    On how this situation's to be met.
ORGON: That strong-box has me utterly upset;
5   This is the worst of many, many shocks.
CLÉANTE: Is there some fearful mystery in that box?
ORGON: My poor friend Argas brought that box to me

With his own hands, in utmost secrecy;
'Twas on the very morning of his flight.
10   It's full of papers which, if they came to light,
Would ruin him—or such is my impression.
CLÉANTE: Then why did you let it out of your possession?
ORGON: Those papers vexed my conscience, and it seemed best
To ask the counsel of my pious guest.
15   The cunning scoundrel got me to agree
To leave the strong-box in his custody,
So that, in case of an investigation,
I could employ a slight equivocation
And swear I didn't have it, and thereby,
20   At no expense to conscience, tell a lie.
CLÉANTE: It looks to me as if you're out on a limb.
Trusting him with that box, and offering him
That deed of gift, were actions of a kind
Which scarcely indicate a prudent mind.
25   With two such weapons, he has the upper hand,
And since you're vulnerable, as matters stand,
You erred once more in bringing him to bay.
You should have acted in some subtler way.
ORGON: Just think of it: behind that fervent face,
30   A heart so wicked, and a soul so base!
I took him in, a hungry beggar, and then . . .
Enough, by God! I'm through with pious men:
Henceforth I'll hate the whole false brotherhood,
And persecute them worse than Satan could.
CLÉANTE: Ah, there you go—extravagant as ever!
Why can you not be rational? You never
Manage to take the middle course, it seems,
But jump, instead, between absurd extremes.
You've recognized your recent grave mistake
40   In falling victim to a pious fake;
Now, to correct that error, must you embrace
An even greater error in its place,
And judge our worthy neighbors as a whole
By what you've learned of one corrupted soul?
45   Come, just because one rascal made you swallow
A show of zeal which turned out to be hollow,
Shall you conclude that all men are deceivers,
And that, today, there are no true believers?
Let atheists make that foolish inference;
50   Learn to distinguish virtue from pretense,
Be cautious in bestowing admiration,
And cultivate a sober moderation.
Don't humor fraud, but also don't asperse
True piety; the latter fault is worse,
55   And it is best to err, if err one must,
As you have done, upon the side of trust.

Scene 2

Damis, Orgon, Cléante

DAMIS: Father, I hear that scoundrel's uttered threats
　　　Against you; that he pridefully forgets
　　　How, in his need, he was befriended by you,
　　　And means to use your gifts to crucify you.
ORGON: It's true, my boy. I'm too distressed for tears.
DAMIS: Leave it to me, Sir; let me trim his ears.
　　　Faced with such insolence, we must not waver.
　　　I shall rejoice in doing you the favor
　　　Of cutting short his life, and your distress.
CLÉANTE: What a display of young hotheadedness!
　　　Do learn to moderate your fits of rage.
　　　In this just kingdom, this enlightened age,
　　　One does not settle things by violence.

Scene 3

Madame Pernelle, Mariane, Elmire, Dorine, Damis, Orgon, Cléante

MADAME PERNELLE: I hear strange tales of very strange events.
ORGON: Yes, strange events which these two eyes beheld.
　　　The man's ingratitude is unparalleled.
　　　I save a wretched pauper from starvation,
5　　House him, and treat him like a blood relation,
　　　Shower him every day with my largesse,
　　　Give him my daughter, and all that I possess;
　　　And meanwhile the unconscionable knave
　　　Tries to induce my wife to misbehave;
10　　And not content with such extreme rascality,
　　　Now threatens me with my own liberality,
　　　And aims, by taking base advantage of
　　　The gifts I gave him out of Christian love,
　　　To drive me from my house, a ruined man,
15　　And make me end a pauper, as he began.
DORINE: Poor fellow!
MADAME PERNELLE: No, my son, I'll never bring
　　　Myself to think him guilty of such a thing.
ORGON: How's that?
MADAME PERNELLE: The righteous always were maligned.
ORGON: Speak clearly, Mother. Say what's on your mind.
MADAME PERNELLE: I mean that I can smell a rat, my dear.
　　　You know how everybody hates him, here.
ORGON: That has no bearing on the case at all.
MADAME PERNELLE: I told you a hundred times, when you were small,
　　　That virtue in this world is hated ever;
25　　Malicious men may die, but malice never.
ORGON: No doubt that's true, but how does it apply?
MADAME PERNELLE: They've turned you against him by a clever lie.

ORGON: I've told you, I was there and saw it done.

MADAME PERNELLE: Ah, slanderers will stop at nothing, Son.

ORGON: Mother, I'll lose my temper . . . For the last time,
    I tell you I was witness to the crime.

MADAME PERNELLE: The tongues of spite are busy night and noon,
    And to their venom no man is immune.

ORGON: You're talking nonsense. Can't you realize
35   I saw it; saw it; saw it with my eyes?
    Saw, do you understand me? Must I shout it
    Into your ears before you'll cease to doubt it?

MADAME PERNELLE: Appearances can deceive, my son. Dear me,
    We cannot always judge by what we see.

ORGON: Drat! Drat!

MADAME PERNELLE: One often interprets things awry;
    Good can seem evil to a suspicious eye.

ORGON: Was I to see his pawing at Elmire
    As an act of charity?

MADAME PERNELLE: Till his guilt is clear,
    A man deserves the benefits of the doubt.
45   You should have waited, to see how things turned out.

ORGON: Great God in Heaven, what more proof did I need?
    Was I to sit there, watching, until he'd . . .
    You drive me to the brink of impropriety.

MADAME PERNELLE: No, no, a man of such surpassing piety
50   Could not do such a thing. You cannot shake me.
    I don't believe it, and you shall not make me.

ORGON: You vex me so that, if you weren't my mother,
    I'd say to you . . . some dreadful thing or other.

DORINE: It's your turn now, Sir, not to be listened to;
55   You'd not trust us, and now she won't trust you.

CLÉANTE: My friends, we're wasting time which should be spent
    In facing up to our predicament.
    I fear that scoundrel's threats weren't made in sport.

DAMIS: Do you think he'd have the nerve to go to court?

ELMIRE: I'm sure he won't: they'd find it all too crude
    A case of swindling and ingratitude.

CLÉANTE: Don't be too sure. He won't be at a loss
    To give his claims a high and righteous gloss;
    And clever rogues with far less valid cause
65   Have trapped their victims in a web of laws.
    I say again that to antagonize
    A man so strongly armed was most unwise.

ORGON: I know it; but the man's appalling cheek
    Outraged me so, I couldn't control my pique.

CLÉANTE: I wish to Heaven that we could devise
    Some truce between you, or some compromise.

ELMIRE: If I had known what cards he held, I'd not
    Have roused his anger by my little plot.

ORGON [To Dorine, as M. Loyal enters.]:

What is that fellow looking for? Who is he?
75   Go talk to him—and tell him that I'm busy.

Scene 4

Monsieur Loyal, Madame Pernelle, Orgon, Damis, Mariane, Dorine, Elmire, Cléante

MONSIEUR LOYAL: Good day, dear sister. Kindly let me see
    Your master.
DORINE: He's involved with company,
    And cannot be disturbed just now, I fear.
MONSIEUR LOYAL: I hate to intrude; but what has brought me here
5   Will not disturb your master, in any event.
    Indeed, my news will make him most content.
DORINE: Your name?
MONSIEUR LOYAL: Just say that I bring greetings from
    Monsieur Tartuffe, on whose behalf I've come.
DORINE [*To Orgon*]:
    Sir, he's a very gracious man, and bears
10   A message from Tartuffe, which, he declares,
    Will make you most content.
CLÉANTE: Upon my word,
    I think this man had best be seen, and heard.
ORGON: Perhaps he has some settlement to suggest.
    How shall I treat him? What manner would be best?
CLÉANTE: Control your anger, and if he should mention
    Some fair adjustment, give him your full attention.
MONSIEUR LOYAL: Good health to you, good Sir. May Heaven confound
    Your enemies, and may your joys abound.
ORGON [*Aside, to Cléante*]:
    A gentle salutation: it confirms
20   My guess that he is here to offer terms.
MONSIEUR LOYAL: I've always held your family most dear;
    I served your father, Sir, for many a year.
ORGON: Sir, I must ask your pardon; to my shame,
    I cannot now recall your face or name.
MONSIEUR LOYAL: Loyal's my name; I come from Normandy,
    And I'm a bailiff, in all modesty.
    For forty years, praise God, it's been my boast
    To serve with honor in that vital post,
    And I am here, Sir, if you will permit
30   The liberty, to serve you with this writ . . .
ORGON: To—*what?*
MONSIEUR LOYAL: Now, please, Sir, let us have no friction:
    It's nothing but an order of eviction.
    You are to move your goods and family out
    And make way for new occupants, without
35   Deferment or delay, and give the keys . . .
ORGON: I? Leave this house?

MONSIEUR LOYAL: Why yes, Sir, if you please.
    This house, Sir, from the cellar to the roof,
    Belongs now to the good Monsieur Tartuffe,
    And he is lord and master of your estate
40   By virtue of a deed of present date,
    Drawn in due form, with clearest legal phrasing . . .
DAMIS: Your insolence is utterly amazing!
MONSIEUR LOYAL: Young man, my business here is not with you,
    But with your wise and temperate father, who,
45   Like every worthy citizen, stands in awe
    Of justice, and would never obstruct the law.
ORGON: But . . .
MONSIEUR LOYAL: Not for a million, Sir, would you rebel
    Against authority; I know that well.
    You'll not make trouble, Sir, or interfere
50   With the execution of my duties here.
DAMIS: Someone may execute a smart tattoo
    On that black jacket[2] of yours, before you're through.
MONSIEUR LOYAL: Sir, bid your son be silent. I'd much regret
    Having to mention such a nasty threat
55   Of violence, in writing my report.
DORINE [Aside]: This man Loyal's a most disloyal sort!
MONSIEUR LOYAL: I love all men of upright character,
    And when I agreed to serve these papers, Sir,
    It was your feelings that I had in mind.
60   It couldn't bear to see the case assigned
    To someone else, who might esteem you less
    And so subject you to unpleasantness.
ORGON: What's more unpleasant than telling a man to leave
    His house and home?
MONSIEUR LOYAL: You'd like a short reprieve?
65   If you desire it, Sir, I shall not press you,
    But wait until tomorrow to dispossess you.
    Splendid. I'll come and spend the night here, then,
    Most quietly, with half a score of men.
    For form's sake, you might bring me, just before
70   You go to bed, the keys to the front door.
    My men, I promise, will be on their best
    Behavior, and will not disturb your rest.
    But bright and early, Sir, you must be quick
    And move out all your furniture, every stick:
75   The men I've chosen are both young and strong,
    And with their help it shouldn't take you long.
    In short, I'll make things pleasant and convenient,
    And since I'm being so extremely lenient,

---

2. In the original, *justaucorps à langues bargues,* a close-fitting, long black coat with skirts, the customary dress of a bailiff.

Please show me, Sir, a like consideration,
80   And give me your entire cooperation.
ORGON [*Aside.*]: I may be all but bankrupt, but I vow
    I'd give a hundred louis, here and now,
    Just for the pleasure of landing one good clout
    Right on the end of that complacent snout.
CLÉANTE: Careful; don't make things worse.
DAMIS: My bootsole itches
    To give that beggar a good kick in the breeches.
DORINE: Monsieur Loyal, I'd love to hear the whack
    Of a stout stick across your fine broad back.
MONSIEUR LOYAL: Take care: a woman too may go to jail if
90   She uses threatening language to a bailiff.
CLÉANTE: Enough, enough, Sir. This must not go on.
    Give me that paper, please, and then begone.
MONSIEUR LOYAL: Well, *au revoir*. God give you all good cheer!
ORGON: May God confound you, and him who sent you here!

Scene 5

Orgon, Cléante, Mariane, Elmire, Madame Pernelle, Dorine, Damis

ORGON: Now, Mother, was I right or not? This writ
    Should change your notion of Tartuffe a bit.
    Do you perceive his villainy at last?
MADAME PERNELLE: I'm thunderstruck. I'm utterly aghast.
DORINE: Oh, come, be fair. You mustn't take offense
    At this new proof of his benevolence.
    He's acting out of selfless love, I know.
    Material things enslave the soul, and so
    He kindly has arranged your liberation
10   From all that might endanger your salvation.
ORGON: Will you not ever hold your tongue, you dunce?
CLÉANTE: Come, you must take some action, and at once.
ELMIRE: Go tell the world of the low trick he's tried.
    The deed of gift is surely nullified
15   By such behavior, and public rage will not
    Permit the wretch to carry out his plot.

Scene 6

Valère, Orgon, Cléante, Elmire, Mariane, Madame Pernelle, Damis, Dorine

VALÈRE: Sir, though I hate to bring you more bad news,
    Such is the danger that I cannot choose.
    A friend who is extremely close to me
    And knows my interest in your family
5   Has, for my sake, presumed to violate
    The secrecy that's due to things of state,
    And sends me word that you are in a plight
    From which your one salvation lies in flight.

That scoundrel who's imposed upon you so
10   Denounced you to the King an hour ago
And, as supporting evidence, displayed
The strong-box of a certain renegade
Whose secret papers, so he testified,
You had disloyally agreed to hide.
15   I don't know just what charges may be pressed,
But there's a warrant out for your arrest;
Tartuffe has been instructed, furthermore,
To guide the arresting officer to your door.
CLÉANTE: He's clearly done this to facilitate
20   His seizure of your house and your estate.
ORGON: That man, I must say, is a vicious beast!
VALÈRE: You can't afford to delay, Sir, in the least.
My carriage is outside, to take you hence;
This thousand louis should cover all expense.
25   Let's lose no time, or you shall be undone;
The sole defense, in this case, is to run.
I shall go with you all the way, and place you
In a safe refuge to which they'll never trace you.
ORGON: Alas, dear boy, I wish that I could show you
30   My gratitude for everything I owe you.
But now is not the time; I pray the Lord
That I may live to give you your reward.
Farewell, my dears; be careful . . .
CLÉANTE: Brother, hurry.
We shall take care of things; you needn't worry.

Scene 7

The Officer, Tartuffe, Valère, Orgon, Elmire, Mariane, Madame Pernelle, Dorine, Cléante, Damis

TARTUFFE: Gently, Sir, gently; stay right where you are.
No need for haste; your lodging isn't far.
You're off to prison, by order of the Prince.
ORGON: This is the crowning blow, you wretch; and since
5   It means my total ruin and defeat,
Your villainy is now at last complete.
TARTUFFE: You needn't try to provoke me; it's no use.
Those who serve Heaven must expect abuse.
CLÉANTE: You are indeed most patient, sweet, and blameless.
DORINE: How he exploits the name of Heaven! It's shameless.
TARTUFFE: Your taunts and mockeries are all for naught;
To do my duty is my only thought.
MARIANE: Your love of duty is most meritorious,
And what you've done is little short of glorious.
TARTUFFE: All deeds are glorious, Madam, which obey
The sovereign prince who sent me here today.
ORGON: I rescued you when you were destitute;

Have you forgotten that, you thankless brute?

TARTUFFE: No, no, I well remember everything;

20   But my first duty is to serve my King.

That obligation is so paramount

That other claims, beside it, do not count;

And for it I would sacrifice my wife,

My family, my friend, or my own life.

ELMIRE: Hypocrite!

DORINE: All that we most revere, he uses

To cloak his plots and camouflage his ruses.

CLÉANTE: If it is true that you are animated

By pure and loyal zeal, as you have stated,

Why was this zeal not roused until you'd sought

30   To make Orgon a cuckold, and been caught?

Why weren't you moved to give your evidence

Until your outraged host had driven you hence?

I shan't say that the gift of all his treasure

Ought to have damped your zeal in any measure;

35   But if he is a traitor, as you declare,

How could you condescend to be his heir?

TARTUFFE: [*To the Officer.*]

Sir, spare me all this clamor; it's growing shrill.

Please carry out your orders, if you will.

OFFICER:[3] Yes, I've delayed too long, Sir. Thank you kindly.

40   You're just the proper person to remind me.

Come, you are off to join the other boarders

In the King's prison, according to his orders.

TARTUFFE: Who? I, Sir?

OFFICER: Yes.

TARTUFFE: To prison? This can't be true!

OFFICER: I owe an explanation, but not to you.

45   [*To Orgon.*] Sir, all is well; rest easy, and be grateful.

We serve a Prince to whom all sham is hateful,

A Prince who sees into our inmost hearts,

And can't be fooled by any trickster's arts.

His royal soul, though generous and human,

50   Views all things with discernment and acumen;

His sovereign reason is not lightly swayed,

And all his judgments are discreetly weighed.

He honors righteous men of every kind,

And yet his zeal for virtue is not blind,

55   Nor does his love of piety numb his wits

And make him tolerant of hypocrites.

'Twas hardly likely that this man could cozen

A King who's foiled such liars by the dozen.

With one keen glance, the King perceived the whole

---

3. In the original, *un exempt*. He would actually have been a gentleman from the king's personal body-guard with the rank of lieutenant colonel or "master of the camp."

60 Perverseness and corruption of his soul,
  And thus high Heaven's justice was displayed:
  Betraying you, the rogue stood self-betrayed.
  The King soon recognized Tartuffe as one
  Notorious by another name, who'd done
65 So many vicious crimes that one could fill
  Ten volumes with them, and be writing still.
  But to be brief: our sovereign was appalled
  By this man's treachery toward you, which he called
  The last, worst villainy of a vile career,
70 And bade me follow the impostor here
  To see how gross his impudence could be,
  And force him to restore your property.
  Your private papers, by the King's command,
  I hereby seize and give into your hand.
75 The King, by royal order, invalidates
  The deed which gave this rascal your estates,
  And pardons, furthermore, your grave offense
  In harboring an exile's documents.
  By these decrees, our Prince rewards you for
80 Your loyal deeds in the late civil war,[4]
  And shows how heartfelt is his satisfaction
  In recompensing any worthy action,
  How much he prizes merit, and how he makes
  More of men's virtues than of their mistakes.

DORINE: Heaven be praised!

MADAME PERNELLE: I breathe again, at last.

ELMIRE: We're safe.

MARIANE: I can't believe the danger's past.

ORGON [*To Tartuffe.*]: Well, traitor, now you see . . .

CLÉANTE: Ah, Brother, please
  Let's not descend to such indignities.
  Leave the poor wretch to his unhappy fate,
90 And don't say anything to aggravate
  His present woes; but rather hope that he
  Will soon embrace an honest piety,
  And mend his ways, and by a true repentance
  Move our just King to moderate his sentence.
95 Meanwhile, go kneel before your sovereign's throne
  And thank him for the mercies he has shown.

ORGON: Well said: let's go at once and, gladly kneeling,
  Express the gratitude which all are feeling.
  Then, when that first great duty has been done,
100 We'll turn with pleasure to a second one,
  And give Valère, whose love has proven so true,
  The wedded happiness which is his due.

---

4. A reference to Orgon's role in supporting the king during the *Frondes.*

✦ PERSPECTIVES ✦
Court Culture and Female Authorship

The prevailing view of the period on the question of the education of women was that they should be kept in ignorance, as much as practicable, of everything other than housewifery and marital duties. In particular, they were to be kept innocent of literary and higher learning. The Enlightenment was characterized, however, by the beginnings of a modern challenge to such traditional attitudes. As in Heian Japan, women's writing flourished especially in court circles. While aristocratic culture placed exceptionally severe restrictions on women's conduct, aristocratic privilege could also allow individual women exceptional power and freedoms of other kinds—including freedom to learn, think, and write.

In France, women's writing flourished in the context of the first literary salons, established by aristocratic women as a kind of alternative court: one dominated by women instead of men, and by the aristocracy (and later by the bourgeoisie) instead of the monarchy. The Marquise de Rambouillet opened her famous "Blue Room" around 1608. One of her great social innovations was to raise women and bourgeois intellectuals to the level of male aristocrats, who subjected themselves increasingly to her salon's prestige until, during the period of its greatest influence (1630–1648), it was frequented even by the *grands seigneurs,* or peers of the realm. Indeed the aristocracy gathered there to oppose the increasingly absolutist power of the monarchy during the first half of the seventeenth century. When this resistance erupted in the rebellion called the *Fronde* (1648–1653), princesses and duchesses led armies in battle against the forces of monarchy. Their defeat effectively put an end to the world of the Blue Room.

Salon culture did not end with the Fronde, however. Indeed, the salons remained female-centered forums for powerful political opposition for two hundred years, from the opening of the Blue Room to Germaine de Staël's Napoleonic-era gatherings. The first salons' valuation of restrained conduct, refined wit, and aesthetic taste over the older aristocratic values of military valor and masculine honor became a cultural movement that spread throughout France over the course of the entire seventeenth century, under the untranslatable name of *préciosité.* The *précieuses,* as its female exponents were called—women like Rambouillet, Scudéry, and Lafayette—capitalized on the older courtly ideals of women as unattainable, idealized beings to be served and courted through a lifetime of deference rather than subjugated by tyrannical husbands, but translated these ideals into a realm where men proved their worth by demonstrating their wit and sensitivity rather than their military prowess. Thus "ladies made gentlemen," as the critic Carolyn Laugee has put it.

The real work, however, was in the women's task of making themselves ladies. The fact that Marie de Lafayette, born into the lower echelons of aristocracy, was described as "a *précieuse* of the highest rank," shows how salon culture created an alternative hierarchy to the class system. This culture of *préciosité* combined the cultivation of rarefied wit and sensibility with a resistance to marriage. Julie d'Angennes, daughter of the Marquise de Rambouillet, married her lover only after seventeen years of courtship, while Madeleine de Scudéry never married her lifelong lover (or anyone else). It was Scudéry who coined the phrase "Platonic love" still current today, to designate emotionally, spiritually, and even erotically intense, but sexually unconsummated, relationships between members of either sex. The greater freedom to be had in such love relationships appealed to many women in an era when, aristocrats or bourgeoises, they were married off very young to promote their families' interests in wealth or status and expected to produce heirs through multiple, life-threatening childbirths.

In their efforts to think their way around the problem of inequality in marriage, the *précieuses* proposed many radical alternatives to the celibacy of Platonic love: temporary or

Art d'Écrire, illustrative plate
from Denis Diderot's
Encyclopédie, 1751–1772.

trial marriage, renewable each year; divorce (illegal at the time); limitation or spacing of preg-
nancies; ending marriage with the birth of the first child; free love; and claiming for women the
right of vengeance against unfaithful husbands (husbands had the right to kill adulterous wives
but not vice versa). Samuel Richardson's devilish rake, Lovelace, later shocked English sensi-
bilities by voicing these same solutions (all except the last) to the problem of monogamous
marriage. Seventeenth-century courtly women's resistance to the restrictions marriage traditionally placed on them finds many other echoes in literature of the period. Female protagonists
in Zayas's *The Disenchantments of Love* (1647), like the title characters of Lafayette's *Princess
of Clèves* (1678) Graffigny's *Letters of a Peruvian Woman* (1747), and Richardson's *Clarissa*
(1747–1748), all refuse attractive suitors, preferring the freedom of a single life. In addition to
the salon gatherings, prominent *précieuses* held weekly audiences in their bedrooms, in which,
decked out like goddesses enthroned on beds of brocade, they would receive specially favored
visitors (called "alcovists" from the alcoves in which beds were placed). In fact the word

"salon" was not used until much later; more common was *ruelle*: literally the narrow space between the bed and the wall. Intense female friendships were an equally important part of *préciosité*, and it was more often in this sense that Platonic love was adopted in seventeenth-century England, where Katherine Philips was the first to promote it both in her circle of literary friends and in her poetry.

Devoted to pleasure, beauty, love, and play, the *précieuses* fostered wit, feeling, and culture—not scholarly learning. It was an aesthetic and social rather than an intellectual movement. It also fostered community and collaborative authorship, and the writing of long, witty letters to be circulated among friends, as well as elaborate verbal games. These allowed the salons' members to engage creatively with one another while showing off their individual wit and sensibility, all the while denying that they were engaged in anything more than a game or trifle—for anything more admittedly serious might smack too much of ungenteel labor or unfeminine learning. The game from Scudéry's *Clélie*, the *Carte de Tendre*, really was played like a board game in her salon. It is of a piece with language games like competing to come up with witty maxims or amusing tales, which resulted in works such as the *Maxims* of La Rochefoucauld (developed in the salon of Mme de Sablé), or literary collections of fairy tales. Many current French idioms were invented by the *précieuses;* "Platonic love" is only one example of terms that penetrated the English language as well. None of their works, however, were written entirely in such idioms—such excessively elaborate language is actually the invention of the satirists. Thanks to the satires of Molière and others, the word "precious" in this sense developed pejorative connotations in French as well as English by the nineteenth century. Nevertheless, besides enriching the language, the *précieuses* brought to prominence in modern literature numerous literary genres, including the "character" or "moral portrait," the literary maxim, literary letters and the epistolary form in fiction, and the psychological novel.

Just after Molière had published *The Ridiculous Précieuses* in Paris, the English monarchy was restored (1660) in the person of King Charles II, after more than a decade of Puritan rule. Charles brought home from his French exile a taste for much of what the *précieuses* stood for, and the Puritans abhorred: pleasure, beauty, wit, frivolity, and foppery. In England the French models for these were transposed into a cultural milieu that was more mercantile and commercialized, as well as less extremely politically centralized. It was possible for a middle-class woman like Aphra Behn, associated with the theater, to become a successful professional writer, in part by translating and elaborating upon French models—even though she was frequently charged with indecency in both her life and works. It may seem odd to modern readers that most of the early professional women writers in England, although not aristocrats, passionately held to Tory or monarchist politics, which today seems a conservative stance at odds with their struggle for greater freedom of expression as women. Yet in the Restoration context, loyalty to the monarchy was associated with relative artistic and sexual freedom, whereas the more politically democratic or leveling forces of Puritanism were accompanied by severe repression of such freedoms.

French salon literature included a strong element of the pastoral—the idealization of the simple life of shepherds in the countryside as antidote to the pressures and hypocrisies of urban court life—inherited from classical literature. Given that salon culture was so Paris-centered, this idealization of rural simplicity was actually the height of urban artifice and refinement. This pastoral aspect was also adopted by the Englishwomen who were inspired by the *précieuses*. Nearly every Englishwoman who wrote poetry in the later seventeenth or early eighteenth centuries adopted a pen name in the pastoral style, beginning with Katherine Philips, "the Matchless Orinda," poet and translator of Corneille. Professional writers like Aphra Behn and Eliza Haywood had to stay in London to earn a living, but those from the landed classes were more able to imitate that aspect of *préciosité* that celebrated leisure, the pleasures of society, intimate friendships outside marriage, and the posture of writing for a cabal of like-minded friends rather than for public consumption. These women established coteries that were very much like the salons, with the important exception of being nearly always centered in a rural estate. The poetry that emerged from these literary coteries celebrated the pleasures of "retirement" from the whirl of urban and courtly distractions, consumption, and display, alongside Scudéry's ideal of Platonic love, especially (though not exclusively) between female friends. Katherine Philips was the first to do this, establishing her "Society of Friendship" in remote Wales.

Despite their success and recognition, all these women still saw themselves as exceptions, as swimming upstream. This remains true even by the end of the period, with writers like Anna Letitia Barbauld and Mary Wollstonecraft; in fact, in important ways, more conservative attitudes about women's proper role and restriction to the domestic sphere predominated in the late eighteenth and the nineteenth centuries than in the seventeenth and early eighteenth centuries—in part because of the demise of courtly culture and the prerogatives and permissions it had lent certain individual women.

PRONUNCIATIONS:
  Préciosité: pray-see-oh-see-TAY
  Précieuses: pray-see-UHZ

━•━ ⇥✦⇤ ━•━

Madeleine de Scudéry
1607–1701

Madeleine de Scudéry invented the *roman à clef,* or novel recognizably portraying living people. Its vogue, and her fame, were immediate and international. She published over thirty works; many were signed by her brother Georges, but her readers always recognized her—and themselves—in her fiction.

Scudéry's father supplemented his inadequate pay as governor of the port of Le Havre through piracy; Madeleine was soon orphaned. Her brother Georges inherited everything, and supported her. At twenty-nine she was an old maid when he took her to Paris and the famous Blue Room. Madeleine and her writings were well received, but Georges took her off to a distant fortress in 1644. In this exile she conceived *The Great Cyrus* (1650–1653), circulated during the Fronde uprising. Readers loved recognizing the Duke of Condé in "Cyrus" and Scudéry herself in "Sapho," as she was called thereafter.

The rebels and their Blue Room were in disarray by the time Scudéry returned to Paris. She opened her own salon, corresponded with other famous writers like Corneille, Leibniz, and Queen Christina of Sweden, and wrote *Clélie* (1654–1660) about herself. Its first of ten volumes contains the "Carte de Tendre," guiding the platonic lover through the pitfalls of sexuality on the one hand and passionlessness marriage on the other. The map was used in her salon like a board game of love, meant to amuse while instructing gentlemen how best to win the heart of a sensitive woman—the only kind worth winning. Combining ideals of chivalric romance with classical historical settings, Scudéry's novels elaborated the profoundly influential salon culture of *préciosité.* Translated into English, German, Italian, and Arabic, they made her publishers rich. Meanwhile a royal pension kept her alive. The *Académie Française* made her its first female laureate in 1671. (An offer of membership was also considered, but no woman would be admitted until 1980.) In her seventies Scudéry was still writing to support herself—mostly moral essays, in defense against Church accusations that she'd written too much about love.

Standing up in her Paris home on 2 June 1701, Scudéry announced, "One must die," and did so.

PRONUNCIATIONS:
Aronce: ah-RONS
Clélie: klay-LEE
Cumae: KEU-may
de Scudéry: duh scoo-day-REE
Herminius: ehr-mee-nee-YEUS

from Clélie[1]

[THE MAP OF TENDER[2]]

No doubt you recall, Madame, that Herminius asked Clélie to teach him how to get from New Affection to Tender. This is the way: you have to begin at the former city, which is at the bottom of this map, in order to get to the others; for in order to comprehend Clélie's design you must understand that she has imagined tenderness may arise from any of three different causes: out of great esteem, or out of gratitude, or out of inclination; and that is why she placed these three cities of Tender on three rivers which bear these three names, and also created three different routes leading to them. Just as one says "Cumae on the Ionian Sea" and "Cumae on the Tyrrhenian Sea,"[3] she has one say Tender-on-Inclination, Tender-on-Esteem, and Tender-on-Gratitude. She assumes, however, that the tenderness born of inclination or fondness has no need of any other assistance; and so as you can see, Madame, Clélie has not put a single village along the shores of that river, which flows so swiftly that one has only to take lodgings along its banks in order to get from New Affection to Tender.

To get to Tender-on-Esteem it is quite otherwise, however, for Clélie has ingeniously made as many villages as there are things great and small that can contribute to enkindle by means of esteem the kind of tenderness she means to describe here. Thus you can see that from New Affection one passes to a place called Fine Wit, since that is how esteem or admiration ordinarily begins; beyond it you see these pleasant villages of Pretty Verses and Flirtatious Letter and Love Letter, which are the most common productions of a fine wit at the beginning of a friendship. Afterwards, in order to make further progress on this route, you see Sincerity, Big Heart, Integrity, Generosity, Respect, Correctness and Goodness, which is right next to Tender, showing that there can be no true esteem without goodness, and that no one can get to Tender from that side without possessing that precious quality.

Now you must, Madame—if you please—return to New Affection in order to find out by which route one can go from there to Tender-on-Gratitude. Please observe how you must proceed first from New Affection to Solicitousness; then to that little village named Submissiveness, which is next to a very pleasant one called Little Attentions. Notice, moreover, that from there you have to pass by Assiduity; this helps us understand that it is not enough to provide all those obliging little attentions that

---

1. Translated by April Alliston. *Clélie* is a multivolume novel set in ancient Roman times but describing seventeenth-century Parisian salon culture in idealized terms. The author represents herself under the guise of the title character, and gives similarly classical-sounding fictional names to various members of her circle. In the dialogue excerpted in this section, a gentleman explains to a lady how to play the game of tenderness using the ingenious map invented by "Clélie," and describes the sensation it caused in the salons.
2. "The Map of Tenderness" might sound more natural,

but the French deliberately—and just as oddly—uses the adjective *tendre* here. The realm of Tender is distinguished from a village within it called *Tendresse* (Tenderness; see map on next page).
3. The ancient city of Cumae was the first Greek colony in Italy, located on its west coast by the Tyrrhenian Sea, near modern Naples. It is strongly associated with the mythical Sybil of Cumae, best known from Virgil's *Aeneid*. Scudéry imagines a second ancient city also called Cumae but located on the east coast of Italy, by the Ionian or Adriatic Sea.

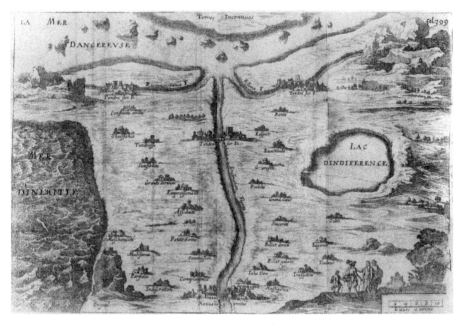

La Carte du pays de Tendre, from Madeleine de Scudéry's *Clélie*, 1660.

cause gratitude for just a few days; one has to offer them assiduously. Next, you see, you must pass on to another village called Eagerness, and not act like those placid souls who never hurry themselves up by one minute no matter how anyone may beg them, and who are incapable of showing this eagerness that can be so engaging. After that, if you look at the map you'll see you have to continue on to Important Favors; but in order to indicate that there are few people who offer them, this village is smaller than the others. From there one must move on to Sympathy; this allows us to recognize how important it is to share in even the smallest sorrows of those we love. From there one must pass by Tenderness in order to get to Tender, for affection attracts affection. From there you go on to Obedience; for blind obedience can engage a heart more completely than almost anything else. And to arrive at last where you wish to go you must pass through Constant Friendship, which is without a doubt the surest way to arrive at Tender-on-Gratitude.

But since there is no such thing as a path from which one cannot stray, Madame, Clélie has designed the map so that if those who begin at New Affection were to wander a little more to the right or a little more to the left, they would soon get lost, as you can see: for if on leaving Fine Wit one went to Neglect, which you see right next to it on this map, and if from there, continuing in this error, one went to Inconsistency; from there to Lukewarmness, to Fickleness and to Oblivion, instead of arriving in Tender-on-Esteem one would soon find oneself in the Lake of Indifference, which you see marked on this map and which, by its tranquil waters, doubtless represents vividly the very thing of which it bears the name. On the other side, starting again at New Affection, if one went a little too far to the left and came to Indiscretion, to Perfidy, to Pride, to Slander or to Malice, instead of getting to Tender-on-Gratitude one would find oneself in the Sea of Enmity, where all vessels are shipwrecked and which, by the roughness of its waves, corresponds precisely to the impetuous passion Clélie wishes it to represent. Thus she reveals by these different routes that a person must have a thousand good qualities to inspire any tender affection in her, and that those who have any bad ones can expect only her hatred or her indifference. This wise girl, wishing also to let everyone know by means of this map that she has never felt love, and that she will never harbor any feeling in her heart other than tenderness, has made the river Inclination flow straight into the Dangerous Sea, because it is rather dangerous for a woman to go even a little beyond the last bounds of friendship; and she has also drawn beyond this Sea what we call the Unknown Lands, because in fact we know nothing at all about what is there, just as we do not believe anyone has ever journeyed farther than the Pillars of Hercules.[4] So in this manner she has found a way to give us all a pleasing moral about the affections by means of a simple pastime and flight of her fancy, and to illustrate in a very intimate and extraordinary way that she has never felt love and cannot feel it.

Aronce, Herminius, and I found this map so elegantly and precisely witty that we were able to understand it immediately, before we parted. Clélie nevertheless insistently begged the person for whom she had made it not to show it to anyone, except five or six people for whom she cared enough to let them see it too; for it was only a game and a simple flight of fancy, so she did not want vulgar people who would not know the origin of the thing, and who would not be capable of understanding such unusual refinements, to go around talking about it guided only by the interpretations of their own unsophisticated minds. She could not be obeyed in this, however; for her stars ordained that even though no one wanted to show it to more than a few people, it soon created such a stir in society that people talked of nothing but the Map of Tender. All the wits in Capua[5] wrote something in praise of this map either in verse or in prose; it was the subject of a very ingenious poem, some other very elegant verses, some very beautiful letters, some quite pleasant messages, and some conversations so entertaining that Clélie insisted all these were a thousand times better than her map. You couldn't run into anyone at that time without asking whether he wanted to go to Tender. Indeed for some time it furnished such a pleasant topic of conversation that there was never anything so entertaining.[6]

At first Clélie was angry that the map was so much talked about, "for after all," she said one day to Herminius, "do you think I like the fact that a trifle I thought would be amusing to the members of our coterie should be made public, and that what I made for the eyes of only five or six persons of the most refined, delicate and discerning wit should be seen by two thousand who have none, who possess only deformed and unenlightened minds and misunderstand the most beautiful things? I know very well," she continued, "that the few who know this all started with a conversation that inspired me to invent this map in an instant will not consider this polite piece of wit chimerical or extravagant; but since there are some very strange people in the world, I'm afraid there might be some who imagine I meant it quite seriously, or that I thought about it for days before coming up with it, or that I believe I've created

4. Rocks standing at either side of the Straits of Gibraltar, where the Mediterranean Sea opens into the Atlantic Ocean. In the ancient Mediterranean world—the setting of this novel—it was commonly believed that no one had ever voyaged beyond them and returned to tell the tale.
5. Another ancient city near Cumae in western Italy, here standing in for Paris.
6. Scudéry's map did in fact cause just such a stir in Parisian society—as indicated by the reference to it in one of the letters of the Duchesse d'Orléans (see page 277)—and it really did inspire just such creative responses, typical of the literary culture of the salons.

something wonderful. It is, however, only the folly of a moment, and I regard it as no more than a trifle—one that might possess some elegance and novelty for those who have the turn of mind to understand it." But Clélie had no reason to worry, Madame, for it's clear that everyone took perfectly well this new invention for finding out how one might earn the tenderness of a good woman—and except for a few vulgar, stupid, malicious, or impertinent people whose approval is of no consequence to Clélie, everyone praises it. It is even possible to derive some amusement from the foolishness of the people who don't, for there was one of them who, after having seen this map—which he had insisted on seeing with strange obstinacy—and after having heard it praised by better men than himself, asked in a vulgar way what it was for, and what use a map like this could possibly have. "I'm not sure," the person he spoke to replied, after having re-folded it very carefully, "that it will be useful to anyone, but I'm very sure that it will never lead *you* to Tender." Thus, Madame, this map had such a fortunate destiny that even those who were too stupid to understand it served to entertain us by giving us cause to make fun of their foolishness.

Marie-Madeleine Pioche de la Vergne, Comtesse de Lafayette
1634–1693

"May God defend all decent people against such a woman as Madame de Lafayette," a victim of her intrigues once complained. She was indeed a mistress of court intrigue, the main subject of her writings. Later in life she even spied for the female Regent of Savoy at Louis XIV's court. Born into a family of intellectual, upwardly mobile courtiers, she grew up in the great salons of Rambouillet and Scudéry. Lafayette's first and only avowed publication was a descriptive "portrait" of her close friend Madame de Sévigné in the *Portrait Gallery* of salon ladies published by the king's sister in 1659. She married the Comte de Lafayette in 1655, following him to his rural estates. Unlike Sévigné's daughter, however, she refused to remain exiled from Paris. After giving the Comte two sons within four years, she returned to her childhood Parisian home. The Duc de la Rochefoucauld visited her there every day until he died in 1680. The salon she opened in 1659 became known as the *Chambre du Sublime* and her circle as the *cabale du sublime*, after a friend, knowing Lafayette's yearning for royal favor, so named a toy replica of the room and its habitués that she showed the king. The best known of the works Lafayette wrote in conversation with her salonniers, *The Princess of Clèves*, called the first modern novel for its psychological interiority, created a moral and aesthetic commotion by featuring a chaste woman's confession of her adulterous desire. *The Countess of Tende*, published posthumously, places a weaker woman in a situation resembling that of the more idealized heroine of her famous novel. She too confesses to her husband, but what she confesses is viewed as a capital crime.

PRONUNCIATIONS:
    Catherine de Médicis: ka-TREEN duh may-dee-SEES
    Condé: kon-DAY
    La Châtre: lah SHAH-truh
    Chevalier de Navarre: shu-val-YAY duh nah-VAHR
    Neufchâtel: noo-shah-TEL
    Maréchale de Saint-André: mah-ray-SHAL duh san-tan-DRAY
    Strozzi: STROT-tsee
    Tende: TOND-uh

The Countess of Tende[1]

Mademoiselle de Strozzi, daughter of the Marshal of France and a close relation of Catherine de Médicis, was married during the first year of that queen's regency to the Count of Tende, of the house of Savoy.[2] Rich and attractive, he lived in greater magnificence than any other lord at court, and was more fitted to win respect than to please. Nevertheless his wife loved him from the first with passion. She was very young; he looked upon her as a mere child, and soon fell in love with another. The Countess of Tende, of ardent nature and Italian descent, became jealous; she gave herself no rest; she left none to her husband; he avoided her presence, and no longer lived with her as one lives with a wife.

The Countess's beauty increased; she showed strength of character; the world looked upon her with admiration; she grew self-absorbed, and was gradually cured both of her jealousy and of her passion.

She became the intimate friend of the Princess of Neufchâtel[3]—young, beautiful, and widowed of the Prince of that name, who had left her at his death a dominion that made her the noblest and most brilliant match at court.

The Chevalier of Navarre,[4] descended from the ancient rulers of that kingdom, was also young at that time—handsome and full of spirit and nobility; but fate had given him no other fortune than his high birth. He cast his eyes upon the Princess of Neufchâtel, whose character he understood as one capable of a violent attachment, and thus suited to make the fortune of a man like himself. With this aim he attached himself to her without being in love with her, and attracted her; she tolerated his attentions, but he found himself still quite far from the success he desired. His plan was unknown to anyone; a single friend had his confidence, and this friend was also an intimate of the Count of Tende. The friend persuaded the Chevalier of Navarre to agree to confide his secret to the Count, thinking thus to enlist the Count to help them with the Princess of Neufchâtel. The Count of Tende already liked the Chevalier of Navarre; he talked the affair over with his wife, for whom he was beginning to have more consideration, and indeed convinced her to do as they wished.

The Princess of Neufchâtel had already confided her feelings for the Chevalier of Navarre to her friend; the Countess encouraged them. The Chevalier went to see the Countess, schemed and planned together with her; but upon seeing her he also conceived a violent passion for her. He did not give himself over to it at first; he saw the obstacles that his feelings, divided between love and ambition, might put in the way of his designs; he resisted; but to resist it would have been necessary not to have seen the Countess of Tende very often, and he saw her every day while visiting the Princess of Neufchâtel; thus he fell desperately in love with the Countess. He could not hide his passion from her entirely; she perceived it; her vanity was flattered, and she felt a violent love for him.

One day as she was talking with him about the great good fortune of marrying the Princess of Neufchâtel, he said to her with a look that declared the full force of his

---

1. Translated by April Alliston.
2. Clarice Strozzi (d. 1564) was the daughter of Pierre Strozzi, Maréchal de France. Her mother was a member of the Medici family, as was Catherine, the queen mother and regent. Clarice married Honorat de Savoie (1538–1572), Count of Tende and Sommerive, Governor and Seneschal of Provence, in 1560.
3. Perhaps modeled on Jacqueline de Rohan, who had

become the widow of François d'Orléans-Longueville in 1548, but by 1560, the year when this story begins, she must have been over forty years old. Marguerite de Navarre called her "the Countess of Neufchâtel" in Story 53 of her *Heptameron*. The Counts of Neufchâtel did not become princes until 1648—so the title itself is fictitious at the date of the narrative.
4. The Chevalier of Navarre is imaginary.

passion: "And do you think, Madame, that there is no fortune I might prefer to that of marrying the Princess?" The Countess of Tende was struck with the looks and words of the Chevalier; she returned his gaze, and there was a troubled silence between them that spoke more than words. From that time the Countess was in such distress that she had no more repose; she felt the remorse of taking from her friend the heart of a man whom she was going to marry only to be loved by him, whom she would wed with the disapproval of all and at the expense of her rank.

This betrayal horrified her. She now saw clearly in her mind the shame and misery of a love affair; she saw the abyss into which she was about to cast herself, and she resolved to avoid it.

She kept her resolution poorly. The Princess had almost determined to marry the Chevalier of Navarre, but she was not sufficiently pleased with his passion for her; despite her own feelings for him and the trouble he took to deceive her, she felt a lack of warmth in his courtship. She complained of this to the Countess of Tende; the Countess reassured her, but the complaints of Mme de Neufchâtel increased the Countess's distress; they showed her the extent of her betrayal, which might cost her lover his fortune. The Countess warned him of the Princess's suspicions. He assured her of his indifference to everything except being loved by her; nevertheless he complied with her orders, and reassured the Princess of Neufchâtel so well that she made it clear to the Countess of Tende that she was perfectly satisfied with the Chevalier of Navarre.

Jealousy then gripped the Countess. She feared that her lover really loved the Princess; she saw all the reasons he had to love her; their marriage, which she herself had wished for, now horrified her; she did not want him to break it off, however, and she found herself caught in a cruel dilemma. She let the Chevalier of Navarre see all her remorse on account of the Princess of Neufchâtel; she resolved to hide only her jealousy from him, and believed she had succeeded in concealing it.

The Princess's passion finally overcame all her doubts; she decided in favor of the marriage, resolving to celebrate it secretly and not to make it public until after it had been concluded.

The Countess of Tende was ready to die of grief. On the same day that was set for the wedding there was a public court ceremony in which her husband participated. She sent all her servants there, announced that she would receive no one, and shut herself up in her study, lying on a couch abandoned to the cruelest pains that remorse, love and jealousy can inflict.

While she was in this state she heard a hidden door in her study open and saw the Chevalier of Navarre appear, adorned with a grace beyond anything she had ever seen. "Chevalier, where are you going?" she cried, "what are you looking for? Have you lost your mind? What has become of your marriage? Have you thought of my reputation?" "Be reassured as to your reputation, Madame," he replied, "no one can possibly know; but there is no question of my marriage, nor of my fortune, but only of your heart, Madame, and of being loved by you; I relinquish all the rest. You have allowed me to see that you do not hate me, but you have tried not to let me know that I am so fortunate that my marriage may cause you some pain. I come to tell you, Madame, that I renounce it, that this marriage would be a torment, and that I want to live only for you. I am expected even as we speak; all is ready, but I will break off everything if, in doing so, I might please you and prove my passion."

The Countess let herself fall back upon the sofa, from which she had half raised herself. Looking at the Chevalier with eyes full of love and tears, she said: "Do you want me to die? Do you think a heart can contain all that you make me feel? To give up for my sake the fortune that awaits you! I can't bear so much as the thought of it. Go to Madame the Princess of Neufchâtel, go to the grandeur to which you are destined; you shall have my heart at the same time. I shall make of my remorse, of my doubts, and of my jealousy, since I must confess it, whatever my feeble reason will counsel me: but I will never see you again if you do not go this instant to conclude your marriage. Go, do not stay a moment longer, but for my sake and yours renounce a passion so unreasonable as the one you bear me, which will lead us, perhaps, into terrible misfortunes."

The Chevalier was at first transported with joy to see himself so truly loved by the Countess of Tende; but the horror of giving himself to another again presented itself to his imagination. He wept, he tormented himself, he promised her all she demanded, on the condition that he would see her again in the same place. Before he left she wanted to know how he had entered. He told her that he had entrusted himself to one of her stablemen who had been in his own service, and that this stableman had let him pass through the stable yard to the small staircase that led to this study, as well as to the stableman's room.

The hour appointed for the wedding approached, however, and the Chevalier, urged by the Countess of Tende, was finally forced to leave. But he went as though to his execution, to accept the greatest good fortune to which a younger son without inheritance had ever been raised. The Countess of Tende spent the night, as one might imagine, tormented by doubts; she called her maids in the morning and, shortly after her door was opened, saw her stableman approach her bed and lay a letter on it in such a way that no one else noticed it. The sight of this letter troubled her since she recognized it as coming from the Chevalier of Navarre, and since it was so unlikely that during this night, which should have been his wedding night, he should have had leisure to write; so that she feared he might have created or found some obstacle to his marriage. She opened the letter with strong emotion, and found more or less these words:

"I think of nothing but you, Madame; I am concerned with nothing but you; in the first moments of possessing the greatest match in France, the day scarcely breaks before I leave the room where I have spent the night to tell you that I have already regretted a thousand times having obeyed you, and not having abandoned it all to live only for you."

This letter and the moment in which it was written touched the Countess of Tende deeply; she went to dine with the Princess of Neufchâtel, who had invited her. Her marriage had been announced. She found an infinite number of people in the room, but as soon as the Princess saw her she left her company and asked her to come into her study. Hardly were they seated before the Princess's face was covered with tears. The Countess thought this was an effect of the announcement of her marriage, that she found it more difficult to bear the humiliation of it than she had expected; but she soon saw her mistake. "Ah! Madame," said the Princess, "what have I done? I have married a man for passion, I have made an unequal match, a match that is disapproved of, and which debases me—and the man I have preferred over everything else loves another!" The Countess of Tende thought she would faint at these words; she thought the Princess could not have discerned the passion of her husband without also having guessed its cause; she was unable to reply. The Princess of Navarre (as she was called since her marriage) noticed nothing, however, and continued: "Monsieur the Prince of Navarre," she said, "Madame, far from showing the impatience that the conclusion of our marriage should have inspired in him, made me wait for him yesterday evening. He came without joy, preoccupied and embarrassed; he left my bedroom at daybreak on some pretext. But he had been writing; I saw it from his hands. To whom could he have written, except to a mistress? Why keep me waiting, and why should he seem so troubled?"

At this moment the conversation was interrupted because the Princess of Condé[5] had arrived; the Princess of Navarre went to receive her, and the Countess of Tende remained beside herself. She wrote that evening to the Prince of Navarre to inform him of his wife's suspicions and to persuade him to restrain himself. Their passion did not lessen with dangers and obstacles; the Countess of Tende found no rest, and sleep no longer came to relieve her sorrows. One morning after she had called for her maids her stableman approached her and said in a whisper that the Prince of Navarre was in her study, and that he begged her to let him tell her something which it was absolutely necessary she should know. One gives in easily to that which pleases; the Countess knew her husband had gone out; she declared that she wanted to sleep and told her servants to close her doors, and not to return until she called them.

The Prince of Navarre entered through this study and threw himself down on his knees by her bed. "What do you have to tell me?" she asked. "That I love you, Madame, that I adore you, that I cannot live with Madame de Navarre. The desire to see you seized me this morning with such violence that I could not resist. I came at the risk of all that might happen without even a hope of speaking with you." The Countess scolded him at first for having compromised her so lightly, and then their passion led them into a conversation so long that the Count of Tende came back from the city. He went to his wife's apartments; he was told that she was not awake. It was late; he went in[6] and found the Prince of Navarre on his knees by her bed, where he had been since he arrived. Never had astonishment been like that of the Count of Tende, and never had consternation equaled that of his wife; only the Prince of Navarre kept his presence of mind, disturbing himself not at all, nor even rising to his feet! "Come, come," he said to the Count of Tende, "help me obtain a favor I am begging for on my knees, but is still refused."

The tone and manner of the Prince of Navarre relieved the surprise of the Count of Tende. "I don't know," he replied in the same tone in which the Prince had spoken, "whether a favor you ask of my wife on your knees, when I am told she is asleep but find you alone with her, with no carriage at my door, would be among those I should wish she might grant you." The Prince of Navarre, reassured and recovered from the embarrassment of the first moment, rose and seated himself with perfect ease, while the Countess of Tende, trembling and wild with fear, concealed her distress in the darkness of the place where she sat. The Prince of Navarre spoke to the Count: "I'm going to surprise you; you'll blame me, but still you have to help me. I am in love with the most charming person at court, and loved by her; I escaped yesterday evening from the Princess of Navarre and all my servants to go to a rendezvous where this person waited for me. My wife, who has already discerned that I am preoccupied with something other than herself, and who spies on my conduct, knew from my servants that I had left them; she is consumed with incomparable jealousy and despair. I told her that I had passed the hours that had caused her distress with the Maréchale de Saint-André,[7] who is indisposed and receives almost no one; I told her that only the

5. Eléonor de Roye (1535–1564) married Louis I de Bourbon, Prince of Condé, in 1551.
6. Such a casual and unannounced entry into his wife's bedchamber was not customary between spouses of high rank. The Count is behaving inappropriately.

7. Marguerite de Lustrac, wife of Jacques d'Albon (d. 1562), named Maréchal de Saint-André by Henri II in 1547 (he plays a significant role in Lafayette's novel, *The Princess of Clèves*). After her husband's death Marguerite became famous as mistress of the Prince of Condé.

Countess of Tende was there with us, and that she could ask her whether she had not seen me there all evening. So I resolved to come and confide in Madame la Comtesse. I went to visit La Châtre,[8] less than a stone's throw from here; I escaped without my servants seeing me, and I was told that Madame was awake. I found no one in her antechamber, and I entered boldly. She refuses to lie in my favor; she says she does not want to betray her friend and gives me very sober reprimands; I have already given them to myself in vain. Madame la Princesse must be spared her present worry and jealousy, and I the mortal bother of her reproaches."

The Countess of Tende was hardly less surprised by the Prince's presence of mind than she had been by the arrival of her husband; she was reassured, however, and the Count no longer entertained the slightest doubt. He joined his wife in reminding the Prince of the abyss of unhappiness into which he would be plunging himself, and how much he owed the Princess. The Countess promised to tell her whatever her husband asked.

As he was about to leave the Count stopped him: "In recompense for the service we are doing you at the expense of the truth, tell us at least who this charming mistress may be. She must not be a very respectable person, to love you and continue relations with you, seeing you take up with a person as beautiful as Madame the Princess of Navarre, seeing you marry her, and knowing what you owe her. She must have neither spirit, courage, nor sensitivity, and really she is not worth your disturbing so great a good fortune as yours, nor your rendering yourself so ungrateful and so guilty." The Prince did not know what to reply; he feigned haste. The Count of Tende saw him out himself, to help him avoid being seen.

The Countess remained shaken by the risk she had run, by the reflections her husband's words had forced her to make, and by the picture of the unhappiness to which her passion exposed her; but she did not have the strength to extricate herself. She continued her relations with the Prince; she saw him sometimes through the mediation of La Lande, her stableman. She considered herself, and in fact she was, one of the unhappiest people in the world. Every day the Princess of Navarre confided in her a jealousy of which she herself was the cause; this jealousy pierced her with remorse; and when the Princess of Navarre was happy with her husband, she was penetrated with jealousy in her turn.

A new torment was added to those she already had: the Count of Tende fell as much in love with her as if she had not been his wife; he never left her alone, and wanted to reclaim all the rights he had disdained.

The Countess resisted him with a force and bitterness approaching contempt: prejudiced in favor of the Prince of Navarre, she was wounded and offended by any passion but his. The Count of Tende felt her conduct in all its severity and, stung to the quick, he assured her he would never trouble her again in his life, and indeed left her very coldly.

War approached; the Prince of Navarre was to leave for the army. The Countess of Tende began to feel the pain of his absence and the fear of the dangers to which he would be exposed; she resolved to spare herself the constraint of hiding her affliction, and decided to spend the summer on an estate she possessed thirty leagues[9] from Paris.

8. Possibly Gaspard de La Châtre (d. 1578), who married a cousin of the Count of Tende in 1570.
9. Ninety miles. The Countess's move resembles that of the Princess of Clèves, who retires to her country house at Coulommiers, at a comparable distance from Paris, for similar reasons.

She put into effect what she had planned; their leave-taking was so sorrowful that they both had to take it as an evil omen.[1] The Count of Tende stayed with the king, where his post obliged him to remain.

The court was to move closer to the army; the house of Mme de Tende was not far away; her husband told her he would visit there for one night, only to see to some projects he had begun. He did not want her to suspect he might be coming to see her; he harbored against her all the spite to which the passions can give rise. In the beginning Mme de Tende had found the Prince so full of respect, and herself so full of virtue, that she had mistrusted neither him nor herself. But time and opportunities had triumphed over virtue and respect, and shortly after she arrived at her country house she perceived that she was pregnant. One need only reflect upon the reputation she had acquired and maintained, and upon the estrangement between her and her husband, to judge of her despair. She was tempted several times to take her own life; however, she conceived some small hope from the visit her husband planned to pay her, and resolved to await what might come of it. In this distress she had the added sorrow of learning that La Lande, whom she had left in Paris to deliver her lover's letters and her own, had died a few days later, and she found herself without assistance at a time when she had much need of it.

The army, meanwhile, had begun a siege.[2] Her passion for the Prince of Navarre caused her continual fears for him, which penetrated even through her mortal terrors for herself.

Her fears were only too well founded; she received letters from the army; she learned of the end of the siege, but learned also that the Prince of Navarre had been killed on the last day. She lost both awareness and reason; for several days she was deprived of both. This extreme of misery seemed to her, at moments, a kind of consolation. She feared no longer for her repose, nor for her reputation, nor for her life; death alone seemed desirable; she hoped it would come of her sorrow, otherwise she was resolved to seek it out herself. A remnant of shame obliged her to say that she felt terrible pains, as a pretext for her cries and tears. If a thousand adversities made her turn upon herself, she saw that she had deserved them, and both nature and Christianity prevented her from becoming her own murderer, suspending the execution of her plan.

She had not been long in this violent distress when the Count of Tende arrived. She thought she recognized in him all the feelings her unfortunate state might inspire; but the arrival of her husband gave her yet another worry, and a new embarrassment. He learned upon arrival that she was ill and, as he had always maintained honest usages in the eyes of the public and of his household, he went first to her bedroom. He found her beside herself, like one gone mad. She could not hold back her tears, which she attributed still to the pains that tormented her. The Count of Tende, touched by the state in which he saw her, softened, and thinking it would distract her from her pain, told her of the Prince of Navarre's death and his wife's grief. That of Madame de Tende could not withstand this conversation; her tears redoubled, so that the Count of Tende was surprised and nearly disabused; he left the chamber full of anxiety and distress; it seemed to him that his wife was not in a state brought on by physical pain; this redoubling of tears when he had spoken to her of the death of the

---

1. The possibility of predicting the future was a subject of heated debate. Evil omens in particular are also a preoccupation in *The Princess of Clèves*.

2. Probably the month-long siege of Rouen in 1562, one of the first conflicts of the wars of religion in France.

Prince of Navarre struck him, and suddenly the incident in which he had discovered him on his knees by her bed came to his mind. He also remembered her behavior toward himself when he had wished to return to her, and finally he thought he saw the truth; but nevertheless that doubt remained with him which self-love always leaves us regarding things it would cost us too much to know.

His despair was extreme and all his thoughts were violent; but as he was wise he withheld his first impulses, and resolved to leave the next morning at break of day without seeing his wife, leaving it to time to give him more certainty and form a resolution.

Plunged as Madame de Tende was in sorrow, she had not failed to notice her own lack of self-control and the manner in which her husband had left her room; she suspected a part of the truth, and, having nothing left but horror of her life, she resolved to lose it in such a way as not to lose her hope for the next.

After having considered well what she was about to do, with deathly trembling, consumed with her misfortunes and with repentance for her life, she determined at last to write these words to her husband:

"This letter will cost me my life; but I deserve death, and I desire it. I am pregnant. The cause of my misfortune is no longer in this world, nor is the only man who knew of our relations; the public never suspected them. I had resolved to end my life by my own hand, but I offer it to God and to you for the expiation of my crime. I did not want to dishonor myself in the eyes of the world because my reputation concerns you; preserve it for your own sake. I shall announce my state; hide the shame of it, and make me perish when and how you will."

The day began to dawn as she wrote this letter, perhaps more difficult to write than any that has ever been written; she sealed it, went to the window, and when she saw the Count of Tende in the courtyard about to get into his carriage, she sent one of her maids to take it to him, and to tell him that it was nothing urgent, that he should read it at his leisure. The Count of Tende was surprised at this letter; it gave him a sort of presentiment, not of all that he would find in it, but that it was related to what he had thought about the evening before. He got into his carriage alone, full of distress and not even daring to open the letter despite his impatience to read it; finally he read it and learned of his misfortune; what did he not think of after having read it! If he had had witnesses, the violent state he was in would have made them think him bereft of reason or about to lose his life. Jealousy and well-founded suspicions ordinarily prepare husbands for their misfortunes; they always have some doubts, but they cannot have the certainty that comes from a confession, which exceeds anything we can discern for ourselves.

The Count of Tende had always found his wife very amiable, although he had not always equally loved her, but she had always seemed to him the most respectable woman he had ever seen; thus his surprise was not less than his fury, and through both those emotions he still felt, in spite of himself, a sorrow in which tenderness had some part.

He stopped at a house along the way where he spent several days, agitated and distressed as one might imagine. At first he thought all that it was natural to think on such an occasion; he thought only of putting his wife to death; but the death of the Prince of Navarre and of La Lande, whom he easily recognized as the confidant, slightly assuaged his fury. He did not doubt that his wife had told the truth in saying that her affair had never been suspected; he judged that the marriage of the Prince of Navarre might have deceived everyone, because he himself had been deceived. After a proof of guilt so strong as the one before his eyes, this entire ignorance of the public concerning his misfortune was a relief to him; but the circumstances, which had shown him to what point and in what manner he had been deceived, pierced him to the heart, and he breathed only vengeance. He considered nevertheless that, if he had his wife killed, and if it should be observed that she was pregnant, the truth would easily be suspected. As he was the proudest of all men he took the course that best suited his honor, and resolved to let nothing be perceived by the public. With this thought he sent a messenger to the Countess of Tende with this note:

"The desire to prevent the scandal of my shame from breaking out overpowers, for the present, my vengeance; I shall see later on what I shall ordain for your unworthy destiny. Conduct yourself as though you had always been as you should have been."

The Countess received this note with joy; she thought it her death sentence, and when she saw that her husband consented to her making her pregnancy known, she felt deeply that shame is the most violent of all passions. She found a kind of calm in believing herself assured of death and seeing her reputation safe; she thought no more of anything but preparing herself for death, and as she was a person in whom all feelings were strong, she embraced virtue and penitence with the same ardor with which she had pursued her passion. Her spirit, moreover, was disillusioned and drowning in affliction; she could see nothing in this life except what seemed more daunting than death itself, so that she saw no other remedy to her misfortunes than the end of her unhappy life. She passed some time in this state, appearing more dead than alive. Toward the sixth month of her pregnancy her body succumbed at last, the fever took hold of her, and she was brought to childbed through the violence of her illness. She had the consolation of seeing her child alive and of being assured that he could not live—that she was not giving her husband an illegitimate heir. She herself expired a few days later, and received death with a joy such as no one has ever felt; she charged her confessor to go and deliver to her husband the news of her death, to ask his pardon on her behalf, and to beg him to forget her, as her memory could only be odious to him.

The Count of Tende received this news without inhumanity, and even with some feelings of pity—but nevertheless with joy. Although he was young he never wanted to remarry, and he lived to an advanced age.[3]

Marie de Rabutin-Chantal, Marquise de Sévigné
1626–1696

Madame de Sévigné never published a word. All she wrote were personal letters, mainly to relatives. Yet she is often considered the greatest stylist of the French language in its golden age, the reign of Louis XIV. The situation that compelled her to write over 1,500 letters reads like the premise of many novels of the subsequent century (when more women started publishing them). She survived a disastrous marriage and entered widowhood at twenty-five, when the Marquis de Sévigné was killed in a duel over his mistress, leaving his family facing financial ruin. She never married again. Beautiful as she was witty and noble, she was offered the greatest matches in France. Wealthy widows, however, were the only women who could enjoy

---

3. The historical Honorat de Savoie was executed by poisoning on 8 September 1572 at the age of 34 for his refusal to participate in the St. Bartholomew's Day massacre of French Protestants. Here he is made to linger on in a long and lonely life after the end of the story, much like the Princess of Clèves.

anything like real independence in her world, and she declined all offers of marriage. When her beloved daughter became Madame de Grignan and followed her husband to his provincial estate, Madame de Sévigné maintained contact mainly through letters. She regaled her effectively exiled daughter with all the gossip from court, source of all news worthy of the name. Her daughter was her primary but not her only correspondent; these included many prominent contemporaries, principally the Marquis de Coulanges and the Comte de Bussy-Rabutin, her cousins and famous fellow wits, as well as her dear friend Madame de Lafayette, a relation by marriage. Sometimes she retired to her own country estate to save money; the displays of wealth required for life at the court of the Sun King were so prohibitive that even the greatest noblemen were often penniless. In fact she was seldom present at court in person, yet she brought it vividly to life for her correspondents, as she does for readers to this day.

PRONUNCIATIONS:

Comte de Bussy-Rabutin: komt duh BEUS-see rah-beu-TANH
Marquis de Coulanges: mahr-KEE duh kOO-LAHNZH
Madame de Grignan: mah-DAHM duh gree-NYAHNH
Langlade: lahn-GLAHD
La Vallière: lah val-YAIR
de Montpensier: duh mohnh-pohnh-SYAY
de Rohan: duh roh-ONH
Marquise de Sévigné: marh-KEEZ duh say-vee-NYAY

from SELECTED LETTERS[1]
To Coulanges

[Paris, Monday 15 December 1670]

What I am about to communicate to you is the most astonishing thing, the most surprising, the most marvellous, the most miraculous, most triumphant, most baffling, most unheard of, most singular, most extraordinary, most unbelievable, most unforeseen, biggest, tiniest, rarest, commonest, the most talked about, the most secret up to this day, the most brilliant, the most enviable, in fact a thing of which only one example can be found in past ages, and, moreover, that example is a false one; a thing nobody can believe in Paris (how could anyone believe it in Lyons?), a thing that makes everybody cry "mercy on us," a thing that fills Mme de Rohan and Mme de Hauterive with joy, in short a thing that will be done on Sunday and those who see it will think they are seeing visions—a thing that will be done on Sunday and perhaps not done by Monday. I can't make up my mind to say it. Guess, I give you three tries. You give up? Very well, I shall have to tell you. M. de Lauzun[2] is marrying on Sunday, in the Louvre[3]—guess who? I give you four guesses, ten, a hundred. Mme de Coulanges will be saying: That's not so very hard to guess, it's Mlle de La Vallière. Not at all, Madame. Mlle de Retz, then? Not at all, you're very provincial. Of course, how silly we are, you say: It's Mlle Colbert. You're still further away. Then it must be Mlle de Créquy? You're nowhere near. I shall have to tell you in the end: he is marrying, on

---

1. Translated by Leonard Tancock.
2. The Duc de Lauzun (1633–1723), a dashing soldier and nobleman in high favor at court at the time.

3. The Louvre in Paris was Louis XIV's official residence until 1682.

Sunday, in the Louvre, with the King's permission, Mademoiselle, Mademoiselle de . . . Mademoiselle . . . guess the name. He's marrying Mademoiselle, of course![4] Honestly, on my honour, on my sworn oath! Mademoiselle, the great Mademoiselle, Mademoiselle, daughter of the late Monsieur, Mademoiselle, granddaughter of Henri IV, Mademoiselle d'Eu, Mademoiselle de Dombes, Mademoiselle de Montpensier, Mademoiselle d'Orléans; Mademoiselle, first cousin of the King, Mademoiselle, destined for a throne, Mademoiselle, the only bride in France worthy of Monsieur. There's a fine subject for conversation. If you shout aloud, if you are beside yourself, if you say we have lied, that it is false, that you are being taken in, that this is a fine old tale and too feeble to be imagined, if, in fine, you should even abuse us, we shall say you are perfectly right. We did as much ourselves.

Good-bye, letters coming by this post will show you whether we are telling the truth or not.

To Coulanges

[Paris, Friday 19 December 1670]

What you might call a bolt from the blue occurred yesterday evening at the Tuileries,[5] but I must start the story further back. You have heard as far as the joy, transports, ecstasies of the Princess and her fortunate lover. Well, the matter was announced on Monday, as you were told. Tuesday was spent in talk, astonishment, compliments. On Wednesday Mademoiselle made a settlement on M. de Lauzun, with the object of bestowing on him the titles, names and honours needed for mention in the marriage contract, and that was enacted on the same day. So, to go on with, she bestowed on him four duchies: first the earldom of Eu, which is the highest peerage in France and gives him first precedence, the duchy of Montpensier, which name he bore all day yesterday, the duchy of Saint-Fargeau and that of Châtellerault, the whole estimated to be worth twenty-two millions. Then the contract[6] was drawn up, in which he took the name of Montpensier. On Thursday morning, that is yesterday, Mademoiselle hoped that the King would sign the contract as he had promised, but by seven in the evening His Majesty, being persuaded by the Queen, Monsieur and divers grey-beards that this business was harmful to his reputation, decided to break it off, and after summoning Mademoiselle and M. de Lauzun, declared to them, in the presence of Monsieur le Prince, that he forbade their thinking any more about this marriage. M. de Lauzun received this order with all the respect, all the submissiveness, all the stoicism and all the despair that such a great fall required. As for Mademoiselle, according to her mood she burst into tears, cries, violent outbursts of grief, exaggerated lamentations, and she remained in bed all day, taking nothing but broth. So much for a beautiful dream, a fine subject for a novel or a tragedy, but above all for arguing and talking for ever and ever. And that is what we are doing day and night, evening and morning, on and on without respite. We hope you will do the same. Upon which I most humbly kiss your hands.

---

4. By convention, the King's brother and his wife were known as Monsieur and Madame, their daughter as Mademoiselle. Sévigné is here referring to Anne Marie Louise d'Orléans, Duchesse de Montpensier (1627–1693), known as la Grande Mademoiselle, daughter of Gaston d'Orléans, brother to the late Louis XIII.

5. The Palais des Tuileries, another royal residence in Paris.
6. Any marriage between highborn or wealthy individuals would be preceded by a legal document laying out the economic terms of the alliance, including dowry and provision for children.

To Coulanges

[Paris, Wednesday 24 December 1670]

You now know the romantic story of Mademoiselle and M. de Lauzun. It is a real subject of tragedy according to all the rules of the theatre. The other day we were plotting out the acts and scenes, giving it four days instead of twenty-four hours, and it made a perfect play. Never have such changes been seen in so short a time, never have you seen such general emotion, never have you heard such extraordinary news. M. de Lauzun has played his part as to the manor born; he has endured this misfortune with a self-control, courage and yet grief mingled with profound respect which have earned him universal admiration. What he has lost is of inestimable value, but the goodwill of the King, which he has kept, is also beyond price, and his fortune seems by no means in a parlous state. Mademoiselle has behaved very well too. She has wept a lot, but today she has returned her duty calls at the Louvre, whence she had been receiving all the visitors. So that is that. Good-bye.

To Madame de Grignan

[Paris, Friday evening, 15 January 1672]

I wrote to you this morning, my dearest, by the post which is bringing you all joys and happiness for your affairs in Provence, but I mean to write again this evening lest it should be said that a post comes without bringing you a word from me. I really think, my dear, that you like my letters. You say you do—why would you want to deceive me as well as yourself? For if by chance it were not so, one would have to pity you for being overwhelmed by the abundance of mine. Yours are a joy to me. I haven't answered about your great soul (it is Langlade who says *great soul* by way of teasing), but honestly you have a very great one. Perhaps it is not one of those souls in the very first class, like that Roman who went back to the Carthaginians to keep his word and was martyred,[7] but below that you can pride yourself on being in the top rank. I find you so perfect and so well thought of that I don't know what to say except admiration, and advice to back up your reason with your courage and your courage with your reason, and to take chocolate, so that the most unpleasant company seems good to you.

◄─•─ ≅◆≡ ─•─►

Elisabeth Charlotte von der Pfalz, Duchesse d'Orléans
1652–1722

Like the Marquise de Sévigné, the Duchess of Orléans has left us one of the finest accounts of the most brilliant European court of their time. While Madame de Sévigné was the greatest prose stylist of the French classical period, Liselotte (as she was called) wrote her best letters in German. Whereas the Marquise wrote letters as a French aristocrat to her daughter exiled from Paris, the Duchess wrote them to her German relatives back home as a foreigner exiled within the very heart of the French court.

---

7. Rome and Carthage were engaged in bitter warfare for many years; this Roman showed he possessed a soul of the first class when he chose to go to his certain death at the hands of his enemies rather than go back on his word.

Born at Heidelberg to the Protestant ruler Karl Ludwig von der Pfalz four years after the Peace of Westphalia had ended the Thirty Years' War, Elisabeth Charlotte witnessed her father's rapid restoration of his devastated kingdom and establishment of the University of Heidelberg. She also witnessed the breakdown of his marriage to her mother, whom he soon repudiated in favor of one of her ladies in waiting, starting a new family without rights of succession. To separate her from her resentful mother, he sent Liselotte away at age seven to live with his sister for several years. That was her first exile, and the beginning of what she would later call her "principal occupation" of writing letters home. As a young woman, although she seemed to prefer a single life, and certainly to remain in Germany, she acquiesced in her father's plan to marry her to the recently widowed brother of Louis XIV, in hopes that such a powerful alliance would forestall a French invasion of his country. No member of the French royal family was allowed to travel without the King, so she never returned home.

The King's brother, known simply as "Monsieur," was well known to be incapable of love for a woman, spending most of his time with male favorites and hangers-on. Despite their mutual physical disgust, Monsieur and Madame produced three children in short order. When he abandoned her bed permanently after the third childbirth, she expressed her relief, writing that she "did not like the business very much." Madame never adapted to French court life any better than she did to married life, but in both she contrived to observe the forms without putting herself out unnecessarily. She despised dressing, dancing, gambling, and court intrigues—everything Monsieur and the other courtiers lived for. Carefully proclaiming her own ignorance, she filled her letters with references to Ovid, Virgil, Petrarch, Montaigne, Rabelais, Cervantes, and Shakespeare, reasoned with living philosophers, and collected art. The one courtly entertainment she loved was the theater, writing, "I'm never tired of the verses of Corneille or Racine, or of the comedies of Molière, as long as they are played well." She learned to ride, and loved to go hunting or walking through the gardens of Versailles with the King, with whom she was a great favorite.

Her friendship with the King was never the same, though, after he destroyed her homeland, the Palatinate, in 1685. When her male relatives died without heirs, Louis XIV claimed the Palatinate in her name, and when it refused to accept French rule he invaded, instituting a ruthless scorched earth policy despite her pleading. Madame describes the nightmares in which she saw her native Heidelberg in flames. She also hated the powerful mistress, the Marquise de Maintenon, whom Louis married secretly after his wife's death. When Louis XIV died in 1715, however, Liselotte became the most powerful woman in France, as mother of the Regent (Monsieur was already dead). Although she wasn't fond of extravagant parties, Madame fostered the arts and literary gatherings at the ducal château of Saint-Cloud, which became an important center for writers of literary fairy tales in particular. Several collections of these, including Perrault's, are dedicated to her. Everyone courted her, but she still refused to meddle in politics, claiming that women had ruled France too long already—disapprovingly echoing Madame de Lafayette's description of a court in which politics and love were always intertwined. Nevertheless her letters continued to be opened and read by her son's censors, as they had been by Louis XIV's. She always had to save her more risqué remarks for letters she could deliver by hand rather than by the post.

PRONUNCIATIONS:
de Conti: duh kohnh-TEE
Dauphin: doh-FANH
D'Effiat: def-FYA
galants: ga-LONH
de la Vallière: duh lah val-YAIR
de Montespan: duh mohnh-tuh-SPAHNH
Liselotte von der Pfalz: lee-zuh-LOT-tuh fon dehr FAHLTS
Marquise de Maintenon: marh-KEEZ duh manh-tuh-NOHNH
de Sévigné: duh say-vee-NYAY

from LETTERS[1]

Versailles 11 May 1685

Today the King sent his confessor to mine, to ask him to reprimand me on three counts. First: I was too free in my speech, and had told the Dauphin[2] that even if I were to see him stark naked from the soles of his feet upward I shouldn't be tempted by him, nor by anyone else. Secondly: I allowed my ladies to have *galants.*[3] And thirdly: I had laughed with the Princesse de Conti[4] about hers. These three things had annoyed the King so much that if I hadn't been his sister-in-law he would have had me banished from the Court. I admitted that the report of my conversation with the Dauphin was quite accurate, and added that I had never thought it a crime not to feel temptation. As for plain speaking, and what I might have said about crapping and pissing, it was more the King's fault than mine, as I had heard him say hundreds of times that within the family one could talk about anything at all. He should have told me if he had changed his mind; it was the easiest thing in the world to correct.

On the second point, my ladies and their lovers: I never meddled in the affairs of my household, and shouldn't begin with the thing hardest to put to rights. But I knew such conduct to be not without precedent, and quite usual at any Court. As long as they did not prejudice their honour, I didn't think they did themselves or me any harm.

As for the third point, concerning his daughter: I was not her governess to stop her from having lovers if she wanted them, and could hardly be expected to weep when she told me of her adventures. But Mme la Duchesse could be my witness: I never interfere, and I felt very hurt at being treated so badly by the King, as though I had committed some frightful crime.

I must say, I am furious that the King should treat me like a chambermaid. That may be perfectly suitable for his Maintenon,[5] who was born to it, but not for me.

Versailles 11 August 1686

Our King is not well, it may turn out to be the four-day fever. God help us if it does, for it will make him a hundred times crosser still. He imagines that he is being devout because he no longer sleeps with young women, but his piety consists of nothing but being ill-tempered and employing spies everywhere, who falsely accuse everyone, flatter his brother's favourites and pester everybody. The old hag, the Maintenon, amuses herself by ruling over the royal family. She makes the King hate every member of it except Monsieur. In order to make the latter live on good terms with her, and do whatever she wants, she praises him in front of the King. On the other hand, the old woman fears that people might really believe she likes Monsieur, so as soon as he is mentioned she calls him every horrible name she can think of.

---

1. Translated by Maria Kroll.
2. The King's eldest son, heir to the throne.
3. Admirers and/or lovers.
4. Marie Anne de Bourbon (1666–1709), illegitimate daughter of Louis XIV and Louise de la Vallière, and married to Louis Armand, Prince de Conti.

5. Françoise d'Aubigné, Marquise de Maintenon (1635–1719), another mistress, married privately to Louis XIV sometime after the death of his Queen, Marie-Thérèse, in 1683. The fact that Louis married her although she was not of royal blood irked Madame, who was.

From St. Cloud 5 June 1689

By now I should be used to knowing that my poor mother-country is in flames. I have heard of nothing else for so long, but every time I learn of another place being burnt down I hear it with pain and sorrow.[6]

Monsieur recently told me something I hadn't heard before, which annoyed me extremely. It seems that the King collected money from the Palatinate in my name, and now the poor people must think that I have profited from their misery as well as being the cause of it all. It grieves me bitterly. I wish to God I had been given all the money that has been extracted from the Palatinate to do as I liked with: the poor Raugrave children[7] and the poor Palatines would certainly be the better off for it. But the truth is that I haven't seen a single penny.

Versailles 26 August 1689

You know that my enemies have put it into Monsieur's head to make his first equerry, d'Effiat,[8] my son's governor. Since all France knows as well as I do that this man is the most immoral and depraved fellow in the world, I have asked Monsieur to select someone else.

My reason is that it doesn't seem compatible with my son's honour to be regarded as d'Effiat's mistress, for there is no greater sodomite in the whole of France. It's a poor début for a young prince to start off in life with the greatest debauchee in the world. Monsieur admitted that d'Effiat had been depraved and fond of boys, but said that he had cured himself of his vices long since. I said that only a few years ago a good-looking German who was staying here had excused himself from coming to see me as often as he would have liked because d'Effiat pestered him whenever he set foot in the Palais-Royal. So he can't have changed as long ago as his friends claim. And even supposing that he hadn't practised his vices for a few years, I don't consider it is necessary to use one's only son to test whether or not the Herr equerry has renounced boys. I said that Monsieur was, of course, the lord and master of his house, and at liberty to put my son in the hands of whomever he pleased, but that I couldn't approve of d'Effiat as long as I lived, and I should make this fact known.

St. Cloud 21 September 1689

Now for the continuation of this story. I have spoken to the King. His Majesty said it was pure invention that he wanted d'Effiat to be his nephew's governor; on the contrary, he had spent all last year trying to dissuade Monsieur from his choice. Whereupon I humbly begged his Majesty to find an honest man for my son and propose him to Monsieur, which he promised to do. Since then all has been quiet. I have found out that the King is keeping his word, and there is reason to hope that my son will soon have a new preceptor. God grant that we may be given an honest man.

St. Cloud 30 October 1689

Yesterday I was told something which moved me so much that it made me cry. I heard that the poor people of Mannheim have returned to their ruined town. They have moved into their cellars, and live there as though they were in their old homes.

6. France invaded the Palatinate in 1688.
7. The children of Liselotte's father's second wife, disinherited when the Electorate passed to a different branch of the family.
8. Antoine René, Marquis d'Effiat (1683–1719), master of the horse to Philippe I d'Orléans.

They even hold their daily market just as if the town were still standing. And whenever a Frenchman comes to Heidelberg, the poor citizens crowd round him to ask after me. Then they begin to talk of His Grace, my late father the Elector, and of my late brother, and they weep bitterly. They have no love for the present Elector.

Versailles 1 January 1693

I can't resist telling you of a splendid conversation I had with Monsieur. I hope it will amuse you as much as it did my two children. There were just the four of us in my apartments after supper: Monsieur, me, my son and my daughter. Monsieur, who didn't consider us fine enough company to trouble himself by talking, after a long silence let off a great long fart (by your leave, by your leave). He turned to me and said, "What was that, Madame?" I turned my behind in his direction, let off in the same tone and said, "That, Monsieur." My son said, "If it comes to that, I can do as well as Monsieur and Madame," and let off a good one, too. Then we all laughed and left the room. These are, as you see, princely conversations, and should anyone still be sufficiently inquisitive to open my letters to you, I offer the first one who does so this incense for the New Year.

Versailles 18 January 1693

I'm glad that our cracking conversation made you laugh. My son has so much wind that he can produce any kind of note, which is why he now plays the flute. I think that if he held it against his behind instead of his mouth, it would sound equally musical.

Versailles 16 December 1694

Salut, sermon and Mass may have their point so far as the next world is concerned, but for this one they are bitterly dreary. If by experiencing little joy and great tribulation one earns the right to go to heaven, my earnings should be enough to make me a great saint.

If the rumours are to be believed, our tedium will become greater still, because we hear that all operas and plays are to be abolished. The Sorbonne[9] has instructions to take the matter in hand. What seems so astonishing to me is that they concentrate on such innocent things while all the vices are in full swing. No one says a single word against poisoning, violence and that horrible sodomy; all the clergy preach against the poor theatre, which does nobody any harm, and where vice is punished and virtue rewarded. It makes me furious.

Versailles 19 December 1694

I see that you like wearing heavy clothes as little as I do. When I order anything new I always ask for it to be kept light. There is no pleasure in walking when one is heavily dressed. You could afford to wear heavy clothes more easily than I can because you are slim, but I, with my large hips and (by your leave) larger behind, have enough of a job to carry myself about. Velvet trimmed with gold must be very heavy. I wear my velvet plain, but then they will give one trimmed underskirts, which often weigh far too much.

Paris 23 December 1694

Thank the Lord, the theatre is to stay. This greatly annoys the great man's old hag, as she was responsible for the proposed ban. But the clergy may shout against it from

9. The theological faculty at the University of Paris, a powerful body in 17th-century France.

their pulpits as much as they like; as long as there are plays, I shall continue to go to see them. When there was a sermon against the theatre a fortnight ago and the preacher said that it inflamed the passions, the King turned to me and remarked, "He doesn't mean me—I don't go to the theatre any longer. He means all of you who love it and do." I said, "I may enjoy the theatre, but M. d'Agen isn't referring to me—he is speaking of the people whose passions are aroused there, and I only go to be entertained. That is no sin." The King was as quiet as a mouse, then.

Versailles 6 February 1695

Two days ago I heard of another mean, spiteful thing the old whore has done. Two years ago the Dauphin wanted to marry my daughter, and mentioned this to the old Kunkunkel. She made no objection, for fear that, if she did, he would be more likely to tell the King of his intentions: instead she sent for the Princesse de Conti and her confidante Mlle de Choin. She ordered them both not to give the Dauphin a minute's peace until he promised to dismiss any such idea entirely from his mind. The two of them gave him no rest for two whole months, until he gave them his promise. And he has kept it, too. So you see how much I am in debt to this old witch. She not only bribed my son to marry badly, she also ruined my daughter's chances. I really have no reason to spare her feelings, and if she should open this letter she will find nothing in it but the truth, and I don't care anyway, she can do nothing worse than she has done already, and I hope that for this she will go to hell, and be conducted there by the Father, the Son and the Holy Ghost.

Versailles 13 February 1695

You would never believe how vulgar and ill-mannered the French have become in the course of the last twelve or thirteen years. You won't find two young people of quality who know how to be polite in word or deed. There are two reasons for this: the piety prevailing at Court, and the excesses amongst the men. For one thing, it is no longer seemly for men and women to be seen speaking together; for another, men no longer wish to please anyone but each other, and the more debauched and impertinent they are, the more they are admired.

It may be a great honour to sit next to the King in church, but I would gladly relinquish it because His Majesty won't let me sleep. As soon as I doze off he nudges me with his elbow and wakes me up again, so that I am neither wholly asleep nor wholly awake. It gives me a headache.

Paris 14 May 1695

Dancing must be out of fashion everywhere. Here at parties people do nothing but play *lansquenet*,[1] that is the game chiefly *en vogue* at the moment. Even the young people don't dance any more. I do neither the one nor the other. I am much too old to dance, and I don't gamble for two very good reasons: I haven't the money, and I don't enjoy it. The stakes are enormously high, and people behave like lunatics when they play. One will bawl, another bang the table so that the room shakes, a third blaspheme to make your hair stand on end—in short, they are like desperate madmen, it is frightening just to look at them.

---

1. A card game of German origin.

St. Cloud 15 September 1695

What happened at St. Cyr[2] was much worse and rather funnier: some of the young ladies there had fallen in love with one another; they were caught committing all sorts of indecencies. Mme de Maintenon is supposed to have cried her eyes out. She had all the relics put on display to drive out the devils of lechery. Also, she sent for a priest to preach against lewdness, but he talked about such hideous things that none of the modest ladies could bear to listen; they all left the church, but the culprits were overcome by uncontrollable fits of the giggles.

Fontainebleau 25 October 1698

My daughter's journey is progressing happily. I had a letter from her today which she wrote in Châlons. It will be a hard day for her today, because this is where she officially leaves the King's house and becomes a wife in earnest. She and her husband are to sleep together tonight. That will seem very peculiar to her. Although my daughter finds her Duke attractive, she says she is feeling very apprehensive at his coming to collect her; she says she's so beside herself with fear about the night that she is all of a tremble and hardly knows what she is saying. She may not be all that wrong, one hears such strange reports of our son-in-law. Apparently once, when he was taking a bath, the man who was washing him said, "Would His Grace move his arm so that I can wash His Grace?" It turned out that it wasn't his arm that was in the way at all, but, by your leave, quite a different thing. I am incredibly impatient to hear how the first night passed.

Fontainebleau 5 November 1698

The Duc de Lorraine seems very fond of my daughter, and if only their love lasts they should be happy enough. "*Mais hélas, il n'est point d'éternelles amours,*" as they say in *Clélie.*[3]

Paris 16 November 1698

My daughter has soon become used to her new state, and it is reported from Nancy that the Duke is extraordinarily keen on married life. After the entry into the town, my daughter was obliged to change her clothes because her dress was so heavy that she couldn't stand up in it, and just as she had taken off her skirts, along came the Duke and paid her one of his visits. She's quite used to it by now, and doesn't dislike that business as much as I did.

It isn't at all surprising that Monsieur had the dressing-table things melted down, for they were his own property. But one day, although I implored him not to, he took all the silver that had come from Heidelberg, as well as all the silver things that used to decorate my rooms and look so pretty, and had them melted down too. He put the money into his own pocket. He hasn't left me so much as one poor little box for my bits and pieces.

Marly 6 February 1699

I enjoy your letters very much. Do go on writing like that, quite naturally and *sans façon:* I can't stand compliments. If only you could write something to make me

---

2. A convent school founded by Madame de Maintenon and the King for the education of poor but nobly born young women.

3. "Alas, there is no such thing as eternal love." *Clélie* is a novel by Madeleine de Scudéry (1607–1701; see page 257).

laugh! Laughter has become rare in my life during the last few years, I am quite getting out of the habit and my spleen is none the better for it. Do not think, dear Ameliese, that cleverness consists in being able to pay compliments. The silliest people in the world can memorize compliments and write them down, but to write well on ordinary subjects and to have a readable style is far rarer than you seem to think, and it is your great humility that is at fault if you think you don't write well.

Your life, as you describe it, sounds quite pleasant to me. Here one soon regrets frank speaking, and that is why I live in solitude.

Versailles 29 December 1701

I'm sure you have fewer wrinkles than I have. Mine come from many years of exposure to the sun while hunting, but I don't mind about them at all. Never having had good looks, I didn't have much to lose, and I see that those who used to be beauties in the past are now as plain as I am. Not a soul could recognize Mme de la Vallière now, and Mme de Montespan's skin looks like paper which children have folded over and over, for her face is covered with minute lines, so close together that it is astonishing. Her beautiful hair is as white as snow, and her face is quite red, no longer pretty at all. I am quite content never to have had what after all passes so quickly.

You possess more lasting beauty: your intelligence, your vivacity, your generosity and goodness, your constancy to those to whom you have once given your friendship, are all qualities that serve to make your friends' attachment to you so strong that they remain devoted to you all their lives.

Versailles 23 July 1702

The Dutch understand cleanliness better than anyone in the world. Things are very different in France. There is one dirty thing at Court that I shall never get used to: the people stationed in the galleries in front of our rooms piss into all the corners. It is impossible to leave one's apartments without seeing somebody pissing. This would be a better thing to abolish than plays and operas.

St. Cloud 29 September 1718

All Frenchmen love Paris above everything. I am fond of the Parisians, but I don't like Paris; everything there is unpleasant. The kind of life they lead there, and everything one hears and sees, is unbearable. It is quite true that women have their veins painted blue now, to make people believe their skin is so transparent that the veins show through. Another thing that is true is that there are fewer beautiful people now than there used to be. I think they ruin their looks with all their paint.

St. Cloud 8 June 1719

Writing is my favourite occupation, because I don't like needlework; to my mind there is nothing more tedious in the world than putting in a needle and pulling it out again.

You did make me laugh, dear Luise, when you said that my letters do you as much good as "balsam on your head." It is to be hoped at least that this balsam won't flow from your head into your beard, as it did with Aaron.[4]

---

4. A humorous reference to Psalm 133:2, which compares brotherly love to an anointing with fine oil.

St. Cloud 27 August 1719

Everywhere you go you hear people complaining about two things: the heat and the damnable bedbugs, which plague me all night long. The Princess of Wales says in her letter that all London is suffering, too, and the Queen of Sicily writes that her bed was overrun.

St. Cloud 26 April 1721

M. Teray[5] knows his business, and inspires confidence. I do as I'm told, but I am absolutely convinced that our hours are numbered, and that we can't exceed the limit. So long as I am meant to be alive the doctors will find every possible cure, but once the fatal hour comes which the Almighty has ordained for taking me out of this life, they will be quite powerless. I view the prospect with indifference. I know that I was born only to die, and await the time without impatience or fear, and pray to God to let me have a peaceful end. Nothing you read in the Bible about the time before the Flood, or Sodom and Gomorrah,[6] comes anywhere near the life people lead in Paris. Of nine young people of quality who dined with my grandson, the Duc de Chartres, a few days ago, seven had the French *malaise*.[7] Isn't that disgusting?

St. Cloud 11 May 1721

It suits me to be out of Paris. My health is much improved. When I open my window the air here is scented like a bouquet of flowers, very different from Paris, where you smell nothing but emptied close-stools and chamberpots, which have not an agreeable perfume.

━━ ▧◈▤ ━━

Katherine Philips
1631–1664

Katherine Philips performed the remarkable feat of importing French-style, aristocratic female-centered literary salon culture to an England without a royal court, transforming herself in the process into "the Matchless Orinda." English culture under the Puritan leader Oliver Cromwell during the "Interregnum" (1649–1660) between the execution of Charles I and the restoration of his son Charles II could not have been more different from the contemporary French culture, centered around the court of Louis XIV. At sixteen this daughter of a London merchant married an older, wealthy Puritan, James Philips, who supported her literary aspirations. Following one's husband to his provincial estate could kill the career of any French salonnière, yet Philips established her famous "Society of Friendship" *with* her husband (a notion unheard of in France) at his remote Welsh home, Cardigan Priory. Like the salons, this was a literary and intellectual coterie in which both sexes took on pastoral pseudonyms, but which centered around intense friendships between women, expressed in letters, poems, and other literary forms. Katherine became "Orinda," her husband became "Antenor," and her friend Anne Owen, Viscountess Dungannon, became the "Lucasia" to whom she addresses the poem below. Like the French salonnières, Philips hesitated to publish her original work, but her translations of the plays of Corneille were performed publicly during her lifetime. All the famous English writers of her day admired her privately circulated poems, and eulogized her upon her early death of

---

5. Liselotte's personal physician.
6. Outrageously sinful behavior on a mass scale, punished

by the wrath of God (Genesis 6).
7. Syphilis. The Duc de Chartres was 17 at the time.

the smallpox. "All laurels to her laurel bowed," the poet Anne Killigrew wrote when her works were published posthumously. She was imitated by English women poets throughout the eighteenth century.

To My Excellent Lucasia, on Our Friendship

I did not live until this time
  Crowned my felicity,
When I could say without a crime,
  I am not thine, but thee.

5 This carcase breathed, and walked, and slept,
  So that the world believed
There was a soul the motions kept;
  But they were all deceived.

For as a watch by art° is wound   *artificial means*
10   To motion, such was mine:
But never had Orinda found
  A soul till she found thine;

Which now inspires,° cures and supplies,   *animates*
  And guides my darkened breast:
15 For thou art all that I can prize,
  My joy, my life, my rest.

No bridegroom's nor crown-conqueror's mirth
  To mine compared can be:
They have but pieces of this earth,
20   I've all the world in thee.

Then let our flames still light and shine,
  And no false fear control,
As innocent as our design,°   *intentions*
  Immortal as our soul.

An Answer to Another Persuading a Lady to Marriage

I

Forbear,° bold youth, all's Heaven here,   *hold back, desist*
  And what you do aver,°   *propose*
To others courtship may appear,
  'Tis sacrifice to her.

II

5 She is a public deity,
  And were't not very odd
She should depose herself to be
  A petty household god?

III

First make the sun in private shine,
10 And bid the world adieu,
That so he may his beams confine
  In compliment° to you.   *homage*

IV

But if of that you do despair,
Think how you did amiss,
15   To strive to fix her beams, which are
More bright and large than his.

Mary, Lady Chudleigh
1656–1710

Lady Chudleigh spent her entire life in the rural solitude of Devonshire, England. There, at seventeen, the young Mary Lee married thirty-year-old George Chudleigh, who succeeded to his father's baronetcy in 1691. Mary spent most of her time alone in her study: "there I meet with nothing to disturb me, nothing to render me uneasy; I find my Books and my Thoughts to be the most agreeable Companions." Her readings literally were her companions, for from her country solitude she exchanged writings with authors including the poet laureate John Dryden and the proto-feminist Mary Astell. It was the fashion in those days to slander the entire female sex in sermons or pamphlets recommending that their excesses be controlled through complete subordination to their husbands. Lady Chudleigh was "troubl'd to see [women] made the Jest of every vain Pretender to Wit." Encouraged by her literary coterie, she ventured in 1701 to publish *The Ladies Defence,* a debate in verse in which a female speaker argues about the nature, education, and duties of women with three variously censorious male characters. Through print she imagines herself addressing a wider coterie of ladies who would join with her to "make it our whole business to be wise."

PRONUNCIATION:
Chudleigh: CHUD-lee

from The Ladies Defence

'Tis hard we should be by the men despised,
Yet kept from knowing what would make us prized;
Debarred from knowledge, banished from the schools,
And with the utmost industry bred fools;
5   Laughed out of reason, jested out of sense,
And nothing left but native° innocence;   *innate*
Then told we are incapable of wit,°   *intelligence*
And only for the meanest drudgeries fit;
Made slaves to serve their luxury and pride,
10   And with innumerable hardships tried,
Till pitying heaven release us from our pain,
Kind heaven, to whom alone we dare complain.
Th' ill-natured world will no compassion show:
Such as are wretched it would still have so.
15   It gratifies its envy and its spite:
The most in others' miseries take delight.
While we are present, they some pity spare,
And feast us on a thin repast° of air;   *meal*
Look grave and sigh, when we our wrongs relate,

20	And in a compliment accuse° our fate;	*deplore*
	Blame those to whom we our misfortunes owe,	
	And all the signs of real friendship show,	
	But when we're absent, we their sport are made,	
	They fan the flame, and our oppressors aid;	
25	Join with the stronger, the victorious side,	
	And all our sufferings, all our griefs deride.	
	Those generous few whom kinder thoughts inspire,	
	And who the happiness of all desire,	
	Who wish we were from barbarous usage free,	
30	Exempt from toils and shameful slavery,	
	Yet let us, unreproved,° mis-spend our hours,	*undisciplined, uncriticized*
	And to mean purposes employ our nobler powers.	
	They think, if we our thoughts can but express,	
	And know but how to work, to dance and dress,	
35	It is enough, as much as we should mind,	
	As if we were for nothing else designed,	
	But made, like puppets, to divert mankind.	
	O that my sex would all such toys despise,	
	And only study to be good and wise;	
40	Inspect themselves, and every blemish find,	
	Search all the close° recesses of the mind,	*hidden*
	And leave no vice, no ruling passion there,	
	Nothing to raise a blush, or cause a fear;	
	Their memories with solid notions fill,	
45	And let their reason dictate to their will;	
	Instead of novels, histories peruse,	
	And for their guides the wiser ancients choose;	
	Through all the labyrinths of learning go,	
	And grow more humble, as they more do know.	
50	By doing this they will respect procure,	
	Silence the men, and lasting fame secure;	
	And to themselves the best companions prove,	
	And neither fear their malice, nor desire their love.	

Anne Finch, Countess of Winchilsea
1661–1720

When Anne Kingsmill was invited in 1682 to become Maid of Honor to Mary of Modena, Duchess of York, "eager from the rural seat [she] came." She abandoned the obscure life of rural gentry only to experience the dangers of politics and develop the appreciation for country "retirement" that marks her poetry. At court she soon met Colonel Heneage Finch, marrying him in 1684. She considered herself extraordinarily blessed in a husband who encouraged her writing: "They err, who say that husbands can't be lovers." In 1685 the Duke of York became King James II and the Finches became prominent courtiers until the "Glorious Revolution" of 1688 drove James and his loyal followers into exile. The couple sought refuge with friends, eventually settling with a nephew, the Earl of Winchilsea, at Eastwell Park in Kent. Anne idealized this estate as "Arcadia," a pastoral retreat from a society where "all's confused." There she gathered an intellectual circle of friends, inspired, like Katherine Philips (see page 279), by the French salons, and under the pastoral pseudonym of Ardelia circulated her manuscripts among this coterie. These brought her a reputation such that writers like Swift and Pope encouraged her to publish. Being talked about at all was risky for ladies, however; Swift and Pope themselves cruelly satirized female authors.

In 1702 Queen Anne brought Finch back to court as Lady of the Bedchamber. She became Countess of Winchilsea upon the death of her nephew in 1712, and the next year anonymously published her collected works, after at least thirty years of writing. The work was admired by contemporaries, and by later writers from Wordsworth to Woolf. "The Introduction," which opened this volume of her poetry, poignantly voices Finch's fears of the censures awaiting women authors. "The Spleen," a subject about which Pope also wrote in *The Rape of the Lock* (see page 524), vividly describes her experience of a disorder that was widespread, not to say fashionable, in their day: partly physical and partly emotional, somewhere between malaise and ennui. "Friendship Between Ephelia and Ardelia" exemplifies the passionate, intellectual friendships between women that characterized salon and coterie culture.

The Introduction

Did I my lines intend for public view,
How many censures would their faults persue,
Some would, because such words they do affect,
Cry they're insipid, empty, uncorrect.
5   And many, have attain'd, dull and untaught,
The name of Wit,° only by finding fault.   *cleverness*
True judges might condemn their want of wit,
And all might say, they're by a Woman writ.
Alas! a woman that attempts the pen,
10   Such an intruder on the rights of men,
Such a presumptuous creature is esteem'd,
The fault can by no virtue be redeem'd.
They tell us, we mistake our sex and way;
Good breeding, fashion, dancing, dressing, play
15   Are the accomplishments we should desire;
To write, or read, or think, or to inquire
Would cloud our beauty and exhaust our time,
And interrupt the conquests of our prime;
Whilst the dull manage of a servile house
20   Is held by some, our outmost art and use.
    Sure 'twas not ever thus, nor are we told
Fables of women that excell'd of old;
To whom, by the diffusive hand of Heaven
Some share of wit and poetry was given.
25   On that glad day on which the Ark return'd,[1]
The holy pledge for which the Land had mourn'd,
The joyful Tribes attend it on the way,
The Levites do the sacred charge convey,
Whilst various instruments before it play;

---

1. The Ark of the Covenant, recovered by the Israelites from the Philistines (2 Samuel 6).

30   Here, holy Virgins in the concert join,
       The louder notes to soften and refine,
       And with alternate verse, complete the hymn divine.
       Lo! the young Poet, after God's own heart,
       By Him inspired, and taught the Muses' art,
35   Return'd from conquest, a bright chorus meets,
       That sing his slain ten thousand in the streets.
       In such loud numbers they his acts declare,
       Proclaim the wonders of his early war,
       That Saul upon the vast applause does frown,
40   And feels its mighty thunder shake the Crown.[2]
       What, can the threaten'd judgment now prolong?
       Half of the kingdom is already gone;
       The fairest half, whose influence guides the rest,
       Have David's empire, o'er their hearts confess't.
45   A woman here leads fainting Israel on,
       She fights, she wins, she triumphs with a song,[3]
       Devout, majestic, for the subject fit,
       And far above her arms exalts her wit,
       Then, to the peaceful, shady palm withdraws,
50   And rules the rescu'd nation with her laws.
       How are we fallen, fallen by mistaken rules?
       And education's, more then nature's, fools,
       Debar'd from all improvements of the mind,
       And to be dull, expected and designed;
55   And if someone would soar above the rest,
       With warmer fancy,° and ambition press't,   *imagination*
       So strong, th' opposing faction still appears,
       The hopes to thrive, can ne'er outweigh the fears,
       Be caution'd then, my Muse, and still retir'd;
60   Nor be despis'd, aiming to be admir'd;
       Conscious of wants, still with contracted wing,
       To some few friends, and to thy sorrows sing;
       For groves of laurel, thou wert never meant;
       Be dark enough thy shades, and be thou there content.

Friendship Between Ephelia and Ardelia

Eph.   What friendship is, Ardelia, show.
Ard.   'Tis to love, as I love you.
Eph.   This account, so short (though kind)
          Suits not my inquiring mind.
5   Therefore farther now repeat;
          What is friendship when complete?

2. King Saul became murderously jealous of his young warrior David when David returned from a victory over the Philistines and the Israelites greeted him by singing, "Saul has killed his thousands, but David his tens of thousands" (1 Samuel 18:7).

3. The judge and prophetess Deborah guided the Israelites to a major victory, and praised God in a poem, "The Song of Deborah" (Judges 5).

	Ard.	'Tis to share all joy and grief;
		'Tis to lend all due relief
		From the tongue, the heart, the hand;
10		'Tis to mortgage house and land;
		For a friend be sold a slave;
		'Tis to die upon a grave,
		If a friend therein do lie.
	Eph.	This indeed, though carried high,
15		This, though more than e'er was done
		Underneath the rolling sun,
		This has all been said before.
		Can Ardelia say no more?
	Ard.	Words indeed no more can show:
20		But 'tis to love, as I love you.

from The Spleen

1

What art thou, *Spleen,* which every thing dost ape?°   mimic
      Thou Proteus[1] to abuse mankind,
        Who never yet thy hidden cause could find,
Or fix thee to remain in one continu'd shape;
5   Still varying thy perplexing form,
      Now a dead sea thoul't represent
        A calm of stupid discontent,
Then dashing on the rocks wilt rage into a storm:
Trembling sometimes thou dost appear,
10   Dissolv'd into a panic fear.
On sleep intruding dost thy shadows spread,
      Thy gloomy terrors round the silent bed,
And crowd with boding dreams the melancholy head.
Or when the midnight hour is told,
15   And drooping lids thou still dost waking hold,
      Thy fond delusions cheat the eyes;
      Before 'em antic spectres dance,
Unusual fires their pointed heads advance,
      And aery phantoms rise.
20   Such was the monstrous vision seen,
When Brutus (now beneath his cares opprest,
And all Rome's fortunes rolling in his breast,
      Before Philippi's latest field
Before his fate did to Octavius yield)[2]
25   Was vanquish'd by the Spleen.

2

      Falsly the mortal part we blame
      Of our depress'd and pond'rous frame,

---

1. A Greek sea god who could change shape at will.
2. See Shakespeare's *Julius Caesar,* 4.3, in which Brutus is visited by the ghost of the murdered Caesar the night before he will lose his own life in battle at Philippi.

Which till the first degrading sin
Let thee its dull attendant in,
30   Still with the other did comply;
Nor clogg'd the active soul, dispos'd to fly,
And range the mansions of its native sky:
          Nor whilst in his own heaven he dwelt,
          Whilst man his paradise possest,
35   His fertile garden in the fragrant east,
                    And all united odours smelt,
          No pointed sweets° until thy reign   *potent perfumes*
          Could shock the sense, or in the face
A flush, unhandsome colour place:
40   Now the Jonquil° o'ercomes the feeble brain,   *a sweet-scented daffodil*
          We faint beneath the aromatic pain,
          Till some offensive scent° thy powers appease,   *smelling salts*
And pleasure we resign for short and nauseous ease.

3

          New are thy motions and thy dress,
45   In every one thou dost possess:
          Here some attentive secret friend
Thy false suggestions must attend,
Thy whisper'd griefs, thy fancy'd sorrows hear,
Breath'd in a sigh, and witness'd by a tear:
50   Whilst in the light and vulgar crowd
          Thy slaves more clamorous and loud,
By laughter unprovok'd thy influence too confess.
          In the imperious Wife thou vapours art,
                    Which from o'er-heated passions rise
55   In clouds to the attractive° brain,   *attracting*
                    Until descending thence again
                    Thro' the o'ercast and show'ring eyes,
                              Upon the Husband's soft'ned heart,
                    He the disputed point must yield,
60   Something resign of the contested field;
'Till lordly Man, born to imperial sway,
Compounds for peace, to make his right away
And Woman arm'd with Spleen does servilely obey.

4

                    The fool, to imitate the wits,
65   Complains of thy pretended fits;
          And dulness, born with him, would lay°   *blame*
                    Upon thy accidental sway;
          Because thou dost sometimes presume
                    Into the ablest heads to come,
70   That often men of thoughts refin'd,
                    Impatient of unequal sense,
          Such slow returns, where they so much dispense,
Retiring from the crowd, are to thy shades confin'd,
In me alas! thou dost too much prevail,

75 I feel thy force, while I against thee rail;
I feel my verse decay, and my crampt numbers fail.
Through thy black jaundies[3] I all objects see,
As dark and terrible as thee;
My lines decry'd, and my employment thought
80 An useless folly, or presumptuous fault,
While in the Muses' paths I stray.
While in their groves, and by their springs,
My hand delights to trace unusual things,
And deviates from the known and common way
85 Nor will in fading silks compose
Faintly th'inimitable rose:
Fill up an ill-drawn bird, or paint on glass
The Sovereign's blur'd and undistinguish'd face,
The threatning angel, and the speaking ass.[4]

5

90 Patron thou art of every gross abuse,
The sullen Husband's feign'd excuse,
When the ill humour with his Wife he spends,
And bears recruited wit and spirits to his friends.
The son of Bacchus[5] pleads thy power,
95 As to the glass he still repairs,
Pretends but to remove thy cares;
Snatcht from thy shades one gay and smiling hour,
And drown thy Kingdom with a purple show'r.
When the coquet° whom every fool admires,   *flirtatious woman*
100 Would in variety be fair,
And shifting hastily the scene,
From light impertinent and vain,
Assumes a soft and melancholy air,
And of her eyes rebates° the wand'ring fires,   *abates*
105 The careless posture, and the head reclin'd;
The thoughtful and composed face
Proclaiming the withdrawn and absent mind,
Allows the Fop more liberty to gaze;
Who gently for the tender cause inquires:
110 The cause indeed is a defect in sense;
But still the Spleen's alledg'd, and still the dull pretence.

6

But these are thy fantastic° harms,   *imagined*
The tricks of thy pernicious rage,
Which do the weaker sort engage;
115 Worse are the dire effects of thy more powerful charms.
By thee Religion all we know

---

3. Black jaundice, a disease described by analogy to yellow jaundice (obstruction of the bile), which reportedly caused yellowed vision.
4. A pious biblical scene, in which the prophet Balaam's donkey urges him not to serve a heathen king (Numbers 22).
5. Bacchus is the Roman god of wine; hence, a drinker of wine.

That should enlighten here below,
Is veil'd in darkness, and perplext
With anxious doubts, with endless scruples vext,
120   And some restraint implied from each perverted Text.
Whilst taste not, touch not what is freely given,
Is but the niggard's° voice, disgracing bounteous Heaven.   *the stingy person's*
From speech restrain'd, by thy deceits abus'd,°   *misled*
To deserts banish'd and in cells reclus'd;°   *confined*
125   Mistaken votaries to the Powers Divine,
While they a purer sacrifice design
Do but the Spleen adore, and worship at thy shrine.

7

In vain to chase thee, every art we try;
In vain all remedies apply;
130   In vain the Indian leaf° infuse,   *tea*
Or the parch'd Eastern berry° bruise;   *coffee*
Some pass in vain those bounds, and nobler liquors use.
Now harmony in vain we bring,
Inspire the flute, and touch the string;
135   From harmony no help is had:
Music but soothes thee, if too sweetly sad;
And if too light, but turns thee gladly mad.
Not skilful Lower[6] thy source could find,
Or through the well-dissected body trace
140   The secret and mysterious ways,
By which thou dost destroy and prey upon the mind;
Tho' in the search, too deep for humane thought,
With unsuccessful toil he wrought,
'Till in pursuit of thee himself was by thee caught;
145   Retain'd thy prisoner, thy acknowledg'd slave,
And sunk beneath thy weight to a lamented grave.

+·+·=◆=·+·+

Jonathan Swift
1667–1745

"The Lady's Dressing Room" is the earliest of the scatological poems for which Swift is distinguished, although it recalls previous descriptions of female bodies in his novel *Gulliver's Travels* (page 349). In it he takes up the same popular theme that Pope explores in *The Rape of the Lock* (page 524)—the mysterious operation of dressing, by which, with the aid of "puffs, powders, and patches," imperfect bodies of flesh and blood were transformed into dazzling objects of desire. But Swift takes us from Pope's airy realm, where the battle of the sexes is fought by sylphs and gnomes, back to the physical world where the divinest pleasures of love remain always disturbingly close to less romanticized bodily functions. Swift's obscenity shocked many contemporaries and later readers, but it is not so different from such verses of the libertine poet Rochester's as, "Fair nasty nymph, be clean and kind / And all my joys restore / By using paper

---

6. Richard Lower (1631–1691), an early English anatomist and experimental physiologist.

still behind / And sponges for before." The discoveries of Swift's Strephon in Celia's chamber pot come as a shock only to one who buys into representations of upper-class women not as mortal human subjects, but as fantastic creatures somewhere between goddesses and dolls. For more on Swift, see his principal listing, page 346.

The Lady's Dressing Room

Five hours (and who can do it less in?)
By haughty Celia spent in dressing;
The goddess from her chamber issues,
Arrayed in lace, brocade, and tissues:
5   Strephon,[1] who found the room was void,
And Betty[2] otherwise employed,
Stole in, and took a strict survey,
Of all the litter as it lay:
Whereof, to make the matter clear,
10   An *inventory* follows here.

    And first, a dirty smock appeared,
Beneath the arm-pits well besmeared;
Strephon, the rogue, displayed it wide,
And turned it round on every side.
15   In such a case few words are best,
And Strephon bids us guess the rest;
But swears how damnably the men lie,
In calling Celia sweet and cleanly.

    Now listen while he next produces
20   The various combs for various uses,
Filled up with dirt so closely fixed,
No brush could force a way betwixt;
A paste of composition rare,
Sweat, dandruff, powder, lead,[3] and hair,
25   A forehead cloth with oil upon't
To smooth the wrinkles on her front;
Here alum flour[4] to stop the steams,
Exhaled from sour, unsavory streams;
There night-gloves made of Tripsy's[5] hide,
30   Bequeathed by Tripsy when she died;
With puppy water,[6] beauty's help,
Distilled from Tripsy's darling whelp.
Here gallipots° and vials placed,   *ointment jars*
Some filled with washes, some with paste;
35   Some with pomatum,° paints, and slops,   *hair ointment*
And ointments good for scabby chops.°   *lips or cheeks*

---

1. Strephon and Celia are names usually associated with pastoral poetry, and are therefore used mockingly here.
2. A typical maidservant's name.
3. White lead face paint, used to whiten the skin.
4. Powdered alum used like modern antiperspirant.
5. Celia's lapdog; no fashionable lady was without such a pet.
6. A recipe for this cosmetic, made from the innards of a pig or a fat puppy, was given in the "Fop's Dictionary" in *Mundus Muliebris* [Womanly Make-up]: *Or, the Ladies' Dressing Room Unlocked* (1690), which Swift also used for other terms.

Hard° by a filthy basin stands,   close
Fouled with the scouring of her hands;
The basin takes whatever comes,
40   The scrapings of her teeth and gums,
A nasty compound of all hues,
For here she spits, and here she spews.

But oh! it turned poor Strephon's bowels,
When he beheld and smelt the towels;
45   Begummed, bemattered, and beslimed;
With dirt, and sweat, and ear-wax grimed.
No object Strephon's eye escapes,
Here, petticoats in frowzy° heaps;   unkempt
Nor be the handkerchiefs forgot,
50   All varnished o'er with snuff[7] and snot.
The stockings why should I expose,
Stained with the moisture of her toes;
Or greasy coifs and pinners° reeking,   night caps
Which Celia slept at least a week in?
55   A pair of tweezers next he found
To pluck her brows in arches round,
Or hairs that sink the forehead low,
Or on her chin like bristles grow.

The virtues we must not let pass
60   Of Celia's magnifying glass;
When frighted Strephon cast his eye on't,
It showed the visage of a giant:[8]
A glass that can to sight disclose
The smallest worm in Celia's nose,
65   And faithfully direct her nail
To squeeze it out from head to tail;
For catch it nicely by the head,
It must come out alive or dead.

Why, Strephon, will you tell the rest?
70   And must you needs describe the chest?
That careless wench! no creature warn her
To move it out from yonder corner,
But leave it standing full in sight,
For you to exercise your spite!
75   In vain the workman showed his wit
With rings and hinges counterfeit
To make it seem in this disguise
A cabinet to vulgar eyes;

7. Powdered tobacco, sniffed by fashionable men and women alike.
8. Cf. *Gulliver's Travels,* Part 2, "A Voyage to Brobding-nag," ch. 1: "This made me reflect upon the fair skins of our *English* ladies, who appear so beautiful to us, only because they are of our own size, and their defects not to be seen but through magnifying glass, where we find by experiment that the smoothest and whitest skins look rough and coarse, and ill colored."

Which Strephon ventured to look in,
80 Resolved to go through *thick and thin;*
He lifts the lid: there need no more,
He smelt it all the time before.

As, from within Pandora's box,
When Epimethus oped the locks,
85 A sudden universal crew
Of human evils upward flew;[9]
He still was comforted to find
That hope at last remained behind.

So, Strephon, lifting up the lid
90 To view what in the chest was hid,
The vapors flew from out the vent,
But Strephon cautious never meant
The bottom of the pan to grope,
And foul his hands in search of hope.

95 O! ne'er may such a vile machine°   *construction*
Be once in Celia's chamber seen!
O! may she better learn to keep
"Those secrets of the hoary deep."[1]

As mutton cutlets, prime of meat,
100 Which though with art you salt and beat
As laws of cookery require,
And roast them at the clearest fire;
If from adown the hopeful chops
The fat upon a cinder drops,
105 To stinking smoke it turns the flame
Poisoning the flesh from whence it came;
And up exhales a greasy stench
For which you curse the careless wench:
So things which must not be expressed,
110 When plumped° into the reeking chest,   *dropped*
Send up an excremental smell
To taint the parts from which they fell:
The petticoats and gown perfume,
And waft a stink round every room.

115 Thus finishing his grand survey,
The swain disgusted slunk away,
Repeating in his amorous fits,
"Oh! Celia, Celia, Celia shits!"

But Vengeance, goddess never sleeping,
120 Soon punished Strephon for his peeping.

---

9. In Greek mythology, Epimetheus, acting against advice, opened the box Jove had given his wife Pandora, and all the evils and vices of the world flew out, leaving only hope in the box.
1. Quoting Milton's *Paradise Lost* 2.891, in which Sin is unleashing the chaotic forces of her infernal realm.

His foul imagination links
Each dame he sees with all her stinks:
And if unsavory odors fly,
Conceives a lady standing by:
125   All women his description fits,
And both ideas jump° like wits   *join together*
By vicious fancy coupled fast,
And still appearing in contrast.

I pity wretched Strephon, blind
130   To all the charms of womankind;
Should I the queen of love refuse,
Because she rose from stinking ooze?[2]
To him that looks behind the scene,
Statira's but some pocky quean.[3]

135   When Celia in her glory shows,
If Strephon would but stop his nose,
Who now so impiously blasphemes
Her ointments, daubs, and paints and creams;
Her washes, slops, and every clout,[4]
140   With which she makes so foul a rout;[5]
He soon would learn to think like me,
And bless his ravished eyes to see
Such order from confusion sprung,
Such gaudy *tulips* raised from *dung*.

Lady Mary Wortley Montagu
1689–1762

Lampooned by Pope for wearing "diamonds with her dirty smock" in his "Epistle II: To a Lady," Lady Mary Wortley Montagu was perhaps particularly sensitive to Swift's unkind reflections on feminine hygiene. In any case, she was not one to let her fellow poets' many satires against women pass in silence without matching wits with them. Her riposte to Swift's "The Lady's Dressing Room" doesn't hesitate to identify, with great comic effect, Dean Swift's well-known lack of ease with women as the source of his unflattering verses. (For more on Lady Mary Wortley Montagu, see the more extensive introduction to her Ottoman writings, page 172.)

The Reasons that Induced Dr. S. to write a Poem called
The Lady's Dressing Room[1]

The Doctor in a clean starched band,
His golden snuff box in his hand,

---

2. Venus, Roman goddess of sexual love and physical beauty, rose from the sea.
3. One of the heroines of Nathaniel Lee's highly popular tragedy *The Rival Queens* (1677); Swift's common slattern (quean) has had either smallpox or venereal disease.
4. Washes were either treated water used for the complexion or stale urine used as a detergent; clouts were rags.
5. Both of her skin and, presumably, of the men.
1. For Jonathan Swift's poem, see page 289. In her riposte, Montagu mimics Swift's iambic tetrameter and other mannerisms.

With care his diamond ring displays
And artful shows its various rays,
5 While grave he stalks down——street
His dearest Betty——to meet.[2]
   Long had he waited for this hour,
Nor gained admittance to the bower,
Had joked and punned, and swore and writ,
10 Tried all his gallantry and wit,[3]
Had told her oft what part he bore
In Oxford's schemes in days of yore,[4]
But bawdy,° politics, nor satire   *obscenity*
Could move this dull hard hearted creature.
15 Jenny her maid could taste° a rhyme   *enjoy*
And, grieved to see him lose his time,
Had kindly whispered in his ear,
"For twice two pound you enter here;
My lady vows without that sum
20 It is in vain you write or come."
   The destined offering now he brought,
And in a paradise of thought,
With a low bow approached the dame,
Who smiling heard him preach his flame.
25 His gold she takes (such proofs as these
Convince most unbelieving shes)
And in her trunk rose up to lock it
(Too wise to trust it in her pocket)
And then, returned with blushing grace,
30 Expects the doctor's warm embrace.
   But now this is the proper place
Where morals stare me in the face,
And for the sake of fine expression
I'm forced to make a small digression.
35 Alas for wretched humankind,
With learning mad, with wisdom blind!
The ox thinks he's for saddle fit
(As long ago friend Horace writ[5])
And men their talents still mistaking,
40 The stutterer fancies his is speaking.
With admiration oft we see
Hard features heightened by toupée,
The beau affects° the politician,   *pretends to be*
Wit is the citizen's ambition,
45 Poor Pope philosophy displays on

2. In Swift's poem, Betty is the maid's name, Celia, the mistress's.
3. Montagu echoes Swift's poem *Cadenus and Vanessa,* where the clumsy lover "Had sighed and languished, vowed, and writ, / For pastime, or to show his wit"
(lines 542–543).
4. Swift had collaborated closely in the political schemes of Robert Harley, first Earl of Oxford (1661–1724).
5. "The ox desires the saddle" (Horace, *Epistles* 1.14.43).

With so much rhyme and little reason,
And though he argues ne'er so long
That all is right, his head is wrong.[6]
   None strive to know their proper merit
50 But strain for wisdom, beauty, spirit,
And lose the praise that is their due
While they've th' impossible in view.
So have I seen the injudicious heir
To add one window the whole house impair.
55 Instinct the hound does better teach,
Who never undertook to preach;
The frighted hare from dogs does run
But not attempts to bear a gun.
Here many noble thoughts occur
60 But I prolixity abhor,
And will pursue th' instructive tale
To show the wise in some things fail.
   The reverend lover with surprise
Peeps in her bubbies, and her eyes,
65 And kisses both, and tries—and tries.
The evening in this hellish play,
Beside his guineas thrown away,
Provoked the priest to that degree
He swore, "The fault is not in me.
70 Your damned close stool° so near my nose,   *chamber pot*
Your dirty smock, and stinking toes
Would make a Hercules as tame
As any beau that you can name."
   The nymph grown furious roared, "By God
75 The blame lies all in sixty odd,"[7]
And scornful pointing to the door
Cried, "Fumbler, see my face no more."
"With all my heart I'll go away,
But nothing done, I'll nothing pay.
80 Give back the money." "How," cried she,
"Would you palm such a cheat on me!
For poor four pound to roar and bellow—
Why sure you want some new Prunella?"[8]
"I'll be revenged, you saucy quean"°   *whore*
85 (Replies the disappointed Dean)
"I'll so describe your dressing room
The very Irish shall not come."
She answered short, "I'm glad you'll write.
You'll furnish paper when I shite."[9]

---

6. Montagu ridicules Pope's conclusion to *An Essay on Man:* "Whatever IS, is RIGHT." See page 521.
7. I.e., Swift's impotence derives not from her odors but from his age (65 at the time the poem was written).
8. "Prunella" is both a fabric used in clergy vestments (Swift was a clergyman), and the name of the promiscuous, low-born heroine in Richard Estcourt's comic interlude *Prunella* (1708).
9. Compare line 118 of Swift's poem, page 291.

↔ ⊯◆⊯ ↔

Ann Yearsley
1752–1806

Known as "the poetical milkwoman of Bristol," Ann Yearsley was no courtly writer, although a bevy of duchesses amused themselves by patronizing "the wild vigor of her rustic muse." She sold milk door to door and collected pig slops from author Hannah More's cook. Her brother had taught her to read, and her milkmaid mother had borrowed books to feed her passion for Milton, Shakespeare, and Pope. Yearsley's six children were starving during the harsh winter of 1783–1784 when she gave the cook some poems to show More, who thought them "extraordinary for a milker of Cows, and a feeder of Hogs, who has never even seen a Dictionary." More signed up a thousand of her aristocratic and literary acquaintance to subsidize a book. Yearsley's debut earned critical praise and £600 over several editions—fabulous wealth for a woman whose husband's yearly income of £6 had made him too good a match to pass up. More, however, said that she never "intended to place her in such a state of independence as might seduce her to devote her time to the idleness of Poetry," investing the money in trust and keeping her protégée on a modest income. Yearsley won the ensuing print battle for independence from her patron. Within a decade she published several collections of poetry, a tragedy and a novel, and opened a circulating library in the fashionable spa at Bristol Hot Wells. In the style of earlier courtly writers, she adopted a pastoral pen name, "Lactilla" (from "milk"). She was admired for writing against slavery and vividly expressing the misery of poverty. "Unlettered poets" like Yearsley—their "natural genius" supposedly unfettered by education—were all the rage in the late eighteenth century; Robert Burns is only the most famous. The "Mr. ****" of the poem below may be Burns himself or John Frederick Bryant (1753–1791), a Bristol tradesman.

To Mr. ****, an Unlettered Poet, on Genius Unimproved

    Florus, canst thou define that innate spark
Which blazes but for glory? Canst thou paint
The trembling rapture in its infant dawn,
Ere young ideas spring; to local thought
5   Arrange the busy phantoms of the mind,
And drag the distant timid shadows forth,
Which, still retiring, glide unformed away,
Nor rush into expression? No; the pen,
Though dipped in awful Wisdom's deepest tint,
10   Can *never* paint the wild ecstatic mood.
    Yet, when the bolder image strikes thine eye,
And uninvited grasps thy strongest thought,
Resolved to shoot into this world of things,
Wide fly the gates of Fancy;° all alarmed,   *imagination*
15   The thin ideal troop in haste advance,
To usher in the substance-seeking shade.
    And what's the shade which rushes on the world
With pow'rful glare, but emblem of the soul?
    Ne'er hail the fabled Nine, or snatch rapt thought
20   From the Castalian spring[1]; 'tis not for *thee*,

---

1. A stream on Mt. Parnassus, sacred to the nine Muses, fabled to endow those who drink of it with poetic gifts.

From embers where the pagan's light expires,
To catch a flame divine. From one bright spark
Of never-erring faith more rapture beams
Than wild mythology could ever boast.
25   Pursue the Eastern Magi[2] through their groves,
Where Zoroaster holds the mystic clue,[3]
Which leads to great Ormazes[4]; there thou'lt find
His god thy own; or bid thy fancy chase
Restless Pythag'ras[5] through his varied forms,
30   And she shall see him sitting on a heap
Of poor absurdity; where cheerful faith
Shall never rest, nor great omniscience claim.
          What are the Muses or Apollo's[6] strains,
But harmony of soul? Like thee, estranged
35   From Science and old Wisdom's classic lore,
I've patient trod the wild entangled path
Of unimproved idea. Dauntless thought
I eager seized, no formal rule e'er awed;
No precedent controlled; no custom fixed
40   My independent spirit: on the wing
She still shall guideless soar, nor shall the fool,
Wounding her pow'rs, e'er bring her to the ground.
          Yet Florus, list! to thee I loudly call;
Dare thee, by all the transport mind can reach,
45   Yea, by the boasted privilege of Man,
To stretch with me the spirit-raising wing
Of artless rapture! Seek earth's farthest bound,
Till Fancy, panting, drops from endless space.
          Deep in the soul live ever-tuneful springs,
50   Waiting the touch of ecstasy, which strikes
Most pow'rful on defenceless, untaught minds;
Then, in soft unison, the trembling strings
All move in one direction. Then the soul
Sails on idea, and would eager dart
55   Through yon ethereal way; restless awhile,
Again she sinks to sublunary° joy.   *earthly*
          Florus, rove on! pluck from the pathless vale
Of Fancy all her loveliest, wildest sweets,
These best can please; but ah! beware, my friend:
60   Timid Idea shrinks, when coldly thou
Would'st hail the tender shade; then strongly clasp
The coy, reluctant fugitive, or seize
The rover as she flies; that breast alone

---

2. Sages or priests of the ancient Zoroastrian religion.
3. Zoroaster is the Greek name for the Persian religious leader Zarathustra (c. 630–c. 553 B.C.E.); a *clue* is a thread that guides a seeker through a labyrinth.
4. Zoroastrianism understood the world as divided in a continual struggle between Good (represented by the creator, Ormuzd or Ormazes) and evil (represented by the demon Ahriman or Ahrimanes).
5. Pythagoras (c. 580–c. 500 B.C.E.), Greek philosopher, mathematician, and mystic, developed a doctrine of the transmigration (metempsychosis) of the soul, thought to be reincarnated in a series of animal and human bodies.
6. Greek god of music and poetry.

Is hers, all glowing with immortal flame;
65   And that be thine.

✤ CROSSCURRENTS: COURT CULTURE AND ✤ FEMALE AUTHORSHIP

- One of the fundamental characteristics of the Enlightenment was the open debate that raged all across Europe during the seventeenth and eighteenth centuries, and well beyond, known as the "Woman Question." The "question" was about women's nature, appropriate education, and proper place in marriage and society. What kinds of answers do the texts gathered in this section offer to that centrally important question? How do their answers compare with those implied in other European works collected elsewhere in this volume, such as Aphra Behn's *Oroonoko*, Alexander Pope's *The Rape of the Lock*, Voltaire's *Candide*, Montesquieu's *Persian Letters*, Denis Diderot's *Supplement to the Voyage of Bougainville*, or any of the works gathered in the Perspectives section, "Liberty and Libertines"?

- The Woman Question persisted and predominated throughout the nineteenth and twentieth centuries, spreading beyond Europe through its former colonies, even though its label fell into disuse during the last century. Do gender roles seem to change significantly in any of the works gathered in the later volumes of this anthology? Consider especially the Perspectives section, "Gendered Spaces," in Volume F.

- The Enlightenment's broad questioning of traditional values, ideas, and social structures made it possible for women to read, write, and publish during the seventeenth and eighteenth centuries in greater numbers than ever before in European history. But as members of a group traditionally forbidden to speak publicly, they still faced special versions of the fundamental challenges involved in any act of writing: how to create compelling authorial voices for themselves and invoke an audience for their works. Can you identify specific strategies by which women writers in this section and beyond, such as Anne Finch, Mary Chudleigh, Katherine Philips, Aphra Behn, Madeleine de Scudéry, or Marie de Lafayette, lay claim to an authorial voice and permission to address a particular kind of audience? What information do they give you about who is speaking, and to whom? How do their strategies compare with those employed by their male contemporaries, by European women of other times (such as the medieval and early modern periods, in Volume B and C), or by writers from non-European cultures gathered elsewhere in the anthology?

- Once we realize that part of the art of writing is constructing a voice or persona through which to address a specific audience, we can begin to analyze how the persona that addresses us is indeed artfully constructed. "Persona" means "mask," originally referring to the masks that amplified the voices of the actors of Greek tragedy and helped their voices to reach their audience from the stage. At the same time, these masks hid their faces and made them into the characters they played instead of the people they were. All writing entails the use of such masks, if only in textual form. How do the writers in this Perspectives section create personae that are gendered feminine? Compare their personae with those of other women writers of the period, such as Aphra Behn, Elisabeth Charlotte von der Pfalz, or Eliza Haywood, all of whom specifically invoke the theater and other places of public display where such personae are costumed and performed. How does the elaborate and theatrical ritual of costuming the seventeenth- and eighteenth-century European woman, as seen in those works and also in Swift's *The Lady's Dressing Room* and Pope's *The Rape of the Lock,* compare with the emphasis on dress in non-European works such as *The Tale of Genji* and the *Tales of the Heike* in Volume B, Cao Xueqin's *The Story of the Stone* in this Volume and many others?

- The themes of domestic life, courtly ritual, and sexual mores form a related, broader basis of comparison between any of the European texts mentioned above and contemporary works from more distant cultural contexts, including not only *The Story of the Stone*, just mentioned, but also Ihara Saikaku's *Life of a Sensuous Woman* and Shen Fu's *Six Records of the Floating Life.* In Volume B there are rich sources of comparison in the sections on China and Japan. *The Tale of Genji* in particular, with its Resonances and its Perspectives section "Courtly Women" provides an excellent comparative example of courtly, vernacular literature in which the status of women and the performance of gender and social status through elaborate dress and ritual are of central importance. Also in Volume B, the special section entitled "Women in Early China" provides another wealth of resources for comparison with the literature on the culture of courtly women in Europe, as do the *Lais* of Marie de France. In Volume C, many of the secular, vernacular novellas and lyric poems collected in the section "Early Modern Europe," from Boccaccio and Marguerite de Navarre to Petrarch, Louise Labé, Shakespeare, and beyond, are also pertinent. What details become important in each of these descriptions of aristocratic daily life, dressing, or courtship rituals? Are such rituals viewed with similar or different attitudes of satire or seriousness? Against what moral standards are characters of different sexes and their actions measured in each? What can we learn from these texts about traditional gender roles in each culture, and about how they are being reinforced or questioned in their respective literatures?

END OF PERSPECTIVES: COURT CULTURE AND FEMALE AUTHORSHIP

Aphra Behn
(1640–1689)

Aphra Behn was the first professional woman of letters in England—and probably in the modern West. Despite an explosive rediscovery of her extensive oeuvre over the past two decades, much remains mysterious about her life, perhaps in part because she was a mistress of masks. Behn flourished in an age of courtly masquerades, when the theater, where she made her name, was the center of literary culture and social life; when noblemen like the Earl of Rochester and even the future king Charles II were not above going incognito to pursue their amorous adventures—or sending young women like Behn, as Charles did in the early years of his reign, to play the spy for him in the Netherlands. Behn very self-consciously manipulated her authorial identity and even her gender as a layered series of masks, in a time when ideas about femininity were particularly unstable, and female authorship almost unheard of.

Was "Aphra Behn" born Behn, Johnson, Amis, or Cooper? What was her social background, and how did she come by an education that allowed her to translate French literature fluently, make frequent allusions to the ancient classics, and contribute to contemporary philosophical, scientific, and political debates? When, if ever, did she marry—and when did she leave or lose—the presumed "Mr. Behn"? Did she travel with her family to the South American colony of Surinam in her early twenties, as she claims in *Oroonoko,* or is that just another part of her elaborate authorial masquerade? Did she also see Virginia, Italy, or Flanders? Probably we will never know. The first thing known of her is that she did work as a spy for a year or two beginning in 1666—the same year in which she started using the name "A. Behn." She was sent by the recently restored monarchy into enemy territory in Antwerp during the second Anglo-Dutch War, on a mission to persuade a former lover to act as a double agent and betray his fellow antimonarchists. Having accumulated debts in this service, on her return to England she was thrown into debtor's prison, and by 1668 she was appealing directly to the King "after more than two years suffering": "I am sick and weak and unfit for a prison . . . Sir, if I have not the money tonight you must send me something to keep me in prison, for I will not starve." It isn't known how she obtained her release; perhaps the King relented. What is certain is that soon thereafter she turned from spying to writing, later remarking that she had been "forced to write for bread," and was "not ashamed to own it."

Behn quickly became the first Englishwoman to make a career as a professional writer. She began with Tory (royalist) political propaganda and plays, the most lucrative literary form of the day. Her first play, *The Forced Marriage* (1670), was performed by the Duke's Company; one of two public London theaters (the King's Company was the other) created a decade previously by royal decree at the restoration of the monarchy, ending the Puritan ban on the theater. From this debut until her death nearly twenty years later, almost every season saw the premiere of one or more of Behn's plays. She flourished at the center of the literary and theatrical culture of the Restoration era, recognized and respected by such prominent writers as John Dryden, Thomas Otway, and the Earl of Rochester (see page 561). Behn remained involved in politics as well, and was briefly imprisoned in the summer of 1682 for too warmly defending Charles II against the pretensions of his illegitimate son, the Duke of Monmouth. At this time of increasing political unrest (as the death of Charles II approached without a legitimate heir) the London theaters began to fall on hard times, politically and financially. The Duke's and King's companies merged, thus reducing the demand for new plays. During the last five years of her life, suffering from illness and poverty, Behn turned to other genres. She began publishing a prodigious quantity of translations from the French, original poetry, and prose fiction that was inspired by contemporary French experiments with the novel form, including one of the earliest epistolary novels in English, *Love-Letters from a Nobleman to his Sister* (1684–1687).

Aphra Behn died on April 16, 1689, in her forties, a few days after the coronation of William III, whose "Glorious Revolution" represented the death of all her party's political hopes. She is buried in Westminster Abbey, under a simple stone inscribed with her name, date of death, and the verses, "Here lies a Proof that Wit can never be / Defense enough against Mortality." Persons of either sex, if so inclined, may there follow the advice of Virginia Woolf: "All women together ought to let flowers fall upon the tomb of Aphra Behn . . . for it was she who earned them the right to speak their minds."

OROONOKO

Oroonoko was one of Behn's last works, and soon became her most enduringly popular one. A dramatic version adapted by Thomas Southerne in 1696 was performed throughout the eighteenth century, even after Behn's original plays had fallen into neglect. The first of seven French translations was published in 1745, and as abolitionist sentiment increased in both France and England, *Oroonoko* came to be read as an antislavery novel. Recent critics disagree about the work's implied commentary on slavery, with its accurate, sympathetic, but passively helpless portrayal of the sufferings of African slaves in the Americas, and its idealization of the character of the "royal slave" in entirely Eurocentric terms. To consider *Oroonoko* an abolitionist tract would be anachronistic at the least, yet it does present a vividly sympathetic account of horrific sufferings that modern historians have documented as anything but imaginary or anachronistic.

R. *Cruikshank, Del.*   G. W. *Bonner, Sc.*

Oroonoko.

Oroonoko. Ha! thou hast roused
The lion in his den, he stalks abroad,
And the wide forest trembles at his roar.

Act III. Scene 2.

Frontispiece to a 1776 edition of *Oroonoko: A Tragedy,* Thomas Southerne's enormously popular stage adaptation of Behn's work.

At the same time, the title character must be understood in terms of the Stuart loyalist cause which Behn served all her life, and which ended disastrously with the Glorious Revolution in the year *Oroonoko* was published (1688). The name "Caesar" given to Oroonoko in the Surinam episode was actually a common slave name, and thus realistic, but it also has symbolic significance: it ironically reminds her audience, in the year of his downfall, of the glorious name Behn had given James II in her ode on his coronation. Like James, Oroonoko dreads the fate of his line. The hero's French connections, courtliness, and idealized European features further associate him with the "black Stuarts," a phrase applied alike to the swarthy James and his father, Charles I—both, in Behn's view, true aristocrats and honorable princes betrayed, like Behn's fictional African, by their social and moral inferiors. Finally, just as the last male heirs of England's royal Stuart line are being ousted in favor of the Dutch Prince William of Orange, Behn laments, at the conclusion of *Oroonoko,* the loss of the English colony in Surinam to the merely mercenary Dutch. (Never mind that the English took Manhattan in exchange. Behn could not see how advantageous was the exchange—from a strategic as well as financial point of view.)

With its nostalgic valuing of aristocratic codes, *Oroonoko* is marked by an ambivalent sense of an encroaching modern commercial culture, beyond the particular horrors of the slave trade. Its hero's aristocratic values are idealized in contrast with a debased, mercenary, and insatiable self-interest that incessantly seeks an elusive gratification in "fresh Diversions every minute, new and strange." The work itself resists classification as a "novel," the new narrative commodity associated with this commercial culture, by drawing heavily upon the rhetoric and conventions of the aristocratic genres of romance and tragedy.

Yet Behn herself had turned to the new prose genre, as she had earlier turned to drama, in large part for commercial motives, and trying to read her personal values or beliefs in *Oroonoko* is as slippery a task as trying to read those of the narrator who bears her name in the novel. The title character is a double for the Stuart kings, but also for Behn's narrator. Besides being linked by sympathy, and as hero and historian, both figures share the paradox of the "royal slave": having to negotiate the difficult position of simultaneously wielding power and being deprived of it. Oroonoko does so with much less moral ambiguity than Behn's narrator. Both, however, claim to tell the truth in a world where no one else does.

Oroonoko
or The Royal Slave: A True History

I do not pretend, in giving you the history of this royal slave, to entertain my reader with the adventures of a feigned hero, whose life and fortunes Fancy may manage at the poet's pleasure; nor in relating the truth, design to adorn it with any accidents, but such as arrived in earnest to him. And it shall come simply into the world, recommended by its own proper merits, and natural intrigues; there being enough of reality to support it, and to render it diverting, without the addition of invention.

I was myself an eyewitness to a great part of what you will find here set down; and what I could not be witness of, I received from the mouth of the chief actor in this history, the hero himself, who gave us the whole transactions of his youth; and though I shall omit, for brevity's sake, a thousand little accidents of his life, which, however pleasant to us, where history was scarce, and adventures very rare, yet might prove tedious and heavy to my reader, in a world where he finds diversions for every minute, new and strange. But we who were perfectly charmed with the character of this great man were curious to gather every circumstance of his life.

The scene of the last part of his adventures lies in a colony in America called Surinam, in the West Indies.

But before I give you the story of this gallant slave, 'tis fit I tell you the manner of bringing them to these new colonies; for those they make use of there, are not natives of the place; for those we live with in perfect amity, without daring to command them; but on the contrary, caress them with all the brotherly and friendly affection in the world, trading with them for their fish, venison, buffaloes, skins, and little rarities; as marmosets, a sort of monkey as big as a rat or weasel, but of a marvelous and delicate shape, and has face and hands like an human creature; and cousheries,[1] a little beast in the form and fashion of a lion, as big as a kitten; but so exactly made in all parts like that noble beast, that it is it in miniature. Then for little parakeets, great parrots, macaws, and a thousand other birds and beasts of wonderful and surprising forms, shapes, and colors. For skins of prodigious snakes, of which there are some threescore yards in length; as is the skin of one that may be seen at His Majesty's Antiquaries,[2] where are also some rare flies,[3] of amazing forms and colors, presented to them by myself, some as big as my fist, some less; and all of various excellencies,

---

1. Other writers mention this animal, but its identity remains uncertain.
2. Probably the "Repository" (museum) of the Royal Society.
3. Butterflies.

such as art cannot imitate. Then we trade for feathers, which they order into all shapes, make themselves little short habits of them, and glorious wreaths for their heads, necks, arms, and legs, whose tinctures are inconceivable. I had a set of these presented to me, and I gave them to the King's Theater, and it was the dress of the *Indian Queen,*[4] infinitely admired by persons of quality, and were inimitable. Besides these, a thousand little knacks and rarities in nature, and some of art; as their baskets, weapons, aprons, etc. We dealt with them with beads of all colors, knives, axes, pins, and needles, which they used only as tools to drill holes with in their ears, noses, and lips, where they hang a great many little things; as long beads, bits of tin, brass, or silver, beat thin, and any shining trinket. The beads they weave into aprons about a quarter of an ell[5] long, and of the same breadth, working them very prettily in flowers of several colors of beads; which apron they wear just before them, as Adam and Eve did the fig leaves; the men wearing a long strip of linen, which they deal with us for. They thread these beads also on long cotton threads, and make girdles to tie their aprons to, which come twenty times or more about the waist and then cross, like a shoulder-belt, both ways, and round their necks, arms, and legs. This adornment, with their long black hair, and the face painted in little specks or flowers here and there, makes them a wonderful figure to behold. Some of the beauties which indeed are finely shaped, as almost all are, and who have pretty features, are very charming and novel; for they have all that is called beauty except the color, which is a reddish yellow; or after a new oiling, which they often use to themselves, they are of the color of a new brick, but smooth, soft, and sleek. They are extreme modest and bashful, very shy, and nice[6] of being touched. And though they are all thus naked, if one lives forever among them, there is not to be seen an indecent action or glance; and being continually used to see one another so unadorned, so like our first parents before the Fall, it seems as if they had no wishes; there being nothing to heighten curiosity, but all you can see, you see at once, and every moment see; and where there is no novelty, there can be no curiosity. Not but I have seen a handsome young Indian, dying for love of a very beautiful young Indian maid; but all his courtship was, to fold his arms, pursue her with his eyes, and sighs were all his language; while she, as if no such lover were present, or rather, as if she desired none such, carefully guarded her eyes from beholding him; and never approached him, but she looked down with all the blushing modesty I have seen in the most severe and cautious of our world. And these people represented to me an absolute idea of the first state of innocence, before man knew how to sin; and 'tis most evident and plain, that simple Nature is the most harmless, inoffensive, and virtuous mistress. 'Tis she alone, if she were permitted, that better instructs the world than all the inventions of man; religion would here but destroy that tranquillity they possess by ignorance, and laws would but teach them to know offense, of which now they have no notion. They once made mourning and fasting for the death of the English governor, who had given his hand to come on such a day to them, and neither came, nor sent; believing, when once a man's word was past, nothing but death could or should prevent his keeping it. And when they saw he was not dead, they asked him, what name they had for a man who promised a thing he did not do? The governor told them, such a man was a liar, which was a word of infamy to a gentleman. Then one of them replied, "Governor, you are a liar, and guilty of that infamy." They have a native justice which knows no fraud, and they understand

---

4. A heroic drama (1664) by Robert Howard and John Dryden, celebrated for its sumptuous costumes and design.

5. Forty-five inches.

6. Shy.

no vice, or cunning, but when they are taught by the white men. They have plurality of wives which, when they grow old, they serve those that succeed them, who are young; but with a servitude easy and respected; and unless they take slaves in war, they have no other attendants.

Those on that continent where I was had no king; but the oldest war captain was obeyed with great resignation.

A war captain is a man who has led them on to battle with conduct[7] and success, of whom I shall have occasion to speak more hereafter, and of some other of their customs and manners, as they fall in my way.

With these people, as I said, we live in perfect tranquillity and good understanding, as it behooves us to do; they knowing all the places where to seek the best food of the country, and the means of getting it; and for very small and invaluable trifles, supply us with what 'tis impossible for us to get; for they do not only in the wood, and over the savannahs, in hunting, supply the parts of hounds, by swiftly scouring through those almost impassable places, and by the mere activity of their feet, run down the nimblest deer, and other eatable beasts; but in the water, one would think they were gods of the rivers, or fellow citizens of the deep, so rare an art they have in swimming, diving, and almost living in water, by which they command the less swift inhabitants of the floods. And then for shooting, what they cannot take, or reach with their hands, they do with arrows, and have so admirable an aim, that they will split almost a hair; and at any distance that an arrow can reach, they will shoot down oranges and other fruit, and only touch the stalk with the darts' points, that they may not hurt the fruit. So that they being, on all occasions, very useful to us, we find it absolutely necessary to caress them as friends, and not to treat them as slaves; nor dare we do other, their numbers so far surpassing ours in that continent.

Those then whom we make use of to work in our plantations of sugar are Negroes, black slaves altogether, which are transported thither in this manner.

Those who want slaves make a bargain with a master, or captain of a ship, and contract to pay him so much apiece, a matter of twenty pound a head for as many as he agrees for, and to pay for them when they shall be delivered on such a plantation. So that when there arrives a ship laden with slaves, they who have so contracted go aboard, and receive their number by lot; and perhaps in one lot that may be for ten, there may happen to be three or four men; the rest, women and children; or be there more or less of either sex, you are obliged to be contented with your lot.

Coramantien,[8] a country of blacks so called, was one of those places in which they found the most advantageous trading for these slaves, and thither most of our great traders in that merchandise trafficked; for that nation is very warlike and brave, and having a continual campaign, being always in hostility with one neighboring prince or other, they had the fortune to take a great many captives; for all they took in battle were sold as slaves, at least, those common men who could not ransom themselves. Of these slaves so taken, the general only has all the profit; and of these generals, our captains and masters of ships buy all their freights.

The King of Coramantien was himself a man of a hundred and odd years old, and had no son, though he had many beautiful black wives; for most certainly, there are beauties that can charm of that color. In his younger years he had had many gallant men to his sons, thirteen of which died in battle, conquering when they fell; and he

---

7. Skillful management.

8. Koromantyn, a fort and trading post on the western coast of Africa (in modern Ghana).

had only left him for his successor one grandchild, son to one of these dead victors; who, as soon as he could bear a bow in his hand, and a quiver at his back, was sent into the field, to be trained up by one of the oldest generals to war; where, from his natural inclination to arms, and the occasions given him, with the good conduct of the old general, he became, at the age of seventeen, one of the most expert captains, and bravest soldiers, that ever saw the field of Mars; so that he was adored as the wonder of all that world, and the darling of the soldiers. Besides, he was adorned with a native beauty so transcending all those of his gloomy race, that he struck an awe and reverence, even in those that knew not his quality; as he did in me, who beheld him with surprise and wonder, when afterwards he arrived in our world.

He had scarce arrived at his seventeenth year when, fighting by his side, the general was killed with an arrow in his eye, which the Prince Oroonoko (for so was this gallant Moor[9] called) very narrowly avoided; nor had he, if the general, who saw the arrow shot, and perceiving it aimed at the Prince, had not bowed his head between, on purpose to receive it in his own body rather than it should touch that of the Prince, and so saved him.

'Twas then, afflicted as Oroonoko was, that he was proclaimed general in the old man's place; and then it was, at the finishing of that war, which had continued for two years, that the Prince came to court, where he had hardly been a month together, from the time of his fifth year to that of seventeen; and 'twas amazing to imagine where it was he learned so much humanity or, to give his accomplishments a juster name, where 'twas he got that real greatness of soul, those refined notions of true honor, that absolute generosity, and that softness that was capable of the highest passions of love and gallantry, whose objects were almost continually fighting men, or those mangled or dead; who heard no sounds but those of war and groans. Some part of it we may attribute to the care of a Frenchman of wit and learning, who finding it turn to very good account to be a sort of royal tutor to this young black, and perceiving him very ready, apt, and quick of apprehension, took a great pleasure to teach him morals, language, and science, and was for it extremely beloved and valued by him. Another reason was, he loved, when he came from war, to see all the English gentlemen that traded thither, and did not only learn their language but that of the Spaniards also, with whom he traded afterwards for slaves.

I have often seen and conversed with this great man, and been a witness to many of his mighty actions, and do assure my reader, the most illustrious courts could not have produced a braver man, both for greatness of courage and mind, a judgment more solid, a wit more quick, and a conversation more sweet and diverting. He knew almost as much as if he had read much: he had heard of, and admired the Romans; he had heard of the late Civil Wars in England, and the deplorable death of our great monarch,[1] and would discourse of it with all the sense, and abhorrence of the injustice imaginable. He had an extreme good and graceful mien, and all the civility of a well-bred great man. He had nothing of barbarity in his nature, but in all points addressed himself as if his education had been in some European court.

This great and just character of Oroonoko gave me an extreme curiosity to see him, especially when I knew he spoke French and English, and that I could talk with him. But though I had heard so much of him, I was as greatly surprised when I saw him as if I had heard nothing of him, so beyond all report I found him. He came

---

9. The word originally meant "Moroccan," but was often used more generally for any person of African descent. Oroonoko's name may echo the river Orinoco in Venezuela, or the African god Oro.

1. Charles I, whose beheading in 1649 by sentence of the House of Commons marked the culmination of the wars between Royalists and Parliament.

into the room, and addressed himself to me, and some other women, with the best grace in the world. He was pretty tall, but of a shape the most exact that can be fancied; the most famous statuary[2] could not form the figure of a man more admirably turned from head to foot. His face was not of that brown, rusty black which most of that nation are, but a perfect ebony, or polished jet. His eyes were the most awful that could be seen, and very piercing, the white of them being like snow, as were his teeth. His nose was rising and Roman, instead of African and flat; his mouth, the finest shaped that could be seen, far from those great turned lips which are so natural to the rest of the Negroes. The whole proportion and air of his face was so noble and exactly formed that, bating[3] his color, there could be nothing in nature more beautiful, agreeable, and handsome. There was no one grace wanting that bears the standard of true beauty. His hair came down to his shoulders by the aids of art, which was, by pulling it out with a quill and keeping it combed, of which he took particular care. Nor did the perfections of his mind come short of those of his person, for his discourse was admirable upon almost any subject; and whoever had heard him speak, would have been convinced of their errors, that all fine wit is confined to the white men, especially to those of Christendom; and would have confessed that Oroonoko was as capable even of reigning well, and of governing as wisely, had as great a soul, as politic maxims,[4] and was as sensible of power as any prince civilized in the most refined schools of humanity and learning, or the most illustrious courts.

This Prince, such as I have described him, whose soul and body were so admirably adorned, was (while yet he was in the court of his grandfather) as I said, as capable of love as 'twas possible for a brave and gallant man to be; and in saying that, I have named the highest degree of love; for sure, great souls are most capable of that passion.

I have already said the old general was killed by the shot of an arrow, by the side of this Prince, in battle; and that Oroonoko was made general. This old dead hero had one only daughter left of his race; a beauty that, to describe her truly, one need say only, she was female to the noble male; the beautiful black Venus to our young Mars; as charming in her person as he, and of delicate virtues. I have seen an hundred white men sighing after her, and making a thousand vows at her feet, all vain and unsuccessful; and she was, indeed, too great for any but a prince of her own nation to adore.

Oroonoko coming from the wars (which were now ended) after he had made his court to his grandfather, he thought in honor he ought to make a visit to Imoinda, the daughter of his foster-father, the dead general; and to make some excuses to her, because his preservation was the occasion of her father's death; and to present her with those slaves that had been taken in this last battle, as the trophies of her father's victories. When he came, attended by all the young soldiers of any merit, he was infinitely surprised at the beauty of this fair Queen of Night, whose face and person was so exceeding all he had ever beheld; that lovely modesty with which she received him, that softness in her look and sighs, upon the melancholy occasion of this honor that was done by so great a man as Oroonoko, and a prince of whom she had heard such admirable things; the awfulness[5] wherewith she received him, and the sweetness of her words and behavior while he stayed, gained a perfect conquest over his fierce heart, and made him feel the victor could be subdued. So that having made his first compli-

---

2. Sculptor.
3. Excepting.

4. Shrewd principles or sayings.
5. Respect.

ments, and presented her a hundred and fifty slaves in fetters, he told her with his eyes that he was not insensible of her charms; while Imoinda, who wished for nothing more than so glorious a conquest, was pleased to believe she understood that silent language of new-born love; and from that moment, put on all her additions to beauty.

The Prince returned to court with quite another humor[6] than before; and though he did not speak much of the fair Imoinda, he had the pleasure to hear all his followers speak of nothing but the charms of that maid; insomuch that, even in the presence of the old king, they were extolling her, and heightening, if possible, the beauties they had found in her; so that nothing else was talked of, no other sound was heard in every corner where there were whisperers, but "Imoinda! Imoinda!"

'Twill be imagined Oroonoko stayed not long before he made his second visit; nor, considering his quality, not much longer before he told her he adored her. I have often heard him say that he admired by what strange inspiration he came to talk things so soft and so passionate, who never knew love, nor was used to the conversation of women; but (to use his own words) he said, most happily, some new, and till then unknown power instructed his heart and tongue in the language of love, and at the same time, in favor of him, inspired Imoinda with a sense of his passion. She was touched with what he said, and returned it all in such answers as went to his very heart, with a pleasure unknown before. Nor did he use those obligations ill that love had done him; but turned all his happy moments to the best advantage; and as he knew no vice, his flame aimed at nothing but honor, if such a distinction may be made in love; and especially in that country, where men take to themselves as many as they can maintain, and where the only crime and sin with woman is to turn her off, to abandon her to want, shame, and misery. Such ill morals are only practiced in Christian countries, where they prefer the bare name of religion; and, without virtue or morality, think that's sufficient. But Oroonoko was none of those professors; but as he had right notions of honor, so he made her such propositions as were not only and barely such; but, contrary to the custom of his country, he made her vows she should be the only woman he would possess while he lived; that no age or wrinkles should incline him to change, for her soul would be always fine, and always young; and he should have an eternal idea in his mind of the charms she now bore, and should look into his heart for that idea, when he could find it no longer in her face.

After a thousand assurances of his lasting flame, and her eternal empire over him, she condescended to receive him for her husband; or rather, received him, as the greatest honor the gods could do her.

There is a certain ceremony in these cases to be observed, which I forgot to ask him how performed; but 'twas concluded on both sides that, in obedience to him, the grandfather was to be first made acquainted with the design; for they pay a most absolute resignation to the monarch, especially when he is a parent also.

On the other side, the old king, who had many wives, and many concubines, wanted not court flatterers to insinuate in his heart a thousand tender thoughts for this young beauty; and who represented her to his fancy as the most charming he had ever possessed in all the long race of his numerous years. At this character his old heart, like an extinguished brand, most apt to take fire, felt new sparks of love and began to kindle; and now grown to his second childhood, longed with impatience to behold this gay thing, with whom, alas, he could but innocently play. But how he should be confirmed she was this wonder, before he used his power to call her to court (where maidens never

6. Frame of mind.

came, unless for the King's private use) he was next to consider; and while he was so doing, he had intelligence brought him, that Imoinda was most certainly mistress to the Prince Oroonoko. This gave him some chagrin; however, it gave him also an opportunity, one day, when the Prince was a-hunting, to wait on a man of quality, as his slave and attendant, who should go and make a present to Imoinda, as from the Prince; he should then, unknown, see this fair maid, and have an opportunity to hear what message she would return the Prince for his present; and from thence gather the state of her heart, and degree of her inclination. This was put in execution, and the old monarch saw, and burned; he found her all he had heard, and would not delay his happiness, but found he should have some obstacle to overcome her heart; for she expressed her sense of the present the Prince had sent her, in terms so sweet, so soft and pretty, with an air of love and joy that could not be dissembled, insomuch that 'twas past doubt whether she loved Oroonoko entirely. This gave the old king some affliction, but he salved it with this, that the obedience the people pay their king was not at all inferior to what they paid their gods, and what love would not oblige Imoinda to do, duty would compel her to.

He was therefore no sooner got to his apartment, but he sent the royal veil to Imoinda, that is, the ceremony of invitation; he sends the lady, he has a mind to honor with his bed, a veil, with which she is covered and secured for the King's use; and 'tis death to disobey; besides, held a most impious disobedience.

'Tis not to be imagined the surprise and grief that seized this lovely maid at this news and sight. However, as delays in these cases are dangerous, and pleading worse than treason, trembling and almost fainting, she was obliged to suffer herself to be covered and led away.

They brought her thus to court; and the King, who had caused a very rich bath to be prepared, was led into it, where he sat under a canopy in state, to receive this longed for virgin; whom he having commanded should be brought to him, they (after disrobing her) led her to the bath and, making fast the doors, left her to descend. The King, without more courtship, bade her throw off her mantle and come to his arms. But Imoinda, all in tears, threw herself on the marble on the brink of the bath, and besought him to hear her. She told him, as she was a maid, how proud of the divine glory she should have been of having it in her power to oblige her king; but as by the laws he could not, and from his royal goodness would not take from any man his wedded wife, so she believed she should be the occasion of making him commit a great sin, if she did not reveal her state and condition, and tell him she was another's, and could not be so happy to be his.

The King, enraged at this delay, hastily demanded the name of the bold man that had married a woman of her degree without his consent. Imoinda, seeing his eyes fierce and his hands tremble, whether with age or anger I know not, but she fancied the last, almost repented she had said so much, for now she feared the storm would fall on the Prince; she therefore said a thousand things to appease the raging of his flame, and to prepare him to hear who it was with calmness; but before she spoke, he imagined who she meant, but would not seem to do so, but commanded her to lay aside her mantle and suffer herself to receive his caresses; or by his gods, he swore, that happy man whom she was going to name should die, though it were even Oroonoko himself. "Therefore," said he, "deny this marriage, and swear thyself a maid." "That," replied Imoinda, "by all our powers I do, for I am not yet known to my husband." "'Tis enough," said the King, "'tis enough to satisfy both my conscience and my heart." And rising from his seat, he went and led her into the bath, it being in vain for her to resist.

In this time the Prince, who was returned from hunting, went to visit his Imoinda, but found her gone; and not only so, but heard she had received the royal veil. This raised him to a storm, and in his madness they had much ado to save him from laying violent hands on himself. Force first prevailed, and then reason. They urged all to him that might oppose his rage; but nothing weighed so greatly with him as the King's old age, incapable of injuring him with Imoinda. He would give way to that hope, because it pleased him most, and flattered best his heart. Yet this served not altogether to make him cease his different passions, which sometimes raged within him, and sometimes softened into showers. 'Twas not enough to appease him, to tell him his grandfather was old, and could not that way injure him, while he retained that awful[7] duty which the young men are used there to pay to their grave relations. He could not be convinced he had no cause to sigh and mourn for the loss of a mistress he could not with all his strength and courage retrieve. And he would often cry, "O my friends! Were she in walled cities, or confined from me in fortifications of the greatest strength; did enchantments or monsters detain her from me, I would venture through any hazard to free her. But here, in the arms of a feeble old man, my youth, my violent love, my trade in arms, and all my vast desire of glory avail me nothing. Imoinda is as irrecoverably lost to me as if she were snatched by the cold arms of death. Oh! she is never to be retrieved. If I would wait tedious years, till fate should bow the old King to his grave, even that would not leave me Imoinda free; but still that custom that makes it so vile a crime for a son to marry his father's wives or mistress would hinder my happiness; unless I would either ignobly set an ill precedent to my successors, or abandon my country and fly with her to some unknown world, who never heard our story."

But it was objected to him that his case was not the same; for Imoinda being his lawful wife, by solemn contract, 'twas he was the injured man, and might, if he so pleased, take Imoinda back, the breach of the law being on his grandfather's side; and that if he could circumvent him, and redeem her from the otan, which is the palace of the King's women, a sort of seraglio, it was both just and lawful for him so to do.

This reasoning had some force upon him, and he should have been entirely comforted, but for the thought that she was possessed by his grandfather. However, he loved so well that he was resolved to believe what most favored his hope, and to endeavor to learn from Imoinda's own mouth what only she could satisfy him in: whether she was robbed of that blessing, which was only due to his faith and love. But as it was very hard to get a sight of the women, for no men ever entered into the otan but when the King went to entertain himself with some one of his wives or mistresses, and 'twas death at any other time for any other to go in, so he knew not how to contrive to get a sight of her.

While Oroonoko felt all the agonies of love, and suffered under a torment the most painful in the world, the old king was not exempted from his share of affliction. He was troubled for having been forced by an irresistible passion to rob his son of a treasure he knew could not but be extremely dear to him, since she was the most beautiful that ever had been seen; and had besides all the sweetness and innocence of youth and modesty, with a charm of wit surpassing all. He found that however she was forced to expose her lovely person to his withered arms, she could only sigh and weep there, and think of Oroonoko; and oftentimes could not forbear speaking of him, though her life were, by custom, forfeited by owning her passion. But she spoke not

7. Reverential.

of a lover only, but of a prince dear to him to whom she spoke; and of the praises of a man, who, till now, filled the old man's soul with joy at every recital of his bravery, or even his name. And 'twas this dotage on our young hero that gave Imoinda a thousand privileges to speak of him without offending, and this condescension in the old king that made her take the satisfaction of speaking of him so very often.

Besides, he many times inquired how the Prince bore himself; and those of whom he asked, being entirely slaves to the merits and virtues of the Prince, still answered what they thought conduced best to his service; which was, to make the old king fancy that the Prince had no more interest in Imoinda, and had resigned her willingly to the pleasure of the king; that he diverted himself with his mathematicians, his fortifications, his officers, and his hunting.

This pleased the old lover, who failed not to report these things again to Imoinda, that she might, by the example of her young lover, withdraw her heart and rest better contented in his arms. But however she was forced to receive this unwelcome news, in all appearance, with unconcern and content, her heart was bursting within, and she was only happy when she could get alone, to vent her griefs and moans with sighs and tears.

What reports of the Prince's conduct were made to the King, he thought good to justify as far as possibly he could by his actions; and when he appeared in the presence of the King, he showed a face not at all betraying his heart; so that in a little time the old man, being entirely convinced that he was no longer a lover of Imoinda, he carried him with him, in his train to the otan, often to banquet with his mistress. But as soon as he entered one day into the apartment of Imoinda with the King, at the first glance from her eyes, notwithstanding all his determined resolution, he was ready to sink in the place where he stood; and had certainly done so, but for the support of Aboan, a young man who was next to him; which, with his change of countenance, had betrayed him, had the King chanced to look that way. And I have observed, 'tis a very great error in those who laugh when one says a Negro can change color; for I have seen them as frequently blush, and look pale, and that as visibly as ever I saw in the most beautiful white. And 'tis certain that both these changes were evident, this day, in both these lovers. And Imoinda, who saw with some joy the change in the Prince's face, and found it in her own, strove to divert the King from beholding either, by a forced caress, with which she met him, which was a new wound in the heart of the poor dying Prince. But as soon as the King was busied in looking on some fine thing of Imoinda's making, she had time to tell the Prince with her angry but love-darting eyes, that she resented his coldness, and bemoaned her own miserable captivity. Nor were his eyes silent, but answered hers again, as much as eyes could do, instructed by the most tender and most passionate heart that ever loved. And they spoke so well, and so effectually, as Imoinda no longer doubted but she was the only delight, and the darling of that soul she found pleading in them its right of love, which none was more willing to resign than she. And 'twas this powerful language alone that in an instant conveyed all the thoughts of their souls to each other, that they both found there wanted but opportunity to make them both entirely happy. But when he saw another door opened by Onahal, a former old wife of the King's who now had charge of Imoinda, and saw the prospect of a bed of state made ready with sweets and flowers for the dalliance of the King, who immediately led the trembling victim from his sight into that prepared repose, what rage, what wild frenzies seized his heart! Which forcing to keep within bounds, and to suffer without noise, it became the more insupportable and rent his soul with ten thousand pains. He was forced to retire to vent his groans, where he fell down on a carpet, and lay struggling a long time, and only breathing now and then, "O Imoinda!" When Onahal had finished her necessary affair within, shutting the door, she came forth to wait till the King called; and hearing some one sighing in the other room, she passed on, and found the Prince in that deplorable condition which she thought needed her aid. She gave him cordials but all in vain, till finding the nature of his disease by his sighs, and naming Imoinda, she told him he had not so much cause as he imagined to afflict himself; for if he knew the King so well as she did, he would not lose a moment in jealousy, and that she was confident that Imoinda bore, at this minute, part in his affliction. Aboan was of the same opinion; and both together persuaded him to reassume his courage; and all sitting down on the carpet, the Prince said so many obliging things to Onahal, that he half persuaded her to be of his party. And she promised him she would thus far comply with his just desires, that she would let Imoinda know how faithful he was, what he suffered, and what he said.

This discourse lasted till the King called, which gave Oroonoko a certain satisfaction; and with the hope Onahal had made him conceive, he assumed a look as gay as 'twas possible a man in his circumstances could do; and presently after, he was called in with the rest who waited without. The King commanded music to be brought, and several of his young wives and mistresses came all together by his command, to dance before him, where Imoinda performed her part with an air and grace so passing all the rest as her beauty was above them, and received the present ordained as a prize. The Prince was every moment more charmed with the new beauties and graces he beheld in this fair one; and while he gazed and she danced, Onahal was retired to a window with Aboan.

This Onahal, as I said, was one of the past mistresses of the old king; and 'twas these (now past their beauty) that were made guardians, or governants, to the new and the young ones; and whose business it was, to teach them all those wanton arts of love with which they prevailed and charmed heretofore in their turn; and who now treated the triumphing happy ones with all the severity, as to liberty and freedom, that was possible, in revenge of those honors they rob them of; envying them those satisfactions, those gallantries and presents, that were once made to themselves, while youth and beauty lasted, and which they now saw pass regardless by, and paid only to the bloomings. And certainly, nothing is more afflicting to a decayed beauty than to behold in itself declining charms that were once adored, and to find those caresses paid to new beauties to which once she laid a claim; to hear them whisper as she passes by, "That once was a delicate woman." These abandoned ladies therefore endeavor to revenge all the despites and decays of time on these flourishing happy ones. And 'twas this severity that gave Oroonoko a thousand fears he should never prevail with Onahal to see Imoinda. But, as I said, she was now retired to a window with Aboan.

This young man was not only one of the best quality, but a man extremely well made and beautiful; and coming often to attend the King to the otan, he had subdued the heart of the antiquated Onahal, which had not forgot how pleasant it was to be in love. And though she had some decays in her face, she had none in her sense and wit; she was there agreeable still, even to Aboan's youth, so that he took pleasure in entertaining her with discourses of love. He knew also, that to make his court to these she-favorites was the way to be great; these being the persons that do all affairs and business at court. He had also observed that she had given him glances more tender and inviting than she had done to others of his quality. And now, when he saw that her favor could so absolutely oblige the Prince, he failed not to sigh in her ear, and to look with eyes all soft upon her, and give her hope that she had made some impressions on his heart. He found her pleased at this, and making a thousand advances to him; but the ceremony ending, and the King departing, broke up the company for that day, and his conversation.

Aboan failed not that night to tell the Prince of his success, and how advantageous the service of Onahal might be to his amour with Imoinda. The Prince was overjoyed with this good news, and besought him, if it were possible, to caress her, so as to engage her entirely; which he could not fail to do, if he complied with her desires. "For then," said the Prince, "her life lying at your mercy, she must grant you the request you make in my behalf." Aboan understood him, and assured him he would make love so effectually, that he would defy the most expert mistress of the art to find out whether he dissembled it or had it really. And 'twas with impatience they waited the next opportunity of going to the otan.

The wars came on, the time of taking the field approached, and 'twas impossible for the Prince to delay his going at the head of his army to encounter the enemy; so that every day seemed a tedious year, till he saw his Imoinda, for he believed he could not live if he were forced away without being so happy. 'Twas with impatience therefore that he expected the next visit the King would make; and, according to his wish, it was not long.

The parley of the eyes of these two lovers had not passed so secretly, but an old jealous lover could spy it; or rather, he wanted not flatterers who told him they observed it. So that the Prince was hastened to the camp, and this was the last visit he found he should make to the otan; he therefore urged Aboan to make the best of this last effort, and to explain himself so to Onahal, that she, deferring her enjoyment of her young lover no longer, might make way for the Prince to speak to Imoinda.

The whole affair being agreed on between the Prince and Aboan, they attended the King, as the custom was, to the otan; where, while the whole company was taken up in beholding the dancing and antic[8] postures the women royal made to divert the King, Onahal singled out Aboan, whom she found most pliable to her wish. When she had him where she believed she could not be heard, she sighed to him, and softly cried, "Ah, Aboan! When will you be sensible of my passion? I confess it with my mouth, because I would not give my eyes the lie; and you have but too much already perceived they have confessed my flame. Nor would I have you believe that because I am the abandoned mistress of a king I esteem myself altogether divested of charms. No, Aboan; I have still a rest of beauty enough engaging, and have learned to please too well, not to be desirable. I can have lovers still, but will have none but Aboan." "Madam," replied the half-feigning youth, "you have already, by my eyes, found you can still conquer; and I believe 'tis in pity of me, you condescend to this kind confession. But, Madam, words are used to be so small a part of our country courtship, that 'tis rare one can get so happy an opportunity as to tell one's heart; and those few minutes we have are forced to be snatched for more certain proofs of love than speaking and sighing; and such I languish for."

He spoke this with such a tone that she hoped it true, and could not forbear believing it; and being wholly transported with joy, for having subdued the finest of all the King's subjects to her desires, she took from her ears two large pearls and commanded him to wear them in his. He would have refused them, crying, "Madam, these

8. Fantastic or grotesque.

are not the proofs of your love that I expect; 'tis opportunity, 'tis a lone hour only, that can make me happy." But forcing the pearls into his hand, she whispered softly to him, "Oh! Do not fear a woman's invention when love sets her a-thinking." And pressing his hand she cried, "This night you shall be happy. Come to the gate of the orange groves, behind the otan, and I will be ready, about midnight, to receive you." 'Twas thus agreed, and she left him, that no notice might be taken of their speaking together.

The ladies were still dancing, and the King, laid on a carpet, with a great deal of pleasure was beholding them, especially Imoinda, who that day appeared more lovely than ever, being enlivened with the good tidings Onahal had brought her of the constant passion the Prince had for her. The Prince was laid on another carpet at the other end of the room, with his eyes fixed on the object of his soul; and as she turned or moved so did they; and she alone gave his eyes and soul their motions. Nor did Imoinda employ her eyes to any other use than in beholding with infinite pleasure the joy she produced in those of the Prince. But while she was more regarding him than the steps she took, she chanced to fall, and so near him as that leaping with extreme force from the carpet, he caught her in his arms as she fell; and 'twas visible to the whole presence, the joy wherewith he received her. He clasped her close to his bosom, and quite forgot that reverence that was due to the mistress of a king, and that punishment that is the reward of a boldness of this nature; and had not the presence of mind of Imoinda (fonder of his safety than her own) befriended him in making her spring from his arms and fall into her dance again, he had at that instant met his death; for the old king, jealous to the last degree, rose up in rage, broke all the diversion, and led Imoinda to her apartment, and sent out word to the Prince to go immediately to the camp; and that if he were found another night in court, he should suffer the death ordained for disobedient offenders.

You may imagine how welcome this news was to Oroonoko, whose unseasonable transport and caress of Imoinda was blamed by all men that loved him; and now he perceived his fault, yet cried that for such another moment, he would be content to die.

All the otan was in disorder about this accident; and Onahal was particularly concerned, because on the Prince's stay depended her happiness, for she could no longer expect that of Aboan. So that e'er they departed, they contrived it so that the Prince and he should come both that night to the grove of the otan, which was all of oranges and citrons, and that there they should wait her orders.

They parted thus, with grief enough, till night, leaving the King in possession of the lovely maid. But nothing could appease the jealousy of the old lover. He would not be imposed on, but would have it that Imoinda made a false step on purpose to fall into Oroonoko's bosom, and that all things looked like a design on both sides, and 'twas in vain she protested her innocence. He was old and obstinate, and left her more than half assured that his fear was true.

The King going to his apartment, sent to know where the Prince was, and if he intended to obey his command. The messenger returned and told him he found the Prince pensive, and altogether unpreparing for the campaign; that he lay negligently on the ground, and answered very little. This confirmed the jealousy of the King, and he commanded that they should very narrowly and privately watch his motions; and that he should not stir from his apartment, but one spy or other should be employed to watch him. So that the hour approaching, wherein he was to go to the citron grove, and taking only Aboan along with him, he leaves his apartment, and was watched to the very gate of the otan, where he was seen to enter, and where they left him, to carry back the tidings to the King.

Oroonoko and Aboan were no sooner entered but Onahal led the Prince to the apartment of Imoinda, who, not knowing anything of her happiness, was laid in bed. But Onahal only left him in her chamber to make the best of his opportunity, and took her dear Aboan to her own, where he showed the height of complaisance[9] for his prince, when, to give him an opportunity, he suffered himself to be caressed in bed by Onahal.

The Prince softly wakened Imoinda, who was not a little surprised with joy to find him there, and yet she trembled with a thousand fears. I believe he omitted saying nothing to this young maid that might persuade her to suffer him to seize his own and take the rights of love; and I believe she was not long resisting those arms where she so longed to be; and having opportunity, night and silence, youth, love and desire, he soon prevailed, and ravished in a moment what his old grandfather had been endeavoring for so many months.

'Tis not to be imagined the satisfaction of these two young lovers; nor the vows she made him, that she remained a spotless maid till that night; and that what she did with his grandfather had robbed him of no part of her virgin honor, the gods in mercy and justice having reserved that for her plighted lord, to whom of right it belonged. And 'tis impossible to express the transports he suffered while he listened to a discourse so charming from her loved lips, and clasped that body in his arms for whom he had so long languished; and nothing now afflicted him but his sudden departure from her; for he told her the necessity and his commands; but should depart satisfied in this, that since the old king had hitherto not been able to deprive him of those enjoyments which only belonged to him, he believed for the future he would be less able to injure him. So that abating the scandal of the veil, which was no otherwise so than that she was wife to another, he believed her safe even in the arms of the King, and innocent; yet would he have ventured at the conquest of the world, and have given it all, to have had her avoided that honor of receiving the royal veil. 'Twas thus, between a thousand caresses, that both bemoaned the hard fate of youth and beauty, so liable to that cruel promotion; 'twas a glory that could well have been spared here, though desired and aimed at by all the young females of that kingdom.

But while they were thus fondly employed, forgetting how time ran on and that the dawn must conduct him far away from his only happiness, they heard a great noise in the otan, and unusual voices of men; at which the Prince, starting from the arms of the frighted Imoinda, ran to a little battle-ax he used to wear by his side; and having not so much leisure as to put on his habit, he opposed himself against some who were already opening the door; which they did with so much violence that Oroonoko was not able to defend it, but was forced to cry out with a commanding voice, "Whoever ye are that have the boldness to attempt to approach this apartment thus rudely, know that I, the Prince Oroonoko, will revenge it with the certain death of him that first enters. Therefore stand back, and know this place is sacred to love and me this night; tomorrow 'tis the King's."

This he spoke with a voice so resolved and assured that they soon retired from the door, but cried, "'Tis by the King's command we are come; and being satisfied by thy voice, O Prince, as much as if we had entered, we can report to the King the truth of all his fears, and leave thee to provide for thy own safety, as thou art advised by thy friends."

9. Desire to please.

At these words they departed, and left the Prince to take a short and sad leave of his Imoinda; who trusting in the strength of her charms, believed she should appease the fury of a jealous king by saying she was surprised, and that it was by force of arms he got into her apartment. All her concern now was for his life, and therefore she hastened him to the camp, and with much ado prevailed on him to go. Nor was it she alone that prevailed; Aboan and Onahal both pleaded, and both assured him of a lie that should be well enough contrived to secure Imoinda. So that at last, with a heart sad as death, dying eyes, and sighing soul, Oroonoko departed, and took his way to the camp.

It was not long after the King in person came to the otan, where beholding Imoinda with rage in his eyes, he upbraided her wickedness and perfidy, and threatening her royal lover, she fell on her face at his feet, bedewing the floor with her tears and imploring his pardon for a fault which she had not with her will committed, as Onahal, who was also prostrate with her, could testify that, unknown to her, he had broke into her apartment, and ravished her. She spoke this much against her conscience; but to save her own life, 'twas absolutely necessary she should feign this falsity. She knew it could not injure the Prince, he being fled to an army that would stand by him against any injuries that should assault him. However, this last thought of Imoinda's being ravished changed the measures of his revenge, and whereas before he designed to be himself her executioner, he now resolved she should not die. But as it is the greatest crime in nature amongst them to touch a woman after having been possessed by a son, a father, or a brother, so now he looked on Imoinda as a polluted thing, wholly unfit for his embrace; nor would he resign her to his grandson, because she had received the royal veil. He therefore removes her from the otan, with Onahal, whom he put into safe hands, with order they should be both sold off as slaves to another country, either Christian or heathen; 'twas no matter where.

This cruel sentence, worse than death, they implored might be reversed; but their prayers were vain, and it was put in execution accordingly, and that with so much secrecy that none, either without or within the otan, knew anything of their absence or their destiny.

The old king, nevertheless, executed this with a great deal of reluctance; but he believed he had made a very great conquest over himself when he had once resolved, and had performed what he resolved. He believed now that his love had been unjust, and that he could not expect the gods, or Captain of the Clouds (as they call the unknown power) should suffer a better consequence from so ill a cause. He now begins to hold Oroonoko excused and to say he had reason for what he did; and now everybody could assure the King, how passionately Imoinda was beloved by the Prince; even those confessed it now who said the contrary before his flame was abated. So that the King being old and not able to defend himself in war, and having no sons of all his race remaining alive but only this to maintain him on the throne; and looking on this as a man disobliged, first by the rape of his mistress, or rather, wife, and now by depriving him wholly of her, he feared, might make him desperate, and do some cruel thing, either to himself, or his old grandfather the offender; he began to repent him extremely of the contempt he had, in his rage, put on Imoinda. Besides, he considered he ought in honor to have killed her for this offense, if it had been one. He ought to have had so much value and consideration for a maid of her quality, as to have nobly put her to death, and not to have sold her like a common slave, the greatest revenge, and the most disgraceful of any, and to which they a thousand times prefer death, and implore it as Imoinda did, but could not obtain that honor. Seeing therefore it was certain that Oroonoko would highly resent this affront, he thought good to make some excuse for his rashness to him, and to that end he sent a messenger to the camp with orders to treat with him about the matter, to gain his pardon, and to endeavor to mitigate his grief; but that by no means he should tell him she was sold, but secretly put to death; for he knew he should never obtain his pardon for the other.

When the messenger came, he found the Prince upon the point of engaging with the enemy, but as soon as he heard of the arrival of the messenger he commanded him to his tent, where he embraced him and received him with joy; which was soon abated, by the downcast looks of the messenger, who was instantly demanded the cause by Oroonoko, who, impatient of delay, asked a thousand questions in a breath, and all concerning Imoinda. But there needed little return, for he could almost answer himself of all he demanded from his sighs and eyes. At last, the messenger casting himself at the Prince's feet and kissing them with all the submission of a man that had something to implore which he dreaded to utter, he besought him to hear with calmness what he had to deliver to him, and to call up all his noble and heroic courage to encounter with his words, and defend himself against the ungrateful things he must relate. Oroonoko replied, with a deep sigh and a languishing voice, "I am armed against their worst efforts—for I know they will tell me, Imoinda is no more—and after that, you may spare the rest." Then, commanding him to rise, he laid himself on a carpet under a rich pavilion, and remained a good while silent, and was hardly heard to sigh. When he was come a little to himself, the messenger asked him leave to deliver that part of his embassy which the Prince had not yet divined, and the Prince cried, "I permit thee." Then he told him the affliction the old king was in for the rashness he had committed in his cruelty to Imoinda, and how he deigned to ask pardon for his offense, and to implore the Prince would not suffer that loss to touch his heart too sensibly which now all the gods could not restore him, but might recompense him in glory which he begged he would pursue; and that death, that common revenger of all injuries, would soon even the account between him and a feeble old man.

Oroonoko bade him return his duty to his lord and master, and to assure him there was no account of revenge to be adjusted between them; if there were, 'twas he was the aggressor, and that death would be just, and, maugre[1] his age, would see him righted; and he was contented to leave his share of glory to youths more fortunate, and worthy of that favor from the gods. That henceforth he would never lift a weapon, or draw a bow, but abandon the small remains of his life to sighs and tears, and the continual thoughts of what his lord and grandfather had thought good to send out of the world, with all that youth, that innocence, and beauty.

After having spoken this, whatever his greatest officers and men of the best rank could do, they could not raise him from the carpet, or persuade him to action and resolutions of life, but commanding all to retire, he shut himself into his pavilion all that day, while the enemy was ready to engage; and wondering at the delay, the whole body of the chief of the army then addressed themselves to him, and to whom they had much ado to get admittance. They fell on their faces at the foot of his carpet, where they lay, and besought him with earnest prayers and tears to lead them forth to battle, and not let the enemy take advantages of them; and implored him to have regard to his glory, and to the world that depended on his courage and conduct. But he made no other reply to all their supplications but this, that he had now no more business for glory; and for the world, it was a trifle not worth his care. "Go," continued he, sighing, "and divide it amongst you; and reap with joy what you so vainly prize, and leave me to my more welcome destiny."

---

1. In spite of; i.e., despite Oroonoko's youth, death will avenge the king by taking Oroonoko first.

They then demanded what they should do, and whom he would constitute in his room, that the confusion of ambitious youth and power might not ruin their order, and make them a prey to the enemy. He replied, he would not give himself the trouble; but wished them to choose the bravest man amongst them, let his quality or birth be what it would. "For, O my friends!" said he, "it is not titles make men brave, or good; or birth that bestows courage and generosity, or makes the owner happy. Believe this, when you behold Oroonoko, the most wretched, and abandoned by fortune of all the creation of the gods." So turning himself about, he would make no more reply to all they could urge or implore.

The army beholding their officers return unsuccessful, with sad faces and ominous looks that presaged no good luck, suffered a thousand fears to take possession of their hearts, and the enemy to come even upon them, before they would provide for their safety by any defense; and though they were assured by some, who had a mind to animate them, that they should be immediately headed by the Prince, and that in the meantime Aboan had orders to command as general, yet they were so dismayed for want of that great example of bravery that they could make but a very feeble resistance, and at last downright fled before the enemy, who pursued them to the very tents, killing them. Nor could all Aboan's courage, which that day gained him immortal glory, shame them into a manly defense of themselves. The guards that were left behind about the Prince's tent, seeing the soldiers flee before the enemy and scatter themselves all over the plain in great disorder, made such outcries as roused the Prince from his amorous slumber, in which he had remained buried for two days without permitting any sustenance to approach him. But in spite of all his resolutions, he had not the constancy of grief to that degree as to make him insensible of the danger of his army; and in that instant he leapt from his couch and cried, "Come, if we must die, let us meet death the noblest way; and 'twill be more like Oroonoko to encounter him at an army's head, opposing the torrent of a conquering foe, than lazily, on a couch, to wait his lingering pleasure, and die every moment by a thousand wrecking thoughts; or be tamely taken by an enemy and led a whining, love-sick slave, to adorn the triumphs of Jamoan, that young victor, who already is entered beyond the limits I had prescribed him."

While he was speaking, he suffered his people to dress him for the field; and sallying out of his pavilion, with more life and vigor in his countenance than ever he showed, he appeared like some divine power descended to save his country from destruction; and his people had purposely put on him all things that might make him shine with most splendor, to strike a reverend awe into the beholders. He flew into the thickest of those that were pursuing his men, and being animated with despair, he fought as if he came on purpose to die, and did such things as will not be believed that human strength could perform, and such as soon inspired all the rest with new courage and new order. And now it was that they began to fight indeed, and so, as if they would not be outdone even by their adored hero, who turning the tide of the victory, changing absolutely the fate of the day, gained an entire conquest; and Oroonoko having the good fortune to single out Jamoan, he took him prisoner with his own hand, having wounded him almost to death.

This Jamoan afterwards became very dear to him, being a man very gallant and of excellent graces and fine parts, so that he never put him amongst the rank of captives, as they used to do, without distinction, for the common sale or market, but kept him in his own court, where he retained nothing of the prisoner but the name, and returned no more into his own country, so great an affection he took for Oroonoko; and by a thousand tales and adventures of love and gallantry, flattered his disease of melancholy and languishment, which I have often heard him say had certainly killed him, but for the conversation of this prince and Aboan, [and] the French governor he had from his childhood, of whom I have spoken before, and who was a man of admirable wit, great ingenuity and learning, all which he had infused into his young pupil. This Frenchman was banished out of his own country for some heretical notions he held; and though he was a man of very little religion, he had admirable morals, and a brave soul.

After the total defeat of Jamoan's army, which all fled, or were left dead upon the place, they spent some time in the camp, Oroonoko choosing rather to remain a while there in his tents, than enter into a palace, or live in a court where he had so lately suffered so great a loss. The officers therefore, who saw and knew his cause of discontent, invented all sorts of diversions and sports to entertain their prince: so that what with those amusements abroad and others at home, that is, within their tents, with the persuasions, arguments, and care of his friends and servants that he more peculiarly prized, he wore off in time a great part of that chagrin and torture of despair which the first effects of Imoinda's death had given him; insomuch as having received a thousand kind embassies from the King, and invitations to return to court, he obeyed, though with no little reluctance; and when he did so, there was a visible change in him, and for a long time he was much more melancholy than before. But time lessens all extremes, and reduces them to mediums and unconcern; but no motives or beauties, though all endeavored it, could engage him in any sort of amour, though he had all the invitations to it, both from his own youth and others' ambitions and designs.

Oroonoko was no sooner returned from this last conquest, and received at court with all the joy and magnificence that could be expressed to a young victor, who was not only returned triumphant but beloved like a deity, when there arrived in the port an English ship.

This person had often before been in these countries, and was very well known to Oroonoko, with whom he had trafficked for slaves, and had used to do the same with his predecessors.

This commander was a man of a finer sort of address and conversation, better bred and more engaging than most of that sort of men are; so that he seemed rather never to have been bred out of a court than almost all his life at sea. This captain therefore was always better received at court than most of the traders to those countries were; and especially by Oroonoko, who was more civilized, according to the European mode, than any other had been, and took more delight in the white nations, and, above all, men of parts and wit. To this captain he sold abundance of his slaves, and for the favor and esteem he had for him made him many presents, and obliged him to stay at court as long as possibly he could. Which the captain seemed to take as a very great honor done him, entertaining the Prince every day with globes and maps, and mathematical discourses and instruments; eating, drinking, hunting, and living with him with so much familiarity that it was not to be doubted but he had gained very greatly upon the heart of this gallant young man. And the captain, in return of all these mighty favors, besought the Prince to honor his vessel with his presence, some day or other, to dinner, before he should set sail; which he condescended to accept, and appointed his day. The captain, on his part, failed not to have all things in a readiness, in the most magnificent order he could possibly. And the day being come, the captain, in his boat richly adorned with carpets and velvet cushions, rowed to the shore to receive the Prince; with another longboat, where was placed all his music and trumpets, with which Oroonoko was extremely delighted, who met him on the shore, attended by his French governor, Jamoan, Aboan, and about an hundred of the noblest of the youths of the court. And after they had first carried the Prince on board, the boats fetched the rest off; where they found a very splendid treat, with all sorts of fine wines, and were as well entertained as 'twas possible in such a place to be.

The Prince having drunk hard of punch, and several sorts of wine, as did all the rest (for great care was taken they should want nothing of that part of the entertainment) was very merry, and in great admiration of the ship, for he had never been in one before; so that he was curious of beholding every place where he decently might descend. The rest, no less curious, who were not quite overcome with drinking, rambled at their pleasure fore and aft, as their fancies guided them: so that the captain, who had well laid his design before, gave the word and seized on all his guests; they clapping great irons suddenly on the Prince when he was leaped down in the hold to view that part of the vessel, and locking him fast down, secured him. The same treachery was used to all the rest; and all in one instant, in several places of the ship, were lashed fast in irons and betrayed to slavery. That great design over, they set all hands to work to hoist sail; and with as treacherous and fair a wind they made from the shore with this innocent and glorious prize, who thought of nothing less than such an entertainment.

Some have commended this act, as brave in the captain; but I will spare my sense of it, and leave it to my reader to judge as he pleases.

It may be easily guessed in what manner the Prince resented this indignity, who may be best resembled to a lion taken in a toil; so he raged, so he struggled for liberty, but all in vain; and they had so wisely managed his fetters that he could not use a hand in his defense, to quit himself of a life that would by no means endure slavery; nor could he move from the place where he was tied to any solid part of the ship against which he might have beat his head, and have finished his disgrace that way; so that being deprived of all other means, he resolved to perish for want of food. And pleased at last with that thought, and toiled and tired by rage and indignation, he laid himself down, and sullenly resolved upon dying, and refused all things that were brought him.

This did not a little vex the captain, and the more so because he found almost all of them of the same humor; so that the loss of so many brave slaves, so tall and goodly to behold, would have been very considerable. He therefore ordered one to go from him (for he would not be seen himself) to Oroonoko, and to assure him he was afflicted for having rashly done so inhospitable a deed, and which could not be now remedied, since they were far from shore; but since he resented it in so high a nature, he assured him he would revoke his resolution, and set both him and his friends ashore on the next land they should touch at; and of this the messenger gave him his oath, provided he would resolve to live. And Oroonoko, whose honor was such as he never had violated a word in his life himself, much less a solemn asseveration, believed in an instant what this man said, but replied he expected for a confirmation of this to have his shameful fetters dismissed. This demand was carried to the captain, who returned him answer that the offense had been so great which he had put upon the Prince, that he durst not trust him with liberty while he remained in the ship, for fear lest by a valor natural to him, and a revenge that would animate that valor, he might commit some outrage fatal to himself and the King his master, to whom his vessel did belong. To this Oroonoko replied, he would engage his honor to behave himself in all friendly order and manner, and obey the command of the captain, as he was lord of the King's vessel, and general of those men under his command.

This was delivered to the still doubting captain, who could not resolve to trust a heathen he said, upon his parole,[2] a man that had no sense or notion of the God that he worshipped. Oroonoko then replied he was very sorry to hear that the captain pretended to the knowledge and worship of any gods who had taught him no better principles, than not to credit as he would be credited; but they told him the difference of their faith occasioned that distrust: for the captain had protested to him upon the word of a Christian, and sworn in the name of a great God, which if he should violate, he would expect eternal torment in the world to come. "Is that all the obligation he has to be just to his oath?" replied Oroonoko. "Let him know I swear by my honor, which to violate, would not only render me contemptible and despised by all brave and honest men, and so give myself perpetual pain, but it would be eternally offending and diseasing all mankind, harming, betraying, circumventing, and outraging all men; but punishments hereafter are suffered by oneself; and the world takes no cognizances whether this god have revenged them, or not, 'tis done so secretly, and deferred so long; while the man of no honor suffers every moment the scorn and contempt of the honester world, and dies every day ignominiously in his fame, which is more valuable than life. I speak not this to move belief, but to show you how you mistake, when you imagine that he who will violate his honor will keep his word with his gods." So turning from him with a disdainful smile, he refused to answer him when he urged him to know what answer he should carry back to his captain; so that he departed without saying any more.

The captain pondering and consulting what to do, it was concluded that nothing but Oroonoko's liberty would encourage any of the rest to eat, except the Frenchman, whom the captain could not pretend to keep prisoner, but only told him he was secured because he might act something in favor of the Prince, but that he should be freed as soon as they came to land. So that they concluded it wholly necessary to free the Prince from his irons that he might show himself to the rest, that they might have an eye upon him, and that they could not fear a single man.

This being resolved, to make the obligation the greater, the captain himself went to Oroonoko; where, after many compliments, and assurances of what he had already promised, he receiving from the Prince his parole, and his hand, for his good behavior, dismissed his irons, and brought him to his own cabin; where, after having treated and reposed him a while, for he had neither eaten nor slept in four days before, he besought him to visit those obstinate people in chains, who refused all manner of sustenance; and entreated him to oblige them to eat, and assure them of their liberty the first opportunity.

Oroonoko, who was too generous not to give credit to his words, showed himself to his people, who were transported with excess of joy at the sight of their darling prince, falling at his feet, and kissing and embracing them, believing, as some divine oracle, all he assured them. But he besought them to bear their chains with that bravery that became those whom he had seen act so nobly in arms; and that they could not give him greater proofs of their love and friendship, since 'twas all the security the captain (his friend) could have against the revenge, he said, they might possibly justly take, for the injuries sustained by him. And they all, with one accord, assured him they could not suffer enough when it was for his repose and safety.

After this they no longer refused to eat, but took what was brought them and were pleased with their captivity, since by it they hoped to redeem the Prince, who, all the

2. Word of honor.

rest of the voyage, was treated with all the respect due to his birth, though nothing could divert his melancholy; and he would often sigh for Imoinda, and think this a punishment due to his misfortune, in having left that noble maid behind him that fatal night in the otan, when he fled to the camp.

Possessed with a thousand thoughts of past joys with this fair young person, and a thousand griefs for her eternal loss, he endured a tedious voyage, and at last arrived at the mouth of the river of Surinam, a colony belonging to the King of England, and where they were to deliver some part of their slaves. There the merchants and gentlemen of the country going on board to demand those lots of slaves they had already agreed on, and amongst those the overseers of those plantations where I then chanced to be, the captain, who had given the word, ordered his men to bring up those noble slaves in fetters, whom I have spoken of; and having put them, some in one, and some in other lots, with women and children (which they call pickaninnies), they sold them off as slaves to several merchants and gentlemen; not putting any two in one lot, because they would separate them far from each other; not daring to trust them together, lest rage and courage should put them upon contriving some great action, to the ruin of the colony.

Oroonoko was first seized on and sold to our overseer, who had the first lot, with seventeen more of all sorts and sizes, but not one of quality with him. When he saw this, he found what they meant; for, as I said, he understood English pretty well; and being wholly unarmed and defenseless, so as it was in vain to make any resistance, he only beheld the captain with a look all fierce and disdainful; upbraiding him with eyes that forced blushes on his guilty cheeks, he only cried in passing over the side of the ship, "Farewell, Sir! 'Tis worth my suffering to gain so true a knowledge both of you and of your gods by whom you swear." And desiring those that held him to forbear their pains, and telling them he would make no resistance, he cried, "Come, my fellow slaves, let us descend, and see if we can meet with more honor and honesty in the next world we shall touch upon." So he nimbly leapt into the boat, and showing no more concern, suffered himself to be rowed up the river with his seventeen companions.

The gentleman that bought him was a young Cornish gentleman, whose name was Trefry, a man of great wit and fine learning, and was carried into those parts by the Lord——, Governor, to manage all his affairs.[3] He reflecting on the last words of Oroonoko to the captain, and beholding the richness of his vest,[4] no sooner came into the boat, but he fixed his eyes on him; and finding something so extraordinary in his face, his shape and mien, a greatness of look, and haughtiness in his air, and finding he spoke English, had a great mind to be inquiring into his quality and fortune; which, though Oroonoko endeavored to hide by only confessing he was above the rank of common slaves, Trefry soon found he was yet something greater than he confessed; and from that moment began to conceive so vast an esteem for him, that he ever after loved him as his dearest brother, and showed him all the civilities due to so great a man.

Trefry was a very good mathematician and a linguist, could speak French and Spanish, and in the three days they remained in the boat (for so long were they going from the ship to the plantation) he entertained Oroonoko so agreeably with his art and discourse, that he was no less pleased with Trefry, than he was with the Prince; and he thought himself, at least, fortunate in this, that since he was a slave, as long as he would

3. John Treffry (d. 1674) supervised the plantation at Parham for Francis, Lord Willoughby (1613?–1686), a nobleman long involved with colonization, who received from Charles II both the governorship and a grant of land in Surinam; his appointment of Behn's father to the post of lieutenant-governor appears to account for her sojourn in the colony (though her father died en route).
4. Robe.

suffer himself to remain so, he had a man of so excellent wit and parts for a master. So that before they had finished their voyage up the river, he made no scruple of declaring to Trefry all his fortunes and most part of what I have here related, and put himself wholly into the hands of his new friend, whom he found resenting all the injuries were done him, and was charmed with all the greatnesses of his actions, which were recited with that modesty and delicate sense, as wholly vanquished him, and subdued him to his interest. And he promised him on his word and honor, he would find the means to reconduct him to his own country again; assuring him, he had a perfect abhorrence of so dishonorable an action; and that he would sooner have died, than have been the author of such a perfidy. He found the Prince was very much concerned to know what became of his friends, and how they took their slavery; and Trefry promised to take care about the inquiring after their condition, and that he should have an account of them.

Though, as Oroonoko afterwards said, he had little reason to credit the words of a backearary,[5] yet he knew not why, but he saw a kind of sincerity and awful truth in the face of Trefry; he saw an honesty in his eyes, and he found him wise and witty enough to understand honor; for it was one of his maxims, "A man of wit could not be a knave or villain."

In their passage up the river they put in at several houses for refreshment, and ever when they landed numbers of people would flock to behold this man; not but their eyes were daily entertained with the sight of slaves, but the fame of Oroonoko was gone before him, and all people were in admiration of his beauty. Besides, he had a rich habit on, in which he was taken, so different from the rest, and which the captain could not strip him of because he was forced to surprise his person in the minute he sold him. When he found his habit made him liable, as he thought, to be gazed at the more, he begged Trefry to give him something more befitting a slave; which he did, and took off his robes. Nevertheless, he shone through all and his osenbrigs (a sort of brown holland suit he had on)[6] could not conceal the graces of his looks and mien; and he had no less admirers than when he had his dazzling habit on. The royal youth appeared in spite of the slave, and people could not help treating him after a different manner without designing it; as soon as they approached him they venerated and esteemed him; his eyes insensibly commanded respect, and his behavior insinuated it into every soul. So that there was nothing talked of but this young and gallant slave, even by those who yet knew not that he was a prince.

I ought to tell you, that the Christians never buy any slaves but they give them some name of their own, their native ones being likely very barbarous, and hard to pronounce; so that Mr. Trefry gave Oroonoko that of Caesar, which name will live in that country as long as that (scarce more) glorious one of the great Roman, for 'tis most evident, he wanted no part of the personal courage of that Caesar, and acted things as memorable, had they been done in some part of the world replenished with people and historians that might have given him his due. But his misfortune was to fall in an obscure world, that afforded only a female pen to celebrate his fame, though I doubt not but it had lived from others' endeavors, if the Dutch, who immediately after his time took that country,[7] had not killed, banished, and dispersed all those that were capable of giving the world this great man's life, much better than I have done. And Mr. Trefry, who designed it, died before he began it, and bemoaned himself for not having undertook it in time.

---

5. An African-derived term for "white master."
6. Osnaburg and holland were thick cotton or linen fabrics.
7. In 1667 Surinam twice changed hands. The Dutch briefly captured the colony and the English won it back, but immediately ceded it to the Dutch (in exchange for New York) at the Treaty of Breda.

For the future therefore, I must call Oroonoko Caesar, since by that name only he was known in our western world, and by that name he was received on shore at Parham House, where he was destined a slave. But if the King himself (God bless him) had come ashore, there could not have been greater expectations by all the whole plantation, and those neighboring ones, than was on ours at that time; and he was received more like a governor than a slave. Notwithstanding, as the custom was, they assigned him his portion of land, his house, and his business, up in the plantation. But as it was more for form than any design to put him to his task, he endured no more of the slave but the name, and remained some days in the house, receiving all visits that were made him, without stirring towards that part of the plantation where the Negroes were.

At last, he would needs go view his land, his house, and the business assigned him. But he no sooner came to the houses of the slaves, which are like a little town by itself, the Negroes all having left work, but they all came forth to behold him, and found he was that prince who had, at several times, sold most of them to these parts; and, from a veneration they pay to great men, especially if they know them, and from the surprise and awe they had at the sight of him, they all cast themselves at his feet, crying out, in their language, "Live, O King! Long live, O King!" And kissing his feet, paid him even divine homage.

Several English gentlemen were with him; and what Mr. Trefry had told them was here confirmed, of which he himself before had no other witness than Caesar himself. But he was infinitely glad to find his grandeur confirmed by the adoration of all the slaves.

Caesar, troubled with their over-joy, and over-ceremony, besought them to rise, and to receive him as their fellow slave, assuring them, he was no better. At which they set up with one accord a most terrible and hideous mourning and condoling, which he and the English had much ado to appease. But at last they prevailed with them, and they prepared all their barbarous music, and everyone killed and dressed something of his own stock (for every family has their land apart, on which, at their leisure times, they breed all eatable things) and clubbing it together, made a most magnificent supper, inviting their grandee captain, their prince, to honor it with his presence, which he did, and several English with him, where they all waited on him, some playing, others dancing before him all the time, according to the manners of their several nations, and with unwearied industry endeavoring to please and delight him.

While they sat at meat Mr. Trefry told Caesar that most of these young slaves were undone in love, with a fine she-slave, whom they had had about six months on their land. The Prince, who never heard the name of love without a sigh, nor any mention of it without the curiosity of examining further into that tale which of all discourses was most agreeable to him, asked, how they came to be so unhappy, as to be all undone for one fair slave? Trefry, who was naturally amorous, and loved to talk of love as well as anybody, proceeded to tell him, they had the most charming black that ever was beheld on their plantation, about fifteen or sixteen years old, as he guessed; that, for his part, he had done nothing but sigh for her ever since she came; and that all the white beauties he had seen never charmed him so absolutely as this fine creature had done; and that no man of any nation ever beheld her, that did not fall in love with her; and that she had all the slaves perpetually at her feet; and the whole country resounded with the fame of Clemene, "for so," said he, "we have christened her. But she denies us all with such a noble disdain, that 'tis a miracle to see that she, who can give such eternal desires, should herself be all ice, and all unconcern. She is adorned with the most graceful modesty that ever beautified youth; the softest sigher—that, if she were capable of love, one would swear she languished for some absent happy man; and so retired, as if she feared a rape even from the God of Day,[8] or that the breezes would steal kisses from her delicate mouth. Her task of work some sighing lover every day makes it his petition to perform for her, which she accepts blushing, and with reluctance, for fear he will ask her a look for a recompense, which he dares not presume to hope, so great an awe she strikes into the hearts of her admirers." "I do not wonder," replied the Prince, "that Clemene should refuse slaves, being as you say so beautiful, but wonder how she escapes those who can entertain her as you can do. Or why, being your slave, you do not oblige her to yield." "I confess," said Trefry, "when I have, against her will, entertained her with love so long as to be transported with my passion even above decency, I have been ready to make use of those advantages of strength and force nature has given me. But oh! she disarms me, with that modesty and weeping so tender and so moving, that I retire, and thank my stars she overcame me." The company laughed at his civility to a slave, and Caesar only applauded the nobleness of his passion and nature, since that slave might be noble, or, what was better, have true notions of honor and virtue in her. Thus passed they this night, after having received from the slaves all imaginable respect and obedience.

The next day Trefry asked Caesar to walk, when the heat was allayed, and designedly carried him by the cottage of the fair slave, and told him, she whom he spoke of last night lived there retired. "But," says he, "I would not wish you to approach, for I am sure you will be in love as soon as you behold her." Caesar assured him he was proof against all the charms of that sex, and that if he imagined his heart could be so perfidious to love again after Imoinda, he believed he should tear it from his bosom. They had no sooner spoke, but a little shock dog,[9] that Clemene had presented her, which she took great delight in, ran out, and she, not knowing anybody was there, ran to get it in again, and bolted out on those who were just speaking of her. When seeing them she would have run in again, but Trefry caught her by the hand and cried, "Clemene, however you fly a lover, you ought to pay some respect to this stranger" (pointing to Caesar). But she, as if she had resolved never to raise her eyes to the face of a man again, bent them the more to the earth when he spoke, and gave the Prince the leisure to look the more at her. There needed no long gazing or consideration to examine who this fair creature was. He soon saw Imoinda all over her; in a minute he saw her face, her shape, her air, her modesty, and all that called forth his soul with joy at his eyes, and left his body destitute of almost life. It stood without motion, and, for a minute, knew not that it had a being. And I believe he had never come to himself, so oppressed he was with overjoy, if he had not met with this allay,[1] that he perceived Imoinda fall dead in the hands of Trefry. This awakened him, and he ran to her aid, and caught her in his arms, where, by degrees, she came to herself; and 'tis needless to tell with what transports, what ecstasies of joy, they both a while beheld each other, without speaking, then snatched each other to their arms, then gaze again, as if they still doubted whether they possessed the blessing they grasped. But when they recovered their speech, 'tis not to be imagined what tender things they expressed to each other, wondering what strange fate had brought them again together. They soon informed each other of their fortunes, and equally bewailed their fate; but at the same time, they mutually protested that even fetters and slavery were soft and easy, and

8. The sun.
9. Poodle.
1. Reduction; release.

would be supported with joy and pleasure, while they could be so happy to possess each other, and to be able to make good their vows. Caesar swore he disdained the empire of the world while he could behold his Imoinda, and she despised grandeur and pomp, those vanities of her sex, when she could gaze on Oroonoko. He adored the very cottage where she resided, and said, that little inch of the world would give him more happiness than all the universe could do, and she vowed, it was a palace, while adorned with the presence of Oroonoko.

Trefry was infinitely pleased with this novel,[2] and found this Clemene was the fair mistress of whom Caesar had before spoke; and was not a little satisfied, that Heaven was so kind to the Prince as to sweeten his misfortunes by so lucky an accident, and leaving the lovers to themselves, was impatient to come down to Parham House (which was on the same plantation) to give me an account of what had happened. I was as impatient to make these lovers a visit, having already made a friendship with Caesar, and from his own mouth learned what I have related, which was confirmed by his Frenchman, who was set on shore to seek his fortunes, and of whom they could not make a slave because a Christian, and he came daily to Parham Hill to see and pay his respects to his pupil prince. So that concerning and interesting myself in all that related to Caesar, whom I had assured of liberty as soon as the governor arrived, I hasted presently to the place where the lovers were, and was infinitely glad to find this beautiful young slave (who had already gained all our esteems, for her modesty and her extraordinary prettiness) to be the same I had heard Caesar speak so much of. One may imagine then, we paid her a treble respect; and though from her being carved in fine flowers and birds all over her body, we took her to be of quality before, yet, when we knew Clemene was Imoinda, we could not enough admire her.

I had forgot to tell you, that those who are nobly born of that country are so delicately cut and raced[3] all over the fore part of the trunk of their bodies, that it looks as if it were japanned;[4] the works being raised like high point[5] round the edges of the flowers. Some are only carved with a little flower or bird at the sides of the temples, as was Caesar; and those who are so carved over the body resemble our ancient Picts,[6] that are figured in the chronicles, but these carvings are more delicate.

From that happy day Caesar took Clemene for his wife, to the general joy of all people, and there was as much magnificence as the country would afford at the celebration of this wedding. And in a very short time after she conceived with child; which made Caesar even adore her, knowing he was the last of his great race. This new accident made him more impatient of liberty, and he was every day treating with Trefry for his and Clemene's liberty; and offered either gold, or a vast quantity of slaves, which should be paid before they let him go, provided he could have any security that he should go when his ransom was paid. They fed him from day to day with promises, and delayed him, till the Lord Governor should come, so that he began to suspect them of falsehood, and that they would delay him till the time of his wife's delivery, and make a slave of that too, for all the breed is theirs to whom the parents belong. This thought made him very uneasy, and his sullenness gave them some jealousies[7] of him, so that I was obliged, by some persons who feared a mutiny (which is very fatal sometimes in those colonies that abound so with slaves that they exceed the whites in vast numbers),

---

2. The unlikely chance reunion of the lovers resembles those common in romances or novels.
3. Carved.
4. Varnished with a glossy black lacquer.
5. Starched lace.

6. Ancient inhabitants of northern Britain, possibly so named by the Romans because of the "pictures" (tattoos and other ornaments) they bore on their skin.
7. Suspicions.

to discourse with Caesar, and to give him all the satisfaction I possibly could. They knew he and Clemene were scarce an hour in a day from my lodgings, that they ate with me, and that I obliged them in all things I was capable of: I entertained him with the lives of the Romans, and great men, which charmed him to my company, and her, with teaching her all the pretty works that I was mistress of, and telling her stories of nuns, and endeavoring to bring her to the knowledge of the true God. But of all discourses Caesar liked that the worst, and would never be reconciled to our notions of the Trinity, of which he ever made a jest; it was a riddle, he said, would turn his brain to conceive, and one could not make him understand what faith was. However, these conversations failed not altogether so well to divert him, that he liked the company of us women much above the men, for he could not drink, and he is but an ill companion in that country that cannot. So that obliging him to love us very well, we had all the liberty of speech with him, especially myself, whom he called his Great Mistress; and indeed my word would go a great way with him. For these reasons, I had opportunity to take notice to him, that he was not well pleased of late, as he used to be, was more retired and thoughtful, and told him, I took it ill he should suspect we would break our words with him, and not permit both him and Clemene to return to his own kingdom, which was not so long away, but when he was once on his voyage he would quickly arrive there. He made me some answers that showed a doubt in him, which made me ask him, what advantage it would be to doubt? It would but give us a fear of him, and possibly compel us to treat him so as I should be very loath to behold: that is, it might occasion his confinement. Perhaps this was not so luckily spoke of me, for I perceived he resented that word, which I strove to soften again in vain. However, he assured me, that whatsoever resolutions he should take, he would act nothing upon the white people. And as for myself, and those upon that plantation where he was, he would sooner forfeit his eternal liberty, and life itself, than lift his hand against his greatest enemy on that place. He besought me to suffer no fears upon his account, for he could do nothing that honor should not dictate, but he accused himself for having suffered slavery so long; yet he charged that weakness on love alone, who was capable of making him neglect even glory itself, and for which now he reproaches himself every moment of the day. Much more to this effect he spoke, with an air impatient enough to make me know he would not be long in bondage, and though he suffered only the name of a slave, and had nothing of the toil and labor of one, yet that was sufficient to render him uneasy, and he had been too long idle, who used to be always in action, and in arms. He had a spirit all rough and fierce, and that could not be tamed to lazy rest, and though all endeavors were used to exercise himself in such actions and sports as this world afforded, as running, wrestling, pitching the bar,[8] hunting and fishing, chasing and killing tigers of a monstrous size, which this continent affords in abundance; and wonderful snakes, such as Alexander[9] is reported to have encountered at the river of Amazons, and which Caesar took great delight to overcome; yet these were not actions great enough for his large soul, which was still panting after more renowned action.

Before I parted that day with him, I got, with much ado, a promise from him to rest yet a little longer with patience, and wait the coming of the Lord Governor, who was every day expected on our shore. He assured me he would, and this promise he desired me to know was given perfectly in complaisance to me, in whom he had an entire confidence.

---

8. Hurling a heavy rod for purposes of exercise or sport.
9. Legends surrounding Alexander the Great included his encounter with the mythical woman warriors called

Amazons, and with the formidable snakes inhabiting their territories.

After this, I neither thought it convenient to trust him much out of our view, nor did the country who feared him; but with one accord it was advised to treat him fairly, and oblige him to remain within such a compass, and that he should be permitted as seldom as could be to go up to the plantations of the Negroes; or if he did, to be accompanied by some that should be rather in appearance attendants than spies. This care was for some time taken, and Caesar looked upon it as a mark of extraordinary respect, and was glad his discontent had obliged them to be more observant to him. He received new assurance from the overseer, which was confirmed to him by the opinion of all the gentlemen of the country, who made their court to him. During this time that we had his company more frequently than hitherto we had had, it may not be unpleasant to relate to you the diversions we entertained him with, or rather he us.

My stay was to be short in that country, because my father died at sea, and never arrived to possess the honor was designed him (which was lieutenant-general of six and thirty islands, besides the continent[1] of Surinam), nor the advantages he hoped to reap by them, so that though we were obliged to continue on our voyage, we did not intend to stay upon the place. Though, in a word, I must say thus much of it, that certainly had his late Majesty,[2] of sacred memory, but seen and known what a vast and charming world he had been master of in that continent, he would never have parted so easily with it to the Dutch. 'Tis a continent whose vast extent was never yet known, and may contain more noble earth than all the universe besides; for they say it reaches from east to west, one way as far as China, and another to Peru. It affords all things both for beauty and use; 'tis there eternal spring, always the very months of April, May, and June. The shades are perpetual, the trees, bearing at once all degrees of leaves and fruit from blooming buds to ripe autumn, groves of oranges, lemons, citrons, figs, nutmegs, and noble aromatics, continually bearing their fragrancies. The trees appearing all like nosegays adorned with flowers of different kind; some are all white, some purple, some scarlet, some blue, some yellow; bearing, at the same time, ripe fruit and blooming young, or producing every day new. The very wood of all these trees have an intrinsic value above common timber, for they are, when cut, of different colors, glorious to behold, and bear a price considerable, to inlay withal. Besides this, they yield rich balm and gums, so that we make our candles of such an aromatic substance as does not only give a sufficient light but, as they burn, they cast their perfumes all about. Cedar is the common firing, and all the houses are built with it. The very meat we eat, when set on the table, if it be native, I mean of the country, perfumes the whole room, especially a little beast called an armadillo, a thing which I can liken to nothing so well as a rhinoceros. 'Tis all in white armor so jointed that it moves as well in it as if it had nothing on. This beast is about the bigness of a pig of six weeks old. But it were endless to give an account of all the diverse wonderful and strange things that country affords, and which we took a very great delight to go in search of, though those adventures are oftentimes fatal and at least dangerous. But while we had Caesar in our company on these designs we feared no harm, nor suffered any.

As soon as I came into the country, the best house in it was presented me, called St. John's Hill. It stood on a vast rock of white marble, at the foot of which the river ran a vast depth down, and not to be descended on that side. The little waves still dashing and washing the foot of this rock made the softest murmurs and purlings in the world, and the opposite bank was adorned with such vast quantities of different

---

1. Mainland.   2. Charles II.

flowers eternally blowing,[3] and every day and hour new, fenced behind them with lofty trees of a thousand rare forms and colors, that the prospect was the most ravishing that sands can create. On the edge of this white rock, toward the river, was a walk or grove of orange and lemon trees, about half the length of the Mall[4] here, whose flowery and fruity branches meet at the top, and hindered the sun, whose rays are very fierce there, from entering a beam into the grove, and the cool air that came from the river made it not only fit to entertain people in at all the hottest hours of the day, but refreshed the sweet blossoms, and made it always sweet and charming, and sure the whole globe of the world cannot show so delightful a place as this grove was. Not all the gardens of boasted Italy can produce a shade to out-vie this, which Nature had joined with Art to render so exceeding fine. And 'tis a marvel to see how such vast trees, as big as English oaks, could take footing on so solid a rock, and in so little earth, as covered that rock, but all things by nature there are rare, delightful, and wonderful. But to our sports.

Sometimes we would go surprising,[5] and in search of young tigers in their dens, watching when the old ones went forth to forage for prey, and oftentimes we have been in great danger, and have fled apace for our lives, when surprised by the dams. But once, above all other times, we went on this design, and Caesar was with us, who had no sooner stolen a young tiger from her nest, but going off, we encountered the dam, bearing a buttock of a cow, which he[6] had torn off with his mighty paw, and going with it towards his den. We had only four women, Caesar, and an English gentleman, brother to Harry Martin, the great Oliverian.[7] We found there was no escaping this enraged and ravenous beast. However, we women fled as fast as we could from it, but our heels had not saved our lives if Caesar had not laid down his cub, when he found the tiger quit her prey to make the more speed towards him, and taking Mr. Martin's sword desired him to stand aside, or follow the ladies. He obeyed him, and Caesar met this monstrous beast of might, size, and vast limbs, who came with open jaws upon him, and fixing his awful stern eyes full upon those of the beast, and putting himself into a very steady and good aiming posture of defense, ran his sword quite through his breast down to his very heart, home to the hilt of the sword. The dying beast stretched forth her paw, and going to grasp his thigh, surprised with death in that very moment, did him no other harm than fixing her long nails in his flesh very deep, feebly wounded him, but could not grasp the flesh to tear off any. When he had done this, he hollowed to us to return, which, after some assurance of his victory, we did, and found him lugging out the sword from the bosom of the tiger, who was laid in her blood on the ground. He took up the cub, and with an unconcern, that had nothing of the joy or gladness of a victory, he came and laid the whelp at my feet. We all extremely wondered at his daring, and at the bigness of the beast, which was about the height of an heifer, but of mighty, great, and strong limbs.

Another time, being in the woods, he killed a tiger, which had long infested that part, and borne away abundance of sheep and oxen and other things, that were for the support of those to whom they belonged. Abundance of people assailed this beast, some affirming they had shot her with several bullets quite through the body, at several times, and some swearing they shot her through the very heart, and they believed she was a devil rather than a mortal thing. Caesar had often said he had a mind to encounter this

---

3. Blossoming.
4. A walk extending alongside London's St. James's Park.
5. I.e., surprise-attacking.
6. The "dam" is the cub's mother, but Behn has surprisingly

shifted the gender of the pronoun from "she" to "he"; she will do so again in reference to another tiger in the next paragraph.
7. Supporter of Oliver Cromwell.

monster, and spoke with several gentlemen who had attempted her, one crying, I shot her with so many poisoned arrows, another with his gun in this part of her, and another in that. So that he remarking all these places where she was shot, fancied still he should overcome her, by giving her another sort of a wound than any had yet done, and one day said (at the table), "What trophies and garlands, ladies, will you make me, if I bring you home the heart of this ravenous beast that eats up all your lambs and pigs?" We all promised he should be rewarded at all our hands. So taking a bow, which he chose out of a great many, he went up in the wood, with two gentlemen, where he imagined this devourer to be. They had not passed very far in it, but they heard her voice, growling and grumbling, as if she were pleased with something she was doing. When they came in view, they found her muzzling in the belly of a new ravished sheep which she had torn open, and seeing herself approached, she took fast hold of her prey with her forepaws, and set a very fierce raging look on Caesar, without offering to approach him, for fear, at the same time, of losing what she had in possession. So that Caesar remained a good while, only taking aim, and getting an opportunity to shoot her where he designed. 'Twas some time before he could accomplish it, and to wound her and not kill her would but have enraged her more, and endangered him. He had a quiver of arrows at his side, so that if one failed he could be supplied. At last, retiring a little, he gave her opportunity to eat, for he found she was ravenous, and fell to as soon as she saw him retire, being more eager of her prey than of doing new mischiefs. When he going softly to one side of her, and hiding his person behind certain herbage that grew high and thick, he took so good aim that, as he intended, he shot her just into the eye, and the arrow was sent with so good a will, and so sure a hand, that it stuck in her brain, and made her caper and become mad for a moment or two, but being seconded by another arrow, he fell dead upon the prey. Caesar cut him open with a knife, to see where those wounds were that had been reported to him, and why he did not die of them. But I shall now relate a thing that possibly will find no credit among men, because 'tis a notion commonly received with us that nothing can receive a wound in the heart and live; but when the heart of this courageous animal was taken out, there were seven bullets of lead in it, and the wounds seamed up with great scars, and she lived with the bullets a great while, for it was long since they were shot. This heart the conqueror brought up to us, and 'twas a very great curiosity, which all the country came to see; and which gave Caesar occasion of many fine discourses, of accidents in war and strange escapes.

At other times he would go a-fishing, and discoursing on that diversion, he found we had in that country a very strange fish, called a numb eel[8] (an eel of which I have eaten), that while it is alive, it has a quality so cold that those who are angling, though with a line of never so great a length, with a rod at the end of it, it shall, in the same minute the bait is touched by this eel, seize him or her that holds the rod with benumbedness, that shall deprive them of sense for a while. And some have fallen into the water, and others dropped as dead on the banks of the rivers where they stood, as soon as this fish touches the bait. Caesar used to laugh at this, and believed it impossible a man could lose his force at the touch of a fish; and could not understand that philosophy, that a cold quality should be of that nature. However, he had a great curiosity to try whether it would have the same effect on him it had on others, and often tried, but in vain. At last, the sought-for fish came to the bait as he stood angling on the bank; and instead of throwing away the rod, or giving it a sudden twitch out of the water, whereby he might have caught both the eel and have dismissed the rod before it could

8. An electric eel.

have too much power over him for experiment sake, he grasped it but the harder, and fainting fell into the river. And being still possessed of the rod, the tide carried him senseless as he was a great way, till an Indian boat took him up, and perceived, when they touched him, a numbness seize them, and by that knew the rod was in his hand, which with a paddle (that is, a short oar) they struck away, and snatched it into the boat, eel and all. If Caesar were almost dead with the effect of this fish, he was more so with that of the water, where he had remained the space of going a league, and they found they had much ado to bring him back to life. But at last they did, and brought him home, where he was in a few hours well recovered and refreshed, and not a little ashamed to find he should be overcome by an eel, and that all the people who heard his defiance would laugh at him. But we cheered him up and he, being convinced, we had the eel at supper, which was a quarter of an ell about, and most delicate meat, and was of the more value, since it cost so dear as almost the life of so gallant a man.

About this time we were in many mortal fears about some disputes the English had with the Indians, so that we could scarce trust ourselves, without great numbers, to go to any Indian towns or place where they abode, for fear they should fall upon us, as they did immediately after my coming away, and that it was in the possession of the Dutch, who used them not so civilly as the English, so that they cut in pieces all they could take, getting into houses, and hanging up the mother, and all her children about her, and cut a footman I left behind me all in joints, and nailed him to trees.

This feud began while I was there, so that I lost half the satisfaction I proposed, in not seeing and visiting the Indian towns. But one day, bemoaning of our misfortunes upon this account, Caesar told us we need not fear, for if we had a mind to go he would undertake to be our guard. Some would, but most would not venture. About eighteen of us resolved, and took barge, and after eight days arrived near an Indian town. But approaching it, the hearts of some of our company failed, and they would not venture on shore, so we polled who would, and who would not. For my part, I said, if Caesar would, I would go. He resolved, so did my brother and my woman, a maid of good courage. Now none of us speaking the language of the people, and imagining we should have a half diversion in gazing only and not knowing what they said, we took a fisherman that lived at the mouth of the river, who had been a long inhabitant there, and obliged him to go with us. But because he was known to the Indians, as trading among them, and being, by long living there, become a perfect Indian in color, we, who resolved to surprise them, by making them see something they never had seen (that is, white people) resolved only myself, my brother, and woman should go. So Caesar, the fisherman, and the rest, hiding behind some thick reeds and flowers, that grew on the banks, let us pass on towards the town, which was on the bank of the river all along. A little distant from the houses, or huts, we saw some dancing, others busied in fetching and carrying of water from the river. They had no sooner spied us but they set up a loud cry, that frighted us at first. We thought it had been for those that should kill us, but it seems it was of wonder and amazement. They were all naked, and we were dressed, so as is most commode for the hot countries, very glittering and rich, so that we appeared extremely fine. My own hair was cut short, and I had a taffeta cap, with black feathers, on my head. My brother was in a stuff[9] suit, with silver loops and buttons, and abundance of green ribbon. This was all infinitely surprising to them, and because we saw them stand still, till we approached them, we took heart and advanced, came up to them, and offered them our hands, which they took, and looked on us round

---

9. Light worsted wool.

about, calling still for more company; who came swarming out, all wondering, and crying out *tepeeme,* taking their hair up in their hands, and spreading it wide to those they called out to, as if they would say (as indeed it signified) "numberless wonders," or not to be recounted, no more than to number the hair of their heads. By degrees they grew more bold, and from gazing upon us round, they touched us, laying their hands upon all the features of our faces, feeling our breasts and arms, taking up one petticoat, then wondering to see another, admiring our shoes and stockings, but more our garters, which we gave them, and they tied about their legs, being laced with silver lace at the ends, for they much esteem any shining things. In fine, we suffered them to survey us as they pleased, and we thought they would never have done admiring us. When Caesar and the rest saw we were received with such wonder, they came up to us, and finding the Indian trader whom they knew (for 'tis by these fishermen, called Indian traders, we hold a commerce with them; for they love not to go far from home, and we never go to them), when they saw him therefore they set up a new joy, and cried, in their language, "Oh! here's our *tiguamy,* and we shall now know whether those things can speak." So advancing to him, some of them gave him their hands, and cried, "*Amora tiguamy,*" which is as much as, "How do you," or "Welcome friend," and all, with one din, began to gabble to him, and asked, If we had sense, and wit? If we could talk of affairs of life, and war, as they could do? If we could hunt, swim, and do a thousand things they use? He answered them, we could. Then they invited us into their houses, and dressed venison and buffalo for us; and, going out, gathered a leaf of a tree, called a sarumbo leaf, of six yards long, and spread it on the ground for a table-cloth, and cutting another in pieces instead of plates, setting us on little bow Indian stools, which they cut out of one entire piece of wood, and paint in a sort of japan work. They serve everyone their mess on these pieces of leaves, and it was very good, but too high seasoned with pepper. When we had eaten, my brother and I took out our flutes and played to them, which gave them new wonder, and I soon perceived, by an admiration that is natural to these people, and by the extreme ignorance and simplicity of them, it were not difficult to establish any unknown or extravagant religion among them, and to impose any notions or fictions upon them. For seeing a kinsman of mine set some paper afire with a burning-glass, a trick they had never before seen, they were like to have adored him for a god, and begged he would give them the characters or figures of his name, that they might oppose it against winds and storms, which he did, and they held it up in those seasons, and fancied it had a charm to conquer them, and kept it like a holy relic. They are very superstitious, and called him the great *peeie,* that is, prophet. They showed us their Indian *peeie,* a youth of about sixteen years old, as handsome as Nature could make a man. They consecrate a beautiful youth from his infancy, and all arts are used to complete him in the finest manner, both in beauty and shape. He is bred to all the little arts and cunning they are capable of, to all the legerdemain tricks and sleight of hand whereby he imposes upon the rabble, and is both a doctor in physic and divinity. And by these tricks makes the sick believe he sometimes eases their pains, by drawing from the afflicted part little serpents, or odd flies, or worms, or any strange thing; and though they have besides undoubted good remedies for almost all their diseases, they cure the patient more by fancy than by medicines, and make themselves feared, loved, and reverenced. This young *peeie* had a very young wife, who seeing my brother kiss her, came running and kissed me; after this, they kissed one another, and made it a very great jest, it being so novel, and new admiration and laughing went round the multitude, that they never will forget that ceremony, never before used or known. Caesar had a mind to see and talk with their war captains, and we were conducted to one of their houses, where we beheld several of the great captains, who had been at council. But so frightful a vision it was to see them no fancy can create; no such dreams can represent so dreadful a spectacle. For my part I took them for hobgoblins, or fiends, rather than men. But however their shapes appeared, their souls were very humane and noble, but some wanted their noses, some their lips, some both noses and lips, some their ears, and others cut through each cheek, with long slashes, through which their teeth appeared; they had several other formidable wounds and scars, or rather dismemberings. They had *comitias,* or little aprons before them, and girdles of cotton, with their knives naked, stuck in it, a bow at their backs, and a quiver of arrows on their thighs, and most had feathers on their heads of diverse colors. They cried "*Amora tiguamy*" to us at our entrance, and were pleased we said as much to them. They feted us, and gave us drink of the best sort, and wondered, as much as the others had done before, to see us. Caesar was marveling as much at their faces, wondering how they should all be so wounded in war; he was impatient to know how they all came by those frightful marks of rage or malice, rather than wounds got in noble battle. They told us, by our interpreter, that when any war was waging, two men chosen out by some old captain, whose fighting was past, and who could only teach the theory of war, these two men were to stand in competition for the generalship, or Great War Captain, and being brought before the old judges, now past labor, they are asked, what they dare do to show they are worthy to lead an army? When he who is first asked, making no reply, cuts off his nose, and throws it contemptibly[1] on the ground, and the other does something to himself that he thinks surpasses him, and perhaps deprives himself of lips and an eye. So they slash on till one gives out, and many have died in this debate. And 'tis by a passive valor they show and prove their activity, a sort of courage too brutal to be applauded by our black hero; nevertheless he expressed his esteem of them.

In this voyage Caesar begot so good an understanding between the Indians and the English, that there were no more fears or heartburnings during our stay, but we had a perfect, open, and free trade with them. Many things remarkable, and worthy reciting, we met with in this short voyage, because Caesar made it his business to search out and provide for our entertainment, especially to please his dearly adored Imoinda, who was a sharer in all our adventures; we being resolved to make her chains as easy as we could, and to compliment the Prince in that manner that most obliged him.

As we were coming up again, we met with some Indians of strange aspects, that is, of a larger size, and other sort of features, than those of our country. Our Indian slaves, that rowed us, asked them some questions, but they could not understand us, but showed us a long cotton string with several knots on it, and told us, they had been coming from the mountains so many moons as there were knots. They were habited in skins of a strange beast, and brought along with them bags of gold dust, which, as well as they could give us to understand, came streaming in little small channels down the high mountains, when the rains fell, and offered to be the convoy to anybody, or persons, that would go to the mountains. We carried these men up to Parham, where they were kept till the Lord Governor came. And because all the country was mad to be going on this golden adventure, the governor, by his letters, commanded (for they sent some of the gold to him) that a guard should be set at the mouth of the river of Amazons (a river so called, almost as broad as the river of Thames), and

1. Contemptuously.

prohibited all people from going up that river, it conducting to those mountains of gold. But we going off for England before the project was further prosecuted, and the Governor being drowned in a hurricane, either the design died, or the Dutch have the advantage of it. And 'tis to be bemoaned what His Majesty lost by losing that part of America.

Though this digression is a little from my story, however since it contains some proofs of the curiosity and daring of this great man, I was content to omit nothing of his character.

It was thus, for some time we diverted him. But now Imoinda began to show she was with child, and did nothing but sigh and weep for the captivity of her lord, herself, and the infant yet unborn, and believed, if it were so hard to gain the liberty of two, 'twould be more difficult to get that for three. Her griefs were so many darts in the great heart of Caesar, and taking his opportunity one Sunday, when all the whites were overtaken in drink, as there were abundance of several trades, and slaves for four years,[2] that inhabited among the Negro houses, and Sunday was their day of debauch (otherwise they were a sort of spies upon Caesar), he went pretending out of goodness to them, to feast amongst them, and sent all his music, and ordered a great treat for the whole gang, about three hundred Negroes. And about a hundred and fifty were able to bear arms, such as they had, which were sufficient to do execution with spirits accordingly. For the English had none but rusty swords, that no strength could draw from a scabbard, except the people of particular quality, who took care to oil them and keep them in good order. The guns also, unless here and there one, or those newly carried from England, would do no good or harm, for 'tis the nature of that country to rust and eat up iron, or any metals but gold and silver. And they are very inexpert at the bow, which the Negroes and Indians are perfect masters of.

Caesar, having singled out these men from the women and children, made a harangue to them of the miseries and ignominies of slavery; counting up all their toils and sufferings, under such loads, burdens, and drudgeries as were fitter for beasts than men, senseless brutes than human souls. He told them it was not for days, months, or years, but for eternity; there was no end to be of their misfortunes. They suffered not like men who might find a glory and fortitude in oppression, but like dogs that loved the whip and bell,[3] and fawned the more they were beaten. That they had lost the divine quality of men, and were become insensible asses, fit only to bear. Nay worse, an ass, or dog, or horse, having done his duty, could lie down in retreat, and rise to work again, and while he did his duty endured no stripes; but men, villainous, senseless men such as they, toiled on all the tedious week till black Friday, and then, whether they worked or not, whether they were faulty or meriting, they promiscuously, the innocent with the guilty, suffered the infamous whip, the sordid stripes, from their fellow slaves till their blood trickled from all parts of their body, blood whose every drop ought to be revenged with a life of some of those tyrants that impose it. "And why," said he, "my dear friends and fellow sufferers, should we be slaves to an unknown people? Have they vanquished us nobly in fight? Have they won us in honorable battle? And are we, by the chance of war, become their slaves? This would not anger a noble heart, this would not animate a soldier's soul. No, but we are bought and sold like apes, or monkeys, to be the sport of women, fools, and

2. I.e., whites who, as punishment for crime or debt, had been forced into service for fixed periods of time.

3. Because rigorous training has taught them to cherish their punishment.

cowards, and the support of rogues, runagades, that have abandoned their own countries, for raping, murders, thefts, and villainies. Do you not hear every day how they
upbraid each other with infamy of life below the wildest savages, and shall we render
obedience to such a degenerate race, who have no one human virtue left to distinguish
them from the vilest creatures? Will you, I say, suffer the lash from such hands?"
They all replied, with one accord, "No, no, no; Caesar has spoke like a great captain,
like a great king."

After this he would have proceeded, but was interrupted by a tall Negro of some
more quality than the rest. His name was Tuscan, who bowing at the feet of Caesar,
cried, "My lord, we have listened with joy and attention to what you have said, and,
were we only men, would follow so great a leader through the world. But oh! consider, we are husbands and parents too, and have things more dear to us than life: our
wives and children unfit for travel, in these impassable woods, mountains, and bogs.
We have not only difficult lands to overcome, but rivers to wade, and monsters to encounter, ravenous beasts of prey—" To this, Caesar replied, that honor was the first
principle in nature that was to be obeyed; but as no man would pretend to that, without all the acts of virtue, compassion, charity, love, justice, and reason, he found it not
inconsistent with that, to take an equal care of their wives and children, as they would
of themselves, and that he did not design, when he led them to freedom and glorious
liberty, that they should leave that better part of themselves to perish by the hand of
the tyrant's whip. But if there were a woman among them so degenerate from love
and virtue to choose slavery before the pursuit of her husband, and with the hazard of
her life to share with him in his fortunes, that such an one ought to be abandoned, and
left as a prey to the common enemy.

To which they all agreed—and bowed. After this, he spoke of the impassable
woods and rivers, and convinced them, the more danger, the more glory. He told them
that he had heard of one Hannibal, a great captain, had cut his way through mountains
of solid rocks,[4] and should a few shrubs oppose them, which they could fire before
them? No, 'twas a trifling excuse to men resolved to die, or overcome. As for bogs,
they are with a little labor filled and hardened, and the rivers could be no obstacle,
since they swam by nature, at least by custom, from their first hour of their birth. That
when the children were weary they must carry them by turns, and the woods and their
own industry would afford them food. To this they all assented with joy.

Tuscan then demanded, what he would do? He said, they would travel towards
the sea; plant a new colony, and defend it by their valor; and when they could find a
ship, either driven by stress of weather, or guided by Providence that way, they would
seize it, and make it a prize, till it had transported them to their own countries. At
least, they should be made free in his kingdom, and be esteemed as his fellow sufferers, and men that had the courage and the bravery to attempt, at least, for liberty. And
if they died in the attempt it would be more brave than to live in perpetual slavery.

They bowed and kissed his feet at this resolution, and with one accord vowed to
follow him to death. And that night was appointed to begin their march; they made it
known to their wives, and directed them to tie their hamaca[5] about their shoulder, and
under their arm like a scarf; and to lead their children that could go, and carry those
that could not. The wives, who pay an entire obedience to their husbands, obeyed, and
stayed for them where they were appointed. The men stayed but to furnish themselves

---

4. The Carthaginian general (247–182 B.C.E.) had accom-   5. Hammock.
plished this while crossing the Alps to invade Rome.

with what defensive arms they could get, and all met at the rendezvous, where Caesar made a new encouraging speech to them, and led them out.

But, as they could not march far that night, on Monday early, when the overseers went to call them all together to go to work, they were extremely surprised to find not one upon the place, but all fled with what baggage they had. You may imagine this news was not only suddenly spread all over the plantation, but soon reached the neighboring ones, and we had by noon about six hundred men, they call the militia of the county, that came to assist us in the pursuit of the fugitives. But never did one see so comical an army march forth to war. The men of any fashion would not concern themselves, though it were almost the common cause, for such revoltings are very ill examples, and have very fatal consequences oftentimes in many colonies. But they had a respect for Caesar, and all hands were against the Parhamites, as they called those of Parham Plantation, because they did not, in the first place, love the Lord Governor, and secondly, they would have it that Caesar was ill used, and baffled with.[6] And 'tis not impossible but some of the best in the country was of his counsel in this flight, and depriving us of all the slaves, so that they of the better sort would not meddle in the matter. The deputy governor,[7] of whom I have had no great occasion to speak, and who was the most fawning fair-tongued fellow in the world, and one that pretended the most friendship to Caesar, was now the only violent man against him, and though he had nothing, and so need fear nothing, yet talked and looked bigger than any man. He was a fellow whose character is not fit to be mentioned with the worst of the slaves. This fellow would lead his army forth to meet Caesar, or rather to pursue him. Most of their arms were of those sort of cruel whips they call cat-with-nine-tails; some had rusty useless guns for show; others old basket-hilts, whose blades had never seen the light in this age, and others had long staffs, and clubs. Mr. Trefry went along rather to be a mediator than a conqueror in such a battle, for he foresaw and knew, if by fighting they put the Negroes into despair, they were a sort of sullen fellows that would drown or kill themselves before they would yield, and he advised that fair means was best. But Byam was one that abounded in his own wit, and would take his own measures.

It was not hard to find these fugitives, for as they fled they were forced to fire and cut the woods before them, so that night or day they pursued them by the light they made, and by the path they had cleared. But as soon as Caesar found he was pursued, he put himself in a posture of defense, placing all the women and children in the rear, and himself, with Tuscan by his side, or next to him, all promising to die or conquer. Encouraged thus, they never stood to parley, but fell on pell-mell upon the English, and killed some, and wounded a good many, they having recourse to their whips, as the best of their weapons. And as they observed no order, they perplexed the enemy so sorely, with lashing them in the eyes. And the women and children, seeing their husbands so treated, being of fearful cowardly dispositions, and hearing the English cry out, "Yield and live, yield and be pardoned," they all ran in amongst their husbands and fathers, and hung about them, crying out, "Yield, yield, and leave Caesar to their revenge," that by degrees the slaves abandoned Caesar, and left him only Tuscan and his heroic Imoinda, who, grown big as she was, did nevertheless press near her lord, having a bow, and a quiver full of poisoned arrows, which she managed with such dexterity that she wounded several, and shot the governor into the shoulder, of which wound he had like

---

6. Cheated.
7. William Byam, who during a decade as administrator in Surinam had acquired a reputation for arrogance and severity.

to have died but that an Indian woman, his mistress, sucked the wound, and cleansed it from the venom. But however, he stirred not from the place till he had parleyed with Caesar, who he found was resolved to die fighting, and would not be taken; no more would Tuscan, or Imoinda. But he, more thirsting after revenge of another sort, than that of depriving him of life, now made use of all his art of talking and dissembling, and besought Caesar to yield himself upon terms which he himself should propose, and should be sacredly assented to and kept by him. He told him, it was not that he any longer feared him, or could believe the force of two men, and a young heroine, could overcome all them, with all the slaves now on their side also, but it was the vast esteem he had for his person, the desire he had to serve so gallant a man, and to hinder himself from the reproach hereafter of having been the occasion of the death of a prince, whose valor and magnanimity deserved the empire of the world. He protested to him, he looked upon this action as gallant and brave, however tending to the prejudice of his lord and master, who would by it have lost so considerable a number of slaves, that this flight of his should be looked on as a heat of youth, and rashness of a too forward courage, and an unconsidered impatience of liberty, and no more; and that he labored in vain to accomplish that which they would effectually perform, as soon as any ship arrived that would touch on his coast. "So that if you will be pleased," continued he, "to surrender yourself, all imaginable respect shall be paid you; and yourself, your wife, and child, if it be here born, shall depart free out of our land." But Caesar would hear of no composition, though Byam urged, if he pursued and went on in his design, he would inevitably perish, either by great snakes, wild beasts, or hunger, and he ought to have regard to his wife, whose condition required ease, and not the fatigues of tedious travel, where she could not be secured from being devoured. But Caesar told him, there was no faith in the white men, or the gods they adored, who instructed them in principles so false that honest men could not live amongst them; though no people professed so much, none performed so little; that he knew what he had to do, when he dealt with men of honor, but with them a man ought to be eternally on his guard, and never to eat and drink with Christians without his weapon of defense in his hand, and, for his own security, never to credit one word they spoke. As for the rashness and inconsiderateness of his action he would confess the governor is in the right, and that he was ashamed of what he had done, in endeavoring to make those free, who were by nature slaves, poor wretched rogues, fit to be used as Christians' tools; dogs, treacherous and cowardly, fit for such masters, and they wanted only but to be whipped into the knowledge of the Christian gods to be the vilest of all creeping things, to learn to worship such deities as had not power to make them just, brave, or honest. In fine, after a thousand things of this nature, not fit here to be recited, he told Byam, he had rather die than live upon the same earth with such dogs. But Trefry and Byam pleaded and protested together so much, that Trefry believing the governor to mean what he said, and speaking very cordially himself, generously put himself into Caesar's hands, and took him aside, and persuaded him, even with tears, to live, by surrendering himself, and to name his conditions. Caesar was overcome by his wit and reasons, and in consideration of Imoinda, and demanding what he desired, and that it should be ratified by their hands in writing, because he had perceived that was the common way of contract between man and man amongst the whites. All this was performed, and Tuscan's pardon was put in, and they surrender to the governor, who walked peaceably down into the plantation with them, after giving order to bury their dead. Caesar was very much toiled with the bustle of the day, for he had fought like a Fury[8], and what mischief was done he and Tuscan performed alone, and gave their enemies a fatal proof that they durst do anything, and feared no mortal force.

But they were no sooner arrived at the place where all the slaves receive their punishments of whipping, but they laid hands on Caesar and Tuscan, faint with heat and toil; and surprising them, bound them to two several stakes, and whipped them in a most deplorable and inhumane manner, rending the very flesh from their bones; especially Caesar, who was not perceived to make any moan, or to alter his face, only to roll his eyes on the faithless governor, and those he believed guilty, with fierceness and indignation. And, to complete his rage, he saw every one of those slaves, who, but a few days before, adored him as something more than mortal, now had a whip to give him some lashes, while he strove not to break his fetters, though if he had, it were impossible. But he pronounced a woe and revenge from his eyes, that darted fire, that 'twas at once both awful and terrible to behold.

When they thought they were sufficiently revenged on him, they untied him, almost fainting with loss of blood from a thousand wounds all over his body, from which they had rent his clothes, and led him bleeding and naked as he was, and loaded him all over with irons, and then rubbed his wounds, to complete their cruelty, with Indian pepper, which had like to have made him raving mad, and in this condition made him so fast to the ground that he could not stir, if his pains and wounds would have given him leave. They spared Imoinda, and did not let her see this barbarity committed towards her lord, but carried her down to Parham, and shut her up, which was not in kindness to her, but for fear she should die with the sight, or miscarry, and then they should lose a young slave, and perhaps the mother.

You must know, that when the news was brought on Monday morning, that Caesar had betaken himself to the woods, and carried with him all the Negroes, we were possessed with extreme fear, which no persuasions could dissipate, that he would secure himself till night, and then, that he would come down and cut all our throats. This apprehension made all the females of us fly down the river, to be secured, and while we were away, they acted this cruelty. For I suppose I had authority and interest enough there, had I suspected any such thing, to have prevented it, but we had not gone many leagues, but the news overtook us that Caesar was taken, and whipped like a common slave. We met on the river with Colonel Martin, a man of great gallantry, wit, and goodness, and, whom I have celebrated in a character of my new comedy,[9] by his own name, in memory of so brave a man. He was wise and eloquent, and, from the fineness of his parts, bore a great sway over the hearts of all the colony. He was a friend to Caesar, and resented this false dealing with him very much. We carried him back to Parham, thinking to have made an accommodation; when we came, the first news we heard was that the governor was dead of a wound Imoinda had given him, but it was not so well. But it seems he would have the pleasure of beholding the revenge he took on Caesar, and before the cruel ceremony was finished, he dropped down, and then they perceived the wound he had on his shoulder was by a venomed arrow, which, as I said, his Indian mistress healed, by sucking the wound.

We were no sooner arrived, but we went up to the plantation to see Caesar, whom we found in a very miserable and inexpressible condition, and I have a thousand times admired how he lived, in so much tormenting pain. We said all things to

---

8. In Greek myth, a demon of vengeance.

9. *The Younger Brother: or the Amorous Jilt,* produced posthumously in 1696.

him that trouble, pity, and good nature could suggest, protesting our innocence of the fact, and our abhorrence of such cruelties; making a thousand professions of services to him, and begging as many pardons for the offenders, till we said so much, that he believed we had no hand in his ill treatment, but told us, he could never pardon Byam. As for Trefry, he confessed he saw his grief and sorrow for his suffering, which he could not hinder, but was like to have been beaten down by the very slaves, for speaking in his defense. But for Byam, who was their leader, their head—and should, by his justice, and honor, have been an example to them—for him, he wished to live, to take a dire revenge of him, and said, "It had been well for him if he had sacrificed me, instead of giving me the contemptible whip." He refused to talk much, but begging us to give him our hands, he took them, and protested never to lift up his, to do us any harm. He had a great respect for Colonel Martin, and always took his counsel, like that of a parent, and assured him, he would obey him in anything but his revenge on Byam. "Therefore," said he, "for his own safety, let him speedily dispatch me, for if I could dispatch myself, I would not, till that justice were done to my injured person, and the contempt of a soldier. No, I would not kill myself, even after a whipping, but will be content to live with that infamy, and be pointed at by every grinning slave, till I have completed my revenge; and then you shall see that Oroonoko scorns to live with the indignity that was put on Caesar." All we could do could get no more words from him, and we took care to have him put immediately into a healing bath, to rid him of his pepper, and ordered a chirurgeon[1] to anoint him with healing balm, which he suffered, and in some time he began to be able to walk and eat. We failed not to visit him every day, and, to that end, had him brought to an apartment at Parham.

The governor was no sooner recovered, and had heard of the menaces of Caesar, but he called his council, who (not to disgrace them, or burlesque the government there) consisted of such notorious villains as Newgate[2] never transported, and possibly originally were such, who understood neither the laws of God or man, and had no sort of principles to make them worthy the name of men, but at the very council table would contradict and fight with one another, and swear so bloodily that 'twas terrible to hear and see them. (Some of them were afterwards hanged, when the Dutch took possession of the place; others sent off in chains.) But calling these special rulers of the nation together, and requiring their counsel in this weighty affair, they all concluded that (damn them) it might be their own cases, and that Caesar ought to be made an example to all the Negroes, to fright them from daring to threaten their betters, their lords and masters, and, at this rate, no man was safe from his own slaves, and concluded, *nemine contradicente,*[3] that Caesar should be hanged.

Trefry then thought it time to use his authority, and told Byam his command did not extend to his lord's plantation, and that Parham was as much exempt from the law as Whitehall; and that they ought no more to touch the servants of the Lord—(who there represented the King's person) than they could those about the King himself; and that Parham was a sanctuary, and though his lord were absent in person, his power was still in being there, which he had entrusted with him, as far as the dominions of his particular plantations reached, and all that belonged to it; the rest of the country, as Byam was lieutenant to his lord, he might exercise his tyranny upon.

---

1. Surgeon.
2. London prison from which convicts were sent to work
in the colonies.
3. No one disagreeing.

Trefry had others as powerful, or more, that interested themselves in Caesar's life, and absolutely said he should be defended. So turning the governor, and his wise council, out of doors (for they sat at Parham House) we set a guard upon our landing place, and would admit none but those we called friends to us and Caesar.

The governor having remained wounded at Parham till his recovery was completed, Caesar did not know but he was still there, and indeed, for the most part, his time was spent there, for he was one that loved to live at other people's expense, and if he were a day absent, he was ten present there, and used to play, and walk, and hunt, and fish, with Caesar. So that Caesar did not at all doubt, if he once recovered strength, but he should find an opportunity of being revenged on him. Though, after such a revenge, he could not hope to live, for if he escaped the fury of the English mobile,[4] who perhaps would have been glad of the occasion to have killed him, he was resolved not to survive his whipping, yet he had, some tender hours, a repenting softness, which he called his fits of coward, wherein he struggled with love for the victory of his heart, which took part with his charming Imoinda there; but, for the most part, his time was passed in melancholy thought, and black designs. He considered, if he should do this deed, and die either in the attempt, or after it, he left his lovely Imoinda a prey, or at best a slave, to the enraged multitude; his great heart could not endure that thought. "Perhaps," said he, "she may be first ravished by every brute, exposed first to their nasty lusts, and then a shameful death." No, he could not live a moment under that apprehension, too insupportable to be borne. These were his thoughts, and his silent arguments with his heart, as he told us afterwards, so that now resolving not only to kill Byam, but all those he thought had enraged him, pleasing his great heart with the fancied slaughter he should make over the whole face of the plantation, he first resolved on a deed that (however horrid it at first appeared to us all), when we had heard his reasons, we thought it brave and just. Being able to walk and, as he believed, fit for the execution of his great design, he begged Trefry to trust him into the air, believing a walk would do him good, which was granted him, and taking Imoinda with him, as he used to do in his more happy and calmer days, he led her up into a wood where, after (with a thousand sighs, and long gazing silently on her face, while tears gushed, in spite of him, from his eyes), he told her his design first of killing her, and then his enemies, and next himself, and the impossibility of escaping, and therefore he told her the necessity of dying. He found the heroic wife faster pleading for death than he was to propose it, when she found his fixed resolution, and on her knees besought him not to leave her a prey to his enemies. He (grieved to death) yet pleased at her noble resolution, took her up, and embracing her with all the passion and languishment of a dying lover, drew his knife to kill this treasure of his soul, this pleasure of his eyes. While tears trickled down his cheeks, hers were smiling with joy she should die by so noble a hand, and be sent in her own country (for that's their notion of the next world) by him she so tenderly loved, and so truly adored in this, for wives have a respect for their husbands equal to what any other people pay a deity, and when a man finds any occasion to quit his wife, if he love her, she dies by his hand; if not, he sells her, or suffers some other to kill her. It being thus, you may believe the deed was soon resolved on, and 'tis not to be doubted, but the parting, the eternal leave-taking of two such lovers, so greatly

4. Mob.

born, so sensible,[5] so beautiful, so young, and so fond, must be very moving, as the relation of it was to me afterwards.

All that love could say in such cases being ended, and all the intermitting irresolutions being adjusted, the lovely, young, and adored victim lays herself down before the sacrificer, while he, with a hand resolved, and a heart breaking within, gave the fatal stroke, first cutting her throat, and then severing her yet smiling face from that delicate body, pregnant as it was with fruits of tenderest love. As soon as he had done, he laid the body decently on leaves and flowers, of which he made a bed, and concealed it under the same coverlid of nature, only her face he left yet bare to look on. But when he found she was dead, and past all retrieve, never more to bless him with her eyes and soft language, his grief swelled up to rage; he tore, he raved, he roared, like some monster of the wood, calling on the loved name of Imoinda. A thousand times he turned the fatal knife that did the deed toward his own heart, with a resolution to go immediately after her, but dire revenge, which now was a thousand times more fierce in his soul than before, prevents him, and he would cry out, "No, since I have sacrificed Imoinda to my revenge, shall I lose that glory which I have purchased so dear, as at the price of the fairest, dearest, softest creature that ever Nature made? No, no!" Then, at her name, grief would get the ascendant of rage, and he would lie down by her side, and water her face with showers of tears, which never were wont to fall from those eyes. And however bent he was on his intended slaughter, he had not power to stir from the sight of this dear object, now more beloved and more adored than ever.

He remained in this deploring condition for two days, and never rose from the ground where he had made his sad sacrifice. At last, rousing from her side, and accusing himself with living too long now Imoinda was dead, and that the deaths of those barbarous enemies were deferred too long, he resolved now to finish the great work; but offering to rise, he found his strength so decayed, that he reeled to and fro, like boughs assailed by contrary winds, so that he was forced to lie down again, and try to summon all his courage to his aid. He found his brains turn round, and his eyes were dizzy, and objects appeared not the same to him as they were wont to do; his breath was short, and all his limbs surprised with a faintness he had never felt before. He had not eaten in two days, which was one occasion of this feebleness, but excess of grief was the greatest; yet still he hoped he should recover vigor to act his design, and lay expecting it yet six days longer, still mourning over the dead idol of his heart, and striving every day to rise, but could not.

In all this time you may believe we were in no little affliction for Caesar and his wife. Some were of opinion he was escaped never to return; others thought some accident had happened to him. But however, we failed not to send out a hundred people several ways to search for him. A party of about forty went that way he took, among whom was Tuscan, who was perfectly reconciled to Byam. They had not gone very far into the wood, but they smelt an unusual smell, as of a dead body, for stinks must be very noisome that can be distinguished among such a quantity of natural sweets, as every inch of that land produces. So that they concluded they should find him dead, or somebody that was so. They passed on towards it, as loathsome as it was, and made such a rustling among the leaves that lie thick on the ground, by continual falling, that Caesar heard he was approached, and though he had, during the space of these eight

5. Sensitive.

days, endeavored to rise, but found he wanted strength, yet looking up, and seeing his pursuers, he rose, and reeled to a neighboring tree, against which he fixed his back. And being within a dozen yards of those that advanced and saw him, he called out to them, and bid them approach no nearer, if they would be safe; so that they stood still, and hardly believing their eyes, that would persuade them that it was Caesar that spoke to them, so much was he altered, they asked him what he had done with his wife, for they smelt a stink that almost struck them dead. He, pointing to the dead body, sighing, cried, "Behold her there." They put off the flowers that covered her with their sticks, and found she was killed, and cried out, "Oh monster! that hast murdered thy wife." Then asking him, why he did so cruel a deed, he replied, he had no leisure to answer impertinent questions. "You may go back," continued he, "and tell the faithless governor he may thank Fortune that I am breathing my last, and that my arm is too feeble to obey my heart in what it had designed him." But his tongue faltering, and trembling, he could scarce end what he was saying. The English taking advantage by his weakness, cried, "Let us take him alive by all means." He heard them; and, as if he had revived from a fainting, or a dream, he cried out, "No, gentlemen, you are deceived, you will find no more Caesars to be whipped, no more find a faith in me. Feeble as you think me, I have strength yet left to secure me from a second indignity." They swore all anew, and he only shook his head, and beheld them with scorn. Then they cried out, "Who will venture on this single man? Will nobody?" They stood all silent while Caesar replied, "Fatal will be the attempt to the first adventurer, let him assure himself," and, at that word, held up his knife in a menacing posture. "Look ye, ye faithless crew," said he, "'tis not life I seek, nor am I afraid of dying," and, at that word, cut a piece of flesh from his own throat, and threw it at them, "yet still I would live if I could, till I had perfected my revenge. But oh! it cannot be. I feel life gliding from my eyes and heart, and, if I make not haste, I shall yet fall a victim to the shameful whip." At that, he ripped up his own belly, and took his bowels and pulled them out, with what strength he could, while some, on their knees imploring, besought him to hold his hand. But when they saw him tottering, they cried out, "Will none venture on him?" A bold English cried, "Yes, if he were the Devil" (taking courage when he saw him almost dead) and swearing a horrid oath for his farewell to the world he rushed on. Caesar with his armed hand met him so fairly, as stuck him to the heart, and he fell dead at his feet. Tuscan seeing that, cried out, "I love thee, oh Caesar, and therefore will not let thee die, if possible." And, running to him, took him in his arms, but at the same time, warding a blow that Caesar made at his bosom, he received it quite through his arm, and Caesar having not the strength to pluck the knife forth, though he attempted it, Tuscan neither pulled it out himself, nor suffered it to be pulled out, but came down with it sticking in his arm, and the reason he gave for it was because the air should not get into the wound. They put their hands across, and carried Caesar between six of them, fainted as he was, and they thought dead, or just dying, and they brought him to Parham, and laid him on a couch, and had the chirurgeon immediately to him, who dressed his wounds, and sewed up his belly, and used means to bring him to life, which they effected. We ran all to see him; and, if before we thought him so beautiful a sight, he was now so altered that his face was like a death's head blacked over, nothing but teeth and eye-holes. For some days we suffered nobody to speak to him, but caused cordials to be poured down his throat, which sustained his life, and in six or seven days he recovered his senses. For you must know, that wounds are almost to a miracle cured in the Indies, unless wounds in the legs, which rarely ever cure.

When he was well enough to speak, we talked to him, and asked him some questions about his wife, and the reasons why he killed her. And he then told us what I have related of that resolution, and of his parting, and he besought us we would let him die, and was extremely afflicted to think it was possible he might live. He assured us, if we did not dispatch him, he would prove very fatal to a great many. We said all we could to make him live, and gave him new assurances, but he begged we would not think so poorly of him, or of his love to Imoinda, to imagine we could flatter him to life again; but the chirurgeon assured him he could not live, and therefore he need not fear. We were all (but Caesar) afflicted at this news; and the sight was gashly.[6] His discourse was sad; and the earthly smell about him so strong, that I was persuaded to leave the place for some time (being myself but sickly, and very apt to fall into fits of dangerous illness upon any extraordinary melancholy). The servants, and Trefry, and the chirurgeons, promised all to take what possible care they could of the life of Caesar, and I, taking boat, went with other company to Colonel Martin's, about three days' journey down the river; but I was no sooner gone, but the governor taking Trefry about some pretended earnest business a day's journey up the river, having communicated his design to one Banister, a wild Irishman, and one of the council, a fellow of absolute barbarity, and fit to execute any villainy, but was rich, he came up to Parham, and forcibly took Caesar, and had him carried to the same post where he was whipped, and causing him to be tied to it, and a great fire made before him, he told him he should die like a dog, as he was. Caesar replied, this was the first piece of bravery that ever Banister did, and he never spoke sense till he pronounced that word, and, if he would keep it, he would declare, in the other world, that he was the only man, of all the whites, that ever he heard speak truth. And turning to the men that bound him, he said, "My friends, am I to die, or to be whipped?" And they cried, "Whipped! no; you shall not escape so well." And then he replied, smiling, "A blessing on thee," and assured them, they need not tie him, for he would stand fixed, like a rock, and endure death so as should encourage them to die. "But if you whip me," said he, "be sure you tie me fast."

He had learned to take tobacco, and when he was assured he should die, he desired they would give him a pipe in his mouth, ready lighted, which they did, and the executioner came, and first cut off his members,[7] and threw them into the fire. After that, with an ill-favored knife, they cut his ears and his nose, and burned them; he still smoked on, as if nothing had touched him. Then they hacked off one of his arms, and still he bore up, and held his pipe. But at the cutting off the other arm, his head sunk, and his pipe dropped, and he gave up the ghost, without a groan, or a reproach. My mother and sister were by him all the while, but not suffered to save him, so rude and wild were the rabble, and so inhuman were the justices, who stood by to see the execution, who after paid dearly enough for their insolence. They cut Caesar in quarters, and sent them to several of the chief plantations. One quarter was sent to Colonel Martin, who refused it, and swore he had rather see the quarters of Banister and the governor himself than those of Caesar on his plantations, and that he could govern his Negroes without terrifying and grieving them with frightful spectacles of a mangled king.

Thus died this great man, worthy of a better fate, and a more sublime wit than mine to write his praise. Yet, I hope, the reputation of my pen is considerable enough to make his glorious name to survive to all ages, with that of the brave, the beautiful, and the constant Imoinda.

---

6. Ghastly.   7. Genitals.

cᗢ⃘

RESONANCE

George Warren: from *An Impartial Description of Surinam*[1]

from CHAPTER 1: OF THE RIVER

The land next the river's mouth is low, woody, and full of swamps; one, but about thirty leagues up, high, and mountainous, having plain fields of a vast extent, here and there beautified with small groves, like islands in a green sea; amongst whose still flourishing trees 'tis incomparably pleasant to consider the delightful handiworks of Nature, expressed in the variety of those pretty creatures, which, with ridiculous antic gestures, disport themselves upon the branches. There is a constant spring and fall, some leaves dropping, and others succeeding in their places; but the trees are never quite divested of their summer livery; some have always blossoms, and the several degrees of fruit at once. The sense of smelling may at any time enjoy a full delight amongst the woods, which disperse their aromatic odors a good distance from the land to the no little pleasure of the sea-tired passenger.

The various productions of insects from the heat and moisture is admirable in that country. I have observed a white speck, at first no bigger than a pin's head, upon a new-sprung soft excrescency from the root of a great tree, which, by degrees in two or three days, has grown to a kind of butterfly, with fair painted black and saffron-colored wings. I have found others not quite perfect sticking upon the bodies of trees, as it were incorporated into the wood itself. There is another, called a cammelfly, from its long neck, how generated I know not, which has its wings like small leaves, and, having lived a while, at length lights upon the ground, takes root, and is transformed into a plant. This I relate, not from any certain knowledge of my own, but I was encouraged to insert it from the information of the Honorable William Byam, Lord General of Guiana and Governor of Surinam, who, I am sure, is too much a gentleman to be the author of a lie.[2] Many more observations of this nature no doubt I might have made, if the vanity of my years would have suffered me to mind it.

The Government is monarchical, an imitation of ours, by a Governor, Council, and Assembly; the laws of England are also theirs, to which are added some by constitutions, no less obliging, proper to the conveniences of that country.

* * *

Of the tigers there are three kinds, black, spotted, and red. The first is accounted[3] fiercest, but he very seldom appears amongst the dwellings. The spotted, which I think are miscalled, being rather leopards than tigers, do no little hurt to plantations, by destroying the cattle and poultry. They are of so vast a strength that one of them will make

---

1. George Warren (second half 17th century) was an English planter in the colony of Surinam in South America. *An Impartial Description of Surinam upon the Continent of Guiana in America, With a History of several strange Beasts, Birds, Fishes, Serpents, Insects, and Customs of that Colony, &c., Worthy the Perusal of all, from the Experience of George Warren Gent.* (1665) stresses his impartiality and accuracy in order to persuade prospective planters that his portrayal of conditions in the colony is objective rather than embellished. Literary critic Ernest Bernbaum identified Warren's pamphlet in 1913 as a source for Behn's *Oroonoko.* Demonstrating a significant overlap between the two texts' accounts of Surinam,

Bernbaum claimed he had proven that Behn was "lying" in her claim to have been there personally. Scholars still debate whether Behn really spent time in Surinam, or only lifted information from Warren's work, but the question can't be decided on the basis of available evidence. It is far more interesting to contrast how the two writers treat shared details and approach the problem of convincing their readers of their credibility as narrators.

2. William Byam, a deputy or lieutenant governor of Surinam in the 1660s; he figures as a character in Aphra Behn's *Oroonoko.*

3. Considered.

nothing to leap over a five or six foot rail with a hog in his mouth. There was once one came into a plantation, killed a bull of two years old, and dragged him above a quarter of a mile into the woods. Unless they be wounded, or very hungry, they will hardly assault a man in the daytime. I never heard of above two or three they have killed one way or other since the settling of the Colony: one of them (who was a huntsman and a lusty fellow) was often heard to wish he could meet with a tiger, and made it a great complaint in all his searches through the woods. It was never his good fortune; at length, one night, lying in his hammock in an open house, a tiger comes, takes him up, and carries him two miles into the woods, in vain crying for help, which was heard by an English woman in a close house hard by[4], who had so much courage (more than is usual in her sex) to fire a musket from the window; but those who have had to do with them know, it is not noise only can scare a tiger from his prey. The man was found next day with his head and shoulders eaten off. They are observed to be not so numerous now as formerly, partly retiring further into the woods, and a great many having been taken by the hunters. There is one John Miller who has killed no fewer than a dozen or fourteen singly with his gun and lance, from some miraculously escaping with his life, and having been dangerously hurt by others. There are not many of the red, and those not so fierce as either of the former. In the woods are a great many land tortoise, but not so big by more than three quarters as the sea ones; their shells are so hard and strong that a laden cart may go over and not crush them, in which, being otherwise defenseless, they secure themselves from any enemies but men and tigers: the first, breaking up their lodgings with an axe; the other, with his teeth. They'll eat almost anything, and are by the planters preserved in pens a great many together, to make use of when they please, being reputed none of the coarsest dishes there. There are also porcupines shaped almost like our English hedgehogs, but larger, and armed all over with black and white quills about two handfuls long, and sharp as needles which Nature has taught them to shoot from their sides with admirable dexterity against a coming enemy.

* * *

CHAPTER 8: OF THE NEGROES OR SLAVES

Who are most brought out of Guinea in Africa to those parts, where they are sold like dogs, and no better esteemed but for their work sake, which they perform all the week with the severest usages for the slightest fault, till Saturday afternoon, when they are allowed to dress their own gardens or plantations, having nothing but what they can produce from thence to live upon; unless perhaps once or twice a year, their Masters vouchsafe them, as a great favor, a little rotten salt-fish, or if a cow or horse die of itself, they get roast-meat. Their lodging is a hard board, and their black skins their covering. These wretched miseries not seldom drive them to desperate attempts for the recovery of their liberty, endeavoring to escape, and, if like to be retaken, sometimes lay violent hands upon themselves; or if the hope of pardon bring them again alive into their Masters' power, they'll manifest their fortitude, or rather obstinacy, in suffering the most exquisite tortures can be inflicted upon them, for a terror and example to others without shrinking. They are there a mixture of several nations which are always clashing with one another, so that no conspiracy can be hatching but 'tis presently detected by some party amongst themselves disaffected to the plot because their enemies have a share in it. They are naturally treacherous and bloody, and practice no religion there, though many of them are circumcised. But they believe the ancient Pythagorean error of the

4. Outhouse nearby.

soul's transmigration out of one body into another,[5] that when they die, they shall return into their own countries and be regenerated, so live in the world by a constant revolution; which conceit makes many of them over-fondly woo their deaths, not otherwise hoping to be freed from that indeed unequalled slavery.

CHAPTER 10: OF THE INDIANS

Who are a People cowardly and treacherous, qualities inseparable: there are several nations which trade and familiarly converse with the people of the Colony, but those they live amongst are the Charibes, or Canibals, who are more numerous than any of the rest, and are settled upon all the islands, and in most of the rivers, from the famous one of Amazons, to that of Oronoque. They go wholly naked, save a flap for modesty, which the women, after having had a child or two, throw off. Their skins are of an orange tawny color, and their hair black, without curls: A happy people as to this world, if they were sensible of their own hap: Nature with little toil providing all things which may serve her own necessities. The women are generally lascivious, and some so truly handsome as to features and proportion, that if the most curious symmetrian[6] had been there, he could not but subscribe to my opinion: and their pretty bashfulness (especially while Virgins) in the presence of a stranger adds such a charming grace to their perfections (too nakedly exposed to every wanton eye) that whoever lives amongst them had need be owner of no less than Joseph's continency[7] not at least to covet their embraces. They have been yet so unfortunately ignorant not to enrich their amorous caresses with that innocent and warm delight of Kissing, but conversing so frequently with Christians, and being naturally docile and ingenious, we have reason to believe they will in time be taught it. Their houses for the night are low thatched cottages with the eaves close to the ground; for the day, they have higher, and open on every side, to defend them from the violence of the sun's rays, yet letting in the grateful[8] coolness of the air. Their household utensils are curiously[9] painted earthen pots and platters, and their napery[1] is the leaves of trees. Their beds or hammocks (which are also used amongst the English) are made of cotton, square like a blanket, and so ordered with strings at each end that, being tied a convenient distance from one another, it opens the full breadth. For bread and drink, they plant gardens of Cassader,[2] and the woods and rivers are their constant suppeditories[3] of flesh and fish. For ornament they color themselves all over into neat works with a red paint called anotta, which grows in cods upon small trees, and the juice of certain weeds. They bore holes also through their noses, lips, and ears, whereat they hang glass pendants, pieces of brass, or any such like baubles their service can procure from the English. They load their legs, necks, and arms too with beads, shells of fish, and almost any trumpery they can get. They have no law nor government but oeconomical[4], living like the Patriarchs of old, the whole kindred in a family, where the eldest son always succeeds his father as the greatest; yet they have some more than ordinary persons who are their Captains, and lead them out to wars, whose courage they first prove by sharply whipping them with rods, which if they endure bravely without crying

---

5. The Greek philosopher and mathematician Pythagoras (late 6th century B.C.E.) espoused the doctrine of metempsychosis, or the transmigration of souls from one being (human or animal) to another in a cycle of retribution or reward.
6. Discriminating judge of symmetry.
7. Joseph is a famous paragon of male chastity because he resisted sexual advances from the wife of his Egyptian master, Potiphar (Genesis 39).
8. Welcome.
9. Intricately.
1. Napkins, table linens.
2. Cassava, a starchy root crop.
3. Repositories, sources.
4. Household-based.

or any considerable motion, they are acknowledged gallant fellows and honored by the less hardy. These chiefs or heads of families have commonly three or four wives apiece, others but one, who may indeed more properly be termed their vassals than companions, being no less subjected to their husbands than the meanest servants amongst us are to their masters. The men rarely oppress their shoulders with a burden, the women carry all, and are so very humble and obedient in their houses that at meals they always wait upon their husbands and never eat till they have done. When a woman is delivered of her first child, she presently goes about her business as before, and the husband feigns himself distempered, and is hanged up to the ridge of the house in his hammock, where he continues certain days dieted with the bread and water of affliction; then, being taken down, is stung with ants (a punishment they usually inflict upon their women, dogs, or children when they are foolish, for that's the term they usually put upon any misdemeanors) and a lusty drinking bout is made at the conclusion of the ceremony.

Their language sounds well in the expression, but is not very easy to be learned because many single words admit of diverse senses, to be distinguished only by the tone or alteration of the voice. When any martial expedition is resolved upon, the General, or chief Captain, summons the towns and families to assemble by a stick with so many notches in it as he intends days before he sets out, which when they have received, they cut out every day one until all are gone, and by that only they know the expiration of the time, for their numbers exceed not twenty, which they want names for too, but express them by their fingers and toes, which they will sometimes double, and triple, but their arithmetic is quickly at a loss, and then they Cry out *Ounsa awara,* that is, like the hair of one's head, innumerable. They go to sea in canoes or boats bravely painted, made of one entire piece, being trees cut hollow like a trough, and some so large that they'll carry five or six tons of goods at once. Their arms are bows, with poisoned arrows, and short clubs of speckle-wood; some, for defense, carry shields made of light wood, handsomely painted and engraved. They observe no order in their fighting, nor, unless upon very great advantages, enterprise anything but by night. The men they take prisoners they put to death with the most barbarous cruelties a coward can invent for an enemy in his power. Women and children they preserve for slaves, and sell them for trifles to the English. They did once cut off some French in Surinam, and made several attempts upon the English at their first settling, which were always frustrated, and they soundly smarted for their folly: now the Colony is grown potent they dare not but be humble. They are highly sensible of an injury amongst themselves, and will, if possible, have revenge at one time or other, which they always effect by treachery, and dare never assault a man to his face.

They have no religion amongst them that ever I could perceive, though they'll talk of a Captain of the Skies, but neither worship him nor any other. They have some knowledge of the Devil, whom they call Yarukin, and their imposters, or, as they call them, Peeies, make them believe they frequently converse with him; whether they do so really or no, I know not, however, it serves to scare the rest, and makes [them] think, death, or any misfortune proceeds immediately from him. They have also a glimpse of an afterlife, in which shall be rewards and punishments for the good and bad, but are wiser than to pretend to any certain knowledge of what or where. The belief of the Peeies' familiarity with the Devil and skill in herbs, to which also they pretend, causes them to be employed by others as physicians, though they need not be over fond of the profession, for one of them being sent for to a sick person, and that, notwithstanding his charms and fooleries the patient die, the surviving friends, if he be not the more wary, will give the poor doctor death also for his fee. They burn the dead body, and with it all the goods he was master of in the world which are combustible, and what is not (as iron-work), they'll destroy by some other means, that no necessaries may be wanting in the other life, and if he had any slaves they are killed also to attend him there. They solemnify the funeral with a drunken feast and confused dancing (in which they are frequent and excessive) while some woman of nearest kin to the deceased sits by, and in a doleful howling tune, lamentably deplores the loss of her relation.

ᗡᘉᗡ

⊷⊶ ⊯⊰⊱ ⊷⊶

Jonathan Swift
1667–1745

Like his fictional creation Lemuel Gulliver, Jonathan Swift was an Englishman who repeatedly found himself stranded on an island peopled by strange inhabitants. The island was called Ireland. It was his luck to be born there; his English father, a lawyer, had moved the family there in an unsuccessful quest for better business, only to die before Jonathan's birth. His wet nurse almost immediately stole away with him back to England, so that he didn't see his mother for the first three years of his life. When he was six and back home in Ireland, his mother sent him away to school near Dublin and promptly moved back to England with his sister.

At twenty-two, Swift was still at his studies in Dublin. It seems he wasn't always the most diligent of students, for Trinity College could grant him a bachelor's degree only by "special favour," meaning he had been unable to earn it by passing his examinations. Dr. Johnson observes that this humiliation taught Swift to study eight hours a day thereafter, and holds him up as an example to all "whose abilities have been made for a time useless by their passions or pleasures." Having lost his source of financial support, Swift found employment in England as a personal secretary to a family friend, Sir William Temple (1628–1699), author and retired Whig statesman. He hoped from this connection to launch a political career and make a noise in the world—which to Swift meant the English world. He would not advance beyond this post, however, before Temple died a decade later. Indeed, Swift's entire career was one of disappointments and frustrated ambition, even though in the end he achieved a great deal. In later years he wrote, "I remember when I was a little boy, I felt a great fish at the end of my line which I drew up almost on the ground, but it dropped in, and the disappointment vexeth me to this day, and I believe it was the type of all my future disappointments."

After several years at Temple's estate of Moor Park in Surrey without sign of the hoped-for political advancement, Swift moved back to Dublin to be ordained in the Church of Ireland, and start afresh what he hoped would be a more promising political career in that branch of the Anglican Church. Again he had little success. Within two years he fled back to England, to Moor Park, and "Stella"—Esther Johnson, the young daughter of a servant of Temple whom he had begun tutoring on his arrival there, when she was eight and he twenty-two. It was a lifelong love affair, and certainly a "marriage of true minds," although it remains uncertain whether it ever involved legal marriage or physical love. In 1701 he invited her and a chaperone to join him in Dublin, having returned there after Temple's death. They accepted and lived in close contact with him there, although in a separate house, for the rest of their lives.

Swift spent many years more pursuing the elusive English preferment, but it proved to be writing, rather than connections or the ecclesiastical hierarchy, that became the key to success for Swift in his desire to distinguish himself politically and socially. He got his first big break in 1701, causing a stir with a political pamphlet defending several Whig lords under threat of impeachment. In 1704 he followed up with two of his most famous works: *A Tale of a Tub* and *The Battle of the Books.* Both show his fondness for elaborately structured prose satires that baffle attempts to decide exactly which side of an issue is coming in for attack, or from what point of view. *A Tale of a Tub* is so ingeniously ambiguous that Swift was later compelled to remark: "Good God! What a genius I had when I wrote that book!" An assault upon religious dissenters and fanatics, it nevertheless savaged the established church sufficiently to harm Swift's long-cherished hopes of advancement in it. It is somewhat easier to see which side Swift is on in *The Battle of the Books,* which compares "modern" writers, those who don't follow classical models, to spiders spinning poison from their own guts.

In 1710 the political tide turned again, and the Tory party coming into power saw in Swift a powerful political tool. For his part Swift was proud to be treated as an intimate by their leaders, and became their best propagandist, notably in the periodical *The Examiner.* He soon became as important in the London literary scene as he now was in politics, hobnobbing with the likes of Alexander Pope, John Gay, and other literary lights of the time.

Around 1708, Swift had met a second young Esther in London: the twenty-year-old Esther Vanhomrigh (rhymes with "flummery"), whom he addressed as "Vanessa" to distinguish her from the other one. He became her mentor as he had become Stella's; again the passions on both sides were complex, and again the relationship lasted for many years. All the while he wrote daily to Stella back in Dublin. Vanessa could not get over her jealousy of Stella, and it was rumored that she died of chagrin when he finally broke with her over it in 1723. Stella herself died in 1728, to Swift's undying regret.

His Tory patrons at last procured for Swift the prestigious Deanery of Saint Patrick's Cathedral in Dublin in 1713. The death of Queen Anne the following year put an abrupt end to the Tory party's power, however, and to all Swift's hopes of continuing a political career in England. In the words of Samuel Johnson, "Swift now, much against his will, commenced Irishman for life, and was to contrive how he might be best accommodated in a country where he considered himself as in a state of exile." Swift threw himself with a vengeance into his new project of accommodating himself to Ireland, tending to his pastoral duties and turning his skills as a satirist to the support of Irish causes. He succeeded so well that, while one contemporary reports his having been "pelted by the populace" upon his taking up the office of Dean of Saint Patrick's, a decade later the people began lighting bonfires annually to celebrate his birthday. (For his own part, Swift always felt so sorry for himself that he marked his own birthdays by reading aloud from the *Book of Job.*) Despite having so successfully "commenced Irishman for life," Swift never ceased corresponding with his literary friends in London, and paid them a long visit in 1726. This meeting of the minds produced three major works: Pope's *Dunciad,* Gay's *Beggar's Opera,* and Swift's own best-loved book, *Gulliver's Travels.*

When he was only fifty Swift predicted he would die like a tree with a withered crown: "from the top." Since youth he had suffered from an intermittent and increasingly debilitating combination of dizziness and deafness caused, he believed, by eating too much fruit as a boy. Modern biographers speculate that his symptoms were caused by Ménière's syndrome, a dysfunction of the inner ear. Whatever the cause, by 1742 Swift was so affected that he could no longer manage his own affairs.

Never rich, Swift was a notoriously frugal man, and his idea about fruit—a luxury in those days—may indicate a guilty reflection on youthful indulgences. Although parsimonious with himself and friends, he was generous to the unfortunate. Living on one-third of his income, he gave an equal amount to charity during his lifetime, and saved the remaining third for the bequest by which he founded Saint Patrick's Hospital for Imbeciles (opened 1757), thus fulfilling his own prophecy in his poem "Verses on the Death of Dr. Swift"—a sardonic auto-obituary—"He gave what little wealth he had / To build a house for fools and mad." This generosity funded by miserliness is of a piece with his misanthropic writings in support of humanitarian causes, and with his contradictory feelings about Ireland, women, and political parties. He could always see both sides of an issue, as his works make so evident, and both sides generally outraged him. One hopes he fulfilled the final prediction for himself that he caused to be engraved on his tombstone, that he would find in the grave a place "Where cruel indignation can tear the heart no further."

GULLIVER'S TRAVELS

Like most of Swift's works, *Gulliver's Travels* (1726) is a political satire; like the best of them, its condemnation of all-too-human corruption is broad and ambiguous enough to transcend its local historical context (criticism of the current prime minister's administration). As is well illustrated by the accompanying political cartoon, printed nearly a century after *Gulliver's* publication, the allegory was flexible enough to be applied to later, entirely different political situations in English history. Again like most of his works, this one was published anonymously. That didn't prevent his being blamed for it by the English government, however, and its jaundiced portrayals of human nature solidified his misanthropic reputation. It was, however, the only one of his many works for which he was actually paid (£200—a large, but hardly princely, sum). Produced during a reunion of the London wits who called themselves the Scriblerus Club, it is very much an expression of the Scriblerian love of satire, parody, and the literary hoax. In many of his works, as here, Swift adopts the voice of a fictional persona and makes the gesture of passing it off as genuine—in this case as the firsthand account of Lemuel Gulliver, ship's surgeon. As in Swift's other works, the narrator is so unlike the author, and moreover so limited and unreliable, that readers must constantly beware of identifying his point of view with their own, or with that of the author.

Gulliver describes his adventures in four bizarre countries: Lilliput, whose people are six inches tall; Brobdingnag—the book illustrated in the cartoon—where he encounters a race of benevolent giants; a third land populated by various types of fools, including philosophers and historians; and finally, the country of the Houyhnhnms (pronounced "whinims"), in the fourth and final book, reprinted here. This book is an allegory not simply of political opposition, but of one of the fundamental conceptual oppositions informing Enlightenment thought: reason versus passion. In the Enlightenment view of humanity, every person was naturally endowed with both; it was usually held that one of the primary functions of reason was to regulate the passions, but how this was to happen, and what role each should play in the conduct of human affairs, were subjects of endless discourse during the period. This of course was not an entirely new problem, although the formulation in terms of "reason" and "passion" is characteristic of the Enlightenment. Indeed Dr. Swift, who refers to Plato in this work, may well have adapted the metaphor of horse and rider from a famous image in Plato's *Phaedrus,* where the soul is likened to a charioteer charged with the difficult task of driving two mismatched horses, one guided by reason (*logos*), the other driven by sexual appetites and controlled only with extreme difficulty. "Houyhnhnm" was Swift's attempt to spell the sound of a horse's whinny, for the Houyhnhnms are horses who behave rationally, while the Yahoos, who have human form, behave like animals. The Houyhnhnms represent the ideal of rational conduct taken to its philosophical extreme; the Yahoos illustrate the effects of acting purely on unbridled passions. What happens to Gulliver upon his return home is a result of his oversimplified interpretation, against which he serves as a caution to the reader.

PRONUNCIATIONS:

Brobdingnag: BRAHB-deeng-nag
Houyhnhnm: WHI-nim
Lilliput: LIL-li-puht

My little friend Grildrig, you have made a most admirable panegyric upon yourself and Country, but from what I can gather from your own relation & the answers I have with much pains wringed & extorted from you, I cannot but conclude you to be one of the most pernicious, little odious reptiles that nature ever suffered to crawl upon the surface of the Earth.

James Gillray, *The King of Brobdingnag and Gulliver,* 1803. George III of England, dressed in military uniform, inspects a miniature version of Napoleon, also in military uniform.

from Gulliver's Travels
Part 4. A Voyage to the Country of the Houyhnhnms

CHAPTER 1

The author sets out as Captain of a ship. His men conspire against him, confine him a long time to his cabin, set him on shore in an unknown land. He travels up into the country. The Yahoos,[1] a strange sort of animal, described. The author meets two Houyhnhnms.

I continued at home with my wife and children about five months in a very happy condition, if I could have learned the lesson of knowing when I was well. I left my poor wife big with child, and accepted an advantageous offer made me to be Captain of the *Adventure,*[2] a stout merchantman of 350 tons: for I understood navigation well, and being grown weary of a surgeon's employment at sea, which however I could exercise upon occasion, I took a skillful young man of that calling, one Robert Purefoy,[3]

---

1. The name may be derived from similarly titled African or Guianan tribes. The animals represent sinful, fallen humanity, and their juxtaposition with the Houyhnhnms is designed to question belief in the innate rationality of humankind and the superiority of humans over other creatures.

2. The name of two ships of the notorious pirate Captain William Kidd (d. 1701). Kidd, originally commissioned to capture pirates, was also subject to a mutiny.
3. "Pure faith," associating Gulliver with the overzealous Puritans.

into my ship. We set sail from Portsmouth upon the seventh day of September, 1710; on the fourteenth, we met with Captain Pocock[4] of Bristol, at Teneriffe,[5] who was going to the bay of Campeche, to cut logwood. On the sixteenth, he was parted from us by a storm; I heard since my return, that his ship foundered, and none escaped, but one cabin boy. He was an honest man, and a good sailor, but a little too positive in his own opinions, which was the cause of his destruction, as it hath been of several others. For if he had followed my advice, he might at this time have been safe at home with his family as well as myself.

I had several men died in my ship of calentures,[6] so that I was forced to get recruits out of Barbados, and the Leeward Islands, where I touched by[7] the direction of the merchants who employed me, which I had soon too much cause to repent; for I found afterwards that most of them had been buccaneers. I had fifty hands on board, and my orders were, that I should trade with the Indians in the South Sea, and make what discoveries I could. These rogues whom I had picked up debauched my other men, and they all formed a conspiracy to seize the ship and secure me; which they did one morning, rushing into my cabin, and binding me hand and foot, threatening to throw me overboard, if I offered to stir. I told them, I was their prisoner, and would submit. This they made me swear to do, and then unbound me, only fastening one of my legs with a chain near my bed, and placed a sentry at my door with his piece charged,[8] who was commanded to shoot me dead, if I attempted my liberty. They sent me down victuals and drink, and took the government of the ship to themselves. Their design was to turn pirates, and plunder the Spaniards, which they could not do till they got more men. But first they resolved to sell the goods in the ship, and then go to Madagascar[9] for recruits, several among them having died since my confinement. They sailed many weeks, and traded with the Indians, but I knew not what course they took, being kept close prisoner in my cabin, and expecting nothing less than to be murdered, as they often threatened me.

Upon the ninth day of May, 1711, one James Welch came down to my cabin; and said he had orders from the Captain to set me ashore. I expostulated with him, but in vain; neither would he so much as tell me who their new captain was. They forced me into the longboat, letting me put on my best suit of clothes, which were good as new, and a small bundle of linen, but no arms except my hanger;[1] and they were so civil as not to search my pockets, into which I conveyed what money I had, with some other little necessaries. They rowed about a league; and then set me down on a strand.[2] I desired them to tell me what country it was. They all swore, they knew no more than myself, but said, that the Captain (as they called him) was resolved, after they had sold the lading,[3] to get rid of me in the first place where they discovered land. They pushed off immediately, advising me to make haste, for fear of being overtaken by the tide, and bade me farewell.

In this desolate condition I advanced forward, and soon got upon firm ground, where I sat down on a bank to rest myself, and consider what I had best to do. When I

---

4. Probably modeled on the dogmatic Captain Dampier (1652–1715), who had spent three years logcutting around the Campeche Bay, on the Yucatan Peninsula, in the Gulf of Mexico. His violent disagreements with his lieutenant led to a court martial.
5. One of the Canary Islands, off the northwestern coast of Africa.
6. Tropical fevers.

7. Landed according to.
8. Gun loaded.
9. A popular meeting place for pirates.
1. A short sword, typically hung from the belt.
2. The shore; in this context, apparently a spit extending into the sea.
3. Cargo.

was a little refreshed, I went up into the country, resolving to deliver myself to the first savages I should meet, and purchase my life from them by some bracelets, glass rings, and other toys,[4] which sailors usually provide themselves with in those voyages, and whereof I had some about me: the land was divided by long rows of trees, not regularly planted, but naturally growing; there was great plenty of grass, and several fields of oats. I walked very circumspectly for fear of being surprised, or suddenly shot with an arrow from behind or on either side. I fell into a beaten road, where I saw many tracks of human feet, and some of cows, but most of horses. At last I beheld several animals in a field, and one or two of the same kind sitting in trees. Their shape was very singular, and deformed, which a little discomposed me, so that I lay down behind a thicket to observe them better. Some of them coming forward near the place where I lay, gave me an opportunity of distinctly marking[5] their form. Their heads and breasts were covered with a thick hair, some frizzled and others lank; they had beards like goats, and a long ridge of hair down their backs, and the foreparts of their legs and feet, but the rest of their bodies were bare, so that I might see their skins, which were of a brown buff color. They had no tails, nor any hair at all on their buttocks, except about the anus; which, I presume, Nature had placed there to defend them as they sat on the ground; for this posture they used, as well as lying down, and often stood on their hind feet. They climbed high trees, as nimbly as a squirrel, for they had strong extended claws before and behind, terminating in sharp points, and hooked. They would often spring, and bound, and leap with prodigious agility. The females were not so large as the males; they had long lank hair on their heads, and only a sort of down on the rest of their bodies, except about the anus, and pudenda.[6] Their dugs[7] hung between their forefeet, and often reached almost to the ground as they walked. The hair of both sexes was of several colors, brown, red, black, and yellow. Upon the whole, I never beheld in all my travels so disagreeable an animal, nor one against which I naturally conceived so strong an antipathy. So that thinking I had seen enough, full of contempt and aversion, I got up and pursued the beaten road, hoping it might direct me to the cabin of some Indian. I had not gone far when I met one of these creatures full in my way, and coming up directly to me. The ugly monster, when he saw me, distorted several ways every feature of his visage, and stared as at an object he had never seen before; then approaching nearer, lifted up his forepaw, whether out of curiosity or mischief, I could not tell. But I drew my hanger, and gave him a good blow with the flat side of it; for I durst not strike him with the edge, fearing the inhabitants might be provoked against me, if they should come to know, that I had killed or maimed any of their cattle. When the beast felt the smart, he drew back, and roared so loud, that a herd of at least forty came flocking about me from the next field, howling and making odious faces; but I ran to the body of a tree, and leaning my back against it, kept them off, by waving my hanger. Several of this cursed brood getting hold of the branches behind leaped up into the tree, from whence they began to discharge their excrements on my head: however, I escaped pretty well, by sticking close to the stem of the tree, but was almost stifled with the filth, which fell about me on every side.

In the midst of this distress, I observed them all to run away on a sudden as fast as they could, at which I ventured to leave the tree, and pursue the road, wondering what it was that could put them into this flight. But looking on my left hand, I saw a

---

4. Trinkets.
5. Observing.

6. Genitals.
7. Breasts (properly an animal's udders).

horse walking softly in the field, which my persecutors having sooner discovered, was the cause of their flight. The horse started a little when he came near me, but soon recovering himself, looked full in my face with manifest tokens of wonder: he viewed my hands and feet, walking round me several times. I would have pursued my journey, but he placed himself directly in the way, yet looking with a very mild aspect, never offering the least violence. We stood gazing at each other for some time; at last I took the boldness to reach my hand towards his neck, with a design to stroke it, using the common style and whistle of jockeys when they are going to handle a strange horse. But this animal, seeming to receive my civilities with disdain, shook his head, and bent his brows, softly raising up his left forefoot to remove my hand. Then he neighed three or four times, but in so different a cadence, that I almost began to think he was speaking to himself in some language of his own.

While he and I were thus employed, another horse came up; who applying[8] himself to the first in a very formal manner, they gently struck each other's right hoof before, neighing several times by turns, and varying the sound, which seemed to be almost articulate. They went some paces off, as if it were to confer together, walking side by side, backward and forward, like persons deliberating upon some affair of weight, but often turning their eyes towards me, as it were to watch that I might not escape. I was amazed to see such actions and behavior in brute beasts, and concluded with myself, that if the inhabitants of this country were endued with a proportionable degree of reason, they must needs be the wisest people upon earth. This thought gave me so much comfort, that I resolved to go forward until I could discover some house or village, or meet with any of the natives, leaving the two horses to discourse together as they pleased. But the first, who was a dapple-grey, observing me to steal off, neighed after me in so expressive a tone, that I fancied myself to understand what he meant; whereupon I turned back, and came near him, to expect[9] his farther commands. But concealing my fear as much as I could, for I began to be in some pain,[1] how this adventure might terminate; and the reader will easily believe I did not much like my present situation.

The two horses came up close to me, looking with great earnestness upon my face and hands. The grey steed rubbed my hat all round with his right forehoof, and discomposed it so much, that I was forced to adjust it better, by taking it off, and settling it again; whereat both he and his companion (who was a brown bay) appeared to be much surprised; the latter felt the lappet[2] of my coat, and finding it to hang loose about me, they both looked with new signs of wonder. He stroked my right hand, seeming to admire the softness, and color; but he squeezed it so hard between his hoof and his pastern,[3] that I was forced to roar; after which they both touched me with all possible tenderness. They were under great perplexity about my shoes and stockings, which they felt very often, neighing to each other, and using various gestures, not unlike those of a philosopher,[4] when he would attempt to solve some new and difficult phenomenon.

Upon the whole, the behavior of these animals was so orderly and rational, so acute and judicious, that I at last concluded, they must needs be magicians, who had thus metamorphosed themselves upon some design, and seeing a stranger in the way,

---

8. Addressing.
9. Await.
1. Began to be worried.
2. Skirts, coattails.

3. Part of a horse's foot between the fetlock (a projection of the lower leg) and the hoof.
4. Scientist.

were resolved to divert themselves with him; or perhaps were really amazed at the sight of a man so very different in habit, feature, and complexion from those who might probably live in so remote a climate.[5] Upon the strength of this reasoning, I ventured to address them in the following manner: Gentlemen, if you be conjurers, as I have good cause to believe, you can understand any language; therefore I make bold to let your Worships know, that I am a poor distressed Englishman, driven by his misfortunes upon your coast, and I entreat one of you, to let me ride upon his back, as if he were a real horse, to some house or village, where I can be relieved. In return of which favor, I will make you a present of this knife and bracelet (taking them out of my pocket). The two creatures stood silent while I spoke, seeming to listen with great attention; and when I had ended, they neighed frequently towards each other, as if they were engaged in serious conversation. I plainly observed that their language expressed the passions[6] very well, and the words might with little pains be resolved into an alphabet more easily than the Chinese.

I could frequently distinguish the word *Yahoo,* which was repeated by each of them several times; and although it were impossible for me to conjecture what it meant, yet while the two horses were busy in conversation, I endeavored to practice this word upon my tongue; and as soon as they were silent, I boldly pronounced *Yahoo* in a loud voice, imitating, at the same time, as near as I could, the neighing of a horse; at which they were both visibly surprised, and the grey repeated the same word twice, as if he meant to teach me the right accent, wherein I spoke after him as well as I could, and found myself perceivably to improve every time, although very far from any degree of perfection. Then the bay tried me with a second word, much harder to be pronounced; but reducing it to the English *orthography,*[7] may be spelled thus, *Houyhnhnm.* I did not succeed in this so well as the former, but after two or three farther trials, I had better fortune; and they both appeared amazed at my capacity.

After some farther discourse, which I then conjectured might relate to me, the two friends took their leaves, with the same compliment of striking each other's hoof; and the grey made me signs that I should walk before him; wherein I thought it prudent to comply, till I could find a better director. When I offered to slacken my pace, he would cry *Hhuun, Hhuun;* I guessed his meaning, and gave him to understand, as well as I could, that I was weary, and not able to walk faster; upon which, he would stand a while to let me rest.

CHAPTER 2

The author conducted by a Houyhnhnm to his house. The house described. The author's reception. The food of the Houyhnhnms. The author in distress for want of meat, is at last relieved. His manner of feeding in that country.

Having traveled about three miles, we came to a long kind of building, made of timber stuck in the ground, and wattled across;[8] the roof was low, and covered with straw. I now began to be a little comforted, and took out some toys, which travelers usually carry for presents to the savage Indians of America and other parts, in hopes the people of the house would be thereby encouraged to receive me kindly. The horse made me a sign to go in first; it was a large room with a smooth, clay floor, and a

5. Region.
6. Emotions.

7. Spelling.
8. Filled in with twigs and branches.

rack[9] and manger extending the whole length on one side. There were three nags,[1] and two mares, not eating, but some of them sitting down upon their hams,[2] which I very much wondered at; but wondered more to see the rest employed in domestic business. The last seemed but ordinary cattle; however, this confirmed my first opinion, that a people who could so far civilize brute animals, must needs excel in wisdom all the nations of the world. The grey came in just after, and thereby prevented any ill treatment, which the others might have given me. He neighed to them several times in a style of authority, and received answers.

Beyond this room there were three others, reaching the length of the house, to which you passed through three doors, opposite to each other, in the manner of a vista;[3] we went through the second room towards the third; here the grey walked in first, beckoning me to attend:[4] I waited in the second room, and got ready my presents, for the master and mistress of the house: they were two knives, three bracelets of false pearl, a small looking glass, and a bead necklace. The horse neighed three or four times, and I waited to hear some answers in a human voice, but I heard no other returns than in the same dialect, only one or two a little shriller than his. I began to think that this house must belong to some person of great note among them, because there appeared so much ceremony before I could gain admittance. But, that a man of quality should be served all by horses, was beyond my comprehension. I feared my brain was disturbed by my sufferings and misfortunes: I roused myself, and looked about me in the room where I was left alone; this was furnished as the first, only after a more elegant manner. I rubbed mine eyes often, but the same objects still occurred. I pinched my arms and sides, to awake myself, hoping I might be in a dream. I then absolutely concluded, that all these appearances could be nothing else but necromancy[5] and magic. But I had no time to pursue these reflections; for the grey horse came to the door, and made me a sign to follow him into the third room, where I saw a very comely mare, together with a colt and foal, sitting on their haunches, upon mats of straw, not unartfully made, and perfectly neat and clean.

The mare, soon after my entrance, rose from her mat, and coming up close, after having nicely[6] observed my hands and face, gave me a most contemptuous look; then turning to the horse, I heard the word *Yahoo* often repeated betwixt them; the meaning of which word I could not then comprehend, although it were the first I had learned to pronounce; but I was soon better informed, to my everlasting mortification: for the horse beckoning to me with his head, and repeating the word *Hhuun, Hhuun,* as he did upon the road, which I understood was to attend him, led me out into a kind of court, where was another building at some distance from the house. Here we entered, and I saw three of those detestable creatures, which I first met after my landing, feeding upon roots, and the flesh of some animals, which I afterwards found to be that of asses and dogs, and now and then a cow dead by accident or disease.[7] They were all tied by the neck with strong withes,[8] fastened to a beam; they held their food between the claws of their forefeet, and tore it with their teeth.

The master horse ordered a sorrel nag, one of his servants, to untie the largest of these animals, and take him into the yard. The beast and I were brought close together, and our countenances diligently compared, both by master and servant, who

9. Hayrack for the feed.
1. Ponies.
2. Buttocks.
3. Long, narrow view (usually between rows of trees).
4. Wait.
5. Sorcery.

6. Closely.
7. The Yahoos eat food listed in Leviticus (11:3, 27, 39–40) as unclean, suggesting that they exemplify the human condition distorted and debased by sin.
8. Shackles of twisted willow.

thereupon repeated several times the word Yahoo. My horror and astonishment are not to be described, when I observed, in this abominable animal, a perfect human figure; the face of it indeed was flat and broad, the nose depressed, the lips large, and the mouth wide. But these differences are common to all savage nations, where the lineaments of the countenance are distorted by the natives suffering[9] their infants to lie groveling on the earth, or by carrying them on their backs, nuzzling with their face against the mother's shoulders. The forefeet of the Yahoo differed from my hands in nothing else but the length of the nails, the coarseness and brownness of the palms, and the hairiness on the backs. There was the same resemblance between our feet, with the same differences, which I knew very well, though the horses did not, because of my shoes and stockings; the same in every part of our bodies, except as to hairiness and color, which I have already described.

The great difficulty that seemed to stick with the two horses, was, to see the rest of my body so very different from that of a Yahoo, for which I was obliged to my clothes, whereof they had no conception: the sorrel nag offered me a root, which he held (after their manner, as we shall describe in its proper place) between his hoof and pastern; I took it in my hand, and having smelt it, returned it to him as civilly as I could. He brought out of the Yahoo's kennel a piece of ass's flesh, but it smelt so offensively that I turned from it with loathing; he then threw it to the Yahoo, by whom it was greedily devoured. He afterwards showed me a wisp of hay, and a fetlock full of oats; but I shook my head, to signify, that neither of these were food for me. And indeed, I now apprehended, that I must absolutely starve, if I did not get to some of my own species: for as to those filthy Yahoos, although there were few greater lovers of mankind, at that time, than myself; yet I confess I never saw any sensitive[1] being so detestable on all accounts; and the more I came near them, the more hateful they grew, while I stayed in that country. This the master horse observed by my behavior, and therefore sent the Yahoo back to his kennel. He then put his forehoof to his mouth, at which I was much surprised, although he did it with ease, and with a motion that appeared perfectly natural, and made other signs to know what I would eat; but I could not return him such an answer as he was able to apprehend; and if he had understood me, I did not see how it was possible to contrive any way for finding myself nourishment. While we were thus engaged, I observed a cow passing by, whereupon I pointed to her, and expressed a desire to let me go and milk her. This had its effect; for he led me back into the house, and ordered a mare-servant to open a room, where a good store of milk lay in earthen and wooden vessels, after a very orderly and cleanly manner. She gave me a large bowl full, of which I drank very heartily, and found myself well refreshed.

About noon I saw coming towards the house a kind of vehicle drawn like a sledge by four Yahoos. There was in it an old steed, who seemed to be of quality; he alighted with his hind feet forward, having by accident got a hurt in his left forefoot. He came to dine with our horse, who received him with great civility. They dined in the best room, and had oats boiled in milk for the second course, which the old horse ate warm, but the rest cold. Their mangers were placed circular in the middle of the room, and divided into several partitions, round which they sat on their haunches upon bosses[2] of straw. In the middle was a large rack with angles answering to every partition of the manger. So that each horse and mare ate their own hay, and their own

9. Allowing.
1. "Having sense or perception, but not reason" (Johnson's

Dictionary).
2. Piles or seats.

mash of oats and milk, with much decency and regularity. The behavior of the young colt and foal appeared very modest, and that of the master and mistress extremely cheerful and complaisant[3] to their guest. The grey ordered me to stand by him, and much discourse passed between him and his friend concerning me, as I found by the stranger's often looking on me, and the frequent repetition of the word Yahoo.

I happened to wear my gloves, which the master grey observing, seemed perplexed, discovering signs of wonder what I had done to my forefeet; he put his hoof three or four times to them, as if he would signify, that I should reduce them to their former shape, which I presently did, pulling off both my gloves, and putting them into my pocket. This occasioned farther talk, and I saw the company was pleased with my behavior, whereof I soon found the good effects. I was ordered to speak the few words I understood, and while they were at dinner, the master taught me the names for oats, milk, fire, water, and some others; which I could readily pronounce after him, having from my youth a great facility in learning languages.

When dinner was done, the master horse took me aside, and by signs and words made me understand the concern he was in, that I had nothing to eat. Oats in their tongue are called *hlunnh*. This word I pronounced two or three times; for although I had refused them at first, yet upon second thoughts, I considered that I could contrive to make of them a kind of bread, which might be sufficient with milk to keep me alive, till I could make my escape to some other country, and to creatures of my own species. The horse immediately ordered a white mare-servant of his family to bring me a good quantity of oats in a sort of wooden tray. These I heated before the fire as well as I could, and rubbed them till the husks came off, which I made a shift[4] to winnow from the grain; I ground and beat them between two stones, then took water, and made them into a paste or cake, which I toasted at the fire, and ate warm with milk. It was at first a very insipid diet, although common enough in many parts of Europe, but grew tolerable by time; and having been often reduced to hard fare in my life, this was not the first experiment I had made how easily nature is satisfied.[5] And I cannot but observe, that I never had one hour's sickness, while I stayed in this island. 'Tis true, I sometimes made a shift to catch a rabbit, or bird, by springes[6] made of Yahoos' hairs, and I often gathered wholesome herbs, which I boiled, or ate as salads with my bread, and now and then, for a rarity, I made a little butter, and drank the whey. I was at first at a great loss for salt; but custom soon reconciled the want of it; and I am confident that the frequent use of salt among us is an effect of luxury, and was first introduced only as a provocative to drink; except where it is necessary for preserving of flesh in long voyages, or in places remote from great markets. For we observe no animal to be fond of it but man:[7] and as to myself, when I left this country, it was a great while before I could endure the taste of it in anything that I ate.

This is enough to say upon the subject of my diet, wherewith other travelers fill their books, as if the readers were personally concerned whether we fared[8] well or ill. However, it was necessary to mention this matter, lest the world should think it impossible that I could find sustenance for three years in such a country, and among such inhabitants.

---

3. Courteous.
4. Managed.
5. A commonplace idea in ancient satire; Swift may here be mocking it.
6. Snares.

7. This is, of course, untrue, but Gulliver's subsequent dislike of salt indicates his dislike of human society in general.
8. A pun on "fare," meaning both food and "to get along."

When it grew towards evening, the master horse ordered a place for me to lodge in; it was but six yards from the house, and separated from the stable of the Yahoos. Here I got some straw, and covering myself with my own clothes, slept very sound. But I was in a short time better accommodated, as the reader shall know hereafter, when I come to treat more particularly about my way of living.

CHAPTER 3

The author studious to learn the language, the Houyhnhnm his master assists in teaching him. The language described. Several Houyhnhnms of quality come out of curiosity to see the author. He gives his master a short account of his voyage.

My principal endeavor was to learn the language, which my master (for so I shall henceforth call him) and his children, and every servant of his house were desirous to teach me. For they looked upon it as a prodigy that a brute animal should discover[9] such marks of a rational creature. I pointed to everything, and inquired the name of it, which I wrote down in my journal book when I was alone, and corrected my bad accent, by desiring those of the family to pronounce it often. In this employment, a sorrel nag, one of the under servants, was very ready to assist me.

In speaking, they pronounce through the nose and throat, and their language approaches nearest to the High Dutch or German, of any I know in Europe; but is much more graceful and significant.[1] The Emperor Charles V made almost the same observation, when he said, that if he were to speak to his horse, it should be in High Dutch.[2]

The curiosity and impatience of my master were so great, that he spent many hours of his leisure to instruct me. He was convinced (as he afterwards told me) that I must be a Yahoo, but my teachableness, civility, and cleanliness astonished him; which were qualities altogether so opposite to those animals. He was most perplexed about my clothes, reasoning sometimes with himself, whether they were a part of my body; for I never pulled them off till the family were asleep, and got them on before they waked in the morning. My master was eager to learn from whence I came, how I acquired those appearances of reason, which I discovered in all my actions, and to know my story from my own mouth, which he hoped he should soon do by the great proficiency I made in learning and pronouncing their words and sentences. To help my memory, I formed all I learned into the English alphabet, and writ the words down with the translations. This last, after some time, I ventured to do in my master's presence. It cost me much trouble to explain to him what I was doing; for the inhabitants have not the least idea of books or literature.

In about ten weeks' time I was able to understand most of his questions, and in three months could give him some tolerable answers. He was extremely curious to know from what part of the country I came, and how I was taught to imitate a rational creature, because the Yahoos (whom he saw I exactly resembled in my head, hands, and face, that were only visible), with some appearance of cunning, and the strongest disposition to mischief, were observed to be the most unteachable of all brutes. I answered, that I came over the sea, from a far place, with many others of my own kind, in a great hollow vessel made of the bodies of trees. That my companions forced me to land on this coast, and then left me to shift for myself. It was with some difficulty,

9. Display.
1. Expressive.
2. Charles V of Spain (1500–1551) was believed to have said that he would address his God in Spanish, his mistress in Italian, and his horse in German.

and by the help of many signs, that I brought him to understand me. He replied, that I must needs be mistaken, or that I *said the thing which was not.* (For they have no word in their language to express lying or falsehood.) He knew it was impossible[3] that there could be a country beyond the sea, or that a parcel of brutes could move a wooden vessel whither they pleased upon water. He was sure no Houyhnhnm alive could make such a vessel, or would trust Yahoos to manage it.

The word *Houyhnhnm,* in their tongue, signifies a *horse,* and in its etymology, the *Perfection of Nature.* I told my master, that I was at a loss for expression, but would improve as fast as I could; and hoped in a short time I should be able to tell him wonders: he was pleased to direct his own mare, his colt and foal, and the servants of the family to take all opportunities of instructing me, and every day for two or three hours, he was at the same pains himself: several horses and mares of quality in the neighborhood came often to our house upon the report spread of a wonderful Yahoo, that could speak like a Houyhnhnm, and seemed in his words and actions to discover some glimmerings of reason. These delighted to converse with me; they put many questions, and received such answers as I was able to return. By all which advantages, I made so great a progress, that in five months from my arrival, I understood whatever was spoke, and could express myself tolerably well.

The Houyhnhnms who came to visit my master, out of a design of seeing and talking with me, could hardly believe me to be a right[4] Yahoo, because my body had a different covering from others of my kind. They were astonished to observe me without the usual hair or skin, except on my head, face, and hands; but I discovered that secret to my master, upon an accident, which happened about a fortnight before.

I have already told the reader, that every night when the family were gone to bed, it was my custom to strip and cover myself with my clothes: it happened one morning early, that my master sent for me, by the sorrel nag, who was his valet; when he came, I was fast asleep, my clothes fallen off on one side, and my shirt above my waist. I awaked at the noise he made, and observed him to deliver his message in some disorder; after which he went to my master, and in a great fright gave him a very confused account of what he had seen: this I presently discovered; for going as soon as I was dressed, to pay my attendance upon his Honor, he asked me the meaning of what his servant had reported, that I was not the same thing when I slept as I appeared to be at other times; that his valet assured him, some part of me was white, some yellow, at least not so white, and some brown.

I had hitherto concealed the secret of my dress, in order to distinguish myself as much as possible, from that cursed race of Yahoos; but now I found it in vain to do so any longer. Besides, I considered that my clothes and shoes would soon wear out, which already were in a declining condition, and must be supplied by some contrivance from the hides of Yahoos or other brutes; whereby the whole secret would be known: I therefore told my master, that in the country from whence I came, those of my kind always covered their bodies with the hairs of certain animals prepared by art, as well for decency, as to avoid inclemencies of air both hot and cold; of which, as to my own person, I would give him immediate conviction, if he pleased to command me; only desiring his excuse, if I did not expose those parts that Nature taught us to conceal. He said my discourse was all very strange, but especially the last part; for he

---

3. The Houyhnhnm thus shows himself to be so dependent on reason that he is dogmatic in his ignorance, unable (like rationalists in religion) to accept what he does not know by his own reasoning.
4. True.

could not understand why Nature should teach us to conceal what Nature had given. That neither himself nor family were ashamed of any parts of their bodies; but however I might do as I pleased. Whereupon, I first unbuttoned my coat, and pulled it off. I did the same with my waistcoat;[5] I drew off my shoes, stockings, and breeches. I let my shirt down to my waist, and drew up the bottom, fastening it like a girdle about my middle to hide my nakedness.

My master observed the whole performance with great signs of curiosity and admiration. He took up all my clothes in his pastern, one piece after another, and examined them diligently; he then stroked my body very gently, and looked round me several times, after which he said, it was plain I must be a perfect Yahoo; but that I differed very much from the rest of my species, in the softness, and whiteness, and smoothness of my skin, my want of hair in several parts of my body, the shape and shortness of my claws behind and before, and my affectation of walking continually on my two hinder feet. He desired to see no more, and gave me leave to put on my clothes again, for I was shuddering with cold.

I expressed my uneasiness at his giving me so often the appellation of Yahoo, an odious animal, for which I had so utter an hatred and contempt; I begged he would forbear applying that word to me, and take the same order in his family, and among his friends whom he suffered to see me. I requested likewise, that the secret of my having a false covering to my body might be known to none but himself, at least as long as my present clothing should last; for, as to what the sorrel nag his valet had observed, his Honor might command him to conceal it.

All this my master very graciously consented to,[6] and thus the secret was kept till my clothes began to wear out, which I was forced to supply by several contrivances, that shall hereafter be mentioned. In the meantime, he desired I would go on with my utmost diligence to learn their language, because he was more astonished at my capacity for speech and reason, than at the figure of my body, whether it were covered or no; adding, that he waited with some impatience to hear the wonders which I promised to tell him.

From thenceforward he doubled the pains he had been at to instruct me; he brought me into all company, and made them treat me with civility, because, as he told them privately, this would put me into good humor, and make me more diverting.

Every day when I waited on him, beside the trouble he was at in teaching, he would ask me several questions concerning myself, which I answered as well as I could; and by those means he had already received some general ideas, though very imperfect. It would be tedious to relate the several steps, by which I advanced to a more regular conversation: but the first account I gave of myself in any order and length, was to this purpose:

That, I came from a very far country, as I already had attempted to tell him, with about fifty more of my own species; that we traveled upon the seas, in a great hollow vessel made of wood, and larger than his Honor's house. I described the ship to him in the best terms I could, and explained by the help of my handkerchief displayed, how it was driven forward by the wind. That upon a quarrel among us, I was set on shore on this coast, where I walked forward without knowing whither, till he delivered me from the persecution of those execrable Yahoos. He asked me, who made the ship, and how it was possible that the Houyhnhnms of my country would leave it to the

---

5. Vest.

6. The Houyhnhnms may have no word for "lying," but they can hide the truth.

management of brutes? My answer was, that I durst proceed no farther in my relation, unless he would give me his word and honor that he would not be offended, and then I would tell him the wonders I had so often promised. He agreed; and I went on by assuring him, that the ship was made by creatures like myself, who in all the countries I had traveled, as well as in my own, were the only governing, rational animals; and that upon my arrival hither, I was as much astonished to see the Houyhnhnms act like rational beings, as he or his friends could be in finding some marks of reason in a creature he was pleased to call a Yahoo, to which I owned my resemblance in every part, but could not account for their degenerate and brutal nature. I said farther, that if good fortune ever restored me to my native country, to relate my travels hither, as I resolved to do, everybody would believe that I *said the thing which was not;* that I invented the story out of my own head; and with all possible respect to himself, his family, and friends, and under his promise of not being offended, our countrymen would hardly think it probable, that a Houyhnhnm should be the presiding creature of a nation, and a Yahoo the brute.

CHAPTER 4

The Houyhnhnms' notion of truth and falsehood. The author's discourse disapproved by his master. The author gives a more particular account of himself, and the accidents of his voyage.

My master heard me with great appearances of uneasiness in his countenance, because *doubting* or *not believing,* are so little known in this country, that the inhabitants cannot tell how to behave themselves under such circumstances. And I remember in frequent discourses with my master concerning the nature of manhood,[7] in other parts of the world, having occasion to talk of *lying,* and *false representation,* it was with much difficulty that he comprehended what I meant, although he had otherwise a most acute judgment. For he argued thus: that the use of speech was to make us understand one another, and to receive information of facts; now if any one *said the thing which was not,* these ends were defeated; because I cannot properly be said to understand him, and I am so far from receiving information, that he leaves me worse than in ignorance, for I am led to believe a thing *black* when it is *white,* and *short* when it is *long.* And these were all the notions he had concerning that faculty of *lying,* so perfectly well understood, and so universally practiced among human creatures.

To return from this digression; when I asserted that the Yahoos were the only governing animal in my country, which my master said was altogether past his conception, he desired to know, whether we had Houyhnhnms among us, and what was their employment: I told him, we had great numbers, that in summer they grazed in the fields, and in winter were kept in houses, with hay and oats, where Yahoo servants were employed to rub their skins smooth, comb their manes, pick their feet, serve them with food, and make their beds. I understand you well, said my master; it is now very plain, from all you have spoken, that whatever share of reason the Yahoos pretend to, the Houyhnhnms are your masters;[8] I heartily wish our Yahoos would be so tractable. I begged his Honor would please to excuse me from proceeding any farther, because I was very certain that the account he expected from me would be highly displeasing. But he insisted in commanding me to let him know the best and the worst: I

---

7. Human nature.   8. Possibly a satire on the English love of horses.

told him, he should be obeyed. I owned, that the Houyhnhnms among us, whom we called *horses,* were the most generous and comely animal we had, that they excelled in strength and swiftness; and when they belonged to persons of quality, employed in traveling, racing, or drawing chariots, they were treated with much kindness and care, till they fell into diseases, or became foundered in the feet;[9] but then they were sold, and used to all kind of drudgery till they died; after which their skins were stripped and sold for what they were worth, and their bodies left to be devoured by dogs and birds of prey.[1] But the common race of horses had not so good fortune, being kept by farmers and carriers and other mean people, who put them to greater labor, and fed them worse. I described as well as I could, our way of riding, the shape and use of a bridle, a saddle, a spur, and a whip, of harness and wheels. I added, that we fastened plates of a certain hard substance called *iron* at the bottom of their feet, to preserve their hoofs from being broken by the stony ways on which we often traveled.

My master, after some expressions of great indignation, wondered how we dared to venture upon a Houyhnhnm's back, for he was sure that the weakest servant in his house would be able to shake off the strongest Yahoo, or by lying down, and rolling upon his back, squeeze the brute to death. I answered, that our horses were trained up from three or four years old to the several uses we intended them for; that if any of them proved intolerably vicious, they were employed for carriages; that they were severely beaten while they were young, for any mischievous tricks; that the males, designed for the common use of riding or draft, were generally *castrated* about two years after their birth, to take down their spirits, and make them more tame and gentle; that they were indeed sensible of rewards and punishments; but his Honor would please to consider, that they had not the least tincture of reason any more than the Yahoos in this country.

It put me to the pains of many circumlocutions to give my master a right idea of what I spoke; for their language doth not abound in variety of words, because their wants and passions are fewer than among us. But it is impossible to express his noble resentment at our savage treatment of the Houyhnhnm race, particularly after I had explained the manner and use of *castrating* horses among us, to hinder them from propagating their kind, and to render them more servile. He said, if it were possible there could be any country where Yahoos alone were endued with reason, they certainly must be the governing animal, because reason will in time always prevail against brutal strength. But, considering the frame of our bodies, and especially of mine, he thought no creature of equal bulk was so ill-contrived for employing that reason in the common offices of life; whereupon he desired to know whether those among whom I lived, resembled me or the Yahoos of his country. I assured him, that I was as well shaped as most of my age, but the younger and the females were much more soft and tender, and the skins of the latter generally as white as milk. He said, I differed indeed from other Yahoos, being much more cleanly, and not altogether so deformed, but in point of real advantage, he thought I differed for the worse. That my nails were of no use either to my fore or hinder feet; as to my forefeet, he could not properly call them by that name, for he never observed me to walk upon them; that they were too soft to bear the ground; that I generally went with them uncovered, neither was the covering I sometimes wore on them of the same shape, or so strong as

---

9. Lamed.
1. Swift mockingly paraphrases the *Iliad* 1.4–6: "The souls of mighty Chiefs untimely slain; / Whose limbs unburied on the naked shore, / Devouring dogs and hungry vultures tore" [Pope's translation].

that on my feet behind. That I could not walk with any security, for if either of my hinder feet slipped, I must inevitably fall. He then began to find fault with other parts of my body, the flatness of my face, the prominence of my nose, mine eyes placed directly in front, so that I could not look on either side without turning my head, that I was not able to feed myself, without lifting one of my forefeet to my mouth, and therefore Nature had placed those joints to answer that necessity. He knew not what could be the use of those several clefts and divisions in my feet behind; that these were too soft to bear the hardness and sharpness of stones without a covering made from the skin of some other brute; that my whole body wanted a fence against heat and cold, which I was forced to put on and off every day with tediousness and trouble. And lastly, that he observed every animal in this country naturally to abhor the Yahoos, whom the weaker avoided, and the stronger drove from them. So that supposing us to have the gift of reason, he could not see how it were possible to cure that natural antipathy which every creature discovered[2] against us; nor consequently, how we could tame and render them serviceable. However, he would (as he said) debate that matter no farther, because he was more desirous to know my own story, the country where I was born, and the several actions and events of my life before I came hither.

I assured him, how extremely desirous I was that he should be satisfied in every point; but I doubted much, whether it would be possible for me to explain myself on several subjects whereof his Honor could have no conception, because I saw nothing in his country to which I could resemble[3] them. That, however, I would do my best, and strive to express myself by similitudes, humbly desiring his assistance when I wanted proper words; which he was pleased to promise me.

I said, my birth was of honest parents, in an island called England, which was remote from this country, as many days' journey as the strongest of his Honor's servants could travel in the annual course of the sun. That I was bred a surgeon, whose trade it is to cure wounds and hurts in the body, got by accident or violence; that my country was governed by a female man, whom we called a *Queen*. That I left it to get riches,[4] whereby I might maintain myself and family when I should return. That in my last voyage, I was commander of the ship, and had about fifty Yahoos under me, many of which died at sea, and I was forced to supply[5] them by others picked out from several nations. That our ship was twice in danger of being sunk; the first time by a great storm, and the second, by striking against a rock. Here my master interposed, by asking me, how I could persuade strangers out of different countries to venture with me, after the losses I had sustained, and the hazards I had run. I said, they were fellows of desperate fortunes, forced to fly from the places of their birth, on account of their poverty or their crimes. Some were undone by lawsuits; others spent all they had in drinking, whoring, and gaming; others fled for treason; many for murder, theft, poisoning, robbery, perjury, forgery, coining false money, for committing rapes or sodomy, for flying from their colors,[6] or deserting to the enemy, and most of them had broken prison; none of these durst return to their native countries for fear of being hanged, or of starving in a jail; and therefore were under a necessity of seeking a livelihood in other places.

During this discourse, my master was pleased often to interrupt me. I had made use of many circumlocutions in describing to him the nature of the several crimes, for

2. Displayed.
3. Compare.
4. Gulliver originally stated that he undertook his second and third voyages out of a desire to travel: he now reads all human motivation in the worst possible light.
5. Replace.
6. Deserting their regiment in the army.

which most of our crew had been forced to fly their country. This labor took up several days' conversation before he was able to comprehend me. He was wholly at a loss to know what could be the use or necessity of practicing those vices. To clear up which I endeavored to give him some ideas of the desire of power and riches, of the terrible effects of lust, intemperance, malice, and envy. All this I was forced to define and describe by putting of cases, and making suppositions. After which, like one whose imagination was struck with something never seen or heard of before, he would lift up his eyes with amazement and indignation. Power, government, war, law, punishment, and a thousand other things had no terms, wherein that language could express them, which made the difficulty almost insuperable to give my master any conception of what I meant. But being of an excellent understanding, much improved by contemplation and converse, he at last arrived at a competent knowledge of what human nature in our parts of the world is capable to perform, and desired I would give him some particular account of that land, which we call Europe, but especially, of my own country.

CHAPTER 5

The author at his master's commands informs him of the state of England. The causes of war among the princes of Europe. The author begins to explain the English Constitution.

The reader may please to observe, that the following extract of many conversations I had with my master, contains a summary of the most material points, which were discoursed at several times for above two years; his Honor often desiring fuller satisfaction[7] as I farther improved in the Houyhnhnm tongue. I laid before him, as well as I could, the whole state of Europe; I discoursed of trade and manufactures, of arts and sciences; and the answers I gave to all the questions he made, as they arose upon several subjects, were a fund of conversation not to be exhausted. But I shall here only set down the substance of what passed between us concerning my own country, reducing it into order as well as I can, without any regard to time or other circumstances, while I strictly adhere to truth. My only concern is, that I shall hardly be able to do justice to my master's arguments and expressions, which must needs suffer by my want of capacity, as well as by a translation into our barbarous English.[8]

In obedience therefore to his Honor's commands, I related to him the Revolution under the Prince of Orange,[9] the long war with France[1] entered into by the said Prince, and renewed by his successor the present Queen, wherein the greatest powers of Christendom were engaged, and which still continued: I computed, at his request, that about a million of Yahoos might have been killed in the whole progress of it, and perhaps a hundred or more cities taken, and five times as many ships burnt or sunk.

He asked me what were the usual causes or motives that made one country go to war with another. I answered they were innumerable, but I should only mention a few of the chief. Sometimes the ambition of princes, who never think they have land or people enough to govern; sometimes the corruption of ministers, who engage their

7. Better explanation.
8. Presumably "barbarous," because English both lacks appropriate words to express Houyhnhnm concepts and has concepts (e.g., of lust, malice, envy) for which the other language has no words.
9. The Glorious Revolution of 1688 by which William of

Orange, and his wife, Mary Stuart, ascended to the English throne in 1689.
1. The War of the League of Augsburg (1689–1697) and the War of the Spanish Succession (1701–1713), which Swift (as a good Tory) opposed.

master in a war in order to stifle or divert the clamor of the subjects against their evil administration. Difference in opinions[2] hath cost many millions of lives: for instance, whether *flesh* be *bread,* or *bread* be *flesh;* whether the juice of a certain *berry* be *blood* or *wine;* whether *whistling* be a vice or a virtue; whether it be better to *kiss a post,* or throw it into the fire; what is the best color for a *coat,* whether *black, white, red,* or *grey;* and whether it should be *long* or *short, narrow* or *wide, dirty* or *clean,* with many more. Neither are any wars so furious and bloody, or of so long continuance, as those occasioned by difference in opinion, especially if it be in things indifferent.[3]

Sometimes the quarrel between two princes is to decide which of them shall dispossess a third of his dominions, where neither of them pretend to any right. Sometimes one prince quarrels with another, for fear the other should quarrel with him. Sometimes a war is entered upon, because the enemy is too *strong,* and sometimes because he is too *weak.* Sometimes our neighbors *want* the *things* which we *have,* or *have* the *things* which we *want;* and we both fight, till they take ours or give us theirs. It is a very justifiable cause of war to invade a country after the people have been wasted by famine, destroyed by pestilence, or embroiled by factions amongst themselves.[4] It is justifiable to enter into a war against our nearest ally, when one of his towns lies convenient for us, or a territory of land, that would render our dominions round and compact. If a prince send forces into a nation where the people are poor and ignorant, he may lawfully put half of them to death, and make slaves of the rest, in order to civilize and reduce[5] them from their barbarous way of living. It is a very kingly, honorable, and frequent practice, when one prince desires the assistance of another to secure him against an invasion, that the assistant, when he hath driven out the invader, should seize on the dominions himself, and kill, imprison, or banish the prince he came to relieve. Alliance by blood or marriage is a sufficient cause of war between princes, and the nearer the kindred is, the greater is their disposition to quarrel: *poor* nations are *hungry,* and *rich* nations are *proud,* and pride and hunger will ever be at variance. For these reasons, the trade of a *soldier* is held the most honorable of all others: because a *soldier* is a Yahoo hired to kill in cold blood as many of his own species, who have never offended him, as possibly he can.

There is likewise a kind of beggarly princes in Europe, not able to make war by themselves, who hire out their troops to richer nations, for so much a day to each man; of which they keep three fourths to themselves, and it is the best part of their maintenance; such are those in Germany and other northern parts of Europe.[6]

What you have told me (said my master), upon the subject of war, doth indeed discover most admirably the effects of that reason you pretend to: however, it is happy that the *shame* is greater than the *danger;* and that Nature hath left you utterly uncapable of doing much mischief. For your mouths lying flat with your faces, you can hardly bite each other to any purpose, unless by consent. Then as to the claws upon your feet before and behind, they are so short and tender, that one of our Yahoos would drive a dozen of yours before him. And therefore in recounting the numbers of those who have been killed in battle, I cannot but think that you have *said the thing which is not.*

---

2. Religious controversies, over the doctrine of transsubstantiation, the place of music (whistling) and images (the post) in church, and the color and style of liturgical vestments.
3. Of no importance either way.

4. Probably a reference to the English Civil War of 1642–1648.
5. Convert.
6. George I employed German mercenaries in his defense of Hannover.

I could not forbear shaking my head and smiling a little at his ignorance. And, being no stranger to the art of war, I gave him a description of cannons, culverins,[7] muskets, carabines,[8] pistols, bullets, powder, swords, bayonets, battles, sieges, retreats, attacks, undermines, countermines,[9] bombardments, seafights; ships sunk with a thousand men, twenty thousand killed on each side; dying groans, limbs flying in the air, smoke, noise, confusion, trampling to death under horses' feet; flight, pursuit, victory; fields strewed with carcasses left for food to dogs, and wolves, and birds of prey; plundering, stripping, ravishing, burning, and destroying. And to set forth the valor of my own dear countrymen, I assured him, that I had seen them blow up a hundred enemies at once in a siege, and as many in a ship, and beheld the dead bodies drop down in pieces from the clouds, to the great diversion of all the spectators.

I was going on to more particulars, when my master commanded me silence. He said, whoever understood the nature of Yahoos might easily believe it possible for so vile an animal to be capable of every action I had named, if their strength and cunning equaled their malice. But as my discourse had increased his abhorrence of the whole species, so he found it gave him a disturbance in his mind, to which he was wholly a stranger before. He thought his ears being used to such abominable words, might by degrees admit them with less detestation. That although he hated the Yahoos of this country, yet he no more blamed them for their odious qualities, than he did a *gnnayh* (a bird of prey) for its cruelty, or a sharp stone for cutting his hoof. But when a creature pretending to reason could be capable of such enormities, he dreaded lest[1] the corruption of that faculty might be worse than brutality itself. He seemed therefore confident, that instead of reason, we were only possessed of some quality fitted to increase our natural vices; as the reflection from a troubled stream returns the image of an ill-shapen body, not only *larger,* but more *distorted.*

He added, that he had heard too much upon the subject of war, both in this, and some former discourses. There was another point which a little perplexed him at present. I had said, that some of our crew left their country on account of being ruined by *law;* that I had already explained the meaning of the word; but he was at a loss how it should come to pass, that the *law* which was intended for *every* man's preservation, should be any man's ruin. Therefore he desired to be farther satisfied what I meant by *law,* and the dispensers thereof, according to the present practice in my own country; because he thought Nature and reason were sufficient guides for a reasonable animal, as we pretended to be, in showing us what we ought to do, and what to avoid.

I assured his Honor, that law was a science wherein I had not much conversed,[2] further than by employing advocates in vain, upon some injustices that had been done me; however, I would give him all the satisfaction I was able.

I said there was a society of men among us, bred up from their youth in the art of proving by words multiplied for the purpose, that white is black, and black is white, according as they are paid.[3] To this society all the rest of the people are slaves. For example, if my neighbor hath a mind to my cow, he hires a lawyer to prove that he ought to have my cow from me. I must then hire another to defend my right, it being

---

7. Large cannons.
8. Short firearms.
9. Digging under fortification walls, and counter-digging by those inside the fort to stop the besiegers.
1. Worried that.

2. Had not had much instruction.
3. Swift's satirical treatment of lawyers probably stems from his dislike of Lord Chief Justice Whitehead, who tried to force juries to give verdicts against Swift and the printer of two of his political pamphlets.

against all rules of law that any man should be allowed to speak for himself.[4] Now in this case, I who am the true owner lie under two great disadvantages. First, my lawyer, being practiced almost from his cradle in defending falsehood, is quite out of his element when he would be an advocate for justice, which as an office unnatural, he always attempts with great awkwardness, if not with ill will. The second disadvantage is, that my lawyer must proceed with great caution, or else he will be reprimanded by the judges, and abhorred by his brethren, as one who would lessen the practice[5] of the law. And therefore I have but two methods to preserve my cow. The first is to gain over my adversary's lawyer with a double fee, who will then betray his client by insinuating that he hath justice on his side. The second way is for my lawyer to make my cause appear as unjust as he can, by allowing the cow to belong to my adversary; and this if it be skillfully done will certainly bespeak[6] the favor of the Bench.

Now, your Honor is to know that these judges are persons appointed to decide all controversies of property, as well as for the trial of criminals, and picked out from the most dexterous lawyers who are grown old or lazy, and having been biased all their lives against truth and equity, lie under such a fatal necessity of favoring fraud, perjury, and oppression, that I have known several of them refuse a large bribe from the side where justice lay, rather than injure the *Faculty*[7] by doing anything unbecoming their nature or their office.

It is a maxim among these lawyers, that whatever hath been done before, may legally be done again; and therefore they take special care to record all the decisions formerly made against common justice and the general reason of mankind. These, under the name of *precedents,* they produce as authorities to justify the most iniquitous opinions; and the judges never fail of directing accordingly.

In pleading, they studiously avoid entering into the *merits* of the cause; but are loud, violent, and tedious in dwelling upon all *circumstances* which are not to the purpose. For instance, in the case already mentioned; they never desire to know what claim or title my adversary hath to my cow, but whether the said cow were red or black, her horns long or short, whether the field I graze her in be round or square, whether she were milked at home or abroad, what diseases she is subject to, and the like; after which they consult *precedents,* adjourn the cause from time to time, and in ten, twenty, or thirty years come to an issue.

It is likewise to be observed that this society hath a peculiar cant[8] and jargon of their own, that no other mortal can understand, and wherein all their laws are written, which they take special care to multiply; whereby they have wholly confounded the very essence of truth and falsehood, of right and wrong; so that it will take thirty years to decide whether the field, left me by my ancestors for six generations, belong to me or to a stranger three hundred miles off.

In the trial of persons accused for crimes against the state the method is much more short and commendable: the judge first sends to sound the disposition of those in power, after which he can easily hang or save the criminal, strictly preserving all the forms of law.

---

4. One of Swift's many references to Thomas More's *Utopia* (1516) in this discussion of the ideals of human and Houyhnhnm society. *Utopia* suggests that it is "better for each man to plead for his own cause, and tell the judge the same story he'd otherwise tell his lawyer."

5. Both profession and morally questionable dealing.
6. Gain.
7. Legal profession.
8. Both insincere and specialist language.

Here my master, interposing, said it was a pity, that creatures endowed with such prodigious abilities of mind as these lawyers, by the description I gave of them, must certainly be, were not rather encouraged to be instructors of others in wisdom and knowledge. In answer to which, I assured his Honor, that in all points out of their own trade they were usually the most ignorant and stupid generation among us, the most despicable in common conversation, avowed enemies to all knowledge and learning, and equally disposed to pervert the general reason of mankind in every other subject of discourse, as in that of their own profession.

CHAPTER 6

A continuation of the state of England. The character of a first Minister.[9]

My master was yet wholly at a loss to understand what motives could incite this race of lawyers to perplex, disquiet, and weary themselves by engaging in a confederacy of injustice, merely for the sake of injuring their fellow animals; neither could he comprehend what I meant in saying they did it for *hire.* Whereupon I was at much pains to describe to him the use of *money,* the materials it was made of, and the value of the metals; that when a Yahoo had got a great store of this precious substance, he was able to purchase whatever he had a mind to, the finest clothing, the noblest houses, great tracts of land, the most costly meats and drinks, and have his choice of the most beautiful females. Therefore since *money* alone was able to perform all these feats, our Yahoos thought they could never have enough of it to spend or to save, as they found themselves inclined from their natural bent either to profusion or avarice. That the rich man enjoyed the fruit of the poor man's labor, and the latter were a thousand to one in proportion to the former.[1] That the bulk of our people was forced to live miserably, by laboring every day for small wages to make a few live plentifully. I enlarged myself[2] much on these and many other particulars to the same purpose: but his Honor was still to seek:[3] for he went upon a supposition that all animals had a title to their share in the productions of the earth, and especially those[4] who presided over the rest. Therefore he desired I would let him know, what these costly meats were, and how any of us happened to want them. Whereupon I enumerated as many sorts as came into my head, with the various methods of dressing them, which could not be done without sending vessels by sea to every part of the world, as well for liquors to drink, as for sauces, and innumerable other conveniencies. I assured him, that this whole globe of earth must be at least three times gone round, before one of our better female Yahoos could get her breakfast, or a cup to put it in.[5] He said, that must needs be a miserable country which cannot furnish food for its own inhabitants. But what he chiefly wondered at was how such vast tracts of ground as I described should be wholly without *fresh water,* and the people put to the necessity of sending over the sea for drink. I replied, that England (the dear place of my nativity) was computed to produce three times the quantity of food more than its inhabitants are able to consume, as well as liquors extracted from grain, or pressed out of the fruit of certain trees, which made excellent drink, and the same proportion in every other convenience

---

9. Swift's first printer/publisher, Benjamin Motte, prudently added "under Queen Anne" and "in the Courts of Europe" at the end of these two sentences, respectively, to remove some of the sting from this satire on George I's reign.
1. A theme of Thomas More's *Utopia.*

2. Explained myself further.
3. Unable to understand.
4. The ruling species.
5. Coffee, tea, and chocolate were relatively new (and highly fashionable) drinks; chinaware was also imported.

of life. But in order to feed the luxury and intemperance of the males, and the vanity of the females, we sent away the greatest part of our necessary things to other countries, from whence in return we brought the materials of diseases, folly, and vice, to spend among ourselves. Hence it follows of necessity, that vast numbers of our people are compelled to seek their livelihood by begging, robbing, stealing, cheating, pimping, forswearing,[6] flattering, suborning,[7] forging, gaming, lying, fawning, hectoring,[8] voting, scribbling, stargazing,[9] poisoning, whoring, canting,[1] libeling, freethinking,[2] and the like occupations: every one of which terms, I was at much pains to make him understand.

That *wine* was not imported among us from foreign countries to supply the want of water or other drinks, but because it was a sort of liquid which made us merry, by putting us out of our senses; diverted all melancholy thoughts, begat wild extravagant imaginations in the brain, raised our hopes, and banished our fears, suspended every office of reason for a time, and deprived us of the use of our limbs, till we fell into a profound sleep; although it must be confessed, that we always awaked sick and dispirited, and that the use of this liquor filled us with diseases, which made our lives uncomfortable and short.[3]

But beside all this, the bulk of our people supported themselves by furnishing the necessities or conveniencies of life to the rich, and to each other. For instance, when I am at home and dressed as I ought to be, I carry on my body the workmanship of an hundred tradesmen; the building and furniture of my house employ as many more, and five times the number to adorn my wife.

I was going on to tell him of another sort of people, who get their livelihood by attending the sick, having upon some occasions informed his Honor that many of my crew had died of diseases. But here it was with the utmost difficulty that I brought him to apprehend what I meant. He could easily conceive, that a Houyhnhnm grew weak and heavy a few days before his death, or by some accident might hurt a limb. But that Nature, who worketh all things to perfection, should suffer any pains to breed in our bodies, he thought impossible, and desired to know the reason of so unaccountable an evil. I told him, we fed on a thousand things which operated contrary to each other; that we ate when we were not hungry, and drank without the provocation of thirst; that we sat whole nights drinking strong liquors without eating a bit, which disposed us to sloth, inflamed our bodies, and precipitated or prevented digestion. That prostitute female Yahoos acquired a certain malady, which bred rottenness in the bones of those who fell into their embraces; that this and many other diseases were propagated from father to son, so that great numbers come into the world with complicated maladies upon them; that it would be endless to give him a catalog of all diseases incident to human bodies; for they could not be fewer than five or six hundred, spread over every limb, and joint; in short, every part, external and intestine, having diseases appropriated to each. To remedy which, there was a sort of people bred up among us, in the profession or pretense of curing the sick. And because I had some skill in the faculty, I would, in gratitude to his Honor, let him know the whole mystery[4] and method by which they proceed.

---

6. Perjury.
7. Inducing through bribery.
8. Bullying.
9. Sensationalist popular astrology of the type Swift mocked when writing as "Isaac Bickerstaff" in 1708.

1. Using jargon, often for deceit.
2. Freethinkers rejected religious authority and dogma in favor of rational inquiry and speculation.
3. Swift, however, was a great wine drinker.
4. Medical secrets.

Their fundamental is, that all diseases arise from *repletion,* from whence they conclude, that a great *evacuation* of the body is necessary, either through the natural passage, or upwards at the mouth. Their next business is, from herbs, minerals, gums, oils, shells, salts, juices, seaweed, excrements, barks of trees, serpents, toads, frogs, spiders, dead men's flesh and bones, birds, beasts and fishes, to form a composition for smell and taste the most abominable, nauseous, and detestable that they can possibly contrive, which the stomach immediately rejects with loathing; and this they call a *vomit;*[5] or else from the same storehouse, with some other poisonous additions, they command us to take in at the orifice *above* or *below* (just as the physician then happens to be disposed), a medicine equally annoying and disgustful to the bowels, which, relaxing the belly, drives down all before it; and this they call a *purge,* or a *clyster.*[6] For Nature (as the physicians allege) having intended the superior anterior orifice[7] only for the *intromission* of solids and liquids, and the inferior posterior for ejection, these artists ingeniously considering that in all diseases Nature is forced out of her seat; therefore to replace her in it, the body must be treated in a manner directly contrary, by interchanging the use of each orifice, forcing solids and liquids in at the anus, and making evacuations at the mouth.

But, besides real diseases, we are subject to many that are only imaginary, for which the physicians have invented imaginary cures; these have their several names, and so have the drugs that are proper for them, and with these our female Yahoos are always infested.

One great excellency in this tribe is their skill at *prognostics,* wherein they seldom fail; their predictions in real diseases, when they rise to any degree of malignity, generally portending *death,* which is always in their power, when recovery is not: and therefore, upon any unexpected signs of amendment, after they have pronounced their sentence, rather than be accused as false prophets, they know how to approve their sagacity to the world by a seasonable dose.[8]

They are likewise of special use to husbands and wives who are grown weary of their mates, to eldest sons, to great ministers of state, and often to princes.[9]

I had formerly upon occasion discoursed with my master upon the nature of *government* in general, and particularly of our own *excellent Constitution,* deservedly the wonder and envy of the whole world. But having here accidentally mentioned a *Minister of State,* he commanded me some time after to inform him, what species of Yahoo I particularly meant by that appellation.

I told him, that a *First* or *Chief Minister of State,*[1] whom I intended to describe, was a creature wholly exempt from joy and grief, love and hatred, pity and anger; at least made use of no other passions but a violent desire of wealth, power, and titles; that he applies his words to all uses, except to the indication of his mind;[2] that he never tells a *truth,* but with an intent that you should take it for a *lie;* nor a *lie,* but with a design that you should take it for a *truth;* that those he speaks worst of behind their backs are in the surest way to preferment;[3] and whenever he begins to praise you

5. Dr. John Woodward (1665–1728), a leading member of the Royal Society, was noted for believing this method a cure for virtually all ills.

6. Enema.

7. The mouth.

8. As Swift wrote in his *Verses on the Death of Dr. Swift,* lines 131–132: "He'd rather choose that I should die / Than his prediction prove a lie."

9. The references are to Queen Caroline, Prince Frederick, and Walpole.

1. A satire on Robert Walpole, then the First Minister or "Prime Minister."

2. Real thoughts or intentions.

3. Most likely to receive a government position or promotion.

to others or to yourself, you are from that day forlorn.[4] The worst mark you can receive is a *promise,* especially when it is confirmed with an oath; after which every wise man retires, and gives over all hopes.

There are three methods by which a man may rise to be Chief Minister: the first is, by knowing how with prudence to dispose of a wife, a daughter, or a sister; the second, by betraying or undermining his predecessor; and the third is, by a *furious zeal* in public assemblies against the corruptions of the Court. But a wise prince would rather choose to employ those who practice the last of these methods; because such zealots prove always the most obsequious and subservient to the will and passions of their master. That the *Ministers* having all employments[5] at their disposal, preserve themselves in power by bribing the majority of a senate or great council; and at last, by an expedient called an *Act of Indemnity*[6] (whereof I described the nature to him) they secure themselves from after-reckonings, and retire from the public, laden with the spoils of the nation.

The palace of a *Chief Minister* is a seminary to breed up others in his own trade: the pages, lackeys, and porter, by imitating their master, become *Ministers of State* in their several districts, and learn to excel in the three principal *ingredients,* of *insolence, lying,* and *bribery.* Accordingly, they have a *subaltern*[7] court paid to them by persons of the best rank, and sometimes by the force of dexterity and impudence arrive through several gradations to be successors to their lord.

He is usually governed by a decayed wench[8] or favorite footman, who are the tunnels[9] through which all graces[1] are conveyed, and may properly be called, *in the last resort,* the governors of the kingdom.

One day my master, having heard me mention the nobility of my country, was pleased to make me a compliment which I could not pretend to deserve: that he was sure I must have been born of some noble family, because I far exceeded in shape, color, and cleanliness, all the Yahoos of his nation, although I seemed to fail in strength and agility, which must be imputed to my different way of living from those other brutes; and besides, I was not only endowed with a faculty of speech, but likewise with some rudiments of reason, to a degree, that with all his acquaintance I passed for a prodigy.

He made me observe, that among the Houyhnhnms, the white, the *sorrel,* and the *iron-grey* were not so exactly shaped as the *bay,* the *dapple-grey,* and the *black;* nor born with equal talents of mind, or a capacity to improve them; and therefore continued always in the condition of servants, without ever aspiring to match[2] out of their own race, which in that country would be reckoned monstrous and unnatural.

I made his Honor my most humble acknowledgments for the good opinion he was pleased to conceive of me; but assured him at the same time, that my birth was of the lower sort, having been born of plain, honest parents, who were just able to give me a tolerable education; that *nobility* among us was altogether a different thing from the idea he had of it; that our young *noblemen* are bred from their childhood in idleness and luxury; that as soon as years will permit, they consume their vigor and

---

4. Forsaken, ruined.
5. Government positions.
6. Swift here suggests that corrupt government ministers make themselves secure from any future legal prosecution for their illegal dealings. He refers to the Act of Indemnity and Oblivion of 1660, which pardoned almost all those who had taken part in the English Civil War (1642–1646, 1648), or the subsequent Commonwealth

government (1649–1660).
7. Lower-ranking.
8. The government minister's mistress is "decayed" either in age or in morals.
9. Routes or conduits.
1. Favors.
2. Mate.

contract odious diseases among lewd females; and when their fortunes are almost ruined, they marry some woman of mean birth, disagreeable person, and unsound constitution, merely for the sake of money, whom they hate and despise. That the productions of such marriages are generally scrofulous,[3] rickety,[4] or deformed children, by which means the family seldom continues above three generations, unless the wife take care to provide a healthy father among her neighbors or domestics, in order to improve and continue the breed. That a weak diseased body, a meager countenance, and sallow complexion are the true marks of *noble blood;* and a healthy robust appearance is so disgraceful in a man of quality, that the world concludes his real father to have been a groom, or a coachman. The imperfections of his mind run parallel with those of his body, being a composition of spleen, dullness, ignorance, caprice, sensuality, and pride.

Without the consent of this *illustrious body* no law can be enacted, repealed, or altered, and these nobles have likewise the decision of all our possessions without appeal.[5]

CHAPTER 7

The author's great love of his native country. His master's observations upon the Constitution and Administration of England, as described by the author, with parallel cases and comparisons. His master's observations upon human nature.

The reader may be disposed to wonder how I could prevail on myself to give so free a representation of my own species, among a race of mortals who were already too apt to conceive the vilest opinion of humankind from that entire congruity betwixt me and their Yahoos. But I must freely confess, that the many virtues of those excellent *quadrupeds,* placed in opposite view to human corruptions, had so far opened mine eyes and enlarged my understanding, that I began to view the actions and passions of man in a very different light, and to think the honor of my own kind not worth managing;[6] which, besides, it was impossible for me to do before a person of so acute a judgment as my master, who daily convinced me of a thousand faults in myself, whereof I had not the least perception before, and which with us would never be numbered even among human infirmities. I had likewise learned from his example an utter detestation of all falsehood or disguise; and *truth* appeared so amiable to me, that I determined upon sacrificing everything to it.

Let me deal so candidly with the reader, as to confess, that there was yet a much stronger motive for the freedom I took in my representation of things. I had not been a year in this country before I contracted such a love and veneration for the inhabitants, that I entered on a firm resolution never to return to humankind, but to pass the rest of my life among these admirable Houyhnhnms in the contemplation and practice of every virtue; where I could have no example or incitement to vice. But it was decreed by Fortune, my perpetual enemy, that so great a felicity should not fall to my share. However, it is now some comfort to reflect, that in what I said of my countrymen, I *extenuated* their faults as much as I durst before so strict an examiner, and upon every article gave as *favorable* a turn as the matter would bear. For, indeed, who is there alive that will not be swayed by his bias and partiality to the place of his birth?

---

3. Afflicted by scrofula which causes swollen glands, rashes, and scarring.
4. Having crooked bones deformed by rickets, a form of malnutrition.

5. Swift here refers to the House of Lords, the upper house of Parliament and the highest law court in the land.
6. Maintaining.

I have related the substance of several conversations I had with my master, during the greatest part of the time I had the honor to be in his service, but have indeed for brevity sake omitted much more than is here set down.

When I had answered all his questions, and his curiosity seemed to be fully satisfied, he sent for me one morning early, and commanding me to sit down at some distance (an honor which he had never before conferred upon me), he said, he had been very seriously considering my whole story, as far as it related both to myself and my country: that he looked upon us as a sort of animals to whose share, by what accident he could not conjecture, some small pittance of *reason* had fallen, whereof we made no other use than by its assistance to aggravate our *natural* corruptions, and to acquire new ones which Nature had not given us. That we disarmed ourselves of the few abilities she had bestowed, had been very successful in multiplying our original wants, and seemed to spend our whole lives in vain endeavors to supply them by our own inventions. That as to myself, it was manifest I had neither the strength or agility of a common Yahoo, that I walked infirmly on my hinder feet, had found out a contrivance to make my claws of no use or defense, and to remove the hair from my chin, which was intended as a shelter from the sun and the weather. Lastly, that I could neither run with speed, nor climb trees like my *brethren* (as he called them) the Yahoos in this country.

That our institutions of *government* and *law* were plainly owing to our gross defects in *reason,* and by consequence, in *virtue;* because *reason* alone is sufficient to govern a *rational* creature; which was therefore a character we had no pretense to challenge,[7] even from the account I had given of my own people, although he manifestly perceived, that in order to favor them I had concealed many particulars, and often *said the thing which was not.*

He was the more confirmed in this opinion, because he observed, that as I agreed in every feature of my body with other Yahoos, except where it was to my real disadvantage in point of strength, speed, and activity, the shortness of my claws, and some other particulars where Nature had no part; so from the representation I had given him of our lives, our manners, and our actions, he found as near a resemblance in the disposition of our minds. He said the Yahoos were known to hate one another more than they did any different species of animals; and the reason usually assigned, was, the odiousness of their own shapes, which all could see in the rest, but not in themselves. He had therefore begun to think it not unwise in us to *cover* our bodies, and, by that invention, conceal many of our deformities from each other, which would else be hardly supportable. But, he now found he had been mistaken, and that the dissensions of those brutes in his country were owing to the same cause with ours, as I had described them. For if (said he) you throw among five Yahoos as much food as would be sufficient for fifty, they will, instead of eating peaceably, fall together by the ears, each single one impatient to *have all to itself;* and therefore a servant was usually employed to stand by while they were feeding abroad, and those kept at home were tied at a distance from each other; that if a cow died of age or accident, before a Houyhnhnm could secure it for his own Yahoos, those in the neighborhood would come in herds to seize it, and then would ensue such a battle as I had described, with terrible wounds made by their claws on both sides, although they seldom were able to kill one another, for want of such convenient instruments of death as we had invented. At other times the like battles have been fought between the Yahoos of several neighborhoods without any

7. We had no right to claim to be rational creatures.

visible cause: those of one district watching all opportunities to surprise the next before they are prepared. But if they find their project hath miscarried, they return home, and for want of enemies, engage in what I call a civil war among themselves.

That in some fields of his country there are certain *shining stones* of several colors, whereof the Yahoos are violently fond, and when part of these *stones* are fixed in the earth, as it sometimes happens, they will dig with their claws for whole days to get them out, and carry them away, and hide them by heaps in their kennels; but still looking round with great caution, for fear their comrades should find out their treasure. My master said, he could never discover the reason of this unnatural appetite, or how these *stones* could be of any use to a Yahoo; but now he believed it might proceed from the same principle of *avarice* which I had ascribed to mankind; that he had once, by way of experiment, privately removed a heap of these *stones* from the place where one of his Yahoos had buried it: whereupon, the sordid animal, missing his treasure, by his loud lamenting brought the whole herd to the place, there miserably howled, then fell to biting and tearing the rest, began to pine away, would neither eat, nor sleep, nor work, till he ordered a servant privately to convey the *stones* into the same hole, and hide them as before; which when his Yahoo had found, he presently recovered his spirits and good humor, but took care to remove them to a better hiding place, and hath ever since been a very serviceable brute.

My master farther assured me, which I also observed myself, that in the fields where these *shining stones* abound, the fiercest and most frequent battles are fought, occasioned by perpetual inroads of the neighboring Yahoos.[8]

He said, it was common, when two Yahoos discovered such a *stone* in a field, and were contending which of them should be the proprietor, a third would take the advantage,[9] and carry it away from them both; which my master would needs contend to have some resemblance with our *suits at law;* wherein I thought it for our credit not to undeceive him; since the decision he mentioned was much more equitable than many decrees among us: because the plaintiff and defendant there lost nothing beside the *stone* they contended for, whereas our *Courts of Equity*[1] would never have dismissed the cause while either of them had anything left.

My master, continuing his discourse, said, there was nothing that rendered the Yahoos more odious, than their undistinguishing appetite to devour everything that came in their way, whether herbs, roots, berries, the corrupted flesh of animals, or all mingled together; and it was peculiar in their temper, that they were fonder of what they could get by rapine or stealth at a greater distance, than much better food provided for them at home. If their prey held out, they would eat till they were ready to burst, after which Nature had pointed out to them a certain *root* that gave them a general evacuation.

There was also another kind of *root* very *juicy,* but something rare and difficult to be found, which the Yahoos sought for with much eagerness, and would suck it with great delight; and it produced in them the same effects that wine hath upon us. It would make them sometimes hug, and sometimes tear one another; they would howl and grin, and chatter, and reel, and tumble, and then fall asleep in the mud.

I did indeed observe, that the Yahoos were the only animals in this country subject to any diseases; which, however, were much fewer than horses have among us, and contracted not by any ill treatment they meet with, but by the nastiness and greediness

8. Neighboring Yahoos attempt invasions to steal these stones.
9. Opportunity.

1. Courts that decide on general (rather than common) principles of law. Swift ironically plays on the name of the court.

of that sordid brute. Neither has their language any more than a general appellation for those maladies, which is borrowed from the name of the beast, and called *hnea-Yahoo,* or the *Yahoo's-evil,* and the cure prescribed is a mixture of *their own dung* and *urine* forcibly put down the Yahoo's throat. This I have since often known to have been taken with success, and do here freely recommend it to my countrymen, for the public good, as an admirable specific against all diseases produced by repletion.[2]

As to learning, government, arts, manufactures, and the like, my master confessed he could find little or no resemblance between the Yahoos of that country and those in ours. For, he only meant to observe what parity there was in our natures. He had heard indeed some curious Houyhnhnms observe, that in most herds there was a sort of ruling Yahoo (as among us there is generally some leading or principal stag in a park), who was always more *deformed* in body, and *mischievous* in *disposition,* than any of the rest. That this *leader* had usually a favorite as *like himself* as he could get, whose employment was to *lick his master's feet and posteriors, and drive the female Yahoos to his kennel;* for which he was now and then rewarded with a piece of ass's flesh. This *favorite* is hated by the whole herd, and therefore to protect himself, keeps always *near the person of his leader.* He usually continues in office till a worse can be found; but the very moment he is discarded, his successor, at the head of all the Yahoos in that district, young and old, male and female, come in a body, and discharge their excrements upon him from head to foot. But how far this might be applicable to our *Courts* and *favorites,* and *Ministers of State,* my master said I could best determine.

I durst make no return to this malicious insinuation, which debased human understanding below the sagacity of a common *hound,* who hath judgment enough to distinguish and follow the cry of the *ablest dog in the pack,* without being ever mistaken.

My master told me, there were some qualities remarkable in the Yahoos, which he had not observed me to mention, or at least very slightly, in the accounts I had given him of humankind: he said, those animals, like other brutes, had their females in common;[3] but in this they differed, that the she-Yahoo would admit the male while she was pregnant, and that the hes[4] would quarrel and fight with the females as fiercely as with each other. Both which practices were such degrees of infamous brutality, that no other sensitive[5] creature ever arrived at.

Another thing he wondered at in the Yahoos, was their strange disposition to nastiness and dirt, whereas there appears to be a natural love of cleanliness in all other animals. As to the two former accusations, I was glad to let them pass without any reply, because I had not a word to offer upon them in defense of my species, which otherwise I certainly had done from my own inclinations. But I could have easily vindicated humankind from the imputation of singularity upon the last article, if there had been any *swine* in that country (as unluckily for me there were not), which although it may be a *sweeter quadruped* than a Yahoo, cannot, I humbly conceive, in justice pretend to more cleanliness; and so his Honor himself must have owned, if he had seen their filthy way of feeding, and their custom of wallowing and sleeping in the mud.

My master likewise mentioned another quality which his servants had discovered in several Yahoos, and to him was wholly unaccountable. He said, a fancy would sometimes take a Yahoo to retire into a corner, to lie down and howl, and groan, and spurn away all that came near him, although he were young and fat, and wanted neither food nor water; nor did the servants imagine what could possibly ail him. And the

---

2. Congestion. See p. 375.
3. Implying that English society did the same.
4. The males.
5. Feeling.

only remedy they found was to set him to hard work, after which he would infallibly come to himself. To this I was silent out of partiality to my own kind; yet here I could plainly discover the true seeds of *spleen*,[6] which only seizeth on the *lazy,* the *luxurious,* and the *rich;* who, if they were forced to undergo the *same regimen,* I would undertake for[7] the cure.

His Honor had farther observed, that a female Yahoo would often stand behind a bank or a bush, to gaze on the young males passing by, and then appear, and hide, using many antic gestures and grimaces, at which time it was observed, that she had a most *offensive smell;* and when any of the males advanced, would slowly retire, looking often back, and with a counterfeit show of fear, run off into some convenient place where she knew the male would follow her.[8]

At other times if a female stranger came among them, three or four of her own sex would get about her, and stare and chatter, and grin, and smell her all over, and then turn off with gestures that seemed to express contempt and disdain.

Perhaps my master might refine a little in these speculations, which he had drawn from what he observed himself, or had been told him by others; however, I could not reflect without some amazement, and much sorrow, that the rudiments of *lewdness, coquetry, censure,* and *scandal,* should have place by instinct in womankind.

I expected every moment that my master would accuse the Yahoos of those unnatural appetites in both sexes, so common among us. But Nature it seems hath not been so expert a schoolmistress; and these politer pleasures are entirely the productions of art and reason, on our side of the globe.

CHAPTER 8

The author relateth several particulars of the Yahoos. The great virtues of the Houyhnhnms. The education and exercise of their youth. Their general Assembly.

As I ought to have understood human nature much better than I supposed it possible for my master to do, so it was easy to apply the character he gave of the Yahoos to myself and my countrymen, and I believed I could yet make farther discoveries from my own observation. I therefore often begged his Honor to let me go among the herds of Yahoos in the neighborhood, to which he always very graciously consented, being perfectly convinced that the hatred I bore those brutes would never suffer me to be corrupted by them; and his Honor ordered one of his servants, a strong sorrel nag, very honest and good-natured, to be my guard, without whose protection I durst not undertake such adventures. For I have already told the reader how much I was pestered by those odious animals upon my first arrival. I afterwards failed very narrowly three or four times of falling into their clutches, when I happened to stray at any distance without my hanger. And I have reason to believe they had some imagination that I was of their own species, which I often assisted myself, by stripping up my sleeves, and showing my naked arms and breast in their sight, when my protector was with me. At which times they would approach as near as they durst, and imitate my actions after the manner of monkeys, but ever with great signs of hatred, as a tame *jackdaw*,[9] with cap and stockings, is always persecuted by the wild ones, when he happens to be got among them.

---

6. Depression with physical symptoms.
7. Guarantee.
8. The sort of seduction tactics used by female characters

in literary pastoral.
9. Small crow, often kept as a pet.

They are prodigiously nimble from their infancy; however, I once caught a young male of three years old, and endeavored by all marks of tenderness to make it quiet; but the little imp fell a squalling, and scratching, and biting with such violence, that I was forced to let it go, and it was high time, for a whole troop of old ones came about us at the noise, but finding the cub was safe (for away it ran), and my sorrel nag being by, they durst not venture near us. I observed the young animal's flesh to smell very rank, and the stink was somewhat between a *weasel* and a *fox,* but much more disagreeable. I forgot another circumstance (and perhaps I might have the reader's pardon, if it were wholly omitted), that while I held the odious vermin in my hands, it voided its filthy excrements of a yellow liquid substance all over my clothes; but by good fortune there was a small brook hard by, where I washed myself as clean as I could, although I durst not come into my master's presence, until I were sufficiently aired.

By what I could discover, the Yahoos appear to be the most unteachable of all animals, their capacities never reaching higher than to draw or carry burdens. Yet I am of opinion this defect ariseth chiefly from a perverse, restive[1] disposition. For they are cunning, malicious, treacherous, and revengeful. They are strong and hardy, but of a cowardly spirit, and by consequence insolent, abject, and cruel. It is observed, that the *red-haired* of both sexes are more libidinous and mischievous than the rest, whom yet they much exceed in strength and activity.[2]

The Houyhnhnms keep the Yahoos for present[3] use in huts not far from the house; but the rest are sent abroad to certain fields, where they dig up roots, eat several kinds of herbs, and search about for carrion, or sometimes catch weasels and *luhimuhs* (a sort of wild rat), which they greedily devour. Nature hath taught them to dig deep holes with their nails on the side of a rising ground, wherein they lie by themselves, only the kennels of the females are larger, sufficient to hold two or three cubs.

They swim from their infancy like frogs, and are able to continue long under water, where they often take fish, which the females carry home to their young. And upon this occasion, I hope the reader will pardon my relating an odd adventure.

Being one day abroad with my protector the sorrel nag, and the weather exceeding hot, I entreated him to let me bathe in a river that was near. He consented, and I immediately stripped myself stark naked, and went down softly into the stream. It happened that a young female Yahoo, standing behind a bank, saw the whole proceeding, and inflamed by desire, as the nag and I conjectured, came running with all speed, and leaped into the water within five yards of the place where I bathed. I was never in my life so terribly frighted; the nag was grazing at some distance, not suspecting any harm. She embraced me after a most fulsome manner; I roared as loud as I could, and the nag came galloping towards me, whereupon she quitted her grasp, with the utmost reluctancy, and leaped upon the opposite bank, where she stood gazing and howling all the time I was putting on my clothes.

This was matter of diversion to my master and his family, as well as of mortification to myself. For now I could no longer deny, that I was a real Yahoo in every limb and feature, since the females had a natural propensity to me as one of their own species; neither was the hair of this brute of a red color (which might have been some excuse for an appetite a little irregular) but black as a sloe,[4] and her countenance did not make an appearance altogether so hideous as the rest of the kind; for, I think, she could not be above eleven years old.[5]

---

1. Stubborn.
2. A prejudice dating back to medieval times.
3. Daily.
4. A wild berry.

5. The disparity in age between Gulliver and the Yahoo may suggest a grotesque parody of Esther Vanhomrigh's pursuit of Swift, she being 21 years his junior.

Having already lived three years in this country, the reader I suppose will expect that I should, like other travelers, give him some account of the manners and customs of its inhabitants, which it was indeed my principal study to learn.

As these noble Houyhnhnms are endowed by Nature with a general disposition to all virtues, and have no conceptions or ideas of what is evil in a rational creature, so their grand maxim is, to cultivate *Reason,* and to be wholly governed by it. Neither is *Reason* among them a point problematical as with us, where men can argue with plausibility on both sides of a question, but strikes you with immediate conviction, as it must needs do where it is not mingled, obscured, or discolored by passion and interest.[6] I remember it was with extreme difficulty that I could bring my master to understand the meaning of the word opinion, or how a point could be disputable, because *Reason* taught us to affirm or deny only where we are certain, and beyond our knowledge we cannot do either.[7] So that controversies, wranglings, disputes, and positiveness[8] in false or dubious propositions are evils unknown among the Houyhnhnms. In the like manner, when I used to explain to him our several systems of *natural philosophy,* he would laugh that a creature pretending to *Reason* should value itself upon the knowledge of other people's conjectures, and in things where that knowledge, if it were certain, could be of no use. Wherein he agreed entirely with the sentiments of Socrates, as Plato delivers them;[9] which I mention as the highest honor I can do that prince of philosophers. I have often since reflected what destruction such a doctrine would make in the libraries of Europe, and how many paths to fame would be then shut up in the learned world.

Friendship and benevolence are the two principal virtues among the Houyhnhnms, and these not confined to particular objects,[1] but universal to the whole race. For a stranger from the remotest part is equally treated with the nearest neighbor, and wherever he goes, looks upon himself as at home. They preserve *decency* and *civility* in the highest degrees, but are altogether ignorant of *ceremony.*[2] They have no fondness for their colts or foals, but the care they take in educating them proceedeth entirely from the dictates of *Reason.* And I observed my master to show the same affection to his neighbor's issue that he had for his own.[3] They will have it that *Nature* teaches them to love the whole species, and it is *Reason* only that maketh a distinction of persons, where there is a superior degree of virtue.

When the matron Houyhnhnms have produced one of each sex, they no longer accompany with[4] their consorts, except they lose one of their issue by some casualty, which very seldom happens: but in such a case they meet again. Or when the like accident befalls a person,[5] whose wife is past bearing, some other couple bestow him one of their own colts, and then go together a second time, till the mother be pregnant. This caution is necessary to prevent the country from being overburdened with numbers.[6] But the race of inferior Houyhnhnms bred up to be servants is not so strictly limited upon this article; these are allowed to produce three of each sex, to be domestics in the noble families.

6. Prejudice based on interest in personal benefit. Both Descartes (*Discourse on Method*) and Locke (*Essay Concerning Human Understanding*) wrote of the intuitive nature of some knowledge.
7. Gulliver's master has clearly expressed "opinion" (i.e., prejudice) himself, however.
8. Assertiveness.
9. I.e., that ethics (human nature) is worth studying, while the physical world is not, as we can never have certain knowledge of it: "Socrates: I am a friend of learning—the trees and the countryside won't teach me anything, but the people in the city do" (*Phaedrus* 230d3–5).
1. To other, particular Houyhnhnms.
2. As are the Utopians.
3. As do men in Plato's *Republic* (461d).
4. Have sex with.
5. A male Houyhnhnm.
6. The Utopians are under no such restriction, knowing (as the Houyhnhnms do not) of other lands to which they can send their excess population.

In their marriages they are exactly careful to choose such colors as will not make any disagreeable mixture in the breed.[7] *Strength* is chiefly valued in the male, and *comeliness* in the female, not upon the account of *love,* but to preserve the race from degenerating; for where a female happens to excel in strength, a consort is chosen with regard to *comeliness.* Courtship, love, presents, jointures,[8] settlements, have no place in their thoughts, or terms whereby to express them in their language. The young couple meet and are joined, merely because it is the determination of their parents and friends: it is what they see done every day, and they look upon it as one of the necessary actions in a reasonable being. But the violation of marriage, or any other unchastity, was never heard of, and the married pair pass their lives with the same friendship, and mutual benevolence that they bear to others of the same species who come in their way; without jealousy, fondness, quarreling, or discontent.

In educating the youth of both sexes, their method is admirable, and highly deserveth our imitation. These are not suffered to taste a grain of *oats,* except upon certain days, till eighteen years old; nor *milk,* but very rarely; and in summer they graze two hours in the morning, and as many in the evening, which their parents likewise observe, but the servants are not allowed above half that time, and a great part of their grass is brought home, which they eat at the most convenient hours, when they can be best spared from work.

Temperance, industry, exercise, and *cleanliness,* are the lessons equally enjoined to the young ones of both sexes, and my master thought it monstrous in us to give the females a different kind of education from the males, except in some articles of domestic management;[9] whereby as he truly observed, one half of our natives were good for nothing but bringing children into the world, and to trust the care of their children to such useless animals, he said, was yet a greater instance of brutality.

But the Houyhnhnms train up their youth to strength, speed, and hardiness, by exercising them in running races up and down steep hills, or over hard stony grounds, and when they are all in a sweat, they are ordered to leap over head and ears into a pond or a river. Four times a year the youth of certain districts meet to show their proficiency in running, and leaping, and other feats of strength or agility, where the victor is rewarded with a song made in his or her praise. On this festival the servants drive a herd of Yahoos into the field, laden with hay, and oats, and milk for a repast to the Houyhnhnms; after which, these brutes are immediately driven back again, for fear of being noisome to the assembly.

Every fourth year, at the *vernal equinox,* there is a Representative Council of the whole nation, which meets in a plain about twenty miles from our house, and continueth about five or six days. Here they inquire into the state and condition of the several districts, whether they abound or be deficient in hay or oats, or cows or Yahoos? And wherever there is any want (which is but seldom) it is immediately supplied by unanimous consent and contribution. Here likewise the regulation of children is settled: as for instance, if a Houyhnhnm hath two males, he changeth one of them with another who hath two females: and when a child hath been lost by any casualty, where the mother is past breeding, it is determined what family in the district shall breed another to supply the loss.

---

7. In Plato's *Republic* (458d–461e), eugenic principles also control mating.
8. Marriage settlements for wives, should they survive their husbands.

9. In both Plato's *Republic* (451e6–7) and *Utopia,* the sexes receive the same education; Swift also began (but never completed) an essay entitled *Of the Education of Ladies* (c. 1728).

CHAPTER 9

A grand debate at the general Assembly of the Houyhnhnms, and how it was deter-mined. The learning of the Houyhnhnms. Their buildings. Their manner of burials. The defectiveness of their language.

One of these grand Assemblies was held in my time, about three months before my departure, whither my master went as the Representative of our district. In this Coun-cil was resumed their old debate, and indeed, the only debate that ever happened in their country; whereof my master after his return gave me a very particular account.

The question to be debated, was, whether the Yahoos should be exterminated from the face of the earth. One of the *members* for the affirmative offered several arguments of great strength and weight, alleging, that as the Yahoos were the most filthy, noisome, and deformed animal which Nature ever produced, so they were the most restive and in-docible,[1] mischievous, and malicious: they would privately suck the teats of the Houy-hnhnms' cows, kill and devour their cats, trample down their oats and grass, if they were not continually watched, and commit a thousand other extravagancies. He took notice of a general tradition, that Yahoos had not been always in their country, but, that many ages ago, two of these brutes appeared together upon a mountain,[2] whether pro-duced by the heat of the sun upon corrupted mud and slime, or from the ooze and froth of the sea, was never known.[3] That these Yahoos engendered, and their brood in a short time grew so numerous as to overrun and infest the whole nation. That the Houy-hnhnms, to get rid of this evil, made a general hunting, and at last enclosed the whole herd; and destroying the elder, every Houyhnhnm kept two young ones in a kennel, and brought them to such a degree of tameness, as an animal so savage by nature can be ca-pable of acquiring; using them for draft and carriage. That there seemed to be much truth in this tradition, and that those creatures could not be *ylnhniamshy* (or *aborigines* of the land) because of the violent hatred the Houyhnhnms, as well as all other animals, bore them; which although their evil disposition sufficiently deserved, could never have arrived at so high a degree, if they had been *aborigines,* or else they would have long since been rooted out. That the inhabitants taking a fancy to use the service of the Ya-hoos, had very imprudently neglected to cultivate the breed of *asses,* which were a comely animal, easily kept, more tame and orderly, without any offensive smell, strong enough for labor, although they yield to the other in agility of body; and if their braying be no agreeable sound, it is far preferable to the horrible howlings of the Yahoos.[4]

Several others declared their sentiments to the same purpose, when my master proposed an expedient to the assembly, whereof he had indeed borrowed the hint from me. He approved of the tradition, mentioned by the Honorable Member who spoke before, and affirmed, that the two Yahoos said to be first seen among them had been driven thither over the sea; that coming to land, and being forsaken by their companions, they retired to the mountains, and degenerating by degrees, became in process of time, much more savage than those of their own species in the country from whence these two originals came. The reason of his assertion was, that he had now in his possession a certain wonderful[5] Yahoo (meaning myself), which most of

1. Unteachable.
2. Probably Milton's "steep savage Hill," the garden of Eden (*Paradise Lost,* 4.172).
3. Humans are supposed to be of divine origin, but the Yahoos represent such a degraded form of humanity that they (like, it was believed, insects on the Nile's banks)

were formed from the action of the sun on mud.
4. The commonplace comparison of humans to asses was one Swift had previously used in *A Tale of a Tub* (1704) and *The Battle of the Books* (1704).
5. Amazing, unusual.

them had heard of, and many of them had seen. He then related to them, how he first found me: that my body was all covered with an artificial composure of the skins and hairs of other animals; that I spoke in a language of my own, and had thoroughly learned theirs; that I had related to him the accidents which brought me thither; that when he saw me without my covering, I was an exact Yahoo in every part, only of a whiter color, less hairy, and with shorter claws. He added, how I had endeavored to persuade him, that in my own and other countries the Yahoos acted as the governing, rational animal, and held the Houyhnhnms in servitude; that he observed in me all the qualities of a Yahoo, only a little more civilized by some tincture of reason, which however was in a degree as far inferior to the Houyhnhnm race, as the Yahoos of their country were to me;[6] that, among other things, I mentioned a custom we had of *castrating* Houyhnhnms when they were young, in order to render them tame; that the operation was easy and safe; that it was no shame to learn wisdom from brutes, as industry is taught by the ant, and building by the swallow. (For so I translate the word *lyhannh*, although it be a much larger fowl.) That this invention might be practiced upon the younger Yahoos here, which, besides rendering them tractable and fitter for use, would in an age put an end to the whole species without destroying life. That, in the meantime the Houyhnhnms should be exhorted to cultivate the breed of asses, which, as they are in all respects more valuable brutes, so they have this advantage, to be fit for service at five years old, which the others are not till twelve.

This was all my master thought fit to tell me at that time, of what passed in the grand Council. But he was pleased to conceal[7] one particular, which related personally to myself, whereof I soon felt the unhappy effect, as the reader will know in its proper place, and from whence I date all the succeeding misfortunes of my life.

The Houyhnhnms have no letters, and consequently their knowledge is all traditional. But there happening few events of any moment among a people so well united, naturally disposed to every virtue, wholly governed by reason, and cut off from all commerce with other nations, the historical part is easily preserved without burdening their memories. I have already observed, that they are subject to no diseases, and therefore can have no need of physicians. However, they have excellent medicines composed of herbs, to cure accidental bruises and cuts in the pastern or frog of the foot by sharp stones, as well as other maims and hurts in the several parts of the body.

They calculate the year by the revolution of the sun and the moon, but use no subdivisions into weeks. They are well enough acquainted with the motions of those two luminaries, and understand the nature of eclipses; and this is the utmost progress of their astronomy.

In poetry they must be allowed to excel all other mortals; wherein the justness of their similes, and the minuteness, as well as exactness of their descriptions, are indeed inimitable. Their verses abound very much in both of these, and usually contain either some exalted notions of friendship and benevolence, or the praises of those who were victors in races, and other bodily exercises.[8] Their buildings, although very rude and simple, are not inconvenient, but well contrived to defend them from all injuries of cold and heat. They have a kind of tree, which at forty years old loosens in the root, and falls with the first storm; it grows very straight, and being pointed like stakes with

---

6. Gulliver falls between the Houyhnhnms and the Yahoos in reason, as he did between the Lilliputians and the Brobdingnagians in size.

7. Another indication that the Houyhnhnms are not completely honest or candid.

8. The type of poetry advocated in Plato's *Republic* (390d1–3) and practiced in Sparta.

a sharp stone (for the Houyhnhnms know not the use of iron), they stick them erect in the ground about ten inches asunder,[9] and then weave in oat-straw, or sometimes wattles betwixt them. The roof is made after the same manner, and so are the doors.

The Houyhnhnms use the hollow part between the pastern and the hoof of their forefeet as we do our hands, and this with greater dexterity than I could at first imagine. I have seen a white mare of our family thread a needle (which I lent her on purpose) with that joint. They milk their cows, reap their oats, and do all the work which requires hands, in the same manner. They have a kind of hard flints, which by grinding against other stones, they form into instruments, that serve instead of wedges, axes, and hammers. With tools made of these flints they likewise cut their hay, and reap their oats, which there groweth naturally in several fields: the Yahoos draw home the sheaves in carriages, and the servants tread them in certain covered huts, to get out the grain, which is kept in stores. They make a rude kind of earthen and wooden vessels, and bake the former in the sun.

If they can avoid casualties, they die only of old age, and are buried in the obscurest places that can be found, their friends and relations expressing neither joy nor grief at their departure; nor does the dying person discover the least regret that he is leaving the world, any more than if he were upon returning[1] home from a visit to one of his neighbors;[2] I remember, my master having once made an appointment with a friend and his family to come to his house upon some affair of importance, on the day fixed, the mistress and her two children came very late; she made two excuses, first for her husband, who, as she said, happened that very morning to *lhnuwnh.* The word is strongly expressive in their language, but not easily rendered into English; it signifies, *to retire to his first mother.* Her excuse for not coming sooner, was, that her husband dying late in the morning, she was a good while consulting her servants about a convenient place where his body should be laid; and I observed she behaved herself at our house as cheerfully as the rest; she died about three months after.

They live generally to seventy or seventy-five years, very seldom to fourscore; some weeks before their death they feel a gradual decay, but without pain. During this time they are much visited by their friends, because they cannot go abroad with their usual ease and satisfaction. However, about ten days before their death, which they seldom fail in computing, they return the visits that have been made them by those who are nearest in the neighborhood, being carried in a convenient sledge drawn by Yahoos, which vehicle they use, not only upon this occasion, but when they grow old, upon long journeys, or when they are lamed by an accident. And therefore when the dying Houyhnhnms return those visits, they take a solemn leave of their friends, as if they were going to some remote part of the country, where they designed to pass the rest of their lives.

I know not whether it may be worth observing, that the Houyhnhnms have no word in their language to express anything that is *evil,* except what they borrow from the deformities or ill qualities of the Yahoos. Thus they denote the folly of a servant, an omission of a child, a stone that cuts their feet, a continuance of foul or unseasonable weather, and the like, by adding to each the epithet of *yahoo.* For instance, *hhnm yahoo, whnaholm yahoo, ynlhmnawihlma yahoo,* and an ill-contrived house, *ynholmhnmrohlnw yahoo.*

I could with great pleasure enlarge farther upon the manners and virtues of this excellent people; but intending in a short time to publish a volume by itself expressly

9. Apart.
1. About to return.

2. This attitude toward death is characteristic of both the Stoics and the Utopians.

upon that subject, I refer the reader thither. And in the meantime, proceed to relate my own sad catastrophe.

CHAPTER 10

The author's economy[3] and happy life among the Houyhnhnms. His great improvement in virtue, by conversing with them. Their conversations. The author hath notice given him by his master that he must depart from the country. He falls into a swoon for grief, but submits. He contrives and finishes a canoe, by the help of a fellow servant, and puts to sea at a venture.[4]

I had settled my little economy to my own heart's content. My master had ordered a room to be made for me after their manner, about six yards from the house, the sides and floors of which I plastered with clay, and covered with rush mats of my own contriving; I had beaten hemp, which there grows wild, and made of it a sort of ticking;[5] this I filled with the feathers of several birds I had taken with springes made of Yahoos' hairs, and were excellent food. I had worked[6] two chairs with my knife, the sorrel nag helping me in the grosser[7] and more laborious part. When my clothes were worn to rags, I made myself others with the skins of rabbits, and of a certain beautiful animal about the same size, called *nnuhnoh,* the skin of which is covered with a fine down. Of these I likewise made very tolerable stockings. I soled my shoes with wood which I cut from a tree, and fitted to the upper leather, and when this was worn out, I supplied it with the skins of Yahoos dried in the sun. I often got honey out of hollow trees, which I mingled with water,[8] or ate it with my bread. No man could more verify the truth of these two maxims, *That nature is very easily satisfied;* and, *That necessity is the mother of invention.* I enjoyed perfect health of body and tranquillity of mind; I did not feel the treachery or inconstancy of a friend, nor the injuries of a secret or open enemy. I had no occasion of bribing, flattering, or pimping, to procure the favor of any great man or of his minion. I wanted no fence[9] against fraud or oppression; here was neither physician to destroy my body, nor lawyer to ruin my fortune; no informer to watch my words and actions, or forge accusations against me for hire; here were no jibers, censurers, backbiters, pickpockets, highwaymen, housebreakers, attorneys, bawds, buffoons, gamesters, politicians, wits, splenetics, tedious talkers, controvertists, ravishers, murderers, robbers, virtuosos;[1] no leaders or followers of party and faction; no encouragers to vice, by seducement or examples; no dungeon, axes, gibbets, whipping posts, or pillories; no cheating shopkeepers or mechanics;[2] no pride, vanity, or affectation; no fops, bullies, drunkards, strolling whores, or poxes;[3] no ranting, lewd, expensive wives; no stupid, proud pedants; no importunate, overbearing, quarrelsome, noisy, roaring, empty, conceited, swearing companions; no scoundrels, raised from the dust upon the merit of their vices, or nobility thrown into it on account of their virtues; no lords, fiddlers, judges, or dancing masters.[4]

I had the favor of being admitted to[5] several Houyhnhnms, who came to visit or dine with my master; where his Honor graciously suffered me to wait in the room,

---

3. Method of living.
4. Without further planning.
5. Sturdy material used for making mattress covering.
6. Made.
7. Heavier, larger.
8. Honey-sweetened water was a Utopian drink.
9. Defense.
1. One knowledgeable or interested in apparently trivial

"scientific" pursuits.
2. Laborers.
3. Venereal diseases.
4. That necessary tutor for the socially aspiring, the dancing master (usually French), was a particular figure of fun; he usually accompanied himself on the fiddle.
5. Allowed to meet.

and listen to their discourse. Both he and his company would often descend to ask me questions, and receive my answers. I had also sometimes the honor of attending my master in his visits to others. I never presumed to speak, except in answer to a question, and then I did it with inward regret, because it was a loss of so much time for improving myself; but I was infinitely delighted with the station of a humble auditor in such conversations, where nothing passed but what was useful, expressed in the fewest and most significant words; where (as I have already said) the greatest *decency* was observed, without the least degree of ceremony; where no person spoke without being pleased himself, and pleasing his companions; where there was no interruption, tediousness, heat,[6] or difference of sentiments. They have a notion, that when people are met together, a short silence doth much improve conversation: this I found to be true, for during those little intermissions of talk, new ideas would arise in their minds, which very much enlivened the discourse. Their subjects are generally on friendship and benevolence, or order and economy, sometimes upon the visible operations of Nature, or ancient traditions, upon the bounds and limits of virtue, upon the unerring rules of reason, or upon some determinations to be taken at the next great Assembly, and often upon the various excellencies of *poetry.* I may add without vanity, that my presence often gave them sufficient matter for discourse, because it afforded my master an occasion of letting his friends into the history of me and my country, upon which they were all pleased to descant in a manner not very advantageous to humankind; and for that reason I shall not repeat what they said: only I may be allowed to observe, that his Honor, to my great admiration, appeared to understand the nature of Yahoos much better than myself. He went through all our vices and follies, and discovered many which I had never mentioned to him, by only supposing what qualities a Yahoo of their country, with a small proportion of reason, might be capable of exerting; and concluded, with too much probability, how vile as well as miserable such a creature must be.

I freely confess, that all the little knowledge I have of any value, was acquired by the lectures I received from my master, and from hearing the discourses of him and his friends; to which I should be prouder to listen, than to dictate to the greatest and wisest assembly in Europe. I admired the strength, comeliness, and speed of the inhabitants; and such a constellation of virtues in such amiable persons produced in me the highest veneration. At first, indeed, I did not feel that natural awe which the Yahoos and all other animals bear towards them, but it grew upon me by degrees, much sooner than I imagined, and was mingled with a respectful love and gratitude, that they would condescend to distinguish me from the rest of my species.

When I thought of my family, my friends, my countrymen, or human race in general, I considered them as they really were, Yahoos in shape and disposition, perhaps a little more civilized, and qualified with the gift of speech, but making no other use of reason, than to improve and multiply those vices, whereof their brethren in this country had only the share that Nature allotted them. When I happened to behold the reflection of my own form in a lake or a fountain, I turned away my face in horror and detestation of myself,[7] and could better endure the sight of a common Yahoo, than of my own person. By conversing with the Houyhnhnms, and looking upon them with delight, I fell to imitate their gait and gesture, which is now grown into a habit, and my friends often tell me in a blunt way, that *I trot like a horse;* which, however, I take

---

6. Heat of argument.

7. A mocking reversal both of a common pattern in pastoral love poetry and of the Greek myth of Narcissus.

for a great compliment; neither shall I disown, that in speaking I am apt to fall into the voice and manner of the Houyhnhnms, and hear myself ridiculed on that account without the least mortification.

In the midst of all this happiness, when I looked upon myself to be fully settled for life, my master sent for me one morning a little earlier than his usual hour. I observed by his countenance that he was in some perplexity, and at a loss how to begin what he had to speak. After a short silence, he told me, he did not know how I would take what he was going to say; that in the last general Assembly, when the affair of the Yahoos was entered upon, the representatives had taken offense at his keeping a Yahoo (meaning myself) in his family more like a Houyhnhnm, than a brute animal. That he was known frequently to converse with me, as if he could receive some advantage or pleasure in my company; that such a practice was not agreeable to reason or Nature, or a thing ever heard of before among them. The Assembly did therefore *exhort* him, either to employ me like the rest of my species, or command me to swim back to the place from whence I came. That the first of these expedients was utterly rejected by all the Houyhnhnms who had ever seen me at his house or their own, for they alleged, that because I had some rudiments of reason, added to the natural pravity[8] of those animals, it was to be feared, I might be able to seduce them into the woody and mountainous parts of the country, and bring them in troops by night to destroy the Houyhnhnms' cattle, as being naturally of the ravenous[9] kind, and averse from labor.

My master added, that he was daily pressed by the Houyhnhnms of the neighborhood to have the Assembly's *exhortation* executed, which he could not put off much longer. He doubted[1] it would be impossible for me to swim to another country, and therefore wished I would contrive some sort of vehicle resembling those I had described to him, that might carry me on the sea, in which work I should have the assistance of his own servants, as well as those of his neighbors. He concluded, that for his own part he could have been content to keep me in his service as long as I lived, because he found I had cured myself of some bad habits and dispositions, by endeavoring, as far as my inferior nature was capable, to imitate the Houyhnhnms.

I should here observe to the reader, that a decree of the general Assembly in this country is expressed by the word *hnhloayn,* which signifies an *exhortation,* as near as I can render it, for they have no conception how a rational creature can be *compelled,* but only advised, or *exhorted,* because no person can disobey reason, without giving up his claim to be a rational creature.

I was struck with the utmost grief and despair at my master's discourse, and being unable to support the agonies I was under, I fell into a swoon at his feet; when I came to myself, he told me, that he concluded I had been dead. (For these people are subject to no such imbecilities of nature.) I answered, in a faint voice, that death would have been too great an happiness; that although I could not blame the Assembly's *exhortation,* or the urgency[2] of his friends, yet in my weak and corrupt judgment, I thought it might consist[3] with reason to have been less rigorous. That I could not swim a league, and probably the nearest land to theirs might be distant above a hundred; that many materials, necessary for making a small vessel to carry me off, were wholly wanting in this country, which, however, I would attempt in obedience and gratitude to his Honor, although I concluded the thing to be impossible, and

8. Depravity.
9. Rapacious, predatory, or greedy.
1. Feared.

2. Urging.
3. Be consistent.

therefore looked on myself as already devoted to destruction. That the certain prospect of an unnatural death was the least of my evils: for, supposing I should escape with life by some strange adventure, how could I think with temper[4] of passing my days among Yahoos, and relapsing into my old corruptions, for want of examples to lead and keep me within the paths of virtue? That I knew too well upon what solid reasons all the determinations of the wise Houyhnhnms were founded, not to be shaken by arguments of mine, a miserable Yahoo; and therefore after presenting him with my humble thanks for the offer of his servants' assistance in making a vessel, and desiring a reasonable time for so difficult a work, I told him I would endeavor to preserve a wretched being; and, if ever I returned to England, was not without hopes of being useful to my own species, by celebrating the praises of the renowned Houyhnhnms, and proposing their virtues to the imitation of mankind.

My master in a few words made me a very gracious reply, allowed me the space of two *months* to finish my boat; and ordered the sorrel nag, my fellow servant (for so at this distance I may presume to call him) to follow my instructions, because I told my master, that his help would be sufficient, and I knew he had a tenderness for me.

In his company my first business was to go to that part of the coast, where my rebellious crew had ordered me to be set on shore. I got upon a height, and looking on every side into the sea, fancied I saw a small island, towards the northeast: I took out my pocket glass, and could then clearly distinguish it about five leagues off, as I computed; but it appeared to the sorrel nag to be only a blue cloud: for, as he had no conception of any country beside his own, so he could not be as expert in distinguishing remote objects at sea, as we who so much converse[5] in that element.

After I had discovered this island, I considered no farther; but resolved it should, if possible, be the first place of my banishment, leaving the consequence to Fortune.

I returned home, and consulting with the sorrel nag, we went into a copse at some distance, where I with my knife, and he with a sharp flint fastened very artificially, after their manner, to a wooden handle, cut down several oak wattles about the thickness of a walking staff, and some larger pieces. But I shall not trouble the reader with a particular description of my own mechanics; let it suffice to say, that in six weeks' time, with the help of the sorrel nag, who performed the parts that required most labor, I finished a sort of Indian canoe, but much larger, covering it with the skins of Yahoos well stitched together, with hempen threads of my own making. My sail was likewise composed of the skins of the same animal; but I made use of the youngest I could get, the older being too tough and thick, and I likewise provided myself with four paddles. I laid in a stock of boiled flesh, of rabbits and fowls, and took with me two vessels, one filled with milk, and the other with water.

I tried my canoe in a large pond near my master's house, and then corrected in it what was amiss; stopping all the chinks with Yahoos' tallow, till I found it staunch,[6] and able to bear me and my freight. And when it was as complete as I could possibly make it, I had it drawn on a carriage very gently by Yahoos, to the seaside, under the conduct of the sorrel nag, and another servant.

When all was ready, and the day came for my departure, I took leave of my master and lady, and the whole family, mine eyes flowing with tears, and my heart quite sunk with grief. But his Honor, out of curiosity, and perhaps (if I may speak it without vanity) partly out of kindness, was determined to see me in my canoe, and got several

4. Calmness.
5. Are familiar with.
6. Watertight.

of his neighboring friends to accompany him. I was forced to wait above an hour for the tide, and then observing the wind very fortunately bearing towards the island, to which I intended to steer my course, I took a second leave of my master, but as I was going to prostrate myself to kiss his hoof, he did me the honor to raise it gently to my mouth. I am not ignorant how much I have been censured for mentioning this last particular. For my detractors are pleased to think it improbable, that so illustrious a person should descend to give so great a mark of distinction to a creature so inferior as I. Neither have I forgot, how apt some travelers are to boast of extraordinary favors they have received.[7] But if these censurers were better acquainted with the noble and courteous disposition of the Houyhnhnms, they would soon change their opinion.

I paid my respects to the rest of the Houyhnhnms in his Honor's company; then getting into my canoe, I pushed off from shore.

CHAPTER 11

The author's dangerous voyage. He arrives at New Holland, hoping to settle there. Is wounded with an arrow by one of the natives. Is seized and carried by force into a Portuguese ship. The great civilities of the captain. The author arrives at England.

I began this desperate voyage on February 15, 1715, at 9 o'clock in the morning. The wind was very favorable; however, I made use at first only of my paddles, but considering I should soon be weary, and that the wind might probably chop about,[8] I ventured to set up my little sail; and thus, with the help of the tide, I went at the rate of a league and a half an hour, as near as I could guess. My master and his friends continued[9] on the shore, till I was almost out of sight; and I often heard the sorrel nag (who always loved me) crying out, *Hnuy illa nyha maiah Yahoo,* Take care of thyself, gentle Yahoo.

My design was, if possible, to discover some small island uninhabited, yet sufficient by my labor to furnish me with the necessaries of life, which I would have thought a greater happiness than to be first minister in the politest court of Europe; so horrible was the idea I conceived of returning to live in the society and under the government of Yahoos. For in such a solitude as I desired, I could at least enjoy my own thoughts, and reflect with delight on the virtues of those inimitable Houyhnhnms, without any opportunity of degenerating into the vices and corruptions of my own species.

The reader may remember what I related when my crew conspired against me, and confined me to my cabin. How I continued there several weeks, without knowing what course we took, and when I was put ashore in the longboat, how the sailors told me with oaths, whether true or false, that they knew not in what part of the world we were. However, I did then believe us to be about ten degrees southward of the Cape of Good Hope, or about 45 degrees southern latitude, as I gathered from some general words I overheard among them, being I supposed to the southeast in their intended voyage to Madagascar. And although this were but little better than conjecture, yet I resolved to steer my course eastward, hoping to reach the southwest coast of New Holland, and perhaps some such island as I desired, lying westward of it. The wind was full west, and by six in the evening I computed I had gone eastward at least eighteen leagues, when I spied a very small island about half a league off, which I soon

---

7. Swift heightens the absurdity of Gulliver's action, and draws attention to his later misanthropy.

8. Change direction.
9. Stayed.

reached. It was nothing but a rock, with one creek, naturally arched by the force of tempests. Here I put in my canoe, and climbing a part of the rock, I could plainly discover[1] land to the east, extending from south to north. I lay all night in my canoe, and repeating my voyage early in the morning, I arrived in seven hours to the southwest point of New Holland.[2] This confirmed me in the opinion I have long entertained, that the maps and charts place this country at least three degrees more to the east than it really is;[3] which thought I communicated many years ago to my worthy friend Mr. Herman Moll, and gave him my reasons for it, although he hath rather chosen to follow other authors.[4]

I saw no inhabitants in the place where I landed, and being unarmed, I was afraid of venturing far into the country. I found some shellfish on the shore, and ate them raw, not daring to kindle a fire, for fear of being discovered by the natives. I continued three days feeding on oysters and limpets,[5] to save my own provisions, and I fortunately found a brook of excellent water, which gave me great relief.

On the fourth day, venturing out early a little too far, I saw twenty or thirty natives upon a height, not above five hundred yards from me. They were stark naked, men, women, and children, round a fire, as I could discover by the smoke. One of them spied me, and gave notice to the rest; five of them advanced towards me, leaving the women and children at the fire. I made what haste I could to the shore, and getting into my canoe, shoved off: the savages observing me retreat, ran after me; and before I could get far enough into the sea, discharged an arrow, which wounded me deeply on the inside of my left knee (I shall carry the mark to my grave). I apprehended the arrow might be poisoned, and paddling out of the reach of their darts (being a calm day) I made a shift to suck the wound, and dress it as well as I could.

I was at a loss what to do, for I durst not return to the same landing place, but stood[6] to the north, and was forced to paddle; for the wind though very gentle was against me, blowing northwest. As I was looking about for a secure landing place, I saw a sail to the north-north-east, which appearing every minute more visible, I was in some doubt, whether I should wait for them or no; but at last my detestation of the Yahoo race prevailed, and turning my canoe, I sailed and paddled together to the south, and got into the same creek from whence I set out in the morning, choosing rather to trust myself among these *barbarians,* than live with European Yahoos. I drew up my canoe as close as I could to the shore, and hid myself behind a stone by the little brook, which, as I have already said, was excellent water.

The ship came within a half a league of this creek, and sent out her longboat with vessels to take in fresh water (for the place it seems was very well known) but I did not observe it till the boat was almost on shore, and it was too late to seek another hiding place. The seamen at their landing observed my canoe, and rummaging it all over, easily conjectured that the owner could not be far off. Four of them well armed searched every cranny and lurking hole, till at last they found me flat on my face behind the stone. They gazed a while in admiration[7] at my strange uncouth dress, my

---

1. Discern.
2. New Holland was the name the explorer Abel Tasman originally gave to the western coast of Australia. Gulliver seems to place the land of the Houyhnhnms west of southwestern Australia, in which case the distance he covers to reach New Holland is improbable (1,500 to 2,000 nautical miles in 16 hours). It is possible, however, that Gulliver is meant to have landed on Tasmania, thus putting the Houyhnhnms a short distance west of this island.

3. Dampier claimed that he had found New Holland further west than indicated in Tasman's charts.
4. This geographer's *New and Correct Map of the Whole World* (1719) was probably the basis for Swift's geography in *Gulliver's Travels.*
5. Small mollusks that attach themselves to rocks.
6. Steered.
7. Wonder, amazement.

coat made of skins, my wooden-soled shoes, and my furred stockings; from whence, however, they concluded I was not a native of the place, who all go naked. One of the seamen in Portuguese bid me rise, and asked who I was. I understood that language very well, and getting upon my feet, said, I was a poor Yahoo, banished from the Houyhnhnms, and desired they would please to let me depart. They admired to hear me answer them in their own tongue, and saw by my complexion I must be a European; but were at a loss to know what I meant by Yahoos and Houyhnhnms, and at the same time fell a laughing at my strange tone in speaking, which resembled the neighing of a horse. I trembled all the while betwixt fear and hatred: I again desired leave to depart, and was gently moving to my canoe; but they laid hold on me, desiring to know, what country I was of? whence I came? with many other questions. I told them, I was born in England, from whence I came about five years ago, and then their country and ours were at peace. I therefore hoped they would not treat me as an enemy, since I meant them no harm, but was a poor Yahoo, seeking some desolate place where to pass the remainder of his unfortunate life.

When they began to talk, I thought I never heard or saw anything so unnatural; for it appeared to me as monstrous as if a dog or a cow should speak in England, or a Yahoo in Houyhnhnmland. The honest Portuguese were equally amazed at my strange dress, and the odd manner of delivering my words, which however they understood very well. They spoke to me with great humanity, and said they were sure their captain would carry me *gratis* to Lisbon, from whence I might return to my own country; that two of the seamen would go back to the ship, to inform the captain of what they had seen, and receive his orders; in the meantime, unless I would give my solemn oath not to fly,[8] they would secure me by force. I thought it best to comply with their proposal. They were very curious to know my story, but I gave them very little satisfaction; and they all conjectured, that my misfortunes had impaired my reason. In two hours the boat, which went loaden with vessels of water, returned with the captain's commands to fetch me on board. I fell on my knees to preserve my liberty; but all was in vain, and the men having tied me with cords, heaved me into the boat, from whence I was taken into the ship, and from thence into the captain's cabin.

His name was Pedro de Mendez; he was a very courteous and generous person; he entreated me to give some account of myself, and desired to know what I would eat or drink; said, I should be used as well as himself, and spoke so many obliging things, that I wondered to find such civilities from a Yahoo. However, I remained silent and sullen; I was ready to faint at the very smell of him and his men. At last I desired something to eat out of my own canoe; but he ordered me a chicken and some excellent wine, and then directed that I should be put to bed in a very clean cabin. I would not undress myself, but lay on the bed clothes, and in half an hour stole out, when I thought the crew was at dinner, and getting to the side of the ship was going to leap into the sea, and swim for my life, rather than continue among Yahoos. But one of the seamen prevented me, and having informed the captain, I was chained to my cabin.

After dinner Don Pedro came to me, and desired to know my reason for so desperate an attempt: assured me he only meant to do me all the service he was able, and spoke so very movingly, that at last I descended[9] to treat him like an animal which had some little portion of reason. I gave him a very short relation of my voyage, of the conspiracy against me by my own men, of the country where they set me on shore, and of my three years' residence there. All which he looked upon as if it were a dream

---

8. Attempt to escape.   9. Condescended.

or a vision; whereat I took great offense; for I had quite forgot the faculty of lying, so peculiar to Yahoos in all countries where they preside, and consequently the disposition of suspecting truth in others of their own species. I asked him, whether it were the custom of his country to *say the thing that was not?* I assured him I had almost forgot what he meant by falsehood, and if I had lived a thousand years in Houyhnhnmland, I should never have heard a lie from the meanest servant; that I was altogether indifferent whether he believed me or no; but however, in return for his favors, I would give so much allowance to the corruption of his nature, as to answer any objection he would please to make, and then he might easily discover the truth.

The captain, a wise man, after many endeavors to catch me tripping in some part of my story, at last began to have a better opinion of my veracity.[1] But he added, that since I professed so inviolable an attachment to truth, I must give him my word of honor to bear him company in this voyage without attempting anything against my life, or else he would continue[2] me a prisoner till we arrived at Lisbon. I gave him the promise he required; but at the same time protested that I would suffer the greatest hardships rather than return to live among Yahoos.

Our voyage passed without any considerable accident.[3] In gratitude to the captain I sometimes sat with him at his earnest request, and strove to conceal my antipathy against human kind, although it often broke out, which he suffered to pass without observation. But the greatest part of the day, I confined myself to my cabin, to avoid seeing any of the crew. The captain had often entreated me to strip myself of my savage dress, and offered to lend me the best suit of clothes he had. This I would not be prevailed on to accept, abhorring to cover myself with anything that had been on the back of a Yahoo. I only desired he would lend me two clean shirts, which having been washed since he wore them, I believed would not so much defile me. These I changed every second day, and washed them myself.

We arrived at Lisbon, Nov. 5, 1715. At our landing the captain forced me to cover myself with his cloak, to prevent the rabble from crowding about me. I was conveyed to his own house, and at my earnest request, he led me up to the highest room backwards.[4] I conjured[5] him to conceal from all persons what I had told him of the Houyhnhnms, because the least hint of such a story would not only draw numbers of people to see me, but probably put me in danger of being imprisoned, or burnt by the Inquisition.[6] The captain persuaded me to accept a suit of clothes newly made, but I would not suffer the tailor to take my measure; however, Don Pedro being almost of my size, they fitted me well enough. He accoutered[7] me with other necessaries all new, which I aired for twenty-four hours before I would use them.

The captain had no wife, nor above three servants, none of which were suffered to attend at meals, and his whole deportment was so obliging, added to very good *human* understanding, that I really began to tolerate his company. He gained so far upon me,

1. In the first edition, the sentence continues: "and the rather, because he confessed, he met with a Dutch Skipper, who pretended to have landed with five others of his crew upon a certain island or continent south of New Holland, where they went for fresh water, and observed a horse driving before him several animals exactly resembling those I had described under the name of Yahoos, with some other particulars, which the captain said he had forgot, because he then concluded them all to be lies." In 1735 Swift's Dublin publisher, George Faulkener, omitted these lines, probably because they contradicted Gulliver's later statement that no other European had visited this land.
2. Keep.
3. Incident.
4. At the back of the house.
5. Appealed earnestly to.
6. Either because the Houyhnhnm hierarchy contradicted Genesis, in which man has dominion over the earth, or because Gulliver had been associating with diabolical powers, who could make humans appear to be horses (as Gulliver himself had first believed).
7. Equipped.

that I ventured to look out of the back window. By degrees I was brought into another room, from whence I peeped into the street, but drew my head back in a fright. In a week's time he seduced me down to the door. I found my terror gradually lessened, but my hatred and contempt seemed to increase. I was at last bold enough to walk the street in his company, but kept my nose well stopped with rue,[8] or sometimes with tobacco.

In ten days Don Pedro, to whom I had given some account of my domestic affairs, put it upon me as a point of honor and conscience, that I ought to return to my native country, and live at home with my wife and children. He told me, there was an English ship in the port just ready to sail, and he would furnish me with all things necessary. It would be tedious to repeat his arguments, and my contradictions. He said, it was altogether impossible to find such a solitary island as I had desired to live in; but I might command in my own house, and pass my time in a manner as recluse as I pleased.

I complied at last, finding I could not do better. I left Lisbon the 24th day of November, in an English merchantman, but who was the master I never inquired. Don Pedro accompanied me to the ship, and lent me twenty pounds. He took kind leave of me, and embraced me at parting, which I bore as well as I could. During this last voyage I had no commerce[9] with the master or any of his men, but pretending I was sick kept close in my cabin. On the fifth of December, 1715, we cast anchor in the Downs[1] about nine in the morning, and at three in the afternoon I got safe to my house at Redriff.

My wife and family received me with great surprise and joy, because they concluded me certainly dead; but I must freely confess the sight of them filled me only with hatred, disgust, and contempt, and the more by reflecting on the near alliance I had to them. For, although since my unfortunate exile from the Houyhnhnm country, I had compelled myself to tolerate the sight of Yahoos, and to converse with Don Pedro de Mendez, yet my memory and imaginations were perpetually filled with the virtues and ideas of those exalted Houyhnhnms. And when I began to consider, that by copulating with one of the Yahoo species, I had become a parent of more, it struck me with the utmost shame, confusion, and horror.

As soon as I entered the house, my wife took me in her arms, and kissed me, at which, having not been used to the touch of that odious animal for so many years, I fell in a swoon for almost an hour. At the time I am writing it is five years since my last return to England: during the first year I could not endure my wife or children in my presence, the very smell of them was intolerable, much less could I suffer them to eat in the same room. To this hour they dare not presume to touch my bread, or drink out of the same cup, neither was I ever able to let one of them take me by the hand.[2] The first money I laid out was to buy two young stone-horses,[3] which I keep in a good stable, and next to them the groom is my greatest favorite; for I feel my spirits revived by the smell he contracts in the stable. My horses understand me tolerably well; I converse with them at least four hours every day. They are strangers to bridle or saddle, they live in great amity with me, and friendship to each other.

CHAPTER 12

The author's veracity. His design in publishing this work. His censure of those travelers who swerve from the truth. The author clears himself from any sinister ends in writing. An objection answered. The method of planting Colonies. His native country commended. The right of the Crown to those countries described by the author is

---

8. Strong-smelling shrub, used for medicinal purposes.
9. Interaction.
1. The sea off the North Downs in East Kent.

2. Gulliver's unwillingness to share his bread or cup with his wife or children emphasizes his unchristian behavior.
3. Stallions.

justified. The difficulty of conquering them. The author takes his last leave of the reader, proposeth his manner of living for the future, gives good advice, and concludeth.

Thus, gentle reader,[4] I have given thee a faithful history of my travels for sixteen years, and above seven months, wherein I have not been so studious of ornament as of truth. I could perhaps like others have astonished thee with strange improbable tales; but I rather chose to relate plain matter of fact in the simplest manner and style, because my principal design was to inform, and not to amuse thee.

It is easy for us who travel into remote countries, which are seldom visited by Englishmen or other Europeans, to form descriptions of wonderful animals both at sea and land. Whereas a traveler's chief aim should be to make men wiser and better, and to improve their minds by the bad as well as good example of what they deliver concerning foreign places.[5]

I could heartily wish a law were enacted, that every traveler, before he were permitted to publish his voyages, should be obliged to make oath before the Lord High Chancellor that all he intended to print was absolutely true to the best of his knowledge; for then the world would no longer be deceived as it usually is, while some writers, to make their works pass the better upon the public, impose the grossest falsities on the unwary reader. I have perused several books of travels with great delight in my younger days; but having since gone over most parts of the globe, and been able to contradict many fabulous accounts from my own observation, it hath given me a great disgust against this part of reading, and some indignation to see the credulity of mankind so impudently abused. Therefore since my acquaintance were pleased to think my poor endeavors might not be unacceptable to my country, I imposed on myself as a maxim, never to be swerved from, that I would *strictly adhere to truth;* neither indeed can I be ever under the least temptation to vary from it, while I retain in my mind the lectures and example of my noble master, and the other illustrious Houyhnhnms, of whom I had so long the honor to be an humble hearer.

    —Nec si miserum Fortuna Sinonem

    Finxit, vanum etiam mendacemque improba finget.[6]

I know very well how little reputation is to be got by writings which require neither genius nor learning, nor indeed any other talent, except a good memory or an exact journal. I know likewise, that writers of travels, like dictionary-makers, are sunk into oblivion by the weight and bulk of those who come last, and therefore lie uppermost.[7] And it is highly probable, that such travelers who shall hereafter visit the countries described in this work of mine, may, by detecting my errors (if there be any), and adding many new discoveries of their own, jostle me out of vogue, and stand in my place, making the world forget that ever I was an author. This indeed would be too great a mortification if I wrote for fame; but, as my sole intention was the PUBLIC GOOD,[8] I cannot be altogether disappointed. For who can read of the virtues I have

---

4. Highly ironic, since the "gentle" readers must be Yahoos.

5. More's *Utopia* also argues that accounts of distant travels should provide useful lessons rather than fabulous tales.

6. "Nor, if cruel Fortune has made Sinon miserable, shall he also make him false and deceitful" (Virgil, *Aeneid* 2.79–80). Swift cleverly employs the words that the Greek Sinon, the most famous liar in antiquity, used in

the fraudulent tale he told to fool the Trojans into accepting *his* (wooden) horse.

7. The most current dictionary is the one most frequently used.

8. The English buccaneer and navigator William Dampier professes a similar aim in the dedication to his *New Voyage Round the World* (1697).

mentioned in the glorious Houyhnhnms, without being ashamed of his own vices, when he considers himself as the reasoning, governing animal of his country? I shall say nothing of those remote nations where Yahoos preside, amongst which the least corrupted are the Brobdingnagians, whose wise maxims in morality and government it would be our happiness to observe. But I forbear descanting further, and rather leave the judicious reader to his own remarks and applications.

I am not a little pleased that this work of mine can possibly meet with no[9] censurers: for what objections can be made against a writer who relates only plain facts that happened in such distant countries, where we have not the least interest with respect either to trade or negotiations? I have carefully avoided every fault with which common writers of travels are often too justly charged. Besides, I meddle not the least with any party, but write without passion, prejudice, or ill-will against any man or number of men whatsoever. I write for the noblest end, to inform and instruct mankind, over whom I may, without breach of modesty, pretend to some superiority from the advantages I received by conversing so long among the most accomplished Houyhnhnms. I write without any view towards profit or praise. I never suffer a word to pass that may look like reflection,[1] or possibly give the least offense even to those who are most ready to take it. So that I hope I may with justice pronounce myself an author perfectly blameless, against whom the tribe of answerers, considerers, observers, reflecters, detecters, remarkers, will never be able to find matter for exercising their talents.[2]

I confess, it was whispered to me, that I was bound in duty as a subject of England, to have given in a memorial to a Secretary of State, at my first coming over; because, whatever lands are discovered by a subject belong to the Crown. But I doubt whether our conquests in the countries I treat of, would be as easy as those of Ferdinando Cortez over the naked Americans.[3] The Lilliputians, I think, are hardly worth the charge of a fleet and army to reduce them, and I question whether it might be prudent or safe to attempt the Brobdingnagians. Or whether an English army would be much at their ease with the Flying Island over their heads.[4] The Houyhnhnms, indeed, appear not to be so well prepared for war, a science to which they are perfect strangers, and especially against missive weapons.[5] However, supposing myself to be a minister of State, I could never give my advice for invading them. Their prudence, unanimity, unacquaintedness with fear, and their love of their country would amply supply all defects in the military art. Imagine twenty thousand of them breaking into the midst of an European army, confounding the ranks, overturning the carriages, battering the warriors' faces into mummy,[6] by terrible yerks[7] from their hinder hoofs. For they would well deserve the character given to Augustus; *Recalcitrat undique tutus.*[8] But instead of proposals for conquering that magnanimous nation, I rather wish they were in a capacity or disposition to send a sufficient number of their inhabitants for civilizing

---

9. Cannot possibly encounter any.
1. Criticism.
2. At this time it was common for historical and fictional accounts to be "applied" to contemporary situations or persons; by having Gulliver deny at such length that he is doing this, Swift draws attention to the possibility of making such connections.
3. In the 1520s, Cortés and 400 soldiers rapidly conquered the Aztec empire in Mexico.
4. These sentences refer to Gulliver's other travels: in Lilliput he encountered a miniature people; in Brobdingnag he met with giants; and in Laputa he encountered the

Flying Island (able to force inhabitants below to submit either through starving them by blocking out the sun or by crushing them).
5. Anything thrown or shot through the air.
6. Pulp.
7. Kicks.
8. "He kicks back, well protected on every side" (Horace, *Satires* 2.i.20). While Gulliver refers admiringly to the horse's ability to defend itself, Swift recalls the context for Horace's decision to use satire (rather than praise) when writing about Augustus: according to Horace, Augustus would kick out like a horse if he sensed servile flattery.

Europe, by teaching us the first principles of honor, justice, truth, temperance, public spirit, fortitude, chastity, friendship, benevolence, and fidelity. The *names* of all which virtues are still retained among us in most languages, and are to be met with in modern as well as ancient authors; which I am able to assert from my own small reading.

But I had another reason which made me less forward[9] to enlarge his Majesty's dominions by my discoveries. To say the truth, I had conceived a few scruples with relation to the distributive justice[1] of princes upon those occasions. For instance, a crew of pirates[2] are driven by a storm they know not whither, at length a boy discovers land from the topmast, they go on shore to rob and plunder; they see a harmless people, are entertained with kindness, they give the country a new name, they take formal possession of it for the king, they set up a rotten plank or a stone for a memorial, they murder two or three dozen of the natives, bring away a couple more by force for a sample, return home, and get their pardon. Here commences a new dominion acquired with a title by *divine right*. Ships are sent with the first opportunity, the natives driven out or destroyed, their princes tortured to discover their gold;[3] a free license given to all acts of inhumanity and lust, the earth reeking with the blood of its inhabitants; and this execrable crew of butchers employed in so pious an expedition, is a *modern colony* sent to convert and civilize an idolatrous and barbarous people.

But this description, I confess, doth by no means affect the British nation, who may be an example to the whole world for their wisdom, care, and justice in planting colonies;[4] their liberal endowments for the advancement of religion and learning; their choice of devout and able pastors to propagate Christianity; their caution in stocking their provinces with people of sober lives and conversations from this the mother kingdom;[5] their strict regard to the distribution of justice, in supplying the civil administration through all their colonies with officers of the greatest abilities, utter strangers to corruption; and to crown all, by sending the most vigilant and virtuous governors, who have no other views than the happiness of the people over whom they preside, and the honor of the King their master.

But, as those countries which I have described do not appear to have any desire of being conquered, and enslaved, murdered, or driven out by colonies, nor abound either in gold, silver, sugar, or tobacco; I did humbly conceive they were by no means proper objects of our zeal, our valor, or our interest. However, if those whom it more concerns, think fit to be of another opinion, I am ready to depose, when I shall be lawfully called, that no European did ever visit those countries before me. I mean, if the inhabitants ought to be believed.[6]

But as to the formality of taking possession in my Sovereign's name, it never came once into my thoughts; and if it had, yet as my affairs then stood, I should perhaps in point of prudence and self-preservation, have put it off to a better opportunity.

Having thus answered the *only* objection that can ever be raised against me as a traveler, I here take a final leave of my courteous readers, and return to enjoy my own

---

9. Eager.
1. Fairness with regard to the rights of the native people.
2. Referring to the first Spanish colonizers of America.
3. Montezuma was tortured by Cortés, and the Incan emperor Atahuallpa by Pizarro (1533).
4. Intended ironically.
5. Felons were commonly given a sentence of mandatory "transportation" to Britain's colonies.
6. The first edition continued: "unless a dispute may arise

about the two Yahoos, said to have been seen many Ages ago on a mountain in Houyhnhnm-land, from whence the opinion is, that the race of those brutes hath descended; and these, for anything I know, may have been English, which indeed I was apt to suspect from the lineaments of their posterity's countenances, although very much defaced. But how far that will go to make out a title, I leave to the learned in colony law." Faulkener omitted this passage in the 1735 edition.

speculations in my little garden at Redriff, to apply those excellent lessons of virtue which I learned among the Houyhnhnms, to instruct the Yahoos of my own family as far as I shall find them docible[7] animals, to behold my figure often in a glass, and thus if possible habituate myself by time to tolerate the sight of a human creature, to lament the brutality of Houyhnhnms in my own country, but always treat their persons with respect, for the sake of my noble master, his family, his friends, and the whole Houyhnhnm race, whom these of ours[8] have the honor to resemble in all their lineaments, however their intellectuals[9] came to degenerate.

I began last week to permit my wife to sit at dinner with me, at the farthest end of a long table, and to answer (but with the utmost brevity) the few questions I ask her. Yet the smell of a Yahoo continuing very offensive, I always keep my nose well stopped with rue, lavender, or tobacco leaves. And although it be hard for a man late in life to remove old habits, I am not altogether out of hopes in some time to suffer a neighbor Yahoo in my company, without the apprehensions I am yet under of his teeth or his claws.

My reconcilement to the Yahoo-kind in general might not be so difficult if they would be content with those vices and follies only, which Nature hath entitled them to. I am not in the least provoked at the sight of a lawyer, a pickpocket, a colonel, a fool, a lord, a gamester, a politician, a whoremonger, a physician, an evidence,[1] a suborner,[2] an attorney, a traitor, or the like: this is all according to the due course of things; but when I behold a lump of deformity and diseases both in body and mind, smitten with *pride,* it immediately breaks all the measures of my patience; neither shall I be ever able to comprehend how such an animal and such a vice could tally together. The wise and virtuous Houyhnhnms, who abound in all excellencies that can adorn a rational creature, have no name for this vice in their language, which hath no terms to express anything that is evil, except those whereby they describe the detestable qualities of their Yahoos, among which they were not able to distinguish this of pride, for want of thoroughly understanding human nature, as it showeth itself in other countries, where that animal presides. But I, who had more experience, could plainly observe some rudiments of it among the wild Yahoos.

But the Houyhnhnms, who live under the government of Reason, are no more proud of the good qualities they possess, than I should be for not wanting a leg or an arm, which no man in his wits would boast of, although he must be miserable without them. I dwell the longer upon this subject from the desire I have to make the society of an English Yahoo by any means not insupportable, and therefore I here entreat those who have any tincture of this absurd vice, that they will not presume to appear in my sight.

FINIS

---

7. Teachable.
8. I.e., horses.
9. Intellects.

1. A (false) witness.
2. One who bribes another to commit a misdeed.

⇒ PERSPECTIVES ⇐
Journeys in Search of the Self

The Enlightenment saw an intensification of the global exploration and colonization begun in the early modern period. There was competition among European nations to sponsor ambitious voyages of discovery and lay claim to new territories, not unlike the space race of the twentieth century. Then as now, such voyages were inspired by a desire for knowledge, but also by competition for economic advantage. The possibilities of colonial exploitation resulted in wild business speculation in both France and England, each of which experienced stock crashes when bubbles of speculation in the Pacific and Louisiana burst in 1720. Exploration continued apace despite the financial ruin.

Many accounts were published of the journeys of exploration that opened up these new worlds to European trade. Among these, the most important were arguably the narratives of Cook's and Bougainville's voyages around the world, published within two years of each other in the 1770s. Both accounts focused on their explorations in the South Pacific, the least explored remaining frontier. The principal voyages of the renowned English explorer Captain James Cook (1728–1779) were publicized in several highly popular works both before and after Cook was killed by Hawaiians during a return South Seas voyage in 1779. Louis Antoine de Bougainville (1729–1811), like Cook a professional military man, undertook a three-year voyage around the world in 1766–1769. The last year of Bougainville's voyage coincided with the first year of Cook's. It made Bougainville the first Frenchman to circumnavigate the globe, and in 1768, as Cook was just setting out, he became only the second European to visit Tahiti. He was also the first to bring a Tahitian to the West. Aotourou, the first Polynesian to see Europe, became a human curiosity—much like Françoise de Graffigny's fictional captive, the Peruvian princess causing a sensation in Parisian society. Above all he impressed Parisians with the lack of restraint with which he expressed his attraction to numerous women. The impression Aotourou created in France helped popularize Bougainville's own impression of Tahiti described in his *Voyage around the World* (1771). The fruitfulness of the soil, the pleasantness of the climate, and the comparative sexual frankness he found among the Tahitians led Bougainville to believe he had found the true Eden.

The accounts of these and other voyages were read avidly, and many imaginative writers borrowed from them, responded to them, or critiqued them in creative ways. The most interesting and enduring of the imaginary travel accounts of the time took a distinctly more anticolonial stance than the nonfictional originals. The naive European hero of Voltaire's *Candide* (page 453), witnessing the sufferings of plantation slaves during his imaginary voyage, is instructed, "This is the price at which you eat sugar in Europe." Similarly, in his reworking of Bougainville in the selection given here, Denis Diderot shows deep sympathy for the Tahitians and is openly critical of European exploitation of the peoples encountered in explorations. Yet Diderot shares Bougainville's fantasy of Tahiti as a sexual utopia. Thus, like all the European travel accounts of the time, fictional or otherwise, Diderot's *Supplement* is much more a reflection upon his own culture than it is an accurate representation of the foreign world itself. Montesquieu's *Persian Letters* makes such self-reflection its main point, although he, too, paints lively pictures of the worlds from which his fictional outsiders have traveled. The former slave Olaudah Equiano, whose narrative closes this section, really did come from another world, but in becoming an author of a complex work in English for an English audience, he adopted European conventions. His book follows the narrative patterns of fiction writers like Behn in first describing an idyllic life untouched by corrupt Western customs or values, from which the narrator is violently wrested when he is taken captive by European invaders. His rhetorical goal is the same as theirs: to persuade Europeans to take a long, hard look at themselves and their actions.

Other works in this period feature both Western and non-Western travelers on a journey to little known parts of the world, such as the Ottoman traveler Evliya Çelebi, whose *Book of Travels* covers lands and peoples across the Ottoman Empire and beyond. Conversely, an outsider's view into the Ottoman Empire is shown in Lady Mary Wortley Montagu's *Turkish Embassy Letters* (page 173).

Aphra Behn's *Oroonoko* (page 301) and Jonathan Swift's *Gulliver's Travels* (page 349) make fully fictional use of voyages to distant lands that provide a vantage point on life back in the writer's homeland. In this game of mirrors where self and other are so closely identified, it is significant that female figures and sexuality play an ambiguously central role in so many of them. Women in this period often served as emblems of the other within the self: from the perspective of the European male explorer, Woman is one who is a European like oneself and yet not quite identical with Man, the new center of the universe. Women writers like Behn imply similar connections. Behn's narrator in *Oroonoko,* one of the most complex voices in fiction, is another European female figure who in many ways serves as a symbolic double of the African title character. Female characters in these and many contemporary works embody the impossibility of keeping the other safely separate from the self.

Enlightenment voyages of exploration, real and fictional, have to be understood as quests for knowledge—and thus of a piece with the era's fascination with scientific experimentation, its encyclopedic quest to unify all human knowledge, and even with libertinism, which can also be understood as a restless quest for a kind of knowledge. In each case, the knowledge sought is knowledge of some external object seen as distinctly separate from the inquiring self—be that object Woman, Nature, or a non-European people. But in the end, the real object of knowledge is always primarily the self, or at least it inevitably and centrally includes the self. This section begins with two actual travel accounts by sophisticated non-European writers. First is the Turkish traveler Evliya Çelebi, who surveys the Ottoman Empire's far-flung territories—from eastern Europe to the eastern Mesopotamia. While Montesquieu's *Persian Letters* later in this section openly ask "How can one be Persian?" Çelebi implicitly asks himself and his readers just how one can be an Ottoman, once the empire has grown to include so many and so varied peoples. In the readings that follow Çelebi, the great Japanese poet and travel writer Matsuo Bashō undertakes directly spiritual and poetic journeys in search of the self. Many of his most famous short poems (haiku) were written on the road, and fill the pages of his haunting travel memoir *The Narrow Road to the Deep North.* Bashō's works reflect a much older sense of the term "enlightenment"—a Buddhist ideal of self-awareness and self-renunciation. Yet Bashō is as self-consciously modern as Diderot and Voltaire, and his works like theirs are built on layers of earlier travel narratives and poetic responses preceding his own. All the writers in this section travel through time as well as space, interior as well as exterior landscapes, testing themselves and their readers against the limits of the known world.

Evliya Çelebi
(1611–1684)

Evliya Çelebi is the pen name of the major Turkish travel writer of the Ottoman period, who was born in Istanbul in 1611. He adopted the name Evliya in veneration of his teacher, the religious scholar Evliya Mehmet Efendi. His first name is unknown, for he adopted the name Evliya in an early stage of his life. His father was the chief jeweler of the Ottoman court. Çelebi was also an amiable and learned man and a minor poet, who knew a great deal of poetry by heart and used to recite it at social occasions. His father's position provided Çelebi with a solid education, exposure to the learned elite of his time, and the favor of the court. As a chief jeweler, descending from a wealthy jeweler family, his father had many houses and estates in different parts of Turkey, and the moves among them aroused in the young Çelebi the wanderlust that was the stimulus for his life and travels.

After he completed his elementary schooling, he joined a distinguished religious school, where he learned the Qur'an by heart, then attended another Qur'anic school for eleven years to become a reciter. He soon distinguished himself as a Qur'anic reciter and was presented at the age of twenty-five to the Sultan, Murad IV, on whose command he was admitted to the palace. At the palace he received extensive training in calligraphy, music, Arabic grammar, and the art of Qur'anic recitation. On account of his pleasant disposition, common sense, good voice, learning, and skill as narrator, he was often summoned to the Sultan's presence to entertain his guests. This enabled him to gain access to many of the dignitaries of the empire and to become part of their retinues when they traveled. From an early age travel was his passion, and he is known to have undertaken many trips both on his own and also in the retinues of Ottoman dignitaries.

His major work is the ten-volume *Seyahatname* or *Book of Travels,* which is recognized as one of the major travel books of the seventeenth century. It explores many lands of the Ottoman Empire and some countries beyond its dominion from Russia to Hungary, from Iraq to Moldavia, and from Egypt to Abyssinia. The selections given here describe territories at the far ends of the Ottoman Empire: Kosovo in Albania in eastern Europe, and Kurdistan in northern Iraq. Çelebi took extensive notes during his many travels, and was writing them up in Constantinople at the time of his death. The manuscript still has gaps where Çelebi intended to go back and fill in names, dates, or figures.

Çelebi's account provides insights into the nature of the world of that time, offering a wealth of information on cultural history, folklore, and geography. Çelebi was an imaginative writer with an eye for detail and a penchant for the wonderful and adventurous. His book is full of anecdotes and demonstrates his sense of humor. Written for Turkish intellectuals of the time, the book reflects the mentality of the Ottomans of the seventeenth century and also provides an acute insight into the inner dynamics of the Ottoman Empire and its organization. With its narrative technique and eye for the ornate, it gives an unparalleled panorama of a far-flung empire and its varied populations.

PRONUNCIATIONS:
> *Diyarbekir:* dee-YAHR-bay-keer
> *Evliya Çelebi:* ev-LEE-ah CHEL-ah-bee
> *Kosovo:* KAH-so-vo
> *Seyahatname:* say-ah-HAHT-nah-may

from The Book of Travels

from JOURNEY THROUGH KOSOVO, 1660[1]

From there [Novi Pazar], in —— hours, we arrived at the lofty fortress of Mitrovica. The name is Latin[2] meaning ——. It was built by King Seleshti, one of the kings of Serbia. This town was conquered in person by Ghazi Khudavendigar, Sultan Murad I son of Orhan Ghazi, in the year ——. During the battle of Kosovo Polje, Sultan Murad put 700,000 infidels to the sword. While he was going about the battlefield on foot, and the bodies of his martyred soldiers were being piled up on the bank of the Llap

---

1. Translated by Robert Dankoff and Robert Elsie.   2. Çelebi uses "Latin" to include "Slavic."

river, an inauspicious infidel named Koblaki rose from among the carcasses of the infidel soldiers and slew him. According to another version the assassination took place
after the battle, when the aforementioned infidel, pretending to be an envoy, approached to kiss the hand of the Sultan, but then drew his dagger and slew him. He
then mounted his horse and set off in flight. A huge number of Ottoman troops rushed
around him with their weapons, yet no one was able to knock the assassin off his
horse. An old woman cried out: "Oh warriors, strike his horse on the hoof, for both he
and his horse are entirely covered in mail." As soon as she said this, a strong-armed
bowman shot at the horse's hoof, and horse and rider both came tumbling down. The
soldiers crowded around, broke through his mail collar and slit his throat. Ever since
that time, whenever an envoy approaches one of the Ottoman dynasty, the sultan sits
on his throne and the envoy kisses a long sleeve attached to the sultan's robe while
being held tightly on both sides. The envoy is first made to kiss the ground and then
the sleeve, which is eight paces in length, and he is not allowed any nearer. That has
been the custom under Ottoman law since the day on which Ghazi Khudavendigar
was murdered.

Because of that incident, this lofty fortress of Mitrovica is called The Inauspicious Fortress. Situated at the extreme western point of the Kosovo plain, it is not
dominated by any higher ground. It is oval shaped and constructed of chiselled
stonework. It is extremely solid and cannot be undermined with trenches or tunnels.
There is a single gate. Inside, there are no memorable buildings. * * * We set out from
this town following the banks of the Llap across the Kosovo plain heading south.

The radiant shrine of the martyr Sultan, Ghazi Khudavendigar, *may his earth be sweet, may God hallow his mystery.*

We visited the site, situated in a wilderness on the banks of the Llap, where the noble
heart and other internal organs of our martyred Sultan Murad I lie buried in a high
domed mausoleum. As I indicated above, a great battle took place here in the year 792
(1389) in which the damned and inauspicious Koblaki martyred such a marvelous sultan. The Sultan's belly was slit open and his kidneys, liver, and heart were removed
and buried here. Later this lofty mausoleum was constructed by Sultan Bayezid I the
Thunderbolt.

There have been seven great battles in the Ottoman empire. The first was this one
of Kosovo Polje. Another was the battle of Sultan Bayezid I the Thunderbolt.[3] Another was the battle of Murad II father of Mehmed the Conqueror, against the Vlachs
and Moldavians in the Ughrash valley near Varna. Another was the great battle which
took place in the valley of Tercan near Erzurum between Mehmed the Conqueror and
Sultan Uzun Hasan, king of Azerbaidjan, in the year —— dated according to the
chronogram *Batlan keydu al-hayinin* ("Void is the scheme of the traitors").[4] Another
was the noteworthy battle of Chaldiran in the year —— between Shah Ismail and Selim
Shah. Another was the battle of Mohács in the year —— when Suleyman Khan slew
king Lajos along with 700,000 infidels. Another was the battle on the Mező-Keresztes
plateau near Erlau in the year —— when seven kings perished along with 700,000
infidels. Praise be to God that in the seven aforementioned battles, the infidel kings

---

3. The battle of Nicopolis (1396) when Bayezid defeated
the Crusading army led by King Sigismund of Hungary.
4. A chronogram is a way of dating using Arabic words,
since every letter of the Arabic alphabet has a numerical
value. The numerical value of this phrase would be 878,
which is the date in the Muslim reckoning corresponding
to 1473 C.E.

were all slain. After the battle of Kosovo Polje, however, Ghazi Murad Khan was slain by a ruse as he took his rest, and his noble heart was placed in this radiant shrine. As for his blessed body, it now lies buried in the sublime mausoleum that is in the courtyard of the Great Mosque in the place called Eski Kaplica (Old Hotspring) in Bursa and is a place of pilgrimage.

A strange thing occurred as we entered this mausoleum of Kosovo Polje. Even the skirt of our master Melek Ahmed Pasha was besmirched with filth. It seems that all the rayah infidels from the surrounding villages used to stop at this mausoleum on their way to Prishtina and Vushtrria and, as an insult, use it as a privy. Melek Ahmed Pasha became enraged when he saw the stench and the filth.

"My lord," said I, "the inauspicious infidel who slew this sultan lies in a monastery on yonder mountain in a fine mausoleum, lit with jewelled lamps and scented with ambergris and musk. It is supported by wealthy endowments and ministered by priests who every day and night play host to passing visitors, infidel and Muslim alike. The mausoleum of our victorious sultan, on the other hand, has no such institution or keeper to tend to it, and thus all the infidels come and treacherously deposit their excrement in it. You ought to summon the infidels from the surrounding villages and have them clean and repair the mausoleum. With one load of *akçe*[5] drawn from the district of Zveçan, strong walls could be built around it and a keeper could be appointed to live here with his family."

Thereupon the Pasha gave the populace of the province two purses of silver coins and summoned the rayah from the surrounding area to clean up the mausoleum. In one week they built a high wall with a lofty gate around the mausoleum so that people on horseback could not get in. They also planted 500 fruit trees and dug a well. A keeper was appointed to live there with his family, receiving a regular salary from the governor's agent of Zveçan. His duty was to care for the silk carpets, candlesticks, censers, rose-water containers and lamps in the radiant mausoleum. At the same time, the notables of the province appointed an official to oversee this charitable institution. Thus a great act of charity was accomplished, and now it has become a pilgrimage site—God's mercy be upon him!

* * *

from THE CITY OF DIYARBEKIR[6]

On the location, the lay-out and the circumference of the walled city of Diyarbekir

To begin with, the city of Qara Amid is a widely renowned fortification and firm barrier, a solid bulwark of black basalt built on top of a high hill that soars up to the zenith on the bank of the Tigris and is widely renowned in this world under the name of *Fıs Qayası* ("Cliff of Whispers"). This robust stronghold is a towering castle under the wryly rotating spheres of heaven. Although it is situated on a steep rock, the top of this mighty mountain is a vast plain with tulip-hued meadows. The fortified city's northeastern quarter is situated on rocks that tower to the zenith, and beneath this high fortification are the cliff caves among which is the station of His Eminence the Prophet Jonah—Peace be upon him. Looking down from here demands more courage

---

5. Silver coins.

6. Translated by Martin van Bruinessen. Diyarbekir is a city in the Kurdish territory of northern Iraq.

than a man can muster; this abyss is, so to speak, another deepest Pit of Hell. Down there the great river flows, and on both banks there are lush flowerbeds, vineyards, regularly laid-out vegetable gardens and plots of basil providing the picnic spots where, for five or six months each year, the people of Diyarbekir can enjoy their riverside-season banquets. This recreational region is a widely renowned beauty spot among the places of pleasure and merriment of this earth. When one looks down from the bastions and ramparts of the city walls to the mighty Tigris the river appears like a mere ditch, so high-soaring, up to the peak of heaven's sphere, is the fortification on that side. On its northern, western and southern sides, however, the terrain is flat.

The walls are everywhere a full forty royal cubits high, and have a base ten cubits wide. All along the circumference there are lofty towers, and there are altogether —— battlements. This beautiful fortification is entirely built of hewn black stone, which is why the city is called Qara Amid (Black Amid). A master of engineering constructed this fortification in the form of a square somewhat elongated towards the north and south. All the towers and crenellated battlements face each other so that in case of danger they can protect one another. * * * The basalt out of which the walls of Diyarbekir are built is a heavy, black stone, on which flintstone is unable to make a scratch. Nor does fire affect it and turn it into lime. It is a strange, wondrous mineral, which the human tongue fails to describe.

* * *

Description of the buildings of the mosques in the ancient city of Diyarbekir *(may God protect it from disaster and deceit)*

[THE GREAT MOSQUE]

Firstly, precisely in the centre of the town is the ancient place of worship, the lofty mosque, the pride of Diyarbekir, namely the Great Mosque. Whether it be the historians of Anatolia (Rum) or [other] sages of intelligence and [deep] insight, all agree that this ancient place of worship was probably built as far back as the blessed time of His Eminence [the prophet] Moses (upon whom be peace). On a white column, on the right-hand side of the columns of the courtyard, is its chronogram in Hebrew. No matter which dynasties controlled the city, this ancient building has never been anything but a place of worship. Here even nowadays the spiritual atmosphere is such that when a worshipper performs his prostrations, his heart testifies that they have been accepted. Like the Great Mosque of Aleppo, the Umayyad Mosque of Damascus, the al-Aqsa Mosque in Jerusalem the Noble, the al-Azhar Mosque of Cairo and the Great Aya Sofya of Istanbul, this Great Mosque of Diyarbekir is one of those where God grants all requests made in it.

In its architectural elements are thousands of clear proofs that the mosque was previously a church.[7] For instance, since its minaret is quadrangular, it obviously was the bell-house when the mosque was a church of old. * * * In short, in Diyarbekir is no other mosque of such greatness. It can accommodate 10,000 men. All its architectural elements and all its vaulted domes are entirely covered with lead of fine quality. In the Friday sermon the preacher here still mentions Sultan Selim the Conqueror since it was Sultan Selim, who, at the hand of Bıyıqlı Mehmed Paşa conquered Amid.

* * *

---

7. In fact, the building was built as a mosque, but in a style unfamiliar to Çelebi.

Description of the excursion spots of the city of Diyarbekir the unparallelled

[THE BANKS OF THE TIGRIS]

Well, we have seen, and accordingly described, all such farfamed parks as the Meram gardens of Qonya in the territory of Greek-inhabited Rum, the Istanaz gardens near Adalya, the Fayyum gardens in Egypt, the Manjik gardens of Damascus, the Darende gardens at Darende, and the Aspuzan gardens near Malatya. But Diyarbekir's basil gardens and regularly laid out vegetable plots on the bank of the Tigris have no equal in Rum or the Arab lands or Iran. When, in the spring season, the flood period of the Tigris has passed and its limpid waters begin to flow again in a stable current, all Diyarbekir's inhabitants, rich and poor alike, move with their entire families to the bank of the Tigris. They settle down under tents and pavilions along this wide water, on the plots that they have inherited from their fathers and ancestors, and they sow and cultivate in their gardens melons, watermelons, various vegetables and flowers. They cultivate here a special type of basil, which everyone plants along the borders of his plot. In a month's time it becomes dense like a forest and as high as spear's length so that it is impossible to look through the basil and see what is inside. The doors and walls, the gates and roofs of all these makeshift habitations on the bank of the Tigris are entirely made out of basil. All these basil stems remain rooted in the earth, and all their leaves remain green throughout the year; continually finding humidity in the soil they go on growing. It is impossible to see from one house to the next through these walls of basil. These pavilions are so densely overgrown with basil that the nostrils of the men and women living in them are scented night and day with the fragrance of basil and the other flowers in these gardens, such as roses, Judas-trees and hyacinth. The women's quarters of each garden are also such open-air pavilions of basil. The ponds and fountains in each pavilion all receive their water from the river Tigris. Between all these gardens and vegetable plots run numerous canals and watercourses which people have diverted from the Tigris to their regularly laid-out vegetable gardens.

For a full seven months a merry tumult, with music and friendly talk, is so going on night and day here on the bank of the river Tigris, as in each pavilion people are passing their time with their beloved and close friends, in jollity and drinking, enjoying concert sessions [like those] of Huseyn Bayqara['s court]. All the artisans however remain busy with their crafts during this garden season; all sorts of food and drink are available. Thousands go to the city and pursue their respective jobs; and in the late afternoon they return in swarms to the gardens on the bank of the Tigris, to indulge in pleasure and enjoyment.

Such juicy melons as grow in these gardens have no match, except perhaps the melons of Bohtan in the province of Van. The melons of Diyarbekir are huge, most juicy and tasty, and they have a delicious aroma as of pure musk and amber, so that whoever eats of them only once will surely keep the fragrance of melons in his nostrils for a full week. There is even a saying among the scholars of Kurdistan and the knowledgeable men of the land of Soran that "the fragrance of the venerable Abu Bakr the Faithful was like that of melons," and the religious scholars of Diyarbekir claim that this must have been the fragrance of their melons of the Tigris. They have such a strong aroma that the nostrils of those who eat or even only smell them would seem to be imbued with the fragrance of ambergris. Some of these melons of Diyarbekir attain a weight of a hundred pounds or more. They all have a green colour. People take them as presents to many various lands, as far as they remain fresh. Many use them to prepare a yellow-rice dish, with cinnamon and cloves and rice, as prescribed by His Highness Mu'awiya. Not even with honey of Athens in Rum can a yellow-rice dish become so fragrant as this musk-scented yellow-rice dish with melons. The watermelons however do not deserve much praise. The basil on the other hand grows into such huge trees that in seven or eight months they can be used as tent-poles and stakes. When one burns them in a fire they smell like hyacinths of China. In short, the people of Diyarbekir arouse the envy of the whole world because of the pleasures and enjoyments that they have on the bank of the Tigris for seven or eight months of the year, their nights being like the Night of Power, and their days like the Feast of Sacrifice. They hold banquets like Husayn Bayqara's, thinking to snatch a bit of pleasure from this transitory world. Each night the banks of the Tigris are illuminated with oil lamps, lanterns, wind tapers and torches, and people arrange in thousands of artful ways oil lamps and wax candles on boards which they then put to float on the Tigris, so that the lights are drifting from one side to the other, and the darkest night becomes like a brilliant day. In each pavilion meanwhile singers and musicians, clowns, minstrels and storytellers perform, players of the lute (*'ud*), the *çartar*, the *şeştar*, the *berbut*, the *qanun*, the *çeng*, the *rebab*, the *musiqar*, the *tanbur*, the *santur*, the *nefir*, the *balaban*, the *ney* and the *dehenk*, in short all sorts of musicians with string and wind instruments give performances like those at Bayqara's court, continuing until the break of dawn, when the Muslim *muezzins* chant with their sorrowful voices the glories of God, as if to apologize, and all followers of the [mystic] path and faithful lovers [of God] begin their recitations in praise of Oneness, in the spirit of Pythagoras the Pantheist.[8] For since the people of Diyarbekir all belong to the order of the Khwajagan and the Gülşeni order they do not miss the ecstatic joy and delight of the ritual chantings. In conclusion one may say that while busy activities and buzzing conversation go on in these Iram-like gardens,[9] the people continually pray for the welfare of the imperial state. May God elevate their station!

[THE QAVS GARDEN]

Another excursion spot is the Qavs garden. This too is one of the Iram-like parks that have great local renown. When the conqueror of Baghdad, the Ghazi, Sultan Murad, came to this garden after his conquest of Baghdad, it was here that, after having attended to the affairs of equity and justice, he engaged in jollity and drinking. This place recreation and repose on the opposite side of the Tigris is a territory of parks giving a foretaste of the gardens of Paradise, so that the tongue is lost for words when trying to describe it.

Additional remarks to complete our review of the city

Among the lands of the House of Osman the city of Diyarbekir stands out for the fact that, thanks to His Holiness Jonah's blessings, it was animated by people of all races; but its Muslim inhabitants are mainly Kurds, Turcomans, Arabs and "Ajams,"[1] while its subjects, those tied to the land as well as the free ones, are all Armenians. For this reason the area is considered part of Armenia.

The walled city itself, on the bank of the Tigris, is deemed to belong to Mesopotamia (the island of the Dijla) for the entire area between the Euphrates and

---

8. The ancient Greek philosopher, who saw God in everything.
9. Iram was an ancient Arabian city supposedly built in

imitation of Paradise.
1. People of Persian origin.

the Tigris is considered as Mesopotamia. Due to the pleasantness of the climate the people are very intelligent, and their young sons are very well-behaved and polite. All the people speak Kurdish, Turkish, Arabic, Ajami (Azeri and/or Persian) and Armenian. As for readiness of tongue, some persons are highly proficient in correctness and elegance of speech. There are men here who are most hospitable and charitable. They are all merry and saucy, mirthful and witty people, with sociable and ingenious, sagacious and quick-witted persons among them. In dignity, strength and courage each of them equals Rustam.[2] Some men and some women have reached very old age. Truly, there are nowhere else people of such pleasant character and with the general elegance of this country's inhabitants, it is said.

All people here are true believers, monotheists of unspoilt creed, given to the contemplation of Oneness, and full of piety. Among their women-folk there are extremely chaste, devout and beautiful ladies of the rank of Rabi'a of the 'Adawiya.[3] In the market streets one does not even see a decrepit old woman. If people were to see a young girl in public they would kill her or at least reprimand her father. To such a degree does Diyarbekir observe the code of respectability.

The shrines of saintly gnostics and pious mystics (may Allah be pleased with them all and bless us with His revealed mystery!)

[THE SHRINE OF THE DISTINGUISHED COMPANIONS]

First, and the oldest of all, is the shrine of the Distinguished Companions, in the citadel, near the pasha's palace, in the mosque of His Eminence Khalid ibn Walid (upon whom be God's mercy), that Guide of the Ardent and Patron of the Discerning, that Noble Warrior and Martyr of the Faith. In this illustrious grave His Eminence —— lies buried, the son of His Eminence Khalid, whereas the latter himself lies buried in Homs. After he had captured Diyarbekir from the Armenian emperors he ruled it independently for several years. During that period his noble son passed away, and he buried him in the mosque here in the citadel, which is now a popular place of pilgrimage. When I, the fault-ridden and humble present author, paid my respects at this tomb a verse came to my mind and I wrote the following lines, composed by myself, on the wall there:

(By the author:)

> The rasp of death cuts even into iron
> And so did it erase the "Eternal Son" of ibn Walid.

[THE SHRINE OF HAMZA BABA]

Next, outside the city walls, is the shrine of the venerable Hamza Baba (may God bless us through his occult saintly powers).

[THE SHRINE OF THE SHAYKH OF URMIA, ŞEYH 'AZIZ MAHMUD]

Next, also outside the Rum gate, is the shrine of the Protector of Reason and Law, the Well-versed in the Fixed Principles and their derivations, the Shaykh of the religious Community and the Pole of the State, the Mine of Divine Mysteries, the Struggler [on the Road] to Boundless Enlightenment, namely the Shaykh of

---

2. A legendary Persian hero.   3. A famous mystical woman poet.

Urmia. His noble name was ——. His birthplace was the city of Urmia in Azarbayjan. The graves of his ancestors, Qoçağa Sultan and Şevri Sultan, are still to be found in Urmia. When we shall describe that place we shall, God willing, also review these. The reason why people call this saint the "shaykh of Urmia" is that his original homeland was the city of Urmia. Because this saint was a wealthy and saintly person, over 40,000 loyal dervishes had become strongly attached to him. Due to this abundance of dervishes he increased the fame of the order of the Khwajagan.

[WHY THE SHAYKH OF URMIA WAS EXECUTED]

[Thus it happened that] intriguers slandered the Shaykh in front of Sultan Murad [IV] Han when the latter was besieging the castle of Yerevan: "Majesty, to all appearances (but God knows best), in Diyarbekir the Shaykh of Urmia might start a great rebellion, claiming to be the Mahdi.[4] He has 40,000 disciples, ragged and sun-blackened people, crying out in divine love, strong and violent." Murad Han replied nothing but a short "May it all turn out for the best!" Three years later Sultan Murad Han set out for the conquest of Baghdad the Paradisiacal, and when after many days' march he reached the vicinity of Diyarbekir and all the prominent notables went out to the banks of the Euphrates to welcome the sultan, the shaykh also appeared, in pomp and magnificence, accompanied by 3,000 finely dressed dervishes. He went without fear and awe into the presence of Murad Han and said "Peace upon you, my *Hunkar* (Sovereign)," somewhat drawing out the syllable *hun* (blood). Murad Han remarked, "My dear [shaykh], you pronounced that syllable *hun* rather long . . ." The shaykh replied: "Yes my *Hunkar!* When you proceed, with good luck, from here to Baghdad and lay siege to that city, you will, after forty days have been completed, on the ——th day of the exalted month of *Sha'ban,* conquer Baghdad the Paradisiacal and cut the heads of the Redheads (*Qızılbaş*) in that city with your fiery sword, causing their blood to flow like torrents, thus taking revenge for the blood of the Sunnis who were slain in Yerevan when it was in the Persians' hands. That is why I drew out the first syllable when calling you 'my Hunkar.'" Upon hearing from the saint this good tiding that he was to conquer Baghdad, Sultan Murad was filled with joy, and said "Well, Efendi! Shall I, after this conquest, return in good health to my Abode of Felicity?" "Yes, after the conquest you will return here to Diyarbekir and, led astray by calumniators and slanderers, once more show yourself a *Hun-kar,* unjustly this time. Having aggrieved many hearts you will arrive in Istanbul. But God knows—another gate yet will be opened for you!"[5]

Sultan Murad did not heed the allusions hidden in these words and said: "If God permits, Efendi, I shall after the conquest of Baghdad set out against the Island of Malta." The saint immediately retorted: "It would be even better, my lord, if you would from now on study the *Books of Muhammad's Path* and follow this religion!"[6] Murad Han replied: "I am certainly, God willing, going to teach the German king who is Austria's emperor a lesson, for as you were pleased to say, the Austrian unbelievers are apparently despatching gangs of infidel raiders, marauders

---

4. Revolutionary spiritual leader.
5. The saint is referring to the gate to heaven, but the sultan assumes he is predicting another earthly conquest.

6. "This religion" is *bu din,* but the sultan hears this as "Buda" (modern Budapest), long disputed between the Ottomans and the Austro-Hungarian Empire.

and hussars against the fortress of my dear Buda!" The saint replied at once: "Whatever you wish, my Lord, if only you liberate our Supreme Imam from the hands of the Redheads. After that, take care of protecting this your religion, and be always on the alert!" He said many more such words, containing treasures of hidden meaning.

When they arrived in Diyarbekir the sultan made rich presents to the saint, but the latter accepted nothing, requesting instead a reduction in the number of Diyarbekir's levyhouses and of the oppressive poll-tax. His requests were favourably received, and then Murad left for Baghdad with the saint's blessings. And, as God's Wisdom would have it, when the day His Eminence the Saint had specified arrived, Baghdad was captured by surrender, at the very moment that Tayyar Mehmed Pasha was killed. But after innumerable soldiers had entered the city those treacherous Redheads barricaded themselves under the Dark Gate and resumed fighting, while those entrenched within the citadel set fire to the arsenal, so that several thousands of Muslim warriors as well as thousands of the heretics were scorched in that Nimrodian fire and flew through the air like the birds *Ababil*.[7] Enraged at this, Murad Han forthwith ordered "Hey, let them put to the sword those Redheads who have surrendered!" whereupon within seven hours the heads of 42,000 Redheads were cut by the sword of Islam.

Murad Han said to himself: "God is Great! In Diyarbekir the shaykh of Urmia foretold that the campaign was going to take this course! He is truly not a vain pretender! I shall, God willing, reward him richly for having foretold the happy tidings of this most glorious of conquests!"

When he returned victorious to Diyarbekir he offered His Eminence the Saint presents in abundance, but the latter refused to accept even the least bit, and just kept praying. Again people told the sultan slanderous stories: "Majesty, the saintly shaykh is a master of alchemy. He owns 10,000 purses in gold, and is capable of turning all his followers' copper utensils into gold if he wishes. It is to be feared that this shaykh will revolt [and set himself up as an independent ruler], like the sinister Timur or like the Mahdi destined to appear [towards the end of time]." Murad Han again paid no attention but one day, in the course of a conversation with the shaykh he asked the latter: "My dear [shaykh], would there be any truth in the science of alchemy?" The saint responded: "Certainly my sovereign, but it is the domain of shaykhs. These have developed it [just] for their physical needs, making little pills of pure gold and eating these. Thereby the true mystics appease their hunger, but it is not for the purpose of acquiring treasures like Korah's that they learn alchemy." Murad Han said: "Ah Efendi, if only I could see people who have mastered this science! I am very sceptical about it." At once the saint retorted: "My lord, if you give me a free hand, let them practice in your presence, so that you may witness miracles." Murad Han went with the saint to the latter's private quarters, where they secluded themselves.

In those days, as God's wisdom would have it, there lived in the women's quarters of the saint's residence a daughter of Ma'anoğlu, the widely known chieftain of the Druzes in the province of Syria. She was an accomplished witch, as aged as the world. She was admitted to the sultan's presence and kissed the ground in front of his feet. After lengthy conversation the deceitful wench lit—just as she had learnt from her father Ma'anoğlu—a Nimrodian fire, and as she added one ounce of elixir to a

---

7. Legendary birds, so powerful that they destroyed an infidel army.

hundred pounds of unmixed copper, its color immediately changed to yellow, and it became unalloyed gold of such high quality that it was "aurum purum" as soft as beeswax. The saint made of it a few pills, which he ate himself. Murad Han also ate three pills, which filled his stomach so well that for a full day and night he had no appetite for food at all. The moment Sultan Murad returned to his pavilion tent he began pondering the fact that the slanderers' claims had proven to be right. He at once sent —— Aga to the shaykh's private quarters, and had both the saint and Ma'anoğlu's daughter strangled; they were buried outside the Rum gate.

After that, Sultan Murad returned to Istanbul, but he did not live very long. With the lament "Aah, Shaykh of Urmia! Aah, ——!" on his lips, he passed away. This humble author has recorded these episodes [of the shaykh's life] as he heard them from his lord Melek Ahmed Pasha. For the latter was Sultan Murad's sword bearer in those years, and after the conquest of Baghdad became the governor of Diyarbekir. He believed in the saint and used to visit his grave frequently. God's mercy be upon him. The shaykh lies buried in the Muslim cemetery outside the Rum gate, in a grave without a dome or any structure. May God bless us through this saint's miraculous powers! This humble author wrote the following lines on his tombstone:

> We came as pilgrims to this station
> where reposes the great guide, the Shaykh of Urmia.

Matsuo Bashō
1644–1694

Matsuo Bashō was born in the castle town of Ueno, southeast of Kyōto. Bashō's grandfather and great-grandfather belonged to the samurai class, but by Bashō's generation, the family had fallen so low that they had become farmers with only tenuous ties to the samurai class. Bashō at first served as a domestic employee of the Tōdō house, presumably as a companion to the son of the Tōdō lord. During this time, Bashō began to write linked verse (*haikai*). The linked verse sequence, usually consisting of 36 or 100 linked verses, began with the seventeen-syllable poetic form now known as haiku.

In the spring of 1672, at the age of twenty-nine, Bashō moved to Edo to establish himself as a linked-verse and haiku master who could charge fees for his services. By the mid-1670s Bashō had attracted the nucleus of his disciples and patrons who played a major role in the formation of what came to be known as the Bashō circle. In the winter of 1680, at the age of thirty-seven, Bashō left Edo and retreated to Fukagawa, on the banks of the Sumida River, on the outskirts of Edo. During the next four years he wrote in the so-called Chinese style, creating the persona of the recluse poet who was opposed to the materialism and social ambitions of the new urban culture. One of Bashō's literary achievements was fusing the earlier recluse poet tradition with the new commoner genre of haiku. He took his poetic name from the *bashō* plant, or Japanese plantain, whose large leaves sometimes tear in the wind, thus representing the fragility of the hermit-traveler's life.

In the fall of 1684, Bashō began the first of a series of journeys that occupied much of the remaining ten years of his life. On his first journey, commemorated in his travel diary *Skeleton in the Fields*, Bashō traveled to several western provinces, recruiting followers before returning to Edo in the summer of 1685. In the spring of 1689, Bashō departed once again, this time with his disciple Sora, for Michinoku ("Deep North") in the northeast, in an expedition later commemorated in *Narrow Road to the Deep North*. For the next two years, Bashō remained in the Kyōto-Ōsaka area. Together with two disciples in Kyōto, Bashō then edited *Monkey's Straw Coat*, the magnum opus of the Bashō school, which was published in the summer of 1691. Bashō died in 1694 on a journey to Ōsaka.

BASHŌ AND THE ART OF HAIKU

The seventeen-syllable haiku, which is usually translated into English in three lines, requires a cutting word and a seasonal word. The cutting word, often indicated in English translation by a dash, divides the haiku into two parts, which constitute two parts of the same scene while at the same time resonating with each other (often in a contrastive or parallel structure). The seasonal word is a word that, as a result of a long tradition of poetic use, not only indicates a specific season but usually possesses a cluster of associations that the poet draws on to widen the scope and complexity of the poem. For example, the seasonal word "evening in autumn" (*aki no kure*), which can also be translated as "end of autumn," is associated in the Japanese poetic tradition with loneliness. In the following haiku by Bashō, the cutting word, marked by a dash, creates a resonance between the implicit loneliness of the crow(s) on a withered branch and the implicit loneliness of an autumn evening or the end of autumn (also implying the end of life).

> *kareeda ni*   On a withered branch
> *karasu no tomarikeri*   a crow comes to rest—
> *aki no kure*   evening in autumn

In Bashō's time, the spirit of haiku meant taking pleasure in seeing things freshly: both dislocating habitual, conventionalized perceptions *and* also recasting established poetic topics into contemporary language and culture. In the previous haiku, the topic of "evening in autumn," which classical poets from the Heian and medieval periods had composed on, is given new life by juxtaposing it with the surprising image of "crows on a withered branch," which had hitherto appeared only in Chinese ink painting.

Of particular interest here is the complex relationship between haiku and tradition. Bashō looked to classical and medieval poets for poetic and spiritual inspiration. He especially admired Saigyō (1118–1190) and Sōgi (1421–1502)—who were travelers and poet-priests—and he was strongly influenced by Chinese poetry and poetics. At the same time, Bashō was a poet of haiku (called haikai at the time), which, by its very nature, was parodic, oppositional, and immersed in popular culture. One result was the emergence in the seventeenth century of a culture of *mitate* (literally, seeing by comparison), which moved back and forth between the two starkly different worlds, that of the Japanese classics and that of the new popular literature and drama, each providing a lens or filter with which to view the other. Artists such as Hishikawa Moronobu (1618–1694), a pioneer of *ukiyo-e* prints, used the technique of *mitate* in the visual arts, both alluding to and radically transforming the topics and imagery of the classical tradition into a contemporary form.

Bashō's haiku differed from the *mitate* found in Moronobu's *ukiyo-e* woodblock prints in that the popular culture in his poetry and prose was not that of the stylish men and women of the great urban centers but, rather, that of the mundane, everyday lives of farmers and fishermen in the provinces. Bashō himself was a socially marginal figure, and his poetry and prose are pervaded by marginal figures such as the beggar, the old man, the outcast, and the traveler, no doubt reflecting his own provincial origins. Likewise, his allusions were not to famous lovers like the shining Genji but, rather, to medieval traveler poets such as Saigyō and Sōgi.

A *haiga* (haikai sketch), on the
Chinese painting theme of cold
crows on a withered branch.
The painting is by Morikawa
Kyoriku, 1656–1715, Bashō's
disciple and his painting instructor, and the calligraphy
and poem are by Bashō:
"On a withered branch
a crow comes to rest—
evening in autumn"
(*Kareeda ni / karasu no
tomarikeri / aki no kure*).
Probably done around
1692/1693 while Kyoriku, a
samurai from Hikone, was in
Edo. Signed "Bashō Tōsei."
(42.1 in. × 12.2 in.)

In the seventeenth century, the popular vernacular genres such as Saikaku's tales frequently parodied their classical predecessors by borrowing the elegant, aristocratic forms of traditional literature and giving them a popular, vulgar, or erotic content. In a reverse movement, Bashō gave a popular, vernacular genre (haiku) a spiritual or refined content, or more accurately, he sought out the spiritual and poetic in commoner culture, giving to contemporary language and provincial subject matter the kind of nuances and sentiments hitherto found only in classical or Chinese poetry. In this way, Bashō was able to raise haiku—which until then had been considered a form of light entertainment—into a serious literary genre and a vehicle for cultural transmission.

[Selected Haiku][1]

kareeda ni	On a withered branch
karasu no tomarikeri	a crow comes to rest—
aki no kure	evening in autumn[2]

Going out on the beach while the light is still faint:

akebono ya—	early dawn—
shirauo shiroki	whitefish, an inch
koto issun	of whiteness[3]

Having stayed once more at the residence of Master Tōyō, I was about to leave for the Eastern Provinces.

botan shibe fukaku	From deep within
wakeizuru hachi no—	the peony pistils, withdrawing
nagori kana	regretfully, the bee[4]

Spending a whole day on the beach:

umi kurete	The sea darkening—
kamo no koe	the voice of a wild duck
honoka ni shiroshi	faintly white[5]

1. Translated by Haruo Shirane.
2. Bashō first composed this haiku in the spring of 1681, during his late Chinese-style period. *Aki no kure* can be read as either "end of autumn" or "autumn nightfall." In a 1698 collection of Bashō's haiku, this haiku is preceded by the title "On Evening in Autumn" (*aki no kure to wa*), indicating that the poem was written on a seasonal topic closely associated with Fujiwara Shunzei (d. 1204) and his medieval aesthetics of quiet, meditative loneliness. Crows perched on a withered branch, on the other hand, was a popular subject in Chinese ink painting. In this context, Bashō's haiku juxtaposes a medieval poetic topic with a Chinese painting motif, causing the two to resonate in montage fashion.
3. Bashō composed this haiku in the Eleventh Month of 1684 while visiting the Ise area during the *Skeleton in the Fields* journey. Drawing on the phonic connotations of *shirauo* (literally, white fish), Bashō establishes a connotative correspondence between the semi-translucent "whiteness" (*shiroki koto*) of the tiny fish and the pale,

faint light of early dawn (*akebono*). The poem has a melodic rhythm, resulting from the repeated "o" vowel mixed with the consonantal "s."
4. This is a good example of a semi-allegorical poetic greeting. Bashō composed the haiku, which appears in *Skeleton in the Fields*, when he left the house of his friend Tōyō in the Fourth Month of 1685. The bee, representing Bashō, is resting peacefully in the peony, an elegant summer flower that symbolizes Tōyō's residence, joyfully imbibing the rich pollen of the pistils, but now, with much reluctance, it must leave. The haiku is an expression of gratitude and a farewell not only to Tōyō but to all the Nagoya-area poets who have hosted him on this journey.
5. The opening verse of a linked-verse sequence composed in Atsuta, in Nagoya, in 1685. The poet looks out toward the voice of the wild duck (*kamo*), which has disappeared with the approaching darkness, and sees only a faint whiteness (*shiroshi* implies a kind of translucency), which may be the waves or the reflection of the sea in the dusk. *Kamo* is a seasonal word for winter.

furuike ya
kawazu tobikomu
mizu no oto

An old pond—
a frog leaps in,
the sound of water[6]

On the road:

kutabirete
yado karu koro ya
fuji no hana

Exhausted,
time to find a lodging—
hanging wisteria[7]

Lodging for the night at Akashi:

takotsubo ya
hakanaki yume o
natsu no tsuki

Octopus traps—
fleeting dreams
under the summer moon[8]

hototogisu
kieyuku kata ya
shima hitotsu

The cuckoo—
where it disappears
a single island[9]

While sleeping in a lodge in the capital and hearing each night the sorrowful chanting of the Kūya pilgrims:

karazake mo
Kūya no yase mo
kan no uchi

Dried salmon
the gauntness of a Kūya pilgrim
in the cold season[1]

6. Written in 1686 and collected in *Spring Days*. Since the ancient period, the frog had been admired for its singing and its beautiful voice. In the Heian period it became associated with spring, the *yamabuki*—the bright yellow globeflower—and limpid mountain streams. According to one source, Kikaku, one of Bashō's disciples, suggested that Bashō use *yamabuki* in the opening phrase. Instead, Bashō works against the classical associations of the frog. In place of the plaintive voice of the frog singing in the rapids or calling out for its lover, Bashō evokes the sound of the frog jumping into the water. And instead of the elegant image of a frog in a fresh mountain stream beneath the *yamabuki*, the haiku presents a stagnant pond. At the same time, the haiku offers a fresh twist to the seasonal association of the frog with spring: the sudden movement of the frog, which suggests rebirth and the awakening of life in spring, is contrasted with the implicit winter stillness of the old pond.

7. This haiku, which Bashō composed in 1688, appears in *Backpack Notes*. The wisteria (*fuji no hana*), with its long drooping flowers, is blooming outside the lodge even as it functions as a metaphor for the traveler's heart.

8. Bashō composed this poem, which appears in *Backpack Notes*, in the Fourth Month of 1688. The octopus traps were lowered in the afternoon and raised the next morning, after the octopus had crawled inside. The octopus in the jars implicitly suggest the troops of the Heike clan that were massacred on these shores at the end of the 12th century and whose ghosts subsequently appear before the traveler in *Backpack Notes*. Now these octopi are having "fleeting dreams," not knowing they are about to be harvested. Bashō juxtaposes the "summer moon" (*natsu no tsuki*), which the classical tradition deemed to be as brief as the summer night and thus associated with ephemerality, and the "octopus traps" (*takotsubo*), a vernacular word, giving new life to the theme of impermanence.

The poem is intended to be humorous and sad at the same time.

9. Diverging from the classical poetic association of the cuckoo (*hototogisu*), which was its singing, Bashō focuses here on its arrow-like flight. In this poem, which Bashō wrote in 1688 during his *Backpack Notes* journey, the speaker implicitly hears the cuckoo, but by the time he looks up, it has disappeared, replaced by a single island, presumably Awajishima, the small island across the bay from Suma and Akashi, where the speaker stands. The haiku is also parodic, twisting a well-known classical poem in the *Senzaishū* (1188): "When I gaze in the direction of the crying cuckoo, only the moon lingers in the dawn." Another possible pretext is the following poem in the classic collection: "Faintly, in the morning mist on Akashi Bay, it disappears behind an island, the boat I long for." In Bashō's haiku, the flight of the disappearing cuckoo, which the poet implicitly longs to see, becomes the path of the ship, which "disappears behind" (*shimagakureyuku*) Awajishima, the "one island."

1. Bashō composed this haiku while visiting Kyōto in the Twelfth Month of 1690 and later included it in *Monkey's Straw Coat*. Kūya were lay monks or pilgrims who commemorated the anniversary of the death of Priest Kūya by begging and chanting Buddhist songs in the streets of Kyōto for 48 days beginning in the middle of the Eleventh Month. *Kan* (cold season), a roughly 30-day period from the Twelfth Month through the beginning of the First Month (February), was the coldest part of the year. The three parts—dried salmon (*karazake*), the gauntness of the Kūya pilgrim (*Kūya no yase*), and the cold season (*kan no uchi*), each of which is accentuated by a hard beginning "k" consonant and by the repeated *mo* (also)—suggest three different dimensions (material, human, and seasonal) of the loneliness of a traveler on a distant journey.

kogarashi ya
hohobare itamu
hito no kao

Withering winds—
the face of a man
pained by swollen cheeks[2]

mugimeshi ni
yatsururu koi ka
neko no tsuma—

A cat's wife—
grown thin from
love and barley?[3]

hototogisu
koe yokotau ya
mizu no ue

A cuckoo—
the voice lies stretched
over the water[4]

hiyahiya to
kabe o fumaete
hirune kana

Taking a midday nap
feet planted
on a cool wall[5]

kiku no ka ya
Nara ni wa furuki
hotoketachi

Chrysanthemum scent—
in Nara ancient statues
of the Buddha[6]

aki fukaki
tonari wa nani o
suru hito zo

Autumn deepening—
my neighbor
how does he live, I wonder?[7]

2. Composed in the winter of 1691. The two parts of the haiku—separated by the cutting word *ya*—can be read together as one continuous scene or separately as two parts reverberating against each other. In the first part, a person suffering from mumps (*hohobare,* literally, swollen cheeks) stands outside, his or her face contorted by the *kogarashi,* the strong winds that blow the leaves off the trees in the winter. In the second part, the person's face inflamed by and suffering from mumps echoes the cold, stinging wind. The expectations generated by withering winds, a classical seasonal topic associated with cold winter landscapes, are humorously undercut by the haiku phrase *hohobare itamu* (pained by swollen cheeks), which then leads to a double reversal: after the initial collision, the reader discovers a fusion between the withering winds and the painfully swollen cheeks.
3. "Cat's love for its mate" (*neko no tsumagoi*), later simply called cat's love (*neko no koi*), was a haiku seasonal topic that became popular in the Edo period. Bashō composed this haiku in 1691 and included it in *Monkey's Straw Coat.* Bashō humorously depicts a female cat that has grown emaciated not only from being fed only barley—a situation that suggests a poor farmhouse—but from intense lovemaking. (*Yatsururu* modifies both *mugimeshi* and *koi,* implying "emaciating barley and love.")
4. Bashō apparently wrote this haiku in the Fourth Month of 1693 after being urged by his disciples to compose on the topic of "cuckoos on the water's edge." As the cuckoo flies overhead, it makes a sharp penetrating cry, which "lies sideways" (*yokotau*), hanging over the quiet surface of the water, probably at dusk or night when it traditionally sings. The cuckoo quickly disappears, but the sound lingers, like an overtone.

5. This haiku appears in *Backpack Diary;* Bashō composed it in 1694 at the residence of Mokusetsu in Ōtsu (near Lake Biwa). This poem uses *hiyahiya* (cool) as a seasonal word for autumn. The speaker, cooling the bottoms of his bare feet on the wall, has fallen asleep on a hot afternoon. The implied topic is lingering summer heat (*zansho*), which is captured from a humorous, haiku angle, in the feet, through which the speaker feels the arrival of autumn.
6. Bashō composed this haiku in 1694, on Chrysanthemum Festival Day (Chōyō), which fell on the ninth day of the Ninth Month, while stopping at Nara on the way to Ōsaka on his last journey. Nara, the capital of Japan in the 8th century, is known for its many temples and buddha statues. The chrysanthemum, considered the aristocrat of flowers in classical poetry and a seasonal word for late autumn, possess a strong but refined fragrance. The many buddhas in the ancient capital of Nara evoke a similar sense of dignity, solemnity, and refinement as well as nostalgia for a bygone era.
7. Bashō composed this haiku, which appears in *Backpack Diary,* in the autumn of 1694, shortly before he died in Ōsaka. Bashō had been invited to a poem party at the home of one of his close followers, but he didn't feel well enough to go and instead sent a poem which subtly expresses his deep regret at not being able to meet his friends. In highly colloquial language, the poem suggests the loneliness of a traveler implicitly seeking companionship, or the loneliness of those who live together and yet apart in urban society, or the loneliness of life itself, particularly in the face of death—all of which resonate with late autumn (*aki fukaki*), associated in classical poetry with loneliness and sorrow.

kono michi ya	This road—
yuku hito nashi ni	no one goes down it
aki no kure	autumn's end[8]

Composed while ill:

tabi ni yande	Sick on a journey
yume wa kareno o	dreams roam about
kakemeguru	on a withered moor[9]

NARROW ROAD TO THE DEEP NORTH

In the spring of 1689, Bashō and his companion Sora departed for Michinoku, or Oku (Interior), the relatively unsettled northeastern area of Honshū, Japan's largest and main island. Bashō traveled north to present-day Sendai, crossed west over the mountains to the Japan Sea side, then moved south, down the coast, through Kanazawa, and arrived at Ōgaki in Mino Province (Gifu), after a five-month journey (see map on page 414). Although *Narrow Road to the Deep North* is often read as a faithful travel account, it is best regarded as a kind of fiction loosely based on the actual journey. Bashō depicts an ideal world in which the traveler devotes himself to poetic life in a manner that Bashō himself probably aspired to but found impossible in the busy world of a linked-verse and haiku master.

The text consists of fifty or so discrete sections strung together like a linked-verse sequence. They describe a series of interrelated journeys: a search for noted poetic places, especially the traces of ancient poets such as Saigyō, the medieval poet-priest to whom this account pays special homage; a journey into the past to such historical places as the old battlefield at Hiraizumi; an ascetic journey and a pilgrimage to sacred places; and interesting encounters with individuals and poetic partners, with whom he exchanges poetic greetings.

The interest of travel literature, at least in the Anglo-European tradition, generally lies in the unknown, new worlds, new knowledge, new perspectives, and new experiences. But for Japanese medieval poets, the object of travel was to confirm what already existed, to reinforce the roots of cultural memory. By visiting noted poetic locales, the poet-traveler hoped to relive the experience of his or her literary predecessors, to be moved to compose poetry on the same landscape, thereby joining his or her cultural forebears. The travel diary itself became a link in a chain of poetic and literary transmission.

In contrast to medieval Japanese poets, however, who attempted to preserve the classical associations of the poetic topics, Bashō sought out new poetic associations in classic sites and discovered new poetic places. In the passage on Muro-no-yashima, toward the beginning, Bashō suggests that *Narrow Road* will take a new approach, exploring both the local place and its historical and poetic roots in an effort to re-envision the landscape. A contrast can be seen between the places visited in the first half of *Narrow Road*, which tend to be major poetic sites and which bear the weight of the classical tradition, and those found along the Japan Sea side in the second half, such as Kisagata, which tend to be lesser poetic locales or even unknown in the classical tradition. In writing *Narrow Road*, Bashō sought a Chinese poetic ideal of "landscape in human emotion, and human emotion in landscape," in which the landscape becomes infused with

---

8. Bashō composed this in the late autumn of 1694, at the end of his life, at a large haiku gathering. The poem can be read as an expression of disappointment that, at the end of his life, in the autumn of his career—*aki no kure* can mean either "autumn's end" or "autumn evening"—he is alone, and/or as an expression of disappointment at the lack of sympathetic poetic partners, as an expression of desire for those who can engage in the poetic dialogue necessary to continue on this difficult journey.

9. Bashō's last poem, written four days before his death on the twelfth day of the Tenth Month of 1694, during a journey in Ōsaka.

cultural memory and a wide variety of human emotions and associations, from the sensual to the spiritual.

A number of the early sections imply that the journey also is a form of ascetic practice. The title of *Narrow Road to the Deep North* (*Oku no hosomichi*) implies not only the narrow and difficult roads (*hosomichi*) of Michinoku but the difficulty of the spiritual journey "within" (*oku*). Pilgrimages to sacred places, to temples and shrines, were popular from as early as the medieval Heian period and formed an integral part of travel literature, particularly those written by hermit-priests, a persona that Bashō adopts here. *Narrow Road,* in fact, has far more sections on this topic than usually found in medieval travel diaries. A typical passage begins with a description of the place and a history of the shrine or temple, usually giving some detail about the founder or the name. The climactic haiku, which may be a poetic greeting to the divine spirit or head of the temple/shrine, usually conveys a sense of the sacred quality or efficacy of the place.

Bashō wrote *Narrow Road* a considerable time after the actual journey, probably in 1694 at the end of his life, when he was developing his new ideal of *haibun,* or haiku-prose, in which haiku was embedded in poetic prose. *Narrow Road to the Deep North* is marked by a great variety of prose styles, and it may best be understood as an attempt to reveal the different possibilities of *haibun* in the form of travel literature. The resulting fusion of vernacular Japanese, classical Japanese, and classical Chinese, with its parallel and contrastive couplet-like phrases, had a profound impact on the development of Japanese prose. Of particular interest is the close fusion between the prose and the poetry, in which the prose creates a dramatic context for many of the best haiku that Bashō wrote.

PRONUNCIATIONS:
>*Hiraizumi:* hee-rye-zou-mee
>*Ise:* ee-say
>*Matsuo Bashō:* mah-tsu-oh bah-show
>*Saigyō:* sigh-gyoh

from Narrow Road to the Deep North[1]

>The months and days, the travelers of a hundred ages;
>the years that come and go, voyagers too.
>floating away their lives on boats,
>growing old as they lead horses by the bit,
>for them, each day a journey, travel their home.
>Many, too, are the ancients who perished on the road.

Some years ago, seized by wanderlust, I wandered along the shores of the sea. Then, last autumn, I swept away the old cobwebs in my dilapidated dwelling on the river's edge.

As the year gradually came to an end and spring arrived, filling the sky with mist, I longed to cross the Shirakawa Barrier, the most revered of poetic places. Somehow or other, I became possessed by a spirit, which crazed my soul. Unable to sit still, I accepted the summons of the Deity of the Road. No sooner had I repaired the holes in my trousers, attached a new cord to my rain hat, and cauterized my legs with moxa than my thoughts were on the famous moon at Matsushima. I turned my dwelling over to others and moved to Sanpū's villa.

---

1. Translated by Haruo Shirane.

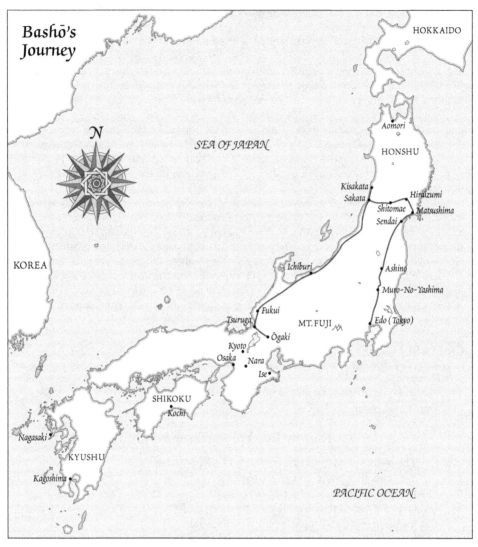

In spring 1687, Bashō and his disciple Sora departed Edo, the capital of Tokugawa Japan, for Michinoku (Deep North). Their five month journey concluded at Ōgaki.

kusa no to mo	Time even for the grass hut
sumikawaru yo zo	to change owners—
hina no ie	house of dolls[2]

I left a sheet of eight linked verses on the pillar of the hermitage.

I started out on the twenty-seventh day of the Third Month.

2. *Hina* (dolls), a new seasonal word for late spring, meant Hinamatsuri, the girls' festival on the third of the Third Month, when families with daughters displayed dolls in their houses. The time has come for even the recluse hut—symbolized by the "grass door"—to become a domestic, secular dwelling, with family and daughter(s).

The dawn sky was misting over; the moon lingered, giving off a pale light; the peak of Mount Fuji appeared faintly in the distance. I felt uncertain, wondering whether I would see again the cherry blossoms on the boughs at Ueno and Yanaka. My friends had gathered the night before to see me off and joined me on the boat. When I disembarked at a place called Senju, my breast was overwhelmed by thoughts of the "three thousand leagues ahead," and standing at the crossroads of the illusory world, I wept at the parting.

yuku haru ya	Spring going—
tori naki uo no	birds crying and tears
me wa namida	in the eyes of the fish[3]

Making this my first journal entry, we set off but made little progress. People lined the sides of the street, seeing us off, it seemed, as long as they could see our backs.

Was it the second year of Genroku? On a mere whim, I had resolved that I would make a long journey to the Deep North. Although I knew I would probably suffer, my hair growing white under the distant skies of Wu, I wanted to view those places that I had heard of but never seen and placed my faith in an uncertain future, not knowing if I would return alive. We barely managed to reach the Sōka post station that night. The luggage that I carried over my bony shoulders began to cause me pain. I had departed on the journey thinking that I need bring only myself, but I ended up carrying a coat to keep me warm at night, a night robe, rain gear, inkstone, brush, and the like, as well as the farewell presents that I could not refuse. All these became a burden on the road.

We paid our respects to the shrine at Muro-no-yashima, Eight Islands of the Sealed Room. Sora, my travel companion, noted: "This deity is called the Goddess of the Blooming Cherry Tree and is the same as that worshiped at Mount Fuji. Since the goddess entered a sealed hut and burned herself giving birth to Hohodemi, the God of Emitting Fire, and proving her vow, they call the place Eight Islands of the Sealed Room. The custom of including smoke in poems on this place also derives from this story. It is forbidden to consume a fish called *konoshiro,* or shad, which is thought to smell like flesh when burned. The essence of this shrine history is already known to the world."[4]

On the thirtieth, stopped at the foot of Nikkō Mountain. The owner said, "My name is Buddha Gozaemon. People have given me this name because I make honesty my first concern in all matters. As a consequence, you can relax for one night on the road. Please stay here." I wondered what kind of buddha had manifested itself in this soiled world to help someone like me, traveling like a beggar priest on a pilgrimage. I observed the actions of the innkeeper carefully and saw that he was neither clever nor calculating. He was nothing but honesty—the type of person that Confucius referred to when he said, "Those who are strong in will and without pretension are close to humanity." I had nothing but respect for the purity of his character.

3. The birds and fish mourn the passing of spring and, by implication, the departure of the travelers. Some commentators see the fish as the disciples left behind and the birds as the departing travelers (Bashō and Sora); others interpret the departing spring as the traveler. *Yuku,* a key word in *Narrow Road,* means both "to go" and "to pass time," thereby fusing passings in time and in space.
4. A typical classical poem on Muro-no-yashima, by Fujiwara Sanekata, reads: "How could I let you know of my longing were it not for the smoke of Muro-no-yashima?" Classical poets believed that the steam from a stream in Muro-no-yashima looked like smoke. However, Sora, who came from a family of Shintō priests, presents here a different explanation, taking a revisionary approach to *utamakura,* or poetic places.

On the first of the Fourth Month, we paid our respects to the holy mountain. In the distant past, the name of this sacred mountain was written with the characters Nikkōzan, Two Rough Mountain, but when Priest Kūkai established a temple here, he changed the name to Nikkō, Light of the Sun. Perhaps he was able to see a thousand years into the future. Now this venerable light shines throughout the land, and its benevolence flows to the eight corners of the earth, and the four classes—warrior, samurai, artisan, and merchant— all live in peace. Out of a sense of reverence and awe, I put my brush down here.

aratōto	Awe inspiring!
aoba wakaba no	on the green leaves, budding leaves
hi no hikari	light of the sun

Black Hair Mountain, enshrouded in mist, the snow still white.

sorisutete	Shaving my head
Kurokamiyama ni	at Black Hair Mountain—
koromogae	time for summer clothes[5]

[Sora]

Sora's family name is Kawai; his personal name is Sōgoro. He lived near me, helping me gather wood and heat water, and was delighted at the thought of sharing with me the sights of Matsushima and Kisagata. At the same time, he wanted to help me overcome the hardships of travel. On the morning of the departure, he shaved his hair, changed to dark black robes, and took on the Buddhist name of Sōgo. That is why he wrote the Black Hair Mountain poem. I thought that the words "time for summer clothes" were particularly effective.

Climbing more than a mile up a mountain, we came to a waterfall. From the top of the cavern, the water flew down a hundred feet, falling into a blue pool of a thousand rocks. I squeezed into a hole in the rocks and entered the cavern: they say that this is called Back-View Falls because you can see the waterfall from the back, from inside the cavern.

shibaraku wa	Secluded for a while
taki ni komoru ya	in a waterfall—
ge no hajime	beginning of summer austerities[6]

There is a mountain-priest temple called Kōmyōji. We were invited there and prayed at the Hall of Gyōja.

natsuyama ni	Summer mountains—
ashida o ogamu	praying to the tall clogs
kadode kana	at journey's start[7]

---

5. Embarking on a journey becomes synonymous with entering the Buddhist path: both imply a firm resolve and a new life, symbolized here by the seasonal word *koromogae* (change of clothes at the beginning of summer).

6. This line refers both to the beginning of summer and to the Buddhist austerities of summer, in which Buddhist practitioners remained indoors for three months fasting, reciting sutras, and carrying out such ascetic and purification practices as standing under a waterfall. The traveler stands behind the waterfall, which gives him the cool, pure feeling of being cleansed of the dirt of the world.

7. At the beginning of the journey, the traveler bows before the high clogs, a prayer for the foot strength of En no Gyōja, the founder of a mountain priest sect and an "austerity man" (gyōja) believed to have acquired superhuman power from rigorous mountain training.

The willow that was the subject of Saigyō's poem, "Where a Crystal Stream Flows,"[8] still stood in the village of Ashino, on a footpath in a rice field. The lord of the manor of this village had repeatedly said, "I would like to show you this willow," and I had wondered where it was. Today I was able to stand in its very shade.

> *ta ichimai* Whole field of
> *uete tachisaru* rice seedlings planted—I part
> *yanagi kana* from the willow[9]

The days of uncertainty piled one on the other, and when we came upon the Shirakawa Barrier, I finally felt as if I had settled into the journey. I can understand why that poet had written, "Had I a messenger, I would send a missive to the capital!" One of three noted barriers, the Shirakawa Barrier captured the hearts of poets. With the sound of the autumn wind in my ears and the image of the autumn leaves in my mind, I was moved all the more by the tops of the green-leafed trees.[1] The flowering of the wild rose amid the white deutzia clusters made me feel as if I were crossing over snow.

At the Sukagawa post station, we visited a man named Tōkyū. He insisted that we stay for four or five days and asked me how I had found the Shirakawa Barrier. I replied, "My body and spirit were tired from the pain of the long journey; my heart overwhelmed by the landscape. The thoughts of the distant past tore through me, and I couldn't think straight." But feeling it would be a pity to cross the barrier without producing a single verse, I wrote:

> *fūryū no* Beginnings of poetry—
> *hajime ya oku no* rice-planting songs
> *taue uta* of the Deep North[2]

This opening verse was followed by a second verse and then a third; before we knew it, three sequences.

The next day we went to Shinobu Village and visited Shinobu Mottling Rock. The rock was in a small village, half buried, deep in the shade of the mountain. A child from the village came and told us, "In the distant past, the rock was on top of this mountain, but the villagers, angered by the visitors who had been tearing up the

---

8. Poem by Saigyō in the *Shinkokinshū* collection (1205): "I thought to pause on the roadside where a crystal stream flows beneath a willow and stood rooted to the spot."

9. The entire passage alludes to *The Wandering Priest and the Willow,* a nō play based on Saigyō's poem just referred to, in which an itinerant priest, retracing the steps of Saigyō through the Deep North, meets an old man who shows him the withered willow about which Saigyō wrote his famous poem. The old man later turns out to be the spirit of that willow. At the end of the play the priest offers prayers to the spirit of the willow, thereby enabling it to achieve salvation. When the district officer offers to introduce Saigyō's willow to the traveler, the passage takes on the atmosphere of a nō dream play in which the traveler encounters the spirit of Saigyō, embodied in the willow. In contrast to Saigyō's classical poem, in which time passes as the traveler rests near a beautiful stream, in Bashō's haiku, time passes as the traveler journeys to meet Saigyō's spirit.

1. The Shirakawa Barrier here exists almost entirely in the traveler's imagination as a circle of poetic associations. Taira Kanemori (d. 990), referred to as "that poet," was the first in a long line of classical poets to compose on the

barrier: "Had I a messenger I would send a missive to the capital!" A poem by Priest Nōin, who first traveled to the Deep North in 1025, created the association of the Shirakawa Barrier with autumn wind. At a poetry contest in 1170, Minamoto Yorimasa composed a variation on Nōin's poem that also linked the Shirakawa Barrier with bright autumn leaves: "In the capital the leaves were still green when I saw them, but bright autumn leaves now scatter at the Shirakawa Barrier." Now Bashō follows the traces of Saigyō, Yorimasa, and others who had earlier sought the traces of Nōin, who in turn had followed the traces of Kanemori.

2. This haiku, which Bashō composed in the summer of 1689 and later placed in *Narrow Road*, is a greeting to his friend and host Tōkyō (1638–1715), a station master at Sukagawa, at the entrance to the Deep North (*oku*), the northeast region. Hearing the rice-planting songs in the fields (probably owned by Tōkyō), Bashō composes a poem that compliments the host on the elegance of his home and region. The poem also expresses Bashō's joy and gratitude at being able to compose linked verse for the first time in the Interior.

barley grass to test the rock, pushed it down into the valley, where it lies face down."
Perhaps that was the way it had to be.

sanae toru	Planting rice seedlings
temoto ya mukashi	the hands—in the distant past pressing
shinobuzuri	the grass of longing[3]

* * *

The Courtyard Inscribed-Stone was in Taga Castle in the Village of Ichikawa.
More than six feet tall and about three feet wide; the moss had eaten away the rock,
and the letters were faint. On the memorial, which listed the number of miles to the
four borders of the province: "This castle was built in 724 by Lord Ōno Azumabito,
the Provincial Governor and General of the Barbarian-Subduing Headquarters. In
762, on the first of the Twelfth Month, it was rebuilt by the Councillor and Military
Commander of the Eastern Seaboard, Lord Emi Asakari." The memorial belonged to
the era of the sovereign Shōmu.[4] Famous places in poetry have been collected and
preserved; but mountains crumble, rivers shift, roads change, rock are buried in dirt;
trees age, saplings replace them; times change, generations come and go. But here,
without a doubt, was a memorial of a thousand years: I was peering into the heart of
the ancients. The virtues of travel, the joys of life, forgetting the weariness of travel, I
shed only tears. * * *

It was already close to noon when we borrowed a boat and crossed over to Matsushima. The distance was more than two leagues, and we landed on the shore of
Ojima. It has been said many times, but Matsushima is the most beautiful place in all
of Japan. First of all, it can hold its head up to Dongting Lake or West Lake. Letting
in the sea from the southeast, it fills the bay, three leagues wide, with the tide of Zhejiang.
Matsushima has gathered countless islands: the high ones point their fingers to
heaven; those lying down crawl over the waves. Some are piled two deep; some, three
deep. To the left, the islands are separated from one another; to the right, they are
linked. Some seem to be carrying islands on their backs; others, to be embracing them
like a person caressing a child. The green of the pine is dark and dense, the branches
and leaves bent by the salty sea breeze—as if they were deliberately twisted. A soft,
tranquil landscape, like a beautiful lady powdering her face. Did the god of the mountain create this long ago, in the age of the gods? Is this the work of the Creator? What
words to describe this?

The rocky shore of Ojima extended out from the coast and became an island protruding in the sea. Here were the remains of Priest Ungo's dwelling and the rock on
which he meditated. Again, one could see, scattered widely in the shadow of the
pines, people who had turned their backs on the world. They lived quietly in grass
huts, the smoke from burning rice ears and pinecones rising from the huts. I didn't
know what kind of people they were, but I was drawn to them, and when I approached,

---

3. Shinobu was the most famous *utamakura,* or poetic
place, in the Deep North. Women there would rub ferns
onto woven cloth so as to create a wild pattern or design,
which became associated with uncontrolled longing. The
traveler in *Narrow Road* is disappointed to discover that
an *utamakura* that had given birth to countless poems has

been neglected and abused, but the powerful memory of
that poetic place enables the poet to find new poetry in the
mundane, as Bashō sees the women's hands planting
seedlings instead of rubbing the famous ferns.
4. Emperor Shōmu, r. 724–748. In actuality, Shōmu
wasn't alive at the time of this memorial.

the moon was reflected on the sea, and the scenery changed again, different from the afternoon landscape. When we returned to the shore and took lodgings, I opened the window. It was a two-story building, and I felt like a traveler sleeping amid the wind and the clouds: to a strange degree it was a good feeling.

> *Matsushima ya*   Matsushima—
> *tsuru ni mi kare*   borrow the body of a crane
> *hototogisu*   cuckoo!!
>
>   [Sora]

I closed my mouth and tried to sleep but couldn't. When I left my old hermitage, Sodō had given me a Chinese poem on Matsushima, and Hara Anteki had sent me a waka on Matsugaurashima. Opening my knapsack, I made those poems my friends for the night. There also were hokku by Sanpū and Jokushi.

On the eleventh, made a pilgrimage to Zuiganji temple. Thirty-two generations ago, Makabe Heishirō took holy vows, went to China, returned, and founded this temple. Owing to his good works, the seven halls of the temple have been splendidly rebuilt, the gold-foiled walls and the grand decorations casting a light on everything. The temple, a realization of the land of the buddha in this world. Wondered where that temple of the famous Kenbutsu sage was.

On the twelfth we headed for Hiraizumi. We had heard of such places as the Pine at Anewa and the Thread-Broken Bridge, but there were few human traces, and finding it difficult to recognize the path normally used by the rabbit hunters and woodcutters, we ended up losing our way and came out at a harbor called Ishi no maki. Across the water we could see Kinkazan, the Golden Flower Mountain, where the "Blooming of the Golden Flower" poem had been composed as an offering to the emperor. Several hundred ferry boats gathered in the inlet; human dwellings fought for space on the shore; and the smoke from the ovens rose high. Never occurred to me I would come across such a prosperous place. Attempted to find a lodging, but no one gave us a place for the night. Finally, spent the night in an impoverished hovel and, at dawn, wandered off again onto an unknown road. Looking afar at Sode no watari, Obuchi no maki, Mano no kayahara, and other famous places, made our way over a dike that extended into the distance. Followed the edge of a lonely and narrow marsh, lodged for the night at a place called Toima and then arrived at Hiraizumi: a distance, I think, of more than twenty leagues.

The glory of three generations of Fujiwara vanished in the space of a dream; the remains of the Great Gate stood two miles in the distance. Hidehira's headquarters had turned into rice paddies and wild fields. Only Kinkeizan, Golden Fowl Hill, remained as it was. First, we climbed Takadachi, Castle-on-the Heights, from where we could see the Kitakami, a broad river that flowed from the south. The Koromo River rounded Izumi Castle, and at a point beneath Castle-on-the-Heights, it dropped into the broad river. The ancient ruins of Yasuhira and others, lying behind Koromo Barrier, appear to close off the southern entrance and guard against the Ainu barbarians. Selecting his loyal retainers, Yoshitsune fortified himself in the castle, but his glory quickly turned to grass. "The state is destroyed; rivers and hills remain. The city walls turn to spring; grasses and trees are green." With these lines from Du Fu in my head, I lay down my bamboo hat, letting the time and tears flow.

natsugusa ya Summer grasses—
tsuwamonodomo ga the traces of dreams
yume no ato of ancient warriors[5]

unohana ni In the deutzia
Kanefusa miyuru Kanefusa appears
shiraga kana white haired[6]

[Sora]

The two halls about which we had heard such wonderful things were open. The Sutra Hall held the statues of the three chieftains, and the Hall of Light contained the coffins of three generations, preserving three sacred images. The seven precious substances were scattered and lost; the doors of jewels, torn by the wind; the pillars of gold, rotted in the snow. The hall should have turned into a mound of empty, abandoned grass, but the four sides were enclosed, covering the roof with shingles, surviving the snow and rain. For a while, it became a memorial to a thousand years.

samidare no Have the summer rains
furinokoshite come and gone, sparing
hikaridō the Hall of Light?

Gazing afar at the road that extended to the south, we stopped at the village of Iwade. We passed Ogurazaki and Mizu no ojima, and from Narugo Hot Springs we proceeded to Passing-Water Barrier and attempted to cross into Dewa Province. Since there were few travelers on this road, we were regarded with suspicion by the barrier guards, and it was only after considerable effort that we were able to cross the barrier. We climbed a large mountain, and since it had already grown dark, we caught sight of a house of a border guard and asked for lodging. For three days, the wind and rain were severe, forcing us to stay in the middle of a boring mountain.

nomi shirami Fleas, lice—
uma no shito suru a horse passes water
makuramoto by my pillow

I visited a person named Seifū at Obanazawa. Though wealthy, he had the spirit of a recluse. Having traveled repeatedly to the capital, he understood the tribulations of travel and gave me shelter for a number of days. He eased the pain of the long journey.

---

5. The four successive heavy "o" syllables in *tsuwamonodomo* ("warriors") suggest the ponderous march of soldiers or the thunder of battle. This haiku depends on multiple meanings: *ato* can mean "site," "aftermath," "trace," or "track"; and *yume* can mean "dream," "ambition," or "glory." The traveler here takes on the aura of the traveling priest in a nō warrior play who visits the site of a former battlefield and then, as if in a dream, watches the ghost of the slain warrior reenact his most tragic moments on the battlefield. Through the reference to Tang Dynasty poet Du Fu's noted Chinese poem on the impermanence of civilization—"The state is destroyed, rivers and hills remain / The city walls turn to spring, grasses and trees are green"—Bashō transforms these classical associations of eroticism and fertility into those of battle and the larger theme of the ephemerality of human ambitions.

6. The white flowers of the deutzia, a kind of brier, appear in the midst of a field of summer grass, from which the figure of Kanefusa rises like a ghost. According to the *Record of Yoshitsune*, Kanefusa, Yoshitsune's loyal retainer, helped Yoshitsune's wife and children commit suicide; saw his master to his end; set fire to the fort at Takadachi; slew an enemy captain; and then leaped into the flames—a sense of frenzy captured in the image of the white hair.

> *suzushisa o*
> *waga yado ni shite*
> *nemaru nari*

Taking coolness
for my lodging
I relax[7]

In Yamagata there was a mountain temple, the Ryūshakuji, founded by the high priest Jikaku, an especially pure and tranquil place. People had urged us to see this place at least once, so we backtracked from Obanazawa, a distance of about seven leagues. It was still light when we arrived. We borrowed a room at a temple at the mountain foot and climbed to the Buddha hall at the top. Boulders were piled on boulders; the pines and cypress had grown old; the soil and rocks were aged, covered with smooth moss. The doors to the temple buildings at the top were closed, not a sound to be heard. I followed the edge of the cliff, crawling over the boulders, and then prayed at the Buddhist hall. It was a stunning scene wrapped in quiet—I felt my spirit being purified.

> *shizukasa ya*
> *iwa ni shimiiru*
> *semi no koe*

Stillness—
sinking deep into the rocks
cries of the cicada[8]

The Mogami River originates in the Deep North; its upper reaches are in Yamagata. As we descended, we encountered frightening rapids with names like Scattered Go Stones and Flying Eagle. The river skirts the north side of Mount Itajiki and then finally pours into the sea at Sakata. As I descended, passing through the dense foliage, I felt as if the mountains were covering the river on both sides. When filled with rice, these boats are apparently called "rice boats." Through the green leaves, I could see the falling waters of White-Thread Cascade. Sennindō, Hall of the Wizard, stood on the banks, directly facing the water. The river was swollen with rain, making the boat journey perilous.

> *samidare wo*
> *atsumete hayashi*
> *Mogamigawa*

Gathering the rains
of the wet season—swift
the Mogami River[9]

Haguroyama, Gassan, and Yudono are called the Three Mountains of Dewa. At Haguroyama, Feather Black Mountain—which belongs to the Tōeizan Temple in Edo, in Musashi Province—the moon of Tendai concentration and contemplation shines, and the lamp of the Buddhist Law of instant enlightenment glows. The temple quarters stand side by side, and the ascetics devote themselves to their calling. The efficacy of the divine mountain, whose prosperity will last forever, fills people with awe and fear.

On the eighth, we climbed Gassan, Moon Mountain. With purification cords around our necks and white cloth wrapped around our heads, we were led up the mountain by a person called a "strongman." Surrounded by clouds and mist, we walked over ice and snow and climbed for twenty miles. Wondering if we had passed Cloud Barrier, beyond which the sun and moon move back and forth, I ran out of breath, my body

7. Bashō, exhausted from a difficult journey, finds Seifū's residence and hospitality to be "coolness" itself and "relaxes" (*nemaru*)—a word in the local dialect—as if he were at home. In an age without air conditioners, the word "cool" (*suzushisa*), a seasonal word for summer, was the ultimate compliment that could be paid to the host of a summer's lodging.
8. In classical poetry, the cicada was associated with its raucous, unpleasant cries. In a paradoxical twist, the sharp, high-pitched cries of the cicada deepen the stillness by penetrating the rocks on top of the mountain.
9. Here Bashō gives a new "poetic essence," based on personal experience, to the Mogami River, an *utamakura* (poetic place) long associated with rice-grain boats, which were thought to ply the river.

frozen. By the time we reached the top, the sun had set and the moon had come out. We spread bamboo grass on the ground and lay down, waiting for the dawn. When the sun emerged and the clouds cleared away, we descended to Yudono, Bathhouse Mountain.

On the side of the valley were the so-called Blacksmith Huts. Here blacksmiths collect divine water, purify their bodies and minds, forge swords admired by the world, and engrave them with "Moon Mountain." I hear that in China they harden swords in the sacred water at Dragon Spring, and I was reminded of the ancient story of Gan Jiang and Mo Ye, the two Chinese who crafted famous swords. The devotion of these masters to the art was extraordinary. Sitting down on a large rock for a short rest, I saw a cherry tree about three feet high, its buds half open. The tough spirit of the late-blooming cherry tree, buried beneath the accumulated snow, remembering the spring, moved me. It was as if I could smell the "plum blossom in the summer heat," and I remembered the pathos of the poem by Priest Gyōson.[1] Forbidden to speak of the details of this sacred mountain, I put down my brush.

When we returned to the temple quarters, at priest Egaku's behest, we wrote down verses about our pilgrimage to the Three Mountains.

suzushisa ya	Coolness—
hono mikazuki no	faintly a crescent moon over
Haguroyama	Feather Black Mountain[2]
kumo no mine	Cloud peaks
ikutsu kuzurete	crumbling one after another—
tsuki no yama	Moon Mountain[3]
katararenu	Forbidden to speak—
yudono ni nurasu	wetting my sleeves
tamoto kana	at Bathhouse Mountain![4]

Left Haguro and at the castle town of Tsurugaoka were welcomed by the samurai Nagayama Shigeyuki. Composed a round of haikai. Sakichi accompanied us this far. Boarded a boat and went down to the port of Sakata. Stayed at the house of a doctor named En'an Fugyoku.

---

1. "Plum blossoms in summer heat" is a Zen phrase for the unusual ability to achieve enlightenment. The plum tree blooms in early spring and generally never lasts until the summer. The poem by the priest Gyōson (1055–1135) is "think of us as feeling sympathy for each other! Mountain cherry blossoms! I know of no one beside you here." 2. Greetings to the spirit of the land often employed complex wordplay and associative words, which interweave the place-name into the physical description. Here the prefix *hono* (faintly or barely) and *mikazuki* (third-day moon) create a visual contrast between the thin light of the crescent moon and the blackness of the night, implied in the name Feather Black Mountain. The silver hook of the moon, which casts a thin ray of light through the darkness, brings a sense of "coolness" amid the summer heat, suggesting both the hospitality and the spiritual purity of the sacred mountain. 3. *Kumo no mine* (literally, cloud peak) is a high, cumulus cloud that results from intense moisture and heat. The mountain-shaped clouds, which have gathered during midday at the peak of Gassan, or Moon Mountain, crumble or collapse one after another until they are finally gone, leaving the moon shining over the mountain (*tsuki no yama*), a Japanese reading for "Gassan." Movement occurs from midday, when the clouds block the view, to night, when the mountain stands unobscured, and from mental obscurity to enlightenment. 4. In contrast to the first two mountains, which never appeared in classical poetry, Yudono (literally, Bathhouse) was often referred to in classical poetry as Koi-no-yama, Mountain of Love. The body of the Yudono deity was a huge red rock that spouted hot water and was said to resemble sexual organs. "Forbidden to speak" refers to the rule that all visitors to Yudono are forbidden to speak about the appearance of the mountain to others. The wetting of the sleeves echoes the erotic association with love and bathing and also suggests the speaker's tears of awe at the holiness of the mountain.

Atsumiyama ya	From Hot Springs Mountain
Fukuura kakete	to the Bay of Breezes,
yusuzumi	the evening cool

atsuki hi o	Pouring the hot day
umi ni iretari	into the sea—
Mogamigawa	Mogami River[5]

Having seen all the beautiful landscapes—rivers, mountains, seas, and coasts—I now prepared my heart for Kisagata. From the port at Sakata moving northeast, we crossed over a mountain, followed the rocky shore, and walked across the sand—all for a distance of ten miles. The sun was on the verge of setting when we arrived. The sea wind blew sand into the air; the rain turned everything to mist, hiding Chōkai Mountain. I groped in the darkness. Having heard that the landscape was exceptional in the rain, I decided that it must also be worth seeing after the rain, too, and squeezed into a fisherman's thatched hut to wait for the rain to pass.

By the next morning the skies had cleared, and with the morning sun shining brightly, we took a boat to Kisagata. Our first stop was Nōin Island, where we visited the place where Nōin had secluded himself for three years. We docked our boat on the far shore and visited the old cherry tree on which Saigyō had written the poem about "a fisherman's boat rowing over the flowers."[6] On the shore of the river was an imperial mausoleum, the gravestone of Empress Jingū. The temple was called Kanmanju Temple. I wondered why I had yet to hear of an imperial procession to this place.

We sat down in the front room of the temple and raised the blinds, taking in the entire landscape at one glance. To the south, Chōkai Mountain held up the heavens, its shadow reflected on the bay of Kisagata; to the west, the road came to an end at Muyamuya Barrier; and to the east, there was a dike. The road to Akita stretched into the distance. To the north was the sea, the waves pounding into the bay at Shiogoshi, Tide-Crossing. The face of the bay, about two and a half miles in width and length, resembled Matsushima but with a different mood. If Matsushima was like someone laughing, Kisagata resembled a resentful person filled with sorrow and loneliness. The land was as if in a state of anguish.

Kisagata ya	Kisagata—
ame ni Seishi ga	Xi Shi asleep in the rain
nebu no hana	flowers of the silk tree[7]

---

5. The first version was composed by Bashō at the residence of Terajima Hikosuke, a wealthy merchant at Sakata: "Coolness— / pouring into the sea, / Mogami River." The haiku praises the view from Hikosuke's house, which overlooks the great Mogami River where it flows into the Japan Sea. In the revised version, the Mogami River is pouring the *atsuki hi*, "hot sun" or "hot day," suggesting both a setting sun washed by the waves at sea and a hot summer's day coming to a dramatic close in the sea. Bashō drops the word "coolness" and the constraints of the greeting to his host to create a more dramatic image, one that suggests coolness without using the word.

6. The poem attributed to Saigyō is "The cherry trees at Kisakata are buried in waves—a fisherman's boat rowing over the flowers."

7. Kisagata was an *utamakura* (poetic place) associated, particularly as a result of the famous poem by Nōin (d. 1050), with wandering, the thatched huts of fisherfolk, lodgings, and a rocky shore. The traveler relives these classical associations, but in the end, he draws on Chinese poet Su Dongpo's "West Lake," which compares the noted lake to Xi Shi, a legendary Chinese beauty who was forced to debauch an enemy emperor and cause his defeat. She was thought to have a constant frown, her eyes half closed, as a result of her tragic fate. Dampened and shriveled by the rain, the silk tree flower echoes the resentful Chinese consort: both in turn became a metaphor for the rain-enshrouded, emotionally dark bay.

shiogoshi ya	In the shallows—
tsuru hagi nurete	cranes wetting their legs
umi suzushi	coolness of the sea[8]

Reluctant to leave Sakata, the days piled up; now I turn my gaze to the far-off clouds of the northern provinces. Thoughts of the distant road ahead fill me with anxiety; I hear it is more than 325 miles to the castle town in Kaga. After we crossed Nezu-no-seki, Mouse Barrier, we hurried toward Echigo and came to Ichiburi, in Etchū Province. During these nine days, I suffered from the extreme heat, fell ill, and did not record anything.

fumizuki ya	The Seventh Month—
muika mo tsune no	the sixth day, too, is different
yo ni wa nizu	from the usual night[9]

araumi ya	A wild sea—
Sado ni yokotau	stretching to Sado Isle
Amanogawa	the River of Heaven[1]

Today, exhausted from crossing the most dangerous places in the north country— places with names like Children Forget Parents, Parents Forget Children, Dogs Turn Back, Horses Sent Back—I drew up my pillow and lay down to sleep, only to hear in the adjoining room the voices of two young women. An elderly man joined in the conversation, and I gathered that they were women of pleasure from a place called Niigata in Echigo Province. They were on a pilgrimage to Ise Shrine, and the man was seeing them off as far as the barrier here at Ichiburi. They seemed to be writing letters and giving him other trivial messages to take back to Niigata tomorrow. Like "the daughters of the fishermen, passing their lives on the shore where the white waves roll in,"[2] they had fallen low in this world, exchanging vows with every passerby. What terrible lives they must have had in their previous existence for this to occur. I fell asleep as I listened to them talk. The next morning, they came up to us as we departed. "The difficulties of road, not knowing our destination, the uncertainty and sorrow—it makes us want to follow your tracks. We'll be inconspicuous. Please bless us with your robes of compassion, link us to the Buddha," they said tearfully.

"We sympathize with you, but we have many stops on the way. Just follow the others. The gods will make sure that no harm occurs to you." Shaking them off with these remarks, we left, but the pathos of their situation lingered with us.

hitotsu ya ni	Under the same roof
yūjo mo netari	women of pleasure also sleep—
hagi to tsuki	bush clover and moon[3]

I dictated this to Sora, who wrote it down.

---

8. Bashō here describes Kisagata after the rains, closing out a series of contrasts: between lightness and darkness, laughter and resentment, the dark brooding atmosphere of Kisagata during the rains and the cool, light atmosphere that follows.

9. The seventh night of the Seventh Month was when the legendary constellations, the Herd Boy and Weaver Girl, two separated lovers, cross over the Milky Way for their annual meeting. Even the night before is unusual.

1. Sado, an island across the water from Izumozaki (Izumo Point), was known for its long history of political exiles. Here the island, standing under the vast River of

Heaven or Milky Way, comes to embody the feeling of loneliness, both of the exiles and of the traveler himself.

2. From the anonymous *Shinkokinshū* poem "Since I am the daughter of a fisherman, passing my life on the shore where the white waves roll in, I have no home."

3. The haiku suggests Bashō's surprise that two very different parties—the young prostitutes and the male priest-travelers—have something in common, implicitly the uncertainty of life and of travel. The bush clover (*hagi*), the object of love in classical poetry, suggests the prostitutes, while the moon, associated with enlightenment and clarity, may imply Bashō and his priest friend.

We visited Tada Shrine where Sanemori's helmet and a piece of his brocade robe were stored. They say that long ago when Sanemori belonged to the Genji clan, Lord Yoshitomo offered him the helmet. Indeed, it was not the armor of a common soldier. A chrysanthemum and vine carved design inlaid with gold extended from the visor to the ear flaps, and a two-horn frontpiece was attached to the dragon head. After Sanemori died in battle, Kiso Yoshinaka attached a prayer sheet to the helmet and offered it to the shrine. Higuchi Jirō had acted as Kiso's messenger. It was as if the past were appearing before my very eyes.

muzan ya na	"How pitiful!"
kabuto no shita no	beneath the warrior helmet
kirigirisu	cries of a cricket[4]

The sixteenth. The skies had cleared, and we decided to gather little red shells at Iro-no-hama, Color Beach, seven leagues across the water. A man named Ten'ya made elaborate preparations—lunch boxes, wine flasks, and the like—and ordered a number of servants to go with us on the boat. Enjoying a tailwind, we arrived quickly. The beach was dotted with a few fisherman's huts and a dilapidated Lotus Flower temple. We drank tea, warmed up saké, and were overwhelmed by the loneliness of the evening.

sabishisa ya	Loneliness—
Suma ni kachitaru	an autumn beach judged
hama no aki	superior to Suma's[5]
nami no ma ya	Between the waves—
kogai ni majiru	mixed with small shells
hagi no chiri	petals of bush clover

I had Tōsai write down the main events of that day and left it at the temple.

Rotsū came as far as the Tsuruga harbor to greet me, and together we went to Mino Province. With the aid of horses, we traveled to Ōgaki. Sora joined us from Ise. Etsujin galloped in on horseback, and we gathered at the house of Jokō. Zensenshi, Keiko, Keiko's sons, and other intimate acquaintances visited day and night. For them, it was like meeting someone who had returned from the dead. They were both overjoyed and sympathetic. Although I had not yet recovered from the weariness of the journey, we set off again on the sixth of the Ninth Month. Thinking to pay our respects to the great shrine at Ise, we boarded a boat.

hamaguri no	Autumn going—
futami ni wakare	parting for Futami
yuku aki zo	a clam pried from its shell[6]

4. In *The Tales of Heike*, Saitō Sanemori, not wanting other soldiers to realize his advanced age, dyed his white hair black and fought valiantly before being slain by the retainers of Kiso Yoshinaka (1154–1184). According to legend, Yoshinaka, who had been saved by Sanemori as a child, wept at seeing the washed head of the slain warrior and subsequently made an offering of the helmet and brocade to Tada Shrine. The cricket, a seasonal word for autumn, was associated in classical poetry with pathos and the loneliness that comes from inevitable decline.

5. Suma was closely associated with the poetry of Ariwara no Yukihira (d. 893), who was exiled to Suma, and the hero of *The Tale of Genji*, who was also exiled there, and so it was considered to be the embodiment of loneliness in the classical tradition.

6. Bashō's closing haiku turns on a series of puns: *wakaru* means both "to depart for" and "to tear from," and Futami refers to a noted place on the coast of Ise Province (the traveler's next destination and a place known for clams) as well as the shell (*futa*) and body (*mi*) of the clam (*hamaguri*). The phrase "autumn going" (*yuku aki*) directly echoes the phrase "spring going" (*yuku haru*) in the poem at the beginning of the narrative.

Charles de Secondat, Baron de la Brède et de Montesquieu
1689–1755

"How can anyone be Persian?" wonder Montesquieu's Parisian elite on meeting Usbek, their fictional foreign visitor. Montesquieu was himself an outsider in Paris—a member of the provincial minor aristocracy who began frequenting Paris at twenty-eight after having dutifully entered an arranged marriage, produced an heir, and taken up his tediously bureaucratic inherited post in the Parliament of Bordeaux. Like Usbek, Montesquieu was seduced by the debauched, ruinously expensive but brilliant Parisian high society he satirized, abandoning his intellectual wife, children, and estates, and squandering his fortune to spend most of his prime years there. He entered on the Parisian scene soon after the death of Louis XIV in 1715, brought in to advise the Regent on how to clean up the financial mess Louis had left behind. His *Persian Letters* is much more about the decadence of Regency Paris than it is about Persia. Its publication in 1721 opened the floodgates to the anti-Catholic pamphlets that increased throughout the century, and provoked numerous responses and sequels.

While his real subject is the critique of Parisian society, Montesquieu did draw upon all the authentic sources on Persia and the Near East available to him in the long-established French tradition of travel writing, as well as on earlier fictions of oriental travelers observing the absurdities of Western culture, and a whole genre of oriental tales inspired by *The Thousand and One Nights,* first translated into French between 1704 and 1717 by Galland. *Persian Letters* was intended not as a novel, but as something more serious than what that age saw as mere entertainment. Nevertheless Montesquieu was pleased his readers found in it "without expecting to, a kind of novel." He claimed that the epistolary form allowed him to combine philosophy with story and character, and inadvertently influenced the development of the novel: "My Persian Letters," he wrote, "taught how to write novels in letter form."

How can anyone be himself? is the question poet Paul Valéry identified as the serious subject of *Persian Letters*. The death of Louis XIV was a milestone in the long dying of absolutism and absolute values in Europe, and Montesquieu led the move from justifying the status quo to the study of societies in relative terms. Nevertheless his project was not a relativist one, although it entails a recognition that only by accepting cultural relativity is a society truly civilized. Ultimately it represents a search for a more comprehensive absolute; Montesquieu pursued this further in his *On the Spirit of the Laws* (1748), which undertook, from a comparative and historical study of laws, to distill underlying truths about man beyond cultural difference. Thus his work is part of the encyclopedic pursuit that characterizes the rest of the century, culminating with that of Rousseau and Diderot.

Montesquieu died in 1755, confessing his faith in the Catholic Church but defending his writings to the end. The only literary man who dared to attend his funeral was Diderot, who had learned much from him.

PRONUNCIATION:
Montesquieu: MON-tehs-cue

from Persian Letters[1]

LETTER 24

Rica to Ibben in Smyrna[2]

We have been in Paris for a month and have been continually in motion. It takes much doing to find a place to live, to meet people to whom you are recommended, and to provide yourself with necessities all at the same time.

Paris is as large as Ispahan.[3] The houses here are so high that you would swear they were all inhabited by astrologers. You can readily understand that a city built up in the air, with six or seven houses built one on top of the other, is an extremely populous city, and that when everyone is down in the streets, there is great confusion.

Perhaps you will not believe this, but for the month I have been here, I have seen nobody walking. There are no people in the world who get so much out of their carcasses as the French: they run; they fly. The slow carriages of Asia, the regular pace of our camels, would make them swoon. As for myself, I am not built that way, and when I go walking, as I do often, without changing my pace, I sometimes fume and rage like a Christian. For, passing over the fact that I am splashed from head to foot, still I cannot forgive the elbowings in my ribs that I collect regularly and periodically. A man walking behind me, passes me and turns me half-around; then another, coming toward me from the opposite direction, briskly puts me back into the position where the first fellow hit me. I have barely made a hundred paces before I am more bruised than if I had gone ten leagues.

Do not expect me to be able just now to talk to you seriously about European usages and customs. I have only a faint idea of them myself and have barely had time to be amazed by them.

The King of France[4] is the most powerful prince of Europe. Unlike his neighbor the King of Spain, he has no gold mines. Yet he possesses greater riches, for he draws from the vanity of his subjects a wealth more inexhaustible than mines. He has been known to undertake and wage great wars with no other funds than honorary titles to sell, and by reason of this miracle of human pride, his troops are paid, his fortresses armed, and his navies fitted out.

Moreover, this king is a great magician. He exercises his empire over the very minds of his subjects and makes them think as he likes. If he has only one million crowns in his treasury and he needs two million, he has only to convince them that one crown equals two, and they believe him. If he is involved in a war that is difficult in the waging and finds himself short of money, he has only to put into their heads the notion that a slip of paper is money, and they are immediately convinced. He even goes so far as to make them believe that he can cure them of all manner of disease by touching them,[5] so great is his strength and dominion over their minds.

What I am telling you about this prince ought not astonish you. For there is another magician even more powerful than the first and who has no less dominion over the mind of the first than that one has over the minds of others. This magician is called the Pope. Sometimes he has the King believing that three are only one, sometimes that the bread he eats is not bread and the wine he drinks not wine, and a thousand other things of the sort.

And, in order to keep up his second wind and not let the prince lose the habit of believing, this magician occasionally gives him certain articles of faith for exercise. Two years ago, he sent him a great writ, which he called the *Constitution*,[6] and at all costs, wanted to make the prince and all his subjects believe everything that was contained therein. He succeeded with the prince, who submitted immediately and gave a good example to his subjects. But some of them rebelled and said they weren't going to believe a single word of what was in the writ. Women were behind this revolt, which divided the whole court, the whole kingdom, and every family. This Constitution forbids the people to read a book that all the Christians claim was brought down from heaven; it is, properly speaking, their Koran. The women, outraged at this insult to their sex, aroused everyone and everything against the Constitution. They have managed to bring the men around to their side, and in this case, the men do not choose to exercise their prerogative. It must be admitted, all the same, that this mufti does not reason badly, and by the great Ali, he must have been instructed in the principles of our holy law. For, since women are inferior to us by creation and since our prophets tell us that they won't enter into paradise, why should they get involved with reading a book that was written solely to teach the way to paradise?

I have heard stories that sound miraculous, told about the King, and I have no doubt you will hesitate to believe them.

They say that while he was making war on his neighbors, all allied against him, he was surrounded in his own kingdom by a countless number of invisible enemies.[7] They add that he had been seeking them out for thirty years and that in spite of the untiring efforts of certain dervishes[8] in his trust, he could not find a single one of them. They are living with him, they are at his court, in his capital city, in his armies, in his law courts, and yet it is said that he will suffer the vexation of dying without having found them out. One might say that they exist in general and yet no longer have any identity in particular. They form a body with no members. No doubt heaven chooses to punish the prince for not having been moderate enough against his conquered enemies, for it provides him with invisible ones whose jinni and destiny are superior to his own.

I shall continue to write to you, and I shall teach you things far removed from Persian character and spirit. It is certainly the same earth carrying both countries, but the men of this country where I am and those of the country where you are are quite different.

From Paris, the 4th of the Moon of Rebiab II, 1712

LETTER 26

Usbek to Roxane in the seraglio[9] at Ispahan

How fortunate you are, Roxane, to be in the gentle country of Persia and not in these poisonous climes where decency and virtue are unknown! How happy for you! You dwell in my seraglio as in a continuing state of innocence, far from the reaches of all human beings. You are in a joyful state of happy inability to transgress: no man

---

6. The papal bull *Unigenitus,* passed in 1713 by Pope Clement XI to suppress Jansenist writings and a vernacular New Testament with Jansenist notes serving as aids to meditation. Jansenism was a Roman Catholic movement that advocated a return to the teachings of St. Augustine. Jansenists emphasized personal holiness and believed in extreme predeterminism, bringing them into conflict with the established Catholic church.
7. Jansenists.
8. Jesuits.
9. Harem.

has ever soiled you with his lascivious regard. Even your father-in-law, in the relaxed freedom of banquets, has not seen your lovely mouth. You have never forgotten to attach the holy band that conceals it. O happy Roxane! Whenever you go to the country, you have always had eunuchs to walk ahead of you and reduce to death all such insolent ones as fail to avoid sight of you. And I myself, to whom heaven has vouchsafed you for my happiness, what great difficulty I had to take possession of that treasure you defended so steadfastly! What frustration for me in the first days of our marriage, what vexation not to see you! And what impatience when I had seen you! Yet you did not satisfy that impatience; on the contrary, you provoked it all the more by an obstinate refusal occasioned by alarmed chastity. You confused me with all those other men from whom you constantly conceal your person. Do you remember the day when I lost sight of you among your treacherous slaves as they whisked you away from my pursuit? Do you remember that other day, when seeing the powerlessness of your tears, you used your mother's authority to put a halt to the fury of my love? Do you remember how, when all other resource failed you, you fell back on the resources of your courage? You seized a dagger and threatened to immolate the husband who loved you if he continued to demand of you what you cherished more than that husband himself. Two months went by in this battle of love and virtue. You pushed your chaste scruples too far; you did not surrender even after you had been vanquished. You defended to the last moment your expiring virginity. You looked upon me as an enemy who had outraged you and not as a husband who had loved you. You were three months without being able to look upon me unblushingly. Your uneasy expression seemed to reproach me for the advantage I had taken. Not even my moments of possession were calm. You withheld from me all you could of your charms and graces, and I was intoxicated with the greatest favors without ever having obtained the lesser.

If you had been educated in this country, you would not have been so troubled; women here have lost all reserve. They appear before men with faces uncovered, as if they sought to request their own downfall. They seek them out with their glances; they see them in the mosques, on their walks, and even in their homes. The usage of having eunuchs for servants is unknown to them. In place of that noble simplicity and lovable modesty which reigns among you, there is to be seen here a brutish impudence to which it is impossible to grow accustomed.

Yes, my Roxane, if you were here, you would feel outraged by the frightful shamelessness into which your sex has slipped. You would flee these abominable places; you would sigh with regret for that sweet retreat where you meet with innocence, where you are sure of yourself, where no danger causes you to tremble, where, finally, you can love me without any fear of ever losing the love you owe me.

When you enhance the beauty of your complexion with the most beautiful of colors, when you perfume your whole body with the most precious of essences, when you embellish yourself in your finest raiment, when you seek to make yourself stand out from your companions by the grace of your dancing or the sweetness of your voice, when you gracefully vie with them in charm, gentleness, and sprightliness—I cannot imagine that you have any other motive save that of pleasing me. And when I see you blush modestly, when your eyes seek mine, when you steal your way into my heart with your sweet and flattering words, then, Roxane, I could not possibly doubt your love.

But what must I think of European women? The art of caring for their complexion, the finery in which they dress, the pains they take with their person, this continual desire to please that possesses them—all these are so many blemishes to their virtue, and insults to their husbands.

It is not that I believe, Roxane, that these women push their outrageous enterprise as far as such conduct might lead one to think; I doubt that they carry debauch to the horrible excess—which strikes terror in the heart—of completely violating conjugal fidelity. There are certainly few women so abandoned as to go that far. They all carry graven within their hearts a certain image of virtue, given by birth, weakened by worldly education, but not destroyed by it. They may quite possibly relax the superficial duties that decency demands. But when it comes to taking the last step, nature revolts. Thus when we shut you away so tightly and have you guarded by slaves, when we interfere so powerfully with your desires should they soar too far, it is not because we fear any final infidelity. But we know that purity can never be too great and that the least stain can corrupt it.

I pity you, Roxane. Your chastity, for so long put to the test, deserved a husband who would never have left you and who could personally repress those desires that now only your virtue manages to subjugate.

From Paris, the 7th of the Moon of Rhegeb, 1712

LETTER 29

Rica to Ibben in Smyrna

The Pope is the head of the Christians. He is an old idol worshipped out of habit. Formerly he was to be feared even by kings, for he deposed them as easily as our magnificent sultans depose the kings of Imirette and Georgia.[1] But now he is no longer feared. He claims that he is the successor of one of the first Christians, who is called Saint Peter, and his is most certainly a rich succession, for he has immense treasures and a great country under his domination.

Bishops are lawyers subordinate to him, and they have, under his authority, two quite different functions. When they are assembled together they create, as does he, articles of faith. When they are acting individually they have scarcely any other function except to give dispensation from fulfilling the law. For you must know that the Christian religion is weighed down with an infinity of very difficult practices. And since it has been decided that it is less easy to fulfill these duties than to have bishops around who can dispense with them, this last alternative was chosen out of a sense of common good. In this way, if you don't wish to keep Ramadan, if you don't choose to be subjected to the formalities of marriage, if you wish to break your vows, if you would like to marry in contravention of the prohibitions of the law, even sometimes if you want to break a sworn oath—you go to the bishop or the Pope and you are given immediate dispensation.

Bishops do not create articles of faith by their own decision. There are countless doctors, most of them dervishes, who introduce among themselves thousands of new questions touching upon religion. They are allowed to dispute at great length, and the war goes on until a decision comes along to finish it.

And thus I can assure you that there never has been a kingdom where there are so many civil wars as in the Kingdom of Christ.

---

1. Small Caucasian kingdoms that were tributaries of Persia.

Those who propose some new proposition are called at first *heretics*. Each heresy has its own name, and this name becomes for those who are involved, something like a rallying cry. But no one has to be a heretic. One needs only split the difference in half and give some distinction to those who make accusations of heresy, and whatever the distinction—logical or not—it makes a man white as snow, and he may have himself called *orthodox*.

What I am telling you is valid for France and Germany, for I have heard it said that in Spain and Portugal there are certain dervishes who stand for no nonsense and will have a man burned as if he were straw. When people fall into the hands of those fellows, happy is he who has always prayed to God with little wooden beads in his hand, who has worn on his person two strips of cloth attached to two ribbons, or who has at some time been in a province called Galicia.[2] Without that, the poor devil is in bad straits. Even should he swear like a pagan that he is orthodox, they might quite possibly disagree with him on his qualifications and burn him for a heretic. He could talk all he likes of distinctions to be made—there is no distinction, for he would be in ashes before they even considered listening to him.

Other judges assume that an accused man is innocent until proved guilty; these judges always assume him guilty. When in doubt, they have as their rule always to decide on the side of severity, apparently because they believe men to be bad. But then, from another point of view, they have such a good opinion of men that they never judge them capable of lying, for they receive the testimony of professed enemies, of women of evil repute, of those who ply an infamous profession. In their sentences they include a little compliment for those clad in the brimstone shirt by telling them that they are very vexed to see them so badly dressed, that they as judges are gentle people and abhor blood and are truly grieved to have condemned them. However, to console their grief, they confiscate all the property of these wretches to their own advantage.

Happy the land inhabited by the sons of the prophets! These sad spectacles are unknown there. The holy religion brought to that land by the angels is protected by its very truth; it needs none of these violent means to preserve itself.

From Paris, the 4th of the Moon of Shalval, 1712

Letter 30

Rica to the same in Smyrna

The inhabitants of Paris are curious to the point of extravagance. When I arrived, they looked upon me as if I had been sent from heaven: old men, young men, women, children—they all wanted to see me. Whenever I went out, everybody appeared at the windows. If I were in the Tuileries, I would see a group circle about me immediately: the women formed a rainbow, shaded through a thousand colors, as they surrounded me. If I were to go to the theater, I would immediately find a hundred lorgnettes[3] turned on me. In short, no man was ever more looked at than myself. I would sometimes smile to hear people who had practically never strayed from their rooms say among themselves: "You must admit that he looks very Persian." What an admirable business! I found portraits of myself everywhere; I saw myself multiplied in every shop, on every mantel. So frightened were they not to have their fill of seeing enough of me.

2. That is, who say the Catholic rosary, dress as priests, or make pilgrimages to the Catholic shrine of St. James of Compostela.

3. Pairs of eyeglasses or opera glasses.

So much honor cannot go long without becoming a burden. I did not think of myself as being such a curious and rare man, however good the opinion I may have of myself. I should never have imagined that I was to upset the tranquillity of a big city where I was totally unknown. All this made me decide to put off the Persian costume and change over to one in European style, just to see if there would remain anything admirable in my face. That test made me understand what I was really worth. Free of all foreign embellishment, I found that I was more soberly judged. I had every reason to complain of my tailor, who in one moment, made me lose the attentions of public esteem, for I immediately fell into a frightful void. I could stay sometimes for a whole hour in a social gathering without being looked at, without being given any occasion to open my mouth. But if, by chance, someone in the group learned that I was Persian, I would immediately hear a humming all about me: "Ah, ah! So Monsieur is a Persian? What an extraordinary thing! How can anyone be a Persian?"

From Paris, the 6th of the Moon of Shalval, 1712

LETTER 38

Rica to Ibben in Smyrna

It is a great question among males to know whether it is better to deprive a woman of her freedom or let her keep it. It seems to me there are many things to be said for and against. If the Europeans can say it is no mark of nobility to make the persons we love miserable, our Asiatics can answer that there is a certain baseness involved in a man's renouncing the dominion over women given him by nature. If they are told that the great number of women shut up by them is embarrassing, they can reply that ten women who obey are less embarrassing than one who does not. Let them object in their turn that Europeans could not possibly be happy with women who are not faithful to them, it could be countered that their much-boasted fidelity does not obviate the disgust that always follows on the satisfaction of the passions, that our women belong too strictly to us, that such calm possession leaves us nothing to desire or fear, and that a bit of coquetry is the salt that adds savor and prevents corruption. A wiser man than myself might find it difficult to decide the issue, for if the Asiatics do well to seek means aimed at calming their uneasiness, the Europeans do well not to have any uneasiness at all.

"After all," they say, "even were we to be unhappy in our status as husbands, we should always find some way of making up for it in our status as lovers. To enable a man to complain with justification of his wife's infidelity, there would have to be only three persons in the world. Things will always be evened out when there are four."

It is quite another question to know whether the natural law subjects women to men. "No," a philosopher with a great penchant for the ladies told me the other day.[4] "Nature never dictated such a law. The dominion we hold over them is a veritable tyranny. They have allowed us to hold it only because they are more gentle than we are, and consequently, possess more humanity than reason. These advantages over us, which ought no doubt to have secured superiority for them if we had been reasonable, have made them lose it because we are not.

---

4. Most likely Bernard le Bovier de Fontenelle (1657–1757), writer-philosopher and nephew of Corneille, a frequenter of Madame de Lambert's literary salon.

"Now, however, if it is true that we have only a tyrannical power over women, it is no less true that they possess a natural dominion over us—their beauty, which is irresistible. Our domination is not the fact in every country, but the domination of beauty is universal. Why, then, should we have any advantage? Is it because we are the stronger? But that would make it a true injustice. We use all manner of means to humble their courage. Their strength would be equal if their education were also equal. Let us put them to the test in the matter of talents not enfeebled by their present education, and we shall soon see if we are so strong."

We must admit it even though it shocks our way of life: among more refined peoples women have always had authority over their husbands. It was established by law with the Egyptians, in honor of Isis; and with the Babylonians, in honor of Semiramis. It was said of the Romans that they commanded all nations but that they obeyed their wives. I do not even mention the Sarmatians,[5] who were bound in veritable servitude to that sex. They were too barbarous to justify my citing their example.

You can see, my dear Ibben, that I have developed a taste for this country where people like to argue extraordinary opinions and reduce everything to paradox. The Prophet has decided the question and laid down the rights of both sexes. "Wives," he said, "should honor their husbands. Husbands should honor wives, but they have the advantage of one degree over them."

From Paris, the 26th of the Moon of Gemmadi II, 1713

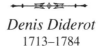

Denis Diderot
1713–1784

Born into a well-to-do provincial family of artisans and clergymen, Denis Diderot was destined for the priesthood. Instead he became perhaps the most irreverent of the anti-clerical Enlightenment philosophers. Educated by Jesuits, he received the monk's tonsure at thirteen, continuing his education at Paris. After earning a master's degree he stayed there, living hand to mouth by tutoring children and writing sermons for hire, and running with a crowd of whom his family would not have approved. During this time he met Rousseau as well as his future wife, and began writing and translating. When his father learned of his bohemian life, he refused to continue his financial support and sent one of their clerical relations to spy on him. In 1743—at thirty—instead of entering a seminary, Diderot published his first book (a translation of an English history of Greece) and sought his father's permission to marry—and was locked up in a monastery.

Escaping to Paris, an impoverished Diderot married Antoinette Champion in a secret midnight ceremony. He didn't inform his family of the event for six years. Within two years of his marriage he had started the first of many affairs with literary women. Within three he had established his literary notoriety. His *Philosophical Reflections* (*Pensées philosophiques,* 1746) were burned by order of the Parliament of Paris. In 1747 he was publicly denounced by the clergy; the associated booksellers of Paris promptly put him and his friend d'Alembert in charge of the great *Encyclopedia* project (1751–1765). The following year Diderot published a pornographic Orientalist novel, *The Indiscreet Jewels* (1748), which was denounced to the police by a rival bookseller. He spent half of 1749 in prison. The first two volumes of the *Encyclopedia* appeared in 1751 and 1752 but were suppressed. In the

---

5. Matriarchal society reported by the Greek historian Herodotus (484?–425? B.C.E.) to be the descendants of Amazons and Scythian men.

midst of this trouble some joy came to Diderot when in 1753 his wife bore their fourth child, a daughter—the only one to survive. He named her after a sister of his who had become a nun and died insane a few years earlier. With Rousseau in 1756 he visited Empress Catherine the Great of Russia, who became his patron for the rest of his life. By 1759 the Parliament of Paris had formally condemned the *Encyclopedia,* and the royal permission to publish it was revoked. Within a few years, though, the Parliament also suppressed the Jesuit order of priests, and Diderot rejoiced: "I am delivered from a great number of powerful enemies."

Diderot's works in fiction, drama, literary and art criticism, Roman history, philosophy, and mathematics are too many to list here. His *Supplement* was a response to Louis Antoine de Bougainville's *Voyage around the World* (1771). Bougainville, the first Frenchman to sail around the world, described Tahiti as a paradise of innocence and sexual freedom. Diderot built ironically on this description, highlighting the discomfort of a priest as he discovers the island's delights, which the priest debates with a Tahitian named Orou. Their discussion in turn is conveyed in a philosophical debate between two unnamed Frenchmen called "A" and "B." Diderot's witty, provocative dialogue succinctly combines the most characteristic aspects of all his writing: anticlerical, anticolonial, liberal, and utilitarian, with a keen interest in the tension between natural sexuality and social mores.

PRONUNCIATIONS:

Bougainville: bou-gahn-VEEL
Denis Diderot: duh-NEE DEE-deh-row
Orou: oh-RUE

from Supplement to the Voyage of Bougainville[1]

THE CONVERSATION BETWEEN THE CHAPLAIN AND OROU

In the division of Bougainville's crew by the Tahitians, the chaplain[2] was allotted to Orou. They were roughly the same age, around thirty-five or thirty-six years old. At the time Orou had only his wife and three children, who were called Asto, Palli and Thia. They undressed the chaplain, washed his face, hands and feet, and served him a wholesome and frugal meal. When he was about to go to bed, Orou, who had stepped out with his family, reappeared, presented him with his wife and three daughters, each of them naked,[3] and said, "You have eaten, you are young and in good health; if you go to bed alone, you will sleep badly. At night a man needs a companion beside him. Here is my wife; here are my daughters. Choose whomever you prefer; but if you wish to oblige me you will select the youngest of my daughters, who is still childless." "Alas," added the mother. "I don't hold it against her, poor Thia! It's not her fault."

The chaplain replied that his religion, his holy orders, morality and decency all prohibited him from accepting Orou's offer.

Orou answered: "I don't know what you mean by religion, but I can only think ill of it, since it prevents you from enjoying an innocent pleasure to which Nature, that sovereign mistress, invites every person: that is, of bringing into the world one of your own kind; rendering a service which the father, mother and children all ask of you; repaying a gracious host, and enriching a nation by adding one more subject to it. I don't know what you mean by 'holy orders,' but your first duty is to be a man and to show

---

1. Translated by John Hope Mason and Robert Wokler.
2. Bougainville says nothing about his ship's chaplain

other than that his name was La Vèze.
3. This rite of hospitality was recorded by Bougainville.

gratitude. I'm not asking you to take back the ways of Orou to your country, but Orou, your host and friend, begs that here you accept the ways of Tahiti. Whether the ways of Tahiti are better or worse than yours is an easy question to settle. Has the land of your birth more people than it can feed? In that case your ways are neither worse nor better than ours. Can it feed more than it has? In that case our ways are better than yours. As for the decency which holds you back, I quite understand. I admit I'm wrong and ask that you forgive me. I don't insist that you put your health in danger. If you are tired, you must rest; but I trust that you will not continue to disappoint us. Look at the sorrow you've brought to all these faces. They're afraid you have detected blemishes in them which have aroused your distaste. But even if that were so, wouldn't the pleasure of doing a good deed, of ensuring that one of my daughters was honoured among her companions and sisters—wouldn't that suffice for you? Be generous."

The chaplain—"It's not that. They are all four of them equally beautiful. But my religion! My holy orders!"

Orou—"They are mine, and I'm offering them to you. They are their own as well and give themselves up to you freely. Whatever purity of conscience is prescribed to you by that thing you call 'religion'[4] and that thing you call 'holy orders,' you may accept them without scruple. I am in no way exceeding my authority, and you may be sure that I know and respect the rights of individuals."

At this point the truthful chaplain acknowledges that Providence had never exposed him to such strong temptation. He was young, agitated, vexed. He averted his eyes from the delightful supplicants and then gazed at them again; he raised his eyes and hands to the heavens. Thia, the youngest, threw her arms around his knees and said to him, "Stranger, do not make my father unhappy, nor my mother, nor me. Honour me in this hut and within my family. Lift me up to the status of my sisters, who make fun of me. Asto, the eldest, already has three children; Palli, the second, has two; but Thia has none. Stranger, good stranger, do not reject me. Make me a mother. Make me bear a child whom I can one day lead by the hand, by my side, in Tahiti, who in nine months' time will be seen suckling at my breast, who will make me proud and who will be a part of my dowry, when I pass from my father's hut to another. I may be more fortunate with you than with our young Tahitians. If you grant me this favour, I shall never forget you. I shall bless you all my life; I shall write your name on my arm and on that of your son. We shall forever utter it with joy; and when you leave these shores my prayers will accompany you across the seas, until you reach your own land."

The artless chaplain says that she clasped his hands, that she fastened her eyes on his with glances so touching and expressive that she wept, that her father, mother and sisters withdrew, that he remained alone with her, and that, still calling out "But my religion, but my holy orders," he found himself at dawn lying beside this young girl who overwhelmed him with caresses and who invited her father, mother and sisters, when in the morning they came to his bed, to add their own gratitude to hers.

Asto and Palli, after withdrawing for a time, returned with native food, drinks and fruits. They embraced their sister and wished her good fortune. They breakfasted together; then Orou remained alone with the chaplain and said to him, "I see that my daughter is pleased with you, and I thank you. But could you tell me just what is the meaning of the word 'religion' which you have expressed so many times and with such sadness?"

---

4. Diderot casts the Tahitians as atheists, but according to Bougainville they in fact recognized a sun-god and a moon-god and venerated idols, sometimes even with human sacrifices.

The chaplain, after reflecting for a moment, replied, "Who made your hut and all the things that furnish it?"

OROU: I did.

THE CHAPLAIN: Well, we think that this world and everything in it is the work of one craftsman.

OROU: Does he then have feet, hands, a head?

THE CHAPLAIN: No.

OROU: Where does he live?

THE CHAPLAIN: Everywhere.

OROU: Here, even?

THE CHAPLAIN: Here.

OROU: We have never seen him.

THE CHAPLAIN: He cannot be seen.

OROU: What a poor father. He must be aged, because he must be at least as old as what he's made.

THE CHAPLAIN: He never grows old. He spoke to our ancestors; he gave them laws; he prescribed the way he wished to be honoured; he ordained that certain actions were good and forbade others as evil.

OROU: I understand. And one of those actions he forbade as evil is to lie with a woman or girl. But why then did he make two sexes?

THE CHAPLAIN: So that they may be united, but subject to certain conditions, following preliminary ceremonies, by virtue of which a man belongs to a woman and only to her; and a woman belongs to a man and only to him.

OROU: For as long as they live?

THE CHAPLAIN: For as long as they live.

OROU: So that if a woman should happen to lie with someone other than her husband, or a husband should lie with someone other than his wife . . . But that doesn't happen, since he's there and whatever displeases him he knows how to stop.

THE CHAPLAIN: No, he lets them do it, and so they sin against the law of God, for that is the name we give to the great craftsman. What we commit against the law of the country is a crime.

OROU: I should be sorry to offend you by what I say, but if you'll permit me, let me tell you what I think.

THE CHAPLAIN: Speak.

OROU: I find these strange precepts contrary to Nature, an offence against reason, certain to breed crime and bound to exasperate at every turn the old craftsman who, without a head, hand or tools has made everything; and who is everywhere but nowhere to be seen; who exists today and endures tomorrow without ever ageing a single moment; who commands and is not obeyed; who does not prevent occurrences which it is in his power to stop. Contrary to Nature, because they assume that a being which feels, thinks and is free may be the property of another being like himself. On what could such a right be based? Don't you see that in your country you have confused something which cannot feel or think or desire or will; which one takes or leaves, keeps or sells, without it suffering or complaining, with a very different thing that cannot be exchanged or acquired; which *does* have freedom, will, desire; which has the ability to give itself up or hold itself back forever; which complains and suffers; and which can never be an article of exchange unless its character is forgotten and violence is done to its nature. Such rules are contrary to the general order of things. What could seem more ridiculous than a precept which forbids any change of our affections, which commands that we show a constancy of which we're not capable, which violates the nature and liberty of male and female alike in chaining them to one another for the whole of their lives? What could be more absurd than a fidelity restricting the most capricious of our pleasures to a single individual; than a vow of immutability taken by two beings formed of flesh and blood, under a sky that doesn't remain fixed for an instant, beneath caverns poised on the edge of collapse, under a cliff crumbling into dust, at the foot of a tree shedding its bark, beneath a quivering stone? Believe me, you have made the plight of man worse than that of an animal. I've no understanding of your great craftsman, but I rejoice in his never having addressed our forefathers, and I hope he will never speak to our children; for he might by chance tell them the same nonsense, and they might commit the folly of believing him.

Yesterday at supper you talked to us about magistrates and priests. I don't know what you mean by 'magistrates' and 'priests,' who have the authority to regulate your conduct, but tell me, are they masters of good and evil? Can they make what is just unjust, and transform what is unjust into what's just? Can they make harmful actions good, and innocent and useful ones evil? One would hardly think so, since nothing could then be true or false, good or evil, beautiful or ugly, unless it pleased your great craftsman and his magistrates and priests to deem them so; in which case you'd be obliged, from one moment to another, to change your beliefs and conduct. One day, on behalf of one of your three masters you'd be told, 'Kill,' and you'd then be obliged in conscience to kill; another day, 'Steal,' and you'd then have to steal; or 'Do not eat this fruit,' and you wouldn't dare eat it; 'I forbid you this plant or animal,' and you'd refrain from touching them. There's nothing good that couldn't be forbidden, nothing evil that might not be required of you. And where would you be if your three masters, out of sorts with one another, took it upon themselves to permit you, command you, and forbid you the very same thing, as I suspect must happen often? Then, to please the priest, you'll be forced to oppose the magistrate; to satisfy the magistrate, you'll be forced to displease the great craftsman; and to satisfy the great craftsman, you'll have to abandon Nature. And do you know what will happen then? You'll come to despise all three of them, and you'll be neither a man, nor a citizen, nor a true believer. You'll be nothing. You'll be out of favour with each form of authority, at odds with yourself, malicious, tormented by your heart, miserable and persecuted by your senseless masters, as I saw you yesterday when I offered my daughters and wife to you, and you cried out, 'But my religion; but my holy orders!'

Would you like to know what's good and what's bad at all times and in all places? Stick to the nature of things and of actions, to your relations with your fellow man, to the effect of your conduct on your own well-being and on the general welfare. You're mad if you suppose there can be anything high or low in the universe which can add to or take away from the laws of Nature. Her eternal will is that good should be preferred to evil and the general good to the particular. You may decree the opposite, but you will not be obeyed. You will merely breed rascals and wretches, inspired by fear, punishment and remorse, depraving their conscience, corrupting their character. People will no longer know what they should do and what they should avoid. Anxious when innocent, calm only in crime, they will have lost sight of the pole star which should have guided their way.

* * *

The good chaplain reports that he spent the rest of the day wandering about the island and viewing the huts; and that in the evening, after supper, when the father and mother implored him to lie with the second of their daughters, Palli offered herself to him in the same state of undress as Thia before; that during the night he cried out several times, 'But my religion! But my holy orders!'; that on the third night he was struck by the same remorse in the arms of Asto, the eldest; and that out of courtesy he granted the fourth night to the wife of his host.

CONTINUATION OF THE DIALOGUE BETWEEN A AND B

A: I warm to this polite chaplain.

B: And I much more to the manners of the Tahitians and the remarks of Orou.

A: Though they show a rather European influence.

B: I don't doubt it.

The good chaplain complains here of the brevity of his stay in Tahiti, and of the difficulty of coming to terms with the customs of a people wise enough to have stopped their development at an early stage, or happy enough to live in a climate under which the soil's fertility assures a long quiescence; a people sufficiently active to secure relief from life's basic needs, and sufficiently indolent to ensure that their innocence, tranquillity and contentment remain unperturbed by too rapid an advance of knowledge. Nothing there was deemed evil by sentiment or law apart from what was evil by nature. Work and harvesting were there undertaken in common. Their notion of property was very limited. The attraction of love, reduced to a simple physical appetite, gave rise among them to none of our disorders. The whole island seemed like one large family, in which every hut is like an apartment of one of our great houses. The chaplain concludes by declaring that these Tahitians will always be in his thoughts; that he was tempted to throw his vestments into the ship and pass the rest of his days among them; and that he fears he would often rue his failure to do so.

A: Despite such tribute, what useful consequences can be drawn from the manners and strange customs of these uncivilised people?

B: It seems to me that as soon as physical factors, such as the need to overcome the infertility of the soil, have brought man's ingenuity into play, the momentum drives him well beyond his immediate objective; so that when his need has elapsed he comes to be swept into the great ocean of fantasy from which he cannot pull out. May the happy Tahitian stop where he is! I can see that, except in this remote corner of the globe, there's never been any morality and perhaps never will be.

A: What do you mean by morality?

B: I mean a general obedience to laws, either good or bad, and such conduct as follows from that obedience. If the laws are good, morality is good. If the laws are bad, morality's bad. If the laws, either good or bad, are not observed, which is the worst condition possible for a society, there are no morals. Now how do you suppose that the laws can be obeyed when they contradict one another?[5] Study the history of epochs, and of nations old and new, and you'll find men subject to three codes of law—the natural code, the civil code and the religious code—which they're obliged to breach in turn, since these codes are never in agreement. From

---

5. The idea that laws should be coherent and noncontradictory was an essential point of Diderot's moral doctrine.

this it follows that there has never been in any country, as Orou guessed of ours, a true man, or a citizen or a pious believer.

A: From which you no doubt conclude that if morality were based on men's eternal relations with one another, religious law would be superfluous and civil law would merely articulate the law of nature.

B: Indeed, lest we breed evil instead of good.

A: Or, if it's judged necessary to retain all three, the last two should be strictly patterned on the first, which we carry with us engraved in our hearts, and which is always the strongest.

B: That's not quite right. We have no more in common with other human beings at birth than an organic similarity of form, the same need, an attraction to the same pleasures and a shared aversion to the same pains. These are the things which make man what he is, and which should form the basis of the morality suited to him.

A: That's not easily achieved.

B: It's so difficult, in fact, that I venture to guess that the most savage people on earth, the Tahitians, who have kept strictly to the law of nature, are nearer to having good laws than any civilised people.

A: Because it's easier to abandon one's excessively primitive ways than to retrace one's steps and reform one's abuses.

B: Especially those to do with the relations between man and woman.

* * *

A: And modesty?

B: You're engaging me in a course on the principles of seduction. A man doesn't wish to be disturbed or distracted while he pursues his pleasures. Those of love are followed by a period of weakness which would expose him to the mercy of his enemies. Apart from this there's nothing natural in modesty; all the rest is convention. The chaplain remarks in a third fragment which I've not read to you that the Tahitian doesn't blush on account of an involuntary movement to which he's subject when aroused when near his wife, surrounded by his daughters; and that at the sight of such an occurrence the women are sometimes moved, but never flustered. It was only when a woman became the property of a man, and another man's furtive enjoyment came to be regarded as theft, that the terms 'modesty,' 'discretion' and 'propriety' were born along with imaginary virtues and vices: in effect, those barriers between sexes which would hinder them from tempting one another to violate the laws imposed upon them, but which often produce an opposite effect, in stirring the imagination and exciting desire. When I see how we plant trees round our palaces, or how a woman's bodice at once hides and exposes her breast, I seem to detect a secret wish to return to the forest, a recollected longing for the freedom of our first habitat.[6] The Tahitian would say to us, 'Why do you hide your body? What are you ashamed of? Is it wrong to submit to the most noble impulse of nature? Man, show yourself openly if you're attractive. Woman, if this man pleases you, receive him with the same candour.'

A: Don't get vexed. Even if we begin by behaving like civilised men, it's rare that we don't end like the Tahitian.

---

6. These ideas are closely related to those of Rousseau. In his philosophical novels, *Julie, or The New Héloïse* (1761) and *Emile* (1762), he makes much of the artifice of imitating nature in gardens as well as the artifice of inspiring desire by means of the bodice that reveals as much as it conceals.

B: Perhaps, but the preliminaries required by convention consume the life of a man of genius.

* * *

A: But how has it come to pass that an act of such solemn purpose, and to which Nature beckons us by such a powerful attraction—that the deepest, sweetest and most innocent of pleasures—has become the most potent source of our evils and depravity?

B: Orou explained it ten times over to the chaplain. Listen once more to what he said, and try to remember it:

It's the tyranny of man which converted the possession of woman into property.

It's morals and customs which have encumbered the union of man and wife with too many conditions.

It's civil laws which have subjected marriage to endless formalities.

It's the nature of our society and the disparity of wealth and rank which have given rise to our proprieties and improprieties.

It's on account of a strange contradiction common to all existing societies, according to which the birth of a child, while always regarded as adding to the wealth of the nation as a whole, more often and more certainly adds to the poverty of its family.

It's on account of the political views of sovereigns, who regard everything only in the light of their own interest and security.

It's on account of religious institutions, which have attached the names of vice and virtue to actions which were not susceptible of moral judgement.

How far we are from both nature and happiness! Yet nature's empire cannot be destroyed; whatever obstacles are put in its way, it will survive. Inscribe as much as you like, on tablets of bronze, that—if I may borrow the expression of the wise Marcus Aurelius[7]—the sensual rubbing together of two intestines is a crime. The heart of man will only be torn between the threat of your inscription and the intensity of its desires. The untamed heart will never cease to crave, and a hundred times in the course of a lifetime your fearsome engraving will fade from our eyes. Chisel upon marble, 'Thou shalt not eat of either kite or vulture'; 'Thou shalt know only thy wife'; 'Thou shalt not take thy sister in marriage' . . . Of course, don't forget to increase the severity of punishments in accordance with the absurdity of your prescriptions. Cruel as you become, you'll never succeed in rooting out my nature.

A: How brief would be the codes of nations, if only they conformed rigorously to that of Nature! How many vices and errors would man have been spared! . . . What then shall we do? Return to nature? Submit to laws?

B: We must speak out against senseless laws until they're reformed and, in the meanwhile, abide by them. Anyone who on the strength of his own personal authority violates a bad law thereby authorises everyone else to violate the good. Less harm is suffered in being mad among madmen than in being wise on one's own. We should both tell ourselves and cry out incessantly that shame, punishment and dishonour have been administered for actions quite innocent in themselves; but let's

---

7. Roman emperor, reigning from 161–180 C.E., a true philosopher-king, who recorded reflections on his Stoic beliefs in a series of *Meditations*.

not perform such actions ourselves, because shame, punishment and dishonour are the worst evils of all. Let's follow the good chaplain's example and be monks in France and savages in Tahiti.

A: Wear the costume of the country you visit, but keep your own clothes for the journey home.

B: And above all be most scrupulously honest and sincere with those frail creatures who can't delight us without sacrificing the most precious advantages of our societies.

Olaudah Equiano
c. 1745–1797

It was Olaudah Equiano's curious fate to be born into a slaveholding family, become enslaved himself, profit from the slave trade enough to purchase his own freedom, and contribute to the eventual abolition of slavery in Britain. Born to a prosperous Ebo family in present-day Nigeria, Equiano was kidnapped by African slavers at about age ten, and for a decade endured slavery in virtually every possible context: in Africa, on a Virginia plantation, in the British Navy (where he served in the Mediterranean and the Seven Years' War in Canada), in England, in Philadelphia, and aboard slave ships trading with the West Indies. As a freed man he extended his travels, establishing a plantation on Central America's Mosquito Coast, touring the Mediterranean, working to establish an African colony for freed slaves, and even joining an Arctic expedition. Finally settling in London, he became a committed Christian working for abolition. In 1792 he married Susanna Cullen, an Englishwoman, and at his death in 1797 was wealthy enough to leave a substantial inheritance of £950 to their surviving daughter. His freedom had cost £70 in 1766. Equiano's glowing portrait (see the cover of this volume) shows him as an established Enlightenment gentleman, the measured directness of his gaze resembling that of his prose in the memoir that made him famous.

The *Interesting Narrative* (1789) invokes the discourse of *sensibility* that became central to abolitionist movements. Its title announces its power to elicit sympathetic *interest* in the narrator revealing his life story. Designed to move the British Parliament investigating slave trading practices in 1788 and 1789 to sympathize with slaves as fellow humans and act to relieve their sufferings, it became an international sensation, translated into Dutch, German, and Russian, with thirty-five editions over fifty years. The vividness of detail and feeling with which Equiano recounts the horrors of slavery and the persecutions experienced even by freed blacks can still move readers two centuries later to sympathize deeply with the unspeakable sufferings of which he reminds us.

PRONUNCIATION:
Olaudah Equiano: oh-LAU-dah eh-key-AH-noh

from The Interesting Narrative of the Life of Olaudah Equiano
or Gustavus Vassa, the African
[THE SLAVE SHIP AND ITS CARGO]

The first object that saluted my eyes when I arrived on the coast was the sea, and a slave ship, which was then riding at anchor, and waiting for its cargo.[1] These filled

---

1. Captured by slavers along with his sister, Equiano was soon separated from her and sold to different African masters over a period of several months before reaching the African coast for shipment to Barbados.

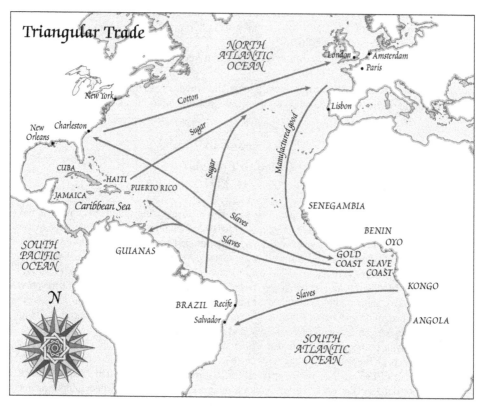

The Atlantic Slave Trade was fueled by triangular trade between Europe, Africa, and the Americas. Olaudah Equiano, himself from a slave-holding family in Benin, was but one of an estimated 11 million Africans caught up in the trade between 1500 and 1870.

me with astonishment, that was soon converted into terror, which I am yet at a loss to describe, and much more the then feelings of my mind when I was carried on board. I was immediately handled and tossed up to see if I was sound, by some of the crew; and I was now persuaded that I had got into a world of bad spirits, and that they were going to kill me. Their complexions too, differing so much from ours, their long hair, and the language they spoke, which was very different from any I had ever heard, united to confirm me in this belief. Indeed such were the horrors of my views and fears at the moment, that if ten thousand worlds had been my own, I would have freely parted with them all to have exchanged my condition with the meanest slave in my own country. When I looked round the ship too, and saw a large furnace or copper boiling and a multitude of black people, of every description, chained together, every one of their countenances expressing dejection and sorrow, I no longer doubted of my fate; and, quite overpowered with horror and anguish, I fell motionless on the deck, and fainted. When I recovered a little, I found some black people about me, who I believed were some of those who brought me on board, and had been receiving their pay: they talked to me in order to cheer me, but all in vain. I asked them if we were not to be eaten by those white men with horrible looks, red faces, and long hair. They told me I was not: and one of the crew brought me a small portion of spirituous liquor in a wine glass; but, being afraid of him, I would not take it out of his hand. One of the blacks therefore took it from him and gave it to me, and I took a little down my palate, which, instead of reviving me, as they thought it would, threw me into the greatest consternation at the strange feeling it produced, having never tasted any such liquor before.

Soon after this the blacks who brought me on board went off, and left me abandoned to despair. I now saw myself deprived of all chance of returning to my native country, or even the least glimpse of gaining the shore, which I now considered as friendly; and I even wished for my former slavery, in preference to my present situation, which was filled with horrors of every kind, still heightened by my ignorance of what I was to undergo. I was not long suffered to indulge my grief. I was soon put down under the decks, and there I received such a salutation in my nostrils as I had never experienced in my life: so that, with the loathsomeness of the stench, and with my crying together, I became so sick and low that I was not able to eat, nor had I the least desire to taste any thing. I now wished for the last friend, death, to relieve me; but soon, to my grief, two of the white men offered me eatables; and, on my refusing to eat, one of them held me fast by the hands, and laid me across, I think, the windlass, and tied my feet, while the other flogged me severely. I had never experienced any thing of this kind before, and although, not being used to the water, I naturally feared that element the first time I saw it, yet nevertheless, could I have got over the nettings, I would have jumped over the side, but I could not; and besides the crew used to watch us very closely, who were not chained down to the decks, lest we should leap into the water. I have seen some of these poor African prisoners most severely cut for attempting to do so, and hourly whipped for not eating. This indeed was often the case with myself. In a little time after, amongst the poor chained men, I found some of my own nation, which in a small degree gave ease to my mind. I inquired of these what was to be done with us. They gave me to understand we were to be carried to these white people's country to work for them. I was then a little revived, and thought if it were no worse than working, my situation was not so desperate. But still I feared I should be put to death, the white people looked and acted, as I thought, in so savage a manner; for I had never seen among any people such instances of brutal cruelty: and this is not only shewn towards us blacks, but also to some of the whites themselves. One white man in particular I saw, when we were permitted to be on deck, flogged so unmercifully with a large rope near the foremast, that he died in consequence of it; and they tossed him over the side as they would have done a brute. This made me fear these people the more; and I expected nothing less than to be treated in the same manner. I could not help expressing my fearful apprehensions to some of my countrymen; I asked them if these people had no country, but lived in this hollow place, the ship. They told me they did not, but came from a distant one. "Then," said I, "how comes it, that in all our country we never heard of them?" They told me, because they lived so very far off. I then asked, where their women were: had they any like themselves. I was told they had. "And why," said I, "do we not see them?" They answered, because they were left behind. I asked how the vessel could go. They told me they could not tell; but that there was cloth put upon the masts by the help of the ropes I saw, and then the vessel went on; and the white men had some spell or magic they put in the water, when they liked, in order to stop the vessel. I was exceedingly amazed at this account, and really thought they were spirits. I therefore wished much to be from amongst them, for I expected they would sacrifice me; but my wishes were in vain, for we were so quartered that it was impossible for any of us to make our escape.

[Equiano, Age 12, Reaches England]

One morning, when I got upon deck, I perceived it covered over with the snow that fell overnight. As I had never seen any thing of the kind before, I thought it was salt; so I immediately ran down to the mate and desired him, as well as I could, to come and see how somebody in the night had thrown salt all over the deck. He, knowing what it was, desired me to bring some of it down to him; accordingly I took up a handful of it, which I found very cold indeed; and when I brought it to him he desired me to taste it. I did so, and was surprised above measure. I then asked him what it was; he told me it was snow; but I could not by any means understand him. He asked me if we had no such thing in our country; and I told him "No." I then asked him the use of it, and who made it; he told me a great man in the heavens, called God: but here again I was to all intents and purposes at a loss to understand him; and the more so, when a little after I saw the air filled with it, in a heavy shower, which fell down on the same day.

After this I went to church; and having never been at such a place before, I was again amazed at seeing and hearing the service. I asked all I could about it; and they gave me to understand it was "worshiping God, who made us and all things." I was still at a loss, and soon got into an endless field of inquiries, as well as I was able to speak and ask about things. However, my dear little friend Dick[2] used to be my best interpreter; for I could make free with him and he always instructed me with pleasure. And from what I could understand by him of this God, and in seeing that these white people did not sell one another as we did, I was much pleased: and in this I thought they were much happier than we Africans. I was astonished at the wisdom of the white people in all things which I beheld; but I was greatly amazed at their not sacrificing, not making any offerings, and at their eating with unwashen hands, and touching of the dead. I also could not help remarking the particular slenderness of their women, which I did not at first like, and I thought them not so modest and shamefaced as the African women.

I had often seen my master Dick employed in reading; and I had a great curiosity to talk to the books, as I thought they did; and so to learn how all things had a beginning. For that purpose I have often taken up a book and talked to it, and then put my ears to it, when alone, in hopes it would answer me; and I have been very much concerned when I found it remaining silent.

[Reading the Bible; Finding a "Father"; Sold Again into Slavery]

There was also one Daniel Queen, about forty years of age, a man very well educated, who messed with me on board this ship,[3] and he likewise dressed and attended the captain. Fortunately this man soon became very much attached to me, and took great pains to instruct me in many things. He taught me to shave, and dress hair a little, and also to read in the Bible, explaining many passages to me, which I did not comprehend. I was wonderfully surprised to see the laws and rules of my own country written almost exactly here; a circumstance which, I believe, tended to impress our manners

---

2. Richard Baker, an American boy four or five years older than Equiano.

3. The *Etna,* of which Pascal had been given command in 1759. Messed: ate.

and customs more deeply on my memory. I used to tell him of this resemblance, and many a time we have sat up the whole night together at this employment. In short, he was like a father to me; and some used even to call me after his name: they also styled me "the black Christian." Indeed I almost loved him with the affection of a son. Many things I have denied myself, that he might have them; and when I used to play at marbles or any other game, and won a few halfpence, or got some money for shaving any one, I used to buy him a little sugar or tobacco, as far as my stock of money would go. He used to say that he and I never should part, and that when our ship was paid off, as I was free as himself or any other man on board, he would instruct me in his business, by which I might gain a good livelihood. This gave me new life and spirits; and my heart burned within me, while I thought the time long till I obtained my freedom. For though my master had not promised it to me, yet, besides the assurances I had often received that he had no right to detain me,[4] he always treated me with the greatest kindness, and reposed in me an unbounded confidence. He even paid attention to my morals, and would never suffer me to deceive him, or tell lies, of which he used to tell me the consequences; and that if I did so, God would not love me. So that from all this tenderness I had never once supposed, in all my dreams of freedom, that he would think of detaining me any longer than I wished.

In pursuance of our orders we sailed from Portsmouth for the Thames, and arrived at Deptford the 10th of December, where we cast anchor just as it was high water. The ship was up about half an hour, when my master ordered the barge to be manned; and, all in an instant, without having before given me the least reason to suspect any thing of the matter, he forced me into the barge, saying, I was going to leave him, but he would take care that I did not. I was so struck with the unexpectedness of this proceeding, that for some time I did not make a reply, only I made an offer to go for my books and chest of clothes, but he swore I should not move out of his sight; and if I did, he would cut my throat, at the same time taking out his hanger.[5] I told him that I was free, and he could not by law serve me so. But this only enraged him the more; and he continued to swear, and said he would soon let me know whether he would or not, and at that instant sprung himself into the barge, from the ship, to the astonishment and sorrow of all on board.

The tide, rather unluckily for me, had just turned downward, so that we quickly fell down the river along with it, till we came among some outwardbound West Indiamen; for he was resolved to put me on board the first vessel he could get to receive me. The boat's crew, who pulled against their will, became quite faint at different times, and would have gone ashore, but he would not let them. Some of them strove then to cheer me, and told me he could not sell me, and that they would stand by me, which revived me a little, and I still entertained hopes; for as they pulled me along he asked some vessels to receive me, and they refused.

But, just as we had got a little below Gravesend, we came alongside of a ship going away the next tide for the West-Indies; her name was the Charming Sally, Captain James Doran. My master went on board and agreed with him for me; and in little time I was sent for into the cabin. When I came there Captain Doran asked me if I knew him; I answered I did not: "Then," said he, "you are now my slave." I told him my master could not sell me to him nor to any one else. "Why," said he, "did not your master buy you?" I confessed he did. "But I have served him," said I, "many years,

---

4. Even before the Mansfield Decision of 1772, contemporary opinion held that Royal Navy ships were British

territory, on which slavery was inappropriate.
5. Short sword.

and he has taken all my wages and prize-money,[6] for I only got one sixpence during the war. Besides this I have been baptized; and, by the laws of the land, no man has a right to sell me." And I added, that I had heard a lawyer, and others, at different times tell my master so. They both then said, that those people who told me so, were not my friends: but I replied—it was very extraordinary that other people did not know the law as well as they. Upon this, Captain Doran said I talked too much English, and if I did not behave myself well and be quiet, he had a method on board to make me. I was too well convinced of his power over me to doubt what he said; and my former sufferings in the slave-ship presenting themselves to my mind, the recollection of them made me shudder. However, before I retired I told them, that as I could not get any right among men here, I hoped I should hereafter in Heaven, and I immediately left the cabin, filled with resentment and sorrow.

The only coat I had with me my master took away with him, and said, "if your prize-money had been £10,000, I had a right to it all, and would have taken it." I had about nine guineas, which, during my long sea-faring life, I had scraped together from trifling perquisites and little ventures; and I hid it that instant, lest my master should take that from me likewise, still hoping that, by some means or other, I should make my escape to the shore. Indeed some of my old shipmates told me not to despair, for they would get me back again; and that, as soon as they could get their pay, they would immediately come to Portsmouth to me, where this ship was going. But, alas, all my hopes were baffled, and the hour of my deliverance was, as yet, far off. My master, having soon concluded his bargain with the captain, came out of the cabin, and he and his people got into the boat and put off. I followed them with aching eyes as long as I could, and when they were out of sight I threw myself on the deck, with a heart ready to burst with sorrow and anguish.

[EMPLOYMENT IN THE WEST INDIES]

I had the good fortune to please my master[7] in every department in which he employed me; and there was scarcely any part of his business, or household affairs, in which I was not occasionally engaged. I often supplied the place of a clerk, in receiving and delivering cargoes to the ships, in tending stores, and delivering goods; and, besides this, I used to shave and dress my master, when convenient, and take care of his horse; and when it was necessary, which was very often, I worked likewise on board of his different vessels. By these means I became very useful to my master, and saved him, as he used to acknowledge, above a hundred pounds a year. Nor did he scruple to say I was of more advantage to him than any of his clerks; tho' their usual wages in the West-Indies are from sixty to a hundred pounds current a year.

I have sometimes heard it asserted that a negro cannot earn his master the first cost; but nothing can be further from the truth. I suppose nine-tenths of the mechanics throughout the West-Indies are negro slaves; and I well know the coopers[8] among them earn two dollars a-day; the carpenters the same, and oftentimes more; also the masons, smiths, and fishermen, &c. and I have known many slaves whose masters would not take a thousand pounds current for them. But surely this assertion refutes itself: for, if it be true, why do the planters and merchants pay such a price for slaves? And, above all,

---

6. Profits from an enemy ship and its cargo seized during war, traditionally shared among the victorious crew.
7. In 1763 Equiano was sold to Robert King, a Quaker merchant, and thereafter served in the West Indies in one of his ships under Captain Thomas Farmer.
8. Barrel-makers.

why do those, who make this assertion, exclaim the most loudly against the abolition of the slave trade? So much are men blinded, and to such inconsistent arguments are they driven by mistaken interest! I grant, indeed, that slaves are sometimes, by half-feeding, half-clothing, over-working, and stripes,[9] reduced so low, that they are turned out as unfit for service, and left to perish in the woods, or to expire on a dunghill.

My master was several times offered by different gentlemen one hundred guineas[1] for me; but he always told them he would not sell me, to my great joy: and I used to double my diligence and care for fear of getting into the hands of these men, who did not allow a valuable slave the common support of life. Many of them used to find fault with my master for feeding his slaves so well as he did; although I often went hungry, and an Englishman might think my fare very indifferent: but he used to tell them he always would do it, because the slaves thereby looked better and did more work.

While I was thus employed by my master, I was often a witness to cruelties of every kind, which were exercised on my unhappy fellowslaves. I used frequently to have different cargoes of new negroes in my care for sale; and it was almost a constant practice with our clerks, and other whites, to commit violent depredations on the chastity of the female slaves; and to these atrocities I was, though with reluctance, obliged to submit at all times, being unable to help them. When we have had some of these slaves on board my master's vessels to carry them to other islands, or to America, I have known our mates commit these acts most shamefully, to the disgrace not of christians only, but of men. I have even known them gratify their brutal passion with females not ten years old; and these abominations some of them practised to such a scandalous excess, that one of our captains discharged the mate and others on that account. And yet in Montserrat[2] I have seen a negro-man staked to the ground, and cut most shockingly, and then his ears cut off, bit by bit, because he had been connected with a white woman, who was a common prostitute! As if it were no crime in the whites to rob an innocent African girl of her virtue; but most heinous in a black man only to gratify a passion of nature, where the temptation was offered by one of a different colour, though the most abandoned woman of her species.

[THE PERILS OF BEING A FREEMAN]

I have since often seen in Jamaica and other islands, free men, whom I have known in America, thus villainously trepanned[3] and kept in bondage. I have heard of two similar practices even in Philadelphia: and were it not for the benevolence of the Quakers in that city, many of the sable race, who now breathe the air of liberty, would, I believe, be groaning under some planter's chains. These things opened my mind to a new scene of horror, to which I had been before a stranger. Hitherto I had thought only slavery dreadful; but the state of a free negro appeared to me now equally so at least, and in some respects even worse; for they live in constant alarm for their liberty, which is but nominal; and they are universally insulted and plundered without the possibility of redress; such being the equity of the West-Indian laws, that no free negro's evidence will be admitted in their courts of justice. * * *

I determined to make every exertion to obtain my freedom, and to return to Old England. For this purpose I thought a knowledge of Navigation might be of use to me;

---

9. Lashings and the welts they leave.
1. The guinea coin, first struck in 1663 by a company of merchants chartered by the British crown to obtain slaves from the Guinea coast of Africa (hence the name), was worth 21 shillings; made of gold, it often traded for more than its face value and connoted a certain prestige.
2. Island in the British West Indies.
3. Betrayed.

for, though I did not intend to run away unless I should be ill used, yet, in such a case, if I understood navigation, I might attempt my escape in our sloop, which was one of the swiftest sailing vessels in the West-Indies, and I could be at no loss for hands to join me. Had I made this attempt, I had intended to go in her to England; but this, as I said, was only to be in the event of my meeting with any ill usage. I therefore employed the mate of our vessel to teach me Navigation, for which I agreed to give him twenty-four dollars, and actually paid him part of the money down; though when the captain, some time after, came to know that the mate was to have such a sum for teaching me, he rebuked him, and said it was a shame for him to take any money from me. However, my progress in this useful art was much retarded by the constancy of our work.

Had I wished to run away I did not want opportunities, which frequently presented themselves; and particularly at one time, soon after this. When we were at the island of Guadaloupe there was a large fleet of merchantmen bound for Old France; and seamen then being very scarce, they gave from fifteen to twenty pounds a man for the run. Our mate and all the white sailors left our vessel on this account, and went aboard of the French ships. They would have had me also to go with them, for they regarded me, and swore to protect me, if I would go: and, as the fleet was to sail the next day, I really believe I could have got safe to Europe at that time. However, as my master was kind, I would not attempt to leave him; still remembering the old maxim, that *honesty is the best policy,* I suffered them to go without me. Indeed my captain was much afraid of my leaving him and the vessel at that time, as I had so fair an opportunity: but, I thank God, this fidelity of mine turned out much to my advantage hereafter, when I did not in the least think of it; and made me so much in favour with the captain, that he used now and then to teach me some parts of Navigation himself. But some of our passengers, and others, seeing this, found much fault with him for it, saying it was a very dangerous thing to let a negro know Navigation; and thus I was hindered again in my pursuits.

[FREEDOM]

When we had unladen the vessel, and I had sold my venture,[4] finding myself master of about forty-seven pounds, I consulted my true friend, the Captain, how I should proceed in offering my master the money for my freedom. He told me to come on a certain morning, when he and my master would be at breakfast together. Accordingly, on that morning I went, and met the Captain there, as he had appointed. When I went in I made my obeisance to my master, and with my money in my hand, and many fears in my heart, I prayed him to be as good as his offer to me, when he was pleased to promise me my freedom as soon as I could purchase it. This speech seemed to confound him; he began to recoil; and my heart that instant sunk within me. "What," said he, "give you your freedom? Why, where did you get the money? Have you got forty pounds sterling?" "Yes, sir," I answered. "How did you get it?" replied he. I told him, "very honestly." The Captain then said he knew I got the money very honestly and with much industry, and that I was particularly careful. On which my master replied, I got money much faster than he did; and said he would not have made me the promise which he did, had he thought I should have got the money so soon. "Come, come," said my worthy Captain, clapping my master on the back, "Come, Robert, (which was his name) I think you must let him have his freedom. You have laid your money out very

4. The stock he was permitted to trade for himself.

well; you have received good interest for it all this time, and here is now the principal at last. I know GUSTAVUS has earned you more than a hundred a year, and he will still save you money, as he will not leave you. Come, Robert, take the money." My master then said, he would not be worse than his promise; and, taking the money, told me to go to the Secretary at the Register Office, and get my manumission[5] drawn up.

These words of my master were like a voice from heaven to me: in an instant all my trepidation was turned into unutterable bliss, and I most reverently bowed myself with gratitude, unable to express my feelings, but by the overflowing of my eyes, and a heart replete with thanks to God; while my true and worthy friend, the Captain, congratulated us both with a peculiar degree of heartfelt pleasure. As soon as the first transports of my joy were over, and that I had expressed my thanks to these my worthy friends in the best manner I was able, I rose with a heart full of affection and reverence, and left the room, in order to obey my master's joyful mandate of going to the Register Office. As I was leaving the house I called to mind the words of the Psalmist, in the 126th Psalm, and like him, "I glorified God in my heart, in whom I trusted." These words had been impressed on my mind from the very day I was forced from Deptford[6] to the present hour, and I now saw them, as I thought, fulfilled and verified.

My imagination was all rapture as I flew to the Register Office; and in this respect, like the apostle Peter (whose deliverance from prison was so sudden and extraordinary, that he thought he was in a vision)[7] I could scarcely believe I was awake. Heavens! who could do justice to my feelings at this moment? Not conquering heroes themselves, in the midst of a triumph—Not the tender mother who has just regained her long-lost infant, and presses it to her heart—Not the weary, hungry mariner, at the sight of the desired friendly port—Not the lover, when he once more embraces his beloved mistress, after she has been ravished from his arms!—All within my breast was tumult, wildness, and delirium! My feet scarcely touched the ground; for they were winged with joy, and, like Elijah, as he rose to Heaven, they "were with lightning sped as I went on."[8] Every one I met I told of my happiness, and blazed about the virtue of my amiable master and Captain. * * *

In short, the fair as well as black people immediately styled me by a new appellation,—to me the most desirable in the world,—which was "Freeman," and, at the dances I gave, my Georgia superfine blue clothes made no indifferent appearance, as I thought. Some of the sable females, who formerly stood aloof, now began to relax and appear less coy; but my heart was still fixed on London, where I hoped to be ere long. So that my worthy Captain, and his owner, my late master, finding that the bent of my mind was towards London, said to me, "We hope you won't leave us, but that you will still be with the vessels." Here gratitude bowed me down; and none but the generous mind can judge of my feelings, struggling between inclination and duty. However, notwithstanding my wish to be in London, I obediently answered my benefactors that I would go in the vessel, and not leave them; and from that day I was entered on board as an able-bodied seaman, at thirty-six shillings per month, besides what perquisites I could make.[9] My intention was to make a voyage or two, entirely to please these my honoured patrons; but I determined that the year following, if it pleased God, I would see Old England once more, and surprise my old master, Captain Pascal, who was hourly in my mind: for I

5. The formal liberation of a slave.
6. A borough southeast of London, where in 1762 Captain Michael Henry Pascal sold Equiano back into slavery, after several years' service.
7. Acts 12:9 [Equiano's note].

8. In 2 Kings 2, Elijah has a vision of a chariot of fire and is carried to Heaven in a whirlwind.
9. Equiano has the right to trade for himself and to receive tips.

still loved him, notwithstanding his usage to me, and I pleased myself with thinking of what he would say when he saw what the Lord had done for me in so short a time, instead of being, as he might perhaps suppose, under the cruel yoke of some planter.

❈ CROSSCURRENTS: JOURNEYS IN ❈ SEARCH OF THE SELF

- Some of the works included in this section, such as Aphra Behn's *Oroonoko,* Voltaire's *Candide,* Montesquieu's *Persian Letters,* and Denis Diderot's *Supplement to the Voyage of Bougainville,* ventriloquize non-European points of view in order to critique European customs. How do these mimicked perspectives on Europe and other societies compare with the views reflected in Near Eastern, Asian, African, or American works collected in this and other volumes?

- How do the descriptions of peoples viewed as less "civilized" than the narrator's own people in some works in this section compare with representations of distant or "primitive" societies in works collected elsewhere in this anthology, such as the *Memoirs of Babur,* Voltaire's *Candide,* or Rousseau's *The Social Contract* in this volume; Montaigne's *Of Cannibals,* Shakespeare's *The Tempest,* and Césaire's *A Tempest,* or the writings of Christopher Columbus, Vasco de Gama, Jean de Léry, and the Spanish conquistadores represented in Volume C; or Flaubert's *Travels in Egypt* in Volume E?

- Numerous works throughout this anthology, fictional or otherwise, take the form of travel narratives, and thus lend themselves perfectly to interesting comparisons with any of the works excerpted in this Perspectives section. Looking beyond this section and its anchoring texts by Swift and Behn, travel narratives in the present volume include Voltaire's *Candide,* Lady Mary Wortley Montagu's *Turkish Embassy Letters,* and the *Memoirs of Babur.* The Chinese narrative *Journey to the West,* the travel accounts of Christopher Columbus, Vasco de Gama, and Jean de Léry, as well as Thomas More's *Utopia,* all in Volume C, would also fit such a comparison—as would Homer's *Odyssey,* Virgil's *Aeneid,* and Herodotus' *History* in Volume A; the writings of Marco Polo, and *The Travels of Ibn Battuta* in Volume B; and in Volume E, *Travels in Egypt,* or anything in its Perspectives section, "Occidentalism," as well as Byron's *Don Juan.* What differing lessons are learned from the encounter with alien cultures and mores in these many and varied travel narratives?

- Think about the character and function of the figure of the narrator who is relating these encounters with alien cultures. Many of the works gathered in this section, like Çelebi's *Book of Travels,* Bashō's *Narrow Road to the Deep North,* Swift's *Gulliver's Travels,* Behn's *Oroonoko,* Equiano's *Interesting Narrative,* and Montesquieu's *Persian Letters,* feature first-person narrators. How does the role of the narrator in each differ from or resemble the others, and how do their roles compare with those of first-person narrators in other kinds of works throughout the anthology? In works that do not use first-person narrators, such as *Candide* or the *Supplement to the Voyage of Bougainville,* how does the change of narrative perspective affect a reader's response to what is narrated about worlds that the implied author, like the implied reader, has not experienced directly? The way the structure of the narrative and narratorial voice(s) work to produce ironic and satiric effects could also be fruitfully discussed in a comparison of these last two works. The question of the narrator's voice and role, and the way it shapes interpretation, is important in any of the travel narratives from other periods and volumes of the anthology, as listed above.

⇒+ END OF PERSPECTIVES: JOURNEYS IN SEARCH OF THE SELF +⇒

+·+ ⩲⧫⩱ +·+

François-Marie Arouet [Voltaire]
1694–1778

Voltaire's life and writings embody the philosophy of the Enlightenment—yet his contemporaries in the Age of Reason forced him into a life of exile. Like his fellow *philosophes* Diderot and Rousseau, François-Marie Arouet was born into a middle-class family. Finding an entrée into aristocratic Parisian society—where wit sparkled, ideas were circulated, and connections were made—was therefore a challenge. The Arouets were engaged in farming and trade, but François's father had become a lawyer and minor government official in Paris, and his son was meant to follow in his footsteps. He received a Jesuit education—the best to be had—but soon thereafter abandoned the study of law, pursuing literary satire as a better way to get the attention of Parisian high society. When he was only twenty-two he began unleashing his satirical wit in anti-aristocratic verses and was exiled from Paris on suspicion of having written a satire against Philippe d'Orléans, Regent of France since the death the previous year of Louis XIV. The next year he did it again, and on this second offense the regent, ready to display some wit of his own, wagered that he could show the unruly author something he had never seen before. When young Arouet asked, "What is that?" he received the reply, "The inside of the Bastille." He spent nearly a year studying the interior of this famous dungeon for political prisoners. He was allowed to bring his books with him, however, to dine frequently with the prison governor, and to write his tragedy *Oedipe* there.

Upon his release in 1718, exiled again to the suburbs outside Paris, Arouet adopted the pen name Voltaire, staged the play he had written in prison, and upon its brilliant success received a gold medal and an annuity from the very Regent who had imprisoned him. In 1723 he cemented his literary reputation with the publication of a poem received as both a masterpiece and the first French national epic, *La Henriade,* a work on the theme of religious tolerance centered around Henri IV, the great Protestant king of the previous century. The same year Voltaire almost died of smallpox, a disease that ravaged Europe and the Americas; he claimed to have saved himself by drinking two hundred pints of lemonade. Over the next several years he added wealth to his new fame and social status by shrewd investments in the period's colonial exploitations. Yet in 1726, just at the moment when his speculations in the stock of the Compagnie des Indes were making him a rich man, Voltaire was forced to renew his acquaintance with the inside of the Bastille. The Chevalier de Rohan, insulted by Voltaire in return for having cast aspersions on the celebrated author's humble origins, retorted by ordering his footmen to beat up the young upstart as he watched from his carriage, and then had him thrown once more into prison. This time Voltaire was released only on condition of exile, not just from Paris but from France.

Far from teaching him to keep to his proper station, his time in prison made Voltaire realize that he would forever remain an outsider to French society, grounded as it was in inherited privilege and unquestioned authority. Having begun as something of a social climber, he became a leader in the great Enlightenment battle against *préjugé,* or "prejudice," in the original sense of that word: literally pre-judgment, the blind acceptance of received ideas without having subjected them to the judgment of reason. Like many other thinkers of the period, Voltaire devoted his career to the critique of traditional, received authority, whether intellectual, religious, or political, which culminated in the American and French revolutions toward the end of the century. He adopted the motto *Ecrasez l'infame!* (Crush infamy!) by which he meant the infamous injustices perpetrated in the name of organized religion—whether Roman Catholicism or Calvinist Protestantism—and of absolute power.

Voltaire spent his exile in London, where he found himself welcomed at all levels of society. The English had beheaded their king nearly a century earlier, and although the monarchy had been restored it clung to legitimacy through anxious attempts to square its authority with the principles of individual freedom from tyranny. By the eighteenth century England had an international reputation for religious and political liberty, and especially for freedom of speech. By contrast with France and many other European countries, this reputation was deserved. Voltaire saw literary men like Joseph Addison entrusted with political responsibilities, and Sir Isaac Newton honored in Westminster Abbey for his scientific achievements. He met John Locke, his predecessor among the foremost philosophers of political liberty and human reason, as well as Pope and Swift, who preceded him as the most important satirists of the age. King George I, who had given Voltaire a gold medal and a watch on the success of *Oedipe,* also welcomed him to England.

Allowed to return to France after several years, Voltaire published his *Letters Concerning the English Nation,* begun in exile. This book appeared first in England (1733) and the following year in a French version. This time his French publisher was thrown into the Bastille, the books condemned by the Parliament of Paris and burnt. Voltaire himself retreated to the château of the philosopher Madame du Châtelet at Cirey in Champagne, where he spent much of his time over the next fifteen years living in a ménage à trois with her and her husband. In the 1740s he gained the protection of the king's mistress, Madame de Pompadour, and was again received at court—even appointed Historiographer to the King (1745) and elected to the Académie Française (1746), as he had been to the Royal Society in London in 1743. Shortly after Madame du Châtelet's death in childbirth, Voltaire left France again in 1750 to accept an invitation to the court of Prussia's King Frederick the Great. Within a few years he had angered this king too, fleeing Prussia in 1753, but detained for a time in Germany by Frederick's soldiers on his way back to France. After his experiences at royal courts Voltaire bought two houses near the republic of Geneva during the later 1750s, Les Délices (1755) and later Ferney, just over the Swiss border in France (1759). There he held court himself, continuing to disseminate his revolutionary ideas. It was the custom for young men of the upper crust to crown their educations with the Grand Tour of Europe, and many visited Voltaire at Ferney to learn the new ideas of the Enlightenment firsthand from one of its most famous exponents.

Voltaire returned to Paris one last time in 1778 for the production of his final tragedy, *Irène.* He arrived to find himself celebrated by the entire capital; saw the opening of his play, met Benjamin Franklin, and addressed the Académie Française. All this overwhelmed the aged exile, who died shortly thereafter. Back at Ferney he had already made plans for his tomb to be placed half in and half out of the chapel he had built there and engraved with the dedication, "Deo erexit Voltaire" ("Voltaire erected [it] to God")—"a fine word between two great names," as he quipped. He was never to rest there, however, as neither transportation nor embalming were quite what they are now. The Archbishop of Paris refused him Christian burial, as it had been refused to Molière; Voltaire's body was disguised and smuggled under cover of darkness to be buried at an abbey outside the city limits. The itinerary of Voltaire's corpse reflects that of his life: at first seemingly exiled forever, in the end he was brought back to Paris in triumph—where his remains are still enshrined in the Pantheon, a neoclassical secular temple dedicated on its frieze AUX GRANDS HOMMES. Voltaire's status as the original "Great Man" is literally written in stone.

CANDIDE, OR OPTIMISM, TRANSLATED FROM THE GERMAN OF DOCTOR RALPH WITH THE ADDITIONS FOUND IN THE DOCTOR'S POCKET WHEN HE DIED AT MINDEN IN THE YEAR OF OUR LORD 1759

This is the full title readers found when they opened the first edition of *Candide* in 1759. Even though he at first denied authorship of the work, no one who read it had much trouble guessing that it was written by Voltaire, who was already well known for using pseudonyms. This was a strategy to protect himself while publishing his merciless satires exposing established religious and secular power structures—and even the thought of some of his fellow Enlightenment philosophers—as irrational and absurd. Like his other works, *Candide* champions the cause of reason and freedom against superstition, intolerance, and privilege. When he published *Candide* at the age of sixty-five, Voltaire was perhaps the most famous living author in Europe. He had already distinguished himself in all the most respected literary genres—tragedy, history, and epic—and was renowned also for his satires and philosophical works. In an encyclopedic age he had written a dictionary and contributed to Diderot's *Encyclopédie*. He had even previously invented the philosophical tale with *Zadig* (1748) and *Micromégas* (1750), perfecting this new genre in *Candide*. It was an immediate bestseller, reprinted about forty times during its first year and soon translated into several European languages.

The eighteenth century was fond of tales of simpleton protagonists whose misadventures expose the folly and vice of all they encounter and the absurdities of the philosophical systems they take to heart. Such, for example, are Sarah Fielding's *The Adventures of David Simple* and Henry Mackenzie's *The Man of Feeling*. The type goes back much further, however, the most famous example being Cervantes' *Don Quixote* (1605); even earlier, several of the tales in Boccaccio's *Decameron* relate the adventures of fools in order to poke fun at the corrupt clergy who take advantage of them. Voltaire also mocks the church, but like other eighteenth-century writers, he used the device of the foolish protagonist to expose the dangers of contemporary philosophical systems. *Candide* attacks the widespread idealist system of philosophical optimism, which could be seen as justifying human suffering as a necessary part of a cosmic order beyond human ken, implicitly condoning a passive resistance to the effort required to prevent or alleviate suffering. The Resonances following *Candide* give famous expressions of such ideas by the philosopher G. W. von Leibniz, who argued that God has created "the best of all possible worlds," and the poet Alexander Pope, who roundly declared that "Whatever Is, is RIGHT."

The age was also fond of romance, a genre of prose fiction going back to late antiquity, featuring amazing adventures, disguises, enslavements, escapes, and world-wanderings, and often winding up with miraculous reunions under the most unlikely circumstances. Probability is not necessary in a world ordered by Providence. In *Candide* Voltaire exposes the irrationality of this form of narrative, which was beginning to be challenged by the novel, an emerging form of fiction governed by standards of verisimilitude, or plausibility. By putting his tale in romance form, however, he is also taking advantage of its lingering popularity.

The parody of romance in *Candide* also helps Voltaire make a point shared by Cervantes and by the authors of many novels in their attack on romance: an emphasis on firsthand experience, rather than idealism, reading or instruction, as the ultimate means to truth. Romance was the product of an aesthetic that held that art should represent the world as it should be, rather than as it is. Everything Candide's teacher Dr. Pangloss tells him about the "best of all possible worlds" is belied by Candide's own experiences of the world he actually inhabits. This stress on individual experience and judgment as the only true path to knowledge characterizes the Enlightenment's more general challenge to received wisdom and authority, as well as its reliance on the senses, rather than the soul, as the way to truth: a vast shift that gave us, among other things, the scientific method. It also gave us one of the Western world's most enduringly delightful and instructive fictions.

PRONUNCIATIONS:

Abare: ah-BAHRH
François-Marie Arouet: frahnh-SWAH mah-REE ah-ROO-AY
Cacambo: kah-KAHM-boh
Candide: cahn-DEED
Madame du Châtelet: mah-DAHM deu SHAH-te-LAY
Cunégonde: keu-nay-GOND
Giroflée: zhee-roh-FLAY
Issachar: ee-sah-KAHR
Pangloss: PAN-gloss
Paquette: pah-KET
Pococurante: poh-koh-keu-RAHN-tay
Thunder-Ten-Tronckh: TUHN-dayr-ten-TROHNK

Candide, or Optimism[1]
Translated from the German of Dr. Ralph
Together with the addenda which were found in the Doctor's pocket when he died at Minden in the year of grace 1759

CHAPTER 1

*How Candide was brought up in a beautiful castle,
and how he was kicked out of the same*

Once upon a time in Westphalia,[2] in the castle of Baron Thunder-ten-tronckh, there lived a young boy whom nature had endowed with the gentlest of dispositions. His soul was written upon his countenance. He was quite sound in his judgement, and he had the most straightforward of minds. It is for this reason, I believe, that he was called Candide. The older servants of the household suspected that he was the son of the Baron's sister by a kind and upright gentleman of the neighbourhood, a man whom this lady had consistently refused to marry because he had only ever been able to establish seventy-one heraldic quarterings,[3] the rest of his family tree having been destroyed by the ravages of time.

The Baron was one of the most powerful noblemen in Westphalia, for his castle had a door and windows. His great hall was even adorned with a tapestry. All the dogs in his farmyards would combine, when the need arose, to make up a pack of hounds: his grooms were his whippers-in, and the local vicar his great almoner.[4] They all called him "Your Lordship," and laughed at his jokes.

The Baroness, who weighed approximately 350 pounds, therefore enjoyed a large measure of public esteem; and she performed the honours of the house with a degree of dignified aplomb that rendered her all the more respectable. Her daughter Cunégonde,[5] being seventeen and of a high complexion, looked fresh, chubby, and toothsome. The Baron's son seemed in every way worthy of his father. Pangloss,[6] the tutor, was the oracle of the household, and little Candide would listen to his lessons with all the good faith of his age and character.

---

1. Translated by Roger Pearson.
2. Region of western Germany.
3. Each quartering or division of a coat of arms represented a separate line of noble ancestry.
4. Grooms care for horses, but here have to double as the beaters who scare small game animals and birds out of the underbrush during a hunt. A truly powerful nobleman would also maintain a separate servant to distribute his alms to the poor.
5. This name puns on the French and Latin words for female genitalia.
6. All tongues (Greek).

Pangloss taught metaphysico-theologico-cosmo-codology. He could prove wonderfully that there is no effect without cause and that, in this best of all possible worlds, His Lordship the Baron's castle was the most beautiful of castles and Madam the best of all possible baronesses.

"It is demonstrably true," he would say, "that things cannot be other than as they are. For, everything having been made for a purpose, everything is necessarily for the best purpose. Observe how noses were made to bear spectacles, and so we have spectacles. Legs are evidently devised to be clad in breeches, and breeches we have. Stones were formed in such a way that they can be hewn and made into castles, and so His Lordship has a very beautiful castle. The greatest baron in the province must be the best lodged. And since pigs were made to be eaten, we eat pork all the year round. Consequently, those who have argued that all is well have been talking nonsense. They should have said that all is for the best."

Candide would listen attentively, and innocently he would believe: for he found Miss Cunégonde extremely beautiful, though he had never made bold to tell her so. His conclusion was that, next to the happiness of being born Baron Thunder-ten-tronckh, the second degree of happiness was being Miss Cunégonde, the third was seeing her every day, and the fourth was listening to Maître Pangloss, the greatest philosopher in the province and therefore in the whole world.

One day, as Cunégonde was taking a stroll near the castle in the little wood they referred to as their "parkland," she caught a glimpse through the bushes of Dr. Pangloss giving a lesson in applied physiology to her mother's maid, a very pretty and very receptive little brunette. As Miss Cunégonde had quite a gift for science, she noted in breathless silence the repeated experiments to which she was witness. She saw clearly the doctor's sufficient reason, the effects and the causes, and returned home all agitated, her thoughts provoked, and filled with desire to be a scientist, musing that she might well be able to be young Candide's sufficient reason, just as he could well be hers.

She met Candide on her return to the castle and blushed. Candide blushed too. She greeted him in a choked voice, and Candide spoke to her without knowing what he was saying. The next day after dinner, as they were leaving the table, Cunégonde and Candide found themselves behind a screen. Cunégonde dropped her handkerchief, Candide picked it up. Innocently she took his hand, innocently the young man kissed the young lady's hand, and with quite singular vivacity, sensibility, and grace. Their mouths met, their eyes shone, their knees trembled, their hands strayed. Baron Thunder-ten-tronckh passed by the screen and, seeing this cause and this effect, chased Candide out of the castle with a number of hefty kicks up the backside. Cunégonde fainted. As soon as she recovered her senses, the Baroness slapped her. And all was consternation in the most beautiful and most agreeable of all possible castles.

CHAPTER 2

What became of Candide among the Bulgars

Candide, thus expelled from paradise on earth, walked on for a long time, not knowing where he was going, weeping, raising his eyes to heaven, and turning them often in the direction of the most beautiful of castles, which contained the most beautiful of barons' daughters. He went to sleep in the middle of the fields, supperless, in a furrow. The snow fell in large flakes. Next day, soaked to the skin, Candide dragged himself as far as the neighbouring town, which was called

Wald-berghoff-trarbk-dikdorff. He had no money, and he was dying of hunger and exhaustion. He stopped wistfully at the door of a small hostelry. Two men dressed in blue spotted him.

"Comrade," said one, "there's a fine figure of a young man, and he's the right height."

They went up to Candide and very civilly invited him to dine with them.

"Gentlemen," said Candide with charming modesty, "you do me great honour, but I have not the means to pay my corner."

"Oh, sir," replied one of the men in blue, "people of your looks and quality[7] never pay. Are you not five feet five inches tall?"

"Yes, gentlemen, that is my height," he said with a bow.

"Oh sir, come, do sit yourself down at the table. Not only will we pay for you, but we will not see a man such as yourself go short either. Man was made that he might help his fellow-man."

"You are right," said Candide. "That's what Mr. Pangloss always told me, and I can see that everything is for the best."

They pressed him to accept a few crowns. He took them and wanted to make out a receipt. It was not required. They all sat down at the table.

"Don't you love . . .?"

"Oh, yes," he replied. "I love Miss Cunégonde."

"No," said one of the gentlemen, "what we want to know is whether you love the King of the Bulgars[8] or not."

"Not in the least," he said, "for I have never met him."

"What! He is the most charming of kings and we must drink to his health."

"Oh, very willingly, gentlemen," and he drank.

"That will do nicely," he was told. "That makes you a supporter, a defender, a champion, nay a hero of the Bulgars. Your fortune is made and your glory assured."

His feet were promptly clapped in irons and he was taken off to the regiment. They made him do right turns, left turns, draw ramrods, replace ramrods, take aim, fire, quick march, and then they gave him thirty strokes of the birch. Next day he performed the drill a little less badly, and he received only twenty. The next day they gave him only ten, and his comrades thought him a prodigy.

Candide, totally bewildered, could not yet quite make out how he was a hero. One fine day in spring he took it into his head to go for a stroll, simply walking straight ahead, in the belief that it was the privilege of the human, as of the animal species to use its legs how it wanted. He had not gone two leagues when up came four other heroes, each six feet tall, who tied him up and carted him off to a dungeon. They asked him which, juridically speaking, he preferred: whether to run the gauntlet of the entire regiment thirty-six times, or to have twelve lead bullets shot through his brains at one go. It did no good his talking about the freedom of the individual and saying that, personally, he wished for neither: a choice had to be made. He resolved, by virtue of that gift of God called "freedom," to run the gauntlet thirty-six times. He managed two. The regiment numbered two thousand men. For him that meant four thousand birch strokes, which laid bare every muscle and sinew in his body from the nape of his neck right down to his butt. As they were preparing for his third run, Candide, quite done for, implored them to be so kind as to do him the favour of bashing his head in.

---

7. Social class.

8. An allusion to Frederick the Great, 1712–1786, King of Prussia.

This favour was granted. His eyes were bandaged, he was made to kneel. At that moment the King of the Bulgars passed by and inquired what crime the condemned man had committed. As this King was a great genius, he understood from everything that Candide told him that here was a young metaphysician much in ignorance of the ways of the world: and he pardoned him with a clemency that will be praised in every newspaper and in every century. A splendid surgeon cured Candide in three weeks with the emollients prescribed by Dioscorides.[9] He already had a little skin and could walk when the King of the Bulgars joined battle with the King of the Abars.[1]

CHAPTER 3

How Candide escaped from the Bulgars and what became of him

Never was there anything so fine, so dashing, so glittering, or so well-regulated as those two armies. The trumpets, the fifes, the oboes, the drums, and the cannon produced a harmony such as was never heard in hell. First the cannon felled about six thousand men on each side. Then the musketry removed from the best of all worlds nine or ten thousand ruffians who were polluting its surface. The bayonet, too, was the sufficient reason for the death of a few thousand. The sum total may well have come to about thirty thousand souls. Candide, who was trembling like a philosopher, hid himself as best he could during this heroic butchery.

At length, while the two Kings were having *Te Deums*[2] sung in their respective camps, he made up his mind to go and think about cause and effect elsewhere. He climbed over the heaps of dead and dying, and came first to a neighbouring village. It was in ashes. This was an Abar village which the Bulgars had burnt to the ground in accordance with international law. In one part, old men riddled with shot looked on as their wives lay dying, their throats slit, and clutching their children to blood-spattered breasts. In another, young girls lay disembowelled, having satisfied the natural urges of a hero or two, breathing their last; others, half burnt to death, cried out for someone to finish them off. Brains lay scattered on the ground beside severed arms and legs.

Candide fled as fast as he could to another village. It belonged to Bulgars, and Abar heroes had given it the same treatment. Candide, continually stepping over quivering limbs or through the midst of ruins, eventually left the battlefield behind, taking with him some few provisions in his bag and with Miss Cunégonde never far from his thoughts. His provisions had run out by the time he reached Holland but, having heard that the people there were all rich and all Christians, he had no doubt that he would be treated as well as he had been in the Baron's castle before he had been turned out on account of Miss Cunégonde's pretty eyes.

He begged alms of several solemn personages, who all replied that if he continued in this occupation, he would be locked up in a house of correction and taught how to earn a living.

He then spoke to a man who, all on his own, had just been addressing a large gathering for a whole hour on the subject of charity. This orator scowled at him and said.

"What are you doing here? Do you support the good cause?"

"There is no effect without a cause," replied Candide humbly. "Everything is connected in a chain of necessity, and has all been arranged for the best. It was necessary

---

9. Famous ancient Greek doctor.
1. Likely a reference to the Seven Years' War, with the "Bulgars" and the "Abars" representing the Prussians and the French.
2. Hymns of thanks to God.

that I should be separated from Miss Cunégonde and that I should run the gauntlet, and it is necessary that I should beg for my bread until such time as I can earn it. All this could not have been otherwise."

"My friend," said the orator, "do you believe that the Pope is the Antichrist?"

"I've never heard that before," replied Candide. "But whether he is or he isn't, I need bread."

"You don't deserve to eat it," said the other. "Be off with you, you rogue! Away with you, you miserable wretch! And don't you come near me ever again."

The orator's wife, having stuck her head out of the window and set eyes on a man who could doubt that the Pope was the Antichrist, poured a pot full of . . . over his head. Heavens! To what lengths the ladies do carry their religious zeal!

A man who had never been baptized, a worthy Anabaptist named Jacques,[3] saw the cruel and ignominious treatment being meted out in this way to one of his brothers, a living being with two feet, no feathers, and possessed of a soul.[4] He took him home with him, cleaned him up, gave him some bread and beer, presented him with two florins, and even wanted to train him for work in his factories, which produced that "Persian" material[5] that is made in Holland. Candide, almost prostrate before him, exclaimed:

"Maître Pangloss was quite right when he told me that everything in this world is for the best. For I am infinitely more touched by your extreme generosity than by the harshness of that gentleman with the black hat and his lady wife."

The next day, while out walking, he met a beggar all covered in sores. His eyes were glazed, the end of his nose was eaten away, his mouth was askew, his teeth black, and he spoke from the back of his throat. He was racked by a violent cough and spat out a tooth with every spasm.

Chapter 4

How Candide chanced upon his old philosophy tutor,
Dr. Pangloss, and what came of it

Candide, again more moved by compassion than by disgust, gave this appalling beggar the two florins which he had received from his worthy Anabaptist, Jacques. The phantom stared at him, wept, and fell upon his neck. Candide, startled, recoiled.

"Alas!" said the one unfortunate to the other, "do you no longer recognize your dear Pangloss?"

"What do I hear? You? My dear tutor?! You in this dreadful state?! But what misfortune has befallen you? Why are you no longer in the most beautiful of castles? What has become of Miss Cunégonde, that pearl of a daughter, that masterpiece of nature?"

"I'm famished," said Pangloss.

Whereupon Candide took him to the Anabaptist's stable, where he gave him a little bread to eat and, when Pangloss had recovered, said:

"Well? What about Cunégonde?"

"She is dead," replied the other.

Candide fainted on hearing this. His friend brought him round with some old vinegar that was lying about in the stable. Candide opened his eyes.

3. Anabaptists, known for their peacefulness and chari-
tability, rejected infant baptism.
4. Jacques follows Aristotle's definition of common

humanity.
5. Silk.

"Cunégonde is dead! Ah, best of all worlds, where are you now? But what did she die of? It wouldn't have been at seeing me kicked out of her father's beautiful castle, would it?"

"No," said Pangloss. "She was eviscerated by Bulgar soldiers after they'd raped her as many times as anyone can be. They smashed the Baron's head in as he tried to protect her, the Baroness was hacked to pieces, my poor pupil received precisely the same treatment as his sister, and as for the castle, not one stone remains standing on another. Not a single barn, or sheep, or duck, or tree is left. But we had our revenge, for the Abars did exactly the same to the neighbouring barony of a Bulgar lord."

At this account Candide fainted again. But having recovered his senses and said everything one should say in such circumstances, he enquired as to the cause and the effect and the sufficient reason which had reduced Pangloss to such a woeful state.

"Alas," said the other, "the answer is love: love, the solace and comfort of the human race, the preserver of the universe, the soul of all sentient beings, tender love."

"Alas," said Candide, "I too have known it, this love of yours, this sovereign ruler of the heart, this soul of our soul. All the good it ever did me was one kiss and a score of kicks up the backside. How can this fine cause have had such an abominable effect on you?"

Pangloss replied in these terms:

"O my dear Candide! You knew Paquette, that pretty lady's maid to our noble Baroness. In her arms I tasted the delights of paradise, and in turn they have led me to these torments of hell by which you see me now devoured. She had the disease,[6] and may have died of it by now. Paquette was made a present of it by a very knowledgeable Franciscan who had traced it back to its source. For he had got it from an old countess, who had contracted it from a captain in the cavalry, who owed it to a marchioness, who had it from a page, who had caught it from a Jesuit, who, during his noviciate, had inherited it in a direct line from one of Christopher Columbus's shipmates. For my part I shall give it to no one, because I'm dying."

"O Pangloss!" cried Candide. "What a strange genealogy! Was it not the devil who began it?"

"Not at all," replied the great man. "It was an indispensable part of the best of all worlds, a necessary ingredient. For if Columbus, on an island in the Americas, had not caught this disease which poisons the spring of procreation, which often even prevents procreation, and which is evidently the opposite of what nature intended, we would have neither chocolate nor cochineal.[7] Moreover one must remember that up till now this disease has been unique to the inhabitants of our continent, like controversy. The Turks, the Indians, the Persians, the Chinese, the Siamese, the Japanese, they have all yet to know it. But there is sufficient reason for them to know it in their turn a few centuries hence. In the mean time it is making spectacular progress among our population, and especially among those great armies of fine, upstanding, well-bred mercenaries who decide the destiny of nations. One can be sure that when thirty thousand soldiers are fighting against a similar number in pitched battle, there are about twenty thousand cases of the pox on either side."

---

6. Syphilis.

7. A scarlet dye, imported, like chocolate, from the Americas.

"Well, isn't that extraordinary," said Candide. "But you must go and get treated."

"And how am I supposed to do that?" said Pangloss. "I haven't a penny, my friend, and in the whole wide world you can't so much as be bled or have an enema without paying for it, or without someone else paying for you."

These last remarks decided Candide. He went and threw himself at the feet of his charitable Anabaptist, Jacques, and painted such a poignant picture of the state to which his friend was reduced that the good fellow did not hesitate to take Dr. Pangloss under his roof: and he had him cured at his own expense. In the process Pangloss lost but one eye and one ear. He could write well and had a perfect grasp of arithmetic. Jacques the Anabaptist made him his bookkeeper. Two months later, having to go to Lisbon on business, he took his two philosophers with him on the ship. Pangloss explained to him how things could not be better. Jacques was not of this opinion.

"Men must surely have corrupted nature a little," he would say, "for they were not born wolves, and yet wolves they have become. God gave them neither twenty-four pounders nor bayonets, and they have made bayonets and twenty-four pounders in order to destroy each other. I could also mention bankruptcies, and the courts who seize the assets of bankrupts and cheat their creditors of them."

"That was all indispensable," was the one-eyed doctor's reply. "Individual misfortunes contribute to the general good with the result that the more individual misfortunes there are, the more all is well."

While he was presenting his argument, the air grew thick, the winds blew from the four corners of the earth, and the ship was assailed by the most terrible storm, within sight of the port of Lisbon.

CHAPTER 5

Storm, shipwreck, earthquake, and what became of Dr. Pangloss,
Candide, and Jacques the Anabaptist

Half the passengers on board, weakened and near dead from those unimaginable spasms that the rolling of a ship can induce in every nerve and humour of the body by tossing them in opposite directions, did not even have the strength to worry about the danger. The other half shrieked and prayed. The sails were rent, the masts were smashed, the ship broke up. Work as they might, no one could make himself understood, and there was no one in charge. The Anabaptist was helping out with the rigging down on the decks. Furious, a sailor came up, gave him a good clout, and laid him flat on the boards. But the force of the blow jerked him so violently that he himself fell head first overboard and ended up suspended in mid-air, hanging from a piece of broken mast. Kind Jacques ran to his rescue, helped him back on board, and in the process was precipitated into the sea in full view of the sailor—who left him to perish without so much as a backward glance. Along came Candide, saw his benefactor momentarily reappear on the surface and then sink without trace, and wanted to jump in after him. Pangloss the philosopher prevented him, arguing that Lisbon harbour had been created expressly so that the Anabaptist would be drowned in it. While he was proving this a priori,[8] the ship foundered and everyone perished, except for Pangloss, Candide, and

---

8. By logic as opposed to experience.

the brute of a sailor who had drowned the virtuous Anabaptist. The blackguard swam safely to the very shore where Pangloss and Candide were also carried on a plank.

When they had recovered a little, they proceeded on foot towards Lisbon. They had some money left and hoped with this to escape hunger, just as they had survived the storm.

Scarcely had they set foot in the city, still weeping over the death of their benefactor, than they felt the earth quake beneath their feet. In the port a boiling sea rose up and smashed the ships lying at anchor. Whirlwinds of flame and ash covered the streets and public squares: houses disintegrated, roofs were upended upon foundations, and foundations crumbled.

Thirty thousand inhabitants of both sexes and all ages were crushed beneath the ruins. The sailor said with a whistle and an oath:

"There'll be some rich pickings here."

"What can be the sufficient reason for this phenomenon?" wondered Pangloss.

"The end of the world is come!" Candide shouted.

The sailor forthwith dashed into the midst of the rubble, braving death in search of money; he duly found some, grabbed it, got drunk and, having slept it off, bought the favours of the first willing girl he met among the remains of the ruined houses, among the dying and the dead.

Pangloss, however, took him aside:

"My friend," he said, "this is not right. You are in breach of universal reason, and this is hardly the moment."

"Hell's teeth!" replied the other. "I'm a sailor and I come from Batavia. Four times I've trampled on the crucifix, on four separate voyages to Japan.[9] You've picked the wrong man, you and your universal reason!"

One or two fragments of stone had injured Candide. He was lying in the street covered in rubble. He kept calling out to Pangloss:

"Help! Get me some wine and oil. I'm dying."

"This earthquake is nothing new," replied Pangloss. "The city of Lima felt the same tremors in America last year. Same causes, same effects. There must be a vein of sulphur running underground from Lima to Lisbon."[1]

"Nothing is more probable," said Candide, "but for God's sake get me some oil and wine."

"What do you mean, probable?" the philosopher retorted. "I maintain that the thing is proven."

Candide lost consciousness, and Pangloss brought him some water from a nearby fountain.

The next day, having located some food by crawling about among the rubble, they recovered their strength a little. Then they worked like everyone else at giving assistance to the inhabitants who had survived. One group of citizens they had helped gave them as good a dinner as was possible in such a disaster. It is true that the meal was a sad one, and the company wept over their bread; but Pangloss consoled them by assuring them that things could not be otherwise:

"For all this is the best there is. If the volcanic activity is in Lisbon, it means it could not have been anywhere else. For it is impossible for things not to be where they are. For all is well."

---

9. In the 18th century Dutch traders could enter Japan only after renouncing Christianity in this way.

1. Lima was destroyed by an earthquake in 1746, and Lisbon suffered a catastrophic earthquake in 1755.

A little man in black, an agent of the Inquisition,[2] was sitting next to him. He intervened politely and said:

"Apparently sir does not believe in original sin. For if everything is as well as can be, there has been neither Fall nor punishment."

"I most humbly beg Your Excellency's pardon," replied Pangloss even more politely, "but the Fall of man and the curse entered necessarily into the scheme of the best of all possible worlds."

"So sir does not believe in freedom?" said the agent.

"Your Excellency will forgive me," said Pangloss. "Freedom can exist alongside absolute necessity, for it was necessary for us to be free. For ultimately, the will once determined . . ."

Pangloss was in the middle of his sentence when the agent nodded to his henchman, who was pouring him some port, or rather Oporto, wine.

CHAPTER 6

How they had a splendid auto-da-fé[3] to prevent earthquakes, and how Candide was flogged

After the earthquake which had destroyed three quarters of Lisbon, the wise men of the country had not been able to come up with any more effective means of preventing total ruin than to give the people a splendid *auto-da-fé*. It was decided by the University of Coimbra that the spectacle of a few people being ceremonially burnt over a low flame is the infallible secret of preventing earthquakes.

Consequently they had arrested a man from Biscay who had been found guilty of marrying his fellow godparent, and two Portuguese who had removed the bacon when eating a chicken.[4] After dinner men came and tied up Dr. Pangloss and his disciple Candide, one for what he had said, and the other for having listened with an air of approval. Both were led away to separate apartments, which were extremely cool and where the sun was never troublesome. A week later they were both dressed in a *san-benito*,[5] and paper mitres were placed upon their heads. Candide's mitre and *san-benito* were painted with flames that were upside down and with devils which had neither claws nor tails, but Pangloss's devils had claws and tails, and his flames were the right way up. So dressed, they walked in procession and listened to a very moving sermon, followed by a beautiful recital of plainchant. Candide was flogged in time to the singing; the man from Biscay and the two men who had not wanted to eat bacon were burned; and Pangloss was hanged, despite the fact that this was not the custom. The very same day the earth quaked once more: the din was fearful.

Terrified, confounded, thoroughly distraught, all bleeding and trembling, Candide reflected to himself:

"If this is the best of all possible worlds, then what must the others be like? I wouldn't mind if I'd only been flogged. That happened with the Bulgars. But, o my dear Pangloss! You, the greatest of philosophers! Did I have to see you hanged without my knowing why?! O my dear Anabaptist! You, the best of men! Did you have to

---

2. The tribunal that violently persecuted persons accused of religious heresy.
3. "Act of faith," the public judgment (and often burning) of an accused authorized by the Inquisition.
4. Implying that they were Jewish; chickens were frequently

covered with bacon strips to keep the meat moist while roasting.
5. A shirt worn by condemned heretics, usually with painted flames to indicate whether the heretic had confessed (upside down) or remained unrepentant (upright).

drown in the port?! O Miss Cunégonde! You pearl among daughters! Did you have to get your stomach slit open?!"

He was just leaving the scene afterwards, scarcely able to stand up, and having been preached at, flogged, absolved, and blessed, when an old woman came up to him and said:

"Take courage, my son, follow me."

CHAPTER 7

How an old woman took care of Candide, and
how he was reunited with the one he loved

Candide did not take courage, but he did follow the old woman into a hovel. She gave him a pot of ointment to rub on himself, set things out for him to eat and drink, and indicated a small, moderately clean bed, beside which lay a full set of clothes.

"Eat, drink, and sleep," she said, "and may Our Lady of Atocha, His Eminence Saint Anthony of Padua, and His Eminence Saint James of Compostella[6] watch over you. I'll be back tomorrow."

Candide, still astonished at all he had seen and suffered, and even more astonished at the charity of the old woman, wanted to kiss her hand.

"It's not my hand you should be kissing. I'll be back tomorrow. Rub yourself with ointment, eat, and sleep."

Candide, despite so many misfortunes, ate and slept. The next day the old woman brought him breakfast, inspected his back, and rubbed a different ointment on it herself. Then she brought him dinner, and in the evening she returned with supper. The day after that she went through the same ritual again.

"Who are you?" Candide kept asking her. "What has made you so kind? How can I repay you?"

The good woman did not answer. She returned that evening bringing nothing for supper.

"Come with me," she said, "and not a word."

She took him by the arm and walked with him for about a quarter of a mile into the country. They arrived at a house standing on its own, surrounded by gardens and waterways. The old woman knocked at a little door. Someone opened it. She led Candide up a secret staircase into a small gilded room, left him sitting on a brocaded couch, shut the door after her, and departed. Candide thought he was dreaming; his whole life seemed to him like a bad dream, and the present moment a sweet one.

The old woman soon reappeared. She was supporting with some difficulty the trembling figure of a majestic-looking woman, all sparkling with jewels and hidden by a veil.

"Remove this veil," the old woman told Candide.

The young man drew near. With a timid hand he lifted the veil. What a moment! What a surprise! He thought he was looking at Miss Cunégonde. He was indeed looking at her, for it was she. His strength failed him, words failed him, and he fell at her feet. Cunégonde fell on the couch. The old woman showered them with various waters. They came to their senses. They spoke to each other. At first it was all half-finished sentences, and questions and answers getting crossed, and sighs,

6. Patron saints of Portugal and Spain.

and tears, and exclamations. The old woman suggested they make less noise and left them to it.

"What! It is you!" said Candide. "You're alive! To think that I should find you in Portugal! So you weren't raped? So you didn't have your stomach slit open as Pangloss the philosopher assured me you did?"

"I certainly was, and did," said the fair Cunégonde. "But those two particular misfortunes are not always fatal."

"But were your father and mother killed?"

"That is only too true," said Cunégonde tearfully.

"And your brother?"

"My brother was killed, too."

"And why are you in Portugal? And how did you know that I was here? And how on earth did you arrange to have me brought to this house?"

"I will tell you all these things," the young lady replied. "But first you must tell me all that has happened to you since that innocent kiss you gave me and those kicks you got."

With deep respect Candide obeyed her, and although he was at a loss for words, and his voice was weak and quavering, and his spine still hurt a little, he gave her the most artless account of all that had happened to him since the moment of their separation. Cunégonde raised her eyes to heaven, and she shed tears at the deaths of the good Anabaptist and Pangloss; after which she spoke in these terms to Candide, who missed not a word and devoured her with his eyes.

CHAPTER 8

Cunégonde's story

"I was in bed fast asleep when it pleased heaven to send the Bulgars into our beautiful castle of Thunder-ten-tronckh. They slit the throats of my father and brother, and hacked my mother to pieces. A great big Bulgar, six feet tall, seeing that I had passed out at the sight of all this, began to rape me. That brought me round. I came to, screamed, struggled, bit him, scratched him. I wanted to tear that big Bulgar's eyes out, little realizing that what was taking place in my father's castle was standard practice. The brute knifed me in the left side, and I still have the scar."

"Dear, oh dear! I hope I may see it," said the guileless Candide.

"You shall," said Cunégonde, "but let me continue."

"Go on," said Candide.

She took up the thread of her story thus:

"A Bulgar captain came into the room and saw me all covered in blood. The soldier didn't take any notice. The captain became angry at this lack of respect being shown him by the brute and killed him where he lay on top of me. Then he had me bandaged up and took me to his quarters as a prisoner of war. I used to wash what few shirts he had, and I cooked for him. He found me very pretty, I must admit, and I won't deny he was a good-looking man himself, with skin that was white and soft. Apart from that, not much brain, not much of a thinker. You could tell he hadn't been educated by Dr. Pangloss. Three months later, having lost all his money and grown tired of me, he sold me to a Jew called Don Issacar, who was a dealer in Holland and Portugal, and who was passionately fond of women. This Jew became much attached to my person, but he was unable to get the better of it. I resisted his advances more successfully than I had the Bulgar soldier's. A woman of honour may be raped once, but her virtue is all the stronger for it. In an attempt to win me over, the Jew brought me here to this country house. I had previously thought that there was nothing in the world as beautiful as the castle of Thunder-ten-tronckh. I have been disabused.

"The Grand Inquisitor noticed me one day during Mass. He kept eyeing me, and then sent word that he had to speak to me on a confidential matter. I was taken to his palace. I told him who I was. He pointed out how far beneath my station it was to belong to an Israelite. It was suggested on his behalf to Don Issacar that he should cede me to His Eminence. Don Issacar, who is the Court's banker and a man of some influence, would have none of it. The Inquisitor threatened him with an *auto-da-fé*. In the end, under intimidation, my Jew agreed to a deal whereby the house and I would belong to both of them jointly. The Jew would have Mondays, Wednesdays, and the sabbath, and the Inquisitor would have the other days of the week. This convention has been operating for six months now. It has not been without its quarrels, for it has often been a moot point which sabbath the period from Saturday night to Sunday morning belongs to, the Old Testament one or the New. For my own part I have resisted both men up till now, and I'm sure that's why they still love me.

"Anyway, in order to ward off the scourge of the earthquakes and to intimidate Don Issacar, it pleased my lord and master the Inquisitor to celebrate an *auto-da-fé*. He did me the honour of inviting me. I had a very good seat, and the ladies were served refreshments between the Mass and the execution. I was horrified, it must be said, to see those two Jews being burnt, as well as that nice man from Biscay who had married his fellow godparent. But how surprised, how shocked, how upset I was to see someone that looked like Pangloss in a *san-benito* and wearing a mitre! I rubbed my eyes, stared, saw him hanged, and fainted. I had hardly come to when I saw you standing there stark naked. That was my moment of greatest horror and consternation, the moment of greatest pain and despair. I can tell you truthfully, your skin is even fairer and more perfectly pink than my Bulgar captain's. The sight of it lent added force to all the feelings which were surging through me and devouring me. I screamed, I wanted to shout out: 'Stop, you animals!,' but nothing came out, and anyway my screaming and shouting would have done no good. 'How is it,' I said to myself, when you had been well and truly flogged, 'that nice Candide and wise Pangloss come to be in Lisbon, and that one of them gets a hundred lashes, and the other is hanged by order of His Eminence the Inquisitor, who in turn is in love with me? So Pangloss deceived me cruelly when he told me that all was well with the world.'

"Distressed, agitated, beside myself with anger one minute and ready to faint clean away the next, all I could think about was the massacre of my father and mother and brother, the insolence of my ugly Bulgar soldier, and the knife wound he gave me, my bondage, my menial work as a cook, my Bulgar captain, my ugly Don Issacar, my abominable Inquisitor, the hanging of Dr. Pangloss, that great *Miserere* they sang in plainchant while you were being flogged, and above all that kiss I gave you behind a screen the day I last saw you. I praised God for bringing you back to me after so many trials and tribulations. I instructed my old servant to tend to you and to bring you here as soon as she could. She has carried out my commission most capably. I have had the indescribable pleasure of seeing you again, of hearing you and speaking to you. You must have a terrible hunger, and I have a large appetite. Let's begin with supper."

With which they both sat down to eat. After supper they resumed their positions on the aforementioned beautiful couch. There they were when Señor Don Issacar, one of the masters of the house, arrived. It was the sabbath. He had come to enjoy his rights and press his suit.

CHAPTER 9

What became of Cunégonde, Candide, the Grand Inquisitor, and a Jew

This Issacar was the most irascible Hebrew in the tribe of Israel since the time of the Captivity in Babylon.[7]

"What!" he said, "you whore of Galilee! So Mr. Inquisitor isn't enough for you then? I've got to share you with this infidel too?"

With these words he drew a long dagger which he always carried with him and, not thinking his adversary would be armed, attacked Candide. But the old woman had given our good Westphalian a fine sword with his suit of clothes. Gentle though his disposition was, he drew his sword, and that was it: one Israelite stone dead on the floor at the feet of the fair Cunégonde.

"Holy Virgin!" cried she. "What is to become of us? A man killed in my house! If the police come, we're lost!"

"If Pangloss had not been hanged," said Candide, "he would have given us some good advice in this predicament, for he was a great philosopher. Since he's not here, let's ask the old woman."

She was a most prudent sort, and was just beginning to give her opinion when another little door opened. It was one hour after midnight: Sunday was beginning. This day belonged to His Eminence the Inquisitor. In he came to find Candide, who had been flogged, now standing sword in hand, with a corpse stretched out on the ground, Cunégonde in a fluster, and the old woman giving advice.

Here is what went through Candide's mind at that moment, and how he reasoned:

"If this holy man calls for help, he will certainly have me burned. He may well do the same to Cunégonde. He has already had me mercilessly whipped. He is my rival. I've already started killing. There's nothing else for it."

This reasoning was clear and quick, and without giving the Inquisitor the time to recover from his surprise, he ran him through and hurled him down beside the Jew.

"Well, here's a fine mess," said Cunégonde. "There's no going back now. That's us excommunicated. Our last hour has come. How is it that someone as soft-hearted as you can have ended up killing a Jew and a prelate in a matter of minutes?"

"My dear girl," replied Candide, "when a man's in love, jealous, and flogged by the Inquisition, there's no knowing what he may do."

The old woman then broke in and said:

"There are three Andalusian horses in the stable, as well as saddles and bridles. Let brave Candide get them ready. Madam has moidores[8] and diamonds. Let us mount quickly—though my seat is but one buttock—and ride to Cadiz.[9] The weather is of the best, and it is always a great pleasure to travel in the cool of the night."

At once Candide saddled up the three horses. Cunégonde, the old woman, and he covered thirty miles without stopping. While they were making their escape, the Holy Hermandad[1] reached the house. They buried His Eminence in a beautiful church, and threw Issacar on to the rubbish-heap.

Candide, Cunégonde, and the old woman had by this time reached the small town of Avacena, in the middle of the Sierra Morena mountains, where they had the following conversation in an inn.

---

7. The period of Hebrew captivity in the 6th century B.C.E.   9. Coastal town in southwestern Spain.
8. Portuguese coins.   1. The "Holy Brotherhood," agents of the Inquisition.

CHAPTER 10

In what distress Candide, Cunégonde, and the old woman
arrived in Cadiz, and of their embarkation

"But who can possibly have stolen my pistoles[2] and diamonds?" sobbed Cunégonde. "What will we live on? How shall we manage? Where will I find the Inquisitors and the Jews to replace them?"

"Alas!" said the old woman, "I have a strong suspicion it was that Franciscan monk who spent yesterday night in the same inn as us in Badajoz. God preserve me from jumping to conclusions, but he did come into our room twice and he did leave long before us."

"Oh dear!" said Candide. "Good Pangloss often used to argue that the fruits of the earth are common to all and that everyone has an equal right to them. According to his principles, that Franciscan ought to have left us enough money behind to finish our journey. Have you really not got anything left, my fair Cunégonde?"

"Not a maravedi,"[3] said she.

"What shall we do?" said Candide.

"Let's sell one of our horses," said the old woman. "I can ride behind Miss Cunégonde, even though I have only one buttock to sit on, and we'll make it to Cadiz."

There was a Benedictine prior staying in the same hostelry. He bought the horse cheaply. Candide, Cunégonde, and the old woman passed through Lucena, Chillas, and Lebrija, and came at last to Cadiz. There a fleet was being fitted out and troops were being mustered to go and knock some sense into the Jesuit reverend fathers in Paraguay, who were accused of having incited one of their local native hordes to revolt against the Kings of Spain and Portugal near the town of San Sacramento.[4] Candide, having served with the Bulgars, performed the Bulgar drill for the general of this little army with so much grace, speed, skill, agility, and panache that he was given command of a company of foot. So there he was a captain. He boarded ship with Miss Cunégonde, the old woman, two valets, and the two Andalusian horses which had belonged to the Grand Inquisitor of Portugal.

During the crossing they discussed poor Pangloss's philosophy a great deal.

"We're going to another world," Candide would say. "I expect it must be there that all is well. For you have to admit, one could grumble rather at what goes on in our one, both physically and morally."

"I love you with all my heart," Cunégonde would say, "but my soul is still in something of a state, what with all I've seen and been through."

"All will be well," was Candide's reply. "Already the sea in this new world is better than those we have in Europe. It's calmer, and the winds are more constant. It is assuredly the new world which is the best of all possible worlds."

"God willing!" said Cunégonde. "But I have been so horribly unfortunate in my own that my heart is almost closed to hope."

"*You're* complaining!" said the old woman. "Alas! You haven't had the misfortunes I have."

---

2. Spanish gold coins.
3. Spanish copper coin.
4. Jesuit missionaries who controlled Paraguay resisted Spain's attempt to transfer this territory to Portugal. Spain sent troops from Cadiz to crush the rebellion; Voltaire invested in this expedition as part owner of one of the ships.

Cunégonde almost burst out laughing and found it extremely droll of this little old woman to claim to be more unfortunate than she.

"I'm afraid, my good woman," she said to her, "that unless you have been raped by two Bulgars, stabbed twice in the stomach, had two of your castles demolished, seen two mothers' and two fathers' throats slit before your very eyes, and watched two of your lovers being flogged at an *auto-da-fé,* then I don't see you bettering me. Added to which, I was born a Baroness with seventy-two heraldic quarterings and yet I have been a cook."

"My young lady," replied the old woman, "you do not know who I am by birth, and if I were to show you my bottom, you would not speak as you do, and you would reserve judgement."

This declaration aroused the deepest curiosity in the minds of Cunégonde and Candide. The old woman had this to say to them.

CHAPTER 11

The old woman's story

"My eyes haven't always been bloodshot and red-rimmed, my nose hasn't always come down to my chin, and I haven't always been a servant. I am the daughter of Pope Urban X[5] and the Princess of Palestrina. Until the age of fourteen I was brought up in a palace, next to which not one of your German barons' castles would even have done as a stable. And any single one of my dresses was worth more than all the treasures of Westphalia put together. As I grew older, so I grew in beauty, grace, and fine accomplishments. I took pleasure in life; I commanded respect; I had prospects. I was already able to inspire love, and my breasts were forming. And what breasts they were! White and firm, just like those of the Medici Venus.[6] And what eyes! What eyelids! What black eyebrows! What fire burned in my pupils and outshone the sparkling of the stars, as the poets in that part of the world used to tell me. The women who dressed and undressed me would go into ecstasies when they saw me, back and front, and all the men would love to have changed places with them.

"I was engaged to be married to a sovereign prince of Massa-Carrara. What a prince! As handsome as I was beautiful, gentle and charming to a fault, brilliant in mind and ardent in love. I loved him as one does love for the first time, I worshipped him with passionate abandon. Arrangements were made for the wedding. The pomp and magnificence of it! No one had seen their like before. It was one continual round of entertainments, tournaments, opera buffa. And all Italy composed sonnets for me, though not one of them was any good. My moment of bliss was at hand when an old marchioness, who had been my prince's mistress, invited him to take chocolate with her. He died less than two hours later after appalling convulsions. But that was a trifle. My mother, being in despair and yet much less grief-stricken than I, wanted to absent herself for a time from so dreadful a scene. She had a very fine property near Gaeta.[7] We took ship on a local galley, which was all covered in gilt like the altar of Saint Peter's in Rome. What happens but a corsair from Salé[8] makes straight for us and boards us. Our soldiers defended themselves as if they were the Pope's own: they all knelt down, cast their weapons aside, and asked the corsair for absolution *in articulo mortis.*[9]

---

5. A fictional pope (the joke is that popes were of course expected to remain celibate).
6. A famous white marble sculpture.
7. A port in southern Italy.

8. A port in Morocco which was a center of piracy in the 18th century.
9. "At the point of death."

"At once they were stripped as naked as monkeys, as were my mother, and our ladies-in-waiting, and I also. It is a remarkable thing, the eagerness of these gentlemen to undress everybody. But what surprised me more was that they put a finger up all of us in a place where we women ordinarily allow only enema nozzles to enter. This ritual struck me as being most odd. But that's how one judges everything when one's never been abroad. I soon gathered that it was to see if we'd hadn't hidden any diamonds up there. It has been established practice among civilized seafaring nations since time immemorial. I discovered that those religious gentlemen, the Knights of Malta,[1] never fail to do it when they capture any Turks, men or women. It is one article of the law of nations which has never been infringed.

"I needn't tell you how hard it is for a young princess to be taken to Morocco as a slave with her mother. You can well imagine all we had to suffer on the pirate ship. My mother was still very beautiful. Our ladies-in-waiting, even our maids, had more charms than are to be found in the whole of Africa. As for me, I was ravishing. I was beauty, grace itself, and I was a virgin. I wasn't one for long. The flower which had been kept for the handsome prince of Massa-Carrara was ravished by the pirate captain. He was a loathsome Negro, who even thought he was doing me a great honour. Yes indeed, the Princess of Palestrina and I had to be extremely tough to survive everything we went through up until our arrival in Morocco. But enough of this. Such things are so commonplace they're not worth talking about.

"Morocco was bathed in blood when we arrived. The fifty sons of the Emperor Muley-Ismael each had his own followers, which in effect meant fifty civil wars— blacks against blacks, blacks against browns, browns against browns, mulattos against mulattos. It was one long bloodbath from one end of the empire to the other.

"We had scarcely disembarked when some blacks belonging to a faction opposed to that of my pirate appeared on the scene wanting to relieve him of his booty. After the diamonds and the gold, we were the most precious things he had. I was witness to a fight the like of which you in your European climates just never see. The Northern races are simply not hot-blooded enough. They don't have that thirst for women that they have in Africa. It's as if you Europeans had milk in your veins, whereas it is vitriol, fire, that flows in the veins of the inhabitants of Mount Atlas and that part of the world. They fought with the fury of the lions and tigers and serpents of their own country to decide which of them should have us. A Moor grabbed my mother by the right arm, my pirate's lieutenant held on to her left, a Moorish soldier took her by one leg, and one of our other pirates held her by the other. In an instant almost all our ladies-in-waiting found themselves being torn like this between four soldiers. My captain kept me hidden behind him. Scimitar in hand, he was killing anything that stood in the way of his own particular thirst. In the end I saw all our Italian women and my mother torn apart, cut to pieces, massacred by the monsters who were fighting over them. My fellow captives and their captors, soldiers, sailors, blacks, browns, whites, mulattos, and finally my captain, all were killed, and I lay dying on top of a pile of corpses. Similar scenes were taking place, as you know, over an area more than three hundred leagues across: and never once did they fail to say the five daily prayers ordered by Mahomet.

"I extricated myself with great difficulty from the piled heap of all these blood-soaked corpses, and dragged myself over to a tall orange-tree next to a nearby stream.

---

1. An old religious order active in the Crusades.

There I collapsed in shock, exhaustion, horror, hunger, and despair. Soon afterwards my shattered senses gave themselves up to a sleep that was more like unconsciousness than rest. I was in this enfeebled and insensible state, halfway between life and death, when I felt myself being pressed down on by something squirming on my body. I opened my eyes and saw a white man with a friendly face sighing and muttering between his teeth: '*O che sciagura d'essere senza coglioni!*'[2]

CHAPTER 12

The continuing story of the old woman's misfortunes

"Astonished and delighted to hear my native tongue, and no less surprised at the words the man was uttering, I replied that there were greater misfortunes than that of which he complained. I informed him in a few words of the horrors to which I had been subjected, and passed out. He carried me to a house nearby, had me put to bed and given something to eat, waited on me, comforted me, flattered me, told me that he had never seen anything so beautiful, and that never had he so much regretted the loss of that which no one could restore to him.

"'I was born in Naples,' he told me. 'They castrate two or three thousand children every year there. Some die, some develop a voice more beautiful than any woman's, and some go off and govern the Papal States.[3] They carried out this operation most successfully on me, and I sang in the chapel of the Princess of Palestrina.'

"'My mother!' cried I.

"'Your mother!' cried he, with tears in his eyes. 'What! Then you would be that young princess I taught till she was six, and who promised even then to be as beautiful as you are?'

"'I am she. My mother lies not four hundred yards from here, in four pieces, beneath a pile of corpses . . .'

"I told him everything that had happened to me. He told me his adventures too, and about how one of the Christian powers had sent him as an envoy to sign a treaty with the King of Morocco, whereby this monarch would be supplied with powder, cannon, and ships to assist him in putting an end to the trading of the other Christian powers.

"'My mission is complete,' the worthy eunuch told me. 'I am on my way to board ship at Ceuta, and I will take you back to Italy. *Ma che sciagura d'essere senza coglioni!*'

"I thanked him with tears of tender gratitude: instead of taking me to Italy, he took me to Algiers and sold me to the local dey.[4] Hardly had I been sold than the plague which was going round Africa, Asia, and Europe broke out with a vengeance in Algiers. You have seen earthquakes; but you, my young lady, have you ever had the plague?"

"Never," the Baron's daughter replied.

"If you had," the old woman went on, "you would agree that it comes well above an earthquake. It is extremely rife in Africa, and I caught it. Can you imagine? What a situation for the fifteen-year-old daughter of a pope to be in, and for one who in the

---

2. "O what calamity it is to lack testicles" (editions after 1759 usually abbreviated the last word); many Italian boys were castrated to give them a future as male sopranos.
3. In the 18th century Farinelli, a castrato, became a top

adviser to the king of Spain. At this time, much of northern Italy was governed by the Pope and known as the Papal States.
4. A ruling official of the Ottoman Empire.

space of three months had suffered poverty and enslavement, been raped almost daily, seen her mother torn limb from limb, survived starvation and war, and was now dying of the plague in Algiers. Die, however, I did not. But my eunuch and the dey and almost the entire seraglio at Algiers perished.

"When the first wave of this appalling plague had passed, they sold the dey's slaves. A merchant bought me and took me to Tunis. He sold me to another merchant who in turn sold me in Tripoli. After Tripoli I was resold in Alexandria, after Alexandria I was resold in Smyrna, and after Smyrna in Constantinople. In the end I became the property of an aga in the janissaries,[5] who shortly afterwards received orders to go and defend Azov against the Russians, who were laying siege to it.[6]

"This aga, who was quite a ladies' man, took his whole seraglio with him, and housed us in a little fort on the Palus-Meotides under the guard of two black eunuchs and twenty soldiers. An enormous number of Russians were killed, but they gave as good as they got. Azov was put to fire and sword, and no quarter was given either as to sex or to age. All that was left was our little fort. The enemy determined to starve us out. The twenty janissaries had sworn not to surrender. The extremes of hunger to which they were reduced forced them to eat our two eunuchs, for fear of breaking their oath. After a few days they decided to eat the women.

"We had a very pious and very understanding imam,[7] who preached a fine sermon to them persuading them not to kill us outright.

"'Cut off one buttock from each of these ladies,' he said, 'and you will eat well. If you have to come back for more in a few days' time, you'll still be able to have the same again. Heaven will be grateful to you for such a charitable deed, and you will be saved.'

"He was very eloquent: he convinced them. They performed this dreadful operation on us. The imam rubbed on us the ointment they use on children who have just been circumcised. We were all at death's door.

"Hardly had the janissaries finished the meal with which we'd provided them than the Russians turn up in flat-bottomed boats. Not one janissary got away. The Russians paid not a blind bit of notice to the state we were in. There are French surgeons all over the world, and a very skilful one took charge of us and made us better. And I shall never forget how, once my wounds were well and truly healed, he then propositioned me. That apart, he told us all to cheer up and assured us that this sort of thing happened in lots of sieges, and that it was one of the laws of warfare.

"As soon as my companions could walk, they were sent to Moscow. I was part of a boyar's share of the spoils, and he put me to work in his garden and gave me twenty lashes a day. But after this nobleman was broken on the wheel two years later, along with thirty other boyars, because of some trouble or other at court, I took my chance and made my escape. I crossed the whole of Russia. For a long time I served in inns, first in Riga, then in Rostock, Wismar, Leipzig, Kassel, Utrecht, Leiden, The Hague, and Rotterdam. I grew old in poverty and dishonour, having but half a bottom, yet always mindful that I was the daughter of a pope. A hundred times I wanted to kill myself, but still I loved life. This ridiculous weakness for living is perhaps one of our most fatal tendencies. For can anything be sillier than to insist on carrying a burden one would continually much rather throw to the ground? Sillier than to feel disgust at

---

5. Turkish soldiers; an aga is a commanding officer.
6. In the 17th century the Russians invaded the sea of Azov, the northern arm of the Black Sea, which contained the islands of Palus-Meotides.
7. Leader of a mosque.

one's own existence and yet cling to it? Sillier, in short, than to clasp to our bosom the serpent that devours us until it has gnawed away our heart? In the countries through which it has been my fate to travel and in the inns where I have served, I have seen a huge number of people who felt abhorrence for their own lives. But I've seen only a dozen voluntarily put an end to their wretchedness: three Negroes, four Englishmen, four Genevans, and a German professor called Robeck.[8]

"In the end I finished up as one of the servants in the household of Don Issacar the Jew. He gave me to you, my fair young lady, as your maid. I have become involved in your destiny and been more concerned with your adventures than with my own. Indeed I would never have mentioned my misfortunes if you hadn't provoked me to it a little, and if it were not the custom on board ship to tell stories to pass the time. So there you are, Miss. I have lived, and I know the world. Just for fun, why not get each passenger to tell you the story of his life, and if there is one single one of them who hasn't often cursed the day he was born and hasn't often said to himself that he was the most unfortunate man alive, then you can throw me into the sea head first."

CHAPTER 13

How Candide was obliged to part from fair Cunégonde and the old woman

Fair Cunégonde, having heard the old woman's story, treated her with all the civilities due to a person of her rank and quality. She accepted her suggestion and got all the passengers one after another to tell her their adventures. Candide and she conceded that the old woman was right.

"It's a great pity," said Candide, "that wise Pangloss was hanged, contrary to the usual custom, during an *auto-da-fé*. He would have some remarkable things to tell us about the physical and moral evil that prevails over land and sea—and I would feel able to venture a few respectful objections."

While each person told his story, the ship continued on its way. They docked at Buenos Aires. Cunégonde, Captain Candide, and the old woman went to call on the Governor, Don Fernando d'Ibaraa y Figueora y Mascarenes y Lampourdos y Souza. This grandee had a pride to match his many names. He spoke to people with the most noble disdain, sticking his nose so far in the air, speaking in such a mercilessly loud voice, adopting so high and mighty a tone, and affecting so haughty a gait, that all who greeted him were also tempted to hit him. He loved women to distraction. Cunégonde seemed to him more beautiful than any he had ever seen. The first thing he did was to ask if she were not by any chance the Captain's wife. The air with which he put this question alarmed Candide. He did not dare say she was his wife, because in fact she was not. He did not dare say she was his sister, because she was not that either. And although this white lie had once been very fashionable among the Ancients,[9] and could still come in very useful to the Moderns, his soul was too pure to be unfaithful to the truth.

"Miss Cunégonde," he said, "is to do me the honour of marrying me, and we humbly beseech Your Excellency to condescend to officiate at our wedding."

With a twirl of his moustache Don Fernando d'Ibaraa y Figueora y Mascarenes y Lampourdos y Souza smiled a bitter smile, and ordered Captain Candide to go and review his company. Candide obeyed. The Governor remained with Miss Cunégonde.

---

8. Author of a book promoting suicide who drowned himself in 1739.

9. The patriarchs Abraham and Isaac passed off their wives as their sisters when in hostile territory (Genesis 12 and 26).

He declared his love for her and made protestations that on the morrow he would marry her, in the eyes of the Church or anyone else's, just as it might please her lovely self. Cunégonde asked him for a quarter of an hour in which to collect herself, consult with the old woman, and come to a decision.

The old woman said to Cunégonde:

"Miss, you have seventy-two quarterings, and not a penny to your name. You can be the wife of the greatest nobleman in South America, who also has a very fine moustache. Are you in any position to make a point of unswerving fidelity? You have been raped by the Bulgars. A Jew and an Inquisitor have enjoyed your favours. Misfortune does give people some rights. Frankly, if I were in your position, I would have no scruples about marrying the Governor and making Captain Candide's fortune for him."

While the old woman was speaking with all the prudence of age and experience, a small ship was seen entering the port. On board were an alcalde and some alguazils:[1] what had happened was this.

The old woman had quite rightly guessed that it had been the Cordelier[2] with the loose sleeves who had stolen the money and jewels from Cunégonde in the town of Badajoz, when she was making her rapid escape with Candide. This monk tried to sell some of the stones to a jeweller. The merchant recognized them as belonging to the Grand Inquisitor. The Franciscan, before being hanged, confessed that he had stolen them. He gave a description of the people concerned and the route they were taking. Cunégonde and Candide were already known to have escaped. They were followed to Cadiz. No time was lost in sending a ship after them, and this ship was already in the port of Buenos Aires. Rumour spread that an alcalde was about to come ashore, and that they were after the Grand Inquisitor's murderers. The prudent old woman saw at once what was to be done.

"You cannot run away," she told Cunégonde, "and you have nothing to fear. It wasn't you who killed His Eminence and, anyway, the Governor loves you and won't allow any harm to come to you. Stay here."

Whereupon she rushed off to Candide: "Quick, off you go," she said, "or in an hour you'll be burnt."

There was not a moment to lose. But how could he leave Cunégonde, and where was he to hide?

CHAPTER 14

How Candide and Cacambo were received by the Jesuits of Paraguay

Candide had brought a manservant with him from Cadiz of the kind frequently found along the coasts of Spain and in the colonies. He was a quarter Spanish, the son of a half-breed in the Tucuman.[3] He had been a choir-boy, sexton, sailor, monk, commercial agent, soldier, and lackey. His name was Cacambo, and he loved his master very much, because his master was a very good man. He saddled up the two Andalusian horses as quickly as he could.

"Come on, master, let's do as the old woman says and be off. Let's ride away, and no looking back."

Candide burst out crying.

---

1. A Spanish mayor and some officers.
2. A Franciscan friar who typically wore a loose habit as a

sign of poverty.
3. Region in Argentina.

"O my darling Cunégonde! Must I abandon you just when the Governor was going to marry us! Cunégonde, what will become of you so far from home?"

"She'll become what she can," said Cacambo. "Women are never stuck. God sees to that. Let's go."

"Where are you taking me? Where are we going? What will we do without Cunégonde?" said Candide.

"By Saint James of Compostella," said Cacambo, "you were going to fight against the Jesuits. Let's go and fight for them instead. I know the roads well enough. I'll take you to their kingdom. They'll be delighted to have a captain who can do drill the Bulgar way. You'll be all the rage. If one doesn't get what one wants in one world, one can always get it in another. It's always a great pleasure to see new places and do different things."

"So you've already been to Paraguay then?" said Candide.

"I've been there all right!" said Cacambo. "I used to be a servant at the College of the Assumption, and I know los Padres' way of running things like I know the streets of Cadiz. It's a wonderful way of governing they have. Their kingdom is already more than three hundred leagues wide, and it's been divided into thirty provinces. Los Padres own everything in it, and the people nothing—a masterpiece of reason and justice. If you ask me, nothing could be more divine than los Padres making war on the Kings of Spain and Portugal over here and being confessors to the very same Kings back in Europe, or than killing Spaniards here and speeding them on their way to heaven back in Madrid. It appeals to me, that does. Come on, let's go. You're about to become the happiest man alive. How pleased los Padres are going to be when they discover there's a captain coming who knows the Bulgar drill!"

The moment they arrived at the first border post, Cacambo told the advance guard that a captain was asking to speak to His Eminence, the commanding officer. The main guard was notified. A Paraguayan officer made haste to go and kneel at the feet of the commanding officer and inform him of the news. Candide and Cacambo were first disarmed, and then their two Andalusian horses were taken from them. Both strangers were ushered between two lines of soldiers. The commanding officer was standing at the far end, with the three-cornered hat on his head, his cassock hitched up, a sword at his side, and a halberd in his hand. He made a sign. Instantly twenty-four soldiers surrounded the two newcomers. A sergeant told them they must wait, that the commanding officer could not speak to them, that the Reverend Father Provincial did not permit Spaniards to open their mouths unless he was present, or to remain in the country for more than three hours.

"And where is the Reverend Father Provincial?" asked Cacambo.

"He has said Mass, and now he's taking parade," replied the sergeant. "And you won't be able to kiss his spurs for another three hours yet."

"But," said Cacambo, "the Captain—who incidentally is dying of hunger, as indeed I am—isn't Spanish. He's German. Couldn't we have lunch while we wait for His Reverence?"

With this the sergeant went off to tell the commanding officer what had been said.

"May God be praised!" said this reverend gentleman. "Since he's German, I can speak to him. Show him to my arbour."

At once Candide was led into a closet of greenery, embellished with a very pretty colonnade of green and gold marble, and trellis-work containing parrots, colibris, humming-birds, guinea-fowl, and all manner of rare birds. An excellent lunch had been laid out in vessels of gold, and while the Paraguayans ate maize from wooden bowls out in the open in the full glare of the sun, the reverend father-in-command entered the arbour.

He was a very handsome young man, rather pale-skinned, with a round, ruddy face, arched eyebrows, a keen gaze, red ears, vermilion lips, and a proud demeanour—though proud in a way quite unlike a Spaniard or a Jesuit. Candide and Cacambo were given back the weapons which had been taken from them, as well as their two Andalusian horses. Cacambo gave the latter their oats near the arbour and kept a watchful eye on them in case of surprise.

First Candide kissed the hem of the commanding officer's cassock, and then they all sat down to table.

"So you're German, you say?" said the Jesuit in that language.

"Yes, reverend father," said Candide.

As they uttered these words, they looked at each other in absolute astonishment and with a degree of emotion which it was beyond them to control.

"And from which part of Germany do you come?" said the Jesuit.

"From the filthy province of Westphalia," said Candide. "I was born in the castle of Thunder-ten-tronckh."

"Good heavens! It's not possible?" exclaimed the commanding officer.

"It's a miracle!" exclaimed Candide.

"Can it really be you?" said the commanding officer.

"It's impossible," said Candide.

They both fell back in amazement, and kissed each other, and wept buckets of tears.

"What! Can it really be you, reverend father? You, the brother of the fair Cunégonde! You who were killed by the Bulgars! You the son of the Baron! You a Jesuit in Paraguay! The world really is a very strange place, I must say. O Pangloss! Pangloss! how pleased you would be now if you hadn't been hanged!"

The commanding officer dismissed the Negro slaves and the Paraguayans who were serving drinks in goblets of rock-crystal. He thanked God and Saint Ignatius[4] a thousand times, and he hugged Candide. Their faces were bathed in tears.

"You will be even more astonished, even more moved, even more beside yourself," said Candide, "when I tell you that Miss Cunégonde, your sister whom you thought disembowelled, is in the best of health."

"Where?"

"Not far from here, with the Governor of Buenos Aires. And I was coming over here to fight against you."

Each word they uttered in this long conversation piled wonder upon wonder. The soul of each took wing upon his tongue, paid careful heed with either ear, and sparkled in his eyes. Being Germans, they sat on at table for a long time; and while they waited for the Reverend Father Provincial, the commanding officer spoke thus to his dear Candide.

CHAPTER 15

How Candide killed the brother of his dear Cunégonde

"For as long as I live I shall always remember that dreadful day when I saw my father and mother killed and my sister raped. When the Bulgars had gone, my adorable sister was nowhere to be found, and my mother and father and I, together with two servant

---

4. Ignatius of Loyola (1491–1556), founder of the Jesuit order.

girls and three little boys who'd had their throats slit, were placed on a cart to be taken for burial at a Jesuit chapel two leagues from our ancestral home. A Jesuit threw some holy water over us. It was horribly salty. A few drops of it went in my eyes. The reverend father saw my eyelids quiver. He put his hand on my heart and felt it beating. I was saved, and three weeks later you wouldn't have known there'd been anything the matter. You know how good-looking I was, my dear Candide. I became even more so, with the result that the reverend father Croust,[5] who was Father Superior, developed the most tender affection for me. He initiated me as a novice. Some time later I was sent to Rome. The Father General had need of a batch of young German Jesuit recruits. The rulers of Paraguay admit as few Spanish Jesuits as they can. They prefer foreign ones in the belief that they can control them better. The Father General thought I was just the right sort of person to go and toil in this particular vineyard. So off we went, a Pole, a Tyrolean,[6] and myself. On arrival I had the honour of being made sub-deacon and lieutenant. Today I am colonel and priest. We shall give the King of Spain's troops a warm reception. They will be excommunicated and beaten, I can promise you. Providence has sent you here to help us. But is it really true that my dear sister Cunégonde is not far away, at the Governor's in Buenos Aires?"

Candide swore to him that nothing could be more true. Their tears began once more to flow.

The Baron could not desist from embracing Candide. He called him his brother, his saviour.

"Ah, my dear Candide," he said, "perhaps we can enter the city as victors, the two of us together, and rescue my dear sister Cunégonde."

"There's nothing I'd like better," said Candide, "for I was intending to marry her, and I still hope to."

"You insolent man!" retorted the Baron. "You would have the audacity to marry my sister who has seventy-two quarterings! I consider it great effrontery on your part to dare speak to me of so rash an intention!"

Candide's blood turned to stone at such a statement. He answered him:

"Reverend father, all the quarterings in the world have nothing to do with it. I have rescued your sister from the arms of a Jew and an Inquisitor. She owes me a number of debts, and she intends to marry me. Maître Pangloss always told me that men are equal, and marry her I most assuredly will."

"We'll see about that, you scoundrel!" said the Jesuit Baron of Thunder-ten-tronckh and, so saying, struck him a heavy blow across the face with the flat of his sword.

Candide, quick as a flash, drew his own and plunged it up to the hilt into the Jesuit Baron's gut. But as he withdrew it, all steaming, he began to cry.

"Dear God," he said, "I've killed my former master, my friend, my brother-in-law. I am the best fellow in the world, and already that makes three men I've killed, and two of them priests!"

Cacambo, who had been standing guard at the door of the arbour, came running.

"There's nothing for it but to sell our lives dearly," his master said to him. "They're bound to come into the arbour, so we'll have to die fighting."

5. Name of a Jesuit who had helped drive Voltaire from Colmar in 1754.

6. Tyrol: Alpine region in present-day Austria and Italy.

Cacambo, who had seen a thing or two, kept his head. He removed the Baron's Jesuit cassock, put it on Candide, handed him the dead man's biretta,[7] and made him mount his horse. This was all done in a trice.

"Quickly, master, at the gallop. Everyone will take you for a Jesuit dashing off to give orders, and we'll have passed the frontier before they can give chase."

He was already riding like the wind when he said this, shouting out in Spanish: "Make way, make way for the reverend father colonel."

CHAPTER 16

What became of the two travellers with two girls, two monkeys,
and the savages called the Lobeiros

Candide and his manservant were past the frontier, and still no one in the camp knew the German Jesuit was dead. The vigilant Cacambo had taken care to fill his bag with bread, chocolate, ham, fruit, and a quantity of wine. They rode their Andalusian horses deep into unknown country where they found no sign of a track. Eventually a beautiful stretch of grassland, criss-crossed with streams, opened up before them. Our two travellers halted to allow their mounts to graze. Cacambo suggested to his master that they eat something and duly set him an example.

"How do you expect me to eat ham," said Candide, "when I have killed the Baron's son and see myself doomed never to see fair Cunégonde again in my life? What's the use of prolonging my miserable existence if I must drag it out, far away from her, in remorse and despair? And what will the *Journal de Trévoux* say?"[8]

So saying, he did not abstain from eating. The sun was setting. The two lost travellers heard one or two faint cries which sounded as though they came from women. They could not tell if they were cries of joy or pain, but they quickly sprang to their feet, full of that apprehension and alarm which anything in a strange land can arouse. The clamour was emanating from two completely naked girls who were scampering along the edge of the meadow pursued by two monkeys who were nibbling at their bottoms. Candide was moved to pity. He had learnt to shoot with the Bulgars, and he could have downed a hazelnut in a thicket without so much as touching a single leaf. He raised his Spanish double-barrelled gun, fired, and killed the two monkeys.

"God be praised, my dear Cacambo! I have delivered those two poor creatures from great peril. If it was a sin to kill an Inquisitor and a Jesuit, I've certainly atoned for it by saving the lives of these two girls. Perhaps the two young ladies are well-to-do and this chance episode will prove to be of great advantage to us hereabouts."

He was about to continue, but he was struck dumb when he saw the two girls throw loving arms around the two monkeys, dissolve into tears over their dead bodies, and rend the air with wails of utmost grief.

"I didn't expect the kindness of their hearts to go that far," Candide said at last to Cacambo, who replied:

"A fine thing you've done there, master. You've just killed those two young ladies' lovers."

"Their lovers! Impossible! You're joking, Cacambo. How can they possibly be?"

---

7. Priest's square hat.

8. This was a Jesuit publication that had been critical of Voltaire.

"My dear master," continued Cacambo, "you're always surprised by everything. Why do you find it so strange that in some countries monkeys should enjoy the favours of the ladies? They're a quarter human, just as I am a quarter Spanish."

"Oh, dear!" replied Candide, "I remember now Maître Pangloss saying that such accidents did use to happen once upon a time, and that these couplings produced centaurs, fauns, and satyrs, and that several of the great names of antiquity had seen them. But I used to think that it only happened in fables."

"Well, you ought to be convinced now that it's true," said Cacambo. "You see how people behave when they haven't had a bit of education. All I hope is that these ladies don't cause us any trouble."

These solid reflections persuaded Candide to leave the meadow and plunge into a wood. There he supped with Cacambo and, having cursed the Inquisitor of Portugal, the Governor of Buenos Aires, and the Baron, they both fell asleep on some moss. When they awoke, they felt unable to move. The reason was that during the night the Lobeiros,[9] who inhabit that country, and to whom the two ladies had denounced them, had pinioned them with rope made of bark. They were surrounded by some fifty naked Lobeiros armed with arrows, cudgels, and hatchets made of flint. Some of them were warming a large cauldron, others were preparing skewers, and they were all chanting:

"It's a Jesuit! It's a Jesuit! We will be avenged, our stomachs will be full. Let's eat Jesuit! Let's eat Jesuit!"

"I told you so, my dear master," cried Cacambo sadly. "I told you those two girls would play us false."

Candide, seeing the cauldron and the skewers, exclaimed:

"We're going to be roasted or boiled, that's for certain. Ah! what would Maître Pangloss say if he could see how human nature is in its pure state? All is well. So it may be. But I must say it's pretty rotten to have lost Miss Cunégonde and be spit-roasted by Lobeiros."

Cacambo was not one to lose his head.

"Don't despair," he said to the disconsolate Candide. "I know these people's lingo a bit. I'll have a word with them."

"Make sure you point out to them," said Candide, "how frightfully inhuman it is to cook people, and how unchristian it is too."

"So, gentlemen," said Cacambo, "you think you're going to have Jesuit today. That's fine by me. Nothing could be fairer than to treat your enemies this way. The laws of nature do indeed tell us to kill our neighbour, and that is the way people behave throughout the world. If we ourselves do not exercise our right to eat our neighbour, that's because we've got better things to eat. But you haven't the same resources as we have. Certainly it is better to eat one's enemies than to leave the fruits of one's victory for the rooks and the crows. But, gentlemen, you would not want to eat your friends. You think you're about to skewer a Jesuit, while in fact it's your defender, the enemy of your enemies, that you'll be roasting. Me, I was born in these parts. This gentleman here is my master and, far from being a Jesuit, he has just killed a Jesuit and is wearing the spoils of combat. That's how you came to be mistaken. If you want to check the truth of what I say, take his cassock to the nearest frontier post of the kingdom of los Padres. Ask them if my master didn't kill a Jesuit officer. It

9. Tribe in Paraguay.

won't take you long, and you'll always be able to eat us anyway if you discover I've lied to you. But if I've told you the truth, you are too well acquainted with the principles, articles, and procedures of international law not to pardon us."

The Lobeiros found this speech very reasonable. They deputed two eminent persons to proceed post-haste to find out the truth. The two deputies carried out their commission like intelligent men and soon returned bearing good tidings. The Lobeiros untied their two prisoners, did them all kinds of honour, offered them girls, gave them refreshments, and escorted them back to the boundary of their lands merrily chanting: "He isn't a Jesuit, he isn't a Jesuit!"

Candide could not get over the manner of his deliverance.

"What a people!" he was saying. "What men! What manners! If I hadn't had the good fortune to run Miss Cunégonde's brother through with a hefty thrust of my sword, I would have been eaten, and without remission of sentence. But human nature in its pure state is good after all, since these people, instead of eating me, were all sweetness and light the minute they knew I wasn't a Jesuit."

CHAPTER 17

The arrival of Candide and his manservant in Eldorado,[1] and what they saw there

When they reached the Lobeiro frontier, Cacambo said to Candide:

"You see, this half of the world is no better than the other. Take my advice, let's head back to Europe by the shortest route possible."

"But how?" said Candide, "and where to? If I go back to my own country, I'll find the Bulgars and Abars busy cutting everyone's throats. If I return to Portugal, I'll be burnt at the stake. And if we stay here, we may end up on a spit at any moment. But how can I bring myself to leave the part of the world that contains Miss Cunégonde?"

"Let's make for Cayenne,"[2] said Cacambo. "We'll find the French there. They travel all over the place. They'll be able to help us. Perhaps God will have pity on us."

Getting to Cayenne was no simple matter. They knew roughly which direction to take, but what with mountains, rivers, precipices, brigands, and savages, terrible obstacles presented themselves at every turn. Their horses died of exhaustion, they ran out of provisions, and for a whole month they survived on wild fruits, before they eventually found themselves by a small river lined with coconut palms, which kept both them and their hopes alive.

Cacambo, whose advice was always as good as the old woman's had been, said to Candide:

"We've had it, we've walked as far as we can. I see an empty canoe on the bank. Let's fill it with coconuts, get in and let the current take us. A river always leads to some kind of habitation. If we don't find anything nice, at least we'll find something new,"

"All right," said Candide. "Let's trust in Providence."

They drifted downstream for a few leagues between riverbanks now covered in flowers, now bare of vegetation, now flat, now steep. The river grew wider and wider. At length it ran under a vault of fearsome-looking rocks that reached high into the

---

1. A rumored city of gold deep in the interior, sought by Sir Walter Raleigh and others. Voltaire's description draws heavily from Garcilaso de la Vega's *History of the Inca.*
2. The capital of French Guiana.

sky. The two travellers had the pluck to let the water carry them under this vault. The river, which narrowed at this point, swept them along with horrifying speed and made a terrifying din. Twenty-four hours later they saw the light of day once more, but their boat was dashed to pieces in the rapids. They had to drag themselves from rock to rock for a whole league. Eventually they came to a vast open space surrounded by impassable peaks. The land had been cultivated as much to give pleasure as to serve a need. Everywhere whatever was useful was also agreeable. The roads were covered, or rather adorned, with conveyances of the most lustrous form and substance, bearing men and women of singular beauty, and drawn at great speed by large red sheep who could outpace the finest horses in Andalusia, Tetuan, or Mequinez.[3]

"This, on the other hand," said Candide, "is something of an improvement on Westphalia."

He and Cacambo stepped ashore at the first village they came to. A few village children, covered in tattered gold brocade, were playing quoits[4] at the entrance to the settlement. Our two men from the other world stopped to watch them. Their quoits were fairly large round objects, some of them yellow, some red, some green, and they gleamed in an odd way. The travellers were prompted to pick some of them up. They were pieces of gold, emerald, and ruby, and the smallest of them would have been the greatest ornament on the Mogul's throne.

"No doubt," said Candide, "these children playing quoits are the sons of the King of this country."

The village schoolmaster appeared at that moment to call them back to the classroom.

"That," said Candide, "must be the royal family's private tutor."

The little urchins stopped their game at once, leaving their quoits and everything else they had been playing with lying on the ground. Candide picked them up, ran to the tutor, and humbly presented him with them, explaining in sign language that their Royal Highnesses had forgotten their gold and their precious stones. The village schoolmaster threw them on the ground with a smile, stared at Candide for a moment in great surprise, and walked off.

The travellers did not fail to gather up the gold, rubies, and emeralds.

"Where can we be?" exclaimed Candide. "The royal children here must be very well brought up if they're taught to turn their noses up at gold and precious stones."

Cacambo was just as surprised as Candide. At length they drew near to the first house in the village. It was built like a European palace. There was a crowd of people at the door, and an even bigger one inside. Some very pleasant music could be heard, and there was a mouth-watering smell of cooking. Cacambo went up to the door and heard Peruvian being spoken. This was his native tongue; for, as everyone knows, Cacambo was born in the Tucuman in a village where this was the only language they knew.

"I'll interpret for you," he told Candide. "Let's go inside. This is an inn."

At once two waiters and two waitresses, dressed in cloth of gold and wearing ribbons in their hair, showed them to a table and offered them the table d'hôte. The meal consisted of four different soups, each garnished with a couple of parrots, then a boiled condor weighing two hundred pounds, two excellent roast monkeys, one platter of three hundred colibris, and another of six hundred humming-birds, some exquisite casseroles, and delicious pastries. Everything was served on dishes made of a

---

3. These last two are towns in Morocco.   4. A game similar to ring toss.

kind of rock-crystal. The waiters and waitresses poured out a variety of liqueurs made from sugar-cane.

The guests were tradesmen and waggoners for the most part, all of them extremely polite. They asked Cacambo one or two questions with the most scrupulous discretion, and returned full answers to those he put to them.

When the meal was over, Cacambo thought, as Candide did, that he could more than cover the cost of their meal by tossing two of the large pieces of gold he had picked up on to the table. The landlord and his wife burst out laughing and held their sides for a long time. Finally they recovered themselves:

"Gentlemen," said the host, "we can see you're strangers. We're not used to them here. Forgive us if we started laughing when you offered to pay with the stones off our roads. Presumably you don't have any of the local currency, but you don't need any to dine here. All inns set up for the convenience of those engaged in commerce are paid for by the government. The meal wasn't very good here because this is a poor village, but anywhere else you'll get the kind of reception you deserve."

Cacambo interpreted for Candide all that the landlord had said, and Candide was as amazed and bewildered to hear it as Cacambo was to tell it.

"What is this place," said one to the other, "which is unknown to the rest of the world and where the whole nature of things is so different from ours? It's probably the place where all goes well, for there absolutely must be such a place. And whatever Maître Pangloss might have said, I often observed that everything went rather badly in Westphalia."

CHAPTER 18

What they saw in the land of Eldorado

Cacambo gave the landlord to understand how curious he was to know more. The landlord said:

"I know very little about things, and that suits me well enough. But we have an old man living in the village who used to be at court and who is the most knowledgeable man in the kingdom, as well as the most communicative."

Thereupon he took Cacambo to see the old man. Candide was playing second fiddle now, and it was he who accompanied his servant. They entered a house of a very modest sort, for its front door was only of silver and the panelling of its room merely gold, though the workmanship was in such good taste that more opulent panelling could not have outshone it. It has to be said that the antechamber was studded only with rubies and emeralds, but the pattern in which they had all been arranged more than made up for this extreme simplicity.

The old man received the two strangers on a sofa stuffed with colibri feathers and gave orders for them to be served various liquors in diamond goblets. After which he satisfied their curiosity in the following fashion:

"I am one hundred and seventy-two years old, and I learnt from my late father, who was a crown equerry,[5] of the extraordinary upheavals which he witnessed in Peru. This kingdom we are in now is the former homeland of the Incas, who most imprudently left it to go and conquer another part of the world and ended up being wiped out by the Spanish.

---

5. Master of the royal horses.

"The princes of their race who remained behind in their native country were wiser. They ordained, with the consent of the nation, that no inhabitant was ever to leave our little kingdom. And that's how we've managed to remain innocent and happy. The Spanish knew vaguely about the place and called it Eldorado, and an English knight called Raleigh even came fairly near it about a hundred years ago. But since we are surrounded by unclimbable rocks and cliffs, we have always hitherto been safe from the rapacity of European nations with their unaccountable fondness for the pebbles and dirt off our land, and who would kill us to the very last man just to lay their hands on the stuff."

Their conversation was a long one and touched on the form of government there, on local customs, on women, public entertainment, and the arts. Eventually Candide, ever one for metaphysics, asked through Cacambo if there was a religion in this country.

The old man flushed a little.

"But how could you suppose there might not be?" he said. "What do you take us for? Ungrateful wretches?"

Cacambo humbly asked what the religion of Eldorado was. The old man flushed again.

"Can there be more than one religion?" he asked. "As far as I know, we have the same religion as everyone else. We worship God from dusk till dawn."

"Do you worship only one God?" asked Cacambo, who was still acting as interpreter to the doubting Candide.

"Obviously," said the old man. "There aren't two Gods, or three, or four. I must say people from your part of the world do ask some very strange questions."

Candide persisted in having further questions put to this genial old man. He wanted to know how they prayed to God in Eldorado.

"We don't pray to God," said the good and worthy sage. "We have nothing to ask him for. He has given us all we need, and we never cease to thank him."

Candide was curious to see the priests. He had Cacambo ask where they were. The kindly old man smiled.

"My friends," he said, "we are all priests. The King and the head of each family sing hymns of thanksgiving solemnly every morning, to the accompaniment of five or six thousand musicians."

"What! You mean you don't have any monks to teach and dispute and govern and intrigue and burn people to death who don't agree with them?"

"We'd be mad to," said the old man. "We're all of like mind here, and we can't see the point of your monks."

Each of these remarks left Candide in raptures, and he kept thinking to himself:

"This is all rather different from Westphalia and His Lordship's castle. If our friend Pangloss had seen Eldorado, he would no longer have said that the castle of Thunder-ten-tronckh was the best place on earth. It just goes to show: travel's the thing."

After this long conversation the kind old man had six sheep harnessed to a carriage and lent the two travellers twelve of his servants to take them to the court.

"Forgive me," he said to them, "if my advancing years deprive me of the honour of accompanying you. You will not be dissatisfied with the way the King receives you, and I am sure you will be tolerant of our customs if any are not to your liking."

Candide and Cacambo stepped into the carriage. The six sheep went like the wind, and in less than four hours they had arrived at the palace of the King, situated at one end of the capital. The main entrance was two hundred and twenty feet high and one hundred wide. There are no words to describe what it was made of, which in itself gives some idea of just how prodigiously superior it was to the sand and pebbles we call "gold" and "precious stones."

Twenty beautiful guardswomen received Candide and Cacambo upon arrival, escorted them to the baths, and dressed them in robes of humming-bird down, after which the Grand Officers and the Grand Dames of the Crown led them to His Majesty's apartments between two lines of musicians each a thousand strong, in accordance with normal protocol. As they approached the throne-room, Cacambo asked one of the Grand Officers what to do when being presented to His Majesty. Should one fall on one's knees or flat on the ground; should one put one's hands on one's head or over one's backside; should one lick the dust off the floor? In a word, what was the done thing?

"It is customary," said the Grand Officer, "to embrace the King and kiss him on both cheeks."

Candide and Cacambo fell upon His Majesty's neck. He welcomed them with all imaginable graciousness and politely asked them to supper.

Before then they were shown round the city, with its public buildings raised (and praised) to the skies, its market-places decorated with a thousand columns, its fountains of spring-water and rose-water and sugar-cane liquors, all playing ceaselessly in the middle of large squares paved with special stones which gave off an aroma similar to that of clove and cinnamon. Candide asked to see the law courts. He was told there weren't any, and that there were never any cases to hear. He asked if there were any prisons, and he was told there weren't. What surprised him most and gave him the greatest pleasure was the Palace of Science, in which he saw a gallery two thousand feet long all full of instruments for the study of mathematics and physics.

Having seen about a thousandth part of the city in the course of the entire afternoon, they were then brought back to the King. Candide sat down to table next to His Majesty, his servant Cacambo, and several ladies. Never did anyone dine better, and never was anyone wittier at supper than His Majesty. Cacambo interpreted the King's 'bons mots'[6] for Candide, and even in translation they still seemed "bons." Of all the things that surprised Candide, this was not what surprised him the least.

They spent a month in this hospice. Candide never stopped saying to Cacambo: "It's true, my friend, and I'll say it again. The castle where I was born is nothing compared to this place. But still, Miss Cunégonde isn't here, and doubtless you have some sweetheart back in Europe. If we stay on here, we'll simply be the same as everyone else, whereas if we return to Europe with even a mere dozen sheep loaded up with Eldorado pebbles, then we'll be richer than all the kings put together, we'll have no more inquisitors to worry about, and we'll easily be able to get Miss Cunégonde back."

Cacambo liked what he heard. Such is the desire to be always on the move, to be somebody, and to show off about what you've seen on your travels, that the two happy men resolved to be happy no longer and to ask leave of His Majesty to depart.

"You're making a great mistake," the King told them. "I know my country isn't up to much, but when one is reasonably content in a place, one ought to stay there. But I certainly have no right to stop strangers from leaving. That is a piece of tyranny which has no part in our customs or our laws. All men are free. Leave when you wish, though getting out is difficult. It is impossible to return up the rapids which, by a

---

6. Witty remarks.

miracle, you managed to come down: the river runs under vault after vault of rock. The mountains which surround my kingdom are ten thousand feet high and as sheer as a city wall. Each one is about ten leagues thick, and the only way down the other side is one long cliff-face. However, since you are absolutely determined to leave, I shall give orders for the machine intendants to make one which will transport you in comfort. When they've got you to the other side of the mountains, no one will be able to accompany you any further, for my subjects have vowed never to set foot outside these boundaries, and they are too sensible to break their vow. Apart from that you can ask me for whatever you want."

"All we ask of Your Majesty," said Cacambo, "is a few sheep laden with provisions and pebbles and some of the local dirt."

The King laughed.

"I really don't understand this passion you Europeans have for our yellow dirt," said the King, "but take all you want, and much good may it do you."

He immediately ordered his engineers to make a machine to windlass these two extraordinary men out of his kingdom. Three thousand of the best scientists worked on it. It was ready in a fortnight and cost no more than the equivalent of twenty thousand pounds sterling in local currency. Candide and Cacambo were installed on the machine, together with two large red sheep saddled up for them to ride when they had crossed the mountains, twenty pack-sheep laden with provisions, thirty carrying a selection of the best local curios and gifts the country could offer, and fifty loaded up with gold, diamonds, and other precious stones. The King embraced the two wanderers and bid them a fond farewell.

They presented quite a sight as they departed, as did the ingenious way in which they were hoisted, men and sheep together, to the top of the mountains. The scientists took their leave of them once they were safely across, and Candide was left with no other desire or object but to go and present Miss Cunégonde with his sheep.

"We have the wherewithal to pay the Governor of Buenos Aires now," he said, "if a price can be put on Miss Cunégonde, that is. Let's head for Cayenne and take ship there, and then we'll see what kingdom we're going to buy."

CHAPTER 19

What happened to them in Surinam and how Candide met Martin

For our two travellers the first day's journey passed pleasantly enough. They were spurred on by the prospect of themselves as owners of more treasures than Asia, Europe, and Africa can muster between them. Candide, quite carried away, carved the name of Cunégonde on trees as he passed. On the second day, two of their sheep became bogged down in a swamp and were swallowed up with their entire load. A few days afterwards two more sheep died of exhaustion. Seven or eight then starved to death in a desert. Others fell down some mountain-sides a day or two later. In the end, after a hundred days of journeying, they had only two sheep left.

Said Candide to Cacambo:

"My friend, you see how perishable are the riches of this world. The only sure thing is virtue and the happiness of seeing Miss Cunégonde again."

"I'm sure," said Cacambo. "But we do still have two sheep left and more treasure than the King of Spain will ever have, and in the distance I can see a town which, I suspect, is Surinam, where the Dutch are. Our troubles are over and the good times are just beginning."

As they drew near to the town, they came on a Negro lying on the ground half-naked, which in his case meant in half a pair of short denim breeches. The poor man was missing his left leg and his right hand.

"My God!" said Candide in Dutch, "what are you doing lying here, my friend, in this dreadful state?"

"I'm waiting for my master, Mr. Van der Hartbargin,[7] the well-known trader," replied the Negro.

"And is it Mr. Van der Hartbargin," said Candide, "who has treated you like this?"

"Yes, sir," said the Negro, "it is the custom. We are given one pair of short denim breeches twice a year, and that's all we have to wear. When we're working at the sugar-mill and catch our finger in the grinding-wheel, they cut off our hand. When we try to run away, they cut off a leg. I have been in both these situations. This is the price you pay for the sugar you eat in Europe. However, when my mother sold me for ten Patagonian crowns on the coast of Guinea, she said to me: 'My dear child, bless our fetishes,[8] worship them always, they will bring you a happy life. You have the honour of being a slave to our lords and masters the Whites and, by so being, you are making your father's and mother's fortune.' Alas! I don't know if I made their fortune, but they didn't make mine. Dogs, monkeys, parrots, they're all a thousand times less wretched than we are. The Dutch fetishes who converted me tell me every Sunday that we are all the sons of Adam, Whites and Blacks alike. I'm no genealogist, but if these preachers are right, we are all cousins born of first-cousins. Well, you will grant me that you can't treat a relative much worse than this."

"O Pangloss!" cried Candide, "this is one abomination you never thought of. That does it. I shall finally have to renounce your Optimism."

"What's Optimism?" asked Cacambo.

"I'm afraid to say," said Candide, "that it's a mania for insisting that all is well when things are going badly."

And he began to weep as he gazed at his Negro, and he entered Surinam in tears.

The first thing they enquired about was whether there were a ship in the port which could be sent to Buenos Aires. The person they approached happened to be a Spanish skipper, who offered to name them a fair price himself. He arranged to meet them in an inn. Candide and the faithful Cacambo went to wait for him there along with their two sheep.

Candide, whose heart was always on his lips, told the Spaniard all about his adventures and confessed that he wished to carry off Miss Cunégonde.

"I'm not taking you to Buenos Aires, that's for sure," said the skipper. "I'd be hanged, and so would you. The fair Cunégonde is His Excellency's favourite mistress."

This came as a bolt from the blue to Candide. He wept for a long time. Eventually he took Cacambo to one side:

"Look, my dear friend," he said to him, "this is what you must do. We've each got about five or six million in diamonds in our pockets. You're cleverer than I am. Go and fetch Miss Cunégonde from Buenos Aires. If the Governor makes difficulties about it, give him a million. If he won't budge, give him two. You haven't killed any

7. In the original French Voltaire has "Vanderdendur," thought to be a dig at a Dutch bookseller, Van Duren, who had driven a hard bargain with Voltaire over a

manuscript.
8. Objects thought to possess magical protective power.

inquisitors, they won't be suspicious of you. I'll have another ship made ready. I'll go and wait for you in Venice. Theirs is a free country where one has nothing to fear from Bulgars or Abars or Jews or Inquisitors."

Cacambo applauded this wise decision. He was in despair at the thought of parting from so good a master, who had become his close friend. But the pleasure of being of use to him outweighed the pain of leaving him. They tearfully embraced each other. Candide told him to make sure and not forget the kind old woman. Cacambo left the same day. He was a very fine fellow, Cacambo.

Candide stayed some while longer in Surinam, waiting to find another skipper who would be prepared to take him and his two remaining sheep to Italy. He engaged servants and bought everything he needed for a long voyage. At last Mr. Van der Hartbargin, the master of a large ship, came and introduced himself.

"How much will you charge," he asked this man, "to take myself, my servants, my baggage, and these two sheep directly to Venice?"

The master asked ten thousand piastres. Candide did not hesitate.

"Hallo," the careful Van der Hartbargin said to himself, "this stranger parts with ten thousand piastres just like that! He must be pretty rich."

He came back at him a moment later and indicated that he could not sail for less than twenty thousand.

"Very well, then, you shall have them," said Candide.

"Blow me!" said the merchant under his breath. "This man parts with twenty thousand piastres as easily as ten."

He came back at him once more and said that he could not take him to Venice for less than thirty thousand piastres.

"Then thirty thousand it is," replied Candide.

"Hallo, indeed!" the Dutch merchant said to himself again. "Thirty thousand piastres are nothing to this man. Those two sheep must be carrying immense treasures. Better not press things any further. Let's get paid the thirty thousand piastres first, and then we'll see."

Candide sold two little diamonds, the smaller of which was worth more than all the money the shipmaster was asking. He paid him in advance. The two sheep were loaded on board. Candide was following behind in a small boat to join the ship moored out in the roads,[9] when the master calmly set his sails and weighed anchor. The wind favoured him. Candide, helpless and quite flabbergasted, soon lost sight of him.

"Alas!" he lamented, "that's just the kind of dirty trick you'd expect from the old world."

He returned to the shore deep in misery, for, after all, he had lost what would have been enough to make the fortune of twenty monarchs.

He took himself off to the Dutch Resident Magistrate and, as he was a little upset, knocked rather peremptorily on the door. In he went, explained what had happened to him, and shouted rather more loudly than was proper. The magistrate began by fining him ten thousand piastres for the noise he had made. Then he listened to him patiently, promised to look into his case as soon as the merchant returned, and charged a further ten thousand piastres for the cost of the hearing.

This treatment was the last straw for Candide in his despair. To be sure, he had suffered misfortunes a thousand times more grievous, but the sang-froid of the magistrate, and of that shipmaster who had robbed him, stirred his bile and plunged

9. Sheltered water near shore.

him into a black melancholy. The wickedness of men struck him in all its ugliness, and his mind fed on images of gloom. Finally, there being a French vessel all ready to sail for Bordeaux, and as he had no more sheep laden with diamonds to place aboard, he paid for a cabin on the ship at the standard price, and made it known in the town that he would pay passage and board for, and give two thousand piastres to, any respectable person who would make the journey with him, on condition that this person was the most disgusted with his lot and the unhappiest man in the province.

A crowd of applicants came forward such as an entire fleet could not have carried. Wanting to choose among the most likely candidates, Candide selected twenty who seemed to him fairly companionable and who all claimed to deserve preference. He got them together in his inn and gave them supper on condition that each would swear to give a faithful version of his story. He undertook to choose the one who would seem to him most to be pitied and to have the greatest reason for being the most dissatisfied with his lot. To the others he promised a small consideration.

The session lasted until four o'clock in the morning. Candide, as he listened to all their adventures, recalled what the old woman had said to him on their way to Buenos Aires and how she had wagered that not a single person on board would not have suffered very great misfortunes. He thought of Pangloss with every story he was told.

"Pangloss," he said, "would be hard put to it to prove his system. I wish he were here. One thing's certain: if all is going well, it's happening in Eldorado and not in the rest of the world."

In the end he decided in favour of a poor scholar who had spent ten years working for the publishing houses of Amsterdam. He took the view that there was no form of employment in the world with which one could possibly be more disgusted.[1]

This man of learning, who was a perfectly decent fellow moreover, had been robbed by his wife, assaulted by his son, and abandoned by his daughter, who had eloped with a Portuguese. He had just been removed from a small post which had provided him with a living, and the preachers of Surinam were persecuting him because they took him for a Socinian.[2] It must be admitted that the other applicants were at least as unhappy as him, but Candide hoped that the scholar would keep him amused on the voyage. All his rivals considered that Candide was doing them a great injustice, but he pacified them by giving them a hundred piastres each.

CHAPTER 20

What happened to Candide and Martin at sea

So the old scholar, who was called Martin, took ship for Bordeaux with Candide. Both had seen much and suffered much, and even if the ship had had to sail all the way from Surinam to Japan via the Cape of Good Hope, they would still have had matter enough to sustain their discussion of physical and moral evil throughout the entire voyage.

However, Candide had one great advantage over Martin, which was that he was still hoping to see Miss Cunégonde again, while Martin had nothing to hope for. Moreover, he had gold and diamonds, and although he had lost a hundred large sheep laden with the greatest treasure on earth, and although the Dutch master's villainy still

---

1. Voltaire had had difficult dealings with Dutch publishers.   2. A sect resembling present-day Unitarians who denied the Trinity and Christ's divinity.

rankled, nevertheless when he thought about what he had left in his pockets, and when he talked about Cunégonde, especially at the end of a meal, then he would be inclined to favour the philosophical system of Pangloss.

"But you, Mr. Martin," he said to the scholar, "what are your thoughts on all this? How do you see physical and moral evil?"

"Sir," replied Martin, "my priests accused me of being a Socinian, but the fact of the matter is that I am a Manichean."[3]

"You're pulling my leg," said Candide. "There aren't any Manicheans left any more."

"There's me," said Martin. "I can't help it. I just can't see things any other way."

"It's the devil in you," said Candide.

"He's mixed up in the affairs of this world to such an extent," said Martin, "that he may well be in me, just as he's in everything else. But to be frank, when I look about me on this globe, or rather this globule, I begin to think God has abandoned it to some malign being—apart from Eldorado, that is. I've scarcely seen one town that did not wish the ruination of its neighbour, or one family that did not want to see the end of another. Everywhere you look, the weak execrate the strong while they grovel at their feet, and the strong treat them like so many sheep, providing wool and meat to be sold. One million regimented assassins, rushing from one end of Europe to the other, commit murder and brigandage by the rule book in order to earn their daily bread, because there is no more respectable profession; and in the cities, where people appear to live in peace and the arts flourish, men are devoured by more envy, worry, and dissatisfaction than all the scourges of a city under siege. Secret sorrows are more cruel even than public tribulations. In short, I have seen so many of them, and suffered so many, that I am a Manichean."

"Yet there is good," Candide would answer.

"That's as may be," Martin would say, "but I've never met it."

In the middle of this debate, they heard the sound of cannon fire. The noise increased by the moment. Each of them grabbed his telescope. Two ships were to be seen engaging at a distance of about three miles. The wind brought both of these ships so close to the French vessel that they had the pleasure of seeing the engagement in perfect comfort. Eventually one ship let fly a broadside at the other that was so low and so accurate that it sank it. Candide and Martin could distinctly see a hundred men on the deck of the ship which was going down. They were all raising their hands heavenwards and letting out the most appalling screams. In an instant everything disappeared beneath the waves.

"Well, there you are," said Martin. "That's how men treat each other."

"It is true," said Candide. "The devil has had a hand in this business."

So saying, he noticed something bright red swimming near their ship. The ship's launch was lowered to go and see what it could be. It was one of his sheep. There was more joy in Candide at finding this one sheep than there had been sorrow at losing an hundredfold all laden with large Eldorado diamonds.

The French captain soon observed that the captain of the sinker was Spanish, while the captain of the sunk was a Dutch pirate. It was the very man who had robbed Candide. The immense riches with which this villain had absconded had gone down with him, and all that had been saved was one sheep.

---

3. Ancient religious philosophy that posits two equal forces of good and evil governing the world; one of the earliest Christian heresies.

"You see," Candide said to Martin, "crime is sometimes punished. That scoundrel of a Dutch skipper got the fate he deserved."

"Yes," said Martin, "but did the passengers on his ship have to perish also? God punished the rogue: the devil drowned the rest."

Meanwhile the French and Spanish ships resumed their voyages, and Candide and Martin their conversations. They argued for a solid fortnight, and at the end of the fortnight they were as far forward as the day they began. But, well, they talked, and exchanged ideas, and consoled each other. Candide would stroke his sheep and say:

"I have found you, so I may well be able to find Cunégonde."

CHAPTER 21

Candide and Martin approach the French coast and reason together

At last they came in sight of the French coast.

"Have you ever been to France, Mr. Martin?" said Candide.

"Yes," said Martin, "I've travelled through several of its provinces. There are some where half the inhabitants are mad, one or two where they're too clever by half, some where they're generally quite gentle and rather stupid, and others where they try to be witty. And in all of them the principal occupation is love. Next comes slander and gossip, and third comes talking nonsense."

"But, Mr. Martin, have you been to Paris?"

"Yes, I've been to Paris. There they have all of these types. It's chaos there, a throng in which everyone is searching for pleasure and where practically no one finds it, at least not as far as I could see. I haven't spent much time there. When I arrived, I was robbed of everything I had by pickpockets at the Saint-Germain fair. I myself was taken for a thief and spent a week in prison, after which I did some proof-reading to earn enough to be able to return to Holland on foot. I got to know the pen-pushing brigade, and the political intriguers, and the religious convulsions crowd.[4] They say there are some very well-mannered people in that city. I dare say there are."

"Personally I have no desire to see France," said Candide. "As I'm sure you can imagine, when one's spent a month in Eldorado, there's nothing in the world one much wants to see other than Miss Cunégonde. I'm on my way to wait for her in Venice. We will be going through France to get to Italy. Why don't you come with me?"

"Delighted to," said Martin. "They say Venice is only fit to live in if you're a Venetian nobleman, but that foreigners are well looked after none the less, providing they have a lot of money. I haven't, you have; I'll follow you anywhere."

"Incidentally," said Candide, "do you believe the Earth was originally a sea, as they say it was in that big book the captain has?"[5]

"I don't believe anything of the sort," said Martin, "no more than I believe any of the other rubbish they've been coming out with recently."

"But for what purpose was this world created then?" said Candide.

"To drive us mad," replied Martin.

"Don't you find it absolutely amazing," Candide went on, "the way the two girls I told you about, the ones who lived in the land of the Lobeiros, loved those two monkeys?"

---

4. Jansenist extremists, who were known for convulsions and trances, through which they supposedly performed miracles.

5. Probably the Bible, in which God creates the sea before dry land (Genesis 1).

"Not at all," said Martin. "I don't see what's odd about that particular passion. I've seen so many extraordinary things that nothing's extraordinary any more."

"Do you think," said Candide, "that men have always massacred each other the way they do now? that they've always been liars, cheats, traitors, ingrates, brigands? that they've always been feeble, fickle, envious, gluttonous, drunken, avaricious, ambitious, bloodthirsty, slanderous, debauched, fanatical, hypocritical, and stupid?"

"Do you think," said Martin, "that hawks have always eaten pigeons when they find them?"

"Yes, no doubt," said Candide.

"Well, then," said Martin, "if hawks have always had the same character, why do you expect men to have changed theirs?"

"Oh!" said Candide, "there's a big difference, because free will . . ." Arguing thus the while, they arrived in Bordeaux.

CHAPTER 22

What happened to Candide and Martin in France

Candide broke his journey in Bordeaux just long enough to sell a few Eldorado pebbles and to procure a good post-chaise with two seats, for he could no longer be without Martin, his philosopher. He was only very sorry to be parted from his sheep, which he left with the Academy of Science at Bordeaux. They set as the subject of that year's prize the question why the wool of this sheep was red, and the prize was awarded to a scientist from the North[6] who proved by A plus B minus C divided by Z that the sheep had necessarily to be red, and to die of sheep-pox.

Meanwhile all the travellers Candide met in the inns along the way told him: "We're off to Paris." In the end this universal eagerness made him want to see that capital city. It would not take him much out of his way on his journey to Venice.

He entered by the Faubourg Saint-Marceau and thought he was in the ugliest village in Westphalia.

Scarce had Candide put up at his inn than he was laid low by a minor indisposition brought on by his exertions. As he had an enormous diamond on his finger, and as an extremely heavy strong box had been noticed among his luggage, he soon had by him two doctors whom he had not sent for, a number of bosom companions who never left his side, and two ladies of good works who were heating up his broth.

Martin said:

"I remember being ill on my first trip to Paris too. I was very poor, so I had no friends or do-gooders or doctors, and I got better."

Meanwhile, by dint of many potions and bloodlettings, Candide's illness became serious. A local priest came and kindly asked him for a confessional note payable to bearer in the other world.[7] Candide would have none of it. The ladies of good works assured him that it was the new fashion. Candide replied that he was not a one for fashion. Martin was for throwing the priest out of the window. The cleric swore that Candide would not be granted burial. Martin swore that he would bury the cleric if he continued to bother them. The quarrel grew more heated. Martin took him by the

---

6. A reference to Maupertuis, the president of Frederick the Great's Berlin Academy of Sciences, who was often ridiculed by Voltaire.

7. In order to receive the last sacraments, Parisians were required to present a note from their confessor indicating they had subscribed to the Papal Bull *Unigenitus*, which condemned the Jansenist heresy.

shoulders and unceremoniously ejected him. This caused a great scandal, which was the subject of an official enquiry.

Candide recovered, and during his convalescence he had some very fine company to supper with him. There was gambling for high stakes. Candide was most surprised never to get a single ace, and Martin was not surprised.

Among those who did him the honours of the city was a little abbé[8] from Périgord, one of those busy little, pushy, fawning, frightfully accommodating types, always on the make, always ready to please, who lie in wait for strangers passing through and give them all the local gossip and scandal and offer them entertainments at all sorts of prices. This one took Candide and Martin to the theatre first. A new tragedy was on. Candide found himself sitting next to some of the intellectual smart set. This did not prevent him from crying at scenes that were played to perfection.

One of these arbiters of taste sitting near him said to him during an interval:

"You are quite wrong to cry. That actress is very bad. The actor playing opposite her is still worse. The play is even worse than the actors. The author doesn't know a word of Arabic, and yet the play is set in Arabia.[9] And what's more, the man doesn't believe in innate ideas. Tomorrow I can bring you twenty pamphlets criticizing him."

"Sir, how many plays do you have in France?" Candide asked the abbé, who replied:

"Five or six thousand."

"That's a lot," said Candide. "How many of them are any good?"

"Fifteen or sixteen," was the answer.

"That's a lot," said Martin.

Candide was much taken with an actress who was playing Queen Elizabeth in a rather dull tragedy which is sometimes put on.

"I do like that actress," he said to Martin. "She looks a bit like Miss Cunégonde. I should be rather pleased to call on her."

The abbé from Périgord offered to effect an introduction. Candide, brought up in Germany, asked what the form was and how queens of England were treated in France.

"We must distinguish," said the abbé. "In the provinces you take them to an inn. In Paris you respect them when they're beautiful, and you throw them on to the rubbish-heap when they're dead."[1]

"Queens on the rubbish-heap!" said Candide.

"Yes, really," said Martin. "The abbé is right. I was in Paris when Mlle Monime passed, as they say, from this life to the next. She was refused what people here call 'the honours of the grave,' that is to say of rotting in a filthy cemetery with all the beggars of the neighbourhood. Unlike the rest of her troupe she was buried alone at the corner of the rue de Bourgogne, which must have pained her exceedingly, for she thought very nobly."

"That's not a very nice way to treat people," said Candide.

"What can you expect?" said Martin. "That's the way they are round here. Take any contradiction or inconsistency you can think of, and you will find it in the government, the courts, the churches, or the theatres of this strange nation."

"Is it true that people in Paris are always laughing?" enquired Candide.

---

8. French clergyman.
9. Voltaire himself had written a play, *Mahomet*, set in Arabia.

1. Actors and actresses were denied Christian burial in France at this time; Voltaire had assisted in the secret burial of an actress in 1730.

"Yes," said the abbé, "but through gritted teeth. For they complain about every-thing with great gales of laughter, and they laugh even when doing the most de-testable things."

"Who," asked Candide, "was the fat pig who was telling me so many bad things about that play I cried such a lot at, and about those actors I liked so much?"

"He is evil incarnate," replied the abbé. "He earns his living by decrying all new plays and books. He hates the up-and-coming writer, just as eunuchs hate the up-and-coming lover. He's one of those vipers of literature that feeds off filth and venom. He's a hack."

"What do you mean by 'hack'?" said Candide.

"I mean," said the abbé, "someone who churns out articles by the dozen, a Fréron."[2]

Such was the discussion between Candide, Martin, and the man from Périgord as they stood on the staircase, watching people pass by on their way out after the play.

"Although I can't wait to see Miss Cunégonde again," said Candide, "neverthe-less I would like to have supper with Mlle Clairon,[3] for she did seem quite admirable to me."

The abbé was not the right man for an approach to Mlle Clairon, who moved only in the best circles.

"She has a prior engagement this evening," he said, "but if you will allow me the honour of taking you to a lady of quality, there you will get to meet Paris society as if you'd already been living here for years."

Candide, who was curious by nature, allowed himself to be taken to the lady, at the bottom end of the Faubourg Saint-Honoré.[4] There they were busy playing faro.[5] Twelve sad punters each held a small hand of cards, the dog-eared register of their misfortunes. A profound silence reigned; pallor was upon the punters' brows, anxiety upon that of the banker; and the lady of the house, seated beside this implacable banker, noted with the eyes of a lynx all the doubling up and any illegal antes when-ever each player turned down the corner of his card. She would make them turn the corners back with firm but polite insistence, and never lost her temper for fear of los-ing her clients. This lady called herself the Marchioness of Dubelauchwitz. Her daughter, aged fifteen, was one of the punters and would indicate with a wink any cheating on the part of these poor people endeavouring to repair the cruel blows of fate. The abbé from Périgord, Candide, and Martin walked in. No one got up, or greeted them, or looked at them; they were all deeply engrossed in their cards.

"The Baroness of Thunder-ten-tronckh was more civil," said Candide.

Meanwhile the abbé had a word in the ear of the Marchioness, who half rose and honoured Candide with a gracious smile and Martin with a thoroughly grand tilt of the head. She had Candide given a seat and dealt a hand: he lost fifty thousand francs in two rounds. Afterwards they supped merrily, and everyone was surprised that Candide was not more upset about his losses. The lackeys said to each other in their own lackey language:

"He must be one of your English lords."

The supper was like most suppers in Paris. First, silence; then a cacaphonous welter of words which no one can make out; and then jokes, which mostly fall flat,

2. Name of one of Voltaire's harshest critics, who had panned his play *Tancrède*.
3. An actress who often performed in Voltaire's plays.

4. A wealthy section of Paris.
5. Popular card game in which "punters" bet against the bank.

false rumours, false arguments, a smattering of politics, and a quantity of slander. They even talked about the latest books.

"Have you read," said the abbé from Périgord, "that nonsense by Master Gauchat,[6] doctor of theology?"

"Yes," replied one of the party, "but I couldn't finish it. There's enough irrelevant rubbish in print as it is, but the whole lot put together doesn't come anywhere near the irrelevance of Master Gauchat, doctor of theology. I'm so sick of this great flood of detestable books that I've taken to punting at faro."

"And the *Miscellany* of Archdeacon T . . .?[7] What do you think of that?" said the abbé.

"Oh," said the Marchioness of Dubelauchwitz, "that crashing bore! The way he tells you with great interest what everybody knows already! The ponderous discussion of points that aren't even worth a passing reference! The witless way he borrows other people's wit! How he ruins what he filches! How he disgusts me! But he won't disgust me any further. One or two pages of the archdeacon are quite enough."

At table there was a man of taste and learning, who agreed with what the Marchioness was saying. Conversation then moved on to tragedies. The lady asked why it was that some tragedies were staged from time to time but were totally unreadable. The man of taste explained very well how a play could be of some interest but of almost no merit. He showed in a few words how it was not enough to contrive one or two of the stock situations which can be found in any novel, and which always captivate the audience, but that one had to be original without being far-fetched; often sublime and always natural; to know the human heart and to make it speak; to be a great poet without any of the characters in the play appearing to be poets themselves; to have perfect command of one's own language, and to use it with fluent euphony, without forcing it, and without ever sacrificing the sense to the rhyme.

"Whoever fails to follow every one of these rules," he added, "may produce one or two tragedies that are applauded in the theatre, but he will never be counted a good writer. There are very few good tragedies. Some are simply idylls in a dialogue that happens to be well-written and well-rhymed; some have political messages, and send you to sleep, while others are so overdone they fail to move; and some are the fantasies of fanatics, written in a barbarous style with broken-off sentences and long speeches to the gods—because they don't know how to communicate with human beings—and full of false maxims and pompous platitudes."

Candide listened attentively to these remarks and formed a high opinion of the speaker. As the Marchioness had taken good care to place Candide next to her, he took the liberty of asking, by means of a whisper in her ear, who this man was who spoke so well.

"He's a man of learning," said the lady, "who doesn't gamble and whom the abbé brings to supper sometimes. He knows all about tragedies and books, and he has himself written a tragedy, which was whistled off the stage, and a book, of which but one copy has ever been seen outside a bookshop, and that was the one he presented to me with a dedication."

"A great man!" said Candide. "He's another Pangloss."

Then, turning to him, he said:

6. Author of a series of refutations of Voltaire's *Encyclopédie*.

7. Trublet, another critic of Voltaire.

"Sir, doubtless you think that everything is for the best in the physical and moral worlds, and that things could not be other than as they are?"

"I, sir?" replied the man of learning. "I don't think anything of the sort. I find that everything in our world is amiss, that nobody knows his place or his responsibility, or what he's doing or what he should do, and that, except for supper parties, which are quite jolly and where people seem to get on reasonably well, the rest of the time is spent in pointless quarrelling: Jansenists with Molinists,[8] parliamentarians with churchmen, men of letters with men of letters, courtiers with courtiers, financiers with the general public, wives with husbands, relatives with relatives. It's one battle after another."

Candide answered him:

"I've seen worse ones. But a wise man, who has since had the misfortune to be hanged, told me that that's all fine. Those are just the shadows in a beautiful painting."

"Your hanged man was having people on," said Martin. "What you call shadows are horrible stains."

"It's human beings who make the stains," said Candide. "They can't help it."

"So it's not their fault," said Martin.

The majority of the punters, who did not understand a word of all this, were drinking. Martin had a discussion with the man of learning; and Candide recounted some of his adventures to the lady of the house.

After supper the Marchioness took Candide to her room and bid him be seated on a couch.

"Well, then," she said to him, "so you're still madly in love with Miss Cunégonde de Thunder-ten-tronckh?"

"Yes, madame."

The Marchioness returned a tender smile:

"You answer like the young man from Westphalia you are. A Frenchman would have said to me: 'It is true that I did once love Miss Cunégonde, but on seeing you, madame, I fear that I love her no longer.'"

"Oh, dear," said Candide. "Madame, I shall answer as you please."

"Your passion for her began," said the Marchioness, "when you picked up her handkerchief. I want you to pick up my garter."

"With all my heart," said Candide, and he picked it up.

"But I want you to put it back for me," said the lady, and Candide put it back for her.

"You see," she said, "you are a foreigner. Sometimes I make my Parisian lovers wait a whole fortnight, but here I am giving myself to you on the very first night, because one must do the honours of one's country to a young man from Westphalia."

The fair lady, having noticed two enormous diamonds on the hands of her young foreigner, enthused about them with such sincerity that from Candide's fingers they passed on to the fingers of the Marchioness.

Candide, as he returned home with his abbé from Périgord, felt some remorse at having been unfaithful to Miss Cunégonde. The abbé commiserated with him; he was only slightly responsible for the fifty thousand francs Candide had lost at cards and the value of the two brilliants which had been half given and half extorted. His object was to profit as much as he possibly could from the advantages that knowing Candide

8. Followers of Luis Molina (1535–1600), a Spanish Jesuit who promoted the doctrine of free will. Jansenists, on the other hand, believed in predestination.

might bring him. He asked him all about Cunégonde, and Candide told him that he would certainly beg that fair lady's pardon for his infidelity when he saw her in Venice.

The man from Périgord became even more courteous and attentive and took a touching interest in everything that Candide said, or did, or wanted to do.

"So you have arranged to meet in Venice then, sir?" he said.

"Yes, Monsieur l'abbé," said Candide. "I really must go and find Miss Cunégonde."

Then, drawn on by the pleasure of talking about the one he loved, he recounted, as was his wont, a part of his adventures with this illustrious Westphalian lady.

"I expect Miss Cunégonde is witty and clever," said the abbé, "and that she writes charming letters?"

"I've never had any from her," said Candide. "The thing is, you see, having been kicked out of the castle for loving her, I couldn't write to her, and then I learnt soon afterwards that she was dead, and then I found her again, and then I lost her, and then I sent an express messenger two thousand five hundred leagues to her, and I am still awaiting a reply."

The abbé listened attentively and seemed somewhat lost in thought. Soon he took his leave of the two strangers, after embracing them warmly. The next day, upon waking, Candide received the following letter:

> My very dear and beloved sir, I have been lying ill in this city for the past week. I discover that you are here too. I would fly to your arms if I could move. I heard in Bordeaux that you had passed through. I left the faithful Cacambo there and the old woman, and they are soon to follow on after me. The Governor of Buenos Aires took everything, but I still have your heart. Come to me. Your presence will restore me to life, or make me die of pleasure.

This charming, this unexpected letter sent Candide into transports of inexpressible joy, while the illness of his dear Cunégonde weighed him down with grief. Torn between these two emotions, he grabbed his gold and diamonds and had someone take him and Martin to the hotel where Miss Cunégonde was staying. He entered the room trembling with emotion, his heart aflutter, his voice choked. He made to open the curtains round the bed and was about to send for a lamp.

"Do no such thing," said the maid, "the light will kill her." And at once she shut the curtains:

"My dear Cunégonde," wept Candide, "How are you? If you cannot look at me, at least speak to me."

"She cannot speak," said the maid. The lady then drew from the bedclothes a chubby little hand, which Candide bathed with his tears for a long time and subsequently filled with diamonds, leaving a pouch full of gold on the chair.

In the midst of his transports an officer of the watch arrived, followed by the abbé from Périgord and a squad of men.

"Are these the two suspicious foreigners then?" he said.

He had them arrested on the spot and ordered his lads to haul them off to prison.

"This is not how they treat travellers in Eldorado," said Candide.

"I feel more Manichean than ever," said Martin.

"But, sir, where are you taking us?" said Candide.

"To the deepest of dark dungeons," said the officer.

Martin, having recovered his sang-froid, judged that the lady claiming to be Cunégonde was a fraud, the abbé from Périgord a scoundrel who had taken advantage of Candide's innocence at the earliest opportunity, and the officer another scoundrel, whom it would be easy to be rid of.

Rather than be exposed to the process of law, Candide, enlightened by Martin's counsel and, more especially, ever impatient to see the real Miss Cunégonde again, offered the officer three little diamonds worth about three thousand pistoles each.

"Ah, sir," the man with the ivory baton said to him, "had you committed every crime in the book, you'd still be the most honest man alive. Three diamonds! And each worth three thousand pistoles! Sir, I'd sooner die for you than take you to a dungeon. There are orders to arrest all foreigners, but leave it to me. I have a brother in Normandy, in Dieppe, I'll take you there. And if you have a diamond or two to give him, he'll take care of you as if it were myself he was looking after."

"And why are they arresting all foreigners?" says Candide.

The abbé from Périgord intervened:

"It's because a wretch from Atrabatia listened to some silly talk, which was all it took to make him commit parricide—not like the one in May 1610 but like the one in December 1594, and like several others committed in other months and other years by other wretches who had listened to similar silly talk."[9]

The officer then explained what this was all about.

"Ah, the monsters!" exclaimed Candide. "What! Such horrors, and from a people that loves singing and dancing! Can't I leave this very minute? Let me out of this country where monkeys provoke tigers. I have seen bears in my own country; I have seen men only in Eldorado. In the name of God, officer, take me to Venice, where I am to wait for Miss Cunégonde."

"Lower Normandy is the best I can do," said the right arm of the law.

Thereupon he had his irons removed, said he must have made a mistake, dismissed his men, and took Candide and Martin to Dieppe and left them in the hands of his brother. There was a small Dutch ship out in the roads. The Norman, who with the help of three more diamonds had now become the most obliging of men, put Candide and his servants aboard the ship, which was about to set sail for Portsmouth in England. It was not the way to Venice, but Candide felt as though he was being delivered from hell, and he fully intended to rejoin the route to Venice at the first opportunity.

CHAPTER 23

Candide and Martin proceed to the shores of England; what they see there

"Ah, Pangloss! Pangloss! Ah, Martin! Martin! Ah, my dear Cunégonde! What sort of a world is this?" Candide was asking on board the Dutch ship.

"A rather mad and rather awful one," answered Martin.

"You know England. Are they as mad there as they are in France?"

"It's a different kind of madness," said Martin. "As you know, the two countries are at war over a few acres of snow across in Canada, and they're spending more on this war than the whole of Canada is worth.[1] To tell you exactly if there are more people who should be locked up in one country than in the other is something my feeble

9. Atrabatia is the Latin name for the French province Artois, the birthplace of Damiens, who attempted to assassinate Louis XV in 1757. Châtel attempted to assassinate Henry IV in December 1594, and in May 1610 Ravaillac assassinated Henry IV.

1. This colonial struggle between Britain and France culminated in the French and Indian War. It was resolved in 1763 by the Treaty of Paris, which transferred Canada from French to British control.

lights do not permit. All I know is that, by and large, the people we are going to see are extremely glum."[2]

Thus conversing, they landed at Portsmouth. A multitude of people covered the shore, all gazing intently at a rather stout man who was kneeling blindfold on the deck of one of the naval ships. Four soldiers, posted opposite this man, each fired three shots into his skull, as calmly as you please, and the assembled multitude then dispersed, thoroughly satisfied.

"What is all this?" said Candide. "And what demon is it that holds such universal sway?"

He asked who this stout man was who had just been ceremonially killed.

"He's an admiral," came the answer.[3]

"And why kill this admiral?"

"Because he didn't kill enough people," Candide was told. "He gave battle to a French admiral, and it has been found that he wasn't close enough."

"But," said Candide, "the French admiral was just as far away from the English admiral as he was from him!"

"Unquestionably," came the reply. "But in this country it is considered a good thing to kill an admiral from time to time so as to encourage the others."

Candide was so dumbfounded and so shocked by what he was seeing and hearing that he refused even to set foot ashore, and he negotiated with the Dutch master of the ship (it was just too bad if he fleeced him like the one in Surinam) to take him to Venice as soon as possible.

The master was ready in two days. They sailed down the French coast. They passed within sight of Lisbon, and Candide shuddered. They entered the straits and the Mediterranean. At last they put in at Venice.

"God be praised!" said Candide, embracing Martin. "This is where I shall see fair Cunégonde again. I trust Cacambo as I would myself. All is well, all is going well, all is going as well as it possibly can."

CHAPTER 24

Of Paquette and Brother Giroflée

As soon as he reached Venice, he instigated a search for Cacambo in every inn and coffee house, and in all the brothels. He was nowhere to be found. Each day he had enquiries made of every new ship or boat that came in. No sign of Cacambo.

"I don't know," he was saying to Martin. "I have had time to cross from Surinam to Bordeaux, to go from Bordeaux to Paris, from Paris to Dieppe, from Dieppe to Portsmouth, to sail the length of Portugal and Spain, to cross the entire Mediterranean, to spend several months in Venice, and fair Cunégonde has still not got here! All I've encountered instead is some hussy and an abbé from Périgord. Cunégonde is probably dead, so I may as well die too. Ah! it would have been better to remain in the paradise of Eldorado than come back to this accursed Europe. How right you are, my dear Martin! All is but illusion and calamity."

2. The British were thought to be characteristically melancholic.
3. Admiral Byng. who had been in charge of British naval forces during their defeat by the French in a battle off Minorca, was court-martialed and tried for cowardice. He was executed by firing squad on his own quarterdeck in 1757; Voltaire had unsuccessfully attempted to intercede on Byng's behalf.

He sank into a dark melancholy and took no part in the opera *alla moda* or in any of the other carnival entertainments. Not a single lady caused him a moment's temptation.

Martin said to him:

"You really are rather simple to imagine that a half-caste[4] manservant with five or six millions in his pocket will go and look for your lady-love on the other side of the world and bring her to you in Venice. He'll take her for himself if he finds her. If he doesn't find her, he'll take somebody else. My advice to you is to forget your manservant Cacambo and your beloved Cunégonde."

Martin was not consoling. Candide's melancholy deepened, and Martin kept on proving to him that there was little virtue and little happiness in this world—except perhaps in Eldorado, where no one could ever go.

While they disputed this important subject and waited for Cunégonde, Candide noticed a young Theatine[5] monk in Saint Mark's Square, who was walking with a girl on his arm. The Theatine had a fresh, chubby, robust appearance. His eyes shone, and there was an air of assurance about him. His expression was haughty, his gait proud. The girl, who was very pretty, was singing. She gazed lovingly at her Theatine, and tweaked his pudgy cheeks from time to time.

"You'll grant me at least," Candide said to Martin, "that those two are happy. So far, throughout the inhabited world, I have encountered only unfortunates—except in Eldorado, that is. But as for that girl and her Theatine, I bet they are very happy creatures."

"I bet they're not," said Martin.

"All we have to do is to invite them to dinner," said Candide, "and you'll see if I'm wrong."

Thereupon he went up to them, presented his compliments, and invited them back to his hostelry for some macaroni, Lombardy partridge, and caviar, washed down with Montepulciano, lachryma Christi,[6] and some of the wines of Cyprus and Samos. The young lady blushed, the Theatine accepted the invitation, and the girl followed him, glancing at Candide with eyes wide in surprise and embarrassment and clouded with tears.

Scarcely had she entered Candide's room than she said to him:

"Well? Doesn't Master Candide recognize Paquette any more?"

At these words Candide, who had not looked at her closely until then (because he had thoughts only for Cunégonde), said to her:

"Oh dear, my poor girl, so you are the one who got Dr. Pangloss into the fine state I saw him in?"

"Alas, sir, I am indeed," said Paquette. "I see you know all about it. I heard about the dreadful misfortunes that befell Her Ladyship's household and the fair Miss Cunégonde. I swear to you, my own fate has hardly been less wretched. I was utterly innocent when last you saw me. A Franciscan monk who was my confessor had no difficulty in seducing me. The consequences were terrible. I was obliged to leave the castle not long after His Lordship kicked you up the backside and sent you packing. If a famous doctor had not taken pity on me, I'd have had it. For a time I became the doctor's mistress, as a way of showing my gratitude. His wife, who was madly jealous, beat me every day without mercy. She was a fury. This doctor was the ugliest of men, and I the unhappiest of creatures to be continually beaten for a man I did not love. As you know, sir, it's very dangerous for a shrewish woman to have a doctor for a husband. One day, sick and tired of the way his wife was behaving, he treated her for a slight cold by giving her some medicine, which proved so effective that within two hours she was dead, having had some horrible convulsions. The mistress's family brought an action against the master. He upped and fled, and I was put in prison. My innocence would not have saved me had I not been reasonably pretty. The judge let me go on condition that he would succeed the doctor. I was soon supplanted by a rival, dismissed without a penny, and obliged to continue in this unspeakable profession which seems so harmless to you men, and which for us is nothing but a vale of tears. I chose Venice to practise my profession in. Oh, sir, if you could imagine what it's like having to caress just anybody, an old merchant, a lawyer, a monk, a gondolier, an abbé; to be exposed to all manner of insult and degradation; to be reduced often to having to borrow a skirt, only then to go and have it lifted up by some disgusting man or other; to be robbed by one of what one's earned with another; to be held to ransom by officers of the law, and to have nothing to look forward to but a gruesome old age, the workhouse, and the rubbish-heap; then you would agree that I am one of the unhappiest and most unfortunate creatures alive."

This was how, in a private room in the hostelry, Paquette opened her heart to good Candide in the presence of Martin, who said to Candide:

"You see, I've already won half my bet."

Brother Giroflée had remained in the dining-room, and was having a drink as he waited for dinner.

"But," Candide said to Paquette, "you were looking so gay, so happy, when I ran into you. You were singing, you were fondling the Theatine quite naturally and willingly. You seemed to me every bit as happy as you say you are unhappy."

"Ah, sir," replied Paquette, "that's another of the awful things about our profession. Yesterday I was robbed and beaten by an officer, and today I have to appear to be in a good mood just to please a monk."

That was enough for Candide; he admitted that Martin was right. They sat down to dinner with Paquette and the Theatine. The meal was quite good-humoured, and at the end they were all talking to each other with some degree of freedom.

"Father," Candide said to the monk, "you seem to me to be enjoying the kind of life everyone must envy. You are the picture of health, you have a happy face, you have a very pretty girl to keep you amused, and you seem perfectly content with your monastic condition."

"By my faith, sir," said Brother Giroflée, "I wish all Theatines were at the bottom of the sea. I've been tempted a hundred times to set fire to the monastery and to go and turn Turk.[7] My parents forced me to don this detestable habit at the age of fifteen so that I would leave a bigger fortune for my damned elder brother, may God confound him! The monastery is rife with jealousy, and backbiting, and bad feeling. It's true that I have preached a few miserable sermons that have brought me in some money, half of which the Prior steals—the rest I use for keeping girls. But when I get back to the monastery in the evening, I'm ready to beat my head in on the dormitory walls. And all the brothers feel the same way."

---

7. A common expression signifying the ultimate infidelity or treachery.

Martin turned to Candide with his usual sang-froid:

"Well?" he said. "Have I not won the whole bet?"

Candide gave Paquette two thousand piastres, and Brother Giroflée a thousand.

"I guarantee you," he said, "that with this money they'll be happy."

"I shouldn't think so for a minute," said Martin. "With these piastres you may make them even more unhappy still."

"Whatever shall be, shall be," said Candide. "But one thing consoles me. I see that people one never thought to see again often do turn up. It may well turn out that, having run into my red sheep and Paquette, I will also run into Cunégonde."

"I wish," said Martin, "that she may one day make you happy. But I very much doubt she will."

"You are a bit hard," said Candide.

"That's because I've lived," said Martin.

"But look at those gondoliers," said Candide. "They're always singing, aren't they?"

"You don't see them at home with their wives and screaming children," said Martin. "The doge[8] has his problems, the gondoliers have theirs. It is true that, all things considered, the life of a gondolier is preferable to that of a doge, but I think there's so little in it that it's not worth arguing about."

"I've heard people talk," said Candide, "about a Senator Pococurante[9] who lives in that beautiful palace on the Brenta, and who's very hospitable to visiting foreigners. They say he's a man who's never had any troubles."

"I'd like to meet such a rare breed," said Martin.

Candide at once sent someone to ask the noble Signor Pococurante's permission to call on him the following day.

CHAPTER 25

The visit to Signor Pococurante, a Venetian nobleman

Candide and Martin proceeded down the Brenta by gondola and came to the palace of the noble Pococurante. The gardens were well laid out and embellished with beautiful marble statues, while the palace itself was a fine piece of architecture. The master of the house, a man of sixty, and very rich, received the two curious visitors most politely but with very little fuss, which disconcerted Candide and did not displease Martin.

First, two pretty and neatly dressed girls poured out some chocolate, managing to give it a good frothy top. Candide could not help but compliment them on their beauty, their kindness, and their skill.

"They're not bad creatures," said Senator Pococurante. "I have them sleep with me sometimes, because I'm rather tired of the society ladies here with all their flirting, and their jealousy, and their quarrelling, and their moods, and their petty-mindedness, and their arrogance, and their silliness, not to mention the sonnets you have to compose, or have composed, for them. But, well, in the end I'm beginning to find these two girls exceedingly boring too."

Candide, walking in a long gallery after lunch, was surprised at the beauty of the paintings. He asked which master had painted the first two.

"They're by Raphael,"[1] said the Senator. "I bought them out of vanity some years ago for a considerable amount of money. They are said to be the finest in Italy, but I

---

8. Chief magistrate of Venice.
9. "Caring little."

1. Famous Renaissance painter whose works were known for their clarity of form and subtle gravity.

don't like them at all. The colouring is very dark, the faces aren't sufficiently rounded and don't stand out enough, and the draperies don't bear the slightest resemblance to any real cloth. Basically, whatever anyone may say, I don't consider they're a true imitation of nature. You'll only get me to like a picture when I think I'm looking at nature itself—and there aren't any like that. I have lots of paintings, but I don't look at them any more."

As they waited for dinner, Pococurante gave orders for a concerto to be played. Candide found the music delightful.

"This sort of noise helps pass the odd half-hour," said Pococurante, "but if it goes on any longer, everybody finds it tedious, though no one dares say so. Nowadays music is simply nothing more than the art of playing difficult pieces, and that which is merely difficult gives no pleasure in the end.

"Perhaps I'd prefer opera, if they hadn't found a way of turning it into a monstrous hybrid which I find quite repugnant. Let anyone who wishes go and see bad tragedies set to music, with all those scenes that have been put together simply as pretexts—and pretty poor ones at that—for two or three ridiculous songs which allow an actress to show off her vocal cords. Let anyone that wants to—and that can—go and swoon away with ecstasy at the sight of a *castrato* humming the roles of Caesar and Cato[2] and strutting about the stage in that ungainly fashion. For my part I have long since given up going to these paltry affairs, even though nowadays they are the glory of Italy and put its ruling princes to so much expense."

Candide demurred somewhat, though with tact. Martin was entirely of the Senator's opinion.

They sat down to eat, and after an excellent dinner, they went into the library. Candide, on seeing a magnificently bound edition of Homer, complimented his most illustrious host on his good taste.

"This book," he said, "used to delight the great Pangloss, the finest philosopher in Germany."

"It doesn't delight me," said Pococurante coolly. "They did once have me believe that I took pleasure in reading it. But that endless repetition of combats which all seem the same, those gods who are always doing things but never getting anywhere, that Helen who causes the war and then plays scarcely any part in the thing, that Troy they besiege and never take, I found all that deadly boring. I've sometimes asked men of learning if they found reading it as boring as I did. The honest ones admitted that the book used to drop from their hands, but said that you had to have it in your library, like an ancient monument, or like those rusty medals that have no commercial value."

"Your Excellency doesn't think the same about Virgil?" said Candide.

"I agree that the second, fourth, and sixth books of the *Aeneid* are excellent," said Pococurante. "But as for his pious Aeneas, and valiant Cloanthus, and faithful Achates, and little Ascanius, not to mention half-witted King Latinus, and parochial Amata, and insipid Lavinia, I can think of nothing more disagreeable or more likely to leave one absolutely cold. I prefer Tasso and those improbable tales of Ariosto."[3]

"Dare I ask, sir," said Candide, "whether Horace does not afford you considerable pleasure?"

---

2. Caesar and Cato are the two principal roles in Vivaldi's 1735 opera *Catone in Utica;* such serious heroic roles were commonly sung by castrati. The joke is that Roman statesmen are represented by eunuchs.
3. Voltaire faithfully traces the history of the epic here.

Homer's *Iliad* (which recounts the Trojan War) and *Odyssey* were imitated by Virgil's *Aeneid*. Ariosto's *Orlando Furioso* and Tasso's *Gerusalemme Liberata* in turn were partly modeled on the *Aeneid*.

"There are one or two maxims," said Pococurante, "which a man of the world may profit by, and which fix themselves more readily in the memory for being compressed in powerful verse. But I care very little for his journey to Brindisi, or the description of that poor dinner he had, or that foulmouthed quarrel between someone or other called Pupilus, whose language, he says, 'was full of pus,' and someone else whose language 'was like vinegar.' It was only with extreme distaste that I read his crude verses against old women and witches, and I cannot see what merit there can be in telling his friend Maecenas that if he were to place him among the ranks of the lyric poets, he would bang his sublime forehead on the stars in the heavens.[4] Fools admire everything in a respected author. I read only for myself. I like only what may be of use to me."

Candide, who had been brought up never to judge things for himself, was much astonished by what he heard; and Martin found Pococurante's way of thinking rather sensible.

"Oh, look! Here's a copy of Cicero," said Candide. "I'm sure when it comes to this great man, you never tire of reading him?"

"I never read him," replied the Venetian. "What does it matter to me whether he defended Rabirius or Cluentius?[5] What with the cases I try myself, I have quite enough of all that as it is. I might have got on better with his philosophical works, but when I saw that he doubted everything, I decided that I knew as much as he did, and that I didn't need anyone else's help if I was going to be ignorant."

"Ah, look, eighty volumes of the proceedings of an Academy of Science," exclaimed Martin. "There may be something worthwhile there."

"There would be," said Pococurante, "if but one of the authors of all that rubbish had so much as invented the art of making pins. But in every one of those books there's nothing but pointless theorizing, and not a single thing that's useful."

"What a lot of plays there are!" said Candide; "in Italian, in Spanish, in French!"

"Yes," said the Senator, "there are three thousand of them, and not three dozen good ones. As for the collected sermons, which between them aren't worth one page of Seneca, and all those fat tomes on theology, well, you can be sure I never open them, not I, not anyone."

Martin noticed some shelves full of English books.

"I imagine," he said, "that a republican[6] must find most of these enjoyable to read, given how free the authors were to write them?"

"Yes," answered Pococurante, "it is a fine thing to write what one thinks. It is man's privilege. Throughout this Italy of ours, people write only what they do not think. Those who live in the land of the Caesars and the Antonines dare not have an idea without obtaining permission from a Dominican friar. I would be content with the freedom which inspires these English men of genius if their passion for the party interest didn't spoil all the estimable things that would otherwise flow from this precious freedom."

Candide, catching sight of a copy of Milton, asked him if he did not regard this author as a great man.

"Who?" said Pococurante, "that barbarian with his long commentary on the first book of *Genesis* in ten books of difficult verse?[7] That crude imitator of the Greeks who

---

4. These refer to passages in Horace's *Satires* 1.5, 2.8, 1.7 (Voltaire changes Rupilius to Pupilus), *Epodes* 5, 8, 12, and *Odes* 1.1.
5. Referring to orations by Cicero.
6. A citizen of a free republic like Venice.
7. *Paradise Lost,* the first edition of which was in ten

books, and later in 12 books. As Pococurante implies, Milton's poem at points imitates the epics of Tasso and Ariosto (as well as those of Homer and Virgil). Voltaire criticized Milton along similar lines in his *Essay on Epic Poetry* and *Age of Louis XIV*.

gives such a distorted view of the Creation and, where Moses shows the Eternal Being producing the world with the spoken word, has the Messiah take a great big compass out of a tool-chest in heaven and start drawing a plan? Me, admire the man who ruined Tasso's vision of hell and the devil; who has Lucifer appear disguised variously as a toad or a pygmy; who makes him say the same things over and over again; who makes him discuss theological points; who takes Ariosto's bit of comic invention about the fire-arms seriously and has the devils firing the cannon into heaven? Neither I nor anyone else in Italy has ever been able to enjoy all these extravagant absurdities. The marriage of Sin and Death, and the adders to which Sin gives birth, are enough to make anyone with a delicate stomach vomit. And his long description of a hospital is fit only for a grave-digger. That obscure, bizarre, disgusting poem was spurned at birth. Now I treat it the way it was treated in its own time by the readers in its own country. Anyway, I say what I think, and I couldn't care less whether anyone thinks the way I do or not."

Candide was distressed to hear all this. He admired Homer, and he had a sneaking fondness for Milton.

"Oh, dear!" he said to Martin under his breath, "I'm very much afraid that this man may have a sovereign disregard for our German poets."

"There would be no great harm in that," said Martin.

"Oh, what a great man!" Candide continued to mutter to himself. "What a great genius this Pococurante is! There is no pleasing him."

Having thus inspected all the books, they went down into the garden. Candide praised all its finer features.

"I know of nothing that could be in worse possible taste," said the master of the house. "All you see here are just pretty bits and pieces. But, as from tomorrow, I'm going to have a new one planted along much nobler lines."

When the two curious visitors had taken their leave of His Excellency, Candide turned to Martin:

"Well, there you are," he said. "You will agree that there is the happiest of men, for he is above all that he owns."

"Don't you see", said Martin, "that he's sated on everything he owns? Plato said a long time ago that the best stomachs are not those which reject all foods."

"But," said Candide, "isn't there pleasure in criticizing everything, in finding fault where other men think they find beauty?"

"Which is to say," rejoined Martin, "that there's pleasure in not having pleasure?"

"Oh, all right. Have it your way then," said Candide. "So the only one who's happy is me, when I see Miss Cunégonde again."

"One does well to hope," said Martin.

Meanwhile the days, the weeks went by. Still Cacambo did not return, and Candide was so sunk in misery that it did not even occur to him that Paquette and Brother Giroflée had not so much as come to thank him.

CHAPTER 26

Of a supper that Candide and Martin ate in the company
of six strangers, and who they were

One evening as Candide, accompanied by Martin, was about to sit down to table with the other passing strangers staying in the same hostelry, a man with a face the colour of soot came up behind him and, taking him by the arm, said:

"Be ready to leave when we do, and do not fail."

He turned round: it was Cacambo. Only the sight of Cunégonde could have surprised and pleased him more. He went nearly mad with joy. He embraced his dear friend.

"Cunégonde must be here, then. Where is she? Take me to her. Let me die of joy with her."

"Cunégonde is not here," said Cacambo. "She's in Constantinople."

"Ah, heavens! In Constantinople! But were she in China, I should fly to her! Let's go!"

"We will leave after supper," replied Cacambo. "I can't say any more. I'm a slave and my master's waiting for me. I've got to go and wait on him at table. Don't breathe a word. Have supper, and then be ready and waiting."

Candide, torn between joy and pain, absolutely delighted to have seen his faithful agent again, surprised to see him now a slave, full of the idea of being reunited with his beloved, his heart in tumult and his mind in a spin, sat down to eat in the company of Martin, who was watching all these goings-on with equanimity, and of the six strangers who had come to spend carnival in Venice.

Cacambo, who was filling the glass of one of these strangers, drew near to his master's ear at the end of the meal and said to him:

"Sire, Your Majesty may depart when he wishes. The ship is ready."

Having said this, he left the room. Astonished, the supper guests were exchanging silent glances, when another servant came up to his master and said:

"Sire, Your Majesty's carriage is at Padua, and the boat is ready."

His master made a sign, and the servant left. All the guests stared at each other again, and the general amazement increased. A third servant, coming up to a third stranger, said to him:

"Believe me, Sire, Your Majesty must not stay here a moment longer. I shall go and get everything ready."

And he disappeared at once.

Candide and Martin now had no doubt that this was some masquerade to do with the carnival. A fourth servant said to a fourth master:

"Your Majesty may depart at his convenience," and left the room like the others.

The fifth servant said the same to the fifth master. But the sixth servant spoke differently to the sixth stranger, who was sitting next to Candide.

He said to him:

"Lor me, Sire, they're refusing to let Your Majesty have any more credit, nor me neither, and the pair of us'll as like be carted off to the clink this very night. I'm off to look after number one, thank you very much. Good-bye."

The servants having all vanished, the six strangers, Candide and Martin remained deep in silence. Finally Candide broke it:

"Gentlemen," he said, "this is some strange joke. How is it that you are all Kings? For my part I must tell you that neither I nor Martin are anything of the sort."

Cacambo's master then intervened gravely and said in Italian:

"I am no joke, my name is Achmed III.[8] I was Grand Sultan for several years; I dethroned my brother; my nephew has dethroned me; my viziers have had their heads cut off; I am spending the rest of my days in the old seraglio; my nephew the Grand

---

8. Sultan of the Ottoman Empire from 1703 until 1730, when he was deposed by a military coup.

Sultan Mahmood occasionally allows me to travel for my health, and I have come to spend carnival in Venice."

A young man who was next to Achmed spoke after him and said:

"My name is Ivan, I was Emperor of all the Russias.[9] I was dethroned in my cradle; my father and mother were locked up; I was brought up in prison; I occasionally get permission to travel, accompanied by my guards, and I have come to spend carnival in Venice."

The third said:

"I am Charles Edward, King of England.[1] My father renounced his claim to the throne in my favour; I have fought many battles to make good my claim; eight hundred of my supporters had their hearts ripped out and their cheeks slapped with them; I was put in prison; I am on my way to Rome to visit my father the King, dethroned like me and my grandfather, and I have come to spend carnival in Venice."

The fourth then spoke up and said:

"I am the King of Poland.[2] The fortunes of war have dispossessed me of my ancestral domains; my father suffered the same reverses; I am resigned to Providence like Sultan Achmed, Emperor Ivan, and King Charles Edward, whom God preserve, and I have come to spend carnival in Venice."

The fifth said: "I too am the King of Poland.[3] I have lost my kingdom twice; but Providence has given me another domain, in which I have done more good than all the Kings of Sarmatia put together have ever been able to manage on the banks of the Vistula. I too am resigned to Providence, and I have come to spend carnival in Venice."

It remained for the sixth monarch to speak.

"Gentlemen," he said, "I am not so great a lord as any of you but, well, I have been a King just like everyone else. I am Theodore;[4] I was elected King in Corsica; they called me 'Your Majesty,' and now they hardly call me 'Sir'; once I minted money, and now I haven't a penny; once I had two secretaries of state, and now I have scarcely a valet; I once sat on a throne, and I have spent a long time in prison in London, with straw for a bed. I am much afraid I shall be treated in the same way here, although I came like Your Majesties to spend carnival in Venice."

The other five Kings listened to this speech with a noble compassion. Each of them gave King Theodore twenty sequins[5] to buy coats and shirts, and Candide made him a present of a diamond worth two thousand sequins.

"Who can this be then," said the five Kings, "a mere private individual who is in a position to give a hundred times as much as each of us, and who gives it?"

Just as they were leaving the table, there arrived in the same hostelry four Serene Highnesses who had also lost their domains through the fortunes of war, and who were coming to spend what was left of the carnival in Venice. But Candide did not even notice these new arrivals. All he could think about was going to find his dear Cunégonde in Constantinople.

9. Ivan VI, whom Catherine the Great imprisoned and ultimately put to death in 1764.
1. The "Young Pretender" (1720–1788), son of James Stuart (the "Old Pretender") and grandson of King James II of England; called "Bonnie Prince Charlie" by the Scots supporters of the uprising he led against the English crown, disastrously defeated at the Battle of Culloden in 1746.
2. Augustus III, Elector of Saxony and King of Poland, was driven from Saxony by Frederick the Great in 1756.

His father Augustus II had similarly been dispossessed by Charles XII of Sweden.
3. Stanislas Lesczinski, King of Poland from 1704 to 1709, when he was driven out by the Russians. He unsuccessfully attempted to regain the Polish throne in 1733 and was made Duke of Lorraine in 1735.
4. The representative of Holy Roman Emperor Charles VI, who led a revolt in Corsica against the Genoese in the 1730s.
5. Venetian coins.

CHAPTER 27

Candide's journey to Constantinople

Faithful Cacambo had already obtained permission from the Turkish captain who was to take Sultan Achmed back to Constantinople for Candide and Martin to join them on board. Together they made their way to the ship, having prostrated themselves before His unhappy Highness.

On the way Candide was saying to Martin:

"There you are, you see. That was six dethroned Kings we had supper with. And that's not all. Among those six Kings there was one I could give alms to. Perhaps there are lots more princes who are even more unfortunate. Whereas me, all I've lost is a hundred sheep, and I'm flying to the arms of Cunégonde. My dear Martin, once more, Pangloss was right: all is well."

"I certainly hope so," said Martin.

"But," said Candide, "that was a pretty unlikely adventure we had in Venice. Who ever saw or heard tell of six dethroned kings having supper together in a tavern."

"It's no more extraordinary," said Martin, "than most of the things that have happened to us. It's very common for kings to be dethroned, and as for the honour of having supper with them, there's nothing special about that."

Scarce was Candide aboard than he fell upon the neck of his former manservant, his friend Cacambo.

"Well, then," said Candide, "what's Cunégonde doing? Is she still a paragon of beauty? Does she still love me? How is she? Presumably you bought her a palace in Constantinople?"

"My dear master," replied Cacambo, "Cunégonde is washing dishes on the shores of the Sea of Marmara for a prince who has very few dishes. She's a slave in the household of an ex-ruler called Ragotsky,[6] to whom in his exile the Grand Turk gives three crowns a day. But, worse than that, she has lost her beauty and become horribly ugly."

"Ah, beautiful or ugly," said Candide, "I'm a man of honour, and my duty is to love her always. But how can she possibly have fallen so low with the five or six millions you took her?"

"Look here," said Cacambo. "Didn't I have to give two million to Señor don Fernando d'Ibaraa y Figueora y Mascarenes y Lampourdos y Souza, Governor of Buenos Aires, for permission to take Miss Cunégonde back? And didn't a pirate very kindly relieve us of the rest? And didn't the same pirate take us to Cape Matapan, Milo, Nicaria, Samos, Petra, the Dardanelles, Marmara, and Scutari? Cunégonde and the old woman are now working as servants to the prince I told you about, and I am a slave of the dethroned sultan."

"What a chain of appalling calamities one after another," said Candide. "But after all, I do still have some diamonds left. I will easily secure Cunégonde's release. It really is a pity that she has become so ugly."

Then, turning to Martin:

"Who do you think one should feel most sorry for," he said, "Emperor Achmed, Emperor Ivan, King Charles Edward, or me?"

"I've no idea," said Martin. "I'd have to see inside all your hearts to know the answer to that."

---

6. Rákóczy (1676–1735), prince of Transylvania, led an unsuccessful uprising against Joseph I in Hungary in the early 1700s and subsequently fled to the Sea of Marmara.

"Ah!" said Candide, "if Pangloss were here, he would know, he would tell us the answer."

"I don't know what sort of scales your Pangloss could have used to weigh the misfortunes of men and calculate their sufferings," said Martin. "All I presume is that there are millions of people on this earth one might feel a hundred times sorrier for than King Charles Edward, Emperor Ivan, and Sultan Achmed."

"That may well be so," said Candide.

In a few days they reached the channel leading to the Black Sea. The first thing Candide did was to buy Cacambo back at a very high price, and then without delay he and his companions quickly boarded a galley and made for the shores of the Sea of Marmara in search of Cunégonde, ugly though she might be.

Amongst the galley-slaves were two prisoners who rowed extremely badly, and to whose naked shoulders the Levantine captain would periodically apply a few lashes of his bull's pizzle. Candide's natural reaction was to pay more attention to them than to the other galley-slaves, and he drew near them with compassion. One or two features on their disfigured faces seemed to him to bear some resemblance to those of Pangloss and that unfortunate Jesuit, Miss Cunégonde's brother, the Baron. The thought touched and saddened him. He watched them even more closely.

"Quite honestly," he said to Cacambo, "if I hadn't seen Maître Pangloss hanged and if I hadn't had the misfortune to kill the Baron, I could swear it was them rowing on this galley."

On hearing the names of the Baron and Pangloss, the two galley-slaves gave a great shout, stopped still on their bench, and dropped their oars. The Levantine captain rushed up to them, and the lashes from his bull's pizzle rained down anew.

"Stop, stop, good sir," screamed Candide. "I will give you all the money you want."

"Why, it's Candide!" said one of the two galley-slaves.

"Why, it's Candide!" said the other.

"Am I dreaming all this?" said Candide. "Am I awake? Am I really here on this galley? Is that the Baron I killed? Is that the Maître Pangloss I saw hanged?"

"It is we, it is we," they replied.

"What, so that's the great philosopher?" said Martin.

"Look here, Mr. Levantine captain," said Candide, "how much ransom do you want for Mr. von Thunder-ten-tronckh, one of the foremost barons of the Empire, and for Mr. Pangloss, the profoundest metaphysician in Germany?"

"You Christian cur," replied the Levantine slave-driver. "Since these two Christian slave dogs are barons and metaphysicians, which is no doubt a great honour where they come from, you can give me fifty thousand sequins."

"You shall have them, sir. Get me to Constantinople as fast as you possibly can, and you will be paid on the spot. On second thoughts, take me to Miss Cunégonde."

The Levantine captain, at Candide's first offer, had already altered course for the city, and he bid the crew row faster than a bird may cleave the air.

Candide embraced the Baron and Pangloss a hundred times.

"And how did I not kill you, my dear Baron? And you, my dear Pangloss, how is it that you are alive after being hanged? And what are you both doing on a galley in Turkey?"

"Is it really true that my dear sister is here in this country?" said the Baron.

"Yes," replied Cacambo.

"So here is my dear Candide again," exclaimed Pangloss.

Candide introduced them to Martin and Cacambo. They all embraced; everybody talked at once. The galley was flying along; they were already in port. A Jew was summoned, to whom Candide sold a diamond worth a hundred thousand sequins for fifty thousand, and who swore by Abraham that he could offer not a sequin more. Thereupon Candide paid the ransom for the Baron and Pangloss. The latter threw himself at the feet of his liberator and bathed them in tears; the other thanked him with a nod of his head and promised to reimburse him at the earliest opportunity.

"But can it really be that my sister is in Turkey?" he said.

"It really can," retorted Cacambo, "seeing as how she's washing dishes for a Prince of Transylvania."

At once two Jews were sent for. Candide sold some more diamonds, and they all left by another galley to go and deliver Cunégonde from bondage.

CHAPTER 28

What happened to Candide, Cunégonde, Pangloss, Martin, and co.

"Once more, forgive me," Candide said to the Baron. "Forgive me, reverend father, for running you through with my sword like that."

"We'll say no more about it," said the Baron. "I did speak rather sharply, I admit. But since you want to know how you came to find me on a galley, I will tell you that after being cured of my wounds by the college's apothecary monk, I was set upon and abducted by a group of Spaniards. I was put in prison in Buenos Aires just after my sister left there. I asked to be allowed to return to Rome to be with the Father General: I was appointed almoner to His Excellency the ambassador of France in Constantinople. I hadn't been in post more than a week when one evening I ran into a young icoglan,[7] who was very good-looking. It was extremely hot: the young man wanted to go for a swim; I took the opportunity to go swimming too. I did not know that it was a capital offence for a Christian to be found stark naked with a young Muslim. A cadi[8] had me birched a hundred times on the soles of the feet and sent me to the galleys. I don't believe there's ever been a more ghastly miscarriage of justice. But what I'd like to know is why my sister is working in the kitchens of a Transylvanian ruler in exile among the Turks."

"But you, my dear Pangloss," said Candide, "how is it that we meet again?"

"It is true that you did see me hanged," said Pangloss. "I was, of course, to have been burned but, as you will remember, it poured with rain just as they were about to roast me. The storm was so violent that they gave up trying to light the fire, and I was hanged for want of a better alternative. A surgeon bought my body, took me home with him, and dissected me. First he made a cruciform incision in me from my navel to my collar-bone. One can't have a worse hanging than I'd had. The executive arm of the high works of the Holy Inquisition, namely a sub-deacon, certainly did a splendid job when it came to burning people, but he wasn't used to hanging. The rope was wet and wouldn't slip through properly, and it got caught. So I was still breathing. The crucial incision made me give such an enormous shriek that my surgeon fell over backwards and, thinking it was the devil himself he was dissecting, rushed away, nearly dying of fright, and then, to cap it all, fell down the stairs in his flight. His wife came running from the next room at the noise, saw me stretched out on the table with my crucial incision, took even greater fright than her husband, fled, and fell over him.

7. A page of the Sultan, often employed in the seraglio.   8. A ranking Muslim official.

"When they had collected their wits a little, I heard the surgeon's wife say to her husband: 'My dear, what on earth were you thinking of, dissecting a heretic like that? Don't you know those sort of people always have the devil in them? I'm going to fetch a priest this minute to exorcize him.' I shuddered to hear this, and I mustered what little strength I had left and cried out: 'Have mercy on me!' In the end the Portuguese barber plucked up courage.[9] He sewed me up again, and his wife even nursed me. I was up and about again in a fortnight. The barber found me a position and made me lackey to a Knight of Malta who was going to Venice. But since my master had not the means to pay me, I entered service with a merchant of Venice and followed him to Constantinople.

"One day I happened to enter a mosque. There was no one in there apart from an old imam and a very pretty young worshipper, who was saying her paternosters. Her bosom was uncovered for all to see, and in her cleavage was a lovely posy of tulips, roses, anemones, buttercups, hyacinths, and auriculas. She dropped her posy; I picked it up and replaced it for her with respectful zeal. I took so long about replacing it that the imam became angry and, seeing I was a Christian, called for help. I was taken to the cadi, who sentenced me to a hundred strokes of the lash on the soles of my feet and sent me to the galleys. I was chained up in precisely the same galley and on precisely the same bench as His Lordship the Baron. On the galley were four young men from Marseilles, five Neapolitan priests, and two monks from Corfu, who all told us that this sort of thing happened every day. His Lordship claimed he'd been more unjustly treated than I had. I maintained for my part that it was much more permissible putting a posy back on a woman's bosom than being stark naked with an icoglan. We used to argue the whole time, and were getting twenty lashes a day with the bull's pizzle when, by a turn in the chain of events that governs this universe, you were led to our galley and bought us back."

"Now then, my dear Pangloss!" Candide said to him. "When you were being hanged, and dissected, and beaten, and made to row in a galley, did you continue to think that things were turning out for the best?"

"I still feel now as I did at the outset," replied Pangloss. "I am a philosopher after all. It wouldn't do for me to go back on what I said before, what with Leibniz not being able to be wrong, and pre-established harmony being the finest thing in the world, not to mention the *plenum* and *materia subtilis.*"[1]

CHAPTER 29

How Candide was reunited with Cunégonde and the old woman

While Candide, the Baron, Pangloss, Martin, and Cacambo were recounting their adventures, and philosophizing about which events in the universe are contingent and which not contingent, and arguing about effects and causes, moral and physical evil, freedom and necessity, and about what consolations are to be had on board a Turkish galley, they landed on the shores of the Sea of Marmara at the house of the Prince of Transylvania. The first thing they saw was Cunégonde and the old woman hanging towels out on a line to dry.

The Baron went pale at the sight. Candide, the tender-hearted lover, on seeing his fair Cunégonde all brown, with her eyes bloodshot, her bosom shrivelled, her cheeks

---

9. Barbers often did minor surgery.
1. Leibniz posited the idea of a pre-established harmony to describe the correspondence between the physical and spiritual realms. Leibniz and Descartes argued that the universe was a *plenum* ("fullness"), meaning there is no empty space in the universe, and that the space between planets was filled by an ethereal *materia subtilis* ("fine matter"). This philosophy was discredited by Newton.

wrinkled, and her arms red and peeling, recoiled three paces in horror, and then went forward out of sheer good manners. She embraced Candide and her brother. They embraced the old woman. Candide bought them both free.

There was a small farm in the vicinity. The old woman suggested to Candide that it would do them nicely while they waited for the whole company to fall on better times. Cunégonde did not know that she had become ugly; no one had told her. She reminded Candide of his promises in such a firm tone that good Candide did not dare refuse her. He intimated to the Baron, therefore, that he was going to marry his sister.

"I will not tolerate such a demeaning act on her part," he said, "nor such insolence from you. Never shall it be said that I allowed such infamy: my wife's children would never be able to mix in Germany's noble chapters.[2] No, my sister will marry no one but a baron of the Empire."

Cunégonde threw herself at his feet and bathed them with her tears; he was inflexible.

"You great numskull," said Candide, "I've saved you from the galleys, I've paid your ransom, and I've paid your sister's. She was washing dishes here, she's ugly, I have the goodness to make her my wife, and you still think you're going to stand in our way! I'd kill you all over again if I let my anger have its way."

"You can kill me all over again if you want," said the Baron, "but you won't marry my sister so long as I live."

CHAPTER 30

Conclusion

Candide, in his heart of hearts, had no desire to marry Cunégonde. But the extreme impertinence of the Baron made him decide to go through with the marriage, and Cunégonde was pressing him so keenly that he could not go back on his word. He consulted Pangloss, Martin, and the faithful Cacambo. Pangloss wrote a fine dissertation in which he proved that the Baron had no rights over his sister, and that it was open to her, under all the laws of the Empire, to marry Candide with the left hand.[3] Martin was for throwing the Baron into the sea. Cacambo decided they should return him to the Levantine captain and have him put back in the galleys, after which he was to be packed off to the Father General in Rome on the first available ship. This view of the matter was thought to be very sound. The old woman approved, nothing was said to his sister, the thing was done with the help of a little money, and they had the pleasure of bettering a Jesuit and punishing the arrogance of a German baron.

It was quite natural to imagine that, after so many disasters, Candide, now married to his sweetheart and living with the philosophical Pangloss, the philosophical Martin, the prudent Cacambo and the old woman and, moreover, having brought back so many diamonds from the land of the ancient Incas, would be leading the most agreeable of all possible lives. But he was swindled so many times by the Jews that all he had left in the end was his little farm; his wife, who grew uglier with every day that passed, became shrewish and impossible to live with; the old woman was infirm and even more bad-tempered than Cunégonde; Cacambo, who worked in the garden and travelled to Constantinople to sell vegetables, was worn out with work and cursed his fate; Pangloss was in despair at not being a luminary in some German

---

2. Assemblies of the nobility.

3. A marriage between persons of different rank in which the inferior's status is not raised.

university. As for Martin, he was firmly persuaded that one is just as badly off wherever one is; he put up with things as they were. Candide, Martin, and Pangloss would argue sometimes about metaphysics and ethics. They would often see boats passing beneath the windows of the farm-house laden with effendis, pashas, and cadis,[4] who were being exiled to Lemnos or Mytilene or Erzerum. They would see more cadis, more pashas, and more effendis coming to take the place of those who had been expelled, and being themselves in their turn expelled. They would see heads duly stuffed with straw being taken for display before the Sublime Porte.[5] Such sights would give rise to yet further disquisitions, and when they were not arguing, the boredom was so excessive that the old woman made bold to say to them one day:

"I would like to know which is worse: being raped a hundred times by negro pirates, having a buttock chopped off, running the gauntlet of the Bulgars, being flogged and hanged in an *auto-da-fé*, being dissected, rowing in a galley, in short, suffering all the misfortunes we've all suffered, or simply being stuck here doing nothing?"

"That is a good question," said Candide.

This speech gave rise to renewed speculation, and Martin in particular came to the conclusion that man was born to spend his life alternately a prey to the throes of anxiety and the lethargy of boredom. Candide did not agree, but asserted nothing. Pangloss admitted that he had always suffered horribly; but having once maintained that everything was going marvellously, he still maintained it, and believed nothing of the sort.

One thing finally confirmed Martin in his detestable principles, gave Candide more than ever pause, and embarrassed Pangloss. This was the sight one day of Paquette and Brother Giroflée arriving at their farm in a state of extreme wretchedness. They had very quickly gone through their three thousand piastres, left each other, patched things up, quarrelled again, been put in prison, escaped; and in the end Brother Giroflée had turned Turk. Paquette still pursued her profession, and no longer earned any money at it.

"I told you so," Martin said to Candide. "I knew what you gave them would soon be gone and would only make them even more wretched. You had more piastres than you knew what to do with, you and Cacambo, and you are no happier than Brother Giroflée and Paquette."

"Aha!" said Pangloss to Paquette, "so heaven brings you back here among us, my poor child! Do you know, you've cost me the tip of my nose, an eye and an ear? And you, just look at the state you're in! What a world we live in!"

This new turn of events led them to philosophize more than ever.

There lived in the neighbourhood a very famous dervish,[6] who passed for the greatest philosopher in Turkey. They went to consult him. Pangloss acted as their spokesman and said to him:

"Master, we have come to ask you to tell us why such a strange animal as man was created."

"What's that to you?" said the dervish. "Is it any of your business?"

"But, reverend father," said Candide, "there's an awful lot of evil in the world."

---

4. Men of high rank.
5. The gate of the Turkish court.

6. Muslim holy man.

"What does it matter whether there's evil or there's good," said the dervish. "When His Highness sends a ship to Egypt, does he worry whether the mice on board are comfortable or not?"

"So what must we do then?" said Pangloss.

"Be silent," said the dervish.

"I had flattered myself," said Pangloss, "that we might have a talk about effects and causes, the best of all possible worlds, the origin of evil, the nature of the soul, and pre-established harmony."

The dervish, at these words, slammed the door in their faces.

During this conversation news had spread that two viziers of the bench and the mufti[7] had been strangled in Constantinople, and several of their friends impaled. This catastrophe made a great stir everywhere for some hours. On their way back to the farm Pangloss, Candide, and Martin met a kindly old man who was taking the air at his door beneath an arbour of orange-trees. Pangloss, who was as curious as he was prone to philosophizing, asked him the name of the mufti who had just been strangled.

"I have no idea," replied the fellow, "and I never have known what any mufti or vizier was called. What you have just told me means absolutely nothing to me. I have no doubt that in general those who get involved in public affairs do sometimes come to a sad end and that they deserve it. But I never enquire what's going on in Constantinople. I am content to send my fruit for sale there from the garden I cultivate."

Having said this, he invited the strangers into his house. His two daughters and two sons offered them several kinds of sorbet which they made themselves, some kaïmak[8] sharpened with the zest of candied citron, some oranges, lemons, limes, pineapple, and pistachio nuts, and some Mocha coffee which had not been blended with that awful coffee from Batavia and the islands. After which the two daughters of this good Muslim perfumed the beards of Candide, Pangloss, and Martin.

"You must have a vast and magnificent property," said Candide to the Turk.

"I have but twenty acres," replied the Turk. "I cultivate them with my children. Work keeps us from three great evils: boredom, vice, and need."

Candide, on his way back to his farm, thought long and hard about what the Turk had said, and commented to Pangloss and Martin:

"That kind old man seems to me to have made a life for himself which is much preferable to that of those six Kings with whom we had the honour of having supper."

"High rank can be very dangerous," said Pangloss; "all the philosophers say so. For the fact is, Eglon, King of the Moabites, was slain by Ehud; Absalom was hanged by the hair on his head and had three darts thrust through his heart; King Nadab, son of Jeroboam, was smitten by Baasha; King Elah by Zimri; Joram by Jehu; Athaliah by Jehoiada; and Kings Jehoiakim, Jehoiachin, and Zedekiah entered into captivity.[9] You know what sort of deaths befell Croesus, Astyages, Darius, Dionysius of Syracuse, Pyrrhus, Perseus, Hannibal, Jugurtha, Ariovistus, Caesar, Pompey, Nero, Otho, Vitellius, Domitian, Richard II of England, Edward II, Henry VI, Richard III, Mary Stuart, Charles I, France's three Henris, and the Emperor Henri IV? You know . . ."

"I also know," said Candide, "that we must cultivate our garden."

---

7. Judge.
8. Sweet cream.

9. Having given a string of biblical examples, Pangloss next turns to classical and then modern cases.

"You're right," said Pangloss; "for when man was placed in the garden of Eden, he was placed there *ut operaretur eum*—that he might work[1]—which proves that man was not born to rest."

"Let's get down to work and stop all this philosophizing," said Martin. "It's the only way to make life bearable."

The little society all fell in with this laudable plan. Each began to exercise his talents. Their small amount of land produced a great deal. Cunégonde was in truth very ugly, but she became an excellent pastry-cook. Paquette embroidered. The old woman took care of the linen. Everyone made himself useful, including Brother Giroflée; he was a very fine carpenter, and even became quite the gentleman. And sometimes Pangloss would say to Candide:

"All events form a chain in the best of all possible worlds. For in the end, if you had not been given a good kick up the backside and chased out of a beautiful castle for loving Miss Cunégonde, and if you hadn't been subjected to the Inquisition, and if you hadn't wandered about America on foot, and if you hadn't dealt the Baron a good blow with your sword, and if you hadn't lost all your sheep from that fine country of Eldorado, you wouldn't be here now eating candied citron and pistachio nuts."

"That is well put," replied Candide, "but we must cultivate our garden."

RESONANCES

Gottfried Wilhelm von Leibniz, from Theodicy[1]

Summary of the Controversy Reduced to Formal Arguments

Some persons of discernment have wished me to make this addition. I have the more readily deferred to their opinion, because of the opportunity thereby gained for meeting certain difficulties, and for making observations on certain matters which were not treated in sufficient detail in the work itself.

OBJECTION I

Whoever does not choose the best course is lacking either in power, or knowledge, or goodness.

1. Genesis 2:15.

1. Translated by E. M. Huggard. A theodicy is a vindication of divine justice in allowing for the existence of physical and moral evil. Gottfried Wilhelm, Freiherr von Leibniz (1646–1716), coined the term in this work. The first great German philosopher of the Enlightenment, Leibniz was by profession a historian and diplomat. After earning a doctorate in law, he worked most of his life as librarian to three Dukes of Hanover, the last of whom became George I of England in 1714. As a diplomat Leibniz helped try to persuade Louis XIV to attack Egypt instead of Germany, proposing that Catholics and Protestants should unite against Muslims rather than fighting each other. As a historian, he authored a history of the Dukes of Braunschweig, linking them to the Italian d'Este family. As a mathematician, he developed infinitesimal calculus independently of Newton. He helped establish the Berlin Academy (1700), of which he remained president for life.

Leibniz is now best known for his metaphysics, in which he set out to solve the mind-body problem left open by Descartes' influential philosophy: if all matter, including the human body, is mechanical, and yet human beings also have mind or spirit, what connects the two? Leibniz hypothesized that the smallest, indivisible units of matter were themselves imbued with primitive mind, spirit, or consciousness. These "monads" were bound together as substance according to a "pre-established harmony" orchestrated by God, the ultimate mind/spirit in the great chain. This harmony of the universe, in which each single element reflects, or "represents" all the others, is ultimately the effect of divine will, and so Leibniz calls it "the best of all possible worlds," even though he sees evil as a necessary element in it.

God did not choose the best course in creating this world.
Therefore God was lacking in power, or knowledge, or goodness.

ANSWER

I deny the minor, that is to say, the second premise of this syllogism,[2] and the opponent proves it by this

PROSYLLOGISM[3]

Whoever makes things in which there is evil, and which could have been made without any evil, or need not have been made at all, does not choose the best course.

God made a world wherein there is evil; a world, I say, which could have been made without any evil or which need not have been made at all.

Therefore God did not choose the best course.

ANSWER

I admit the minor of this prosyllogism: for one must confess that there is evil in this world which God has made, and that it would have been possible to make a world without evil or even not to create any world, since its creation depended upon the free will of God. But I deny the major, that is, the first of the two premises of the prosyllogism, and I might content myself with asking for its proof. In order, however, to give a clearer exposition of the matter, I would justify this denial by pointing out that the best course is not always that one which tends towards avoiding evil, since it is possible that the evil may be accompanied by a greater good. For example, the general of an army will prefer a great victory with a slight wound to a state of affairs without wound and without victory. I have proved this in further detail in this work by pointing out, through instances taken from mathematics and elsewhere, that an imperfection in the part may be required for a greater perfection in the whole. I have followed therein the opinion of St. Augustine, who said a hundred times that God permitted evil in order to derive from it a good, that is to say, a greater good; and Thomas Aquinas says (in libr. 2, *Sent. Dist.* 32, qu. 1, art. 1) that the permission of evil tends towards the good of the universe. I have shown that among older writers the fall of Adam was termed *felix culpa*, a fortunate sin, because it had been expiated with immense benefit by the incarnation of the Son of God: for he gave to the universe something more noble than anything there would otherwise have been amongst created beings. For the better understanding of the matter I added, following the example of many good authors, that it was consistent with order and the general good for God to grant to certain of his creatures the opportunity to exercise their freedom, even when he foresaw that they would turn to evil: for God could easily correct the evil, and it was not fitting that in order to prevent sin he should always act in an extraordinary way. It will therefore sufficiently refute the objection to show that a world with evil may be better than a world without evil. But I have gone still further in the work, and have even shown that this universe must be indeed better than every other possible universe.

---

2. An argument supported by two premises, statements that together lead to a single conclusion, but only if both premises are accepted as true.

3. A syllogism whose conclusion is used as the premise of another syllogism.

Alexander Pope: from *An Essay on Man*

In Four Epistles to Henry St. John, Lord Bolingbroke[1]

from Epistle I

	Awake, my ST. JOHN! leave all meaner° things	*base*
	To low ambition, and the pride of kings.	
	Let us (since life can little more supply	
	Than just to look about us and to die)	
5	Expatiate° free o'er all this scene of man;	*wander; speak*
	A mighty maze! but not without a plan;	
	A wild, where weeds and flow'rs promiscuous° shoot,	*randomly mixed*
	Or garden, tempting with forbidden fruit.	
	Together let us beat this ample field,	
10	Try what the open, what the covert yield;[2]	
	The latent tracts, the giddy heights explore	
	Of all who blindly creep, or sightless soar;[3]	
	Eye nature's walks,° shoot folly as it flies,	*behaviors*
	And catch the manners living as they rise;	
15	Laugh where we must, be candid° where we can;	*generous*
	But vindicate the ways of God to Man.[4]	
	1. Say first, of God above, or Man below,	
	What can we reason, but from what we know?	
	Of Man what see we, but his station here,	
20	From which to reason, or to which refer?	
	Through worlds unnumbered though the God be known,	
	'Tis ours to trace him only in our own.	
	He, who through vast immensity can pierce,	
	See worlds on worlds compose one universe,	
25	Observe how system into system runs,	
	What other planets circle other suns,	
	What varied being peoples° ev'ry star,	*inhabits*
	May tell why Heav'n has made us as we are.	
	But of this frame the bearings, and the ties,	
30	The strong connections, nice dependencies,	

1. Alexander Pope's ambitious philosophical poem is divided into separate "epistles" contemplating humankind in relation to the universe, itself, society, and happiness. His plan to expand it and the *Four Moral Essays* (1731–1735) into a grand sequence investigating human nature in all its aspects was never completed. Nevertheless, *An Essay on Man*, published anonymously in 1733–1734, stands monumentally alone as an elaboration of Pope's own system of ethics. Contemporaries, however, thought Pope a better poet than philosopher. Voltaire satirized his simplified Leibnizian optimism at length in *Candide*. Wortley Montagu mocked: "Poor Pope philosophy displays on / With so much rhyme and little reason, / And though he argues ne'er so long / That all is right, his head is wrong" (see pages 293–294). Dr. Johnson concurred: "Never was penury of knowledge and vulgarity of sentiment so happily disguised." Nevertheless, the philosophy required of a man who thought his life a "long disease" to declare that

"Whatever IS, is RIGHT" should not be underestimated. The *Essay* is addressed to Henry St. John, first Viscount Bolingbroke (1678–1751), a leading Tory statesman and political writer whom Pope described as "my guide, philosopher, and friend." For more on Pope, see his principal listing, page 521.

2. "Beat," "open," "covert" are all hunting terms: Pope imagines them to be searching out game by walking back and forth across open and wooded land.

3. There is a middle way appropriate to man between ignorance and presumption.

4. Echoing *Paradise Lost,* 1.24–26: "That to the highth of this great argument / I may assert eternal providence, / And justify the ways of God to men." Pope's mention of the "garden, tempting with forbidden fruit" (line 8) also calls to mind the opening lines of Milton's epic. There is also a reference here to the Theodicy, or "justifcation of God," of Leibniz. See page 513, n. 1.

Gradations just,[5] has thy° pervading soul   *the reader's*
Looked through? or can a part contain the whole?
   Is the great chain,[6] that draws all to agree,
And drawn supports, upheld by God, or thee?

35   2. Presumptuous Man! the reason wouldst thou find,
Why formed so weak, so little, and so blind!
First, if thou canst, the harder reason guess,
Why formed no weaker, blinder, and no less!
Ask of thy mother earth, why oaks are made
40   Taller or stronger than the weeds they shade?
Or ask of yonder argent fields above,
Why Jove's satellites° are less than Jove?   *Jupiter's moons*
   Of systems possible, if 'tis confest
That wisdom infinite must form the best,
45   Where all must full or not coherent be,
And all that rises, rise in due degree;
Then, in the scale of reas'ning life, 'tis plain
There must be, somewhere, such a rank as Man;
And all the question (wrangle e'er so long)
50   Is only this, if God has placed him wrong?
* * *

     5. Ask for what end th' heav'nly bodies shine,
Earth for whose use? Pride answers, "'Tis for mine:
For me kind Nature wakes her genial° pow'r,   *generating*
Suckles each herb, and spreads out ev'ry flow'r;
135   Annual for me, the grape, the rose renew
The juice nectareous, and the balmy dew;
For me, the mine a thousand treasures brings;
For me, health gushes from a thousand springs;
Seas roll to waft me, suns to light me rise;
140   My foot-stool earth, my canopy the skies."
   But errs not Nature from this gracious end,
From burning suns when livid deaths descend,
When earthquakes swallow, or when tempests sweep
Towns to one grave, whole nations to the deep?
145   "No" ('tis replied) "the first Almighty cause°   *God the creator*
Acts not by partial, but by gen'ral laws;
Th' exceptions few; some change since all began,
And what created perfect?"—Why then Man?
If the great end be human happiness,
150   Then Nature deviates; and can Man do less?
As much that end a constant course requires
Of show'rs and sunshine, as of Man's desires;
As much eternal springs and cloudless skies,
As men for ever temp'rate, calm, and wise.

---

5. "Connections," "dependencies," and "gradations" were
key terms of the new sciences.

6. The Great Chain of Being linked all levels of creation,
at the same time maintaining a fixed hierarchy.

155   If plagues or earthquakes break not Heav'n's design,
Why then a Borgia, or a Catiline?[7]
Who knows but he, whose hand the light'ning forms,
Who heaves old ocean, and who wings the storms,
Pours fierce ambition in a Caesar's mind,

160   Or turns young Ammon[8] loose to scourge mankind?
From pride, from pride, our very reas'ning springs;
Account for moral as for nat'ral things:
Why charge we Heav'n in those, in these acquit?
In both, to reason right is to submit.

165   Better for us, perhaps, it might appear,
Were there all harmony, all virtue here;
That never air or ocean felt the wind;
That never passion discomposed the mind:
But all subsists by elemental strife;

170   And passions are the elements of life.
The gen'ral ORDER, since the whole began,
Is kept in Nature, and is kept in Man.

* * *

    7. Far as creation's ample range extends,
The scale of sensual, mental pow'rs ascends:
Mark how it mounts, to Man's imperial race,

210   From the green myriads in the peopled grass:
What modes of sight betwixt each wide extreme,
The mole's dim curtain, and the lynx's beam:
Of smell, the headlong lioness between,[9]
And hound sagacious on the tainted[1] green:

215   Of hearing, from the life that fills the flood,
To that which warbles through the vernal wood:
The spider's touch, how exquisitely fine!
Feels at each thread, and lives along the line:
In the nice° bee, what sense so subtly true   *discriminating*

220   From pois'nous herbs extracts the healing dew:[2]
How instinct varies in the grov'ling swine,
Compared, half-reas'ning elephant, with thine:
"Twixt that, and reason, what a nice barrier;[3]
Forever sep'rate, yet forever near!

225   Remembrance and reflection how allied;
What thin partitions sense from thought divide:
And middle natures, how they long to join,
Yet never pass th' insuperable line!
Without this just gradation, could they be

7. Cesare Borgia (1476–1507), an Italian duke from a notoriously ruthless family. Lucius Sergius Catiline (d. 62 B.C.E.) plotted unsuccessfully against the Roman state.
8. Alexander the Great, King of Macedonia (336–323 B.C.E.) and conqueror of Asia Minor, Syria, Egypt, Babylonia, and Persia.

9. According to Pope, lions were believed to hunt "by the ear, and not by the nostril."
1. The hound is perceptive in following the "taint" or smell of the hunted animal.
2. Honey was used for medicinal purposes.
3. Fine distinction. "Barrier" is pronounced "bar-REAR."

230   Subjected these to those, or all to thee?
       The pow'rs of all subdued by thee alone,
       Is not thy reason all these pow'rs in one?

       8. See, through this air, this ocean, and this earth,
       All matter quick,° and bursting into birth.   *living*
235   Above, how high progressive life may go!
       Around, how wide! how deep extend below!
       Vast chain of being, which from God began,
       Natures ethereal, human, angel, Man,
       Beast, bird, fish, insect! what no eye can see,
240   No glass° can reach! from infinite to thee,   *magnifying glass*
       From thee to nothing!—On superior pow'rs
       Were we to press, inferior might on ours:
       Or in the full creation leave a void,
       Where, one step broken, the great scale's destroyed:
245   From nature's chain whatever link you strike,
       Tenth or ten thousandth, breaks the chain alike.
          And if each system in gradation roll,
       Alike essential to th' amazing whole;
       The least confusion but in one, not all
250   That system only, but the whole must fall.
       Let earth unbalanced from her orbit fly,[4]
       Planets and suns run lawless through the sky,
       Let ruling angels from their spheres be hurled,[5]
       Being on being wrecked, and world on world,
255   Heav'n's whole foundations to their center nod,
       And Nature tremble to the throne of God:
       All this dread ORDER break—for whom? for thee?
       Vile worm!—oh madness, pride, impiety!

       9. What if the foot, ordained the dust to tread,
260   Or hand to toil, aspired to be the head?
       What if the head, the eye, or ear repined
       To serve mere engines to the ruling mind?
       Just as absurd for any part to claim
       To be another, in this gen'ral frame:
265   Just as absurd, to mourn the tasks or pains
       The great directing MIND of ALL ordains.
          All are but parts of one stupendous whole,
       Whose body, Nature is, and God the soul;
       That, changed through all, and yet in all the same,
270   Great in the earth, as in th' ethereal frame,
       Warms in the sun, refreshes in the breeze,
       Glows in the stars, and blossoms in the trees,
       Lives through all life, extends through all extent,
       Spreads undivided, operates unspent,

---

4. Recalling *Paradise Lost* 7.242, where "Earth, self-balanced, on her center hung."

5. According to Thomas Aquinas (c. 1225–1274), a sign of the end of the world.

275 Breathes in our soul, informs° our mortal part,   *permeates*
As full, as perfect, in a hair as heart;
As full, as perfect, in vile Man that mourns,
As the rapt seraph that adores and burns;
To him no high, no low, no great, no small;
280 He fills, he bounds, connects, and equals all.

    10. Cease then, nor ORDER imperfection name:
Our proper bliss depends on what we blame.
Know thy own point: This kind, this due degree
Of blindness, weakness, Heav'n bestows on thee.
285 Submit—In this, or any other sphere,
Secure to be as blest as thou canst bear:
Safe in the hand of one disposing Pow'r,
Or° in the natal, or the mortal hour.   *either*
All nature is but art, unknown to thee;
290 All chance, direction, which thou canst not see;
All discord, harmony, not understood;
All partial evil, universal good:
And, spite of pride, in erring reason's spite,
One truth is clear, "Whatever Is, is RIGHT."

TRANSLATIONS: VOLTAIRE'S *CANDIDE*

Translators make many choices as they devise a translation, some of them linguistic and some of them social. Here are two brief passages from *Candide*. Each appears first in French, then in the first English translation of 1759, then in a Victorian translation, and finally in two recent translations. The later translators are probably partly dependent on the earlier ones, and yet each translation shows its own approach to Voltaire's lively language and his treatment of the body.

    In this passage from Chapter 9, Candide's young love Cunégonde has been forced to divide her time between Spain's Grand Inquisitor and a rich Jewish merchant, Issachar. The merchant has reluctantly accepted the arrangement with the Inquisitor but flies into a rage when Candide appears on the scene:

VOLTAIRE'S ORIGINAL

Cet Issachar était le plus colérique Hébreu qu'on eût vu dans Israël, depuis la captivité en Babylone. "Quoi! dit-il, chienne de galiléenne, ce n'est pas assez de monsieur l'inquisiteur? Il faut que ce coquin partage aussi avec moi?"

ANONYMOUS 1759 TRANSLATION

This said Issachar was the most choleric Hebrew that had been ever seen in Israel since the captivity of Babylon. What! said he, thou b—h of a Galilean, was not the inquisitor enough for thee? Must this rascal also come in for a share with me?

This Issachar was the most choleric Hebrew that had been seen in Israel since the captivity in Babylon. "What," said he, "you dog of a Galilean, is it not enough to share with Monsieur the inquisitor? but must this varlet also share with me?"

ROBERT M. ADAMS TRANSLATION (1991)

This Issachar was the most choleric Hebrew seen in Israel since the Babylonian captivity.—What's this, says he, you bitch of a Christian, you're not satisfied with the Grand Inquisitor? Do I have to share you with this rascal, too?

DANIEL GORDON TRANSLATION (1998)

This Issachar was the most hot-tempered Hebrew seen in Israel since the Babylonian captivity. "What!" he said. "You Christian bitch, you are not satisfied with the Inquisitor? I have to share you with this scoundrel too?"

What shifting norms are suggested by the changing translation of "chienne" as "b—h," then "dog," and then "bitch"? Though generally similar, the two recent translations differ in that Robert Adams keeps a degree of period flavor while Daniel Gordon strives for a fast-paced, modern effect. What choices does each of them make for these purposes?

Candide and Cunégonde are helped by an old woman, who tells her story in Chapter 11. As in the first passage, here again the translators can be seen to make choices that reflect their values of candor or modesty, literalness or flexibility, modern or period atmosphere. What social or verbal values underlie a pope's turning into a king, or a neck becoming a breast, or eyes looking crusty and bloodshot, bleared and scarlet, or simply sore?

VOLTAIRE'S ORIGINAL

Je n'ai pas eu toujours les yeux éraillés et bordés d'écarlate; mon nez n'a pas toujours touché à mon menton, et je n'ai pas toujours été servante. Je suis la fille du pape Urbain X et de la princesse de Palestrine. On m'éleva jusqu'à quatorze ans dans un palais .... J'inspirais déjà de l'amour; ma gorge se formait; et quelle gorge! blanche, ferme, taillée comme celle de la Vénus de Médicis ... Les femmes qui m'habillaient et qui me déshabillaient tombaient en extase en me regardant par-devant et par-derrière; et tous les hommes auraient voulu être à leur place.

1759 TRANSLATION

I had not always sore eyes; neither did my nose always touch my chin; nor was I always a servant: I am the daughter of pope Urban X and of the princess of Palestrina. To the age of fourteen, I was brought up in a palace .... Now I began to inspire the men with love. My neck was come to its right shape: and such a neck! white, erect, and exactly formed like that of the Venus of Medicis. ... My waiting-women, in dressing and undressing me, used to fall into an ecstasy, whether they viewed me before or behind: and how glad would the gentlemen have been to perform that office for them!

VICTORIAN TRANSLATION

My eyes have not always been bleared, and bordered with scarlet; my nose has not always touched my chin; nor have I always been a servant. I am the daughter of a king, and the Princess of Palestrina. I was brought up, till I was fourteen, in a palace. . . . I began to captivate every heart. My neck was formed—oh, what a neck! white, firm, and shaped like that of the Venus de Medici. . . . The maids who dressed and undressed me fell into an ecstasy when they viewed me, and all the men would gladly have been in their places.

ROBERT M. ADAMS TRANSLATION (1991)

My eyes were not always bloodshot and red-rimmed, my nose did not always touch my chin, and I was not born a servant. I am in fact the daughter of Pope Urban the Tenth and the Princess of Palestrina. Till the age of fourteen, I lived in a palace. . . . Already I was inspiring the young men to love; my breast was formed— and what a breast! white, firm, with the shape of the Venus de Medici. . . . The women who helped me dress and undress fell into ecstasies, whether they looked at me from in front or behind; and all the men wanted to be in their place.

DANIEL GORDON TRANSLATION (1998)

My eyes were not always crusty and bloodshot, my nose did not always touch my chin, and I was not always a servant. I am the daughter of Pope Urban X and the Princess of Palestrina. I lived until the age of fourteen in a palace .. . . I was beginning to inspire love. My bosom was forming, and what a bosom! White, firm, sculptured like the ancient statue of Venus. . . . The women who dressed and undressed me fell into ecstasies when they beheld me from the front and from the rear, and any man would have desired to be in their place.

━━ ▆◆▆ ━━

Alexander Pope
1688–1744

Alexander Pope was perhaps the most celebrated poet of the eighteenth century. He was also a tiny hunchback and a Catholic during a rabidly anti-Catholic time in England. The sufferings he endured because of his deformity and religion jaundiced his view of humanity. Satire became his preferred mode. Yet this "hunch-backed toad," as one critic called him (toads were believed to spit poison) was also known for his "general benevolence and particular fondness," in the words of another. Like the philosopher Kant, he cultivated close friendships in the absence of sexual relationships. Aside from his satiric genius, he was acknowledged a master of all the neoclassical genres that predominated in the poetic practice of his age. Through them all he developed what remains his signature style: the rhyming "heroic couplets" in which he delivers nuggets of wisdom.

For Pope, Fate took the form of a wayward cow. He was trampled by one at age twelve, severely wounded, and thereafter developed a spinal infection that within a few years transformed a pretty child into a "little, tender, and crazy Carcass," as one of his early mentors, the playwright William Wycherley, lamented. Thus began what Pope later described as "this long disease, my life." His weakness and deformity made him unable to dress or undress himself; a maid had to help him in and out of the fur undergarment he wore because of his extreme sensitivity to cold, lace up the corset without which he could not stand upright, and cover it all with a warm shirt and flannel waistcoat, shortened on one side. At table he had to have his seat raised, like a child's. Worse than all this, he was in constant pain. He suffered especially from headaches, which he tried to treat by inhaling coffee vapors (like his character the Baron in his great mock-epic satire, *The Rape of the Lock*).

It was no mere accident that the young Alexander was out roaming the countryside, dangerously exposed to rural misadventures. His parents, a London linen merchant and his second wife, had just been forced to leave the city for the country village of Binfield, near Windsor. They were complying with recent laws designed to bar Catholics like themselves from any significant resources or advantages, and especially from government—so that they were no longer allowed to live within ten miles of the royal seat in London. The Protestant rulers William and Mary, who ousted Mary's Catholic father King James II in their "Glorious Revolution" the year of Pope's birth, intended to end forever the long and bloody history of struggle between Catholic and Protestant factions for control of the English throne, which stretched back to the heirs of Henry VIII in the sixteenth century. They succeeded—partly by encouraging the enactment of particularly harsh anti-Catholic legislation. In addition to being exiled from London and forbidden to celebrate mass in public, Catholics were excluded from attending public schools or universities, from holding public office or voting in elections, and from owning real estate or inheriting it. The severity of these restrictions varied even during Pope's lifetime, but Catholics would not regain equal rights with other British subjects until 1829: one year after Protestant dissenters, four years before slaves, and eighty-nine years before women of any persuasion or social standing. Meanwhile widespread prejudice saw all Catholics in Britain as potential traitors. Pope suffered as much under this social disability as he did under his physical one.

Luckily young Alexander encountered some human neighbors in the countryside who influenced the course of his life in positive ways. There he met William Wycherley and through him his fellow-dramatist William Congreve, the poet William Walsh, and the statesman Sir William Trumbull. With a little help from these and other friends Pope continued his study of classical languages and literature on his own, and traveled to London to study French and Italian. By these efforts he became as able a classicist as any trained at Oxford or Cambridge. When Pope was still only seventeen, through the good offices of Walsh and Congreve his poetry came to the attention of prominent publisher Jacob Tonson, who brought out Pope's first publication several years later. Several early publications, including a first version of *The Rape of the Lock,* gave him an entree to London literary circles, and he tried to maintain good relations with the Whig associates of the essayists Addison and Steele even as he became closely associated with Jonathan Swift and the other Tory members of the Scriblerus Club, a short-lived but influential group of satirists.

It is a tried–and–true strategy of writers who would become great men to edit or translate the great men of yore, thus elevating themselves by association. This strategy worked brilliantly for Pope. By 1713, having made enough of a name for himself with his first publications to attract subscribers to his next, he agreed to translate Homer's *Iliad* and *Odyssey.* "What terrible moments does one feel, after one has engaged for large work!" he later wrote. "In the beginning of my translating the *Iliad,* I wished anybody would hang me, a hundred times." The hard work paid off, however, for it was this translation that made Pope truly famous, and moreover made him rich. It made him the first commercially successful English poet: the first, that is, to earn enough from the sale of his published works to dispense with the previously indispensable noble patrons, royal pension, or politically appointed sinecure. "Thanks to Homer," as he acknowledged in his *Imitations of Horace* (*Epistle* 2.2), he could henceforth "live and thrive, / Indebted to no Prince or Peer alive."

So established was Pope's reputation by the first volumes of his *Iliad* that he soon ventured to publish his collected *Works of Alexander Pope* (1717), though he was still in his twenties. That same year Pope's father died, and during the next he moved into a rented villa called Twickenham, at the regulation distance from London. It became famous for the gardens he created there. Its five acres of land were unfortunately separated from the house by the highway to London, and Pope, declaring that "what we cannot *overcome,* we must *undergo,*" caused the two areas to be joined by a tunnel, which he grandiosely christened his "Grotto of Friendship and Liberty." This burrow actually became the most elaborate and most celebrated part of his whole landscape garden. He decorated its surfaces with semiprecious and other exotic stones, marble, glass, and shells. Comparing it favorably to his poetic creations, he called it his "best imitation of nature," and invited only his best friends to share this favorite retreat from the outside world.

While finishing his translation of the *Odyssey* Pope tried to repeat the marketing strategy that had worked so well for him, by editing the works of Shakespeare (1725). He thought even less of this type of literary labor than he had of translating, lamenting that he had sunk, "by due gradation of dulness, from a poet a translator, and from a translator, a mere editor." Indeed his bowdlerized versions of the plays were soon discredited by contemporary Shakespeare scholars. Pope lashed out in revenge against anyone who had ever made him feel small in *The Dunciad* (1728), in which he attacked his former friend Lady Mary Wortley Montagu, the popular novelist Eliza Haywood, and nearly every other writer alive. This satirical mock-epic purported to trace "the Progress of Dulness" in the characters of the hack writers, or "dunces" of the day—authors who, like Pope himself, were attempting to make writing a commercially successful enterprise. Pope continued another fifteen years engaged in his brilliantly successful manipulation of the medium of print to disparage other writers and enhance his own image. He published *An Essay on Man* anonymously in 1733–1734, for fear of attacks by the hordes of literary enemies he'd made with his earlier satires, and even got his friends to rally his enemies to support its unknown author as a new "rival" to Pope's literary supremacy. He then published his own letters while he was still alive (1737), after strategically editing them. Not many years later he died, surrounded by friends in spite of his printed vituperations. Some of these friends feared that he had hastened his demise by his habit of using a silver saucepan to heat his favorite dish of potted lampreys. When asked on his deathbed by a Catholic friend whether a priest should be called so that he could "die like his father and mother," Pope replied, "I do not think it essential, but it will be very right; and I thank you for putting me in mind of it." He left the fortune he had amassed to his dear friend Martha Blount, with whom he had been in love all his life.

THE RAPE OF THE LOCK (1712–1717)

The Rape of the Lock is Pope's mocking response to a real-life incident in which two Catholic families of high standing feuded after the scion of one, Robert, Lord Petre, snipped a love-lock from the unwilling daughter of the other, Miss Arabella Fermor. Their mutual friend John Caryll asked Pope to try and "laugh them together again" by writing a poem that would make a joke of the whole affair.

Pope's method was to highlight the absurdity of this tempest in a teapot by comparing small things to great: writing an epic on the model of Homer and Virgil with this minor social squabble as its subject and the trivial, domestic world of English high society as its setting. In this plan he had in mind recent models of comic mock-epics, notably Boileau's *Le Lutrin,* (1674, 1683), which similarly satirized a dispute among priests over an object of little more than symbolic significance (a lectern). Pope published his first version in 1712, which seemed only to aggravate the original quarrel by the public attention it attracted. In 1714 and 1717, as he progressed in his work of translating Homer, he offered the public revised and expanded versions, each time adding more specific—and thus more ludicrous—parallels to the classical epics. The Homeric rape of Helen—the abduction that led to the Trojan War—becomes the violation of a modern society belle's elaborate coiffure. Her lament, "Oh hadst thou, cruel! been content to seize / Hairs less in sight, or any hairs but these!" exposes with ribald humor the misplaced value with which, Pope implies, his contemporaries invested outward signs of honor and status to the neglect of real virtue. In keeping with its original conciliatory intent, however, this poem is far lighter in tone, less bitter and brittle than more ruthless satires like *The Dunciad*. As Pope himself described it to friend, "'Tis a sort of writing very like tickling."

The Rape of the Lock
An Heroi-Comical Poem in Five Cantos

Nolueram, Belinda, *tuos violare capillos*
Sed juvat hoc precibus me tribuisse tuis.

Martial[1]

TO MRS. ARABELLA FERMOR

MADAM,

It will be in vain to deny that I have some regard for this piece, since I dedicate it to you. Yet you may bear me witness, it was intended only to divert a few young ladies, who have good sense and good humour enough to laugh not only at their sex's little unguarded follies, but at their own.[2] But as it was communicated with the air of a secret, it soon found its way into the world. An imperfect copy having been offered to a bookseller, you had the good-nature, for my sake, to consent to the publication of one more correct. This I was forced to, before I had executed half my design, for the machinery was entirely wanting to complete it.

The machinery, Madam, is a term invented by the critics, to signify that part which the deities, angels, or demons, are made to act in a poem. For the ancient poets are in one respect like many modern ladies, let an action be never so trivial in itself, they always make it appear of the utmost importance. These machines I determined to raise on a very new and odd foundation, the Rosicrucian[3] doctrine of spirits.

I know how disagreeable it is to make use of hard words before a lady; but it is so much the concern of a poet to have his works understood, and particularly by your sex, that you must give me leave to explain two or three difficult terms.

The Rosicrucians are a people I must bring you acquainted with. The best account I know of them is in a French book, called Le Comte de Gabalis,[4] which both in its title and size is so like a novel, that many of the fair sex have read it for one by mistake. According to these gentlemen the four elements are inhabited by spirits, which they call sylphs, gnomes, nymphs, and salamanders.[5] The gnomes or demons of earth delight in mischief; but the sylphs, whose habitation is in the air, are the best conditioned[6] creatures imaginable. For they say, any mortals may enjoy the most intimate familiarities with these gentle spirits, upon a condition very easy to all true adepts, an inviolate preservation of chastity.

As to the following cantos, all the passages of them are as fabulous,[7] as the vision at the beginning, or the transformation at the end, except the loss of your hair, which I always mention with reverence. The human persons are as fictitious as the airy ones; and the character of Belinda, as it is now managed, resembles you in nothing but in beauty.

If this poem had as many graces as there are in your person, or in your mind, yet I could never hope it should pass through the world half so uncensured as you have

---

1. "I did not wish, [Belinda,] to violate your locks, but I rejoice to have yielded this to your wishes" (Martial, *Epigrams* 12.84). Pope has substituted "Belinda" for Martial's "Polytimus."
2. I.e., at their own individual follies as well.
3. A secret society of the 17th and 18th centuries, devoted to the study of ancient religious, philosophical, and mystical doctrines.
4. Written in 1670 by the Abbé de Monfaucon de Villars, its approach to Rosicrucian philosophy was lighthearted.
5. Elemental spirits living in fire.
6. Best natured.
7. Fictional.

done. But let its fortune be what it will, mine is happy enough, to have given me this occasion of assuring you that I am, with the truest esteem,

Madam,
Your most obedient, humble servant,
A. POPE

CANTO 1

WHAT dire offence from am'rous causes springs,
What mighty contests rise from trivial things,
I sing[8]—This verse to Caryll,[9] Muse! is due:
This, ev'n Belinda may vouchsafe to view:
5 Slight is the subject, but not so the praise,
If she inspire, and he approve my lays.°   *verses*
    Say what strange motive, goddess!° could compel   *his Muse*
A well-bred lord t' assault a gentle belle?
O say what stranger cause, yet unexplored,
10 Could make a gentle belle reject a lord?
In tasks so bold, can little men engage,
And in soft bosoms, dwells such mighty rage?
    Sol through white curtains shot a tim'rous ray,
And ope'd those eyes that must eclipse the day:
15 Now lap-dogs[1] give themselves the rousing shake,
And sleepless lovers, just at twelve, awake:
Thrice rung the bell, the slipper knocked the ground,[2]
And the pressed watch returned a silver sound.[3]
Belinda still her downy pillow pressed,
20 Her guardian sylph prolonged the balmy rest:
'Twas he had summoned to her silent bed
The morning dream that hovered o'er her head,
A youth more glitt'ring than a birth-night beau,[4]
(That ev'n in slumber caused her cheek to glow)
25 Seemed to her ear his winning lips to lay,
And thus in whispers said, or seemed to say.[5]
    "Fairest of mortals, thou distinguished care
Of thousand bright inhabitants of air!
If e'er one vision touched thy infant thought,
30 Of all the nurse and all the priest have taught;[6]
Of airy elves by moonlight shadows seen,

---

8. Pope begins with the ancient epic formula of "proposition" of the work as a whole, and "invocation" of the gods' assistance, continuing with the traditional epic questions.
9. John Caryll, a mutual friend of Pope and the Fermor family. See page 523.
1. Small dogs imported from Asia were highly fashionable ladies' pets at this time.
2. Belinda rings the bell and then finally bangs her slipper on the floor to call her maid.

3. The popular "pressed watch" chimed the hour and quarter hours when its stem was pressed, saving its owner from striking a match to see the time.
4. On a royal birthday, courtiers' clothes were particularly extravagant.
5. His whispering recalls the serpent's temptation of Eve in Milton's *Paradise Lost.*
6. The nurse and priest were seen as two standard sources of superstition.

The silver token, and the circled green,[7]
Or virgins visited by angel-pow'rs[8]
With golden crowns and wreaths of heav'nly flow'rs;
35   Hear and believe! thy own importance know,
Nor bound thy narrow views to things below.
Some secret truths, from learned pride concealed,
To maids alone and children are revealed.
What though no credit doubting wits may give?[9]
40   The fair and innocent shall still believe.
Know then, unnumbered spirits round thee fly,
The light militia of the lower sky:
These, though unseen, are ever on the wing,
Hang o'er the box, and hover round the ring.[1]
45   Think what an equipage[2] thou hast in air,
And view with scorn two pages and a chair.[3]
As now your own, our beings were of old,
And once inclosed in woman's beauteous mould;
Thence, by a soft transition, we repair
50   From earthly vehicles[4] to these of air.
Think not, when woman's transient breath is fled,
That all her vanities at once are dead;
Succeeding vanities she still regards,
And though she plays no more, o'erlooks the cards.
55   Her joy in gilded chariots, when alive,
And love of ombre,[5] after death survive.
For when the fair in all their pride expire,
To their first elements,[6] their souls retire:
The sprites of fiery termagants° in flame   *scolding women*
60   Mount up, and take a salamander's name.
Soft yielding minds to water glide away,
And sip, with nymphs, their elemental tea.
The graver prude sinks downward to a gnome,
In search of mischief still on earth to roam.
65   The light coquettes in sylphs aloft repair,
And sport and flutter in the fields of air.
    "Know further yet; whoever fair and chaste
Rejects mankind, is by some sylph embraced:
For spirits, freed from mortal laws, with ease
70   Assume what sexes and what shapes they please.[7]

---

7. Withered circles in the grass and silver coins were supposed to be signs of fairies' presence.
8. Belinda is reminded of the many virgin saints, and particularly the Annunciation of the Virgin Mary.
9. Religious skepticism was on the increase.
1. The theater box and the equally fashionable drive round Hyde Park.
2. Carriage, horses, and attendants.
3. A sedan chair, carried by two chairmen.
4. Both the carriage, and the physical body.

5. Ombre (pronounced "Omber") was an elaborate card game. Pope may also be punning on the origin of the word "Ombre," from the Spanish *hombre*, meaning "man."
6. The four elements of fire, water, earth, and air were thought to make up all things; so an individual's character was determined by whichever element dominated his or her soul.
7. Cf. *Paradise Lost*, "For spirits when they please / Can either sex assume, or both" (1.423–24).

What guards the purity of melting maids,
In courtly balls, and midnight masquerades,
Safe from the treach'rous friend, the daring spark,°   *bold young man*
The glance by day, the whisper in the dark,
75   When kind occasion prompts their warm desires,
When music softens, and when dancing fires?
"'Tis but their sylph, the wise celestials know,
Though honour is the word with men below.
      "Some nymphs there are, too conscious of their face,
80   For life predestined to the gnomes' embrace.
These swell their prospects and exalt their pride,
When offers are disdained, and love denied:
Then gay ideas crowd the vacant brain,
While peers° and dukes, and all their sweeping train,   *aristocrats*
85   And garters, stars, and coronets[8] appear,
And in soft sounds 'Your Grace'[9] salutes their ear.
'Tis these that early taint the female soul,
Instruct the eyes of young coquettes to roll,
Teach infant-cheeks a bidden° blush to know,   *deliberate*
90   And little hearts to flutter at a beau.
      "Oft, when the world imagine women stray,
The sylphs through mystic mazes guide their way,
Through all the giddy circle they pursue,
And old impertinence° expel by new.   *frivolity*
95   What tender maid but must a victim fall
To one man's treat, but for another's ball?
When Florio speaks, what virgin could withstand,
If gentle Damon did not squeeze her hand?
With varying vanities, from ev'ry part,
100   They shift the moving toyshop[1] of their heart;
Where wigs with wigs, with sword-knots sword-knots strive,[2]
Beaux banish beaux, and coaches coaches drive.[3]
This erring mortals levity may call;
Oh blind to truth! the sylphs contrive it all.
105   "Of these am I, who thy protection claim,
A watchful sprite, and Ariel is my name.
Late, as I ranged the crystal wilds of air,
In the clear mirror of thy ruling star
I saw, alas! some dread event impend,
110   Ere to the main° this morning sun descend.   *sea*
But heaven reveals not what, or how, or where:
Warned by the sylph, oh pious maid, beware!
This to disclose is all thy guardian can:
Beware of all, but most beware of man!"

---

8. Emblems of noble rank.
9. Form of address for a duke or a duchess.
1. Where toys and trinkets are sold; "moving" here means easily changed, unstable.

2. Most men wore wigs in public; formally dressed men tied ribbons to the hilt of their swords.
3. These two lines mimic both Homer's and Ovid's description of heroic combat.

115	He said; when Shock,° who thought she slept too long,	*her poodle*
	Leaped up, and waked his mistress with his tongue;	
	'Twas then, Belinda, if report say true,	
	Thy eyes first opened on a billet-doux;°	*love letter*
	Wounds, charms, and ardours, were no sooner read,	
120	But all the vision vanished from thy head.	
	And now, unveiled, the toilet° stands displayed,	*dressing table*
	Each silver vase in mystic order laid.	
	First, robed in white, the nymph intent adores,	
	With head uncovered, the cosmetic pow'rs.	
125	A heav'nly image⁴ in the glass appears,	
	To that she bends, to that her eyes she rears°	*raises*
	Th' inferior priestess,⁵ at her altar's side,	
	Trembling begins the sacred rites of pride.	
	Unnumbered treasures ope at once, and here	
130	The various off'rings of the world appear;	
	From each she nicely culls with curious° toil,	*careful*
	And decks the goddess with the glitt'ring spoil.	
	This casket India's glowing gems unlocks,	
	And all Arabia° breathes from yonder box.	*eastern perfume*
135	The tortoise here and elephant unite,	
	Transformed to combs, the speckled, and the white.⁶	
	Here files of pins extend their shining rows,	
	Puffs, powders, patches, bibles,⁷ billets-doux.	
	Now awful° beauty puts on all its arms;	*awe-inspiring*
140	The fair each moment rises in her charms,	
	Repairs her smiles, awakens ev'ry grace,	
	And calls forth all the wonders of her face;	
	Sees by degrees a purer blush° arise,	*rouge*
	And keener lightnings⁸ quicken in her eyes.	
145	The busy sylphs surround their darling care,	
	These set the head, and those divide the hair,	
	Some fold the sleeve, whilst others plait° the gown;	*pleat*
	And Betty's praised for labours not her own.	

Canto 2

	Not with more glories, in th' ethereal plain,°	*sky*
	The sun first rises o'er the purpled main,	
	Than, issuing forth, the rival of his beams	
	Launched on the bosom of the silver Thames.¹	
5	Fair nymphs, and well-dressed youths around her shone,	
	But ev'ry eye was fixed on her alone.	

---

4. I.e., Belinda herself.
5. Belinda's maid, Betty.
6. Tortoise-shell and ivory.
7. Patches were small beauty spots of black silk, pasted onto the face to make the skin appear whiter. It was fashionable to own Bibles in very small format.

8. Caused by drops of belladonna (deadly nightshade), which dilates the pupils.
1. Belinda takes a boat from London to Hampton Court, avoiding the dirt and squalor of the streets; her voyage compares with Aeneas's up the Tiber (*Aeneid* 7), or Cleopatra's up the Nile (*Antony and Cleopatra* 2.2).

On her white breast a sparkling cross she wore,
Which Jews might kiss, and infidels adore.
Her lively looks a sprightly mind disclose,
10   Quick as her eyes, and as unfixed as those;
Favours to none, to all she smiles extends;
Oft she rejects, but never once offends.
Bright as the sun, her eyes the gazers strike,
And, like the sun, they shine on all alike.
15   Yet graceful ease, and sweetness void of pride,
Might hide her faults, if belles had faults to hide;
If to her share some female errors fall,
Look on her face, and you'll forget 'em all.
     This nymph, to the destruction of mankind,
20   Nourished two locks, which graceful hung behind
In equal curls, and well conspired to deck,
With shining ringlets, the smooth iv'ry neck.
Love in these labyrinths his slaves detains,
And mighty hearts are held in slender chains.
25   With hairy springes° we the birds betray,   *noose traps*
Slight lines° of hair surprise the finny prey,   *fishing lines*
Fair tresses man's imperial race insnare,
And beauty draws us with a single hair.
     Th' advent'rous baron[2] the bright locks admired;
30   He saw, he wished, and to the prize aspired.
Resolved to win, he meditates the way,
By force to ravish, or by fraud betray;
For when success a lover's toil attends,
Few ask, if fraud or force attained his ends.
35   For this, ere Phoebus[3] rose, he had implored
Propitious heav'n, and ev'ry pow'r adored,°   *worshipped*
But chiefly Love—to Love an altar built,
Of twelve vast French romances, neatly gilt.
There lay three garters, half a pair of gloves,
40   And all the trophies of his former loves;
With tender billets-doux he lights the pyre,
And breathes three am'rous sighs to raise the fire.
Then prostrate falls, and begs with ardent eyes
Soon to obtain, and long possess the prize:
45   The pow'rs gave ear, and granted half his pray'r,
The rest, the winds dispersed in empty air.[4]
     But now secure the painted vessel glides,
The sun-beams trembling on the floating tides:
While melting music steals upon the sky,
50   And softened sounds along the waters die;
Smooth flow the waves, the zephyrs° gently play,   *breezes*

2. Robert, Lord Petre (1690–1713), responsible for the original incident.
3. Phoebus Apollo, Greek sun god.

4. Cf. *The Aeneid* 2.794–95, which Dryden translated: "Apollo heard, and granting half his pray'r, / Shuffled in winds the rest, and toss'd in empty air."

Belinda smiled, and all the world was gay.
All but the sylph—with careful° thoughts oppressed,   *worried*
Th' impending woe sat heavy on his breast.
He summons straight his denizens° of air;   *residents*
The lucid squadrons round the sails repair:
Soft o'er the shrouds° aërial whispers breathe,   *ropes*
That seemed but zephyrs to the train beneath.
Some to the sun their insect-wings unfold,
Waft on the breeze, or sink in clouds of gold;
Transparent forms, too fine for mortal sight,
Their fluid bodies half dissolved in light.
Loose to the wind their airy garments flew,
Thin glitt'ring textures of the filmy dew,
Dipped in the richest tincture of the skies,
Where light disports in ever-mingling dyes;
While ev'ry beam new transient colours flings,
Colours that change whene'er they wave their wings.
Amid the circle, on the gilded mast,
Superior by the head, was Ariel placed;[5]
His purple pinions opening to the sun,
He raised his azure wand, and thus begun.
        "Ye sylphs and sylphids,° to your chief give ear!   *female sylphs*
Fays, fairies, genii, elves, and demons, hear!
Ye know the spheres, and various tasks assigned
By laws eternal to th' aërial kind.
Some in the fields of purest ether[6] play,
And bask and whiten in the blaze of day.
Some guide the course of wand'ring orbs° on high,   *comets*
Or roll the planets through the boundless sky.
Some less refined, beneath the moon's pale light
Pursue the stars that shoot athwart the night,
Or suck the mists in grosser° air below,   *heavier*
Or dip their pinions in the painted bow,°   *rainbow*
Or brew fierce tempests on the wintry main,
Or o'er the glebe° distil the kindly rain.   *farmland*
Others on earth o'er human race preside,
Watch all their ways, and all their actions guide:
Of these the chief the care of nations own,
And guard with arms divine the British throne.
        "Our humbler province is to tend the fair,
Not a less pleasing, though less glorious care;
To save the powder from too rude° a gale,   *rough*
Nor let th' imprisoned essences° exhale;   *perfumes*
To draw fresh colours from the vernal flow'rs;
To steal from rainbows ere they drop in show'rs
A brighter wash[7]; to curl their waving hairs,

5. Heroes of epics were typically taller than their men.   7. A cosmetic rinse.
6. Air beyond the moon.

Assist their blushes, and inspire their airs;
Nay oft, in dreams, invention we bestow,
100   To change a flounce, or add a furbelow.°   *ruffle*
       "This day, black omens threat the brightest fair
That e'er deserved a watchful spirit's care;
Some dire disaster, or° by force, or slight;°   *either / trick*
But what, or where, the fates have wrapped in night.
105   Whether the nymph shall break Diana's law,°   *virginity*
Or some frail china jar receive a flaw;
Or stain her honour, or her new brocade;
Forget her pray'rs, or miss a masquerade;
Or lose her heart, or necklace at a ball;
110   Or whether heav'n has doomed that Shock must fall.
Haste then, ye spirits! to your charge° repair: *duty*
The flutt'ring fan be Zephyretta's care;
The drops° to thee, Brillante, we consign;   *earrings*
And, Momentilla, let the watch be thine;
115   Do thou, Crispissa,[8] tend her fav'rite lock;
Ariel himself shall be the guard of Shock.
       "To fifty chosen Sylphs, of special note,
We trust th' important charge, the petticoat:
Oft have we known that seven-fold fence[9] to fail,
120   Though stiff with hoops and armed with ribs of whale;
Form a strong line about the silver bound,
And guard the wide circumference around.
       "Whatever spirit, careless of his charge,
His post neglects, or leaves the fair at large,
125   Shall feel sharp vengeance soon o'ertake his sins,
Be stopped in vials, or transfixed with pins;
Or plunged in lakes of bitter washes lie,
Or wedged, whole ages, in a bodkin's[1] eye:
Gums and pomatums° shall his flight restrain,   *ointments*
130   While clogged he beats his silken wings in vain;
Or alum styptics[2] with contracting pow'r
Shrink his thin essence like a rivelled° flow'r: *shriveled*
Or, as Ixion fixed, the wretch shall feel
The giddy motion of the whirling mill,[3]
135   In fumes of burning chocolate shall glow,
And tremble at the sea that froths below!"
       He spoke; the spirits from the sails descend:
Some, orb in orb, around the nymph extend;
Some thrid° the mazy ringlets of her hair;   *slid through*

---

8. The Latin *crispere* means "to curl."
9. Serving Belinda like the epic warrior's shield, her petticoat has seven layers bound together with a silver band (cf. *Iliad* 18 or *Aeneid* 8).
1. Blunt, thick needle; the Sylph, like the camel in Matthew 19:24, has difficulty getting through. Pope later plays on the various meanings of "bodkin," which also include a hair ornament and a dagger.
2. Astringents that stopped bleeding.
3. For grinding cocoa beans for chocolate, a new and highly fashionable drink. Ixion was punished by being tied to a revolving wheel of fire, after trying to seduce the goddess Hera.

140   Some hang upon the pendants of her ear;
       With beating hearts the dire event they wait,
       Anxious, and trembling for the birth of fate.

Canto 3

       Close by those meads, for ever crowned with flow'rs,
       Where Thames with pride surveys his rising tow'rs,
       There stands a structure of majestic frame,
       Which from the neighb'ring Hampton takes its name.[1]
5   Here Britain's statesmen oft the fall foredoom
       Of foreign tyrants, and of nymphs at home;
       Here thou, great ANNA! whom three realms obey,[2]
       Dost sometimes counsel take—and sometimes tea.
           Hither the heroes and the nymphs resort,
10   To taste awhile the pleasures of a court;
       In various talk th' instructive hours they passed,
       Who gave the ball, or paid the visit last;
       One speaks the glory of the British Queen,
       And one describes a charming Indian screen;
15   A third interprets motions, looks, and eyes;
       At ev'ry word a reputation dies.
       Snuff, or the fan, supply each pause of chat,
       With singing, laughing, ogling, and all that.
           Meanwhile, declining from the noon of day,
20   The sun obliquely shoots his burning ray;
       The hungry judges soon the sentence sign,
       And wretches hang that jury-men may dine;
       The merchant from th' Exchange° returns in peace,   *market*
       And the long labours of the toilet cease.
25   Belinda now, whom thirst of fame invites,
       Burns to encounter two advent'rous knights,
       At ombre[3] singly to decide their doom;
       And swells her breast with conquests yet to come.
       Straight the three bands prepare in arms to join,
30   Each band the number of the sacred nine.[4]
       Soon as she spreads her hand, th' aërial guard
       Descend, and sit on each important card:
       First Ariel perched upon a Matadore,[5]
       Then each according to the rank they bore;
35   For sylphs, yet mindful of their ancient race,
       Are, as when women, wondrous fond of place.°   *rank*

---

1. Hampton Court, about 15 miles upriver from London, was built in the 16th century by Cardinal Wolsey, and by Queen Anne's day was associated with wits as well as with statesmen.
2. England, Scotland, and Ireland.
3. A card game played with 40 cards, similar to modern bridge: three players hold nine cards each and bid for tricks, with the highest bidder becoming the "ombre" (man) and choosing trumps.
4. Pope links the nine Muses to the nine cards each player holds.
5. The Matadores are the three cards of highest value; Belinda holds all three: when trumps are black, they are the Spadillio (ace of spades), Manillio (deuce of spades), and Basto (ace of clubs).

Behold, four kings, in majesty revered,
With hoary whiskers[6] and a forky beard;
And four fair queens whose hands sustain° a flow'r,   *hold*
40 Th' expressive emblem of their softer pow'r;
Four knaves in garbs succinct,° a trusty band;   *girded up*
Caps on their heads, and halberts in their hand;
And parti-coloured troops, a shining train,
Draw forth to combat on the velvet plain.[7]
45   The skilful nymph reviews her force with care:
Let spades be trumps! she said, and trumps they were.[8]
    Now move to war her sable Matadores,
In show like leaders of the swarthy Moors.
Spadillio first, unconquerable lord!
50 Led off two captive trumps, and swept the board.
As many more Manillio forced to yield,
And marched a victor from the verdant field.
Him Basto followed, but his fate more hard
Gained but one trump and one plebeian card.
55 With his broad sabre next, a chief in years,
The hoary majesty of spades appears,
Puts forth one manly leg, to sight revealed,
The rest, his many-coloured robe concealed.
The rebel knave, who dares his prince engage,
60 Proves the just victim of his royal rage.
Ev'n mighty Pam,[9] that kings and queens o'erthrew,
And mowed down armies in the fights of loo,
Sad chance of war! now destitute of aid,
Falls undistinguished by the victor spade!
65   Thus far both armies to Belinda yield;
Now to the baron fate inclines the field.
His warlike Amazon her host invades,
Th' imperial consort of the crown of spades.
The club's black tyrant first her victim died,
70 Spite of his haughty mien, and barb'rous pride:
What boots the regal circle on his head,
His giant limbs, in state unwieldy spread;
That long behind he trails his pompous robe,
And of all monarchs only grasps the globe?
75   The baron now his diamonds pours apace!
Th' embroidered king who shows but half his face,
And his refulgent queen, with pow'rs combined,
Of broken troops, an easy conquest find.
Clubs, diamonds, hearts, in wild disorder seen,

6. Gray mustache. The royal figures on the cards now conduct a mock-epic review of their forces, and the whole game is described as an epic battle, with the characters appearing as on the cards.
7. The green velvet card table.
8. "Then God said, 'Let there be light'; and there was light" (Genesis 1:3).
9. The knave or jack of clubs, which took precedence over all trumps in the game of Lu, or Loo.

80   With throngs promiscuous strew the level green.
        Thus when dispersed a routed army runs,
        Of Asia's troops, and Afric's sable sons,
        With like confusion different nations fly,
        Of various habit, and of various dye;
85   The pierced battalions disunited fall,
        In heaps on heaps; one fate o'erwhelms them all.
            The knave of diamonds tries his wily arts,
        And wins (oh shameful chance!) the queen of hearts.
        At this, the blood the virgin's cheek forsook,
90   A livid paleness spreads o'er all her look;
        She sees, and trembles at th' approaching ill,
        Just in the jaws of ruin, and codille.[1]
        And now (as oft in some distempered state)
        On one nice trick[2] depends the gen'ral fate:
95   An ace of hearts steps forth: the king[3] unseen
        Lurked in her hand, and mourned his captive queen:
        He springs to vengeance with an eager pace,
        And falls like thunder on the prostrate ace.
        The nymph exulting fills with shouts the sky;
100   The walls, the woods, and long canals reply.
            Oh thoughtless mortals! ever blind to fate,
        Too soon dejected, and too soon elate.
        Sudden these honours shall be snatched away,
        And cursed for ever this victorious day.
105   For lo! the board with cups and spoons is crowned;
        The berries crackle, and the mill turns round;[4]
        On shining altars of japan[5] they raise
        The silver lamp; the fiery spirits blaze:
        From silver spouts the grateful° liquors glide,   *pleasing*
110   While China's earth receives the smoking tide:
        At once they gratify their scent and taste,
        And frequent cups prolong the rich repast.
        Straight° hover round the fair her airy band;   *immediately*
        Some, as she sipped, the fuming liquor fanned,
115   Some o'er her lap their careful plumes displayed,
        Trembling, and conscious of the rich brocade.
        Coffee (which makes the politician wise,
        And see through all things with his half-shut eyes)
        Sent up in vapours[6] to the baron's brain
120   New stratagems, the radiant lock to gain.
        Ah cease, rash youth! desist ere 'tis too late,
        Fear the just gods, and think of Scylla's fate![7]

---

1. Literally "elbow": the defeat suffered by the ombre if another player wins more tricks.
2. Trick applies in both its technical and general senses as Belinda makes this careful maneuver.
3. The King of Hearts.
4. Grinding coffee beans.
5. Lacquered tables.
6. Both steam and vain imaginations.
7. Scylla plucked purple hair from the head of her father, King Nisus, to offer to her lover, Minos, so destroying her father's power. Minos rejected her impiety, and Scylla was transformed into a bird.

Changed to a bird, and sent to flit in air,
She dearly pays for Nisus' injured hair!
125   But when to mischief mortals bend their will,
How soon they find fit instruments of ill!
Just then, Clarissa drew with tempting grace
A two-edged weapon from her shining case:
So ladies in romance assist their knight,
130 Present the spear, and arm him for the fight.
He takes the gift with rev'rence, and extends
The little engine° on his fingers' ends;   *instrument*
This just behind Belinda's neck he spread,
As o'er the fragrant steams she bends her head.
135 Swift to the lock a thousand sprites repair,
A thousand wings, by turns, blow back the hair;
And thrice they twitched the diamond in her ear;
Thrice she looked back, and thrice the foe drew near.
Just in that instant, anxious Ariel sought
140 The close recesses of the virgin's thought:
As on the nosegay in her breast reclined,
He watched th' ideas rising in her mind,
Sudden he viewed in spite of all her art,
An earthly lover° lurking at her heart.   *Lord Petre*
145 Amazed, confused, he found his pow'r expired,
Resigned to fate, and with a sigh retired.
    The peer now spreads the glitt'ring forfex° wide,   *scissors*
T' inclose the lock; now joins it, to divide.
Ev'n then, before the fatal engine closed,
150 A wretched sylph too fondly interposed;
Fate urged the shears, and cut the sylph in twain,
(But airy substance soon unites again,)[8]
The meeting points the sacred hair dissever
From the fair head, for ever, and for ever!
155   Then flashed the living lightning from her eyes,
And screams of horror rend th' affrighted skies,
Not louder shrieks to pitying heav'n are cast,
When husbands, or when lap-dogs breathe their last;
Or when rich china vessels fall'n from high,
160 In glitt'ring dust, and painted fragments lie!
    "Let wreaths of triumph now my temples twine,"
(The victor cried,) "the glorious prize is mine!
While fish in streams, or birds delight in air,
Or in a coach and six[9] the British fair,
165 As long as Atalantis shall be read,[1]

8. *Milton* lib. 6 [Pope's note], citing *Paradise Lost* 6.329–31, "The girding sword with discontinuous wound / Passed through him, but the ethereal substance closed / Not long divisible. . . ."
9. A carriage drawn by six horses; a symbol of wealth and prestige.
1. The scandalous *Atalantis: Secret Memoirs and Manners of Several Persons of Quality* (1709), by Mary Delarivière Manley.

Or the small pillow grace a lady's bed,[2]
While visits shall be paid on solemn days,
When num'rous wax-lights[3] in bright order blaze,
While nymphs take treats, or assignations give,
170   So long my honour, name, and praise shall live!"
　　　What time would spare, from steel receives its date,°　　　　　*end*
And monuments, like men, submit to fate!
Steel could the labour of the gods destroy,
And strike to dust th' imperial tow'rs of Troy,[4]
175   Steel could the works of mortal pride confound,
And hew triumphal arches to the ground,
What wonder then, fair nymph! thy hairs should feel
The conqu'ring force of unresisted steel?

CANTO 4

BUT anxious cares the pensive nymph oppressed,
And secret passions laboured in her breast.
Not youthful kings in battle seized alive,
Not scornful virgins who their charms survive,
5   Not ardent lovers robbed of all their bliss,
Not ancient ladies when refused a kiss,
Not tyrants fierce that unrepenting die,
Not Cynthia when her manteau's° pinned awry,　　　　　*gown's*
E'er felt such rage, resentment, and despair,
10   As thou, sad virgin! for thy ravished hair.
　　　For, that sad moment, when the sylphs withdrew,
And Ariel weeping from Belinda flew,
Umbriel, a dusky, melancholy sprite,
As ever sullied the fair face of light,
15   Down to the central earth, his proper scene,
Repaired to search the gloomy cave of Spleen.[1]
　　　Swift on his sooty pinions flits the gnome,
And in a vapour[2] reached the dismal dome.
No cheerful breeze this sullen region knows,
20   The dreaded east[3] is all the wind that blows.
Here in a grotto, sheltered close from air,
And screened in shades° from day's detested glare,　　　　　*shadows*
She sighs for ever on her pensive bed,
Pain at her side, and Megrim° at her head.　　　　　*migraine*
25   　　　Two handmaids wait' the throne: alike in place,
But diff'ring far in figure and in face.
Here stood Ill-nature like an ancient maid,

---

2. Said to be a place where ladies hid romance novels and other contraband.
3. Candles made of wax, rather than the cheaper tallow. Evening social visits were an essential part of the fashionable woman's routine.
4. Even Troy, fabled to have been built by Apollo and Poseidon, was destroyed by arms.

1. Named after the bodily organ, "spleen" was the current name for the fashionable affliction of melancholy or ill-humor. Umbriel's descent into the womb-like Cave of Spleen suggests the epic commonplace of the journey to the underworld.
2. "The spleen" was also called "the vapors."
3. The east wind was supposed to induce fits of spleen.

Her wrinkled form in black and white arrayed;
With store of pray'rs, for mornings, nights, and noons,
30   Her hand is filled; her bosom with lampoons.
      There Affectation with a sickly mien,
Shows in her cheek the roses of eighteen,
Practised to lisp, and hang the head aside,
Faints into airs, and languishes with pride,
35   On the rich quilt sinks with becoming woe,
Wrapped in a gown, for sickness, and for show.
The fair ones feel such maladies as these,
When each new night-dress gives a new disease.
      A constant vapour o'er the palace flies;
40   Strange phantoms rising as the mists arise;
Dreadful, as hermits' dreams in haunted shades,
Or bright, as visions of expiring maids.[4]
Now glaring fiends, and snakes on rolling spires,°   *coils*
Pale spectres, gaping tombs, and purple fires:
45   Now lakes of liquid gold, Elysian scenes,[5]
And crystal domes, and angels in machines.
      Unnumbered throngs, on ev'ry side are seen,
Of bodies changed to various forms by Spleen.[6]
Here living tea-pots stand, one arm held out,
50   One bent; the handle this, and that the spout:
A pipkin[7] there, like Homer's tripod walks;
Here sighs a jar, and there a goose-pye talks;[8]
Men prove with child, as pow'rful fancy works,
And maids turned bottles, call aloud for corks.
55   Safe past the gnome through this fantastic band,
A branch of healing spleenwort in his hand.[9]
Then thus addressed the pow'r—"Hail, wayward queen!
Who rule the sex to fifty from fifteen:
Parent of vapours and of female wit,
60   Who give th' hysteric, or poetic fit,
On various tempers act by various ways,
Make some take physic,° others scribble plays;[1]   *medicine*
Who cause the proud their visits to delay,
And send the godly in a pet° to pray;   *ill-humor*
65   A nymph there is, that all thy pow'r disdains,
And thousands more in equal mirth maintains.
But oh! if e'er thy gnome could spoil a grace,
Or raise a pimple on a beauteous face,
Like citron-waters° matrons' cheeks inflame,   *flavored brandy*

---

4. Religious visions of hell and heaven.
5. Elysium was the classical paradise, but this also recalls contemporary theater, which made much of scenic spectacle and the use of machinery.
6. Hallucinations similar to those described in the following lines were common to those afflicted with spleen.
7. Small pot or pan. Hephaistos's "walking" tripods are

described in the *Iliad* 18.439ff.
8. Alludes to a real fact, a Lady of distinction imagin'd herself in this condition [Pope's note].
9. Pope changes the golden bough that protected Aeneas on his trip through the underworld into an herb that was supposed to be good for the spleen.
1. Melancholy was associated with artistic creativity.

70 Or change complexions at a losing game;
    If e'er with airy horns I planted heads,[2]
    Or rumpled petticoats, or tumbled beds,
    Or caused suspicion when no soul was rude,
    Or discomposed the head-dress of a prude,
75 Or e'er to costive° lap-dog gave disease,   *constipated*
    Which not the tears of brightest eyes could ease:
    Hear me, and touch Belinda with chagrin,
    That single act gives half the world the spleen."
        The goddess with a discontented air
80 Seems to reject him, though she grants his pray'r.
    A wondrous bag with both her hands she binds,
    Like that where once Ulysses held the winds;[3]
    There she collects the force of female lungs,
    Sighs, sobs, and passions, and the war of tongues.
85 A phial next she fills with fainting fears,
    Soft sorrows, melting griefs, and flowing tears.
    The gnome rejoicing bears her gifts away,
    Spreads his black wings, and slowly mounts to day.
        Sunk in Thalestris'[4] arms the nymph he found,
90 Her eyes dejected, and her hair unbound.
    Full o'er their heads the swelling bag he rent,
    And all the furies issued at the vent.
    Belinda burns with more than mortal ire,
    And fierce Thalestris fans the rising fire.
95 "O wretched maid!" she spread her hands, and cried,
    (While Hampton's echoes, "Wretched maid!" replied)
    "Was it for this you took such constant care
    The bodkin, comb, and essence to prepare?
    For this your locks in paper durance° bound?   *curling papers*
100 For this with tort'ring irons wreathed around?
    For this with fillets[5] strained your tender head,
    And bravely bore the double loads of lead?°   *curl fasteners*
    Gods! shall the ravisher display your hair,
    While the fops envy, and the ladies stare!
105 Honour forbid! at whose unrivalled shrine
    Ease, pleasure, virtue, all our sex resign.
    Methinks already I your tears survey,
    Already hear the horrid things they say,
    Already see you a degraded toast,[6]
110 And all your honour in a whisper lost!
    How shall I, then, your helpless fame defend?
    'Twill then be infamy to seem your friend!
    And shall this prize, th' inestimable prize,

---

2. A sign that a husband had been cuckolded.
3. Given to him by the wind god Aeolus (*Odyssey* 10.19ff.).
4. A queen of the Amazons; here Mrs. Morley, Arabella's

second cousin.
5. Headbands, with reference to priestesses in the *Aeneid*.
6. A woman whose toast is often drunk, and who by implication is all too well known to her (male) toasters.

Exposed through crystal to the gazing eyes,
115 And heightened by the diamond's circling rays,
On that rapacious hand for ever blaze?[7]
Sooner shall grass in Hyde-Park Circus grow,[8]
And wits take lodgings in the sound of Bow;[9]
Sooner let earth, air, sea, to chaos fall,
120 Men, monkeys, lap-dogs, parrots, perish all!"
      She said; then raging to Sir Plume[1] repairs,
And bids her beau demand the precious hairs:
(Sir Plume, of amber snuff-box justly vain,
And the nice conduct of a clouded cane)[2]
125 With earnest eyes, and round unthinking face,
He first the snuff-box opened, then the case,
And thus broke out—"My Lord, why, what the devil!
Zounds![3] damn the lock! 'fore Gad, you must be civil.
Plague on't! 'tis past a jest—nay prithee, pox!
130 Give her the hair"—he spoke, and rapped his box.
      "It grieves me much," replied the peer again,
"Who speaks so well should ever speak in vain,
But by this lock, this sacred lock I swear,
(Which never more shall join its parted hair;
135 Which never more its honours shall renew,
Clipped from the lovely head where late it grew)
That while my nostrils draw the vital air,
This hand, which won it, shall for ever wear."
He spoke, and speaking, in proud triumph spread
140 The long-contended honours of her head.[4]
      But Umbriel, hateful gnome! forbears not so;
He breaks the phial whence the sorrows flow.
Then see! the nymph in beauteous grief appears,
Her eyes half languishing, half drowned in tears;
145 On her heaved bosom hung her drooping head,
Which, with a sigh, she raised; and thus she said.
      "For ever cursed be this detested day,[5]
Which snatched my best, my fav'rite curl away!
Happy! ah ten times happy had I been,
150 If Hampton-Court these eyes had never seen!
Yet am not I the first mistaken maid,
By love of courts to num'rous ills betrayed.
Oh had I rather unadmired remained
In some lone isle, or distant northern land;
155 Where the gilt chariot never marks the way,
Where none learn ombre, none e'er taste bohea!°   *the finest tea*

---

7. I.e., mounted in a ring.
8. The fashion for driving coaches around Hyde Park prevented grass from growing there.
9. A commercial area around St. Mary-le-Bow, and not at all fashionable.
1. Sir George Browne, cousin of Arabella's mother.

2. Skilled use of a cane with a head of dark polished stone.
3. A Corruption of "God's wounds," a mild oath.
4. Her beautiful hair.
5. Echoing Achilles' lament for his slain friend Patroclus (*Iliad* 18.107ff.).

There kept my charms concealed from mortal eye,
Like roses, that in deserts bloom and die.
What moved my mind with youthful lords to roam?
160   O had I stayed, and said my pray'rs at home!
'Twas this the morning omens seemed to tell,
Thrice from my trembling hand the patch-box fell;
The tott'ring china shook without a wind,
Nay, Poll° sat mute, and Shock was most unkind!   *her parrot*
165   A sylph too warned me of the threats of fate,
In mystic visions, now believed too late!
See the poor remnants of these slighted hairs!
My hands shall rend what ev'n thy rapine spares:
These in two sable ringlets taught to break,°   *divide*
170   Once gave new beauties to the snowy neck;
The sister-lock now sits uncouth, alone,
And in its fellow's fate foresees its own;
Uncurled it hangs, the fatal shears demands,
And tempts, once more, thy sacrilegious hands.
175   Oh hadst thou, cruel! been content to seize
Hairs less in sight, or any hairs but these!"

CANTO 5

SHE said: the pitying audience melt in tears,
But Fate and Jove had stopped the baron's ears.
In vain Thalestris with reproach assails,
For who can move when fair Belinda fails?
5   Not half so fixed the Trojan could remain,[1]
While Anna begged and Dido raged in vain.
Then grave Clarissa[2] graceful waved her fan;
Silence ensued, and thus the nymph began.
      "Say, why are beauties praised and honoured most,
10   The wise man's passion, and the vain man's toast?
Why decked with all that land and sea afford,
Why angels called, and angel-like adored?
Why round our coaches crowd the white-gloved beaux,
Why bows the side-box from its inmost rows?[3]
15   How vain are all these glories, ill our pains,
Unless good sense preserve what beauty gains:
That men may say, when we the front box grace,
Behold the first in virtue as in face!
Oh! if to dance all night, and dress all day,
20   Charmed the small-pox,[4] or chased old age away;

---

1. Aeneas, fixed on his decision to leave Carthage and abandon Dido despite her pleas and those of her sister Anna (*Aeneid* 4.269–449).
2. A new character introduced . . . to open more clearly the moral of the poem, in a parody of the speech of Sarpedon to Glaucus in Homer [Pope's note in the 1717

edition]. Sarpedon's speech (*Iliad* 12) is a famous reflection on glory.
3. At the theater, gentlemen sat in the side boxes, ladies in the front boxes facing the stage.
4. A common disease, which often left permanent facial scars.

Who would not scorn what housewifes' cares produce,
Or who would learn one earthly thing of use?
To patch, nay ogle, might become a saint,
Nor could it sure be such a sin to paint.
25 But since, alas! frail beauty must decay,
Curled or uncurled, since locks will turn to grey;
Since painted, or not painted, all shall fade,
And she who scorns a man, must die a maid;
What then remains but well our pow'r to use,
30 And keep good humour still, whate'er we lose?
And trust me, dear! good humour can prevail,
When airs, and flights, and screams, and scolding fail.
Beauties in vain their pretty eyes may roll;
Charms strike the sight, but merit wins the soul."
35   So spoke the dame, but no applause ensued;
Belinda frowned, Thalestris called her prude.
To arms, to arms! the fierce virago[5] cries,
And swift as lightning to the combat flies.
All side in parties, and begin th' attack;
40 Fans clap, silks rustle, and tough whalebones crack;
Heroes' and heroines' shouts confus'dly rise,
And base and treble voices strike the skies.
No common weapons in their hands are found,
Like gods they fight, nor dread a mortal wound.
45   So when bold Homer makes the gods engage,
And heav'nly breasts with human passions rage;
'Gainst Pallas,° Mars; Latona,[6] Hermes arms;   *Athena*
And all Olympus rings with loud alarms:
Jove's thunder roars, heav'n trembles all around,
50 Blue Neptune storms, the bellowing deeps resound:
Earth shakes her nodding tow'rs, the ground gives way,
And the pale ghosts start at the flash of day!
    Triumphant Umbriel on a sconce's[7] height
Clapped his glad wings, and sate to view the fight.
55 Propped on their bodkin spears, the sprites survey
The growing combat, or assist the fray.
    While through the press enraged Thalestris flies,
And scatters death around from both her eyes,
A beau and witling° perished in the throng,   *little wit*
60 One died in metaphor, and one in song.
"O cruel nymph! a living death I bear,"
Cried Dapperwit, and sunk beside his chair.
A mournful glance Sir Fopling upwards cast,
"Those eyes are made so killing"[8]—was his last.

---

5. Woman who behaves like a man.
6. Mother of Diana and Apollo.
7. Candlestick attached to the wall.

8. A line from Giovanni Bononcini's opera, *Camilla* (1696), popular in London.

65   Thus on Maeander's flow'ry margin lies
      Th' expiring swan, and as he sings he dies.[9]
          When bold Sir Plume had drawn Clarissa down,
      Chloe stepped in, and killed him with a frown;
      She smiled to see the doughty hero slain,
70   But, at her smile, the beau revived again.
          Now Jove suspends his golden scales in air,[1]
      Weighs the men's wits against the lady's hair;
      The doubtful beam long nods from side to side;
      At length the wits mount up, the hairs subside.
75   See fierce Belinda on the baron flies,
      With more than usual lightning in her eyes:
      Nor feared the chief th' unequal fight to try,
      Who sought no more than on his foe to die.[2]
      But this bold lord with manly strength endued,
80   She with one finger and a thumb subdued;
      Just where the breath of life his nostrils drew,
      A charge of snuff the wily virgin threw;
      The gnomes direct, to ev'ry atom just,
      The pungent grains of titillating dust.
85   Sudden, with starting tears each eye o'erflows,
      And the high dome re-echoes to his nose.[3]
          "Now meet thy fate," incensed Belinda cried,
      And drew a deadly bodkin[4] from her side.
      (The same, his ancient personage to deck,
90   Her great great grandsire wore about his neck,
      In three seal-rings; which after, melted down,
      Formed a vast buckle for his widow's gown:
      Her infant grandame's° whistle next it grew,   *grandmother's*
      The bell she jingled, and the whistle blew;
95   Then in a bodkin graced her mother's hairs,
      Which long she wore, and now Belinda wears.)
      "Boast not my fall," he cried, "insulting foe!
      Thou by some other shalt be laid as low:
      Nor think, to die dejects my lofty mind;
100   All that I dread is leaving you behind!
      Rather than so, ah let me still survive,
      And burn in Cupid's flames—but burn alive."
          "Restore the Lock!" she cries; and all around
      "Restore the Lock!" the vaulted roofs rebound.
105   Not fierce Othello in so loud a strain
      Roared for the handkerchief that caused his pain.
      But see how oft ambitious aims are crossed,
      And chiefs contend till all the prize is lost!
      The lock, obtained with guilt, and kept with pain,

9. Meander: a river in Asia Minor. Swans were believed   both Homer and Virgil.
to sing only on their death. This simile refers to Ovid's   2. A standard metaphor for sexual climax.
Heroides 7, a lament from Dido to Aeneas.   3. See his boast, 4.133–38.
1. To determine victory in battle; a convention found in   4. A decorative pin, shaped like a dagger.

110   In ev'ry place is sought, but sought in vain:
      With such a prize no mortal must be blessed,
      So heav'n decrees! with heav'n who can contest?
      Some thought it mounted to the Lunar sphere,⁵
      Since all things lost on earth are treasured there.
115   There heroes' wits are kept in pond'rous vases,
      And beaus' in snuff-boxes and tweezer-cases.
      There broken vows, and death-bed alms are found,
      And lovers' hearts with ends of ribbon bound,
      The courtier's promises, and sick man's pray'rs,
120   The smiles of harlots, and the tears of heirs,
      Cages for gnats, and chains to yoke a flea,
      Dried butterflies, and tomes of casuistry.⁶
          But trust the muse—she saw it upward rise,
      Though marked by none but quick, poetic eyes:
125   (So Rome's great founder to the heav'ns withdrew,
      To Proculus alone confessed in view)⁷
      A sudden star, it shot through liquid air,
      And drew behind a radiant trail of hair.
      Not Berenice's locks first rose so bright,⁸
130   The heav'ns bespangling with dishevelled light.
      The sylphs behold it kindling as it flies,
      And pleased pursue its progress through the skies.
          This the beau monde shall from the Mall⁹ survey,
      And hail with music its propitious ray;
135   This the bless'd lover shall for Venus° take,   *the planet*
      And send up vows from Rosamonda's lake;¹
      This Partridge² soon shall view in cloudless skies,
      When next he looks through Galileo's eyes;°   *a telescope*
      And hence th' egregious wizard shall foredoom
140   The fate of Louis, and the fall of Rome.
          Then cease, bright nymph! to mourn thy ravished hair,
      Which adds new glory to the shining sphere!
      Not all the tresses that fair head can boast,
      Shall draw such envy as the lock you lost.
145   For after all the murders of your eye,
      When, after millions slain, yourself shall die;
      When those fair suns° shall set, as set they must,   *her eyes*
      And all those tresses shall be laid in dust,
      This lock the muse shall consecrate to fame,
150   And 'midst the stars inscribe Belinda's name.

5. In Ariosto's *Orlando Furioso* (1516–1532), Orlando's lost wits are sought on the moon.
6. Subtle reasoning (often used of arguments justifying immoral conduct).
7. When Romulus was killed mysteriously, Proculus soothed popular grief by asserting that he had been taken up to heaven.
8. The Egyptian queen Berenice made an offering of her hair after her husband returned victorious from the wars;

when it disappeared from the temple, the court astronomer claimed it had been made into a new constellation.
9. A fashionable walk in St. James's Park.
1. Where lovers met in St. James's Park.
2. John Partridge was a ridiculous star-gazer, who in his almanacs every year never failed to predict the downfall of the Pope and the King of France, then at war with the English [Pope's note].

➤ PERSPECTIVES ➤

Liberty and Libertines

The word "libertine," like the related "rakehell" (later shortened simply to "rake"), began among the many slurs hurled back and forth between Protestants and Catholics during the sixteenth-century European wars of religion. A "libertine" was originally a member of a French Protestant sect that believed that individuals should be guided in matters of religious faith by their own lights—"lights," that is, of reason, direct divine inspiration, or independent interpretation of holy scripture—rather than exclusively by the clergy or established church dogma. The word entered the English language at the tail end of the sixteenth century as a near synonym for the native, somewhat earlier "rakehell"—a freethinker in religion whose behavior is generally unconstrained by social norms or ethical considerations.

In France the word soon came to be applied by the police to any act deemed an "outrage to public morality," so that the original religious sense tended to become obscured by a newer, specifically sexual one. The first notorious libertines in this more modern sense were such great noblemen as the Prince de Conti—who, very much like Don Juan at the beginning of Mozart's famous opera, boasted that he had collected 2,000 rings as tokens of fidelity from as many abandoned mistresses—and the Duc de Richelieu (1696–1788), who, frustrated in one of his amorous pursuits, burned down the house that stood in his way.

Despite growing impulses toward democracy, greater social equality, and religious freedom, at the beginning of the Enlightenment period it was still mainly the upper classes who enjoyed any real freedoms at all. Thus libertinism, while expressing a general cultural drive toward breaking out of the bondage of traditional authority of all kinds, was nevertheless associated with the persistent privileges of the aristocracy, and of aristocratic men in particular. Libertinage mainly meant the aristocratic male's freedom to do whatever he could—regardless of the needs (not yet conceived of as rights) of women or of men of the lower classes, and in flagrant disregard, moreover, of the honor of his peers, vested as that was in their ability to preserve the chastity of their wives, daughters, and sisters.

Robert Lovelace, the protagonist of Samuel Richardson's novel *Clarissa* (1747–1748) and one of the greatest libertines in literature, justifies with cynical clarity in a letter to his friend Belford his culture's sexual double standard:

> Nor say thou that virtue, in the eye of heaven, is as much a *manly* as a *womanly* grace (by virtue in this place I mean chastity, and to be superior to temptation . . .). Nor ask thou: Shall the man be guilty, yet expect the woman to be guiltless, and even unsuspectable?— Urge thou not these arguments, I say, since the wife by a failure may do much more injury to the husband, than the husband can do to the wife, and not only to the husband, but to all his family, by obtruding another man's children into his possessions, perhaps to the exclusion (and at least to a participation with) his own; he believing them all the time to be his. In the eye of heaven therefore, the sin *cannot* be equal. Besides, I have read in some place [I Corinthians 2:9] *that the woman was made for the man*, not *the man for the woman*.

Despite this double standard, though, especially during the first half of the Enlightenment period women were still acknowledged to be not merely objects of exchange between families but desiring subjects at the same time. The mere possibility of their sexual desire was seen as potentially threatening to the maintenance of the social order, however, and therefore requiring the ultimate restraint and vigilance. The works of Aphra Behn and Eliza Haywood in particular give voice to a proscribed female sexual desire that provoked the pervasive cultural anxieties so well expressed in Alexander Pope's famous pronouncement in his "Epistle II: To a Lady": "ev'ry Woman is at heart a Rake."

The Enlightenment project of liberation led immediately to a question that still vexes societies today: At what point does individual freedom from political tyranny, religious dogma, or unexamined prejudice become merely unchecked liberty to do anything one can get away with, regardless of the needs, benefit, or rights of others? On what basis can moral principles be established once the traditional authority of church, state, and custom are no longer seen as absolute, and how can individual freedoms be justly limited for the benefit of society as a whole? Rousseau's *The Social Contract* (1762) grapples with these questions directly in philosophical terms, arguing that the moment a solitary individual turns to others for the gratification of his needs or wants, he enters implicitly into a contract with them that limits the freedoms of each for the mutual benefit and protection of all. Wollstonecraft's *A Vindication of the Rights of Woman* (1792) and Barbauld's *The Rights of Woman* (1795) debate the proper place, liberties, rights, and responsibilities of women in the post-Revolutionary commonweal. In *Philosophy in the Boudoir,* the Marquis de Sade, the last and most excessive embodiment of the true Enlightenment aristocratic rake, attacked Rousseau's argument directly, rejecting the idea that simply being born into any social group constitutes a contract willingly engaged in, and promulgating the notion that the true liberty for which the French Revolution was fought must be absolute and unmitigated individual freedom, to the point of flying in the face of any and all laws formulated to "enslave" mankind.

Societies elsewhere in the world were struggling with comparable problems of individual and social liberty, as old court cultures entered the modern world. This section begins with striking selections from two Asian sources, both dealing with the intimate overlap of religious and sexual concerns—fictionally portrayed in Ihara Saikaku's *Life of a Sensuous Woman* and poetically expressed in the surprisingly erotic love poems of the sixth Dalai Lama.

Ihara Saikaku
1642–1693

Ihara Saikaku wrote *Life of a Sensuous Woman* (1686) at the peak of his career. Published in Osaka, the work marks one of the last in a series of "books on love," a sub-genre of tales of the floating world, which began with *Life of a Sensuous Man. Life of a Sensuous Woman* is an aging woman's extended confession to two young men. She describes her various experiences, beginning with her childhood (as the daughter of a former aristocrat in Kyoto) and her life as an attendant in the imperial palace, through a series of increasingly low positions, until in the end she falls to the position of a streetwalker. *Life of a Sensuous Woman* can be seen as a seventeenth-century version of the legendary Ono no Komachi, known for her transformation from a stunning beauty with many lovers to an unattractive old woman. Saikaku here looks at the world of love and sexuality from the perspective of a woman who is growing older and whose outlook is becoming increasingly bleak.

The only major narrative that Saikaku wrote in the first person, *Life of a Sensuous Woman,* structurally echoes Buddhist confession narratives, in which someone who has become a priest or nun recounts a past life of sin, particularly the crisis that led to spiritual awakening. Instead of a religious confession, however, the aged woman narrator is implicitly initiating her young visitors into the secrets of the way of love, describing a life of vitality and sexual desire. It is not until the end, when the sight of the statues of the five hundred disciples in a Buddhist temple causes the woman to have a vision of many of the men with whom she has had relations, that the narrative takes the form of a Buddhist confession.

Significantly, the two young male listeners ask the aged woman to tell them about her past experience in "the style of the present." Instead of describing her life in the past as it happened, she transforms it into the present, telling it as if she were repeatedly living "today." In this fashion

Saikaku explores many of the positions that a woman could have at the time—as a palace attendant, a dancer, a mistress of a domain lord, a high-ranking licensed courtesan, a priest's wife, a teacher of calligraphy and manners, a nun who performs Buddhist chants, a hairdresser, a seasonal house cleaner, a go-between for marital engagements, a seamstress, a waitress at a teahouse, a streetwalker, and many other professions—providing a remarkable portrayal of contemporary commoner society. *Life of a Sensuous Woman* has in fact been described by modern scholars as a novel of manners. Sometimes with the names of actual people barely disguised, Saikaku satirically reveals the underside of the lives of domain lords, powerful samurai, wealthy priests, and upper-level merchants. Throughout the work, Saikaku's main interest remains the woman's resourcefulness and imagination in these concrete social circumstances, and he explores how these contexts evoke or frustrate her irrepressible desire.

PRONUNCIATION:
   Ihara Saikaku: EE-ha-ra SIGH-kah-ku

from Life of a Sensuous Woman[1]

AN OLD WOMAN'S HERMITAGE (1:1)

A beautiful woman, many ages have agreed, is an ax that cuts down a man's life. No one, of course, escapes death. The invisible blossoms of the mind[2] finally fall and scatter; the soul leaves; and the body is fed like kindling into a crematorium fire in the night. But for the blossoms to fall all too soon in a morning storm—ah, how foolish are the men who die young of overindulgence in the way of sensuous love. Yet there is no end of them.

On the seventh of the First Month, the day people go out to have their fortunes told, I had to visit Saga[3] in northwest Kyōto. As if to show that spring had truly come, the plums at Umezu Crossing were just breaking into blossom. On the eastbound ferry to Saga I saw an attractive young man dressed in the latest style but unmistakably disheveled. His face was pale, and he was thin and worn, obviously from too much lovemaking. He looked as if he didn't have much time left and was getting ready to leave his inheritance to his own parents.

"I've never lacked anything at all," he said to the man with him. "But there's one thing I really would like. I wish my pledging liquid could keep flowing on and on like this river and never stop."

His friend was startled. "What I'd like," he said, "is a country without women. I'd go there and find a quiet place to live, far from any town. There I'd take good care of myself, so I could live to a decent old age. The world keeps changing, and I'd really like to see a lot of different things."

The two men had opposite attitudes toward life and death. One sought as much sensual pleasure as he could get, even though he knew that it was shortening his life, and the other wanted to give up love altogether and live many more years. Both longed for the impossible, and they talked in a dazed way, halfway between dreaming and waking.

After we reached the other side, the men joked and horsed around, staggering along the path on the bank and stamping without a thought on the parsley and thistles that were coming into leaf. Finally they turned away from the river, left the last houses

---

1. Translated by Chris Drake.
2. Alludes to a poem by Ono no Komachi, *Kokinshū:* "They fade invisibly and change, these blossoms of the

mind in our human world."
3. A wooded area of temples and the huts of recluses.

behind, and entered the shadows of the mountains to the north. I felt curious about them and followed at a distance. Eventually we came to a grove of red pines and, within it, an old fence made of bundled bush-clover stalks that were beginning to come apart. Beside the braided bamboo gate a gap had been opened so a dog could pass through. Inside the fence, in deep silence, stood a meditation hut, its front roof sloping down from a boulder above the mouth of a natural cave. Ferns grew in its thatched eaves, and vines clung to the roof, their leaves still tinted with last fall's colors.

To the east stood a willow tree, and from below it came a soft sound. Clear, pure water was flowing naturally through a raised pipe of split bamboo from a source nearby. I looked around for the venerable monk that I assumed must live there and was surprised to see an old woman, one whose face the years had given a refined beauty. Her back was bent, but her frost-touched hair was well combed. Her eyes were as soft and hazy as the moon low on the western horizon. Over an old-style sky blue wadded-silk robe embroidered with gold thread, she wore another splashed with a dappled pattern of thickly petaled chrysanthemums. Her medium-width sash, with flowers in a lozenge design, was tied in front—stylish even at her age. To the cross-beam above the front of what seemed to be her bedroom was attached a weathered plaque that read "Hut of a Sensuous Hermit." A scent of incense lingered in the air. I think it must have been First Warbler's Cry, a very fine aloeswood.[4]

I found a place outside a window and stood there, so overcome with curiosity that my mind strained to leap out of myself and into the hermitage. As I watched, the two men, looking thoroughly at home, went right inside without even announcing themselves.

"So, you've come again today," the woman said smiling. "There are so many pleasures in the world to captivate you men. Why have you come all the way here to see me, like wind visiting a rotting old tree? My ears are bad, and words no longer come easily. It's just too difficult for me now to keep up relationships properly, the way I'd need to do if I wanted to stay in the world. I've been living in this place for seven years already, and the plum trees are my calendar. When they bloom, I know spring's come. When the mountains are white with snow, I know it's winter. I almost never see anyone any more. Why do you keep coming here?"

"He's being tortured by love," said one of the men. "And I get very depressed. Neither of us understands the way of sensuous love deeply enough yet. We've heard many things about you, and we've followed the same path you've traveled. Right here to your door. You're so very experienced, won't you please tell us the story of your life in the words people use now? Please do it in a way that will help us understand more about life and the world today."

One of the men poured some fine saké into a beautiful gold wine cup and strongly urged the old woman to drink. She relented and gradually lost her reserve and began to play on her koto. She was so skillful it was obvious she played it often. For a while she sang a short song about deep love. Then overcome with emotion, she began to relate, as if in a dream, all the loves in her own life and the various things that had happened to her.

I didn't come from a low-class family, she began. My mother was a commoner, but my father was descended from middle-ranking aristocrats who mixed with high

---

4. Temple incense chosen to match the early spring season, when the warblers return.

officials at the court of Emperor Go-Hanazono.[5] Families, like everything else in the world, go up and down. Mine came down very hard, and we were so miserable we didn't want to go on living. But I happened to be born with a beautiful face, so I went to Kyōto to serve a court lady of the highest rank, and I learned most of those elegant, refined ways of aristocrats. If I'd continued to serve there for a few more years, I'm sure I would have had a very happy future.

From the beginning of the summer when I was eleven, I became very loose and forgot I was supposed to concentrate on serving my employer. When people did my hair, I wouldn't be satisfied and I'd redo it myself. I was the one, you know, who invented the version of the Shimada hairstyle that has the hair swept up behind and the chignon tied and folded flat in back. It became quite stylish. I also created that way of tying the topknot without showing the cord that became so popular. I'm sure you know the white silk robes with colorful Gosho-dyed patterns. Well, in the beginning only court ladies wore them. But I spent all my time and energy making new patterns and colors for them, and soon they became quite popular with ordinary women.

Aristocrats, you know, are always thinking about love, whether they're composing poems or playing kickball. Those women's pillows, why, they're always in use. Whenever I saw women and men lying together, I'd feel excited, and when I'd hear them in the dark, my heart pounded. Naturally I began to want to make love myself. Just when I was beginning to feel love was the most important thing in my life, I also began to get love letters from a lot of men. They all were full of deep feelings and tender thoughts, but I got so many I had no way to get rid of them all. I had to ask a guard to burn them for me. Of course I made him promise to keep it secret. Later, you know, he told me something strange. The places in the letters where the men swore by their patron gods that their love for me was true and would never change, those places, he said, didn't burn. They rose up with the smoke and came down in the Yoshida Shrine, where all the gods of Japan gather together.[6] There's nothing as strange as love. Every one of the men who longed for me was handsome and knew how to look attractive, but I didn't have special feelings for any of them. I was interested in a young samurai who was working for one of the aristocrats. He was of low rank and wasn't good-looking, but his writing, even in his very first letter, sent me into another world. He kept on writing more and more letters, and before I knew it I was beginning to suffer and yearn for him, too.

It was hard for us to meet, but I managed to arrange things sometimes, and we were able to make love. Rumors started, but I couldn't stop myself. In the faint light early one morning, someone saw both of us together out in the shifting mist,[7] as they say, and while the mist swirled ever more thickly, my employer secretly fired me and had me discreetly left beside the road at the end of Uji Bridge. I was merely punished, but the man—how cruel they were! He lost his life for what we'd done.

For four or five days I couldn't tell whether I was sleeping or awake. I couldn't sleep, but I couldn't get up either. Several times I was terrified when I saw the man's resentful-looking shape in front of me. It refused to even speak. I was in complete shock, and I thought about killing myself. But the days went by, and you know, I

5. Presumably she is referring to Emperor Go-Hanazono both while he reigned (1429–1464) and while he was a cloistered emperor until his death in 1470.
6. The Yoshida Shrine, in Kyōto, claimed to include all

3,132 gods in Japan.
7. Ironically alludes to a poem by Sadayori, *Senzaishū* no. 420: "In faint early light, mist on the Uji River begins to break, and through its gaps: weir poles in the shallows."

completely forgot about that man. It's amazing how quickly a woman's mind can change. But I was thirteen at the time, and people looked on me leniently. Ridiculous, they'd think, surely she hasn't done *that* already. And what could have been more ridiculous than their own thoughts!

In the old days, when it came time for a bride to leave for the groom's house, she would grieve at leaving her parents' house and cry at the gate until her sleeves were all wet. But these days young women know a lot more about lovemaking. They grow impatient with the slow bargaining of the go-between woman, rush to get their trousseaus ready, and can't wait for the fancy palanquin to come and take them away. When it arrives, they practically leap in, excitement glowing everywhere, to the tips of their noses. Until forty years ago, young women used to play horse outside their front doors until they were eighteen or nineteen. And young men didn't have their coming-of-age ceremonies until they were twenty-five. My goodness, the world certainly does change quickly!

I was very young when I learned about love. I was still a flower in bud, you could say. And after that I had so many experiences that the pure water of my mind turned completely the color of sensuous love, like the water in the Uji River where it turns yellow from all the mountain roses on the banks. I just followed my desires wherever they went—and I ruined myself. The water will never be clear again. There's no use regretting it now, though. I certainly have managed to live a long time, but my life, well, it wasn't what you'd call exemplary.

MISTRESS OF A DOMAIN LORD (1:3)

The land was at peace, and calm breezes drifted through the pines of Edo. One year the daimyō lord of a certain rural domain was in Edo spending his obligatory year living near the castle of the shōgun. There he was able to be with his wife, who was required to live permanently in Edo, but during the year she died. Since she'd left no male heir, the lord's worried retainers gathered more than forty beautiful young women from leading warrior families in Edo, hoping one of them would bear a boy baby for the lord and ensure the continued rule of the lord's clan over the domain— and the retainers' own employment. The head chambermaid was resourceful, and whenever she saw the lord feeling good, she brought a young woman near his sleeping chamber and did her best to put him in the mood. All the women were fresh as budding cherry blossoms, ready to burst into full bloom if wet by the slightest rain. Most men would have gazed at any of these women and never grown tired, yet not a single one suited the lord, and his retainers began to grow anxious.[1]

The retainers didn't bother to look for other women among the commoners in Edo. Ordinary women raised in the eastern provinces, you know, they're rough and insensitive.[2] They have flat feet and thick necks, and their skin is hard. They're honest and straightforward, but they don't feel deep passion and don't know how to express their desire to men or attract them by acting afraid. Their minds are sincere, but they're ignorant of the way of sensuous love and can't share it with a man who knows it.

I've never heard of any women more attractive than those in Kyōto. For one thing, Kyōto women have a beautiful way of speaking. It's not something they study.

1. If a daimyō lord died without a male heir, the domain administration was transferred to a new clan, forcing the retainers to become unemployed.

2. Edo was located in the eastern provinces, an area considered by Kyōto people to be rustic and unrefined.

They pick it up naturally living in the capital, where women have talked that way for centuries. Just look at how different Kyōto is from Izumo Province. In Izumo they have an ancient tradition of love and courtship going back to the days of the gods, but the men and women there slur their words so badly it's hard to understand them. But then just go offshore from Izumo to Oki Island. The islanders there look like country people, but they speak the way people do in the capital. And Oki women are gentle and know how to play the koto, play *go*, distinguish fine incense, and compose and appreciate waka poems. That's because long ago Emperor Go-Daigo was exiled to Oki with his entourage,[3] and the islanders maintain the customs from that time even now.

So the daimyō's councillors thought that in Kyōto, at least, there must be a woman their lord would like. To look for one, they sent the lord's old and trusted retainer, the overseer of the inner chambers. The overseer was more than seventy. He couldn't see a thing without glasses and had only few front teeth. He'd forgotten what octopus tasted like, and the only pickled vegetables he could still eat were finely grated radishes. Day after day he lived without any pleasure, and as for sensuous love, well, he did wear a loincloth, but he might as well have been a woman. The best he could do was excitedly tell a few sexy stories. As a samurai, he wore formal divided skirts and robes with starched, high shoulders, but since he served in his lord's wife's private chambers and in the women's quarters, he wasn't allowed to wear either a long or a short sword. Too old to be a warrior, he was put in charge of watching the silver lock on the doors to the inner chambers. That's why the councillors chose him to go to Kyōto to find a mistress—and to chaperon her all the way back to Edo. It would be like putting a precious buddha statue in front of a puzzled cat. You just can't let a young man alone with a woman, you know, even if he's Shakyamuni Buddha.

The old retainer finally arrived in the capital, which looked to him like the Pure Land paradise on earth. He went directly to one of the exclusive Sasaya clothiers on Muromachi Avenue that caters to aristocrats and warrior lords. There he announced himself and was led to a private room.

"I cannot discuss my business with any of the young clerks," he told the person who received him. "I need to talk very confidentially with the owner's retired parents."

The old retainer, who knew nothing of how things worked, felt uneasy as he waited. Finally the retired shop owner and his wife appeared. With a grave expression on his face, the old retainer said, "I've come to choose a mistress for my lord." "But of course," the retired owner said. "All the daimyō lords have them. Exactly what kind of woman are you looking for?"

The retainer opened a paulownia-wood scroll box and took out a painting of a woman. "We want to find someone," he said, "who looks like this."

The retired couple saw a woman between fifteen and eighteen with a full, oval face of the kind so popular then, skin the light color of cherry blossoms, and perfect facial features. The lord's councillors wanted round eyes; thick eyebrows with plenty of space between them; a gradually rising nose; a small mouth with large, even white teeth; ears a bit long but not fleshy and with clearly formed earlobes; a natural forehead and unaltered hairline; as well as a long, slender nape with no loose hairs. Her fingers were to be long and delicate with thin nails, and her feet, about seven inches long, with the large toes naturally curved the way a truly sensuous woman's are and with arched soles. Her torso was to be longer than most women's, her waist firm and

---

3. Go-Daigo was exiled to Oki in 1332.

slim, and her hips full. She should move and wear her clothes gracefully, and her figure should show dignity and refinement. She was to have a gentle personality, be
skilled at all the arts that women learn, and know something about everything. The
old retainer added that she was not to have a single mole on her body.

"The capital is a big place," the retired owner said, "and a lot of women live here.
Even so, it won't be easy to find a woman who meets all these requirements. But it's
for a domain lord, and expense is no concern. If the woman exists, we'll find her for
you." The retired couple then went to see an experienced employment agent named
Hanaya Kakuemon on Takeyamachi Street. They discreetly explained all the conditions and asked him to search for suitable candidates.

Employment agencies live off commissions. If an employer pays one hundred
large gold coins as a down payment, the agency takes ten. This is broken down into
silver coins, and even the errand woman gets 2 percent. An applicant for a mistress
job has to have an interview, and if she has no proper clothes, she has to rent what she
wants. For two and a half ounces of silver a day, she can rent a white silk robe or one
of figured black satin, a dapple-dyed robe to wear over that, a wide brocade sash, a
scarlet crepe underskirt, a colorful dye-pattern shawl to cover her head like an elegant
lady, and even a mat to sit on in her hired palanquin. If the young woman makes a
good impression and is hired, she has to pay the agency a large silver coin as its fee.

A woman from a poor family needs to have a new set of foster parents who own
property and will vouch for her. The agency negotiates with the owners of a small
house, and the young woman formally becomes their daughter. In return, the foster
parents receive money and gifts from the lord or rich merchant who employs their
new daughter. If the woman works for a lord and bears a baby boy, she becomes an
official domain retainer, and the lord gives a regular rice stipend to her foster parents.

Competition is intense, and candidates try very hard to make a good impression
at the interview. In addition to renting clothes, they have to spend half an ounce of silver for a palanquin and two carriers—no matter how short the ride is, the rate is the
same to anywhere in Kyōto. And the woman needs a girl helper at two grams of silver
a day and an older maid at three. She also has to pay for their two meals. After all this,
if the woman is not hired, not only does she still have no job, but she's lost well over
three ounces of silver. It's a very hard way to make a living.

And that's not the only thing the woman has to worry about. Well-off merchants
from Ōsaka and Sakai constantly come to Kyōto to visit the Shimabara licensed quarter or party with boy kabuki actors near the theaters along the river by the Fourth
Avenue Bridge. Sometimes these men have some free time and prey on women applicants to amuse themselves. The merchant pays a jester with a shaved head to pretend
to be a wealthy visitor from the western provinces and has him ask women from all
over Kyōto to come interview to be his mistress. The merchant attends the interview,
and if a woman catches his eye, he asks her to stay and secretly negotiates with the
owner of the house for a secluded room. Then he asks the woman to sleep with him
for just that one time. The surprised woman is terribly angry and disappointed, but
when she tries to leave, he says all sorts of things to persuade her. Finally he mentions
money, and since the woman has paid so much for the interview, she gives in. For
selling herself, she gets two small gold pieces. There's nothing else she can do. But
women who aren't from poor families don't do that.

The employment agency carefully chose more than 170 attractive young women
and sent them to the old retainer for interviews, but he wasn't satisfied with a single
one. Desperately, the agency kept on searching, and when they heard about me, they

contacted someone in the village of Kohata on the Uji River. Together they came to see me at my parents' house in an out-of-the-way part of Uji, where we were trying to live inconspicuously away from the world until people had forgotten what I'd done. But I agreed to an interview, and I went right back to Kyōto with the anxious agents just as I was, without putting on good clothes or makeup. When I got there, the old retainer thought I was even better than the woman in the painting, so the search was called off. Everything was decided on the spot, and I got to set the conditions myself. I became an official domain mistress.[4]

And so I went with the retainer all the way to Edo, far off in Musashi Province in the east. There I lived very happily day and night in the lord's third mansion[5] in Asakusa, on the outskirts of the city. Everything was so luxurious, well, in the day I couldn't believe my eyes. I felt I must be seeing the most beautiful cherry blossoms in the world on the Mount Yoshino in China[6] that people talk about. And at night they had top kabuki actors from Sakai-chō come, and we'd watch their plays and variety shows and laugh hour after hour. Everything was so luxurious you couldn't imagine anything else you'd want.

But women, you know, are very basic creatures. They just can't forget about physical love, even though warriors have very strict rules keeping women and men apart. The serving women who live in the inner rooms of those mansions almost never even see a man and don't have the slightest idea what the scent of a man's loincloth is like. Whenever they look at one of Moronobu's suggestive prints, they'll feel a rush and go dizzy with desire. Without even imagining they're really making love, they'll twist and push their own heels or middle fingers way around and move their implements. And when they're finished, they still feel unsatisfied. They want to make love with a flesh-and-blood man all the more.

Daimyō lords usually spend most of their time in the front rooms of their mansions overseeing domain business, and without knowing it, they become attracted to the young pages with long hair who are constantly waiting on them. The love a lord feels for a page is deeper than anything he feels for a woman. His wife is definitely in second place. In my opinion, this is because a lord's wife isn't allowed to show her jealousy the way commoner women do. Men, high or low, fear a jealous woman more than anything else in the world, and those warriors take strict precautions.

I've always been an unlucky woman, but with the lord I was fortunate. He was tender to me, and we enjoyed our lovemaking. But things didn't work out. Before I could get pregnant, he started taking herbal pills. They didn't do much good, though. He was still young, but in bed he just couldn't do anything anymore. It was just extremely bad luck. I couldn't talk about it with anyone, so I spent all my time regretting what had happened. The lord kept losing weight, and finally he became so weak and haggard he was just awful to look at.

I was amazed to discover that the councillors thought it was my fault. They said I was a woman from the capital who liked fancy sex and had worn out their lord. Those old men didn't know the first thing about love, but they made the decisions. I was suddenly dismissed and sent all the way back to my parents—again. If you look

---

4. She becomes the daimyō lord's semiofficial second wife. Normally the mistress would live with the daimyō while he was in his home domain on alternate years, but in this case the lord's wife has died, so she goes to Edo.
5. A daimyō lord usually had three mansions in Edo: the first was for his family and formal audiences; the second

was for emergencies; and the third was for relaxation and a mistress.
6. Mount Yoshino, south of Nara, was believed to have the most beautiful cherry blossoms in Japan—prompting the belief in an even more beautiful, ideal Mount Yoshino in China.

closely at the world, you'll see that a man who's born sexually weak is a very sad thing for a woman.

A MONK'S WIFE IN A WORLDLY TEMPLE (2:3)

I have a small build, so I unstitched the sewn-up openings under the arms of the robes I'd worn as a girl[1] and put them on again. I looked so young people called me a female version of the Daoist wizard Tie-guai.[2]

In those days Buddhism was at its proverbial high noon, and truly, even in broad daylight, women dressed as temple pages[3] would walk right into temple precincts and visit the monks there. I, too, finally overcame my shame and had my hair done up like a boy, with thick, long hair in front and the top of my head shaved. I learned to speak like a boy and move my body almost like one, too. When I put on a loincloth, I was surprised to see how much like a boy I looked! I also changed to a boy's narrow sash, but the first time I stuck long and short swords through it, they were so heavy I couldn't keep my waist and legs steady. And when I put on a boy's cloak and wide-rimmed sedge hat, I began to wonder whether I was really myself.

I hired a young man with a long ink moustache painted on his face to carry my spare sandals and other things, and I set out together with a professional jester from the licensed quarter who knew a lot about how things worked in Kyōto. We asked around and found a temple known to have wealth and a sex-loving head monk. We walked right through the gate in the earth walls surrounding the temple, pretending we were going inside to see the small cherry tree in the temple garden. Then the jester went to the head monk's quarters and began whispering with the monk, who seemed to have a lot of free time on his hands. Soon I was called into the reception room, where the jester introduced me to the monk.

"This young warrior," the jester said, "has lost his lord, and he has no one to depend on. He's been able to make some contacts, but while he's waiting for an offer from another lord, he'll drop in here from time to time for a little recreation. I most sincerely ask you to take care of him to the best of your ability." He went on and on about a lot of similar things.

The head monk was flushed with excitement. "Just last night," he blurted out, "I got someone to teach me how to make an herbal mixture to induce abortions. It's something you women really need to. . . ." Then he clapped his hand on his mouth. It was all quite amusing.

Later we drank some saké and spoke more freely. As we savored the smells of meat and fish coming from the temple kitchen, my fee was set at two small gold coins per night. Later, the jester and I went around to temples of every persuasion suggesting they switch to the Woman-Loving sect, and we didn't find a single monk who didn't convert.

Eventually the head priest of one temple fell in love with me, and I agreed to become his temporary wife for three years in exchange for twenty-five pounds of silver.

---

1. Girls wore long, loose sleeves with an opening under the arms, which was sewn up when they became adults, usually in their late teens. In this chapter, the woman is about 25 or 26 years of age.
2. A Daoist wizard from the Sui dynasty who, according to legend, was able to breathe out earlier versions of himself from his own mouth.
3. Boys serving as assistants to high-ranking monks. They often were sexual partners of the older men, but in the 17th century, women were able to enter temples more easily, and a new type of page "flourished."

I became what people call an "oven god."[4] As the days went by, I was more and more amazed by what I saw and heard at this floating-world temple. In the past, a group of monk friends who lived in various halls around the temple compound had gotten together on the six days a month when special purifications and austerities are required. They all solemnly pledged that on days except for these six, they would strictly obey their abstentions. And they vowed to rigorously limit their fish and poultry and their sex with women to the nights of these six days, except, of course, when the days fell on the memorial days for various buddhas and the sect founder. To pursue their pleasures, they went all the way to Third Avenue in downtown Kyōto and visited places like the Koiya Inn.[5] On other days, the men acted like model monks. The buddhas, who know all, looked on them leniently, and everything went smoothly.

But in the last few years, this large temple had been growing very prosperous, and the monks were losing all restraint. At night they replaced their black robes with long cloaks and went to the licensed quarter pretending to be shaven-headed herbal doctors. And the head priest would bring his secret wife of the moment right into the monks' living quarters. He'd had his monks dig far down below one corner of the main living room and built a secret underground room for the wife. Between the ground and the raised floor of the quarters, they'd constructed a narrow window in a place that no one could see from the outside. That way the woman could have a little light. They'd also filled the space between the ceiling of the underground room and the quarters floor with earth and constructed soundproof walls more than a foot thick all the way around to the back of the room. During the day the head priest forced me down into this underground cell. When the sun went down, I was allowed up and could go as far as his bedroom.

Living like this was depressing enough, but sleeping with the priest made me even sadder. It was just a job, and there was no love in it. I had to give myself to that disgusting priest day and night, whenever he wanted to have sex, and I began to lose interest in living. Nothing gave me pleasure any more, and I gradually lost weight and grew weaker. But the priest didn't let up in the least. His expression showed that as far as he was concerned, if I died he'd just have me secretly buried somewhere on the temple grounds without even a proper cremation. And that would be that. It was frightening.

Later I got used to the situation, and I even came to enjoy it. When the priest went out to chant sutras at a parishioner's house on the night after a death or on a memorial day, I found myself waiting up late, wishing he would come back. And when he went out at dawn to pray over the ashes of a cremated person, I felt as if we were saying good-bye to each other, and I hated for him to be away, no matter how short a time it was. Even the smell of incense on his white robe clung to my body and seemed dear to me. After a while I forgot my loneliness, and I started to like the sounds of gongs and cymbals at the ceremonies. At first, you know, I would hold my hands over my ears whenever I heard them. And my nose got used to the smell from the crematory. The more deaths there were, well, the happier I was, since they meant more offerings for the temple. Early each evening, I called in fish peddlers and made suppers of duck meat with and without bones, blowfish soup, cedar-broiled fish, and

---

4. Daikoku, one of the seven gods of fortune, was often worshiped as a kitchen or oven god. The term was also a euphemism for a woman living and cooking in a temple, a custom that was widespread but officially forbidden. The priest pays the woman a substantial sum.
5. Koiya Inn, a popular seafood restaurant, had many private rooms where the monks could meet women.

other fine seafood.[6] I did take one small precaution, though. I always put a cover on the brazier so the nice smells wouldn't escape.

The young monks in training saw our loose way of living and imitated us. They hid salted red herrings in their sleeve pockets and wrapped them in pieces of old calligraphy practice paper covered with half-written buddha names. After soaking the papers, they would place them in warm ashes to bake and would eat herrings from morning till night. It gave them wonderful complexions and lustrous skin and kept them vigorous and healthy. Some monks go off for long periods to a mountain or forest where they eat only berries and plants. Other monks are so poor they have no choice but to eat only vegetables. You can spot these kinds of monks right away from their lifeless expressions. They look like rotting trees.

I'd worked at the temple from spring until early fall. At first the priest was terribly afraid I would run away, and while I was up out of my underground room, he would lock the living quarters each time he went out. But later he came to trust me and just glanced in at me from the kitchen from time to time. Gradually I became bolder, and when parishioners came to visit the priest I no longer rushed underground but simply slipped out of sight into another room.

One evening I went out onto the bamboo verandah to get some fresh air, and a strong wind was moaning in the trees and ripping the thin leaves of the plantains in the garden. It was an eerie sight. Everything in the world really does change, I felt, just as they preach. I lay down on the porch with my head on my arm and was soon very drowsy. Then I saw what looked like a phantom shape. Her hair was completely gray, and her face was covered with wrinkles. Her pathetic arms and legs were thin as tongs, and she was bent over with a crooked back. She came toward me crawling on all fours.

"I've lived in this temple for many, many years," she said in a voice so full of sorrow I could hardly bear to listen. "The priest told people I was his mother. I'm not from a low-class family, but I decided to do a disgraceful thing, and I came here. I was twenty years older than he was, and I'm ashamed to say I was so poor I couldn't get by any more, and I began to sleep with him. Later we became close and exchanged many pledges, but they. . . . For him, all those pledges were nothing, nothing at all. When I got old like this, he pushed me into a dark corner of the temple. He gives me nothing but old rice offerings he's taken down from the altars. And now he sees I'm not about to die eating only that, so he glares resentfully at me. He's treated me terribly, but still, you know, it isn't really so bad. There's something else that gnaws at me until I can't stand it. Every single day. It's you! You don't know anything about me, but whenever I hear you and the priest saying little things to each other in bed, well, you see, even at my age I just can't forget sex. So I've decided to get rid of this terrible longing I have and feel good again. I'm going to bite right into you. Tonight!"

I was completely shaken. I knew I had no business being in that temple a minute longer. Finally I devised a method of escape that impressed even me. I stuffed a lot of cotton wadding between the outer and inner layers in the front part of my robe. That made me look quite heavy. Then I went to see the head priest.

"I haven't told you until now," I said, "but I'm several months pregnant. I'm not sure exactly when, but the baby could come any time now."

6. All prohibited foods.

The priest lost his usual composure. "Please go back to your parents' house," he said. "Have a safe delivery and then come back here." He gathered up a lot of offertory coins from different places and gave them to me, swearing he was very worried about all the needs I'd have at home. Then he gave me some tiny silk robes that grief-stricken parents had left as offerings after their babies died. The priest said he couldn't stand to look at them any more, and he gave me all he had, telling me to sew them into things for his baby instead. Then he began celebrating and named the child Ishijiyo—Everlasting Rock—a boy's name, even though it hadn't been born yet.

I'd had enough of that temple. There was a lot of time left on my contract, but I never went back. The priest must have been very upset, but in a situation like that, well, there was no legal action he could take.

FIVE HUNDRED DISCIPLES OF THE BUDDHA—I'D KNOWN THEM ALL (6:4)

In winter the mountains sleep beneath leafless trees, and the bare limbs of the cherries turn white only with snow at dusk. Then spring dawns come once more, filled with blossoms. Only humans get old as the years pass and lose all pleasure in living. I especially. When I recalled my own life, I felt thoroughly ashamed.

I thought I at least ought to pray for the one thing I could still wish for—to be reborn in Amida Buddha's Pure Land paradise. So I went back to Kyōto one more time and made a pilgrimage to the Daiunji temple[1] in the northern hills. It was supposed to be a visible Pure Land right here in this world. My mind was filled with pious feelings, and I'd chosen a good time to visit. It was the end of the Twelfth Month, when people gathered to chant the names of all the buddhas and to confess the bad deeds they'd done during the year and ask for forgiveness.[2] I joined in their chanting.

Afterward, as I walked down the steps of the main hall, I noticed a smaller hall devoted to the Five Hundred Disciples of Shakyamuni Buddha.[3] All were wise and worthy men who had achieved enlightenment, and I went over and looked inside. Each virtuous disciple was distinctly individual and differed from all the others. I wondered what marvelous sculptor could have carved all these many unique statues.

People say there are so many disciples that if you search hard enough, you're bound to find someone you know. Wondering if it might be true, I looked over the wooden statues and saw disciples who obviously were men with whom I'd shared my pillow when I was younger. I began to examine them more closely and found a statue that looked like Yoshi from Chōjamachi in Kyōto.[4] When I was working in the Shimabara quarter, we exchanged very deep vows, and he tattooed my name on his wrist where no one would notice. I was beginning to remember all the things that had happened between us when I saw another disciple sitting under a large rock. He looked exactly like the owner of the house in uptown Kyōto where I worked as a parlor maid. He loved me in so many ways that even after all those years I couldn't forget him.

On the other side of the hall I saw Gohei. Even the disciple's high-ridged nose was exactly his. I once lived together with him. We loved each other from the bottoms of our hearts for several years, and he was especially dear to me. Then, closer to me, I

1. A temple in the northern hills of Kyōto, believed to be a place where the bodhisattva Kannon manifested herself, making it a Pure Land on earth. The temple was famed for cures of mental problems and was a refuge for those considered mentally ill.
2. A ceremony held annually between the 19th day and the end of the 12th Month.
3. The original disciples of Shakyamuni Buddha who propagated his doctrines after his death.
4. A wealthy area of uptown Kyōto west of the imperial palace famous for its many money brokers.

saw a wide-bodied disciple in a blue green robe with one shoulder bared. He was working very hard—and he looked familiar. Yes, yes, it was definitely Danpei, the man who did odd jobs for a warrior mansion in Kōjimachi.[5] While I was working in Edo, I used to meet him secretly six nights a month.

Up on some rocks in back was a handsome man with light skin and the soft, gentle face of a buddha. Finally I remembered. He was a kabuki actor from the theaters down along the riverbank near the Fourth Avenue in Kyōto who'd started out as a boy actor selling himself to men on the side. We met while I was working at a teahouse, and I was the first woman with whom he'd ever made love. I taught him all the different styles women and men use, and he learned well, but pretty soon he just folded up. He grew weaker and weaker, like a flame in a lantern, and then he was gone. He was only twenty-four when they took his body to the crematory at Toribe Mountain. The disciple I saw had just his hollow jaw and sunken eyes. There was no doubt about it.

Farther on was a ruddy-faced disciple with a mustache and bald head. Except for the mustache, he looked just like the old chief priest who'd kept me in his temple as his mistress and treated me so badly. By the time I met him I was used to every kind of sex, but he came at me day and night until I was so worn down I lost weight and had fevers and coughs and my period stopped. But even he had died. Endless storehouse of desire that he was, he, too, finally went up in crematory smoke.

And there, under a withered tree, a disciple with a fairly intelligent face and prominent forehead was shaving the top of his head. He seemed to be on the verge of saying something, and his legs and arms looked as though they were beginning to move. As I gazed at him, I gradually realized he, too, resembled someone I'd loved. While I was going around dressed up like a singing nun, I would meet a new man every day, but there was one who became very attached to me. He'd been sent from a western domain to help oversee the domain's rice warehouse sales in Ōsaka, and he loved me so much he risked his life for me. I could still remember everything about him. The sad things as well as the happy ones. He was very generous with what people begrudge the most,[6] and I was able to pay back everything I owed my manager.

Calmly I examined all five hundred disciples and found I recognized every single one! They all were men I'd known intimately. I began to remember event after event from the painful years when I was forced to work getting money from men. Women who sold themselves, I was sure, were the most fearful of all women, and I began to grow frightened of myself. With this single body of mine I'd slept with more than ten thousand men. It made me feel low and ashamed to go on living so long. My heart roared in my chest like a burning wagon in hell,[7] and hot tears poured from my eyes and scattered in every direction like water from one of hell's cauldrons. Suddenly I went into a sort of trance and no longer knew where I was. I collapsed on the ground, got up, and fell down again and again.

Many monks had apparently come to where I was, and they were telling me that the sun was going down. Then the booming of the big temple bell finally returned my soul to my body and startled me back to my senses.

"Old woman, what grieves you so?"

"Does one of these five hundred disciples resemble your dead child?"

"Is one your husband?"

"Why were you crying so hard?"

---

5. The narrator lived there herself as a seamstress.
6. That is, money.
7. The woman fears she will soon go to Buddhist hell, not the Pure Land. Fiery carts were believed to carry condemned souls to the assigned part of hell.

Their gentle voices made me feel even more ashamed. Without replying, I walked quickly out the temple gate. As I did, I suddenly realized the most important thing there is to know in life. It was all actually true![8] The Pure Land, I was sure then, really does exist. And our bodies really do disappear completely. Only our names stay behind in the world. Our bones turn to ash and end up buried in wild grass near some swamp.[9]

Some time later I found myself standing in the grass at the edge of Hirosawa Pond. And there, beyond it, stood Narutaki Mountain. There was no longer anything at all keeping me from entering the mountain of enlightenment on the far side. I would leave all my worldly attachments behind and ride the Boat of the Buddhist Dharma across the waters of worldly passions all the way to the Other Shore. I made up my mind to pray, enter the water, and be reborn in the Pure Land.[1]

I ran toward the pond as fast as I could. But just then someone grabbed me and held me back. It was a person who'd known me well many years before.[2] He persuaded me not to end my own life and fixed up this hermitage for me.

"Let your death come when it comes," he said. "Free yourself from all your false words and actions and return to your original mind. Meditate and enter the way of the Buddha."

I was very grateful for this advice, and I've devoted myself to meditation ever since. From morning to night I concentrate my mind and do nothing but chant Amida Buddha's name. Then you two men came to my old door, and I felt drawn to you. I have so few visitors here. Then I let you pour me some saké, and it confused my mind. I actually do realize how short life is, you know, though I've gone on and on, boring you with the long story of my own.

Well, no matter. Think of it as my sincere confession of all the bad things I've ever done. It's cleared the clouds of attachment from me, and I feel my mind now shining bright as the moon. I hope I've also managed to make this spring night pass more pleasantly for you. I didn't hide anything, you know. With no husband or children, I had no reason to. The lotus flower in my heart[3] opened for you, and before it closed it told everything, from beginning to end. I've certainly worked in some dirty professions, but is my heart not pure?

Tsangyang Gyatso
1683–1706

After Buddhism was introduced into Tibet following the seventh century, the Himalayan kingdom became a center for monastic culture and religious thought and poetry. Over time, the major priests or lamas came to have wide political influence as well, often supported by Chinese emperors to the east or Mongol khans to the north. In the sixteenth century, the Mongol leader

---

8. The woman cites the Nō play *Tomonaga*, in which a monk prays for the soul of the dead warrior Tomonaga. Tomonaga's soul returns and exclaims that the Pure Land, Kannon's mercy, and other Buddhist beliefs are "actually true!"
9. The woman alludes to the Nine Stages of the Corpse, a meditative Buddhist poem on the reality of death attributed to Su Dongpo, and then literally arrives at some swamp grass.
1. Buddhist teachings are commonly compared with a boat. To the woman, the pond looks like the sea of existence itself. In the medieval period, many people believed

that one could reach the Pure Land by sailing out to sea in a small boat or by jumping into rivers or ponds while meditating on Amida and Kannon. It was a form of religious suicide chosen most commonly by outcasts, sick people, or monks.
2. Gender unspecified; "he" is used because the person has enough money to buy the woman a hut.
3. A Buddhist metaphor. Just as the lotus rises from the mud, the pure mind experiences enlightenment amid the delusions of the world. Exemplified by Kannon, the lotus-holding female bodhisattva.

proclaimed the head of a major sect the Dalai Lama, recognizing him as the legitimate successor of the previous chief lama (whose name, Gyatso, means "ocean" in Tibetan; "dalai" was the Mongol equivalent, which came to serve as a formal title). In 1642, the fifth Dalai Lama became the country's effective ruler, presiding over a united and prosperous nation for forty years. Each Dalai Lama was believed to be the reincarnation of his predecessor, and a year after one died, a national search would be launched for a newborn who would be revealed to be his reincarnation. A regent would then rule the country until the new (or newly reborn) lama came of age, a system still used in 1939 to discover the present, fourteenth Dalai Lama, who has been recognized worldwide as a spiritual leader as well as the voice of Tibet's struggle for independence in the decades since its absorption by China in 1950.

Though the fifth Dalai Lama codified this system of selection, it was disrupted upon his own death in 1682, when the ambitious regent took effective power, actually concealing news of the lama's death from the outside world. Tsangyang Gyatso was eventually located, at the age of five, as the reincarnated Dalai Lama, but he was brought up in private; he wasn't publicly proclaimed the Sixth Dalai Lama until 1696, and even then he was kept under the regent's thumb. Deprived of real authority, Tsangyang Gyatso devoted himself to the study of Buddhist scriptures, to archery, and to love affairs. His visits were said to be considered a great honor by the young women in the village of Shol, beneath the walls of the towering Potala monastery where he lived, and families would repaint their white houses yellow in honor of his visits. Farther afield, though, the young Dalai Lama's activities shocked monks who held more strictly to their vows, particularly when Tsangyang Gyatso gained a reputation for writing love songs to his sweethearts. Tibet's neighbors took the opportunity to intervene: with the approval of China's Manchu emperor, the Mongol khan invaded, killed the aging regent, and deposed Tsangyang Gyatso, asserting that he wasn't the true reincarnation of the Fifth Dalai Lama at all. The Mongol ruler attempted to install his own son in his place, and the twenty-three-year-old Tsangyang Gyatso was sent over the mountains toward exile in China. He never reached his destination but disappeared en route, most likely assassinated by his guards—though according to popular tradition, still widely believed by Tibetans, he escaped and lived out his life as a wandering religious mendicant.

Some seventy short poems survive, attributed to him since the eighteenth century, though their authorship can't be proven. Some treat strictly religious themes, but most take erotic love as their subject. The examples given here offer a striking self-portrait of a libertine who chafes under extreme social constraint, yet also playfully exploits the physical and emotional opportunities his exceptional situation offers.

PRONUNCIATION:
Tsangyang Gyatso: TSANG-yang g'YAHT-SO

from Love Poems of the Sixth Dalai Lama[1]

1

I sought my lover at twilight
Snow fell at daybreak.
Secret or not, no matter.
Footprints have been left in the snow.

2

Residing at the Potala
I am Rigdzin Tsangyang Gyatso
But in the back alleys of Shol-town

1. Translated by Rick Fields and Brian Cutillo (poems 1–3 and 10); G. W. Houston (poems 4, 9, 12); Coleman Barks (poems 5, 7, 8); and Per K. Sorensen (poems 6, 11, 13, 14).

I am rake and stud.

3

Lover met by chance on the road,
Girl with delicious-smelling body –
Like picking up a small white turquoise
Only to toss it away again.

4

Small written letters
Destroyed by water drops.
Unwritten memories
Never could be so erased.

5

If the one I love gives up everything
to study the teachings,
I'll take the holy path too.
I'll live in a secluded retreat
and forget how young I am.

6

During meditation my lama's face
Will not come forth in my mind;
But my lover's face, unmeditated,
So clear, so clear in my mind.

7

If I could meditate as deeply
on the sacred texts as I do
on you, I would clearly be
enlightened in this lifetime!

8

Pure snow-water from the holy mountain.
Dew of the rare Naga Vajra grass.[2]
These essences make a nectar
which is fermented by one
who has incarnated as a maiden.
Her cup's contents can protect you
from rebirth in lower form,
if it is tasted in the state
of awareness it deserves.

9

Someone has stolen from me
That one with conch-white heart.
Astrologer, to you I come.
She still invades my dreams.

---

2. A plant growing on the slopes of a holy mountain in southeast Tibet, sacred to "the Sow-headed Goddess." Drinking the elixir made from this herb would bring the adept into symbolic union with the goddess and produce enlightenment.

10

Wild horses running in the hills
Can be caught with snares or lassoes
But not even magic charms can stop
A lover's heart that's turned away.

11

Rock and wind kept tryst
To abrade the vulture's plumage;
People fraught with deceptive schemes
Fray me to the very bone.[3]

12

Snowy cloud with dark inside
Is the home of frost and hail,
While the monk not white nor yellow[4]
Is the foe of Buddha's teaching.

13

Beyond death, in the Realm of Hell,
The karma-mirror of Yama[5] stands:
Judge me, but yield me fairness in the hereafter
Because this life paid me none!

14

In this life's short walk
We have faced up to so much.
Let us now see whether we shall meet again
In the young years of our next life!

John Wilmot, Earl of Rochester
1647–1680

Surely Lord Rochester was the greatest rake of the Restoration—which invented rakes—and probably of all time. Born during the dour and democratic administration of Puritan Oliver Cromwell, he came of age just in time for the triumphant restoration of monarchy, pleasure, and extravagance. For Rochester, liberty *was* libertinage: the freedom of the rich aristocrat to do whatever he pleased. Even in that permissive age he was often punished for his excesses, but he always found pardon. When at eighteen he tried to abduct Elizabeth Malet, "melancholy heiress," poet, and much sought-after match, he was imprisoned in the Tower of London—but he married her two years later. He boxed the ears of a fellow courtier in the King's presence, yet was pardoned. He broke the King's valuable clock and was banished from court for brawling, yet the King still drank with him afterward. Elizabeth Malet had to forgive him an unthinkable variety of infidelities—but his tender love letters to her imply she did. One assumes that God too forgave him when he embraced the Church of England in the end, after a life of violating

---

3. This and the next poem have traditionally been read as expressing Tsangyang Gyatso's frustration with the double-dealing of the Regent who kept him from full power.
4. A pure heart would be white; a monk's robes were yellow.

The Regent often dressed as a monk, though he hadn't taken vows and himself had mistresses.
5. Lord of the Underworld, and holder of the mirror in which one's destiny was reflected.

its tenets daily. In the words of contemporary dramatist Nathaniel Lee, "He was the Spirit of Wit—and had such an art in gilding his Failures, that it was hard not to love his faults." He versified furiously but, as a nobleman, was above publishing, and had his irreverent manuscripts burnt during a fit of deathbed piety. Rochester died in his new-found faith at age thirty-three, having, according to Samuel Johnson, "blazed out his youth and health in lavish voluptuousness." His surviving poems still betray the witty contradictions of his spirit.

The Imperfect Enjoyment

Naked she lay, clasped in my longing arms,
I filled with love, and she all over charms;
Both equally inspired with eager fire,
Melting through kindness, flaming in desire.
5   With arms, legs, lips close clinging to embrace,
She clips me to her breast, and sucks me to her face.
Her nimble tongue, Love's lesser lightning, played
Within my mouth, and to my thoughts conveyed
Swift orders that I should prepare to throw
10   The all-dissolving thunderbolt below.
My fluttering soul, sprung with the pointed kiss,
Hangs hovering o'er her balmy brinks of bliss.
But whilst her busy hand would guide that part
Which should convey my soul up to her heart,
15   In liquid raptures I dissolve all o'er,
Melt into sperm, and spend at every pore.
A touch from any part of her had done 't:
Her hand, her foot, her very look's a cunt.
       Smiling, she chides in a kind murmuring noise,
20   And from her body wipes the clammy joys,
When, with a thousand kisses wandering o'er
My panting bosom, "Is there then no more?"
She cries. "All this to love and rapture's due;
Must we not pay a debt to pleasure too?"
25   But I, the most forlorn, lost man alive,
To show my wished obedience vainly strive:
I sigh, alas! and kiss, but cannot swive.°   screw
Eager desires confound my first intent,
Succeeding shame does more success prevent,
30   And rage at last confirms me impotent.
Ev'n her fair hand, which might bid heat return
To frozen age, and make cold hermits burn,
Applied to my dead cinder, warms no more
Than fire to ashes could past flames restore.
35   Trembling, confused, despairing, limber, dry,
A wishing, weak, unmoving lump I lie.
This dart of love, whose piercing point, oft tried,
With virgin blood ten thousand maids have dyed,
Which nature still directed with such art
40   That it through every cunt reached every heart—
Stiffly resolved, 'twould carelessly invade

Woman or man, nor ought° its fury stayed:°   *anything / stopped*
Where'er it pierced, a cunt it found or made—
Now languid lies in this unhappy hour,
45   Shrunk up and sapless like a withered flower.
     Thou treacherous, base deserter of my flame,
False to my passion, fatal to my fame,
Through what mistaken magic dost thou prove
So true to lewdness, so untrue to love?
50   What oyster-cinder-beggar-common whore
Didst thou e'er fail in all thy life before?
When vice, disease, and scandal lead the way,
With what officious haste doest thou obey!
Like a rude, roaring hector° in the streets   *bully*
55   Who scuffles, cuffs, and justles all he meets,
But if his king or country claim his aid,
The rakehell villain shrinks and hides his head;
Ev'n so thy brutal valor is displayed,
Breaks every stew,° does each small whore invade,   *brothel*
60   But when great Love the onset does command,
Base recreant to thy prince, thou dar'st not stand.
Worst part of me, and henceforth hated most,
Through all the town a common fucking post,
On whom each whore relieves her tingling cunt
65   As hogs on gates do rub themselves and grunt,
Mayst thou to ravenous chancres° be a prey,   *syphilis sores*
Or in consuming weepings waste away;
May strangury and stone[1] thy days attend;
May'st thou never piss, who didst refuse to spend
70   When all my joys did on false thee depend.
     And may ten thousand abler pricks agree
To do the wronged Corinna right for thee.

A Satyr[1] Against Reason and Mankind

     Were I (who to my cost already am
One of those strange, prodigious creatures, man)
A spirit free to choose, for my own share,
What case of flesh and blood I pleased to wear,
5   I'd be a dog, a monkey, or a bear,
Or anything but that vain animal
Who is so proud of being rational.
     The senses are too gross, and he'll contrive
A sixth, to contradict the other five,
10   And before certain instinct, will prefer
Reason, which fifty times for one does err;
Reason, an *ignis fatuus*[2] in the mind,

1. Painful diseases of the bladder and urinary tract that
block the flow of urine.
1. Possibly a pun, identifying both the genre (satire) and
the speaker (a satyr: lascivious half-man, half-animal).

2. Literally "foolish fire": a marshland phosphorescence
that, appearing now here and now there, was thought to be
created by sprites to mislead night travelers.

Which, leaving light of nature, sense, behind,
Pathless and dangerous wandering ways it takes
15 Through error's fenny bogs and thorny brakes;
Whilst the misguided follower climbs with pain
Mountains of whimseys, heaped in his own brain;
Stumbling from thought to thought, falls headlong down
Into doubt's boundless sea, where, like to drown,
20 Books bear him up awhile, and make him try
To swim with bladders of philosophy;
In hopes still to o'ertake th' escaping light,
The vapor dances in his dazzling sight
Till, spent, it leaves him to eternal night.
25 Then old age and experience, hand in hand,
Lead him to death, and make him understand,
After a search so painful and so long,
That all his life he has been in the wrong.
Huddled in dirt the reasoning engine lies,
30 Who was so proud, so witty, and so wise.
    Pride drew him in, as cheats their bubbles° catch,   *victims*
And made him venture to be made a wretch.
His wisdom did his happiness destroy,
Aiming to know that world he should enjoy.
35 And wit was his vain, frivolous pretense
Of pleasing others at his own expense,
For wits are treated just like common whores:
First they're enjoyed, and then kicked out of doors.
The pleasure past, a threatening doubt remains
40 That frights th' enjoyer with succeeding pains.
Women and men of wit are dangerous tools,
And ever fatal to admiring fools:
Pleasure allures, and when the fops escape,
'Tis not that they're belov'd, but fortunate,
45 And therefore what they fear at heart, they hate.
    But now, methinks, some formal band and beard[3]
Takes me to task. Come on, sir; I'm prepared.
    "Then, by your favor, anything that's writ
Against this gibing, jingling knack called wit
50 Likes° me abundantly; but you take care   *pleases*
Upon this point, not to be too severe.
Perhaps my muse were fitter for this part,
For I profess I can be very smart
On wit, which I abhor with all my heart.
55 I long to lash it in some sharp essay,
But your grand indiscretion bids me stay
And turns my tide of ink another way.

---

3. I.e., clergyman, wearing these marks of office. In 1675 one clergyman in particular, the king's chaplain Edward Stillingfleet, had denounced in a sermon an earlier version of Rochester's *Satyr*, prompting the poet to alter and add some portions of the dialogue that follows.

     "What rage ferments in your degenerate mind
     To make you rail at reason and mankind?
60   Blest, glorious man! to whom alone kind heaven
     An everlasting soul has freely given,
     Whom his great Maker took such care to make
     That from himself he did the image take
     And this fair frame in shining reason dressed
65   To dignify his nature above beast;
     Reason, by whose aspiring influence
     We take a flight beyond material sense,
     Dive into mysteries, then soaring pierce
     The flaming limits of the universe,
70   Search heaven and hell, find out what's acted there,
     And give the world true grounds of hope and fear."
       Hold, mighty man, I cry, all this we know
     From the pathetic pen of Ingelo,
     From Patrick's *Pilgrim,* Stillingfleet's replies,[4]
75   And 'tis this very reason I despise:
     This supernatural gift, that makes a mite
     Think he's the image of the infinite,
     Comparing his short life, void of all rest,
     To the eternal and the ever blest;
80   This busy, puzzling stirrer-up of doubt
     That frames deep mysteries, then finds 'em out,
     Filling with frantic crowds of thinking fools
     Those reverend bedlams,° colleges and schools;   *madhouses*
     Borne on whose wings, each heavy sot can pierce
85   The limits of the boundless universe;
     So charming ointments make an old witch fly
     And bear a crippled carcass through the sky.
     'Tis this exalted power, whose business lies
     In nonsense and impossibilities,
90   This made a whimsical philosopher
     Before the spacious world, his tub prefer,[5]
     And we have modern cloistered coxcombs who
     Retire to think, 'cause they have nought to do.
       But thoughts are given for action's government;
95   Where action ceases, thought's impertinent.
     Our sphere of action is life's happiness,
     And he who thinks beyond, thinks like an ass.
     Thus, whilst against false reasoning I inveigh,
     I own[6] right reason, which I would obey:
100   That reason which distinguishes by sense
     And gives us rules of good and ill from thence,

4. Rochester names three pious inspirational writers: Nathaniel Ingelo (?1621–1683); Simon Patrick, whose *Parable of the Pilgrim* appeared in 1664; and Stillingfleet, Rochester's clerical critic.
5. Diogenes (c. 400–325 B.C.E.), Greek philosopher who supposedly lived in an earthenware tub, as an emblem of his scorn for the shallowness of more opulent modes of life.
6. Acknowledge. "Right reason" refers to natural instinct or common sense, as opposed to the more elaborate modes of thought Rochester is attacking.

That bounds desires with a reforming will
To keep 'em more in vigor, not to kill.
Your reason hinders, mine helps to enjoy,
105   Renewing appetites yours would destroy.
My reason is my friend, yours is a cheat;
Hunger calls out, my reason bids me eat;
Perversely, yours your appetite does mock:
This asks for food, that answers, "What's o'clock?"
110   This plain distinction, sir, your doubt secures:
'Tis not true reason I despise, but yours.
    Thus I think reason righted, but for man,
I'll ne'er recant; defend him if you can.
For all his pride and his philosophy,
115   'Tis evident beasts are, in their degree,
As wise at least, and better far than he.
Those creatures are the wisest who attain,
By surest means, the ends at which they aim.
If therefore Jowler[7] finds and kills his hares
120   Better than Meres[8] supplies committee chairs,
Though one's a statesman, th' other but a hound,
Jowler, in justice, would be wiser found.
    You see how far man's wisdom here extends;
Look next if human nature makes amends:
125   Whose principles most generous are, and just,
And to whose morals you would sooner trust.
Be judge yourself, I'll bring it to the test:
Which is the basest creature, man or beast?
Birds feed on birds, beasts on each other prey,
130   But savage man alone does man betray.
Pressed by necessity, they kill for food;
Man undoes man to do himself no good.
With teeth and claws by nature armed, they hunt
Nature's allowance, to supply their want.
135   But man, with smiles, embraces, friendship, praise,
Inhumanly his fellow's life betrays;
With voluntary pains works his distress,
Not through necessity, but wantonness.
    For hunger or for love they fight and tear,
140   Whilst wretched man is still in arms for fear.
For fear he arms, and is of arms afraid,
By fear to fear successively betrayed;
Base fear, the source whence his best passions came:
His boasted honor, and his dear-bought fame;
145   That lust of power, to which he's such a slave,
And for the which alone he dares be brave;
To which his various projects are designed;

---

7. A dog's name, emphasizing the animal's appetites.
8. Sir Thomas Meres (1634–1715), politician noted for his energy, efficacy, and self-serving flexibility in questions of party allegiance.

Which makes him generous, affable, and kind;
For which he takes such pains to be thought wise,
150 And screws his actions in a forced disguise,
Leading a tedious life in misery
Under laborious, mean hypocrisy.
Look to the bottom of his vast design,
Wherein man's wisdom, power, and glory join:
155 The good he acts, the ill he does endure,
'Tis all from fear, to make himself secure.
Merely for safety, after fame we thirst,
For all men would be cowards if they durst.
　　And honesty's against all common sense:
160 Men must be knaves, 'tis in their own defense.
Mankind's dishonest; if you think it fair
Amongst known cheats to play upon the square,
You'll be undone.
Nor can weak truth your reputation save:
165 The knaves will all agree to call you knave.
Wronged shall he live, insulted o'er, oppressed,
Who dares be less a villain than the rest.
　　Thus, sir, you see what human nature craves:
Most men are cowards, all men should be knaves.
170 The difference lies, as far as I can see,
Not in the thing itself, but the degree,
And all the subject matter of debate
Is only: Who's a knave of the first rate?
　　All this with indignation have I hurled
175 At the pretending part of the proud world,
Who, swollen with selfish vanity, devise
False freedoms, holy cheats, and formal lies
Over their fellow slaves to tyrannize.
　　But if in court so just a man there be
180 (In court a just man, yet unknown to me)
Who does his needful flattery direct,
Not to oppress and ruin, but protect
(Since flattery, which way soever laid,
Is still a tax on that unhappy trade);
185 If so upright a statesman you can find,
Whose passions bend to his unbiased mind,
Who does his arts and policies apply
To raise his country, not his family,
Nor, whilst his pride owned avarice withstands,
190 Receives close bribes through friends' corrupted hands—
　　Is there a churchman who on God relies;
Whose life, his faith and doctrine justifies?
Not one blown up with vain prelatic pride,
Who, for reproof of sins, does man deride;
195 Whose envious heart makes preaching a pretense,
With his obstreperous, saucy eloquence,

To chide at kings, and rail at men of sense;
None of that sensual tribe whose talents lie
In avarice, pride, sloth, and gluttony;
200   Who hunt good livings, but abhor good lives;
Whose lust exalted to that height arrives
They act adultery with their own wives,
And ere a score of years completed be,
Can from the lofty pulpit proudly see
205   Half a large parish their own progeny;
Nor doting bishop who would be adored
For domineering at the council board,
A greater fop in business at fourscore,
Fonder of serious toys, affected more,
210   Than the gay, glittering fool at twenty proves
With all his noise, his tawdry clothes, and loves;
  But a meek, humble man of honest sense,
Who, preaching peace, does practice continence;
Whose pious life's a proof he does believe
215   Mysterious truths, which no man can conceive.
If upon earth there dwell such God-like men,
I'll here recant my paradox to them,
Adore those shrines of virtue, homage pay,
And, with the rabble world, their laws obey.
220   If such there be, yet grant me this at least:
Man differs more from man, than man from beast.

Eliza Haywood
c. 1693–1756

Eliza Haywood was possibly the most prolific writer in a century of prolific writers, and also one of the most famous and widely read. She was so good at constructing fictional personae, however, and masking her private identity—much like her character, "Fantomina"—that virtually nothing is known for certain about her life. That she was born, married, and divorced or separated in England in the early part of the century are uncontested, but where and to whom, and whether she had children, are matters of debate. Like many women novelists of her century, she began her public career as an actress, first in Dublin at the Smock Alley Theatre and then in London. She soon tried her hand at fiction, and her first novel, *Love in Excess* (1719), was one of three major bestsellers published in English within the next few years, alongside Defoe's *Robinson Crusoe* (1719) and Swift's *Gulliver's Travels* (1726). Over the next forty years she published more than sixty titles in many genres: novels, short fiction, plays, poetry, translations, political tracts, and entire periodical series that she wrote and edited herself.

Haywood became so successful during the 1720s as a writer of "scandalous" narratives that she was mocked by fellow novelist Henry Fielding as "Mrs. Novel," and viciously lampooned by Pope in his *Dunciad* (1728). These attacks had their effect on Haywood, and she temporarily stopped publishing novels. Moreover, the general tone of British fiction changed markedly in the direction of moralizing prudishness after the success of Samuel Richardson's sentimental novels of the 1740s, which Haywood first satirized (as did Fielding), and then imitated. "Fantomina" (1724) characterizes Haywood's best early fiction, with its open expression of female sexual desire—which, nevertheless, must always be masked, and finally punished.

PRONUNCIATIONS:
Beauplaisir: BOH-play-ZEER
Fantomina: fan-to-MAI-nah

Fantomina: Or, Love in a Maze

Being a Secret History of an Amour Between Two Persons of Condition[1]

In love the victors from the vanquished fly.
They fly that wound, and they pursue that die.

—Waller[2]

A young lady of distinguished birth, beauty, wit, and spirit, happened to be in a box one night at the playhouse; where, though there were a great number of celebrated toasts,[3] she perceived several gentlemen extremely pleased themselves with entertaining a woman who sat in a corner of the pit,[4] and, by her air and manner of receiving them, might easily be known to be one of those who come there for no other purpose than to create acquaintance with as many as seem desirous of it. She could not help testifying her contempt of men who, regardless either of the play or circle, threw away their time in such a manner, to some ladies that sat by her: but they, either less surprised by being more accustomed to such sights than she who had been bred for the most part in the country, or not of a disposition to consider anything very deeply, took but little notice of it. She still thought of it, however; and the longer she reflected on it, the greater was her wonder that men, some of whom she knew were accounted to have wit,[5] should have tastes so very depraved.—This excited a curiosity in her to know in what manner these creatures were addressed:[6]—she was young, a stranger to the world, and consequently to the dangers of it; and having nobody in town at that time to whom she was obliged to be accountable for her actions, did in everything as her inclinations or humors rendered most agreeable to her: therefore thought it not in the least a fault to put in practice a little whim which came immediately into her head, to dress herself as near as she could in the fashion of those women who make sale of their favors, and set herself in the way of being accosted as such a one, having at that time no other aim, than the gratification of an innocent curiosity.— She no sooner designed this frolic than she put it in execution; and muffling her hoods over her face, went the next night into the gallery-box, and practicing as much as she had observed at that distance the behavior of that woman, was not long before she found her disguise had answered the ends she wore it for.—A crowd of purchasers of all degrees and capacities were in a moment gathered about her, each endeavoring to

---

1. Upper-class rank.
2. The final lines of Edmund Waller's "To a Friend, on the different success of their loves" (1645), in which a man describes how his infatuation with a proud woman named Celia met with her rejection, while his subsequent loss of interest turned the tables and made her solicitous of him. "To die" here also means "to experience orgasm."
3. Belles, fine young ladies (whose health was commonly

drunk by gentlemen in toasts).
4. The area below the stage generally occupied by gentlemen, law students, professional or literary types, and (in this case) prostitutes. Aristocracy generally sat in the boxes above.
5. Intelligence, good taste, judgment.
6. Creatures: common term of disrespect for women of low birth or reputation. Addressed: approached, solicited.

outbid the other in offering her a price for her embraces.—She listened to 'em all, and was not a little diverted in her mind at the disappointment she should give to so many, each of which thought himself secure of gaining her.—She was told by 'em all that she was the most lovely woman in the world; and some cried, *Gad, she is mighty like my fine Lady Such-a-one*—naming her own name. She was naturally vain, and received no small pleasure in hearing herself praised, though in the person of another, and a supposed prostitute; but she dispatched as soon as she could all that had hitherto attacked her, when she saw the accomplished *Beauplaisir*[7] was making his way through the crowd as fast as he was able, to reach the bench she sat on. She had often seen him in the drawing-room, had talked with him; but then her quality[8] and reputed virtue kept him from using her with that freedom she now expected he would do, and had discovered something in him which had made her often think she should not be displeased, if he would abate some part of his reserve.—Now was the time to have her wishes answered:—he looked in her face, and fancied, as many others had done, that she very much resembled that lady whom she really was; but the vast disparity there appeared between their characters prevented him from entertaining even the most distant thought that they could be the same.—He addressed her at first with the usual salutations of her pretended profession, as, *Are you engaged, Madam?—Will you permit me to wait on you home after the play?—By Heaven, you are a fine girl!—How long have you used this house?*—and such like questions; but perceiving she had a turn of wit, and a genteel manner in her raillery, beyond what is frequently to be found among those wretches, who are for the most part gentlewomen but by necessity, few of 'em having had an education suitable to what they affect to appear, he changed the form of his conversation, and showed her it was not because he understood no better that he had made use of expressions so little polite.—In fine, they were infinitely charmed with each other: he was transported to find so much beauty and wit in a woman, who he doubted not but on very easy terms he might enjoy; and she found a vast deal of pleasure in conversing with him in this free and unrestrained manner. They passed their time all the play with an equal satisfaction; but when it was over, she found herself involved in a difficulty, which before never entered into her head, but which she knew not well how to get over.—The passion he professed for her, was not of that humble nature which can be content with distant adorations:—he resolved not to part from her without the gratifications of those desires she had inspired; and presuming on the liberties which her supposed function allowed of, told her she must either go with him to some convenient house of his procuring, or permit him to wait on her to her own lodgings.—Never had she been in such a *dilemma:* three or four times did she open her mouth to confess her real quality; but the influence of her ill stars prevented it, by putting an excuse into her head, which did the business as well, and at the same time did not take from her the power of seeing and entertaining him a second time with the same freedom she had done this.—She told him, she was under obligations to a man who maintained her, and whom she durst not disappoint, having promised to meet him that night at a house hard by.[9]—This story so like what those ladies sometimes tell was not at all suspected by *Beauplaisir;* and assuring her he would be far from doing her a prejudice,[1] desired that in return for the pain he should suffer in being deprived of her company that night, that she would order her affairs, so as not to render him unhappy the next. She gave a solemn promise

7. Lovely pleasure (French).
8. High social station.

9. Nearby.
1. Injury.

to be in the same box on the morrow evening; and they took leave of each other; he to the tavern to drown the remembrance of his disappointment; she in a hackney-chair[2] hurried home to indulge contemplation on the frolic she had taken, designing nothing less on her first reflections than to keep the promise she had made him, and hugging herself with joy, that she had the good luck to come off undiscovered.

But these cogitations were but of a short continuance; they vanished with the hurry of her spirits, and were succeeded by others vastly different and ruinous:—all the charms of *Beauplaisir* came fresh into her mind; she languished, she almost died for another opportunity of conversing with him; and not all the admonitions of her discretion were effectual to oblige her to deny laying hold of that which offered itself the next night.—She depended on the strength of her virtue, to bear her fate through trials more dangerous than she apprehended this to be, and never having been addressed by him as Lady —— was resolved to receive his devoirs[3] as a town-mistress, imagining a world of satisfaction to herself in engaging him in the character of such a one, observing the surprise he would be in to find himself refused by a woman, who he supposed granted her favors without exception.—Strange and unaccountable were the whimsies she was possessed of—wild and incoherent her desires—unfixed and undetermined her resolutions, but in that of seeing *Beauplaisir* in the manner she had lately done. As for her proceedings with him, or how a second time to escape him, without discovering who she was, she could neither assure herself, nor whether or not in the last extremity she would do so.—Bent, however, on meeting him, whatever should be the consequence, she went out some hours before the time of going to the playhouse, and took lodgings in a house not very far from it, intending, that if he should insist on passing some part of the night with her, to carry him there, thinking she might with more security to her honor entertain him at a place where she was mistress, than at any of his own choosing.

The appointed hour being arrived, she had the satisfaction to find his love in his assiduity: he was there before her; and nothing could be more tender than the manner in which he accosted her: but from the first moment she came in, to that of the play being done, he continued to assure her no consideration should prevail with him to part from her again, as she had done the night before; and she rejoiced to think she had taken that precaution of providing herself with a lodging, to which she thought she might invite him, without running any risk, either of her virtue or reputation.— Having told him she would admit of his accompanying her home, he seemed perfectly satisfied; and leading her to the place, which was not above twenty houses distant, would have ordered a collation[4] to be brought after them. But she would not permit it, telling him she was not one of those who suffered themselves to be treated at their own lodgings; and as soon she was come in, sent a servant, belonging to the house, to provide a very handsome supper, and wine, and everything was served to table in a manner which showed the director neither wanted money, nor was ignorant how it should be laid out.

This proceeding, though it did not take from him the opinion that she was what she appeared to be, yet it gave him thoughts of her, which he had not before.—He believed her a *mistress*, but believed her to be one of a superior rank, and began to imagine the possession of her would be much more expensive than at first he had expected: but not being of a humor to grudge anything for his pleasures, he gave himself no farther

2. Hired sedan chair carried by two men.   4. Light meal.
3. Respects.

trouble than what were occasioned by fears of not having money enough to reach her price, about him.

Supper being over, which was intermixed with a vast deal of amorous conversation, he began to explain himself more than he had done; and both by his words and behavior let her know he would not be denied that happiness the freedoms she allowed had made him hope.—It was in vain; she would have retracted the encouragement she had given:—in vain she endeavored to delay, till the next meeting, the fulfilling of his wishes:—she had now gone too far to retreat:—he was bold;—he was resolute: *she* fearful—confused, altogether unprepared to resist in such encounters, and rendered more so, by the extreme liking she had to him.—Shocked, however, at the apprehension of really losing her honor, she struggled all she could, and was just going to reveal the whole secret of her name and quality, when the thoughts of the liberty he had taken with her, and those he still continued to prosecute, prevented her, with representing[5] the danger of being exposed, and the whole affair made a theme for public ridicule.—Thus much, indeed, she told him, that she was a virgin, and had assumed this manner of behavior only to engage him. But that he little regarded, or if he had, would have been far from obliging him to desist;—nay, in the present burning eagerness of desire, 'tis probable, that had he been acquainted both with who and what she really was, the knowledge of her birth would not have influenced him with respect sufficient to have curbed the wild exuberance of his luxurious wishes, or made him in that longing—that impatient moment, change the form of his addresses. In fine, she was undone; and he gained a victory, so highly rapturous, that had he known over whom, scarce could he have triumphed more. Her tears, however, and the distraction she appeared in, after the ruinous ecstasy was past, as it heightened his wonder, so it abated his satisfaction:—he could not imagine for what reason a woman, who, if she intended not to be a *mistress,* had counterfeited the part of one, and taken so much pains to engage him, should lament a consequence which she could not but expect, and till the last test, seemed inclinable to grant; and was both surprised and troubled at the mystery.—He omitted nothing that he thought might make her easy; and still retaining an opinion that the hope of interest had been the chief motive which had led her to act in the manner she had done, and believing that she might know so little of him, as to suppose, now she had nothing left to give, he might not make that recompense she expected for her favors: to put her out of that pain, he pulled out of his pocket a purse of gold, entreating her to accept of that as an earnest of what he intended to do for her; assuring her, with ten thousand protestations, that he would spare nothing, which his whole estate could purchase, to procure her content and happiness. This treatment made her quite forget the part she had assumed, and throwing it from her with an air of disdain, Is this a reward (*said she*) for condescensions,[6] such as I have yielded to?—Can all the wealth you are possessed of make a reparation for my loss of honor?—Oh! no, I am undone beyond the power of heaven itself to help me!—She uttered many more such exclamations; which the amazed *Beauplaisir* heard without being able to reply to, till by degrees sinking from that rage of temper, her eyes resumed their softening glances, and guessing at the consternation he was in, No, my dear *Beauplaisir,* (*added she*) your love alone can compensate for the shame you have involved me in; be you sincere and constant, and I hereafter shall, perhaps, be satisfied with my fate, and forgive myself the folly that betrayed me to you.

---

5. By calling to mind.   6. Unworthiness, vice.

Beauplaisir thought he could not have a better opportunity than these words gave him of inquiring who she was, and wherefore she had feigned herself to be of a profession which he was now convinced she was not; and after he had made her a thousand vows of an affection, as inviolable and ardent as she could wish to find in him, entreated she would inform him by what means his happiness had been brought about, and also to whom he was indebted for the bliss he had enjoyed.—Some remains of yet unextinguished modesty, and sense of shame, made her blush exceedingly at this demand; but recollecting herself in a little time, she told him so much of the truth, as to what related to the frolic she had taken of satisfying her curiosity in what manner *mistresses,* of the sort she appeared to be were treated by those who addressed them; but forbore discovering her true name and quality, for the reasons she had done before, resolving, if he boasted of this affair, he should not have it in his power to touch her character: she therefore said she was the daughter of a country gentleman, who was come to town to buy clothes, and that she was called *Fantomina.* He had no reason to distrust the truth of this story, and was therefore satisfied with it; but did not doubt by the beginning of her conduct, but that in the end she would be in reality, the thing she so artfully had counterfeited; and had good nature enough to pity the misfortunes he imagined would be her lot: but to tell her so, or offer his advice in that point, was not his business, at least, as yet.

They parted not till towards morning; and she obliged him to a willing vow of visiting her the next day at three in the afternoon. It was too late for her to go home that night, therefore contented herself with lying there. In the morning she sent for the woman of the house to come up to her; and easily perceiving, by her manner, that she was a woman who might be influenced by gifts, made her a present of a couple of broad pieces,[7] and desired her, that if the gentleman, who had been there the night before, should ask any questions concerning her, that he should be told, she was lately come out of the country, had lodged there about a fortnight, and that her name was *Fantomina.* I shall (*also added she*) lie but seldom here; nor, indeed, ever come but in those times when I expect to meet him: I would, therefore, have you order it so, that he may think I am but just gone out, if he should happen by any accident to call when I am not here; for I would not, for the world, have him imagine I do not constantly lodge here. The landlady assured her she would do everything as she desired, and gave her to understand she wanted not the gift of secrecy.

Everything being ordered at this home for the security of her reputation, she repaired to the other, where she easily excused to an unsuspecting aunt, with whom she boarded, her having been abroad all night, saying, she went with a gentleman and his lady in a barge, to a little country seat of theirs up the river, all of them designing to return the same evening; but that one of the bargemen happening to be taken ill on the sudden, and no other waterman to be got that night, they were obliged to tarry till morning. Thus did this lady's wit and vivacity assist her in all, but where it was most needed.—She had discernment to foresee, and avoid all those ills which might attend the loss of her *reputation,* but was wholly blind to those of the ruin of her *virtue;* and having managed her affairs so as to secure the *one,* grew perfectly easy with the remembrance she had forfeited the *other.*—The more she reflected on the merits of *Beauplaisir,* the more she excused herself for what she had done; and the prospect of that continued bliss she expected to share with him took from her all remorse for having engaged in an affair which promised her so much satisfaction, and in which she found not the least danger of misfortune.—If he is really (*said she, to herself*) the faithful, the

7. Gold coins.

constant lover he has sworn to be, how charming will be our amor?—And if he should
be false, grow satiated, like other men, I shall but, at the worst, have the private vexation
of knowing I have lost him;—the intrigue being a secret, my disgrace will be so too:—I
shall hear no whispers as I pass—She is forsaken:—the odious word *forsaken* will never
wound my ears; nor will my wrongs excite either the mirth or pity of the talking
world:—it would not be even in the power of my undoer himself to triumph over me;
and while he laughs at, and perhaps despises the fond, the yielding *Fantomina,* he will
revere and esteem the virtuous, the reserved lady.—In this manner did she applaud her
own conduct, and exult with the imagination that she had more prudence than all her sex
beside. And it must be confessed, indeed, that she preserved an economy in the management of this intrigue beyond what almost any woman but herself ever did: in the first
place, by making no person in the world a confidant in it; and in the next, in concealing
from *Beauplaisir* himself the knowledge who she was; for though she met him three or
four days in a week, at that lodging she had taken for that purpose, yet as much as he
employed her time and thoughts, she was never missed from any assembly she had been
accustomed to frequent.—The business of her love has engrossed her till six in the
evening, and before seven she has been dressed in a different habit, and in another
place.—Slippers, and a night-gown loosely flowing, has been the garb in which he has
left the languishing *Fantomina;*—laced and adorned with all the blaze of jewels has he,
in less than an hour after, beheld at the royal chapel, the palace gardens, drawing-room,
opera, or play, the haughty awe-inspiring lady—a thousand times has he stood amazed
at the prodigious likeness between his little mistress and this court beauty; but was still
as far from imagining they were the same as he was the first hour he had accosted her in
the playhouse, though it is not impossible but that her resemblance to this celebrated
lady might keep his inclination alive something longer than otherwise they would have
been; and that it was to the thoughts of this (as he supposed) unenjoyed charmer she
owed in great measure the vigor of his latter caresses.

But he varied not so much from his sex as to be able to prolong desire to any great
length after possession: the rifled charms of *Fantomina* soon lost their potency, and
grew tasteless and insipid; and when the season of the year inviting the company to the
Bath,[8] she offered to accompany him, he made an excuse to go without her. She easily
perceived his coldness, and the reason why he pretended her going would be inconvenient, and endured as much from the discovery as any of her sex could do: she dissembled it, however, before him, and took her leave of him with the show of no other concern than his absence occasioned: but this she did to take from him all suspicion of her
following him, as she intended, and had already laid a scheme for.—From her first
finding out that he designed to leave her behind, she plainly saw it was for no other
reason, than that being tired of her conversation, he was willing to be at liberty to pursue new conquests; and wisely considering that complaints, tears, swoonings, and all
the extravagancies which women make use of in such cases, have little prevalence over
a heart inclined to rove, and only serve to render those who practice them more contemptible, by robbing them of that beauty which alone can bring back the fugitive
lover, she resolved to take another course; and remembering the height of transport she
enjoyed when the agreeable *Beauplaisir* kneeled at her feet, imploring her first favors,
she longed to prove the same again. Not but a woman of her beauty and accomplishments might have beheld a thousand in that condition *Beauplaisir* had been; but with
her sex's modesty, she had not also thrown off another virtue equally valuable, though

---

8. Town in southwestern England, popular as a resort because of its hot springs.

generally unfortunate, *constancy:* she loved *Beauplaisir;* it was only he whose solicitations could give her pleasure; and had she seen the whole species despairing, dying for her sake, it might, perhaps, have been a satisfaction to her pride, but none to her more tender inclination.—Her design was once more to engage him, to hear him sigh, to see him languish, to feel the strenuous pressures of his eager arms, to be compelled, to be sweetly forced to what she wished with equal ardor, was what she wanted, and what she had formed a stratagem to obtain, in which she promised herself success.

She no sooner heard he had left the town, than making a pretense to her aunt, that she was going to visit a relation in the country, went towards *Bath,* attended but by two servants, who she found reasons to quarrel with on the road and discharged: clothing herself in a habit she had brought with her, she forsook the coach, and went into a wagon, in which equipage she arrived at *Bath.* The dress she was in was a round-eared cap,[9] a short red petticoat, and a little jacket of gray stuff;[1] all the rest of her accoutrements were answerable to these, and joined with a broad country dialect, a rude unpolished air, which she, having been bred in these parts, knew very well how to imitate, with her hair and eye-brows blacked, made it impossible for her to be known, or taken for any other than what she seemed. Thus disguised did she offer herself to service in the house where *Beauplaisir* lodged, having made it her business to find out immediately where he was. Notwithstanding this metamorphosis she was still extremely pretty; and the mistress of the house happening at that time to want a maid was very glad of the opportunity of taking her. She was presently received into the family; and had a post in it (such as she would have chose, had she been left at her liberty), that of making the gentlemen's beds, getting them their breakfasts, and waiting on them in their chambers. Fortune in this exploit was extremely on her side; there were no others of the male-sex in the house than an old gentleman, who had lost the use of his limbs with the rheumatism, and had come thither for the benefit of the waters, and her beloved *Beauplaisir;* so that she was in no apprehensions of any amorous violence, but where she wished to find it. Nor were her designs disappointed: He was fired with the first sight of her; and though he did not presently take any farther notice of her, than giving her two or three hearty kisses, yet she, who now understood that language but too well, easily saw they were the prelude to more substantial joys.—Coming the next morning to bring his chocolate, as he had ordered, he catched her by the pretty leg, which the shortness of her petticoat did not in the least oppose; then pulling her gently to him, asked her, how long she had been at service?—How many sweethearts she had? If she had ever been in love? and many other such questions, befitting one of the degree she appeared to be: all which she answered with such seeming innocence, as more enflamed the amorous heart of him who talked to her. He compelled her to sit in his lap; and gazing on her blushing beauties, which, if possible, received addition from her plain and rural dress, he soon lost the power of containing himself.—His wild desires burst out in all his words and actions: he called her little angel, cherubim, swore he must enjoy her, though death were to be the consequence, devoured her lips, her breasts with greedy kisses, held to his burning bosom her half-yielding, half-reluctant body, nor suffered her to get loose, till he had ravaged all, and glutted each rapacious sense with the sweet beauties of the pretty *Celia,*[2] for that was the name she bore in this

9. Style of cap associated with country women.
1. Coarse wool fabric.
2. In Renaissance literature the name Celia is frequently associated with vanity or pride, as in Lyly's *Love's Metamorphosis* as well as Waller's "To Phyllis" and "To a Friend" (quoted in the epigraph); similarly, in Swift's "The Lady's Dressing Room" (see page 289) Celia is the woman who spends five hours in her dressing room each day in an effort to conceal her natural nastiness.

second expedition.—Generous as liberality itself to all who gave him joy this way, he gave her a handsome sum of gold, which she durst not now refuse, for fear of creating some mistrust, and losing the heart she so lately had regained; therefore taking it with an humble courtesy, and a well counterfeited show of surprise and joy, cried, O law, Sir! what must I do for all this? He laughed at her simplicity, and kissing her again, though less fervently than he had done before, bad her not be out of the way when he came home at night. She promised she would not, and very obediently kept her word.

His stay at *Bath* exceeded not a month; but in that time his supposed country lass had persecuted him so much with her fondness, that in spite of the eagerness with which he first enjoyed her, he was at last grown more weary of her, than he had been of *Fantomina;* which she perceiving, would not be troublesome, but quitting her service, remained privately in the town till she heard he was on his return; and in that time provided herself of another disguise to carry on a third plot, which her inventing brain had furnished her with, once more to renew his twice-decayed ardors. The dress she had ordered to be made, was such as widows wear in their first mourning, which, together with the most afflicted and penitential countenance that ever was seen, was no small alteration to her who used to seem all gaiety.—To add to this, her hair, which she was accustomed to wear very loose, both when *Fantomina* and *Celia,* was now tied back so straight, and her pinners[3] coming so very forward, that there was none of it to be seen. In fine, her habit and her air were so much changed, that she was not more difficult to be known in the rude country *girl,* than she was now in the sorrowful *widow.*

She knew that *Beauplaisir* came alone in his chariot to the *Bath,* and in the time of her being servant in the house where he lodged, heard nothing of any body that was to accompany him to *London,* and hoped he would return in the same manner he had gone: She therefore hired horses and a man to attend her to an inn about ten miles on this side of *Bath,* where having discharged them, she waited till the chariot should come by; which when it did, and she saw that he was alone in it, she called to him that drove it to stop a moment, and going to the door saluted the master with these words:

The distressed and wretched, Sir (*said she*), never fail to excite compassion in a generous mind; and I hope I am not deceived in my opinion that yours is such:—You have the appearance of a gentleman, and cannot, when you hear my story, refuse that assistance which is in your power to give to an unhappy woman, who without it, may be rendered the most miserable of all created beings.

It would not be very easy to represent the surprise, so odd an address created in the mind of him to whom it was made.—She had not the appearance of one who wanted charity; and what other favor she required he could not conceive: but telling her she might command any thing in his power gave her encouragement to declare herself in this manner: You may judge (*resumed she*), by the melancholy garb I am in, that I have lately lost all that ought to be valuable to womankind; but it is impossible for you to guess the greatness of my misfortune, unless you had known my husband, who was master of every perfection to endear him to a wife's affections.—But, notwithstanding, I look on myself as the most unhappy of my sex in out-living him, I must so far obey the dictates of my discretion, as to take care of the little fortune he left behind him, which being in the hands of a brother of his in *London,* will be all carried off to *Holland,*[4] where he is going to settle; if I reach not the town before he leaves it, I am undone for ever.—To which end I left *Bristol,* the place where we lived, hoping to

---

3. The side flaps of a close-fitting hat, usually worn by women of higher rank.

4. Holland had been a frequent destination for English religious dissenters in exile.

get a place in the stage at *Bath,* but they were all taken up before I came; and being, by a hurt I got in a fall, rendered incapable of traveling any long journey on horseback, I have no way to go to *London,* and must be inevitably ruined in the loss of all I have on earth, without you have good nature enough to admit me to take part of your chariot.

Here the feigned widow ended her sorrowful tale, which had been several times interrupted by a parenthesis of sighs and groans; and *Beauplaisir,* with a complaisant and tender air, assured her of his readiness to serve her in things of much greater consequence than what she desired of him; and told her it would be an impossibility of denying a place in his chariot to a lady who he could not behold without yielding one in his heart. She answered the compliments he made her but with tears, which seemed to stream in such abundance from her eyes, that she could not keep her handkerchief from her face one moment. Being come into the chariot, *Beauplaisir* said a thousand handsome things to persuade her from giving way to so violent a grief; which, he told her, would not only be destructive to her beauty, but likewise her health. But all his endeavors for consolement appeared ineffectual, and he began to think he should have but a dull journey, in the company of one who seemed so obstinately devoted to the memory of her dead husband, that there was no getting a word from her on any other theme:—but bethinking himself of the celebrated story of the *Ephesian* matron,[5] it came into his head to make trial, she who seemed equally susceptible of *sorrow,* might not also be so too of *love:* and having began a discourse on almost every other topic, and finding her still incapable of answering, resolved to put it to the proof, if this would have no more effect to rouse her sleeping spirits:—with a gay air, therefore, though accompanied with the greatest modesty and respect, he turned the conversation, as though without design, on that joy-giving passion, and soon discovered that was indeed the subject she was best pleased to be entertained with; for on his giving her a hint to begin upon, never any tongue run more voluble than hers, on the prodigious power it had to influence the souls of those possessed of it, to actions even the most distant from their intentions, principles, or humors.—From that she passed to a description of the happiness of mutual affection;—the unspeakable ecstasy of those who meet with equal ardency; and represented it in colors so lively, and disclosed by the gestures with which her words were accompanied, and the accent of her voice so true a feeling of what she said, that *Beauplaisir,* without being as stupid, as he was really the contrary, could not avoid perceiving there were seeds of fire, not yet extinguished, in this fair widow's soul, which wanted but the kindling breath of tender sighs to light into a blaze.—He now thought himself as fortunate, as some moments before he had the reverse; and doubted not, but, that before they parted, he should find a way to dry the tears of this lovely mourner, to the satisfaction of them both. He did not, however, offer, as he had done to *Fantomina* and *Celia,* to urge his passion directly to her, but by a thousand little softening artifices, which he well knew how to use, gave her leave to guess he was enamored. When they came to the inn where they were to lie, he declared himself somewhat more freely, and perceiving she did not resent it past forgiveness, grew more encroaching still:—he now took the liberty of kissing away her tears, and catching the sighs as they issued from her lips; telling her if grief was infectious, he was resolved to have his share; protesting he would gladly exchange passions with her, and be content to bear her load of *sorrow,* if she would as willingly ease the burden of his *love.*—She said little in answer to the strenuous pressures

---

5. In Petronius's *Satyricon,* the Ephesian matron is a faithful wife who stays by her dead husband's burial vault day and night until she is seduced by a soldier who guards the nearby bodies of crucified criminals. When one of the bodies is stolen, the matron gives her own husband's body to the soldier to save him from punishment.

with which at last he ventured to enfold her, but not thinking it decent, for the character she had assumed, to yield so suddenly, and unable to deny both his and her own inclinations, she counterfeited a fainting, and fell motionless upon his breast.—He had no great notion that she was in a real fit, and the room they supped in happening to have a bed in it, he took her in his arms and laid her on it, believing, that whatever her distemper was, that was the most proper place to convey her to.—He laid himself down by her, and endeavored to bring her to herself; and she was too grateful to her kind physician at her returning sense, to remove from the posture he had put her in, without his leave.

It may, perhaps, seem strange that *Beauplaisir* should in such near intimacies continue still deceived: I know there are men who will swear it is an impossibility, and that no disguise could hinder them from knowing a woman they had once enjoyed. In answer to these scruples, I can only say, that besides the alteration which the change of dress made in her, she was so admirably skilled in the art of feigning, that she had the power of putting on almost what face she pleased, and knew so exactly how to form her behavior to the character she represented, that all the comedians at both playhouses[6] are infinitely short of her performances: she could vary her very glances, tune her voice to accents the most different imaginable from those in which she spoke when she appeared herself.—These aids from nature, joined to the wiles of art, and the distance between the places where the imagined *Fantomina* and *Celia* were, might very well prevent his having any thought that they were the same, or that the fair *widow* was either of them: it never so much as entered his head, and though he did fancy he observed in the face of the latter, features which were not altogether unknown to him, yet he could not recollect when or where he had known them;—and being told by her, that from her birth, she had never removed from *Bristol*, a place where he never was, he rejected the belief of having seen her, and supposed his mind had been deluded by an idea of some other, whom she might have a resemblance of.

They passed the time of their journey in as much happiness as the most luxurious gratification of wild desires could make them; and when they came to the end of it, parted not without a mutual promise of seeing each other often.—He told her to what place she should direct a letter to him; and she assured him she would send to let him know where to come to her, as soon as she was fixed in lodgings.

She kept her promise; and charmed with the continuance of his eager fondness, went not home, but into private lodgings, whence she wrote to him to visit her the first opportunity, and inquire for the Widow *Bloomer*.—She had no sooner dispatched this billet,[7] than she repaired to the house where she had lodged as *Fantomina*, charging the people if *Beauplaisir* should come there, not to let him know she had been out of town. From thence she wrote to him, in a different hand, a long letter of complaint, that he had been so cruel in not sending one letter to her all the time he had been absent, entreated to see him, and concluded with subscribing herself his unalterably affectionate *Fantomina*. She received in one day answers to both these. The first contained these lines:

To the Charming Mrs. Bloomer,

It would be impossible, my Angel! for me to express the thousandth part of that infinity of transport, the sight of your dear letter gave me.—Never was woman formed to charm like you: never did any look like you,—write like you,—bless like you;—nor did ever man adore as I do.—Since yesterday we parted, I have seemed a body without a soul; and had you not by this inspiring billet, gave me new life, I know not what by tomorrow I

---

6. Comedians are actors. There were only two public playhouses in London, established by royal decree in 1660.   7. Note, brief letter.

*should have been.—I will be with you this evening about five:—O, 'tis an age till then!—
But the cursed formalities of duty oblige me to dine with my lord —— who never rises
from table till that hour;—therefore adieu till then sweet lovely mistress of the soul and all
the faculties of*

Your most faithful,
Beauplaisir.

The other was in this manner:

To the Lovely Fantomina,

*If you were half so sensible as you ought of your own power of charming, you would
be assured, that to be unfaithful or unkind to you, would be among the things that are in
their very natures impossibilities.—It was my misfortune, not my fault, that you were not
persecuted every post with a declaration of my unchanging passion; but I had unluckily
forgot the name of the woman at whose house you are, and knew not how to form a direction that it might come safe to your hands.—And, indeed, the reflection how you might
misconstrue my silence, brought me to town some weeks sooner than I intended—If you
knew how I have languished to renew those blessings I am permitted to enjoy in your society, you would rather pity than condemn*

Your ever faithful,
Beauplaisir.

P.S. *I fear I cannot see you till tomorrow; some business has unluckily fallen out that will
engross my hours till then.—Once more, my dear,* Adieu.

Traitor! (*cried she*) as soon as she had read them, 'tis thus our silly, fond, believing sex are served when they put faith in man: so had I been deceived and cheated, had
I like the rest believed, and sat down mourning in absence, and vainly waiting recovered tendernesses.—How do some women (*continued she*) make their life a hell, burning in fruitless expectations, and dreaming out their days in hopes and fears, then wake
at last to all the horror of despair?—But I have outwitted even the most subtle of the
deceiving kind, and while he thinks to fool me, is himself the only beguiled person.

She made herself, most certainly, extremely happy in the reflection on the success
of her stratagems; and while the knowledge of his inconstancy and levity of nature kept
her from having that real tenderness for him she would else have had, she found the
means of gratifying the inclination she had for his agreeable person, in as full a manner
as she could wish. She had all the sweets of love, but as yet had tasted none of the gall,
and was in a state of contentment, which might be envied by the more delicate.

When the expected hour arrived, she found that her lover had lost no part of the
fervency with which he had parted from her; but when the next day she received him
as *Fantomina,* she perceived a prodigious difference; which led her again into reflections on the unaccountableness of men's fancies, who still prefer the last conquest,
only because it is the last.—Here was an evident proof of it; for there could not be a
difference in merit, because they were the same person; but the Widow *Bloomer* was
a more new acquaintance than *Fantomina,* and therefore esteemed more valuable.
This, indeed, must be said of *Beauplaisir,* that he had a greater share of good nature
than most of his sex, who, for the most part, when they are weary of an intrigue, break
it entirely off, without any regard to the despair of the abandoned nymph. Though he
retained no more than a bare pity and complaisance for *Fantomina,* yet believing she
loved him to an excess, would not entirely forsake her, though the continuance of his
visits was now become rather a penance than a pleasure.

The Widow *Bloomer* triumphed some time longer over the heart of this inconstant, but at length her sway was at an end, and she sunk in this character, to the same degree of tastelessness, as she had done before in that of *Fantomina* and *Celia*.—She presently perceived it, but bore it as she had always done; it being but what she expected, she had prepared herself for it, and had another project in embryo, which she soon ripened into action. She did not, indeed, complete it altogether so suddenly as she had done the others, by reason there must be persons employed in it; and the aversion she had to any confidants in her affairs, and the caution with which she had hitherto acted, and which she was still determined to continue, made it very difficult for her to find a way without breaking through that resolution to compass what she wished.—She got over the difficulty at last, however, by proceeding in a manner, if possible, more extraordinary than all her former behavior:—muffling herself up in her hood one day, she went into the park about the hour when there are a great many necessitous gentlemen,[8] who think themselves above doing what they call little things for a maintenance, walking in the *Mall*,[9] to take a *Camelion* Treat,[1] and fill their stomachs with air instead of meat. Two of those, who by their physiognomy she thought most proper for her purpose, she beckoned to come to her; and taking them into a walk more remote from company, began to communicate the business she had with them in these words: I am sensible, gentlemen (*said she*), that, through the blindness of fortune, and partiality of the world, merit frequently goes unrewarded, and that those of the best pretentions meet with the least encouragement:—I ask your pardon (*continued she*), perceiving they seemed surprised, if I am mistaken in the notion, that you two may, perhaps, be of the number of those who have reason to complain of the injustice of fate; but if you are such as I take you for, I have a proposal to make you, which may be of some little advantage to you. Neither of them made any immediate answer, but appeared buried in consideration for some moments. At length, We should, doubtless, madam (*said one of them*), willingly come into any measures to oblige you, provided they are such as may bring us into no danger, either as to our persons or reputations. That which I require of you (*resumed she*), has nothing in it criminal: All that I desire is *secrecy* in what you are entrusted, and to disguise yourselves in such a manner as you cannot be known, if hereafter seen by the person on whom you are to impose.—In fine, the business is only an innocent frolic, but if blazed abroad, might be taken for too great a freedom in me:—Therefore, if you resolve to assist me, here are five pieces to drink my health, and assure you, that I have not discoursed you[2] on an affair, I design not to proceed in; and when it is accomplished fifty more lie ready for your acceptance. These words, and, above all, the money, which was a sum which, 'tis probable, they had not seen of a long time, made them immediately assent to all she desired, and press for the beginning of their employment: but things were not yet ripe for execution; and she told them, that the next day they should be let into the secret, charging them to meet her in the same place at an hour she appointed. 'Tis hard to say, which of these parties went away best pleased; *they,* that fortune had sent them so unexpected a windfall; or *she,* that she had found persons, who appeared so well qualified to serve her.

Indefatigable in the pursuit of whatsoever her humor was bent upon, she had no sooner left her new-engaged emissaries, than she went in search of a house for the completing of her project.—She pitched on one very large, and magnificently furnished, which she hired by the week, giving them the money beforehand, to prevent any

---

8. Poor men.
9. A popular walk in St. James's Park.

1. Chameleons were thought to subsist on air.
2. Talked to you.

inquiries. The next day she repaired to the park, where she met the punctual 'squires of low degree; and ordering them to follow her to the house she had taken, told them they must condescend to appear like servants, and gave each of them a very rich livery. Then writing a letter to *Beauplaisir,* in a character vastly different from either of those she had made use of, as *Fantomina,* or the fair Widow *Bloomer,* ordered one of them to deliver it into his own hands, to bring back an answer, and to be careful that he sifted out nothing of the truth.—I do not fear (*said she*), that you should discover to him who I am, because that is a secret, of which you yourselves are ignorant; but I would have you be so careful in your replies, that he may not think the concealment springs from any other reasons than your great integrity to your trust.—Seem therefore to know my whole affairs; and let your refusing to make him partaker in the secret, appear to be only the effect of your zeal for my interest and reputation. Promises of entire fidelity on the one side, and reward on the other, being past, the messenger made what haste he could to the house of *Beauplaisir;* and being there told where he might find him, performed exactly the injunction that had been given him. But never astonishment exceeded that which *Beauplaisir* felt at the reading this billet, in which he found these lines:

> To the All-conquering Beauplaisir.
>
> *I imagine not that 'tis a new thing to you, to be told, you are the greatest charm in nature to our sex: I shall therefore, not to fill up my letter with any impertinent praises on your wit or person, only tell you, that I am infinite in love with both, and if you have a heart not too deeply engaged, should think myself the happiest of my sex in being capable of inspiring it with some tenderness.—There is but one thing in my power to refuse you, which is the knowledge of my name, which believing the sight of my face will render no secret, you must not take it ill that I conceal from you.—The bearer of this is a person I can trust; send by him your answer; but endeavor not to dive into the meaning of this mystery, which will be impossible for you to unravel, and at the same time very much disoblige me:—But that you may be in no apprehensions of being imposed on by a woman unworthy of your regard, I will venture to assure you, the first and greatest men in the kingdom would think themselves blessed to have that influence over me you have, though unknown to yourself, acquired.—But I need not go about to raise your curiosity, by giving you any idea of what my person is; if you think fit to be satisfied, resolve to visit me tomorrow about three in the afternoon; and though my face is hid, you shall not want sufficient demonstration, that she who takes these unusual measures to commence a friendship with you, is neither old, nor deformed. Till then I am,*
>
> Yours,
> Incognita.[3]

He had scarce come to the conclusion, before he asked the person who brought it, from what place he came;—the name of the lady he served;—if she were a wife, or widow, and several other questions directly opposite to the directions of the letter; but silence would have availed him as much as did all those testimonies of curiosity: no *Italian Bravo,*[4] employed in a business of the like nature, performed his office with more artifice; and the impatient inquirer was convinced, that nothing but doing as he was desired, could give him any light into the character of the woman who declared so violent a passion for him; and little fearing any consequence which could ensue from such an encounter, resolved to rest satisfied till he was informed of everything from herself, not imagining this *Incognita* varied so much from the generality of her sex, as to be able to refuse the knowledge of anything to the man she loved with that transcendency of passion she professed, and which his many successes with the ladies

3. Unknown woman (Latin); i.e., a woman in disguise.   4. Hired assassin.

gave him encouragement enough to believe. He therefore took pen and paper, and answered her letter in terms tender enough for a man who had never seen the person to whom he wrote. The words were as follows:

> To the Obliging and Witty Incognita.
>
> *Though to tell me I am happy enough to be liked by a woman, such, as by your manner of writing, I imagine you to be, is an honor which I can never sufficiently acknowledge, yet I know not how I am able to content myself with admiring the wonders of your wit alone: I am certain, a soul like yours must shine in your eyes with a vivacity, which must bless all they look on.—I shall, however, endeavor to restrain myself in those bounds you are pleased to set me, till by the knowledge of my inviolable fidelity, I may be thought worthy of gazing on that heaven I am now but to enjoy in contemplation.—You need not doubt my glad compliance with your obliging summons: there is a charm in your lines, which gives too sweet an idea of their lovely author to be resisted.—I am all impatient for the blissful moment, which is to throw me at your feet, and give me an opportunity of convincing you that I am,*

Your everlasting slave,
Beauplaisir.

Nothing could be more pleased than she, to whom it was directed, at the receipt of this letter; but when she was told how inquisitive he had been concerning her character and circumstances, she could not forbear laughing heartily to think of the tricks she had played him, and applauding her own strength of genius, and force of resolution, which by such unthought-of ways could triumph over her lover's inconstancy, and render that very temper, which to other women is the greatest curse, a means to make herself more blessed.—Had he been faithful to me (*said she, to herself*), either as *Fantomina,* or *Celia,* or the Widow *Bloomer,* the most violent passion, if it does not change its object, in time will wither: possession naturally abates the vigor of desire, and I should have had, at best, but a cold, insipid, husband-like lover in my arms; but by these arts of passing on him as a new mistress whenever the ardor, which alone makes love a blessing, begins to diminish, for the former one, I have him always raving, wild, impatient, longing, dying.—O that all neglected wives, and fond abandoned nymphs would take this method!—Men would be caught in their own snare, and have no cause to scorn our easy, weeping, wailing sex! Thus did she pride herself as if secure she never should have any reason to repent the present gaiety of her humor. The hour drawing near in which he was to come, she dressed herself in as magnificent a manner, as if she were to be that night at a ball at court, endeavoring to repair the want of those beauties which the vizard[5] should conceal, by setting forth the others with the greatest care and exactness. Her fine shape, and air, and neck appeared to great advantage; and by that which was to be seen of her, one might believe the rest to be perfectly agreeable. *Beauplaisir* was prodigiously charmed, as well with her appearance, as with the manner she entertained him: but though he was wild with impatience for the sight of a face which belonged to so exquisite a body, yet he would not immediately press for it, believing before he left her he should easily obtain that satisfaction.—A noble collation being over, he began to sue for the performance of her promise of granting everything he could ask, excepting the sight of her face, and knowledge of her name. It would have been a ridiculous piece of affectation in her to have seemed coy in complying with what she herself had been the first in desiring:

---

5. Mask or veil.

she yielded without even a show of reluctance: and if there be any true felicity in an amour such as theirs, both here enjoyed it to the full. But not in the height of all their mutual raptures, could he prevail on her to satisfy his curiosity with the sight of her face: she told him that she hoped he knew so much of her, as might serve to convince him, she was not unworthy of his tenderest regard; and if he could not content himself with that which she was willing to reveal, and which was the conditions of their meeting, dear as he was to her, she would rather part with him for ever, than consent to gratify an inquisitiveness, which, in her opinion, had no business with his love. It was in vain that he endeavored to make her sensible of her mistake; and that this restraint was the greatest enemy imaginable to the happiness of them both: she was not to be persuaded, and he was obliged to desist his solicitations, though determined in his mind to compass what he so ardently desired, before he left the house. He then turned the discourse wholly on the violence of the passion he had for her; and expressed the greatest discontent in the world at the apprehensions of being separated;—swore he could dwell for ever in her arms, and with such an undeniable earnestness pressed to be permitted to tarry with her the whole night, that had she been less charmed with his renewed eagerness of desire, she scarce would have had the power of resisting him; but in granting this request, she was not without a thought that he had another reason for making it besides the extremity of his passion, and had it immediately in her head how to disappoint him.

The hours of repose being arrived, he begged she would retire to her chamber, to which she consented, but obliged him to go to bed first; which he did not much oppose, because he supposed she would not lie in her mask, and doubted not but the morning's dawn would bring the wished discovery.—The two imagined servants ushered him to his new lodging; where he lay some moments in all the perplexity imaginable at the oddness of this adventure. But she suffered not these cogitations to be of any long continuance: she came, but came in the dark; which being no more than he expected by the former part of her proceedings, he said nothing of; but as much satisfaction as he found in her embraces, nothing ever longed for the approach of day with more impatience than he did. At last it came; but how great was his disappointment, when by the noises he heard in the street, the hurry of the coaches, and the cries of penny-merchants,[6] he was convinced it was night nowhere but with him? He was still in the same darkness as before; for she had taken care to blind the windows in such a manner, that not the least chink was left to let in day.—He complained of her behavior in terms that she would not have been able to resist yielding to, if she had not been certain it would have been the ruin of her passion:—she, therefore, answered him only as she had done before; and getting out of the bed from him, flew out of the room with too much swiftness for him to have overtaken her, if he had attempted it. The moment she left him, the two attendants entered the chamber, and plucking down the implements which had screened him from the knowledge of that which he so much desired to find out, restored his eyes once more to day:—they attended to assist him in dressing, brought him tea, and by their obsequiousness, let him see there was but one thing which the mistress of them would not gladly oblige him in.—He was so much out of humor, however, at the disappointment of his curiosity, that he resolved never to make a second visit.—Finding her in an outer room, he made no scruple of expressing the sense he had of the little trust she reposed in him, and at last plainly told

6. Street vendors of cheap wares.

her, he could not submit to receive obligations from a lady, who thought him uncapable of keeping a secret, which she made no difficulty of letting her servants into.—
He resented—he once more entreated—he said all that man could do, to prevail on
her to unfold the mystery; but all his adjurations were fruitless; and he went out of the
house determined never to re-enter it, till she should pay the price of his company
with the discovery of her face and circumstances.—She suffered him to go with this
resolution, and doubted not but he would recede from it, when he reflected on the
happy moments they had passed together; but if he did not, she comforted herself
with the design of forming some other stratagem, with which to impose on him a
fourth time.

She kept the house, and her gentlemen-equipage[7] for about a fortnight, in
which time she continued to write to him as *Fantomina* and the Widow *Bloomer,*
and received the visits he sometimes made to each; but his behavior to both was
grown so cold, that she began to grow as weary of receiving his now insipid caresses as he was of offering them: she was beginning to think in what manner she
should drop these two characters, when the sudden arrival of her mother, who had
been some time in a foreign country, obliged her to put an immediate stop to the
course of her whimsical adventures.—That lady, who was severely virtuous, did not
approve of many things she had been told of the conduct of her daughter; and
though it was not in the power of any person in the world to inform her of the truth
of what she had been guilty of, yet she heard enough to make her keep her afterwards in a restraint, little agreeable to her humor, and the liberties to which she had
been accustomed.

But this confinement was not the greatest part of the trouble of this now afflicted
lady: she found the consequences of her amorous follies would be, without almost a
miracle, impossible to be concealed:—she was with child; and though she would easily have found means to have screened even this from the knowledge of the world,
had she been at liberty to have acted with the same unquestionable authority over herself, as she did before the coming of her mother, yet now all her invention was at a
loss for a stratagem to impose on a woman of her penetration:—by eating little, lacing
prodigious straight, and the advantage of a great hoop-petticoat, however, her bigness
was not taken notice of, and, perhaps, she would not have been suspected till the time
of her going into the country, where her mother designed to send her, and from
whence she intended to make her escape to some place where she might be delivered
with secrecy, if the time of it had not happened much sooner than she expected.—A
ball being at court, the good old lady was willing she should partake of the diversion
of it as a farewell to the town.—It was there she was seized with those pangs, which
none in her condition are exempt from:—she could not conceal the sudden rack which
all at once invaded her; or had her tongue been mute, her wildly rolling eyes, the dis-
tortion of her features, and the convulsions which shook her whole frame, in spite of her,
would have revealed she labored under some terrible shock of nature.—Everybody
was surprised, everybody was concerned, but few guessed at the occasion.—Her
mother grieved beyond expression, doubted not but she was struck with the hand of
death; and ordered her to be carried home in a chair, while herself followed in another.—A physician was immediately sent for: but he presently perceiving what was
her distemper, called the old lady aside, and told her, it was not a doctor of his sex,

---

7. Retinue of footmen.

but one of her own, her daughter stood in need of.—Never was astonishment and horror greater than that which seized the soul of this afflicted parent at these words: she could not for a time believe the truth of what she heard; but he insisting on it, and conjuring her to send for a midwife, she was at length convinced of it.—All the pity and tenderness she had been for some moment before possessed of now vanished, and were succeeded by an adequate[8] shame and indignation:—she flew to the bed where her daughter was lying, and telling her what she had been informed of, and which she was now far from doubting, commanded her to reveal the name of the person whose insinuations had drawn her to this dishonor.—It was a great while before she could be brought to confess anything, and much longer before she could be prevailed on to name the man whom she so fatally had loved; but the rack of nature growing more fierce, and the enraged old lady protesting no help should be afforded her while she persisted in her obstinacy, she, with great difficulty and hesitation in her speech, at last pronounced the name of *Beauplaisir.* She had no sooner satisfied her weeping mother, than that sorrowful lady sent messengers at the same time, for a midwife, and for that gentleman who had occasioned the other's being wanted.—He happened by accident to be at home, and immediately obeyed the summons, though prodigiously surprised what business a lady so much a stranger to him could have to impart.—But how much greater was his amazement, when taking him into her closet, she there acquainted him with her daughter's misfortune, of the discovery she had made, and how far he was concerned in it?—All the idea one can form of wild astonishment, was mean to what he felt:—he assured her, that the young lady her daughter was a person whom he had never, more than at a distance, admired:—that he had indeed, spoke to her in public company, but that he never had a thought which tended to her dishonor.—His denials, if possible, added to the indignation she was before enflamed with:—she had no longer patience; and carrying him into the chamber, where she was just delivered of a fine girl, cried out, I will not be imposed on: the truth by one of you shall be revealed.—*Beauplaisir* being brought to the bedside, was beginning to address himself to the lady in it, to beg she could clear the mistake her mother was involved in; when she, covering herself with the cloths, and ready to die a second time with the inward agitations of her soul, shrieked out, Oh, I am undone!—I cannot live, and bear this shame!—But the old lady believing that now or never was the time to dive into the bottom of this mystery, forcing her to rear her head, told her, she should not hope to escape the scrutiny of a parent she had dishonored in such a manner, and pointing to *Beauplaisir,* Is this the gentleman (*said she*), to whom you owe your ruin? or have you deceived me by a fictitious tale? Oh! no (*resumed the trembling creature*), he is, indeed, the innocent cause of my undoing:—Promise me your pardon (*continued she*), and I will relate the means. Here she ceased, expecting what she would reply, which, on hearing *Beauplaisir* cry out, What mean you, madam? I your undoing, who never harbored the least design on you in my life, she did in these words, Though the injury you have done your family (*said she*), is of a nature which cannot justly hope forgiveness, yet be assured, I shall much sooner excuse you when satisfied of the truth, than while I am kept in a suspense, if possible, as vexatious as the crime itself is to me. Encouraged by this she related the whole truth. And 'tis difficult to determine, if *Beauplaisir,* or the lady, were most surprised at what they heard; he, that he should have been blinded so often by her artifices; or she, that so young a

---

8. Equal.

creature should have the skill to make use of them. Both sat for some time in a profound reverie; till at length she broke it first in these words: Pardon, sir (*said she*),[9] the trouble I have given you: I must confess it was with a design to oblige you to repair the supposed injury you had done this unfortunate girl, by marrying her, but now I know not what to say:—The blame is wholly hers, and I have nothing to request further of you, than that you will not divulge the distracted folly she has been guilty of.—He answered her in terms perfectly polite; but made no offer of that which, perhaps, she expected, though could not, now informed of her daughter's proceedings, demand. He assured her, however, that if she would commit the newborn lady to his care, he would discharge it faithfully. But neither of them would consent to that; and he took his leave, full of cogitations,[1] more confused than ever he had known in his whole life. He continued to visit there, to inquire after her health every day; but the old lady perceiving there was nothing likely to ensue from these civilities, but, perhaps, a renewing of the crime, she entreated him to refrain; and as soon as her daughter was in a condition, sent her to a monastery in *France,* the abbess of which had been her particular friend. And thus ended an intrigue, which, considering the time it lasted, was as full of variety as any, perhaps, that many ages have produced.

•+ ═╪═ +•

Jean-Jacques Rousseau
1712–1778

Philosopher, novelist, and composer, Jean-Jacques Rousseau was among the most troubled and troubling figures of the Enlightenment. Reared by his father, a Genevan watchmaker, at sixteen he fled an apprenticeship to live with Françoise-Louise de Warens. "Mamma" encouraged his talents, his conversion to Catholicism, and eventually his sexual education by becoming his lover. In 1742 Rousseau moved to Paris, where Diderot admired his new system of musical notation and invited him to contribute to the *Encyclopédie*. He became a leading contributor, alongside Voltaire and Diderot himself. In 1745 he reconverted to Protestantism and took up with Thérèse Levasseur, an illiterate servant girl with whom he had five illegitimate children, all of whom he abandoned in orphanages. He married her in 1768 when he decided she was the only person he could trust; by then he had fallen out with most of his fellow intellectuals. Like Voltaire, Rousseau was frequently forced into exile. In 1766 he went to England with philosopher David Hume, but he fled after becoming convinced that the English intelligentsia secretly mocked him. Allowed back in Paris on condition that he stop criticizing church or state, he ended his days writing various unreliable, self-justifying memoirs—most famously his scandalous and brilliant *Confessions.*

Rousseau's life and works express the defining oppositions of the Enlightenment: emotion versus reason, individualism versus social welfare, faith versus skepticism, political liberty versus moral libertinage. Although he died before the French Revolution, he was probably the single most important intellectual influence on the Revolution and the Romantic movement that followed. *The Social Contract* (1762) reflects his view that European civilization had become decadent and that individual freedom, just political systems, and sound aesthetics could be achieved only by flouting institutions while cherishing social principles and individual emotions arising from a state of nature.

---

9. I.e., the elder lady.   1. Anxious thoughts.

from The Social Contract[1]

THE SUBJECT OF THE FIRST BOOK

Man was born free, and everywhere he is in chains. There are some who may believe themselves masters of others, and are no less enslaved than they. How has this change come about? I do not know. How can it be made legitimate? That is a question which I believe I can resolve.

If I were to consider force alone, and the effects that it produces, I should say: for so long as a nation is constrained to obey, and does so, it does well; as soon as it is able to throw off its servitude, and does so, it does better; for since it regains freedom by the same right that was exercised when its freedom was seized, either the nation was justified in taking freedom back, or else those who took it away were unjustified in doing so. Whereas the social order is a sacred right, and provides a foundation for all other rights. Yet it is a right that does not come from nature; therefore it is based on agreed conventions. Our business is to find out what those conventions are. Before we come to that, I must make good the assertion that I have just put forward.

THE FIRST SOCIETIES

The most ancient of all societies, and the only one that is natural, is the family. Even in this case, the bond between children and father persists only so long as they have need of him for their conservation. As soon as this need ceases, the natural bond is dissolved. The children are released from the obedience they owe to their father, the father is released from the duty of care to the children, and all become equally independent. If they continue to remain living together, it is not by nature but voluntarily, and the family itself is maintained only through convention.

This shared freedom is a result of man's nature. His first law is his own conservation, his first cares are owed to himself; as soon as he reaches the age of reason, he alone is the judge of how best to look after himself, and thus he becomes his own master.

If we wish, then, the family may be regarded as the first model of political society: the leader corresponds to the father, the people to the children, and all being born free and equal, none alienates his freedom except for reasons of utility. The sole difference is that, in the family, the father is paid for the care he takes of his children by the love he bears them, while in the state this love is replaced by the pleasure of being in command, the chief having no love for his people.

SLAVERY

Since no man has a natural authority over his fellow, and since strength does not confer any right, it follows that the basis remaining for all legitimate authority among men must be agreed convention.

If, says Grotius, an individual is able to transfer his liberty, and become the slave of a master, why should an entire nation not transfer its liberty and become subject to a king?[2] Here we have several equivocal words that need elucidation, but let us keep to the term *transfer*. To transfer is to give or to sell. Now a man who becomes the slave of another does not give himself: he sells himself, in exchange, at the very least,

1. Translated by Christopher Betts. These selections come from Book 1, chapters 1–8.
2. Hugo Grotius, or de Groot was an advocate of the "Natural Law" school of political theory. In this section Rousseau makes repeated references to Grotius's *On the Law of War and Peace* (1625).

for his subsistence. But in exchange for what does a nation sell itself? A king, far from providing subsistence to his subjects, takes it all from them, and as Rabelais says, a king doesn't live cheaply.[3] So will his subjects give him their persons on condition that he will take their property also? I cannot see what they still have to keep.

It will be objected that a despot ensures civil peace for his subjects. Very well; but what do they gain thereby, if the wars that his ambition brings down on them, his insatiable greed, and the troubles inflicted by his administrators, plague them more sorely than their dissensions would? What do they gain thereby, if civil peace itself is a source of misery? Prisoners live peacefully in their dungeons; is that enough for them to feel comfortable there? The Greek captives in the cave of the Cyclops lived there peacefully, while awaiting their turn to be devoured.[4]

To say that a man gives himself for nothing is an absurd and incomprehensible statement; such an action is illegitimate and void, simply because anyone who does it is not in his right mind. To say the same about an entire people is to imagine a nation of madmen, and madness does not make rights.

Even if each person could transfer himself, he could not transfer his children; they are born men, and free; their freedom belongs to them, and nobody except them has the right to dispose of it. Until they reach the age of reason, their father can stipulate, in their name, the conditions for their conservation and well-being, but he cannot make a gift of them, irrevocably and without condition; such a gift is contrary to the purposes of nature and exceeds the rights of fatherhood. In order, then, for an arbitrary government to be legitimate, it would be necessary for the people, at every new generation, to have the power to accept it or reject it; but in that case the government would no longer be arbitrary.

To renounce our freedom is to renounce our character as men, the rights, and even the duties, of humanity. No compensation is possible for anyone who renounces everything. It is incompatible with the nature of man; to remove the will's freedom is to remove all morality from our actions. Finally, a convention is vain and contradictory if it stipulates absolute authority on one side and limitless obedience on the other. Is it not obvious that we have no obligations towards a person from whom we can demand anything, and that this condition, requiring nothing in return or exchange, is enough to render the covenant null? For what right can my slave have against me, since everything he has belongs to me? His rights being mine, a right of mine against myself is a word without a meaning.

Grotius and the others take war to be another origin of the so-called right of slavery.[5] The conqueror having the right, according to them, to kill the conquered, the latter may redeem his life at the expense of his freedom; an agreement that is the more legitimate because it is to the advantage of both parties.

But it is clear that this so-called right to kill the conquered does not derive in any way from the state of war. For the simple reason that men who are living in their original condition of independence are not in a sufficiently continuous relationship with each other for a state either of peace or war to exist, they are not naturally enemies. It is the relationship of things, not of men, that constitutes a state of war, and since the state of war cannot be engendered merely by personal relationships but only by relationships between things, a private war between man and

---

3. François Rabelais (c. 1494–c. 1553), French humanist and satirist.
4. Homer's *Odyssey*, Book 9; echoing John Locke's use of the same reference in his *Second Treatise of Civil Government* (1690).
5. Slavery as a right of war had also been proposed by Thomas Hobbes in his *Of the Citizen* (1642), and by Samuel von Pufendorf (1632–1694).

man cannot exist—either in the state of nature, in which there is no permanent possession of property, or in the social state, in which everything is controlled by laws.

Single combat, duels, and chance encounters are actions which do not produce a state of affairs; and with respect to private wars, which were authorized by the Establishments of Louis IX of France and abrogated by the Peace of God,[6] they were an abuse due to feudal government, an absurd system if ever there was one, contrary both to the principles of natural law and all good polity.

War is not, therefore, a relationship between man and man, but between state and state, in which individuals become enemies only by accident, not as men, nor even as citizens,[7] but as soldiers; not even as members of their own nation, but as its defenders. Furthermore each state can be enemy only to other states, and not to men, given that between things diverse in nature no true relationship can be established.

The principle involved conforms, moreover, to maxims accepted in every age, and to the constant practice of every politically organized nation. Declarations of war are notices given less to national powers than to their subjects. A foreign king, or private individual, or people, who pillages, kills or detains a ruler's subjects, without declaring war on the ruler, is not an enemy, but a brigand. Even in war proper, a just ruler will indeed take possession, when he is in enemy territory, of anything belonging to the public, but will respect the person and property of individuals; he is respecting the rights on which his own are founded. The purpose of war being to destroy the enemy state, its defenders may rightfully be killed so long as they are carrying arms; but as soon as they lay them down and surrender, ceasing to be enemies or agents of the enemy, they become simply men again, and there is no longer any right over their lives. On occasion it is possible to kill the state without killing any of its members; war confers no rights that are not necessary to its purpose. These are not Grotius's principles; they are not based on the authority of poets, but derive from the nature of things, and are based on reason.[8]

As regards the right of conquest, its only foundation is the right of the strongest. If war does not give the victor the right to massacre the vanquished people, this right that he does not possess cannot create the right to enslave them. One has the right to kill an enemy only when it is impossible to make a slave of him: therefore the right to enslave him does not come from the right to kill him; therefore it is an iniquitous exchange to make him pay with his freedom for his life, over which one has no right. Is it not plain that there is a vicious circle in basing the right of life and death on the right to enslave, and the right to enslave on the right of life and death?

Even if we were to admit this terrible right of massacre, I say that men enslaved in war, or a conquered people, have no obligation at all to their masters, beyond obeying them to the extent that they are forced to do so. The conqueror has not spared the

6. The Establishments were a collection of laws attributed to Louis IX (1214–1270); the Peace of God was a series of Church decrees attempting to restrict feudal warfare.
7. The Romans, who understood and observed the laws of war better than any other nation on earth, carried their scruples on this point so far that citizens were not allowed to serve as volunteers unless they committed themselves to fighting against the enemy, and an enemy specifically named. When the legion in which the younger Cato had fought his first campaign was disbanded, the elder Cato wrote to Popilius to say that if he wished his son to continue to serve with him he would have to take the military

oath again, because, once the first oath had been cancelled, he could no longer bear arms against the enemy. And Cato also wrote to his son telling him to take care not to go into battle without taking the new oath. I know that the siege of Clusium and other particular incidents could be used against my argument, but for my part I am citing laws and customs. Of all peoples the Romans transgressed their laws least often, and their laws were the finest of all [Rousseau's note, added in 1782].
8. Montesquieu made a similar argument in *The Spirit of Laws,* 10.3, "The Right of Conquest."

slave's life when he has taken the equivalent of life: instead of killing him without profit he has killed him usefully. So far from any authority having been added to the power that the one has over the other, the state of war continues between them, and their relation is the consequence of it. The enforcement of a right of war does not create the assumption that a peace treaty has been made. An agreement has indeed been reached, but this covenant is far from destroying the state of war, and makes the assumption that it still continues.

From whatever angle the question is considered, then, the right of slavery is void, not only because it is illegitimate, but because of its absurdity and meaninglessness. The words *slavery* and *right* contradict each other; they are mutually exclusive. Whether made by one man addressing another, or by a man addressing a nation, this statement will always be equally senseless: "I make a covenant between us which is entirely at your expense and entirely for my good, which I will observe as long as I please, and which you will observe as long as I please."

THE SOCIAL PACT

I make the assumption that there is a point in the development of mankind at which the obstacles to men's self-preservation in the state of nature are too great to be overcome by the strength that any one individual can exert in order to maintain himself in this state. The original state can then subsist no longer, and the human race would perish if it did not change its mode of existence.

Now as men cannot generate new strength, but only unify and control the forces already existing, the sole means that they still have of preserving themselves is to create, by combination, a totality of forces sufficient to overcome the obstacles resisting them, to direct their operation by a single impulse, and make them act in unison.

The totality of forces can be formed only by the collaboration of a number of persons; but each man's strength and freedom being the main instruments of his preservation, how can he commit them to others without harming himself, and without neglecting the duty of care to himself? The difficulty as it relates to my subject may be defined in the following terms:

"Find a form of association which will defend and protect, with the whole of its joint strength, the person and property of each associate, and under which each of them, uniting himself to all, will obey himself alone, and remain as free as before." This is the fundamental problem to which the social contract gives the answer.

The clauses of this contract are so closely determined by the nature of the act in question that the slightest modification would make them empty and ineffectual; whence it is that, although they may perhaps never have been formally pronounced, they are the same everywhere, and everywhere tacitly recognized and accepted, until, should the social pact be violated, each associate thereupon recovers his original rights and takes back his natural freedom, while losing the freedom of convention for which he gave it up.

Properly understood, the clauses can all be reduced to one alone, namely, the complete transfer of each associate, with all his rights, to the whole community. For in the first place, each giving himself completely, the condition is the same for all; and the condition being the same for all, none has any interest in making it burdensome to the others.

Further, the transfer being carried out unreservedly, the union between the associates is as perfect as it can be, and none of them has any further requirements to add.

For if individuals retained some rights, there being no common superior to give judgement between them and the public, each would make his own judgement on certain points, and would soon aspire to do so on all of them: the state of nature would remain in force, and the association would become, necessarily, either tyrannical or meaningless.

Finally, each in giving himself to all gives himself to none, and since there are no associates over whom he does not acquire the same rights as he cedes, he gains the equivalent of all that he loses, and greater strength for the conservation of what he possesses.

If therefore we set aside everything that is not essential to the social pact, we shall find that it may be reduced to the following terms. *Each of us puts his person and all his power in common under the supreme direction of the general will; and we as a body receive each member as an indivisible part of the whole.*

Immediately, this act of association produces, in place of the individual persons of every contracting party, a moral and collective body, which is composed of as many members as there are votes in the assembly, and which, by the same act, is endowed with its unity, its common self, its life, and its will. The public person that is formed in this way by the union of all the others once bore the name *city,*[9] and now bears that of *republic* or *body politic;* its members call it *the state* when it is passive, *the sovereign* when it is active, and a *power* when comparing it to its like. As regards the associates, they collectively take the name of *people,* and are individually called *citizens* as being participants in sovereign authority, and *subjects* as being bound by the laws of the state.

THE CIVIL STATE

This passage from the state of nature to the civil state produces in man a very remarkable change, replacing instinct by justice in his behaviour, and conferring on his actions the moral quality that they had lacked before. It is only now, as the voice of duty succeeds to physical impulse and right to appetite, that man, who had previously thought of nothing but himself, is compelled to act on other principles, and to consult his reason before he attends to his inclinations. Although, in the civil state, he deprives himself of a number of advantages which he has by nature, the others that he acquires are so great, so greatly are his faculties exercised and improved, his ideas amplified, his feelings ennobled, and his entire soul raised so much higher, that if the abuses that occur in his new condition did not frequently reduce him to a state lower than the one he has just left, he ought constantly to bless the happy moment when he was taken from it for ever, and which made of him, not a limited and stupid animal, but an intelligent being and a man.

---

9. The true sense of this word has almost disappeared in modern writers. Most of them take a town to be a city and a town-dweller to be a citizen. They are unaware that it is houses that make a town, but citizens who make the City. The same error once cost the Carthaginians dear [when their general underestimated the loyalty of Roman citizens]. In my reading I have not seen the title of *cives* [citizen] given to the subjects of any ruler, not even to the Macedonians in ancient times, nor to the English nowadays, although they are nearer to being free than any others. The French alone call themselves *citizens* as a matter of course, because they have no idea of what it means, as can be seen from their dictionaries; otherwise, they would be guilty of treason in usurping it. Among them, the name expresses a virtue, not a right. Bodin, meaning to discuss our citizens and burgesses [city-dwellers], made a sad blunder in taking the one for the other. M. d'Alembert did not make the same mistake in his article *Geneva,* where he correctly distinguished the four orders (or even five, if you count those who are simply foreigners) to which those living in our city belong, only two of them constituting the Republic. No other French author, to my knowledge, has understood the true sense of the word *citizen* [Rousseau's note]. Rousseau is referring to Jean Bodin's *Six Books of the Republic* (1576); d'Alembert's "Geneva" appeared in Volume 7 (1757) of Diderot and d'Alembert's *Encyclopédie.*

Let us convert the balance of gains and losses into terms that are easy to compare. What man loses by the social contract is his natural freedom and an unlimited right to anything by which he is tempted and can obtain; what he gains is civil freedom and the right of property over everything that he possesses.

In order not to be misled over the compensating advantages, we must clearly distinguish natural freedom, which is limited only by the strength of the individual, from civil freedom, which is limited by the general will; and possession, which is merely the effect of force or the right of the first occupant, from property, which can be founded only on positive entitlement.

To the acquisition of moral status could be added, on the basis of what has just been said, the acquisition of moral liberty, this being the only thing that makes man truly the master of himself; for to be driven by our appetites alone is slavery, while to obey a law that we have imposed on ourselves is freedom.

Mary Wollstonecraft
1759–1797

Mary Wollstonecraft proclaimed what everyone already knew: that "female character" was an artificial construct. For centuries "conduct books" had been sold to educate naturally depraved females into modest, obedient ladies. The revolutionary principles of equality and universal human reason, however, allowed Wollstonecraft to argue that the female "nature" beneath the veneer of education was not depraved but rational, and that conduct-book education itself made women silly and vain. In response she was labeled a "hyena in petticoats" by conservatives relying on prevalent models of femininity. Wollstonecraft made an easy target, for she flouted conventional morality in both her life and works. Her life reads like the contemporary novels she ridiculed (and wrote): her drunken father squandered the family fortune, while her abused mother favored her irresponsible eldest son. Forced to earn her living, Mary, sustained by female friendships, worked as a lady's companion, seamstress, governess, and schoolmistress. Her revolutionary lover abandoned her and their child, and Mary twice attempted suicide. Afterward she married the philosopher William Godwin, bearing him the future novelist Mary Godwin (Shelley). She died of this childbirth, receiving relief only from wine and the puppies brought in to draw the milk from her breasts. What no contemporary novel would have included was that in the midst of this romantic heroine's life Wollstonecraft also had a brilliant career as a journalist, novelist, and political thinker. Her most famous book is *A Vindication of the Rights of Woman* (1792), a response to the French "Declaration of the Rights of Man and Citizen" and Olympe de Gouges' "Declaration of the Rights of Woman" (for which Gouges was beheaded by the revolutionary government), and to Rousseau's *The Social Contract* (see page 587) and *Emile*. This work has earned Wollstonecraft the title of "mother of modern feminism."

from A Vindication of the Rights of Woman

from *Introduction*

After considering the historic page, and viewing the living world with anxious solicitude, the most melancholy emotions of sorrowful indignation have depressed my spirits, and I have sighed when obliged to confess, that either nature has made a great difference between man and man, or that the civilization which has hitherto taken place in the world has been very partial. I have turned over various books written on the subject of education, and patiently observed the conduct of parents and the management of schools; but what has been the result?—a profound conviction that the neglected education of my fellow-creatures is the grand source of the misery I deplore; and that women, in particular, are rendered weak and wretched by a variety of concurring causes, originating from one hasty conclusion. The conduct and manners of women, in fact, evidently prove that their minds are not in a healthy state; for, like the flowers which are planted in too rich a soil, strength and usefulness are sacrificed to beauty; and the flaunting leaves, after having pleased a fastidious eye, fade, disregarded on the stalk, long before the season when they ought to have arrived at maturity.—One cause of this barren blooming I attribute to a false system of education, gathered from the books written on this subject by men who, considering females rather as women than human creatures, have been more anxious to make them alluring mistresses than affectionate wives and rational mothers; and the understanding of the sex has been so bubbled[1] by this specious homage, that the civilized women of the present century, with a few exceptions, are only anxious to inspire love, when they ought to cherish a nobler ambition, and by their abilities and virtues exact respect. * * *

My own sex, I hope, will excuse me, if I treat them like rational creatures, instead of flattering their *fascinating* graces, and viewing them as if they were in a state of perpetual childhood, unable to stand alone. I earnestly wish to point out in what true dignity and human happiness consists—I wish to persuade women to endeavour to acquire strength, both of mind and body, and to convince them that the soft phrases, susceptibility of heart, delicacy of sentiment, and refinement of taste, are almost synonymous with epithets of weakness, and that those beings who are only the objects of pity and that kind of love, which has been termed its sister, will soon become objects of contempt.

Dismissing then those pretty feminine phrases, which the men condescendingly use to soften our slavish dependence, and despising that weak elegancy of mind, exquisite sensibility, and sweet docility of manners, supposed to be the sexual characteristics of the weaker vessel, I wish to shew that elegance is inferior to virtue, that the first object of laudable ambition is to obtain a character as a human being, regardless of the distinction of sex; and that secondary views should be brought to this simple touchstone.

from *Chapter 2. The Prevailing Opinion of a Sexual Character Discussed*

To account for, and excuse the tyranny of man, many ingenious arguments have been brought forward to prove, that the two sexes, in the acquirement of virtue, ought to aim at attaining a very different character: or, to speak explicitly, women are not allowed to have sufficient strength of mind to acquire what really deserves the name of virtue. Yet it should seem, allowing them to have souls, that there is but one way appointed by Providence to lead *mankind* to either virtue or happiness. * * *

In fact, it is a farce to call any being virtuous whose virtues do not result from the exercise of its own reason. This was Rousseau's opinion respecting men: I extend it to women, and confidently assert that they have been drawn out of their sphere by false refinement, and not by an endeavour to acquire masculine qualities. Still the regal homage which they receive is so intoxicating, that till the manners of the times are changed, and formed on more reasonable principles, it may be impossible to convince them that the illegitimate power, which they obtain, by degrading themselves, is a curse, and that they must return to nature and equality, if they wish to secure the placid satisfaction that unsophisticated affections impart. But for this epoch we must wait—wait, perhaps, till kings and nobles, enlightened by reason, and, preferring the real dignity of man to childish

1. Gas-filled; deluded.

state, throw off their gaudy hereditary trappings: and if then women do not resign the arbitrary power of beauty—they will prove that they have *less* mind than man.

I may be accused of arrogance; still I must declare what I firmly believe, that all the writers who have written on the subject of female education and manners from Rousseau to Dr. Gregory, have contributed to render women more artificial, weak characters, than they would otherwise have been; and, consequently, more useless members of society.[2] * * * My objection extends to the whole purport of those books, which tend, in my opinion, to degrade one half of the human species, and render women pleasing at the expense of every solid virtue.

Though, to reason on Rousseau's ground, if man did attain a degree of perfection of mind when his body arrived at maturity, it might be proper, in order to make a man and his wife *one,* that she should rely entirely on his understanding; and the graceful ivy, clasping the oak that supported it, would form a whole in which strength and beauty would be equally conspicuous. But, alas! husbands, as well as their helpmates, are often only overgrown children; nay, thanks to early debauchery, scarcely men in their outward form—and if the blind lead the blind, one need not come from heaven to tell us the consequence.[3]

from *Chapter 3. The Same Subject Continued*

If it be granted that woman was not created merely to gratify the appetite of man, or to be the upper servant, who provides his meals and takes care of his linen, it must follow, that the first care of those mothers or fathers, who really attend to the education of females, should be, if not to strengthen the body, at least, not to destroy the constitution by mistaken notions of beauty and female excellence; nor should girls ever be allowed to imbibe the pernicious notion that a defect can, by any chemical process of reasoning, become an excellence. * * *

The mother, who wishes to give true dignity of character to her daughter, must, regardless of the sneers of ignorance, proceed on a plan diametrically opposite to that which Rousseau has recommended with all the deluding charms of eloquence and philosophical sophistry: for his eloquence renders absurdities plausible, and his dogmatic conclusions puzzle, without convincing, those who have not ability to refute them.

Throughout the whole animal kingdom every young creature requires almost continual exercise, and the infancy of children, conformable to this intimation, should be passed in harmless gambols, that exercise the feet and hands, without requiring very minute direction from the head, or the constant attention of a nurse. In fact, the care necessary for self-preservation is the first natural exercise of the understanding, as little inventions to amuse the present moment unfold the imagination. But these wise designs of nature are counteracted by mistaken fondness or blind zeal. The child is not left a moment to its own direction, particularly a girl, and thus rendered dependent—dependence is called natural.

To preserve personal beauty, woman's glory! the limbs and faculties are cramped with worse than Chinese bands,[4] and the sedentary life which they are condemned to

2. In *Émile,* ch. 5, "Sophy or Woman," Rousseau advises that a "woman's education must . . . be planned in relation to man. To be pleasing in his sight, to win his respect and love, to train him in childhood, to tend him in manhood, to counsel and console, to make his life pleasant and happy"; at any state of life, she "will always be in subjection to a man, or to man's judgment, and she will never be free to set her own opinion above his." Dr. John Gregory wrote a popular English conduct book, *A Father's Legacy to His Daughters* (1774).
3. See Jesus' admonition, "if the blind lead the blind, both shall fall into the ditch" (Matthew 15:14). "Rousseau's ground" is given in *Émile,* ch. 5.
4. The Chinese practice of binding girls' feet to keep them delicately small often left them crippled for life, reinforcing dependency.

live, whilst boys frolic in the open air, weakens the muscles and relaxes the nerves.—As for Rousseau's remarks, which have since been echoed by several writers, that they have naturally, that is from their birth, independent of education, a fondness for dolls, dressing, and talking—they are so puerile as not to merit a serious refutation. That a girl, condemned to sit for hours together listening to the idle chat of weak nurses, or to attend at her mother's toilet,[5] will endeavour to join the conversation, is, indeed, very natural; and that she will imitate her mother or aunts, and amuse herself by adorning her lifeless doll, as they do in dressing her, poor innocent babe! is undoubtedly a most natural consequence. For men of the greatest abilities have seldom had sufficient strength to rise above the surrounding atmosphere; and, if the page of genius have always been blurred by the prejudices of the age, some allowance should be made for a sex, who, like kings, always see things through a false medium.

Pursuing these reflections, the fondness for dress, conspicuous in women, may be easily accounted for, without supposing it the result of a desire to please the sex on which they are dependent. The absurdity, in short, of supposing that a girl is naturally a coquette, and that a desire connected with the impulse of nature to propagate the species, should appear even before an improper education has, by heating the imagination, called it forth prematurely, is so unphilosophical, that such a sagacious observer as Rousseau would not have adopted it, if he had not been accustomed to make reason give way to his desire of singularity, and truth to a favorite paradox. * * *

I have, probably, had an opportunity of observing more girls in their infancy than J. J. Rousseau[6]—I can recollect my own feelings, and I have looked steadily around me; yet, so far from coinciding with him in opinion respecting the first dawn of the female character, I will venture to affirm, that a girl, whose spirits have not been damped by inactivity, or innocence tainted by false shame, will always be a romp, and the doll will never excite attention unless confinement allows her no alternative. Girls and boys, in short, would play harmlessly together, if the distinction of sex was not inculcated long before nature makes any difference.—I will go further, and affirm, as an indisputable fact, that most of the women, in the circle of my observation, who have acted like rational creatures, or shewn any vigour of intellect, have accidentally been allowed to run wild—as some of the elegant formers of the fair sex would insinuate.

The baneful consequences which flow from inattention to health during infancy, and youth, extend further than is supposed—dependence of body naturally produces dependence of mind; and how can she be a good wife or mother, the greater part of whose time is employed to guard against or endure sickness? Nor can it be expected that a woman will resolutely endeavour to strengthen her constitution and abstain from enervating indulgencies, if artificial notions of beauty, and false descriptions of sensibility, have been early entangled with her motives of action. Most men are sometimes obliged to bear with bodily inconveniencies, and to endure, occasionally, the inclemency of the elements; but genteel women are, literally speaking, slaves to their bodies, and glory in their subjection.

I once knew a weak woman of fashion, who was more than commonly proud of her delicacy and sensibility. She thought a distinguishing taste and puny appetite the height of all human perfection, and acted accordingly.—I have seen this weak sophisticated being neglect all the duties of life, yet recline with self-complacency on a sofa, and boast of her want of appetite as a proof of delicacy that extended to, or, perhaps, arose from, her exquisite sensibility: for it is difficult to render intelligible such ridiculous

---

5. Grooming and dressing.

6. Wollstonecraft was the eldest sister in a family with three girls and had also worked as a governess.

jargon.—Yet, at the moment, I have seen her insult a worthy old gentlewoman, whom unexpected misfortunes had made dependent on her ostentatious bounty, and who, in better days, had claims on her gratitude. Is it possible that a human creature could have become such a weak and depraved being, if, like the Sybarites,[7] dissolved in luxury, every thing like virtue had not been worn away, or never impressed by precept, a poor substitute, it is true, for cultivation of mind, though it serves as a fence against vice?

Such a woman is not a more irrational monster than some of the Roman emperors, who were depraved by lawless power. Yet, since kings have been more under the restraint of law, and the curb, however weak, of honour, the records of history are not filled with such unnatural instances of folly and cruelty, nor does the despotism that kills virtue and genius in the bud, hover over Europe with that destructive blast which desolates Turkey, and renders the men, as well as the soil, unfruitful.[8] * * *

It is time to effect a revolution in female manners—time to restore to them their lost dignity—and make them, as a part of the human species, labour by reforming themselves to reform the world. It is time to separate unchangeable morals from local manners.

from Chapter 13. Some Instances of the Folly Which the Ignorance of Women Generates; with Concluding Reflections on the Moral Improvement That a Revolution in Female Manners Might Naturally Be Expected to Produce

[CONCLUDING REFLECTIONS]

That women at present are by ignorance rendered foolish or vicious, is, I think, not to be disputed; and, that the most salutary effects tending to improve mankind might be expected from a REVOLUTION in female manners, appears, at least, with a face of probability, to rise out of the observation. For as marriage has been termed the parent of those endearing charities which draw man from the brutal herd, the corrupting intercourse that wealth, idleness, and folly, produce between the sexes, is more universally injurious to morality than all the other vices of mankind collectively considered. To adulterous lust the most sacred duties are sacrificed, because before marriage, men, by a promiscuous intimacy with women, learned to consider love as a selfish gratification—learned to separate it not only from esteem, but from the affection merely built on habit, which mixes a little humanity with it. Justice and friendship are also set at defiance, and that purity of taste is vitiated which would naturally lead a man to relish an artless display of affection rather than affected airs. But that noble simplicity of affection, which dares to appear unadorned, has few attractions for the libertine, though it be the charm, which by cementing the matrimonial tie, secures to the pledges of a warmer passion the necessary parental attention; for children will never be properly educated till friendship subsists between parents. Virtue flies from a house divided against itself—and a whole legion of devils take up their residence there.[9]

The affection of husbands and wives cannot be pure when they have so few sentiments in common, and when so little confidence is established at home, as must be the case when their pursuits are so different. That intimacy from which tenderness should flow, will not, cannot subsist between the vicious.

Contending, therefore, that the sexual distinction which men have so warmly insisted upon, is arbitrary, I have dwelt on an observation, that several sensible men,

---

7. The inhabitants of a 5th-century Greek colony in Italy famed for luxurious decadence.
8. Both the hot, dusty winds from the deserts to the south and the despotic Ottoman Empire.
9. An allusion to Jesus' lesson that "if a house be divided against itself, that house cannot stand" (Mark 3:25).

with whom I have conversed on the subject, allowed to be well founded; and it is simply this, that the little chastity to be found amongst men, and consequent disregard of modesty, tend to degrade both sexes; and further, that the modesty of women, characterized as such, will often be only the artful veil of wantonness instead of being the natural reflection of purity, till modesty be universally respected.[1]

From the tyranny of man, I firmly believe, the greater number of female follies proceed; and the cunning, which I allow makes at present a part of their character, I likewise have repeatedly endeavoured to prove, is produced by oppression.

Were not dissenters,[2] for instance, a class of people, with strict truth, characterized as cunning? And may I not lay some stress on this fact to prove, that when any power but reason curbs the free spirit of man, dissimulation is practised, and the various shifts of art are naturally called forth? Great attention to decorum, which was carried to a degree of scrupulosity, and all that puerile bustle about trifles and consequential solemnity, which Butler's caricature of a dissenter, brings before the imagination, shaped their persons as well as their minds in the mould of prim littleness.[3] I speak collectively, for I know how many ornaments to human nature have been enrolled amongst sectaries; yet, I assert, that the same narrow prejudice for their sect, which women have for their families, prevailed in the dissenting part of the community, however worthy in other respects; and also that the same timid prudence, or headstrong efforts, often disgraced the exertions of both. Oppression thus formed many of the features of their character perfectly to coincide with that of the oppressed half of mankind; or is it not notorious that dissenters were, like women, fond of deliberating together, and asking advice of each other, till by a complication of little contrivances, some little end was brought about? A similar attention to preserve their reputation was conspicuous in the dissenting and female world, and was produced by a similar cause.

Asserting the rights which women in common with men ought to contend for, I have not attempted to extenuate their faults; but to prove them to be the natural consequence of their education and station in society. If so, it is reasonable to suppose that they will change their character, and correct their vices and follies, when they are allowed to be free in a physical, moral, and civil sense.[4]

Let woman share the rights and she will emulate the virtues of man; for she must grow more perfect when emancipated, or justify the authority that chains such a weak being to her duty.—If the latter, it will be expedient to open a fresh trade with Russia for whips; a present which a father should always make to his son-in-law on his wedding day, that a husband may keep his whole family in order by the same means; and without any violation of justice reign, wielding this sceptre, sole master of his house, because he is the only being in it who has reason:—the divine, indefeasible earthly sovereignty breathed into man by the Master of the universe. Allowing this position, women have not any inherent rights to claim; and, by the same rule, their duties vanish, for rights and duties are inseparable.

---

1. By chastity and modesty, Wollstonecraft means sexual self-control and self-discipline; male chastity entails fidelity, not sexual self-denial, in marriage.
2. Those who dissented from the established Church of England to form independent religious sects; many of Wollstonecraft's friends were dissenters.
3. Samuel Butler's mock-heroic, satirical poem *Hudibras* (1663–1678) takes aim at Puritans (dissenters who formed the commonwealth government after the execution of Charles I); Sir Hudibras, pedant and hypocrite, is a country justice who sets out to reform England of various popular entertainments.
4. I had further enlarged on the advantages which might reasonably be expected to result from an improvement in female manners, towards the general reformation of society; but it appeared to me that such reflections would more properly close the last volume [Wollstonecraft's note; no further volumes were published].

Be just then, O ye men of understanding! and mark not more severely what women do amiss, than the vicious tricks of the horse or the ass for whom ye provide provender—and allow her the privileges of ignorance, to whom ye deny the rights of reason, or ye will be worse than Egyptian task-masters, expecting virtue where nature has not given understanding!

Anna Letitia Barbauld
1743–1825

Anna Letitia Barbauld was an influential professional woman of letters who believed women should not be educated for literature or professions. She herself received an education rarely available to women. Her father, a tutor in literature at prestigious Warrington Academy for Dissenters, near Liverpool, taught her Greek, Latin, French, and Italian. Two other Warrington tutors, her brother John Aikin (physician, author, editor) and Joseph Priestley (discoverer of oxygen, founder of modern Unitarianism) encouraged her to publish her poetry; her first volume (1773) ran through five editions over four years. At the advanced age of thirty-one she married Warrington graduate Rochemont Barbauld, opening a boys' school with him. She refused an invitation to open a girls' school, arguing that women should be only "good wives or agreeable companions." Her husband's increasing mental instability forced them to sell their school in 1785. By 1808 he became so violent toward her that he had to be restrained, but escaping his keepers, he drowned himself.

Always prolific, Anna published more than ever. Her magisterial fifty-volume *British Novelists* (1810) established the canon of the English novel and the literary seriousness of the genre. She wrote "The Rights of Woman" in 1795 in reaction to Wollstonecraft's *Vindication of the Rights of Woman* (see page 592), which had criticized her for her Rousseau-inspired verses instructing women: "Your BEST, your SWEETEST empire is—TO PLEASE." Barbauld and Wollstonecraft agreed that women should be housewives and mothers, and that to fill those roles effectively they must be educated as "rational beings," but Barbauld thought it fruitless to "provoke a war with the other sex." That war, however, was already underway: one of her most important poems, "Eighteen Hundred and Eleven" (1812), criticizing British imperialism, was reviewed so harshly as the trivial "intervention of a lady-author" into political concerns that she never published another word in her long lifetime. (A further selection of Barbauld's poems can be found in Volume E.)

The Rights of Woman

Yes, injured Woman! rise, assert thy right!
Woman! too long degraded, scorned, opprest;
O born to rule in partial° Law's despite,   *one-sided*
Resume thy native empire o'er the breast!

5 Go forth arrayed in panoply° divine;   *armor*
That angel pureness which admits no stain;
Go, bid proud Man his boasted rule resign,
And kiss the golden sceptre of thy reign.

Go, gird thyself with grace; collect thy store
10 Of bright artillery glancing from afar;
Soft melting tones thy thundering cannon's roar,
Blushes and fears thy magazine° of war.   *storehouse*

Thy rights are empire: urge no meaner° claim,—   *lower*
Felt, not defined, and if debated, lost;
15   Like sacred mysteries, which withheld from fame,
Shunning discussion, are revered the most.

Try all that wit and art suggest to bend
Of thy imperial foe the stubborn knee;
Make treacherous Man thy subject, not thy friend:
20   Thou mayst command, but never canst be free.

Awe the licentious, and restrain the rude;
Soften the sullen, clear the cloudy brow:
Be, more than princes' gifts, thy favours sued;—
She hazards all, who will the least allow.

25   But hope not, courted idol of mankind,
On this proud eminence secure to stay;
Subduing and subdued, thou soon shalt find
Thy coldness soften, and thy pride give way.

Then, then, abandon each ambitious thought,
30   Conquest or rule thy heart shall feebly move,
In Nature's school, by her soft maxims taught,
That separate rights are lost in mutual love.

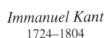

Immanuel Kant
1724–1804

Immanuel Kant spent all his eighty years without leaving Königsberg (now Kaliningrad, Russia), a Baltic port city in what was then the powerful German kingdom of Prussia. Fortunately the world came to him, for Königsberg was the center of a thriving trade in goods and ideas with other northern countries, from England to Russia. Although his parents were poor harness-makers who raised him in strict Christian Pietism (anticlerical Protestantism) and died when he was in his teens, the small, ill-favored Kant gained entrance to the Albertus University and was transformed into a dandy who loved clothes, gambling, and Enlightenment philosophy. He gave up on his early ambitions of becoming a doctor or writer around the same time he gave up hustling billiards, and instead taught philosophy—which in those days included everything from politics to physics, with logic and metaphysics in between—at his university for more than forty years. He thought of proposing marriage once or twice, but he always thought too long. He was sociable and enjoyed a good dinner party, but his only intensive, long-term relationship seems to have been his friendship with one Mr. Green, an English merchant, whom he visited every afternoon so punctually and for so many years that Green's neighbors adjusted their erratic eighteenth-century timepieces by Professor Kant's comings and goings. For Green impressed upon Kant the importance of regulating one's life, without deviating from clocks or principles, an emphasis that would come to characterize the philosopher's ethical thought. Green shared Kant's enthusiasm for the thought of Rousseau and Hume, and talked over with him the ideas Kant finally published in his first major philosophical contribution, *Critique of Pure Reason* (1781). This was soon followed by the *Groundwork of the Metaphysics of Morals* (1785), the *Critique of Practical Reason* (1788), and the *Critique of Judgment* (1790), to name only some of the highest points. Kant's "critical" opus explores the *limitations* of the faculties central to Enlightenment definitions of humanity: reason, free will, (aesthetic) judgment, and sensibility (including both perception and emotion). Its influence on subsequent philosophy and imaginative literature, from the Romantics onward, cannot be underestimated.

"An Answer to the Question: What Is Enlightenment?" was first published in the *Berlin Monthly* in 1784—not coincidentally, between the American and French Revolutions. Like his hero Rousseau, Kant favored revolutionary principles, but as the servant of one of the most enlightened despots of the era—Frederick the Great of Prussia—he is careful in this essay not to advocate the direct overthrow of monarchies. Rather, he places his hopes for the liberation of humanity in a combination of individual responsibility and free exchange of ideas in a republic of letters that transcends political boundaries.

An Answer to the Question: What Is Enlightenment?[1]

Enlightenment is the human being's emergence from his self-incurred minority.[2] *Minority* is inability to make use of one's own understanding without direction from another. This minority is *self-incurred* when its cause lies not in lack of understanding but in lack of resolution and courage to use it without direction from another. *Sapere aude!*[3] Have courage to make use of your *own* understanding! is thus the motto of enlightenment.

It is because of laziness and cowardice that so great a part of humankind, after nature has long since emancipated them from other people's direction (*naturaliter maiorennes*),[4] nevertheless gladly remains minors for life, and that it becomes so easy for others to set themselves up as their guardians. It is so comfortable to be a minor! If I have a book that understands for me, a spiritual advisor who has a conscience for me, a doctor who decides upon a regimen for me, and so forth, I need not trouble myself at all. I need not think, if only I can pay; others will readily undertake the irksome business for me. That by far the greatest part of humankind (including the entire fair sex) should hold the step toward majority to be not only troublesome but also highly dangerous will soon be seen to by those guardians who have kindly taken it upon themselves to supervise them; after they have made their domesticated animals dumb and carefully prevented these placid creatures from daring to take a single step without the walking cart[5] in which they have confined them, they then show them the danger that threatens them if they try to walk alone. Now this danger is not in fact so great, for by a few falls they would eventually learn to walk; but an example of this kind makes them timid and usually frightens them away from any further attempt.

Thus it is difficult for any single individual to extricate himself from the minority that has become almost nature to him. He has even grown fond of it and is really unable for the time being to make use of his own understanding, because he was never allowed to make the attempt. Precepts and formulas, those mechanical instruments of a rational use, or rather misuse, of his natural endowments, are the ball and chain of an everlasting minority. And anyone who did throw them off would still make only an uncertain leap over even the narrowest ditch, since he would not be accustomed to free movement of this kind. Hence there are only a few who have succeeded, by their own cultivation of their spirit, in extricating themselves from minority and yet walking confidently.

---

1. Translated by Mary J. Gregor.
2. Legal status of dependency on a parent or other guardian. The German term is *unmündigkeit,* which literally means the inability to speak for oneself.
3. Dare to know; from Horace, *Epodes,* 1.2.40. This phrase had been adopted by the Society of the Friends of Truth, a prominent organization of the German Enlightenment.
4. Literally "those who have become mature through nature" (Latin); i.e. reached physical adulthood.
5. A support for children learning to walk.

But that a public should enlighten itself is more possible; indeed this is almost inevitable, if only it is left its freedom. For there will always be a few independent thinkers, even among the established guardians of the great masses, who, after having themselves cast off the yoke of minority, will disseminate the spirit of a rational valuing of one's own worth and of the calling of each individual to think for himself. What should be noted here is that the public, which was previously put under this yoke by the guardians, may subsequently itself compel them to remain under it, if the public is suitably stirred up by some of its guardians who are themselves incapable of any enlightenment; so harmful is it to implant prejudices, because they finally take their revenge on the very people who, or whose predecessors, were their authors. Thus a public can achieve enlightenment only slowly. A revolution may well bring about a falling off of personal despotism and of avaricious or tyrannical oppression, but never a true reform in one's way of thinking; instead new prejudices will serve just as well as old ones to harness the great unthinking masses.

For this enlightenment, however, nothing is required but *freedom,* and indeed the least harmful of anything that could even be called freedom: namely, freedom to make *public use* of one's reason in all matters. But I hear from all sides the cry: *Do not argue!* The officer says: Do not argue but drill! The tax official: Do not argue but pay! The clergyman: Do not argue but believe! (Only one ruler in the world says: *Argue* as much as you will and about whatever you will, *but obey!*[6]) Everywhere there are restrictions on freedom. But what sort of restriction hinders enlightenment, and what sort does not hinder but instead promotes it?—I reply: The *public* use of one's reason must always be free, and it alone can bring about enlightenment among human beings; the *private use* of one's reason may, however, often be very narrowly restricted without this particularly hindering the progress of enlightenment. But by the public use of one's own reason I understand that use which someone makes of it *as a scholar* before the entire public of the *world of readers.* What I call the private use of reason is that which one may make of it in a certain *civil* post or office with which he is entrusted. Now, for many affairs conducted in the interest of a commonwealth a certain mechanism is necessary, by means of which some members of the commonwealth must behave merely passively, so as to be directed by the government, through an artful unanimity, to public ends (or at least prevented from destroying such ends). Here it is, certainly, impermissible to argue; instead, one must obey. But insofar as this part of the machine also regards himself as a member of a whole commonwealth, even of the society of citizens of the world, and so in his capacity of a scholar who by his writings addresses a public in the proper sense of the word, he can certainly argue without thereby harming the affairs assigned to him in part as a passive member. Thus it would be ruinous if an officer, receiving an order from his superiors, wanted while on duty to engage openly in subtle reasoning about its appropriateness or utility; he must obey. But he cannot fairly be prevented, as a scholar, from making remarks about errors in the military service and from putting these before his public for appraisal. A citizen cannot refuse to pay the taxes imposed upon him; an impertinent censure of such levies when he is to pay them may even be punished as a scandal (which could occasion general insubordination). But the same citizen does not act against the duty of a citizen when, as a scholar, he publicly expresses his thoughts about the inappropriateness or even injustice of such decrees. So too, a clergyman is

6. Referring to Frederick the Great, King of Prussia 1740–1786.

bound to deliver his discourse to the pupils in his catechism class and to his congregation in accordance with the creed of the church he serves, for he was employed by it on that condition. But as a scholar he has complete freedom and is even called upon to communicate to the public all his carefully examined and well-intentioned thoughts about what is erroneous in that creed and his suggestions for a better arrangement of the religious and ecclesiastical body. And there is nothing in this that could be laid as a burden on his conscience. For what he teaches in consequence of his office as carrying out the business of the church, he represents as something with respect to which he does not have free power to teach as he thinks best, but which he is appointed to deliver as prescribed and in the name of another. He will say: Our church teaches this or that; here are the arguments it uses. He then extracts all practical uses for his congregation from precepts to which he would not himself subscribe with full conviction but which he can nevertheless undertake to deliver because it is still not altogether impossible that truth may lie concealed in them, and in any case there is at least nothing contradictory to inner religion present in them. For if he believed he had found the latter in them, he could not in conscience hold his office; he would have to resign from it. Thus the use that an appointed teacher makes of his reason before his congregation is merely a *private use;* for a congregation, however large a gathering it may be, is still only a domestic gathering; and with respect to it he, as a priest, is not and cannot be free, since he is carrying out another's commission. On the other hand as a scholar, who by his writings speaks to the public in the strict sense, that is, the world—hence a clergyman in the *public use* of his reason—he enjoys an unrestricted freedom to make use of his own reason and to speak in his own person. For that the guardians of the people (in spiritual matters) should themselves be minors is an absurdity that amounts to the perpetuation of absurdities.

But should not a society of clergymen, such as an ecclesiastical synod or a venerable classis (as it calls itself among the Dutch), be authorized to bind itself by oath to a certain unalterable creed, in order to carry on an unceasing guardianship over each of its members and by means of them over the people, and even to perpetuate this? I say that this is quite impossible. Such a contract, concluded to keep all further enlightenment away from the human race forever, is absolutely null and void, even if it were ratified by the supreme power, by imperial diets and by the most solemn peace treaties. One age cannot bind itself and conspire to put the following one into such a condition that it would be impossible for it to enlarge its cognitions (especially in such urgent matters) and to purify them of errors, and generally to make further progress in enlightenment. This would be a crime against human nature, whose original vocation lies precisely in such progress; and succeeding generations are therefore perfectly authorized to reject such decisions as unauthorized and made sacrilegiously. The touchstone of whatever can be decided upon as law for a people lies in the question: whether a people could impose such a law upon itself. Now this might indeed be possible for a determinate short time, in expectation as it were of a better one, in order to introduce a certain order; during that time each citizen, particularly a clergyman, would be left free, in his capacity as a scholar, to make his remarks publicly, that is, through writings, about defects in the present institution; meanwhile, the order introduced would last until public insight into the nature of these things had become so widespread and confirmed that by the union of their voices (even if not all of them) it could submit a proposal to the crown, to take under its protection those congregations that have, perhaps in accordance with their concepts of better insight, agreed to an altered religious institution, but without hindering those that wanted to acquiesce in the old one. But it is absolutely impermissible to agree, even for a single lifetime, to a permanent religious constitution not to be doubted publicly by anyone and thereby, as it were, to nullify a period of time in the progress of humanity toward improvement and make it fruitless and hence detrimental to posterity. One can indeed, for his own person and even then only for some time, postpone enlightenment in what it is incumbent upon him to know; but to renounce enlightenment, whether for his own person or even more so for posterity, is to violate the sacred right of humanity and trample it underfoot. But what a people may never decide upon for itself, a monarch may still less decide upon for a people; for his legislative authority rests precisely on this, that he unites in his will the collective will of the people. As long as he sees to it that any true or supposed improvement is consistent with civil order, he can for the rest leave it to his subjects to do what they find it necessary to do for the sake of their salvation; that is no concern of his, but it is indeed his concern to prevent any one of them from forcibly hindering others from working to the best of their ability to determine and promote their salvation. It even infringes upon his majesty if he meddles in these affairs by honoring with governmental inspection the writings in which his subjects attempt to clarify their insight, as well as if he does this from his own supreme insight, in which case he exposes himself to the reproach *Caesar non est super grammaticos,*[7] but much more so if he demeans his supreme authority so far as to support the spiritual despotism of a few tyrants within his state against the rest of his subjects.

If it is now asked whether we at present live in an *enlightened* age, the answer is: No, but we do live in an *age of enlightenment.* As matters now stand, a good deal more is required for people on the whole to be in the position, or even able to be put into the position, of using their own understanding confidently and well in religious matters, without another's guidance. But we do have distinct intimations that the field is now being opened for them to work freely in this direction and that the hindrances to universal enlightenment or to humankind's emergence from its self-incurred minority are gradually becoming fewer. In this regard this age is the age of enlightenment or the century of Frederick.

A prince who does not find it beneath himself to say that he considers it his *duty* not to prescribe anything to human beings in religious matters but to leave them complete freedom, who thus even declines the arrogant name of *tolerance,* is himself enlightened and deserves to be praised by a grateful world and by posterity as the one who first released the human race from minority, at least from the side of government, and left each free to make use of his own reason in all matters of conscience. Under him, venerable clergymen, notwithstanding their official duties, may in their capacity as scholars freely and publicly lay before the world for examination their judgments and insights deviating here and there from the creed adopted, and still more may any other who is not restricted by any official duties. This spirit of freedom is also spreading abroad, even where it has to struggle with external obstacles of a government which misunderstands itself. For it shines as an example to such a government that in freedom there is not the least cause for anxiety about public concord and the unity of the commonwealth. People gradually work their way out of barbarism of their own accord if only one does not intentionally contrive to keep them in it.

I have put the main point of enlightenment, of people's emergence from their self-incurred minority, chiefly in *matters of religion* because our rulers have no interest in playing guardian over their subjects with respect to the arts and sciences and also

---

7. [Even] Caesar does not rule the grammarians; Marcus Pomponius Marcellus, 1st century C.E.

because that minority, being the most harmful, is also the most disgraceful of all. But the frame of mind of a head of state who favors the first goes still further and sees that even with respect to his *legislation* there is no danger in allowing his subjects to make *public* use of their own reason and to publish to the world their thoughts about a better way of formulating it, even with candid criticism of that already given; we have a shining example of this, in which no monarch has yet surpassed the one whom we honor.

But only one who, himself enlightened, is not afraid of phantoms, but at the same time has a well-disciplined and numerous army ready to guarantee public peace, can say what a free state may not dare to say: *Argue as much as you will and about what you will; only obey!* Here a strange, unexpected course is revealed in human affairs, as happens elsewhere too if it is considered in the large, where almost everything is paradoxical. A greater degree of civil freedom seems advantageous to a people's freedom of *spirit* and nevertheless puts up insurmountable barriers to it; a lesser degree of the former, on the other hand, provides a space for the latter to expand to its full capacity. Thus when nature has unwrapped, from under this hard shell, the seed for which she cares most tenderly, namely the propensity and calling to *think* freely, the latter gradually works back upon the mentality of the people (which thereby gradually becomes capable of *freedom* in acting) and eventually even upon the principles of *government*, which finds it profitable to itself to treat the human being, *who is now more than a machine,* in keeping with his dignity.[8]

Königsberg in Prussia, 30th September, 1784[9]

❦ CROSSCURRENTS: LIBERTY AND LIBERTINES ❦

- The European Enlightenment ideal of individual liberty inevitably begged a series of questions that still vex many societies today: At what point does individual freedom from political tyranny, religious dogma, or unexamined prejudice become merely unchecked liberty to do anything one can get away with, regardless of the needs, benefit, or rights of others? On what basis can moral principles be established once the traditional authority of church, state, and custom are no longer seen as absolute, and how can individual freedoms be justly limited for the benefit of society as a whole? All the texts in this section explore some aspect of these questions.

- Societies around the world were struggling with problems of individual and social liberty comparable to those treated in the works in this section, as old court cultures entered the modern world as a result of the globalization first brought about by the explosion of exploration and imperialism that began in the sixteenth century and continued into the twentieth. This section begins with striking selections from two Asian sources, both of them dealing with the intimate overlap of religious and sexual concerns—fictionally portrayed in Ihara Saikaku's *Life of a Sensuous Woman* and poetically expressed in the surprisingly erotic love poems of the sixth Dalai Lama. How do other texts, beyond the present section and volume, deal with similar issues arising from the conflict of traditional culture with

---

8. A jab at the mechanistic view of human nature prevalent since Descartes.
9. Today, on September 30th, I read in *Büsching's Weekly News* of 13th September a notice concerning this month's *Berlin Monthly,* which mentions Mendelssohn's answer to the same question. I have not yet seen this journal; otherwise I should have held back the present essay, which may now stand only in order to find out to what extent chance may bring about agreement in thoughts [Kant's note].

new values of increased individual freedoms? Places to look would include, in Volume C: the poems of Kshetrayya; Boccaccio's *Decameron*; Marguerite de Navarre's *Heptameron*; the sonnets of Louise Labé; François Rabelais' *Gargantua and Pantagruel*; as well as "Attacking and Defending the Vernacular Bible." The many writings in Volume E that engage in the struggle of changing and clashing cultures and values in the movements toward greater individual liberty during the nineteenth century include Byron's *Don Juan*; Flaubert's *Travels in Egypt*, Frederick Douglass's *Narrative of the Life of Frederick Douglass*, Elizabeth Barrett Browning's *Aurora Leigh*, Harriet Jacobs's *Incidents in the Life of a Slave Girl*; and any of the works collected under "Occidentalism." Volume F continues to reflect similar, ongoing upheavals in the twentieth century especially in Mina Loy's *Feminist Manifesto* and the selections in the sections entitled "Gendered Spaces" and "Postcolonial Conditions."

END OF PERSPECTIVES: LIBERTY AND LIBERTINES

BIBLIOGRAPHY

The Seventeenth and Eighteenth Centuries

General Background • Linda Colley, *Britons: Forging the Nation, 1707–1837*, 1992. • Christine Guth, *Art of Edo Japan: The Artist and the City, 1615–1868*, 1996. • John Whitney Hall, ed. *The Cambridge History of Japan.* Vol. 4, *Early Modern Japan*, 1988. • Julie C. Hayes, *Reading the French Enlightenment: System and Subversion*, 1999. • Donald Keene, *World Within Walls: Japanese Literature of the Pre-Modern Era, 1600–1868*, 1976. • Chie Nakane and Shinzaburō Ōishi, eds. *Tokugawa Japan: The Social and Economic Antecedents of Modern Japan*, 1991. • Matsunosuke Nishiyama, *Edo Culture: Daily Life and Diversions in Urban Japan, 1600–1868*, 1997. • Felicity Nussbaum and Laura Brown, eds., *The New Eighteenth Century*, 1987. • James Sambrook, *The Eighteenth Century: The Intellectual and Cultural Context of English Literature, 1700–1789*, 1986. • Conrad Totman, *Early Modern Japan*, 1993. • Steven N. Zwicker, *The Cambridge Companion to English Literature, 1650–1740*, 1998.

The World the Mughals Made • Muzaffar Alam, "The Culture and Politics of Persian in Pre-Colonial Hindustan," in *Literary Cultures in History: Reconstructions from South Asia*, ed. Sheldon Pollock, 2003. • Muzaffar Alam and Sanjay Subrahmanyam, eds. *The Mughal State 1526–1750*, 1998. • Shamsur Rahman Faruqi, "A Long History of Urdu Literary Culture—Part 1: Naming and Placing a Literary Culture," in *Literary Cultures*, ed. Pollock, 2003. • Mukund Lath, *Half a Tale: A Study in the Interrelationship Between Autobiography and History*, 1981. • Stuart McGregor, "The Progress of Hindi—Part 1: The Development of a Transregional Idiom," in *Literary Cultures*, ed. Pollock, 2003. • C. M. Naim, *Zikr-i Mir: The Autobiography of the Eighteenth-century Mughal Poet*, 1999. • Francis W. Pritchett, "A Long History of Urdu Literary Culture—Part 2: Histories, Performances, and Masters," in *Literary Cultures*, ed. Pollock, 2003. • Ralph Russell and Khurshidul Islam, *Three Mughal Poets: Mir, Sauda, Mir Hasan*, 1968. • Wheeler M. Thackston, *The Baburnama: Memoirs of Babur, Prince and Emperor*, 1996. • Wheeler M. Thackston, *The Jahangirnama: Memoirs of Jahangir, Emperor of India*, 1999.

Chikamatsu Mon'zaemon • Barbara Curtis Adachi, *Backstage at Bunraku: A Behind the Scenes Look at Japan's Traditional Puppet Theater*, 1985. • Barbara Curtis Adachi, *The Voices and Hands of Bunraku*, 1978. • C. U. Dunn, *The Early Japanese Puppet Drama*, 1966. • C. Andrew Gerstle, trans. *Chikamatsu: Five Late Plays*, 2001. • C. Andrew Gerstle, *Circles of Fantasy: Convention in the Plays of Chikamatsu*, 1986. • C. Andrew Gerstle, "Hero as Murderer in Chikamatsu," *Monumenta Nipponica*, vol. 51, 1996, 317–356. • C. Andrew Gerstle, "Heroic Honor: Chikamatsu and the Samurai Ideal," *Harvard Journal of Asiatic Studies*, vol. 57, 1997, 307–382. • Donald Keene, *Bunraku: The Art of the Japanese Puppet Theatre*, 1965. • Donald Keene, trans. *Four Major Plays of Chikamatsu*, 1969. • Donald Keene, trans. *Major Plays of Chikamatsu*, 1961. • Adolphe Clarence Scott, *The Puppet Theater of Japan*, 1963. • Donald H. Shively, trans. *The Love Suicides at Amijima*, 1953.

Cao Xueqin and Shen Fu • Cao Xueqin, *The Story of the Stone: A Chinese Novel in Five Volumes*, trans. David Hawkes, 1973–1986. • Louise P. Edwards, *Men and Women in Qing China: Gender in the Red Chamber Dream*, 1994. • Martin Huang, *Desire and Fictional Narrative in Late Imperial China*, 2001. • Martin Huang, *Literati and Self-Re/Presentation: Autobiographical Sensibility in the Eighteenth-Century Chinese Novel*, 1995. • Jeanne Knoerle, *The Dream of the Red Chamber: A Critical Study*, 1972. • Dore Jesse Levy, *Ideal and Actual in the Story of the Stone*, 1999. • Florence and Isabel McHugh, trans. *The Dream of the Red Chamber*, 1958. • Lucien Miller, *Masks of Fiction in Dream of the Red Chamber: Myth, Mimesis and Persona*, 1975. • Andrew H. Plaks, *Archetype and Allegory in the Dream of the Red Chamber*, 1976. • Shen Fu, *Six Records of a Floating Life*, trans. Leonard Pratt and Chiang Su-hui, 1983. • C. C. Wang, trans. *Dream of the Red Chamber*, 1958. • Jing Wang, *The Story of Stone: Intertextuality, Ancient Chinese Stone Lore, and the Stone Symbolism in Dream of the Red Chamber, Water Margin, and The Journey to the West*, 1992. • Chi Xiao, *The Chinese Garden as Lyric Enclave: A Generic Study of "The*

Story of the Stone," 2001. • Xianyi and Gladys Yang, trans. *A Dream of Red Mansions,* 1999. • Anthony C. Yu. *Rereading the Stone: Desire and the Making of Fiction in "Dream of the Red Chamber,"* 2001.

The Ottoman Empire • M. S. Anderson, *The Eastern Question,* 1966. • F. E. Bailey, *British Policy and the Turkish Reform Movement,* 1942. • D. C. Blaisdell, *European Financial Control in the Ottoman Empire,* 1929. • Ferdinand Braudel, *The Mediterranean and the Mediterranean World in the Age of Philip II,* 1976. • S. N. Fisher, *The Foreign Relations of Turkey: 1481–1512,* 1948. • H. A. R. Gibb and H. Bowen, *Islamic Society and the West: Islamic Society in the Eighteenth Century, Parts I and II,* 1950, 1957. • P. M. Holt, *Egypt and the Fertile Crescent, 1516–1922,* 1966. • A. H. Lybyer, *The Government of the Ottoman Empire in the Time of Suleiman the Magnificent,* 1915. • S. Runciman, *The Fall of Constantinople 1453,* 1965. • K. M. Setton et al., *A History of the Crusades,* 2 vols., 1955, 1962. • D. M. Vaughan, *Europe and the Turk: A Pattern of Alliance 1350–1700,* 1954. • P. Wittek, *The Rise of the Ottoman Empire,* 1938.

The Age of the Enlightenment • John Bender, *Imagining the Penitentiary: Fiction and the Architecture of Mind in Eighteenth-Century England,* 1987. • Linda Colley, *Britons: Forging the Nation, 1707–1837,* 1992. • Robert Darnton, *George Washington's False Teeth: An Unconventional Guide to the Eighteenth Century,* 2003. • Joan DeJean, *Ancients Against Moderns: Culture Wars and the Making of a Fin de Siècle,* 1997. • Catherine Gallagher, *Nobody's Story: The Vanishing Acts of Women Writers in the Marketplace, 1670–1820,* 1994. • Julie C. Hayes, *Reading the French Enlightenment: System and Subversion,* 1999. • David Marshall, *The Surprising Effects of Sympathy: Marivaux, Diderot, Rousseau, and Mary Shelley,* 1988. • Michael McKeon, *The Origins of the English Novel, 1600–1740,* 1987. • Nancy K. Miller, *The Heroine's Text: Readings in the French and English Novel, 1722–1782,* 1980. • Dorothea E. von Mücke, *Virtue and the Veil of Illusion: Generic Innovation and the Pedagogical Project in Eighteenth-Century Literature,* 1991. • Felicity Nussbaum and Laura Brown, eds. *The New Eighteenth Century,* 1987. • William Ray, *Story and History: Narrative Authority and Social Identity in the Eighteenth-Century*

French and English Novel, 1990. • James Sambrook, *The Eighteenth Century: The Intellectual and Cultural Context of English Literature, 1700–1789,* 1986. • Londa Schiebinger, *Nature's Body: Gender in the Making of Modern Science,* 1993. • Stuart Sherman, *Telling Time: Clocks, Diaries, and English Diurnal Form, 1660–1785,* 1996. • Julia Simon, *Mass Enlightenment: Critical Studies in Rousseau and Diderot,* 1995. • Aram Vartanian, *Science and Humanism in the French Enlightenment,* 1999. • Anne C. Vila, *Enlightenment and Pathology: Sensibility in the Literature and Medicine of Eighteenth-Century France,* 1998. • Ian Watt, *The Rise of the Novel: Studies in Defoe, Richardson, and Fielding,* 1957. • Steven N. Zwicker, *The Cambridge Companion to English Literature, 1650–1740,* 1998.

Perspectives: Court Culture and Female Authorship • April Alliston, *Virtue's Faults: Correspondences in Eighteenth-Century British and French Women's Fiction,* 1996. • Carol Barash, *English Women's Poetry, 1649–1714: Politics, Community, and Linguistic Authority,* 1996. • Joan DeJean, *Tender Geographies: Women and the Origins of the Novel in France,* 1991. • Peter France, *Politeness and Its Discontents: Problems in French Classical Culture,* 1992. • Elizabeth C. Goldsmith, *Exclusive Conversations: The Art of Interaction in Seventeenth-Century France,* 1988. • Elizabeth C. Goldsmith and Dena Goodman, eds., *Going Public: Women and Publishing in Early Modern France,* 1995. • Floyd Gray, *Gender, Rhetoric, and Print Culture in French Renaissance Writing,* 2000. • Isobel Grundy and Susan Wiseman, eds. *Women, Writing, and History: 1640–1799,* 1992. • Nicholas Hammond, *Creative Tension: An Introduction to Seventeenth-Century French Literature,* 1997. • Michael Moriarty, *Taste and Ideology in Seventeenth-Century France,* 1988. • Joan Hinde Stewart, *Gynographs: French Novels by Women of the Late Eighteenth Century,* 1993. • Harriet Amy Stone, *The Classical Model: Literature and Knowledge in Seventeenth-Century France,* 1996. • Janet Todd, *The Sign of Angellica: Women, Writing, and Fiction, 1660–1800,* 1989.

Perspectives: Journeys in Search of the Self • Srinivas Aravamudan, *Tropicopolitans: Colonialism and Agency, 1688–1804,* 1999. • Pamela Cheek, *Sexual Antipodes: Enlightenment,*

Globalization and the Placing of Sex, 2003. • Julia V. Douthwaite, *Exotic Women: Literary Heroines and Cultural Strategies in Ancien Régime France,* 1992. • Richard Drayton, *Nature's Government: Science, Imperial Britain, and the "Improvement" of the World,* 2000. • Stephen Greenblatt, *Marvelous Possessions: The Wonder of the New World,* 1991. • Richard Grove, *Green Imperialism: Colonial Expansion, Tropical Island Edens, and the Origins of Environmentalism, 1600–1860,* 1995. • Suvir Kaul, *Poems of Nation, Anthems of Empire: English Verse in the Long Eighteenth Century,* 2000. • Jonathan Lamb, *Preserving the Self in the South Seas, 1680–1840,* 2001. • Felicity A. Nussbaum, *Torrid Zones: Maternity, Sexuality, and Empire in Eighteenth-Century English Narratives,* 1995. • Bridget Orr, *Empire on the English Stage, 1660–1714,* 2001. • Anthony Pagden, *European Encounters with the New World: From Renaissance to Romanticism,* 1993. • Mary Louise Pratt, *Imperial Eyes: Travel Writing and Transculturation,* 1992.

Perspectives: Liberty and Libertines • G. J. Barker-Benfield, *The Culture of Sensibility: Sex and Society in Eighteenth-Century Britain,* 1992. • Warren Chernaik, *Sexual Freedom in Restoration Literature,* 1995. • Catherine Cusset, *No Tomorrow: The Ethics of Pleasure in the French Enlightenment,* 1999. • Claudia Johnson, *Equivocal Beings: Politics, Gender, and Sentimentality in the 1790s,* 1995. • Robert W. Jones, *Gender and the Formation of Taste in Eighteenth-Century Britain: The Analysis of Beauty,* 1998. • Vivien Jones, ed., *Women and Literature in Britain, 1700–1800,* 2000. • Nancy K. Miller, *French Dressing: Women, Men, and Ancien Régime Fiction,* 1995. • William Stafford, *English Feminists and Their Opponents in the 1790s: Unsex'd and Proper Females,* 2002. • Harold Weber, *The Restoration Rake-Hero: Transformations in Sexual Understanding in Seventeenth-Century England,* 1986.

Anna Laetitia Barbauld • Stuart Curran, "Dynamics of Female Friendship in the Later Eighteenth Century," *Nineteenth-Century Contexts,* vol. 23, 2001, 221–29. • William Keach, "A Regency Prophecy and the End of Anna Barbauld's Career," in *Studies in Romanticism,* 1994, 569–577. • William McCarthy and Elizabeth Kraft, eds., *The Poems of Anna Laetitia Barbauld,* 1994. • Josephine McDonagh, "Barbauld's Domestic Economy,"

Essays and Studies, vol. 51, 1998, 62–77. • Jerome Murch, *Mrs. Barbauld and Her Contemporaries: Sketches of Some Eminent Literary and Scientific Englishwomen,* 1877. • Betsy Rodgers, *Georgian Chronicle: Mrs. Barbauld and Her Family,* 1958. • Daniel E. White, "The 'Joineriana': Anna Barbauld, the Aikin Family Circle, and the Dissenting Public Sphere," *Eighteenth-Century Studies,* vol. 32, 1999, 511–533. • Jonathan Wordsworth, *The Bright Work Grows: Women Writers of the Romantic Age,* 1997.

Aphra Behn • April Alliston, "Gender and the Rhetoric of Evidence in Early-Modern Historical Narratives," *Comparative Literature Studies,* vol. 33, 1996, 233–257. • Ros Ballaster, "New Hystericism: Aphra Behn's *Oroonoko:* The Body, the Text and the Feminist Critic," in *New Feminist Discourses: Critical Essays on Theories and Texts,* ed. Isobel Armstrong, 1992. • Brown, Laura, "The Romance of Empire: Oroonoko and the Trade in Slaves," in *The New Eighteenth Century: Theory, Politics, English Literature,* ed. Felicity Nussbaum and Laura Brown 1987. (pp. 41–61). • Robert L. Chibka, "'Oh! Do Not Fear a Woman's Invention': Truth, Falsehood, and Fiction in Aphra Behn's *Oroonoko,"* Texas Studies in Literature and Language,* vol. 30, 1988, 510–537. • Maureen Duffy, *The Passionate Shepherdess: Aphra Behn, 1640–1689,* 1977. • Margaret W. Ferguson, "Juggling the Categories of Race, Class, and Gender," in *Women, "Race," and Writing in the Early Modern Period,* ed. Margo Hendricks and Patricia Parker, 1994, 209–224. • Angeline Goreau, *Reconstructing Aphra: A Social Biography of Aphra Behn,* 1980. • David E. Hoegberg, "Caesar's Toils: Allusion and Rebellion in Oroonoko," *Eighteenth-Century Fiction,* vol. 7, 1995, 239–258. • Heidi Hutner, ed., *Rereading Aphra Behn: History, Theory, and Criticism,* 1993. • Joanna Lipking, "Confusing Matters: Searching the Backgrounds of Oroonoko," in *Aphra Behn Studies,* ed. Janet Todd, 1996. • Joanna Lipking, ed., Oroonoko: *An Authoritative Text, Historical Backgrounds, Criticism,* 1997. • Joseph M. Ortiz, "Arms and the Woman: Narrative Imperialism and Virgilian *Memoria* in Aphra Behn's *Oroonoko,"* Studies in the Novel,* vol. 34, 2002, 119–136. • Janet Todd, ed., *Works of Aphra Behn,* 7 vols., 1992–1996. • Janet Todd, *The Secret Life of Aphra Behn,* 1997.

Evliya Çelebi • Robert Dankoff and Robert Elsie, *Evliya Çelebi in Albania and Adjacent Regions*, 2000. • Robert Dankoff, *The Intimate Life of an Ottoman Statesman*, 1991. • Martin Van Bruinessen and Hendrik Boeschoten, *Evliya Çelebi in Diyarbekir*, 1988.

Mary, Lady Chudleigh • Margaret J. M. Ezell, ed. *The Poems and Prose of Mary, Lady Chudleigh*, 1993. • Ann Messenger, *Pastoral Tradition and the Female Talent: Studies in Augustan Poetry*, 2001.

Denis Diderot • Wilda Anderson, *Diderot's Dream*, 1990. • Julie Wegner Arnold, *Art Criticism as Narrative: Diderot's Salon de 1767, Vol. 13*, 1996. • Daniel Brewer, *The Discourse of Enlightenment in Eighteenth-Century France: Diderot and the Art of Philosophising*, 1993. • Rosalina de la Carrera, *Success in Circuit Lies: Diderot's Communicational Practice*, 1991. • Denis Diderot, *Thoughts on the Interpretation of Nature, and Other Philosophical Works*, ed. David Adams, 2000. • Denis Diderot, *Selected Writings on Art and Literature*, ed. and trans. Geoffrey Bremner, 1994. • Denis Diderot, *This Is Not a Story and Other Stories*, ed. and trans. P. N. Furbank, 1993. • Denis Diderot, *The Indiscreet Jewels*, ed. Aram Vartanian, trans. Sophie Hawkes, 1993. • Philip Furbank, *Diderot: A Critical Biography*, 1992. • Charles C. Gillispie, ed. *A Diderot Pictorial Encyclopedia of Trades and Industry: Manufacturing and the Technical Arts in Plates Selected from "L'Encyclopédie, ou dictionnaire raisonné des sciences, des arts, et des métiers" of Denis Diderot*, 1993. • John Goodman, ed. and trans. *Diderot on Art:Selections*, 1995. • Stephanie Barbé Hammer, *Satirizing the Satirist: Critical Dynamics in Swift, Diderot, and Jean Paul*, 1990. • Julie Candler Hayes, *Identity and Ideology: Diderot, Sade and the Serious Genre*, 1991. • Erik MacPhail, "Diderot and the Plot of History," *New Literary History*, vol. 30, 1999, 439–452. • Claudia Moscovici, "An Ethics of Cultural Exchange: Diderot's *Supplement au Voyage de Bougainville*," *Clio*, vol. 30, 2001, 289–307. • Bo G. Oranzon, ed. *Skill, Technology, and Enlightenment: On Practical Philosophy*, 1994. • James L. Schor, "Caverns and the Dialogic Structure of *Le Supplément au voyage de Bougainville*," in *Diderot Studies* 1993, 109–118. • Stephen Werner, *Blueprint: A Study of Diderot and the "Encyclopédie" Plates*, 1993.

Olaudah Equiano • William L. Andrews, *To Tell a Free Story: The First Century of Afro-American Autobiography*, 1986. • Angelo Costanzo, *Surprising Narrative: Olaudah Equiano and the Beginnings of Black Autobiography*, 1987. • Olaudah Equiano, *The Interesting Narrative and Other Writings*, ed. Vincent Carretta, 1995. • Henry Louis Gates, ed., *The Classic Slave Narratives*, 1987. • Susan M. Marren, "Between Slavery and Freedom: The Transgressive Self in Olaudah Equiano's Autobiography," *PMLA*, 1993. • Geraldine Murphy, "Olaudah Equiano, Accidental Tourist," in *Eighteenth-Century Studies*, 1994, 551–568. • Adam Potkay, "Olaudah Equiano and the Art of Spiritual Autobiography," in *Eighteenth-Century Studies*, 1994, 677–692. • Gordon M. Sayre, ed., *American Captivity narratives: Olaudah Equiano, Mary Rowlandson, and Others*, 2000. • James Walvin, *An African's Life: The Life and Times of Olaudah Equiano, 1745–1797*, 1998.

Anne Finch, Countess of Winchilsea • Jean M. Ellis D'Alessandro, *When in the Shade: Imaginal Equivalents in Anne the Countess of Winchilsea's Poetry*, 1989. • Anne Finch, *Selected Poems of Anne Finch, Countess of Winchilsea*, ed. Katherine M. Rogers, 1979. • Anne Finch, *Selected Poems*, ed. Denys Thompson, 1987. • Desiree Hellegers, *Handmaid to Divinity: Natural Philosophy, Poetry, and Gender in Seventeenth-Century England*, 2000. • Charles H. Hinnant, *The Poetry of Anne Finch: An Essay in Interpretation*, 1994. • Barbara McGovern, *Anne Finch and Her Poetry: A Critical Biography*, 1992. • Barbara McGovern and Charles H. Hinnant, eds. *The Anne Finch Wellesley Manuscript Poems*, 1998. • Ann Messenger, ed. *Gender at Work: Four Women Writers of the Eighteenth Century*, 1990. • Ann Messenger, *Pastoral Tradition and the Female Talent: Studies in Augustan Poetry*, 2001.

Eliza Haywood • Ros Ballaster, *Seductive Forms: Women's Amatory Fiction from 1684 to 1740*, 1992. • Christine Blouch, "Eliza Haywood and the Romance of Obscurity," *Studies in English Literature*, vol. 31, 1991, 535–552. • Catherine Craft-Fairchild, *Masquerade and Gender: Disguise and Female Identity in Eighteenth-Century Fictions by Women*, 1993. • Eliza Haywood, *Selections from "The Female Spectator*," ed. Gabrielle M. Firmager, 1993. • Eliza Haywood, *The Plays of Eliza Haywood*, ed. Valerie C. Rudolph, 1983. • Kirsten T. Saxton and Rebecca P. Bocchicchio, eds. *The Passionate Fictions of Eliza Haywood*, 2000. • Mary Anne Schofield, *Eliza Haywood*, 1985. • Eliza Haywood, *The Masquerade Novels of Eliza Haywood*, ed. Mary Anne Schofield, 1986. • Mary Ann Schofield, *Masking and Unmasking the Female Mind: Disguising Romances in Feminine Fiction, 1713–1799*, 1990. • Jane Spencer, *The Rise of the Woman Novelist: From Aphra Behn to Jane Austen*, 1986. • William B. Warner, *Licensing Entertainment: The Elevation of Novel Reading in Britain, 1684–1750*, 1957. • George Frisbie Whicher, *The Life and Romances of Mrs. Eliza Haywood*, 1915.

Ihara Saikaku • *Five Women Who Loved Love*, trans. William Theodore de Bary, 1956. • Howard S. Hibbett, *The Floating World in Japanese Fiction*, 1959. • Ihara Saikaku, *Worldly Mental Calculations: An Annotated Translation of Ihara Saikaku's "Seken munezan'yo,"* trans. Ben Befu, 1976. • Ihara Saikaku, *Tales of Samurai Honor*, trans. Caryl Ann Callahan, 1981. • Ihara Saikaku, *The Life of an Amorous Man*, trans. Kengi Hamada, 1964. • Ihara Saikaku, *The Life of an Amorous Woman*, trans. Ivan Morris, 1963. • Ihara Saikaku, *Some Final Words of Advice*, trans. Peter Nosco, 1980. • Ihara Saikaku, *The Japanese Family Storehouse or the Millionaire's Gospel Modernized*, trans. G. W. Sargent, 1959. • Ihara Saikaku, *The Great Mirror of Male Love*, trans. Paul Gordon Schalow, 1990.

Immanuel Kant • William James Booth, *Interpreting the World: Kant's Philosophy of History and Politics*, 1986. • Arsenij Gulyga, *Immanuel Kant: His Life and Thought*, 1987. • Immanuel Kant, *On History*, ed. and trans. Lewis White Beck, trans. Robert E. Anchor and Emil L. Fackenheim, 1963. • Immanuel Kant, *Political Writings*, ed. Hans Reiss, trans. H. B. Nisbet, 1991. • Manfred Kuehn, *Kant: A Biography*, 2002. • Peter Lassman, "Enlightenment, Cultural Crisis, and Politics: The Role of Intellectuals from Kant to Habermas," *The European Legacy*, vol. 5, 2000, 815–828. • Susan Neiman, *The Unity of Reason: Rereading Kant*, 1994. • Arthur Strum, "What Enlightenment Is(*)," *New German Critique*, vol. 79, 2000, 106–136. • Ralph C. S. Walker, *Kant*, 1978. • Yirmiahu Yovel, *Kant and the Philosophy of History*, 1980.

Matsuo Bashō • Dorothy Britton, trans. *A Haiku Journey: Bashō's "Narrow Road to a Far Province,"* 1980. • Cid Corman and Susumu Kamaike, trans. *Back Roads to Far Towns*, 1968. • Koji Kawamoto, *The Poetics of Japanese Verse: Imagery, Structure, Meter*, 2000. • Donald Keene, "Bashō's Diaries," *Japan Quarterly*, vol. 32, 1985, 374–383. • Donald Keene, "Bashō's Journey of 1684," *Asia Major*, vol. 7, 1959, 131–144. • Donald Keene, trans. *The Narrow Road to Oku*, 1996. • Helen McCullough, trans. "The Narrow Road of the Interior," in *Classical Japanese Prose: An Anthology*, ed. Helen McCullough, 1990. • Hiroaki Sato, trans. *Bashō's "Narrow Road": Spring and Autumn Passages: Two Works*, 1996. • Haruo Shirane, *Traces of Dreams: Landscape, Cultural Memory, and the Poetry of Bashō*, 1997. • Makoto Ueda, trans. *Bashō and His Interpreters: Selected Hokku with Commentary*, 1992. • Makoto Ueda, *Matsuo Bashō: The Master Haiku Poet*, 1982. • Nobuyuki Yuasa, trans. *Bashō: The Narrow Road to the Deep North and Other Travel Sketches*, 1968.

Marie-Madeleine Pioche de la Vergne, Comtesse de Lafayette • Ruth Carver Capasso, "The Letter in Lafayette's 'La Comtesse de Tende,'" *Romance Notes*, vol. 38, 1997, 111–118. • Anne Green, *Privileged Anonymity: The Writings of Madame de Lafayette*, 1996. • Stirling Haig, *Madame de Lafayette*, 1970. • Carleen S. Leggett, "The Woman in Love in Lafayette, Villedieu, Segrais, and Saint-Réal," *Journal of the Association for the Interdisciplinary Study of the Arts*, vol. 1, 1995, 83–91. • Marie-Madeleine Pioche de la Vergne, Comtesse de Lafayette, *The Princesse de Clèves; The Princesse de Montpensier; The Comtesse de Tende*, ed. and trans. Terence Cave, 1992. • Marie-Madeleine Pioche de la Vergne, Comtesse de Lafayette, *The Princess of Clèves*, ed. and trans. John D. Lyons, 1994.

Jean Baptiste Poquelin (Molière) • David Bradby and Andrew Calder, *The Cambridge Companion to Molière*, 2006. • Thomas P. Finn, "Dueling Capitalism in Molière: Cornering the Corner Markets," *Papers on French Seventeenth Century Literature* 29 (2002): 23–32. • J. F. Gaines, *Social Structures in Molière's Theater*, 1984. • Lionel Gossman, *Men and Masks: A Study of Molière*, 1963. • N. Gross, *From Gesture to Idea: Esthetics and*

Ethics in Molière's Comedy, 1982. • Jacques Guicharnaud, ed. *Molière: A Collection of Critical Essays*, 1964. • W. D. Howarth, *Molière: A Playwright and His Audience*, 1984. • Harold C. Knutson, *The Triumph of Wit*, 1988. • L. F. Norman, *The Public Mirror: Molière and the Social Commerce of Depiction*, 1999. • Molière, *The Misanthrope, Tartuffe, and Other Plays*, trans. Maya Slater, 2001. • Martin Turnell, *The Classical Moment: Studies of Corneille, Molière, and Racine*, 1975. • H. Walker, *Molière*, 1990.

Lady Mary Wortley Montagu • Elizabeth A. Bohls, "Aesthetics and Orientalism in Lady Mary Wortley Montagu's Letters," *Studies in Eighteenth-Century Culture*, vol. 23, 1994, 179–205. • Isobel Grundy, *Lady Mary Wortley Montagu*, 1999. • Robert Halsband, *The Life of Lady Mary Wortley Montagu*, 1956. • Donna Landry, "Alexander Pope, Lady Mary Wortley Montagu, and the Literature of Social Comment," in *English Literature 1650–1740*, ed. Steven N. Zwicker, 1998. • Cynthia Lowenthal, *Lady Mary Wortley Montagu and the Eighteenth-Century Familiar Letter*, 1994. • Lady Mary Wortley Montagu, *Selected Letters of Mary Wortley Montagu*, ed. Isobel Grundy, 1997. • Lady Mary Wortley Montagu, *The Complete Letters of Lady Mary Wortley Montagu*, ed. Robert Halsband, 3 vols., 1965–1967. • Lady Mary Wortley Montagu, *The Selected Letters of Lady Mary Wortley Montagu*, ed. Robert Halsband, 1970. • Lady Mary Wortley Montagu, *Turkish Embassy Letters*, eds. Malcolm Jack and Anita Desai, 1993. • Lady Mary Wortley Montagu, *Embassy to Constantinople: The Travels of Lady Mary Wortley Montagu*, eds. Christopher Pick and Dervla Murphy, 1988. • George Paston, *Lady Mary Wortley Montagu and Her Times*, 1907.

Charles de Secondat, Baron de la Brède et de Montesquieu • Dena Goodman, *Criticism in Action: Enlightenment Experiments in Political Writing*, 1989. • Norman Hampson, *Will and Circumstance: Montesquieu, Rousseau, and the French Revolution*, 1983. • Elizabeth Heckendorn Cook, *Epistolary Bodies: Gender and Genre in the Eighteenth-Century Republic of Letters*, 1996. • Montesquieu, *The Persian Letters*, ed. and trans. J. Robert Loy, 1961. • Diana J. Schaub, *Erotic Liberalism: Women and Revolution in Montesquieu's* Persian Letters, 1995. • Robert Shackleton, *Montesquieu: A Critical Biography*, 1961.

Elisabeth Charlotte Von Der Pfalz, Duchesse d'Orléans • W. S. Brooks and P. J. Yarrow, *The Dramatic Criticism of Elizabeth Charlotte, Duchesse d'Orleans: With an Annotated Chronology of Performances of the Popular and Court Theatres in France 1671–1722, Reconstructed from Her Letters*, 1996. • Harold Donaldson Eberlein, *The Rabelaisian Princess: Madame Royale of France*, 1931. • Elborg Forster, trans. *A Woman's Life in the Court of the Sun King: Letters of Liselotte von der Pfalz, 1652–1722, Elisabeth Charlotte, Duchesse d'Orléans*, 1984. • Maria Kroll, ed. and trans. *Letters from Liselotte, Elisabeth Charlotte, Princess Palatine and Duchess of Orléans, "Madame," 1652–1722*, 1970. • Claude Pasteur, *La Princesse Palatine: Une Allemande à la Cour de Louis XIV*, 2001. • Gertrude Scott Stevenson, ed. and trans. *The Letters of Madame: The Correspondence of Elizabeth-Charlotte of Bavaria, Princess Palatine, Duchess of Orleans, Called "Madame" at the Court of King Louis XIV*, 2 vols., 1924–1925. • Dirk van der Cruysse, *Madame Palatine, Princesse Européenne*, 1988.

Katherine Philips • Celia A. Easton, "Excusing the Breach of Nature's Laws: The Discourse of Denial and Disguise in Katherine Philips' Friendship Poetry," *Early Women Writers: 1600–1720*, ed. Anita Pacheco, 1998. • Elaine Hobby, *Virtue of Necessity: English Women's Writing, 1646–1688*, 1988. • Dorothy Mermin, "Women Becoming Poets: Katherine Philips, Aphra Behn, Anne Finch," *English Literary History*, vol. 57, 1990, 335–355. • Fidelis Morgan, *The Female Wits*, 1981. • Katherine Philips, *Collected Works of Katherine Philips, the "Matchless Orinda,"* eds. Patrick Thomas, G. Greer, and R. Little, 3 vols., 1990. • Arlene Stiebel, "Subversive Sexuality: Masking the Erotic in Poems by Katherine Philips and Aphra Behn," *Renaissance Discourses of Desire*, eds. Claude J. Summers and Ted Larry Pebworth, 1993. • Philip Webster Sower, *The Matchless Orinda*, 1931.

Alexander Pope • Rueben Brower, *Alexander Pope: The Poetry of Allusion*, 1959. • Laura Brown, *Alexander Pope*, 1985. • Morris Brownell, *Alexander Pope and the Arts of Georgian England*, 1978. • Alexander Pope, *The Poems of Alexander Pope*, ed. John Butt, 1963. • Alexander Pope, *The Twickenham Edition of the Poems of Alexander Pope*, eds.

John Butt et al., 11 vols., 1940–1969. • Helen Deutsch, *Resemblance and Disgrace: Alexander Pope and the Deformation of Culture*, 1996. • Margaret Anne Doody, *The Daring Muse: Augustan Poetry Reconsidered*, 1985. • H. H. Erskine-Hill, *The Social Milieu of Alexander Pope*, 1978. • David Fairer, ed. *Pope: New Contexts*, 1990. • David Fairer, *Pope's Imagination*, 1984. • David F. Foxon, *Pope and the Eighteenth-Century Book Trade*, 1991. • Bertrand A. Goldgar, *Literary Criticism of Alexander Pope*, 1965. • Dustin Griffin, *Alexander Pope: The Poet in the Poems*, 1978. • Brean Hammond, ed. *Longman Critical Readers: Pope*, 1966. • J. Paul Hunter, "Pope and the Ideology of the Couplet," *Ideas*, vol. 4, 1996. • Maynard Mack, *Alexander Pope: A Life*, 1985. • Maynard Mack, *The Garden and the City: Retirement and Politics in the Later Poetry of Pope*, 1969. • David B. Morris, *Alexander Pope: The Genius of Sense*, 1984. • Marjorie Hope Nicolson and G. S. Rousseau, *"This Long Disease, My Life": Alexander Pope and the Sciences*, 1968. • Valerie Rumbold, *Women's Place in Pope's World*, 1989. • Alexander Pope, *The Correspondence of Alexander Pope*, ed. George Sherburn, 5 vols., 1956. • George Sherburn, *The Early Career of Alexander Pope*, 1934. • Patricia Meyer Spacks, *An Argument of Images; the Poetry of Alexander Pope*, 1971. • Joseph Spence, *Observations, Anecdotes, and Characters of Books and Men*, ed. James M. Osborn, 2 vols., 1966. • Geoffrey Tillotson, *On the Poetry of Pope*, 1950. • Alexander Pope, *The Rape of the Lock*, ed. Cynthia Wall, 1998. • Howard Weinbrot, *Alexander Pope and the Tradition of the Formal Verse Satire*, 1982. • Alexander Pope, *Poetry and Prose of Alexander Pope*, ed. Aubrey Williams, 1969.

Jean-Jacques Rousseau • Maurice Cranston, *Jean-Jacques: The Early Life and Work of Jean-Jacques Rousseau, 1712–1754*, 1983. • Alessandro Ferrara, *Modernity and Authenticity: A Study in the Social and Ethical Thought of Jean-Jacques Rousseau*, 1993. • Frederick Charles Green, *Jean-Jacques Rousseau: A Critical Study of his Life and Writings*, 1955. • Arthur Melzer, *The Natural Goodness of Man: On the System of Rousseau's Thought*, 1990. • Mira Morgenstern, *Rousseau and the Politics of Ambiguity: Self, Culture, and Society*, 1996. • Timothy O'Hagan, *Rousseau*, 1999. • Helena Rosenblatt, *Rousseau and*

Geneva: From the First Discourse to the Social Contract, 1749–1762, 1997. • Jean-Jacques Rousseau, *Discourse on Political Economy and The Social Contract*, ed. and trans. Christopher Betts, 1994. • Jean-Jacques Rousseau, *The Social Contract; and, The Discourses*, eds. J. H. Brumfitt and John C. Hall, trans. G. D. H. Cole, 1993. • Jean-Jacques Rousseau, *The Social Contract; and The First and Second Discourses*, ed. Susan Dunn, 2002. • Jean-Jacques Rousseau, *The Social Contract and Other Later Political Writings*, ed. and trans. Victor Gourevitch, 1997. • Jean Starobinski, *Jean-Jacques Rousseau, Transparency and Obstruction*, trans. Arthur Goldhammer, 1988.

Madeleine de Scudéry • Nicole Aronson, *Mademoiselle de Scudéry*, trans. Stuart R. Aronson, 1978. • Joanne Davis, *Mademoiselle de Scudéry and the Looking-Glass Self*, 1993. • Madeleine de Scudéry, *Clélie, Histoire Romaine*, 10 vols., 1973. • Dorothy McDougall, *Madeleine de Scudéry: Her Romantic Life and Death*, 1972. • James S. Munro, *Mademoiselle de Scudéry and the Carte de Tendre*, 1986.

Marie de Rabutin-Chantal, Marquise de Sévigné • Harriet Ray Allentuch, *Madame de Sévigné: A Portrait in Letters*, 1963. • Philip Elwyn Arsenault, *The Literary Opinions of Madame de Sévigné*, 1959. • Michèle Longino Farrell, *Performing Motherhood: The Sévigné Correspondence*, 1991. • Violet Hammersley, ed. and trans. *Letters from Madame La Marquise de Sévigné*, 1955. • *Letters from the Marchioness de Sévigné to Her Daughter the Countess of Grignan*, 10 vols., 1927. • Frances Mossiker, *Madame de Sévigné: A Life and Letters*, 1983. • A. Edward Newton, ed. *The Letters of Madame de Sévigné*, 7 vols., 1927. • Jeanne A. Ojala and William T. Ojala, *Madame de Sévigné: A Seventeenth-Century Life*, 1990. • Jo Ann Marie Recker, *"Appelle-moi Pierrot": Wit and Irony in the Letters of Madame de Sévigné*, 1986. • Leonard Tancock, trans. *Selected Letters*, 1982.

Jonathan Swift • Frank Boyle, *Swift as Nemesis: Modernity and Its Satirist*, 2000. • J. A. Downie, *Jonathan Swift: Political Writer*, 1985. • Irvin Ehrenpreis, *Swift: The Man, His Works, and the Age*, 3 vols., 1962–1983. • Robert C. Elliott, *The Power of Satire: Magic, Ritual, Art*, 1960. • Oliver W. Ferguson, *Jonathan Swift and Ireland*, 1962. • H. J. Real Fischer and J. Wooley, eds. *Swift and His*

Contexts, 1989. • John Irwin Fischer and Donald C. Mell Jr., eds. *Contemporary Studies of Swift's Poetry*, 1980. • Victoria Glendinning, *Jonathan Swift: A Portrait*, 1999. • Carol Houlihan Flynn, *The Body in Swift and Defoe*, 1990. • Christopher Fox, ed. *Walking Naboth's Vineyard: New Studies of Swift*, 1995. • Nora Crow Jaffe, *The Poet. Swift*, 1977. • David Nokes, *Jonathan Swift, A Hypocrite Reversed: A Critical Biography*, 1985. • Ellen Pollak, *The Poetics of Sexual Myth: Gender and Ideology in the Verse of Swift and Pope*, 1985. • Martin Price, *Swift's Rhetorical Art: A Study in Structure and Meaning*, 1953. • C. J. Rawson, ed. *The Character of Swift's Satire*, 1983. • Richard H. Rodino, *Swift Studies, 1965–1980: An Annotated Bibliography*, 1984. • Edward W. Rosenheim, *Swift and the Satirist's Art*, 1963. • Edward W. Said, "Swift as Intellectual" and "Swift's Tory Anarchy," *The World, the Text, and the Critic*, 1983. • Brian Vickers, ed. *The World of Jonathan Swift: Essays for the Tercentenary*, 1968. • David M. Vieth, *Swift's Poetry 1900–1980: An Annotated Bibliography of Studies*, 1982. • Kathleen Williams, ed. *Swift: The Critical Heritage*, 1970.

Tsangyang Gyatso • Coleman Barks, trans. *Stallion on a Frozen Lake: Love Songs of the Sixth Dalai Lama*, 1992. • Rick Fields and Brian Cutillo, *The Turquoise Bee: The Lovesongs of the Sixth Dalai Lama*, 1990. • Per K. Sorensen, *Divinity Secularized: An Inquiry into the Nature and Form of the Songs Ascribed to the Sixth Dalai Lama*, 1995.

François Marie Arouet (Voltaire) • T. Besterman, *Voltaire*, 1969. • William Bottiglia, *Voltaire's Candide: Analysis of a Classic*, 1964. • William Bottiglia, ed. *Voltaire: A Collection of Critical Essays*, 1968. • Maxine G. Cutler, ed. *Voltaire, the Enlightenment, and the Comic Mode: Essays in Honor of Jean Sareil*, 1990. • Diane Fourny, "Literature of Violence or Literature on Violence? The French Enlightenment on Trial," *SubStance: A Review of Theory and Literary Criticism*, vol. 27, 1998, 43–60. • Voltaire, *Candide*, ed. D. Gordon, 1999. • M. Hayden, *Voltaire: A Biography*, 1981. • F. M. Keener, *The Chain of Becoming*, 1983. • Susan Klute, "The Admirable Cunegonde," *Eighteenth-Century Women: Studies in Their Lives, Work, and Culture*, vol. 2, 2002, 95–107. • Bettina L. Knapp, *Voltaire Revisited*, 2000. • Haydn Mason, *Candide:*

Optimism Demolished, 1992. • Voltaire, *Candide and Other Stories*, ed. and trans. Roger Pearson, 1998. • P. E. Richter and Ilona Ricardo, *Voltaire*, 1980. • R. S. Ridgway, *Voltaire and Sensibility*, 1973. • I. O. Wade, *Voltaire and "Candide,"* 1959. • Voltaire, *The Complete Tales of Voltaire*, trans. William Walton, 1990. • D. Williams, *Candide*, 1997. • Voltaire, *Candide and Related Texts*, ed. and trans. David Wooton, 2000.

John Wilmot, Earl of Rochester • John Adlard, *The Debt to Pleasure*, 1974. • David Farley-Hills, ed., *Rochester: The Critical Heritage*, 1972. • David Farley-Hills, *Rochester's Poetry*, 1978. • Graham Greene, *Lord Rochester's Monkey; Being the Life of John Wilmot, Second Earl of Rochester*, 1974. • Dustin Griffin, *Satires Against Man: The Poems of Rochester*, 1973. • Jeremy Lamb, *So Idle a Rogue: The Life and Death of Lord Rochester*, 1993. • Vivian de Sola Pinto, *Enthusiast in Wit: A Portrait of John Wilmot, Earl of Rochester*, 1962. • Marianne Thromahlen, *Rochester: The Poems in Context*, 1993. • Jeremy Treglown, ed. *Spirit of Wit: Reconsiderations of Rochester*, 1982. • David M. Vieth, ed. *John Wilmot, Earl of Rochester: Critical Essays*, 1988. • John Wilmot, Earl of Rochester, *The Complete Works*, ed. Frank H. Ellis, 1994. • John Wilmot, Earl of Rochester, *The Letters of John Wilmot, Earl of Rochester*, ed. Jeremy Treglown, 1980. • John Wilmot, Earl of Rochester, *The Complete Poems of John Wilmot, Earl of Rochester*, ed. David M. Vieth, 1968. • John Wilmot, Earl of Rochester, *The Poems of John Wilmot, Earl of Rochester*, ed. Keith Walker, 1984.

Mary Wollstonecraft • William Godwin, *Memoirs of the Author of a Vindication of the Rights of Woman*, 1798. • Gary Kelly, *Revolutionary Feminism: The Mind and Career of Mary Wollstonecraft*, 1992. • Jennifer Lorch, *Mary Wollstonecraft: The Making of a Radical Feminist*, 1990. • Anne K. Mellor, *Romanticism and Gender*, 1993. • Timothy J. Reiss, "Revolution in Bounds: Wollstonecraft, Women, and Reason," in *Gender and Theory: Dialogues on Feminist Criticism*, ed. Linda Kauffman, 1989. • Virginia Sapiro, *A Vindication of Political Virtue: The Political Theory of Mary Wollstonecraft*, 1992. • Emily Sunstein, *A Different Face—the Life of Mary Wollstonecraft*, 1975. • Claire Tomalin, *The Life and Death of*

Mary Wollstonecraft, 1974. • Mary Wollstonecraft, *A Critical Edition of Mary Wollstonecraft's "A Vindication of the Rights of Woman," with Strictures on Political and Moral Subjects*, ed. Ulrich H. Hardt, 1982. • Mary Wollstonecraft, *A Vindication of the Rights of Woman*, ed. Carol H. Poston, 1988 [1975]. • Mary Wollstonecraft, *Political Writings: A Vindication of the Rights of Men, A Vindication of the Rights of Woman, an Historical and Moral View of the French Revolution*, ed. Janet Todd, 1993. • Mary Wollstonecraft *Collected Letters of Mary Wollstonecraft*, ed. Ralph M. Wardle, 1979.

Ann Yearsley • Tim Burke, "Ann Yearsley and the Distribution of Genius in Early Romantic Culture," in *Early Romantics: Perspectives in British Poetry from Pope to Wordsworth*, ed. Thomas Woodman, 1998. • T. M. Brunk, "'A hurly-burly in this poor woman's head'": The Gothic Character of Ann Yearsley's Authorial Identity," *English Language Notes*, vol. 37, 2000, 29–52. • W. J. Christmas, *The Lab'ring Muses: Work, Writing, and the Social Order in English Plebeian Poetry, 1730–1830*, 2001.

• Moira Ferguson, *Eighteenth-Century Women Poets: Nation, Class, and Gender*, 1995. • A. D. Harvey, "Working-Class Poets and Self-Education," *Contemporary Review*, vol. 274, 1999, 252–263. • Greg Kucich, "Women's Historiography and the (Dis)Embodiment of Law: Ann Yearsley, Mary Hays, Elizabeth Benger," *Wordsworth Circle*, vol. 33, 2002, 3–7. • Donna Landry, *The Muses of Resistance: Laboring-Class Women's Poetry in Britain, 1739–1796*, 1990. • Alan Richardson, "Women Poets and Colonial Discourse: Teaching More and Yearsley on the Slave Trade," *Approaches to Teaching British Women Poets of the Romantic Period*, eds. Stephen C. Behrendt and Harriet Kramer Linkin, 1997. • Mary Waldron, *Lactilla, Milkwoman of Clifton: The Life and Writings of Ann Yearsley, 1753–1806*, 1996. • Mary Waldron, "'This Muse-Born Wonder', The Occluded Voice of Ann Yearsley, Milkwoman and Poet of Clifton," in *Women's Poetry in the Enlightenment, The Making of a Canon, 1730–1820*, eds. Isobel Armstrong and Virginia Blain, 1999. • Ann Yearsley, *Poems on Various Subjects, 1787*, 1994.

CREDITS

Tsangyang Gyatso: Poems from *The Turquoise Bee: Love Poems of the Sixth Dalai Lama* translated by Rick Fields, Brian Cutillo, and Mayumi Oda. Copyright © 1994 by Rick Fields, Brian Cutillo, and Mayumi Oda. Reprinted by permission of HarperCollins Publishers, Inc.

Tsangyang Gyatso: From *Wings of the White Crane: Poems of Tshangs dbyangs rgya mtsho (1683–1706)*, translated by G. W. Houston (Delhi: Motilal Banarsidass, 1982).

Tsangyang Gyatso: From *Divinity Secularized: An Inquiry into the Nature and Form of the Songs Ascribed to the Sixth Dalai Lama*, translated by Per K. Sorensen. Reprinted by permission of Per K. Sorensen and Ernst Steinkellner.

Tsangyang Gyatso: From *Stallion on a Frozen Lake: Love Songs of the Sixth Dalai Lama*, translated by Coleman Barks. Copyright © 1992 by Coleman Barks. Reprinted by permission of Coleman Barks.

Voltaire: *Candide* from *Voltaire: Candide and Other Stories*, translated by Roger Pearson. Translation and editorial material copyright © 1990 by Roger Pearson. Reprinted by permission of Oxford University Press.

ILLUSTRATION CREDITS

Cover image: Detail from *Portrait of a Negro Man, Olaudah Equiano*, 1780s, English school, 18th century, previously attributed to Joshua Reynolds. Royal Albert Memorial Museum, Exeter, Devon, UK/The Bridgeman Art Library. **Inside front cover image:** Map of the Eastern Hemisphere, China, 1790. Ruth Schacht/Staatsbibliothek zu Berlin Preussischer Kulturbesitz. Kartenabteilung/Art Resource, New York. **Page xxx:** Anonymous drawing of Louis XIV as the "Sun King." Snark/Art Resource, New York. **Page 12:** The Taj Mahal. Jean-Louis Nou/AKG Images. **Page 45:** Puppeteers performing *The Love Suicides at Amijima*. Photograph courtesy of Barbara Curtis/Adachi Collection, C. V. Starr East Asian Library, Columbia University. **Page 173:** Title page of Baudier's *General History of the Seraglio and of the Court of the Noble Lord Emperor of the Turks*,1631. Rare Books Division, Department of Rare Books and Special Collections, Princeton University Library. **Page 184:** Execution of Louis XVI (period engraving). Musée de la Révolution Française, Vizille, France/The Bridgeman Art Library. **Page 188:** *An Emblematical View of the Constitutions of England and France*. Division of Rare and Manuscript Collections, Cornell University, Olin Library. **Page 190:** Babylonian and Egyptian antiquities, from Denis Diderot's *Encyclopédie*, 1751–1772. Public domain. **Page 254:** *Art d'Écrire*, illustrative plate from Denis Diderot's *Encyclopédie*, 1751–1772. The Granger Collection, New York. **Page 258:** *La Carte du pays de Tendre*, from Madeleine de Scudéry's *Clélie*, 1660. Department of Rare Books and Special Collections, Princeton University Library. **Page 300:** Frontispiece to a 1776 edition of *Oroonoko: A Tragedy in Five Acts*, by Thomas Southern; printed from the acting copy, with remarks, biographical and critical, by D.—G. Based on Aphra Behn's novel of the same name. Drawing by R. Cruikshank. Private collection/New York Public Library. **Page 349:** James Gillray, *The King of Brobdingnag and Gulliver*, 1803. The Granger Collection, New York. **Page 408:** A *haiga* (haikai sketch), Courtesy of Idemitsu Museum of Arts.

FONTS CREDIT

The EuroSlavic, AfroRoman, Macron, TransIndic, Semitic Transliterator, and ANSEL fonts used to publish this work are available from Linguist's Software, Inc., PO Box 580, Edmonds, WA 98020-0580 USA, tel (425) 775-1130, www.linguistsoftware.com.

INDEX